W9-AMU-481

CUBA

CHRISTOPHER P. BAKER

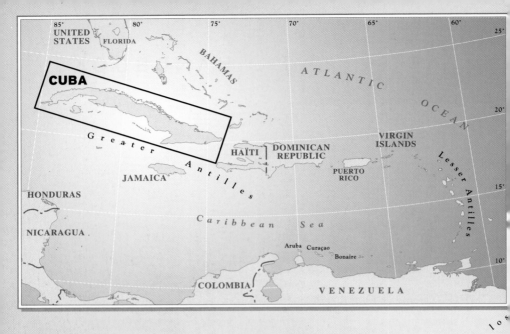

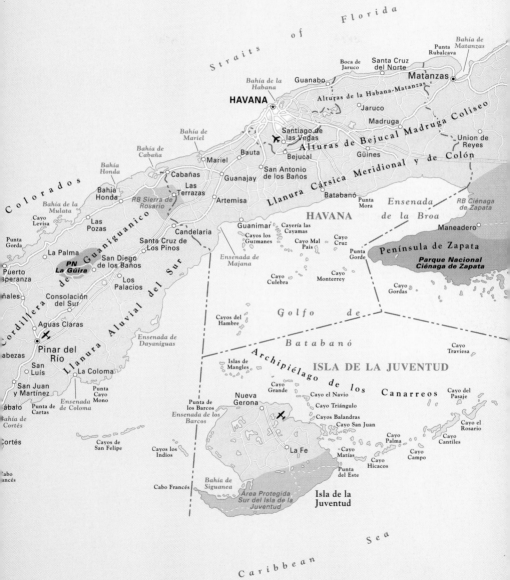

CUBA

Straits of *Florida*

Bahía de Matanzas
Punta Rubalcava

Boca de Jaruco · Santa Cruz del Norte · **Matanzas**

Bahía de la Habana · Guanabo

HAVANA

Alturas de la Habana-Matanzas

Jaruco

Santiago de las Vegas · Madruga · Alturas de Bejucal Madruga Coliseo

Bahía de Mariel

Union de Reyes

Bahía de Cabaña

Mariel · Bauta · Bejucal · Güines · de Colón

Bahía Honda

Cabañas · Guanajay · San Antonio de los Baños

Colorados

Las Terrazas · Artemisa · Batabanó · Punta Mora

Bahía Honda

Ensenada de la Broa

RB Sierra de Rosario

Llanura Cársica Meridional y de Colón

HAVANA

RB Ciénaga de Zapata

Bahía de la Mulata

Cayo Levisa

Guanimar · Cayería las Cayamas

Península de Zapata

Las Pozas

Candelaria · Cayos los Guzmanes · Cayo Mal País · Cayo Cruz

Maneadero

Punta Gorda

Santa Cruz de Los Pinos

Cayo Gorde

Parque Nacional Ciénaga de Zapata

La Palma

San Diego de los Baños

Ensenada de Majana

Cayo Monterrey

Puerto esperanza

PN La Güira

Cayo Culebra

Cayo Gordas

ñales

Consolación del Sur

Los Palacios

Cordillera del Sur

Aguas Claras

Ensenada de Dayaniguas

Cayos del Hambre

Golfo de

Cayo Traviesa

abezas

Pinar del Río

Batabanó

San Luís

La Coloma

Archipiélago

ISLA DE LA JUVENTUD

San Juan y Martínez

Punta Cayo Mono

Islas de Mangles

de los

Canarreos

Cayo del Pasaje

ábalo

Punta de Cartas

Ensenada de Coloma

Cayo Grande · Cayo el Navio

Nueva Gerona

Cayo Triángulo

Cayo del Rosario

Bahía de Cortés

Punta de los Barcos

Cayos Balandras · Cayo San Juan

Cayo el Rosario

ortés

Ensenada de los Barcos

Cayo Palma · Cayo Cantiles

Cayos de San Felipe

Cayos los Indios

La Fe · Cayo Matías · Cayo Campo

abo ancés

Cayo Hicacos

ahía de Cortés

Cabo Francés

Bahía de Siguanea

Punta del Este

Área Protegida Sur del Isla de la Juventud

Isla de la Juventud

Sea

Caribbean

Archipiélago de Sabana

Punta de Morlas
Cayos Blancos
Cayo Cruz del Padre
Cayos Juan Carito
Cayos Falcones
Cayo Blanquizal
Cayos Dromedarios
Cayos del Pajonal
Cayo Fragoso

Península de Hicacos
Cayos de las Cinco Leguas
Bahía de Santa Clara
Cayo las Picuas
Isabela de Sagua
Cayo la Vaca
Emilio Córdova
Cayo del Santo

Bahía de Matanzas
Varadero
Bahía de Cárdenas
La Teja
Corralillo
Rancho Velóz
Sagua la Grande
Llanuras del Norte de Las Villas
El Santo

Cárdenas
Martí
Alturas del Nordeste
Cifuentes
VILLA CLARA
Remedios

Limonar
Máximo Gómez
Los Arabos
Cascajal
Presa Alacranes
San Diego del Valle
San Antonio de las Vueltas
Buena Vista

Perico
Manacas
Jicotea
Presa Minerva
Zulueta

San Miguel de los Baños
Jovellanos
Colón
Esperanza
Santa Clara
Placetas

Unión de Reyes
Pedro Betancourt
Agramonte
Ranchuelo
Alturas de Santa Clara
Mataguá
Fomento

MATANZAS
Jagüey Grande
Calimete
Rodas
Cartagena
CIENFUEGOS
Manicaragua

Reserva de la Biosfera Ciénaga de Zapata
Aguada de Pasajeros
Palmira
Cumanayagua
Sierra del Escambray

Maneadero
Santo Tomás
Yaguaramas
Cienfuegos
Pepito Tey
Presa del Hanabanilla
Topes de Collantes

Llanura de Zapata
Playa Larga
San Blás
Jagua
Alturas de Trinidad

Parque Nacional Ciénaga de Zapata
Playa Girón
Bahía de Cienfuegos
Trinidad
San Pedro

Cayo del Macio
Bahía de Cochinos (Bay of Pigs)
Punta Palmillas
Península de Ancón
Bahía de San Pedro

Cayo Diego Pérez
Cayo Ernest Thaelmann
Ensenada de Casilda

Cayo Traviesa

Cayo Rico
Cayo Largo

Cayo el Rosario

Caribbean

| 0 | 25 mi |
| 0 | 25 km |

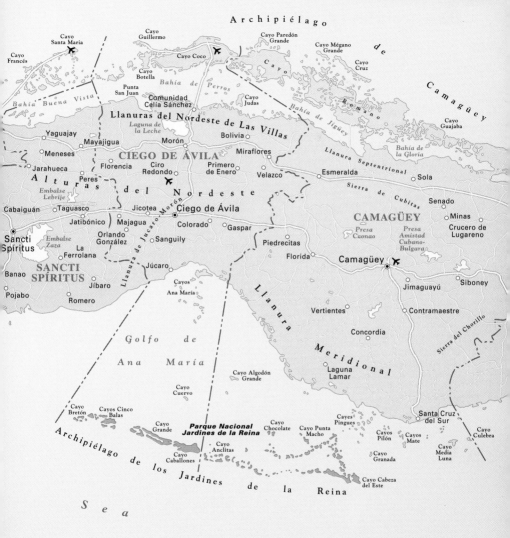

Archipiélago

Cayo
Santa María

Cayo
Francés

Cayo
Guillermo

Cayo Paredón
Grande

Cayo Mégano
Grande

Cayo
Cruz

de

Camagüey

Cayo Coco

Cayo
Botella

Punta
San Juan

Bahía de Perros

Comunidad
Celia Sánchez

Cayo
Judas

Bahía Buena Vista

C a y o

Bahía de Jigüey

R o m a n o

Cayo
Guajaba

Llanuras del Nordeste de Las Villas

Yaguajay

Meneses

Jarahueca

Mayajigua

Florencia

Laguna de
la Leche

Morón

Bolivia

Miraflores

Bahía de
la Gloria

CIEGO DE ÁVILA

Ciro
Redondo

Primero
de Enero

Llanura Septentrional

Esmeralda

Sola

A l t u r a s

Peres

d e l

N o r d e s t e

Velazco

Sierra de Cubitas

Senado

Embalse
Lebrije

Cabaiguán

Taguasco

Jatibónico

Jicotea

Majagua

Ciego de Ávila

Colorado

Gaspar

CAMAGÜEY

Presa
Caonao

Presa
Amistad
Cubano-
Bulgara

Minas

Crucero de
Lugareno

Sancti
Spíritus

Embalse
Zaza

Orlando
González

La
Ferrolana

Sanguily

Piedrecitas

Camagüey

SANCTI
SPÍRITUS

Júcaro

Florida

Banao

Jíbaro

Cayos
Ana María

Jimaguayú

Siboney

Pojabo

Romero

G o l f o   d e

Vertientes

Contramaestre

A n a   M a r í a

Concordia

Sierra del Chorrillo

L l a n u r a

M e r i d i o n a l

Laguna
Lamar

Cayo Algodón
Grande

Cayo
Cuervo

Cayo
Bretón

Cayos Cinco
Balas

Cayo
Grande

Parque Nacional
Jardines de la Reina

Cayo
Chocolate

Cayo Punta
Macho

Cayes
Pingues

Santa Cruz
del Sur

Cayo
Culebra

Archipiélago

Cayo
Caballones

Cayo
Anclitas

Cayos
Pilón

Cayos
Mate

Cayo
Granada

Cayo
Media
Luna

d e   l o s

J a r d i n e s

d e   l a   R e i n a

Cayo Cabeza
del Este

S e a

CUBA (continued)

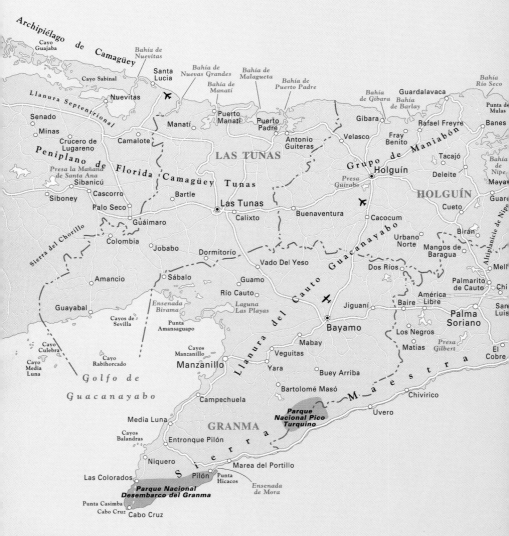

A T L A N T I C

Archipiélago de Camagüey

Cayo Guajaba

Cayo Sabinal

Santa Lucia

Bahía de Nuevitas

Bahía de Nuevas Grandes

Bahía de Manatí

Bahía de Malagueta

Bahía de Puerto Padre

Bahía Río Seco

Nuevitas

Llanura Septentrional

Senado

Minas

Crucero de Lugareno

Camalote

Peniplano de Florida

Presa la Mañana de Santa Ana

Sibanicú

Siboney

Cascorro

Palo Seco

Guáimaro

Colombia

Jobabo

Dormitorio

Amancio

Sábalo

Guamo

Río Cauto

Ensenada Birama

Cayos de Sevilla

Punta Amansaguapo

Guayabal

Cayo Culebra

Cayo Media Luna

Cayo Rabihorcado

Golfo de Guacanayabo

Cayos Manzanillo

Manzanillo

Veguitas

Yara

Mabay

Los Negros

Matias

Presa Gilbert

El Cobre

Media Luna

Cayos Balandras

Campechuela

GRANMA

Entronque Pilón

Niquero

Las Colorados

Punta Casimba

Cabo Cruz

Parque Nacional Desembarco del Granma

Pilón

Punta Hicacos

Marea del Portillo

Ensenada de Mora

Bartolomé Masó

Parque Nacional Pico Turquino

Buey Arriba

Chivirico

Uvero

Sierra Maestra

Manatí

Puerto Manatí

Puerto Padre

Antonio Guiteras

LAS TUNAS

Camagüey

Bartle

Las Tunas

Calixto

Buenaventura

Tunas

Cacocum

Urbano Norte

Dos Ríos

Jiguaní

Baire

Baire

América Libre

Palma Soriano

San Luis

Vado Del Yeso

Laguna Las Playas

Bayamo

Velasco

Fray Benito

Gibara

Bahía de Gibara

Bahía de Barlay

Guardalavaca

Rafael Freyre

Banes

Punta de Mulas

Grupo de Maniabón

Holguín

Tacajó

Deleite

Bahía de Nipe

Maya

HOLGUÍN

Cueto

Guar

Birán

Mangos de Baragua

Mell

Palmarito de Cauto

Chi

Altiplanicie de Nipe

Presa Guirabo

Sierra del Chorillo

Llanura del Cauto

Guacanayabo

© AVALON TRAVEL PUBLISHING, INC

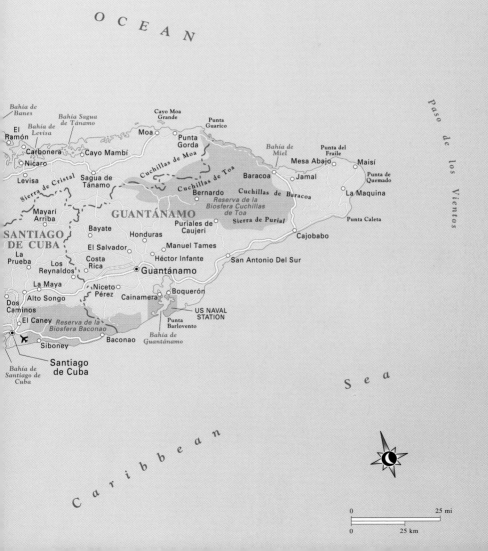

O C E A N

Bahía de Banes

Bahía Sagua de Tánamo

Cayo Moa Grande

Punta Guarico

Bahía de Levisa

El Ramón

Moa

Punta Gorda

Bahía de Miel

Punta del Fraile

Carbonera

Cayo Mambí

Mesa Abajo

Maisí

Nicaro

Cuchillas de Moa

Cuchillas de Toa

Baracoa

Jamal

Punta de Quemado

Levisa

Sagua de Tánamo

Sierra de Cristal

Bernardo

Cuchillas de Baracoa

La Maquina

Mayarí Arriba

GUANTÁNAMO

Reserva de la Biosfera Cuchillas de Toa

Puriales de Caujeri

Sierra de Purial

Punta Caleta

SANTIAGO DE CUBA

Bayate

Honduras

La Prueba

El Salvador

Manuel Tames

Cajobabo

Costa Rica

Héctor Infante

San Antonio Del Sur

Los Reynaldos

Guantánamo

La Maya

Niceto Pérez

Boquerón

Dos Caminos

Alto Songo

Cainamera

US NAVAL STATION

El Caney

Reserva de la Biosfera Baconao

Punta Barlovento

Siboney

Baconao

Bahía de Guantánamo

Santiago de Cuba

Bahía de Santiago de Cuba

Paso de los Vientos

S e a

C a r i b b e a n

0   25 mi

0   25 km

DISCOVER CUBA

In October 1959 Fidel Castro spoke to the
American Society of Travel Agents (ASTA) convention, held in the old
Blanquita Theater (now the Karl Marx) in Havana. "We have sea," said
Castro. "We have bays, we have beautiful beaches, we have medicinal
waters in our hotels, we have mountains, we have game and we have
fish in the sea and the rivers, and we have sun. Our people are noble,
hospitable, and most important, they hate no one. They love visitors,
so much in fact that our visitors feel completely at home."

Normal relations with the United States still existed back then,
and the U.S. ambassador, Philip Bonsai, also lauded Cuban tourism
at the ASTA convention: "Cuba is one of the most admirable countries in the world from the point of view of North American tourism
and from many other points of view."

Almost five decades have passed. Nothing has changed but
the politics.

A steam train runs from Guachinango to Trinidad.

© CHRISTOPHER P. BAKER

Travelers visiting Cuba today do so at a fascinating historical moment, as Cuba becomes increasingly dependent on tourism. Four decades after Castro closed the doors to outsiders, his country is enjoying cult status again. In 2004, more than two million visitors vacationed in Cuba.

Deluxe all-inclusive resorts are well-established. Even boutique hotels are emerging. And U.S. trade embargo notwithstanding, there's no shortage of modern tour buses, nor of Mercedes taxis, and even BMWs and Audis for rent. With all the hoopla about politics, it's easy to overlook the sheer beauty and delight of the place.

Cuba is made for tropical tourism: the diamond-dust beaches and bathtub-warm seas the color of peacock feathers; the bottle-green mountains and jade valleys full of dramatic formations; the ancient cities, with their flower-bedecked balconies, rococo churches, and palaces and castles evocative of the once mighty power of Spain;

Traditional colonial architecture is a highlight of Gibara's *casas particulares.*

and, above all, the sultriness and spontaneity of a country called the most emotionally involving in the Western hemisphere. No matter what the state of political tensions, there is *santería* and salsa, and sunny days on talcum beaches. Whatever the temperature a fresh breeze is sure to be blowing, carrying tropical aromas through cobbled colonial plazas. There are *mojitos* and *cuba libres* to enjoy, and the world's finest cigars to smoke fresh from the factory as you rumble down the lonesome highways in a chrome-spangled '55 Cadillac to the rhythm of the rumba on the radio.

The country is blessed with possibility. Divers are delirious over Cuba's wealth of deep-sea treasures. Sportfishing is also relatively advanced and has far more fish than fishhooks. Laguna del Tesoro, part of the swampy Zapata Peninsula National Park, is one of several premier bird-watching sites. There are crocodiles, too, lurking leery-eyed in well-preserved everglades. Horseback-riding options abound. Cuba is a prime destination for bicycle touring, and hikers can head for the Sierra Maestra to tread trails trod by Fidel Castro and Che Guevara.

A 1951 Chevy Bel Air reflects the cool blues of *azulejo* tiles, Havana.

Cuba's greatest, most enigmatic appeal, however, is that while traveling through it you sense you are living inside an unfolding drama. Cuba is still intoxicating, still laced with the sharp edges and sinister shadows that made Federico García Lorca, the Spanish poet, write to his parents, "If I get lost, look for me in Cuba," and that made Ernest Hemingway want "to stay here forever." No other Western nation offers such uniquely sensual and surreal sensations, made more poignant by Cuba's romantic caught-in-a-time-warp setting and a demimonde bubbling just beneath the surface. Walking Havana's streets you sense you are living inside a romantic thriller. You don't want to sleep for fear of missing a vital experience. Before the Revolution, Cuba had a reputation as a place of intrigue and tawdry romance. The whiff of conspiracy, the intimation of liaison, is still in the air. For foreign visitors, it is heady stuff.

The "real" Cuba isn't easy to fathom, however. In this twilight land, everything appears twice: once as the government likes to present it, and once as it really is. An open-minded visitor is torn two ways; Cuba is both disheartening and uplifting. You'll most probably

Soldiers in period costume prime a cannon at El Morro castle.

fall madly in love with the country, while being thankful you don't have to live in it.

To the international visitor, the frustrations of life for the average Cuban need be no more than a slight inconvenience. Tourists are free to go wherever they wish, and there are few visible hallmarks of a totalitarian system, which is well hidden from tourists – the secret police lurk in the shadows. And though the government tries to erect barriers between tourists and Cubans as much as possible (for example, an apartheid policy denies Cubans access to hotels and beaches reserved for tourists – a humiliation that angers most Cubans), interacting with the vivacious, self-assured Cubans is one of the greatest pleasures.

The compellingly warm-hearted Cubans relish a passion for pleasure despite (or because of) their hardships. Salsa and irresistible rumbas pulse through the streets, and throngs of people congregate at nightclubs and cabarets. Cubans you have met only moments previously may invite you into their homes, where rum and beer are passed around and you are lured to dance by narcotic rhythms.

fishing, Cayo Santa María

Contents

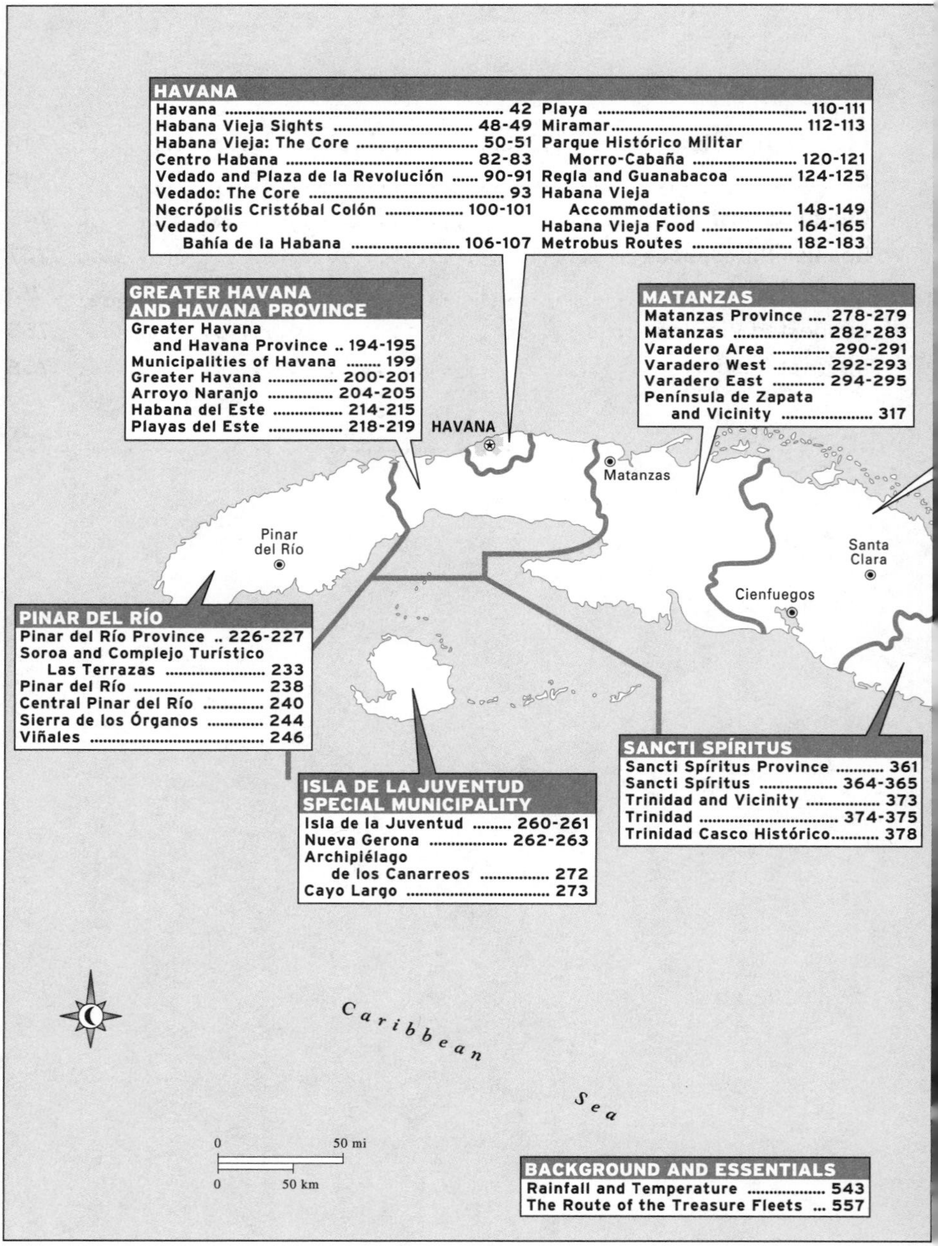

HAVANA
Havana ... 42
Habana Vieja Sights ... 48-49
Habana Vieja: The Core ... 50-51
Centro Habana ... 82-83
Vedado and Plaza de la Revolución ... 90-91
Vedado: The Core ... 93
Necrópolis Cristóbal Colón ... 100-101
Vedado to Bahía de la Habana ... 106-107
Playa ... 110-111
Miramar ... 112-113
Parque Histórico Militar Morro-Cabaña ... 120-121
Regla and Guanabacoa ... 124-125
Habana Vieja Accommodations ... 148-149
Habana Vieja Food ... 164-165
Metrobus Routes ... 182-183
GREATER HAVANA AND HAVANA PROVINCE
Greater Havana and Havana Province .. 194-195
Municipalities of Havana ... 199
Greater Havana ... 200-201
Arroyo Naranjo ... 204-205
Habana del Este ... 214-215
Playas del Este ... 218-219
MATANZAS
Matanzas Province 278-279
Matanzas ... 282-283
Varadero Area ... 290-291
Varadero West ... 292-293
Varadero East ... 294-295
Península de Zapata and Vicinity ... 317
HAVANA
Matanzas
Pinar del Río
Santa Clara
Cienfuegos
PINAR DEL RÍO
Pinar del Río Province .. 226-227
Soroa and Complejo Turístico Las Terrazas ... 233
Pinar del Río ... 238
Central Pinar del Río ... 240
Sierra de los Órganos ... 244
Viñales ... 246
SANCTI SPÍRITUS
Sancti Spíritus Province ... 361
Sancti Spíritus ... 364-365
Trinidad and Vicinity ... 373
Trinidad ... 374-375
Trinidad Casco Histórico ... 378
ISLA DE LA JUVENTUD SPECIAL MUNICIPALITY
Isla de la Juventud ... 260-261
Nueva Gerona ... 262-263
Archipiélago de los Canarreos ... 272
Cayo Largo ... 273
Caribbean Sea
0 50 mi
0 50 km
BACKGROUND AND ESSENTIALS
Rainfall and Temperature ... 543
The Route of the Treasure Fleets ... 557

MAP CONTENTS

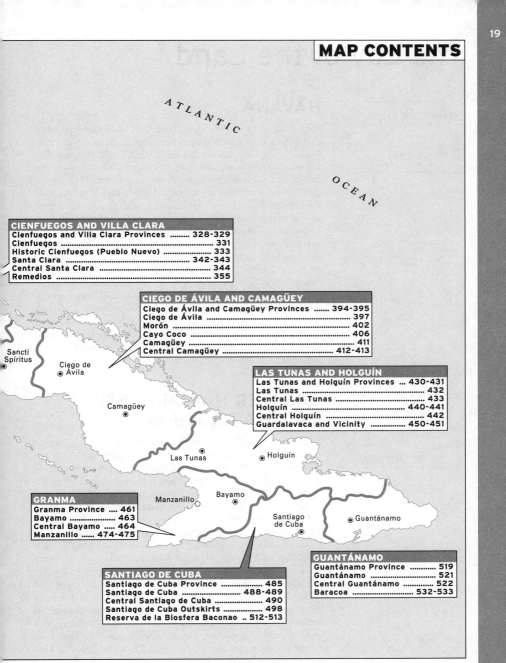

ATLANTIC

OCEAN

Sancti
Spíritus

Ciego de
Ávila

Camagüey

Las Tunas

Holguín

Manzanillo

Bayamo

Santiago
de Cuba

Guantánamo

The Lay of the Land

HAVANA

A destination in its own right, this city of two million people is enthralling. Compact and ideal for walking, Habana Vieja (Old Havana), the historic core, is a UNESCO World Heritage Site, full of fabulous plazas, cathedrals, castles, and colonial mansions; fans of Ernest Hemingway can follow the informal Hemingway trail. To the west, the leafy streets of Vedado and Miramar boast thousands of Beaux-Arts, art nouveau, and art deco structures, as well as modernist hotels from the heyday of Mafia sin, plus Cementerio Colón, a vast cemetery with astonishing tombs and mausoleums. Intriguing museums include those dedicated to the Revolution and nationalist hero José Martí, and the Parque Histórico Militar Morro-Cabaña preserves the largest castle in the Americas. The art scene is vibrant and includes street markets, plus galleries with world-class collections. Though nightlife is somewhat desultory compared to prerevolutionary days, there is still no shortage of classical concerts, Las Vegas–style cabarets such as the kaleidoscopic Tropicana, jazz venues, and earthy clubs playing sizzling *son* and salsa rhythms. One week is barely sufficient; two weeks is required to do Havana justice.

GREATER HAVANA AND HAVANA PROVINCE

Most of Havana Province should be treated as a place to pass through en route to provinces farther afield; the majority is given entirely to agriculture, and the southern coast has no beaches of any appeal. Suburban Havana is best experienced on short excursions from the city. Playas del Este—a string of gorgeous palm-shaded beaches—provide a superb weekend escape for *habaneros.* Southeast of the city is Ernest Hemingway's former house, now a museum maintained as he left it. Nearby, the fishing village of Cojímar has a fine restaurant where Hemingway ate. Worth a visit is Iglesia de Santa María del Rosario, a quaint 18th-century church in historic Santa María del Rosario containing a lavishly gilt baroque altar. It makes for a good day's excursion combined with Museo Ernest Hemingway, the Santuario de San Lázaro pilgrimage site outside Rincón, and the nearby mausoleum of national hero General Antonio Maceo. If you're traveling with children, consider an excursion to Parque Lenin (with horseback riding, rowboats, and more), the national zoo, and ExpoCuba (an expo touting Cuba's accomplishments in every field), all within a small distance of one another and the national botanical garden.

PINAR DEL RÍO

Almost every visitor to Cuba sets their sights on Pinar del Río, known for its spectacular limestone *mogotes*. These rounded free-standing mountains frame the Valle de Viñales, where Cuba's finest tobacco is grown. Famed for the most magnificent scenery on the entire island, the valley can be visited on a day trip from Havana, just three hours' drive, but it is well worth lingering, not least because Viñales village is a time-warp charmer. The valley also offers preeminent climbing and caving. Scuba divers rave about the waters off Cayo Levisa, and at María la Gorda, where the nearby Parque de Guanahacabibes is being developed and offers potential bird-watching. Otherwise the north coast is undeveloped for tourism; likewise the marshy southern shore. Bird-watchers and nature lovers are lured to Las Terrazas, Cuba's most developed eco-resort, where vacationers can stay at a de-lightful hotel and partake of horseback rides and hiking. Other sites of interest are few, although the scenic drives along the Carretera Central, fringing the Sierra del Rosario, are splendid. Visitors in a hurry can access Pinar del Río via the Autopista. Three days is sufficient time for seeing this province.

ISLA DE LA JUVENTUD SPECIAL MUNICIPALITY

Slung beneath the underbelly of Cuba, this archipelago draws few visitors. The exception is Cayo Largo, a tiny coral jewel with stupendous beaches, warm turquoise waters, and a choice of all-inclusive accommodations (the downside is that this is a tourists-only enclave; no Cubans are allowed to visit). Isla de la Juventud, the main island, was once famous for schooling students from developing nations. It, too, has fine beaches, though they are not developed and are off-limits except by permit (eas-ily obtained on the island). The sole historical attraction is the Presidio Modelo prison, today a museum, where Fidel Castro and fellow revolutionaries of the Moncada assault were briefly imprisoned. The wildlands of Refugio Ecológico Los Indios offer fabulous bird-watching, and a nearby crocodile farm proves intriguing. The main incentive, however, is for scuba divers. The waters off Punta Francés are renowned for some of the fin-est coral reefs and sponges, and remains of Spanish galleons and contemporary warships to explore. Two days is all that's required to explore Isla de la Juventud, plus two days more for Cayo Largo.

MATANZAS

The setting for Cuba's premier beach resort, Varadero, this province receives more visitors than anywhere else in Cuba. Miles-long Varadero beach is a stunner, scuba diving is offered, Cuba's sole 18-hole golf course is here, and some of the dozens of all-inclusive hotels are world-class. Stray from the reclusive Varadero Peninsula (off-limits to ordinary Cubans) to discover the real Cuba beyond. The province is mostly flat with sugar cane and citrus plantations in the north and the Caribbean's largest swamp—the Ciénaga de Zapata—in the south. The latter offers fantastic bird-watching, crocodile-viewing, and sportfishing. Nearby, Playa Girón was the site of the Bay of Pigs invasion in 1961; a museum recalls the event, while the beach is now developed for tourists. Snorkeling and scuba diving off this southern coast are excellent. The city of Matanzas is a center for Afro-Cuban music and dance and has an outlet of the Tropicana cabaret nightclub, plus some intriguing colonial architecture. On the outskirts of town, Cuevas de Bellamar, a cavern with dripstone formations, is worth an excursion, as is the nearby colonial spa town of San Miguel de los Baños. Two or three days in Varadero plus three days for Matanzas and the Ciénaga de Zapata region should suffice.

CIENFUEGOS AND VILLA CLARA

Cut through by the Autopista, these contiguous provinces are superbly scenic. Bird-watchers and hikers are particularly enamored of the Sierra Escambray, where forest trails lead to waterfalls. The provincial capital of Santa Clara figured prominently in the battles to topple Batista; in December 1958, Che Guevara's army "liberated" the city. His remains are interred in a mausoleum-museum beneath the Plaza de la Revolución. During Christmas week, visitors pour in to the otherwise sleepy towns of Remedios, Caibarién, and Zulueta for the region's unique *parrandas*—fireworks battles of almost unimaginable ferocity. Caibarién is the gateway to Cayo Santa María, a series of exquisite coral cays fringed by white-sand beaches and turquoise waters. To the south, the bayside city of Cienfuegos is worth a day or two for its colonial architecture. Outside town, Jardín Botánico Soledad is a world-class botanical garden, while the nearby beach at Rancho Luna has a small *delfinario* where dolphin shows are given. Most visitors stop over in this region en route between Havana and more easterly provinces. The entire region can be explored in five days.

SANCTI SPÍRITUS

Spanning the Atlantic shore to the Caribbean, Sancti Spíritus, in the center of Cuba, is synonymous with the colonial town of Trinidad. A UNESCO World Heritage Site, this charming hill town founded in 1514 is a crown jewel of colonial architecture, set at the base of the Sierra Escambray just minutes away from Playa Ancón. This beautiful beach has a choice of international-standard accommodation, while Trinidad offers scores of *casas particulares* that put you in touch with local life. Scuba diving is popular off Ancón, where sailboats can be rented, and local excursions include steam-train rides, plus former sugar planta-tions in the Valle de los Ingenios slated to become museums. The eponymous provincial capital, Sancti Spíritus, also has a colonial core worth exploring. Nearby, Zaza is a center for bird-watching and fishing. On the north shore, Parque Nacional Caguanas is being developed for ecotourism. The province can be accessed swiftly from Havana by the Autopista, which peters out near the border with Ciego de Ávila Province. You'll want to concentrate on Trinidad, which requires at least two days to savor, plus two additional days for Playa Ancón and the Valle de los Ingenios.

CIEGO DE ÁVILA
AND CAMAGÜEY

Forming the slender waist of Cuba, Ciego de Ávila, the island's smallest and narrowest province, is also its least appealing. The notable exception is Cayo Coco, the most developed of the chain of offshore cays that form the Jardines del Rey archipelago. Accessed by a 17-mile-long causeway, the cay is fringed by spec-tacular white-sand beaches—the setting for more than a dozen all-inclusive resort hotels, with more going up every year. Like Varadero (in Matanzas), Cayo Coco is off-limits to Cubans other than tourism workers. The cays stretch east into the province of Camagüey, though as yet none of its cays are developed (Cayo Sabinal does have one very rustic albeit delightful place to stay). The same is true of the Jardines de la Reina, a sprawling chain of smaller cays scattered across shallow turquoise waters off the southern coast of both provinces. Yachters will appreciate these waters, as do fisherfolk and scuba divers, who also thrill to the reefs off Playa Santa Lucía. The city of Camagüey boasts quaint cobbled plazas and a distinct colonial architecture worthy of two days' perusal. You can pack it all into five days.

LAS TUNAS AND HOLGUÍN

This region is noticeably more barren than more westerly provinces, with large swathes given over to raising beef cattle. Las Tunas is the least interesting of the twin provinces, and you can safely pass through without fear of missing something vital. By contrast, Holguín Province packs in much that is of interest in Cuba: fabulous beaches (centered on the resort complex of Guardalavaca and nearby Playas Esmeralda and Pesquero), splendid scenery (especially the *mogotes* of the Grupo de Maniabon), interesting colonial architecture (in Holguín city), archaeological sites (at Museo Aborigen Chorro de Maísa, and at Parque Monumento Nacional Bariay, where Christopher Columbus supposedly landed), and opportunities for bird-watching and hiking (at Pinares de Mayarí). Fidel Castro's birthplace and boyhood home is even open for view under strict security at Sitio Histórico Birán. It is worth lingering around Holguín, where the capital city makes a good base. Plan on four days to see all the sights.

GRANMA

Far from the beaten tourist path, Granma Province is dominated by the Sierra Maestra chain. Spanning the province east–west, this vast complex was the base for Fidel Castro's guerrillas during the years preceding the Revolution. The hale and hearty can traipse mountain trails to reach his headquarters, La Comandancia de la Plata, and even continue to the summit of Pico Turquino, Cuba's highest peak. The Wars of Independence were launched in the town of Bayamo, which contains a colonial plaza with church and other edifices of historical import. Granma has additional sites associated with leading figures in the quest for independence: the farm of Carlos Manuel de Céspedes, who launched the wars; and Dos Ríos, where nationalist leader José Martí was killed. And Parque Nacional Desembarco del Granma is the site where Fidel Castro and his guerrilla band landed in 1956 to launch the Revolution (there's an exact replica of the vessel), but is more rewarding for hiking through the rare tropical dry forest ecosystem. For stupendous scenery, the lonesome coast road from Marea del Portillo to Santiago de Cuba is unsurpassed in Cuba. Other than a choice of mediocre all-inclusive resorts at Marea, the province lacks services, including quality accommodations. You'll need two days minimum to tackle the Turquino hike; otherwise you can breeze through Granma in two or three days.

SANTIAGO DE CUBA

Cuba's second city and the province to which it lends its name are a world apart from Havana. The city of Santiago de Cuba, founded in 1514, predates Havana and looks and feels more "Caribbean" than Havana, which, architecturally, is quintessentially Spanish. Santiago is also more African, with strong hints of French, Haitian, and even Jamaican influence in the people and their culture. Much of Cuba's musical heritage was birthed here. So, too, the Revolution. Museums, mausoleums, and other sites recalling the city's revolutionary fervor abound, as do traditional cultural centers. Other sites include a cigar factory, the former Bacardi rum factory (now producing Havana Club), and Castillo de San Pedro del Morro. Santiago is also the setting for Cuba's preeminent carnival, as well as a regional outlet of the Tropicana nightclub. There are several handsome beaches close by in Reserva de la Biosfera Baconao, as well as forested mountains, though they still await development for ecotourists (El Salton is a second-tier spa resort in the mountains). Four days are required to do the city in-depth.

GUANTÁNAMO

The nation's Cinderella province is synonymous with the U.S. Naval Base, which occupies land outside the namesake capital city. Perhaps Cuba's most oddball tourist experience, the base can be viewed from the adjacent Cuban military base, from the hilltop Mirador de Malones. The town of Guantánamo is rather dreary, with little appeal--but well worth the drive into the hills north of town, the Zoológico Piedra is literally a stone zoo, with every variety of animal carved out of rock. Most visitors to the province head to Baracoa, the oldest settlement in Cuba. This venerable town has a unique aura, not least thanks to its tumbledown wooden structures in a regional vernacular style. The surrounding forest-clad mountains are at the forefront of Cuba's ecotourism drive, and several national parks are being developed with trails; in time, even whitewater rafting may be offered. The drive over La Farola to reach isolated Baracoa is Cuba's most daunting (and one of its most beautiful). You can even drive from Baracoa to land's end, where a lighthouse pins Punta Maisí. Four days is all that's required to see the sights, but you may want to add on several days to laze in Baracoa.

Planning Your Trip

Arranging a visit to Cuba takes more forethought than most destinations. For Americans, the first question is "can I go legally?" A four-decades-old trade embargo denies most U.S. citizens and residents the right to travel to Cuba, although there are exceptions, and the restrictions loosen and tighten with shifts in the political breeze (the Clinton administration created a category of travel that essentially permitted *anyone* to visit Cuba; George W. Bush rescinded this "person-to-person exchange" allowance and flipped to a more harshly restrictive extreme). Understandably, thousands of U.S. citizens simply hop a plane to Cuba via Canada, Mexico, or other countries. Citizens of other nations don't have this concern.

Cuba is a large island (almost 1,000 miles east–west) and many of the most popular destinations are far apart. In Havana, getting around is simple, thanks to an efficient taxi system. Traveling between cities by public transportation, however, can be a challenge. Domestic flights are best avoided, as safety is a great concern. Fortunately, tourists receive preferential treatment: modern air-conditioned buses connect the major cities, for example. And the country's road network is well developed, although much deteriorated, poorly lit, and with unique hazards (such as lumbering ox carts). You can easily drive yourself around. Renting a car is recommended for anyone seeking serendipitous travel; cars are widely available, although their maintenance is usually very iffy and rental prices are outrageous.

In fact, Cuba is now vastly overpriced in almost every regard. Recently considered a bargain, the island is today one of the most expensive destinations in the Caribbean. Cuba's financial institutions are not as progressive as those in Europe and North America, and you should not rely on being able to get by with your credit card. A good deal of cash is essential. U.S. citizens will need to operate on a cash-only basis, as credit cards issued by U.S. institutions cannot be used. (Also, notwithstanding Cuba's vaunted health system, medicines are rarely available except in Havana and other key tourist venues, so come prepared with aspirin and other essentials.)

Be prepared for boring food and some sub-par accommodation. With few exceptions, food island-wide is uniformly bland (Cuba is well suited to anyone contemplating a diet). At the beach, most hotels operate as all-inclusive resorts, from which Cubans are barred. Havana has some splendid boutique hotels and several outwardly attractive but otherwise second-rate "deluxe" hotels dating back to the Mafia heyday. Cuba's hotels are recommended only if you've little interest in engaging with Cubans. Far more rewarding and enlightening is to stay with a Cuban family in a licensed *casa particular*. Make reservations well before arriving in Cuba—but don't expect your reservations to be honored (except at *casas particulares*).

Cuba's strongest suit is its vibrant culture. The vast majority of visitors to Cuba come for the vivacious music and dance; the historic architecture; and, of course, a chance to experience life under the only Communist regime in the Western hemisphere before it all changes. Others are content sampling the beautiful beaches and bucolic landscapes. For active travelers, bicycling, horseback riding, scuba diving, and sportfishing are the most developed pursuits. Ecotourism is only now beginning to be developed and facilities and knowledgeable guides are few and far between.

WHEN TO GO

Cuba has fairly distinct seasons: a relatively dry and mild winter (November–April) and hot and wet summer (May–October). Early spring is the ideal time to travel, especially in the Oriente (the eastern provinces), which can be insufferably hot in summer. Christmas and New Year's are the busiest periods, and many accommodations and car rental agencies sell out during this period, while finding a domestic flight is near impossible. Hotel prices are usually lower in summer—the low season (*temporada baja*)—when hurricanes are a slim possibility. Tropical storms can lash the island even in winter, however.

You might want to time your visit to coincide with a major festival, such as carnival in Santiago de Cuba, or the Festival of New Latin American Cinema in Havana.

WHAT TO TAKE

Dress for a tropical climate. Pack items that work in various combinations—preferably darker items that don't show the inevitable dirt and stains you'll quickly collect on your travels (Cuba's laundry and dry-cleaning services are untrustworthy). However, dark clothes tend to be hotter than khaki or light-colored clothing. White T-shirts are perfect for reflecting the harsh sunlight. A pair of cargo shorts or pants and a photographer's jacket with heaps of pockets is handy.

Pack a warm sweater and a windbreaker for winter visits, as brief spells of cold weather can occur. Eschew a raincoat for a breathable Gore-Tex jacket. A small umbrella is also a good idea at any time of year (they're almost impossible to find in Cuba, so bring your own). In summer, the weather is hot and humid: You'll want light, loose-fitting shirts and shorts. Knee-length shorts for men are acceptable almost everywhere. Save your shorter running shorts for the track. For longer visits, pack a regular change of socks and underpants. Wash them frequently to help keep athlete's foot and other fungal growths at bay. Denim jeans and other thick cottons take forever to dry when wet, so light cotton/polyester blend clothes are preferred; they're cooler and dry quickly. Ideally, everything should be drip-dry, wash-and-wear.

Cubans are fastidious about dressing well, especially when going out to the theater or dinner, and for business functions. You may wish to take a dress jacket or cocktail dress for dinners in more expensive hotel restaurants, and for that unexpected meeting with Fidel. However, most Cubans dress informally, though neatly, for all occasions.

Two T-shirts plus two dressier shirts (including a *guayabera*), a sweater, photographer's jacket, pair of jeans, cargo pants, lightweight sweatpants, two pairs of shorts, and a pair of dress pants suffice for me. Women may wish to substitute blouses and mid-length skirts. Don't forget your bathing suit.

A comfortable, well-fitting pair of sneakers will work for most occasions. Pack a pair of dress shoes for your evening ensemble. You'll want lightweight canvas hiking boots with ankle protection for hiking muddy trails in the mountains.

Take all the toiletries you think you'll need, including some toilet paper, a towel, and face cloth. Bring any specific medications you think you'll need. If you bring prescription drugs, be sure the druggist's identification label is on the container. Women should pack extra tampons.

Writing materials are hard to come by; take pens, pencils, and notepads (these make great gifts for children). An English/Spanish dictionary is handy and makes a good parting gift.

Space on buses and planes is limited. Limit yourself to one bag or suitcase, plus a small daypack and/or camera bag. Avoid backpacks with external appendages; they catch and can easily break. A small daypack allows you to pack everything you need for a one- or two-day side-trip and leave the rest of your luggage in storage at a Havana hotel. However, do not leave items in exterior pockets, and always ensure that your bag or suitcase is securely locked.

Explore Cuba

THE 21-DAY BEST OF CUBA

Cuba is a large island—much larger than most visitors imagine—and exploring the isle fully would take a month. Few visitors have time to explore Cuba from end to end. I do not recommend domestic flights for reasons of safety, and given the dire state of public transport, your best options are either self-drive or the Víazul bus service, designed for tourists. Unless your intent is to explore as comprehensively as possible, with lots of time on the road, concentrate your time in no more than three or four places. You'll want at least four days to sample Havana before heading out to the provinces (don't underestimate how much there is to see in the capital city). The following itinerary combines a sampling of the best scenery, beaches, and cities for those intent on seeing the island end to end.

DAY 1

Arrive **Havana**'s José Martí International Airport; transfer to a hotel or *casa particular* in the Habana Vieja or Vedado districts.

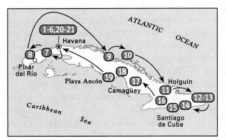

DAY 2

Take a self-guided walking tour of **Habana Vieja,** to include the **Plaza de Armas** and **Plaza de la Catedral** and the museums, galleries, and shops along surrounding streets. Return at night to savor the plazas lit by traditional gas lanterns. Don't fail to sip a *mojito* at La Bodeguita del Medio (I also recommend lunch here).

DAY 3

Continue exploring Habana Vieja, to include the **Plaza de San Francisco** and **Plaza Vieja** and surrounding area, being sure not to miss the **Museo de Ron.** In late afternoon, head to the **Parque Histórico Militar Morro-Cabaña,** being sure not to miss the *cañonazo* ceremony.

DAY 4

This morning, concentrate your time around **Parque Central** and **Paseo de Martí.** Be sure to visit the **Capitolio Nacional, Partagás cigar factory,** the **Museo Nacional de Bellas Artes,** and the **Museo de la Revolución.** A daiquiri at El Floridita is a must! At dusk, walk the **Malecón.**

DAY 5

Spend the morning exploring the streets of **Vedado,** being sure to call in at the **Hotel Nacional,** the **Hotel Tryp Habana Libre,** and **University of Havana.** After cooling off with an ice cream at Coppelia (with pesos in hand, stand in line with the Cubans), walk along Calle 17, calling in at the **Museo de Artes Decorativas.** Then hail a taxi to take you to **Cementerio Colón** and **Plaza de la Revolución.**

DAY 6

Rent a car and set out on a tour of **suburban Havana,** calling in at **Iglesia Santa María del Rosario** and **Museo Ernest Hemingway.** Continue to the village of **Cojímar** for lunch at La Terraza, then head to **Playas del Este** for time on the beach. I recommend the Playa Mégano section at Tarará.

DAY 7

Head west along the Circuito Norte highway to **Las Terrazas,** an eco-resort and rural community in the heart of the Sierra del Rosario. Hike the trails and visit the artists' studios. Overnight at Hotel La Moka.

DAY 8

Continue west to **Valle de Viñales.** Spend the afternoon exploring Viñales village, the Cuevo del Indio, and tobacco fields. Overnight either in a *casa particular* or at the Hotel La Ermita.

DAY 9

This morning head to the town of Pinar del Río and take the Autopista east to Havana and onwards to **Santa Clara** (yes, it's a long drive, but there's no alternative). Visit the mausoleum and museum of Che Guevara, then continue to the historic town of **Remedios.** During Christmas week, overnight in Remedios to enjoy the local fireworks battles called *parrandas.*

DAY 10

Continue east via Morón to **Cayo Coco,** arriving mid-afternoon with time to enjoy the beach and water sports.

DAY 11

Follow the Circuito Norte east to Las Tunas, then continue along the Carretera Central to **Holguín.** I recommend staying at a *casa particular.*

DAY 12

After walking the main plazas, set out for **Sitio Histórico Birán,** birthplace of Fidel Castro, before following the coast road east via Moa to **Baracoa,** arriving in this isolated and charming town in early evening. Overnight at Hotel El Castillo or a *casa particular.*

DAY 13

Stroll the streets of Baracoa, savoring its unique laid-back flavor. This afternoon head to **El Yunque,** where you can hike to the summit of this fantastic mountain formation.

DAY 14

Continue over **La Farola,** a switchback mountain road, dropping to the city of **Guantánamo.** En route, be sure to visit the **Zoológico Piedra.** Continue to **Santiago de Cuba,** arriving early evening. Check into the Hotel Casa Grande or a *casa particular.*

DAY 15

After visiting the **Cuartel Moncada** and **Museo de la Revolución,** spend the balance of the day exploring the historic quarter of Santiago de Cuba, being sure to include the **Cementerio de Santa Ifigenia.** Before dusk, head out to **El Morro** castle to watch the *cañonazo* ceremony, when soldiers in period costume put a light to an ancient cannon. This evening, call in at the Casa de la Trova to hear traditional Cuban music at its best.

DAY 16

This morning depart Santiago and follow the Carretera Central northwest to the town of **Bayamo.** En route, call in at **El Cobre** to visit the shrine of the Virgen de la Caridad. After sightseeing around the main plaza of Bayamo, continue northwest via Yasa to Las Tunas. Overnight at a *casa particular.*

DAY 17

Continue west along the Carretera Central to Camagüey, arriving midday with time to explore the three major colonial plazas. For digs, I recommend the charmingly restored 18th-century Gran Hotel, which also has one of the best eateries in town.

DAY 18

Get an early start today for the drive west via the provincial capitals of Ciego de Ávila and Sancti Spíritus, then through the Valle de los Ingenios, where you should have lunch at Hacienda Iznaga. Arriving in Trinidad, spend the rest of the afternoon perambulating the ancient plazas.

DAY 19

After further walking the cobbled colonial heart of Trinidad, drive out to Playa Ancón for beach time and perhaps even some scuba diving. Tonight check out an Afro-Cuban performance, then head to the Disco Ayala, set in a cave.

DAY 20

Up early again to follow the long and winding road up over the Sierra Escambray to Topes de Collantes. Continue north to Santa Clara, then head back to Havana via the Autopista. This evening, visit the Tropicana cabaret, being sure to have made reservations.

DAY 21

Transfer to the airport for your departure flight.

CUBA BY BICYCLE

In many ways, Cuba is a cyclist's delight. Many Cubans rely on bicycles for getting around. The scenery is magnificent, and the roads are relatively light on traffic. That said, cyclists face all sorts of hazards (potholes, errant vehicles, etc.), and refreshments (and sometimes accommodation) of any sort are often very far between. You'll want to come fully supplied with spare parts, including inner tubes, and stock up with plenty of snacks and drinks for each day's journey. A mountain bike is essential.

DAY 1

Arrive Havana's José Martí International Airport; transfer to a hotel or *casa particular* in the Habana Vieja or Vedado districts.

DAY 2

Spend the day exploring Habana Vieja, concentrating your time around Parque Central, Plaza de Armas, and Plaza de la Catedral.

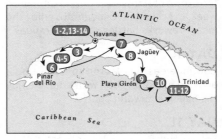

DAY 3

Set out from Havana west along the coast road via Playa Baracoa and Mariel to Las Terrazas. Overnight at the Hotel La Moka.

DAY 4

Today head south via Soroa to the Carretera Central, then cycle west to San Diego de los Baños. Either overnight here, being sure to steep in the local thermal mineral baths, or if you have energy, continue uphill through Parque Nacional La Güira and San Andrés to Viñales.

DAY 5

Today you'll want to soak in the atmosphere of the Valle de Viñales, with forays through the valley to Cuevas del Indio and other key local sights.

DAY 6

South to Pinar del Río, where the sights are few. Continue west to San Juan y Martínez to visit Finca El Pinar San Luís to learn the fine art of tobacco-growing from world-renowned farmer Alejandro Robaina.

DAY 7

Catch an early morning Víazul bus to Havana then transfer via Víazul or the Hershey train to Matanzas, with time for exploring the colonial core. Overnight at a *casa particular*.

DAY 8

Head east along the Carretera Central to Jovellanos, making a detour en route to see San Miguel de los Baños. Turn south at Jovellanos and cycle through citrus plantations to Jagüey Grande, where you can overnight at Motel Batey Don Pedro.

DAY 9

Today head south through the Ciénaga de Zapata. Sights en route include Museo Memorial Comandancia FAR, a small museum at the former Australia sugar-processing factory, and a crocodile farm at La Boca, where a pleasant restaurant serves decent meals. Passing through Playa Larga, you'll arrive at Playa Girón (setting for the Bay of Pigs invasion of 1961) with time to explore the museum and relax on the beach.

DAY 10

Eastward, the road gives way to dirt as you pass Caleta Buena (good for snorkeling). Continue along the coast (you'll need a mountain bike for the track) to Jagua, where you can catch a ferry across the mouth of Cienfuegos Bay. Head east a short distance to Finca las Colorados, a superb *casa particular*.

DAY 11

Follow the coast road (Costanera Sur) east via Arimao and Guajimico. You can eat midway at Hacienda La Vega. The Sierra Escambray loom to the north as the road runs along the shore. Eventually you'll cycle the hill into Trinidad, your destination.

DAY 12

You deserve a rest today. Spend the day exploring the colonial plazas of Trinidad on foot.

DAY 13

Either cycle to Playa Ancón for a day at the beach, returning via Boca, where you can spend beachtime among Cubans; or take a round-trip into the Valle de los Ingenios, with lunch at Hacienda Iznaga. This afternoon, return to Havana on a Víazul bus.

DAY 14

Transfer to the airport for your departure flight.

¡VIVA LA REVOLUCIÓN!

Many a traveler to Cuba arrives, and/or departs, toting a T-shirt emblazoned with the world-renowned image of Che. That doesn't necessarily indicate a fondness for Castro or socialism. Still, thousands of visitors *do* arrive every year to pay homage to the *revolución*. Numerous North American and European organizations offer "solidarity" tours, often with a work component in which tour participants contribute labor to a local community, if only for a day. These tours are designed to show you the positive side of the Revolution, and most participants are already firmly enamored of the socialist system and its successes in education and health. A few make a pilgrimage along the revolutionary trail. Whatever your politics, following the footsteps of Fidel Castro & Co. from youthful zealots to eventual power makes for a fascinating historical journey.

DAY 1

Arrive Havana's José Martí International Airport; transfer to a hotel or *casa particular* in the Habana Vieja or Vedado districts.

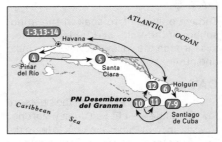

DAY 2

Start the day with a visit to the Museo de la Revolución, housed in the former presidential palace of corrupt dictator Fulgencio Batista, whom the revolution overthrew. Of course, you'll want to spend some time viewing the other fascinating sites nearby. In the afternoon, your tour of Habana Vieja should include the Museo Casa Natal de José Martí, birthplace of the national hero whom Fidel Castro named the "intellectual author" of the revolution; and Museo de Che, in Fortaleza de la Cabaña.

DAY 3

Today, concentrate your sightseeing around Vedado. Must-see sights include the Museo Abel Santamaría, a former apartment that was the secret headquarters for Castro's 26th of July Movement; the university, where the *Escaleras* (steps) were a venue for clashes with Batista's police; Galería 23 y 12, where Castro first announced that Cuba was socialist; and Plaza de la Revolución, the seat of Communist government.

DAY 4

Head west from Havana to Pinar del Río Province to visit Cuevas de los Portales, used as Che Guevara's command center during the "Missile Crisis." Continue to Viñales to visit the tobacco fields and overnight.

DAY 5

Depart Pinar del Río along the Autopista for the town of Santa Clara, setting for the seminal battle that toppled the Batista regime. Your tour of town should include the Tren Blindado (a troop train destroyed by Che Guevara's troops) and the Monumento Ernesto Che Guevara and, below it, the Museo de Che, devoted to the Argentinian revolutionary whose remains are interred here.

DAY 6

A long day's drive today along the Carretera Central to reach Holguín, with time for exploring the colonial heart of the city.

DAY 7

Leaving the city, take Avenida Simón Bolívar, lined with monuments to nationalist and revolutionary heroes, including a pop-art rendition of Che. Your destination is Sitio Histórico Birán, Fidel Castro's birthplace and home into adolescence. Afterwards, continue via Palma Soriano, arriving in Santiago de Cuba in the afternoon.

DAY 8

First stop today is Cuartel Moncada, site of the attack in 1953 that launched the revolution; today the former barracks holds the Museo de la Revolución. Nearby is the Museo Abel Santamaría, named for a prominent revolutionary tortured to death following the failed attack. This afternoon, tour the historic town center, including Parque Céspedes (where Fidel Castro gave his victory speech after Batista was toppled); the Colegio Jesuita Dolores, where Fidel attended school; and the Museo Lucha Clandestina, recalling the clandestine war in the cities.

DAY 9

Head out to Siboney to visit the farmhouse from where Castro and his revolutionaries set out to attack the Moncada barracks. The route is lined with monuments to those who died in the attack. Afterwards, head into the mountains to Mayarí Arriba and the Museo Comandancia del Segundo Frente (Museum of the Second Front) and the nearby mausoleum. Return to Santiago for the evening.

DAY 10

Head west along the coast via Chivírico – a stupendous drive! Beyond Ocujal, visit La Comandancia de la Plata, which regales the tale of the revolutionary war in the mountains. Nearby, in Pilón, call in at the Casa Museo Celía Sánchez, from which the revolutionary heroine ran the secret supply line to Fidel's army in the Sierra Maestra. Continue to the Parque Nacional Desembarco del Granma, site of the landing of Fidel's army in 1956. Overnight in Niquero.

DAY 11

Call in at Media Luna to view the birthplace of Celía Sánchez en route to Manzanillo. Here, visit the statue of Celía then continue via Bartolomé Masó to Santo Domingo, where a small museum features a 3-D map of the war in the Sierra Maestra. Overnight in Santo Domingo.

DAY 12

This morning hike to Comandancia de la Plata, Fidel's headquarters deep in the Sierra Maestra. In the afternoon, continue via Bayamo, arriving in Las Tunas in late afternoon.

DAY 13

A long drive back to Havana today via the Carretera Central and Autopista.

DAY 14

Transfer to the airport for your departure flight.

THE BEACH LOVER'S TOUR

Cuba boasts glorious beaches. Many feature sugarcane-white sands shelving into waters of Maxfield Parrish blues. Most are scattered along the north shore, with concentrations immediately east of Havana; in Varadero; Cayo Largo; the Jardines del Rey (Ciego de Ávila and Camagüey Provinces); and Holguín. Many of the best beaches have been developed for tourism and at most, ordinary Cubans are not allowed. The south coast has relatively few noteworthy beaches; most are of an unappealing taupe color and backed by mangroves. Some beaches are used by marine turtles for laying eggs, although few of these are accessible to tourists and equally few are otherwise appealing for nature viewing, other than snorkeling and scuba diving. Likewise, surfers will find very few beaches where the waves come rolling in, with the exception being around Baracoa. Swimming requires caution, as many beaches are known for riptides, dangerous undertows that can sweep unwary swimmers out to see. Arrive with plenty of mosquito repellent, and avoid most beaches at dusk, when minuscule but ferocious no-see-ums are active.

By combining the following beaches on a 10-day holiday, you'll pass through much of Cuba's most beautiful scenery.

DAY 1

Arrive **Havana**'s José Martí International Airport; transfer to a hotel or *casa particular* in the Habana Vieja or Vedado districts.

DAY 2

This morning, make your way to **Playas del Este** for a day with the locals at the capital city's beaches. The best section by far is **Playa Mégano.** Return to Havana for the evening.

DAY 3

Hire a car or transfer by Víazul bus or train then taxi to **Cayo Coco.** You have a wide choice of all-inclusive resorts, all supplied with water sports from Jet Skis to Hobie Cats.

DAY 4

Relax all day on Cayo Coco, perhaps with time for some scuba diving.

DAY 5

If you arrived in Cayo Coco by bus, rent a scooter or car for a day excursion to neighboring **Cayo Guillermo,** where the best of several beaches is Playa El Paso.

DAY 6

With your hired car (there are plenty available on Cayo Coco), head east to **Cayo Sabinal.** After the luxe of Cayo Coco, Sabinal might seem like a comedown, but I adore its reclusive setting, with only a collection of extremely rustic huts for accommodation, and a simple thatched restaurant where basic seafood is served. Scuba divers might want to skip Sabinal and head the short distance to **Playa Santa Lucía,** renowned for its spectacular marine life.

DAY 7

Today, head west via the Carretera Central and the cities of Camagüey, Ciego de Ávila, and Sancti Spíritus. Arrive in **Trinidad** in the late afternoon, with time to explore this quintessentially colonial city.

DAY 8

This morning you'll want to explore Trinidad some more before making the short journey to nearby **Playa Ancón.** The scuba diving here is superb, and there's a dive shop at the Hotel Playa Ancón. Return to Trinidad via the small beach at **Boca,** where the mood is entirely different. Though the beach is less appealing, the setting across the bay, with the Sierra Maestra as a backdrop, is fabulous, and the scene is lively, as Boca is the beach for *trinitarios.*

DAY 9

Today, return to Havana.

DAY 10

Transfer to the airport for your departure flight. Or, if you choose to extend your stay, fly to **Cayo Largo** for one or two days at this tiny cay where the beaches are as good as any in Cuba. There are plenty of water sports, but no Cubans are allowed.

CARS, CIGARS, AND CABARETS

So you enjoy indulging your fancies and fantasies à la Ernest Hemingway? Nothing wrong with that. Cuba is the mother lode for anyone who loves classic American autos, fine cigars, quality rums, and Las Vegas–style cabaret revues. Before 1959, Havana was the hottest spot in the Caribbean, notorious for its glittering cabarets, smooth rum, and chrome-laden Cadillacs. The good news is that the tail fins of '57 Eldorados still glint beneath the floodlit mango trees of nightclubs such as the Tropicana, the open-air extravaganza now in its seventh decade of stiletto-heeled paganism. OK, big spender, let the fun begin.

DAY 1

Arrive **Havana**'s José Martí International Airport; transfer to a hotel or *casa particular* in the Habana Vieja or Vedado districts.

DAY 2

This morning concentrate your focus around **Parque Central,** where the highlight will be a guided tour of the **Partagás cigar factory.** After buying some premium smokes, head to either the earthy art deco bar in the **Edificio Bacardí** or the sophisticated bar in the **Hotel Saratoga**

to enjoy your stogie with a Cuba libre, then rent a classic 1950s auto from Gran Car and set out for a tour of the city. This evening, enjoy dinner at the Comedor de Aguiar restaurant in the Hotel Nacional, then thrill to the sexy spectacle of the hotel's Cabaret Parisien.

DAY 3

Today, follow Hemingway's ghost. Drive out to the village of San Miguel del Padrón and the Museo Ernest Hemingway, in the author's former home. Afterwards, head to Cojímar for a seafood lunch at La Terraza restaurant, once popular with Papa and his former skipper, the late local resident Gregorio Fuentes. Return to Havana for a *mojito* and stogie at La Bodeguita del Medio. Explore Plaza de la Catedral and Plaza de Armas, being sure to stop in at the Hotel Ambos Mundos (Room 511, where Hemingway was a long-time guest, is a museum) and the Museo de Ron, a splendid museum giving insight into production of Cuba's fine rums. This evening, sample the daiquiris at El Floridita.

DAY 4

Rent an Audi from Rex car rental (the company has chauffeur service) for a day trip to Pinar del Río. Visit the tobacco fields of Valle de Viñales, and the Finca El Pinar San Luís, *finca* of Alejandro Robaina, a living legend after whom the Cuban state even named a brand of cigar. Return to Havana this evening and dinner at El Aljibe. Share fine cigars and *añejo* rums with connoisseur cigar lovers at the Casa del Habano, in Miramar.

DAY 5

Head out to Marina Hemingway for a full-day sportfishing for blue marlin in Hemingway's "great blue river." This evening, enjoy dinner at La Guarida, Havana's chicest private restaurant. If you still have energy after a day battling game fish, take a taxi to the Macumba Habana cabaret and disco.

DAY 6

This morning visit Fábrica El Laguito, where Cohibas (Cuba's premier cigar) are handmade. Then head to nearby Club Habana, a private and very chic members club (open to nonmembers for a fee) where you can relax on the fine beach, partake of water sports, and sample cocktails and fine cigars. After dinner at Cocina de Lilliam *paladar* head to the Tropicana nightclub for the most sizzling, sauciest cabaret in Cuba.

DAY 7

Transfer to the airport for your departure flight.

10 BEST SCENIC DRIVES

Cuba is a visual delight and anyone who enjoys driving (and can handle the sometimes daunting obstacles that pave the way) will thrill to the following scenic drives.

Pinar del Río Province

Mariel to Valle de Viñales via Circuito Norte: Winding ridge-top drive between mountain and sea, with quintessential rural scenery. The jade-colored waters make a startling contrast to the forested Sierra del Rosario. At San Vicente, turn south for Viñales, passing between *mogotes* to enter the most beautiful setting in Cuba. You might break this five-hour drive with a detour to Las Terrazas for a meal (there are few other dining options en route), or even overnight at the Hotel La Moka, with time for visiting the local artisan community and hiking the forested trails.

Viñales to Guane via Sumidero: This mountain drive through a valley farmed with tobacco shows off rural Cuba at its most scenic. Much of the terrain resembles that of Viñales, with ox-drawn ploughs and thatched *bohíos* (peasant homes) adding to the romantic time-warp effect. The road is badly potholed, however, and there are no restaurants or places to buy food whatsoever. And don't forget your camera!

Sancti Spíritus Province

Chambas to Caibarién via Circuito Norte: This route (which begins in Ciego de Ávila Province and ends in Villa Clara Province, or vice versa) offers quintessentially Cuban rural scenery: tobacco fields tended by ox-drawn plows, shaded by royal palms, with rustic *bohíos* in the lee of mountains. En route, stop at Jaguajay to visit the Monumento y Museo Camilo Cienfuegos. Westbound, end your trip with an overnight in Cayo Santa María, partaking of the gorgeous beaches.

Trinidad to Sancti Spíritus via Circuito Sur: This roller-coaster ride leads through swathes of lime-green sugarcane in the Valle de los Ingenios, where you should call in to climb the tower at Hacienda Iznaga. Here, a former hacienda now serves traditional Cuban meals. Further east you'll pass the rugged heights of the Alturas de Banao.

Cienfuegos and Villa Clara Provinces

Trinidad to Santa Clara via Manicaragua: Mountain drive with steep climbs and hairpin turns winds through forests (south side) and rolling tobacco country (north side). The distance is short, so you don't need to worry about accommodation en route. Drive cautiously on the ascent to Topes de Collantes, as the switchback road can be treacherous in the bends.

Holguín Province

Rafael Freyre to Flor Pérez: Wheel-bending potholes don't deter from the enjoyment of this short drive past dramatic *mogotes,* palm-shaded *bohíos,* and tobacco fields tended by *guajiros* in straw hats and linens. It's a lonesome drive (you don't want a flat tire!). Westbound, you can overnight in Holguín or Gibara; eastbound head for Guardalavaca.

Guardalavaca to Banes via Carretera 6-241: This road wends between soaring *mogotes,* with stands of royal palms in the vales, and more ox-drawn plows and endearing rusticity than you can shake a stick at. An interesting stop en route is the Museo Aborigén Chorro de Maíta, Cuba's most important aboriginal site.

Granma Province

Bartolomé Masó to Marea del Portillo: A four-wheel drive challenge via the Sierra Maestra, with steep, looping road in awful condition, but the staggering mountain vistas are topped by views down over the coast and sea. The beach "resort" of Marea del Portillo offers a choice of accommodations, plus food (there is otherwise none en route).

Granma and Santiago Provinces

Marea del Portillo to Santiago de Cuba: A lonesome drive featuring awesome coastal scenery, with the jade-colored sea hemmed in by cloud-tipped mountains. Copper-colored cliffs loom massively out of the sea, with Cuba's highest peaks within fingertip distance beyond the stark low-desert plains. There is no habitation, not a single hamlet, for miles, but food (and accommodation, if you wish) are eventually available at the town of Chivírico, two-thirds of the way to Santiago de Cuba.

Guantánamo Province

Cajobabo to Baracoa via La Farola: An awesomely steep ascent through the pine-clad Sierra Cristal, with snaking bends and occasional pullouts for savoring the vistas. On the north side of the mountain, the road loops down through more jungly terrain. The weather is often inclement, and it can be cold near the summit, where the only food en route is available (sometimes) at a roadside shack billing itself as a café.

HAVANA

Havana (pop. 2.2 million), political, cultural, and industrial heart of the nation, lies 150 kilometers (93 miles) due south of Florida on Cuba's northwest coast. It is built on the west side of a sweeping bay with a narrow funnel entrance—Bahía de la Habana—and extends west 12 kilometers to the Río Jaimanitas and south for an equal distance.

Countless writers have commented on the exhilarating sensation that engulfs visitors to this most beautiful and beguiling of Caribbean cities. The potency of Havana's appeal is owed to a quality that "runs deeper than the stuff of which travel brochures are made. It is irresistible and intangible," writes Juliet Barclay—as if, adds Arnold Samuelson, recalling his first visit to Havana in 1934, "everything you have seen before is forgotten, everything you see

and hear then being so strange you feel… as if you had died and come to life in a different world." The city's ethereal mood, little changed today, is so pronounced that it finds its way into novels. "I wake up feeling different, like something inside me is changing, something chemical and irreversible. There's a magic here working its way through my veins," says Pilar, a Cuban-American character from New York who returns to Havana in Cristina García's novel *Dreaming in Cuban*. Set foot one time in Havana and you can only succumb to its enigmatic allure. It is impossible to resist the city's mysteries and contradictions.

Havana has a flavor all its own; a strange amalgam of colonialism, capitalism, and Communism merged into one. One of the great historical cities of the New World,

HIGHLIGHTS

((Museo Nacional de Bellas Artes: Divided into national and international sections, this art gallery competes with the world's finest (pages 53, 57).

((Capitolio Nacional: Cuba's former congressional building is an architectural glory reminiscent of Washington's own Capitol (page 54).

((Museo de la Revolución: The former presidential palace now tells the tale of the Revolution in gory detail (page 56).

((Plaza de la Catedral: This small, atmospheric plaza is hemmed in by colonial mansions and a baroque cathedral (page 59).

((Plaza de Armas: The restored cobbled plaza at the heart of Old Havana features a castle, museums, and heaps of charm (page 64).

((Plaza Vieja: Still undergoing restoration, this antique plaza offers offbeat museums, Havana's only brewpub, flashy boutiques, and heaps of ambience (page 71).

((Hotel Nacional: A splendid landmark with magnificent architecture and oodles of history, this hotel is a great place to relax with a *mojito* and cigar while soaking in the heady atmosphere of the past (page 92).

((Necrópolis Cristóbal Colón: This is one of the New World's great cemeteries, with dramatic tombstones that comprise a who's who of Cuban history (page 99).

((Parque Histórico Militar Morro-Cabaña: An imposing castle complex contains the restored Castillo de los Tres Reyes del Morro and massive Fortaleza de San Carlos de la Cabaña, with cannons in situ, soldiers in period costume, and various museums (page 119).

((Tropicana: Havana at its most sensual, the Tropicana is home to a spectacular cabaret with more than 200 performers and dancers in fantastic costumes (page 137).

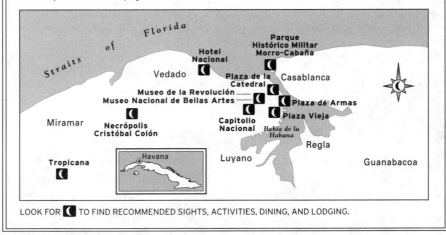

LOOK FOR ((TO FIND RECOMMENDED SIGHTS, ACTIVITIES, DINING, AND LODGING.

Havana is a far cry from the Caribbean backwaters that call themselves capitals elsewhere in the Antilles. It is obvious that Cuba was wealthy years ago to a degree that most South American and Caribbean cities were not. Havana is a city, notes architect Jorge Rigau, "upholstered in columns, cushioned by colonnaded arcades." The buildings come in a spectacular amalgam of styles—from the academic classicism of aristocratic homes, rococo residential exteriors, Moorish interiors, and art deco and art nouveau to stunning exemplars of 1950s moderne.

At the heart of the city is enchanting Habana Vieja (Old Havana), a living museum inhabited by 60,000 people and containing perhaps the finest collection of Spanish-colonial buildings in all the Americas. Baroque churches, convents, and castles that could have been transposed from Madrid or Cádiz still reign majestically over squares embraced by the former palaces of Cuba's ruling gentry and cobbled streets still haunted by Ernest Hemingway's ghost.

Hemingway's house, Finca Vigía, is one of dozens of museums dedicated to the memory of great men and women. And although most of the older monuments—those of politically incorrect heroes—were pulled down, at least they were replaced by dozens of grandiose monuments to those on the correct side of history.

Street names and monuments may have been changed, but balmy city streets with walls in faded tropical pastels still smolder gold in the waxing sun. Sunlight still filters through stained-glass *mediopuntos* to dance on the cool marble floors. And time cannot erase the sound of the "jalousies above the colonnades creaking in the small wind from the sea," in the words of Graham Greene. "True, [Havana] was

disheveled and shabby," wrote Brenda Loree, "but in the manner of a beautiful woman who had let herself go. You could still tell that she had good bones."

Fortunately, the heart of Habana Vieja has been in the midst of an impressive restoration for over a decade, and most of the historically important structures have been given facelifts, or better. Some have even metamorphosed into boutique hotels. Nor is there a shortage of 1950s-era modernist hotels steeped in Mafia associations. And hundreds of *casas particulares* provide an opportunity to live life at least partially alongside the *habaneros* themselves. There's something for every budget, although most hotels are overpriced, some outrageously so. As for food, Havana is the only place in Cuba where you can dine well every night of the week (for a price).

Then there's the arts scene, perhaps unrivaled in Latin America. The city offers some first-rate museums and galleries. Not only formal galleries, but informal ones where contemporary artists produce unique works of amazing profundity and appeal. There are some tremendous crafts markets, and boutique stores selling hand-made Cuban perfumes. Afro-Caribbean music is everywhere, quite literally on the streets. Lovers of sizzling *salsa* have dozens of venues from which to choose. Havana even has a hot jazz scene. Classical music and ballet is world class, with numerous venues to choose from. There's even hip-hop, though the past few years have seen a cooling of the scene as the government has brought its displeasure to bear. And neither Las Vegas, Paris, or Rio de Janeiro can compare with Havana for sensational and sexy cabarets (to be sure, some venues are cheesy), with top billing now, as back in the day, being the Tropicana, with a sensational show.

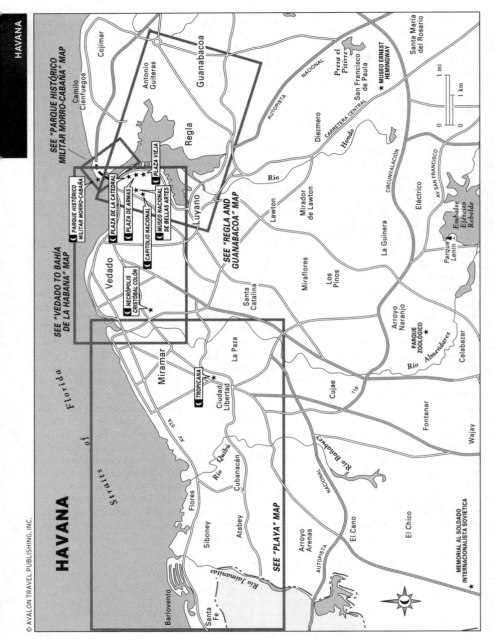

HAVANA

SEE "PARQUE HISTÓRICO MILITAR MORRO-CABAÑA" MAP

SEE "VEDADO TO BAHÍA DE LA HABANA" MAP

SEE "REGLA AND GUANABACOA" MAP

SEE "PLAYA" MAP

Straits of Florida

■ PARQUE HISTÓRICO MILITAR MORRO-CABAÑA
■ PLAZA DE LA CATEDRAL
■ PLAZA DE ARMAS
■ CAPITOLIO NACIONAL
■ MUSEO NACIONAL DE BELLAS ARTES
■ NECRÓPOLIS CRISTÓBAL COLÓN
■ TROPICANA

★ MUSEO ERNEST HEMINGWAY

★ PARQUE ZOOLÓGICO

★ MEMORIAL AL SOLDADO INTERNACIONALISTA SOVIÉTICA

Barlovento · Santa Fe · Siboney · Atabey · Flores · Cubanacán · Río Quibú · Río Jaimanitas · Miramar · Ciudad Libertad · Vedado · La Paza · Santa Catalina · Plaza Vieja · Luyano · Regla · Guanabacoa · Cojimar · Camilo Cienfuegos · Antonio Guiteras · Río · Lawton · Mirador de Lawton · Miraflores · Los Pinos · La Guinera · Arroyo Naranjo · Almendares · Río · Calabazar · Cujae · Fontanar · Wajay · El Cano · El Chico · Arroyo Arenas · Río Bumbuey

Presa el Pitirre · San Francisco de Paula · Diezmero · Hondo · CARRETERA CENTRAL · CIRCUNVALACIÓN · Eléctrico · AV SAN FRANCISCO · Embalse Ejército Rebelde · Parque Lenin · Santa María del Rosario

AUTOPISTA NACIONAL

1 mi
1 km
0   0

N

Planning Your Time

The vast majority of visitors to Cuba spend at least some time in Havana (beachgoers who visit Havana for a cursory visit may regret not spending longer). For many, the city is a worthy destination unto itself, like London or Paris. Havana is so large and ancient, and the sights to be seen so many, that one week is the bare minimum needed.

Metropolitan Havana sprawls over 740 square kilometers (286 square miles) and incorporates 15 *municipios* (municipalities). Like all fine cities, Havana is a collection of neighborhoods, each with its own distinct character that owes much to the century that each developed. Since the city is so spread out, it is best to explore Havana in sections, concentrating your time on the three main districts of touristic interest—Habana Vieja, Vedado, and Miramar—in that order.

If you have only one or two days in Havana, then I recommend an organized city tour offered by Havanatur or a similar agency. This will provide an overview of all the major sites. Concentrate the balance of your time around Parque Central, **Plaza de la Catedral,** and **Plaza de Armas.** Your checklist of must-sees should include the **Capitolio Nacional,** Gran Teatro, Partagás cigar factory, **Museo de la Revolución, Museo Nacional de Bellas Artes,** the Catedral de la Habana, and the Museo de la Ciudad de la Habana (in the Palacio de los Capitanes Generales).

For visitors who intend to linger in the city, give most of your time to Habana Vieja (Old Havana), the original colonial city within the 17th-century city walls (now demolished). The area deserves a minimum of three or four days; more if you want to see every museum, castle, and other place of interest lining its cobbled streets and plazas. You might base yourself here in one of the charming historic hotel conversions close to the main sights of interest. Be sure to journey across the harbor to visit **Parque Histórico Militar**

the Capitolio Nacional, from the roof of the Hotel Saratoga

© CHRISTOPHER P. BAKER

Morro-Cabaña, featuring two restored castles attended by soldiers in period costume.

Centro Habana has many *casas particulares* but few sites of interest and its rubble-strewn, dimly lit streets aren't the safest. Skip Centro for Vedado, the modern heart of the city that evolved in the early 20th century, with many ornate mansions in Beaux-Arts and art nouveau style. Its leafy streets make for great walking. Many of the city's best *casas particulares* are here, as are a majority of businesses, *paladares,* hotels, and nightclubs. The **Hotel Nacional,** Universidad de la Habana, Cementerio Colón, and Plaza de la Revolución are among the prime sights not to miss.

If you're interested in Beaux-Arts, art deco, or even 1950s moderne architecture, then once-glamorous Miramar, Cubanacán, and Siboney regions, west of Vedado, are worth exploring. Miramar also has several excellent restaurants, deluxe hotels, and fine beaches, plus Cuba's preeminent cigar factory and some of my favorite nightspots.

Most other sections of Havana are run-down residential districts of little interest to tourists. A few exceptions lie on the east side of Havana harbor. Regla and neighboring Guanabacoa are together a center of *santería* and Afro-Cuban music. The 18th-century fishing village of Cojímar has Hemingway associations, and the nearby community of San Miguel de Padrón is where the great author lived for twenty years. A visit to his home, Finca Vigía, today the Museo Ernest Hemingway, is de rigueur. About 15 kilometers east of the city, a series of long, white-sand beaches—the Playas del Este—prove tempting on hot summer days. (For more information about Cojímar, San Miguel de Padrón, Playas del Este, and other sites that lie beyond the *circunvalación*—a freeway that rings the city—see the *Greater Havana and Havana Province* chapter.)

Despite Havana's great size, most sights of interest are highly concentrated, and most exploring is best done on foot. Ideally you'll want wheels for touring beyond Habana Vieja. The taxi system is efficient and fairly priced, although public transport is mostly a nightmare, as elsewhere in Cuba.

Don't restrict your wandering to daylight hours. There is always life on the streets, 24/7.

All touristed areas are patrolled by police.

History

The city was founded in July 1515 as San Cristóbal de la Habana, and was located on the south coast, where Batabanó stands today. The site was a disaster. On November 25, 1519, the settlers moved to the shore of the flask-shaped Bahía de la Habana. Its location was so advantageous that in July 1553 the city replaced Santiago de Cuba as the capital of the island.

Havana's sheltered harbor became the key to the New World. Every spring and summer, Spanish treasure ships returning from the Americas crowded into Havana's harbor before setting off for Spain in an armed convoy—*la flota*. By the turn of the 18th century, Havana was the third-largest city in the New World after Mexico City and Lima. The 17th and 18th centuries saw a surge of pious energy and ecclesiastical construction. The wealth of the Americas helped fill the churches and convents with gold and silver.

In 1762, the English captured Havana but ceded it back to Spain the following year. The Spanish lost no time in building the largest fortress in the Americas—San Carlos de la Cabaña. Under the supervision of the new Spanish governor, the Marqués de la Torre, the city attained a new focus and rigorous architectural harmony. The first public gas lighting arrived in 1768, along with a workable system of aqueducts. Most of the streets were cobbled. Along them, wealthy merchants and plantation owners erected beautiful mansions graced with baroque stonework fitted inside with every luxury in European style.

By the mid-19th century, Havana was bursting its seams. In 1863, the city walls came tumbling down, less than a century after they were completed. New districts went up, and graceful boulevards pushed into the surrounding countryside, lined with a parade of *quintas* fronted by classical columns. By the mid-1800s, Havana had achieved a level of modernity that surpassed that of Madrid. (Havana owes much of its modern face to Governor Miguel Tacón y Rosique, who initiated a brisk program of unbridled construction. Tacón had a rival: the Conde de Villanueva, the *criollo*, or Cuban-born, administrator of the royal estates. Their unquenchable animosity fueled a contest to erect public and rival edifices as expressions of Spanish and disaffected *criollo* pride.)

Following the Spanish-Cuban-American War, Havana entered a new era of prosperity.

THE MOB IN HAVANA

For three decades, the Mafia had dealings in Cuba, and prerevolutionary Havana will forever be remembered for its presence.

During U.S. Prohibition (1920–33), mobsters such as Al Capone had contracted with Cuban refineries to supply molasses for their illicit rum factories. When Prohibition ended, the Mob turned to gambling. The Mafia's interests were represented by Meyer Lansky, the Jewish mobster from Miami who arrived in 1939 and struck a deal with Fulgencio Batista, Cuba's strongman president – "the best thing that ever happened to us," Lansky told national crime syndicate boss Salvatore "Lucky" Luciano. Lansky, acting as lieutenant for Luciano, took over the Oriental Park racetrack and the casino at Havana's Casino Nacional, where he ran a straight game that attracted high rollers.

World War II effectively put an end to the Mob's business, which was relatively small scale at the time. Lansky returned to Florida; Batista followed him in 1944 when he lost to Ramón Grau in the national election. Lansky's aboveboard operation soon withered in the Mob's absence, replaced by rigged casinos, and Havana's gambling scene developed a bad reputation.

Following the war, the United States deported Luciano to Italy. In 1946, he moved to Cuba, where he intended to establish a gambling and narcotics operation and regain his status as head of the U.S. Mob. He called a summit in Havana's Hotel Nacional. The meeting was immortalized in *The Godfather*, and the official cover, records Alan Ryan, "was that it was meant to honor a nice Italian boy from Hoboken called Frank Sinatra," who went down to Havana to say thanks. The United States, however, pressured Grau to deport Luciano back to Italy. Before leaving, Luciano named Lansky head of operations in Cuba.

The Mob's Cuba presence was given a boost when Florida's casinos were closed down, followed by a federal campaign to suppress the Mob. Mobsters decided Cuba was the place to be. A new summit was called at Batista's house in Daytona Beach, attended by Cuban politicians and military brass. A deal was struck: Batista would return to Cuba, regain power, and open the doors to large-scale gambling. In return, he and his crooked pals would receive a piece of the take. A gift of US$250,000 personally delivered by Lansky helped convince President Grau to step aside, and on March 10, 1952, Batista again occupied the presidential palace. New laws were quickly enacted to attract investment in hotels and casinos, and banks were set up as fronts to channel money into the hands of Cuban politicos.

The "family" headed by Cuban-Italian Amleto Batistti controlled the heroin and cocaine routes to the United States and an emporium of illegal gambling from Batistti's base at the Hotel Sevilla. Tampa's Mafia boss, Santo Trafficante Jr., operated the Sans Souci casino-nightclub, plus the casinos in the Capri, Comodoro, Deauville, and Sevilla-Biltmore Hotels. Watching over everyone was Lansky, who ran the Montmartre Club and the Internacional Club of the Hotel Nacional. Anything was permissible: gambling, pornography, drugs. Nonetheless, no frivolities were allowed. Games were regulated, and cardsharps and cheats were sent packing, although cocaine and prostitutes were supplied to high rollers. (In 1957, Mob boss Santo Trafficante claims to have set John F. Kennedy up with a private party, supplying three prostitutes in a special suite in the Hotel Comodoro.)

The tourists flocked. Lansky's last act was to build the ritziest hotel and casino in Cuba – the US$14 million Hotel Riviera and Gold Leaf Casino, which opened on December 10, 1958. Once Castro took power, the casinos were closed down and in June 1959, Lansky, Trafficante, and other "undesirable aliens" were kicked out of Cuba. Said Lansky: "I crapped out."

The city spread out, its perimeter enlarged by parks, boulevards, civic spaces, and dwellings in eclectic, neoclassical, and revivalist styles, while older residential areas settled into an era of decay.

By the 1950s Havana was a wealthy and thoroughly modern city on a par with Buenos Aires and Montevideo, and had acquired skyscrapers such as the Focsa building and the Hilton (now the Habana Libre). Ministries were being moved to a new center of construction, the Plaza de la República (today the Plaza de la Revolución), inland from Vedado. Gambling found a new lease on life, and casinos flourished.

Following the Revolution, a mass exodus of the wealthy and the middle class began, inexorably changing the face of Havana. Tourists also got the message, dooming Havana's hotels, restaurants, and other businesses to bankruptcy.

In 1959 Havana was a highly developed city with a large and prospering middle class and vigorous culture. Nonetheless, festering slums and shanty towns marred the suburbs. The government ordered them razed. Concrete high-rise apartment blocks were erected on the outskirts, especially in Habana del Este. That accomplished, the Revolution turned its back on the city. Havana's aged housing and infrastructure, much of it already decayed, have ever since suffered benign neglect. Even the mayor of Havana has admitted that "the Revolution has been hard on the city."

Meanwhile, tens of thousands of poor peasant migrants poured into Havana from Oriente, shipped in by the Castro government to bolster Fidel's natural base of support. The settlers changed the city's demographic profile, as most of the immigrants were black (as many as 400,000 *"palestinos,"* immigrants from Santiago and the eastern provinces, live in Havana, their presence resented by a large segment of *habaneros*).

The revolutionary government has since established a preservation program for Habana Vieja and the Centro Nacional de Conservación, Restauración, y Museología was created to inventory Havana's historic sites and implement a restoration program that would return much of the ancient city to pristine splendor (see the sidebar *Restoring Old Havana* in this chapter).

Sights – Habana Vieja

Habana Vieja (4.5 square km) is defined by the limits of the early colonial settlement that lay within fortified walls. The legal boundary of Habana Vieja includes the Paseo de Martí (colloquially called the Prado) and everything east of it.

Habana Vieja is roughly shaped like a diamond, with the Castillo de la Punta its northerly point. The Prado runs south at a gradual gradient from the Castillo de la Punta to Parque Central and, beyond, Parque de la Fraternidad, from where Avenida de la Bélgica runs southeast, tracing the old city wall to the harborfront at the west end of Desamparados. East of Castillo de la Punta, Avenida Carlos Manuel de Céspedes (Avenida del Puerto) runs along the harbor channel and curls south to Desamparados.

The original settlement developed along an axis that extended roughly north–south from Castillo de la Real Fuerza to Plaza Vieja. Here are the major sites of interest, centered on the Plaza de Armas and the smaller but more imposing Plaza de la Catedral. Each square has its own flavor. The plazas and surrounding streets shine after a complete restoration, their structures newly painted, like confections in stone.

The restoration now extends to the area east of Avenida de Bélgica and southwest of Plaza Vieja, between Calles Brasil and Merced. This was the great ecclesiastical center of colonial Havana and is replete with churches and convents.

In the 20th century, many grandiose structures went up around Parque Central. Today, the park is the social hub of Habana Vieja, and forms a nexus for sightseeing in the region.

Habana Vieja is a living museum—as many as 60,000 people live within the confines of the old city wall—and suffers from inevitable ruination brought on by the tropical climate, hastened since the Revolution by years of neglect. The grime of centuries has been soldered by tropical heat into the chipped cement and faded pastels. Beyond the restored areas, Habana Vieja is a quarter of sagging, mildewed walls and half-collapsed balconies. You'll frequently find humble and haughty side by side, since for most of the colonial period, areas were socially mixed.

The much-deteriorated (mostly residential) southern half of Habana Vieja has relatively few sights; take care with your possessions when walking this area.

PASEO DE MARTÍ (PRADO)

Paseo de Martí, colloquially known as the Prado, is a kilometer-long tree-lined boulevard that slopes southward, uphill, from the harbor mouth to Parque Central.

The beautiful boulevard was initiated by the Marquis de la Torre in 1772 and completed in 1852, when it had the name Alameda de Isabella II. It lay *extramura* (outside the old walled city) and was Havana's most notable thoroughfare. Mansions of aristocratic families rose on each side and it was a sign of distinction to live here. The *paseo*—the daily carriage ride—along the boulevard was an important social ritual, with bands positioned at regular intervals to play to the colorful parade of *volantas* (carriages). In time, the Prado lost its luster as the rich moved to new neighborhoods.

French landscape artist Forestier remodeled the Prado to its present form in 1929. It is guarded by eight bronze lions, and its central median is an elevated walkway. An ornate wall borders the path, with alcoves inset into each side containing marble benches carved with scroll motifs. At night it is lit by brass gas lamps with globes atop wrought-iron lampposts in the shape of griffins. Schoolchildren sit beneath shade trees, listening attentively to lessons presented alfresco. An art fair is held on Sundays.

© CHRISTOPHER P. BAKER

bronze lion at the base of the Prado

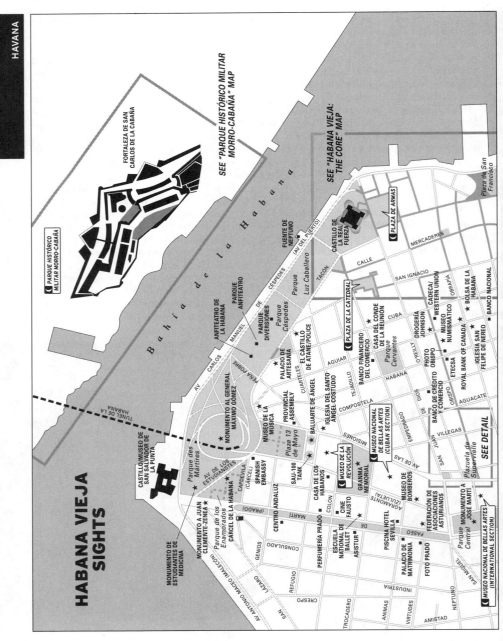

HABANA VIEJA SIGHTS

PARQUE HISTÓRICO MILITAR MORRO-CABAÑA

FORTALEZA DE SAN CARLOS DE LA CABAÑA

SEE "PARQUE HISTÓRICO MILITAR MORRO-CABAÑA" MAP

SEE "HABANA VIEJA: THE CORE" MAP

Bahía de la Habana

Plaza de San Francisco

MERCADERES

PLAZA DE ARMAS

CASTILLO DE LA REAL FUERZA

FUENTE DE NEPTUNO

CALLE

SAN IGNACIO

Parque Luz Caballero

TACÓN (AV. DEL PUERTO)

CÉSPEDES

PLAZA DE LA CATEDRAL

CASA DEL CONDE DE LA REUNIÓN

CUBA

DROGERÍA JOHNSON

PARQUE ANFITEATRO

ANFITEATRO DE LA HABANA

Parque Céspedes

PARQUE DIVERSIONES

BANCO FINANCIERO DEL COMERCIO

AGUIAR

Parque Cervantes

MUSEO NUMISMÁTICO

O'REILLY

PHOTO OBISPO

IGLESIA SAN FELIPE DE NEREO

MANUEL DE

MUSEO

PALACIO DE ARTESANÍA

CUARTELES EL CASTILLO DE ATANE/POLICE

ETECSA

ROYAL BANK OF CANADA

BANCO NACIONAL

AV. CARLOS

PEÑA POBRE

HABANA

BANCO DE CRÉDITO Y COMERCIO

OBISPO

AGUACATE

BALUARTE DE ÁNGEL

IGLESIA DEL SANTO ÁNGEL COSTUDIO

TEJADILLO

MUSEO DE LA MÚSICA

PROVINCIAL ASSEMBLY

COMPOSTELA

DIOS

EMPEDRADO

MONUMENTO AL GENERAL MÁXIMO GÓMEZ

Plaza 13 de Mayo

MUSEO NACIONAL DE BELLAS ARTES (CUBAN SECTION)

SAN JUAN

VILLEGAS

SEE DETAIL

MISIONES

AV. DE LOS ESTUDIANTES

CAPDEVILA

SPANISH EMBASSY

SAU-100 TANK

MUSEO DE LA REVOLUCIÓN

AV. DE LAS

SAN

Plazuela de Supervielle

Parque des Mártires

(CÁRCEL)

MUSEO DE BOMBEROS

AGRAMONTE (ZULUETA)

GRANMA MEMORIAL

CASTILLO/MUSEO DE SAN SALVADOR DE LA PUNTA

CASA DE LOS HABANOS

COLÓN

CINE FAUSTO

FEDERACIÓN DE ASOCIACIONES ASTURIANOS

AV. DE LOS ESTUDIANTES

CENTRO ANDALUZ

MARTÍ (PRADO)

Parque MONUMENTO A JOSÉ MARTÍ

MONUMENTO A JUAN CLEMENTE ZENEA

Parque de los Enamorados

CÁRCEL DE LA HABANA

ESCUELA NATIONAL DE BALLET ASISTUR

PISCINA HOTEL SEVILLA

Parque Central

PERFUMERÍA PRADO

PALACIO DE MATRIMONIA

PASEO DE

MUSEO NACIONAL DE BELLAS ARTES (INTERNATIONAL SECTION)

MONUMENTO DE ESTUDIANTES DE MEDICINA

FOTO PRADO

GENIOS

CONSULADO

CAPDEVILA

AV. ANTONIO MACEO (MALECÓN)

SAN LÁZARO

REFUGIO

CRESPO

TROCADERO

ANIMAS

VIRTUDES

INDUSTRIA

AMISTAD

NEPTUNO

SAN MIGUEL

SAN

TÚNEL DE LA HABANA

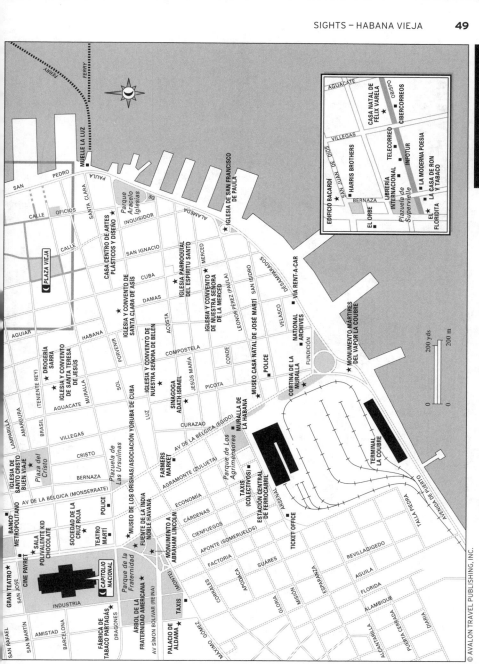

© AVALON TRAVEL PUBLISHING, INC.

HABANA VIEJA: THE CORE

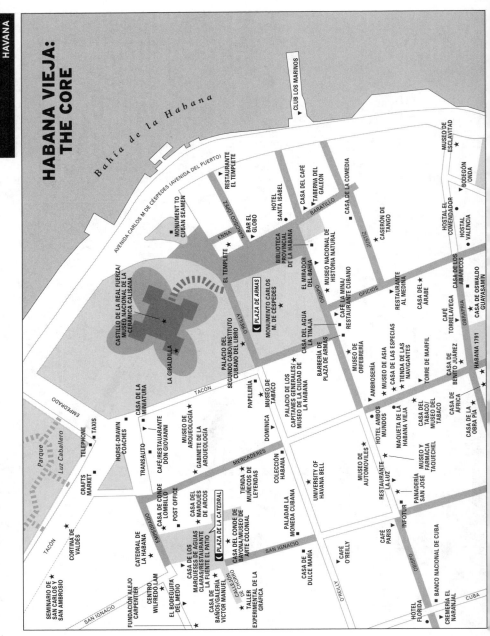

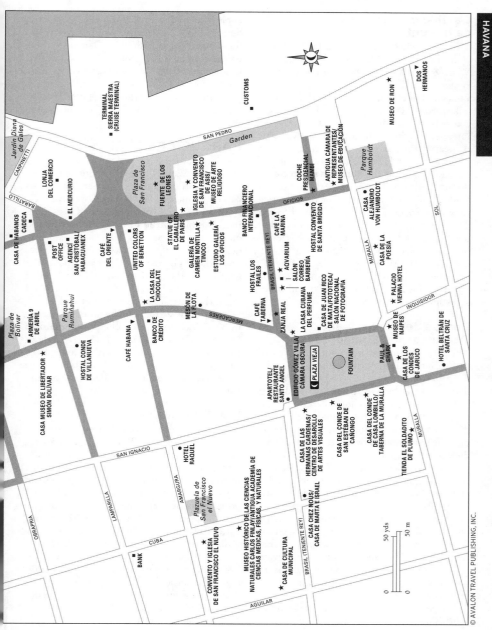

TERMINAL (SIERRA MAESTRA (CRUISE TERMINAL))

CUSTOMS

DOS HERMANOS ★

MUSEO DE RON ★

SAN PEDRO

Garden

Jardin Diana de Gales

CARPINETTI

BARATILLO

Plaza de San Francisco

LONJA DEL COMERCIO ■

EL MERCURIO ■

FUENTE DE LOS LEONES ★

IGLESIA Y CONVENTO DE SAN FRANCISCO DE ASÍS/ MUSEO DE ARTE RELIGIOSO ★

COCHE PRESIDENCIAL MAMBÍ

ANTIGUA CÁMARA DE REPRESENTANTES/ MUSEO DE EDUCACIÓN ★

Parque Humboldt

CASA ALEJANDRO VON HUMBOLDT ●

SOL

CASA DE HABANOS ■ CADECA ■

POST OFFICE ■

AGENCI ■ SAN CRISTÓBAL HABAGUANEX

CAFÉ DEL ORIENTE ■

UNITED COLORS OF BENETTON ●

STATUE OF EL CABALLERO DE PARÍS ★

GALERÍA DE CARMEN MONTILLA TIÑOCO ★

ESTUDIO GALERÍA LOS OFICIOS ★

BANCO FINANCIERO INTERNACIONAL

OFICIOS

CAFÉ LA MARINA ▼

HOSTAL CONVENTO DE SANTA BRÍGIDA ■

CASA DE LA POESÍA ★

MURALLA

PALACIO VIENNA HOTEL ★

INQUISIDOR

Plaza de Bolívar

ARMERÍA 9 DE ABRIL ■

Parque Rumiñahui

LA CASA DEL CHOCOLATE ●

MESÓN DE LA FLOTA ●

CAFÉ TABERNA ▼

HOSTAL LOS FRAILES ★

BRASIL (TENIENTE REY)

ZANJA REAL

AQUARIUM ★

SALON CORREO BARBERÍA

LA CASA CUBANA DEL PERFUME ★

CASA DE JUAN RICO DE MATA/FOTOTECA/ SALÓN NACIONAL DE FOTOGRAFÍA ★

MERCADERES

CASA MUSEO DE LIBERTADOR ★ SIMÓN BOLÍVAR

HOSTAL CONDE DE VILLANUEVA ★

CAFÉ HABANA ▼

BANCO DE CRÉDITO ●

EDIFICIO GÓMEZ VILA/ CÁMARA OSCURA

ⓘ PLAZA VIEJA

FOUNTAIN

PAUL & SHARK ●

CASA DE LOS CONDES DE JARUCO ★

MUSEO DE NAIPES ★

HOTEL BELTRÁN DE SANTA CRUZ ★

APARTOTEL/ RESTAURANTE SANTO ÁNGEL ★

HOTEL RAQUEL ●

SAN IGNACIO

AMARGURA

Plazuela de San Francisco el Nuevo

CASA DE LAS HERMANAS CÁRDENAS/ CENTRO DE DESARROLLO DE ARTES VISUALES ★

CASA DEL CONDE DE SAN ESTEBAN DE CAÑONGO ★

CASA DEL CONDE DE CASA LOMBILLO/ TABERNA DE LA MURALLA ★

TIENDA EL SOLDADITO DE PLOMO ★

MURALLA

LAMPARILLA

OBRAPRIA

CUBA

BANK ■

CASA CHEZ NOUS/ CASA DE MARTÍ E ISRAEL ●

MUSEO HISTÓRICO DE LAS CIENCIAS NATURALES CARLOS FINLAY/ANTIGUA ACADEMIA DE CIENCIAS MÉDICAS, FÍSICAS, Y NATURALES ★

CASA DE CULTURA MUNICIPAL ★

CONVENTO Y IGLESIA ★ DE SAN FRANCISCO EL NUEVO ■

BRASIL (TENIENTE REY)

AGUILAR

50 yds

50 m

0

0

© AVALON TRAVEL PUBLISHING, INC.

Castillo de San Salvador de la Punta

This charming fortress (Av. Carlos M. de Céspedes, esq. Prado y Malecón, tel. 07/860-3196; Wed.–Sun. 10 A.M.–6 P.M.; entrance CUC3, cameras CUC2) guards the entrance to Havana's harbor channel at the base of the Prado. The fortress was initiated in 1589 directly across from the Morro castle so that the two fortresses might catch invaders in a crossfire. A great chain was slung between them each night to secure Havana harbor. Recently restored, it contains the **Museo de San Salvador de la Punta,** displaying treasures from the golden age when the riches of the Americas flowed to Spain. The air-conditioned Sala de Tesoro gleams with gold bars, chains, coins, toothpicks, and brooches, plus precious jewels, bronze astrolabes, pewter dishes, rosary beads, clay pipes, and silver *reales* ("pieces of eight"). Labels are in Spanish only. Another *sala* has naval uniforms, swords, pistols, and model ships spanning three centuries.

Parque de Mártires and Parque de los Enamorados

The parkland immediately south of the castle, on the south side of Avenida Carlos Manuel de Céspedes, at the base (and east) of the Prado, is divided in two by Avenida de los Estudiantes.

Parque de los Enamorados (Park of the Lovers), on the north side of Avenida de los Estudiantes, features a statue of an Indian couple, plus the **Monumento de Estudiantes de Medicina,** a small Grecian-style temple shading the remains of a wall used by Spanish-colonial firing squads. Here on November 27, 1871, eight medical students met their deaths after being falsely accused of desecrating the tomb of a prominent loyalist, Gonzalo Castañón. A trial found them innocent, but enraged loyalist troops—the Spanish Volunteers—held their own trial and shot the students. Elevated to the pantheon of revolutionary martyrs, the students are commemorated with a national holiday each November 27.

Parque de Mártires (Martyr's Park), on the south side of Avenida de los Estudiantes, oc-cupies the ground of the former Tacón prison, built in 1838. Nationalist hero José Martí was imprisoned here in 1869–70. The prison was demolished in 1939, and the park dedicated in memory of all those who suffered for their ideals. Preserved for posterity were two of the punishment cells and the chapel used by condemned prisoners before being marched to the firing wall.

PARQUE CENTRAL

Spacious Parque Central is the social epicenter of Habana Vieja. The park—bounded by the Prado, Neptuno, Zulueta, and San Martín—is paved in pink slabs and presided over by stately royal palms, poinciana, and almond trees shading a marble **statue of José Martí.** Erected on the 10th anniversary of the national hero's death, it was sculpted by José Vilalta de Saavedra and inaugurated in 1905. Baseball fanatics gather near the Martí statue at a point called *esquina caliente* ("hot corner") to discuss and argue the intricacies of *pelota* (baseball).

The park is surrounded by hotels of historic import, including the ocher-colored **Hotel Plaza** (Zulueta #267), built as a triangle in 1909, on the northeast face of the square. Babe Ruth stayed in room 216 in 1920; the room is preserved as a museum, with his signed bat and ball in a glass case.

Hotel Inglaterra

Much of the social action happens in front of the Hotel Inglaterra (Paseo de Martí #416), which opened in 1856 and is today the oldest Cuban hotel still extant. The Café Louvre, in front of the hotel, was known in colonial days as the Acera del Louvre and was a focal point for bohemian society and for rebellion against Spanish rule. A plaque outside the hotel entrance honors the "lads of the Louvre sidewalk" who died for Cuban independence.

Inside, the hotel boasts elaborate wrought-ironwork and exquisite Mudejar-style detailing, including arabesque archways and *azulejos* (patterned tile). A highlight is the sensuous life-size bronze statue of a Spanish dancer—*La Sevillana*—in the main bar.

A WALK DOWN THE PRADO

Begin your walk of the Prado at Parque Central and Neptuno. Heading downhill, the first building of interest, the **Palacio de Matrimonio** (Prado #306, esq. Ánimas, tel. 07/862-5781; Tues.-Fri. 10 A.M.-5 P.M., Sat.-Sun. 4-5:30 P.M.), on the west side, at the corner of Ánimas, is where many of Havana's wedding ceremonies are performed. The palace boasts a magnificent neo-baroque facade and an ornate stuccoed interior that at last visit was in a desperate state of disrepair.

Up and down the Prado you'll see tiled mosaics reflecting the Moorish style that has influenced Havana's architecture through the centuries. The most stunning example is the lobby of the **Hotel Sevilla** (Trocadero #55), which is like entering a Moroccan medina. It was inspired by the Patio of the Lions at the Alhambra in Granada, Spain. The hotel opened in 1908 and became a place of repose for fashionable society. The gallery walls are festooned with black-and-white photos of famous figures who have stayed here, from singer Josephine Baker and boxer Joe Louis to Al Capone, who took the entire sixth floor (Capone occupied Room 615). The top-story restaurant is a magnificent exemplar of neo-

classical decor – perfect for sampling a Mary Pickford (rum, pineapple juice, and grenadine), invented here. The Sevilla was the setting for the comical intrigues of Wormold in Graham Greene's *Our Man in Havana*.

At Trocadero, budding dancers train for potential ballet careers in the **Escuela Nacional de Ballet** (National School of Ballet, Prado #207, e/ Colón y Trocadero, tel. 07/862-7053; call 07/803-0817 for permission to visit). Across the street, on the west side, the **Casa de los Científicos** (Prado #212, esq. Trocadero, tel. 07/862-1607), the former home of President José Miguel Gómez, first president of the Republic, is now a hotel, but you can pop in to admire the fabulous stained-glass work and chapel where locals come to make offerings.

At Prado and Colón, note the **Cine Fausto,** a modernist building with an ornamental band on its upper facade harking back to art deco; and, two blocks north, the mosaic mural of a Nubian beauty on the upper wall of the **Centro Cultural de Árabe** (between Refugio and Trocadero).

The bronze **statue of Juan Clemente-Zenea** (1832-71), at the base of the Prado, honors a patriotic poet shot for treason in 1871.

Gran Teatro

Immediately south of the Inglaterra, the Gran Teatro (Paseo de Martí #452, e/ San Rafael y Neptuno, tel. 07/861-3077; daily 9 A.M.–5 P.M.; CUC2 with guided tour) originated in 1837 as the Teatro Tacón, drawing operatic luminaries such as Enrico Caruso and Sarah Bernhardt. The current neo-baroque structure dates from 1915, when a social club—the Centro Gallego—was built around the old Teatro Tacón for the Galician community (the theater was renamed Gran Teatro).

Its exorbitantly baroque facade drips with caryatids and has four towers, each tipped by a white marble angel reaching gracefully for heaven. The entire edifice is crumbling dangerously, however, though it still functions as a theater for the National Ballet and Opera.

The main auditorium—the exquisitely decorated 2,000-seat Teatro García Lorca—features a painted dome and huge chandelier. Smaller performances are hosted in the 500-seat Sala Alejo Carpentier and the 120-seat Sala Artaud.

◖ Museo Nacional de Bellas Artes (International Section)

The international section of the National Fine Arts Museum (San Rafael, e/ Zulueta y Monserrate, tel. 07/863-9484 or 862-0140, www.museonacional.cult.cu; Tues.–Sat. 10 A.M.–6 P.M., Sun. 10 A.M.–2 P.M.; entrance CUC5, or CUC8 for both sections; guided tour CUC2) occupies the Centro Asturiano, on the southeast side of the square. The building, lavishly decorated with neoclassical motifs, was erected in 1885 but rebuilt in Renaissance style in 1927 following a fire and until recently housed the postrevolutionary People's Supreme Court, where a questionable version of justice was dispensed. A highlight is the stained-glass window above the main staircase showing Columbus's three caravels.

The art collection is displayed on five floors covering 4,800 square meters. The works are separated by nationality and span the United States, Latin America, Asia, and European masters—including Gainsborough, Goya, Murillo, Rubens, and Velásquez, and various Impressionists. The museum also boasts Latin America's richest trove of classical antiquities, including Roman, Greek, and Egyptian statuary and artworks.

A 248-seat theater hosts cultural activities.

【 Capitolio Nacional

This statuesque building (Paseo de Martí, e/ San Martín y Dragones, tel. 07/861-5519; daily 9 A.M.–7 P.M.; entrance CUC3, guided tours CUC1, cameras CUC2), one block south of Parque Central, dominates Havana's skyline. It was built between 1926 and 1929 as Cuba's Chamber of Representatives and Senate and was obsequiously designed after Washington's own Congress building. The 692-foot-long edifice is supported by flanking colonnades of Doric columns, with semicircular pavilions at each end of the building. The lofty stone cupola rises 61.75 meters, topped by a replica of 16th-century Florentine sculptor Giambologna's famous bronze Mercury in the Palazzo de Bargello.

A massive stairway—flanked by neoclassical figures in bronze by Italian sculptor Angelo Zanelli and representing Labor and Virtue—leads steeply up to a 40-meter-wide entrance portico with three tall bronze doors sculpted with 30 bas-reliefs that depict important events of Cuban history.

Inside, facing the door is the **Estatua de la República** (Statue of the Republic), a massive bronze sculpture (also by Zanelli) of Cuba's voluptuous Indian maiden. At 17.54 meters (56 feet) tall, she is the world's third-largest indoor statue (the other two are the gold Buddha in Nava, Japan, and the Lincoln Memorial in Washington, D.C.). In the center of the floor is a 24-carat diamond that marks Kilometer 0—the point from which all distances on the island are calculated. The diamond, alas, is a replica—rumor has it that the original is kept securely in Fidel's office. Above your head is the dome with its gilt-covered, barrel-vaulted ceiling carved in refulgent relief.

The 394-foot-long **Salón de los Pasos Perdidos** (Great Hall of the Lost Steps), so named because of its acoustics (the sound of your footfalls seems to retreat behind you), is inlaid with patterned marble motifs and features bronze bas-reliefs, green marble pilasters, and massive lamps on tall carved pedestals of glittering copper. Renaissance-style candelabras dangle from the arched frescoed ceiling. The semicircular Senate chamber and Chamber of Representatives are at each end; former congressional offices line the hallway; and there's a mahogany-paneled former congressional library.

The Capitolio is the headquarters of the **Academía de Ciencias** (Academy of Sciences); the library—the **Biblioteca Nacional de Ciencias y Naturales**—is on the ground floor on the Capitolio's south side (Mon.–Sat. 8 A.M.–5 P.M.).

PARQUE DE LA FRATERNIDAD AND VICINITY

Paseo de Martí (Prado) runs south from Parque Central three blocks, where it ends at the junction with Avenida Máximo Gómez (Monte). Here rises the **Fuente de la India Noble Habana**, a fountain in the middle of the Prado. Erected in 1837, the fountain is surmounted by a Carrara-marble statue of the legendary Indian queen after whom the province is named. In one hand she bears a cornucopia, in the other a shield with the arms of Havana. Four great fishes lie at her feet and occasionally spout water.

The **Asociación Cultural Yoruba de Cuba** (Prado #615, e/ Dragones y Monte, tel. 07/863-5953; Mon.–Sat. 9 A.M.–4 P.M.; CUC6) has a **Museo de los Orishas** dedicated to the various *orishas* of *santería*. It's upstairs.

VISITING HAVANA'S CIGAR FACTORIES

You'll forever remember the pungent aroma of a cigar factory, a visit to which is de rigueur. The factories, housed in fine old colonial buildings, remain much as they were in the mid-19th century. Though now officially known by ideologically sound names, they're still commonly referred to by their prerevolutionary names, which are displayed on old signs outside. Each specializes in a number of cigar brands of a particular flavor – the government assigns to certain factories the job of producing particular brands. Revolutionary slogans exhort workers to maintain strict quality.

Two antique cigar factories in Havana were recently closed. The six remaining major factories welcome visitors. Unfortunately, the tours are not well organized and often crowded with tour groups. Explanations of tobacco processes and manufacturing procedures are also sparse. Tours usually bypass the tobacco preparations and instead begin in the *galeras* (rolling rooms), then pass to the quality-control methods. Visitors therefore miss out on seeing the stripping, selecting, and dozens of other steps that contribute to producing a handmade cigar.

Tabacuba (Virtudes #609, e/ Escobar y Gervasio, Centro Habana, tel. 07/877-6861) is in charge of the industry.

THE FACTORIES

Fábrica Partagás (Calle Industria #502, e/ Dragones y Barcelona, Habana Vieja, tel. 07/862-0086 or 878-4368; 9-11 A.M. and noon-3 P.M.) offers 40-minute guided tours (CUC10).

Fábrica Corona (20 de Mayo #520, e/ Marta Abreu y Línea, Cerro, tel. 07/873-0131; Mon.-Fri. 9:30 A.M.-2:30 P.M.; CUC10 with guide) has guided tours. No cameras are permitted.

Fábrica H. Upmann (Calle 23, e/ 14 y 16) makes the famous H. Upmann brand of cigars, plus cigarettes, and is open by appointment. Visits can be arranged via Tabacuba. Note that this is *not* the original H. Upmann factory (Amistad #407, e/ Barcelona y Dragones), which no longer manufactures cigars.

Fábrica Romeo y Julieta (Padre Varela, e/ Desague y Peñal Verno, Centro Habana, tel. 07/878-1058 or 879-3927; Mon.-Fri. 8:30-11 A.M. and noon-3 P.M.; CUC10) has 30-minute tours.

Fábrica El Laguito (Av. 146 #2302, e/ 21 y 21A, Cubanacán, tel. 07/208-2486), which makes Cohibas, allows visits by appointment only. Visits can be arranged via Tabacuba.

Fábrica Héroes del Moncada (Av. 57 #13403, e/ 134 y 136, Marianao, tel. 07/260-6723) makes most major brands of export cigars, including Cohibas. Visits, by appointment only, can be arranged via Tabacuba.

The Constitution for the Republic was signed in 1901 in the **Teatro Martí** (Dragones, esq. Zulueta), one block west of the Prado. It has fallen into virtual ruin since the Revolution and awaits restoration. Around the corner, the **Sociedad de la Cruz Roja** (Red Cross Society, Zulueta, e/ Muralla y Brasil) is housed in an exquisite classical building.

Parque de la Fraternidad

This park was laid out in 1892 on an old military drill square, the Campo de Marte, to commemorate the fourth centennial of Columbus's discovery of America. By the mid-1850s, it was the site of the city's train station, terminating the railway that ran along today's Zanja and Dragones. The current layout by Forestier dates from 1928, with a redesign to celebrate the sixth Pan-American Conference, held in Havana that year.

The **Árbol de la Fraternidad Americana** (the Friendship Tree) was planted at its center on February 24, 1928, to cement goodwill between the nations of the Americas. Busts of oustanding American leaders such as Simón Bolívar as well as a statue of Abraham Lincoln look out over the comings and goings.

Palacio de Aldama

The Palacio de Aldama, on the park's far southwest corner, is a grandiose mansion built in neoclassical style in 1844 for a wealthy Basque, Don Domingo Aldama y Arrechaga. Its facade is lined by Ionic columns; its interior features murals of scenes from Pompeii; the garden courtyard features ornamental fountains. When the owner's nationalist feelings became known it was ransacked and the interior defaced in 1868 by the Spanish Volunteers militia.

Today, duly restored, it houses the **Instituto de la História del Movimiento Comunista y de la Revolución Socialista de Cuba** (Institute of the History of the Communist Movement and the Socialist Revolution of Cuba, Amistad #510, e/ Reina y Estrella, tel. 07/862-2076; Mon.–Fri. 8 A.M.–4:30 P.M.; CUC2).

Fábrica de Tabaco Partagás

A highlight of any visit to Havana is a visit to the Partagás cigar factory (Industria #502, e/ Dragones y Barcelona, tel. 07/862-0086; 9–11 A.M. and noon–3 P.M.; guided tour CUC10), on the west side of the Capitolio. The classical Spanish-style facade of this four-story structure is capped by a roofline of baroque curves topped by lions. An interior patio is surrounded by colored glass windows. Here you can see Cuba's premium cigars being hand-rolled for export. The factory specializes in full-bodied cigars such as the spicy, strongly aromatic La Gloria Cubana, Ramón Allones, the Montecristo, and, of course, the Partagás, one of the oldest of the Havana brands, started in 1843 by Catalan immigrant Don Jaime Partagás Ravelo. Partagás was murdered in 1868—some say by a rival who discovered that Partagás was having an affair with his wife—and his ghost is said to haunt the factory. The factory's showroom displays a cigar measuring 50 inches.

Guided tours (40 minutes) are offered every 15 minutes.

CALLE AGRAMONTE (ZULUETA)

Calle Agramonte, more commonly referred to by its colonial name of Zulueta, parallels the Prado and slopes gently upward from Avenida de los Estudiantes to the northeast side of Parque Central. Traffic runs one-way uphill.

On the north side of Avenida de los Estudiantes (Cárcel) is the **Monumento al General Máximo Gómez.** This massive monument of white marble by sculptor Aldo Gamba was erected in 1935 to honor the Dominican-born hero of the Cuban Wars of Independence who led the Liberation Army as commander-in-chief. Generalissimo Gómez (1836–1905) is cast in bronze, reining in his horse. Its base, supported by classical columns, features three bas-reliefs.

C Museo de la Revolución

The ornate building facing north over Plaza 13 de Mayo was initiated in 1913 to house the provincial government. Before it could be finished (in 1920), it was earmarked as the Palacio Presidencial (Presidential Palace), and Tiffany's of New York was entrusted with its interior decoration. It was designed by Belgian Paul Belau and Cuban Carlos Maruri in an eclectic style, with a lofty dome. It was from here that a string of corrupt presidents spun their webs of dissolution.

Following the Revolution, the three-story palace was converted into the Museum of the Revolution (Refugio #1, e/ Zulueta y Monserrate, tel. 07/862-4091; daily 10 A.M.–5 P.M.; CUC5, cameras free). The marble staircase leads upstairs to the Salón de los Espejos (the Mirror Room), a replica of that in Versailles (replete with paintings by Armando Menocal and other notable Cuban painters); and Salón Dorado (the Gold Room), decorated with yellow marble and gold leaf and highlighted by its magnificently decorated dome.

Rooms are divided chronologically, from the colonial period to the modern day. Maps describe the progress of the revolutionary war. Guns and rifles are displayed alongside grisly photos of dead and tortured heroes. One section is dedicated to the revolutionaries who died in an assault on the palace on March 13, 1957, when Batista escaped through a secret door, frustrating an action that turned into a bloody debacle. Don't miss the *Rincón de los Cretinos*

A WALK DOWN ZULUETA AND MONSERRATE

A stroll down Zulueta from Parque Central, returning via Monserrate, reveals several sites of interest, in addition to the "must-sees."

One block north of Parque Central, at the corner of Zulueta and Ánimas, a mosaic on the paving announces your arrival at **Sloppy Joe's,** commemorated as Freddy's Bar in Hemingway's *To Have and Have Not.* At last visit, the near-derelict building remained shuttered, its interior a dusty shambles, awaiting the restoration now sweeping Habana Vieja. Across the way is the old Cuartel de Bomberos fire station, slated in due course to house the **Museo de Bomberos** (Museum of Firemen, Zulueta #257, e/ Neptuno y Ánimas)

Immediately west of the Museo de la Revolución (see the main text) is the three-story green facade of the former **Fábrica de Tabaco La Corona** (Zulueta #106, e/ Refugio y Colón, tel./fax 07/862-6173), dating from 1888, when this cigar factory was built by the American Tobacco Company. Though the factory closed in 2004, the cigar store is still a favorite on the package-tour circuit.

As you cross Refugio, on your right is an **SAU-100 Stalin tank** fronting the Museo de la Revolución. It was supposedly used by Fidel Castro himself at the Bay of Pigs, according to the plaque. Immediately beyond is **Plaza 13 de Mayo,** a grassy park named to commemorate the ill-fated attack of the presidential palace by student martyrs on March 13, 1957. It was

laid out by French landscaper Forestier. At the base of Zulueta, at the junction with Cárcel, note the flamboyant art nouveau building housing the **Spanish Embassy.**

Turn right and cross Plaza 13 de Mayo to reach Monserrate.

At the base of Monserrate, at its junction with Calle Tacón, is the **Museo y Archivo de la Música** (Capdevila #1, tel. 07/861-9846 and 863-0052; Mon.-Sat. 10 A.M.-5:45 P.M.; CUC2), housed in the sober Casa de Pérez de la Riva, built in Italian Renaissance style in 1905. The museum traces the evolution of Cuban music since early colonial days; its collection of antique instruments includes venerable pianos and drums. In a separate room, you can listen to old scores drawn from the record library.

Following Monserrate uphill, southward, you'll pass the Iglesia del Santo Ángel Custodio (see the main text). Opposite, a semi-derelict watchtower – **Baluarte de Ángel** – erected in 1680 stands in front of Museo de la Revolución. Monserrate continues south three blocks to Edifico Bacardí and **Plazuela de Supervielle,** commemorating Dr. Manuel Fernández Supervielle, mayor of Havana during the 1940s.

One block south brings you to **Plazuela de Albear,** with a bust of Francisco de Albear, who last century engineered the Malecón and Havana's first water-drainage system. On its south side, adjoining El Floridita, is the **Casa del Ron,** where free rum samples are given.

("Corner of Cretins"), which pokes fun at Batista, Ronald Reagan, and George Bush.

The **Sala al gesto boliviano del Che y sus compañeros,** to the right of the entrance, celebrates the ill-fated efforts of Che to inspire a revolution in Bolivia.

At the rear, in the former palace gardens, is the **Granma Memorial,** preserving the vessel that brought Castro, Guevara, and other revolutionaries from Mexico to Cuba in 1956. The *Granma* is encased in a massive glass structure. It's surrounded by vehicles used in the revolutionary war: armored vehicles, the bullet-

riddled "Fast Delivery" truck used in the student commandos' assault on the Presidential Palace in 1957, and Castro's green Land Rover from the Sierra Maestra. There's also a turbine from the U-2 spy plane downed during the missile crisis in 1962, plus a naval Sea Fury and a T-34 tank.

◖ Museo Nacional de Bellas Artes (Cuban Section)

The Cuban section of the National Fine Arts Museum is housed in the soberly classical Palacio de Bellas Artes (Trocadero, e/ Zulueta y

Monserrate; tel. 07/863-9484 or 862-0140, www .museonacional.cult.cu; Tues.–Sat. 10 A.M.– 6 P.M., Sun. 10 A.M.–2 P.M.; entrance CUC5, or CUC8 for both sections; guided tour CUC2), immediately south of the Granma memorial. The museum features an atrium garden from which ramps lead up to two floors exhibiting more than 1,200 works of art; a complete spectrum of Cuban paintings, engravings, sketches, and sculptures laid out according to eight themes in 24 *salas*. Works representing the vision of early 16th- and 17th-century travelers merge into colonial-era pieces, early 20th-century Cuban interpretations of Impressionism and Surrealism, thence into works spawned by the Revolution and contemporary works, including René Portocarrero, Amelia Paláez, and Wilfredo Lam.

Also see *Museo Nacional de Bellas Artes (International Section)* in the *Parque Central* section in this chapter.

AVENIDA DE LOS MISIONES (MONSERRATE)

Avenida de los Misiones, or Monserrate as everyone knows it, parallels Zulueta one block to the east (traffic is one-way, downhill) and follows the space left by the ancient city walls after they were demolished last century. There are three sights of import.

Iglesia del Santo Ángel Custodio

This church (Monserrate y Cuarteles), immediately east of the Palacio Presidencial, sits atop a rock known as Angel Hill. The lavish Gothic church was founded in 1687 by builder-bishop Diego de Compostela. The tower dates from 1846, when a hurricane toppled the original, while the facade was reworked in neo-Gothic style in the mid-19th century. It's immaculate yet simple within: gray marble floor, modest wooden Gothic altar, statues of saints all around, pristine stained-glass windows. Cuba's national hero, José Martí, was baptized here on February 12, 1853.

The church was the setting for both the opening scene and tragic marriage scene that ends in the violent denouement on the steps of the church in the 19th-century novel *Cecilia Valdés* by Cirilo Villaverde. A bust of the author stands in the *plazuela* outside the main entrance, to the rear of the church, on the corner of Calles Compostela and Cuarteles.

Edificio Bacardí

The Bacardí Building (Monserrate #261, esq. San Juan de Díos), former headquarters of the Bacardi rum empire, is a stunning exemplar of art deco design. Designed by Cuban architect Esteban Rodríguez and finished in December 1929, it is clad in Swedish granite and local limestone. Terra-cotta of varying hues accents the design, with motifs showing Grecian nymphs and floral patterns. It is crowned by a Lego-like pyramidal bell tower topped in turn by a wrought-iron, brass-winged bat—the famous Bacardi motif.

The building now houses various offices. Access is restricted to a bar—a true gem of art deco design—to the right of the lobby, up the stairs.

The best perspectives are from the roof of the Hotel Parque Central or Hotel Plaza.

El Floridita

This famous restaurant and bar (corner of Monserrate and Calle Obispo, tel. 07/867-1300; noon–11 P.M.) has been serving food since 1819, when it was called Pina de Plata. It is haunted by Ernest Hemingway's ghost. You expect a spotlight to come on and Desi Arnaz to appear conducting a dance band, and Hemingway to stroll in as he would every morning when he lived in Havana and drank with Honest Lil, the Worst Politician, and other real-life characters from his novels.

The novelist's seat is preserved as a shrine (a chain prevents anyone from sitting on it), while a bronze bust watches over things from its pedestal beside the dark mahogany bar where Constante Ribailagua once served frozen daiquiris to the great writer (Hemingway immortalized both the drink and the venue in his novel *Islands in the Stream*) and such illustrious guests as Gary Cooper, Tennessee Williams, Marlene Dietrich, and Jean-Paul

Sartre. There's even a life-size bronze statue of Hemingway, by sculptor José Villa, leaning with its elbow upon the bar.

El Floridita has been spruced up for tourist consumption with a 1930s art deco polish. They've overpriced the place for the package-tourist crowd, but sipping a daiquiri at El Floridita is a must.

THE HARBOR CHANNEL

Throughout most of the colonial era, sea waves washed up on a beach that lined the southern shore of the harbor channel, known as the Playa de las Tortugas for the marine turtles that came ashore to lay eggs. The beach bordered what is today Calle Cuba and, eastward, Calle Tacón, which runs along the site of the old city walls forming the original waterfront. In the early 19th century, the area was extended with landfill, and a broad boulevard—**Avenida Carlos Manuel de Céspedes** (Avenida del Puerto)—was laid out along the new harborfront. **Parque Luz Caballero,** between the Avenida and Calle Tacón, is pinned by a statue of José de la Luz Caballero (1800–62), a philosopher and nationalist.

Overlooking the harborfront at the foot of Empedrado is the **Fuente de Neptuno** (Neptune Fountain), erected in 1838.

Calles Cuba and Tacón

Calle Cuba extends east from the foot of Monserrate. At the foot of Calle Cuarteles is the **Palacio de Mateo Pedroso y Florencia** (Cuba #64, e/ Tacón y Peña Pobre; free), a magnificent mansion built in Moorish style for nobleman Don Mateo Pedroso (a slave trader and former mayor) around 1780. Pedroso's home displays the typical architectural layout of period houses, with stores on the ground floor, slave quarters on the mezzanine, and the owner's dwellings above. Today it houses the **Palacio de Artesanía,** with craft shops, boutiques, and folkloric music daily 3–8 P.M.

Immediately east is **Plazuela de la Maestranza,** where a remnant of the old city wall is preserved. On its east side, in the triangle formed by the junction of Cuba, Tacón, and Chacón, is a medieval-style fortress, **El Castillo de Atane,** that today houses a police headquarters, as it has since it was built in 1941 as a pseudo-colonial confection.

The **Seminario de San Carlos y San Ambrosio** (e/ Chacón y Empedrado), a massive seminary running the length of Tacón east of El Castillo de Atane, was established by the Jesuits in 1721 and ever since has been a center for young men studying for an ecclesiastical career. Each first Sunday of October, the doors swing open and the public is admitted for the day. Mass is held Monday, Tuesday, Thursday, and Friday at 7:15 A.M. and 8:15 P.M., and Sunday 8:30 A.M. and 10:30 A.M.

A large artisans' market takes up the length of Tacón directly in front of the seminary, where an excavated site shows the foundations of the original seafront section of the city walls—here called the **Cortina de Valdés.**

Tacón opens to a tiny *plazuela* at the junction with Empedrado, where horse-drawn cabs called *calezas* offer guided tours to tourists. From here, Tacón leads to Plaza de Armas. The **Museo de Arqueología** (Tacón #12, e/ O'Reilly y Empedrado, tel. 07/861-4469; Tues.–Sat. 9 A.M.–5 P.M., Sun. 9 A.M.–1 P.M.; CUC1), displays pre-Columbian artifacts, plus a miscellany of ceramics and other household items from the early colonial years. The museum occupies Casa de Juana Carvajal, a beautiful mansion first mentioned in documents in 1644. Its most remarkable feature is a series of eccentric floor-to-ceiling murals depicting life as it was lived at the time they were painted between 1763 and 1767.

◀ PLAZA DE LA CATEDRAL

This exquisite cobbled square was the last square to be laid out in Habana Vieja. It occupied a lowly quarter where rainwater drained and refuse collected and rotted (it was originally known as the Plazuela de la Ciénaga—Little Square of the Swamp). A cistern was built here in 1587, and only in the following century was the area drained for construction. Its present texture dates from the 18th century.

The square is Habana Vieja at its most

This *santera* in her white robes adds to the atmosphere of the Plaza de la Catedral.

quintessential, the atmosphere enhanced by mulattas in traditional costume who will happily preen and pose for your camera (for a small fee). At night the setting is enhanced by the soft glow of wan lanterns. One Saturday a month, the plaza is one of the venues for the **Noche en las Plazas** *espectáculo* (see the *Entertainment and Events* section of this chapter).

Catedral San Cristóbal de la Habana

This intimate cathedral, on the north side of the plaza, is known colloquially as Catedral Colón (Columbus Cathedral) but is officially called the Catedral de la Virgen María de la Concepción Inmaculada (tel. 07/861-7771), or Virgin of the Immaculate Conception, whose statue is installed in the High Altar. The cathedral was initiated by the Jesuits in 1748. The order was kicked out of Cuba by Carlos III in 1767, but the building was eventually completed in 1777 and altered again in the early 19th century. Thus the original baroque inte-

rior (including the altar) is gone, replaced in 1814 by a new classical interior.

The baroque facade is adorned with clinging columns and ripples like a great swelling sea; Cuban novelist Alejo Carpentier thought it "music turned to stone." A royal decree of December 1793 elevated the church to a cathedral because "the beautifully carved stones of the church… are clamouring from their walls for the distinction of cathedral." On either side of the facade are mismatched towers (one fatter and taller than the other) containing bells supposedly cast with a dash of gold and silver, said to account for their musical tone.

Columns divide the rectangular church into three naves. The neoclassical main altar is very simple and made of wood. The murals above the main altar by Italian painter Guiseppe Perovani are badly deteriorated. The chapel immediately to the left has several altars, including one of Carrara marble inlaid with gold, silver, onyx, and carved hardwoods. Note, too, the wooden image of Saint Christopher, patron saint of Havana, dating to 1633.

The Spanish believed that a casket brought to Havana from Santo Domingo in 1796 and that resided in the cathedral for more than a century held the ashes of Christopher Columbus. Casket and ashes were returned to Spain in 1899. All but the partisan *habaneros* now believe that the ashes were those of Columbus's son Diego.

The cathedral is officially open Monday–Saturday 10:30 A.M.–2 P.M., Sunday 9 A.M.–noon. However, more often than not it is closed except for Mass (Mon., Tues., Thurs., and Fri. at 7:15 A.M. and 8:15 P.M., and Sun. at 8:30 A.M.).

Casa de los Marqueses de Aguas Claras

This splendid old mansion, on the northwest side of the plaza, was built during the 16th century by Governor General Gonzalo Pérez de Angulo and has since been added to by subsequent owners. Today a café occupies the *portico,* while the inner courtyard, with its fountain and grand piano amid lush palms and clinging vines, houses the Restaurante La Fuente del Patio. The restaurant extends upstairs, where members of the middle classes once dwelled in apartments. Sunlight pouring in through stained-glass *mediopuntos* saturates the floors with shifting fans of red and blue.

Casa del Conde de Bayona

This simple two-story structure faces the cathedral on the south side of the square. It's a perfect example of the traditional Havana merchant's house of the period, with side stairs and an *entresuelo* (mezzanine of half-story proportions). It was built in the 1720s for Governor General Don Luis Chacón and later passed to Pancho Marty, a former smuggler-turned-entrepreneur. In the 1930s, it housed the Havana Club Bar, which was used by Graham Greene as the setting for Wormold's meeting with Captain Segura (based on Batista's real-life police chief, Ventura) in *Our Man in Havana*. Today it houses the **Museo de Arte Colonial** (San Ignacio #61, tel. 07/862-6440; daily 9 A.M.– 5:45 P.M.; entrance CUC2, cameras CUC2, guides CUC1), which re-creates the lavish interior of an aristocratic colonial home. One room is devoted to colorful stained-glass *vitrales* and *mediopuntos*.

Callejón de Chorro

Leading from the southwest corner of the plaza, this short cul-de-sac is where the original cistern was built to supply water to ships in the harbor. The *aljibe* (cistern) marked the terminus of the Zanja Real (the "royal ditch," or *chorro*), a covered aqueduct that brought water from the Río Almendares some 10 kilometers away. A small sink and spigot are all that remain.

The **Casa de Baños**, which faces onto the squares, looks quite ancient but was built in the 20th century in colonial style on the site of a bathhouse erected over the *aljibe*. Today the building contains the **Galería Victor Manuel** (San Ignacio #56, tel. 07/861-2955; daily 9 A.M.–9 P.M.), selling quality arts.

At the far end of Callejón de Chorro is the **Taller Experimental de la Gráfica**

(tel. 07/862-0979, tgrafica@cubarte.cult .cu; Mon.–Fri. 9 A.M.–4 P.M.), where you can watch professional artists making prints as well as purchase them.

Casa de Conde de Lombillo

On the plaza's east side is the Casa de Conde de Lombillo (tel. 07/860-4311; Mon.–Fri. 8:30 A.M.–4:30 P.M., Sat. 9 A.M.–1 P.M.; free). Built in 1741, this former home of a slave trader houses a small post office (Cuba's first), as it has since 1821. Note the mailbox set into the outside wall; it is a grotesque face—that of a tragic Greek mask—carved in stone, with a scowling mouth as its slit. The building now houses historical lithographs, plus an exhibition portraying the restoration project for Habana Vieja.

The Casa de Conde de Lombillo adjoins the **Casa del Marqués de Arcos,** built in the 1740s for the royal treasurer. At last visit the mansion was being restored as a hotel and was not open to visitors. What you see is the rear of the mansion; the entrance is on Calle Mercaderes, where the building facing the entrance is graced by the **Mural Artístico-Histórico,** by Cuban artist Andrés Carrillo.

The two houses are fronted by a wide *portico* supported by thick columns.

Centro Wilfredo Lam

This art center (San Ignacio #22, esq. Empredado, tel. 07/861-2096 and 861-3419, wlam@ artsoft.cult.cu; Mon.–Fri. and alternate Sat. 10 A.M.–5 P.M.; CUC2), on cobbled Empredado, on the northwest corner of the plaza, occupies the former mansion of the Counts of Peñalver. It displays works by the eponymous Cuban artist as well as artists from many developing nations (primarily Latin America). The institution studies and promotes contemporary art from around the world. It also features a library on contemporary art, plus a large music store.

La Bodeguita del Medio

No visit to Havana is complete without a visit to Ernest Hemingway's favorite watering hole

CUBAN COLONIAL ARCHITECTURE

Cuba, one of the world's great architectural troves, boasts the New World's finest assemblage of colonial buildings. Spanning four centuries, these palaces, mansions, churches, castles, and more simple structures catalog an astonishing progression of styles. The academic classicism of aristocratic 18th-century Spanish homes blend with 19th-century French rococo, while art deco and art nouveau exteriors from the 1920s fuse into the cool, columned arcades of ancient palaces in Mudejar style. They were laid out along ruler-straight roads arranged in a grid pattern as decreed by the Laws of the Indies and usually intentionally narrow, conducive to shade. The finest, most fully realized examples are in Habana Vieja, Trinidad, and Santiago de Cuba.

THE COLONIAL HOME

The 17th-century home was made of limestone and modeled on the typical, fairly austere Spanish house, with the only elaboration being a simple portal and balconies with lathe-turned *rejas*. Cuba's colonial mansions – with their tall, generously proportioned rooms and shallow-stepped staircases – were usually built on two main floors (the lower floor for shops and warehouses, the upper floor for the family) with a mezzanine between them or an attic above for the house servants. By the 18th century, those houses that faced onto squares had adopted a portico and loggia (supported by arched columns) to provide shelter from sun and rain.

Colonial homes grew larger with ensuing decades and typically featured two small courtyards, with a dining area between the two, parallel to the street and with a central hallway, or *zaguán*, big enough for carriages and opening directly from the street. Arrayed around the ground floor courtyard were warehouses, offices, and other rooms devoted to the family business, with stables and servants' quarters to the rear, while the private family quarters were sequestered above around the galleried second story reached by a stately inner stairway. The design was unique to Havana houses. Commercial activity on the ground floor was relegated to those rooms (*dependencias*) facing the street (these were usually rented out to merchants). Laundry and other household functions were relegated to the inner, second patio, or *traspatio*, hidden behind massive wooden doors often flanked by pillars that in time developed ornate arches. The formal layout of rooms on the ground floor was usually repeated on the main, upper story. Another design borrowed from Jerez and Cádiz was the *entresuelo*, a mezzanine of half-story proportions tucked between the two stories and used to house servants and slaves (and sometimes rented out).

By the 19th century, the wealthy were building summer homes in Havana's hilly suburbs. These *quintas* were typically in neoclassical style, with extensive front porticos and gardens to the rear. Many, however, were influenced by the Palladian style, fashionable in Europe.

Throughout the colonial period, windows evolved as one of the most decorative elements. Ground floor windows were full height from ground level and featured shutter-doors to permit a free flow of air. The earliest homes were protected by wooden shutter panels. Later windows acquired ornate grilled wooden balusters, which often protruded where streets

(Empedrado #207, tel. 07/862-6121; daily noon–midnight), half a block west of the cathedral. This neighborhood hangout—Hemingway's "little shop in the middle of the street"—was originally the coach house of the mansion next door. Later it was a *bodega,* a mom-and-pop grocery store where Spanish immigrant Ángel Martínez served food and drinks.

The bar is to the front, with the restaurant behind (note the beautiful tilework along the passageway wall). Troubadours move among the thirsty *turistas.* Between tides, you can still savor the proletarian fusion of dialectics and rum. The house drink is the *mojito,* the rum mint julep that Hemingway brought out of obscurity and turned into the national drink.

were sufficiently wide. In the 19th century, glass was introduced, though usually only for decoration in multicolored stained-glass panes inserted between, or more frequently above, the wooden panels, which were louvered to allow free flow of air. Meanwhile, ornate metal grills called *guardavecinos* were adopted for upper stories to divide balconies of contiguous properties and so prevent intrusion.

Certain styles evolved unique to individual cities, as with the *arco mixtilíneo* (doorway lintel) and projecting turned-wood roof brackets unique to Camagüey; the mail-order gingerbread wooden homes (imported from Key West) common in Varadero; and the tromp l'oeil interior murals found in homes of Sancti Spíritus. Cuban structures were heavily influenced by traditional Spanish and Mudejar (Moorish) styles, and evolved quintessential Cuban features that included:

Alfarje: A pitched wooden roof combining parallel and angled beams, providing a conceptual shift in emphasis to enhance a room's sense of space. Normally found in churches and smaller homes, they adopted a star pattern and often bear a nautical influence (many were made by shipbuilders).

Antepecho: An ornamented window guard flush with the building facade.

Cenefa: Italianate band of colored plasterwork used as decorative ornamentation on interior walls.

Entresuelo: Shallow mezzanine level between ground and upper stories, usually housing slaves' living quarters.

Luceta: Long rectangular window along the edges of a doorway or window, usually containing stained or marbled glass.

Mamparas: Double-swing half doors that serve as room dividers or as partial outer doors to protect privacy while allowing ventilation. Typically they contained colored or frosted glass.

Mediopunto: Stained-glass window (*vitral*) in half-moon shape, normally used above windows or doorways.

Patio: An open space in the center of Spanish buildings – a Spanish adaptation of the classic Moorish inner court – which permits air to circulate through the house. The patios of more grandiose buildings are surrounded by columned galleries.

Persiana: Slatted shutter in tall, glassless windows, designed to let in the breezes while keeping out the harsh light and rain.

Portal: The main doorway to structures. Early *portales* were fairly simple but soon evolved to monumental proportions and featured elaborate stone molding on the lintel and bas-relief columns to each side.

Portico: Galleried exterior walkway fronting mansions and protecting pedestrians from sun and rain. Often these stretch the length of a street, supported by stone Tuscan columns dividing vaulted ceilings and arches. Later, North American influences led to a more sober approach, with square wooden posts (like a porch).

Postigo: Small door set at face level into massive wooden doors of Spanish homes.

Reja: Wooden window screen of rippled, lathe-turned rods called *barrotes* that served to keep out burglars (later *rejas* were made of metal).

Vitral: Window of stained glass in geometric designs that diffuse the sunlight, saturating a room with shifting color.

Adorning the walls are posters, paintings, and faded photos of Papa Hemingway, Carmen Miranda, and other famous visitors. The walls were once decorated with the signatures and scrawlings of visitors dating back decades, as if a swarm of adolescents has been let loose with crayons. Alas, a recent renovation has wiped away much of the original charm (the artwork has been erased and replaced in ersatz style, with visitors being handed blue pens; famous visitors now sign a chalkboard).

The most famous graffiti is credited to Papa: *"Mi Mojito en La Bodeguita, Mi Daiquirí en El Floridita,"* he supposedly scrawled on the sky-blue walls—according to Tom Miller in *Trading with the Enemy,* Martínez concocted the phrase as a marketing gimmick after the writer's death. Errol Flynn thought it "A Great Place to Get Drunk." They are there, these ribald fellows, smiling at the camera through a haze of cigar smoke and rum. Stepping from La Bodeguita with rum in your veins, you may feel an exhilarating sensation, as if Hemingway himself were walking beside you through the cobbled streets of this most literary of Havana's terrain.

Casa del Conde de la Reunión

Built in the 1820s, at the peak of the baroque era, this home has a trefoil-arched doorway opening onto a *zaguán* (courtyard). Exquisite *azulejos* (painted tiles) decorate the walls.

Famed novelist Alejo Carpentier used the house as the main setting for his novel *El siglo de las luces* (The Enlightenment). A portion of the home, which houses the Centro de Promoción Cultural, is dedicated to his memory as the **Fundación Alejo Carpentier** (Empedrado #215, tel. 07/861-5500; Mon.–Fri. 8:30 A.M.–4:30 P.M.; free). One entire wall bears a display of Carpentier's early works. His raincoat is thrown stylishly over his old desk chair, suggesting that the novelist might return home at any moment.

While here, walk one block west to **Plazuela de San Juan de Díos** (Empedrado, e/ Habana y Aguiar), a small plaza centered on a white marble life-size facsimile of Miguel de Cervantes, author of *Don Quixote,* sitting in a chair, book and pen in hand, lending the plaza its colloquial name: Parque Cervantes.

◀ PLAZA DE ARMAS

The most important plaza in Habana Vieja, and the oldest, this handsome square was laid out in 1519 and named Plaza de Iglesia for the church that was demolished in 1741 after an English warship, the ill-named HMS *Invincible,* was struck by lightning and exploded, sending its main mast sailing down on the church. Later, Plaza de Armas evolved to become the settlement's administrative center.

The plaza seems still to ring with the cacophony of the past, when military parades,

extravagant fiestas, and musical concerts were held under the watchful eye of the governor, and the gentry would take their formal evening promenade. Wednesday–Saturday the plaza is ringed by stalls selling tatterdemalion antiquarian books.

At its heart is **Parque Céspedes,** a verdant park shaded by palms and tall kapok (ceiba) trees, and pinned by a white marble **statue of Manuel de Céspedes,** hero of the Ten Years War.

The following buildings are described in clockwise order, beginning on the west side.

Palacio de los Capitanes Generales

This somber yet stately palace was completed in 1791 and became home to 65 governors of Cuba between 1791 and 1898 and, after that, the U.S. governor's residence during Uncle Sam's occupation and, in 1902–20, the early seat of the Cuban government. Between 1920 and 1967, it served as Havana's city hall.

The palace is fronted by a cool loggia shadowed by a facade of Ionic columns, and by "cobblewood" laid instead of stone to soften the noise of carriages and thereby lessen the disturbance of the governors' sleep. The three-story structure surrounds a courtyard that contains a statue of Christopher Columbus by Italian sculptor Cucchiari amid palms and other tropical foliage. Arched colonnades rise on all sides, festooned with vines and bougainvillea. In the southeast corner, a hole containing the coffin of an unknown nobleman is one of several graves from the old Cementerio de Espada.

Today, the palace houses the **Museo de la Ciudad de la Habana** (City of Havana Museum, Tacón #1, e/ Obispo y O'Reilly, tel. 07/861-5779; daily 9 A.M.–6 P.M., last entry at 5:30 P.M.); entrance CUC3, cameras CUC2, videos CUC10, guide CUC1). The great flight of marble stairs leads to palatially furnished rooms. The Salón del Trono (Throne Room), made for the King of Spain but never used, is of breathtaking splendor and brims with treasures. The museum also features the Salón de las Banderas (Hall of Flags), with magnificent artwork that includes *The Death of Antonio*

A WALK ALONG CALLE OBISPO

Pedestrians-only Calle Obispo links Plaza de Armas with Parque Central and is Habana Vieja's busiest street. The name means "Bishop's Street," supposedly because it was the path favored by ecclesiastics of the 18th century. It became Havana's premier shopping street early on and was given a boost when the city walls went up in the mid-1700s, linking the major colonial plaza with the Monserrate Gate, the main entranceway built into the city wall. (*Jiniteros* and *jiniteras* concentrate here. Watch your valuables.)

Begin at Plaza Albear and walk east. Fifty yards on your left you'll pass the Infotur office and one block further, also on your left, the **Casa Natal de Félix Varela** (Obispo, e/ Aguacate y Villegas), the birthplace of the Cuban nationalist philosophy-priest, which was being restored as a museum at last visit.

The next few blocks are lined with boutiques, small art galleries, and simple cafés and bars.

Crossing Havana, five blocks east of Plaza Albear, you arrive at Havana's erstwhile "Wall Street," centered on Calles Obispo, Cuba, and Aguiar, where the main banks were concentrated prior to the Revolution. The former neoclassical Banco Mendoza today houses the **Museo Numismático** (Coin Museum, Obispo, e/ Habana y Aguiar, tel. 07/861-5811; Tues.-Sat. 9 A.M.-4:45 P.M., Sun. 9 A.M.-1 P.M.; CUC1). The broad-ranging collection of coins and banknotes spans the Greco, Roman, and Phoenician epochs, as well as Spanish *reales* and *escudos*, plus Cuban money dating back to the republican era. There are also medals, and gold US$20 pieces.

Passing the **Drogería Johnson** at the corner of Obispo and Aguiar, continue a short distance to the **Hotel Florida** (Obispo #252, esq. Cuba, tel. 07/862-4127), a beautifully restored colonial mansion with a fine bar and restaurant. Cater-corner to the hotel, you'll pass the former **Banco Nacional de Cuba** (Obispo #211, esq. Cuba), in a splendid neoclassical building – today occupied by the Ministerio de Finanzas y Precios (Ministry of Finance and Prices) – fronted by fluted Corinthian columns.

Havana is replete with dusty old apothecaries, but the **Museo y Farmacia Taquechel** (Obispo #155, esq. Aguiar, tel. 07/862-9286; daily 9 A.M.-6 P.M.; free) is surely the most interesting, with its mixing vases, mortars and pestles, and colorful ceramic jars full of herbs and potions. Dating from 1898, it's named for Dr. Francisco Taquechel y Mirabal.

Across the street, on the north side Obispo, is the original site of the University of Havana, founded in January 1728. An antique bell that once tolled to call the students to class has been placed in a campanile on the north side of the new building, still in construction at last visit.

Fifty meters beyond Museo y Farmacia Taquechel you'll arrive at the rose-pink **Hotel Ambos Mundos** (Obispo, esq. Mercaderes, tel. 07/860-9530), dating from the 1920s. Off and on throughout the 1930s, Hemingway laid his head in Room 511, contemplating the plot of *For Whom the Bell Tolls*. Hemingway's quarters – "a gloomy room, 16 square meters, with a double bed made of ordinary wood, two night tables and a writing table with a chair," recalled author Gabriel García Márquez – has been preserved, down to an old Spanish edition of *Don Quixote* on the night table. The room looks out over Plaza de Armas (Mon.-Sat. 10 A.M.-5 P.M.; CUC1).

One block farther brings you to Plaza de Armas.

Maceo by Menocal; plus exquisite collections illustrating the story of the city's (and Cuba's) development and the 19th-century struggles for independence. One top-floor room contains the shattered wings of the eagle that once crested the Monumento del Maine in Vedado, along with other curios suggestive of U.S. voracity. Old horse-drawn carriages and artillery are among the other exhibits.

Girls in crinolines favor the setting for photos, delighting in the ritual of the *quinceañera*, the traditional celebration of a girl's 15th birthday.

To the south side of the palace, along a 50-meter-long cobbled pedestrian section of Calle Obispo, is a row of ancient mansions each today hosting a unique site of interest. For example, the **Casa del Agua la Tinaja** (Obispo #111) sells mineral water (CUC0.25 a glass); and the **Museo de la Orfebrería** (Obispo #113; Tues.–Sat. 9 A.M.–5 P.M., Sun. 9 A.M.– 1 P.M.; CUC1), or Museum of Silverwork, is crammed with silver and gold ornaments from the colonial era. Upstairs you'll find candelabras, a beautiful replica in silver of Columbus's *Santa María,* walking sticks, and a splendid collection of swords and firearms. Next door, the bookstore at Obispo #117–119 is housed in the oldest house in Havana, dating from around 1570.

Palacio del Segundo Cabo

The austere, quasi-Moorish, pseudo-baroque, part neoclassical Palace of the Second Lieutenant (O'Reilly #14, tel. 07/862-8091; Mon.–Fri. 6 A.M.–midnight) dates from 1770, when it was designed as the Casa de Correos (the city post office). Later it became the home of the vice-governor general (Second Lieutenant) and, immediately after independence, the seat of the Senate. Today, it houses the **Instituto Cubano del Libro** (Cuban Book Institute), which hosts readings and cultural events. Upstairs, the mezzanine is occupied by the **Galería Raúl Martínez** (Mon.–Fri. 10 A.M.–5 P.M., Sat. 10 A.M.– 3 P.M.) showing works by prominent painters.

Immediately east of the loggia is a life-size marble **statue of Fernando VII,** holding in one hand a scroll of parchment that from the side appears jauntily cocked and is the butt of ribald jokes among locals.

Castillo de la Real Fuerza

The pocket-size castle (O'Reilly #2; daily 9 A.M.– 7 P.M.; CUC1) on the northeast corner of the plaza was begun in 1558 and completed in 1582. It's the oldest of the four forts that guarded the New World's most precious harbor. Built in medieval fashion, with walls 6 meters wide and 10 meters tall, the castle forms a square with enormous triangular bulwarks

Castillo de la Real Fuerza
© CHRISTOPHER P. BAKER

at the corners, their sharp angles slicing the dark waters of the moat. It was almost useless from a strategic point of view, being landlocked far from the mouth of the harbor channel and hemmed in by surrounding buildings that would have formed a great impediment to its cannons in any attack. The governors of Cuba lived here until 1762.

Visitors enter the fortress via a courtyard full of cannons and mortars. Note the royal coat of arms representing Seville, Spain, carved in stone above the massive gateway as you cross the moat by a drawbridge. The battlements house the **Museo Nacional de la Cerámica Cubana** (tel. 07/861-6130; daily 9 A.M.–7 P.M.; CUC1), featuring pottery both ancient and new.

You can climb to the top of a cylindrical tower rising from the northwest corner and containing a patinated brass bell. The tower is topped by a bronze weathervane called **La Giraldilla de la Habana** showing a voluptuous figure with hair braided in thick ropes, bronze robes fluttering in the wind; in her right hand she holds a palm tree and in her left a cross.

HAVANA

This pathetic-looking figure is the official symbol of Havana. The vane is a copy; the original, which resides in the city museum, was cast in 1631 in honor of Inéz de Bobadilla, the wife of Governor Hernando de Soto, the tireless explorer who fruitlessly searched for the Fountain of Youth in Florida. De Soto named his wife governor in his absence, and she became the only female governor ever to serve in Cuba. Every afternoon for four years she climbed the tower and scanned the horizon in vain for his return, and eventually died of sorrow.

Immediately east of the castle, at the junction of Avenida del Puerto and O'Reilly, is an obelisk to the 77 Cuban seamen killed during World War II by German submarines.

El Templete

A charming copy of a Doric temple, El Templete (daily 9 A.M.–6 P.M.; CUC1, including guide) stands on the square's northeast corner. It was inaugurated on March 19, 1828, on the site where the first mass and town council meeting were held in 1519, beside a massive ceiba tree. The original ceiba was felled by a hurricane in 1828 and replaced by a column fronted by a small bust of Christopher Columbus. A ceiba has since been replanted and today shades the tiny temple, which is cloaked by bougainvillea. Its interior features a wall-to-ceiling triptych depicting the first Mass, the first town council meeting, and the inauguration of the Templete. In the center of the room sits a bust of the artist, Jean-Baptiste Vermay (1786–1833).

Hotel Santa Isabel

The building immediately south of El Templete is the former Palacio del Conde de Santovenia (Baratillo, e/ Narciso López y Baratillo y Obispo). Its quintessentially Cuban-colonial facade is graced by a becolumned portico and, above, wrought-iron railings on balconies whose windows boast stained-glass *mediopuntos*. The *conde* (count) in question was famous for hosting elaborate parties, most notoriously a three-day bash in 1833 to celebrate the accession to the throne of Isabel II that climaxed

with the ascent of a gaily decorated gas-filled balloon. Later that century it served as a hotel, and is touted today as the finest hotel in Habana Vieja. President Carter stayed here during his visit to Havana in 2002.

Half a block east of the hotel, on Calle Baratillo, is the **Casa del Café** (tel. 07/33-8061), serving all kinds of Cuban coffees; next door stands the **Taberna del Galeón** (tel. 07/33-8476; Mon.–Sat. 9 A.M.–5 P.M., Sun. 9 A.M.–3 P.M.), the "House of Rum," where a free *mojito* awaits your arrival.

Museo Nacional de Historia Natural

On the south side of the plaza, this natural history museum (Obispo #61, e/ Oficios y Baratillo, tel. 07/863-9361, museo@mnhnc.inf.cu; Tues.–Fri. 9:30 A.M.–5 P.M., Sat.–Sun. 9 A.M.–5:30 P.M.; CUC3) shows off the rather paltry collection of the Academía de Ciencias and encompasses the Museo de Ciencias Naturales (Museum of Natural Sciences) and the Museo de Ciencias y Técnicas (Museum of Science and Technology), which covers evolution in a well-conceived display. The museum houses collections of Cuban flora and fauna—many in clever reproductions of their natural environments—plus stuffed tigers, apes, and other beasts from around the world. Children will appreciate the interactive displays.

Immediately east, the **Biblioteca Provincial de la Habana** (Mon.–Fri. 8:15 A.M.–7 P.M., Sat. 8:15 A.M.–4:30 P.M., Sun. 8:15 A.M.–1 P.M.) is Havana's provincial library. The building once served as the U.S. Embassy.

Casa del Árabe

Arab House (Oficios #12, tel. 07/861-5868; Tues.–Sat. 9 A.M.–4:30 P.M., Sun. 9 A.M.–1 P.M.; CUC1), fifty meters south of Plaza de Armas and comprising two 17th-century mansions, was formerly the Colegio de San Ambriosio, and is a fine example of Moorish-inspired architecture. It is the only place in Havana where Muslims can practice the Islamic faith (the prayer hall is decorated with hardwoods inlaid with mother-of-pearl). It now houses a museum dedicated to the many Levantine immigrants who settled Cuba throughout the centuries; it displays camel saddles and Oriental carpets, an exact replica of a *souk* (market), models of Arab *dhows* (traditional sailing vessels), and Arab weaponry.

Depósito del Automóvil

The Depository of Automobiles (Oficios #13, tel. 07/863-9942; Tues.–Sat. 9 A.M.–5 P.M., Sun. 9 A.M.–1 P.M.; entrance CUC1, cameras CUC2, videos CUC10), opposite Casa del Árabe, includes an eclectic range of 30 antique automobiles, from a 1905 Cadillac, a 1926 Rolls-Royce Phantom, a 1924 Packard, 1926 Willys Overland Whippet, and 1930 V-6 Cadillac limousine, to a pre-war Dodge hearse and a 1960s-era Daimler limousine gifted by the British Embassy. Che Guevara's 1959 mint green Chevrolet Bel-Air is normally here also but was in the shop at last visit. A number of classic Harley-Davidson motorcycles are also exhibited.

PLAZA DE SAN FRANCISCO

Cobbled Plaza de San Francisco, two blocks south of Plaza de Armas, at Oficios and the foot of Amargura, faces onto Avenida del Puerto. During the 16th century the area was the great waterfront of the early colonial city. Iberian emigrants disembarked, slaves were unloaded, and galleons were replenished for the passage to Spain. A market developed on the plaza, which became the focus of the annual Fiesta de San Francisco each October 3, and a gambling fair was established. At its heart is the **Fuente de los Leones** (Fountain of the Lions) by Giuseppe Gaggini, erected in 1836 and though moved to different locations at various times, finally ensconced where it began.

The five-story neoclassical building on the north side is the **Lonja del Comercio** (Goods Exchange, Amargura #2, esq. Oficios, tel. 07/866-9588; daily 9 A.M.–6 P.M.), dating from 1907, when it was built as a center for commodities trading. Restored, it houses offices of international corporations, news bureaus, and tour companies. The beautiful dome is crowned by a bronze figure of the god Mercury.

Behind the Lonja and entered by a wrought-iron archway topped by a most-uncommunist fairytale crown, is the **Jardín Diana de Gales** (Baratillo, esq. Carpinetti; daily 9 A.M.–6 P.M.), a park unveiled in 2000 in memory of Diana, Princess of Wales. The 10-foot-tall column is by acclaimed Cuban artist Alfredo Sosabravo. There's also an engraved Welsh slate and stone plaque from Althorp, Diana's childhood home, donated by the British Embassy.

The garden backs onto the **Casa de los Esclavos** (Obrapía, esq. Av. del Puerto), a slave-merchant's home that at last visit was being restored as the **Museo de Esclavitud** (Museum of Slavery).

Iglesia y Convento de San Francisco de Asís

Dominating the plaza on the south side is this great church (Oficios, e/ Armagura y Brasil, tel. 07/862-9683; daily 9 A.M.–5:30 P.M.; entrance CUC2, campanile CUC1, guide CUC1, cameras CUC2, videos CUC10), whose construction was launched in 1719. It was reconstructed in 1730 in baroque style with a 40-meter bell tower crowned by St. Helen holding a sacred Cross of Jerusalem. The church was eventually proclaimed a Minorite Basilica, and it was from its chapel that the processions of the *Via Crucis* departed every Lenten Friday, ending at the Iglesia del Santo Cristo del Buen Viaje. The devout passed down Calle Amargura (Street of Bitterness), where Stations of the Cross were set up at street corners and decorated with crucifixes and altars.

The Protestant English used the church briefly for worship during their tenure in Havana in 1762; the Catholics refused thereafter to use it.

The church and adjoining convent were reopened in October 1994 after a complete restoration. The main nave, with its towering roof supported by 12 columns, each topped by an apostle, features a trompe l'oeil that extends the perspective of the nave. The sumptuously adorned altars are gone, replaced by a huge crucifix suspended above a grand piano. Members of the most aristocratic families of the times

RESTORING OLD HAVANA

Old Havana has been called the "finest urban ensemble in the Americas." The fortress colonial town that burst its walls when Washington, D.C., was still a swamp is a 350-acre repository of antique buildings in an astounding amalgam of styles. More than 900 of Habana Vieja's 3,157 structures are of historic importance. Of these, only 101 were built in the 20th century. Almost 500 are from the 19th; 200 are from the 18th; and 144 are from the 16th and 17th. Alas, many buildings are crumbling into ruins around the people who occupy them.

In 1977, the Cuban government named Habana Vieja a National Monument. In 1982, UNESCO's Inter-Governmental Committee for World Cultural and Natural Protection named Habana Vieja a World Heritage Site worthy of international protection. Cuba formalized a plan to rescue much of the old city from decades of neglect under the guidance of Eusebio Leal Spengler, the charismatic official city historian, who runs the **Oficina del Historiador de la Ciudad de La Habana** (Calle de los Oficios #110, e/ Lamparilla y Amargura, Habana Vieja, tel. 07/861-5001, www.ohch.cu) and has been granted an unusual degree of autonomy. Leal, who grew up in Habana Vieja, is a member of Cuba's National Assembly, the Central Committee of the Communist Party, and the all-important Council of State.

The ambitious plan stretches into the future and has concentrated on four squares: Plaza de Armas, Plaza de la Catedral, Plaza Vieja, and Plaza de San Francisco. The most important buildings have received major renovations; others have been given face-lifts – symbols of triumph over horrendous shortages of materials and money. Structures are ranked into one of four levels according to historical and physical value. The top level is reserved for museums; the second level for hotels, restaurants, offices, and schools; and the bottom levels for housing. Priority is given to edifices with income-generating tourist value.

Leal selects sites for renovation, supervises the construction teams, and chooses the entities that will occupy the restored buildings. Restoration is being run as a self-financing business. **Habaguanex** (Calle Oficios #110, Plaza de San Francisco, Havana, tel. 07/67-1039, www.habaguanex.cu) has responsibility for opening and operating commercial entities such as hotels, restaurants, cafés, and shops. The profits help finance further infrastructural improvements; 33 percent of revenues are supposedly devoted to social projects. Not every palace ends up converted for tourist use, however; some become schools, while one restored mansion is now a pediatric rehabilitation center.

Still, there is little evidence of actual homes being restored. In southern Habana Vieja, where there are relatively few structures of touristic interest, talk of restoration raises hollow laughs from the inhabitants. Because of overcrowding, some 30,000 longtime residents will be moved out for good. Many occupants have already been moved to new apartments in Alamar, the monstrous housing project east of the city; those who've been moved complain about having been transferred from ancient slum quarters to what many consider a modern and soulless slum.

---

were buried in the crypt; some bodies are open to view. You can climb the campanile for a panoramic view over Habana Vieja.

The nave opens to the cloisters of a convent that today contains the **Museo de Arte Religioso,** featuring fabulous silverwork and other treasures of the Spanish epoch. Recent additions are the lectern and armchairs used by Fidel and the pope during the latter's visit in 1998. A music school occupies part of the building.

The cathedral serves as a concert hall. Classical music performances are hosted each Saturday at 6 P.M. and Sunday at 11 A.M. (except July and August).

A life-size bronze statue (by José Villa Soberón) of an erstwhile and once-renowned tramp known as **El Caballero de París** graces the sidewalk in front of the cathedral entrance. Many Cubans believe that touching his beard of fingers will bring good luck.

Calle Oficios

The west side of cobbled Calle Oficios facing the cathedral is lined with 17th-century colonial buildings that possess a marked Mudejar style, exemplified by their wooden balconies. The entire block has been magnificently restored and many of the buildings converted into art galleries. One of the gems is the **Galería de Carmen Montilla Tinoco** (Oficios #162, tel. 07/866-8768; Mon.–Sat. 9 A.M.– 5 P.M.; free). Only the front of the house remains, but the architects have made creative use of the empty shell. Next door, **Estudio Galería Los Oficios** (Oficios #166, tel. 07/863-0497; Mon.–Sat. 9:30 A.M.–5 P.M., Sun. 9 A.M.–1 P.M.; free) displays works by renowned artist Nelson Domínguez.

Midway down the block, Calle Brasil extends west about 80 meters to Plaza Vieja. Portions of the original colonial-era aqueduct (the Zanja Real) are exposed beneath the cobbled street. It's worth the brief detour to visit the **Aqvarium** (Brasil #9, tel. 07/863-9493; Tues.–Sat. 9 A.M.–5 P.M., Sun. 9 A.M.–1 P.M.; CUC1, children free), displaying tropical freshwater fish. Children's events are hosted each second Wednesday of the month; video screenings each third Wednesday; and lectures each fourth Wednesday. Next door, **La Casa Cubana del Perfume** (Brasil #13, tel. 07/866-3759; Mon.–Sat. 10 A.M.–6 P.M.) displays colonial-era distilleries, has aromatherapy demos, and sells handmade perfumes made on site.

Back on Oficios, you'll pass the former Casa de Don Lorenzo Montalvo, which later housed a convent and is today the **Hostal Convento de Santa Brígida.**

Opposite the hotel, the **Coche Presidencial Mambí** (CUC1) railway carriage stands on rails at Oficios and Churruca. It served as the official presidential carriage of five presidents, beginning in 1902 with Tomás Estrada Palma. Its polished hardwood interior gleams with brass fittings.

Immediately beyond is the **Antigua Cámara de Representantes** (Oficios #211, esq. Muralla). This 19th-century building housed the Chamber of Representatives during the early Republic. Later it served as the Ministerio de Educación (1929–60) and following the Revolution it housed the Asemblea Provincial Poder Popular (Havana's local government office). The interior lobby is striking for its ornate baroque and neoclassical stucco work, including a magnificent stained-glass skylight. Today it houses a concert hall and the **Museo de Educación** (tel. 07/862-4076; Mon.–Sat. 9 A.M.–5 P.M.).

Cater-corner to the Asemblea, on the southeast side of Oficios and Muralla, is **Casa Alejandro Von Humboldt** (Oficios #254, tel. 07/863-1144; Tues.–Sat. 9 A.M.–5 P.M., Sun. 9 A.M.–noon; CUC1), a museum dedicated to the famous German explorer (1769–1854) who lived here during his investigations of Cuba in 1800–01.

Museo de Ron

The Fundación Destilería Havana Club, or Museo de Ron (Museum of Rum, Av. San Pedro #262, e/ Muralla y Sol, tel. 07/861-8051, www.havanaclubfoundation.com; Mon.–Fri. 9 A.M.–5 P.M., Sat. 9 A.M.–4 P.M., Sun. 10 A.M.–4 P.M.; CUC5 including guide and drink), two blocks south of Plaza San Francisco, occupies the former harborfront colonial mansion of the Conde de la Mortera. It's a must-see and provides an introduction to the mystery and manufacture of Cuban rum. Your tour begins with an audiovisual presentation. Exhibits include a mini-cooperage, *pailes* (sugar boiling pots), original wooden *trapiches* (sugarcane presses), and *salas* dedicated to an exposition on sugarcane, and to the colonial sugar mills and factories where the cane was pressed and the liquid processed. An operating mini-production unit replete with bubbling vats and copper stills demonstrates the process that results in some of the world's finest rums.

The highlight is a model of an early 20th-century sugar plantation at 1:22.5 scale, complete with milling machines and plantation grounds with workers' dwellings, a church, hotel, and working steam locomotives. Your tour ends in the Bar Havana Club.

On the rum theme, Hemingway once favored **Dos Hermanos** (Av. San Pedro #304, esq. Sol, tel. 07/861-3514), a simple bar immediately south of the museum. A strong *mojito* will provide a pick-me-up and steel you for a close look at the polluted harbor (it is now being cleaned up, with plans to move all cargo ships to the port of Mariel).

CALLE MERCADERES

Cobbled Calle Mercaderes between Obispo and Plaza Vieja, four blocks south, is full of major and minor attractions. Not least is the **Maqueta de la Habana Vieja** (Mercaderes #114, tel. 07/866-4425; daily 9 A.M.–6 P.M.; entrance CUC1, guide CUC1, cameras CUC3, videos CUC10), half a block south of Obispo. This 1:500 scale model of Habana Vieja measures eight by four meters, with every building delineated and color coded by use. Guides give a spiel.

Museo de Ásia

This charming museum (Mercaderes #111, tel. 07/863-9740; Tues.–Sat. 9 A.M.–5 P.M., Sun. 9 A.M.–1 P.M.; entrance CUC1, cameras CUC2, videos CUC10) displays a collection of Asiatica comprising gifts to Fidel from Asian nations. The best rooms are upstairs, containing an array of carved ivory, silverware, mother-of-pearl furniture, kimonos, and Oriental armaments. The museum also includes a small bonsai garden, and one of the rooms downstairs doubles as a school classroom, reminding visitors of the success of Cuba's education program.

Casa de la Obra Pía

One of the most important buildings in the region, the House of Charitable Works (Obrapía #158, tel. 07/861-3097; Tues.–Sat. 9 A.M.–4:30 P.M., Sun. 9:30 A.M.–12:30 P.M.; CUC1), 20 meters west of Mercaderes, comprises two adjacent houses that were later combined. This splendid mansion with lemon-yellow walls was built in 1665 by Capitán Martín Calvo de la Puerta y Arrieta, the Cuban solicitor general (the house and street are named for the *obra pía,* or pious act, of Don Martín Calvo de la Puerta, who devoted a portion of his wealth to sponsoring five orphan girls every year). The Calvo de Puertas family built additions in baroque style. The family coat of arms, surrounded by exuberant baroque stonework, is emblazoned above the massive *portal,* brought from Cádiz in 1686. The mansion exemplifies the Spanish adaptation of a Moorish inner courtyard, with a serene, scented coolness illuminated by daylight filtering through *mediopuntos* fanning out like a peacock's tail. It features a permanent exhibition of works by Alejo Carpentier in the foyer (including, rather incongruously, his blue Volkswagen brought back from Paris after his tenure as Cuban ambassador to UNESCO); other rooms contain miscellaneous art.

Casa de África

Dedicated to a celebration of African culture, Africa House (Obrapía #157, e/ Mercaderes y San Ignacio, tel. 07/861-5798; Tues.–Sat. 9:30 A.M.–4:30 P.M., Sun. 9:30 A.M.–12:30 P.M.; CUC2), opposite Casa de la Obra Pía, is full of African artwork and artifacts. On the third floor, you'll find a collection of paraphernalia used in *santería,* including statues of the leading deities in the Yoruban pantheon, plus dancing costumes of the Abakuá. Much of the collection was contributed by various African embassies in Havana.

◖ PLAZA VIEJA AND VICINITY

The last of the four main squares to be laid out in Habana Vieja, the old commercial square (bounded by Calles Mercaderes, San Ignacio, Brasil, and Muralla) originally hosted a covered market. It is surrounded by mansions and apartment blocks from where in colonial times residents looked down on processions, executions, bullfights, and fiestas.

Time and neglect brought near ruin this century,

A WALK DOWN CALLE MERCADERES

Setting out toward Plaza Vieja from the Hotel Ambos Mundos, after 20 meters you'll pass the **Museo de Ásia** (see the main text) on your left. Next door, the **Casa de las Especias** (Mon.-Sat. 9 A.M.-5 P.M., Sun. 9 A.M.-4 P.M.) sells natural herbs, such as anise, oregano, and laurel, in cloth bags. The scent upon entering is worth the visit.

Nearby, be sure to call in to the **Maqueta de la Habana Vieja** (see main text). On the west side, 20 meters farther south, are the **Casa de Puerto Rico** and **Casa del Tabaco,** both at Mercaderes #120. Besides a fine stock of cigars, the latter houses the **Museo del Tabaco** (tel. 07/861-5795; Tues.-Sat. 10 A.M.- 5 P.M., Sun. 9 A.M.-1 P.M.; free), a cigar museum upstairs.

At the end of the block, at the corner of Obrapía, the pink building with the Mexican flag fluttering above the doorway is the **Casa de Benito Juárez** (also called Casa de México, Mercaderes #116, tel. 07/861-8186; Tues.-Sat. 9:30 A.M.-4:45 P.M., Sun. 9:30 A.M.-1 P.M.; entrance by donation), displaying artwork and costumes from Mexico, including a collection of priceless Aztec jewelry.

Turn west onto Obrapía to visit the Casa de la Obra Pía and Casa de África (see the main text). One block east, between Mercaderes and Oficios, is the **Casa de Oswaldo Guayasamín** (Obrapía #112, tel. 07/861-3843; Tues.-Sat. 10:15 A.M.-5:45 P.M., Sun. 9 A.M.-12:30 P.M.; free), housing a museum of art and photographs from Latin America. Guayasamín, a famous Ecuadorian painter called the "Artist of the Americas," lived and worked here for many years; you can see his works – many are portraits of Fidel – on the upper story, where his living quarters are displayed as he left them upon his death in 1999.

Next door is the **Casa de los Abanicos** (Obrapía #107, tel. 07/863-4452; Mon.-Fri.

9 A.M.-5 P.M., Sat. 9 A.M.- 2 P.M.; free), where traditional Spanish fans (abanicos) are handmade and painted.

Return to Mercaderes and pop into **Habana 1791** (Mercaderes #176, tel. 07/861-3525; 10 A.M.- 6 P.M. daily), on the southwest corner of Obrapía, where traditional fragrances are made and sold. Continue south half a block to **Casa-Museo del Libertador Simón Bolívar** (Mercaderes #160, tel. 07/861-3988; Tues.-Sat. 9 A.M.-5 P.M., Sun. 9 A.M.-1 P.M.; CUC1), displaying cultural works and art from Venezuela. The collection includes portraits of the "Great Liberator," ceremonial swords, coins minted in his honor, and paintings by contemporary Venezuelan and Cuban artists. Bolívar stayed here in March 1799 and is commemorated in the small Plaza de Bolívar at the corner of Mercaderes and Obrapía.

Across the street is the **Armería 9 de Abril** (Mercaderes #157, tel. 07/861-8080; Mon.-Sat. 9 A.M.-5 P.M.; CUC1), a museum that commemorates four members of Castro's 26th July Movement killed in an assault on the armory on April 9, 1958.

Crossing Lamparilla, peek in at the **Hostal Conde de Villanueva,** one of Havana's finest boutique hotels. One block south, the corner of Mercaderes and Amargura is known as the Cruz Verde – green cross – as it was the first stop on the annual Via Crucis pilgrimage. Today it houses the **Casa del Chocolate** (tel. 07/866-4431; daily 10 A.M.-8:30 P.M.), selling chocolate rolls and beverages and featuring a museum collection of porcelains and wall pieces relating anecdotes and the history of chocolate.

Midway down this curling block you'll pass **Mesón de la Flota,** a Spanish bodega with live flamenco. About 75 meters beyond, you'll arrive at Plaza Vieja.

and many of the square's beautiful buildings sank into disrepair. At last visit it was in the final stages of being restored. Even the white Carrara marble fountain—an exact replica of the original by Italian sculptor Giorgio Mas-sari—has reappeared, now gurgling clear water. The upper stories of many buildings still house tenement apartments, although tenants are gradually being moved out as the buildings are restored as boutiques, restaurants, and so on.

A WALK AROUND PLAZA VIEJA

After visiting the **Cámara Oscura** (see the main text), begin your clockwise tour by following the shaded arcade along the east side of the plaza. Midway, you'll pass the **Casa de Juan Rico de Mata,** today the headquarters of **Fototeca** (Mercaderes #307, tel. 07/862-2530; Tues.-Sat. 10 A.M.-5 P.M.), the state-run agency that promotes the work of Cuban photographers. It offers international photo exhibitions in the Salón Nacional de Fotografía. Note the ceramic wall mural designed by Amelia Peláez.

The old **Palacio Vienna Hotel** (also called the Palacio Cueto), on the southeast corner of Plaza Vieja, is a phenomenal piece of Gaudíesque art nouveau architecture dating from 1906. At last visit it was being restored as a deluxe hotel.

Moving to the south side, the Casa de Marqués de Prado Amero today houses the **Museo de Naipes** (Museum of Playing Cards, Muralla #101, tel. 07/860-1534; Tues.-Sat. 9 A.M.-4:45 P.M., Sun. 9 A.M.-2:45 P.M.; entrance by donation), displaying playing cards through the ages.

On the plaza's southwest corner, call in at the **Casa de los Condes de Jaruco** (see the main text) to view the various art galleries, then cross San Ignacio and follow Muralla half a block to the **Tienda El Soldadito de Plumo** (Muralla #164; Mon.-Fri. 9 A.M.-5 P.M., Sat. 9 A.M.-

1:30 P.M.), selling miniature metal soldiers. A large glass window lets you watch artists painting the pieces.

Return to the plaza, turn left to follow San Ignacio north, and cool off with a chilled beer brewed on-site in the **Taberna de la Muralla** (San Ignacio #364; daily 11 A.M.-1 A.M.), in the former **Casa del Conde de Casa Lombillo.** The copper stills are displayed in the main bar, where an antique delivery truck now sits as a museum piece.

Fifty meters to the north, the somewhat forlorn **Casa del Conde de San Estéban de Cañongo** (San Ignacio #356) was awaiting restoration at the time of writing. Adjoining, on the northwest corner of the plaza, is the **Casa de las Hermanas Cárdenas,** recently restored and today housing the **Centro de Desarollo de Artes Visuales** (San Ignacio #352, tel. 07/862-3533 or 862-2611; Tues.-Sat. 10 A.M.-5 P.M.). The inner courtyard is dominated by an intriguing sculpture by Alfredo Sosabravo. Art education classes are given on the second floor, reached via a wide wooden staircase that leads to the top story, where you'll find an art gallery.

Well worth the side trip is **Hotel Raquel** (San Ignacio, esq. Amargura, tel. 07/860-8280), one block north of the plaza. This recently restored hotel is an art deco and neoclassical jewel.

The tallest building in the square is the **Edificio Gómez Villa,** on the northeast corner. Be sure to take the elevator to the top floor for views over the plaza and to visit the **Cámara Oscura** (daily 9 A.M.–5 P.M.; CUC1), an optical reflection camera that revolves through 360 degrees and projects a real-time picture of Havana at 30-times magnification onto a two-meter-wide parabola housed in a completely darkened room.

Casa de los Condes de Jaruco

The most important building on the square is the House of the Counts of Jaruco (Muralla #107), on the southeast corner. This restored 18th-century mansion, "La Casona," as it is colloquially known, was built between 1733 and 1737 by the father of the future Count of Jaruco and is highlighted by mammoth doors opening into a cavernous courtyard surrounded by lofty archways festooned with hanging vines. Whimsical murals are painted on the walls, touched in splashy color by the undulating play of light through *mediopuntos* and by the shifting of shadows through *rejas*. Art galleries occupy the downstairs rooms (Tues.–Sat. 9 A.M.–5 P.M.).

JEWS IN CUBA

Today, Havana's Jewish community is thought to number only about 1,300, about five percent of its prerevolutionary size, when it supported five synagogues, several schools, and a college.

The first Jew in Cuba, Luis de Torres, arrived with Columbus in 1492 as the explorer's translator. He was followed in the 16th century by Jews escaping persecution at the hands of the Spanish Inquisition. Later, Ashkenazic Jews from Florida founded the United Hebrew Congregation in 1906, and Turkish Jews flocking to avoid World War I concentrated in southern Habana Vieja, many starting out in Cuba selling ties and cloth. Other Jews emigrating from Eastern Europe passed through Cuba en route to the United States in significant numbers until the United States slammed its doors in 1924, after which they settled in Cuba. Arriving during a time of destitution, they were relatively poor compared to the earlier Jewish immigrants and were disparagingly called *polacos*.

Sephardic Jews came later and were profoundly religious. They formed social clubs, opened their own schools, and married their own. By contrast, many Ashkenazic men married Cuban (Catholic) women and eventually were assimilated into Cuban society, says author Robert M. Levine. The Ashkenazim were fired with socialist ideals and were prominent in the founding of both the labor and Cuban Communist movements.

Cuba seems to have been relatively free of anti-Semitism (Batista was a friend to Jews fleeing Nazi Europe). Levine, researching records how during the late 1930s the U.S. government bowed to isolationist, labor, and anti-Semitic pressures at home and convinced the Cuban government to turn back European Jews. This sordid chapter in U.S. history is reflected in the tragic story of the SS *St. Louis* and its 937 passengers trying to escape Nazi Germany in 1939. The ship languished in Havana harbor for a week while U.S. and Cuban officials deliberated on letting passengers disembark; tragically, entry was refused, and the passengers were sent back to Europe and their fate.

By the 1950s, about 20,000 Jews lived in Havana, concentrated around Calle Belén and Calle Acosta — still widely known as the capital's "Jewish Street." Acosta bustled with kosher bakeries, cafés, and clothes stores. The Jewish quarter, however, began its decline even before the Revolution, when Jews began migrating to North America. Jews knew the lessons of Nazi Germany and the totalitarian regimes of Eastern Europe and so, following the Revolution, became part of the Cuban diaspora. About 95 percent of them fled, although a few joined the Castro government; two became early cabinet members. Some 500 Cuban Jews were secretly allowed to emigrate to Israel beginning in 1994.

Although the Castro government discouraged Jews from practicing their faith, Jewish religious schools were the only parochial schools allowed to remain open after the Revolution and the government even provided school buses. The government has always made matzo available and even authorized a kosher butcher shop on Calle Acosta to supply meat for observant Jews. And Jews are the only Cubans permitted to buy beef, a nod to restrictions on pork. The Jewish community also has its own cemetery, in Guanabacoa, dating from 1910. However, the community has no rabbi and marriages and circumcisions must often wait for foreign religious officials passing through Havana.

Still, a renaissance in the Jewish faith is occurring. Synagogues have been refurbished and new ones opened, and the faithful are returning in larger numbers and observing Shabbat. In 1994, the first bar mitzvah took place in over 12 years and the first formal bris in over five years. And the Hebrew Sunday School in the Patronato teaches Hebrew and Yiddish.

JEWISH HERITAGE SITES

The Cuban government proposes to reconstruct Habana Vieja's Jewish quarter, having made a start by rehabilitating the **Sinagoga Adath Israel** (Picota #52, esq. Acosta, tel. 07/861-3495; daily 8 A.M.-noon and 5-8 P.M.), which now sports a new wooden altar carved

entrance to the United Hebrew
Congregation Cemetery, Guanabacoa

with scenes from Jerusalem and historic Havana. Services are Monday–Friday 8 A.M. and 6 P.M., Saturday at 9 A.M. and 6 P.M., and Sunday at 9 A.M.

Chevet Achim (Inquisidor, e/ Luz y Santa Clara, tel. 07/832-6623) was built in 1914 and is the oldest synagogue in Cuba. The building is owned and maintained by the Centro Sefardi, but is not used for ritual or community purposes. It can be viewed by appointment. A Jewish museum is slated.

In Vedado, the **Casa de la Comunidad Hebrea de Cuba** (Calle I #241, e/ 13 y 15, tel. 07/832-8953; Mon.-Sat. 9:30 A.M.-5 P.M.) works to preserve Cuba's Hebrew traditions and contains an active community center and a large library on Judaica. Services at the adjacent **Bet Shalon Sinagogo** are Friday at 7:30 P.M. (May-Sept.) or 6 P.M. (Oct.-Apr.) and Saturday at 10 A.M. (year-round). Nearby, the **Centro Sefardí** (Calle 17 #462, esq. E, tel. 07/832-6623) is a Conservative Jewish synagogue completed in 1960.

Guanabacoa, on the east side of Havana harbor, has two Jewish cemeteries. The **Cementerio de la Comunidad Religiosa Ebrea Adath Israel** (Av. de la Independencia Este, e/ Obelisco y Puente, tel. 07/97-6644; Mon.-Fri. 8-11 A.M. and 2-5 P.M.), also known as the United Hebrew Congregation Cemetery, is for Ashkenazim. It dates from 1912 and is entered by an ocher-colored Spanish-colonial frontispiece with a Star of David. A **Holocaust**

memorial immediately to the left of the gate stands in somber memory of the millions who lost their lives to the Nazis, with emotionally stirring text: "Buried in this place are several cakes of soap made from Hebrew human fat, a fraction of the six million victims of Nazi savagery in the 20th century. May their remains rest in peace."

Behind the Ashkenazic cemetery is the **Cementerio de la Unión Hebrea Chevet Ahim** (Calle G, e/ 5ta y Final, tel. 07/97-5866; daily 7 A.M.- 5 P.M.), for Sephardic Jews. It too has a memorial to the Holocaust victims; turn north off Avenida de la Independencia Este at Avenida de los Mártires (4ta) to reach it.

JEWISH AID ORGANIZATIONS

The following organizations send humanitarian aid to Cuba and/or offer organized trips: the **B'nai B'rith Cuban Jewish Relief Project** (1831 Murray Ave. #208, Pittsburgh, PA 15217, 412/521-2390, http://jewishcuba.org/bnaibrith); the **Cuba-America Jewish Mission** (1442A Walnut St. #224, Berkeley, CA 94709, www.thecajm.org); the **Jewish Cuba Connection** (4 Lighthouse St. #4, Marina Del Rey, CA 90292, 202/232-3317, www.jewban.org); **Jewish Solidarity** (100 Beacom Blvd., Miami, FL 33135, 305/642-1600, http://jewishcuba.org/solidarity); and **Sephardic Friendship Committee** (2012 Lerner Ln., Santa Ana, CA 92705, 800/335-4109, www.sephardicfriends.com).

RESOURCES

Books on the subject include *Jewish Community of Cuba: The Golden Years, 1906-1958,* by Jay Levinson (Westview Publishing, 2006); *The Chosen Island: Jews in Cuba,* by Maritza Corrales (Salsedo Press, 2005); and *Tropical Diaspora: The Jewish Experience in Cuba,* by Robert M. Levine (University Press of Florida, 1993).

Also look for screenings of the documentary films *Havana Nagila: The Jews of Cuba,* by Laura Paull, and *Next Year in Havana,* by Lori Beraha.

HAVANA'S CITY WALLS

Construction of Havana's fortified city walls began on February 3, 1674. They ran along the western edge of the bay and, on the landward side, stood between today's Calle Egido, Monserrate, and Zulueta. Under the direction of engineer Juan de Siscaras, African slaves labored for 23 years to build the 1.4-meter-thick, 10-meter-tall city wall that was intended to ring the entire city, using rocks hauled in from the coast. The 4,892-meter-long wall was completed in 1697, with a small opening for the mooring of ships, and a perimeter of five kilometers. The damage inflicted by the British artillery in 1762 was repaired in 1797, when the thick wall attained its final shape. It formed an irregular polygon with nine defensive bastions with sections of wall in between, and moats and steep drops to delay assault by enemy troops. It was protected by 180 cannons and garrisoned with 3,400 troops. In its first stage it had just two entrances (nine more were added later), opened each morning upon the sound of a single cannon and closed at night the same way.

As time went on, the *intramuros* (the city within the walls) burst its confines. In 1841, Havana authorities petitioned the Spanish Crown for permission to demolish the walls. Just 123 years after the walls went up, they came down again. The demolition began in 1863, when African slave-convicts were put to work to destroy what their forefathers had built. The demolition wasn't completed until well into the 20th century.

Only fragments remain.

Museo Histórico de las Ciencias Naturales Carlos Finlay

Physicians and scientists inclined to a busman's holiday might walk one block west and one north of the plaza and check out the Museum of Natural History (Cuba #460, e/ Amargura y Brasil, tel. 07/863-4824; Mon.–Fri. 8:30 A.M.–5 P.M., Sat. 9 A.M.–3 P.M.; CUC2). Dating from 1868 and once the headquarters of the Academy of Medical, Physical, and Natural Sciences, today it contains a pharmaceutical collection and tells the tales of Cuban scientists' discoveries and innovations. The Cuban scientist Dr. Finlay is honored, of course; it was he who on August 14, 1881, discovered that yellow fever is transmitted by the *Aedes aegipti* mosquito. The museum also contains a medical library of 95,000 volumes and, on the third floor, a reconstructed period pharmacy. It has a rooftop bar with a good view of the harbor. It was being renovated at last visit.

Adjoining the museum to the north is the **Convento y Iglesia de San Francisco el Nuevo** (Cuba, esq. Amargura, tel. 07/861-8490; Mon.–Thurs. 9 A.M.–6 P.M., Sun. 8 A.M.–1 P.M.; free), completed in 1633 for the Augustine friars. It was consecrated anew in 1842 when it was given to the Franciscans, who rebuilt it in renaissance style in 1847. The church has a marvelous domed altar and nave, plus a fine organ. Mass is at 10 A.M.

SOUTHERN HABANA VIEJA

The mostly residential southern half of Habana Vieja, south of Calle Brasil, was the ecclesiastical center of Havana during the colonial era and is studded with churches and convents. Most have been restored, or are in the process of being so. Before the Revolution, this was also Havana's Jewish quarter (see the sidebar *Jews in Cuba*) and also a disreputable center for bars and brothels.

Southern Habana Vieja is enclosed by Avenida del Puerto, which swings along the harborfront and becomes Avenida San Pedro, then Avenida Leonor Pérez, then Avenida Desamparados as it curves around to Avenida de Bélgica (colloquially called Egido). The waterfront boulevard is overshadowed by warehouses. Here were the old P&O docks where the ships from Miami and Key West used to dock and where Pan American World Airways

© CHRISTOPHER P. BAKER

a 1951 Chevrolet Bel Air in Plaza del Cristo

tion, designed in 1910 by a North American architect, blending Spanish Revival and Italian Renaissance styles, and featuring twin towers displaying the shields of Havana and Cuba. It is built atop the former Arsenal, or Spanish naval shipyard.

On the station's north side is a small shady plaza—**Parque de los Agrimensores** (Park of the Surveyors)—pinned by a large remnant of the **Cortina de la Habana,** the old city wall. *Colectivo* taxis—old *yanqui* jalopies—park here, awaiting custom.

Plaza del Cristo

Plaza del Cristo lies at the west end of Amargua, between Lamparilla and Brasil, two blocks east of Avenida de Bélgica (Monserrate). It was here that Wormold, the vacuum-cleaner salesman turned secret agent, was "swallowed up among the pimps and lottery sellers of the Havana noon" in Graham Greene's *Our Man in Havana*. Wormold and his wayward daughter Millie lived at 37 Lamparilla. Alas, the house was fictional.

The plaza is dominated by the tiny **Iglesia de Santo Cristo Buen Viaje** (Villegas, e/ Amargura y Lamparilla, tel. 07/863-1767; daily 9 A.M.–noon), one of Havana's oldest churches, dating from 1732, but with a Franciscan hermitage—called Humilladero chapel—dating from 1640. Buen Viaje was the final point of the *Via Crucis* (the Procession of the Cross) held each Lenten Friday and beginning at the Iglesia de San Francisco de Asís. The church, which was named for its popularity among sailors and travelers who used to pray here for safe voyages, has an impressive cross-beamed wooden ceiling, stained-glass windows, and exquisite altars, including one to the Virgen de la Caridad showing the three boatmen being saved from the tempest.

had its terminal when it was still flying the old clipper flying-boats. Before World War II, when the U.S. Navy took over the docks, Calle San Isidro, which runs inland perpendicular to Desamparados, had been lined with brothels.

Egido follows the hollow once occupied by Habana Vieja's ancient walls. It is a continuation of Monserrate and flows downhill to the harbor. The **Puerta de la Tenaza** (Egido, esq. Fundición) is the only ancient city gate still standing; a plaque inset within a still extant remnant of the wall shows a map of the old city and walls. About 100 meters south, on Avenida de Puerto, is the **Monumento Mártires del Vapor La Coubre,** made of twisted metal fragments of *La Coubre,* the French cargo ship that exploded in Havana harbor on March 4, 1960 (the vessel was carrying armaments for the Castro government). The monument honors the seamen who died in the explosion.

Egido is lined with once-beautiful buildings constructed during the mid-19th century, and today greatly dilapidated. Egido's masterpiece is the **Estación Central de Ferrocarril** (esq. Arsenal), Havana's Venetian-style railway sta-

Iglesia y Convento de Santa Teresa de Jesús

This handsome church and adjoining convent (Brasil, esq. Compostela), two blocks east of Plaza del Cristo, was built by the Carmelites in 1705, with separate baroque doorways for each.

GRAHAM GREENE: OUR MAN IN HAVANA

No contemporary novel quite captures the tawdry intrigue and disreputable aura of Batista's Havana than does Graham Greene's *Our Man in Havana*, published in 1958 and set amid the torrid events of Havana in 1957.

The comic tale tells of Wormold, an English vacuum-cleaner salesman based in Havana and short of money. His daughter has reached an expensive age, so when approached by Hawthorne, he accepts the offer of £300 a month and becomes Agent 59200/5, MI6's man in Havana. To keep his job, he files bogus reports and dreams up military apparatuses from vacuum-cleaner parts. Unfortunately, Wormold becomes trapped by his own deceit and the workings of a hopelessly corrupt city and society.

Graham Greene (1904-91) was already a respected author when he was recruited to work for the Foreign Office, serving the years 1941-43 in Sierra Leone, Africa. In the last years of the war, he worked for the British Secret Service dealing with counterespionage on the Iberian Peninsula, where he learned how the Nazi Abwehr (the German Secret Service) sent home false reports – perfect material for his novel. He traveled widely and based many of his works, including *Our Man in Havana*, on his experiences. He visited Havana several times in the 1950s and was disturbed by the mutilations and torture practiced by Batista's police officers and by social ills such as racial discrimination: "Every smart bar and restaurant was called a club so that a Negro could be legally excluded." But he confessed to enjoying the "louche atmosphere" of Havana and seems to have savored the fleshpots completely. "I came there... for the brothel life, the roulette in every hotel," he later wrote.

Castro condoned *Our Man in Havana* but complained that it didn't do justice to the ruthlessness of the Batista regime. Greene agreed: "Alas, the book did me little good with the new rulers in Havana. In poking fun at the British Secret Service, I had minimized the terror of Batista's rule. I had not wanted too black a background for a light-hearted comedy, but those who had suffered during the years of dictatorship could hardly be expected to appreciate that my real subject was the absurdity of the British agent and not the justice of a revolution." Nonetheless, Castro permitted the screen version, starring Alec Guinness as Wormold, to be filmed in Havana in 1959.

Greene returned to Cuba in the years 1963-66. Although initially impressed by Castro's war on illiteracy (he called it "a great crusade"), he later soured after witnessing the persecution of homosexuals, intellectuals, and Catholics. Perhaps for this reason, the author isn't commemorated in Cuba in any way.

The church still performs its original function, although the convent ceased to operate as such in 1929, when the nuns were moved out and the building was converted into a series of homes. On Saturday afternoon, Afro-Cuban music and dance is hosted.

Across the road is the **Drogería Sarrá** (Brasil, e/ Compostela y Habana, tel. 07/866-7554; daily 9 A.M.–6 P.M.; free), a historic pharmacy—also known as Farmacia La Reunión—with paneled cabinets still stocked with herbs and pharmaceuticals in colorful old bottles and ceramic jars. Duly restored, it now serves as a fascinating apothecary museum.

Iglesia y Convento de Nuestra Señora de Belén

The Church and Convent of Our Lady of Bethlehem (Compostela y Luz, tel. 07/860-3150) is the largest religious complex in Havana, occupying an entire block. The convent, completed in 1718, was built to house the first nuns to arrive in Havana and later served as a refuge for convalescents. In 1842, Spanish authorities ejected the religious order and turned the church into a government office before making it over to the Jesuits. They in turn established a college for the sons of the aristocracy. The Jesuits were the nation's official weather forecasters and in 1858 erected the Observatorio Real (Royal Observatory) atop the tower. It was in use until 1925. At last visit, the convent was still in the process of being renovated.

The church and convent are linked to contiguous buildings across the street by an arched walkway—the Arco de Belén (Arch of Bethlehem)—spanning Acosta.

Iglesia y Convento de Santa Clara de Asís

The Convent of Saint Clair of Assisi (Cuba #610, e/ Luz y Sol, tel. 07/861-3335; Mon.–Fri. 8:30 A.M.–5 P.M.; CUC2), two blocks east of Belén, is a massive former nunnery completed in 1644. The nuns moved out in 1922. It is a remarkable building, with a lobby full of beautiful period pieces. Its inner and outer cloistered courtyard, awash in divine light, is surrounded by columns, one of which is entwined by the roots of a *capulí* tree. Note the 17th-century fountain of a Samaritan woman, and the beautiful cloister roof carved with geometric designs—a classic *alfarje*—in the Salón Plenario, a marble-floored hall of imposing stature. Wooden carvings abound. The second cloister contains the so-called Sailor's House, built by a wealthy ship owner for his daughter, whom he failed to dissuade from a life of asceticism.

Iglesia Parroquial del Espíritu Santo

The Parish Church of the Holy Ghost (Acosta #161, esq. Cuba, tel. 07/862-3410; daily 8 A.M.–noon and 3–6 P.M.), two blocks south of Santa Clara de Asís, is Havana's oldest church, dating from 1638 (the circa-1674 central nave and facade, and circa-1720 Gothic vault are later additions), when it was a hermitage for the devotions of free *negros*. Later King Charles III issued a royal decree giving the right of asylum here to anyone hunted by the authorities, a privilege no longer bestowed.

The church reveals many surprises, including a gilded, carved wooden pelican in a niche in the baptistery. The sacristy, where parish archives dating back through the 17th century

are preserved, boasts an enormous cupboard full of baroque silver staffs and incense holders. Catacombs to each side of the nave are held up by subterranean tree trunks. You can explore the eerie vault that runs under the chapel, with the niches still containing the odd bone as well as the body of Bishop Gerónimo Valdés, who remained in a kind of limbo, his whereabouts unknown, until he turned up, buried under the floor, during a restoration in 1936. The sturdy tower holds four bells; steps lead up to the gallery. Mass is daily at 6 P.M.

Iglesia y Convento de Nuestra Señora de la Merced

Two blocks south of Espíritu Santo is Our Lady of Mercy (Cuba #806, esq. Merced, tel. 07/863-8873; daily 8 A.M.–noon and 3–6 P.M.), a small handsome church and convent with an ornate interior containing romantic dome paintings and the Capilla de Lourdes (Lourdes Chapel), also with early-20th-century religious frescoes. The church, begun in 1755, has strong Afro-Cuban connections (the Virgin of Mercy is also Obatalá, goddess of earth and purity), and it is not unusual to see devotees of *santería* kneeling in prayer. Each September 24, scores of worshippers cram in for the Virgen de la Merced's feast day. More modest celebrations are held on the 24th of every other month. Mass is Monday–Saturday at 9 A.M. and Sunday at 9 A.M. and noon.

Alameda de Paula

This 100-meter-long raised promenade runs alongside the waterfront boulevard between Luz and Leonor Pérez. It is lined with marble and iron street lamps. Midway along the Alameda stands a carved column with a fountain at its base, erected in 1847 in homage to the Spanish navy. It bears an unlikely Irish name: **Columna O'Donnell,** for the Capitán-General of Cuba, Leopoldo O'Donnell, who dedicated the monument. It is covered in relief work on a military theme and crowned by a lion with the arms of Spain in its claws.

At the southern end of the Alameda, **Iglesia de San Francisco de Paula** (San Ignacio y Leonor

Pérez, tel. 07/860-4210; daily 8:30 A.M.–6:30 P.M.) studs circular Plazuela de Paula. The quaint, restored church features marvelous artworks including stained-glass pieces. It is used for baroque and chamber concerts.

Museo Casa Natal de José Martí

The birthplace of the nation's preeminent national hero (Leonor Pérez #314, esq. Av. de Bélgica, tel. 07/861-3778; daily 9 A.M.–6:30 P.M.; entrance CUC1, guide CUC1, cameras CUC2, videos CUC10), one block south of the railway station, sits at the end of a street named after Martí's mother. This simple house—painted ocher, with blue-green window and door frames and terra-cotta tile floors—is a shrine for Cubans who flock to pay homage. The national hero and leader of the independence movement was born on January 28, 1853, and spent the first four years of his life here. The house is splendidly kept, with many of his personal effects, including a beautiful lacquered *escritorio* (writing desk) and a broad-brimmed Panama hat given to him by Ecuadorian President Eloy Alfaro (Panama hats are made in Ecuador). Many of his original texts, poems, and sketches are on display. There's even a lock of the hero's hair from when he was a child.

Sights – Centro Habana and Cerro

Centro Habana (Central Havana—pop. 175,000) lies west of the Paseo del Prado and south of the Malecón. The region is a 19th-century extension of Habana Vieja and evolved following demolition of the city walls in 1863. Prior, it had served as a glacis. The buildings are deep and tall, of four or five stories, built mostly as apartment units, with air shafts instead of interior patios. Hence, the population and street life are denser. Laid out in a near-perfect grid, Centro is mostly residential, with few sights of note. A notable exception is the remnants of Chinatown—Barrio Chino—delineated by Calles Zanja, Dragones, Salud, Rayo, San Nicolás, and Manrique.

The major west–east thoroughfares are the Malecón to the north, and Zanja and Avenida Salvador Allende through the center; plus Calles Neptuno and San Rafael between the Malecón and Zanja. Three major thoroughfares run perpendicular, north–south: Calzada de Infanta, forming the western boundary; Padre Varela, down the center; and Avenida de Italia (Galiano), farther east.

In prerevolutionary days, Centro Habana hosted Havana's red-light district, and prostitutes roamed such streets as the ill-named Calle Virtudes (Virtues). Then, too, Neptuno and San Rafael formed the retail heart of the city. In recent years, they have regained some of their life and the famous department stores of prerevolutionary days have reopened; many still bear prerevolutionary neon signs promoting U.S. brand names from yesteryear.

Many houses, having been battered by waves and salt air over decades, are in a tumbledown state—about one in three houses has collapsed, conjuring up images of what Dresden, Germany, must have looked like after it was bombed in World War II. Take care walking the streets, as pickpockets and muggings commonly occur here.

South of Centro, the land rises gently to Cerro, which developed during the last century as the place to retire for the torrid midsummer months; many wealthy families maintained two homes in Havana—one in town, another on the cooler hill (*cerro* means "hill"). The area is replete with once-stately *casas quintas* (summer homes) in neoclassical, Beaux-Arts, and art nouveau styles. Alas, the region is terribly deteriorated, and the majority of buildings transcend sordid. It is one of the more disreputable areas of the city, and caution is required.

THE MALECÓN

Officially known as Avenida Antonio Maceo, and more properly the Muro de Malecón (literally "embankment," or "seawall"), Havana's seafront boulevard winds sinuously and dramatically along the Atlantic shoreline between the Castillo de San Salvador de la Punta and the Río Almendares. The six-lane seafront boulevard was designed as a jetty wall in 1857 by Cuban engineer Francisco de Albear but not laid out until 1902 by U.S. governor General Woods. It took 50 years to reach the Río Almendares, almost five miles to the west.

"Silver lamé" was what composer Orlando de la Rosa called the boulevard. The metaphor has stuck, although it is today only a ghostly reminder of its former brilliance—what Martha Gellhorn called a "19th century jewel and a joke." The Malecón is lined with once-glorious high-rise houses, each exuberantly distinct from the next. Unprotected by seaworthy paint since the Revolution, they have proven incapable of withstanding the salt spray that crashes over the seawall in great airy clouds and then floats off in rainbows. Their facades are now decrepit, while the broad limestone walkway is pitted and broken. Many buildings have already collapsed.

However, at last visit a restoration of the Malecón (which in 2005 was trashed by Hurricane Wilma) was well under way, while new wrought-iron street lamps in classical style have gone up, adding much-needed beauty. (The renovation, however, betrays shoddy workmanship and the newly restored seawall and sidewalk were crumbling once again and the newly painted houses—green trimmed with purple, pink with blue, yellow with orange—were already peeling, having been painted in haste for the pope's visit in 1998.)

All along the shore are the worn remains of square baths—known as the "Elysian Fields"—hewn from the rocks below the seawall, originally with separate areas for men, women, and *negros*. These **Baños del Mar** preceded construction of the Malecón. Each is about 12 feet square and six to eight feet deep, with rock steps for access and a couple of portholes through which the waves wash in and out.

The Malecón offers a microcosm of Havana life: the elderly walking their dogs; the shift-less selling cigars and cheap sex to tourists; the young passing rum among friends; fishermen (*neumáticos*) tending their lines and casting off on giant inner tubes; and always, scores of couples courting and necking. The Malecón is known as "Havana's sofa" and acts, wrote Claudia Lightfoot, as "the city's drawing room, office, study, and often bedroom." All through the night, lovers' murmurings mingle with the crash of the waves.

The Malecón—the setting for spontaneous riots in the early 1990s—is also a barometer of the political state of Havana. During times of tension, the police presence is abnormally strong and the Malecón becomes eerily empty. At other times, keep one hand on your purse!

Every October 26, schoolchildren are bussed here to throw flowers over the seawall in memory of revolutionary leader Camilo Cienfuegos, killed in a mysterious air crash on that day in 1959.

Parque Maceo

Dominating the Malecón to the west, at the foot of Avenida Padre Varela, is the massive bronze **Monumento Antonio Maceo,** atop a marble base in a plaza with a fountain. The classical monument was erected in 1916 in honor of the mulatto general and hero of the Wars of Independence who was known as the "Bronze Titan" (see the sidebar *Heroes of the Wars of Independence* in the *Background* chapter). The motley tower that stands at the west end of the plaza is the 17th-century **Torreón de San Lázaro,** with loopholes for snipers aiming along the Malecón. Although it looks fairly modern, it was built in 1665 to guard the former cove of San Lázaro.

To the south, the **Hospital Hermanos Almeijeiras** looms over the park. The **Convento y Capilla de la Inmaculada Concepción** (San Lázaro #805, e/ Oquendo y Lucena, tel. 07/878-8404) is immediately west of the hospital. This beautiful church and convent was built in Gothic style in 1874 and features notable stained-glass windows and a painted altar. Services are held Monday, Wednesday, and Friday 7 A.M. and 5 P.M.; Thursday and Saturday 5 P.M.; and Sunday 9 A.M.

BARRIO CAYO HUESO

Immediately west of the Plaza Antonio Maceo is a triangular area bordered by the Malecón, San Lázaro, and Calzada de Infanta, forming the northwest corner of Centro Habana. Known as Barrio Cayo Hueso, the region dates from the early 20th century, when tenement homes were erected atop what had been the Espada cemetery (hence the name, Cay of Bones). It boasts several art deco inspirations, such as the **Edificio Solimar** (Soledad #205, e/ San Lázaro y Ánimas) apartment complex, built in 1944.

Museo Fragua Martiana

Known to very few travelers yet hallowed ground to Cubans, this small museum (Principe #108, esq. Hospital, tel. 07/870-7338; Mon.–Fri. 8 A.M.–4 P.M.; free) occupies the site of the former San Lázaro quarry, where national hero José Martí and fellow prisoners were forced to break rocks. The museum, whose name roughly translates as Museum of Martí's Forging, is dedicated to Martí, and displays manuscripts, and even shackles. To its rear, the quarry has been turned into a garden, with a life-size bronze statue of Martí.

"Salvador's Alley"

Almost every dance enthusiast and budget traveler-in-the-know gravitates at some point during their stay to **Callejón de Hamel** (e/ Aramburu y Hospital), an alley where local artist Salvador González Escalona has adorned walls with evocative murals in sun-drenched yellow, burnt orange, and blazing reds, inspired by *santería*. The alley features a *santería* shrine and fantastical totemic sculptures. González, a bearded artist with an eye for self-promotion, has an eclectic art gallery, **Estudio-Galería Fambá** (Callejón de Hamel #1054, tel. 07/878-1661, eliasasef@yahoo.es; daily 9:30 A.M.–6 P.M.). On Sundays, he hosts Afro-Cuban rumbas (see the *Entertainment* section of this chapter).

HAVANA

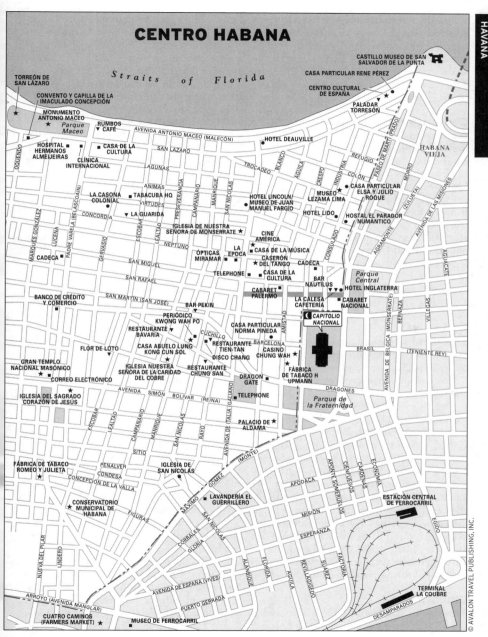

CENTRO HABANA

Straits of Florida

CASTILLO MUSEO DE SAN SALVADOR DE LA PUNTA

CASA PARTICULAR RENE PÉREZ

TORREÓN DE SAN LÁZARO

CENTRO CULTURAL DE ESPAÑA

CONVENTO Y CAPILLA DE LA IMACULADO CONCEPCIÓN

PALADAR TORRESÓN

MONUMENTO ANTONIO MACEO

Parque Maceo

RUMBOS CAFÉ

AVENIDA ANTONIO MACEO (MALECÓN)

HOTEL DEAUVILLE

HABANA VIEJA

HOSPITAL HERMANOS ALMEIJEIRAS

CASA DE LA CULTURA

SAN LÁZARO

CLÍNICA INTERNACIONAL

TROCADERO

LAGUNAS

REFUGIO

COLÓN

ANIMAS

CASA PARTICULAR ELSA Y JULIO ROQUE

LA CASONA COLONIAL

TABACUBA HQ

VIRTUDES

HOTEL LINCOLN/ MUSEO DE JUAN MANUEL FARGIO

MUSEO LEZAMA LIMA

CONCORDIA

LA GUARIDA

HOTEL LIDO

HOSTAL EL PARADOR NUMANTICO

CADECA

IGLESIA DE NUESTRA SEÑORA DE MONSERRATE

CINE AMÉRICA

NEPTUNO

ÓPTICAS MIRAMAR

LA EPOCA

CASA DE LA MÚSICA

SAN MIGUEL

CASERÓN DEL TANGO

CADECA

SAN RAFAEL

TELEPHONE

CASA DE LA CULTURA

Parque Central

HOTEL INGLATERRA

CABARET PALERMO

BAR NAUTILUS

BANCO DE CRÉDITO Y COMERCIO

SAN MARTÍN (SAN JOSÉ)

BAR PEKIN

LA CALESA CAFETERÍA

CABARET NACIONAL

PERIÓDICO KWONG WAH PO

CASA PARTICULAR NORMA PINEDA

CAPITOLIO NACIONAL

RESTAURANTE BAVARIA

CUCHILLO

FLOR DE LOTO

CASA ABUELO LUNG KONG CUN SOL

RESTAURANTE TIEN-TAN

BARCELONA

CASINO CHUNG WAH

BRASIL

(TENIENTE REY)

DISCO CHANG

GRAN TEMPLO NACIONAL MASÓNICO

IGLESIA NUESTRA SEÑORA DE LA CARIDAD DEL COBRE

RESTAURANTE CHUNG SAN

DRAGON GATE

FÁBRICA DE TABACO H UPMANN

CORREO ELECTRÓNICO

AVENIDA SIMÓN BOLIVAR (REINA)

TELEPHONE

DRAGONES

IGLESIA DEL SAGRADO CORAZÓN DE JESÚS

Parque de la Fraternidad

PALACIO DE ALDAMA

SITIO

FÁBRICA DE TABACO ROMEO Y JULIETA

PENALVER

IGLESIA DE SAN NICOLÁS

CONCEPCIÓN DE LA VALLA

CONDESA

CONSERVATORIO MUNICIPAL DE HABANA

FIGURAS

ESTACIÓN CENTRAL DE FERROCARRIL

LAVANDERÍA EL GUERRILLERO

MISIÓN

NUEVA DEL PILAR

LINDERO

CORRALES

GLORIA

ESPERANZA

TERMINAL LA COUBRE

ARROYO (AVENIDA MANGLAR)

AVENIDA DE ESPAÑA (VIVES)

PUERTO GERRADA

DESAMPARADOS

CUATRO CAMINOS (FARMERS MARKET)

MUSEO DE FERROCARRIL

OQUENDO

MARQUÉS GONZÁLEZ

LUCENA

PADRE VARELA (BELASCOAÍN)

GERVASIO

ESCOBAR

LEALTAD

CAMPANARIO

MANRIQUE

SAN NICOLÁS

RAYO

AVENIDA DE ITALIA (GALIANO)

MÁXIMO GOMEZ (MONTE)

APONTE SOMERUELOS

CIENFUEGOS

CÁRDENAS

ECONOMÍA

AVENIDA DE BÉLGICA (MONSERRATE)

BERNAZA

VILLEGAS

AGUACATE

CONSULADO

AGRAMONTE

ZULUETA

AVENIDA DE LAS MISIONES

MORRO

PASEO DE MARTÍ

PRADO

INDUSTRIA

CRESPO

AGUILA

BLANCO

AMISTAD

APODACA

AGUILA

REVILLAGIGEDO

SUÁREZ

FACTORIA

EGIDO

ALAMBIQUE

FLORIDA

© AVALON TRAVEL PUBLISHING, INC.

Nearby, **Parque de los Mártires Universitarios** (Infanta, e/ Calles Jovellar y San Lázaro), one block west of Callejón de Hamel, honors students of the University of Havana who were murdered or otherwise lost their lives during the fights against the Machado and Batista regimes.

Convento y Iglesia del Carmen

Soaring over Calle Infanta, about 100 meters south of San Lázaro, is one of Havana's largest and most impressive churches (Infanta, e/ Neptuno y Concordia, tel. 07/878-5168; Mon.–Sat. 8–10 A.M. and 4–7 P.M., Sun. 7:30 A.M.–12:30 P.M. and 4:30–7:30 P.M.). Built in baroque fashion, the church and convent is capped by a 60.5-meter-tall tower atop which soars a 7.5-meter-tall sculpture of Our Lady of Carmen. Inside, the church features beautiful stained glass and statuary. Mass is held Monday–Saturday at 8 A.M. and 6:30 P.M. and Sundays at 8:30 A.M., 11:30 A.M., and 6:30 P.M.

GALIANO

This broad boulevard, lined with arcaded porticos its entire length, runs south from the Malecón to Avenida Salvador Allende and is Centro's main north–south artery. It has several sights of interest.

The Hotel Lincoln (Galiano, e/ Ánimas y Virtudes) was where Argentina's world-champion racecar driver Fangio was kidnapped by Castro's revolutionaries in 1958 during the Cuban Grand Prix. Room #810 is today the **Museo de Juan Manuel Fangio**, with photos and magazines from the period presenting a predictably one-sided version of the affair. Also on an Argentinian theme, fans of tango might check out the **Caserón del Tango** (Neptuno #303, e/ Águila y Italia, tel. 07/863-0097; 10 A.M.– 8 P.M.), a tiny cultural center-cummuseum run by tango lover Edmundo Daubal in honor of the Argentinian dance.

Cine América

This cinema (Galiano #253, esq. Concordia, tel. 07/862-5416) dates from 1941 and is one of the world's great art deco theaters, albeit severely deteriorated. The foyer features a terrazzo floor with zodiac motifs and an inlaid map of the world, with Cuba, which lies at the very center, picked out in polished brass. Cater-corner, the **Iglesia de Nuestra Señora de Monserrate** dates from 1843.

Museo Lezama Lima

Literature buffs might detour to this museum (Trocadero #162, e/ Crespo y Industria, tel. 07/863-4161), four blocks east of Galiano, in the former home of writer José Lezama Lima. The novelist is most famous for *Paradiso,* an autobiographical, sexually explicit, homoerotic baroque novel that viewed Cuba as a "paradise lost" and was eventually made into a renowned movie. Lima fell afoul of Fidel Castro and became a virtual recluse until his death in 1975.

BARRIO CHINO

The first Chinese immigrants to Cuba arrived in 1847 as indentured laborers. Over ensuing decades, as many as 150,000 Chinese may have arrived to work the fields. They were contracted to labor for eight years for miserable wages insufficient to buy their return. Most stayed, and many intermarried with blacks. The Sino-Cuban descendants of those who worked off their indenture gravitated to Centro Habana, where they settled in the zones bordering the Zanza Real, the aqueduct that channeled water to the city. They were later joined by other Chinese fleeing persecution, including a wealthy group of California Chinese who arrived with investment opportunities in mind. In time Havana's Chinese quarter, Barrio Chino, became the largest in Latin America—a mini-Beijing in the tropics.

In the decades preceding the Revolution, Barrio Chino evolved as a center of opium dens, brothels, peep shows, and sex clubs. Today, Barrio Chino is a mere shadow of its former self, with about 400 native-born Chinese and perhaps 2,000 descendants still resident in the area. The vast majority of Chinese left Cuba in the years immediately following the Revolution. Barrio Chino has since lost most of its person-

the Pórtico Chino, on Calle Dragones, at the entrance to Barrio Chino

ality along with its colorful characters, who were encouraged to become "less Chinese and more Cuban." Nonetheless, there's enough to remind you of how things once were.

In 1995, the government of China funded a **Pórtico Chino** (Dragon Gate) across Calle Dragones, between Amistad and Aguila, announcing visitors' entry from the east.

Nearby, the **Iglesia Nuestra Señora de la Caridad del Cobre** (Manrique #570, esq. Salud, tel. 07/861-0945; Tues.–Fri. 7:30 A.M.– 6 P.M., Sat. 7:30 A.M.–noon, Sun. 7:30 A.M.– noon and 4–6 P.M.) was erected in 1802 and features exquisite statuary, stained-glass windows, and a gilt altar.

Callejón Cuchillo

A lively market is held daily (except Wednesday) on pedestrian-only "Knife Alley," lined with Chinese restaurants and aglow at night with Chinese lanterns. Ernest Hemingway used to eat at Restaurante Pacífico (San Nicolás, esq. Cuchillo), as did Fidel Castro. "To get there," recalls Hemingway's son, Gregory, "you

had to go up in an old elevator with a sliding iron grille for a door. It stopped at every floor, whether you wanted it to or not. On the second floor there was a five-piece Chinese orchestra blaring crazy atonal music. … Then you reached the third floor, where there was a whorehouse. … The fourth floor was an opium den with pitifully wasted little figures curled up around their pipes." The restaurant is no longer open.

Chinese "Casinos"

More than one dozen social associations work to promote Chinese culture (many Cuban-Chinese, for example, worship Cuan Cung, a red-faced, long-bearded deity synchronistically akin to Changó, the African warrior saint in *santería*). Visitors are welcome. The **Casa de Artes y Tradiciones Chinas** (Salud #313, e/ Gervasio y Escobar, tel. 07/863-9632; Mon.– Fri. 8:30 A.M.–5:30 P.M., Sat. 8:30 A.M.–noon) features a small gallery, and tai chi and dance classes are offered. The **Casa Abuelo Lung Kong Cun Sol** (Dragones #364, e/ Manrique y San Nicolás, tel. 07/862-5388 or 863-2061; daily noon–midnight) exists to support elders in the Chinese community. On the third floor is the **Templo San Fan Kong,** with an exquisitely carved, centenary gold-plated altar imported from Canton.

AVENIDAS SIMÓN BOLÍVAR AND SALVADOR ALLENDE (CARLOS III)

Avenida Simón Bolívar (formerly Avenida Reina) runs west from Parque de la Fraternidad. Simón Bolívar is lined with once-impressive colonial-era structures gone to ruin. Beyond Avenida Padre Varela (Belascoain), it broadens into a wide boulevard called Avenida Salvador Allende. The avenue was laid out in the early 19th century by Governor Tacón, when it was known officially as Carlos III.

The **Gran Templo Nacional Masónico** (Av. Salvador Allende, e/ Padre Varela y Lucena) was established in 1951 as Havana's Grand Masonic Temple. Though no longer a Freemason's lodge, it retains a fading mural in the lobby depicting the history of Masonry in Cuba.

Iglesia del Sagrado Corazón de Jesús

One of the few structures not seemingly on its last legs, the Church of the Sacred Heart of Jesus (Simón Bolívar, e/ Padre Varela y Gervasio, tel. 07/862-4979; daily 8 A.M.–noon and 4–7 P.M.) is a Gothic inspiration in stone that could have been transported from medieval England. It was built in 1922 with a beamed ceiling held aloft by great marbled columns. Gargoyles and Christian allegories adorn the exterior, featuring a 77-meter-tall spire topped by a bronze cross. The church boasts stained-glass windows and a soaring altar of carved wood. Services are offered Monday–Saturday 8 A.M. and 4:30 P.M. and Sunday 8 A.M., 9:30 A.M., and 4:30 P.M.

CUATROS CAMINOS AND CERRO

South of Avenidas Simón Bolívar and Salvador Allende, the down-at-the-heels neighborhoods of southern Centro Habana extend into the adjacent and equally squalid *municipalidad* of Cerro. Still, the area has a few sights of interest, although caution is required when walking the streets. I recommend taking a taxi.

Several key arterial roads meet at Cuatros Caminos, an all-important junction.

Cuatros Caminos

A photogenic delight for photographers, the Four Roads Farmers Market (tel. 07/870-5934; Tues.–Sat. 7 A.M.–6:30 P.M., Sun. 7 A.M.–2 P.M.) takes up the entire block between Máximo Gómez and Cristina (also called Avenida de la México), and Manglar Arroyo and Matadero. This much-dilapidated 19th-century market hall has functioned as such for two centuries and is worth a visit for its bustling color and ambience. Here you can buy live goats, geese, pig's heads, and all manner of fruits and veggies.

Museo de Ferrocarril

On the east side of Cristina, facing the market, is the Railway Museum (tel. 879-3546; Tues.–Sun. 8 A.M.–5 P.M.; entrance CUC2), housed in the former Estación Cristina and telling the history of rail in Cuba. You'd have to be a serious rail buff to get a thrill from the exhibits (from model trains to bells, signals, and even telegraph equipment). Sitting on rails in its lobby is an 1843 steam locomotive (Cuba's first) called *La Junta*. Three other antique steam trains are displayed, along with various diesel locomotives, albeit without any information whatsoever.

Fábrica de Tabaco Romeo y Julieta

Cigar connoisseurs the world over know the name Romeo y Julieta, a fine cigar brand made at this factory (Padre Varela, e/ Desagüe y Peñal Verno, tel. 07/878-1058 or 879-3927; Mon.–Fri. 8:30–11 A.M. and noon–3 P.M.; adults CUC10, children free), five blocks northwest of Cuatro Caminos. The factory was founded in 1875 by Inocencia Álvarez and is known officially today as the Antonio Briones Montoto cigar factory. It specializes in medium-flavored brands. Like most Havana cigar factories, duties vary by floor, with leaf handling on the ground floor, and stemming, sorting, rolling, box decorating, and ringing on the upper two floors. Tours are offered every 30 minutes. No cameras.

One block south is the **Conservatorio Municipal de Habana** (Padre Varela, esq. Carmen), a music conservatory boasting a well-preserved classical facade.

Avenida Máximo Gómez and Calzada de Cerro

Avenida Máximo Gómez (popularly called Monte; the name changes to Calzada de Cerro west of Infanta) snakes southwest from Parque de la Fraternidad and connects Habana Vieja with Cerro. During the 19th century, scores of summer homes in classical style were erected here, each more extravagantly Italianate than the next. It has been described by writer Paul Goldberger as "one of the most remarkable streets in the world: three unbroken kilometers of nineteenth-century neoclassical villas, with colonnaded arcades making an urban vista of heartbreaking beauty." Heartbreaking is correct. The avenue ascends southward, marching backward into the past like a classical ruin. Monte's once-stunning arcades are now in desperate condition, and houses are collapsing behind decaying facades.

One of the most splendid mansions still extant is the **Quinta del Conde de Santovenia** (Calzada de Cerro #1424, e/ Patria y Auditor, tel. 07/870-6449), erected in 1845 in subdued neoclassical style, with a 1929 neo-Gothic chapel addition. It has served as a home for the elderly (*hogar de ancianos*) for more than a century.

Farther west, one block south of Calzada de Cerro, is the tiny **Plaza de Galicia** (Peñon, esq. Santo Tomás). Shaded by venerable ceiba trees and bougainvillea bowers, the square features the diminutive **Iglesia de Peñon,** with a Corinthian frontage and round spire. The plaza was dedicated in 1991 to the *pueblo gallego* (Galician people). Ecclesiastics on a busman's holiday might also check out the **Iglesia de**

Fábrica de Ron Bocoy

San Nicolás, on San Nicolás one block west of Monte. This splendidly restored yet tiny church has a circular bell tower.

Fábrica de Ron Bocoy

The most intriguing site in Cerro is this venerable former home turned rum factory (Máximo Gómez #1417, e/ Patria y Auditor, tel. 07/877-5781, bocoy@tuhv.cha.cyt.cu; Mon.–Sat. 9 A.M.–5 P.M., Sun. 9 A.M.–3 P.M.), facing Quinta del Conde de Santovenia. The two-tone pink facade, with the legend BOCOY above the wide, handsome door, is decorated with four dozen cast-iron swans painted blue and white and marching wing to wing, "each standing tall and slim, its long neck bent straight down in mortal combat with an evil serpent climbing up its legs to sink its fangs," wrote James Michener, who chose this building as a setting in his book *Caribbean.* Hence the building's colloquial nickname, *Casa de Culebras* (House of Snakes). The swans were a symbol of wealth that the snakes were meant to guard. It was formerly owned by the Counts of Villanueva.

Today the mansion is a distillery and makes

Cuba's famous Legendario rums and liquors. Bocoy also manufactures one of the choicest rums in Cuba, intended solely for Fidel Castro to give as gifts to notable personalities: The special libation is packaged in a bulbous earthenware bottle inside a miniature pirate's treasure chest labeled La Isla del Tesoro (Treasure Island), on display in the small upstairs museum that boasts an original 19th-century copper distillery.

The vaults contain great oak casks up to seven meters tall stacked in dark recesses. Free tours are offered.

Quinta las Delicias

This art nouveau mansion (Av. Santa Catalina, esq. Palatino, tel. 07/867-0205 or 841-1526; Mon.–Fri. 8 A.M.–5 P.M.), on Calzada Palatino, a westerly extension of Calzada de Cerro, was built in 1905 by Charles Brun for Rosalia Abreu, a socialite who populated the extensive grounds with almost 200 monkeys—hence the popular name, Finca de los Monos (Villa of Monkeys). Beyond the castellated entrance, the vestibule is graced by a mural by Cuban artist Arturo Mendocal, and by a gloriously decorated ceiling and stained-glass *ventrales*. The woodsy gardens contain a neo-Gothic family chapel. It functions today as a youth center. Visits by appointment only.

If you've come this far, you may as well peek at the **Pabellón de los Depósitos del Acueducto de Albear** (Fomento, e/ Chaple y Recreo), two blocks east of Calzada Palatino. This neoclassical aqueduct and reservoir with giant frogs in each corner was designed in 1856 by Francisco de Albear to supply gravity-fed water to the ever-expanding city. It still functions as the modern, albeit much dilapidated, waterworks, and supplies one-fifth of Havana's water. Visitors are not allowed in without special permission.

Sights – Vedado and Plaza de la Revolución

The *municipio* of Plaza de la Revolución (pop. 165,000), west of Centro Habana, comprises the leafy residential streets of Vedado and, to the southwest, the modern enclave of Nuevo Vedado and Plaza de la Revolución.

Vedado—the commercial heart of "modern" Havana—has been described as "Havana at its middle-class best." The University of Havana is here. So are the Cementerio Colón, many of the city's prime hotels and restaurants, virtually all its main commercial buildings, and block after block of handsome mansions and apartment houses in art deco, eclectic, Beaux-Arts, and neoclassical styles—luxurious and humble alike lining streets shaded by stately jagüeys dropping their aerial roots to the ground.

Formerly a vast open space between Centro Habana and the Río Almendares, Vedado ("forest reserve" or "forbidden") served as a buffer zone in case of attack from the west; construction was prohibited. In 1859, how-

ever, plans were drawn up for urban expansion using a grid system. Strict building regulations, for example, defined that there should be 15 feet of gardens between building and street, and more in wider *avenidas*. Regularly spaced parks were mandated, along with an extension of the Malecón. The conclusion of the brief Spanish-American-Cuban War, in 1898, brought U.S. money rushing in. Civic structures, large hotels, casinos, department stores, and lavish restaurants sprouted alongside nightclubs.

The sprawling region is hemmed to the north by the Malecón, to the east by Calzada de Infanta, to the west by the Río Almendares, running in a deep canyon, and to the southeast by the Calzada de Ayestaran and Avenida de la Independencia. Vedado follows a grid pattern aligned north–northwest by south–southeast and laid out in quadrants. Odd-numbered streets (calles) run east–west, parallel to the shore. Even-numbered calles run perpendicular.

TWENTIETH-CENTURY ARCHITECTURAL TREASURES

The turn of the 20th century spawned a desire for modernity. Cuba, a nation seeking to free itself of a parochial past, adopted North American and European influences with remarkable fervor. The arrival of U.S. architects spearheaded an American influence, while Cuba developed its own world-class Cuban School of Architecture, whose graduates showed occasional displays of genuine brilliance. The period 1925–65 was uniquely inventive. Although no uniquely Cuban architecture evolved, a subtle "Cubanization" transformed styles introduced to the island. Modernist designs with a tropical twist, from streamlined art deco apartment blocks to modernist villas, complemented Havana's astonishing trove of colonial structures.

Art nouveau arrived from Europe around 1905, with Franco-Belgian, Viennese, and Catalan versions in overlapping succession, such as the highly decorative, even whimsical, Palacio Cueto (on the southeast corner of Plaza Vieja), built in 1906 in a style influenced by Barcelona's Gaudí-inspired *modernismo*. The 1920s Beaux-Arts style, influenced by the École de Beaux-Arts in Paris, fused baroque, classical, Renaissance, and neoclassical elements. Corinthian columns, Pompeiian fresoes, with a lavish use of symbolic statues (such as those adorning the staircase to the Capitolio Nacional), conveyed a message of Havana's power and grandeur. Purely neo-Renaissance edifices – such as the legendary Hotel Nacional (1930) – also went up in quintessentially Cuban versions of Italian, French, and Spanish styles. Other structures, such as the Palacio Presidencial, completed in 1919, adopted the so-called Eclectic style, which melded revivalist trends to elements of neoclassicism, Renaissance, and Beaux-Arts forms.

Art deco followed and coincided with the heyday of Hollywood movies. Public edifices were adorned with lavish ornamentation inside and out, as with Esteban Rodríguez's masterful Edificio Bacardí (1930), on Monserrate, and the Cine América (1940), on Galiano. This was the great age of transport and Cuban architects were inspired to infuse their art deco buildings with slick streamlined forms. Decorative panels and geometric motifs were relegated to the interiors of buildings, while exteriors were graced by gradually rounded curves and horizontally banded parapets and verandas representing bodies streaking through air. Centro Habana, in particular, boasts many apartment buildings in this streamlined style, such as the Edificio Solimar (Soledad #205, e/ San Lázaro y Ánimas).

MODERNISMO

Wed to a contemporary avant-garde style led by architects Eugenio Batista, Mario Romañach, and Max Borges Recio, "modernism" came into its glory in the 1950s and continued into the early years of the Revolution. Thousands of magnificent homes in experimental contemporary fashion blossomed in Miramar, Cubanacán, and other western suburbs. Back came stained glass, tile detailing, jalousies, and the inner patio, fused with asymmetrical cubist elements, cantilevered stairs, parabolic structures, and cast shell roofs popularized by Borges. His masterpiece is the Tropicana nightclub, combining complexity with a tropical sensuality defined by graceful curves.

Modernismo reached for the sky. Cuba's pioneering architects changed the Vedado skyline with towering hotels and apartment buildings funded, often, by Mafia money, as with the Hotel Capri (1957), Hotel Riviera (1957), and Habana Libre (1958). Meanwhile, the influence of monumentalist edifices associated with European fascist regimes was assimilated into new public structures, such as the Palace of Justice (now the Palace of the Revolution).

Following the Revolution, leading architects fled the country and the closure of the School of Architecture in 1965 spelled the end of a glorious era.

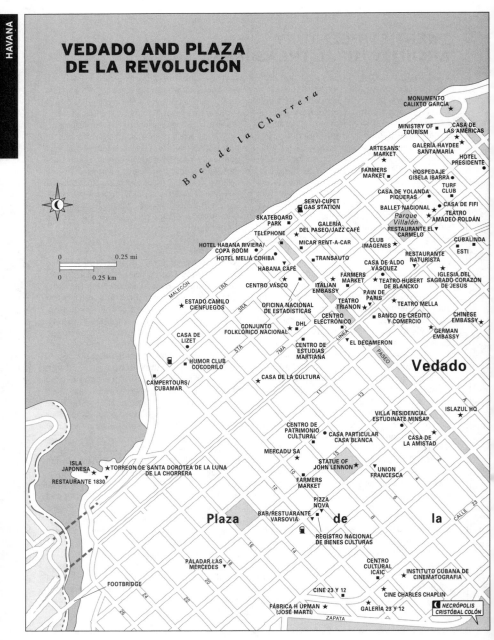

VEDADO AND PLAZA DE LA REVOLUCIÓN

Boca de la Chorrera

MONUMENTO CALIXTO GARCÍA

MINISTRY OF TOURISM
CASA DE LAS AMÉRICAS

ARTESANS' MARKET
GALERÍA HAYDEE SANTAMARÍA
HOTEL PRESIDENTE

FARMERS MARKET
HOSPEDAJE GISELA IBARRA

CASA DE YOLANDA PIQUERAS
TURF CLUB

SERVI-CUPET GAS STATION
BALLET NACIONAL
CASA DE FIFI

SKATEBOARD PARK
Parque Villalón
TEATRO AMADEO ROLDÁN

GALERÍA DEL PASEO/JAZZ CAFÉ
RESTAURANTE EL CARMELO

TELEPHONE
CLUB IMÁGENES
CUBALINDA

HOTEL HABANA RIVIERA/ COPA ROOM
MICAR RENT-A-CAR
RESTAURANTE NATURISTA
ESTI

HOTEL MELIÁ COHIBA
TRANSAUTO
CASA DE ALDO VÁSQUEZ

HABANA CAFÉ
FARMERS MARKET
IGLESIA DEL SAGRADO CORAZÓN DE JESÚS

CENTRO VASCO
ITALIAN EMBASSY
TEATRO HUBERT DE BLANCKO

PAIN DE PARIS

ESTADO CAMILO CIENFUEGOS
OFICINA NACIONAL DE ESTADÍSTICAS
TEATRO TRIANON
TEATRO MELLA

CONJUNTO FOLKLÓRICO NACIONAL
CENTRO ELECTRÓNICO
DHL
BANCO DE CRÉDITO Y COMERCIO
CHINESE EMBASSY

CASA DE LIZET
GERMAN EMBASSY

CENTRO DE ESTUDIAS MARTIANA
EL DECAMERON

HUMOR CLUB COCODRILO

Vedado

CAMPERTOURS/ CUBAMAR

CASA DE LA CULTURA

VILLA RESIDENCIAL ESTUDINATE MINSAP
ISLAZUL HQ

CENTRO DE PATRIMONIO CULTURAL
CASA PARTICULAR CASA BLANCA
CASA DE LA AMISTAD

MERCADU SA

ISLA JAPONESA
TORREON DE SANTA DOROTEA DE LA LUNA DE LA CHORRERA
STATUE OF JOHN LENNON
UNION FRANCESCA

RESTAURANTE 1830
FARMERS MARKET

PIZZA NOVA

Plaza
BAR/RESTUARANTE VARSOVIA
de
la

REGISTRO NACIONAL DE BIENES CULTURAS

PALADAR LAS MERCEDES

CENTRO CULTURAL ICAIC
INSTITUTO CUBANA DE CINEMATOGRAFIA

FOOTBRIDGE

CINE 23 Y 12
CINE CHARLES CHAPLIN

FÁBRICA H UPMAN (JOSÉ MARTI)
GALERÍA 23 Y 12
NECRÓPOLIS CRISTÓBAL COLÓN

ZAPATA

MALECON
1RA
3RA
5TA
7MA
LINEA
PASEO
11
13
15
10
12
18
14
16
20
22
24
26
28
2
4
6
8
CALLE 23

0   0.25 mi
0   0.25 km

HAVANA

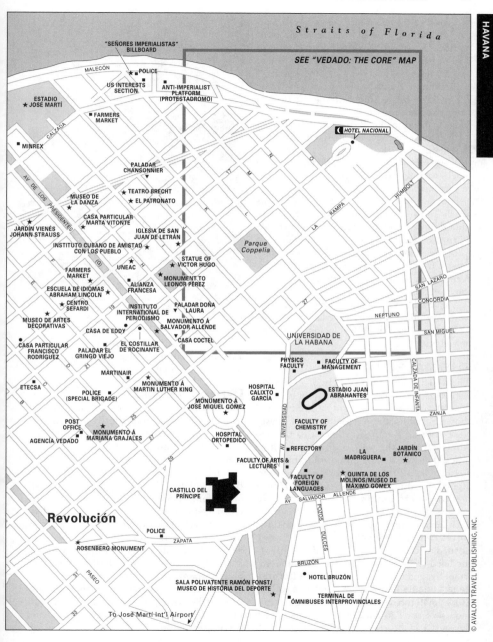

Straits of Florida

SEE "VEDADO: THE CORE" MAP

"SEÑORES IMPERIALISTAS" BILLBOARD

MALECÓN

POLICE

US INTERESTS SECTION

ANTI-IMPERIALIST PLATFORM (PROTESTADROMO)

ESTADIO JOSÉ MARTÍ

CALZADA

FARMERS MARKET

HOTEL NACIONAL

MINREX

AV. DE LOS PRESIDENTES

PALADAR CHANSONNIER

MUSEO DE LA DANZA

TEATRO BRECHT

EL PATRONATO

RAMPA

HUMBOLT

LA

CASA PARTICULAR MARTA VITONTE

JARDÍN VIENÉS JOHANN STRAUSS

IGLESIA DE SAN JUAN DE LETRÁN

Parque Coppelia

INSTITUTO CUBANO DE AMISTAD CON LOS PUEBLO

FARMERS MARKET

UNEAC

STATUE OF VICTOR HUGO

SAN LÁZARO

CONCORDIA

MONUMENTO A LEONOR PÉREZ

ESCUELA DE IDIOMAS ABRAHAM LINCOLN

ALIANZA FRANCESA

NEPTUNO

CENTRO SEFARDI

INSTITUTO INTERNACIONAL DE PERIODISMO

PALADAR DOÑA LAURA

SAN MIGUEL

MUSEO DE ARTES DECORATIVAS

CASA DE EDDY

MONUMENTO A SALVADOR ALLENDE

CASA COCTEL

UNIVERSIDAD DE LA HABANA

CASA PARTICULAR FRANCISCO RODRÍGUEZ

EL COSTILLAR DE ROCINANTE

PALADAR EL GRINGO VIEJO

PHYSICS FACULTY

FACULTY OF MANAGEMENT

CALZADA DE INFANTA

ETECSA

MARTINAIR

MONUMENTO A MARTIN LUTHER KING

POLICE (SPECIAL BRIGADE)

HOSPITAL CALIXTO GARCÍA

ESTADIO JUAN ABRAHANTES

ZANJA

UNIVERSIDAD

FACULTY OF CHEMISTRY

POST OFFICE

MONUMENTO A JOSÉ MIGUEL GOMEZ

AGENCIA VÉDADO

MONUMENTO A MARIANA GRAJALES

HOSPITAL ORTOPEDICO

REFECTORY

LA MADRIGUERA

JARDÍN BOTÁNICO

FACULTY OF ARTS & LECTURES

FACULTY OF FOREIGN LANGUAGES

QUINTA DE LOS MOLINOS/MUSEO DE MÁXIMO GOMEX

CASTILLO DEL PRÍNCIPE

AV. SALVADOR ALLENDE

POZOS

DULCES

Revolución

POLICE

ZAPATA

ROSENBERG MONUMENT

PASEO

BRUZON

HOTEL BRUZON

SALA POLIVATENTE RAMÓN FONST/ MUSEO DE HISTORIA DEL DEPORTE

TERMINAL DE ÓMNIBUSES INTERPROVINCIALES

To José Martí Int'l Airport

© AVALON TRAVEL PUBLISHING, INC.

(To confuse things, some "calles" are "avenidas." In addition, west of Paseo, calles are even-numbered; east of Paseo, calles run from A to P.) The basic grid is overlaid by a larger grid of broad boulevards averaging six blocks apart.

Dividing the quadrants east–west is Calle 23, which rises (colloquially) as La Rampa from the Malecón at its junction with Calzada de Infanta. La Rampa runs uphill to Calle L and continues on the flat as Calle 23. Paralleling it to the north is a second major east–west thoroughfare, Calle 9 (Línea), five blocks inland of the Malecón, which it meets to the northeast.

Four major roadways divide the quadrants north–south: Calle L to the east, and Avenida de los Presidentes, Paseo, and Avenida 12 further west. Vedado slopes gently upward from the shore to Calle 23 and thence gently downward toward the Cerro district. Almost every major avenue in Vedado emerges onto the Malecón.

Avenida de los Presidentes, Paseo, and, to the west, Avenida 26, connect Vedado to Nuevo Vedado and Plaza de la Revolución, southwest of Vedado.

A 1940s Cadillac sweeps along Havana's Malecón boulevard, with the Hotel Nacional behind.

© CHRISTOPHER P. BAKER

THE MALECÓN

The Malecón (see the listing in *Sights—Centro Habana and Cerro* in this chapter for more details) runs along the bulging, wave-battered shorefront of northern Vedado, curling east–west from La Rampa in the east to the Río Almendares in the west, a distance of three miles. The sidewalk is pitted underfoot, but a stroll its full length makes for good exercise while taking in such sites as the **Monumento Calixto García** (Malecón y Av. de los Presidentes), featuring a bronze figure of the 19th-century rebel general on horseback; the **Hotel Habana Riviera** (Malecón y Paseo), opened by the Mafia in 1958 and recently remodeled to show off its spectacular modernist lobby; and the **Torreón de Santa Dorotea de la Luna de la Chorrera** (Malecón y Calle 20), a small fortress built in 1762 to guard the mouth of the Río Almendares. Immediately beyond "La Chorrera," the Restaurante 1830

features a Gaudíesque garden that includes a dramatic cupola and a tiny island—**Isla Japonesa**—in Japanese style.

🄲 Hotel Nacional

The landmark Hotel Nacional (Calles O y 21, tel. 07/33-3564) is dramatically perched atop a small cliff at the junction of La Rampa and the Malecón. Now a national monument, this grande dame hotel was designed by the same architects who designed The Breakers in Palm Beach, which it closely resembles. It opened on December 30, 1930, in the midst of the Great Depression. The elaborately detailed, Spanish-style neoclassical hotel suffered from bad management and by 1955 was greatly in need of refurbishment when mobster Meyer Lansky persuaded General Batista to let him build a grand casino and convert some of the rooms to luxurious suites for wealthy gamblers. The hotel's mob associations run deep; in 1946 Lucky Luciano called a summit here to discuss carving up Havana. Luminaries from Winston

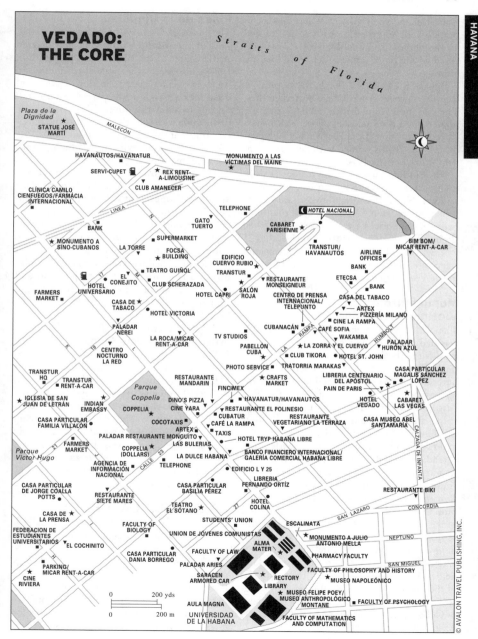

VEDADO: THE CORE

Straits of Florida

Plaza de la Dignidad
★ STATUE JOSÉ MARTÍ

MALECÓN

HAVANAUTOS/HAVANATUR

MONUMENTO A LAS VÍCTIMAS DEL MAINE

SERVI-CUPET ★ REX RENT-A-LIMOUSINE

CLUB AMANECER

CLÍNICA CAMILO CIENFUEGOS/FARMACIA INTERNACIONAL

LINEA

TELEPHONE

GATO TUERTO

HOTEL NACIONAL

BANK

CABARET PARISIENNE

★ MONUMENTO A SINO-CUBANOS

SUPERMARKET

LA TORRE

FOCSA BUILDING

TRANSTUR/ HAVANAUTOS

AIRLINE OFFICES

BIM BOM/ MICAR RENT-A-CAR

EDIFICIO CUERVO RUBIO

BANK

EL CONEJITO

TEATRO GUIÑOL

TRANSTUR

RESTAURANTE MONSEIGNEUR

ETECSA

BANK

HOTEL UNIVERSARIO

CLUB SCHERAZADA

HOTEL CAPRI

SALÓN ROJA

CENTRO DE PRENSA INTERNACIONAL/ TELEPUNTO

CASA DEL TABACO

FARMERS MARKET

CASA DE TABACO

HOTEL VICTORIA

ARTEX
PIZZERÍA MILANO

CINE LA RAMPA

PALADAR NEREI

CUBANACÁN

CAFÉ SOFIA

RAMPA

WAKAMBA

LA ROCA/MICAR RENT-A-CAR

TV STUDIOS

PABELLÓN CUBA

★ LA ZORRA Y EL CUERVO

PALADAR HURÓN AZÚL

HUMBOLT

CENTRO NOCTURNO LA RED

CLUB TIKORA

HOTEL ST. JOHN

TRANSTUR HQ

PHOTO SERVICE

TRATORRIA MARAKAS

CASA PARTICULAR MAGALIS SÁNCHEZ LÓPEZ

RESTAURANTE MANDARIN

CRAFTS MARKET

LIBRERIA CENTENARIO DEL APOSTOL

TRANSTUR RENT-A-CAR

FINCIMEX

PAIN DE PARIS

IGLESIA DE SAN JUAN DE LETRÁN

INDIAN EMBASSY

Parque Coppelia

DINO'S PIZZA

HAVANAR/HAVANAUTOS

HOTEL VEDADO

CABARET LAS VEGAS

COPPELIA

CINE YARA

RESTAURANTE EL POLINESIO

CASA PARTICULAR FAMILIA VILLALÓN

COCOTAXIS

CUBATUR

CAFÉ LA RAMPA

RESTAURANTE VEGETARIANO LA TERRAZA

CASA MUSEO ABEL SANTAMARIA

PALADAR RESTAURANTE MONGUITO

ARTEX

TAXIS

HOTEL TRYP HABANA LIBRE

Parque Victor Hugo

FARMERS MARKET

COPPELIA (DOLLARS)

LAS BULERIAS

LA DULCE HABANA

BANCO FINANCIERO INTERNACIONAL/ GALERIA COMERCIAL HABANA LIBRE

AGENCIA DE INFORMACIÓN NACIONAL

CALLE 23

TELEPHONE

EDIFICIO L Y 25

LIBRERIA FERNANDO ORTÍZ

RESTAURANTE BIKI

CASA PARTICULAR DE JORGE COALLA POTTS

RESTAURANTE SIETE MARES

CASA PARTICULAR BASILIA PÉREZ

HOTEL COLINA

SAN LAZARO

CONCORDIA

CASA DE LA PRENSA

TEATRO EL SÓTANO

STUDENTS' UNION

ESCALINATA

FACULTY OF BIOLOGY

UNION DE JÓVENES COMUNISTAS

MONUMENTO A JULIO ANTONIO MELLA

NEPTUNO

FEDERACIÓN DE ESTUDIANTES UNIVERSITARIOS

EL COCHINITO

ALMA MATER

PHARMACY FACULTY

SAN MIGUEL

CASA PARTICULAR DANIA BORREGO

FACULTY OF LAW

FACULTY OF PHILOSOPHY AND HISTORY

PARKING/ MICAR RENT-A-CAR

PALADAR ARIES

RECTORY

MUSEO NAPOLEÓNICO

CINE RIVIERA

SARACÉN ARMORED CAR

LIBRARY

MUSEO FELIPE POEY/ MUSEO ANTHROPOLÓGICO MONTANE

FACULTY OF PSYCHOLOGY

AULA MAGNA

UNIVERSIDAD DE LA HABANA

FACULTY OF MATHEMATICS AND COMPUTATION

CALZADA DE INFANTA

0 — 200 yds
0 — 200 m

© AVALON TRAVEL PUBLISHING, INC.

Churchill and the Prince of Wales to Marlon Brando have laid their heads here, as attested by the photos in the lobby bar. It is still favored as the hotel par excellence for visiting bigwigs.

Beyond the Palladian porch, the vestibule is lavishly adorned with Mudejar patterned tiles. The sweeping palm-shaded lawns to the rear slope toward the Malecón, above which sits a battery of cannons from the Wars of Independence. The cliff is riddled with defensive tunnels built since the 1970s.

The **Edificio Cuervo Rubio** (Calles 21 y O), cater-corner to the hotel entrance, is an art deco stunner. Nip inside the lobby, which has an Italian marble statue, and look up through the "tube" of the spiral staircase augering up seven flights. The modernist **Hotel Capri** (Calles 21 y N) was built in 1958 by the American gangster Santo Trafficante and was a setting in the movie *The Godfather*.

Monumento a las Víctimas del Maine

The Maine Monument (Malecón y Calle 17) was dedicated by the republican Cuban government to the memory of the 260 sailors who died when the USS *Maine* exploded in Havana harbor in 1898, creating a prelude for U.S. intervention in the Wars of Independence. Two rusting cannons tethered by chains from the ship's anchor are laid out beneath 40-foot-tall Corinthian columns dedicated in 1925 and originally topped by an eagle with wings spread wide. Following the Revolution, the monument was a point for anti-Yankee rallies. Immediately after the failed Bay of Pigs invasion in 1960, it was desecrated by an angry mob that toppled the eagle from its roost and broke its wings—its body is now in the Museum of the City of Havana, while the head hangs on the wall of the cafeteria in the U.S. Interests Section. The Castro government later dedicated a plaque that reads, "To the victims of the *Maine*, who were sacrificed by imperialist voracity in its eagerness to seize the island of Cuba." (See the *History* section in the *Background* chapter for more details.)

Plaza de la Dignidad

The Plaza of Dignity (Malecón y Calzada), west of the Maine Monument, was created at the height of the Elián González fiasco in 1999–2000 from what was a grassy knoll in front of the U.S. Interests Section. A **statue of José Martí** stands at the plaza's eastern end, bearing in one arm a bronze likeness of young Elián while with the other he points an accusatory finger at the Interests Section—*habaneros* joke that Martí is trying to tell them, "Your visas are that way!"

The Cuban government also pumped US$2 million into constructing the **Tribuna Abierta Anti-Imperialista** (José Martí Anti-Imperialist Platform)—called jokingly by locals the *"protestadromo"*—at the west end of the plaza to accommodate the masses bussed in to taunt Uncle Sam. The concrete supports bear plaques inscribed with the names of Communist and revolutionary heroes, plus those of prominent North Americans—from Benjamin Spock to Malcolm X—at the fore of the fight for social reforms.

At the western end of the plaza is the unmarked **U.S. Interests Section** (formerly the U.S. Embassy), where low-profile U.S. diplomats and CIA agents serve Uncle Sam's whims behind a veil of mirrored-glass windows. About 100 meters further west, beyond the police station that is a vision of beaux geste, is a huge, brightly painted billboard showing a fanatical Uncle Sam growling menacingly at a Cuban soldier, who is shouting, *"Señores Imperialistas: ¡No les tenemos absolutamente ningún miedo!"* ("Imperialists: We have absolutely no fear of you!")

LA RAMPA (CALLE 23)

Calle 23 rises from the Malecón to Calle L and climbs steadily past the major airline offices, nightclubs, cinemas, travel agencies, TV studios, and art deco apartment buildings mingling with high-rise office buildings. La Rampa ("the ramp") was the setting of *Three Trapped Tigers*, Guillermo Cabrera Infante's famous novel about swinging 1950s Havana, for it was here that the ritziest hotels, casinos, and

HAVANA

COPPELIA

Coppelia, at the top of La Rampa, esq. Calle L, is the name of a park in Havana, the flying saucer-like structure at its heart, and the brand of excellent ice cream served there. In 1966 the government built this lush park with a parlor in the middle as the biggest ice creamery in the world, serving an estimated 30,000 customers a day. Cuba's rich diversity is to be found standing in line at Coppelia on a sultry Havana afternoon.

Before the Revolution, Cuba relied on its northern neighbor for much of its ice-cream supply and Howard Johnson's (which graced the corner of Calles 23 y G) 28 flavors was the brand of choice. Fidel, however, promised to outdo the Yanks with twenty-nine flavors. Before the Special Period, you used to be able to choose anything from a one-scoop cone to complex sundaes as well as more than two dozen flavors, including exotic tropical fruits that Ben and Jerry have never heard of. Today it can manage only two or three flavors a day.

The strange concrete structure that looms over the park, suspended on spidery legs, shelters a marble-topped bar where Cubans seated atop tall bar stools slurp ice cream from stainless steel bowls. A series of circular rooms is arranged overhead like a four-leaf clover, offering views out over three open-air sections where *helados* (ice cream) can be enjoyed beneath the dappled shade of lush yagüey trees. Each section has its own *cola* (line) proportional in length to the strength of the sun. Even on temperate days the *colas* snake out of the park and onto nearby streets like lethargic serpents. Waitresses serve you at communal tables made of local marble.

Coppelia featured in Tomás Gutiérrez Alea's trenchant classic movie, *Fresa y chocolate*, which was based on Senel Paz's short story, "The Woods, the Wolf, and the New Man." The movie is named for the scene at Coppelia where Diego, a gay man, had ordered strawberry ice cream, much to the consternation of David, a loyal Fidelista: "Although there was chocolate that day, he had ordered strawberry. Perverse." After the success of the movie, Cuban males, concerned with their macho image, avoided ordering *fresa*.

nightclubs were concentrated in the days before the Revolution. Multicolored granite tiles created by Wilfredo Lam, René Portocarrero, and other leading artists are laid at intervals in the sidewalks.

While exploring, be sure to stop at **Parque Coppelia** (Calles 23 y L), a park that takes up an entire block and is exclusively devoted to the consumption of ice cream, of which Cubans are consummate lovers.

Hotel Tryp Habana Libre

The 416-foot-tall "Free Havana Hotel" (Calle L, e/ 23 y 25) was once *the* place to be after opening as the Havana Hilton in April 1958. Castro even had his headquarters here briefly in 1959. For years the hotel teemed with shady foreigners—many of them, reported *National Geographic,* "not strictly tourists" and all "watched by secret police agents from the 'ministry,' meaning MININT, the Ministry of the Interior." The hotel is fronted by a spectacular contemporary mural—**Carro de la Revolución** (the Revolutionary Car)—by ceramist Amelia Peláez, made of 525 pieces in the style of Picasso. The lobby contains many fine contemporary art pieces, including a mosaic mural by René Portocarrero.

Casa Museo Abel Santamaría

Of interest primarily to students of Cuba's revolutionary history, this museum (Calle 25 #164, e/ Infanta y O, tel. 07/835-0891; Mon.–Fri. 10 A.M.–5 P.M., Sat. 10 A.M.–1 P.M.; free) occupies a simple two-room, sixth-floor apartment (#603) where Fidel Castro's revolutionary movement, the M-26-7, had its secret headquarters in the former home of the eponymous martyr. Abel Santamaría was brutally tortured and murdered following the attack on

A WALK ALONG VEDADO'S CALLE 17

Allow one hour for this walk along one of the most astonishing streets in the city.

From the Monumento del Maine, follow Calle 17 west toward the landmark 35-story **Focsa** (Calle 17 e/ M y N), a V-shaped apartment building built 1954-56 as one of the largest reinforced concrete structures in the world. Following the Revolution it was used to house East European and Soviet personnel. Today, it houses Cuban and Venezuelan doctors and nurses.

Continue west two blocks to Calle J. Turn left and after one block turn right onto Calle 19 to view the Gothic **Iglesia San Juan de Letrán,** which dates from the 1880s and is one of Havana's most impressive ecclesiastical edifices, with some of the finest stained-glass windows in Cuba.

One block west of the church is **Parque Victor Hugo** (Calle 19, e/ I y H), centered on a pergola. Circle the park counterclockwise, passing a monument to the 19th-century French novelist (author of *Les Miserables*) on the northeast corner. At the corner of Calles 19 and H is a memorial to Leonor Pérez Cabrera, mother of José Martí, with a letter from

Martí to his dearly beloved *mamá* inscribed in metal. The southeast corner (Calle 21 y I) bears a monument to Bobby Sands and nine other IRA nationalists ("martyrs" says the plaque) who died on hunger strike in Crumlin Road jail, Northern Ireland, in 1981.

Return to Calle 17 and continue westward, passing the **Instituto Cubano de Amistad con los Pueblos** (Cuban Institute for People's Friendship, Calle 17 #301, e/ H y I), occupying a palatial Beaux-Arts villa. One block west, call in at the equally magnificent mansion on the southwest corner of Calle H: The Casa de Juan Gelats, a spectacular exemplar of the Beaux-Arts style, was built in 1920 and today houses the **Unión Nacional de Escritores y Artistas de Cuba** (National Union of Cuban Writers and Artists, UNEAC, Calle 17 #351, esq. H, tel. 07/832-4551, www.uneac.com), which hosts cultural events and is open to the public.

Cross Avenida de los Presidentes and detour 20 meters uphill to the **Escuela de Idiomas Abraham Lincoln** (Presidentes, e/ 17 y 19) to admire a magnificent bronze statue of the former U.S. president in the front garden.

---

the Moncada barracks in 1953 (see the sidebar *Revolutionary Heroes* in the *History* section of the *Background* chapter). The original furnishings are still in place: a sofa bed, a small bookcase, Fidel's work desk with a statue of José Martí, and a kerosene fridge. The adjoining room (#604) has a small exhibition of Abel's sister Haydee Santamaría, Fidel, and other revolutionaries; curiously, the only photo of Abel is as a two-year-old.

UNIVERSIDAD DE LA HABANA AND VICINITY

The **University of Havana** (Calle L y San Lázaro, tel. 07/878-3231, www.uh.cu; Mon.–Fri. 8 A.M.–6 P.M.) was founded by Dominican friars in 1728 and was originally situated on Calle Obispo in Habana Vieja. During the 20th century, the Federación de Estudiantes Universitarios (University Students' Federa-

tion) was an extremely influential group amid the jungle of Cuban politics, and the university was an autonomous "sacred hill" that neither the police nor the army could enter—although gangsters and renegade politicians roamed the campus. (The student federation is in a beautiful Beaux-Arts mansion at the corner of Calles 27 and K.) Visitors are allowed to stroll the grounds, although peeking into the classes requires advance permission, and you'll need authorization to take photos (tel. 07/832-9844). The campus is off-limits on weekends, and the campus and museums are closed July–August.

From Calle L, the university is entered via an immense, 50-meter-wide stone staircase: the famous 88-step *Escalinata* (staircase). The **Monumento a Julio Antonio Mella,** across Calle L at the base of the stairs, contains the ashes of Mella, founder of the University Stu-

Venerable jagüey trees drop their tendrils to the ground, providing shade as you continue west along Calle 17 two blocks to the **Museo de Artes Decorativas** (Museum of Decorative Arts, Calle 17 #502, e/ D y E, tel. 07/832-0924; Tues.-Sat. 10:30 A.M.-6 P.M.; entrance CUC3 with guide, cameras CUC5, videos CUC10), housed in the former mansion of a Cuban countess. It brims with a lavish collection of furniture, paintings, textiles, and chinoiserie from the 18th and 19th centuries. Upstairs, there's a boudoir decorated in Asian style, its furniture inlaid with mother-of-pearl.

At Calle C, turn right and head downhill one block to Calle 15. Turn left and visit the **Galería Marianao** (Calle 15 #607, e/ B y C, tel. 07/55-2702; Tues.-Fri. 10 A.M.-5 P.M., Sat. 10 A.M.-3 P.M.), containing the 6,000-piece Art Collection of New America.

Return to Calle 17 and continue west four blocks to Paseo. Cross this wide boulevard and call in at the **Casa de la Amistad** (Paseo #406, e/ 17 y 19, tel. 07/830-3114; Mon.-Fri. 11 A.M.-11 P.M., Sat. noon-2 P.M., Sun. 11 A.M.-6 P.M.), a "friendship house" that makes a good place to break your perambulations with a *mojito* and a hearty meal while musicians entertain. This generously proportioned mansion is the **Casa de Juan Pedro Baró**, built in 1926 in Italian Renaissance style with a surfeit of Carrara marble.

Refreshed, walk two blocks west along Calle 17 to Calle 6 and **"Parque Lennon."** Following John Lennon's death in 1980, a gathering of Havana bohemia took place at this small quiet park. In 2000, on the 20th anniversary of his death, a life-size bronze statue was unveiled in the presence of Fidel Castro. Lennon, who is dressed in open-neck shirt, sits on a bench, his head slightly tilted, right leg resting on his left knee, with his arm draped casually over the back of the dark-green cast-iron bench, and plenty of room for anyone who wants to join him. The sculpture was rendered by Cuban artist José Villa, who inscribed the words "People say I'm a dreamer, but I'm not the only one," at the foot of the statue. By night, a spotlight shines on Lennon, denying him sleep. A *custodio* is there 24/7.

dents' Federation and, later, of the Cuban Communist Party (see the sidebar *Revolutionary Heroes* in the *History* section of the *Background* chapter). A patinated bronze **statue of the Alma Mater** cast by Czech sculptor Mario Korbel in 1919 sits atop the staircase. The twice-life-size statue of a woman is seated in a bronze chair with six classical bas-reliefs representing various disciplines taught at the university. She is dressed in a long-sleeve tunic and extends her bare arms, beckoning all those who desire knowledge.

The staircase is topped by a porticoed, columned facade beyond which lies a peaceful square—**Plaza Ignacio Agramonte**—surrounded by classical buildings (the tree-shaded campus was loosely modeled after New York's Columbia University). A **Saracen armored car** sits in the quadrant—it was captured in 1958 by students in the fight against Batista.

The **Aula Magna** (Great Hall) features a marble urn containing the ashes of Félix Varela, plus a magnificent mural by Armando Menocal. It is usually only opened for special events.

Museo de Ciencias Naturales Felipe Poey

The Escuela de Ciencias (School of Sciences), on the south side of the quadrant, contains the Felipe Poey Museum of Natural Sciences (tel. 07/832-9000; Mon., Wed., and Fri. 9 A.M.–noon and 1–4 P.M.; entrance CUC1), displaying dozens of endemic species, from alligators to sharks, stuffed or pickled for posterity. The museum dates from 1842 and is named for its French-Cuban founder. Poey (1799–1891) was versed in every field of the sciences and founded the Academy of Medical Sciences, the Anthropological Society of Cuba, and a half-dozen other societies.

A WALK ALONG AVENIDA DE LOS PRESIDENTES

Avenida de los Presidentes (Calle G) runs perpendicular to Calle 23 and climbs from the Malecón toward Plaza de la Revolución. A wide, grassy, tree-lined pedestrian median divides separate roadways running uphill and downhill. The avenue is named for the statues of Cuban presidents that grace its length, along with statues of other notables in American history. (The busts of Tomás Estrada Palma and José Miguel Gómez, the first and second presidents of the Cuban republic, were toppled following the Revolution, as they were accused of being "puppets" of the U.S. government.)

Allow 40 minutes, setting out from the Malecón, where first you should admire the bas-reliefs that adorn the **Monumento Calixto García.** One block south, on your right, is the **Casa de las Américas** (Av. de los Presidentes, esq. 3ra, tel. 07/55-2707, fax 07/33-4554, www.casa.cult.cu; Mon.-Fri. 8 A.M.-4:45 P.M.), a cultural center formed in 1959 to study and promote the cultures of Latin America and the Caribbean. The center contains a shop and hosts concerts and cultural programs. Fifty meters south along Avenida de los Presidentes you'll pass the Casa's **Galería Haydee Santamaría** (e/ 5ta and G; Tues.-Fri. 10 A.M.-5 P.M., Sat. 10 A.M.-3 P.M.).

At 5ta you'll pass the **Hotel Presidente,** an art deco high-rise dating from 1927. Across Avenida de los Presidentes, on the east side, is the headquarters of **MINREX** (Ministerio de Relaciones Exteriores), the Foreign Relations Ministry, taking up two blocks including a beautiful neo-baroque building on the north side of Calzada (7ma Calle).

At Calzada, detour west along 5ta for four blocks to **Parque Villalón** (5ta y D). On its southeast side is the Romanesque **Teatro Amadeo Roldán** (tel. 07/832-4521), recently restored to grandeur as a concert hall. Next door is the headquarters of the **Ballet Nacional de Cuba** (Calzada #510 e/ D y E, Vedado, tel. 07/835-2952, www.balletcuba.cu). The facility is closed to visitors, but sometimes you can spot the dancers practicing their pirouettes if you peek through the gate.

Turn north onto Calle D and walk one block to Línea. Be cautious crossing this busy thoroughfare. On the far side, peek into the 19th-century **Iglesia del Sagrado Corazón de Jesús** (Línea, e/ C y D, tel. 07/832-6807), Vedado's parish church colloquially called Parroquia del Vedado.

Exiting the church, head east one block along Línea to Avenida de los Presidentes, where on the northwest corner is a small triangular park, **Jardín Vienés Johann Strauss** (alas, the life-size gold-painted statue of the composer playing a violin has been stolen). On the south side of Línea note the handsome bronze **statue of Alejandro Rodríguez y Velasco** (Av. de los Presidentes y Línea), a brigadier general in the Cuban Wars of Independence, atop a granite pedestal guarded by a bronze figure of Perseus.

Cross Avenida de los Presidentes to view the **Museo de la Danza** (Calle Línea #365, esq. Av.

The **Museo Antropológico Montane** (Montane Anthropology Museum, tel. 07/879-3488; same hours as above), on the second floor of the Escuela de Ciencias, contains a valuable collection of pre-Columbian artifacts, including carved idols and turtle shells.

Museo Napoleónico

Who would imagine that so much of Napoleon Bonaparte's personal memorabilia would end up in Cuba? But it has, housed in the Napoleonic Museum (San Miguel #1159, e/ Ronda y Masón, tel. 07/879-1460, musnap@cubarte.cult.cu; Mon.–Sat. 10 A.M.–5:30 P.M.; entrance CUC3, guide CUC2) in a Florentine Renaissance mansion on the south side of the university. The collection (7,000 pieces) was the private work of a politician, Orestes Ferrara, one-time Cuban ambassador to France. Ferrara brought back from Europe such precious

de los Presidentes, tel. 07/831-2198 or 836-1636, musdanza@cubarte.cult.cu; Tues.-Sat. 11 A.M.-6:30 P.M.; CUC2, guide CUC1), in a restored mansion on the southeast corner of the junction. The museum has four salons dedicated to Russian ballet, modern dance, the National Ballet of Cuba, and other themes. Exhibits include wardrobes, recordings, manuscripts, and photographs relating to the history of dance. Such oddities as Nijinsky's wedding certificate are displayed.

From here, walk south along the central median. Ascending the avenue southward, you'll pass other statues to Mexican Benito Juárez (e/ 17 y 19), Venezuelan Simón Bolívar (e/ 19 y 21), and Chilean president Salvador Allende (e/ 21 y 23).

Cross Calle 23 and walk west one block to Calle F, where on the southwest corner of the junction the **Monumento a Martin Luther King** is a marble tableaux with a bas-relief bronze of the Afro-American civil rights leader.

Return to Avenida de los Presidentes and continue south. The tree-shaded boulevard climbs two blocks to the **Monumento a José Miguel Gómez** (Calle 29), designed by Italian sculptor Giovanni Nicolini and erected in 1936 in classical style to honor the former Republican president (1909-13). Beyond, the road drops through a canyon lined with giant jagüey trees, which form a glade over the road. Hidden from sight on the bluff to the west is the **Castillo del Príncipe,** built between 1767 and 1779 following the English invasion. The castle is off-limits as it is now a military zone and houses a prison.

Arriving at the junction with Avenida Salvador Allende, Zapata, and Avenida Rancho Boyeros, turn left onto Salvador Allende. After 100 meters, on the north side of the road, you'll arrive at the once-graceful **Quinta de los Molinos** (e/ Infanta y Luaces), reached via a decrepit cobbled, gladed drive. The mansion, built between 1837 and 1840, is named for the royal snuff mills that were built here in 1791 to take advantage of the waters of Zanza Real; you can still see part of the original aqueduct inaugurated in 1592 to the rear of the time-worn *quinta.* The mansion originated as a summer palace for the captains-general and in 1899 was granted as the private residence of General Máximo Gómez, the Dominican-born commander-in-chief of the liberation army. It now houses the motley **Museo de Máximo Gómez** (tel. 07/879-8850; Tues.-Sun. 10 A.M.-6 P.M.; CUC1). His sword and a few other personal effects are on display.

The *quinta* grounds now form the **Jardín Botánico** (Botanical Gardens; Tues.-Sun. 7 A.M.-7 P.M.). Following the Revolution, the once exquisite pleasure gardens of the governor's summer palace were transferred to the University of Havana and are now an overgrown mess littered with tumbledown statues, fountains, and grottoes with giant jagüeys and other trees twining around them, many with voodoo dolls and other *santería* offerings stuffed in their interstices.

items as the French emperor's death mask, toothbrush, and the pistols Napoleon used at the Battle of Borodino. Other items were seized from Julio Lobo, the former National Bank president, when he left Cuba for exile. The museum—housed in Ferrara's former three-story home (Ferrara was also forced out by the Revolution)—is replete with portraits of the military genius. A library is organized chronologically to trace the life of the "Great Corsican."

◖ NECRÓPOLIS CRISTÓBAL COLÓN

Described as "an exercise in pious excesses," this cemetery also known as Cementerio Colón (Columbus Cemetery, Zapata, esq. 12, tel. 07/833-4196 or 832-1050; daily 9 A.M.–5 P.M.; entrance CUC1, guided tours CUC5, cameras CUC5) covers 56 hectares and contains more than 500 major mausoleums, chapels, vaults, tombs, and galleries (in addition to countless gravestones) embellished with angels, griffins,

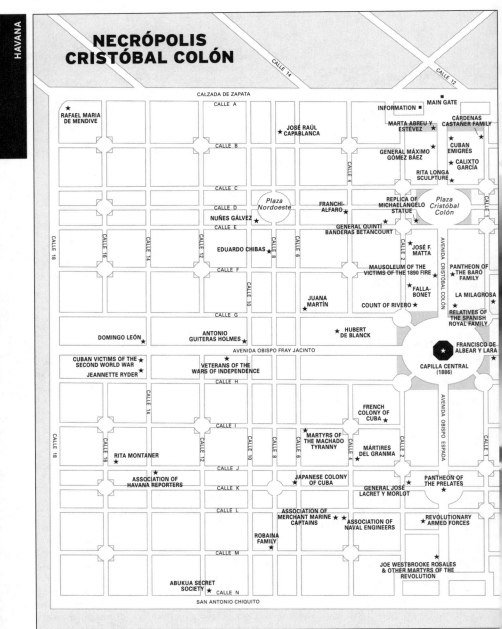

NECRÓPOLIS CRISTÓBAL COLÓN

CALLE 14

CALLE 12

CALZADA DE ZAPATA

CALLE A

★ RAFAEL MARIA DE MENDIVE

INFORMATION ■

■ MAIN GATE

CÁRDENAS CASTAÑER FAMILY ★

★ JOSÉ RAÚL CAPABLANCA

MARTA ABREU Y ESTÉVEZ ★

CALLE B

GENERAL MÁXIMO GÓMEZ BÁEZ ★

CUBAN EMIGRÉS ★

★ CALIXTO GARCÍA

RITA LONGA SCULPTURE ★

CALLE C

Plaza Nordoeste

CALLE D

REPLICA OF MICHAELANGELO STATUE ★

Plaza Cristóbal Colón

FRANCHI-ALFARO ★

NUÑES GÁLVEZ ★

CALLE E

GENERAL QUINTÍ BANDERAS BETANCOURT

CALLE 18

CALLE 16

CALLE 14

CALLE 12

EDUARDO CHIBAS ★

CALLE 8

CALLE 6

★ JOSÉ F. MATTA

CALLE 2

CALLE F

MAUSOLEUM OF THE VICTIMS OF THE 1890 FIRE ★

PANTHEON OF ★ THE BARÓ FAMILY

CALLE 10

★ FALLA-BONET

LA MILAGROSA

JUANA MARTÍN

COUNT OF RIVERO ★

CALLE G

RELATIVES OF THE SPANISH ROYAL FAMILY ★

DOMINGO LEÓN ★

ANTONIO GUITERAS HOLMES ★

★ HUBERT DE BLANCK

AVENIDA OBISPO FRAY JACINTO

FRANCISCO DE ★ ALBEAR Y LARA ★

CUBAN VICTIMS OF THE ★ SECOND WORLD WAR

JEANNETTE RYDER ★

VETERANS OF THE WARS OF INDEPENDENCE

CAPILLA CENTRAL (1886)

CALLE H

CALLE 14

FRENCH COLONY OF CUBA ★

AVENIDA OBISPO ESPADA

CALLE I

CALLE 18

CALLE 16

CALLE 12

CALLE 10

CALLE 8

CALLE 6

★ MARTYRS OF THE MACHADO TYRANNY

CALLE 4

CALLE 2

CALLE 1

RITA MONTANER ★

MÁRTIRES DEL GRANMA ★

CALLE J

ASSOCIATION OF HAVANA REPORTERS ★

JAPANESE COLONY ★ OF CUBA

PANTHEON OF ★ THE PRELATES

CALLE K

GENERAL JOSÉ LACRET Y MORLOT ★

CALLE L

ASSOCIATION OF MERCHANT MARINE ★ ★ CAPTAINS

ASSOCIATION OF NAVAL ENGINEERS ★

REVOLUTIONARY ★ ARMED FORCES

ROBAINA FAMILY ★

CALLE M

JOE WESTBROOKE ROSALES & OTHER MARTYRS OF THE REVOLUTION ★

ABUKUA SECRET SOCIETY ★ CALLE N

SAN ANTONIO CHIQUITO

CALLE 4

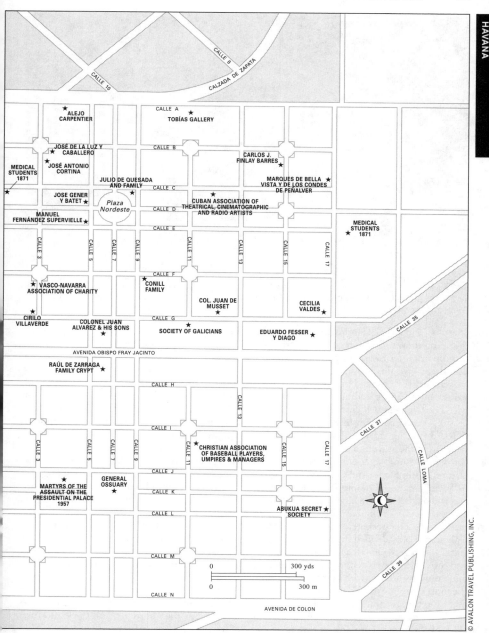

© CHRISTOPHER P. BAKER

The Necrópolis Cristóbal Colón is one of the world's greatest collections of flamboyant funerary architecture.

cherubs, and other flamboyant ornamentation. You'll even find Greco-Roman temples in miniature, an Egyptian pyramid, and medieval castles, plus baroque, Romantic, Renaissance, art deco, and art nouveau art by a pantheon of Cuba's leading sculptors and artists. The triple-arched entrance gate, inspired by the Triumphal Arch in Rome, has marble reliefs depicting the crucifixion and Lazarus rising from the grave and is topped by a marble coronation stone representing the theological virtues: Faith, Hope, and Charity.

Today a national monument, the cemetery was laid out between 1871 and 1886 in 16 rectangular blocks, or *insulae,* like a Roman military camp. The designer, a Spaniard named Calixto de Loira, divided the cemetery by social status, with separate areas for non-Catholics and for victims of epidemics. It was originally open only to nobles, who competed to build the most elaborate tombs, with social standing dictating the size and location of plots.

The cemetery is a petrified version of society of the times, combining, says the *Guía*

Turística (available at the entrance gate), a "grandeur and meanness, good taste and triviality ... and even an unusual black humor, as in the gravestone carved as a double-three, devoted to an emotional elderly lady who died with that domino in her hand, thus losing both game and life at a time." The *doble tres* was that of Juana Martín, a domino fanatic who indeed died as described (Calles 6 y G).

Famous *criollo* patricians, colonial aristocrats, and war heroes such as Máximo Gómez are buried here alongside noted intellectuals, merchants, and politicians. The list goes on and on: José Raúl Capablanca, the world chess champion 1921–27 (his tomb is guarded by a marble bishop); Alejo Carpentier, Cuba's most revered contemporary novelist; Hubert de Blanck, the noted composer; Celia Sánchez; Haydee Santamaría; and a plethora of revolutionaries killed for the cause, and even some of the Revolution's enemies. Many monuments belong to such communities as the Abakuá secret society, the Asturians, and the Galicians, and to groups such as film and radio stars. The

Galería Tobias is one of several underground galleries; this one is 100 meters long and contains 256 niches containing human remains.

The major tombs line Avenida Cristóbal Colón, the main avenue, which leads south from the gate to an ocher-colored, octagonal neo-Byzantine church, the **Capilla Central,** containing a fresco of the Last Judgment.

La Milagrosa

The most visited grave is the flower-bedecked tomb of Amelia Goyri de Hoz (Calles 3 y F), revered as La Milagrosa ("The Miraculous One") and to whom miraculous healings are ascribed. According to legend, she died during childbirth in 1901 and was buried with her stillborn child at her feet. When her sarcophagus was later opened, the baby was supposedly cradled in her arms. Ever since, superstitious Cubans have paid homage by knocking three times on the tombstone with one of its brass rings, before touching the tomb and requesting a favor (one must not turn one's back on the tomb when departing). Many childless women pray here in hopes of a pregnancy.

Cementerio Chino

The Chinese built their own cemetery immediately southwest of Cementerio Colón, on the west side of Avenida 26, e/ 28 y 33. Beyond the circular gateway, traditional lions stand guard over hundreds of graves beneath highly pitched burial chapels with upward-curving roofs of red and green tile in the traditional *xuan-shan* (hanging mountain) gabled style. Entry is free, but the gates are usually locked. To arrange a visit, call the Periódico Kwong Wah Po (tel. 07/52-0522).

Galería 23 y 12

The northwest corner of Calles 23 and 12, one block north of Cementerio Colón, marks the spot where on April 16, 1961, Castro announced (on the eve of the Bay of Pigs invasion) that Cuba was henceforth socialist. The anniversary of the declaration of socialism is marked each April 16th, when Castro speaks here. The facade bears a bronze bas-relief showing Fidel surrounded by the heroes who were killed in the U.S.-sponsored strike on the airfield at Marianao that was a prelude to the invasion.

PLAZA DE LA REVOLUCIÓN

Havana's largest plaza, which occupies the Loma de los Catalanes (Hill of the Catalans), is an ugly tarred square accurately described by P. J. O'Rourke as "a vast open space resembling the Mall in D.C., but dropped into the middle of a massive empty parking lot in a tropical Newark." The trapezoidal complex spanning 11 acres was laid out during the Batista era, when it was known as the Plaza Cívica. It forms the administrative center for Cuba, and all the major edifices date back to the 1950s. Huge rallies are held here on May 1.

Among the important buildings are the **Biblioteca Nacional** (tel. 07/55-5442), Cuba's largest library, built 1955–57 on the east side of the plaza in a similar monumental style as the Palace of Justice; the 21-story **Ministerio de Defensa,** originally built as the municipal seat of government on the plaza's southeast side; and the **Teatro Nacional** (Paseo y Av. Carlos M. de Céspedes, tel. 07/879-6011), one block to the northwest of the plaza, built 1954–60 with a convex glazed facade. Paseo climbs northwest from the plaza to Zapata, where in the middle of the road rises the **Memorial a Ethel y Julius Rosenberg,** bearing cement doves and an inset sculpture of the U.S. couple executed in Sing Sing Prison, New York, in 1953 for passing nuclear secrets to the Soviet Union. An inscription reads, "Assassinated June 19, 1953." The Cuban government holds a memorial service here each June 19.

To the rear of the library is the **Monumento El Legado Cultural Hispánico,** a dramatic, classical-style, larger-than-life bronze statue by American sculptor Anna Hyatt Huntington of two naked men (one on horseback) passing a baton.

One block northeast of the plaza is the **Museo de História del Deporte** (Av. Rancho Boyeros, e/ 19 de Mayo and Bruzón, tel.

JOSÉ MARTÍ

A knowledge of José Martí is an absolute prerequisite to understanding contemporary Cuba. He is the most revered figure in Cuban history… the canonical avatar of Cuba's independence spirit and the "ideological architect" of the Cuban Revolution, claims Castro. His works have been seized upon by Cubans on both sides of the Straits of Florida, being "full of the lament of exile and the passion for the lost homeland," thought Claudia Lightfoot. "Cubans take José Martí into their consciousness with their first breath and their mother's milk." Cubans of every stripe quote their saintly hero by heart. So important is Martí within the Cuban psyche that foreigners who admit to never having heard of him are usually met with a wide-mouthed, uncomprehending stare. There is hardly a quadrant in Havana that does not have a street, square, or major building named in his honor. Every year on January 28 the entire country honors Martí's birth with a national celebration.

José Julian Martí de Pérez was born in 1853 in a small house on Calle Paula (today known as Leonor Pérez, to honor his mother) in Habana Vieja. His father was from Valencia, Spain, and became a policeman in Cuba; his mother came from the Canary Islands. He spent much of his youth in Spain before his parents returned to Cuba. When the War of Independence erupted in 1868, Martí was 15 years old. Already he sympathized with the nationalist cause.

At the age of 16, he published his first newspaper, La Patria Libre (Free Fatherland). He also wrote a letter denouncing a school friend for attending a pro-Spanish rally. The letter was judged to be treasonous, and Martí was sentenced to six years' imprisonment, including six months' hard labor. Martí suffered a hernia, and gained permanent scars from his shackles. In 1871, his sentence was commuted to exile on the Isla de Pinos, and briefly thereafter he was exiled to Spain, where he earned a degree in law and philosophy and gravitated to the revolutionary circles then active in Madrid.

Later, he settled in Mexico, where he became a journalist, and Guatemala, where he taught, but was expelled for incendiary activities by the respective governments. In 1878, as part of a general amnesty, he was allowed to return to Cuba but was then deported again. He traveled through France and Venezuela and, in 1881, to the United States, where he settled in New York for the next 14 years with his wife and son. Here he worked as a reporter and acted as a consul for Argentina, Paraguay, and Uruguay.

THE PEN AND THE SWORD

Dressed in his trademark black frock coat and bow tie, with his thick moustache waxed into

---

07/881-4696; Tues.–Sun. 10 A.M.–5 P.M.; CUC1), the sports museum, in the **Sala Polivatente Ramón Fonst** stadium.

To get from Vedado to the plaza, you can take bus #84 from the bottom of La Rampa, at Calle 0 and Humboldt. The plaza is under close surveillance and loitering is discouraged.

Monumento y Museo José Martí

This massive monument on the south side of the square sits atop a 30-meter-tall base that is shaped as a five-pointed star. It is made entirely of gray granite and marble and was designed by architect Enrique Luis Varela. It predates the Revolution, having been completed in 1958. To each side, great arching stairways lead to an 18-meter-tall (59-foot) gray-white marble statue of national hero José Martí sitting in a contemplative pose, like Rodin's *The Thinker*.

Behind looms a 109-meter-tall marble edifice stepped like a soaring ziggurat from a sci-fi movie. It's the highest point in Havana. The edifice houses the **Museo José Martí** (tel. 07/59-2351; Mon.–Sat. 9 A.M.–4:30 P.M.; entrance CUC3, cameras CUC5, videos

pointy tips, Martí devoted more and more of his time to winning independence for Cuba. He wrote poetry heralding the liberation of his homeland, wedding the rhetoric of nationalism to calls for social justice and fashioning a vision of a free Cuba that broke through class and racial barriers. He was one of the most prolific and accomplished Latin American writers of his day, unsurpassed in the inspiration he ignited. Martí's writing helped define the school of modern Latin American poetry.

He admired the liberty of America but became an arch-anticolonialist, and his voluminous writings are littered with astute critiques of U.S. culture and politics. He despised the expansionist nature of the United States, arguing that U.S. ambitions toward Cuba were as dangerous as the rule of Spain. "It is my duty... to prevent, through the independence of Cuba, the USA from spreading over the West Indies and falling with added weight on other lands of Our America. All I have done up to now and shall do hereafter is to that end."

Prophetically, Martí's writings are full of invocations to death. It was he who coined the phrase *"La Victoria o el Sepulcro"* (Victory or the Tomb), which Fidel Castro has turned into a call for *"Patria o Muerte"* (Patriotism or Death) and more recently *"Socialismo o Muerte."*

THEORY INTO ACTION
In 1892, Martí presented his "Fundamentals and Secret Guidelines of the Cuban Revolutionary Party," outlining the goals of the nationalists: independence for Cuba, equality of all Cubans, and establishment of democratic processes. That year, Martí began publishing *Patria*. Having established himself as the acknowledged political leader of the independence cause, he melded the various exile factions together and integrated the cause of Cuban exile workers into the crusade – they contributed 10 percent of their earnings to his cause. He also founded a revolutionary center, Cuba Libre (Free Cuba), and La Liga de Instrucción, which trained revolutionary fighters.

In 1895, Martí was named major general of the Armies of Liberation; General Máximo Gómez was named supreme commander. On April 11, 1895, Martí, Gómez, and four followers landed at Cajobabo, in a remote part of eastern Cuba. Moving secretly through the mountains, they gathered supporters and finally linked up with Antonio Maceo and his army of 6,000. The first skirmish with the Spanish occurred at Dos Ríos on May 19, 1895. Martí was the first casualty. He had determined on martyrdom and committed sacrificial suicide by riding headlong into the enemy line. Thus, Martí – the "Apostle of the Nation" – brought the republic to birth, says Guillermo Cabrera Infante, "carrying a cadaver around its neck."

CUC10). Among the exhibits are first-edition works, engravings, drawings, and maps, as well as reproductions of significant artifacts in Martí's life. New Age music plays in the background, drawing you to a multiscreen broadcast on the Wars of Independence and the Revolution. An art gallery features portraits of Martí. For an additional CUC2 you can take an elevator to the top of the tower for a 360-degree view over Havana.

Palacio de la Revolución
The center of government is the Palace of the Revolution (tel. 07/879-6551), immediately south of the José Martí monument. This monumental structure was inspired by the architecture then popular in Fascist Europe and was built 1954–57 as the Palace of Justice. Today, it is where Castro and the Council of Ministers work out their policies of state. The labyrinthine, ocher-colored palace adjoins the buildings of the Central Committee of the Communist Party and is fronted by a broad staircase built by Batista for the Cuban Supreme Court and national police headquarters. No visitors are allowed.

HAVANA

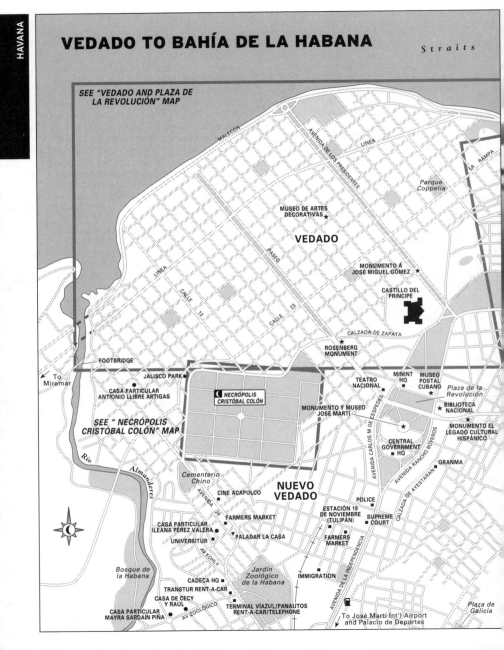

VEDADO TO BAHÍA DE LA HABANA

Straits

SEE "VEDADO AND PLAZA DE
LA REVOLUCIÓN" MAP

MALECÓN

AVENIDA DE LOS PRESIDENTES

LINEA

LA RAMPA

Parque Coppelia

MUSEO DE ARTES
DECORATIVAS ★

VEDADO

PASEO

LINEA

CALLE 12

CALLE 23

MONUMENTO Á
JOSÉ MIGUEL GÓMEZ ★

CASTILLO DEL
PRINCIPE

CALZADA DE ZAPATA

ROSENBERG
MONUMENT ★

FOOTBRIDGE

To
Miramar

JALISCO PARK ■

CASA PARTICULAR
ANTIONIO LLIBRE ARTIGAS ●

MININT
HQ ■

TEATRO
NACIONAL ■

MUSEO
POSTAL
CUBANO ★

*Plaza de la
Revolución*

**NECRÓPOLIS
CRISTÓBAL COLÓN**

BIBLIOTECA
NACIONAL ■

MONUMENTO Y MUSEO
JOSÉ MARTÍ ■

AVENIDA CARLOS M DE CESPEDES

*SEE " NECRÓPOLIS
CRISTÓBAL COLÓN" MAP*

MONUMENTO EL
LEGADO CULTURAL
HISPÁNICO ■

CENTRAL
GOVERNMENT ★
HQ ■

AVENIDA RANCHO BOYEROS

Río

Almendares

*Cementerio
Chino*

GRANMA ■

CINE ACAPULCO ■

NUEVO
VEDADO

AVENIDA 26

POLICE ■

CALZADA DE AYESTARÁN

CASA PARTICULAR
ILEANA PÉREZ VALERA ●

FARMERS MARKET ■

ESTACIÓN 19
DE NOVIEMBRE
(TULIPÁN) ■

SUPREME
COURT ■

UNIVERSITUR ■

PALADAR LA CASA ▼

FARMERS
MARKET ■

AVENIDA DE LA INDEPENDENCIA

AV KOHLY

*Bosque de
la Habana*

*Jardín
Zoológico
de la Habana*

IMMIGRATION ■

CADECA HQ ■

TRANSTUR RENT-A-CAR ■

CASA DE CECY
Y RAÚL ■

CASA PARTICULAR
MAYRA SARDAIN PIÑA ●

AV ZOOLÓGICO

TERMINAL VIAZUL/PANAUTOS
RENT-A-CAR/TELEPHONE ■

*Plaza de
Galicia*

To José Martí Int'l Airport
and Palacio de Deportes

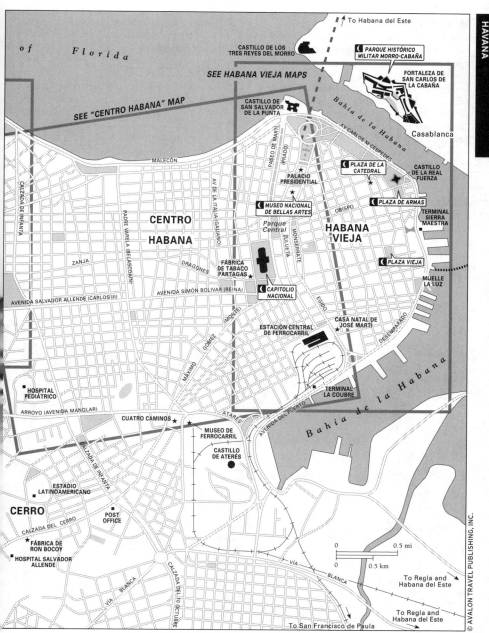

of Florida

To Habana del Este

CASTILLO DE LOS
TRES REYES DEL MORRO

PARQUE HISTÓRICO
MILITAR MORRO-CABAÑA

FORTALEZA DE
SAN CARLOS DE
LA CABAÑA

SEE HABANA VIEJA MAPS

CASTILLO DE
SAN SALVADOR
DE LA PUNTA

Bahía de la Habana

Casablanca

SEE "CENTRO HABANA" MAP

AV CARLOS M CÉSPEDES

MALECÓN

PASEO DE MARTÍ (PRADO)

PALACIO
PRESIDENCIAL

PLAZA DE LA
CATEDRAL

CASTILLO
DE LA REAL
FUERZA

CALZADA DE INFANTA

AV DE LA ITALIA (GALIANO)

MUSEO NACIONAL
DE BELLAS ARTES

PLAZA DE ARMAS

OBISPO

TERMINAL
SIERRA
MAESTRA

PADRE VARELA (BELASCOAÍN)

CENTRO

Parque
Central

ZULUETA

MONSERRATE

**HABANA
VIEJA**

HABANA

ZANJA

DRAGONES

FÁBRICA
DE TABACO
PARTAGÁS

PLAZA VIEJA

AVENIDA SALVADOR ALLENDE (CARLOS III)

AVENIDA SIMÓN BOLÍVAR (REINA)

CAPITOLIO
NACIONAL

MUELLE
LA LUZ

(MONTE)

EGIDO

DESEMPARADO

CASA NATAL DE
JOSÉ MARTÍ

ESTACIÓN CENTRAL
DE FERROCARRIL

MÁXIMO GÓMEZ

HOSPITAL
PEDIÁTRICO

TERMINAL
LA COUBRE

Bahía de la Habana

ARROYO (AVENIDA MANGLAR)

ATARÉS

CUATRO CAMINOS

MUSEO DE
FERROCARRIL

AVENIDA DEL PUERTO

CASTILLO
DE ATERÉS

CALZADA DE INFANTA

ESTADIO
LATINOAMERICANO

CERRO

POST
OFFICE

CALZADA DEL CERRO

FÁBRICA DE
RON BOCOY

HOSPITAL SALVADOR
ALLENDE

VÍA

VÍA BLANCA

CALZADA DE 10 OCTUBRE

BLANCA

0   0.5 mi

0   0.5 km

To Regla and
Habana del Este

To Regla and
Habana del Este

To San Francisco de Paula

© AVALON TRAVEL PUBLISHING, INC.

Ministerio del Interior

Commanding the northwest side of the plaza is the seven-story Ministry of the Interior (the ministry in charge of national security), built in 1953 to be the Office of the Comptroller. On its east side is a windowless horizontal block that today bears a soaring "mural" of Che Guevara—the image is from Alberto "Korda" Gutiérrez's world-renowned photo—and the words Hasta la Victoria Siempre ("Always Toward Victory"), erected in 1995 from steel railings donated by the French government. No visitors are allowed.

Ministerio de Comunicaciones

Immediately east of the Interior Ministry is the Ministry of Communications, bearing the word Venceremos ("We will overcome") on its roof. It contains the **Museo Postal Cubano** (Av. Rancho Boyeros, esq. 19 de Mayo, tel. 07/882-8255; Mon.–Sat. 9 A.M.–5 P.M.; entrance CUC1) on the ground floor. The well-cataloged philatelic collection displays a complete range of Cuban postage stamps (including the first, dating from 1855), plus a large collection of stamps from almost 100 other countries. A well-stocked *filatelica* sells stamps.

NUEVO VEDADO

Nuevo Vedado, which stretches south from Cementerio Colón and southwest of Plaza de la Revolución, is a sprawling complex of mid-20th-century housing, including high-rise, postrevolutionary apartment blocks. There are also some magnificent modern edifices, notably private homes built in modernist style in the 1950s, plus the **Palacio de Deportes** (Sports Palace, but colloquially called "El Coliseo"), on the southeast side of the traffic circle at Avenida 26, Avenida de la Independencia (Rancho Boyeros), and Vía Blanca.

Jardín Zoológico de la Habana

The Havana Zoological Garden (Av. 26 y Zoológico, tel. 07/881-9926 or 881-8915, zoohabana@ch.gov.cu; Tues.–Sun. 9:30 A.M.–5:30 P.M.; CUC2) suffers from poor management and lack of resources. The hippopotamus, crocodiles, caimans, flamingos, and

Visitors admire a leopard in the Jardín Zoológico de la Habana.

other water-loving species wade and wallow in polluted lagoons. It has many monkeys and chimpanzees, but though their cages abut each other, they are separated by walls so that no monkey or ape has a view of its neighbors. Other species on view include Andean condors, water buffalo, jaguars, leopards, lions, and a gorilla.

Bosque de la Habana and Parque Metropolitano de la Habana

From the zoo, you can follow Avenida Zoológica west to the bridge over the Río Almendares to enter the Bosque de la Habana (Havana Forest). This wild woodland stretches alongside the river, forming a ribbon of vine-draped virgin forest that is virtually untouched. There is no path—you must walk along Calle 49C, which parallels the river—and going alone is not advised, as robberies have been known to occur.

To the south, the woods extend to **Los Jardines de la Tropical** (Calle Rizo, tel. 07/881-8767; Tues.–Sun. 9 A.M.–6 P.M.), a landscaped park built 1904–10 on the grounds of a former brewery for promotional purposes. The park found its inspiration in Antoni Gaudí's Parque Güell in Barcelona. Today it is in near-derelict status and looks like an abandoned set from *Lord of the Rings*. The Polar brewing company competed by opening the smaller **Jardines de la Polar,** a short distance further south on the north side of Calzada de Puentes Grandes.

North of Bosque de la Habana, and accessed from Avenida 47, the motley riverside Parque Metropolitano de la Habana has pony rides, row boats, and a short riverside walk.

The headquarters is at **Aula Ecológica** (Ciclovía, tel. 07/881-9979; Mon.–Fri. 9 A.M.–5 P.M.), which features a meager visitor center with a 1:2,000 scale model of the project.

Sights – Playa (Miramar and Beyond)

West of Vedado and the Río Almendares, the *municipio* of Playa extends to the western boundary of Havana as far as the Río Quibú. Many of the areas were renamed following the Revolution. Gone are Country Club and Biltmore, replaced with politically acceptable names such as Atabey, Cubanacán, and Siboney, in honor of Cuba's indigenous past.

MIRAMAR

Leafy Miramar is Havana's upscale residential district, laid out in an expansive grid of tree-shaded streets lined by fine mansions. Most of their original owners fled Cuba following the Revolution and many of the mansions have fallen into ruin. Nonetheless, Miramar is at the forefront of Cuba's quasi-capitalist remake. The best-stocked stores are here, as are the international schools and foreign embassies.

Avenida Primera runs along the shore. It's Havana's answer to South Beach or Santa Monica without the sand and the pier. The

shoreline is comprised of raised coral outcrops and lacks beaches, except to the extreme west. *Balnearios* (bathing areas) are found all along Miramar's waterfront, cut into the coral shore. They're time-worn and of limited appeal to tourists, although they draw Cubans in huge numbers on hot summer days.

Inland, running parallel at intervals of about 100 meters, are 3ra Avenida, 5ta Avenida (the main thoroughfare), and 7ma Avenida.

Tunnels under the Río Almendares connect Miramar to Vedado. The first connects the Malecón with 5ta Avenida; the second connects Línea (Calle 9) with 7ma Avenida and Avenida 31, which leads to the Marianao district. In addition, Calle 23 crosses the river via the Puente Almendares bridge to become Avenida 47, linking Vedado with the Kohly district and Marianao. You can also cross via a steel footbridge (the Puente de Hierro) at the west end of Calle 11.

Buses #132 and 232 run to Miramar from

HAVANA

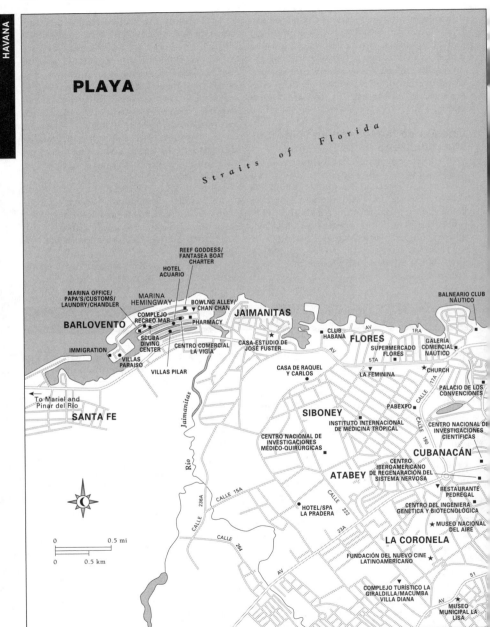

PLAYA

Straits of Florida

REEF GODDESS/
FANTASEA BOAT
CHARTER

HOTEL
ACUARIO

MARINA OFFICE/
PAPA'S/CUSTOMS/
LAUNDRY/CHANDLER

MARINA
HEMINGWAY

BOWLNG ALLEY/
CHAN CHAN

JAIMANITAS

COMPLEJO
RECREO MAR

BARLOVENTO

PHARMACY

BALNEARIO CLUB
NÁUTICO

SCUBA
DIVING
CENTER

CENTRO COMERCIAL
LA VIGÍA

CASA-ESTUDIO DE
JOSÉ FUSTER

CLUB
HABANA

AV

1RA

FLORES

GALERÍA
COMERCIAL
NÁUTICO

IMMIGRATION

VILLAS
PARAISO

VILLAS PILAR

SUPERMERCADO
FLORES

5TA

CHURCH

CALLE 17A

CASA DE RAQUEL
Y CARLOS

LA FEMININA

AV

To Mariel and
Pinar del Río

Jaimanitas

PALACIO DE LOS
CONVENCIONES

SANTA FE

PABEXPO

CALLE 190

CENTRO NACIONAL DE
INVESTIGACIONES
CIENTÍFICAS

SIBONEY

INSTITUTO INTERNACIONAL
DE MEDICINA TROPICAL

Río

CENTRO NACIONAL DE
INVESTIGACIONES
MÉDICO-QUIRÚRGICAS

CUBANACÁN

CENTRO
IBEROAMERICANO
DE REGENARACIÓN DEL
SISTEMA NERVOSA

ATABEY

CALLE 236A

CALLE 15A

CALLE 222

RESTAURANTE
PEDREGAL

CENTRO DEL INGENIERA
GENÉTICA Y BIOTECNOLÓGICA

HOTEL/SPA
LA PRADERA

CALLE 23A

MUSEO NACIONAL
DEL AIRE

LA CORONELA

CALLE 264

FUNDACIÓN DEL NUEVO CINE
LATINOAMERICANO

0   0.5 mi

0   0.5 km

51

COMPLEJO TURÍSTICO LA
GIRALDILLA/MACUMBA
VILLA DIANA

AV

MUSEO
MUNICIPAL LA
LISA

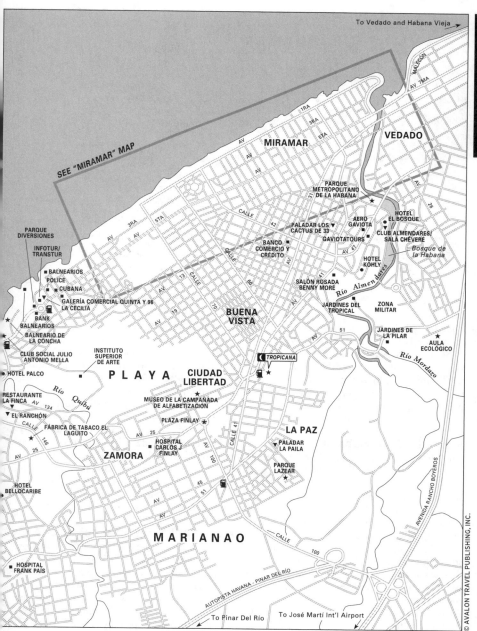

To Vedado and Habana Vieja

MIRAMAR

VEDADO

PARQUE
METROPOLITANO
DE LA HABANA

HOTEL
EL BOSQUE

AERO
GAVIOTA

PALADAR LOS
CACTUS DE 33

CLUB ALMENDARES/
SALA CHÉVERE

GAVIOTATOURS

PARQUE
DIVERSIONES

INFOTUR/
TRANSTUR

BANCO
COMERCIO Y
CRÉDITO

Bosque de
la Habana

HOTEL
KOHLY

BALNEARIOS

POLICE

CUBANA

SALÓN ROSADA
BENNY MORE

GALERÍA COMERCIAL QUINTA Y 96
LA CECILÍA

BANK

BALNEARIOS

JARDINES DEL
TROPICAL

ZONA
MILITAR

BUENA
VISTA

Río Almendares

BALNEARIO DE
LA CONCHA

JARDINES DE
LA PILAR

CLUB SOCIAL JULIO
ANTONIO MELLA

INSTITUTO
SUPERIOR
DE ARTE

AULA
ECOLÓGICO

Río Mordaco

HOTEL PALCO

P L A Y A

CIUDAD
LIBERTAD

TROPICANA

RESTAURANTE
LA FINCA

Río
Quibú

EL RANCHÓN

MUSEO DE LA CAMPAÑADA
DE ALFABETIZACIÓN

LA PAZ

FÁBRICA DE TABACO EL
LAGUITO

PLAZA FINLAY

PALADAR
LA PAILA

ZAMORA

HOSPITAL
CARLOS J
FINLAY

PARQUE
LAZEAR

AVENIDA RANCHO BOYEROS

HOTEL
BELLOCARIBE

M A R I A N A O

HOSPITAL
FRANK PAÍS

SEE "MIRAMAR" MAP

To Pinar Del Río

Autopista Havana - Pinar Del Río

To José Martí Int'l Airport

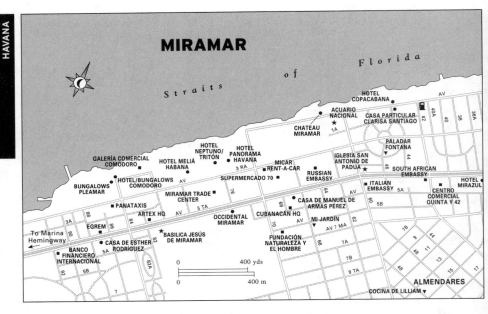

Dragones y Industria, on the northwest side of Parque de la Fraternidad, Habana Vieja. Bus #264 runs to Miramar from Desamparados (e/ Compostela y Picota), near the railway station in Habana Vieja. In Vedado, the P1 runs along Calle 23 to Miramar (you can board at Coppelia, esq. L), where it runs along 4ra Avenida; and the P4 runs along Línea.

Maqueta de la Habana

The Model of Havana (Calle 28 #113, e/ 1ra y 3ra, tel. 07/202-7303, maqueta@gdic.ch.gov.cu; Tues.–Sat. 9:30 A.M.–5 P.M.; adults CUC3; students, seniors, and children CUC1; guided tour CUC1) is a 1:1,000 scale model of the city housed in a hangar-sized, air-conditioned building called the Pabellón. The 22-meter-long, 144-square-meter model represents 144 square kilometers of Havana and its environs. The *maqueta* took nine experts more than 10 years to complete and shows Havana in the most intimate detail. It is color-coded by age. A visit here puts the entire city in accessible 3-D perspective.

Acuario Nacional

The National Aquarium (3ra Av., esq. 62, tel. 07/203-6401 or 202-5872, www.acuarionacional.cu; Tues.–Sun. 10 A.M.–6 P.M.; adults CUC7, children CUC5) exhibits 450 species of sealife, including anemones, corals, exotic tropical fish, sharks, hawksbill turtles, sea lions, and dolphins. Alas, most of the tanks are bare and the displays are disappointing by international standards. Daily activities are offered. The highlights are the sea lion show, held daily at noon, 2 P.M., and 4 P.M.; and dolphin show daily at 11 A.M., 3 P.M., and 5 P.M. A theater show for kids is held every hour on the half hour.

Museo del Ministerio del Interior

The Museum of the Ministry of the Interior (5ta Av., esq. 14, tel. 07/203-4432; Tues.–Fri. 9 A.M.–4:30 P.M., Sat. 9 A.M.–3 P.M.; entrance CUC2, guide CUC1) is dedicated to the CIA's inept efforts to dethrone Fidel. The seal of the CIA looms over a room full of photos and gadgets straight from a spy movie, small arms, ba-

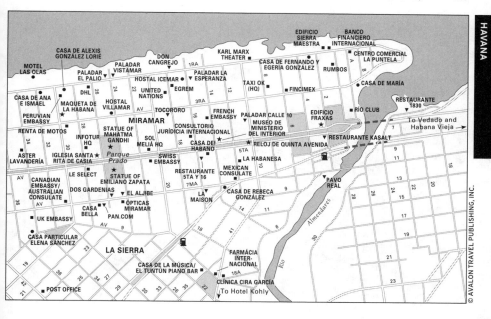

zookas, and the like. It also features exhibits honoring MININT's good work in solving homicides—there's even a stuffed German shepherd that was used by police in their sleuthing. To make things easier for the CIA should it ever take another stab at Fidel, the museum shows a video giving details of Castro's security plans, including tunnels that lead from his residence (one of many) in Jaimanitas to the nearby Ciudad Libertad military airstrip.

Fundación Naturaleza y El Hombre

This institution, the Foundation of Man and Nature (Av. 5B #6611, e/ 66 y 70, tel. 07/204-0438; Mon.–Fri. 10 a.m.–4 p.m.; CUC3) honors Cuban naturalist and explorer Antonio Nuñez Jiménez and features his personal collection. Much of the fascinating and eclectic exhibit is dedicated to the 10,889-mile journey by a team of Cubans (led by Nuñez) that paddled from the source of the Amazon to the Bahamas in dugout canoes in 1996. A replica of the canoe is there, along with a large photo collection, indigenous artifacts such as weapons, headdresses, and a vast collection of ceramics, many showing figures copulating and masturbating. Visits by appointment only.

NÁUTICO, FLORES, AND JAIMANITAS

Beyond Miramar, 5ta Avenida curls around the half-moon Playa Marianao, and passes through the Náutico and Flores districts, setting for Havana's formerly elite social clubs and *balnearios* that date from prerevolutionary days. Following the Revolution they were reopened to the hoi polloi and rechristened. The beaches—collectively known as Playas del Oeste—are popular with Cubans on weekends, when they get crowded. There was even an eponymous mini-version of New York's famous Coney Island theme park; at last visit it was being re-created as Havana's only amusement park with a circus, skate ring, miniature train, and more.

Commanding the scene is the palatial

Bathers cool off in the summer heat at *balnearios* (bathing areas) lining 1ra Avenida, Miramar.

© CHRISTOPHER P. BAKER

Mudejar-style former **Balneario de la Concha** (5ta e/ 112 and 146), and immediately west, the former **Havana Yacht Club** (5ta y 146). The "Yacht," as the latter was colloquially called, was founded in 1886 and became the snootiest place in Havana (it was here that mulatto President Fulgencio Batista was famously refused entry for being too "black") until the Revolution, when it became the Club Social Julio Antonio Mella, for workers.

The area is most famous for Havana's huge yachting marina, **Marina Hemingway** (5ta Av. y Calle 248, tel. 07/204-1150, fax 07/204-1149, comercial@comermh.cha.cyt.cu), one kilometer west of Club Habana in the Jaimanitas district, 15 kilometers west of downtown.

Buses #9 and 420 run to Marina Hemingway from 5ta Avenida and Calle 0.

Club Habana

Beyond the Río Quibu, 5ta Avenida passes into the Flores district. Here was the Havana-Biltmore Yacht and Country Club, dating from 1928, with a grandiose Moorish tower topping archways separated by ornate columns, and a veranda from which a broad stairway swept down to a beautiful expanse of white sand. After the Revolution the beach was opened to all Cubans, black and white, for a peso, while the former casino went for the use of a worker's union and the hotel became the Casa Cultural de Trabajadores de Construcción. Today, as the Club Habana (5ta Av., e/ 188 y 192, Playa, tel. 07/204-5700), it has reverted to its former role as a private club for the social (mostly foreign) elite. Nonmembers are welcome (entrance CUC10 Mon.–Fri., CUC15 Sat.–Sun.).

Casa-Estudio de José Fuster

Artist José R. Fuster, a world-renowned painter and ceramist nicknamed the "Picasso of the Caribbean," has an open-air workshop-gallery at his home (Calle 226, esq. Av. 3A, tel. 07/271-2932 or 264-6051, fuster@cubarte.cult.cu; daily 9 A.M.–5 P.M.). You step through a giant doorway—La Puerta de Fuster—to discover a surreal world made of ce-

A WALK ALONG QUINTA AVENIDA

The wide fig-tree-lined boulevard called Fifth Avenue, or "Quinta," runs ruler-straight through the heart of Miramar. It is flanked by mansions, many of which have been restored and are now occupied by various Cuban commercial agencies or leased to foreign corporations. Quinta Avenida is also "Embassy Row." The broad central median is tailor-made for walking the boulevard's eight-kilometer length.

Begin at the **Edificio Fraxas,** a near-derelict Beaux-Arts mansion on the north side of 5ta at Calle 2. Walking west you'll arrive, after four blocks, at Calle 10, pinned by **Reloj de Quinta Avenida,** a large clock erected in 1924 in the central median. At Calle 12, cross to the north side of the street to visit the **Museo del Ministerio del Interior** (see main text); then, one block west, cross to the south side to admire the stained glass and large cigar collection in the **Casa del Habano** (5ta, e/ 14 y 16).

Continue west four blocks to Calle 24, where **Parque de los Ahorcados** (Park of the Hanged), spanning 5ta between Calles 24 and 26, is shaded by massive jagüey trees, seemingly supported by their aerial roots dangling like cascades of water. On the south side of the road is **Plaza Emiliano Zapata,** with a life-size stone statue of Zapata, Mexico's revolutionary hero; on the north side is **Parque Prado,** with a Romanesque temple and a bronze bust to Mahatma Gandhi.

Rising over the west side of Parque Prado is **Iglesia de Santa Rita de Casia** (5ta, esq. Calle 26, tel. 07/204-2001). This exemplar of modernist church architecture dates from 1942 and mixes neocolonial and modern features. Its main feature is a modernist statue of Santa Rita by Rita Longa.

The next 10 blocks are lined with gracious mansions, many of them now serving as foreign embassies.

Crossing Calle 60, call in at the modernist-style Romanesque **Iglesia San Antonio de Padua** (Calle 60 #316, esq. 5ta, tel. 07/203-5045), which dates from 1951 and boasts a magnificent, albeit non-functional, organ. If the main door is locked, try entering via the sacristy.

One block west, on the south side of the street, you finally pass a monstrous Cubist tower that can be seen virtually the length of the avenue. Formerly the Soviet Embassy, it is now the **Russian Embassy** (5ta, e/ 62 y 66).

Turn left at Calle 70 and walk two blocks to Avenida 5B. Two houses down, on the south side of the street, is the **Fundación Naturaleza y El Hombre** (see the main text). After visiting this intriguing museum (you'll need to call ahead), retrace your steps to 5ta Avenida and continue west. Immediately on your left is the **Occidental Miramar** hotel and, on your right, the **Miramar Trade Center.**

One block farther, on the south side of 5ta, rises the massive Roman-Byzantine-style **Basilica Jesús de Miramar** (5ta #8003, e/ 80 y 82, tel. 07/203-5301; daily 9 A.M.-noon and 4-6 P.M.), built in 1953 with a magnificent organ with 5,000 pipes. Newly restored, the church features 14 splendid oversize paintings of the Stations of the Cross by Spanish artist César Hombrados Oñativa.

One block west of the cathedral, turn right onto Calle 84 and walk the two blocks to the **Hotel Comodoro,** where restaurants, bars, and taxis await.

---

ramics. Many of the naive, childlike works are inspired by farmyard scenes, such as *El torre del gallo* (Rooster's Tower), a 12-foot-tall statement on male chauvinism that also doubles as an oven. Other allegorical, often baroque, creations—puppet-like forms, buses bulging with people—pay tribute to Compay Segundo (of Buena Vista Social Club fame)

and other provincial figures. Call ahead to arrange a visit.

Fuster's creativity now graces the entryways, benches, roofs, and facades of houses throughout his local community.

Fidel Castro's main domicile is nearby, but you can't see it. The home, complete with tennis and basketball courts, is set in an expansive

THE CIA'S ATTEMPTS TO KILL CASTRO

The bitter taste left by the CIA's botched Bay of Pigs invasion led to an all-out secret war against Castro, an effort code-named Operation Mongoose and headed by Bobby Kennedy. Mongoose eventually involved 500 caseworkers handling 3,000 anti-Castro Cubans at an expense of more than US$100 million a year. The CIA's attempts (now defunct) to oust Castro were set in motion by President Eisenhower as early as March 1959. In *Inside the Company: CIA Diary*, ex-CIA agent Philip Agee describes how the dirty-tricks campaign included bombings of public venues meant to discredit Cuba. The agency also invented protest demonstrations, sowed discord in Cuban intelligence by fingering top officials as CIA agents, and even recruited Cuban Embassy staff by "dangling stunning beauties... exceptionally active in amorous adventures."

The CIA's plans read like a James Bond novel... or a comedy of errors. Some plots were straightforward, like the attempt to kill Castro with a bazooka. The CIA's Technical Services Division (TSD) was more imaginative. It impregnated a box of cigars with botulism (they were tested on monkeys and "did the job expected of them") and hoped – in vain – to dupe Castro into smoking one. No one knows whether they reached Castro or whether some innocent victim smoked them. The spooks also tried to damage Castro's image by sprinkling his shoes with thallium salts (a strong depilatory), hoping that his beard would fall out. Another box of Castro's favorite cigars was contaminated with a chemical that produced "temporary disorientation."

Eventually the CIA turned to the Mob. It hired assassins hand-picked by Johnny Rosselli, who had run the syndicate's Sans Souci casino in Havana. The killers were on both the FBI's 10 Most Wanted and Bobby Kennedy's target list of organized crime figures. The marksmen disguised as Marxmen didn't fool Castro – he correctly assumed the CIA would hire assassins, whom he considered inefficient. Several assassins were caught and executed.

---

compound surrounded by pine trees and electrified fences and heavy security. All streets surrounding it are marked as one-way, heading away from the house.

CUBANACÁN AND VICINITY

Cubanacán is—or was—Havana's Beverly Hills, a reclusive area on either side of the Río Quibú. It was developed in the 1920s with winding tree-lined streets and enormous lots on which the most grandiose of Havana's mansions arose. An 18-hole golf course at the Havana Country Club served Havana's wealthy classes, lending the name Country Club Park to what is now called Cubanacán, still the swankiest address in town.

Following the Revolution, most of the area's homeowners decamped and fled Cuba. Their mansions were dispensed to Communist Party officials, many of whom live in a lap of luxury that the vast majority of Cubans can only dream of and, of course, never see. Castro maintains several homes here, and the area is replete with military camps and security personnel. Other homes serve either as "protocol" houses—villas where foreign dignitaries and VIPs are housed during visits to Cuba—or as foreign embassies and ambassadors' homes, among them the U.S. Residency (even the U.S. Marines have a house).

Havana's impressive convention center, the **Palacio de las Convenciones** (Calle 146, e/ 11 y 13, tel. 07/202-6011, fax 07/271-9426, www.complejopalco.com), was built in 1979 for the Non-Aligned Conference. The main hall (one of 15), seating 2,200 delegates, hosts twice-yearly meetings of the Cuban National Assembly. To its rear is **Pabexpo** (Av. 17 y 180, tel. 07/271-6775), with four exhibition halls for hosting trade shows.

Cuba's biotechnology industry is also centered here and extends westward into the

A BIOTECH SUCCESS STORY

Cuba is a biotech minipower. Under Fidel Castro's personal patronage, Cuba has evolved one of the world's most advanced genetic engineering and biotechnology industries, with large-scale investment coming from public sources such as the Pan American Health Organization and the World Food Program.

Cuba has developed some 200 products, both innovative and derivative. It invented and manufactures vaccines for cerebral meningitis, cholera, Hepatitis B, interferon for the treatment of AIDS and cancer, and a skin growth factor to speed the healing of burns. For years, Cuba has touted a cure for the skin disease vitiligo. Recently it developed PPG, a "wonder drug" that reputedly washes cholesterol out of blood (and, incidentally, is Cuba's equivalent of Viagra). In 1996, CIGB scientists even began testing a vaccine to prevent HIV infection. Other advances have been made in agriculture and industrial bioengineering. Unfortunately, U.S. law prevents these lifesaving wonders from being sold in the United States.

The **Centro de Ingeniería Genética y Biotecnología** (Center for Genetic Engineering and Biotechnology, Av. 31, e/ 158 y 190, Havana, tel. 07/271-6413 or 07/271-5149, www.cigb.edu.cu), Cuba's main research facility, is perhaps the most sophisticated research facility in any developing nation.

districts of Atabey and Siboney, earning the area the moniker Scientific City (see the sidebar *A Biotech Success Story).* The convoluted roads of Siboney and Cubanacán follow no logical order.

Bus #32 operates between La Rampa in Vedado and Cubanacán (five pesos).

Instituto Superior de Arte

Following the Revolution, Fidel Castro and Che Guevara famously played a few rounds of golf at the exclusive Havana Country Club before tearing it up and converting the grounds to house Cuba's leading art academy, the National Art Schools (Calle 120 #1110, esq. 9na, tel. 07/208-0017 or 208-0288, isa@cubarte.cult.cu), featuring the Escuela de Música (School of Music), Escuela de Ballet (Ballet School), Escuela de Baile Moderno (School of Modern Dance), and Escuela de Bellas Artes (School of Fine Arts). The school was designed by three young "rebel" architects: Italians Roberto Gottardi and Vittorio Garatti, and Cuban Ricardo Porro. Porro's art school was a deliberate evocation of the female form complete with fountain shaped as a *mamey,* or papaya—an overt reference to the female vulva. Gradually, as the five main buildings emerged, they were thought too sensual, too avant-garde for grim Communist tastes. The project was brought to a halt before completion, though the school did open. Scattered across acres of rough lawn and overgrown forest, the ghostly complex fell into ruin, with long tentacles of branches and roots creeping into the buildings. Amazingly, in 2001 the Cuban government approached the three architects and asked them to complete the project. Restoration was well advanced at last visit.

For the best views, drive along Calles 15 and 134. In summer the facility is closed.

Fábrica El Laguito

Cigar aficionados gravitate to El Laguito (Av. 146 #2302, e/ 21 y 21A, tel. 07/208-4654) like bees to pollen. Incongruously housed in a fabulous mansion built in 1910 for the Marquís de Pinar del Río (it was later adorned with 1930s art deco glass and chrome, a spiral staircase, and abstract floral designs), this cigar factory makes Montecristos and the majority of Cohibas, *the* premium Havana cigar. Since Cohibas are made from only the finest leaves, El Laguito is given first choice from the harvest—"the best selection of the best selection," says factory head Emilia Tamayo. El Laguito also makes the best cigar in the world—the Trinidad, a 7.5-inch-long cigar made exclusively for Castro to present to diplomats and dignitaries. Visits by appointment only.

MARIANAO AND LA CORONELA

This dilapidated *municipio*, on the heights south of Miramar, evolved in the mid-19th century, when wealthy Cubans built fine summer homes along newly laid streets. During the 1920s, Marianao boasted the Marianao Country Club, the Oriental Park racetrack, and Grand Nacional Casino, and was given a further boost on New Year's Eve 1939 when the Tropicana nightclub opened as the ritziest establishment Havana had ever seen. Marianao remained a pleasure center until the Revolution, when the cabarets were shut down.

Following the U.S. occupation of Cuba in 1898, the U.S. military governor, General Fitzhugh Lee, established his headquarters in Marianao and called it Camp Columbia: Campamento Columbia later became headquarters for Batista's army; it was from here that the sergeant effected his *golpes* in 1933 and 1952. Camp Columbia was bombed on April 15, 1960, during the prelude to the CIA-run Bay of Pigs invasion. Five of Castro's planes were destroyed, but the bombers also struck houses in the neighborhood, killing 7 people and wounding 52, giving Castro a grand political victory in his calls for solidarity against U.S. aggression (one of the dying men wrote Castro's name in blood on a wall). The following day he announced for the first time that Cuba was undergoing a "socialist revolution."

A tower in the center of the traffic circle— **Plaza Finlay**—outside the main entrance, at Avenida 31 and Avenida 100, was erected in 1944 as a beacon for the military airfield. In 1948 a needle was added so that today it is shaped like a syringe in honor of Carlos Finlay, the Cuban who in 1881 discovered the cause of yellow fever.

Access from Miramar is via Avenida 31 and Avenida 51, which continues west to the districts of La Lisa and La Coronela.

Bus #34 departs Dragones y Industria, on the northwest side of Parque de la Fraternidad, Habana Vieja, for Marianao.

Museo de la Campaña de Alfabetización

Following the Revolution, Castro turned the barracks of Camp Columbia into a school complex—Ciudad Escolar Libertad—which in 1961 became the headquarters for Castro's national literacy campaign. The Museum of the Literacy Campaign (Av. 29E, esq. 76, tel. 07/260-8054; Mon.– Fri. 8 A.M.–5 P.M., Sat. 8 A.M.–noon; free) is dedicated to the amazing campaign initiated on January 1, 1960, when 120,632 uniformed *brigadistas,* mostly comprising students, spread out across the country to teach illiterate peasantry to read and write. The museum is a fascinating memorial to a splendid achievement.

Tropicana

The Tropicana nightclub (Calle 72 between 41 and 45, tel. 07/207-0110, fax 07/207-0109) is one of Havana's most astonishing exemplars of modernist architecture. Most of the structures date from 1951, when the club was restored with a new showroom—the **Salon Arcos de Cristal** (Crystal Bows)—designed by Max Borges Recio with a stupendous roof of five arcing concrete vaults and curving bands of glass to fill the intervening space. Built in decreasing order of height, they produce a telescopic effect that channels the perspective toward the orchestra platform. Borges also added the famous geometric sculpture that still forms the backdrop to the main stage, in the outdoor *Salón Bajo las Estrellas.*

A ballet dancer (shown pirouetting on the tips of her toes) by the renowned Cuban sculptor Rita Longa dances amid the lush foliage in front of the entrance. The statue, which has become Tropicana's motif, is joined by a fittingly sensuous statue of the Greek maenads by Longa, with the bacchants performing a wild ritual dance to honor Dionysius at night amid the woods.

Visitors can only view the exterior features by day, when the dancers practice. To admire

HAVANA

the Salon Arcos de Cristal, you must visit at night, when the lavishly costumed, statuesque showgirls perform beneath the stars (see the *Entertainment* section and the sidebar *Paradise under the Stars,* both in this chapter).

Museo Nacional del Aire

The National Air Museum (Av. 212, e/ 29 y 31, tel. 07/271-0632; Wed.–Sun. 10 A.M.–5 P.M.; entrance CUC2, guide CUC1, cameras CUC2, videos CUC5), occupying a grassy area in the heart of La Coronela, west of Marianao, displays more than 50 civilian and military aircraft, including helicopters, missiles, bombers, and fighter planes. It features Soviet MiGs, Che Guevara's personal Cessna 310, a P-51 Mustang fighter, a World War II–era AT6, and several biplanes. Three rooms are replete with aviation mementos and include sections dedicated to the Bay of Pigs battle, and to Yury Gagarin and Col. Arnaldo Tamayo Méndez, the first Cuban cosmonaut. It also has a collection of model aircraft, and a planetarium (CUC3 extra).

For a swim and refreshments, call in at **Complejo Turístico La Giraldilla** (Calle 272, e/ 37 y 51, tel. 07/273-0568; Tues.–Sun. 10 A.M.–6 P.M.), a restaurant and entertainment complex occupying a huge 1920s mansion on expansive grounds.

Sights – Across the Harbor

The harbor channel and Bahía de la Habana (Havana Bay) separate Habana Vieja from the communities of Casablanca, Regla, and Guanabacoa. Although run-down, and with relatively few sights of interest, the latter two districts draw tourists interested in *santería* and Afro-Cuban music and dance, while Casablanca is an access point to the Parque Histórico Militar Morro-Cabaña.

Little ferries bob their way across the harbor, connecting Casablanca and Regla with each other and with Habana Vieja.

◖ PARQUE HISTÓRICO MILITAR MORRO-CABAÑA

Looming over Habana Vieja, on the north side of the harbor channel, is the rugged cliff face of the Cabaña, dominated by two great fortresses that constitute El Morro-La Cabaña Historical Military Park (Carretera de la Cabaña, Habana del Este, tel. 07/862-7653; daily 8 A.M.–8 P.M.). Together, the castles comprise the largest and most powerful defensive complex built by the Spanish in the Americas.

Visitors arriving by car reach the complex via the harbor tunnel (no pedestrians or motorcycles without sidecars are allowed) that descends beneath the Máximo Gómez

THE CAÑONAZO

The Ceremonía del Cañonazo (Cannon-Firing Ceremony, tel. 07/862-0671; CUC4, but CUC6 after 6 P.M.) is held nightly at 8:30 P.M. at the Fortaleza de San Carlos de la Cabaña, where troops dressed in 18th-century military garb and led by fife and drum light the fuse of a cannon to announce the closing of the city gates, maintaining a tradition going back centuries. You are greeted at the castle gates by soldiers in traditional uniform, and the place is lit by flaming lanterns. About 8:50 P.M. a cry rings out, announcing the procession of soldiers marching across the plaza bearing muskets, while a torchbearer lights flaming barrels. The soldiers ascend to the cannon, which they prepare with ramrod and live charge. When the soldier puts the torch to the cannon, you have about three seconds before the thunderous boom. Your heart skips a beat. But it's all over in a millisecond, and the troops march away.

Be sure to get there no later than 8 P.M. if you wish to secure a place close to the cannon. Hotel tour desks offer excursions.

Monument off Avenida de Céspedes. Buses from Parque de la Fraternidad pass through the tunnel and will drop you by the fortress access road.

Castillo de Los Tres Reyes del Morro

This handsome castle (tel. 07/863-7941; daily 8 A.M.–8 P.M.; entrance CUC3, guide CUC1, cameras CUC2, videos CUC5) is built into the rocky palisades of Punta Barlovento, crowning a rise that drops straight to the sea at the entrance to Havana's narrow harbor channel. Canted in its articulation, the fort—designed by Italian engineer Juan Bautista Antonelli and initiated in 1589—forms an irregular polygon that follows the contours of the rocky headland on which it was built, with a sharp-angled bastion at the apex, stone walls 10 feet thick, and a series of batteries stepping down to the shore. Hundreds of slaves toiled under the lash of whip and sun to cut the stone in situ, extracted from the void that forms the moats. El Morro took 40 years to complete and served its job well, repelling countless pirate attacks and withstanding for 44 days a siege by British cannon in 1762.

Originally the castle connected with the outside world principally by sea, to which it was linked via the **Plataforma de la Estrella,** the wharf at the southern foot of the cliff. Today you enter via a drawbridge across the deep moat that leads through the **Túnel de Aspillerado** (Tunnel of Loopholes) to vast wooden gates that open to the **Camino de Rondas,** a small parade ground (Plaza de Armas) containing a building atop the cisterns that supplied the garrison of 1,000 men with water. This two-story structure today houses the **Museo de Navegación** (also called Sala de Cristóbal Colón) with expositions on the colonial sea voyages of Columbus and later Portuguese and Spanish explorers; and the **Sala de História del Faro y Castillo,** which profiles the various lighthouses in Cuba.

To the right of the plaza, a narrow entrance leads to the **Baluarte de Austria** (Austrian Bastion), with cannon embrasures for firing down on the moat. A cobbled ramp leads up

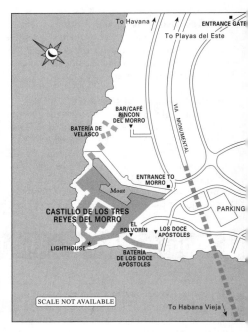

to other *baluartes.* On the seaward side of the Tejeda bastion (named for the governor and military leader who began work on the castle), you can look down into the crevasse caused by the explosion that breached the Caballero del Mar wall in the 1762 siege by the British. Various plaques commemorate heroic figures of the siege—even the Royal Navy is honored. Do not be tempted to walk the wind-battered battlements, which are canted seaward and have no guardrails.

To the left of the Plaza de Armas is the **Surtida de los Tinajones,** where giant earthenware vases are inset in stone. They once contained rapeseed oil as lantern fuel for the 15-meter-tall **Faro del Morro** (10 A.M.–8 P.M.; CUC2 extra), a lighthouse constructed in 1844. Today an electric lantern still flashes every 15 seconds. You can climb to the top for a bird's-eye view of the castle—the last leg of the climb is tight, and not for claustrophobics.

All maritime traffic in and out of Havana harbor is controlled from the **Estación**

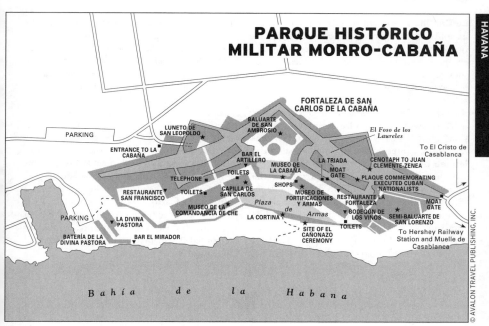

PARQUE HISTÓRICO MILITAR MORRO-CABAÑA

© AVALON TRAVEL PUBLISHING, INC.

Semafórica, the semaphore station atop the castle, accessed via the Baluarte de Tejeda.

Below the castle, facing the city on the landward side and reached by a cobbled ramp, is the **Batería de los Doce Apóstoles** (Battery of the Twelve Apostles). It boasts massive cannons and a little bar—El Polvorín (The Powderhouse).

Fortaleza de San Carlos de la Cabaña

This massive fortress (Carretera de la Cabaña, tel. 07/862-0671; daily 10 A.M.–10 P.M.; entrance CUC4 adults, CUC2 children, CUC6 for the *cañonazo,* guide CUC1, cameras CUC2, videos CUC10), half a kilometer east of the Morro, enjoys a fantastic strategic position, with a clifftop balcony over the city and harbor. It is the largest fort in the Americas, covering 10 hectares and stretching 700 meters in length. It was built 1764–74 following the English invasion, and cost the staggering sum of 14 million pesos—when told the cost, the king after whom it is named reached for a tele-

scope; surely, he said, it must be large enough to see from Madrid. The castle counted some 120 bronze cannons and mortars, plus a permanent garrison of 1,300 men (the castle was designed to hold 6,000 troops in times of need). While never actually used in battle, it has been claimed that its dissuasive presence won all potential battles—a tribute to the French designer and engineer entrusted with its conception and construction. The castle has been splendidly restored.

From the north, you pass through two defensive structures before reaching the monumental baroque portal flanked by great columns with a pediment etched with the escutcheon of Kings Charles III, and a massive drawbridge over a 12-meter-deep moat, one of several moats carved from solid rock and separating individual fortress components.

Beyond the entrance gate, a paved alley leads to the **Plaza de Armas,** centered on a grassy, tree-shaded park fronted by a 400-meter-long curtain wall. The wall—

La Cortina—runs the length of the castle on its south side and formed the main gun position overlooking Havana. It is lined with ceremonial cannons engraved with lyrical names such as *La Hermosa* (The Beautiful). The *cañonazo* ceremony is held here nightly, when soldiers in period costume light a cannon (see the sidebar *The Cañonazo* in this chapter).

To the west, the cobbled street leads past a small **chapel** with baroque facade and charming vaulted interior. Facing the chapel is the **Museo de la Comandancia de Che,** where Che Guevara had his headquarters in the months following the Triunfo del Revolución. Here he set up his revolutionary tribunals for "crimes against the security of the state." The small museum salutes the Argentinian doctor-turned-revolutionary who played such a key part in the Cuban Revolution. His M-1 rifle, submachine gun, radio, and rucksack are among the exhibits.

Calle Marina leads west from the entrance gate to a large cannon-filled courtyard, from where steps lead down to **La Divina Pastora** restaurant, beside the wharf where supply ships once berthed.

On the north side of the plaza is the **Museo Monográfico de la Fortaleza,** tracing the castle's development. The museum features uniforms and weaponry from the colonial epoch, including a representation of the *cañonazo* ceremony. A portal here leads into a garden—**Patio de Los Jagüeyes**—that once served as a *cortadura,* a defensive element packed with explosives that could be ignited to foil the enemy's attempts to gain entry.

Farther east is the **Museo de las Maquetas,** featuring 3-D *maquetas* of each of Cuba's castles, including a detailed model of the Cabaña. Next door, the **Museo de Fortificaciones y Armas** contains an impressive collection of suits of armor and weaponry that spans the ancient Arab and Asian worlds and stretches back through medieval times to the Roman era.

The museums open to the north to an eastern extension of cobbled **Calle Marina,** where converted barracks, armaments stores, and prisoners' cells now contain restaurants and

the **Casa del Tabaco y Ron,** displaying the world's longest cigar (11 meters long).

Midway down Marina, a gate leads down to **El Foso de los Laureles,** a massive moat containing the execution wall where nationalist sympathizers were shot during the Wars of Independence. A cenotaph is dedicated to Juan Clemente Zenea, executed in 1871. Following the Revolution, scores of Batista supporters and "counterrevolutionaries" met a similar fate here.

On the north side of the moat, a separate fortress unit called **San Julián Revellín** contains examples of Soviet missiles installed during the Cuban Missile Crisis (called the October 1962 Crisis or the Caribbean Crisis by Cubans).

The rest of the fortress grounds is still used as a military base and is off-limits. It includes the domed **Observatorio Nacional** (National Observatory).

A ferry (10 centavos) runs to Casablanca every 20 minutes or so from the Muelle Luz (Av. del Puerto y Calle Santa Clara) in Habana Vieja. You can walk uphill from Casablanca to an easterly entrance gate to the Foso de los Laureles. However, this gate closes at dusk, so don't take this route if you plan on seeing the *cañonazo.*

Estatua Cristo de la Habana

A great statue of Jesus Christ on Carretera del Asilo looms over Casablanca, dominating the cliff face immediately east of the Fortaleza. The 15-meter-tall statue, which was unveiled on December 25, 1958 ("just seven days before the triumph of the Antichrist in Cuba," said Fulgencio Batista), stands atop a three-meter-tall pedestal and was hewn from Italian Carrara marble by female Cuban sculptor Jilma Madera. From the *mirador* surrounding the statue, you have a bird's-eye view of the harbor. The views are especially good at dawn and dusk, and it is possible, with the sun gilding the waters, to imagine great galleons slipping in and out of the harbor, laden with treasure en route to Spain.

The statue is a 10-minute uphill walk from the Casablanca dock.

REGLA

Regla, a working-class *barrio* on the eastern shore of Havana harbor, evolved in the 16th century as a fishing village and eventually became Havana's foremost warehousing and slaving center. It developed into a smugglers' port in colonial days, a reputation it maintained until recent days, when pirates (who made their living stealing off American yachts anchored in the harbor) were known as *terribles reglanos*. It was also the setting for Havana's bullfights. Havana's main electricity-generating plant is here, along with petrochemical works, both of which pour bilious plumes over town.

Many slaves settled here, infusing Regla with a profound African heritage. Regla is a center of *santería* and the all-male Abakúa secret society; while walking its streets, you may note tiny shrines outside many houses. Calle Calixto García has many fine examples. Many *babalawos* (*santería* priests) live here and will happily dispense advice for a fee; try **Eberardo Marero** (Ñico López #60, e/ Coyola y Camilo Cienfuegos).

The **Museo Municipal de Regla** (Martí #158, e/ Facciolo y La Piedra, tel. 07/97-6989; Tues. 9 A.M.–6 P.M., Wed. 1–8 P.M., Thurs.–Sat. 9 A.M.–6 P.M., Sun. 9 A.M.–1 P.M.; entrance CUC2, guide CUC1), two blocks east of the harborfront, tells the tale of the town's *santería* associations. Other displays include colonial-era swords, slave shackles, and the like.

Ferries (10 centavos) run between Regla and the Muelle Luz (Av. San Pedro y Santa Clara) in Habana Vieja.

Bus #6 departs for Regla from Agramonte (Zulueta) and Genios in Habana Vieja; bus #106 departs from Agramonte and Refugio.

Iglesia de Nuestra Señora de Regla

The ocher-colored Church of Our Lady of Regla (Sanctuario #11, e/ Máximo Gómez y Litoral, tel. 07/97-6228; daily 7:30 A.M.–5:30 P.M.), built in 1810 on the harborfront, is one of Havana's loveliest churches. Its inner beauty—a blaze of white and sky-blue lit by incandescent light pouring in through the huge studded wooden doors—is highlighted by a fabulous gilt altar beneath an arched ceiling. On holy days, the altar is sumptuously lit with votive candles. Dwelling in alcoves in the wall are figurines of miscellaneous saints, including a statue of St. Anthony leading a wooden suckling pig wearing a dog collar and a large blue ribbon. *Habaneros* flock to pay homage to the black Virgen de Regla, patron saint of sailors and Catholic counterpart to Yemayá, the African goddess of the sea in the Yoruba religion. Time your visit for the seventh of each month, when large masses are held; or September 7, when a pilgrimage draws the devout of Catholicism and *santería* and the Virgin is taken down from her altar and paraded through town. Masses are held Tuesday–Wednesday at 8 A.M., Thursday–Friday at 5 P.M., and Sunday at 8:30 A.M.

Outside, 20 meters to the east and presiding over her own private chapel, is another statue of the Virgen de Regla, with a statue of the Virgen de la Caridad del Cobre, Cuba's patron saint. Syncretized as the *orisha* Ochún, the Virgen de la Caridad del Cobre also draws adherents of *santería*.

Colina de Lenin

Calle Martí, the main street, leads east to the city cemetery where turning north, after two blocks, steps lead up to Lenin Hill (Calle Vieja, e/ Enlase y Rotaria), where a three-meter-tall bronze face of the Communist leader is carved into the cliff face, with a dozen life-size figures (in cement) cheering him from below. A small and rather pitiful museum (tel. 07/97-6899; Tues.–Sat. 9 A.M.–6 P.M.) atop the hill is dedicated to the life of Lenin and various martyrs of the Cuban revolution.

The Colina is more directly reached from Parque Guaycanamar (Calle Martí, six blocks east of the harborfront) via Calle Albuquerque and 24 de Febrero; you'll reach a metal staircase that leads to the park. Bus #29 will also take you there from the Regla dock.

GUANABACOA

Guanabacoa, about three kilometers east of Regla, was founded in 1607 and developed in colonial days as the major trading center for slaves. Thus, an Afro-Cuban culture evolved here, expressed not least in a strong musical heritage. The **Casa de la Trova** (Martí #111, e/ San Antonio y Versalles, tel. 07/97-7687; Tues.–Sun. 9 A.M.–11 P.M.; entrance one peso) hosts performances of Afro-Cuban music and dance, as does **Restaurante Las Orishas** (Calle Martí, e/ Lamas y Cruz Verde, tel. 07/94-7878; daily noon–midnight).

Guanabacoa is also Cuba's most important center of *santería*. So strong is the association that all over Cuba, folks facing extreme adversity will say "I'm going to have to go to Guanabacoa," implying that only the power of a *babalawo* can fix the problem.

Guanabacoa also boasts several important religious sites (most are tumbledown and await restoration), including two Jewish cemeteries on the east side of town. Combined with a visit to Regla, it makes an intriguing excursion from downtown Havana, although restaurants and tourist facilities are virtually nonexistent.

Getting There: Bus #29 runs to Guanabacoa from the Regla dock. Bus #3 departs for Guanabacoa from Máximo Gómez and Aponte, on the south side of Parque de la Fraternidad, in Habana Vieja; and bus #95 from the corner of Corrales and Agramonte (Zulueta). From Vedado, you can take bus #195; from the Plaza de la Revolución, take bus #5.

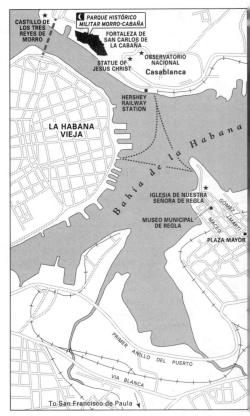

Parque Martí

The sprawling town is centered on this small tree-shaded plaza (Calles Martí, División Pepe Antonio, y Adolfo del Castillo Cadenas). Parque Martí is dominated by the recently restored **Iglesia Nuestra Señora de la Asunción** (División #331, e/ Martí y Cadenas, tel. 07/97-7368; Mon.–Fri. 8:30 A.M.–noon, Sun. 8:30–11:30 A.M.), commonly called the Parroquial Mayor. Completed in 1748, it features a lofty Mudejar-inspired wooden roof and baroque gilt altar dripping with gold, plus 14 Stations of the Cross. If the main doors are locked, try the side entrance on Calle Enrique Güiral.

The **Museo Histórico de Guanabacoa**

(Historical Museum of Guanabacoa, Martí #108, e/ Valenzuela y Quintín Bandera, tel. 07/97-9117; Tues.–Sat. 10 A.M.–6 P.M., Sun. 9 A.M.–1 P.M.; entrance CUC2), one block west of the plaza, tells the tale of Guanabacoa's development and outlines the evolution of Afro-Cuban culture and *santería*. One block farther west, the **Bazar de Reproducciones Artísticas** (Martí #175; Mon.–Sat. 10 A.M.–6 P.M.) has rooms brimming with *santería* regalia, much of it for sale.

One block southwest of the park is the **Convento y Iglesia de San Antonio** (Máximo Gómez, esq. San Antonio, tel. 07/97-7241), begun in 1720 and completed in 1806. The

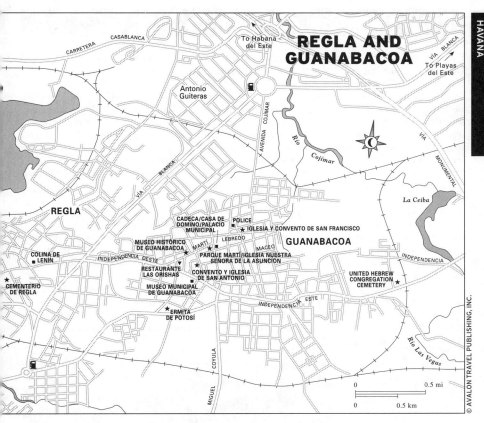

REGLA AND GUANABACOA

convent is now a school but if you ask nicely, the *custodio* will likely let you in to admire the exquisitely decorated *alfarje*.

Convento de Santo Domingo

This convent (Santo Domingo #407, esq. Rafael de Cadena, tel. 07/97-7376; Tues.–Fri. 9–11:30 A.M. and 3:30–5 P.M.) has an impressive neo-baroque facade and was designed in 1728 and constructed by artisans from the Canary Islands. Its church, the **Iglesia de Nuestra Señora de la Candelaria,** boasts a magnificent blue-and-gilt baroque altar plus an intricate *alfarje*. The

door is usually closed, in which case ring the doorbell to the left of the main entrance.

Ermita de Potosí

The only ecclesiastical edifice thus far restored is the tiny hilltop Potosí Hermitage (Calzada Vieja Guanabacoa, esq. Calle Potosí, tel. 07/97-9867; daily 8 A.M.–5 P.M.), the highlight of a visit to Guanabacoa. The simple hermitage dates back to 1644, and is the oldest religious structure still standing in Cuba. It now gleams with fresh whitewash and sky-blue paint. It has an intriguing cemetery. Mass is on Sunday at 8:30 A.M.

Entertainment and Events

Don't believe anything you've read about Communism having killed the capital city's zest. Yes, the city has lost the Barbary Coast spirit of prerevolutionary days, but *habaneros* love to paint the town red (so to speak) as much as their budgets allow. Many venues—particularly those that primarily cater to Cubans—are seedier (albeit without the strippers) than they were four decades ago; in many the decor hasn't changed!

The scene is fluid. Sudden restrictions imposed by the government occasionally put a damper on Havana's nightlife. Nightlife is a lot tamer than it was just a decade ago, not least because the past few years have seen many discos replaced by live-music venues with pricey entrance fees that dissuade Cubans from attending. All of which means that *habaneros* mostly socialize impromptu, on the street, although afternoon discos keep up some of the old abandon. And though Havana has scores of bars, Cubans are even

priced out of most bars (one beer can cost the equivalent of a week's salary), and few have any energy.

For theater, classical concerts, and other live performances it's often difficult to make a reservation by telephone; few box office operators speak English in any event. Instead, you should go to the venue and buy a ticket in advance or just before the performance.

Comedy is exclusively in colloquial Cuban Spanish.

Resources

Havana lacks a reliable, widely circulated forum for announcements of upcoming events. Word of mouth is the best resource. If you read about an event, call ahead to double-check dates, times, and venue.

A good Internet source is www.cubarte.cult.cu/eng/index.php.

The weekly *Cartelera* (tel. 07/55-3840, www.cartelera.com) has information on

© CHRISTOPHER P. BAKER

Karl Marx theater, formerly known as the Blanquita theater

CINEMAS

Most of Havana's cinemas are mid-20th-century gems that have been allowed to deteriorate to the point of near-dilapidation. Movie houses on La Rampa, in Vedado, tend to be less rundown than those in Habana Vieja and Centro Habana. *Granma* and *Cartelera* list what's currently showing. Children under 16 years of age are not allowed in, regardless of movie content. Entrance usually costs two pesos; foreigners are rarely charged in dollars.

The **Sala Glauber Rocha** (Av. 212, esq. 31, La Coronela, tel. 07/271-8967), in the Fundación del Nuevo Cine Latinoamericano, shows mostly Latin American movies Tuesday–Friday at 3 P.M. and 5:30 P.M. (CUC2).

The most important cinemas are:

Cine Acapulco (Av. 26, e/ 35 y 37, Vedado, tel. 07/833-9573) has movies starting at 4:30 P.M.

Cine Astral (Calzada de Infanta #501, esq. San Martín, Centro Habana, tel. 07/878-1001) is the comfiest *cine* in Havana.

Cine Charles Chaplin (Calle 23 #1155, e/ 10 y 12, Vedado, tel. 07/831-1101) shows daily at 5 and 8 P.M. except Tuesday.

Cine La Rampa (Calle 23 #111, e/ O y P, Vedado, tel. 07/878-6146) shows daily from 4:40 P.M. except Wednesday; it mostly shows Cuban and Latin American films, plus the occasional obscure foreign movie, and is one of Havana's more comfy cinemas.

Cine Payret (Prado #503, esq. San José, Habana Vieja, tel. 07/863-3163), opposite the Capitolio Nacional, is Havana's largest (albeit timeworn) cinema and has as many as six showings daily, beginning at 12:30 P.M. It has midnight shows Friday–Sunday.

Cine Riviera (Calles 23, e/ H y G, Vedado, tel. 07/832-9564), has predominantly action or other Hollywood movies daily from 4:40 P.M.

Cine Yara (Calle 23 y Calle L, Vedado, tel. 07/832-9430) opens at 12:30 P.M. and is Havana's "main" theater.

---

exhibitions, galleries, performances, and more in both Spanish and English. It's available in many hotel lobbies, as is the monthly *Guía Cultural de la Habana,* which provides up-to-date information on what's on in town. *Granma,* the daily Communist Party newspaper, also lists the forthcoming week's events.

Radio Taíno (1290 AM and 93.3 FM), serving tourists, offers information on cultural happenings with nightly broadcasts 5–7 P.M., as does Radio Habana (94.9 FM); the TV program Hurón Azul (Cubavision) gives a preview of the next week's top happenings every Thursday at 10:25 P.M.

EVENTS

For a list of forthcoming festivals, conferences, and events, contact **Paradiso** (Calle 19 #560, esq. C, Vedado, Havana, tel. 07/832-6928, fax 07/33-3921, paradis@paradiso.artex.com.cu), or the **Buró de Convenciones** (Hotel Neptuno, Calle 3ra, e/ 70 y 74, 3er. piso, Mira-mar, tel. 07/204-8273, fax 07/204-8162, www.cubameeting.co.cu).

Annual Events
JANUARY
The **Cabildos** festival is held on January 6, when Habana Vieja resounds with festivities recalling the days when Afro-Cuban *cabildos* danced through the streets in vivid costumes. Contact Habaguanex (Oficios #110, e/ Lamparilla y Amargura, tel. 07/867-1034 or 860-6686, www.habaguanex.cu).

FEBRUARY
The **Habanos Festival,** for big-spenders, celebrates Cuban cigars and opens at the Tropicana nightclub. The high point is an elegant dinner and auction, with Fidel Castro usually in attendance.

Literati and bookworms should time their visit to coincide with the **Feria Internacional del Libro de la Habana** (Havana Book Fair), organized by the Instituto Cubano del Libro (Cuban Book Institute, Calle O'Reilly #14, Habana Vieja, tel. 07/862-8091) and held in Plaza de Armas.

APRIL
The **Festival Internacional de Percusión** (International Percussion Festival, tel. 07/203-8808, percuba@mail.com) is held each April.

MAY
When May 1 rolls around, head to the Plaza de la Revolución for the **Primero de Mayo** (May Day Parade). The day is meant to honor workers and is intended to appear as a spontaneous demonstration of revolutionary loyalty. In reality it is a carefully choreographed affair—hundreds of buses bring workers and children from surrounding regions. While loyalists display genuine enthusiasm, the majority of attendees attend for fear of being black-marked by CDRs and party officials at work. Cuban stooges use the loudspeakers to work up the crowd with chants of *"¡Viva Fidel!"* Each year's theme reflects the anti–United States flavor of the day. You'll be surrounded by as many as 500,000 people waving colorful banners and placards and wearing T-shirts painted with revolutionary slogans.

The **Festival Internacional de Guitarra** (International Guitar Festival and Contest), hosted by Instituto Cubano de la Música (ICM), is held at the Teatro Roldán in even-numbered years.

JUNE
The **Festival Internacional Boleros de Oro** (International Boleros Festival), sponsored by the Unión Nacional de Escritores y Artistas de Cuba (National Union of Cuban Writers and Artists, UNEAC, Calle 17 #351, e/ G y H, Vedado, tel. 07/832-4551, www.uneac.com), features traditional folk music from Cuba, Spain, and Latin America.

JULY
The **Carnaval de la Habana** (Carnival in Havana, tel. 07/832-3742, atic@cubarte.cult.cu) is held the last two weekends of July and the first two weekends of August. It's amateurish compared to the more lavish festivals of Rio de Janeiro and Trinidad, but it's fun nonetheless.

The **Coloquio Internacional Hemingway** (International Hemingway Colloquium), takes place in early July every odd-numbered year. The venue changes each year.

AUGUST
Every odd year sees the **Festival Internacional de Música Popular Benny Moré,** named for the popular Cuban composer-singer and featuring a panorama of popular Cuban music. The festival takes place in Havana concurrently with events in Cienfuegos.

The **Festival de Rap de Alamar** (Alamar Rap Festival), in late August, brings U.S. hip-hop groups to perform alongside Cuba's best rap groups in a most unlikely venue: the Anfiteatro de Alamar and the Casa de la Cultura de Alamar (Calle 164, esq. 5taB, Zona 7, Alamar, tel. 07/65-0624).

SEPTEMBER
The 10-day biennial **Festival Internacional de Teatro** (International Theater Festival of Havana), sponsored by the Consejo Nacional de Artes Escénicas (National Council of Scenic Arts, Calle 4 #257, Miramar, tel. 07/832-4126), is held in odd-numbered years and features international theater companies covering drama, street theater, musicals, and dance.

OCTOBER
The annual **Festival de la Habana de Música Contemporánea** (Havana Festival of Contemporary Music) spans a week in early October, with performances ranging from choral to electro-acoustic. Contact UNEAC (Calle 17 #351, e/ G y H, Vedado, tel. 07/832-4551, www.uneac.com).

The **Festival Internacional de Ballet** (International Ballet Festival) features dancers and choreographers from around the world, as well as the acclaimed Ballet Nacional de Cuba (BNC, Calzada #510, e/ D y E, Vedado, Ciudad Habana, C.P. 10400, tel. 907/832-4625, www.balletcuba.cu).

The prestigious **Bienal de la Habana** (Havana Biennial), hosted in even-numbered years by the Centro Wilfredo Lam (Calle San Ignacio #22, tel. 07/861-2096 and 861-3419, www.cnap.cult.cu), features artists from more than 50 countries. It offers workshops and other activities.

DECEMBER

The **Festival del Nuevo Cine Latinoamericano** (Festival of New Latin American Cinema, also known as the Latin American Film Festival) is one of Cuba's most glittering events. Castro is usually on hand, schmoozing with Hollywood actors and directors in the lobbies of the Hotel Nacional and Habana Libre. Movies from throughout the Americas and Europe are shown at cinemas and theaters across the city and the festival culminates with Cuba's own version of the Oscar, the Coral prizes. You buy your tickets for particular cinemas well before the programming is announced; or you can buy a pass (CUC25) good for the duration of the festival. Contact the Instituto de Cinematografía (Calle 23 #1155, Vedado, tel. 07/831-3145, 833-4634, or 55-2418, www.havanafilmfestival.com).

The biennial star-studded **Festival Internacional de Jazz** (International Havana Jazz Festival, Calle 15, esq. F, Vedado, tel. 07/832-8298, icm@cubarte.cult.cu) is held mid-month in even-numbered years, highlighted by the greats of Cuban jazz, such as Chucho Valdés and Irakere and Juan Formell and Los Van Van. Concerts are held at various venues.

HABANA VIEJA
Bars

Every tourist, it seems, wants to sip a *mojito* at **La Bodeguita del Medio** (Empredado #207, e/ Cuba y Tacón, tel. 07/33-8276; daily noon–midnight), as Ernest Hemingway did almost daily. However, the *mojitos* are weak and far too small for the CUC4 tab. Go for the ambience.

Another Hemingway favorite—and one offering far better and cheaper (CUC3) *mojitos*—is the **Dos Hermanos** (Av. San Pedro #304, esq. Sol, tel. 07/861-3514; 24 hours), a down-to-earth wharf-front saloon where Hemingway bent elbows with sailors and prostitutes at the long wooden bar, open to the street through wooden *rejas*. There's often live music and usually more Cubans than tourists—always a good sign.

Hemingway enjoyed his daily daiquiri at **El Floridita** (Obispo, esq. Monserrate, tel. 07/867-1300; bar daily noon–1 A.M.). The frosty daiquiri for which the bar is famous is a perfect pick-me-up after a hot stroll through town. It may not quite live up to its 1950s aura, when *Esquire* magazine named it one of the great bars of the world, but to visit Havana without sipping a daiquiri here would be like visiting France without tasting the wine.

The atmospheric wood-paneled **Bar Monserrate** (Monserrate, esq. Obrapía, tel. 07/860-9751; daily 11 A.M.–3 A.M.), just south of El Floridita, is popular with Cubans and is noted for its Coctel Monserrate (one teaspoon of sugar, two ounces of grapefruit juice, five drops of grenadine, two ounces of white rum, ice, and a sprig of mint; CUC2.20). It's a good spot to while away the afternoon listening to live music that sometimes lasts through the night. It also draws *jiniteros* and *jiniteras*. The staff is no less trustworthy: Count your change!

I love the **Café Barrita** (Monserrate #261, esq. San Juan de Díos, tel. 07/862-9271; Mon.–Sat. 9 A.M.–6 P.M.), in Edificio Bacardí. Formerly the private bar of the Bacardí family, it casts you right back to the 1920s. Snacks are served. It's popular with a cigar-smoking foreign crowd, and the *mojitos* are strong.

Lluvia de Oro (Obispo #316, esq. Habana, tel. 07/862-9870; Mon.–Thurs. 8 A.M.–1 A.M., Sat.–Sun. 8 A.M.–3 A.M.) is a lively, down-to-earth bar popular with foreigners come to sample the live music and meet wayward *cubanas* and *cubanos*. It serves cheap but strong *mojitos* (CUC2.50), and features live *son* music. Its likeness, the nearby **Café París** (San Ignacio #202, esq. Obispo; 24 hours), until recently the liveliest spot in Old Havana, seems to have fallen afoul of the police for the lively mixing of Cubans and tourists; Cubans were absent at last visit, when the place was consistently dead.

Hotel bars are more sedate. The lobby piano-bar in the **Hotel Ambos Mundos** (Obispo, esq. Mercaderes, tel. 07/860-9529) is a delightful place to tipple, as is the **Bar La Marina** (Av. San Pedro, esq. Luz, tel. 07/862-8000) in the Hotel Armadores de Santander. The latter has an upscale mood and nautical motif (including staff in mariners' uniforms), plus live music. The chicest bars in Habana Vieja are in the restaurant of the **Hotel Saratoga** (Paseo del Prado #603, esq. Dragones, tel. 07/868-1000; noon–midnight) and **Hotel Telégrafo** (Paseo del Prado #408, esq. Neptuno, tel. 07/861-1010), whose contemporary ground floor bars would look right at home in New York or LA. I also like the art deco **Bar Lejaim** (San Ignacio, esq. Amargura, tel. 07/860-8280) in the Hotel Raquel, which has an open bar each Wednesday evening, with Cuban cocktails and *bocas* (snacks).

Beer lovers should head to Plaza Vieja, where the **Taberna de la Muralla** (San Ignacio #364; daily 11 A.M.–1 A.M.) is a Viennese-style brewpub run in cooperation with an Austrian company. This converted colonial mansion produces Pilsen (light) and Munich (dark) beer. You can order half-liters (CUC2), liters, or a whopping five-liter dispenser. The bar has live music.

Traditional Cuban Music and Dance

On Monday nights I recommend a soirée called **Encounter with Cuban Music** (Calle San Ignacio #78, e/ O'Reilly y Callejón del Chorro, Habana Vieja, tel. 07/861-0412). The former hostess, Dulce María Baralt, recently died, but her family and band, Son de Cuba, keep alive this magnificent rooftop rumba. Climbing a rickety staircase to the top of the dilapidated three-story building, you emerge on an *azotea* overlooking the Plaza de la Catedral. Hands are extended. You are hugged warmly by Cubans you do not know. The rhythms of the *marimbas, bongos,* and *tres* guitar pulse across the rooftops of Habana Vieja. Rum and beer are passed around, and soon you are clapping and singing to traditional Cuban compositions

until the infectious beat lures you to dance. Entry costs CUC5, including a drink. Feel free to donate a bottle of rum.

Habaguanex (Oficios #110, e/ Lamparilla y Amargura, tel. 07/867-1034 or 860-6686, www.habaguanex.cu) hosts **Noche en las Plazas** (Night in the Plazas) one Saturday per month at 9 P.M. in the Plaza de la Catedral or Plaza de San Francisco, with *criollo* dinners and folkloric *espectáculos* (CUC22 with dinner). Reservations can be made at hotel tour desks. The New Year's Eve special dinner is *the* social event of the city, costing a whopping CUC100.

Every Saturday at 3 P.M. the Compañia "JJ" Túrarte performs Afro-Cuban rumba in the courtyard of the Antigua Capilla San Agustín (Amargura, esq. Aguilar, Habana Vieja; CUC1).

Hotel Santa Isabel, on Plaza de Armas, hosts a rooftop *Noche cubana* each Friday at 8 P.M. (CUC15 including five-course dinner!)

The **Asociación Cultural Yoruba de Cuba** (Prado #615, e/ Dragones y Monte, tel. 07/863-5953) hosts the Peña Oyú Obbá, with traditional Afro-Cuban music and dance, each Sunday, 5–8 P.M. (CUC5).

Cabarets Espectáculos

The rooftop bar of the **Hotel Inglaterra** (Prado #416, esq. San Rafael, tel. 07/860-8594; CUC5) features a small *cabaret espectáculo* on weekends.

Discotheques and Nightclubs

Disco Karaoke, atop the Hotel Plaza (Zulueta #267, esq. Neptuno, tel. 07/860-8583; nightly 11 P.M.–5 A.M.; CUC5), packs Cubans in thick as sardines.

Jazz

A jazz trio performs in the **Café del Oriente** (Oficios #112, esq. Amargura, tel. 07/860-6686), on Plaza de San Francisco, where you can enjoy cocktails at the ritzy marble-top bar.

Another atmospheric bar with live jazz is the **Bar Chico O'Farrill** (Cuba #102, esq. Chacón; tel. 07/860-5080).

HAVANA

Tango and Flamenco

Flamenco is hosted at **Centro Andaluz en Cuba** (Prado #104, e/ Genios y Refugio, tel. 07/863-6745; free) each Wednesday, Friday, and Saturday at 9 P.M. Lessons are offered Tuesday–Thursday 9–11 A.M. (CUC15 per hour).

El Mesón de la Flota (Mercaderes #257, e/ Amargura y Brasil, tel. 07/863-3888; free) hosts flamenco 1–3 P.M., as does the **Bodegón de los Vinos** in the Fortaleza de San Carlos de la Cabaña.

The **Caserón de Tango** (Calle Justíz #21, e/ Baratillo y Oficios, tel. 07/861-0822) has tango *peñas* on Wednesday and Friday at 5 P.M.; shows on Saturday at 10 P.M. and Sunday at 9:30 P.M.; and tango lessons (CUC5) Thursday at 4–6 P.M. and Saturday 2–4 P.M., and other days by arrangement.

Theater, Classical Music, and Ballet

The most important theater in Havana is the **Gran Teatro de la Habana** (Paseo de Martí #458, e/ San Rafael y San Martín, Habana Vieja, tel. 07/861-3077; CUC3, or CUC10 for best orchestra seats), on the west side of Parque Central. It's the main stage for the acclaimed Ballet Nacional de Cuba, Ballet Español de la Habana, and the national opera company. However, anyone used to a live orchestra may be disappointed, as the ballet is usually performed to taped music. The building has three theaters—the Teatro García Lorca, where ballet and concerts are held, and the smaller Sala Alejo Carpentier and Sala Antonin Artaud, for less commercial, experimental performances. Performances are Thursday–Saturday at 8:30 P.M. and Sunday at 5 P.M. A dress code (no shorts or hats) applies.

On Friday afternoons, head to **Plaza de Armas,** where a symphony band strikes up at 4 P.M.

The **Basílica de San Francisco de Asís** (Calle Oficios, e/ Amargura y Brasil, tel. 07/862-9683) hosts classical concerts daily at 6 P.M. (CUC2–10). Classical and ecclesiastical concerts are featured in the **Iglesia de**

the baroque facade of the Gran Teatro – each corner is tipped by an angel

© CHRISTOPHER P. BAKER

San Francisco de Paula (Av. del Puerto, esq. Leonor Pérez, tel. 07/860-4210) on Fridays at 7 P.M. The **Museo de la Música** (Calle Capdevilla #1, tel. 07/861-9846; CUC2), offers classical concerts on Saturday and Sunday at 4 P.M. Classical concerts are also offered in the Sala Teatro of the **Museo Nacional de Bellas Artes** (Trocadero, e/ Zulueta y Monserrate, tel. 07/862-0241).

Other Entertainment

Comedy: The **Casa de la Comedia** (Calle Justíz #18, esq. Baratillo, tel. 07/863-9282; CUC2), one block southeast of Plaza de Armas, hosts comic theater on weekends at 7 P.M.

Teatro Fausto (Prado #201, esq. Colón, Habana Vieja, tel. 07/862-5416) has comedy Friday–Saturday at 8:30 P.M. and Sunday at 5 P.M. **Bar Monserrate** (Av. de Bélgica, Monserrate, esq. Obrapía, tel. 07/860-9751) has comedy each Saturday at 10 P.M. (CUC5.30 *consumo mínimo*).

Poetry Readings and Literary Events: The **La Moderna Poesía** (Calle Obispo #525, esq.

Bernaza, Habana Vieja, tel. 07/861-5600) bookshop hosts literary events, as do UNEAC's **Casa de la Poesía** (Calle Muralla #63, e/ Oficios y Inquisidor, Habana Vieja, tel. 07/861-8251) and the **Fundación Alejo Carpentier** (Empedrado #215, Habana Vieja, tel. 07/861-3667).

CENTRO HABANA
Traditional Cuban Music and Dance

The place to be on Sunday is "Salvador's Alley" for **Rumba del "Salvador's Alley"** (Callejón de Hamel, e/ Aramburo y Hospital, tel. 07/878-1661, eliasasef@yahoo.es), where Salvador González Escalona hosts a weekend rumba with Afro-Cuban music and dance, Sunday noon–3 P.M. González also hosts a traditional music night every last Friday of the month at 9 P.M.

The **Casa de la Trova** (San Lázaro #661, e/ Padre Varela y Gervasio, tel. 07/879-3373l; CUC5) has live music—everything from *filin* to *son* and *nueva trova*—Thursday–Sunday at 7 P.M. Friday evening is best. Adherents of *filin* music flock on Friday 10 P.M.–1 A.M. for **La Peña de Joya** (San Lázaro #667, Apto. 9, e/ Padre Varela y Gervasio), two doors down the street.

Centro Cultural Comunitario (San Nicolás #220, e/ Concordia y Virtudes) hosts a *peña campesina* with country music every Monday at 6 P.M.

Folkloric groups practice *bolero, danzón, guanguancó* and more at the **Salón de Ensayo Benny Moré** (Neptuno #960, e/ Aguila y Galiano, tel. 07/878-8827; Tues.–Sat. 9:30 A.M.–noon and 2–5 P.M.). Visitors are welcome.

Cabarets Espectáculos

Cabaret Nacional (San Rafael, esq. Prado, tel. 07/863-2361; CUC5), in the dingy basement of the Gran Teatro, has a modest *espectáculo* nightly at 10 P.M. The campy show normally doesn't begin until later, and is followed by a disco. It packs in a young Cuban set on weekends for steamy dancing. A dress code applies, and ostensibly only couples are admitted.

Less impressive is the **Disco Ribera Azul**

(Av. de Italia, e/ Malecón y San Lázaro, tel. 07/33-8813), in the basement of the Hotel Deauville. It has a small *cabaret espectáculo* and disco Friday–Sunday at 11 P.M. (CUC5).

Discotheques and Nightclubs

The hottest spot in town at last visit was **Casa de la Música** (Galiano, e/ Concordia y Neptuno, tel. 07/862-4165; daily 4–7 P.M. and 10 P.M.–2 A.M.; CUC10–20), a modern theater known as "Dos" (for Casa de la Música 2, or *dos*) that packs in a mostly Cuban crowd for concerts and dancing.

More down-to-earth, but a favorite of Afro-Cubans, is **La Pampa** (Malecón y Vapor; Tues.–Sun. 7 P.M.–3 A.M.; CUC2 per couple); however, the once-popular hip-hop scene for which the venue was famous is no longer offered.

Rap and Rock

The **Teatro América** (Av. de Italia #253, e/ Concordia y Neptuno, tel. 07/862-4165; CUC5) hosts rap and reggae concerts Tuesday–Sunday 10 A.M.–4 P.M.

Tango and Flamenco

Caserón del Tango (Neptuno #303, e/ Águila y Italia, tel. 07/863-0097) hosts tango *peñas* on Monday, 7–8 P.M.

Other Entertainment

Comedy and vaudeville are staples at **Teatro América** (Av. de Italia, e/ Concordia y Neptuno, tel. 07/862-5416) every Saturday at 8:30 P.M. and Sunday at 5 P.M.

VEDADO AND PLAZA DE LA REVOLUCIÓN
Bars

El Relicario Bar (Paseo, e/ 1ra y 3ra, tel. 07/204-3636), in the Hotel Meliá Cohiba, is popular with a monied, cigar-loving crowd and offers an elegant Edwardian ambience and relative serenity. It has a pool table. I also like the small lobby bar in the **Hotel Habana Riviera** (Malecón y Paseo, tel. 07/836-4051).

The **Bar Vista del Golfo** (Calle O, esq. 21, tel. 07/874-3564), in the Hotel Nacional, has a jukebox and walls festooned with photos of such famous visitors as Errol Flynn and assorted mobsters. Better yet is the hotel's backgarden patio, **Bar La Terraza,** where calming music is offered and you can sit in a sofa chair with a cigar and cocktail in hand.

For superb views of the city, try **Salón Turquino,** on the 25th floor of the Hotel Tryp Habana Libre, or **La Torre** (Calle 17 #55, e/ M y N, tel. 07/55-3089), atop the Focsa building.

Penny-pinchers wanting to sup with Cubans should head to **Casa del Coctel** (Calle 23, esq. Av. de los Presidentes, tel. 07/830-9375; daily 11 A.M.–2 A.M.), serving CUC1 *mojitos* and CUC0.50 rum shots. The surrounds are simple. Also popular with Cubans is **Mesón de la Chorrera** (Malecón y Calle 20; daily noon–midnight), upstairs in the old fortress at the mouth of the Río Almendares; this atmospheric place even has cannons pointing through the windows. It hosts live Spanish music Thursday–Sunday at 9 P.M.

Looking for a Vegas-style lounge? Good luck in Havana! The closest thing these days is the **Opus Bar** (Calzada, esq. D; daily 3 P.M.–3 A.M.), in Teatro Amadeo Roldán, a 1950s retro-themed bar with stuffed sofas that might have appealed to Sammy Davis Jr. and the Rat Pack.

Traditional Cuban Music and Dance

My favorite hangout is **Café Concierto Gato Tuerto** (Calle O #14, e/ 17 y 19, tel. 07/833-2224; CUC2 cover plus CUC3 *consumo mínimo*), a cramped and moody 1950s-style nightclub that hosts *música filin, trova,* and *bolero* nightly until 3 A.M. It gets packed, mostly with middle-aged Cubans (and a smattering of tourists) who like nothing more than to sing along. The show normally doesn't begin until 11 P.M.

In a similar vein, try **Club Imágenes** (Calzada #602, esq. C, tel. 07/833-3606; daily 11 P.M.–3 A.M.; CUC5 cover plus CUC3 *consumo mínimo*), a stylish piano bar hosting *boleros* and other traditional music for the late-night (and more mature) crowd.

El Hurón Azul (UNEAC, Calle 17 #351, esq. H, tel. 07/832-4551; daily 5 P.M.–2 A.M.), in the Unión Nacional de Escritores y Artistas de Cuba, hosts a *peña* with Afro-Cuban music and dance on Wednesday at 5 P.M. (CUC5), *trovas* on Thursday at 5 P.M. (CUC1), plus *boleros* each Saturday at 10 P.M. (CUC1). This is ground zero for bohemian intellectual life in Havana, and many of Cuba's top writers and artists, and even Abel Prieto, the youthful (and long-haired) Minister of Culture, hang out here.

The **Casa de la Amistad** (Paseo #406, e/ 17 y 19, tel. 07/830-3114; Mon.–Fri. 11 A.M.–midnight, Sat. 11 A.M.–2 A.M., Sun. 11 A.M.–6 P.M.; CUC5, including one drink) offers live music nightly, and on Tuesday 9 P.M.–midnight you can listen to the late Compay Segundo's band, Compay y Los Amigos. Rumba is offered on Wednesday, *danzón* on Friday, and a "Noche Cubana" on Saturday.

The Afrocuban Allstars perform *Buena Vista Social Club* numbers every Monday and Wednesday in the **Copa Room** (Hotel Havana Riviera, tel. 07/834-4228, CUC20) at 11:30 P.M., preceded by the cabaret.

Casa de las Américas (3ra Calle, esq. Av. de los Presidentes, tel. 07/55-2706, fax 07/33-4554, www.casa.cult.cu; five pesos), hosts an eclectic range of concerts, Monday–Friday 8 A.M.–4:30 P.M.

Cabarets Espectáculos

The most lavish show is the **Cabaret Parisien** (Calle O, esq. 21, tel. 07/873-3564 or 07/373-4701; CUC35), in the Hotel Nacional. The *Cubano cubano* show is offered nightly at 10 P.M. The dinner special (CUC50–70) is best avoided. The place is cramped and gets filled with smoke, and while the show is nowhere near the scale of the Tropicana, it has plenty of feathers and flesh and sexual energy, and it's handily right in the heart of Vedado.

The small-scale cabaret at **Salón Rojo** (Calle 21, e/ N y O, tel. 07/833-3747 or 832-0511; Thurs.–Sun. 10 P.M.–2 A.M.; CUC10 including two drinks), beside the Hotel Capri, is cheaper albeit far less impressive. It is followed by live performances.

The **Cabaret Copa Room** (Paseo y Malecón, tel. 07/836-4051; CUC20, or CUC45 with dinner and cocktail), in the Hotel Riviera, hosts a cabaret Monday–Saturday at 10:30 P.M. The venue specializes in the Latin beat and often features the top names in live Cuban music, such as Los Van Van. It's Havana's top spot for serious salsa fans, but relies heavily on the tourist trade and there's no shortage of *jiniteras.*

Catering mostly to a tourist crowd, the contrived **Habana Café** (Paseo, e/ 1ra y 3ra, tel. 07/833-3636, ext. 147; nightly 8 P.M.–2:30 A.M.), adjoining the Hotel Meliá Cohiba, offers cabaret. A classic Harley-Davidson, an old Pontiac, and a 1957 open-top canary-yellow Chevy add a dramatic effect, as does an airplane suspended from the ceiling (suddenly the car horns beep and the headlamps flash, you hear the roar of an airplane taking off, then the curtains open and—voilà—the show begins). Entrance is free but a CUC5 *consumo mínimo* applies; entrance costs CUC20 when top bands such as Los Van Van, Charanga Habanera, and—on Sundays—Grupo de Compay Segundo play. It has a disco on Friday nights. You can make a night of it by dining on reasonable quality but overpriced burgers (from CUC5) delivered American style with ketchup and mustard, Caesar salad (CUC7.50), filet mignon (CUC17), and "banana split" (CUC5). Check your bill carefully, as scams are frequent.

Primarily serving impecunious Cubans is the **Cabaret Las Vegas** (Infanta #104, e/ 25 y 27, tel. 07/870-7939; Wed.–Sun. 10 P.M.–3 A.M.; CUC1 Fri.; CUC2 Thurs., Sat., and Sun.; CUC5 Wed.), with a show at 11 P.M. followed by a disco. Author Tom Miller summed up the mood well: "The *chicas* danced in earnest but seldom in sync, their tattered fishnet stockings running before our eyes" while the solo singer "singing off-key into her cordless mike… would have been better served had she carried a mikeless cord."

Similar third-tier venues catering mostly to Cubans are **Karachi Club** (Calles 17 y K, tel. 07/832-3485; nightly 10 P.M.–4 A.M.; CUC5);

Centro Nocturno La Red (Calle 19 #151, esq. L, tel. 07/832-5415; 10 P.M.–4 A.M.; CUC1–2), with karaoke on Monday, Latin music on Wednesday, comedy on Thursday–Saturday, followed by disco; and **Club Amanecer** (Calle 15, e/ O y N; 10 P.M.–3 A.M.; CUC5 *consumo mínimo*), with a small *cabaret espectáculo* on Monday and Tuesday, karaoke on Wednesday and Thursday, and live music Friday and Saturday.

Discotheques and Nightclubs

Salón Turquino (Calle L, e/ 23 y 25, tel. 07/55-4011; nightly 10:30 P.M.–3 A.M.; CUC10 cover), atop the Hotel Habana Libre, offers a medley of entertainment varying nightly, followed by salsa dancing. Top bands often perform, and the place often closes for VIP parties. It's one of the most popular venues, drawing tourists and Cubans with dollars to spend. No single Cubans are allowed, so foreigners are often propositioned at the door by females seeking admission. The hotel's mezzanine-level **Salón de los Embajadores** (nightly 10 P.M.–3 A.M.; free, except CUC5 cover Saturday) has karaoke nightly except Saturday, when there's often live music; there's no point in arriving before midnight, when the music begins.

I also like the **Cabaret Pico Blanco** (Calle O #206, e/ 23 y 25, tel. 07/833-3740; nightly 9:30 P.M.–2:30 A.M.; CUC5), in the glass-enclosed top floor of the Hotel St. John. It features salsa, *boleros,* and *trova* nightly, though the mood runs hot and cold. Occasionally a top name is featured; other times you may have to suffer through karaoke. A disco follows.

Around the corner, Calle 23 between Calles O y N has several dingy clubs drawing a young Cuban crowd for merengue and salsa.

Cubans also flock to **Café Cantante** (Paseo, esq. 39, tel. 07/879-0710; Tues.–Sat. 9 P.M.–5 A.M.; CUC3, or CUC10–20 when top groups perform), one of the city's hottest spots, in the basement of the Teatro Nacional. No hats, T-shirts, or shorts for men. Also go on Fridays for live salsa (4–6 P.M.); only Cubans go and with luck you'll be charged in pesos. The plusher **Delirio Habanero** (tel. 07/873-5713), a lounge on the third floor of the Teatro Nacional, also has afternoon *peñas* (3–7 P.M.) and live music Tuesday–Sunday (10 A.M.–2 A.M.; CUC5–CUC15), when the place can rock to everything from *boleros* to *timba*. Also in the Teatro Nacional, **Mi Habana** has music and dance the same hours.

Jazz

The **Jazz Café** (1ra at the base of Paseo, tel. 07/55-3475; daily noon–2 A.M.; CUC10 *consumo mínimo*), on the third floor of the Galería del Paseo, is a classy supper-club with some of the best live jazz in town, including from resident maestro Chucho Valdés and Irakere. The music doesn't get going until about 11:30 P.M., though the seats usually fill up well before then. There's barely a dance floor.

La Zorra y el Cuervo (Calle 23, e/ N y O, tel. 07/833-2402, zorra@cbcan.cyt.cu; 10 P.M.–2 A.M.; CUC5) is a dedicated jazz club in a dreary basement setting. Occasional foreign bands perform here, as do the Cuban greats such as Chucho Valdés. It has "blues" on Thursdays. The first set normally kicks off at 10:30 P.M. Get there early to guarantee a seat.

Rap and Rock

If ever you doubted that Cuba has a rock scene, head to the colloquially named **Parque de los Roqueros** at the corner of Calle 23 and Avenida de los Presidentes, where the goth (black leather, black eyeliner, pink-tinted hair) crowd gathers nightly.

Roqueros gravitate to **Patio de María** (Calle 37 #262, e/ Paseo y 2, Vedado, tel. 07/881-0722; daily 7:30 A.M.–11 P.M.; five pesos), one block west of Teatro Nacional, where live rock concerts are hosted; there's also a disco Friday and Sunday 9 P.M.–midnight.

Rap concerts are held at **La Madriguera** (Av. Salvador Allende, e/ Infanta y Luaces, tel. 07/879-8175; 5–10 pesos), an unlikely spot in the overgrown former botanical gardens of the Quinta de los Molinos, entered off Infanta. La Madriguera is open Monday–Wednesday and Friday 9 A.M.–7 P.M., and Thursday 9 A.M.–midnight, when a disco is hosted.

Theater, Classical Music, and Ballet

Performances of the National Symphony and Danza Contemporanea de Cuba are hosted at the **Teatro Nacional** (Av. Carlos M. de Céspedes, esq. Paseo, Vedado, tel. 07/879-6011, tnc@cubarte.cult.cu) every Friday–Saturday at 8:30 P.M. and Sunday at 5 P.M. (CUC1.80–8.90). The ticket office is open Tuesday–Thursday 10 A.M.–6 P.M. and Friday–Sunday 3–9 P.M.

The **Teatro Mella** (Línea #657, e/ A y B, Vedado, tel. 07/833-5651) is noted for contemporary dance, theater, and ballet (CUC5–10), and hosts the Conjunto Folklórico Nacional.

Teatro Cine Trianón (Línea #706, e/ Paseo y A, tel. 07/832-9648; five pesos) often features foreign classics, such as the works of Tennessee Williams, performed by the Teatro el Público company.

The **Teatro Amadeo Roldán** (Calzada y D, Vedado, tel. 07/832-4521; CUC5–10), which has two *salas*, features classical concerts year-round. The Orquesta Sinfónica Nacional is based here, with concerts each Sunday at 11 A.M. in season, and many lesser classical groups perform.

Nearby is the **Teatro Hubert de Blanck** (Calzada #657, e/ A y B, tel. 07/830-1011; CUC5), known for both modern and classical plays. It hosts the Teatro Estudio theater company. Shows (in Spanish) are usually Friday–Saturday at 8:30 P.M. and Sunday at 5 P.M.

The 150-seat **Teater Buendía** (Calle Loma y 38, Nuevo Vedado, tel. 07/881-6689; five pesos), in a converted Greek Orthodox church, hosts performances by the eponymous theater company, considered to be Cuba's most innovative and accomplished. It performs here Friday–Sunday at 8:30 P.M.

Other Entertainment

Comedy: The **Teatro Bertolt Brecht** (Calle 13, esq. I, tel. 07/832-9359) specializes in comedy, offered Tuesday at 8:30 P.M.

The **Teatro Guiñol** (Calle M, e/ 17 y 19, tel. 07/832-6262; CUC2), on the west side of the Focsa building, is Cuba's leading children's

HAVANA'S GAY SCENE

Gay life in Havana has expanded noticeably in recent years, although homosexual venues remain subject to police crackdowns. There are no established gay bars or clubs, which are banned, and the gay "scene" typically is relegated to "hangout" street locales. Most venues attract male prostitutes, called *pingueros* (from the Spanish word *pinga*, or prick). Be careful who you give a ride to on 5ta Avenida, Miramar, as *transvesti* prostitutes trawl for clients by night.

Most nights there's one or more gay parties known as *fiestas de diez pesos* at private venues (entrance typically costs 10 pesos, or sometimes CUC1-2). Havana society is non-exclusionary, however; everyone is welcome, and the mix usually includes a sprinkling of straight, lesbian, and even *transvestis*. Private parties often feature drag shows. The "floating party" venues change nightly as they try to stay one step ahead of the police.

To find out where the night's gay party is, head to the **Cine Yara** (La Rampa y L, Vedado), opposite Coppelia, the ice-cream park made famous by the homoerotic Cuban movie *Strawberry and Chocolate*. This is Havana's main cruising spot, particularly for transvestites. Likewise, gays gather at the **Malecón** at the foot of La Rampa, where the party spreads along the seafront boulevard at night.

Cine Yara is also the sole public venue for lesbians, who are less tolerated in this macho society.

BARS, CAFÉS, AND CLUBS

In Habana Vieja, **El Café Mercurio** (Oficios, e/ Lamparilla y Amargura, tel. 07/860-6188; daily 8:30 A.M.-midnight), on Plaza de San Francisco, attracts a gay crowd. A *transvesti* show is hosted at the **Sociedad Cultural Rosalía de Castro** (Av. de Bélgica #504 altos, e/ Máximo Gómez y Dragones, tel. 07/862-3193).

In Centro Habana, the **Castropol** (Malecón #107, esq. Genios, tel. 07/861-4864; CUC1) has a drag cabaret Monday-Thursday at 11:30 P.M.

La Pampa (Marina #102, esq. Vapor, tel. 07/878-3426) is a smoky, down-to-earth disco that draws a mixed bag, including a large gay contingent.

In Vedado, **La Arcada** (Calle M y 23; 24 hours) is effectively the only gay bar in town and is always packed. The cramped, humid **Club Tropical** (Línea, esq. F, tel. 07/832-7361; daily 10 P.M.-3 A.M.) occasionally acts as a gay venue, as does the steamy cellar bar, **Club Saturno** (Línea, e/ 10 y 12, tel. 07/833-7942; daily 11 P.M.-2:30 A.M.).

Bar de las Estrellas (Calle A #507, e/ 15 y 16), in the Lawton district, south of Cerro, is a *paladar* (private restaurant) with a transvestite cabaret at 10 P.M.

---

theater with comedy and puppet shows on Friday at 3 P.M., Saturday at 5 P.M., and Sunday at 10:30 A.M. and 5 P.M.

Comedy is also performed at the **Humor Club Cocodrilo** (Av. 3ra and 10, Vedado; nightly 10 P.M.–3 A.M.; CUC5). Magicians perform there as well.

Aguas Espectáculos: Swimming pool *espectáculos* (also called *ballets acuáticos*) are choreographed water ballets offered at the **Hotel Meliá Cohiba** nightly at 9:30 P.M. (CUC10) and at the **Hotel Nacional** Sunday at 9 P.M. (CUC10).

Poetry Readings and Literary Events:

The **Unión Nacional de Escritores y Artistas de Cuba** (UNEAC, Calle 17, esq. H, Vedado, tel. 07/832-4551) and the **Casa de las Américas** (3ra Calle, esq. Av. de los Presidentes, tel. 07/55-2707, fax 07/33-4554, www.casa.cult.cu) host literary events.

PLAYA (MIRAMAR AND BEYOND)
Bars

This district has very few bars. The most sophisticated are in the Hotel Meliá Habana and Occidental Miramar hotels, though these are devoid of Cubans and lifeless.

Two piano bars to consider are at **Dos Gardenias** (7ma Av. y 26, tel. 07/204-2353) and **Piano Bar Piel Canela** (Calle 16 #701, esq. 7ma, tel. 07/204-1543; Thurs., Sat., and Sun. 3 P.M.– 8 A.M.; entrance CUC1), at La Maison.

Traditional Cuban Music and Dance

The acclaimed **Conjunto Folklórico Nacional** (National Folklore Dance Group, Calle 4 #103, e/ Calzada y 5ta, tel. 07/836-9075; CUC5) performs *Sábado de rumba* alfresco each Saturday at 3 P.M. This is Afro-Cuban music and dance at its best; many of the cast are *santeros*.

For *boleros*, head to **Rincón de Boleros** (7ma Av., esq. 26, tel. 07/204-2353; daily 10:30 P.M.–3 A.M.; CUC10), in the Dos Gardenias complex.

Tropicana

Cuba's premier Las Vegas–style nightclub is the Tropicana (Calle 72 #4504 y Línea del Ferrocarril, Marianao, tel. 07/267-1717, fax 07/267-0119, www.cabaret-tropicana.com; entrance CUC65; cameras CUC5, videos CUC15), boasting more than 200 performers, a fabulous orchestra, and astonishing acrobatic feats (see the sidebar *Paradise under the Stars*). Famous international entertainers occasionally perform. The cabaret takes place in the open-air Salón Bajo Las Estrellas Tuesday–Sunday at 9 P.M. The entrance fee is outrageous, but includes a Cuba libre. You can purchase tickets at the reservation booth (10 A.M.– 6 P.M.) or directly at the entrance from 8:30 P.M. (call ahead to check availability), but it's best to book in advance through your hotel tour desk, as the show often sells out. Whole or partial refunds are offered if the show is rained out. Cocktails cost CUC3, but it's usually best to buy a bottle of rum and a can of Coke to last you all night. The Tropicana features two eateries: the elegant sky-lit Los Jardines, serving tasty continental fare (6 P.M.–1 A.M.); and the 1950s diner–style Rodney Café (noon–2 A.M.).

Other *Cabarets Espectáculos*

Macumba Habana (Calle 222, e/ 37 y 51, tel.

07/273-0568; Mon.–Sat. 9 P.M.–3 A.M., Sun. 5–11 P.M.; CUC10–15), in the La Giraldilla complex in the La Coronela district, offers a top-class, albeit small, *espectáculo* at 10:30 P.M. with a different theme nightly, followed by one of Havana's top discos.

Second-tier venues include the **Hotel Comodoro** (1ra Av. y Calle 84, tel. 07/204-5551); **Hotel Kohly** (Av. 49 y 36A, Rpto. Kohly, Playa, tel. 07/204-0240), on Monday and Friday; and **La Cecilia** (5ta Av. #11010, e/ 1110 y 112, tel. 07/204-1562) on Thursday–Sunday at 9:30 P.M.

Discotheques and Nightclubs

The **Casa de la Música** (Av. 25, esq. 20, tel. 07/204-0447; CUC5 afternoons, CUC15–20 evenings) sometimes has sizzling-hot afternoon salsa sessions as well as nightly (except Monday) performances by such legends as Bamboleo and Chucho Valdés. This is *the* place preferred by Cubans with some money to burn, and the fact that the audience usually includes some of Cuba's hottest performers says it all. The shows are advertised to begin at 10:30 P.M., but the headliner normally doesn't come out until 1 A.M. Also here is the **Tun Tún Piano Bar** (tel. 07/204-0447; Tues.–Sun. 10 P.M.–4 A.M.; CUC10).

The hippest spot in Havana is **Macumba Habana** (see *Other Cabarets Espectáculos*). This open-air disco boasts great music and draws the chic crowd (mostly well-heeled foreign males, monied white Cubans with high-positioned parents, and beautiful *habaneras,* many of them with their eyes on the well-heeled foreign males). The tunes range from Los Van Van to George Michael. There is a dress code. Only couples (*parejas*) are allowed entry, though this can include two women.

Cubans of lesser means head to **Club Río** (Calle A #314, e/ 3ra y 5ta, tel. 07/209-3389; Tues.–Sun. 10 P.M.–4 A.M.; CUC5), colloquially called Johnny's. DJs spin up-to-date tunes. It also has a cabaret on the sunken dance floor. Couples only are permitted. It has a reputation for pickpockets, occasional fights, and scams by bar staff.

PARADISE UNDER THE STARS

Tropicana, the prerevolutionary extravaganza now in its sixth decade of Vegas paganism – girls! girls! girls! – has been in continuous operation since New Year's Eve 1939, when it opened (in the gardens of a mansion – Villa Mina – that once housed the U.S. ambassador) as the most flamboyant nightclub in the world. The club quickly won the favor of the elite of society and soon eclipsed all other clubs in the grandeur and imagination of its productions. The Congo Pantera revue, which simulated a panther's nocturnal hunt in lush jungle, established the Tropicana's trademark, with dancers in the thick vegetation illuminated by colored spotlights – the name Tropicana melds the world *trópico* (tropics) with *palma cana* (fan palm).

In its heyday, the Tropicana spent more than US$12,000 nightly on its flamboyant shows, which ranged from the "Asian Paradise" portraying the exotic Orient, to choreographed Haitian voodoo rituals. International celebrities such as Nat "King" Cole, Josephine Baker, and Carmen Miranda headlined the show, which was so popular that a 50-passenger "Tropicana Special" flew nightly from Miami for an evening of entertainment that ended in the nightclub's casino, where a daily US$10,000-bingo jackpot was offered and a new automobile was raffled every Sunday.

Talent scouts scoured Cuba for the most beautiful models and dancers. The more than 200 performers are still handpicked from the crème de la crème of Cuba's singers and dancers, though the latter no longer dance topless. Patrons watch mesmerized as rainbow-hued searchlights sweep over the hordes of long-legged showgirls, gaudily feathered with sensational headdresses more ostentatious than peacocks, parading twenty feet up among the floodlit palm trees, quivering beseechingly like the most exotic of tropical birds.

In 2005, however, the Ministry of Tourism, headed by a new, austere military figure, took control of Tropicana. Immediately, it was announced that the infamously erotic show would be tamed down and replaced with "Drums in Concert," a theatrical show with more emphasis on stage sets and high-tech lighting. Even the dancers bemoan the change, which means goodbye to the gratuitous skin and erotic gyrations marked by the opening act, when a troupe of near-naked showgirls parades down the aisles wearing see-through body stockings and glowing chandeliers atop their heads.

Salón Chévere (Club Almendares, Calle 49C y 28A, Rpto. Kohly, tel. 07/204-4990; daily 11 A.M.–4 A.M.) has live music and dancing alfresco, with the real action beginning after 10 P.M. The CUC15 entrance includes an open bar.

Farther out, **Salón Rosado Benny Moré** (Av. 41, esq. 48, tel. 07/209-0985 or 07/203-5322; Fri.–Mon. 7 P.M.–2 A.M. with live groups; Tues.–Wed. for cabaret; CUC3–10), an open-air concert arena known as El Tropical, is immensely popular on weekends, when top-billed Cuban salsa bands perform. Probably the wildest place in town on Saturday night, with kick-ass music and dancing, it gets jam-packed, the dancing is salacious (foreign females are fair game for no-holds-barred come-ons), and rum-induced fights often break out. For better or worse, foreigners are sometimes kept apart from *habaneros.*

Cubans without dollars also find their fun at **Juventud 2000 Discoclub** (1ra Av., e/ 8 y 10, tel. 07/203-0801; Fri.–Sun. 9 P.M.–2 A.M.), in the Teatro Karl Marx. Los Van Van, Isaac Delgado, and other big names play here. The cover charge varies, depending on who's performing. The vast theater also plays host to many of the city's big-ticket events (such as the closing galas of the Latin American Film Festival).

If you're hankering for some homegrown music (think Beatles, Bee Gees, or Barry White) mixed in with your salsa, head to **Club Ipanema** (1ra Av., e/ 44 y 46, tel. 07/204-0340; Tues.–Sun. 10 P.M.–3 A.M.; CUC5), adjacent to the Hotel Copacabana.

Jazz

The **Casa de la Música** (see *Discotheques and Nightclubs*) sometimes hosts jazz.

A jazz group performs at the **Tocororo** (Calle 18 y 3ra Av., tel. 07/202-4530) restaurant.

Other Entertainment

Cuba's catwalk divas strut at **La Maison** (Calle 16 #701, esq. 7ma, Miramar, tel. 07/204-1543; CUC10), renowned for its *desfiles de modas* (fashion shows) and *cabaret espectáculo* held nightly at 10 P.M. in the terrace garden of an elegant old mansion. Reservations are recommended. A 4 P.M. matinee show is offered on Wednesday–Thursday and Saturday–Sunday. A disco follows the show.

Shopping

Havana offers superb shopping for art and crafts, as well as hand-crafted scents, Spanish fans, and rum and cigars. Havana has about two dozen Casas del Habano (the official cigar stores), with more being added all the time. Buy at an official store. If you buy off the street, you're almost certainly going to be sold fakes, although you'll be hard-pressed to know this (see *Cigars* in the *Shopping* section of the *Essentials* chapter for more information).

The airport departure lounge has the best-stocked rum and liquor stock in town, as well as a fine cigar selection and a full range of Cuban and import scents and colognes, though don't expect better prices.

HABANA VIEJA
Antiques

Havana's museums and private homes overflow with colonial-era antiques. However, the government recently placed a ban on the sale and export of antiques. Hence, there are no longer any stores selling antiques to tourists. (See *Exporting Arts and Antiques* in the *Shopping* section of the *Essentials* chapter.)

Colección Habana (Mercaderes, esq. O'Reilly, Habana Vieja, tel. 07/861-3388; daily 9 A.M.–6 P.M.) sells antique reproductions and decorative items.

Arts and Crafts

The largest market is the **Feria de la Artesanía** (Tacón; daily 8:30 A.M.–7 P.M.), selling everything from little ceramic figurines, miniature bongo drums, and papier-mâché 1950s autos, to banana-leaf hats, crocheted bikinis, straw hats, and paintings.

Habana Vieja contains dozens of galleries, many selling naive works by the artists themselves; these galleries, called *expo-ventas* (commercial galleries representing freelance artists), concentrate along Calle Obispo. The **Asociación Cubana de Artesana Artistas** (Obispo #411, tel. 07/860-8577; Mon.–Sat. 10 A.M.–8 P.M., Sun. 10 A.M.–6 P.M.) represents various artists.

For information on formal galleries, contact the **Fondo Cubano de Bienes Culturales** (Muralla #107, Habana Vieja, tel. 07/862-2633, galeriahab@cubarte.cult.cu; Mon.–Fri. 10 A.M.–5 P.M., Sat. 10 A.M.–2 P.M.), in Plaza Vieja, which sells quality work in its **Génesis Galerías.** The most creative treasures are in the upstairs galleries.

Nearby, experimental art is for sale at the **Centro de Desarrollo de las Artes Visuales** (Casa de las Hermanas Cárdenas, Plaza Vieja, tel. 07/862-3533).

One of the best galleries is **Galería Forma** (Obispo #255, tel. 07/862-0123; daily 10 A.M.–7 P.M.), selling artwork of international standard, including intriguing sculptures, ceramics, and copper pieces. Similar pieces can be found at **Galería Victor Manuel** (San Ignacio #46, e/ Callejón del Chorro y Empedrado, tel. 07/861-2955; daily 9 A.M.–9 P.M.), on the west side of Plaza de la Catedral. Around the corner is the **Taller Experimental de la Gráfica** (Callejón del Chorro, tel. 07/862-0979, tgrafica@cubarte.cult.cu; Mon.–Fri. 9 A.M.–4 P.M.), which has exclusive lithographic prints for sale upstairs in the **Galería del Grabado.**

Books and Stationery

Havana is desperately in need of a Barnes & Noble, and don't bother looking for newspapers or magazines, which are sold only in a few select tourist hotels.

The **Instituto Cubano del Libro** (Cuban Book Institute, O'Reilly #4, esq. Tacón, tel. 07/861-8585; Mon.–Sat. 9 A.M.–4:30 P.M.), in the Palacio del Segundo Cabo on Plaza de Armas, has three small bookshops, though almost the entire stock is in Spanish.

Plaza de Armas is also the setting for the **Mercado de Libros** (Wed.–Sat. 9 A.M.–7 P.M.), a secondhand book fair where you can rummage through the dreary collection of tattered tomes, but you'll be amazed at the high prices.

Librería La Internacional (Obispo #528, Habana Vieja, tel. 07/861-3238; daily 10 A.M.–5:30 P.M.) stocks a limited selection of texts in English, plus a small selection of English-language novels. **La Moderna Poesía** (Obispo #527, esq. Bernaza, tel. 07/861-6983; Mon.–Sat. 10 A.M.–8 P.M.) is Cuba's largest bookstore, although virtually the entire (albeit limited) stock is in Spanish.

La Papelería (O'Reilly #102, esq. Tacón, Habana Vieja, tel. 07/863-4263; 9 A.M.–6:30 P.M.), cater-corner to the Plaza de Armas, sells pens and other office supplies.

Cigars

The best source is the **Casa del Habano** (Industria #520, e/ Barcelona y Dragones, tel. 07/33-8060; Mon.–Fri. 9 A.M.–7 P.M., Sat. 9 A.M.–5 P.M., Sun. 10 A.M.–4 P.M.), in the Partagás factory. It has a massive walk-in humidor, plus a hidden lounge with a narrow humified walk-in cigar showcase for serious smokers.

My other favorites are the **Casa del Habano** (Mercaderes #202, esq. Lamparilla, tel. 07/862-9682; daily 10:30 A.M.–7 P.M.), in the Hostal Conde de Villanueva; and **Salón Cuba** (Neptuno, e/ Prado y Zulueta, tel. 07/66-6627;

daily 9 A.M.–9 P.M.), in the Hotel Golden Tulip Parque Central. Each has a sumptuous smoker's lounge.

Palacio del Tabaco (Agramonte #106, e/ Colón y Refugio, tel. 07/33-8389; Mon.–Fri. 9 A.M.–6 P.M.), in the former Fábrica La Corona, offers rare cigars and has a small bar. The **Casa del Habano** (Mercaderes #120, esq. Obrapía, tel. 07/861-5795; daily 9 A.M.–5 P.M.) has a selection fairly limited in range but high in quality. And the **Casa del Ron y Tabaco** (Obispo, e/ Monserrate y Bernaza, tel. 07/866-0911; daily 10 A.M.–6 P.M.), above El Floridita, has knowledgeable staff and prices are among the best in town.

Rum and Liquors

Three excellent rum stores offer tasting before you buy: **Casa del Ron** (Obispo, e/ Monserrate y Bernaza, tel. 07/33-8911; daily 10 A.M.– 8 P.M.), above El Floridita; **Taberna del Galeón** (Baratillo, esq. Obispo, tel. 07/33-8476; Mon.–Fri. 9 A.M.–7 P.M.), off the southeast corner of Plaza de Armas (try the house special, *puñetazo,* a blend of rum, coffee, and mint); and the **Fundación Havana Club** (Av. del Puerto #262, e/ Churruca y Sol, tel. 07/861-8051; daily 9 A.M.–9 P.M.), adjoining the Museo de Ron.

Music and Musical Instruments

Longina Música (Obispo #360, tel. 07/862-8371; Mon.–Sat. 10 A.M.–7 P.M., Sun. 10 A.M.–1 P.M.) sells drums, plus guitars, and even trombones (from China), and has a large CD collection.

The **Museo de la Música** (Capdevila #1, tel. 07/861-9846; Mon.–Sat. 10 A.M.–5:45 P.M.) also has a wide selection of CDs.

Perfumes and Toiletries

Havana 1791 (Mercaderes #156, esq. Obrapía, tel. 07/861-3525; daily 10 A.M.– 6 P.M.) sells locally made scents (CUC6–18) in exquisite engraved bottles with not entirely trustworthy cork tops, in an embossed linen bag. The twelve fragrances—*aromas coloniales*—include Tabaco, which smells surprisingly unlike cigars. It also sells brand-name French perfumes at duty-free prices. Yanelda, the official "Alchemist of Old Havana," will make up a fragrance to order.

In a similar vein is **La Casa Cubana del Perfume** (Brasil #13, tel. 07/866-3759; Mon.–Sat. 10 A.M.–6 A.M.), on the south side of Plaza Vieja.

Farmacia Taquechel (Obispo #155, e/ Mercaderes y San Ignacio, tel. 07/862-9286; daily 9 A.M.–6 P.M.) sells face creams, lotions, and other natural products made in Cuba.

Perfumería Prado (Prado, e/ Refugio y Colón, Habana Vieja; 10 A.M.–6 P.M.) has a large selection of imported perfumes, as do boutique stores in most of the city's upscale hotels.

Clothing and Shoes

Men seeking a sexy *guayabera* should head to **El Quitrín** (Obispo #163, e/ San Ignacio y Mercaderes, tel. 07/862-0810; daily 9 A.M.–5 P.M.). For ladies, El Quitrín also sells embroideries and lace, plus chic blouses, skirts, and so on. Most items are Cuban-made, but far above average quality. Items can be made to order.

Nearby, **Sombreros Jipi Japa** (Obispo, esq. Compostela) is the place to go for hats of every shade, and **La Habana** (Obispo, e/ Habana y Compostela, tel. 07/861-5292; and Obispo, esq. Aguacate) offers a reasonable stock of shoes and leather goods.

For hip Italian items head to **Paul & Shark** (Muralla #105, e/ San Ignacio y Mercaderes, tel. 07/866-4326, www.paulshark.it), on Plaza Vieja. This upscale boutique sells quality silk blouses, skirts, and other designer wear, including jackets and pants for men. The only other quality clothes store is Italy's **United Colors of Benetton** (Oficios, esq. Amargura, tel. 07/862-2480; Mon.–Sat. 10 A.M.–6:30 P.M., Sun. 10 A.M.– 1 P.M.); and in **Harris Brothers** (Monserrate #305, e/ O'Reilly y Progreso, Habana Vieja, tel. 07/861-1644; daily 9 A.M.–6 P.M.).

Department Stores and Shopping Centers

Harris Brothers (Monserrate #305, e/ O'Reilly y Progreso, Habana Vieja, tel. 07/861-1644; daily 9 A.M.–6 P.M.) is a Havana institution with four stories of separate stores that sell everything from fashions and children's items to toiletries.

Flowers

Jardín Wagner (Mercaderes #113, e/ Obispo y Obrapía, Habana Vieja, tel. 07/66-9017; 9 A.M.– 5 P.M.) sells domestically grown and imported flowers, but they're ridiculously expensive (it also handles Interflora delivery).

Miscellany

You can buy handmade Spanish fans (*abanicos*) for CUC2–150 at the **Casa del Abanicos** (Obrapía #107, e/ Mercaderes y Oficios, tel. 07/863-4453; Mon.–Sat. 10 A.M.–5 P.M.).

The **Tienda El Soldadito de Plano** (Muralla #164; Mon.–Fri. 9 A.M.–5 P.M., Sat. 9 A.M.–1:30 P.M.) sells miniature metal soldiers, including a 22-piece Wars of Independence collection, for CUC5.45 apiece.

The **Tienda Muñecos de Leyendas** (Mercaderes, e/ O'Reilly y Empedrado; Tues.–Sat. 10 A.M.–5:30 P.M., Sun. 10 A.M.–1 P.M.) sells dolls of *duendes* (goblins).

CENTRO HABANA
Rum and Liquors

Fábrica de Ron Bocoy (Máximo Gómez #1417, e/ Patria y Auditor, Cerro, tel. 07/877-5781; Mon.–Sat. 9 A.M.–5 P.M., Sun. 9 A.M.– 3 P.M.) has a well-stocked store, plus a bar for tasting the goods as a prelude to buying.

Music and Musical Instruments

You can buy instruments at their source at **Industria de Instrumentos Musicales Fernando Ortíz** (Pedroso #12, esq. Nueva, Cerro, tel. 07/879-3161), where guitars, drums, claves, etc. are made.

Department Stores and Shopping Centers

The **Plaza Carlos III** (Av. Salvador Allende, e/ Árbol Seco y Retiro, Centro Habana, tel. 07/873-6370; Mon.–Sat. 10 A.M.–6 P.M.) is intended for Cubans, not tourists. Its many stores range from electronics and clothing to a take on the original Woolworth's dime store (with separate stores where everything costs CUC1, CUC5, or CUC10, respectively).

And the former Woolworth's, today called **Variedades Galiano** (Av. de Italia, esq. San Rafael, tel. 07/862-7717), still has its original lunch counter. This section of San Rafael is a pedestrian-only shopping zone, known colloquially as "El Bulevar," where many department stores were located in prerevolutionary days. Nearby, **La Época** (Av. de Italia, esq. Neptuno, Centro Habana, tel. 07/66-9414; Mon.–Sat. 9:30 A.M.–7 P.M., Sun. 9:30 A.M.– 2 P.M.), also dating back to the 1950s, is a good place for clothing, including kiddie items and designer fashions.

Flowers

One of the most charming aspects of life in Havana are the flower-sellers selling floral arrangements on the street and at major markets, notably **Cuatro Caminos** (Máximo Gómez y Cristina, esq. Manglar Arroyo y Matadero, tel. 07/870-5934; Tues.–Sat. 7 A.M.–6:30 P.M., Sun. 7 A.M.–2 P.M.).

VEDADO AND PLAZA DE LA REVOLUCIÓN

Arts and Crafts

Vedado has two artisans' markets: on La Rampa, e/ M y N (8 A.M.–6 P.M.) and the **Feria del Malecón** (Malecón, e/ D y E; Tues.–Sun. 8:30 A.M.–6 P.M.).

The **Casa de las Américas** (Av. de los Presidentes, esq. 3ra, tel. 07/55-2707, fax 07/33-4554, www.casa.cult.cu; Mon.–Fri. 8 A.M.–4:45 P.M.) hosts exhibitions with works for sale. The small gallery in the lobby of the **Hotel Nacional** and the Hotel Meliá Cohiba's **Galería Cohiba** also exhibit and sell paintings by the Cuban masters.

Books and Stationery

Librería Fernando Ortíz (Calle L, esq. 27, tel. 07/832-9653; Mon.–Sat. 10 A.M.– 5:30 P.M.) is your best bet for English-language books. Its collection is meager but spans a wide range of subjects.

Librería Centenario del Apóstol (Calle 25 #164, e/ Infanta y O, tel. 07/870-7220; daily 9 A.M.–9 P.M.) has a broad selection of used texts.

Cigars

The **Casas del Habano** in the Hotel Nacional, the Hotel Meliá Cohiba, and the Hotel Riviera are well-stocked.

Clothing and Shoes

Galerías Amazonas (Calle 12, e/ 23 y 25, tel. 07/66-2438; Mon.–Sat. 10 A.M.–7 P.M., Sun. 10 A.M.–2 P.M.) is a mall with several shops devoted to fashion. The best store for designer jeans (Calvin Klein, Levi's, etc.) and men's fashions is **Tienda Brava,** which also sells leather goods. For quality imported shoes, try the gallery's **Peletería Claudia.**

Adidas and **Nike** have their own well-stocked branches selling sportswear in the **Galería Habana Libre** (Calle 25, e/ L y M).

You can buy quality homemade sandals at street markets, such as that on Calle 23, e/ M y N.

Department Stores and Shopping Centers

Galerías de Paseo (1ra Calle, e/ Paseo y A, tel. 07/55-3475; Mon.–Sat. 9 A.M.–6 P.M., Sun. 9 A.M.–1 P.M.), at the foot of Paseo, has more than two dozen stores of varying kinds.

Flowers

You'll drop big bucks buying flowers at **Floralia** (1ra Calle, e/ Paseo y A, Vedado, tel. 07/55-3266; Mon.–Sat. 10 A.M.–6 P.M., Sun. 9 A.M.–1 P.M.), in the Galerías Paseo; and **Tropiflora** (Calle 12 #156, e/ Calzada y Línea, Vedado, tel. 07/66-2332; Mon.– Sat. 8 A.M.–8 P.M.), known for its floral arrangements.

Posters and Movie-Related Items

The **Centro Cultural Cinematográfico** (Calle 23 #1155, e/ 10 y 12, tel. 07/833-6430; Mon.– Sat. 9 A.M.–5 P.M.) sells posters and videos of Cuban films; it's on the fourth floor of the Cuban Film Institute (ICAIC).

PLAYA (MIRAMAR AND BEYOND)

Jewelry

Most upscale hotels have quality jewelry stores, as do **La Maison** (Calle 16 #701, esq. 7ma, Miramar, tel. 07/204-1543) and **Le Select** (5ta Av., esq. 30, Miramar, tel. 07/204-7410), plus the Club Habana's **Joyería Bella Cantando** (5ta Av. y 188, tel. 07/204-5700), and **Joyería La Habanera** (Calle 12 #505, e/ 5ta y 7ma, tel. 07/204-2546; Mon.–Sat. 10 A.M.–6 P.M.).

Cigars

Miramar has some of the best cigar stores in town. The **Casa del Habano** (5ta Av., esq. 16, tel. 07/204-7975; Mon.–Sat. 10 A.M.–6 P.M.) boasts a vast humidor, executive rooms, bar and lounge, and good service.

Club Habana's **Casa del Habano** (5ta Av. e/ 188 y 192, tel. 07/204-5700; daily 9 A.M.– 5 P.M.) is run by Enrique Mons, whom *Cigar Aficionado* magazine has termed "the maestro of cigar merchants in Havana," and who for most of the 1970s and '80s was in charge of quality control for the Cuban cigar industry.

Other sources include **Tabaco El Aljibe** (7ma Av., e/ 24 y 26, tel. 07/204-1012); **Tabaco La Giraldilla** (Calle 222 y Av. 37, La Coronela, tel. 07/33-1155); and the tobacco stores in the Hotel Comodoro, Hotel Meliá Habana, and Hotel Occidental Miramar.

Music and Musical Instruments

For the widest CD selection in town, head to the **Casa de la Música Egrem** (Calle 10 #309, tel. 07/202-6900), the sales room of EGREM, the state recording agency. The **Casa de la Música** (Calle 20 #3309, e/ 33 y 35, tel. 07/204-0447; daily 10 A.M.–12:30 P.M.) also has a large selection.

Clothing and Shoes

The **Complejo Comercial Comodoro** (3ra Av., esq. 84, tel. 07/204-5551), adjoining the Hotel Comodoro, has outlets for United Colors of Benetton, Givenchy, Versace, and Yves Saint-Laurent.

La Maison (Calle 16 #701, esq. 7ma, tel. 07/204-1543; Mon.–Sat. 10 A.M.–6:45 P.M.) has boutiques selling upscale imported clothing, shoes, and duty-free items. Likewise, **Le Select** (5ta Av., esq. 30, tel. 07/204-7410; Mon.–Sat. 10 A.M.–8 P.M., Sun. 10 A.M.– 2 P.M.), with its ritzy chandeliers and marble statues, is as close as you'll come to Bond Street or Rodeo Drive. This little Harrods in the tropics even has a ground-floor delicatessen, plus an array of boutiques selling high-fashion, cosmetics, and the like.

Exclusividades Verano (Calle 18 #4106, e/ 41 y 43, tel. 07/203-7040; Mon.–Sat. 10 A.M.–6 P.M., Sun. 9 A.M.–1 P.M.) sells Cuban-designed clothes, including beautiful one-of-a-kind Verano dresses and straw hats; upstairs sells men's fashion, including shoes.

Adidas (3ra Av., e/ 70 y 82; Mon.–Sat. 9:30 A.M.–7 P.M., Sun. 9:30 A.M.–1:30 P.M.), in the Miramar Trade Center, sells sportswear.

Department Stores and Shopping Centers

La Puntilla Centro Comercial (1ra Av., esq. 0, tel. 07/204-7309), is one of the ritziest of plazas, with four floors and stores covering electronics, furniture, clothing, and more; similarly there's **Quinta y 42** (5ta Av. y 42, Miramar, tel. 07/204-7070; Mon.–Sat. 10 A.M.–6 P.M., Sun. 9 A.M.–1 P.M.) and **Complejo Comercial Comodoro** (3ra Av., esq. 84, Miramar, tel. 07/204-5551).

The largest supermarket is **Supermercado 70** (3ra Av., e/ 62 y 70), with all manner of imported foodstuffs.

Sports and Recreation

Havana has many *centros deportivos* (sports centers). The largest are the **Complejo Panamericano** (Vía Monumental Km 1.5, Ciudad Panamericano, Habana del Este, tel. 07/95-4140), with an Olympic athletic stadium, tennis courts, swimming pool, and even a velodrome for cycling; and **Ciudad Deportiva** (Vía Blanca, esq. Av. Rancho Boyeros, tel. 07/54-5022), or Sports City, colloquially called "El Coliseo," in Nuevo Vedado.

See the *Greater Havana and Havana Province* chapter for information on Complejo Panamericano. Also see the *Outdoor Recreation* section as well as *By Organized Tour,* in the *Getting There* section, of the *Essentials* chapter.

PARTICIPATORY ACTIVITIES

Bowling
You can practice your 10-pin bowling in the **Hotel Kohly** (Av. 49, esq. 36A, Rpto. Kohly, Vedado, tel. 07/204-0240; CUC2 per game); or at **La Bolera**, at the Club de Golf Habana (see the *Greater Havana and Havana Province* chapter), with a fully mechanized two-lane bowling alley and full-size pool tables.

Golf
The **Club Habana** (5ta Av., e/ 188 y 192, Rpto. Flores, tel. 07/204-5700, fax 07/204-5705; 7 A.M.–1 A.M.; entrance CUC10 Mon.–Fri., CUC15 Sat.–Sun.) has a practice range. Nonmembers are welcome.

See the *Greater Havana and Havana Province* chapter for information on the Club de Golf Habana.

Gyms and Spas
Upscale hotels have tiny gyms and/or spas, though most are a letdown by international standards. Recommended gyms include the **Gimnasio Sansón** in the Hotel Raquel (CUC5 for use of gym, CUC5 for the sauna; or CUC20 per month); the Hotel NH Parque Central; the Hotel Nacional (which charges nonguests CUC15); the Hotel Meliá Cohiba;

and the Hotel Meliá Habana (see the *Accommodations* listings for contact information).

One of the best facilities is at **Club Habana** (see *Golf*).

Running
The Malecón is a good place to jog, although you need to beware the uneven surface and massive potholes. For wide open spaces, head to Parque Lenin, where the road circuit provides a perfect running track. Runners in search of a track might head to the **Estadio José Martí** (Calle I, e/ 5ta y Malecón, Vedado), **Estadio Juan Abrahantes** (Zapata), south of the university; or **Ciudad Deportiva** (Vía Blanca, esq. Av. Rancho Boyeros, Nuevo Vedado, tel. 07/54-5022).

Annual **road races** include the 5K International Terry Fox Race (February), the 98K Ultra Marabana (April), the 5K Día de la Madre (Mother's Day Race; May), the 10K Clásico Internacional Hemingway (May), and the Habana Marabana (Havana Marathon; November; CUC40 entry fee). Contact the **Comisión Marabana** at the Ciudad Deportiva for information.

Sailing
Yachts and motor vessels can be rented at **Fantasea Boat Charters** (Marina Hemingway, 5ta Av., esq. 248, Santa Fe, tel. 07/204-1150, comercial@comermh.cha.cyt.cu) and **Club Habana** (see *Golf*).

Also see *Tarará* in the *Playas del Este* section of the *Greater Havana and Havana Province* chapter.

Scuba Diving
There's excellent diving offshore of Havana. The Gulf Stream and Atlantic Ocean currents meet west of the city, where many ships have been sunk through the centuries. The so-called "Blue Circuit," a series of dive sites, extends east from Bacuranao, about 10 kilometers east of Havana, to the

Playas del Este, where there's a **decompression chamber** at Hospital Luis Díaz Soto (Vía Monumental y Carretera, Habana del Este, tel. 07/95-4251).

Centro de Buceo La Aguja (Marina Hemingway, 5ta Av. y 248, Santa Fe, tel. 07/204-5088 or 07/271-5277, fax 07/204-6848 or 07/204-1149) rents equipment and charges CUC30 for one dive, CUC50 for two dives, CUC60 for a "resort course," and CUC360 for an open-water certification.

The **Club Habana** (see *Golf*) also has scuba facilities, as does **Centro de Buceo Cocosub** (Carretera Panamericana Km 23.5, Caimito, tel./fax 07/880-5089), at the Hotel Cocomar, 23 kilometers west of Havana.

Also see **Tarará** in the *Playas del Este* section of the *Greater Havana and Havana Province* chapter.

Sportfishing
Marlin, S.A. (Canal B, Marina Hemingway, tel. 07/204-1150, ext. 735) charges from CUC275 for four hours and from CUC375 for eight hours, including skipper and tackle.

Also see the *Outdoor Recreation* section of the *Essentials* chapter.

Swimming
Most large tourist hotels have pools that permit use by nonguests. Many are popular with Cuban families in summer and can be noisy and crowded on weekends.

In Habana Vieja, head to the small rooftop pool of the Hotel NH Parque Central, or to **Piscina Hotel Sevilla** (Prado, esq. Ánimas; 10 A.M.–6 P.M.; entrance CUC8, deductible from the price of drinks and food; free to guests of the hotel).

In Vedado, the **Hotel Nacional** (CUC18 *consumo mínimo* for nonguests) and **Hotel Tryp Habana Libre** (CUC15 *consumo mínimo*) have excellent pools. The Hotel Victoria charges CUC3 to use its small pool.

In Miramar, the Occidental Miramar and Hotel Meliá Habana have excellent pools, and **Club Habana** (see *Golf*) has a large swimming pool, plus a splendid beach that shelves gently

into calm waters. The **Complejo Turístico La Giraldilla** (Calle 222, e/ 37 y 51, tel. 07/33-0568; Tues.–Sun. 10 A.M.–6 P.M.; CUC5 *consumo mínimo*), in La Coronela, has a splendid swimming pool.

The pool at Papa's in **Marina Hemingway** (5ta Av., esq. 248, Santa Fe, tel. 07/204-1150) is very popular with Cubans, as are those at the Hotel Copacabana and Hotel Comodoro and **Club Almendares** (Av. 49C, esq. 28A, Rpto. Kohly, tel. 07/204-4990; daily 11 A.M.–7 P.M.; CUC3 adults, CUC1 children).

SPECTATOR SPORTS
Baseball
Havana has two teams: the Industriales (colloquially called "Los Azules," or "The Blues"), considered the best team in the National League; and the Metropolitanos (known as "Los Metros"). Both teams play at the 60,000-seat **Estadio Latinoamericano** (Consejero Aranjo y Pedro Pérez, Cerro, tel. 07/870-6526), the main baseball stadium. Games are played October–May, Tuesday–Thursday at 7:30 P.M., Saturday at 1:30 and 7:30 P.M., and Sunday at 1:30 P.M. (three pesos). Tickets are sold on a first come first served basis, although a few seats are reserved for foreigners.

Games are also played at the **Estadio Juan Abrahantes** (also called Estadio Universitario, Calzada de Zapata, Vedado).

For further information, contact the **Federación Cubana de Béisbol** (tel. 07/879-7980). (Also see the sidebar *Loco por Béisbol* in the *Essentials* chapter.)

Basketball
The Liga Superior de Baloncesto (National Basketball League) comprises four teams—Havana's team is the Capitalinos—and runs September–November. Games are played at the **Coliseo de Deportes** (Vía Blanca, esq. Av. Rancho Boyeros, Nuevo Vedado, tel. 07/40-5933; Mon.–Fri. 8 A.M.–5 P.M.), at Ciudad Deportiva; and at the **Sala Polivalente Ramón Fonst** (Av. de la Independencia, esq. Bruzón, Plaza de la Revolución, tel. 07/882-0000; Mon.–Sat. 8:30 P.M., Sun. 3 P.M.).

For further information, contact the **Federación Cubana de Baloncesto** (tel. 07/57-7156).

Boxing

Championship matches are hosted at the **Coliseo de Deportes** (see *Basketball*), base for the **Federación Cubana de Boxeo** (tel. 07/57-7047).

The main boxing training center is the **Centro de Entrenmiento de Boxeo** (Carretera Torrens, Wajay, tel. 07/202-0538), in the Boyeros district (see the *Boyeros* section of the *Greater Havana and Havana Province* chapter).

You can watch boxing and martial arts at the **Gimnasio de Boxeo Rafael Trejo** (Calle Cuba #815, Habana Vieja, tel. 07/862-0266; Mon.– Fri. 8 A.M.–5 P.M.) and at **Sala Polivalente Kid Chocolate** (Prado, e/ San Martín y Brasil, Habana Vieja, tel. 07/862-8634).

OTHER SPORTS
Volleyball

Voleibol is a major sport in Cuba; the national women's team—Las Morenas del Caribe (the Caribbean Brown Sugars)—is the best in the world, and took gold at the 2000 Olympics for the fourth time. Volleyball games are hosted at the **Sala Polivalente Kid Chocolate** (see *Boxing*) and **Sala Polivalente Ramón Fonst** (Av. de la Independencia, esq. Bruzón, Plaza de la Revolución, tel. 07/882-0000). Major tournament games are held at the **Coliseo de Deportes** (see *Basketball*), which hosts the Liga Mundial de Voleibol (World Volleyball League) each spring. For further information, contact the **Federación Cubana de Voleibol** (tel. 07/41-3557).

Roller Skating

The **Complejo de Pelota Vasca y Patinodromo,** at Ciudad Deportiva (Vía Blanca, esq. Av. Rancho Boyeros, tel. 07/54-5022), has a roller skating track.

Soccer

Fútbol has a seasonal following and is adopted as the sport of choice by Cubans when baseball season ends. Cuba's soccer league is not well developed, although there *is* a national league. Havana's team is Ciudad Havana (nicknamed "Los Rojos"—"The Reds"). Games are played at the **Estadio Pedro Marrero** (Av. 41 #4409, e/ 44 y 50, Rpto. Kohly, tel. 07/203-4698).

Squash and Tennis

The national *equipo* (team) trains at **Complejo Panamericano** (Vía Monumental Km 4, Ciudad Panamericano, tel. 07/97-4140), where six tennis courts (*canchas de tenis*) can be rented (see *Ciudad Panamericano* in the *Greater Havana and Havana Province* chapter). **Club Habana** (see *Golf*) has squash and tennis courts for rent, as do the **Hotel Copacabana** (squash and tennis); **Hotel Meliá Habana** (tennis); **Hotel Nacional** (tennis); and **Hotel Occidental Miramar** (squash and tennis).

For information, contact the **Federación Cubana de Ténis** (tel. 07/97-2121).

Accommodations

Havana is blessed with accommodations of every stripe. Although budget options are fairly priced, most Havana hotels cost two or three times what they are worth. Some are outrageously overpriced! Even the most up-scale hotels suffer from indifferent staffing, unresponsive management, and lousy food. Scams by staff are endemic. And many of the priciest hotels scream for total refurbishment. For these reasons we strongly recommend *casas particulares,* found throughout the city, with the broadest selection in Vedado.

Which District?

Location is important in choosing your hotel.

Habana Vieja puts you in the heart of the old city, within walking distance of Havana's main touristic sights. Many colonial-era mansions administered by Habaguanex have recently opened after splendid makeovers. Especially noteworthy are exquisite colonial palaces-turned-hotels.

Centro Habana, although offering few sites of interest, has three budget-oriented hotels that lie close to the Prado and Habana Vieja; Cuba's state tour agencies push the Hotel Deauville, used by many budget package-tour companies, but this gloomy cement tower is terrible and everyone who stays here has a complaint. This predominantly run-down residential district also has a large number of reasonably priced *casas particulares,* but safety on the ill-lit, rubble-strewn streets is a concern.

Vedado and Plaza de la Revolución offer mid-20th-century accommodations well situated for sightseeing and including several first-class, albeit overpriced, modernist hotels with modest decor. Vedado also has some of the best *casas particulares.*

Playa (Miramar and Beyond) has a number of moderate hotels popular with tour groups, as well as modern deluxe hotels aimed at business travelers. All are far away from the main tourist sights and you'll need wheels to get around. Otherwise be prepared to spend your money on taxi rides to and fro. One hotel to avoid is the Hotel Neptuno/Triton, dreary siblings that face consistent plumbing and other infrastructural problems.

HABANA VIEJA
Casas Particulares

Casa de Daniel Carrasco Guillén (Cristo #16, 2ndo piso, e/ Brasil y Muralla, tel. 07/866-2106, carrascohousing@yahoo.com; CUC25) is recommended. The owner and his friendly family rent two lofty-ceilinged rooms with modest furnishings. Take a pick from rooms in the colonial home or more modern rooms atop the roof. (They have several rooms from which to choose, but legally they can only offer two for rent.) The rooftop rooms can get hot during midday, but are cross-ventilated. All rooms have air-conditioning and hot water and are clean, but only one has a private bathroom.

Casa de Eugenio Barral García (San Ignacio #656, e/ Jesús María y Merced, tel. 07/862-9877; CUC30), in southern Habana Vieja, is one of the best private room rentals with three air-conditioned bedrooms with fans and refrigerator in an old home graciously and eclectically appointed with antiques and precious ornaments. Rooms share two modern hot-water bathrooms. **Casa de Paula y Norma** (San Ignacio #654, e/ Merced y Jesús María, tel. 07/863-1279; CUC25–30), next door, is an identical home but much more simply furnished.

For historic ambience, I like **Casa de Luis Batista** (Amargura #255, e/ Habana y Compostela, tel. 07/863-0622; CUC30). Beyond its nail-studded door, this 1717 colonial gem has *vitrales* and a stunning *alfarje* ceiling. Four rooms open to a long narrow patio where you can relax on rockers, shaded by an arbor of vines. Three rooms are air-conditioned; two have private bathrooms with hot water; all have fans.

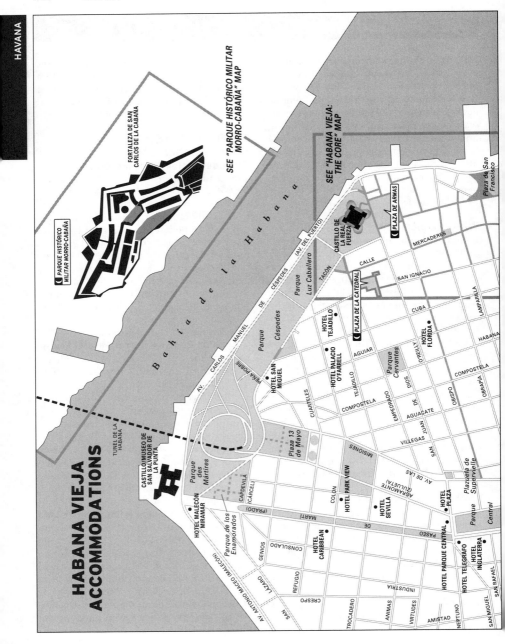

HABANA VIEJA ACCOMMODATIONS

PARQUE HISTÓRICO MILITAR MORRO-CABAÑA

FORTALEZA DE SAN CARLOS DE LA CABAÑA

SEE "PARQUE HISTÓRICO MILITAR MORRO-CABAÑA" MAP

SEE "HABANA VIEJA: THE CORE" MAP

Bahía de la Habana

TUNEL DE LA HABANA

CASTILLO/MUSEO DE SAN SALVADOR DE LA PUNTA

Parque de los Mártires

Parque de los Enamorados

HOTEL MALECON MIRAMAR

Plaza 13 de Mayo

CAPDEVILA

CÁRCEL

MARTI

CASTILLO DE LA REAL FUERZA

PLAZA DE ARMAS

Plaza de San Francisco

MERCADERES

CALLE

SAN IGNACIO

PLAZA DE LA CATEDRAL

HOTEL TEJADILLO

CUBA

LAMPARILLA

HOTEL PALACIO O'FARRELL

AGUIAR

Parque Cervantes

HOTEL FLORIDA

O'REILLY

HABANA

HOTEL SAN MIGUEL

TEJADILLO

DE DIOS

OBISPO

COMPOSTELA

CUARTELES

COMPOSTELA

EMPEDRADO

OBRAPIA

AGUACATE

AGRAMONTE (ZULUETA)

VILLEGAS

SAN JUAN

MISIONES

AV. DE LAS

Plazuela de Supervielle

HOTEL PARK VIEW

COLÓN

HOTEL SEVILLA

HOTEL PLAZA

Parque Central

HOTEL CARIBBEAN

CONSULADO

DE

PASEO

HOTEL PARQUE CENTRAL

GENIOS

REFUGIO

INDUSTRIA

HOTEL TELEGRAFO

HOTEL INGLATERRA

SAN RAFAEL

SAN LAZARO

AV. ANTONIO MACEO (MALECON)

CRESPO

TROCADERO

ANIMAS

VIRTUDES

AMISTAD

NEPTUNO

SAN MIGUEL

Parque Céspedes

Parque Luz Caballero

CÉSPEDES

MANUEL DE CÉSPEDES

PEÑA POBRE

AV. CARLOS MANUEL

TACÓN

AV. DEL PUERTO

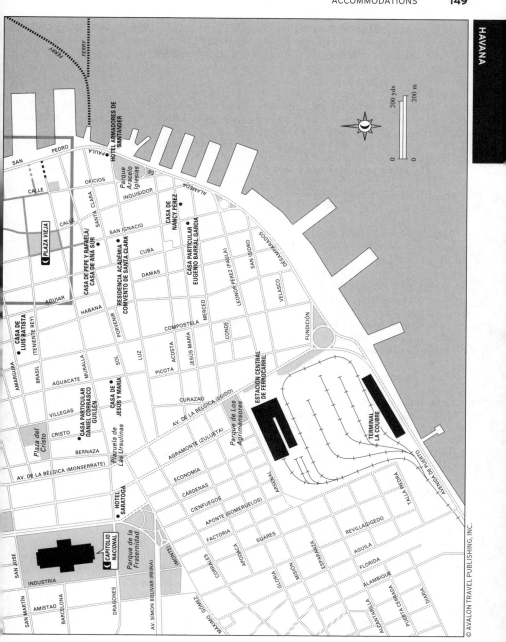

200 yds
200 m

FERRY

FERRY

SAN   PEDRO

CALLE

PLAZA VIEJA

CALLE

OFICIOS

SANTA CLARA

INQUISIDOR

DE PAULA

HOTEL ARMADORES DE SANTANDER

Parque Aracelo Iglesias

SAN IGNACIO

CASA DE PEPE Y RAFAELA/ CASA DE ANA SUR

RESIDENCIA ACADEMIA CONVENTO DE SANTA CLARA

CASA DE NANCY PÉREZ

CUBA

DAMAS

CASA PARTICULAR EUGENIO BARRAL GARCÍA

ALAMEDA

DESAMPARADOS

SAN ISIDRO

LEONOR PÉREZ (PAULA)

VELASCO

AGUIAR

HABANA

PORVENIR

MERCED

CONDE

FUNDICIÓN

CASA DE LUIS BATISTA

(TENIENTE REY)

COMPOSTELA

AMARGURA

BRASIL

AGUACATE

MURALLA

SOL

LUZ

ACOSTA

JESÚS MARÍA

PICOTA

ESTACIÓN CENTRAL DE FERROCARRIL

VILLEGAS

CASA PARTICULAR DANIEL CORRASCO GUILLÉN

CRISTO

CASA DE JESÚS Y MARÍA

Plazuela de Las Ursulinas

BERNAZA

CURAZAO

AV. DE LA BÉLGICA (EGIDO)

Parque de Los Agrimensores

TERMINAL LA COUBRE

Plaza del Cristo

AV. DE LA BÉLGICA (MONSERRATE)

HOTEL SARATOGA

AGRAMONTE (ZULUETA)

ECONOMÍA

CÁRDENAS

CIENFUEGOS

APONTE (SOMERUELOS)

ARSENAL

TALLA PIEDRA

AVENIDA DE PUERTO

SAN JOSÉ

CAPITOLIO NACIONAL

Parque de la Fraternidad

FACTORIA

APODACA

SUÁREZ

REVILLAGIGEDO

AGUILA

SAN MARTÍN

AMISTAD

BARCELONA

INDUSTRIA

DRAGONES

AV. SIMON BOLÍVAR (REINA)

MONTE

CORRALES

GLORIA

MISIÓN

ESPERANZA

FLORIDA

ALAMBIQUE

MÁXIMO GÓMEZ

ALCANTARILLA

PUERTA CERRADA

DIARIA

© AVALON TRAVEL PUBLISHING, INC.

I also recommend **Casa Chez Nous** (Brasil #115, e/ Cuba y San Ignacio, tel. 07/862-6287, cheznous@ceiai.inf.cu; CUC30), one block from Plaza Vieja. This delightful upstairs colonial home has two large air-conditioned rooms with *vitral* windows, fridges, simple antique furnishings, and balconies. They share a spacious bathroom with hot water. There's an airy TV lounge, plus a shaded patio with songbirds. A tight spiral staircase leads to a rooftop terrace with lounge chairs. Adjoining, in the same building, **Casa de Marta e Israel** (tel. 07/862-0948, martha@secomar.telemar.cu; CUC30) is similar, though rooms are smaller, darker, and more simply furnished but have private bathrooms.

Casa de Pepe y Rafaela (San Ignacio #454, e/ Sol y Santa Clara, tel. 07/867-5551; CUC30), on the second floor of a colonial home, has a spacious lounge full of antiques and songbirds. The owners rent two air-conditioned rooms with tall ceilings, fridges, fans, antique beds and furniture, glass chandeliers, and heaps of light pouring in from the balcony windows. Modern bathrooms have large showers. One flight up, **Casa de Ana Sur** (tel. 07/862-2717, sura@web.correosdecuba.cu) is an identical unit with more modern, albeit simpler, furnishings.

Casa Jesús y María (Aguacate #518, e/ Sol y Muralla, tel. 07/861-1378, jesusmaria2003@yahoo.com; CUC25) is a clean home with large TV and stereo in the lounge. It has two spacious and impeccably clean, albeit simply furnished, air-conditioned rooms off a hallway with atrium patio—a nice place for meals. They have ceiling fans and small modern bathrooms.

Casa de Nancy Pérez (Jesús María #23, Apt. F, e/ San Ignacio y Inquisidor, tel. 07/860-1898; CUC20) is a third-floor home with two high-ceilinged, simply furnished air-conditioned rooms off an airy TV lounge with marble columns and rockers. Each has a modern shared bathroom with hot water.

Hotels Under CUC50

Residencia Académica Convento de Santa Clara (Cuba #610, e/ Luz y Sol, tel. 07/861-3335, fax 07/866-5696, reaca@cencrem.cult.cu; CUC25 per person, CUC35 suite, including breakfast), in a former 17th-century convent, is a bargain. It has nine charming, modestly furnished but well-kept dorm rooms plus some private rooms. However, the rooms lack air-conditioning and can be stifling, especially in midsummer. A café serves refreshments. (Habaguanex.)

Hotel Caribbean (Prado #164, e/ Colón y Refugio, tel. 07/860-8241, fax 07/860-9479; CUC36 s, CUC54 d, including breakfast) serves budget travelers with 38 small air-conditioned rooms, meagerly yet adequately furnished in lively Caribbean colors, with tiny satellite TVs, telephones, safe deposit boxes, and small yet pleasant bathrooms. There's a small, simple bar, and the Café del Prado. (Cubanacán.)

Hotels CUC50-100

Hostal Valencia (Oficios #53, e/ Obrapía y Lamparilla, tel. 07/857-1037, fax 07/860-5628, www.habaguanex.cu; CUC62 s, CUC80 d low season; CUC100 s, CUC142 d high season) might induce a flashback to the romantic *posadas* of Spain. The 18th-century mansion-turned-hotel originated as the home of Governor Count Sotolongo. It exudes charm, with its lobby of hefty oak beams, Spanish tiles, and wrought-iron chandeliers. The 12 spacious rooms have cool marble floors, are simply furnished, and have satellite TVs, telephones, refrigerators, and safes, plus private bathrooms (hot water is said to be unreliable). It offers the atmospheric La Paella restaurant and charming Bar Entresuelo. (Habaguanex.)

Hotel El Comendador (Obrapía #55 e/ Baratillo y Oficios; tel. 07/857-1037, fax 07/860-5628, www.habaguanex.cu; CUC62 s, CUC80 d low season; CUC100 s, CUC142 d high season), behind the Hostal Valencia, is another endearingly restored colonial home. Its 14 exquisite rooms feature marble floors, iron-frame beds, antique reproduction furnishings, safe deposit boxes, local TVs, old-style phones, and mini-fridges. Modern bathrooms have claw-foot bathtubs, hairdryers, and toiletries. Rooms on the mezzanine are cramped; take an upper-story room with lofty ceilings. (Habaguanex).

El Mesón de la Flota (Mercaderes #257, e/ Amargura y Brasil, tel. 07/863-3838, habaguanexhmflota@ip.etecsa.cu; CUC53 s, CUC86 d low season; CUC64 s, CUC105 d high season) is a classic Spanish *bodega* bar-restaurant with five intimate rooms, all with private bathrooms and hot water. Each features antique reproductions, and one has a magnificent *vitral*. It's overpriced, despite its charm. (Habaguanex.)

Hotel Park View (Colón, esq. Morro, tel. 07/861-3293, fax 07/863-6036, www.hotelparkview.cu; CUC45 s, CUC80 d low season; CUC50 s, CUC90 d high season, including breakfast), in a sober green-and-ocher color scheme, has 55 lofty-ceilinged rooms, nicely furnished with green marble highlights. Some bathrooms have stand-up showers; others have tubs. Third-floor rooms have balconies. It has minimal facilities, but the Hotel Sevilla is around the corner. It's overpriced. (Habaguanex.)

Work on the **Hotel Convento de Santa Brigida** (on Baratillo, between Plaza de Armas and Plaza de San Francisco), another converted colonial mansion, was being completed at last visit. It promises to be a stylish and exquisite addition.

Hotels CUC100-150

Hotel Plaza (Zulueta #267, esq. Neptuno, tel. 07/860-8583, fax 07/860-8869, reserva@plaza.gca.cma.net; CUC84 s, CUC120 d standard, CUC115 s, CUC145 d suites, year-round), built in 1909, occupies the northeast corner of Parque Central. The lobby is supported by Corinthian columns. A marble stairway leads upstairs to 186 lofty-ceilinged, air-conditioned rooms and suites furnished with simple antique reproductions, satellite TVs, radios, safes, and heaps of closet space. Some rooms are gloomy, and those facing the street can be noisy. Though recently refurbished, the rooms are priced beyond all reason. A pianist hits the ivories in the gracious lobby bar lit by stained-glass skylights and gilt chandeliers. It has a chic restaurant, plus a gift store, pharmacy, and solarium. (Gran Caribe.)

The vastly overpriced **Hotel Inglaterra** (Prado #416, esq. San Rafael, tel. 07/860-8594, fax 07/860-8254, reserva@gcingla.gca.tur.cu; CUC84 s, CUC120 d year-round), on the west side of Parque Central, has an extravagant lobby bar and restaurant that whisk you off to Morocco with their arabesque archways and mosaics. It has 83 air-conditioned rooms with telephones, satellite TVs, safes, hairdryers, and minibars. Noise from the square can be a problem, and many rooms are dark and musty. (Gran Caribe.)

Hotel Ambos Mundos (Obispo #153, e/ San Ignacio y Mercaderes, tel. 07/860-9530, fax 07/860-9532, www.habaguanex.cu; CUC80 s, CUC130 d low season; CUC90 s, CUC150 d high season; CUC105 s, CUC180 d junior suites low season; CUC115 s, CUC200 d junior suites high season), one block west of Plaza de Armas, lets you rest your head where Ernest Hemingway found inspiration in the 1930s. The hotel offers 49 air-conditioned rooms and three junior suites arranged atrium style, each with satellite TV and direct-dial telephone. Most rooms are small and dark, and feature undistinguished furnishings, for which room rates are double what is justified. Those facing the interior courtyard are quieter. It has a pleasant lobby bar, plus modest rooftop restaurant and solarium. Avoid the fifth floor, which is a thoroughfare for sightseeing gawkers. (Habaguanex.)

I like the **Hotel del Tejadillo** (Tejadillo, esq. San Ignacio, tel. 07/863-7283, fax 07/863-8830, www.habaguanex.com; CUC70 s, CUC110 d low season; CUC80 s, CUC135 d high season; CUC77 s, CUC130 d suites low season; CUC97 s, CUC150 d suites high season), another converted colonial mansion. Beyond the huge doors is an airy marble-clad lobby with a quaint dining area. It offers 32 air-conditioned rooms around two courtyards with fountains and plants. The cool, high-ceilinged rooms are graced by *mediopuntos* and modern furniture, and feature safes, minibars, and simple bathrooms. (Habaguanex.)

On the harborfront, **Hotel Armadores de Santander** (Luz #4, esq. San Pedro, tel. 07/862-8000, fax 07/862-8080, www.hotelsantander.cu; CUC90 s, CUC150 d low season; CUC80 s, CUC130 d high season; CUC135 s, CUC225 d junior suite low season; CUC150 s, CUC255 d junior suite high season; CUC300 s/d suite year-round) has 39 spacious rooms, including three duplexes, a junior suite, and a fabulous contemporary suite with a whirlpool tub in the center of the mezzanine bedroom with a four-poster bed. All rooms feature lush hardwoods, colonial tile floors, and handsome furnishings, including state-of-the-art bathrooms. One room is accessible for travelers with disabilities. A rooftop terrace offers views over the harbor, plus there's a 24-hour bar, billiards room, and a fine restaurant. (Habaguanex.)

Playing on a monastic theme, the **Hostal Las Frailes** (Brasil, e/ Oficios y Mercaderes, tel. 07/862-9383, fax 07/862-9718, www.hostalosfrailes.cu; CUC62 s, CUC100 d low season; CUC80 s, CUC125 d high season), another restored historic property, has staff dressed in monks' habits, plus lots of heavy timbers, stained glass, wrought-iron, murals, and earth-tone decor. It has 23 air-conditioned rooms around a patio with an *aljibe* and fountain. The rooms have patterned terra-cotta tile floors, sponge-washed walls, religious prints, plus TVs, period telephones, minibars, safes, and spacious bathrooms. It has a bar, but no restaurant. (Habaguanex.)

❰ Hotel Beltrán de Santa Cruz (San Ignacio #411, e/ Muralla y Sol, tel. 07/860-8330, fax 07/860-8363, reserva@bsantacruz.co.cu; CUC70 s, CUC110 d low season; CUC80 s, 135 d high season) is a handsome conversion of an elegant, three-story 18th-century mansion with exquisite *mediopuntos* and other architectural features (the atrium still features the original *aljibe*). It has 11 air-conditioned rooms plus junior suite exuding historic ambience courtesy of gracious antique reproductions; rooms also have direct phone lines, satellite TVs, minibars, safes, and modern bathrooms.

Another fine colonial conversion, the romantic **Hotel Palacio O'Farrill** (Cuba #102, esq. Chacón, tel. 07/860-5080, habaguanex@ofarrill.co.cu; CUC80 s, CUC130 d standard low season; CUC90 s, CUC150 d standard high season; CUC105 s, CUC180 d suite low season; CUC115 s, CUC200 d suite high season) is centered on a three-story atrium courtyard lit by a skylight. It has 38 rooms, each with satellite TV, safe, and minibar. Facilities include a cybercafé and elegant restaurant.

❰ Hotel Raquel (San Ignacio, esq. Amargura, tel. 07/860-8280, fax 07/860-8275, reservas@hotelraquel.co.cu; CUC105 s, CUC180 d low season; CUC115 s, CUC200 high season, including breakfast), dating to 1905, is a dramatic exemplar of art nouveau styling. The lobby gleams with marble columns and period detailing, including Tiffany lamps and a mahogany art nouveau bar. The theme carries into the charming air-conditioned rooms featuring tile floors, wrought-iron beds, direct-dial phones, satellite TVs, safes, minibars, and hairdryers. It has an elegant restaurant, and there's a rooftop solarium plus gym. (Habaguanex.)

Hotels CUC150-250

Entered via giant brass-studded carriage doors, **❰ Hotel Conde de Villanueva** (Mercaderes #202, esq. Lamparilla, tel. 07/862-9293, fax 07/862-9682, www.habaguanex.com; CUC95 s, CUC140 d, CUC180 suite low season; CUC110 s, CUC175 d, CUC220 high season) is an exquisite conversion of the mansion of the Conde de Villanueva. The spacious lobby-lounge, with its bottle-green sofas and blood-red cushions, terra-cotta floor, and beamed ceiling with chandeliers, opens to an intimate courtyard, with caged birds and tropical foliage. It has nine large, airy, simply appointed air-conditioned rooms and one suite (with whirlpool tub) with 1920s reproduction furnishings, TVs, safes, and minibars. There's a small restaurant and bar. The hotel aims at cigar smokers with a Casa del Habano outlet and a sumptuous smokers' lounge. (Habaguanex.)

❰ Hotel Florida (Obispo #252, esq.

Cuba, tel. 07/862-4127, fax 07/862-4117, www.habaguanex.com; CUC80 s, CUC130 d low season; CUC90 s, CUC150 d high season; CUC105 s, CUC180 d suite low season; CUC115 s, CUC200 d suite high season) is a compact colonial charmer built around an atrium courtyard with rattan lounge chairs, planters, stained-glass skylight, and black-and-white checkered marble floors, found throughout the hotel. Sumptuously furnished, its 25 rooms feature tasteful colonial decor, including marble floors and wrought-iron beds, plus phones, satellite TVs, mini-bars, and safes. The restaurant is elegant and has above-average cuisine, while the upstairs piano bar is a marvelous place for evening cocktails. (Habaguanex.)

On Parque Central, **Hotel Telégrafo** (Paseo del Prado #408, esq. Neptuno, tel. 07/861-1010, fax 07/861-4741, www.hoteltelegrafo.cu; CUC80 s, CUC130 d low season; CUC110 s, CUC175 d high season; CUC105 s, CUC180 d suite low season; CUC150 s, CUC170 d suite high season) melds its classical elements into an exciting contemporary vogue. It has 63 rooms with beautiful furnishings and trendy color schemes, including sponge-washed walls and bare stone, plus marble floors and classy bathrooms. The hip lobby bar is skylit within an atrium framed by colonial ruins. (Habaguanex.)

The **Hotel Sevilla** (Trocadero #55, e/ Prado y Zulueta, tel. 07/860-8560, fax 07/860-8582, reserva@sevilla.gca.tur.cu; CUC138 s, CUC188 d low season; CUC144 s, CUC196 d high season), built in 1924, is famous as the setting for Graham Greene's *Our Man in Havana* (Wormold stayed in room 501). The lobby is straight out of *1,001 Arabian Nights*. Its 178 rooms—recently done up in ocher and red color schemes, with antique reproductions, but still rather modest and vastly overpriced—each have a safe, minibar, telephone, and satellite TV. The sumptuous top-floor restaurant serves continental fare. There's a tour and car rental desk, swimming pool, four bars, a beauty parlor, and assorted shops. (Gran Caribe.)

Hotel Santa Isabel (Baratillo #9, e/ Obispo y Narciso López, tel. 07/860-8201, fax 07/860-8391, www.hotelsantaisabel.cu; CUC190 s, CUC240 d standard; CUC230 s, CUC340 d junior suite), a small and intimate hostelry in the former 18th-century palace of the Countess of Santovenia, enjoys a fabulous setting overlooking Plaza de Armas (some rooms face the harbor). The hotel has 27 lofty-ceilinged, air-conditioned rooms furnished with marble or stone floors, plus four-poster beds, reproduction antique furniture, satellite TVs, direct-dial telephones, Internet access, and safes, plus leather recliners on wide balconies. Suites have whirlpool tubs. There's an elegant restaurant and three bars. President Carter and his entourage stayed here in May 2002. Still, plumbing has been an issue, many rooms have mold, and readers report that staff are indifferent, which makes the rates all the more outrageous. (Habaguanex.)

Hotels CUC250 and Up

◀ **Hotel NH Parque Central** (Neptuno, e/ Prado y Zulueta, tel. 07/866-6627, fax 07/866-6630, www.nh-hotels.cu; CUC205 s, CUC270 d standard, CUC225 s, CUC325 d superior, CUC330 s/d junior suite; CUC375–420 s/d suite year-round) occupies the north side of Parque Central and fuses colonial contemporary styles. This modern, Dutch-managed hotel is one of the most sophisticated in town and is popular with businessfolk. Its 281 air-conditioned rooms are tastefully appointed with antique reproduction furnishings, king-size beds, direct-dial phones, satellite TVs, Internet modems, plus marble-clad bathrooms. Many rooms have no views; be sure to ask for an exterior room. Two choice restaurants and a rooftop grill are among the better dining options in town. Facilities include a cigar lounge-bar, meeting rooms, business center, boutiques, plus rooftop swimming pool, whirlpool tub, and fitness room. At press time, a 150-room annex was being built. (Cubanacán.)

The finest hotel in Havana by far is the ◀ **Hotel Saratoga** (Paseo del Prado #603, esq. Dragones, tel. 07/868-1000, fax 07/868-1001, reservas@saratoga.co.cu; CUC195–385

a standard room in the Hotel Saratoga

© CHRISTOPHER P. BAKER

s/d, CUC385–650 suite, year-round), which opened in late 2005. European architects and designers have turned this colonial edifice into a visual stunner inside. Imbued throughout with a hip aesthetic, the hotel effuses sophistication on a par with New York or London. Guest-room decor varies from colonial inspired to thoroughly contemporary. Most rooms have king-size four-poster beds; all have rich color schemes, gorgeous halogen-lit bathrooms, and 21st-century amenities. A rooftop pool, spa, and gym offer fabulous views over the city. And the bar and restaurant, with their exciting Moorish aesthetic, are surely the place to be. If you can afford it, go for it!

CENTRO HABANA
Casas Particulares

In a high-rise overlooking the Malecón, **Casa de Rene Pérez** (Malecón #51, e/ Tenios y Carcel, tel. 07/861-8108, rmichelpd@yahoo.com; CUC40) is an unusually lavish option with two spacious and romantic air-conditioned rooms decorated with fantastic antiques. They share a mediocre hot-water bathroom, and neither has windows. The vast lounge is sumptuously appointed and has a TV/VCR plus views along the Malecón and toward El Morro. Entry is to the rear, via the parking lot; secure parking is offered (CUC1).

I also recommend **Casa de Elsa y Julio Roque** (Consulado #162, Apto. 2, e/ Colón y Trocadero, tel. 07/861-8027, julioroq@yahoo. com; CUC20, CUC25 with fridge and TV), with a pleasant lounge with leather sofas, a small library, and works of art. Run by erudite and delightful owners, it has two rooms with air-conditioning, fans, wicker furniture, modern private hot-water bathrooms, and each with an independent entrance.

Hostal el Parador Numantino (Consulado #223, e/ Ánimas y Trocadero, tel. 07/863-8733; CUC30) is a contemporary conversion with a spacious air-conditioned lounge with gleaming ceramic floor and comfy leather sofas. The two air-conditioned bedrooms upstairs are small and feature fans, TV, and mini-fridge, plus private hot-water bathrooms. Meals are offered 24 hours.

La Casona Colonial (Gervasio #216, e/ Concordia y Virtudes, tel. 07/862-7109, www .casacolonialcn.com; CUC25) is a gracious place with two spacious and pleasantly furnished bedrooms with fans and air-conditioning, and filled with antiques, but with a shared outside bathroom. It has a nice courtyard plus security. Jorge Díaz, the owner, speaks English, French, Italian, and Russian.

Hotels Under CUC50

Hotel Lincoln (Av. de Italia #164, esq. Virtudes, tel. 07/862-8061; CUC30 s, CUC40 d low season; CUC39 s, CUC46 d high season) dates from 1926 and features graceful public arenas, including a lobby boasting chandeliers and Louis XVI–style furnishings. The 135 clean, air-conditioned rooms have radios, telephones, satellite TVs, and mini-fridges. Facilities include two eateries, a 24-hour rooftop terrace bar, and nightly entertainment. (Islazul.)

While popular with budget travelers, **Hotel Islazul Lido** (Consulado, esq. Ánimas, tel./fax 07/867-1102; CUC26 s, CUC36 d low season; CUC36 s, CUC46 d high season) awaits a thorough renovation, although some rooms had been refurbished at last visit. The 63 modest air-conditioned rooms feature utility furniture, satellite TVs, telephones, radios, and tiny balconies. Safes can be rented (the Lido has a reputation for theft), and a bar serves snacks in the dreary, overly air-conditioned lobby with Internet service. The rooftop restaurant is open 24 hours. (Islazul.)

VEDADO AND PLAZA DE LA REVOLUCIÓN
Casas Particulares
 Casa de Jorge Coalla Potts (Calle I #456, Apto. 11, e/ 21 y 23, Vedado, tel. 07/832-9032 or cell 5283-1237, www.havanaroomrental .com, jorgepotts@correodecuba.cu; CUC30)

is to my mind the best all-around *casa particular* in Havana. This delightful home is run by Jorge and his wife, Marisel, who offer a large, well-lit, and well-furnished air-conditioned bedroom to the rear of their spotless ground-floor apartment home, only two blocks from the Hotel Tryp Habana Libre. The room has a telephone, refrigerator, double bed with a firm orthopedic mattress, a lofty ceiling with a large, silent fan, and a spacious tiled bathroom with plentiful hot water. There's a TV lounge with rockers and a large window facing the street at ground level. The couple and their daughter Jessica are an absolute delight and go out of their way to make you feel at home. Jorge and Jessica speak English. There's secure parking nearby.

Associated with La Chansonnier *paladar* and exuding a New York boutique hotel aesthetic, the **Casa de Niurys Higueras** (Calle J #259, e/ 15 y Línea, tel. 07/832-1576; CUC30, CUC35 including breakfast) offers one air-conditioned room in a gorgeously rehabbed 1905 mansion with tall ceilings, antique furnishings, a gas chandelier, and a beautiful contemporary travertine-clad bathroom with a large walk-in, glass-walled shower. You'll sleep in an antique wooden bed. The restaurant is always busy, so peace and quiet may be a factor.

Casa de Magalis Sánchez López (Calle 25 #156, e/ Infanta y O, tel. 07/870-7613, magalissanlop@web.correosdecuba.cu; CUC30 low season; CUC35 high season) has two air-conditioned rooms to the rear of a patio with arbor. Both have a TV, fridge, and radiocassette player. Guests get use of the centenary home with lofty ceilings, a kitchen, and TV lounge with Mexican decor. There's secure parking.

Casa de Basilia Pérez (Calle 25 #361, Apto. 7, e/ K y L, tel. 07/832-3953, bpcdt@ hotmail.com; CUC25) has two air-conditioned rooms in a pleasant home secluded behind an apartment block. Each has an independent entrance, fridge, fan, TV, telephone, and private hot-water bathroom.

Casa de Dania Borrego (Calle J #564B, e/ 25 y 27, tel. 07/832-9956; CUC30) has two

HOTELS FOR STUDENTS

Various state agencies operate accommodations for visiting students and educators.

In Vedado, **Villa Residencial Estudiantil** (Calle 2, e/ 15 y 17, tel. 07/830-5250; CUC12.50 s, CUC25 d), run by the Ministry of Public Health (MINSAP), is in a converted mansion with simple rooms. It has a small restaurant and a broad, breeze-swept veranda with rockers.

Hotel Universitario (Calle L y 17, tel. 07/55-2323, hoteluni@enet.cu; CUC25 s, CUC34 d), run by the Ministerio de Educación (MINED), is a basic, wood-paneled affair with a gloomy student union-style bar and a pleasant restaurant downstairs behind the glum lobby. Its 21 rooms offer the bare essentials.

In Miramar, **Hostal Icemar** (Calle 16, e/ 1 y 3, tel. 07/203-7735 or 203-6130; CUC22 s, CUC27 d), operated by MINED, is a 1950s Miami-style hotel with 54 large air-conditioned rooms with TV and hot water. Rooms facing the sea have more light. Six apartments across the road at the same rates sleep up to eight people, but are minimally furnished.

MINED also operates **Hotel Universitaria Ispaje** (1ra, esq. 22, tel. 07/203-5370; CUC25), with eight rooms with private baths, plus a swimming pool and bar; **Villa Universitaria Miramar** (Calle 62 #508, e/ 5ta-A y 5ta-B Av., tel. 07/832-1034; CUC18 s, CUC20 d), with 25 rooms with private baths; **Hostal Costa Sol** (3ra y Calle 60, tel. 07/209-0828; CUC22 s, CUC45 d), with 11 air-conditioned rooms, plus a restaurant; and **Hotel Mirazúl** (5ta #3603, e/ 36 y 40, tel. 07/204-0088, fax 07/204-0045, hotelmi@enet.cu; CUC25 s, CUC36 d), with eight spacious rooms with modest bamboo furnishings, satellite TV, air-conditioning, telephone, and hot-water bathroom.

upstairs air-conditioned rooms in the home of this pleasant family. Each has fans, modern furnishings, and private modern hot-water bathroom. Guests get use of a well-lit lounge, plus secure parking.

Casa de Eddy Gutiérrez (Calle 21 #408, e/ F y G, tel. 07/832-5207; CUC35) has two independent apartments to the rear of the owner's colonial mansion with secure parking. Both are air-conditioned and have fans and refrigerators; one has its own small kitchen, while the other is larger and has higher ceilings.

Casa de Marta Vitorte (Av. de los Presidentes #301, e/ 17 y 19, tel. 07/832-6475, martavitorte@hotmail.com; CUC35) is a splendid three-room, two-bath apartment that takes up the entire 14th floor and boasts wraparound glass windows on a balcony that offers fabulous views. The lounge has plump leather sofas, lounge chairs, and antiques. The three rooms, which are rented separately, are clean and beautifully kept and feature antique beds and private bathrooms. Martha is an engaging conversationalist who speaks fluent English. The only drawback is the rickety elevator, and readers have complained about a "snobbish" attitude.

Hospedaje Gisela Ibarra (Calle F #104 altos, e/ 5ta y Calzada, tel. 07/832-3238; CUC30) is a beautiful colonial-era home decorated with antiques and modern art. The delightful elderly owners, Gisela and Daniel, have two air-conditioned rooms with antiques (including antique double beds), safety deposit boxes, and refrigerators. One room has its own modern tiled bathroom; two rooms share a bathroom. There's a roof terrace, plus parking, and a TV lounge gets the breezes. Meals are served in a gracious dining room.

I also like **Casa de Enrique y Mirien** (Calle F #509, e/ 21 y 23, tel. 07/832-4201, mirien@enet.cu; CUC30), a beautiful option with an independent entrance, security box, a nice modern bathroom, a delightful bedroom with TV, and a patio with rockers and a shade tree. Another independent apartment nearby is **Casa de Humberto San Pedro** (Calle 25 #567 e/ G y H, tel. 07/833-9670; CUC30), tucked behind a massive vine. It has a small kitchen and tiny lounge downstairs; the air-conditioned bedroom and small modern bathroom are upstairs; the only drawback is the low ceiling, and it can get hot. The erudite hosts live above and are a delight.

Farther west, I like **Casa de Fifi** (Calzada #508, e/ D y E, tel. 07/832-3133, lacasonacalzada@yahoo.com or fifiacosta@yahoo.com; CUC30), an 1892 house in colonial style entered via a dramatic carriage door, featuring original *mamparasas* and colonial tiles, and opening to an arched terrace with planters. The single air-conditioned room, simply furnished with aged pieces, is spacious and has a lofty ceiling and a large modern shower. The hostess is a delight.

Nearby, a marvelous option, **Casa de Yolanda Piqueras** (Calle E #104, e/ Calzada y 5ta, tel. 07/832-3025; CUC30) is a pleasant colonial home with a shaded patio with rockers and swing chair and an interior with marble columns. The English-speaking family rents two rooms. One has a delightful modern bathroom. The second, a modern addition with its own entrance, is up a dangerous staircase.

Run by a savvy, politically well-placed owner, the nearby **Casa de Aldo Vásquez** (Calle B #154, e/ Línea y Calzada, tel. 07/832-3223; CUC30) is another huge, well-kept colonial home with a wide front porch with rockers, plus a TV lounge full of antiques. The two spacious air-conditioned bedrooms each have TV, fan, and modern clean private bathroom. There's secure parking.

Casa de Lizet (Calle 3ra #580 bajos, e/ 8 y 10, tel. 07/832-1226; CUC30) offers an independent apartment with a garage, spacious lounge, and small kitchen, plus air-conditioned bedroom with two beds, simple 1950s furnishings, a fridge and TV, and small modern bathroom.

Casa de Octavio Fundora (Calle 10 #152, Apto. 1-D, e/ Calzada y Línea, Vedado, tel. 07/833-9769; CUC30) has a nicely furnished apartment with two air-conditioned rooms, each with TV, VCR, CD player, and private bathroom with hot water. The host speaks English.

One of the best options in town, **Casa Blanca** (Calle 13 #917, e/ 6 y 8, tel. 07/833-5697; CUC25), in the heart of western Vedado, is a gracious colonial home with a front garden riotous with bougainvillea. The home is replete with antiques. It has an air-conditioned room with two double beds, stereo, safe deposit box, and a clean, modern private hot-water bathroom. It also has email service for guests.

Casa de Antonio Llibre Artigas (Calle 24 #260, e/ 17 y 19, tel. 07/833-7156; CUC30) offers two rooms in a well-kept, cross-ventilated house with lofty ceilings in western Vedado. There's also a two-bedroom air-conditioned apartment with a small kitchen and TV. It has secure parking. Sr. Llibre was formerly aide-de-camp to Fidel in the Sierra Maestra (as photographs and diplomas in his office attest). Today, he's a lawyer and historian with a much-faded library.

The remarkable art deco Edificio Cuervo Rubio, at the corner of Calles 21 and O, has 14 *casas particulares*. They're more or less identical in layout. Take an east-facing apartment for ocean views. One such is **Casa de Alejandria García** (#42, tel. 07/832-0689; CUC35), on the fourth floor.

In Nuevo Vedado, **Casa Mayra Sardaín Piña** (Av. Zoológico #160, e/ 38 y 40, tel. 07/881-3792; CUC40 low season; CUC50 high season), close to the Víazul bus station, is a graciously decorated house with a sun-kissed lounge with wicker furnishings and modern art. Two pleasingly furnished air-conditioned rooms reached by a spiral staircase have TVs and fridges. Each has a private bathroom. There's a small swimming pool in the rear courtyard.

Nearby, **Casa de Cecy y Raul** (Av. Zoológico #112, e/ 36 y 28, tel. 07/881-3727; CUC40) is a pleasant 1950s home with an independent air-conditioned apartment.

Hotels CUC50–100

Hotel St. John's (Calle O #206, e/ 23 y 25, tel. 07/833-3740, fax 07/833-3561, jrecepci@ stjohns.gca.tur.cu; CUC50 s, CUC67 d low season; CUC56 s, CUC80 d high season) is a popular bargain. Beyond the chill lounge, this 14-story property has 88 air-conditioned rooms, each with radio, telephone, and TV. A cabaret is offered in the rooftop nightclub, plus there's a rooftop swimming pool, a tourism bureau, and the Steak House Toro. (Gran Caribe.)

Nearby, **Hotel Vedado** (Calle O #244, e/ 23 y 25, tel. 07/836-4072, fax 07/834-4186; CUC47 s, CUC67 d low season; CUC56 s, CUC80 d high season) is of similar standard. It has a tiny, uninspired lounge. Its 203 air-conditioned pastel-hued rooms are small, with satellite TV, telephone, tile floors, and small bathrooms. There's a restaurant, disco and cabaret, swimming pool, and tour desk. (Gran Caribe.)

Hotel Victoria (Calle 19 #101, esq. M, tel. 07/833-3510, fax 07/833-3109, reserva@victoria.gca.tur.cu; CUC55 s, CUC70 d low season; CUC65 s, CUC90 d high season; CUC150 suites year-round) is a charming Victorian-style, neoclassical hotel that focuses on a business clientele yet offers a personal feel. It has 31 elegant, albeit somewhat small air-conditioned rooms refurbished with 1970s decor, with hardwoods and antique reproduction furnishings. There's a small swimming pool, intimate lobby bar, and elegant restaurant. It represents a bargain compared to the ludicrous rates of competing hotels. (Gran Caribe.)

Hotels CUC100-150

The art deco high-rise **Hotel Presidente** (Calzada #110, esq. Av. de los Presidentes, tel. 07/55-1801, fax 07/833-3753, reserva@hpdte.gca.tur.cu; CUC90 s, CUC140 d standard, CUC220 s/d suites year-round) was inaugurated in 1927 and retains its maroon and pink interior, with sumptuous Louis XIV–style furnishings and Grecian urns and busts that rise from a beige marble floor. It has 160 spacious rooms with modern tile floors and tasteful contemporary furnishings, including marble bathrooms. One suite is appointed in Louis XIV style. It has an elegant restaurant, an outdoor swimming pool, plus gym and sauna. (Gran Caribe.)

A legacy from the heyday of sin, Mobster Meyer Lansky's 23-story **Hotel Habana Riviera** (Malecón y Paseo, tel. 07/836-4051, fax 07/833-3739, reserva@gcrivie.gca.tur.cu; CUC74 s, CU106 d, CUC150 junior suite year-round) recently underwent restoration to recapture its 1950s luxe, sans casino. The fabulous modernist '50s lobby, with acres of marble and glass, is the high point and has a pleasant cocktail lounge. The 352 spacious air-conditioned rooms, however, have jaded and conservative furniture, plus direct-dial phones, satellite TV, safes, and minibar. Cleanliness and bad plumbing are of concern, and some rooms have mildew. The hotel offers two mediocre restaurants, 24-hour snack bar, mediocre seawater pool, gym with sauna and massage service, tour desk, boutique, cigar store, and the swank Salón Internacional cabaret nightclub. Past guests report that theft from guest rooms is a problem. That said, it's a favorite with tour groups. (Gran Caribe.)

Hotels CUC150-250

Hotel Nacional (Calle O y 21, tel. 07/873-3564, fax 07/873-5054, reserva@gcnacio.gca.tur.cu; CUC120 s, CUC170 d standard, CUC215 s/d one-bedroom suite, CUC390 two-bedroom suite, CUC400–CUC1,000 special suites; all rooms CUC25 more in peak season) is supposedly Havana's flagship hotel, to which celebrities flock. A recent restoration revived much of the majesty of this 1930s eclectic-style gem, perched on a cliff overlooking the Malecón. The 475 large air-conditioned rooms each have satellite TV, telephone, safe, and minibar, although furnishings are dowdy. The Executive Floor has 63 specially appointed rooms and suites. The Comedor de Aguiar (one of four restaurants) is one of the city's most elegant eateries, and the Cabaret Parisien is one of Havana's hottest cabarets. The top-floor cocktail lounge (one of six bars) offers a magical view, and the open-air gallery bar in the rear gardens is a delightful spot for savoring a *mojito* and stogie. There are two swimming pools, plus upscale boutiques, beauty salon, spa, tennis courts, tour desk, bank, and business center. Numerous guests have complained about theft from guest rooms. (Gran Caribe.)

Hotel Tryp Habana Libre (Calle L, e/ 23 y 25, tel. 07/834-6100, fax 07/834-6365, www

.solmeliacuba.com; CUC140 s, CUC160 d, CUC275 s/d junior suite, CUC440 s/d suite, including breakfast), managed by the Spanish Grupo Sol Meliá, is Havana's landmark high-rise hotel. It was built in the 1950s by the Hilton chain and soon became a favorite of mobsters and high rollers. The modernist atrium lobby with glass dome exudes a sexy '50s retro feel. Although the 533 rooms feature satellite TVs, direct-dial telephones, minibars, safes, and hairdryers, furnishings and fabrics are dowdy, the plumbing is finicky to the point of breakdown, and guests complain about poor housekeeping. It also offers 36 junior suites and three suites, plus 24-hour room service. The hotel is loaded with facilities: tour desks, bank, airline offices, boutiques, international telephone exchange, plus 24-hour café, four restaurants (the Polinesio and El Baracón are dismal; the rooftop Las Antillas is recommended), an open-air swimming pool, business center, an underground parking lot, and one of Havana's best nightclubs. (Gran Caribe.)

The business-oriented **Meliá Cohiba** (Paseo, esq. 1ra, tel. 07/833-3636, fax 07/834-4555, www.solmeliacuba.com; CUC180 s/d standard, CUC220 s/d junior suite, CUC325 s/d suite low season; CUC225 s/d standard, CUC275 s/d junior suite, CUC360 s/d suite high season) is a deluxe postmodern hotel also run by Spain's Sol Meliá. The 22-story hotel has first-rate executive services. Its 462 spacious and elegant air-conditioned rooms feature brass lamps, marble floors, and Romanesque chairs with contemporary fabrics in beige, gold, and rust. The bathrooms dazzle with halogen lights and huge mirrors, bidets, hairdryers, and fluffy towels. Avoid south-facing rooms, which can get hot. Facilities include two swimming pools, gym, squash court, solarium, boutiques, business center, five restaurants, four bars, and the Habana Café nightclub.

PLAYA (MIRAMAR AND BEYOND)
Casas Particulares

Casa de Fernando y Egeria González (1ra #205, e/ 2 y 4, Miramar, tel. 07/203-3866; CUC35) is a superb property. This gracious family home offers two spacious and airy air-conditioned rooms with huge and exquisite tiled bathrooms. The family is a delight. There's secure parking, and a patio to the rear.

Further west, **Casa de Clarisa Santiago** (1ra #4407, e/ 44 y 46, tel. 07/209-1739; CUC30) is another excellent option, with an independent air-conditioned apartment in the rear patio. It's modern throughout and has a nicely decorated bedroom with TV and fan, plus a bathroom with a small shower and hot water. A separate, well-stocked kitchen (by Cuban standards) has a tall refrigerator. There's secure parking and daily maid service.

Casa de Alexis González Lorié (1ra #2803, 5ta piso, e/ 28 y 30, tel. 07/209-3955; CUC30) is a splendid, tastefully decorated fifth-floor air-conditioned apartment with one double room with marble floors, rattan furniture, and a whirlpool tub. The lounge has a smoked-glass solarium offering ocean views. It has secure parking.

Inland, **C Casa de Elena Sánchez** (Calle 34 #714, e/ 7ma y 17, tel. 07/202-8969, gerardo@enet.cu; CUC100) is one of the nicest 1950s-style rentals in town. You rent the entire spacious, well-kept, two-story modernist home. It has two air-conditioned rooms, each with TV, fridge, private hot-water bathrooms, and a mix of antiques, 1950s modernist pieces, and contemporary furniture. A large lounge has leather sofas plus rockers and TV, and opens to a garden with a shaded patio, bougainvillea, and rockers. There's secure parking.

Receiving a strong recommendation from past guests, **Casa de Rebeca González** (7ma #1205, e/ 12 y 14, tel. 07/202-7548; CUC35 low season, CUC40 high season) is a 1920s home maintained by a gracious and educated mature couple. The cross-ventilated house has one spacious room with ceiling fan, modest mid-century furnishings, and a large bathroom, plus secure parking.

Casa de María (3ra #37, esq. B, Miramar, tel. 07/209-5297, fffmiramar@yahoo.com; CUC200 to CUC300) is a four-bedroom modernist home circa 1950s that's rented out in its entirety. Downstairs it has a large TV lounge and separate dining room with period pieces. The two upstairs bedrooms, reached by a spiral staircase, each have a large marble-clad bathroom from the era, plus huge walk-in closet with wall safe. The rear garden even has its own swimming pool overlooking the mouth of the Río Almendares. It has secure parking for several cars.

If you want to know how Communist bigwigs live, check out **Casa de Raquel y Carlos** (7ma #21602, e/ 216 y 218, Siboney, tel. 07/271-4319, fax 07/469-5404, figueredos@ hotmail.com; CUC300 daily, CUC5,000 monthly). This fantastic modernist home, built in 1958 and "bequeathed" when its original owner fled Cuba following the revolution, is graciously furnished with rattan furnishings, original Tiffany lamps, Amelia Palaáz *vitrales,* plus paintings and eclectic items such as antique pistols. The vast kitchen features contemporary appliances and would do Betty Crocker proud. It has two huge air-conditioned bedrooms, each with fabulous rattan king-size beds, large satellite TVs, and fans, plus humongous bathrooms with his and hers sinks. The vast garden has a swimming pool with heated whirlpool tub, plus lounge chairs and an arbor. How is all this permitted, you may wonder? Well, the new owner is a former head of MININT, the Ministry of the Interior.

Others to consider include **Casa de Manuel de Armas Pérez** (5ta #6607, e/ 66 y 68, tel. 07/203-7429; CUC50), a beautiful old home with a huge, pleasantly furnished, independent apartment with a patio and parking; **Casa de Esther Rodríguez** (5ta #8609, e/ 86 y 88, tel. 07/203-8480; CUC30), a 1950s home with one room simply furnished with period pieces, plus secure parking; and **Casa de Ana e Ismael** (Calle 32 #101, esq. 1ra, tel. 07/202-9486; CUC120), a two-story 1950s home full of antique furnishings and enclosed in spacious, well-kept grounds with secure parking.

Hotels CUC50-100

Hotel Kohly (Av. 49 y 36A, Rpto. Kohly, Playa, tel. 07/204-0240, fax 07/204-1733, carp2@kohly.gav.tur.cu; CUC50 s, CUC65 d) is a 1970s-style property popular with budget tour groups despite its out-of-the-way location. The 136 air-conditioned rooms have tasteful albeit simple furniture, satellite TVs, radios, telephones, minibars, safes, and spacious showers in handsome bathrooms. Most have a balcony. Facilities include two modest restaurants, a tour desk, car rental, bar, pool tables, and 10-pin bowling alley, plus a twice-weekly cabaret. (Gaviota.)

Nearby, the **Hotel el Bosque** (Calle 28A, esq. Av. 47, tel. 07/204-9232, fax 07/204-5637, reservas@bosque.gav.tur.cu; CUC50 s, CUC65 d) has 62 modestly furnished air-conditioned rooms with satellite TVs, telephones, safes, and French windows opening to balconies (some rooms only). It has car rental, a laundry, and a tour desk. However, there's no restaurant; guests must walk downhill to Club Almendares. (Gaviota.)

Way out west, **Hotel y Villas Marina Hemingway** (5ta Av. y Calle 248, Santa Fe, tel. 07/204-7628, fax 07/204-4379, comercial@comermh.cha.cyt.cu; CUC 49 s, CUC62 d standard low season, CUC60 s, CUC70 d high season; CUC63 s/d junior suite low season, CUC74 s/d high season; CUC73 s/d suite low season, CUC81 s/d high season; CUC81 s/d bungalows low season, CUC90 s/ d high season; from CUC100 year-round for one-bedroom villas, CUC132 two-bedroom, CUC160 three-bedroom), in the Marina Hemingway complex, offers attractive waterfront suites and villas. All have terrace, TV and video, safe deposit box, and kitchen.

Hotels CUC100-150

Used principally by package-tour groups, the **Hotel Copacabana** (1ra Av., e/ 34 y 36, tel. 07/204-1037, fax 07/204-2846, comercio@ copa.gca.tur.cu; CUC63 s, CU90 d low season; CUC70 s, CUC120 d high season) is an oceanfront hotel with a Brazilian flavor: the Itapoa steak house, the Caipirinha bar and grill, and more. The 168 rooms boast hardwood furnishings, floral bedspreads, small TVs, telephones, and safes. Facilities include a swimming pool (popular with locals on weekends), discotheque, tourism bureau, car rental, and boutique. (Cubanacán.)

Hotel Comodoro (1ra Av. y Calle 84, tel. 07/204-5551, fax 07/204-2089, reservas@comodor.cha.cyt.cu; CUC65 s, CUC90 d, CUC135 s/d suite low season; CUC110 d, CUC155 s/d suite high season) is a training school for apprentice Cuban hotel staff. It has 134 spacious air-conditioned rooms, including 15 suites, with modern furnishings plus satellite TV and telephone. Some rooms have a balcony. The contemporary lobby lounge opens to four restaurants, several bars, a small cabaret, plus a bathing area. Yet another much-needed refurbishment was underway at last visit. The adjacent shopping complex has boutiques, a clinic, and beauty salon. A free shuttle runs to Habana Vieja five times daily. The Comodoro's **Bungalows Pleamar** (CUC89 s, CUC118 d one-bedroom, CUC153 s/d two-bedroom low season; CUC98 s, CUC137 d one-bedroom, CUC180 s/d two-bedroom high season) are the closest thing to a beach resort in the city. The 320 aesthetically striking two-story, one-, two-, and three-bedroom villas are built around two sinuous amoeba-shaped swimming pools. Rooms have a balcony or patio, plus kitchen, living room, and minibar. (Cubanacán.)

Cubanacán Boutique Chateau Miramar (1ra Av., e/ 60 y 70, tel. 07/204-1951, fax 07/204-0224, reservas@chateau.cha.cyt.cu; CUC95 s, CUC120 d standard; CUC150 s/d junior suite; CUC170 s/d suite), on the lonesome shorefront, aims at business clientele. The handsome five-story hotel has 50 rather sterile rooms, despite nice furnishings. They feature satellite TV, minibar, radio, and safe, while suites have whirlpool tubs. Facilities include a pool, elegant restaurant, two bars, executive office, massage, and entertainment. (Cubanacán.)

The **Hotel Palco** (Av. 146, e/ 11 y 13, tel. 07/204-7235, fax 07/204-7236, info@hpalco .gov.cu; CUC74 s, CUC94 d low season; CUC91 s, CUC111 d high season; CUC130–150 junior suites year-round), adjoining the

Palacio de Convenciones, aims at convention traffic. The 144 air-conditioned rooms and 36 junior suites are spacious and have modern decor in lively colors, plus satellite TVs, telephones, minibars, safes, and large bathrooms with hairdryers. Facilities include a business center, elegant restaurant, outdoor snack bar, split-level pool, and small sauna and gym.

Hotels CUC150-250

Directly across from the Miramar Trade Center, **Meliá Habana** (3ra Av., e/ 76 y 80, tel. 07/204-8500, fax 07/204-8505, www.solmeliacuba.com; CUC225 s/d standard, CUC500 suites) is a luxury hotel that aims at a business clientele. The expansive lobby is beautiful, with a surfeit of gray and green marbles and ponds. The 405 air-conditioned, marble-clad rooms and four suites are up to international standards and feature satellite TVs, telephones with fax and modem lines, and safes. The executive floor offers more personalized service plus data ports. Facilities include five restaurants, five bars including a cigar lounge, swimming pool, tennis courts, gym, and business center.

The Spanish-managed **C Occidental Miramar** (5ta Av., e/ 72 y 76, tel. 07/204-3584, fax 07/204-9227, www.occidental-hoteles. com/miramar; CUC100 s, CUC130 d standard; CUC130 s, CUC160 d deluxe; CUC160 s, CUC190 d junior suite; CUC300 s/d suite) is one of the few Cuban hotels that lives up to its deluxe billing. This beautiful modern property features a bounty of limestone, marble, and a mix of neoclassical wrought-iron furniture and hip contemporary pieces in the vast lobby. Its 427 cavernous rooms, including eight junior suites, eight suites, and five rooms rigged for travelers with disabilities, are done up in regal dark blue and gold. Cabarets are held beside a huge swimming pool. It has a beauty salon, squash court, health center, tennis courts, business center, three restaurants, and bars. (Gaviota.)

The thoroughly contemporary **Hotel Panorama Havana** (Calle 70, esq. 3ra, tel. 07/204-0100, fax 07/204-4969, comercial@ panorama.co.cu; CUC95 s, CUC120 d standard; CUC142 s, CUC180 d one-bedroom

HAVANA

suite) opened in 2004 as a deluxe option but is garishly gauche for my tastes! Its 317 rooms, junior suites, and suites have ceramic floors, minibars, safes, direct-dial phones, in-teractive TVs, and Internet access. Facilities include a piano bar, squash court, Internet room, and Italian- and German-themed res-taurants. (Gaviota.)

Food

Havana reflects all the horror stories about Cuban dining, but fortunately *does* have some fine restaurants, many in the top-class hotels. The number of private restaurants (*paladares*) had fallen from 600 to fewer than 50 at last visit. Unfortunately, many establishments mentioned in this book may be closed by the time you arrive.

HABANA VIEJA
Breakfasts
Most hotel restaurants are open for breakfast. I recommend the buffet in the **Mediterráneo** (tel. 07/860-6627; daily 7–10 A.M.), in the Hotel NH Parque Central (see the *Nouvelle Cuban* section below).

If all you want is a croissant and coffee, head to **Pastelería Francesca** (Prado #410, e/ Neptuno y San Rafael, tel. 07/862-0739; daily 8 A.M.–11 P.M.), on the west side of Parque Central.

Paladares
The pocket-size **La Moneda Cubana** (San Ignacio #77, e/ O'Reilly y Plaza de la Cat-edral, tel. 07/861-0401 or 867-3852; daily noon–11 P.M.) is a tiny, well-run place with speedy service and huge portions. The menu offers Cuban staples such as grilled chicken or fried fish (CUC9) and even pork chops (CUC10) served with rice and beans, mixed salad, and bread. Take your business card or a foreign banknote (*moneda*) to add to the wall.

La Julia (O'Reilly #506A, e/ Bernaza y Villegas, tel. 07/862-7438; noon–midnight) is tiny, simple, and recommended for tradi-tional cooking. The ambience is kitschy, the family service is friendly, and the prices are right (CUC4–9) for set plates that include pork, chicken, or lamb.

Paladar Don Lorenzo (Acosta #260A, e/ Habana y Compostela, tel. 07/861-6733; daily noon–midnight), a rooftop restaurant with thatched bar, has a large and creative menu that includes stuffed tomatoes (CUC2.50) and octopus vinaigrette (CUC5) appetizers, and main dishes such as squid in ink (CUC14), crocodile in mustard sauce (CUC18), and roast chicken in cider (CUC15).

Criollo
La Bodeguita del Medio (Empedrado #207, e/ San Ignacio y Cuba, tel. 07/862-1374, comercial@bdelm.gca.tur.cu; daily noon–midnight; bar 10:30 A.M.–12:30 A.M.), one block west of Plaza de la Catedral, spe-cializes in traditional Cuban dishes—most famously its roast pork, steeped black beans, flat-fried bananas, garlicky yucca, and sweet guava pudding "overflowing," thought Nicolás Guillén (Cuba's national poet), "with surges of aged rum." Though Ernest Hemingway liked to drink *mojitos* here, today they are the worst in Havana. You may have to wait for an hour or more to be seated, but a tip or friendly ban-ter with Tito or Caesar, the "house captains," should get you a good table. The service is re-laxed to a fault, and the atmosphere bohemian and lively. Troubadours entertain. Some readers report ho-hum fare; the food is generally fresher at lunch than at dinner, for which you'll pay CUC9–20. Reservations are advised.

Restaurant El Patio (tel. 07/867-1035; patio bar 24 hours; main restaurant noon–midnight), on Plaza de la Catedral, has heaps of ambience, as you dine at tables spilling into the plaza, with live jazz and *son,* too. It serves

SELF-CATERING

Farmers markets (*agromercados* or *mercados agropecuarios*) selling fresh produce exist throughout the city. State-run hard-currency groceries charge exorbitantly for packaged goods, but you have no other option.

HABANA VIEJA

The *agromercado* is on Avenida de la Bélgica (Egido), e/ Apodada y Corrales.

Imported meats are sold at **La Monserrate** (Monserrate, e/ Brasil y Muralles), an air-conditioned butcher shop; and at **Harris Brothers** (Monserrate #305, e/ O'Reilly y Progreso, Habana Vieja, tel. 07/861-1644), a department store with various foodstuff sections.

Supermercado Isla de Cuba (Máximo Gómez #213, esq. Factoria, tel. 07/33-8793; Mon.- Sat. 10 A.M.-6 P.M., Sun. 9 A.M.-1 P.M.), on the south side of Parque de la Fraternidad, is reasonably well stocked.

CENTRO HABANA

Havana's largest *agromercado* is **Cuatro Caminos** (Máximo Gómez, esq. Manglar, tel. 07/870-5934; Tues.-Sat. 7 A.M.-6:30 P.M., Sun. 7 A.M.-2 P.M.).

Almacenes Ultra (Av. Simón Bolívar #109, esq. Rayo; Mon.-Sat. 9 A.M.-6 P.M., Sun. 9 A.M.-1 P.M.) is a reasonably well-stocked grocery. Similarly, try the basement supermarket in

La Época (Galiano, esq. Neptuno; Mon.-Sat. 9:30 A.M.-9:30 P.M., Sun. 9 A.M.-1 P.M.).

VEDADO

There are **agromercados** at Calle 15, esq. 10; at Calle 17, e/ K y L; at Calle 19, e/ F y Av. de los Presidentes; and at Calle 21, esq. J.

There's a grocery stocking Western goods, plus a bakery, on Calle 17, e/ M y N (Mon.-Sat. 9 A.M.-6 P.M., Sun. 9 A.M.- 1 P.M.). Also try **Supermercado Meridiano** (1ra, esq. Paseo, in the Galería del Paseo; Mon.-Sat. 10 A.M.-5 P.M., Sun. 10 A.M.-2 P.M.).

The **Pescadería Especial** (Calle 25 e/ N y O) sells fresh seafood.

PLAYA (MIRAMAR AND BEYOND)

Supermercado 70 (3ra Av., e/ 62 y 70, Miramar, tel. 07/204-2890; Mon.-Sat. 9 A.M.-6 P.M., Sun. 9 A.M.-1 P.M.) is Cuba's largest supermarket selling imported foodstuffs. The next best-stocked grocery is **Diplo Mercado Miramar** (Mon.-Sat. 10 A.M.-6 P.M., Sun. 9 A.M.-1 P.M.), in the Havana Trade Center.

You can buy delicious pastries and breads at **Doña Neli Panadería Dulcería** (5ta Av., esq. 42; Mon.-Sat. 7 A.M.-6 P.M., Sun. 7 A.M.-1 P.M.), in the Quinta y 42 shopping complex; and at **La Francesa del Pan** (Calle 42, esq. 19, tel. 07/204-2211).

---

sandwiches (CUC3.50), hamburger (CUC3), and gazpacho (CUC4.50), plus hot dishes such as roasted pork leg (CUC9). The main restaurant inside has three air-conditioned dining rooms, and an upstairs grill where the overpriced dishes (CUC16–28) include shrimp *al ajillo* (in garlic) and T-bone steak. Go for the ambience.

Similar, but facing onto Plaza de Armas, **Café/Restaurante La Mina** (Obispo #109, esq. Oficios, tel. 07/862-0216; noon–midnight) offers shaded patio dining and a menu featuring snacks and salads (CUC3–5), tamales, and Cuban dishes (CUC4–12). The waiters are efficient, the setting is wonderful, and

there's always live music. To the rear, you can dine in a courtyard with an arbor and free-roaming peacocks.

Penny-pinchers know to head to **Restaurante Hanoi** (Brasil, esq. Bernaza, tel. 07/867-1029; noon–midnight). Although it promotes its Vietnamese cuisine, the menu is Cuban (Vietnamese is limited to one rice dish). Imagine, lobster enchiladas for CUC6.50! No single dish costs more than CUC11, and it offers "combination specials" for below CUC3. *Mojitos* cost a mere CUC2. It can get packed.

Another great bargain is the hidden restaurant in the **Asociación Canaria de Cuba** (Monserrate #258, e/ Neptuno y Ánimas, tel.

HAVANA

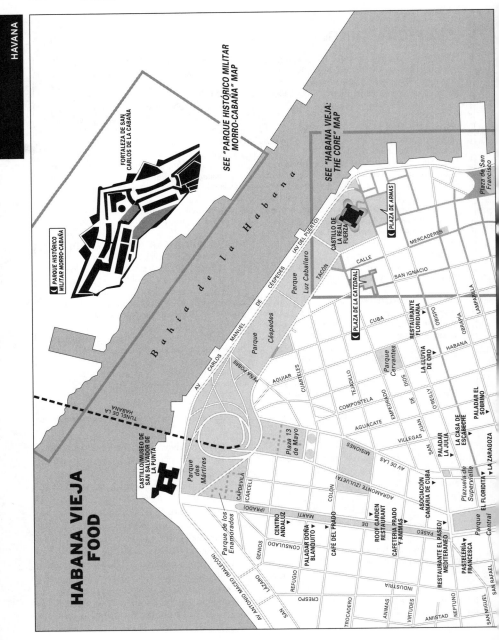

HABANA VIEJA FOOD

PARQUE HISTÓRICO MILITAR MORRO-CABAÑA

FORTALEZA DE SAN CARLOS DE LA CABAÑA

SEE "PARQUE HISTÓRICO MILITAR MORRO-CABAÑA" MAP

SEE "HABANA VIEJA: THE CORE" MAP

Bahía de la Habana

Plaza de San Francisco

PLAZA DE ARMAS

MERCADERES

CASTILLO DE LA REAL FUERZA

CALLE

SAN IGNACIO

RESTAURANTE FLORIDIANA

PLAZA DE LA CATEDRAL

CUBA

OBISPO

OBRAPIA

LAMPARILLA

HABANA

Parque Luz Caballero

Parque Céspedes

Parque Cervantes

TACÓN

(AV. DEL PUERTO)

LA LLUVIA DE ORO

O'REILLY

PALADAR EL SOBRINO

DE

CÉSPEDES

MANUEL

TEJADILLO

DIOS

DE

PALADAR LA JULIA

LA CASA DE ESCABECHE

LA ZARAGOZA

CARLOS

AV

PEÑA POBRE

CUARTELES

COMPOSTELA

AGUACATE

SAN JUAN

VILLEGAS

MISIONES

AV DE LAS

AGUIAR

EMPEDRADO

ASOCIACIÓN CANARIA DE CUBA

EL FLORIDITA

Plazuela de Supervielle

Parque Central

TÚNEL DE LA HABANA

CASTILLO/MUSEO DE SAN SALVADOR DE LA PUNTA

Parque des Mártires

Plaza 13 de Mayo

AGRAMONTE (ZULUETA)

CARDEVILÁ

(CÁRCEL)

COLÓN

ROOF GARDEN RESTAURANT

CAFETERIA PRADO Y ANIMAS

RESTAURANTE EL PASEO/ MEDITERANEO

PASTELERÍA FRANCESCA

DE

PASEO

Parque de los Enamorados

AV ANTONIO MACEO (MALECÓN)

GENIOS

CONSULADO

(PRADO)

MARTÍ

CAFÉ DEL PRADO

PALADAR DOÑA BLANQUITO

CENTRO ANDALUZ

SAN LÁZARO

REFUGIO

CRESPO

TROCADERO

ANIMAS

VIRTUDES

NEPTUNO

AMISTAD

INDUSTRIA

SAN MIGUEL

SAN RAFAEL

HAVANA

FERRY

SAN
PEDRO
PAULA
Parque
Aracelo
Iglesias
CALLE
OFICIOS
SANTA CLARA
INQUISIDOR
DE
ALAMEDA
CALLE
SAN IGNACIO
PLAZA VIEJA
CUBA
DAMAS
SAN ISIDRO
DESAMPARADOS
AGUIAR
HABANA
FARMERS
MARKET
PORVENIR
MERCED
LEONOR PÉREZ (PAULA)
VELASCO
PALADAR
DON LORENZO
(TENIENTE REY)
COMPOSTELA
CONDE
FUNDICIÓN
AMARGURA
BRASIL
SOL
LUZ
ACOSTA
JESÚS MARÍA
MURALLA
AGUACATE
PICOTA
ESTACIÓN CENTRAL
DE FERROCARRIL
VILLEGAS
CURAZAO
RESTAURANTE
PUERTO DE SAGUA
EL BATURRO
BAR MONTSERRATE
Plaza del
Cristo
RESTAURANTE
HANOI
CRISTO
BERNAZA
Plazuela de
Las Ursulinas
AV DE LA BÉLGICA (EGIDO)
Parque de Los
Agrimensores
TERMINAL
LA COUBRE
AV DE LA BÉLGICA (MONSERRATE)
RESTAURANTE
ANACOANA
FARMERS
MARKET
AGRAMONTE (ZULUETA)
AVENIDA DE PUERTO
AV DE LA BÉLGICA (MONSERRATE)
ECONOMÍA
ARSENAL
TALLA PIEDRA
CAPITOLIO
NACIONAL
CÁRDENAS
CIENFUEGOS
Parque de la
Fraternidad
APONTE (SOMERUELOS)
CASA DE
LOS VINOS
SAN JOSÉ
FACTORIA
SUÁRES
REVILLAGIGEDO
INDUSTRIA
CORRALES
APODACA
GLORIA
MISIÓN
ESPERANZA
AGUILA
SAN MARTÍN
AMISTAD
BARCELONA
DRAGONES
MÁXIMO GÓMEZ
AV SIMÓN BOLÍVAR (REINA)
(MONTE)
FLORIDA
ALAMBIQUE
ALCANTARILLA
PUERTA CERRADA
DIARIA

200 yds
200 m
0
0

© AVALON TRAVEL PUBLISHING, INC.

07/862-5284; Wed.–Sun. noon–8:30 P.M.). It serves fruit cocktails (CUC0.50), shredded beef stew (CUC2), shrimp enchiladas (CUC5), and the like amid garish surrounds. It's tucked into the rear at the top of the stairs. The **Centro Andaluz** (Prado #104, e/ Genios y Refugio, tel. 07/863-6745, www.centro-andaluz.galeon .com; Tues.–Sun. 6–11 P.M.) is another colonial Spanish social club with a bargain-priced, albeit no-frills *criollo* restaurant. I recommend the paella (CUC4) followed by a *locura flamenco* cocktail (CUC1.75). Stick around for the flamenco show at 9 P.M.

Café Taberna (Mercaderes #531, esq. Brasil, tel. 07/861-1637; daily 11 A.M.–midnight), on the northeast side of Plaza Vieja, is a lively place serving creative *criollo* fare (CUC5–15), and the long bar is a handsome place to bend an elbow. The walls are festooned with the personal effects of Cuban's renowned singer-composer Beny Moré. A nine-piece band performs. Inspect your bill; I've been scammed by the waiters *every* visit!

Taberna de la Muralla (San Ignacio #364; daily 11 A.M.–1 A.M.) is a great place to sit on the shaded patio overlooking Plaza Vieja. It serves a good cheese and onion soup (CUC1.10), shrimp skewer (CUC8.25), and grilled sausage (CUC2.75), plus burgers, but avoid the *pescado parillada* (grilled fish), which is bony and draws flies.

Nouvelle Cuban

The inspired and colorful Moorish-themed **Restaurante Anacaona** (Paseo del Prado #603, esq. Dragones, tel. 07/868-1000; daily 7 A.M.–midnight), in the Hotel Saratoga, exudes chic. The menu promises cold broccoli soup (CUC5.50), cuttlefish in ink (CUC11), roast beef in coffee sauce (CUC20), and sea bass saffron (CUC29.50). Not cheap, but this is as good as it gets in Cuba.

Restaurante Santo Ángel (Brasil, esq. San Ignacio, tel. 07/861-1626; daily 8 A.M.–11 P.M.), on the northwest corner of Plaza Vieja, is one of my favorite restaurants. The menu features gazpacho (CUC2), garlic mushrooms (CUC3.75), curried shrimp

(CUC15), and pork chops in mustard (CUC10). Fresh-baked breads come with a superb *comport de champiñones* (mushroom paté) in olive oil; the bread is charged extra on your bill, which includes a 10 percent service charge. The tiramisu is first rate. A large wine list includes California labels (CUC14–25). It has troubadours by day and live jazz in the evenings.

The **Roof Garden Restaurant** (Trocadero #55, e/ Prado y Zulueta, tel. 07/860-8560; daily 6:30–10 P.M.), atop the Hotel Sevilla, offers an effusive Renaissance paneled ceiling and marble floors, and tall French doors open to balconies. One reader raves about the food—a fusion of Cuban and French (CUC5–30), but my experience was mediocre, as was service.

The elegant **Restaurante El Paseo** (Neptuno, e/ Prado y Zulueta, tel. 07/866-6627; daily 6–11 P.M.), in the Hotel NH Parque Central, has a creative menu that includes such starters as monkfish ravioli with sweet pepper sauce (CUC14.50) and blackened scallops with anise veloute (CUC20) for a main course. An alternative is the hotel's **Restaurante Mediterráneo** (7–10 A.M. and noon–11 P.M.), serving the likes of shellfish bisque (CUC7.50), Mediterranean salad (CUC8.75), pastas, and continental entrees such as confit legs of duck with gratin potatoes and mushrooms (CUC18.50). Desserts include tiramisu (CUC6.50). The cuisine is well executed, if overpriced, but service can be indifferent.

The elegant **Restaurante Floridiana** (7–10 A.M. and noon–10 P.M.), in the Hotel Florida, also offers well-prepared dishes, such as roast pork (CUC8) and an overpriced lobster with orange (CUC27).

Arabic

Restaurante al Medina (Oficios, e/ Obispo y Obrapía, tel. 07/867-1041; daily noon–midnight), in the Casa de los Árabes, one block south of Plaza de Armas, offers predominantly *criollo* items such as fish and rice (CUC3), salsa chicken (CUC2.50), and vegetarian specialties. But you'll also find couscous and lamb dishes (CUC6), as well as kebabs (CUC5.50), kibbe (minced meatballs, CUC5), and hummus (CUC3).

Continental

Italian: There are several Italian restaurants in Habana Vieja; few can be recommended. An exception is **Dominica** (O'Reilly #108, esq. Mercaderes, tel. 07/860-2918; daily noon–midnight; CUC7–24), serving pastas, pizzas, spaghettis, and more in elegant air-conditioned surroundings. Live musicians perform. The place is foreign managed and the food and service above average.

Spanish: I love the rustic ambience at **El Mesón de la Flota** (Mercaderes #257, e/ Amargura y Brasil, tel. 07/863-3888; daily 9–11 A.M. and 1–3 P.M.; bar 24 hours), a classic Spanish *bodega* with Iberian decor and *tapas,* tortillas, *criollo* entrees (CUC4–18), and Spanish wines (CUC1.50 a glass). It hosts flamenco.

Similarly, the *bodega*-style **(La Paella** (Oficios #53, esq. Obrapía. tel. 07/867-1037; daily noon–11 P.M.), in the Hostal Valencia, serves paella for two people only, although one person could ostensibly eat a double serving, for CUC7–15. The *caldo* (soup) and bread is a meal in itself (CUC3). You can also choose steak, grilled fish, and chicken dishes (CUC2–10), washing them down with Spanish wines (CUC5.30–12). Try the excellent house vegetable soup. The kitchen also serves the **Bodegón Ouda** (Obrapía, esq. Baratillo, tel. 07/867-1037; Mon.–Sat. noon–7 P.M.), a quaint tapas bar around the corner in the Hotel El Comendador. It serves empanadas, tortillas (CUC1–2), *piquillos* (fried green peppers, CUC1.50), pizza slices, and the like, washed down with sangria.

La Zaragoza (Monserrate #352, e/ Obispo y Obrapía, tel. 07/867-1033; daily noon–midnight), a moody Spanish-style *bodega,* serves mostly *criollo* fare but offers seafood such as squid rings (CUC6), garlic shrimp (CUC12), and *ceviche peruano* (CUC2.50), plus lamb stew (CUC9), tortillas (CUC3), and pizza (from CUC2). Cabaret is offered on Thursday and Saturday nights.

Asian

Torre de Márfil (Mercaderes #121, e/ Oficios y Obrapía, tel. 07/867-1038; daily noon–midnight) has all the trappings: the Chinese lanterns, screens, and even a banquet table beneath a pagoda. It's staffed by Chinese waiters, but the service can be excruciatingly slow. The menu includes authentic spring rolls and reasonable chop suey, chow mein, fried wontons (CUC1.50), and shrimp and lobster dishes (CUC14). It serves set dinners from CUC6.

Surf and Turf

El Floridita (Obispo #557, esq. Monserrate, Habana Vieja, tel. 07/867-1299 or 07/867-1300; daily noon–11 P.M.) has a fantastic fin de siècle ambience—the sole reason to dine here—notwithstanding the excessive air-conditioning, ridiculous prices, and surly service. A shrimp cocktail costs CUC15; oyster cocktails cost CUC5. The house special is *langosta mariposa* (lobster grilled with almonds, pineapple, and butter; CUC42). Many of the dishes are disappointing; stick with simple dishes such as prawns flambéed in rum. The wine list is impressive, and cigars are offered. A string trio serenades.

The simple **La Casa del Escabeche** (Obispo, esq. Villegas, tel. 07/863-2660; daily noon–11 P.M.), with flagstone floor and *rejas* open to the street, serves delicious *escabeche* (cube chunks of fish marinated with lime and salsa) for pennies. You can opt for a modern air-conditioned area.

The ritzy **Café del Oriente** (Oficios, esq. Amargura, tel. 07/860-6686; daily 8 P.M.–midnight), on Plaza de San Francisco, has a marbletop bar, tux-clad waiters, and a jazz pianist downstairs in the Bar Café (heck, you could be in New York or San Francisco). Upstairs is even more elegant, with sparkling marble and antiques, French drapes, and a magnificent stained-glass ceiling. It offers mostly steaks and seafood dishes (CUC12–30), including calf's brains with mustard and brandy cream sauce.

Restaurante El Templete (Av. del Puerto, esq. Narciso López, tel. 07/866-8807; daily noon–midnight) is recommended for its harborfront position, where it receives the breezes. Housed in a restored colonial mansion, this seafood restaurant with rustic decor has heaps of ambience, plus a diverse menu that includes an oyster cocktail (CUC5) and octopus (CUC12).

CENTRO HABANA
Paladares

Private restaurants are few and far between in residential Centro, yet the area boasts the best *paladar* in town: 🄲 **La Guarida** (Concordia #418, e/ Gervasio y Escobar, Centro Habana, tel. 07/862-4940 or 264-4940, www .laguarida.com; daily noon–4 P.M. and 7 P.M.–midnight; closed June–July), on the third floor of a once glamorous, now dilapidated, 18th-century townhouse-turned-crowded *ciudadela* (tenement). Don't be put off by the near-derelict staircase, lent an operatic stage-set air by hanging laundry. The place is run jointly with the Ministry of Culture, explaining why there are vastly more seats than the officially permitted 12 for *paladares*. The walls are festooned with period Cuban pieces and giant prints showing famous personages who've dined here, plus fashion shoots on the crumbling stairway. You may recognize it as a setting for scenes in the Oscar-nominated 1995 movie *Fresa y Chocolate*. Owners Enrique and Odeysis Nuñez serve up such treats as gazpacho (CUC4) and *tartar de atún* (CUC6) for starters; and tuna with sugarcane and coconut (CUC13), chicken breast with pepper sauce (CUC12), and desserts such as lemon pie (CUC5). The couple knows how to make their food dance, although quality is far from consistent and there are some duds (the Caesar salad needs work). It has a large wine list, but only house wine by the glass (CUC3). La Guarida is usually jam-packed with diplomats, foreign businessmen, glamorous models, and perhaps even a sprinkling of Hollywood figures. Reservations are essential.

The popular **Paladar Doña Blanquita** (Prado #158, e/ Colón y Refugio, tel. 07/867-4958; daily noon–midnight) offers a choice of dining in the elegant *sala* or on a balcony overlooking the Prado. The *criollo* menu delivers large portions for CUC5–10. The place overflows with whimsical Woolworth's art such as cheap *muñequitas* (dolls), plastic flowers, animals, and cuckoo clocks.

Criollo

Restaurant Colonial (Galiano #164, esq. Virtudes, tel. 07/861-0702; daily 11 A.M.–midnight), in the Hotel Lincoln, is one of the better restaurants in Centro and serves soups, fish, shrimp, and chicken dishes for less than CUC4. The service is swift and conscientious.

Asian

Barrio Chino boasts a score of Chinese restaurants, many with waitstaff in traditional costumes. Most are concentrated along Calle Cuchillo and offer both indoor and patio dining, where *jiniteros* and *jiniteras* (from flower-sellers to not-so-subtle hookers) tout their wares while you dine. However, this isn't Hong Kong or San Francisco, so temper your expectations.

Restaurante Tien-Tan (Cuchillo #17, tel. 07/861-5478, taoqi@net.cu; daily 9 A.M.–midnight) is the best of a dozen options on Cuchillo. The extensive menu includes such tantalizing offerings as sweet-and-sour fried fish balls with vinegar and soy, and pot-stewed liver with seasoning. The budget-minded will find many dishes for around CUC2; but dishes run to CUC18 (medium and large portions are offered). Chef Tao Qi hails from Shanghai and speaks English. A 20 percent service fee is charged.

One of the best bargains in town is **Flor de Loto** (Salud #313, e/ Gervasio y Escobar, no tel.; daily noon–midnight). Though the staff dress in Chinese robes, about the only Asian item on the menu is *maripositas* (fried wontons). However, the *criollo* fare, such as spicy shrimp (CUC6.50) and grill lobster (CUC7.50), is tasty and filling.

Casa Abuelo Lung Kong Cun Sol (Dragones #364, e/ Manrique y San Nicolás, tel. 07/862-5388; daily noon–midnight) has a restaurant upstairs open to Cubans (pesos) and tourists (CUCs). *Maripositas chinas* (fried wontons) cost CUC0.40; chop suey and other entreés range CUC0.40–2.70. This is the real McCoy: Chinese staff, Chinese ambience, Chinese patrons.

VEDADO AND PLAZA DE LA REVOLUCIÓN
Breakfasts

Café La Rampa (Calle 23, esq. L; 24 hours), outside the Hotel Tryp Habana Libre, serves meager American-style breakfasts (CUC2–6), plus tortillas (CUC2.50–4), and has a breakfast special of toast, eggs, bacon, coffee, and juice for CUC7. The hotel also offers a varied breakfast buffet (CUC9) in its mezzanine restaurant, as do all the other upscale tourist hotels in Vedado.

Pain de Paris (Línea, e/ Paseo y A; and at Calle 25 #164, esq. O, tel. 07/33-3347; 24 hours) sells excellent croissants, pastries, and coffees.

Paladares

I regularly dine at **[** **Le Chansonnier** (Calle J #259, e/ 15 y Línea, tel. 07/832-1576; daily 1 P.M.–1 A.M.), located in a venerable home with soaring ceilings and an antique clock collection. I highly recommend it for its warm ambience (aided by tasteful background music) and creative fare inspired by France. Well-prepared trademark sauces highlight tasty and hearty fare such as roasted rabbit in mustard sauce; lamb in tomato sauce, olives, and wine; calamari enchiladas; or duck with *salsa guyabera*. Most main dishes cost CUC10. Portions are generous, and service is efficient, courteous, and friendly. The restaurant draws local gays and resident expats. Reservations recommended.

Another of my favorites, **[** **Paladar Hurón Azul** (Humboldt #153, esq. P, tel. 07/879-1691, dehuronzaul@hotmail.com; daily noon–midnight), is favored by Cuban intelligentsia, reflected in the exceptional decor showing original works of art by Cuba's leading painters. It offers inexpensive but excellent nouvelle Cuban food, including bargain-priced *cajitas*

STUDENT FARE

There's no shortage of in-house cafeterías around the University of Havana, in Vedado.

Penny-pinching pizza hounds should head to **Pizza Celina** (Infanta y San Rafael), alias "Pie-in-the-Sky." Reports student Bridget Murphy: "Celina the capitalist genius hasn't let the fact that she lives on the third floor stop her from running a successful pizza business. Scream up your order from across the street, and then in a few minutes pick up your pizzas from, and drop your pesos into, the plastic basket (complete with red bows) that comes crashing down." It's pretty good pizza, too.

For cajitas (no more than CUC1 in pesos) try **Cajitas** (Calle L, esq. 25; go down the stairs into the home).

And nearby, **Doña Laura's** (Calle H, e/ 21 y 23; 11 A.M.–4 P.M.) is a great bargain. This porch-based cafeteria serves good food, including sandwiches for five pesos. A cajita costs 23 pesos, and the batidos are fabulous.

(box lunches). The *escabeche* (CUC4.50), garbanzo (CUC3.50), and octopus vinaigrette (CUC5.50) starters are superb. Main dishes include oven-roasted chicken with wine and mustard sauce (CUC10.70). Its house combo, *La Guajira* (CUC9), comprises a seasoned pork steak, stuffed corn tamale, fried plantains, *congrí*, and salad. Desserts include trifle (CUC5) and cheesecake (CUC3.50). A six-course "Menu Gourmet" costs CUC20–25, by reservation only. It has a vast wine list. Service is polite and professional, albeit a tad aloof. Take a sweater!

Restaurante Gringo Viejo (Calle 21 #454, e/ E y F, Vedado, tel. 07/831-1946; daily noon–11 P.M.) is another eatery favored by Cuban celebrities and granted extensive leeway by the authorities. However, I've been scammed frequently by the staff (check your bill carefully), so I recommend it only because

FOR VEGETARIANS

Vedado has four vegetarian restaurants. **Restaurante Biki** (Infanta, esq. San Lázaro, tel. 07/879-6406; noon-10 P.M.) is a tremendous vegetarian outlet with an unusually varied buffet including stuffed eggplant (aubergine) and the like, plus salads (4.50-7 pesos), rice with veggies (7 pesos), and a wide range of natural juices (3 pesos). Foreigners can pay in pesos, but if you don't have *moneda nacional*, the bill will be charged in CUC at an exorbitant one-to-one rate.

Restaurante Naturista (Línea, esq. C, tel. 07/830-3453; noon-10 P.M.); **Restaurante El Carmelo de Calzada** (Calzada, esq. D, tel. 07/832-4495; 10 A.M.-10 P.M.); and **La Terraza Vegetariana** (Calle M, e/ 23 y 25; 10 A.M.-10 P.M.) are in the same chain and offer similar options.

it has a consistently great *ropa vieja* (CUC11), and the *flan de la casa* is delicious.

Another place where the owners sometimes scam patrons is **Paladar Nerei** (Calle 19, esq. L, tel. 07/832-7860; Mon.–Fri. noon–midnight, Sat.–Sun. 6 P.M.–midnight), which I'm recommending for its terrace dining and superb grilled calamari (CUC10–18). The wide-ranging menu includes duck with onions (CUC7.50) and lamb in tomato sauce (CUC7.50).

The tiny **Paladar Restaurante Monguito** (Calle L, e/ 23 y 25; Fri.–Wed. 11 A.M.–10 P.M.), directly opposite the Hotel Tryp Habana Libre, is a bargain and for that reason almost always full. "China," your hostess, serves simple but filling Cuban dishes such as *pollo asado,* grilled fish, and pork dishes (CUC3–6).

Further west, **Paladar Las Mercedes** (Calle 18 #204, e/ 15 y 17, tel. 07/831-5706; daily noon–midnight) is a charming option in the style of a thatched rural *bohío*. Excellent quality *criollo* dishes with an imaginative twist are served. I recommend the *pescado a la Mercedes* (two types of fish with cheese sauce,

CUC10.50). The *brocheta* (kebab) is also good. The *paladar* includes a set menu (CUC15) and has a student special for CUC3 before 7 P.M.

In Nuevo Vedado, **La Casa** (Calle 30 #865, e/ 26 y 41, tel. 07/881-7000; daily noon–midnight) is worth the drive. This 1950s modernist house still has its original modish decor and is lush with tropical plantings. An indoor-outdoor patio features waterfalls and pools full of drowsy terrapins. La Casa serves such delicious dishes as octopus and onions (CUC9), fresh prawns sautéed in butter with garlic (CUC10), and caramel flan (CUC1.20). Matt Dillon and the Kennedys are among the famous clientele.

El Decameron (Línea #753, e/ Paseo y 2, tel. 07/832-2444; daily noon–midnight) specializes in Italian fare. You dine on a varied menu of tasty regional staples, surrounded by potted plants and the ticking of antique clocks. The eggplant appetizer is recommended. There's a broad selection of wines, and the place is so popular it has a full bar in the waiting room. Budget about CUC12 per head.

Criollo

El Conejito (Calle M #206, esq. Av. 17, tel. 07/832-4671; daily noon–midnight) is a good option, not least for its Teutonic ambience. A pianist plays while you dine on *conejo* (rabbit) served any of a dozen ways. It also serves beef, chicken, and pasta dishes, plus a decent grilled fish. Entrées average CUC7. It has inexpensive "student nights" on Wednesday and weekends.

Continental

The **Comedor de Aguiar** (Calle O, esq. 21, tel. 07/33-3564; daily 7 A.M.–midnight), in the Hotel Nacional, fairly glitters with chandeliers and silverware and appeals to those with money to burn. The waiters are liveried to the T and trained to provide top-notch service. The well-executed menu featuring creative international cuisine is highlighted by shrimp with rum flambé, and smoked salmon with capers and onion for starters. Main courses are priced CUC13–36.

ICE-CREAM PARLORS

Street stalls sell ice-cream cones for about 2.50 pesos. However, the milk may not be pasteurized, and hygiene is always a question.

Habana Vieja: The **Cremería el Naranjal** (Obispo, esq. Cuba) sells overpriced ice-cream sundaes, including a banana split (CUC1.50-3), as does **Heladería La Mina** (Oficios, esq. Obispo). A better bet is **Cremería Obispo** (Obispo, esq. Villegas), selling various flavors for pesos.

Centro Habana: The **Heladería Sun Wu Kung** (Zanja, esq. Aguila; noon-midnight) sells ice-cream sundaes for the moon.

Vedado: An institution in its own right, **Coppelia** (Calle 23, esq. Calle L, tel. 07/832-6149; daily 10 A.M.-9:30 P.M.) serves ice cream of excellent quality. Tourists are normally steered toward a special section that, though offering immediate service, charges CUC2.60 for an *ensalada* (three scoops), while the half a dozen communal peso sections for Cubans (choose from indoor or outdoor dining) offer larger *ensaladas* (five scoops) for only five pesos, a *jimagua* (two scoops) for two pesos, and a *marquesita* (two scoops plus a sponge cake) for 2.50 pesos. Be prepared for a *long* wait, especially on hot summer days. Some lines are for inferior (lower fat) Veradero ice cream (closed Monday). Also see the sidebar *Coppelia* earlier in this chapter.

Bim Bom (Calle 23, esq. Infanta, tel. 07/879-2892; 10 A.M.-midnight), at the bottom of La Rampa, is run along the lines of Baskin-Robbins and charges accordingly, as does **Dulce Habana** (Calle 25; daily 10 A.M.-9 P.M.), on the south side of the Hotel Tryp Habana Libre.

Playa (Miramar and Beyond): Try **Bosque de la Habana** (3ra Av., e/ 78 y 80, tel. 07/204-8500; 24 hours), in the Hotel Meliá Habana.

La Torre (Calle 17 #155, e/ M y N, tel. 07/832-2451; daily noon-midnight; bar 11:30 A.M.-12:30 A.M.), atop the Focsa building, offers splendid all-around views of the city. Its French-inspired nouvelle cuisine is of acceptable standard: I recommend the prawns and mushrooms in olive oil and garlic starter (CUC9), and salmon in olive oil and mustard sauce (CUC12). Be sure to order the mountainous and delicious profiteroles (CUC5) for dessert! The bar offers reasonably priced cocktails.

The Meliá Cohiba's **El Abanico Restaurante Gourmet** (Paseo, esq. 1ra, tel. 07/833-3636; daily 7-11 P.M.) is one of the most elegant in town. Its nouvelle dishes might seem a bit ambitious, but execution is accomplished. I recommend the medallions of caramelized trout with tarragon starter (CUC7), followed by walnut sole with risotto (CUC17).

The best place for Italian fare is **La Piazza Ristorante** (tel. 07/833-3636; daily 1 P.M.-midnight), in the mezzanine of the Meliá Cohiba. It offers 17 types of pizza (CUC7-20) but also has minestrone (CUC7.50), gnocchi (CUC9.50), and seafoods (from CUC11). Bring a sweater against the air-conditioning. Service can be terribly slow, and the place can get smelly with smoke from the oven.

PLAYA (MIRAMAR AND BEYOND)
Breakfasts

All the tourist hotels have buffet breakfasts. Those of the **Meliá Habana** and **Occidental Miramar** are recommended.

For fresh-baked croissants and good coffee, I like **Pain de Paris** (Calle 26 e/ 5ta y 7ma; daily 8 A.M.-10 P.M.), in the Dos Gardenias complex.

Paladares

🄲 **La Esperanza** (Calle 16 #105, e/ 1ra y 3ra, tel. 07/202-4361; Mon.-Sat. 7-11:30 P.M.) is an exceptional *paladar* inside a 1930s middle-class home with a *sala* full of art nouveau furnishings, antiques, books, and intriguing miscellany. Jazz or classical music is normally playing. Your waiter will read off the day's French inspirations, served with lively sauces. On my last visit, I enjoyed a superb eggplant *de ochún* (in honey) stuffed with chicken. The service is friendly and professional, and prices are fair (budget CUC25 for a meal), although a 10 percent service charge is automatically added. A reservation is essential.

Reservations are also essential at **(Cocina de Lilliam** (Calle 48 #1311, e/ 13 y 15, Miramar, tel. 07/209-6514; Mon.–Sat. noon–3 P.M. and 7–11 P.M.), in the lush grounds of a 1939s era mansion romantically lit at night. The brick-lined patio is shaded by trees, with colonial lanterns and wrought-iron tables and chairs. Lilliam Domínguez conjures up tasty nouvelle Cuban. Her appetizers include tartlets of tuna and onion, and a savory dish of garbanzo beans and ham with onion and red and green peppers. Entrées include such Cuban classics as *ropa vieja* of simmered lamb with onions and peppers; chicken breast with pineapple; plus fresh fish dishes and oven-roasted meats served with creamy mashed potatoes. Budget CUC15–25 apiece. The place has been jam-packed ever since President Jimmy Carter dined here in May 2002. The house often runs out of more popular dishes by 9 P.M. and is closed August 1–15 and the month of December.

Paladar Calle 10 (Calle 10 #314, e/ 3ra y 5ta, tel. 07/209-6702; 11 A.M.–midnight) is to the rear of a mansion and features a dramatic re-creation of a country theme, including thatched roofing and an outdoor *parilla* (grill). Very attractive! The limited menu features 10 house dishes, all creatively prepared and presented. I enjoyed a splendid *filete de salmon al ajillo* (garlic salmon). The portions are huge, and the food tasty and filling. Live music is offered.

By the shore, **Paladar Vistamar** (1ra Av. #2206, e/ 22 y 24, tel. 07/203-8328; noon–midnight), in a modern house on the seafront, is popular for its high-quality cuisine and has the advantage of ocean views. It serves continental fare as well as Cuban staples. Starters include fish cocktail (CUC3) and mushroom soup (CUC3.50), while main dishes include *pescado milanesa* (CUC12), and grilled fish with garlic (CUC11.50). One block west, **Paladar Ristorante El Palio** (1ra Av. #2402, esq.

24, tel. 07/202-9869; noon–midnight) serves Italian-*criollo* cuisine and is popular with elite Cubans. Pastas and seafood dishes average CUC5. You dine on a shaded patio to the rear, with suitably Italian decor.

La Fontana (3ra Av. #305, esq. 46, tel. 07/202-8337; noon–midnight) specializes in barbecued meats from an outdoor grill serving T-bone steak. Starters include salads (CUC1–3), *escabeche* (CUC5), and onion soup (CUC2.50); main dishes include a greasy fillet grilled with garlic (CUC8). Rice and extras cost additional. Review your bill closely! Choose cellar or garden seating in a traditional country *bohío* setting. It has caged birds and animals. Service is hit or miss.

Mi Jardín (Calle 66 #517, esq. 5ta Av. B, tel. 07/203-4627; noon–midnight), in a beautiful 1950s home full of antiques, is run by an affable and conscientious Mexican and his Italian wife. They serve genuine Mexican fare—well, as much as the government prohibition on beef allows. The chicken *molé cubano* and house special fish Veracruz are recommended. You'll also find enchiladas, *totopos* (nachos), and *papas fritas con mojo* (chips with garlic and salsa), plus Italian and *criollo* dishes. You can dine inside, or on a patio beneath an arbor. Budget CUC10 per person.

More expensive than competitors, **Paladar Los Cactus de 33** (Av. 33 #3405, e/ 34 y 36, Rpto. Kohly, tel. 07/203-5139; noon–midnight) justifies the price with splendid fare—they do have off nights, however—such as the grilled snapper with creole sauce, and the house chicken breast with olives, mushrooms, and cheese, plus baked custard (my favorite dessert) enjoyed in an ambience so elegant that the Gothic-style home with a garden garlanded with fairy lights is often used as a backdrop for TV shows and fashion shoots. Budget about CUC25 per head.

Much more reasonably priced, **Paladar La Paila** (Av. 51A #8827, e/ 88B y 88C, Marianao, tel. 07/205-3970; noon–3 P.M. and 6–11 P.M.), hidden in the run-down Pogolotti district but handily close to the Tropicana nightclub, is a romantic charmer with tables in a lantern-lit garden. The house staple is *bistec uruguayano* (stuffed with ham and cheese), but pizzas are also very good, at least by Cuban standards. With drink you can dine for less than CUC10 per peson.

Criollo

I find myself returning time and again to **❮ El Aljibe** (7ma Av., e/ 24 y 26, tel. 07/204-1583; daily noon–midnight), my favorite state-run restaurant in Havana, serving the best Cuban fare in town and popular with the Havana elite and foreign businessmen showing off their trophy Cuban girlfriends. You dine beneath a soaring thatch roof. The superb house dish, the *pollo asado el aljibe,* is glazed with a sweet orange sauce, then baked and served with fried plantain chips, rice, French fries, and black beans served until you can eat no more. It's a tremendous bargain at CUC12; desserts and beverages cost extra. Other *criollo* dishes are served (CUC10–20), but you really should order the house chicken. The bread and side salad delivered to your table will be charged to your bill even if you didn't order it, and a 10 percent service charge is automatically billed. The wine cellar, it is claimed, has almost 27,000 bottles! Service is prompt and ultraefficient.

Restaurant 5ta y 16 (5ta Av., esq. 16, tel. 07/206-9509; daily noon–1 A.M.), formerly El Rachón, is acclaimed as one of Havana's best restaurants, although it serves traditional Cuban cooking, notably grilled fish and meats (the grilled pork chops are particularly good) from a *churrasquería.* More creative dishes include a delicious appetizer of stuffed red peppers with tuna, plus a daily special, from roast beef to lamb chops. The food is well prepared and the portions are huge. Choose from a downstairs buffet or à la carte upstairs. Budget CUC10–20.

El Rancho Palco (Av. 19, esq. 140, tel. 07/208-9346; daily noon–11 P.M.), in jungly surroundings in the heart of Cubanacán, is a handsome, open-sided *bohío* with terra-cotta floor, Tiffany-style lamps, decor featuring saddles, and wooden toucans and parrots on swings. You can opt to dine on a patio or beneath thatch, or in an air-conditioned dining room. It serves meat dishes (CUC10–30), seafood (CUC12–26), and the usual *criollo* fare. Quality is hit or miss, depending on your timing; on a good night it serves the best filet mignon (CUC11) in Cuba. It offers floor shows at night. It is popular among the government elite. Scan your bill carefully as scams are frequent!

Seafood

Don Cangrejo (1ra Av., e/ 16 y 18, tel. 07/204-4169; daily noon–midnight) offers some of the finest seafood in town, served in a converted colonial mansion offering views out to sea. It's popular with the monied Cuban elite. The menu features crab cocktail (CUC6), crab-filled wontons (CUC3), house specialties such as crab claws (CUC15), and garlic shrimp (CUC13); plus paella, lobster, and fish dishes. The wine list runs to more than 150 labels. An open bar is offered on Monday for CUC10. You can use the swimming pool 10 A.M.– 5 P.M. (CUC16 *consumo mínimo*).

Continental

Two favorites of Cuba's political and social elite, the **Tocororo** (Calle 18 #302, esq. 3ra) and **La Ferminia** (5ta Av. #18207, e/ 182 y 184), serve disappointing fare at outrageous prices and are thereby best avoided.

Paleta Bar y Amelia Restaurante (3ra Av., e/ 70 y 82, tel. 07/204-7311; daily 10 A.M.–10 P.M.), on the ground floor of the Miramar Trade Center, is an elegant contemporary restaurant decorated with modern art. The hip marble-topped bar is a fine place to bend your elbow. The fairly simple menu includes sandwiches, burgers (CUC3), steaks, and the likes of shrimp enchiladas (CUC7).

For jungly ambience (and saucy showgirls) try **La Cecilia** (5ta Av. #11010, e/ 110 y 112, tel. 07/204-1562; daily noon–midnight), another elegant option in the middle of a large garden surrounded by bamboo, although it has an air-conditioned section. It serves typical Cuban dishes such as *ajiaco* (a stew, and the national dish), *tasajo* (jerked beef), *churrasco* (broiled steak), and *pollo con mojo* (chicken with onion and garlic), as well as grilled lobster. Entrées cost CUC12–25. It hosts a *cabaret espectáculo* Thursday– Sunday.

 Complejo Turístico La Giraldilla (Calle 222, e/ 37 y 51, tel. 07/27-0568; 10 A.M.–5 A.M.), in La Coronela, is well worth the long journey for recherché nouvelle dishes under the baton of foreign management (Argentinian at last visit). Choose from a selection of dining rooms in the Patio Los Naranjos. I enjoyed a superb creamed vegetable soup (CUC4), sautéed prawns in garlic (CUC17), and sautéed salmon (CUC19). The gazpacho (CUC5) and lobster in Ricard sauce are also recommended. On Saturdays it hosts a CUC18 "La Noche del Búfalo" special for steak lovers. La Bodega del Vino basement tapas bar serves everything from tacos to chicken mole, washed down with sangria. It has an extensive wine list, plus a well-stocked cigar store.

Asian

For sushi and traditional Japanese fare, head to **Sakura** (Calle 18, esq. 3ra, tel. 07/204-2209; daily noon–midnight), in the Tocororo (see listing in *Continental* above). The sushi menu is restricted, but quality is surprisingly good. Miso soup (CUC3), tempura (CUC12), and sashimi (CUC12) are served, as are sake and Japanese beers.

Other

Pan.Com (Calle 26, esq. 7ma; Mon.–Fri. 8 A.M.–2 A.M., Sat.–Sun. 10 A.M.–2 A.M.), pronounced pahn POOHN-to com, makes every kind of sandwich. It also has omelettes, burgers, and tortillas, all for less than CUC5, plus yogurts, fruit juices, *batidos,* and cappuccinos.

Information and Services

MONEY
Banks

The state-run **Banco Financiero Internacional** is the main bank, with eight branches throughout Havana (Mon.–Fri. 8 A.M.–3 P.M., but 8 A.M.–noon only on the last working day of each month). Its main outlet, in the Hotel Tryp Habana Libre, has a special cashiers' desk handling travelers checks and credit card advances up to US$5,000 for foreigners. The state-run Banco de Crédito y Comercio (Bandec), Banco Internacional de Comercio, and Banco Metropolitano also have services for foreigners. The Banco Popular primarily serves Cubans.

The main foreign exchange bureau, **Cadeca** (Obispo, e/ Cuba y Aguiar, Habana Vieja, tel. 07/866-4152; daily 8 A.M.–10 P.M.), represents Western Union (Mon.–Sat. 8 A.M.–5 P.M., Sun. 8:30 A.M.–noon). Cadeca also has a branch on the mezzanine level of the Hotel Nacional, in Vedado (daily 10 A.M.–7 P.M.), good on Sunday when banks are closed.

ATM Cards

ATMs allowing cash advances of Cuban convertible pesos from Visa cards (but not Master-Card or U.S.-issued Visa cards) are located at the Cadeca bureau de change on Calle Obispo (see above); in Etecsa (Obispo esq. Habana, tel. 07/866-0089; daily 8:30 A.M.–9 P.M.); and at the Hotel Golden Tulip Parque Central, Hotel Cohiba, Hotel Nacional, and Miramar Trade Centre; plus the Banco Internacional de Comercio (3ra Av., esq. 78, Miramar) and Banco Metropolitano (5ta Av., esq. 113, Miramar), all of which dispense up to CUC300.

COMMUNICATIONS
Post Offices

Most major tourist hotels have small post offices and will accept your mail for delivery. In Habana Vieja, there are post offices on the northeast corner of the Plaza de la Catedral; at Obispo #102, on the west side of Plaza de San Francisco; at Obispo #518; next to the Gran Teatro on Parque Central; and on the north side of the railway station on Avenida de Bélgica.

In Vedado, there's a small post office inside the lobby of the Hotel Tryp Habana Libre (open 24 hours). Havana's main post office is **Correos de Cuba** (tel. 07/879-6824 or 879-8654; 24 hours) on Avenida Rancho Boyeros, one block north of the Plaza de la Revolución.

The most tourist-friendly facility is **Servi-Postal** (Havana Trade Center, 3ra Av., e/ 76 y 80, Miramar, tel. 07/204-5122; Mon.–Sat. 10 A.M.–6 P.M.), which also has a copy center, DHL, and Western Union agency.

Express Mail Services

DHL Worldwide Express (1ra Av. y Calle 26, Miramar, tel. 07/204-1578; Mon.–Fri. 8 A.M.–8 P.M., Sat. 8 A.M.–4 P.M.) also has offices at Calzada #818, e/ 2 y 4, Vedado (tel. 07/832-2112; Mon.–Fri. 8 A.M.–4 P.M.), and in the Hotel Tryp Habana Libre.

Telephone and Fax Service

The **Empresa de Telecomunicaciones de Cuba** (Etecsa) is headquartered at the Havana Trade Center (3ra Av., e 76 y 80, Miramar). The main international telephone exchange (tel. 07/834-6106; 24 hours) is in the lobby of the Hotel Tryp Habana Libre.

Key *centros telefónicos* (telephone kiosks) are on the ground floor of the Lonja del Comercio (Mon.–Fri. 8:30 A.M.–5:30 P.M.) on Plaza de San Francisco and at Obispo, esq. Habana, in Habana Vieja; and, in Vedado, in the Centro de Prensa Internacional at Calle O; and outside the Hotel Meliá Cohiba at the foot of Paseo.

Cellular Phones: You can rent cellular phones from **Cubacel** (see *Cellular Phones* in the *Communications* section of the *Essentials* chapter).

Internet Access

Most *correos* (post offices) offer email service to the general public for CUC5 for three hours. Foreigners can freely surf the Internet. Most tourist hotels also have Internet access for guests; shop around, as hourly rates vary widely.

Habana Vieja: The best outlet is **Ciber-correo** (Obispo #457, esq. Aguacate; Mon.–Sat. 9 A.M.–8:30 P.M., Sun. 10 A.M.–6:30 P.M.), which charges CUC4.50 per hour. Nearby, **Etecsa** (Obispo, esq. Habana, tel. 07/866-0089; daily 8:30 A.M.–9 P.M.) charges CUC6 per hour.

The business center at the Hotel NH Parque Central charges CUC17.50 per hour (Mon.–Fri. 8 A.M.–8 P.M., Sat.–Sun. 8 A.M.–4 P.M.). The cybercafés at the nearby Hotel Telégrafo and Hotel Santa Isabel are cheaper.

Centro Habana: The **Telecorreo** (Salvador Allende, esq. Padre Varela, tel. 07/879-5795; 24 hours) offers email and Internet access (CUC5 for three hours).

Vedado: Etecsa has Internet service in the **Centro de Prensa Internacional** (Calle 23, e/ N y O; CUC15 for up to five hours).

Most tourist hotels offer Internet service. The business center in the **Hotel Nacional** (Calle O y 21, tel. 07/55-0294; daily 8 A.M.–8 P.M.) charges CUC3.23 per 15 minutes; the center in the **Hotel Tryp Habana Libre** (Calle L, e/ 23 y 25, tel. 07/55-4011; daily 7 A.M.–11 P.M.) charges CUC3 for 15 minutes, and CUC10 per hour; and the center in the **Hotel Meliá Cohiba** (Paseo, e/ 1ra y 3ra, tel. 07/204-3636; Mon.–Sat. 8 A.M.–8 P.M.) charges CUC15 per hour. Avoid the inexpensive hotels, such as the Hotel Vedado, with slow connections.

Correos de Cuba (Av. Rancho Boyeros, tel. 07/66-8249), the main post office, on the northeast side of Plaza de la Revolución, has 24-hour Internet service; as does the **Telecorreo** (Línea, esq. Paseo, tel. 07/830-0809).

Students at the University of Havana have free Internet service in the Biblioteca Central (you can have your home email account forwarded to their telnet account), at the faculty of Artes y Letras (you need to sign up for a slot the day before), and Filosofía y História, which operates on the *último* system, with long lines for use.

Miramar: The **Servi-Postal** in the Havana Trade Center (see *Post Offices*) has an Internet Center charging CUC4.50 per hour.

The Hotel Occidental Miramar, Hotel Meliá Habana, and Hotel Kohly each have a cybercafé.

Photography

The best resource is **Photo Obispo** (Obispo #307, esq. Habana; Mon.–Sat. 9 A.M.–9 P.M., Sun. 9 A.M.–1 P.M.), which develops film, sells digital cameras, makes CDs, and acts as a digital center.

Also try **Agfa Photo Center,** in the Havana Trade Center (3ra Av., e/ 76 y 80, Miramar).

GOVERNMENT OFFICES
Immigration and Customs

Requests for visa extensions (*prórrogas*) and other immigration issues relating to foreigners are handled by **Inmigración** (Calle Factor final, Nuevo Vedado, no tel.; Mon.–Tues. and Thurs.–Fri. 8:30 A.M.–noon). Journalists and others requiring special treatment are handled by the **Ministerio de Relaciones Exteriores** (Ministry of Foreign Relations, Calzada #360, e/ G y H, Vedado, tel. 07/30-5031, fax 07/31-2314).

The main Customs office is on Avenida del Puerto, opposite the Iglesia San Francisco de Asís.

Consulates

See the sidebar *Embassies and Consulates in Havana* in the *Essentials* chapter.

TRAVEL AGENCIES

There are no independent travel agencies. Hotel tour bureaus can make reservations for excursions, car rental, and flights, as can **Cubalinda.com** (Calle E #158, Piso 4-A, esq. 9na, Vedado, tel. 07/264-9034, www.cubalinda. com; Mon.–Sat. 8 A.M.–5 P.M.), a competent U.S.-owned entity with European staff.

San Cristóbal Travel (Oficios #110, e/ Lamparilla y Amargura, tel. 07/860-9585, fax 07/860-9586, reservas@sancrist.get.tur.net; Mon.–Sat. 9 A.M.–6 P.M., Sun. 9:30 A.M.–1 P.M.) specializes in travel in and around Habana Vieja, including hotel reservations.

(See the *Cuban Tour Operators* sidebar in the *Essentials* chapter for a complete list of agencies.)

TOURIST INFORMATION
Information Bureaus

Infotur (tel. 07/866-3333), the government tourist information bureau, has nine information bureaus in Havana, including in the arrivals lounges at José Martí International Airport (see the sidebar *Infotur Bureaus*) and at the Ministerio de Turismo headquarters (Malecón y G, Vedado).

Habaguanex (Oficios #110, on Plaza de San Francisco, tel. 07/33-8693, fax 07/33-8697) provides information on hotels, restaurants, and other places under its umbrella in Habana Vieja.

Maps

Tienda de los Navegantes (Mercaderes #115, e/ Obispo y Obrapía, Habana Vieja, tel. 07/861-3625; Mon.–Fri. 8:30 A.M.–5 P.M., Sat. 8:30 A.M.–noon) has a wide range of tourist maps of Havana and provinces.

MEDICAL SERVICES

Most large tourist hotels have nurses on duty. Other hotels will be able to request a doctor for in-house diagnosis. See *Facilities for Foreigners* in the *Medical Services* section of the *Essentials* chapter for general information on services for tourists.

Hospitals

Tourists needing medical assistance are usually steered to the **Clínica Internacional Cira García** (Calle 20 #4101, esq. Av. 41, Miramar, tel. 07/204-4300 or 204-2811, fax 07/204-2660, ciragcu@infomed.sld.cu; 24 hours), a full-service hospital dedicated to serving foreigners.

The **Centro Internacional Oftalmológica Camilo Cienfuegos** (Calle L, e/ Línea y 13, Vedado, tel. 07/832-5554, fax 07/833-3536, www.retinosis.sld.cu) specializes in eye disorders but also offers a range of medical services running from optometry to odontology.

Hospital Hermanos Almeijeiras (Padre Varela, esq. San Lázaro, Centro Habana, tel. 07/876-1000) offers medical consultations for foreigners Monday–Friday 8 A.M.–4 P.M. (CUC25). Overnight stays cost CUC75.

INFOTUR BUREAUS

Infotur (tel. 07/866-3333, www.infotur.cu), the government tourist information bureau, has 24-hour bureaus in the José Martí International Airport (Terminal Two, tel. 07/55-8733; Terminal Three, tel. 07/641-6101); at the Terminal de Cruceros (Cruise Terminal); plus the following outlets in Havana (8:30 A.M.–8:30 P.M.):

HABANA VIEJA
Calle Obispo, e/ Bernazas y Villegas, tel. 07/866-3333
Calle Obispo, esq. San Ignacio, tel. 07/863-6884

VEDADO
Malecón y G, tel. 07/836-0033

MIRAMAR
5ta Avenida, esq. Calle 112, tel. 07/204-7036
Calle 28 #303, e/ 3ra y 5ta, tel. 07/204-0624

PLAYAS DEL ESTE
Av. Las Terrazas, e/ 10 y12, Playa Santa María, tel. 07/96-1111
5ta-C Avenida, e/ 468 y 470, Guanabo, tel. 07/96-6868

Pharmacies

Local pharmacies serving Cubans are meagerly stocked. For alternative (homeopathic) remedies, try **Farmacia Ciren** (Calle 216, esq. 11B, Playa, tel. 07/271-5044) and **Farmacia las Praderas** (Calle 230, e/ 15A y 17, Siboney, tel. 07/33-7473).

Your best bets are the *farmacias internacionales,* for foreigners only and stocked with imported medicines. They're located at the **Hotel Plaza** (Zulueta #267, esq. Neptuno, Habana Vieja, tel. 07/860-8583), atop the roof; **Farmacia Internacional Camilo Cienfuegos** (Calle L, e/ Línea y 13, Vedado, tel. 07/832-5554 or 07/33-3538, fax 07/33-3536, cirpcc@infomed.sid.cu; 8 A.M.–8 P.M.); the

Galería Comercial Habana Libre (Calle 25 y L, Vedado; Mon.–Sat. 9 A.M.–6 P.M.); the **Clínica Internacional Cira García** (Calle 20 #4101, esq. Av. 41, Miramar, tel. 07/204-4300; 24 hours); the **Farmacia Internacional** (Av. 41, esq. 20, Miramar, tel. 07/204-2051; daily 9 A.M.–7 P.M.); and in the **Habana Trade Center** (3ra Av., e/ 76 y 80, Miramar; Mon.–Fri. 8 A.M.–6 P.M.).

Opticians
Ópticas Miramar (Neptuno #411, e/ San Nicolás y Manrique, Centro Habana, tel. 07/863-2161; and 7ma Av., e/ Calle 24 y 26, Miramar, tel. 07/204-2990) provides full-service optician and optometrist services.

SAFETY
A rash of muggings and petty crime that erupted some years back has been drastically reduced since January 1999, when thousands of policeman took to the streets on a 24-hour basis. Still, Havana is not entirely safe despite this remarkable policing. Most crime is opportunistic, and thieves seek easy targets. Be wary of darker back streets at night (very few streets have lights).

Bad apples hang out at major touristed haunts. Be wary around the Capitolio Nacional and Parque Central, the Paseo de Martí (Prado), and Plaza 13 de Marzo in front of the Museo de la Revolución, once a favorite spot for nocturnal muggings. Other areas that require special caution by day or night are the back streets of southern Habana Vieja and Centro Habana, and anywhere in the Cerro district and other slum districts. I was mugged on a main street in Centro!

Be cautious and circumspect of all *jiniteros.*

Also see the *Safety* section of the *Essentials* chapter.

MISCELLANEOUS PRACTICALITIES
Haircuts
I recommend the **Barbería de Plaza de Armas** (Obispo, e/ Oficios y Mercaderes, Habana Vieja, tel. 07/863-0943; Mon.–Sat.

8 A.M.–noon and 2–5 P.M.) or **Salón Correo Barbería** (Brasil, e/ Oficios y Mercaderes, Habana Vieja; Mon.–Sat. 8 A.M.–6 P.M.), two old-style barber shops.

Laundry

In Habana Vieja, **Lavandería El Guerrillero** (Máximo Gómez #521, e/ San Nicolás y Indio, tel. 07/863-7585; daily 6 A.M.–6 P.M.) offers a wash and dry service for 3 pesos. Another small launderette is at the corner of Villegas and Lamparilla. You drop off your clothes and, hey presto, they're usually ready a few hours later, crisp and folded, for CUC3 a load.

In Miramar, **Aster Lavandería** (Calle 34 #314, e/ 3ra y 5ta, Miramar, tel. 07/204-1622; Mon.–Fri. 8 A.M.–5 P.M., Sat. 8 A.M.–2 P.M.) has a wash-and-dry service (CUC3 per load) and dry cleaning (CUC2 for pants, CUC1.50 for shirts).

Most upscale hotels offer dry-cleaning and laundry service. It's expensive, takes two days, and results can be questionable. Many locals are willing to wash your clothes for a few dollars, but be prepared to have them stretched, beaten, and faded.

Legal Services

Consultoría Jurídica Internacional (CJI, International Judicial Consultative Bureau, Calle 16 #314, e/ 3ra y 5ta, Miramar, tel. 07/204-2490, fax 07/204-2303) provides legal advice and services.

Libraries

The **Biblioteca Nacional** (Av. de la Independencia, esq. 20 de Mayo, tel. 07/55-5442, fax 07/81-6224, fernando@jm.lib.cult.cu or aponce@jm.lib.cult.cu; Mon.–Fri. 8:15 A.M.–6 P.M., Sat. 8:15 A.M.–4 P.M.), on the east side of Plaza de la Revolución, has about 500,000 texts, plus an archive of 100,000 photos. Getting access, however, is another matter. Five categories of individuals are permitted to use the library, including students and professionals, but not lay citizens. Foreigners can obtain a library card valid for one year (CUC3) if they have a letter from a sponsoring Cuban government agency, and/or ID establishing academic credentials, plus two photographs and a passport, which you need to hand over whenever you wish to consult books. The antiquated, dilapidated file system makes research a Kafkaesque experience. There is no open access to books. Instead, individuals must request a specific work, which is then brought to you; your passport or (for Cubans) personal ID is recorded along with the purpose of your request. Big brother at work!

The University of Havana, in Vedado, has several libraries, including the **Biblioteca Central** (San Lázaro, esq. Ronda, tel. 07/878-5573 or 878-3951, ranero@dict.uh.cu).

The **Biblioteca Provincial de la Habana** (Obispo, Plaza de Armas, tel. 07/862-9035; Mon.–Fri. 8:10 A.M.–9 P.M., Sat. 9 A.M.–5:30 P.M.) is a meagerly stocked affair with mostly out-of-date encyclopedias and texts. It has a small magazine room and musical library. It's closed the first Monday of each month.

Toilets

The only modern public toilet to Western standards is in the ground floor of the Lonja del Comercio, Plaza de Armas.

Most hotels and restaurants will let you use their facilities. An attendant usually sits outside the door dispensing a few sheets of toilet paper for pocket change (also note the bowl with a few coins meant to invite a tip).

Getting There

BY AIR

See the *Essentials* chapter for information on flights to and from Havana.

José Martí International Airport

José Martí International Airport (switchboard tel. 07/206-4644 or 07/33-5753) is 25 kilometers southwest of downtown Havana, in the Wajay district. It has five terminals spaced well apart and accessed by different roads (nor are they linked by a connecting bus service).

Terminal One: This terminal serves domestic flights.

Terminal Two: Charter flights originating in Los Angeles, Miami, and New York arrive at Terminal Two (tel. 07/33-5576 or 07/33-5577) carrying passengers with OFAC licenses. Occasionally other flights pull in here, although the outbound flight will invariably depart Terminal Three. There's an Infotur information booth (tel. 07/55-8733) plus car rental outlets.

Terminal Three: All international flights except United States–Havana charters arrive at Terminal Three, on the north side of the airport. For information on arrivals and departures call 07/266-4133 or 07/33-5666.

Immigration and Customs: Immigration proceedings are slow. Travelers arriving without prebooked accommodations are usually made to book—and pay for—at least two nights' hotel stay before being granted entry. You'll be escorted to a tour desk where representatives sell hotel rooms at full price.

Beware porters who grab your bags as you exit the arrivals hall; they'll expect a tip for hauling your bag the few yards to the taxi stands. Some may purposely drop your bag at the wrong tour bus or taxi so that a partner can get another tip for carrying your bags to the correct vehicle.

Information and Services: There's a 24-hour Infotur (tel. 07/66-6101) tourist information office immediately on the left after exiting the customs lounge. You should check in here

if you have prepaid vouchers for accommodations or transfers into town.

There's a foreign exchange counter in the baggage claim area.

Terminal Four: This serves the military.

Terminal Five: Aero Caribbean and Aero-Taxi flights arrive here.

Getting into Town

There is no public bus service from either of the international terminals. A green-and-white public bus marked Aeropuerto departs from Terminal One (domestic flights) for Vedado and Parque Central about 15 minutes after the arrival of domestic flights (one peso). The bus is intended for Cubans, and foreigners may be refused. It only runs about once every two hours.

Alternately, you can catch a "camel bus" (M2 originating in Santiago de las Vegas) or Ómnibus #480 from the east side of Avenida de la Independencia, about a 20-minute walk east of the terminal—no fun with baggage. The bus goes to Parque de la Fraternidad on the edge of Habana Vieja. The journey takes about one hour, but the wait can be just as long; the bus gets incredibly crowded, is renowned for pickpockets, and is one heck of a hassle that will appeal to only the most seasoned, penny-pinching travelers. You'll need 20 pesos for the fare.

Taxis are plentiful outside the arrivals lounges. You'll be charged about CUC10–12 by Cubataxi (yellow and black Ladas) and CUC12–20 by tourist taxis to downtown hotels. Some taxi drivers will not want to use their meter and may ask you how much you're prepared to pay (they reset their meter at a discount rate and pocket the difference), in which case always quote below the fares given here. Avoid private (and illegal) taxis, as several foreigners have been robbed.

Most people arriving on package tours will have been issued prepaid vouchers for a shuttle; drivers are often happy to shuttle individual travelers, too.

Car Rental: The following have booths at Terminal Three: **Havanautos** (tel. 07/649-5197); **Micar** (tel. 07/33-0333); **Rex** (tel. 07/66-6074); and **Transtur** (tel. 07/33-5765). The following have booths at Terminal Two: **Havanautos** (tel. 07/649-5215) and **Transauto** (tel. 07/33-5764).

The cars are poorly maintained and I recommend against renting here.

BY SEA
By Cruise Ship

See *By Cruise Ship* in the *Getting There* section of the *Essentials* chapter for details on cruise ships that call on Cuba.

Havana's **Terminal Sierra Maestra** (Av. del Puerto, tel. 07/862-1925) is a natty conversion of the old customs building. Passengers step through the doorways directly onto Plaza de San Francisco, in the heart of Havana.

By Private Vessel

See the *Essentials* chapter for general information on travel to Cuba by private boat.

Private yachts and motor cruises berth at **Marina Hemingway** (Av. 5ta y Calle 248, Santa Fe, tel. 07/204-1150, fax 07/204-5280, comercial@prto.mh.cyt.cu), 15 kilometers west of downtown. The harbor coordinates are 23° 5'N and 82° 29'W. You should announce your arrival on VHF Channel 16, HF Channel 68, and SSB 2790.

You must clear Immigration and Customs at the wharf just inside the entrance channel. If you plan to dock for less than 72 hours, visas are not required (your passport will suffice). For longer stays you'll need a tourist card (CUC20), issued at the marina. The harbormaster's office (tel. 07/204-1150, ext. 2884), in Complejo Turístico Papa's, at the end of channel B, will facilitate your entry and exit, and visa extensions can also be arranged for CUC25.

The marina has four parallel canals. Docking fees, which include water, electricity, and custodial services, cost CUC0.35 per foot per day. Gasoline and diesel are available 8 A.M.–7 P.M. (tel. 07/204-1150, ext. 450).

The 24-hour medical post (ext. 737) is in Complejo Turístico Papa's, as are a 24-hour launderette (ext. 451), bathrooms with showers, soda bar, and TV lounge, storage room (security boxes can be rented), ship chandler (ext. 2344), plus a beach volleyball court and tennis courts. The post office (ext. 448) is at the entrance of Intercanal C, where you'll also find the Hemingway International Nautical Club (ext. 701), which offers fax and telephone facilities. The shopping mall is at the east end of Intercanal B (ext. 739). The marina even has a scuba diving center (ext. 735) at Complejo Turístico Papa's.

Rental cars are also available (ext. 87), as are microbuses and taxis (ext. 85).

Getting Around

ON FOOT

Havana is a walker's city, easily and best explored on foot. Only when traveling between districts will you need transport. Except in the restored section of Habana Vieja, sidewalks are in atrocious repair. Beware potholes, broken curbs, and dog excrement underfoot. And be wary of walking beneath corroded porticos, which frequently collapse, killing pedestrians. If *habaneros* are walking in the street to avoid certain arcades, so should you.

BY BUS
Tourist Bus

The **Tren Turístico Bella Época** (tel. 07/66-2476) departs from the Terminal Sierra Maestra, located on the east side of Plaza de San Francisco, daily 10 A.M.–1 P.M. (CUC1). This motorized jeep dressed up as a train has shaded open-air carriages and takes in major sights in Habana Vieja and Vedado, where it ends at the Hotel Meliá Cohiba.

CAMELS IN CUBA?

Yes, camels roam the streets of Havana. These giant buses – *camellos* – were designed locally to save the day during the gasoline crisis, when bodies were added to articulated flatbed trucks. They're so named for the shape of the coach: sagging in between two humps like a bactrian camel.

The "camel" is a warehouse on wheels: officially a *supertrenbus*. Designed to carry 220 people, they are usually stuffed with more than 300, so many that the true number can't be untangled. As a popular Cuban joke goes, the always-packed and chaotic *camellos* are like the Saturday-night film on state TV, "because they contain sex, violence, and swear words!" Beware pickpockets!

About half of the one million trips that *habaneros* make daily are aboard the rumbling behemoths, which carry the "M" designation (for Metrobus). Most *camellos* originate from Parque de la Fraternidad. Seven routes span Havana and the most distant suburbs. Two key *camello* routes to know are the M1 (Parque de la Fraternidad to Habana del Este) and M2 (Parque de la Fraternidad to Santiago de las Vegas via the international airport). Most begin operation at 4 A.M., with the last departure at 10 or 11 P.M. A standard 20 centavo fare applies.

M1: Alamar to Vedado
Route: Calle 168 (e/ 5taE y 7taF) – 5ta Av. – Calle 168 – 3ra Av. – Calle 162 – Av. Los Cocos – 7ma Av. – Vía Monumental – Tunnel – Agramonte – Máximo Gómez (Monte) – Simón Bolívar (Reina) – Salvador Allende – Calle G

M2: Santiago de las Vegas (Boyeros) to Parque de la Fraternidad
Route: Av. 349 (y Final) – Calle 17 – Calle 2 – Av. Boyeros – Salvador Allende – Simón Bolívar (Reina)

M3: Alamar to Ciudad Deportiva
Route: Calle 168 (e/ 5taE y 7taF) – 5ta Av. – Calle 168 – 3ra Av. – Calle 160 – 7ma Av. – Av. Cojímar – Vía Blanca – Calzada de Guanabacoa – Lindero – Calzada de Luyanó – Porvenir – Acosta – Mayía Rodríguez – Santa Catalina – Av. Boyeros

M4: San Agustín (Lisa) to Parque de la Fraternidad
Route: Calle 270 (e/ 25 y 27) – Av. 27 – Calle 264 – Av. 31 – Calle 250 – Av. 51 – Calzada de Puentes Grandes – Calzada de Cerro – Máximo Gómez (Monte) – Prado (return to Monte via Dragones and Zulueta)

M5: San Agustín (Lisa) to Vedado
Route: Calle 270 (e/ 25 y 27) – Av. 27 – Calle 264 – Av. 31 – Calle 250 – Av. 23 – Av. 26 – Av. 31 – Av. 41 – Calle 28 – Calle 23 – Malecón – Marina (return to Calle 23 via San Lázaro and Calle L)

M6: Calvario (Arroyo Naranjo) to Vedado
Route: Calzada de Managua (e/ Camilo Cienfuegos y 1ra) – 10 de Octubre – Cristina – Belascosín – San Lázaro – Calle L (return to San Lázaro via Calle L, Línea, Malecón, and Marina)

M7: Alberro (Cotorro) to Parque de la Fraternidad
Route: Av. 99 (y Final) – Carretera de Alberro – Av. 101 – Calzada de Güines – Lindero – Calzada de Luyanó – 10 de Octubre – Cristina – Máximo Gómez (Monte) – Industria (return to Monte via Dragones and Prado)

Public Bus

Havana's crowded and uncomfortable public buses, or *guaguas* (pronounced WAH-wahs), are for stoics. No buses operate within Habana Vieja except along the major peripheral thoroughfares. Buses are usually packed to the gills, especially during rush hours—7–10 A.M. and 3–6 P.M.

In recent years, the overloaded bus system has been relieved by introduction of modern (albeit "pre-owned") Mercedes and Volvo buses from Europe, 400 new Chinese buses,

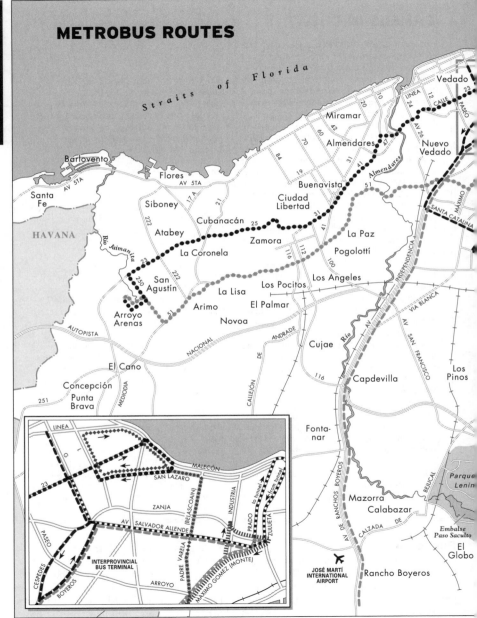

METROBUS ROUTES

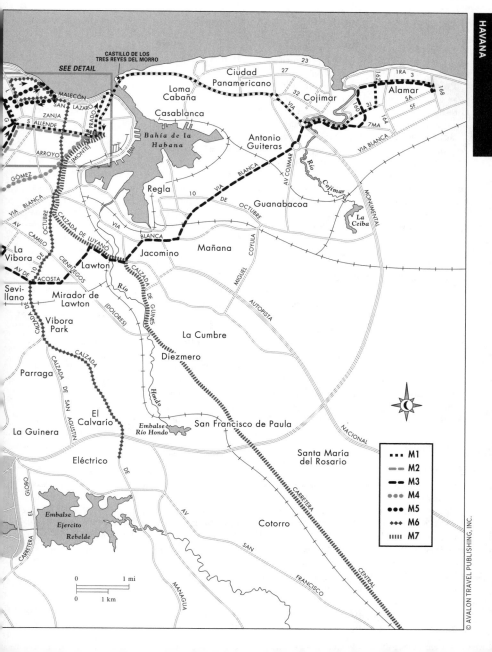

CASTILLO DE LOS
TRES REYES DEL MORRO

SEE DETAIL

MALECÓN

SAN LÁZARO

PRADO

ZANJA

ALLENDE

ARROYO

GÓMEZ

Loma
Cabaña

Ciudad
Panamericano

Cojimar

Alamar

Casablanca

Bahía de la
Habana

Antonio
Guiteras

Regla

Guanabacoa

La
Ceiba

Río
Cojimar

VÍA BLANCA

AV COJIMAR

VÍA

BLANCA

DE

OCTUBRE

MIGUEL

COYULA

MONUMENTAL

AUTOPISTA

VÍA

BLANCA

Jacomino

Mañana

La
Víbora

Lawton

Sevi-
llano

Mirador de
Lawton

Víbora
Park

Parraga

El
Calvario

La Guinera

Eléctrico

La Cumbre

Diezmero

San Francisco de Paula

Santa María
del Rosario

Cotorro

Embalse
Río Hondo

Río

Hondo

Embalse
Ejercito
Rebelde

AV DE 10 DE

ACOSTA

CIENFUEGOS

CALZADA DE

GUINES

(DOLORES)

CALZADA

CALZADA DE SAN AGUSTIN

AV

DE

NACIONAL

CARRETERA

CENTRAL

SAN

FRANCISCO

MANAGUA

AV

CAMILO

VIA BLANCA

CALZADA DE LUYANO

10

23

27

32

1RA

3

5A

5F

7MA

	M1
	M2
	M3
	M4
	M5
	M6
	M7

0   1 mi

0   1 km

© AVALON TRAVEL PUBLISHING, INC.

and by *tren buses* (see the sidebar *Camels in Cuba?*). Bus service is the responsibility of three agencies: Asociación de Transportes de Servicios de Ómnibus (Astro), Transmetro, and Ómnibus Metropolitano.

Public transportation comes to a halt on May 1 and other days of major political celebrations, as buses are redirected to transporting the masses to the demonstrations.

Schedules and Fares: Most *guaguas* run 24 hours, at least hourly during the day but on reduced schedules 11 P.M.–5 A.M. The standard fare for any journey throughout the city is 20 centavos, or 40 centavos on smaller buses called *ómnibuses ruteros,* which have the benefit of being uncrowded. *Taxibuses*— buses that ply a fixed, non-stop route to the airport and bus and train stations—charge one peso. You deposit the money in the box beside the driver.

Routes and Route Maps: Many buses follow a loop route, traveling to and from destinations along different streets. Most buses display the bus number and destination above the front window. Many buses arrive and depart from Parque Central and Parque de la Fraternidad in Habana Vieja and La Rampa (Calle 23) in Vedado, especially at Calle L and at Calzada de Infanta.

Few routes are a circle. If you find yourself going in the wrong direction, don't assume that you'll eventually come around to where you want to get to. You'll more likely end up in the boondocks.

BY TRAIN

Local commuter trains (*ferro-ómnibuses*) operate from **Estación 19 de Noviembre** (Calle Tulipán and Hidalgo, tel. 07/881-4431 or 07/881-3642), also called Estación Tulipán, south of Plaza de la Revolución, to ExpoCuba at 9:35 A.M. Wed.–Sun. (CUC1 each way); to San Antonio de los Baños at 10:05 A.M. and 4:25 and 8:30 P.M. (CUC1.50); to Artemisa at 6 P.M. (CUC2.20); and to Batabanó at 5 P.M. (CUC1.80).

Return trains depart from ExpoCuba at 5:30 P.M.; from San Antonio at 5:35 A.M. and

1:55 and 6:15 P.M.; from Artemisa at 5:30 A.M.; and from Batabanó at 5:25 A.M.

BY TAXI

Modern taxis—including top-of-the-line Mercedes—serve the tourist trade while locals make do with wheezing jalopies. Most taxis lack seatbelts or are otherwise in a poor state of repair.

Dollar Taxis

Turistaxis are operated by state organizations and charge in dollars. Rates vary slightly between companies and, often, the size of the car. Taxis are metered. You will rarely pay more than CUC10 or so for any journey within town. Expect to pay about CUC5 between Habana Vieja and the Hotel Tryp Habana Libre. Nighttime fares cost about 20 percent more.

The cheapest option is **Panataxi** (tel. 07/55-5555, comercial@dcpanatrans.transnet.cu), which provides efficient radio-dispatched taxi service using Ladas (CUC1 at flag drop, then CUC0.45 a kilometer) and slightly more expensive Peugeots.

The following companies operate tourist taxis, which can be found outside any tourist hotel: **Fénix** (tel. 07/863-9580); **Habanataxi** (tel. 07/53-9086); **Taxis-OK** (tel. 07/204-0000); **Transgaviota** (tel. 07/267-1626); and **Transtur** (tel. 07/208-6666).

Classic Cars: Fancy tooling around in a 1950 Studebaker or 1959 Buick Invicta convertible? **Gran Car** (Vía Blanca y Palatino, Cerro, tel. 07/41-7980, grancardp@transnet.cu) rents classic-car taxis for CUC15 per hour (20-km limit the first hour, with shorter limits for extra hour). Daily rates decline from CUC90 for one day to CUC70 per day for five days (120-km daily limit). Set prices apply for provincial touring. They can be found outside major hotels.

See *By Taxi* in the *Getting Around* section of the *Essentials* chapter for general information on taxis.

Peso Taxis

Cubataxi has the cheapest taxis. It uses Ladas, the Russian-made Fiat described by Martha

© CHRISTOPHER P. BAKER

Tourists embark on a tour of Habana Vieja by horse-drawn cab from outside the Capitolio.

Gellhorn as "tough as a Land Rover, with iron-hard upholstery and, judging by sensation, no springs." They're painted black and yellow, with a strange Hebrew-type logo on the sides. They're leased by the state to the drivers for CUC150 monthly and can pick up foreigners, but not within 100 yards of a hotel. You'll be charged in dollars; few drivers will use the meter but will ask you how much you want to pay, or will charge you about the same rate as Panataxi. You can't call for one, but must wave one down on the street. A light above the cab signifies if the taxi is *libre* (free).

The workhorses of the taxi system, the privately owned 1950s-era *colectivos* or *máquinas* run along fixed routes, much like buses, and charge 10 or 50 pesos for a ride anywhere along the route. Parque de las Agrimensores, on the north side of the railway station, is the official starting point for set routes throughout the city. They are officially barred from accepting foreigners, but occasionally will do so.

Bici-taxis

Hundreds of homespun tricycle taxis with shade canopies ply the streets of Habana Vieja and Vedado. The minimum fare is usually CUC1 (or five pesos for Cubans on peso-only *bici-taxis*). You can go the full length of the Malecón, from Habana Vieja to Vedado, for CUC3 or so. Always agree to a fare before setting off.

These jalopies are barred from certain streets, so you might end up taking a zigzagging route to your destination; sometimes walking is quicker!

Coco-taxis

These cutesy three-wheeled eggshells on wheels whiz around the touristed areas of Havana and charge CUC0.50 per kilometer. However, they are inherently unsafe.

Horse-Drawn Buggies

Horse-drawn coaches offer a popular way of exploring the Malecón and Old Havana, although the buggies are barred from entering the pedestrian-only quarter. They're operated by **San Cristóbal Travel** (Oficios #110, e/ Lamparilla y Amargura, Habana Vieja, tel. 07/860-9585). Their official starting point is the junction of Empedrado and Tacón, but you can hail them wherever you see them. Others can be hailed outside the Hotel Inglaterra, on Parque Central. They charge CUC5 for 45 minutes.

BY CAR

The maze of narrow one-way streets in Habana Vieja is purgatory for anyone with a motor vehicle. The main plazas and the streets between them are barred to traffic.

A four-lane freeway—the **Autopista Circular** (route Calle 100 or *circunvalación*)—encircles southern and eastern Havana, linking the arterial highways and separating the core from suburban Havana. It has treacherous potholes, mainly at the equally dangerous intersections.

Parking

A capital city without parking meters? Imagine. Parking meters were detested during the Batista era, mostly because they were a source of *botellas* (skimming) for corrupt officials. After the triumph of the Revolution, *habaneros* rampaged through the city smashing the meters.

Finding parking is rarely a problem, except in Habana Vieja. No Parking zones are well marked. Avoid these like the plague, especially if it's an officials-only zone. Havana has an efficient towing system for the recalcitrant.

Never leave your car parked unguarded. In central Vedado, the Hotel Tryp Habana Libre has an underground car park (CUC0.80 for one hour, CUC0.50 each additional hour; CUC4 maximum for 24 hours).

Rental Companies

See *By Car* in the *Getting Around* section of the *Essentials* chapter for general information on rental car companies, including rates.

Car Repairs

Your car rental company can arrange repairs. However, if you need emergency treatment, **Oro Negro** (5ta Av., esq. 120, Miramar, tel. 07/208-6149; Calle 2, esq. 7ma, Miramar, tel. 07/204-5760; and Av. 13, esq. 84, Playa, tel. 07/204-1938) has *servicentros* open Monday–Saturday 8 A.M.–7 P.M. Cubalse, which

oversees sales of cars in Cuba, has a major automotive repair shop at **Agency Multimarcas** (Av. 222, esq. La Lisa, tel. 07/204-8743).

You can arrange a tow through **Agencia Peugeot** (Vía Blanca y Primelles, Cerro, tel. 07/57-7533 or 879-3854), which charges CUC1 per kilometer outbound and CUC1 per kilometer for the tow.

BY MOTORCYCLE AND SCOOTER

You can rent motorcycles at the Hotel Comodoro. However, they are not in very good condition.

Renta de Motos (3ra Av., e/ 28 y 30, Miramar, tel. 07/204-5491; daily 9 A.M.–9 P.M.) rents scooters for CUC10 one hour, CUC15 three hours, or CUC24 per day (CUC21 per day for rentals of 3–10 days). It does not offer insurance.

If you're staying in Cuba any length of time, consider buying a scooter (from CUC1,300) from **Agencia Vedado** (Calle 23 #753, e/ B y C, Vedado, tel. 07/833-3994, ventas23@23c. automotriz.cubalse.cu).

BY BICYCLE

Bicycling offers a chance to explore the city alongside the Cubans themselves, although the roads are a bit dodgy, with bullying trucks and buses pumping out fumes, plus potholes and other obstacles to contend with (an average of two cyclists are killed in traffic accidents in Havana every three days). A helmet is a wise investment.

The municipal government provides specially converted buses—the **Ciclobus**—to ferry cyclists and their *bicis* through the tunnel beneath Havana harbor (10 centavos). Buses depart from Parque de la Fraternidad, but the location is subject to change.

Renting Bicycles: You can rent bikes from **El Orbe** (Monserrate #304, e/ O'Reilly y San Juan de Díos, Habana Vieja, tel. 07/860-2617 or 860-8532; Mon.–Fri. 9 A.M.–6 P.M., Sat. 9 A.M.–5 P.M.), which has mountain bikes and hybrids for CUC2 hourly, CUC12 daily, CUC70 weekly. Rentals come with racks,

HAVANA

© CHRISTOPHER P. BAKER

Muelle Luz terminal for the ferry to Regla, Avenida San Pedro

locks, and a helmet, and bottle holders and lights can be installed.

Cubalinda (Calle E #158, Piso 4-A, esq. 9na, Vedado, tel. 07/264-9034, www.cubalinda.com; Mon.–Sat. 8 A.M.–5 P.M.) charges CUC11 per day (less for longer periods, declining to CUC7 per day for 15-day rentals) for 21-speed hybrid Peugeot and Norco bicycles. A CUC250 deposit is required.

BY FERRY

Tiny ferries (standing room only—no seats) bob across the harbor between the Havana waterfront and Regla (on the east side of the bay) and Casablanca (on the north side of the bay). The ferries leave on a constant yet irregular basis 24 hours, from a wharf called Muelle Luz on Avenida San Pedro at the foot of Calle Santa Clara in Habana Vieja (tel. 07/97-7473 in Regla); 10 centavos; five minutes.

ORGANIZED EXCURSIONS
City Tours

Havanatur (Calle 23, esq. M, Vedado, tel. 07/830-3107 or 07/833-7907; daily 8 A.M.–8 P.M.) offers a city tour, plus excursions to Finca Vigía, and ExpoCuba and Jardín Bo-

tánico. However, most tours, including guided walking tours, provide only a cursory and poorly informed experience.

Agencia San Cristóbal (Oficios #110, e/ Lamparilla y Amargura, tel. 07/861-9171, www.viajessancristobal.cu; daily 8 A.M.–5 P.M.) offers guided walking tours of Habana Vieja, as does **Infotur** (see the *Infotur Bureaus* sidebar). You can book through hotel tour bureaus.

Private Guides

Cubatur (Calle 23, esq. L, Vedado, tel. 07/33-4120, 07/55-4736, or 07/33-4135, fax 07/33-3142; daily 8 A.M.–5 P.M.) offers guides for CUC25 per day in Havana, CUC30 outside Havana. **Agencia San Cristóbal** (see *City Tours*) also will arrange guides.

Jineteros will offer to be your guide. Although great for showing you the offbeat scene that most tourists miss, they're usually pretty useless as sightseeing guides.

English-speaking professional tour guide **José "Pepe" Alvarez** (Lazada Norte I #182, Santa Catalina, Havana, tel. 07/41-1209, fax 07/33-3921, americuba@yahoo.com) is recommended for walking and other tours. He charges from CUC25 per day for one person to CUC15 per person for larger groups.

Getting Away

DEPARTING CUBA
By Air

Airlines serving Havana have flights that usually depart Havana on the same days they arrive.

Cubana (Calle 23 #64, e/ P y Infanta, Vedado, tel. 07/33-4446, 33-4447, 33-4448, or 33-4449, www.cubana.cu; Mon.–Fri. 8:30 A.M.–4 P.M., Sat. 8 A.M.–1 P.M.) has a fully computerized reservation system. Cubana also has a sales office in Miramar (Calle 110, esq. 5ta, tel. 07/202-9367; Mon.–Fri. 8:30 A.M.–4 P.M.).

See *Getting Away* in the *Essentials* chapter for caveats and details.

José Martí International Airport

The airport, at Wajay, 25 kilometers southwest of downtown Havana, is accessed by Avenida de la Independencia (Avenida Rancho Boyeros). Make sure you arrive at the correct terminal for your departure (see *Arriving in Havana* in the *Getting There* section).

U.S.-bound charter flights depart **Terminal Two** (Terminal Nacional, tel. 07/33-5577), on the north side of the runway.

Terminal Three (switchboard tel. 07/206-4644 or 07/33-5753; tel. 07/33-5666 for flight information), about one kilometer west of Terminal Two, handles all international flights. The departure tax (CUC25) must be paid at a separate counter after you've checked in with the airline. The foreign exchange bank refuses to accept Cuban pesos, so you should spend these in Havana (or give them to a needy Cuban) before leaving for the airport.

Terminal Five (also called Terminal Caribbean), about three kilometers west of the international terminal, at the northwest corner of the airport, handles small-plane flights (mostly domestic) offered by Aero Caribbean.

GETTING TO THE AIRPORT

No buses serve the international terminals. A tourist taxi to the airport will cost about CUC12–20 from Havana. A Lada Panataxi should cost no more than CUC5 using the meter.

A green-and-white bus marked Aeropuerto operates to Terminal One—the domestic terminal—from the east side of Parque Central in Habana Vieja. It's intended for Cubans only. The *cola* begins near the José Martí statue. Note that there are two lines: one for people wishing to be seated (*sentados*) and one for those willing to stand (*de pie*). The journey costs one peso, takes about one hour, and is very unreliable (departures are about every two hours). You can also catch Ómnibus #480 or Metrobus M2 from the west side of Parque de la Fraternidad (you can also get on the M2 near the University of Havana on Avenida Salvador Allende). Both go to Santiago de las Vegas via the domestic terminal (Terminal One), but will let you off about 400 yards east of Terminal Two.

EXPLORING BEYOND HAVANA

Special buses and trains serve foreigners. All other public transport out of Havana is usually booked solid weeks in advance; make your reservations as far ahead as possible.

By Air

Cubana (Calle 23 #64, e/ P y Infanta, Vedado, tel. 07/33-4446, 33-4447, 33-4448, or 33-4449, www.cubana.cu; Mon.–Fri. 8:30 A.M.–4 P.M., Sat. 8 A.M.–1 P.M.) and several other poorly managed Cuban carriers offer service to all major Cuban cities. (Cuban nationals need to purchase their Cubana tickets at Infanta, esq. Humboldt, Havana, tel. 07/33-4949.)

Most domestic flights leave from José Martí International Airport's **Terminal One** (Av. Van Troi, off Av. Rancho Boyeros, tel. 07/33-5753 or 07/33-5777; tel. 07/33-5576 for flight information).

AeroGaviota (Av. 47 #2814, e/ 28 y 34, Rpto. Kohly, tel. 07/203-0668) flights depart from Aeropuerto Baracao, on the Autopista Habana–Mariel, about three kilometers west of Marina Hemingway.

By Bus

Tourist Buses: Modern **Víazul** (Av. 26, esq. Zoológico, Nuevo Vedado, tel. 07/881-1413, fax 07/66-6092, www.viazul.cu; 7 A.M.–9 P.M.) buses serve provincial capitals and major tourist destinations throughout the country. They depart Terminal Víazul; city bus #27 connects the Víazul terminal to Vedado and Centro Habana. The buses make a 10-minute stop at the public bus terminal (see below), where you can also buy a ticket just prior to the bus's arrival. Terminal Víazul has a café and free luggage storage. Children travel at half price. See the *Víazul Bus Schedule* sidebar in the *Essentials* chapter for departures.

Cuban tour agencies such as Havanatur and Veracuba offer transfer seats on tour buses serving key tourist destinations. Check with tour desks in hotel lobbies.

Public Buses: Astro buses to destinations throughout the country leave from the **Terminal de Ómnibuses Nacionales** (Av. Independencia #101, esq. 19 de Mayo), two blocks north of Plaza de la Revolución. The terminal is served by local bus #47 from the Prado (at Ánimas) in Habana Vieja; by bus #265 from the east side of Parque Central; and by buses #67 and 84 from La Rampa in Vedado. Facilities include a bank, snack bars, and an information booth (tel. 07/870-9401).

Foreigners pay in dollars (*especial* fares are about 20 percent less than Víazul) and receive preferential seating. The ticket office (*venta de boletines,* tel. 07/870-3397; daily 7 A.M.–9 P.M.) is to the right of the entrance and has an air-conditioned lounge. The ticket agent will most likely not sell you a ticket until your specific bus departure is confirmed. Only one-way tickets are available. The following fares apply: Baracoa CUC43.50 *regular,* CUC53 *especial,* Bayamo CUC30/36, Camagüey CUC22.50/27, Cárdenas CUC6/7, Cayo Coco CUC44 *regular,* Ciego de Ávila CUC18.50/22, Cienfuegos CUC14/17, Guantánamo CUC38/46, Holguín CUC30/36, Las Tunas CUC27/33, Manzanillo CUC32.50/39, Matanzas CUC4/5, Morón CUC19.50/24, Pinar del Río CUC7/8, Playa Girón CUC10.50/13, Remedios CUC14/17, Sancti Spíritus CUC15.50/19, Santa Clara CUC12/15, Santiago de Cuba CUC35/42, Trinidad CUC17/21, Varadero CUC5.50/6, and Viñales CUC8/10.

Foreign residents in Cuba, including students, with appropriate ID can travel like Cubans for pesos. Make your reservation as early as possible, either at the bus terminal or at the **Agencia Reservaciones de Pasaje** (Factor y Tulipán, Nuevo Vedado, tel. 07/881-5931 or 07/55-5537). Your name will be scrawled on a decrepit pile of parchment and added to the scores of names ahead of you.

If you don't have a reservation or miss your departure, you can try getting on the standby list (*lista de espera*) at **Terminal La Coubre** (Av. del Puerto y Egido, tel. 07/872-3726), in southwest Habana Vieja. Interprovincial buses that have unfilled seats call in here after departing the Terminal de Ómnibus Nacionales to pick up folks on the standby list. The *lista de espera* service is at the western end of the terminal.

Buses to towns throughout Havana Province depart from Calle Apodaca, e/ Agramonte y Avenida de Bélgica.

By Train

See *By Train* in the *Getting Around* section of the *Essentials* chapter for general details on rail service in Cuba. Also see the sidebar *Train Schedules and Fares* in the *Essentials* chapter.

Estación Central de Ferrocarril: The most important station is the Central Railway Station (Egido, esq. Arsenal, Habana Vieja, tel. 07/861-4259 or 861-3047). Trains depart here for major cities.

FerroCuba (Arsenal, e/ Cienfuegos y Apontes, tel. 07/861-4259; daily 8 A.M.–8 P.M.), on the north side of the station, handles ticket sales and reservations for foreigners, who pay in dollars for a guaranteed seat. At last visit, the office was closed, however, and tickets were being sold at the dysfunctional **Terminal La Coubre** (Av. del Puerto, tel. 07/862-1012), 100 meters south of the main railway station at *taquilla* #3. Tickets can be purchased up to 30 minutes prior to departure, but you must purchase your ticket before 8 P.M. for a night-time departure. You may be able to buy tickets in pesos in the main station, but you'll usually need to book days, or weeks, in advance. Terminal La Coubre offers service to Cienfuegos and Matanzas.

Estación 19 de Noviembre: See *By Train,* in the *Getting Around* section in this chapter.

Estación Casablanca: The famous "Hershey Train" operates to Matanzas from Casablanca's harborfront station (tel. 07/862-4888) on the north side of Havana harbor. (See the sidebar *A Sugar of a Journey* in the *Matanzas* chapter.)

By Taxi

Most taxi companies offer chauffeured taxi excursions by car or minivan within a 150-mile radius of Havana. However, touring far from Havana by taxi can be inordinately expensive unless several people are sharing the cost. Typical round-trip prices are: to Varadero CUC180, Bay of Pigs CUC320, and Viñales CUC250. Hourly rates for a chauffeured taxi are on a sliding scale, from about CUC15 the first hour (20-km limit) to CUC80 for eight hours (125-km limit), typically with CUC0.80 per kilometer for extra distance.

Far cheaper is **Cubataxi** (tel. 07/870-1326 or 879-0443), which offers service by Lada. Taxis depart from next to the bus station at 19 de Mayo, esq. Avenida Independencia, in Plaza de la Revolución. Typical fares (at CUC0.35 per km) are Cienfuegos CUC90, Pinar del

Río CUC55, Santa Clara CUC75, Trinidad CUC100, and Varadero CUC45.

Freelance Cabs: Penny-pinchers might try finding a *colectivo* taxi near the central railway. *Colectivo* drivers are officially banned from taking foreigners, but with luck you might find someone willing to take you.

By Rental Car

Most tourist hotels have car rental outlets, and there is no shortage of stand-alone rental outlets. See the *Getting Around* section of the *Essentials* chapter for details, including for fly-drive packages and campervans.

If your budget extends to it, by far the preferred company is **Rex** (reservations tel. 07/683-0303, www.rex-rentacar.com), with offices at Avenida Rancho Boyeros y Calzada de Bejucal, Plaza de la Revolución (tel 07/683-0303); Avenida 194, e/ 15 y 17, Siboney (tel. 07/273-9166); Hotel Tryp Habana Libre (tel. 07/830-5919); Hotel Copacabana (tel. 07/202-7684); and at the cruise terminal (tel. 07/862-6343).

Organized Tours and Excursions

You can book excursions and tours at the tour desk in the lobby of virtually any tourist hotel; also see the *Cuban Tour Operators* sidebar in the *Essentials* chapter.

Belgian-owned **Transnico** (Lonja del Comercio #6D, Habana Vieja, tel. 07/66-9954, fax 07/66-9908, www.transnico.com) specializes in special-interest tours, including bicycle tours, music and dance programs, and train trips.

GREATER HAVANA AND HAVANA PROVINCE

Encircling Havana's heartland is a freeway, the *circunvalación,* beyond which the suburban residential districts gradually merge into the countryside. Suburban Havana has many sights that lure Cuban families (at least those with cars and the money for gas) for day trips on weekends, although few tourists venture this far afield, and fewer still to the outlying eponymous province, which extends 65 kilometers east and west and 40 kilometers south of Havana's city limits. The most popular site, and a must-see, is the Museo Ernest Hemingway, in the bucolic hilltop community of San Francisco de Paula.

Suburban Havana is ringed with small time-worn colonial towns such as San Antonio de los Baños and Artemisa that seem trapped in a centenary time-warp and give a good foretaste of what much of provincial Cuba still looks like. Think of oxen drawing rumbling carts through dusty streets, some still cobbled, lined with simple dwellings with wooden colonnades and red-tile roofs (or even thatch) and walls of wattle-and-daub and you have the picture. Most of Havana province is agricultural, especially the low-lying southern plain, whose rich red soils feed fruit trees and vegetables. This southern half of the province is the bread basket of the city and visually appears to be the wealthiest region in Cuba, as reflected in the many relatively well-maintained homes of local farmers. The southern shore, however, is a soggy no-man's-land of swamp and mangroves, where lowly fishing villages are among the most deprived and down at the heels in Cuba. No road runs along the southern shore

© CHRISTOPHER P. BAKER

GREATER HAVANA

HIGHLIGHTS

◖ **Santuario de San Lázaro:** This national shrine and pilgrimage site is best visited on the 17th of each month and especially on December 17th for the Procession of the Miracles, when thousands of pilgrims come to beseech favors of San Lázaro (page 199).

◖ **ExpoCuba:** This exhibition center provides a tangible expression of Cuba's achievements in the arts, culture, science, and technology (page 203).

◖ **Museo Ernest Hemingway:** "Papa's" former home is preserved as it was on the day

he died. His sportfishing boat, the *Pilar,* stands in the grounds (page 209).

◖ **Iglesia de Santa María del Rosario:** The sleepy colonial village of Santa María del Rosario boasts this simple historic church with priceless murals and an exquisite gilt baroque altar (page 212).

◖ **Playas del Este:** Gorgeous palm-shaded beaches and turquoise seas can be found within a 30-minute drive of downtown Havana (page 216).

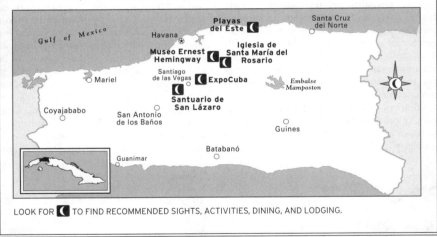

LOOK FOR ◖ TO FIND RECOMMENDED SIGHTS, ACTIVITIES, DINING, AND LODGING.

and I can think of no reason to send you there, other than to the sole coastal township of Batabanó, from where the ferries depart for Isla de la Juventud.

The northern shore east of Havana is another matter. Within a 40-minute drive of downtown Havana, white beaches unfold beneath the shade of coconut palms. Shelving into turquoise waters, these stunning sands lure *habaneros* in droves on weekend, when the music cranks up, spontaneous games of volleyball break out, and many a new romance is formed. Most foreign visitors who spend time in Havana yet seek some beach time tend to head to well-known Varadero, but the beaches of Havana's Playas del Este are nicer, have most of the water sports and services one could need, and benefit from being accessible to ordinary Cubans. En route from Havana city, you'll pass through the district of La Habana del Este, extending east for some 30 kilometers along the shore as far as the Playas del Este and exclusively comprising dreary high-rise postrevolutionary urban enclaves, most famously the urban blight of Alamar.

Inland much of the northern province is hilly and pocked with reservoirs that supply fresh water to *habaneros*. The Escaleras de Jaruco, southeast of the city inland of Playas del Este, is a woodsy bucolic retreat appealing to hikers and popular as a picnic spot for city-folk with wheels. These hills, and those of the Sierra de Camarones, further east, are quite dramatic, with deep canyons and sheer-faced knolls reminiscent of the *mogotes* of world-renowned Valle del Viñales, in Pinar del Río Province. As yet they are untapped for tourism, despite their unique beauty, and exploring along dusty rural roads that cut through these valleys is one of the pleasures of day excursions through Havana Province.

PLANNING YOUR TIME

Fortunately, most of the sites of interest in this region lie close to the city, with shining stars diminishing in number and brilliance with distance. The main sights can be broken into a two-day excursion, with day one concentrating on the neighboring districts of Boyeros and Arroyo Naranjo to the southwest; and a second combining the district of Cotorro and the beaches, southeast and east of Havana. A third day will suffice for exploring the more distant colonial villages.

Though buses run to most villages, few of the stand-alone sites are served by public transport which, in any event, is fickle and often overcrowded. For exploring, you'll need wheels. Scooters are available for hire at Playas del Este and prove perfect for whizzing around (basically, the five miles of beaches are linked by a single road), but should not be hired to get you to and from the city—the roads are far too congested, fast, and dangerous. Hire a taxi or your own rental car.

West of Havana, the coast is visually of little interest, although scuba divers might head to Playa Baracoa, where scuba diving is offered at the run-down hotel of Villa Cocomar.

To experience old-time village life in the 21st century, follow the Carretera Central westward (take Avenida 51 from Marianao) through a string of yesteryear townships: Bauta, Caimito, Guanajay, and Artemisa, where a side trip to Antiguo Cafetal Angerona may interest anyone wishing to see plantation ruins that clearly recall the epoch of slavery. Before arriving at Bauta, a turn-off to the village of El Cano provides an entrée to a lifestyle that has changed little in recent times; many local inhabitants still make pottery in age-old tradition.

In the district of Boyeros, the timeless hamlet of Rincón is the setting for **Santuario de San Lázaro,** an important pilgrimage site. A visit here can be combined with the nearby Mausoleo Antonio Maceo, where the mulatto hero general of the Wars of Independence is buried, near where he fell outside the village of Santiago de las Vegas. A short distance east (but unimaginably hard to reach directly, due to convoluted roads and poor signage), in the Arroyo Naranjo district, are a quartet of attractions for anyone with a specialist interest. If you have children in tow, plan a visit to Parque

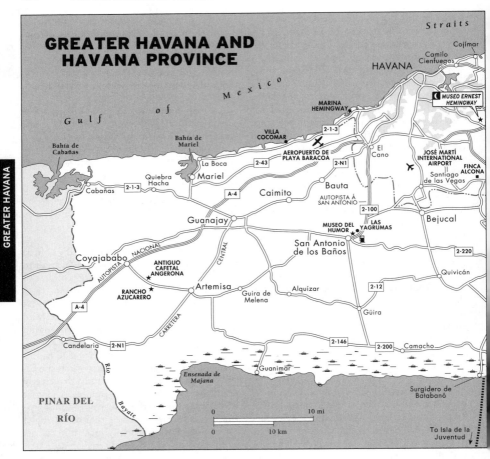

Zoológico, a second-rate zoo but with all the elephants, lions, monkeys, and serpents you and your kids could ever hope to see; and Parque Lenin, a vast park with a small amusement park, horseback rides, boating, and more. A regular excursion for Cuban schoolkids is **ExpoCuba,** a permanent expo touting Cuban achievements in every field. A good two hours or more is required to do it justice. A commuter train from Havana will deliver you there, and enthusiasts of botany can also take it to visit the botanic garden, Jardín Botánico Nacional, across the street

from ExpoCuba. However, the sprawling garden is too vast to explore on foot, and arriving and touring by car is recommended.

A pilgrimage to Ernest Hemingway's former home, Finca Vigía, is an absolute must for anyone spending time in Havana. Now the **Museo Ernest Hemingway,** it is best combined with a visit to the seaside village of Cojímar, with its bust of Hemingway, its tiny fortress, and La Terraza restaurant, once frequented by "Papa" and serving excellent seafood dishes and cocktails. When visiting the museum, however, be sure to journey the

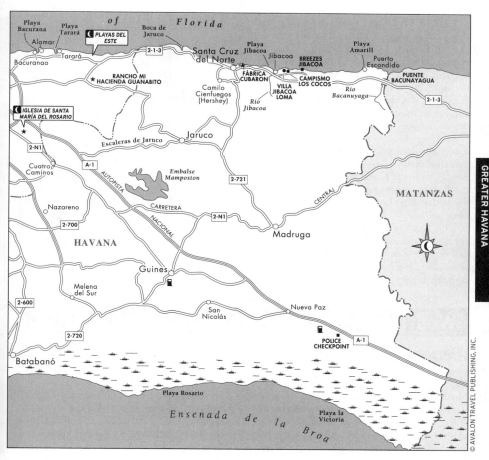

extra five miles to Santa María del Rosario to admire one of the prettiest churches in Cuba, **Iglesia de Santa María del Rosario.**

Beach lovers will want to head east along the coast highway that leads past the eyesore high-rise communities of Alamar and Celimar. Immediately beyond begin the beaches of **Playas del Este.** Unless you want to mingle with a young Cuban crowd, skip the first beach, Bacuranao, in favor of Tarará, which has fantastic sands and good facilities, including restaurants, bars, and water sports. One look at Tarará is enough to make any-

one add an additional day to his or her stay at the beaches of Playas del Este. Eastward, the contiguous beaches of Playa Mégano and Santa María del Mar are lively with Cubans on weekends, though the police presence is significant and Cubans here like to keep to themselves for that reason. Playas del Este has numerous hotels, although they are mostly desultory and I much prefer overnighting in Havana, with day-time forays out to the beach. The last of the Playas del Este is Guanabo, backed by a Cuban village where *casas particulares* are offered.

Beyond Playas del Este, the coast road winds over rugged hills and descends via the industrial port town of Santa Cruz del Norte, with a rum factory (not open to view). Nearby, inland, the small town of Hershey is the decaying setting for a now-closed sugar factory and township founded by the Hershey chocolate company. A short distance beyond, a side road leads off the highway to Playa Jibacoa, a beautiful beach with simple *cabinas* or the option of a relatively ritzy all-inclusive resort. This coastal drive is worth it not least for the fantastic views offered from the Puente Bacunayagua, spanning an eponymous river that is the boundary with Matanzas Province.

The beach resorts have bars and grills serving food, but elsewhere finding food can be a challenge. If you plan on a full day of touring, it pays to plan ahead by stocking up with snacks.

The Monumento Ernest Hemingway in Cojímar features a bronze bust made from items donated by local fishermen.

Western Havana Province

HAVANA TO MARIEL

Beyond Marina Hemingway, you leave Havana behind as Avenida 5ta becomes the coast road (route 2-1-3) to Pinar del Río Province. The shore is unremarkable, except for **Playa Baracoa,** about 16 kilometers west of Havana and popular on hot weekends with Cubans. Some five kilometers further west, the rather dull **Playa Salado** is the setting for a go-kart race track and scuba diving center at Villa Cocomar.

About 45 kilometers beyond the marina, you arrive at **Mariel.** This port city (pop. 29,000), founded in 1792 deep inside a flask-shaped bay, is best known as the site of the famous "boatlift" in April 1980, when 120,000 Cubans departed the island and sailed away to Florida. It's a small and sleepy town despite its polluted port status. Mariel is ringed by docks and factories, including a cement factory that casts a pall of dust over everything for kilometers around. The **Museo Histórico** (Calle 132 #6926, tel.

063/92554), opposite the church, tells of the city's development, but isn't worth making a stop in its own right.

The Moorish-inspired building atop the hill on the outskirts north of town is a vision of beau geste (it's a military zone, and off limits).

Beyond Mariel, Route 2-1-3 continues west to **Cabañas,** beyond which you pass into Pinar del Río Province. It's a stunning drive as you pass through quintessentially Cuban landscapes, with distant *centrales* belching out black smoke above sensuously rolling green hills of cane, the Sierra del Rosario off to the south, and glimpses of the sea glowing in kaleidoscopic blues.

Buses depart and drop off at Calle 71 (tel. 063/92104).

Accommodations and Food

The run-down **Villa Cocomar** (Carretera Panamericano, Km 23.5, tel./fax 07/205-88090, fax 07/205-8889; CUC29 s, CUC36 d low season; CUC32 s, CUC42 d high season), at Playa Salado, has 47 air-conditioned *cabinas* and a scuba diving center, but unless you're a serious diver it is best avoided. (Cubanacán.)

THE CARRETERA CENTRAL

The old Carretera Central—route 2-N1— was the main thoroughfare to Pinar del Río before the Autopista was built. To get there, take Avenida 51 from Marianao to La Lisa and follow the signs. Many of the province's most atmospheric colonial towns line the route, good for a day's foray from Havana. The journey will take you through **Bauta;** nearby **Caimito,** with an attractive ocher-colored colonial-era church fronted by an intriguing mural displaying a fierce bald eagle painted in the Stars and Stripes voraciously attacking a noble Cuban Indian and peasant; and **Guanajay,** with the baroque Teatro Vicente Mora on the town square. South of Guanajay, midway to Artemisa, there's a restored remnant of the **Trocha Mariel-Majana,** a 19th-century fortification built by the Spanish to forestall the Army of Liberation during the Wars of Independence.

EL CANO

This small village, two kilometers east of the Carretera Central, on Havana's southwestern outskirts, was founded in 1723 and has retained elements of its historic charm. Immigrants from the Canary Islands and Majorca brought a tradition of pottery making. Their descendants are still known as skilled potters (*alfareros*), who use local red clays shaped on foot-operated wheels and fired in traditional wood-fired kilns.

ARTEMISA

Artemisa (pop. 35,000), 60 kilometers southwest of Havana, dates from the early 19th century and has a wide main street lined by neoclassical houses fronted with verandas supported by Doric and Ionic columns. The cubist **Mausoleo a las Mártires** (Av. 28 de Enero; Tues.–Sat. 8 A.M.–5 P.M., Sun. 8 A.M.–noon; CUC1) honors 28 Artemisa rebels who participated in the attack on the Moncada bar-

racks in Santiago in 1953; fourteen were killed in the assault or were later tortured to death in captivity and are buried beneath the cube, which features brass bas-reliefs.

Rancho Azucarero

This 2,200-hectare ranch, which serves as Cuba's main horse-breeding and equestrian center, is stocked safari-style with animals— antelopes, wildebeest, zebras, etc.—imported from Africa in the 1970s for the hunting pleasure of Communist bigwigs. Today the facility breeds English purebred horses for international competition. It is slated to become the Havana Polo Club and horse-racing track. Plans call for a golf course, African-style lodge and an equestrian center. Tour agencies in Havana offer excursions for horseback rides.

Antiguo Cafetal Angerona

Cafetal Angerona, five kilometers west of Artemisa, midway to Cayajabos, was founded as a coffee (and, later, sugar) plantation in 1813 by Cornelio Sauchay, who kept almost 500 slaves. It went out of business about 1910 and is now a national monument, albeit in ruins. Novelist James Michener used the site as the setting for his sugar plantation in his novel *The Caribbean.* Following a stream, Michener records in *Six Days in Havana,* how "it was when I climbed out of the cisterns and onto the plateau above that I came upon the salient fact of this great operation: the immense fenced-in area in which the slaves were kept, an area so vast that five or six football fields could have been fitted in. … The mournful place, called a *barracón,* had only one gate, beside which rose a tall stone tower in which men with guns waited day and night for any sign of incipient rebellion."

The watchtower and huge cisterns are still intact. There's no entrance fee, but you should tip any guide.

Getting There

Bus #215 operates from Havana's main bus terminal and runs to Artemisa's **Terminal de**

GREATER HAVANA

Ómnibus (Carretera Central, at Km 58, tel. 063/36-3527). Trains depart Estación Tulipán in Havana at 6 P.M. for Artemisa, where the station is on Avenida Héroes del Moncada, five blocks west of the main plaza (CUC2.20); return trains depart for Havana at 5:30 A.M.

Southwestern Suburbs

SANTIAGO DE LAS VEGAS

This colonial-era rural town in the midst of the country, 20 kilometers south of Havana, is accessed via Avenida de la Independencia, a fast-paced highway that runs south through the industrial area of Rancho Boyeros to the José Martí International Airport, beyond which it becomes Avenida de los Mártires before entering Santiago de las Vegas.

The *circunvalación*—a poorly maintained four-lane freeway—leads east from Avenida de la Independencia, encircles Havana, and connects with the coast road to Playas del Este.

Mausoleo de General Antonio Maceo Grajales

Avenida de los Mártires rises south of San-tiago de las Vegas, passes through pine forests, and deposits you at El Cacahual. Here, Antonio Maceo Grajales (1845–96), the black general and hero of the Wars of Independence (see the sidebar *Heroes of the Wars of Independence* in the *Background* chapter), slumbers in a mausoleum in a circular park the size of a football field. The mausoleum also contains the tomb of Capitán Ayudante (Captain-Adjutant) Francisco Gómez Toro (1876–96), General Máximo Gómez's son, who gave his life alongside Maceo at the Battle of San Pedro on December 7, 1896. The granite tombs are engraved in the style of Mexican artist Diego Rivera. The park forms a giant traffic circle, on the east side of which stands a monument in bronze to

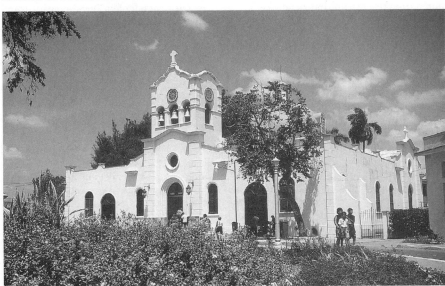

The Iglesia de San Lázaro draws pilgrims who come to request a miracle of the patron saint.

© CHRISTOPHER P. BAKER

MUNICIPALITIES OF HAVANA

© AVALON TRAVEL PUBLISHING, INC.

Coronel (Colonel) Juan Delgado, chief of the Santiago de las Vegas regiment, who recovered Maceo's body.

The tiny main square in Santiago de las Vegas is pinned by the **Monumento a Juan Delgado Gonzáles,** a marble statue of the local hero.

◖ Santuario de San Lázaro

Cuba's most important pilgrimage site is the Sanctuary of San Lázaro (Carretera de San Antonio de los Baños, tel. 0683/2396; daily 7 A.M.–6 P.M.; free), on the west side of Rincón, a rustic hamlet about four kilometers southwest of Santiago de las Vegas. Every day, the church, **Iglesia de San Lázaro,** is busy with mendicants come to have their children baptized while others fill bottles with holy water from a fountain behind the church. Behind the church is a leprosy and AIDS sanatorium, **Los Cocos,** Cuba's first sanatorium built to house patients infected with HIV.

San Lázaro is the patron saint of the sick, and is an immensely popular figure throughout Cuba (in *santería,* his avatar is Babalú Ayé). His symbol is the crutch. His stooped figure is usually covered in sores, and in effigy he goes about attended by his two dogs. Limbless beggars and other unfortunates crowd at the gates and plead for a charitable donation.

A procession to the sanctuary takes place the 17th of each month. The annual **Procesión de los Milagros** (Procession of the Miracles) takes place December 17, drawing thousands of pilgrims to beseech or give thanks to the saint for miracles they imagine he has the power to grant. The villagers of Rincón do a thriving business selling votive candles and flowers to churchgoers. Penitents crawl on their backs and knees, and others walk in front of them and sweep the road ahead with palm fronds.

Getting There: If driving, follow Carretera al Rincón, which begins at the bus station on the southwest edge of Santiago de las Vegas; bus #476 also runs from here.

A three-car train for San Antonio de los Baños departs Havana's Estación 19 de Noviembre (Tulipán) at 10:05 A.M. and 4:25 and 8:30 P.M., stopping at Rincón (CUC1). Trains run continuously on December 17.

Food

The **Tabernita** (Av. de los Mártires, tel.

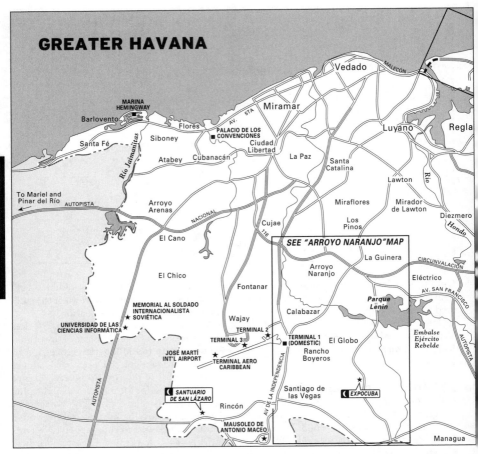

GREATER HAVANA

07/683-2033), a thatched restaurant about one kilometer south of Santiago de las Vegas, serves *criollo* fare and is popular with Cuban families on weekends.

Getting There and Away
Bus M2 runs from Parque de la Fraternidad in Havana to Santiago de las Vegas. Ómnibus #480 also serves Santiago de las Vegas from Havana's main bus terminal (Av. Independencia #101, Plaza de la Revolución, tel. 07/870-3397). The **Terminal de Ómnibus** (Calle al Rincón #43, tel. 07/683-3159) is on the southwest side

of town, on the road to Rincón; you can catch a taxi here to El Cacahual.

ARROYO NARANJO
This *municipio* lies east of Boyeros and due south of Havana.

Parque Zoológico Nacional
Cuba's national zoo, on Avenida Zoo–Lenin (Av. 8, esq. Av. Soto, tel. 07/44-7613, Wed.–Sun. 9:30 A.M.–3:30 P.M.; adults CUC3, children CUC2, vehicles CUC5), southeast of the village of Arroyo Naranjo, about 16 kilome-

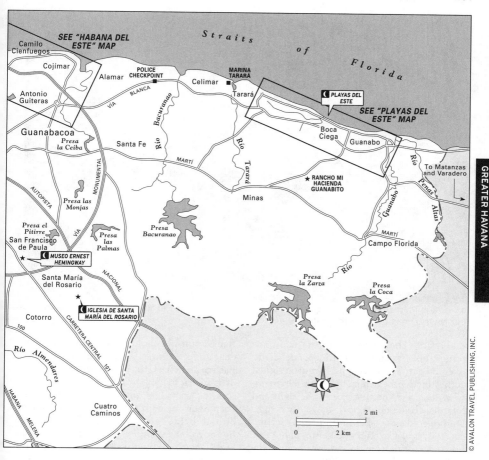

GREATER HAVANA

ters south of central Havana, covers 340 hectares and contains about 1,000 animals and more than 100 species. You can drive your own car through the park. A walk-through section houses a leopard, tiger, chimps, monkeys, and birds, but the cages are small and bare, many of the animals look woefully neglected, and the conditions are deplorable. The zoo also reproduces more than 30 endangered species and includes a taxidermist's laboratory. A children's area provides pony rides.

Tour buses (40 centavos) depart the parking lot about every 30 minutes and run through the African wildlife park—*pradera africana*—taking you through an expansive area not unlike the savanna of east Africa. Elephants come to the bus and stick their trunks in through the window to glean tidbits. There are rhinos, zebra, wildebeests, ostriches, and hippos, which spend most of their daylight hours wallowing in a deep pool. The bus tours also loops through the *foso de leones*—a deep quarry on the north side of the park. Here you can also sit atop the cliff on a viewing platform and look down upon the lions.

© CHRISTOPHER P. BAKER

a thrilling moment for visitors to the Pradera Africana, in the Parque Zoológico, as elephants put their trunks through the tour bus window

Getting There: To get to the main entrance, take Avenida de la Independencia to Avenida San Francisco (the Parque is signed at the junction) which merges with the *circunvalación*. Take the first exit to the right and follow Calzada de Bejucal south. Turn right onto Avenida Zoo–Lenin (signed). A second entrance is at Carretera de Vento, about one kilometer south from the *circunvalación*—the turnoff from the latter is 200 meters east of Avenida de la Independencia.

Buses #31, 73, and 88 operate between La Víbora and Arroyo Naranjo. A taxi will cost about CUC12 each way.

Parque Lenin

Lenin Park (Calle 100 y Carretera de la Presa, tel. 07/44-2721; Tues.–Sun. 9 A.M.–5 P.M.), east of the zoo, was created from a former hacienda and landscaped mostly by volunteer labor from the city. The vast complex features wide rolling pastures and small lakes surrounded by forests and pockets of bamboo, ficus, and flamboyants. What Lenin Park lacks in grandeur and stateliness, it makes up for in scale. Each September 1, the park is packed for a day of special activities.

The park is laid out west of a dam, Presa Paso Sequito, with a huge reservoir—Ejército Rebelde—to the east. The park is bounded by the *circunvalación* to the north and Calzada de Bejucal to the west; there is an entrance off Calzada de Bejucal. A second road—Calle Cortina de la Presa—enters from the *circunvalación,* runs down the center of the park, and is linked to Calzada de Bejucal by a loop road.

Sights, Galleries, and Museums: The **Galería del Arte Amelia Peláez,** at the south end of Cortina, displays works by the eponymous Cuban ceramist. Behind the gallery is a series of bronze busts inset in rock. A short distance to the west is the **Monumento Lenin,** a huge granite visage of the Communist leader and thinker in Soviet-realist style, carved by Soviet sculpture I. E. Kerbel. Further west, you'll pass an **aquarium** (entrance CUC1) displaying freshwater fish and turtles, including the antediluvian garfish (*manjuarí*) and a couple of Cuban crocodiles.

About 400 meters farther west is the **Monumento a Celia Sánchez.** Here, a trail follows a wide apse to a broad amphitheater lined with ferns. At its center is a bronze figure of the national heroine inset in a huge rock (see the sidebar *Revolutionary Heroes* in the *Background* chapter). A small museum honors the heroine.

Also worth a visit are the **Taller Cerámica** (ceramic workshop), on the southwest corner of the park; and, on the north side, the Palacio de Pioneros Che Guevara, displaying stainless-steel sculptures of the revolutionary hero.

Horseback Riding: An equestrian center, **Centro Ecuestre** (tel. 07/44-1058; daily 9 A.M.–5 P.M. June–Aug., Wed.–Sun. 9 A.M.–5 P.M. Sept.–July), also called Club Hípico, immediately east of the entrance off Calzada de Bejucal, offers one-hour trips (CUC15) plus riding lessons, and you can rent horses. Horseback riding is also offered at **El Rodeo** (tel. 07/57-8893), the national rodeo arena, in the southeast corner of the park. El Rodeo offers rodeo (entry costs three pesos) every Sunday, with "Rodeo Pionero" (for youth) at noon and competitive adult rodeo at 3 P.M. The "Feria de Rodeo" (National Championships) is held each August 25.

Train Rides: A narrow-gauge railway circles the park, stopping at four stages. The old steam train dates from 1870 and operates daily 10 A.M.–4 P.M. (four pesos), departing Estación Galapagos de Oro and taking 25 minutes to circle the park. Another old steam train dating from 1915 is preserved under a red-tile canopy in front of the disused **Terminal Inglesa.**

Bicycle and Rowboat Rental: You can rent aquatic bicycles and rowboats on the lake at El Rodeo (five pesos for 30 minutes).

For Children: A *parque de diversiones* located in the northwest quarter includes carousels, a miniature "big dipper," and pony rides.

Swimming Pools: There are swimming pools in the **Palacio de Pioneros Che Guevara**

and east of the community of Calabazar, on the south side of the park (five pesos).

Getting There: See Parque Zoológico, earlier in this section, for directions on getting there by car. Buses #31, 73, and 88 operate between La Víbora and the park entrance, and bus #113 runs from Marianao. A taxi will cost about CUC15 each way.

ⓒ Expocuba

ExpoCuba, on the Carretera del Globo (official address Carretera del Rocío, Km 3.5, Arroyo Naranjo, tel. 07/697-4269; Wed.–Sun. 10 A.M.–5 P.M.; closed Sept.–Dec.; CUC1), three kilometers south of Parque Lenin, houses a permanent exhibition of Cuban industry, technology, sports, and culture touting the achievements of socialism. The facility covers 588,000 square meters and is a museum, trade expo, world's fair, and entertainment hall rolled into one. It has 34 pavilions, including booths that display the crafts, products, music, and dance of each of Cuba's provinces. Railroad buffs might check out the vintage rolling stock on the entrance forecourt. There's an information office at the main entrance, plus a currency exchange and bank.

A three-car train runs to ExpoCuba from Estación 19 de Noviembre (Tulipán, Nuevo Vedado, tel. 07/881-4431; CUC1 each way) every Wednesday–Sunday at 9:35 A.M.; it departs ExpoCuba at 5:30 P.M.

Buses #88 and 113 leave for ExpoCuba from the north side of Havana's main railway station weekends at 10 A.M., noon, and 3 P.M., and from Havana's Terminal de Ómnibus at 9 A.M., 11 A.M., and 4 P.M. Bus #80 also serves the park from Lawton.

Jardín Botánico Nacional

This 600-hectare botanical garden (Carretera del Rocío Km 3.5, Arroyo Naranjo, tel. 07/54-9864, www.uh.cu/centros/jbn; daily 9 A.M.–4 P.M.; entrance CUC1, guide CUC2), directly opposite ExpoCuba, doesn't have the fine-trimmed herbaceous borders of Kew or Butchart, but nonetheless is worth the drive for enthusiasts. Thirty-five kilometers of roads

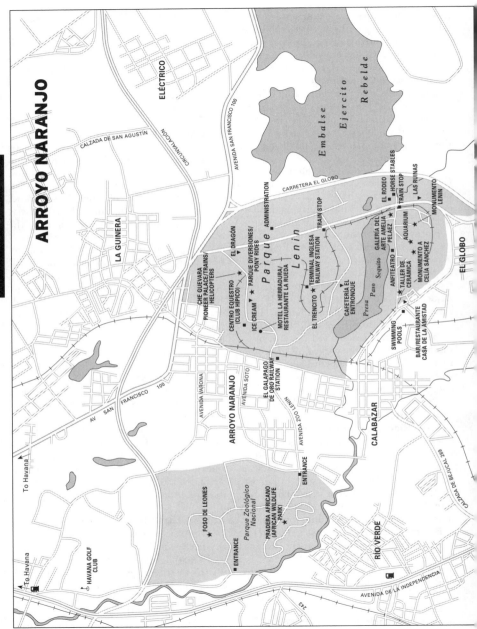

GREATER HAVANA

ARROYO NARANJO

ELÉCTRICO

CALZADA DE SAN AGUSTÍN

CIRCUNVALACIÓN

AVENIDA SAN FRANCISCO 100

Embalse

Ejercito

Rebelde

CARRETERA EL GLOBO

LA GUINERA

ADMINISTRATION

Parque

EL RODEO

HORSE STABLES

TRAIN STOP

LAS RUINAS

MONUMENTO
LENIN

EL DRAGÓN

CHE GUEVARA
PIONEER PALACE/TRAINS/
HELICOPTERS

PARQUE DIVERSIONES/
PONY RIDES

TRAIN STOP

Lenin

GALERIA DEL
ARTE AMELIA
PELAEZ

CENTRO EQUESTRO
(CLUB HIPICO)

ICE CREAM

MOTEL LA HERRADURA/
RESTAURANTE LA RUEDA

TERMINAL INGLESA
RAILWAY STATION

Seguito

AQUARIUM

EL GLOBO

EL TRENCITO

CAFETERIA EL
ENTRONQUE

Paso

ANFITEATRO

MONUMENTO A
CELIA SANCHEZ

Presa

TALLER DE
CERÁMICA

SWIMMING
POOLS

BAR/RESTAURANTE
CASA DE LA AMISTAD

AVENIDA VARONA

ARROYO NARANJO

AVENIDA SOTO

EL GALAPAGO
DE ORO RAILWAY
STATION

LENIN

AVENIDA ZOO

CALABAZAR

AV. SAN FRANCISCO 100

To Havana

FOSO DE LEONES

*Parque Zoológico
Nacional*

PRADERA AFRICANO
(AFRICAN WILDLIFE
PARK)

ENTRANCE

CALZADA DE BEJUCAL 269

To Havana

ENTRANCE

RIO VERDE

HAVANA GOLF
CLUB

To Havana

ENTRANCE

AVENIDA DE LA INDEPENDENCIA

E-3

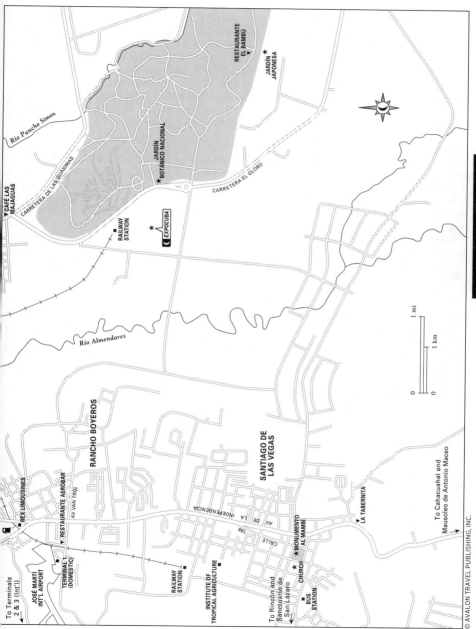

RESTAURANTE EL BAMBÚ

JARDÍN JAPONESA

Río Pancho Simon

CARRETERA DE LAS GUÁSIMAS

CAFÉ LAS MAJAGUAS

JARDÍN BOTÁNICO NACIONAL

CARRETERA EL GLOBO

EXPOCUBA

RAILWAY STATION

Río Almendares

1 mi

1 km

0

0

RANCHO BOYEROS

SANTIAGO DE LAS VEGAS

REX LIMOUSINES

RESTAURANTE AEROBAR

AV VAN TROI

To Terminals 2 & 3 (Int'l)

JOSÉ MARTÍ INT'L AIRPORT

TERMINAL (DOMESTIC)

RAILWAY STATION

INSTITUTE OF TROPICAL AGRICULTURE

AV DE LA INDEPENDENCIA

CALLE 788

788

MONUMENTO AL MAMBÍ

LA TABERNITA

To Cahacuahal and Mausoleo de Antonio Maceo

CHURCH

BUS STATION

To Rincón and Sanctuario de San Lázaro

lead through the park, which was laid out between 1969 and 1984. You can drive your own vehicle, with a guide.

The garden consists mostly of wide pastures planted with copses divided by Cuban ecosystems and by regions of the tropical world (from coastal thicket to Oriental humid forest). The geographic center contains a fascinating variety of palm trees from around the world. There is even an "archaic forest" containing species such as *Microcyca calocom,* Cuba's cork palm. The highlight is the **Jardín Japonés** (Japanese garden) landscaped with tiered cascades, fountains, and a jade-green lake full of koi. The **Invernáculo Rincón Eckman** is a massive greenhouse named after Erik Leonard Eckman (1883–1931), who documented Cuban flora between 1914 and 1924. It is laid out as a triptych: a cactus house; a room full of epiphytes, bromeliads, ferns, and insectivorous plants; and a room containing tropical mountain plants.

Club de Golf Habana

The Havana Golf Club (Carretera de Vento Km 8, Capdevila, Boyeros, tel. 07/649-8918, ext 111) is hidden east of Avenida de la Independencia in the industrial-residential area called Capdevilla, about 20 kilometers south of Havana. The "Diplo Golf Course" was opened as the Rover's Athletic Club in 1948 by the British community and maintained by the British Embassy until given to the Cuban government in 1980. Of four courses in Havana in 1959, this is the only one remaining. The nine-hole course has 18 tees positioned for play to both sides of the fairway. The course, a "woody layout" that is compared to Pinehurst in North Carolina, starts off badly, but the fifth and sixth holes are described as "well-de-signed holes that could hold their own on almost any course of the world." "Golfito" (as the locals know it) has a minimally stocked pro shop, five tennis courts, a swimming pool, and two restaurants. Membership costs CUC70 plus CUC45 monthly. A round costs nonmembers CUC20 for nine holes (CUC30 for 18). You can rent clubs for CUC10. Caddies cost CUC6.

Food

Cubans travel from Havana to dine at **₵ Las Ruinas** (Calle 100 y Cortina, tel. 07/57-8286; Tues.–Fri. noon–8 P.M., Sat.–Sun. 10 A.M.–10 P.M.) in Parque Lenin. Looking like something Frank Lloyd Wright might have conceived, it was designed in concrete and encases the ruins of an old sugar mill. It serves continental and *criollo* cuisine (lobster bellevue is a specialty, CUC20) described by readers as both "reminiscent of school dinners" and "the best in Havana." I enjoyed a tasty shrimp enchilada (CUC12).

Parque Lenin has several other basic restaurants and snack bars of mediocre quality, including **El Dragon,** serving quasi-Chinese fare.

The **₵ Restaurante El Bambú** (tel. 07/54-4106; Tues.–Sun. noon–5 P.M.), overlooking the Japanese garden in the Jardín Botánico Nacional, bills itself as an *eco-restorán* and serves vegetables—beetroot, cassava, pumpkin, spinach, taro, and more—grown right there in the garden. I recommend the *fufo* (mashed boiled banana with garlic), and eggplant cooked in cheese sauce. You're permitted free refills. Locals and foreign students with ID are charged 40 pesos for a meal; other foreigners pay CUC14 for an all-you-can-eat buffet. The restaurant is often booked solid. You can reserve a table by calling ahead.

Southern Havana Province

The landscape of southern Havana Province is intensively farmed. The area is modestly wealthy, with houses that are comfortable by Cuban standards (there are few rustic *bohíos*) and plenty of cars further hint at the regional prosperity. The southern coast is depressingly opposite and melancholic in the extreme.

A network of roads fans out south from Havana, crisscrossed by minor roads that form an unfathomable labyrinth linking small towns of mostly unpretentious appeal. The following are exceptions, worth a day's journey.

SAN ANTONIO DE LOS BAÑOS

This small town (pop. 39,000), founded in 1775 on the banks of the Río Ariguanabo, 30 kilometers southwest of Havana, is appealing, despite its ramshackle state. There is considerable charm to its tiny triangular plaza, ocher church (Calles 66 y 41), and streets lined with colonnaded arcades. The prestigious **Escuela Internacional de Cine y Televisión** (International Cinema and Television School, Carretera Villa Nueva Km 4.5, tel. 0650/38-3152), sponsored by the New Latin American Cinema Foundation, is here, presided over by the great Colombian writer Gabriel García Márquez. The school trains cinema artists from developing nations.

The town boasts a **Museo Municipal** (Calle 66 #4113, e/ 41 y 43, tel. 0650/38-2539, Tues.–Sat. 10 A.M.–6 P.M., Sun. 9 A.M.–noon; free) and a **Casa Bienal del Humor** (aka Museo del Humor, Calle 60 #4116, esq. 45, tel. 0650/38-2817; Tues.–Sat. 10 A.M.–5 P.M., Sun. 9 A.M.–1 P.M.; CUC2) in a beautiful colonial home. The humor museum opened in 1979, when the city hosted the first **Humor Bienal Internacional,** the International Humor Festival, which draws some of the best cartoonists from around the world.

A freeway—the Autopista a San Antonio—links San Antonio with Havana. Midway between the two cities, you'll pass the

Universidad de las Ciencias Informáticas, Cuba's university dedicated to making the country a world power in software technology. On the north side is the gray marble **Memorial al Soldado Internacionalista Soviético,** with an eternal flame dedicated to Soviet military personnel who died in combat.

Accommodations and Food

Hotel Las Yagrumas (Calle 40 y Final Autopista, tel. 0650/38-4460, reservas@yagrumas. isazul.tur.cu; CUC30 s, CUC40 d) overlooks the banks of the Río Ariguanabo one kilometer northeast of town on the Havana road. This colonial-style, red-tile, two-story property has 120 pleasantly decorated air-conditioned rooms with satellite TVs. It has two grills, a café, pool, tennis courts, squash courts, game room, and tour desk. Bicycle and boat rentals, plus boat excursions on the river, are offered. (Islazul.)

The hotel has a good restaurant. Otherwise head to **Tabera del Tío Cabrera** (Calle 56 #3910, e/ 39 y 41; Mon.–Fri. 2–5 P.M., Sat.–Sun. 2 P.M.–1 A.M.), serving *criollo* dishes and hosting an open-air cabaret.

Transportation

Buses serve San Antonio de los Baños from Calle Apodaca, e/ Agramonte y Avenida de Bélgica, Habana Vieja, and arrive or depart San Antonio at the **Terminal de Ómnibus** (Av. 55, tel. 0650/38-2737). Trains serve San Antonio de los Baños from the Estación Tulipán, in Nuevo Vedado, Havana, at 10:05 A.M. and 4:25 and 8:30 P.M. (CUC1.50), returning from San Antonio at 5:35 A.M. and 1:55 and 6:15 P.M.

BATABANÓ

This funky town (pop. 15,000) 51 kilometers due south of Havana was one of the original seven cities, founded in 1515 by Pánfilo de Narváez and named San Cristóbal de la Habana. The settlers lasted only four years before uprooting and establishing a new city on the

© CHRISTOPHER P. BAKER

Memorial al Soldado Internacionalista Soviético

north coast—today's Havana. Batabanó is surrounded by ugly dormitories for agricultural field hands.

About three kilometers south of Batabanó is **Surgidero de Batabanó,** a rundown place of ramshackle wooden houses, of significance only as the port town from which catamarans depart for Isla de la Juventud. There are no accommodations, so plan your arrival and departure accordingly.

Getting There and Away

A bus to Batabanó's ferry terminal departs Havana's Terminal de Ómnibus (Av. de Rancho Boyeros, esq. 19 de Mayo, Plaza de la Revolución) at 8 A.M. Buy your tickets (CUC2.10) at the kiosk marked "NCC," between gates 9 and 10, open Monday–Friday 8 A.M.–noon and Saturday 8–11 A.M. for advance sales (you pay for the catamaran journey separately in Surgidero, however). You must show your passport when buying the ticket. The journey takes 90 minutes.

A train serves Surgidero de Batabanó from Havana's Estación 19 de Noviembre (Calle Tulipán and Hidalgo, tel. 07/881-4431 or 881-3642) at 5 P.M. (CUC1.80). The return train to Havana departs Surgidero at 5:25 A.M. from the rail station at the end of Calle 68.

There's a Cupet gas station in Batabanó, at the junction of Calle 64 (the main street) and Avenida 73.

See *Getting There and Away* in the *Nueva Gerona and Vicinity* section of the *Isla de la Juventud Special Municipality* chapter for information on the catamaran and ferry service.

Southeastern Suburbs

The Carretera Central (Rt. 2-N1) runs southeast through the Havana suburbs of San Francisco de Paula and Cotorro and, beyond, the rolling hills of the **Alturas de Habana-Matanzas** via the provincial town of Madruga. It's a scenic route to the city of Matanzas.

The Autopista (Rt. A-1) also runs southeast from Havana ruler-straight to the border with Matanzas Province, where it continues as far as Sancti Spíritus. It's wide, fast, and devoid of traffic. However, watch for tractors, ox-carts, and even cattle crossing the freeway, which runs parallel to and north of the old Carretera Central (Rt. 2-N1), skirting the towns and villages that line the old road.

SAN MIGUEL DEL PADRÓN

The *municipio* of San Miguel del Padrón, which extends southeast of Habana Vieja, is mostly residential, with ugly modern factory areas in the lowlands by the harbor and timeworn colonial housing on the hills south of town.

The region is accessed from the Vía Blanca or (parallel to it) Calzada de Luyano via the Carretera Central (Calzada de Güines), which ascends to the quintessential colonial village of San Francisco de Paula, on the city's outskirts, 12.5 kilometers south of Habana Vieja.

En route, you pass through the suburb of Luyano, where Cubans come to throw coins (the money goes to pay for the indigent) into the **Fuente de la Virgen del Camino** (Virgin of the Way), a fountain by acclaimed sculptor Rita Longa at the junction of Calzada de Luyano and Carretera Central. Two blocks east is the **Monumento a Doña Leonor Pérez** (Balear, esq. Leonor Pérez), dedicated to José Martí's mother. The patinated bronze figure sits in a dignified pose atop a marble pedestal. Bas-reliefs depict key moments in Martí's life.

◖ Museo Ernest Hemingway

In 1939, Hemingway's third wife, Martha Gellhorn, saw and was struck by Finca Vigía (Vigía y Steinhart, tel. 07/91-0809, mushem@cubart.cult.cu; Wed.–Sun. 9 A.M.–4:30 P.M.; entrance CUC2, rainy days CUC1, guided tours CUC1, cameras CUC5), Lookout Farm, a one-story Spanish-colonial house built in 1887 and boasting a wonderful view of Havana. They rented it for US$100 a month. When Hemingway's first royalty check from *For Whom the Bell Tolls* arrived in 1940, he bought the house for US$18,500. In August 1961, his widow, Mary Welsh, was forced to sign papers handing over the home to the Castro government, along with its contents (see the sidebar *Ernest Hemingway and Cuba*). On July 21, 1994, on the 95th anniversary of Papa's birthday, Finca Vigía reopened its doors as a museum following nearly two years of repairs and remodeling. The house is preserved in suspended animation, just the way the great writer left it.

Bougainvilleas frame the gateway to the 20-acre hilltop estate. Mango trees and sumptuous jacarandas line the driveway leading up to the gleaming white house. No one is allowed inside—reasonably so, since every room can be viewed through the wide-open windows, and the temptation to pilfer priceless trinkets is thus reduced. Through the large windows, you can see trophies, firearms, bottles of spirits, old issues of *The Field, Spectator,* and *Sports Afield* strewn about, and more than 9,000 books and magazines, arranged the way he supposedly liked them, with no concern for authors or subjects. The dining-room table is set with cut crystal, as if guests were expected.

It is eerie being followed by countless eyes—those of the guides (one to each room) and those of the beasts that had found themselves in the crosshairs of Hemingway's hunting scope. "Don't know how a writer could write surrounded by so many dead animals," Graham Greene commented when he visited. There are bulls, too, everywhere bulls, including paintings by Joan Miró and Paul Klee; photographs and posters of bullfighting scenes; and a chalk plate of a bull's head, a gift from Picasso.

ERNEST HEMINGWAY AND CUBA

Ernest Hemingway first set out from Key West to wrestle marlin in the wide streaming currents off the Cuban coast in April 1932. The blue waters of the Gulf Stream, chock-full of billfish, brought him closer and closer until eventually, "succumbing to the other charms of Cuba, different from and more difficult to explain than the big fish in September," he settled on this island of sensual charm. Hemingway loved Cuba and lived there for the better part of 20 years. Once, when Hemingway was away from Cuba, he was asked what he worried about in his sleep. "My house in Cuba," he replied, referring to Finca Vigía, in the suburb of San Francisco de Paula, 12.5 kilometers southeast of Havana.

Walking Havana's streets you can still feel Hemingway's presence. It is easy to imagine the sun-bronzed writer driving in his brand-new Chrysler New Yorker convertible, white mane and beard haloed in tropical light, hoary chest showing beneath khaki shirt, en route for his daily sugarless double daiquiri with his friends.

THE CULT OF HEMINGWAY

Havana's marina is named for the prize-winning novelist. Hemingway's room in the Hotel Ambos Mundos and his former home, Finca Vigía, are preserved as museums. And his likeness adorns T-shirts and billboards. "We admire Hemingway because he understood the Cuban people; he supported us," a friend told me. "His friends were fishermen, jai alai players, bullfighters. He never related

to high society," adds Evelio González, one of the guides at Finca Vigía.

Yet the cult of Hemingway is very real. The novelist's works are required reading in Cuban schools. His books are bestsellers. The Cuban understanding of Hemingway's "Cuban novels" is that they support a core tenet of Communist ideology – that humans are only fulfilled acting in a "socialist" context for a moral purpose, not individualistically. (Many of Hemingway's novels appear to condemn economic and political injustices.) "All the works of Hemingway are a defense of human rights," claims Castro, who knows Papa's novels in depth and once claimed that For Whom the Bell Tolls, Hemingway's fictional account of the Spanish Civil War, inspired his guerrilla tactics. Castro has said the reason he admires Hemingway so much is that he envies the adventures he had. The two headstrong fellows met only once, during the 10th Annual Ernest Hemingway Billfish Tournament in May 1960. As sponsor and judge of the competition, Hemingway invited Cuba's youthful new leader as his guest of honor. Castro was to present the winner's trophy; instead, he hooked the biggest marlin and won the prize for himself. Hemingway surrendered the trophy to a beaming Fidel. They never met again.

With the Cold War and the United States' break with Cuba, Hemingway had to choose. Not being able to return to Cuba contributed to Hemingway's depression, says his son Patrick: "He really loved Cuba, and I think it was a great shock to him at his age to have to choose

Here is where Hemingway wrote *Islands in the Stream, Across the River and into the Trees, A Moveable Feast,* and *The Old Man and the Sea.* The four-story tower next to the house was built at his fourth wife's prompting so that he could write undisturbed. Hemingway disliked the tower and continued writing amid the comings and goings of the house, surrounded by papers, shirtless, in Bermuda shorts, with any of 60 cats

at his feet as he stood barefoot on the hide of a kudu.

Hemingway's legendary cabin cruiser, the *Pilar,* is poised beneath a wooden pavilion on the former tennis court, shaded by bamboo and royal palms. Nearby are the swimming pool where Ava Gardner swam naked, and the graves of four of the novelist's favorite dogs.

Alas, the wooden home is falling apart. In 2004, a restoration was initiated, although

between his country, which was the United States, and his home, which was Cuba."

PAPA AND THE REVOLUTION

There has been a great deal of speculation about Hemingway's attitude toward the Cuban Revolution. Cuba, of course, attempts to portray him as sympathetic, not least because Hemingway's Cuban novels are full of images of prerevolutionary terror and destitution. "There is an absolutely murderous tyranny that extends over every little village in the country," he wrote in *Islands in the Stream*.

Hemingway's widow, Mary Welsh, told the journalist Luis Báez that "Hemingway was always in favor of the Revolution." Another writer, Lisandro Otero, records Hemingway as saying, "Had I been a few years younger, I would have climbed the Sierra Maestra with Fidel Castro." And Papa was away from Cuba all of 1959, but he returned in 1960, recorded *New York Times* correspondent Herbert Matthews, "to show his sympathy and support for the Castro Revolution." Papa even used his legendary 38-foot sportfishing boat, the *Pilar*, to run arms for the rebel army, claimed Gregorio Fuentes, the weatherbeaten sailor-guardian of the *Pilar* for 23 years. Welsh claims, however, to have been on board when Hemingway dumped his stash of sporting guns and ammunition into the sea so that neither side would get them.

Hemingway's enigmatic farewell comment as he departed the island in 1960 is illuminating: "*Vamos a ganar. Nosotros los cubanos vamos a ganar.* [We are going to win. We Cu-

bans are going to win.] I'm not a Yankee, you know." Before leaving Cuba, however, Hemingway expressed hope that the Revolution would not become Communist, claims writer Claudia Lightfoot. Prophetically, in *Islands in the Stream*, a character says: "The Cubans… double cross each other. They sell each other out. They got what they deserve. The hell with their revolutions."

FINCA VIGÍA'S FATE

After Hemingway's death, Finca Vigía was seized by the Castro government, though the writer had willed the property to his fourth wife, Mary Welsh. The Cuban government allowed her to remove 200 pounds of papers, but insisted that most of their home's contents remain untouched, including 3,000 letters and documents, 3,000 photographs, and 9,000 books… all kept secreted in the humid basement, where they have since been allowed to deteriorate to the point of near ruin. Only in 2002 was this invaluable resource opened to scholars.

In his will, the author left his sportfishing vessel, the *Pilar*, to Gregorio Fuentes (the former skipper couldn't afford its upkeep and it, too, became the property of the government). Meanwhile, Hemingway's sleek black 1955 Chrysler New Yorker escaped and apparently passed into the hands of Augustín Nuñez Gutiérrez, a Cuban policeman, according to writer Joann Biondi. Later, Nuñez hid the car and hopped on a raft for Miami. Popular legend says the car's whereabouts are still a mystery and that the Chrysler still awaits discovery.

the Bush administration denied U.S. preservationists a license to travel to Cuba. For more information, visit www.hemingwaypreservationfoundation.org.

Getting There: The M7 *camello* metro-bus departs from Industria, e/ Dragones y Avenida Simón Bolívar, Parque de la Fraternidad, in Habana Vieja. Bus #404 departs from Avenida de Bélgica (Monserrate) and Dragones. Both travel via San Francisco de Paula.

Paradiso: Promotora de Viajes Culturales (Calle 19 #560, esq. C, Vedado, Havana, tel. 07/832-6928, fax 07/33-3921, paradis@paradiso.artex.com.cu) offers excursions from Havana.

SANTA MARÍA DEL ROSARIO

This charming colonial village surrounded by palm-studded farmland, 20 kilometers south of Parque Central, is in the *municipio* of Cotorro, about five kilometers southeast of San

Francisco de Paula, from which it is divided by the *circunvalación.*

The village was founded in 1732 by José Bayona y Chacón, the Conde (Count) de Casa Bayona, who formed the subject of the movie *La última cena* (*The Last Supper,* 1976), by Tomás Gutiérrez Alea. The town, which was an important spa in colonial days, boasts a number of 18th- and 19th-century buildings centered on **Plaza Mayor,** the main square, fronted by the **Casa del Conde Bayona** (Calle 33 #2404, esq. 24, tel. 07/682-3510; daily noon–10 P.M.), the count's former home, comprising three adjacent structures complete with coach house. Part of the home is now occupied by a bar with snacks.

Curative waters have been tapped at **Balneario de Santa María del Rosario** (Calle 30, esq. Final, tel. 07/682-2734; Mon.–Fri. 8 A.M.–4 P.M.), a near-derelict mineral spa; it's about 400 meters southeast of the church. Behind it rises **Loma La Cruz** (Hill of the Cross), named for the large cross erected by the count to honor those killed in a slave rebellion. There is a fine view of the countryside from the hillcrest.

The **Casa de la Cultura** (Calle 33 #202, esq. 24, tel. 07/682-4259) hosts a *peña* with local musicians each Sunday at 8:30 P.M. Note the intriguing mural by the world-renowned Cuban artist Manuel Mendive, who lives in Luyano.

Getting There: Santa María is served by bus #97 from Guanabacoa, or take the M7 from Parque de la Fraternidad to Cotorro, then catch the #97.

◖ Iglesia de Santa María del Rosario

The main reason to visit the village is to view this baroque church (Calle 24, e/ 31 y 33, tel. 07/682-2183; Tues.–Sat. 8 A.M.–noon, Sun. 3:30–6 P.M.), dominating the plaza. One of the nation's finest, this national monument is colloquially called the Catedral del Campo de Cuba (Cathedral of the Fields of Cuba). The highlight is the spectacular baroque altar of cedar dripping with gold leaf, and the resplendent carved ceiling of indigo, plus four priceless art pieces by José Nicolás de Escalera. Mass is Sunday at 5 P.M.

Finca Alcona

This state-run farm 17 kilometers south of Havana, at the village of Las Guasimas, on the Carretera de Managua outside the village of Managua, raises *gallos* (cockerels) for combat and export (US$150–1,000 apiece), and hosts cockfights in the official *valla,* or ring. A grand **Feria de Gallos de Lidia** (Cockfight Fair) is held in early June. The restaurant features musicians performing popular campesino songs.

The easiest route is to take the Carretera Central to Cuatro Caminos, then turn west on the Carretera a Portugaletes for Managua, 15 kilometers west (midway to Santiago de las Vegas), then turn north and drive five kilometers to Las Guasimas. You can book an excursion through **Ecotur** (Santa Catalina y Boyeros, Havana, tel. 07/54-9855 or 07/57-7647, ecotur@teledata.get.tur.cu).

ESCALERAS DE JARUCO

These rolling hills rising east of the Autopista are popular among *habaneros* escaping the heat for walks and horseback rides. The hills are composed of limestone terraces denuded in places into rugged karst formations laced with caves. Take the turnoff for **Tapaste** from the Autopista, about 15 kilometers east of Havana.

Parque Escaleras de Jaruco (tel. 64/32665) is six kilometers west of Jaruco village and makes a scenic day trip, especially if you return via Playas del Este. It has basic cabins, a simple restaurant, a bar situated in a natural cavern, plus swimming pool and horseback riding and draws Cubans for weekend visits.

Habana del Este and Beyond

Beyond the tunnel under Havana harbor, you pass through a heavily policed toll booth (no toll is charged), beyond which the six-lane Vía Monumental freeway leads east to modern Ciudad Panamericano and, immediately beyond, the time-worn fishing village of Cojímar.

CIUDAD PANAMERICANO AND COJÍMAR

Ciudad Panamericano, three kilometers east of Havana, dates from the 1991 Pan-American Games when a high-rise village was built in hurried, jerry-rigged style to accommodate the athletes, spectators, and press. Several massive sports stadiums rise to each side of the Vía Monumental, most significantly the 55,000-seat **Estadio Panamericano** (Vía Monumental Km 4, Ciudad Panamericano, tel. 07/97-4140).

Cuban tour agencies promote stays at the Hotel Panamericano, but anyone who overnights here will find themselves cut off from Havana in a desultory place with no appeal whatsoever. Fortunately, you can walk to Cojímar, a far more interesting place to stay.

Cojímar

Modern Ciudad Panamericano merges eastward into this forlorn fishing village with a waterfront lined with weather-beaten cottages. Whitecaps are often whipped up in the bay, making the Cuban flag flutter above **Fuerte de Cojímar** (locally called El Torreón), a pocket-size fortress guarding the cove's entrance. It was here in 1762 that the English put ashore and marched on Havana to capture Cuba for King George III. The fortress, built in the 1760s to forestall another fiasco, is still in military hands, and you will be shooed away if you get too close.

Cojímar is best known as the place where Ernest Hemingway berthed his sportfishing boat, the *Pilar*. When Hemingway died, every fisherman in the village apparently donated a

GREATER HAVANA

© CHRISTOPHER P. BAKER

the main stadium of the Panamericano sports complex, built in 1991 for the Pan-American Games

brass fitting from his boat. The collection was melted down to create the bust of the author— **Monumento Ernest Hemingway**—that has stared out to sea since 1962 from within a columned rotunda at the base of El Torreón. A plaque reads: "Parque Ernest Hemingway. In grateful memory from the population of Cojímar to the immortal author of *Old Man and the Sea,* inaugurated July 21, 1962, on the 63rd anniversary of his birth."

After exploring, appease your hunger with fisherman's soup and paella at Hemingway's favorite restaurant, **La Terraza** (Calle 152 #161, esq. Candelaria, tel. 07/55-9232). The gleaming mahogany bar at the front, accepting dollars only, gets few locals. You sense that Papa could stroll in at any moment. His favorite corner table is still there. He is there, too, patinated in bronze atop a pedestal, and adorning the walls in black and white, sharing a laugh with Fidel.

Cojímar was most famous as the residence of Gregorio Fuentes, Hemingway's former skipper and friend, and the model for "Antonio" in *Islands in the Stream,* and—albeit more contentiously—for Santiago, the fisherman cursed by *salao* (the worst form of bad luck) in *The Old Man and the Sea.* Fuentes, born in 1897, died in 2002 at the grand old age of 104. From 1938 until Hemingway's death, Fuentes was in charge of the writer's sportfishing boat, the *Pilar.* Cojímar's homegrown hero is venerated by Cubans. The old man, who lived at Calle 98 #209, esq. 3D, could often be found regaling travelers in La Terraza, where you can toast to his memory with a turquoise cocktail—Coctel Fuentes.

Accommodations

Hotel Islazul Panamericano (Calle A y Av. Central, tel. 07/95-1001, fax 07/95-1021; CUC35 s, CUC54 d low season; CUC51 s, CUC58 d high season) is popular with budget-tour operators, but despite a refurbishing it offers nothing but regret for tourists. It has a swimming pool (popular with Cubans on weekends), gym, sauna, car and moped rental, and tourism bureau. **Aparthotel Islazul**

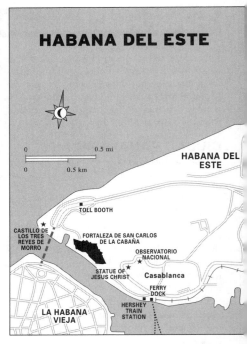

HABANA DEL ESTE

Costazul (tel. 07/95-0763, fax 07/95-4104) is part of the hotel complex and offers 475 meagerly furnished two- and three-bedroom apartments. (Islazul.)

In Cojímar, **Casa Hostal Marlins** (Calle Real #128A, e/ Santo Domingo y Chacón, tel. 07/65-3261, cell 891-4899; CUC20-25) has a nice, independent air-conditioned apartment upstairs with kitchenette, TV, an enclosed dining patio, and modern bathroom. A tight spiral staircase leads to a roof terrace for sunning.

Uphill, inland, **Villa Lennon** (Calle Los Pinos #302, e/ 27 y 28, tel. 07/65-0557; CUC20) is a handsome house where hosts Sonia and Joaquín have an independent apartment with a small lounge and kitchen, plus private bath with hot water. You can use the family TV lounge. Cater-corner, **Casa Particular Arsenio Rivas** (Calle 27 #98, e/

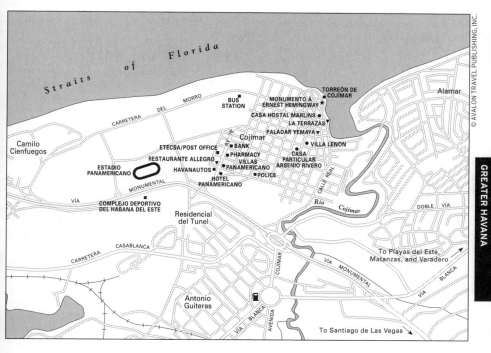

© AVALON TRAVEL PUBLISHING, INC.

GREATER HAVANA

Maceo y Los Pinos, tel. 07/65-2962; CUC20) has a pleasant, cross-ventilated, air-conditioned upstairs apartment with modern furnishings, a small kitchen, and large modern bathroom with hot water (but no toilet seat) and a terrace shaded by an arbor.

Food

Several uninspired restaurants line Avenida 78 (Paseo Panamericano), the main boulevard in Ciudad Panamericano. The best is **Restaurante Allegro** (Av. 78, e/ 5C y 5D), serving pizzas and Italian dishes.

Far better is (**La Terraza** (Calle Real #161, esq. Candelaria, tel. 07/93-9232; 10:30 A.M.– 11 P.M. daily), Ernest Hemingway's old haunt in Cojímar, where the seafood is good, with a wide-ranging menu that includes paella (CUC6– 12), pickled shrimp (CUC6.50), oyster cocktail (CUC2.95), and sautéed calamari (CUC6.15).

Services

Services along Avenida 78 in Ciudad Panamericano include a bank (esq. Calle 5), Cadeca exchange bureau (esq. 5D), post office (e/ 5 y 3), *telecorreo* (esq. 5C), international pharmacy (e/ 7 y 5D), and medical center (esq. 5D).

The **Farmacia Internacional** (tel. 07/95-1157) is at Villa Panamericana.

Getting There and Around

Heading east from Havana on the Vía Monumental, take the first exit marked Cojímar and cross over the freeway to reach Ciudad Panamericano. For Cojímar, take the *second* exit off the freeway.

Metrobus (*camello*) M1 departs the Prado, opposite the Capitolio Nacional, in Habana Vieja, and runs along the Vía Monumental to Ciudad Panamericano. You can also catch it at the corner of Avenida de los Presidentes y

ALAMAR

Immediately east of Cojímar, you'll pass a dormitory city long prized by Fidel Castro as an example of the achievements of socialism. In April 1959, Alamar (pop. 100,000) emerged on the drawing board as the first revolutionary housing scheme in postrevolutionary Cuba. The initial plan for 10,000 people in 4- to 11-story prefabricated concrete apartment blocks was to be fully self-contained in self-sufficient "superblocks." The sea of concrete high-rise complexes (extending east to the adjacent town of Celimar) was built with shoddy materials by microbrigades of untrained "volunteer" workers borrowed from their normal jobs. Castro was a regular visitor during the early years of construction: Alamar was a matter of pride and joy for him.

Though Cuban planners came to acknowledge its isolating nature and overwhelming deficiencies (the plumbing came from the Soviet Union, the wiring from China, the stoves from North Korea; there were no spare parts budgeted for upkeep), Alamar was vastly expanded beginning in 1976 and today covers four square miles. Today it is a virtual slum. Refuse litters the potholed roads, and the roadside parks are untended. There are no jobs here, either, and few stores, nor proper transportation, and no logic to the maze of streets or to the addresses of buildings, so that finding your way around is a study in maddening frustration.

27 in Vedado. Buses #195 and 265 also run to Ciudad Panamericano.

Bus #58 departs Avenida Rancho Boyeros and Bruzón, Plaza de la Revolución, for Cojímar; you can also catch it at the bottom of the Prado, at the junction with Avenida de los Estudiantes (10 centavos). The return bus departs Cojímar from Calle 99 y 3A.

A free shuttle departs the Hotel Panamericano for Havana four times daily.

Havanautos (tel. 07/95-1093), outside the Hotel Panamericano, rents cars and scooters, as does **Transtur** (tel. 07/95-1235), in Villa Panamericana.

◖ PLAYAS DEL ESTE

Cubans are great beachgoers, and nowhere on the island proves the case more than the Playas del Este. On hot summer weekends all of Havana seems to come down to the beach to meet friends, tan their bodies, play soccer or volleyball, and flirt.

The beaches of Playas del Este stretch unbroken for six kilometers east–west. They are divided by name. A nearly constant tropical breeze is usually strong enough to conjure surf from the warm turquoise seas—a perfect scenario for lazing, with occasional breaks for grilled fish or fried chicken from thatch-roofed *ranchitas*, where you can eat practically with your feet in the water.

Playas del Este is pushed as a hot destination for foreign tourists and, in the mid-1990s, enjoyed some success, bringing tourists (predominantly Italian and male) and Cubans (predominantly young and female) together for rendezvous under *palapas* and palms. Then a police crackdown (to temper the foreigner–Cuban coupling) initiated in early 1999 knocked the wind clear out of Playas del Este's sails. By international standards, it's a nonstarter other than for a day visit.

Care should always be taken when swimming: The waves can be powerful and riptides are common. In winter, the seas are full of jellyfish that locals call *agua mala*. The beaches also get terribly littered. Yuck!

When driving from Havana via the Vía Monumental, it's easy to miss the turn-off, one kilometer east of the second (easternmost) turnoff for Cojímar, where the Vía Monumental splits awkwardly. Take the narrow Vía Blanca exit to the left to reach Playas del Este; the main Vía Monumental swings south (you'll end up circling Havana on the *circunvalación*).

Playa Bacuranao

This small horseshoe cove with a white-sand beach lies immediately east of Alamar and is popular on weekends with residents of Alamar escaping city life for a day by the sea in the sun. The wreck of an 18th-century galleon lies just off the tiny beach. Coral grows abundantly on both sides of the bay, so if you have snorkeling gear, bring it. Food and beverages are available at Villa Islazul Bacuranao (see *Accommodations*).

Getting There: Buses #62 and 162 pass by Bacuranao, departing from Parque Central in Havana.

Tarará

Beyond Alamar, you'll cross the Río Tarará and pass Tarará, a villa resort hidden at the far western end of Playas del Este, at Vía Blanca Km 19. Before the Special Period, when it was called Campamento de Pioneros José Martí, it was used by Cuban schoolchildren, who combined study with beachside pleasures. Here, too, several thousand young victims of the 1988 Chernobyl nuclear disaster in the Ukraine have been treated free of charge. (It was here also that Castro operated his secret government in the early stage of the Revolution. Che Guevara was convalescing here after his debilitating years of guerrilla warfare in the Sierra Maestra, and the location away from Havana proved perfect for secret meetings to shape Cuba's future while Castro played puppeteer to the official democratic government of President Urrutia.)

Today it is a tourist villa complex, though the beaches are open to Cubans. To the west is a delightful pocket-size beach that forms a spit at the rivermouth; it has a volleyball court and shady *palapas,* plus a restaurant and marina with water sports. (The rivermouth channel is renowned for its coral, large groupers, and schools of snappers—great for snorkeling and scuba diving.) The main beach, **Playa Mégano,** lies further east. It, too, has a sand volleyball court, shade umbrellas, and lounge chairs, and is served by shops and the **Casa Club Cubanacán** complex, with a swimming pool with grill (entrance CUC5, or CUC20 including all you can eat plus six beers) and an elegant restaurant.

massage on the beach at Playas del Este

Entry is free, but you must show ID—bring your passport in case the occasionally mule-minded *custodios* get a case of *burro-cracia.*

Santa María del Mar

Playa Mégano extends east from Tarará and merges into Playa Santa María del Mar, the broadest and most beautiful swathe, with light golden sand shelving into stunning aquamarine and turquoise waters. The beaches are palm-shaded and studded with shade umbrellas. Most of Playas del Este's tourist facilities are here, including bars and water sports, plus a fistful of tourist hotels. In 2005 it was looking more deteriorated than ever, although the beaches are fabulous.

Playa Santa María runs east for about three kilometers to the mouth of the Río Itabo—a popular bathing spot for Cuban families. A large mangrove swamp centered on **Laguna Itabo** extends inland from the mouth of the river, where waterfowl can be admired. A coral reef runs offshore at a depth of no more than

GREATER HAVANA

20 feet, with lots of brain, elkhorn, and staghorn formations.

Boca Ciega and Guanabo

Beautiful Playa Boca Ciega begins east of the Río Itabo estuary and is popular with Cuban families, many of whom choose to rent simple *cabinas* in the residential and rental complex called Boca Ciega. Playa Boca Ciega merges eastward into Playa Guanabo, the least-attractive beach, but running for several kilometers along the shorefront of Guanabo, a Cuban village with many plantation-style wooden homes. It is the only village at Playas del Este.

For grand views up and down the beaches, head inland of Guanabo to **Mirador de Bellomonte,** where a café and bar (Vía Blanca Km 24.5, tel. 07/96-3431; daily 2 P.M.–2 A.M.) atop the Altura Bellomonte offers fine vistas.

Entertainment

The **Casa Club Cubanacán** (Av. de Terrazas; 10 A.M.–10 P.M. daily) has a pool hall and dance club.

Cabaret Guanimar (3ra Av. y Calle 468; Fri.–Sun. 11 P.M.–3 A.M.; CUC3) has a simple *cabaret espectáculo* followed by a disco. It draws an unsophisticated local crowd.

Recreation

Outlets on the beach rent watercraft (CUC15 for 15 minutes), Hobie-Cats (CUC20 per hour), and beach chairs and lounge chairs (CUC2 per day). **Mi Cayito** rents kayaks and water bikes on the lagoon.

Horses can be rented on the beach in front of Hotel Tropicoco, and are a specialty of **Rancho Mi Hacienda Guanabito** (Calzada de Jústiz, Km 4, Guanabo, tel. 07/96-4711; daily 9 A.M.–8 P.M.), four kilometers inland of Guanabo. This *finca de recreo* (dude ranch) raises animals and features bloodless cockfights (the birds' spurs are covered to prevent them from seriously hurting each other).

Scuba diving is available from the water sports stand on the beach in front of the Hotel Tropicoco, and at **Caribbean Diving Center** (Casa 4, Tarará, tel. 07/96-0201, fax 07/97-1313, www.caribscuba.com) in Tarará.

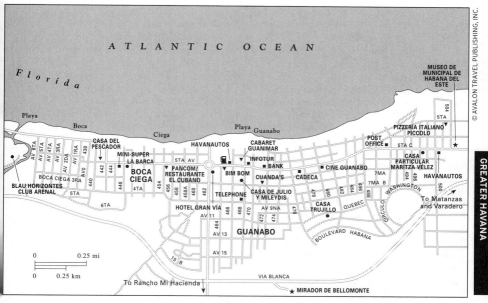

GREATER HAVANA

Marina Tarará (tel. 07/97-1510 or 07/97-1462, fax 07/97-1499, channel VHF 77 or 108, marina@mit.tur.cu), at the Tarará rivermouth, has 50 berths with water and electricity hook-ups, plus diesel and gas. You can rent yachts, pedal boats are available, and sportfishing charters are offered. Boat excursions include six-hour "seafaris" at 9:30 A.M., featuring fishing, snorkeling, and lunch (CUC55 based on a minimum of four passengers); and a three-hour nocturnal cruise.

Accommodations

Casas Particulares: All the *casas particulares* are located in Guanabo.

One of the best options is **Casa de Julio y Mileydis** (Calle 468 #512, e/ 5ta y 7ma, Guanabo, tel. 07/96-0100; CUC30–35). Set in a beautiful garden, this air-conditioned apartment is equipped for people with disabilities and has a security box, large lounge with a kitchen, and a small and simply furnished bedroom. It has a small pool for children. The owners are a delight.

Casa Maritza Vélez (Calle 5D #49610, e/ 496 y 498, Guanabo, tel. 07/96-4389; CUC30–35) is a handsome 1950s house with a beautiful interior in a well-maintained garden. It has two air-conditioned rooms with modern furnishings, old metal-frame beds, soothing pastel colors, and modern tiled bathrooms (but no toilet seats).

Casa Trujillo (Av. Quebec #55, e/ 478 y 482, Guanabo, tel. 07/96-3325, www.cubanasol.com/casatrujillo.htm; CUC30–35) is a two-story family unit with one spacious air-conditioned bedroom, a TV lounge, and a modern kitchen to which guests have access. Miriam Trujillo and Alberto Mendes, your hosts, are fluent in Spanish, French, and English.

Rental Villas: In Boca Ciega, Islazul rents *cabinas,* almost exclusively to Cubans. Few meet international standards.

Hotels: The **Hotel Gran Vía** (Av. 5ta, e/ 502 y 504, tel. 07/96-4300; CUC18 s, CUC21 d low season; CUC22 s, CUC26 d high season) is a simple option catering mostly to Cubans but with three basically furnished rooms for foreigners.

The **Villa Islazul Bacuranao** (Vía Blanca Km 15.5, tel. 07/65-7645, reservas@bacuranao.co.cu; one-bedroom units CUC23 s, CUC25 d low season, CUC26 s, CUC30 d high season; two-bedroom units CUC33 s, CUC38 d low season, CUC38 s, CUC44 d high season) has 52 rooms in air-conditioned, modestly furnished cabanas, each with satellite TV and private bath. Facilities include a restaurant, café, snack bar, swimming pool, and nightly entertainment.

Villas Marina Tarará (Calle 9na, esq. 14, Villa Tarará, tel. 07/97-1462, fax 07/97-1333, comercial@tarara.mit.tur.cu; CUC79 low season, CUC106 high season 2–3 bedrooms; CUC105 low season, CUC132 high season 4–5 bedrooms), run by Cubanacán, offers 94 villas—*casas confort*—with from two to five bedrooms, many with swimming pools. All have satellite TV, radio, telephone, safe, kitchen with fridge, and private parking. No Cuban guests are allowed, and no guests may stay overnight without authority of the management, which even requires a list of guests attending "a social gathering." A grocery, laundry, restaurants, and pharmacy are on-site.

In Santa María, the **Club Amigo Mégano** (Av. de las Terrazas, tel. 07/97-1610, fax 07/97-1624, vmegano@meganohor.tur.cu; CUC32 s, CUC45 d low season; CUC38 s, CUC54 d high season, including breakfast), at the far west end of Playas del Este, is a 10-minute walk from the beach. The 103 air-conditioned cabins are simple yet appealing, with tile floors, bamboo furnishings, tiny satellite TV, small tiled baths with showers, and plate-glass doors opening to verandas. It has a pool. (Cubanacán.)

Hotel Horizontes Tropicoco (Av. de las Terrazas, e/ 5 y 7, tel. 07/97-1371, fax 07/97-1389, recepcion@htropicoco.hor.tur.cu; CUC45 s, CUC75 d low season; CUC55 s, CUC85 d high season) is the most popular place in town. The five-story building was recently renovated and has 188 air-conditioned rooms with simple yet adequate decor and bamboo furniture, plus telephone, radio, and modern bathrooms. Services include a pleasing restaurant, as well as a bar, tour desk, shops, post office, and car rental. (Cubanacán.)

Managed as an all-inclusive property by a Spanish hotel group, the **Blau Horizontes Club Arenal** (Lago de Boca Ciega, tel. 07/97-1272, fax 07/97-1287, www.bla-hotels.com; CUC70 s, CUC100 d standard low season, CUC 95 s, CUC150 d high season; CUC90 s, CUC120 d suite low season, CUC125 s, CUC190 d high season), in the midst of the lagoon between Playas Santa María del Mar and Boca Ciega, has 166 air-conditioned rooms in three categories. Rooms are spacious and eye-pleasing and have satellite TVs, hairdryers, minibars, and safes. They surround a massive pool with thatched restaurant and bar, and the staff tries hard to keep guests amused with *animaciónes*. But the overall effect is desultory, and the grounds are unkempt. (Cubanacán.)

The **Villas los Pinos** (Av. 4ta, tel. 07/97-1361, fax 07/97-1524, recepcion@pinos.gca.tur.cu; CUC120–220 low season; CUC160–250 high season) offers the most elegant option, with 27 two-, three-, and four-bedroom villas. Some appear a bit fuddy-duddy; others are impressive and up to international standards and have their own private pools. They all have TV, VCR, radio, telephone, and kitchen. Visitors are prohibited. (Gran Caribe.)

Food

Several thatched bars and eateries can be found on the beach. **Mi Casita de Coral,** 100 meters east of the Hotel Tropicoco, serves *criollo* fare 24 hours daily and has some appealing seafoods, including grilled fillet of fish (CUC5) plus spicy lobster enchiladas (CUC8). Likewise, **Casa Club Atlántico** (tel. 971344, ext. 178; 24 hours) is a pleasant airy restaurant offering spaghettis and pizzas, plus a chicken *oferta especial* (lunch special) for CUC2. **Parrillada Costarenas** (Av. Norte, esq. Av. de las Terrazas, tel. 07/97-1361; noon–6 P.M., daily) serves inexpensive grilled fare (CUC5) and offers seaviews from its air-conditioned beachside diner.

Restaurante Mi Cayito (Av. las Terrazas, tel. 07/97-1339; daily 10 A.M.–6 P.M.)

is a pleasant thatched restaurant on a small island overhanging the mangroves of Laguna Itabo. It has the usual fare: grilled fish, shrimp, and lobster, but is grossly overpriced (CUC10–26).

In Guanabo, the best place by far is **C Paladar Italiano Piccolo** (5ta Av., e/ 502 y 504, tel. 07/96-4300; noon–midnight daily), a spacious private restaurant with riverstone walls with Greek murals. Run by Greek owners, it offers surprisingly tasty Mediterranean fare, including wood-fired pizzas, served with hearty salads at low prices (CUC5–10).

Giving Piccolo a run for its money is **Casa del Pescador** (5ta Av. #44005, esq. Calle 442, tel. 07/96-3653; noon– 11 p.m. daily), a Spanish-style *bodega* in Boca Ciega, with fishing nets hanging from the ceiling. The menu is huge. Fish dishes average CUC8, including shrimp and lobster. The house specialty is *escabeche* (CUC4).

Pan.Com (5ta Av., esq. 454, tel. 07/94-4061; noon–11 p.m. daily) is a modern, clean eatery in a red-brick building with a choice of airy patio or air-conditioned interior. It serves *criollo* dishes, plus sandwiches, omelettes, burgers, and tortillas.

For ice cream, head to **Bim-Bom,** a clean, modern, well-run operation serving various sundaes and 32 flavors of ice cream along the lines of Baskin-Robbins.

Services

Infotur (Av. Las Terrazas, e/ 11 y 12, tel. 07/97-1261; and 5ta-C Av., e/ 468 y 470, Guanabo, tel. 07/96-3841) tourist information offices offer meager assistance.

In Santa María, the **post office** (Av. de las Terrazas, e/ 10 y 11; 8 a.m.–1 p.m. Mon.–Sat.) is in Edificio Los Corales. In Boca Ciega, the **post office** is at 5ta Avenida and Calle 448; and in Guanabo at 5ta-C Avenida y 492.

The **Clínica Internacional** (Av. de las Terrazas, e/ 8 y 9, tel. 07/97-1032 or 07/96-1810; 24 hours) is 100 yards east of Hotel Tropicoco.

A **Bandec** is at 5ta Avenida, e/ 468 y 470 (tel. 07/96-3320), with a **Cadeca** exchange booth adjacent.

Getting There

Tarará is at Vía Blanca Km 17, 27 kilometers east of Havana. It is signed off the Vía Blanca, as is Playas del Este, with three exits farther east. A taxi will cost about CUC20.

Buses #62, 162, and 262 serve Playas del Este from Parque Central; bus #219 departs from the main bus terminal. Bus #400 serves Guanabo and departs from Parque Taya Piedra, at the junction of Manglar Arroyo and Almanbique, in the Atarés neighborhood.

Warning: If driving, beware the *punto de control* (police control) near Bacuranao. Keep your speed down to 50 kph or you *will* be pulled over and ticketed.

Getting Around

Havanautos has a car and scooter rental office in the parking lot of Hotel Tropicoco, and at 5ta Avenida y Calle 464 (tel. 07/96-3858) and Calle 500-A, e/ 5ta y 7ma (tel. 07/96-3845). **Transautos** (5ta Av., esq. 11), in Santa María, also rents cars. **Vía Rent-a-Car** (5ta Av., e/ 10 y 11, tel. 07/96-1152) is one block west.

SANTA CRUZ DEL NORTE

East of the Playas del Este, the northern shore is hemmed in by low hills. Precious oil lies deep underground, and you'll pass small oil derricks bobbing languidly atop the coral cliff tops. Beyond, Santa Cruz, some 30 kilometers east of Havana, is a ramshackle industrial town steeping in a miasma of photo-chemical fumes and fronted by badly polluted waters. Cuba's largest rum factory, **Fábrica Cubarón,** also known as Ronera Santa Cruz, is here, producing the famous Havana Club (founded in 1878) rums and scenting the air with its own heady aromas. No visits are permitted. The original factory, dating from 1919, stands down by the shore.

About four kilometers south of Santa Cruz and worth the detour is the community of Camilo Cienfuegos, formerly called Hershey and built as a model town by the Hershey chocolate company, which owned the sugar mill now called **Central Camilo Cienfuegos.** Hershey's town had a baseball

GREATER HAVANA

THE MAKING OF RUM

Christopher Columbus introduced sugarcane to Cuba in 1493. *Trapiches* (rudimentary ox-powered mills) squeezed *guarapo* from the cane, which was fermented and mixed with *miel de caña* (molasses), the dark-brown residue left after crystallized sugar has been processed from cane, to produce a crude type of "molasses wine."

The introduction of steam power (and of distilleries in the manufacturing process) in the early 1800s increased sugar production and permitted production of more-refined rum. Havana, Matanzas, Cárdenas, and Santiago de Cuba became major centers for the production of rum. Foremost among the many private companies was Bacardi, founded in Santiago de Cuba in 1868 by Don Facundo Bacardí. (Following the Revolution, the state seized the rum factories and the company today is active in anti-Castroite politics). About one dozen distilleries make about 60 brands of *ron* today.

Production involves fermentation, distillation, aging, and blending. Molasses is first fermented with yeast (which occurs naturally in sugarcane) to transform the sugar into ethanol. The fermented liquid is then heated with compressed vapor and then diluted with distilled water. It is distilled in copper vats to eliminate unpleasant flavors and then aged in oak barrels for one to 15 years. Distilled rums are clear. Darker rums gain their distinct color and flavor from caramels added during the aging process, or naturally from the tannins of the oak barrels. The resulting overproof rum is then diluted and bottled.

field, movie theater, an amusement park, the Hershey Hotel, and scores of wooden homes for workers. The facilities still stand, forming a kind of lived-in museum made more intriguing by the quaint trains that serve the town from Casablanca, north of Havana, and Matanzas. The mill closed in 2002 and is now in a derelict state. The Hershey train stops here between Havana and Matanzas. (See the sidebar *A Sugar of a Journey* in the *Matanzas* chapter.)

PLAYA JIBACOA

This beautiful beach, also known as **Playa Amarillo,** about four kilometers east of Santa Cruz, extends east of the Río Jibacoa for several kilometers. A smaller beach—**Playa Arroyo Bermejo**—lies tucked between cliffs at the mouth of the Río Jibacoa, about three kilometers east of Santa Cruz del Norte, bracketed by rocky headlands. Coral reefs lie close to shore, perfect for snorkeling and scuba diving.

Both beaches are popular with Cubans, who are served by simple *campismos*—holidays camps that may be too basic for most foreign tastes. In time, the master plan for Jibacoa calls for 11 luxury hotels, two 18-hole championship golf courses, health spas, and time-share villas.

Puerto Escondido

About eight kilometers east of the Río Jibacoa, a road leads north to the small coastal village of Puerto Escondido, a "wonderfully cool inlet a few miles down the Cuban coast," wrote Ernest Hemingway, who arrived aboard the *Pilar* to escape the hot summer nights. The spectacular setting—within a wide bend of a deep ravine—is occupied today by **Cubanacán Naútica** (tel. 0692/96-1508, nauhab@cbcan. cyt.cu), offering windsurfing, waterskiing, and excursions by yacht and catamaran, plus diving (CUC25 one dive, CUC35 two dives), snorkeling (CUC10 for two hours), and deep-sea fishing (from CUC75).

Puente Bacunayagua

Camera at the ready? Then take a deep breath for your stop at this bridge, 106 kilometers from Havana and 10 kilometers east of Puerto

Escondido (about 2 km after crossing the Havana–Matanzas provincial boundary; it's 14 km from here to Matanzas). The 313-meter-long bridge (the longest and highest—112 meters—in Cuba) spans the gorge of the Río Bacunayagua, which slices through the narrow coastal mountain chain. The Yumurí Valley rolls away to the south, fanning out spectacularly as if contrived for a travel magazine's double-page spread. The views are incredible.

The bridge is a favorite stop for tour buses, and there are facilities, including a bar and restaurant, on the west bank to cater to the hordes. A *mirador* atop the cliff above the bridge offers the best views. Police are usually stationed at either side of the bridge to catch speeding cars.

Accommodations and Food

Basic *campismos* line Playa Jibacoa. Most are restricted to Cubans, but foreigners are catered to at **Campismo Los Cocos** (tel. 0692/29-5231; reservations c/o Cubamar, 3ra Av., e/ 12 y Malecón, Havana, tel. 07/66-2523, fax 07/33-3111, www.cubamarviajes.cu; CUC18 s, CUC28 d low season; CUC19 s, CUC30 d high season), which has 20 small concrete *cabinas* for foreigners amid well-kept lawns. Painted in canary-yellow and deep-blue color schemes, they feature air-conditioning, fans, local TV, simple furnishings, kitchenettes, and modern bathrooms with hot water. There's a swimming pool, video and games room, plus a restaurant serving mediocre fare. (Cubamar.)

Breezes Jibacoa (Vía Blanca Km 60, tel. 0692/85122, fax 0692/85150, www.superclubscuba.com; per person CUC80 garden view, CUC94 ocean view, CUC125 suite low season; CUC230/245/265 peak season), run by the Jamaican all-inclusive chain SuperClubs, is a splendid four-star resort with a contemporary take on classical architecture. Its 250 spacious and tastefully decorated rooms and 10 suites center on a vast swimming pool. Facilities include five bars, two restaurants, a café, grill, gym, basketball and volleyball courts, beauty store, a souvenir store, a well-stocked humidor and rum store, plus massage, and a medical center. Reservations are required.

The handsome **Villa Loma Jibacoa** (tel. 0692/85316) was reserved for the exclusive use of Cuban military at last visit.

Getting There

Bus #669 departs Terminal La Coubre, on Desamparados in Habana Vieja, and travels to San Cruz del Norte, where you can catch a taxi or bus #126. Alternately, take a Havana–Matanzas bus and ask the driver to let you off. The Hershey Train departs Casablanca and stops at Jibacoa Pueblo, five kilometers from Jibacoa, and at the Arcos de Canasí station, three kilometers from El Abra, but it's a lonesome walk.

PINAR DEL RÍO

Pinar del Río is Cuba's westernmost province and, in many ways, its most scenic. Ox-drawn plows transport you back in time amid quintessentially Cuban landscapes that attain their most dramatic beauty in Viñales Valley, with incredible limestone formations called *mogotes*, plus caves for exploring and a bucolic setting that Hollywood might have conceived for your camera. Here, and in the neighboring region of Vuelta Abajo, the world's finest tobacco is grown.

Pinar del Río is dominated by a low mountain chain—the Cordillera de Guaniguanico—which forms an east–west spine through the province. The chain is divided by the Río San Diego into two mountain ranges—the Sierra del Rosario in the east and the Sierra de los Órganos in the west. The pine-forested mountains, which reach a height of 692 meters atop Pan de Guajaibón, are pimpled with *mogotes*, adding drama to the photogenic effect. Opportunities for ecotourism are being developed, notably at Soroa, known for its orchid garden; and Las Terrazas, a model community with a first-rate hotel (billed, euphemistically as an eco-resort) plus artists studios, nature trails, cascades, thermal pools, and the remains of 18th-century *cafetales* (coffee plantations) and thermal baths. Although undeveloped for tourism, Parque Nacional La Güira is great for bird-watching and for history buffs investigating the history of Che Guevara.

A slender pencil of uninhabited land—the Península de Guanahacabibes—hangs loosely off the western tip of Cuba, jutting west 50 kilometers into the Gulf of Mexico. Smothered

HIGHLIGHTS

◖ Cayo Levisa: Scintillating white-sand beaches and turquoise shallows surround Cayo Levisa; deeper waters offer fantastic diving (page 229).

◖ Orquideario Soroa: Hundreds of orchids species, as well as other botanicals, fill this exquisite hillside garden (page 232).

◖ Complejo Turístico Las Terrazas: The scenic setting of this unique mountain community is home to intriguing art studios, fabulous hiking, thermal baths, and ecotourist excursions (page 232).

◖ Cuevas de los Portales: Che Guevara used this huge cave, adorned with dripstone formations, as his headquarters during the Cuban Missile Crisis (page 237).

◖ Parque Nacional de Viñales: Among Cuba's most famous and fascinating landscapes, skyscraper-scale *mogotes* provide a magnificent backdrop for tobacco fields; there's also great climbing and caving (page 243).

◖ Finca El Pinar San Luis: At the tobacco farm of world-renowned farmer Alejandro Robaina, visitors gain a complete knowledge of tobacco production (page 251).

◖ Diving at María la Gorda: Whale sharks, manta rays, and fantastic coral formations are among the highlights for divers in the Bahía de Corrientes (page 254).

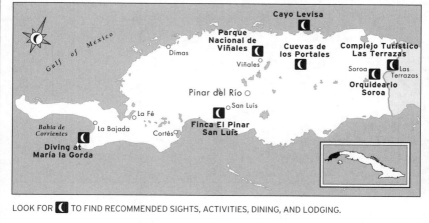

LOOK FOR **◖** TO FIND RECOMMENDED SIGHTS, ACTIVITIES, DINING, AND LODGING.

PINAR DEL RÍO

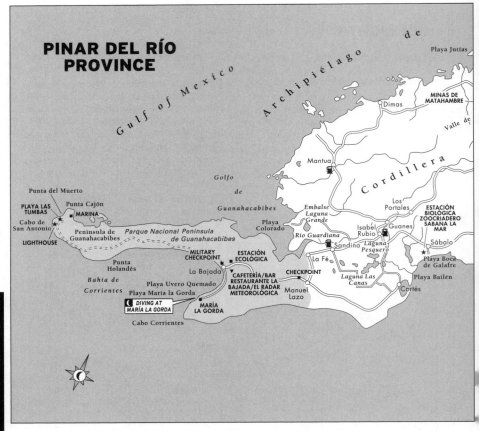

in dense brush and cactus, the peninsula is touted as a nature reserve, while retaining a section where hunters may track down wild pig and deer. Playa María la Gorda, in Bahía de Corrientes, is a center for scuba diving. This area was inhabited at least 4,000 years ago by the Guanahatabey, the island's initial aboriginal settlers; later the region became a last refuge for the Ciboney Indians, who retreated before the advance of the Taíno. Aboriginal sites are being unearthed.

The region is regularly mauled by hurricanes—five have torn through the province since 2002, among them Hurricanes

Ivan and Charlie, in 2004, and Dennis and Wilma in 2005.

PLANNING YOUR TIME

Most visitors to this province justifiably set their sights on Viñales, a rustic time-warp village fully deserving of two days or more. There's plenty to see and do in the national park that bears its name, and you may wish to budget longer to savor Viñales's fabulous scenery, slow pace, and yesteryear way of life.

To get there, most tourists follow the six-lane Autopista, the concrete highway linking the capital city with the provincial capital of

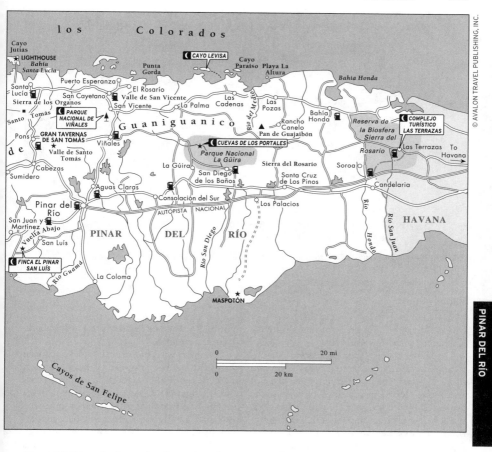

Pinar del Río, which can be skipped without regret. It heads west almost ruler-straight and is in reasonably good condition the entire way. There's relatively little traffic, and the route is pleasingly scenic, notably in the east, where the lowlands are smothered in oceans of green sugarcane; a sweet, cloying odor of molasses wafts across the countryside; and, in season, thick blue-black smoke billows from the tall chimneys of busy *centrales*. There are two refreshment stops along the highway, one about a kilometer east of the turn-off for Las Terrazas, about four kilometers west of Coyajabos, and a second at Las Barrigonas, 27 kilometers

east of Pinar del Río. The only gas station is at the turnoff for Soroa. The highway ends at the town of Pinar del Río, a two-hour drive from Havana.

A more interesting option is to follow the old Carretera Central through sleepy provincial towns such as Candelaria, Santa Cruz de los Pinos, and Consolación del Sur—towns memorable for their old churches, faded pastel houses, and covered walkways with neoclassical pillars. The two-lane highway parallels the Autopista along the southern edge of the mountains and grants easy access to Soroa and Parque Nacional La Güira, which should be visited for the

© CHRISTOPHER P. BAKER

María la Gorda

enormous cavern that once formed a military headquarters for Che Guevara.

For scenery, I prefer the lonesome, undulating Circuito Norte, which follows the picturesque north coast. Offshore, a necklace of cays—the Archipiélago de los Colorados—are protected by a coral reef. There are beaches, though few of great appeal. The star attractions are **Cayo Levisa,** offering fabulous diving, and Cayo Jutía, with a super beach (albeit much denuded by Hurricane Wilma). Cayo Levisa is a short drive from Viñales, and can be enjoyed on a day excursion, although I recommend at least one night on the isle. Scuba enthusiasts should also head west to **María la Gorda,** where the diving is first-rate; and nature enthusiasts might enjoy a day or two exploring **Reserva de la Biosfera Península de Guanahacabibes.**

The northwest coast and broad southern plains can safely be skipped, although anglers might be tempted by lagoons stocked with bass and other game fish. And historical attractions are few (the first Spanish settlement occurred only after 1717), although everywhere modernity overlays a way of life that has changed little since the end of the 19th century. This is especially so in the tobacco fields that are the province's main claim to fame, and never more so than at **Finca El Pinar San Luis,** the *finca* of Alejandro Robaina, renowned worldwide to cigar aficionados. On the outskirts of the sleepy town of San Juan y Martínez, a visit here is de rigueur.

The North Coast

BAHÍA HONDA TO CAYO LEVISA

The coast road west from Havana between Mariel and San Vicente is one of the most scenic in Cuba: a gentle roller-coaster ride. West of San Vicente, the villages thin out and there is little to hold your attention except the deep-shadowed Sierras. The road runs a few miles inland of the coast. There are few beaches of vital appeal.

Beyond the town of Bahía Honda, at the head of a namesake bay 20 kilometers west of Mariel, the road twists and loops and grows ever more scenic. Soon you are edging along beneath the *mogotes,* with lower slopes covered with coffee bushes shaded by royal palms. The sensuously rounded **Pan de Guajaibón** (692 meters; 2,294 feet) looms ahead like the Sugarloaf of Rio de Janeiro. The dramatic peak lies within a protected area known as Mil Cumbres (18,160 hectares), part of the Sierra del Rosario Biosphere Reserve. One kilometer east of Las Pozas, you can turn south from the highway to follow a side road south into the Sierra del Rosario. The road gradually deteriorates and finally fizzles out at the hamlet of **Rancho Canelo,** from where a rough, overgrown track—good for hiking—probes the final few miles to the base of Pan de Guajaibón.

About 10 kilometers west of Bahía Honda and three kilometers east of Las Pozas another side road leads north to the beach of **Playa La Altura.**

West of Las Pozas you'll see the first cays of the Archipiélago de los Colorados beckoning seductively offshore. Scuba diving is sensational. Ernest Hemingway had a fondness for beach-fringed, tousled-palm-shaded **Cayo Paraíso** (also known as Cayo Mégano de Casiguas), linked to the mainland by a seven-kilometer causeway. The only site of interest on the cay is a 42-meter-tall lighthouse atop a skeletal structure. A marina is planned for scuba divers and yachters. The coral is superb, and there's a sunken vessel to explore eight meters down. Hemingway's presence is venerated by a small monument beside the small wooden dock, which reads:

> *From the beginning of the 1940s, this place was the refuge of the great North American author Ernest Hemingway, who visited it assiduously, sometimes remaining on the cay for up to 20 days at a time. Here he wrote, rested, roamed the beach, swam, and loved it so much he used it as a base for antisubmarine operations from his yacht the* Pilar *during the Second World War.*

Cayo Levisa

About 10 kilometers west of Cayo Paraíso is Cayo Levisa, two kilometers offshore and ringed by 3.5 kilometers of sugar-white beaches. Cayo Levisa is popular with divers for its abundant black coral (dives cost CUC25, CUC45 for two dives). There's a 30-meter-long dock on the south side. In October 2005, Hurricane Wilma almost totally destroyed the facilities, which were being rebuilt at last visit. A boat leaves for Cayo Levisa at 10 A.M. and 6 P.M. (CUC10 per person, CUC15 including cocktail) from adjacent to the coast guard station at Palma Rubia: The turnoff from the Circuito Norte is 15 kilometers west of Las Pozas, just west of the village of Las Cadenas. The return boats depart Cayo Levisa at 9 A.M. and 5 P.M. Excursions to Cayo Levisa are offered from tour agencies in Pinar del Río and Viñales.

Accommodations

In Bahía Honda, you can admire the coastal vista from the hilltop **Motel Punta de Piedra** (tel. 086/66-8341, CUC15 s/d May, June, Sept., Oct., and Nov.; CUC19 s/d the rest of the year), about three kilometers north of town. It has 20 basic rooms with private bath and fridge. Bring mosquito repellent.

PINAR DEL RÍO

Campismo La Altura (tel. 086/86470; CUC5 per person), inland of Playa La Altura, has 50 rooms in basic cabins that are popular with Cubans on weekends. You'll need to bring your own food.

Villa Cayo Levisa (tel. 08/66-6075; previous rates were CUC55 s, CUC71 d low season; CUC63 s, CUC81 d high season, including transfer) is a resort and diving center that was being rebuilt at last visit following its destruction by Hurricane Wilma. It formerly offered 20 rustic yet pleasantly furnished, air-conditioned beachfront *cabinas* with satellite TV; plus water sports and a buffet restaurant. (Cubanacán.)

WEST OF CAYO LEVISA

Continuing west, you reach **La Palma,** the only town of consequence in the area, with a tiny museum and shops. A road leads south from here over the mountains to Parque Nacional La Güira and San Diego de los Baños. The scenery continues to inspire, with lonesome *bohíos* and oxen working the palm-studded fields, the sea to the north tantalizingly blue, and—to the south—round-topped *mogotes.*

Ten kilometers west of La Palma is the junction for Viñales and the town of Pinar del Río. Continue straight, though, and you reach **San Cayetano** (handy for its Cupet gas station), beyond which the land takes on a new look, with pine forests and, farther west where the land flattens out, citrus orchards. A turnoff leads north from here to the sleepy fishing village of **Puerto Esperanza.**

From San Cayetano it is 22 kilometers to the small port of **Santa Lucía.** Nearby **Cayo Jutía** (tel. 08/38326) offers superb beaches and swimming. The cay is connected to the shore by a *pedraplén,* accessed by a turnoff from the main highway, four kilometers west of Santa Lucía. In past years a toll booth charged CUC5, but Hurricane Wilma trashed the cay in 2005 and at last visit access was free. It's 13 kilometers from the coast highway to the beach, pinned by a metal *faro* erected in 1902.

West of Baja, there's not a soul for miles until you arrive at the pretty hamlet of **Dimas.** Beyond Dimas you pass around the western edge of the Sierra de los Órganos as the road veers south to Mantua, a pleasant little town that in 1896 was the site of a major battle during the War of Independence. This is a lonesome drive. The parched land is scrub covered and boring. Scattered wrecks lie offshore, caught amid the coral reefs that scuttled them.

Accommodations and Food

Accommodations are few and far between, but several locals rent rooms in Puerto Esperanza. Two to consider are **Casa de Teresa Hernández Martínez** (Calle 4ta #7, tel. 08/79-3803; CUC15) with two clean, simply furnished rooms with shared bath and comfy beds, plus pleasant owners. Nearby, **Casa de Leonila Blanca** (Calle Hermanos Caballeros #41, tel. 08/93843) also has two modestly appointed rooms (CUB15-20) with shared bath and secure parking.

Campismo Popular El Copey (tel. 08/38398; CUC5 per person), about 10 kilometers west of the turnoff for Cayo Jutía and three kilometers from the coast highway, has 2 of its 30 basic concrete *cabinas* set aside for foreigners. There's a meager restaurant. It is usually open only on weekends, when Cubans flock.

Sierra del Rosario

The Sierra del Rosario dominates eastern Pinar del Río Province. Much of the area is encompassed within the **Reserva de la Biosfera Sierra del Rosario**. This 25,000-hectare (61,775-acre) reserve covers the easternmost slopes of the Sierra del Rosario, with most of the area lush, prime forest. Much of the mountain slopes had been transformed by logging following the Spanish arrival. As time progressed, erosion and infertility contributed to abandonment of coffee farms and further denudation by impoverished peasants seeking income through logging. Today the land is given over predominantly to forestry. The area was named a biosphere reserve by UNESCO in 1985, following a decade of efforts at reforestation by the Cuban government.

The reserve protects close to 600 endemic higher plant species and 250 lower plant species. The reserve is covered by montane forest of pine and spruce. In springtime the slopes blaze with bright red blossoms of *flamboyanes,* and *poma rosa* grows wild by the roadside, which is also lined in season with white *yagruma* and the fiery blossoms of *popili.* At any time, the air smells piney fresh.

The 98 bird species (including 11 of Cuba's 24 endemic species) include Cuban trogons, *pedorreras,* woodpeckers, hummingbirds, parrots, and the national bird, the *tocororo.* Terrestrial turtles and frogs are common, including the smallest frog in the world (*Sminthilus limbatus*). There's an outlandish-looking water lizard, found only here, along with bats (five species), deer, and large guinea pig–like rodents called *jutías.*

It can get cool at night—bring a sweater.

SOROA

Most famous of the biosphere reserve's attractions is Soroa, an "eco-retreat" set in a valley at about 250 meters elevation and perfect for nature hikes. Soroa is called the "the Rainbow of Cuba" for its natural beauty, although you need to get above the valley to fully ap-

THE CORK PALM

This shaggy, endemic "palm," found only in Pinar del Río, is a souvenir of the Carboniferous era, when this valley was the ocean floor. The gravely endangered living fossil – *palma corcho,* or *Microcycas calocoma* – isn't a true palm, but rather a member of a primitive cycad family abundant 270 million years ago. It grows to six meters and sheds leaves every other year, leaving a ring around its fuzzy trunk that marks its age. It differs by sex: the masculine and feminine reproductive cells are emitted at different times, thus limiting the plant's propagation. Although some living species are 300 years old, there are no young ones known, suggesting that whichever insect acted as a fertilizing agent may have been wiped out by modern agriculture.

preciate the setting. The resort is named for Jean-Paul Soroa, a Frenchman who owned a coffee estate here two centuries ago. In the 1930s, it became fashionable as a spa with sulfur baths. Since the Revolution, it has gained a new lease on life, with a hotel and other facilities for tourists.

Attractions include **Cascadas El Salto** (entrance CUC5, including drink), a small waterfall reached by deteriorated stairs that descend 400 meters through fragrant woodlands to the bottom of the falls, which tumble 35 meters into pools good for bathing. The waters have medicinal properties. The cascades are at their most postcard-perfect in the early morning. There's a bar and restaurant overlooking the rippling Río Manantiales at the top of the cascades. The **Baños Romanos** (CUC5 per hour; open 9 A.M.–4 P.M.), at the entrance to El Salto, is a dour bathhouse offering massage.

A rugged dirt track leads uphill from the entrance to the El Salto parking lot to **Mirador** de Venus, a hilltop lookout. It's a stiff one-kilometer climb that deposits you far above the valley with stupendous views. Vultures swoop and slide overhead. Another rugged trail from the parking lot leads to the ruins of **Cafetal Independencia,** a French coffee plantation (six hours round-trip).

Orquideario Soroa

Soroa's prize attraction is this orchid garden (tel. 085/2558; daily 8:30 A.M.–5 P.M.; CUC3 with obligatory guide; cameras CUC1, videos CUC2), which covers three hectares and claims to be the world's second-largest. It was created in 1943 by Spaniard Tomás Felipe Camacho, who built the hilltop house—now a beer garden and *mirador*—and planted the craggy hillside with flowers. The garden offers views down the palm-tufted valley. The garden, nourished by the humid climate and maintained by the University of Pinar del Río, contains more than 20,000 plants representing over 700 species—250 of them indigenous to Cuba. Begonias flourish along with other ornamentals beneath the shade of tall palms and towering ephiphyte-clad trees, such as the aptly named elephant's feet.

Accommodations and Food

About a dozen families who live along the road linking Soroa with the Autopista rent rooms. All are similar. **Hospedaje Virginia y Rolando** (Carretera Soroa Km 4.5, no tel; CUC20–25) offers a spacious and attractive room with two beds, air-conditioning, fans, a small TV, and private hot-water bathroom. **Casa de Pepe Hernández** (no tel.; CUC20, CUC25 including breakfast), half a kilometer farther up the road, offers one large, well-lit, simply furnished room with a small TV and a fridge.

Hotel and Villa Turística Soroa (Carretera de Soroa Km 8, Candelaria, tel. 085/3534; CUC 38 s, CUC48 d low season; CUC42 s, CUC52 d high season cabins; from CUC43–72 s/d low season, CUC46–77 s/d high season *casas*) is a delightful resort complex. Stone pathways lead through landscaped grounds to an Olympic-size swimming pool surrounded

by 49 small *cabinas* on slopes backed by forest. The small cabins offer a pleasing ambience, with air-conditioning, cable TV, and handsome hot-water bathrooms. The resort also has 20 one- to four-bedroom houses—Casitas de Soroa—with kitchenettes, TVs, safes, and private pools. Tomás Felipe Camacho's original three-bedroom home can be rented. (Gran Caribe.)

The hotel's **Restaurant Centro** (daily 7:15–9:30 A.M., 12:30–4 P.M., and 7–9:45 P.M.) is attractive and serves continental and *criollo* dishes.

The **Bar y Restaurante El Salto** (daily noon–4 P.M.), by the entrance to the cascade, is a handsome thatched eatery serving fish and meat dishes for US$4–7.

Services

The Hotel Soroa offers hiking, plus horseback riding (CUC3 per hour) and bird-watching (CUC15–25).

A Transtur office in the hotel rents cars.

Getting There

Soroa is seven kilometers north of the Autopista. The turnoff is about 80 kilometers west of Havana. Trains from Havana and Pinar del Río (one per day each direction) stop at Candelaria, from where you can take a taxi or hitch to Soroa, nine kilometers north. The Havana–Pinar Víazul and Astro buses will drop you at the Cupet gas station at the Candelaria junction on the Autopista, from where you can hitch.

Tour companies in Havana offer excursions.

COMPLEJO TURÍSTICO LAS TERRAZAS

This one-of-a-kind model village, 20 kilometers northeast of Soroa and 4 kilometers northwest of the Autopista, is touted as one of Cuba's prime ecotourism sites. Las Terrazas (pop. 1,200; 8 A.M.–5 P.M. for day visits) was founded in 1971 and is situated in a narrow valley above the shores of Lago San Juan with mountains to every side. It lies at the heart of a comprehensive rural development project

SOROA AND COMPLEJO TURÍSTICO LAS TERRAZAS

© AVALON TRAVEL PUBLISHING, INC.

that encompasses 12,355 acres and is better known throughout Cuba as the home of the late singer Polo Montañez.

French settlers who fled Haiti in 1792 planted coffee in these hills. After the plantations failed, the local campesinos continued to fell the trees for export and eke out a living as charcoal burners. Hillside by hillside, much of the region was deforested. In 1967 the government initiated a 5,000-hectare reforestation project, employing the impoverished campesinos and providing them with housing in a prize model village. Las Terrazas is named for the terraces of trees (teak, cedar, mahogany, pine) that were planted two at a time, side by side.

The houses of whitewashed concrete are aligned in terraces that cascade down the hillside to the lake. The village **community center,** facing a tiny *plazuela* with a fountain, houses a cinema, dentists' and doctors' offices, a small store, a post office, and a small **museum** that tells the tale of Las Terrazas' development. There's even a rodeo ring where you can watch *guajiros* tussling with stallions and steers.

Rancho Curijey (tel. 082/77-8555, fax 082/77-8578), the administrative center, about 400 meters east of the village, offers a thatched restaurant and bar over its own lake with geese and an inflatable trampoline. The **Centro Ecológico,** a basic ecological center, gathers scientific information for the reserve. Visitors are welcome.

It gets cool here; bring a sweater.

Cafetal Buenavista

The "Beautiful View Coffee Estate," about two kilometers east of La Moka, preserves the ruins of a French coffee plantation constructed in 1801. The buildings have been lovingly restored. The main building is now a handsome restaurant. Behind the restaurant are stone terraces where coffee beans were laid out to dry, the remains of the old slave quarters, and, on the uppermost terrace, an ox-powered coffee grinder where coffee beans were ground to remove the husks. It is hoped that the land eventually will be restored to the point that this could again become a working coffee plantation.

It's very breezy up here, with spectacular views over the expansive plains. Guides (CUC3 per hour) are available for local hikes.

Ruinas del Cafetal San Pedro y Cafetal Santa Catalina

Beginning about eight kilometers west of Las Terrazas, the **Sendero Cañada del Infierno** follows the Río Bayate south through dense forest to the ruins of San Pedro and the sulfur baths of Santa Catalina (CUC2 Mon.– Thurs., free Fri.–Sun.). It's easy to miss the turnoff; look for the bridge over the Río Bayate. The dirt road follows the river south two kilometers to the ruins of the French coffee plantation. The crumbling remains are overgrown, and climbing figs clamber up the walls. Midway, a faint hint of sulfur lures you downhill to the river, where natural pools encourage swimming.

Baños de San Juan

A paved road leads south from the rodeo ring in Las Terrazas, three kilometers to the San Juan (9 A.M.–7 P.M.; CUC4 entrance Mon.– Thurs., free Fri.–Sun.) cascades and pools. From the parking lot a paved path leads over a small bridge and along the river's edge past deep pools (good for swimming) and sunning platforms to a series of cascades. *¡Que linda!* Thatched *ranchitas,* including a small bar selling burgers and grilled meals, sit above the falls, and there are toilets.

The **Caminata El Contento** trail leads from the San Juan baths to Campismo El Taburete via the ruins of La Victoria coffee plantation.

Entertainment and Events

The two community bars, **El Almacigo** and **Casa de Bota,** down by the lake, usually have someone playing guitar. The touristed **Dos Hermanos** bar in La Moka is plusher but lacks life.

The **Peña de las Terrazas** (10 A.M.–6 P.M.), in the Casa de Cultura, shows a revolving video of Polo Montañez's life.

Recreation

Several poorly marked trails lead into the mountains. Two of import are the **Sendero Las Delicias** and the **Sendero La Serafina.** The former climbs Lomas Las Delicias, from where you have a fine view down the valley. The trip ends at the Buena Vista coffee plantation. La Serafina (4 km) is of particular appeal to bird-watchers. The Cuban trogon, the solitaire, woodpeckers, and the Cuban tody are common. The **Sendero Buenavista** also leads two kilometers to the coffee plantation.

Guided hikes (CUC18–21 per person) and bird-watching trips (CUC16–18 per person) can be booked at La Moka. The Centro Ecológico also rents guides (CUC5 per person, per hour for up to four people; flat fee CUC20 per hour for more than four).

You can rent horses (CUC1 for 20 minutes, CUC15 for three hours). Pedal-boats can be rented on the lake at **Casa de los Botes** (tel. 082/77-8519; CUC2 per hour). You can swim at the Hotel La Moka (CUC3).

Accommodations

In 2004, the government enlarged and furnished five private homes to be rented out by their owners as *casas particulares* (CUC50 s, CUC60 d low season; CUC55 s, CUC70 d high season). They are furnished in similar fashion as the Hotel La Moka, which handles all bookings. Three rooms are with families; two are independent apartments. The government creams the daily charge, and pays the owners 500 pesos—*moneda nacional*—monthly.

Campismo El Taburete (tel. 082/77-8670; CUC5), one kilometer east of Las Terrazas, has 54 two- and four-bed basic concrete cabins beside the forest. Eastern-bloc architecture prevails over good taste, but the woodsy ambience is appealing and they provide a rare chance to mingle with Cubans, who flock on weekends. There's a bar and restaurant, TV room, and ponies for the kids. Camping is permitted (tents can be rented).

You can also rent rustic thatched cabins on stilts (CUC13 s, CUC22 d) or pitch a tent

(CUC5 per person) at **Camping Baños de San Juan** (tel. 082/77-8600, fax 082/77-8136, www.lasterrazas.cu).

 Hotel La Moka (tel. 082/77-8600, fax 082/77-8136, www.lasterrazas.cu; CUC60 s, CUC80 d low season; CUC70 s, CUC95 d high season) is a contemporary interpretation of Spanish-colonial architecture and features an atrium lobby surrounding a lime tree disappearing through the skylight, while the two-story accommodations block has magnificent red-barked trees growing up through the balconies and ceiling. The 26 rooms are designed to international standards. Each has a floor-to-ceiling glass window and French door leading onto a spacious balcony with tables, reclining chairs, and views through the trees to the lake. Take an upper-story room with high sloping wooden ceilings and antique ceiling fans. Facilities include a tennis court, small swimming pool, sundeck, and lido café and bar amid landscaped grounds.

Food

At **La Fondita de Mercedes** (Unit 9; daily 11 A.M.–4 P.M. and 7–9 P.M.), Mercedes Dache cooks fabulous meals enjoyed on a terrace. My beef in a tangy sauce with rice and beans, plantain, and pimento, was excellent (CUC12, including beer and dessert). Most *platos principales* cost CUC4.50–6.

The menu at the upscale **La Moka** restaurant (7:30–10 A.M., noon–4 P.M., and 7–10 P.M.) includes beef stew (CUC6.50), roast chicken (CUC7), and butterfly lobster (CUC6.50).

At **Cafetal Buenavista** (11 A.M.–4 P.M.) you can have lunch on a tree-shaded terrace. A set lunch costs CUC13, including coffee, dessert, and a fabulous main dish of rice, lightly boiled potatoes, vegetables, fried bananas, and baked garlic chicken.

The most atmospheric place is **Casa del Campesino** (radio tel. 082/77-8555; 11 A.M.–4 P.M. and 6:30–9 P.M. daily), two kilometers west of Las Terrazas, a typical peasant's farm on the ruins of the old Hacienda Unión coffee plantation. Here Gustavo Golnega and his family raise fowl and serve traditional meals prepared in the open kitchen with wood-fired oven. Most dishes are overpriced but you can enjoy a hearty meal for around CUC15, including coffee. Reservations are required for meals after 5 P.M. Unfortunately, the place is often packed with tour groups and the kitchen often runs out of everything but pork.

Vegetarians should head to the **Eco-Restaurante El Romero** (tel. 08/77-8555, 9 A.M.–9 P.M. daily).

Shopping

Whether you intend to invest or not, call at **Estudio Lester Campa** (Unit 4, tel. 082/77-8590, lester@terraz.co.cu; 8 A.M.–4 P.M. daily). Lester Campa's fabulous works display staggering detail; his works begin at around CUC300 (Campa's larger paintings fetch thousands of dollars on the international market).

Local artisan Alberto González sells his beautiful kitchen implements handcrafted of local hardwoods at **Taller de Alberto** (8 A.M.–4 P.M. daily). Just up from the rodeo is **Taller de Fibras**, where a women's cooperative makes bargain-priced hats, baskets, and other items of banana leaves and straw. An artist named Duporté specializes in paintings on Cuban flora, especially orchids. There's also a pottery workshop and **Taller de Serigrafo** (8 A.M.–5 P.M. daily), a serigraphy workshop.

Getting There

Las Terrazas, 75 kilometers west of Havana, is four kilometers north of the Autopista, at Km 51 (there's a sign), where a road runs into the mountains. You'll pass a barrier and guard post en route. You can also reach Las Terrazas north from Soroa, and from the Circuito Norte (although the turn-off is unmarked and easily missed).

Tour agencies in Havana offer excursions to Las Terrazas. A taxi costs about CUC40 each way.

The EssTo gas station (8 A.M.–5 P.M. daily) is hidden off the main road, 400 meters west of the turnoff into Las Terrazas.

PINAR DEL RÍO

SAN DIEGO DE LOS BAÑOS

Continuing west along the Autopista or Carretera Central, you'll pass the turnoff for San Diego de los Baños, a small but once important spa town on the banks of the Río San Diego, 120 kilometers west of Havana and 60 kilometers east of Pinar del Río. This endearing village, about 10 kilometers north of the Autopista, is centered on a tree-shaded plaza with a Greek Orthodox–style church. The spa waters of the Templado springs were discovered in the 17th century and launched to fame when a leprous slave was supposedly miraculously cured after bathing here. German scholar and explorer Baron Alexander von Humboldt hyped the San Diego waters. Subsequently, the resort was promoted in the United States as the Saratoga of the Tropics (the historic Hotel Saratoga, one block west of the park, is of interest).

The mineral waters (a near-constant 37°–40°C) are an ideal salve for rheumatism, skin disorders, and other ailments. A modern facility with subterranean whirlpool baths was built after the Revolution. The deteriorated **Balneario San Diego** (tel. 08/37874; daily 8 A.M.–4 P.M.) provides treatments including acupuncture (CUC20) and massage (CUC20). Wheelchairs are provided for visitors with disabilities.

Accommodations and Food

Casa de Caridad y Julio Gutiérrez (Calle 29 #4009, e/ 40 y 42, tel. 082/37811 c/o a neighbor; CUC20), 50 meters west of Hotel Saratoga, has two air-conditioned rooms with refrigerators and private hot-water bathrooms. Meals are served on a shady terrace fronting the pleasant garden.

Hotel El Mirador (Calle 23 final, tel./fax 082/77-8338, carpeta@mirador.sandiego.co.cu; CUC30 s, CUC37 d, CUC46 s/d suite low season; CUC34 s, CUC41 d, CUC50 s/d suite high season including breakfast) is an attractive property with a beautiful setting above landscaped grounds, with a swimming pool and tiled courtyard. You'll find contemporary flourishes inside the colonial-style 1950s-era structures. The 30 large, air-conditioned rooms feature simple albeit attractive decor (rattan and pink floral prints), satellite TVs, direct-dial telephones, and hot water in the showers. The classy restaurant is lit by Tiffany lamps, although the menu is limited to the usual *criollo* staples; plus there's an open-air grill. (Islazul.)

Services

There are a post office and telephone office opposite Hotel Libertad, and a gas station on the east side of town.

The Hotel Mirador offers guided birdwatching (CUC5 per person) and excursions, and the hotel's Transtur branch rents cars.

Getting There and Away

Astro buses depart Havana for San Diego at 8:45 A.M., and San Diego for Havana at 1 P.M., arriving and departing from the southwest side of the plaza.

PARQUE NACIONAL LA GÜIRA

Parque Nacional La Güira protects 54,000 acres of wilderness that rise to pine forests on the higher slopes of the Sierra de los Órganos. The park occupies the former estate of Manuel Cortina, a wealthy landowner who traded in precious woods. Following the Revolution, the land was expropriated and made a preserve for the recreational use of all Cubans, although it sees few visitors.

You enter the park through a mock fortress gate with turrets (4 km west of San Diego de los Baños), beyond which the road rises to Cortina's former mansion—now in ruins—and a series of modest and deteriorated gardens including a Japanese garden, a Cuban garden planted profusely with butterfly jasmine and flame trees, and a formal English garden with statuary and topiary.

A road leads north through the park and continues to La Palma, on the north coast; midway to La Palma, you can turn left via San Andrés to Viñales. Albeit very scenic, the roads are very denuded!

◖ Cuevas de los Portales

This dramatic cave (entrance CUC1, cameras CUC1) on the northwestern edge of the park, about seven kilometers from the main entrance, has a stunning setting beside the Río Caiguanabo flowing beneath a fantastically sculpted natural arch that the river has carved through a great *mogote*. The cave, reaching 30 meters high, lies inside one wall of the arch. The massive chamber's curved walls and vaulted ceilings are stippled with giant stalagmites and stalactites.

The caves' remoteness and superb natural position made them a perfect spot for Che Guevara to establish his staff headquarters during the 1962 Cuban Missile Crisis, when he commanded the Western Army. The cave opens out to the rear, where stands Che's breeze-block office and dormitory, still containing the original table and chairs. Inside, a portal leads to another tiny cave with a floor of rough-hewn boards still supporting Che's narrow, iron bed.

The road to the caves is very eroded; four-wheel drive is preferred.

Accommodations and Food

Campismo Cuevas Portales (tel. 082/32749; CUC5 per person, CUC3 per person camping), beside the river, has spartan concrete *cabinas* with bunks, sofa, and cold-water showers. It also has tent sites with barbecue pits beneath shade trees. There's a basic thatched bar and restaurant. Bring insect repellent. (Cubamar.)

Pinar del Río and Vicinity

PINAR DEL RÍO

Pinar del Río (pop. 125,000), 178 kilometers west of Havana, is named for the native pine trees that once flourished along the banks of the Río Guamá. It was founded in 1669. Tobacco farmers established themselves nearby, in Viñales and Vuelta Abajo, and the city prospered on the tobacco trade—the first tobacco factory was founded nearby in 1761. The town is known for its neoclassical buildings with decorative art nouveau frontages. Tourist literature stretches the truth in touting the city as the "Paradise in the West," as tourist sites of interest are few. However, it makes a good base for exploring the province, and banks, tour agencies, and other tourist services are found here.

Orientation

The town is laid out in a rough grid, but many streets are aligned or curve at odd angles, and it is easy to lose your direction. The Autopista slides into town from the east. It becomes Calle Martí, a wide boulevard dividing the town north and south. Martí is the main street, and most places of interest are here, or along adjacent Calle Máximo Gómez (one block south). The main cross street is Isabel Rubio, which leads north and south to the regions of Viñales and Vuelto Abajo. The city rises westward: at the "top" of Calle Martí is Plaza de la Independencia, a small triangular plaza where the most important historic buildings are found.

Street numbers begin at Calle Martí (which runs east–west) and Calle Gerardo Medina (which runs north–south). Thus addresses suffixed by "Este" lie east of Gerardo Medina, and addresses suffixed by "Oeste" are west of Gerardo Medina. Similarly, any streets suffixed by "Norte" lie north of Calle Martí and those suffixed by "Sur" lie south of Calle Martí.

Museo de Ciencias Naturales

The small and mediocre Museum of Natural Sciences (Calle Martí Este #202, esq. Av. Comandante Pinares, tel. 082/75-3087; Mon.– Sat. 9 A.M.–4:45 P.M., Sun. 9 A.M.–12:45 P.M.; CUC1) displays the natural history of the province and includes stuffed mammals, birds, fish, and a collection of seashells. Concrete dinosaurs stand transfixed in the

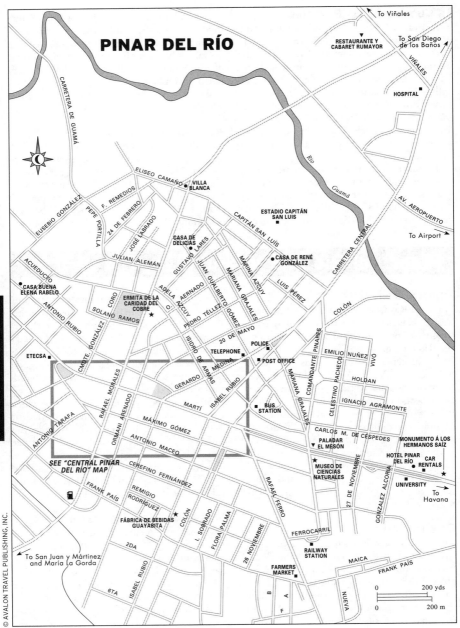

PINAR DEL RÍO

To Viñales

RESTAURANTE Y
CABARET RUMAYOR

To San Diego
de los Baños

CARRETERA DE GUAMÁ

VIÑALES

HOSPITAL

Río Guamá

AV. AEROPUERTO

To Airport

ELISEO CAMAÑO

VILLA
BLANCA

EUSEBIO GONZÁLEZ

F. REMEDIOS

PEPE PORTILLA

24 DE FEBRERO

JOSÉ LABRADO

JULIAN ALEMÁN

ACUEDUCTO

CASA DE
DELICIAS

GUSTAVO LARES

ESTADIO CAPITÁN
SAN LUIS

CAPITÁN SAN LUIS

CASA DE RENÉ
GONZÁLEZ

MARINA AZCUY

MARIANA GRAJALES

LUIS PÉREZ

CARRETERA CENTRAL

CASA BUENA
ELENA RABELO

CORO

SOLANO RAMOS

ADELA AZCUY

ERMITA DE LA
CARIDAD DEL
COBRE

JUAN GUALBERTO GÓMEZ

JUAN AERNADO

PEDRO TÉLLEZ

COLÓN

ANTONIO RUBIO

CMTE. GONZÁLEZ

ISIDRO DE ARMAS

20 DE MAYO

POLICE

TELEPHONE

POST OFFICE

EMILIO NUÑEZ

VIVÓ

COMANDANTE PINARES

CELESTINO PACHECO

HOLDAN

IGNACIO AGRAMONTE

ETECSA

RAFAEL MORALES

GERARDO

ISABEL RUBIO

MARTÍ

BUS
STATION

MARIANA GRAJALES

ANTONIO TARAFA

ORMANI ARNADO

MÁXIMO GÓMEZ

ANTONIO MACEO

CARLOS M. DE CÉSPEDES

PALADAR
EL MESÓN

MONUMENTO Á LOS
HERMANOS SAÍZ

SEE "CENTRAL PINAR
DEL RÍO" MAP

CEREFINO FERNÁNDEZ

MUSEO DE
CIENCIAS
NATURALES

27 DE NOVIEMBRE

HOTEL PINAR
DEL RÍO

CAR
RENTALS

GONZÁLEZ ALCORA

UNIVERSITY

To
Havana

FRANK PAÍS

REMIGIO
RODRÍGUEZ

COLÓN

RAFAEL FERRO

FÁBRICA DE BEBIDAS
GUAYABITA

I. SOBRADO

FLORA/PALMA

26 NOVIEMBRE

FERROCARRIL

2DA

To San Juan y Mártinez
and María La Gorda

ISABEL RUBIO

RAILWAY
STATION

MAICA

FRANK PAÍS

FARMERS
MARKET

6TA

B   A

F

NUEVA

0   200 yds

0   200 m

WALKING TOUR OF PINAR DEL RÍO

The city's few sites of interest, concentrated within a few blocks, can be explored on foot in half a day.

Begin at the Museo de Ciencias Naturales, handily situated at the foot of Calle Martí. After perusing the museum, follow Martí west two blocks to the **Teatro José Jacinto Milanés** (Calle Martí, esq. Calle Colón, tel. 082/75-3871; Mon.-Fri. 9 A.M.-5 P.M.; CUC1) to admire its ornate circular, tiered interior made entirely of wood. The first theater here was dedicated in 1845, though the current theater dates to 1898. A recent restoration has resurrected its fin-de-siècle splendor. Immediately west is the **Museo Provincial de Historia** (Calle Martí Este #58, e/ Isabel Rubio y Colón, tel. 082/75-4300; Mon.-Fri. 8 A.M.-6:30 P.M., Sat. 8 A.M.-noon; CUC1), which traces local history. Aboriginal artifacts (including a mock cave dwelling) are displayed, along with antique furniture and weaponry.

Turn left onto Isabel Rubio and walk four blocks to the **Fábrica de Bebidas Guayabita** (Isabel Rubio Sur #189, e/ Cerefino Fernández y Frank País, tel. 082/75-2966; Mon.-Fri. 10 A.M.-4 P.M., alternate Sat. 9 A.M.-1 P.M.), which since 1892 has made guayabita, a spicy, brandy-like alcoholic drink made from rum and guava and produced exclusively in Pinar del Río. It is made from the fruit of a wild bush – Psidium guayabita – that grows only in Pinar del Río. There are two kinds: a sweet licor de guayabita and a dry guayabita seca brandy. Tours are offered (CUC1). In the tasting room, you can tipple various versions, including guayabita served with a shot of crème de menthe.

Retrace your steps two blocks to Antonio Maceo. Turn left and walk west to the **Catedral de San Rosendo** (Calle Maceo Este #2, esq. Gerardo Medina; Mon.-Fri. 2-6 P.M.), which dates from 1833 and has a barrel vaulted wooden ceiling and fine gilt altar. Mass is held Wednesday-Friday at 5:30 P.M.; Tuesday, Thursday, and Saturday at 8 A.M.; and Sunday at 7:30 A.M. and 10 A.M.

Continuing west, uphill, call in at the **Galería Korda** (Maceo #21, esq. Ormani Arenado). Art is also displayed in the **Casa Natal de Antonio Guiteras Holmes** (Maceo Este #52, e/ San Juan y Ormani Avenado), in the former house of a local pharmacist and revolutionary hero brutally murdered in 1935 by the Machado regime.

One block farther west you come to the **Fábrica de Tabacos Francisco Donatién** (Calle Antonio Maceo Oeste #157, esq. Ajete, tel. 082/75-3069; Mon.-Fri. 9 A.M.-noon and 1-4 P.M., Sat.-Sun. 9 A.M.-noon; guided tour CUC5), a quaint cigar factory housed in the former jail. You can peer through glass windows to watch the 30 or so tabaqueros, who sit in two aisles, sorting their leaves and rolling, trimming, and gluing labels onto cigars.

End your walking tour one block west at **Plaza Independencia.** Those with a religious bent might turn east down Calle Martí and follow Rafael Morales west three blocks to the little **Ermita de la Caridad del Cobre** (Rafael Morales, e/ Ramos y Isidro de Armas; daily 8 A.M.-noon and 3-5:30 P.M.), a small church with a splendid classical aesthetic.

courtyard, including a plesiosaur (a giant marine reptile) and a *Megalocnus rodens* (an extinct oversized rodent once found in Cuba). The museum is housed in an ornately stuccoed building, the Palacio Gausch, built in 1914 by a Spanish doctor to reflect elements from his travels around the world. Thus, the columned entrance is supported by Athenian columns bearing Egyptian motifs, while Gothic griffins and gargoyles adorn the facade.

Entertainment

Pinar hosts a four-day **Carnaval** in early July, when *carrozas* (floats) and *comparsas* (costumed troupes) followed by conga lines of revel-making locals wind through the streets, beginning in Plaza de la Independencia.

Cabaret Rumayor (Carretera Viñales, tel. 082/76-3007; Thurs.–Sun. at 10 P.M.; CUC3 including one drink), one kilometer north of town, offers a modest two-hour-long *cabaret*

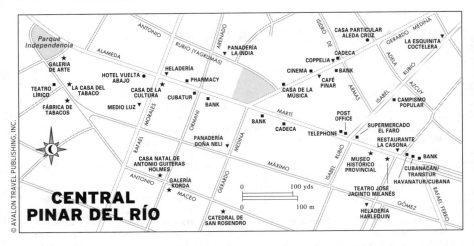

CENTRAL PINAR DEL RÍO

espectáculo. The show begins at 11 P.M. and is followed by a disco. It's the liveliest spot in town, and gets packed on weekends. You need to show ID to enter.

Disco Azul, in the Hotel Pinar del Río, hosts a *cabaret espectáculo* (Tues.–Sun. at 10 P.M.; CUC2), preceded by karaoke.

The small **Café Pinar** (Gerardo Medina Norte #34, tel. 08/77-8199; CUC3 including one drink) also draws the young crowd for live music nightly, from bolero to rap. Again, you need ID to get in.

For traditional music, try the **Casa de Cultura** (Máximo Gómez #108, tel. 082/75-2324), with live music nightly at 9 P.M. The folkloric dances feature the *punta campesina,* in which *guajiros* recite poetry to each other in conversational fashion, each building on the work of the other in a form known as *controversias.* Children's programs are offered on weekends at 2 P.M. Live music is also featured nightly in the patio at the **Casa de la Música** (Gerardo Medina Norte #21 y Antonio Rubio; CUC1).

For a quiet drink, head to **La Esquinita Coctelera** (Isabel Rubio Norte, esq. Juan Gualberto Gómez, no tel.; noon–midnight, daily), which serves *guayabita* and the house special, vermouth and rum.

The Vegueros, the local **baseball team,** hosts visiting teams at the Estadio Capitán San Luis (Calle Capitán San Luis), three blocks west of the Carretera Central for Viñales (Oct.–Mar.).

Accommodations

Casas Particulares: There are dozens to choose from. **Villa Blanca** (Rafael Morales #233, esq. Horriman, tel. 082/75-2012; CUC20) offers one air-conditioned room with independent entrance and a private hot-water bath. Guests have use of a pleasantly furnished TV lounge.

Casa de Elena Rabelo (Antonio Rubio #284, e/ Méndez Capote y Coronel Pozo, tel. 082/75-4295, ghernandez@princesa.pri.sld.cu; CUC20) has two pleasantly furnished rooms with private bathrooms, plus secure parking. Elena charges CUC1 for the garage.

Casa de Aleda Cruz (Gerardo Medina 67, tel. 082/75-3133; CUC15 with fans, CUC20 with a/c) is a venerable colonial home with a choice of eight basically furnished rooms that differ in size. Each has private hot-water bathroom. A patio to the rear has an exquisite little garden and secure parking.

Casa Las Delicias (Delicias #206, e/ Justo Hidalgo y Marina, tel. 082/77-1678, marguy48@princesa.pri.sld.cu; CUC20 low season, CUC25 high season) is a complete air-conditioned apartment with a telephone, patio with rockers, and hot water in a clean bathroom lacking a toilet seat. It offers secure parking. The owners are educated and good conversationalists.

Casa de René González (Calle Unión #13, e/ Capitán San Luis y Carmen, Rpto. Villamil, tel. 082/75-5196; CUC20) has two air-conditioned rooms upstairs, each with independent entrance, spacious balcony, and separate lounge. They're clean and have fans, fridges, and clean hot-water bathrooms. There's secure parking. Meals are offered.

Hotels: The newly restored **Hotel Vuelta Abajo** (Martí #103, esq. Rafael Morales, tel. 082/75-9387, suset@vueltabajo.pinar.cu; CUC40 s, CUC52 d low season; CUC45 s, CUC62 d high season) is a charming historic hotel done up in pinks and ochers. A marble staircase leads to 24 lofty-ceilinged rooms with simple antique furnishings. Street noise is a factor here. Public arenas feature beautiful antiques and stained glass. It has the best restaurant in town, plus an Internet café.

Hotel Pinar del Río (Martí y Final Autopista, tel. 082/75-5070, fax 082/77-1699, isidro@hpt.co.cu; CUC24 s, CUC34 d low season; CUC29 s, CUC38 d high season), on the eastern fringe of town, is a depressingly post-Stalinist structure. Its 149 large, air-conditioned rooms are modestly furnished and have private baths, satellite TVs, telephones, radios, and safes. It has car rental, a boutique, nightclub, game room, restaurant, poolside grill, café, and lobby bar. The swimming pool is a gathering spot for locals on weekends.

Villa Aguas Claras (Carretera de Viñales Km 7.5, tel. 08/77-8426; CUC21 s/d including breakfast) is eight kilometers north of town on the road to Viñales; bus #7 from town passes by. It bills itself as an eco-resort and has 50 thatched and modestly furnished air-conditioned *cabinas* spread amid landscaped grounds. Folkloric shows are performed. Facilities include a swimming pool, restaurant, snack bar, and tourism bureau. Guides are available for hikes, and horses can be rented (CUC3.60 per hour; CUC8.90 for a guided excursion). Loud music is a problem when Cuban groups are in, and mosquitoes thrive. **Camping** is also allowed.

Food

The best place in town is the **Restaurant Vuelta Abajo** (7:15–9:30 A.M., noon–3 P.M., and 6–10 P.M. daily), in the Hotel Vuelta Abajo. It serves *criollo* staples for below CUC5 but is clean and has efficient air-conditioning.

Paladar El Mesón (Calle Martí Este #205, tel. 082/75-2867; Mon.–Sat noon–10 P.M.), opposite the Museo de Ciencias Naturales, serves the usual *criollo* fare for CUC4–6. The tablecloths were dirty at last visit, the food mediocre, and flies were abundant, but this is the only *paladar* in the center of town.

For ambience, try the **Restaurante y Cabaret Rumayor** (tel. 082/76-3007; daily noon–midnight), one kilometer north of town on Carretera Viñales. The thatch-and-log dining room is decorated with African drums, shields, and religious icons. Service is keen, but the food is mediocre at best. *Criollo* dishes include the famous house special, *pollo ahumado* (smoked chicken, CUC5) and *chirna frita* (fish sautéed with garlic, CUC7).

Restaurante La Casona (Calle Martí y Colón, tel. 08/77-8263; daily 11 A.M.–11 P.M.) is a large, airy option serving simple spaghetti and *criollo* dishes for less than CUC1.

Coppelia (Gerardo Medina Norte #33; Tues.–Sun. noon–midnight), one block east of Martí, has ice cream for 60 centavos per scoop.

For baked goods, head to **Panadería La India Moderna** (Antonio Rubio y 20 de Mayo; daily 7 A.M.–noon and 5–7 P.M.) or **Panadería Doña Neli** (Gerado Medina Sur y Máximo Gómez; daily 7 A.M.–10 P.M.).

You can buy produce at the *mercado agropecuario* (Rafael Ferro y Ferrocarril), four blocks south of Martí.

Shopping

La Casa del Tabaco (Antonio Maceo Oeste, tel. 082/77-2244; daily 8:30 A.M.–4:30 P.M.) is well stocked with export-quality cigars, as is the humidor in the **Fábrica de Tabacos Francisco Donatién** (Calle Antonio Maceo Oeste

#157, esq. Ajete, tel. 082/75-3424, 9 A.M.–noon and 1 P.M.–4 P.M. Mon.–Fri., 9 A.M.–noon Sat.–Sun.). And you can buy bottles of *guayabita* at the **Fábrica de Bebidas Guayabita** (Isabel Rubio Sur #189, e/ Cerefino Fernández y Frank País, tel. 082/75-2966).

Information and Services

There's a post office and DHL station in the Hotel Pinar del Río (tel. 082/75-5070, ext. 251). The main post office is at Calle Martí Este #49, esq. Isabel Rubio. **Etecsa** *telepunto* (Gerardo Medina, esq. Juan Gualberto Gómez; daily 8:30 A.M.–6:30 P.M.) has international phone plus Internet service.

Banks include **Bandec** (Martí Este #32, e/ Rafael Morales y Ormani Arenado) and **Banco Financiero Internacional** (Gerardo Medina Norte #44, esq. Isidro de Armas). You can change foreign currency at **Cadeca** (Gerardo Medina Norte #35, esq. Isidro de Armas; and Martí, e/ Medina y Isabel Rubio).

The **Hospital León Cuevo Rubio** (Gerardo Medina, tel. 082/75-2229) is about one kilometer northeast of town; and **Hospital Abel Santamaria** (tel. 082/76-3113) is nearby, on the Carretera Central near the junction for Viñales.

Basic cabins at *campismos* throughout the province can be reserved through **Campismo Popular** (Isabel Rubio Norte #20, tel. 08/75-5316; Mon.–Fri. 8 A.M.–noon and 1–5 P.M., Sat. 8 A.M.–noon).

Getting There and Away

By Air: The **Aeropuerto Álvaro Barba** (tel. 08/76-3196) is two miles northeast of town. At last visit, the airport was dormant. In the past, flights have occasionally used La Coloma airstrip (tel. 08/75-5545), about 13 kilometers southeast of town.

By Bus: Buses arrive and depart the **Terminal de Ómnibus** (Calle Adela Azcuy, e/ Colón y Comandante Pinares, tel. 082/75-

2571). **Víazul** (tel. 082/75-2572) buses connect Pinar del Río, departing from Havana at 9 A.M. and 2 P.M. and continuing to Viñales at 11:30 A.M. and 4:30 P.M.; and to Havana from Pinar at 8:50 A.M. and 2:50 P.M. (CUC11). The Víazul office (8 A.M.–7 P.M.) is upstairs.

Astro bus #100 departs Pinar del Río for Havana at 3, 5:20, and 7:20 A.M., noon, and 4 P.M.; and for Viñales at 10 A.M., 11 A.M., and 6:20 P.M. (CUC8).

Colectivo taxis and *camiones* also leave from the bus station for Havana.

By Train: The railway station (Calle Comandante Pinares y Ferrocarril, tel. 082/75-2272) is three blocks south of Calle Martí. Trains depart Havana's main railway station daily at 10:13 P.M. (six hours, CUC6.50). Trains depart Pinar del Río for Havana at 8:15 A.M.

Tour Agencies: Tour agencies offer excursions and can make air and hotel reservations nationwide. These include **Cubatur** (Calle Martí #115, esq. Ormani Arenado, tel. 082/77-8405; Mon.–Fri. 8 A.M.–5 P.M., Sat. 8 A.M.–noon); **Cubanacán** (Martí #109, esq. Colón, tel. 082/75-0178 8 A.M.–5 P.M. daily); and, next door, **Havanatur** (tel. 082/77-8494).

EcoTur (Carretera a Luis Lazo Km 21.5, tel. 082/75-3844, ecoturpr@enet.cu) offers ecotourism excursions.

Getting Around

Pinar is small enough to walk virtually everywhere. You can flag down *bici-taxis* virtually anywhere. Horse-drawn taxis gather on Máximo Gómez between Rafael Ferro and Ciprian Valdes. Tourist taxis are based at the Hotel Pinar del Río, where car rental agencies include **Transtur** (tel. 082/77-8278), **Havanautos** (tel. 082/77-8015), and **Micar** (tel. 082/76-1454).

There's a gas station at the bottom of Rafael Morales on the south side of town, and two more stations northeast of town, on the Carretera Central, beyond the turnoff for Viñales.

Sierra de los Órganos

Northwest Pinar del Río Province is dominated by the Sierra de los Órganos range of mountains, boasting the most spectacular scenery in Cuba. The dramatic karst scenery is most fantastic and fascinating within the Valle de Viñales. The valley (about 11 km long and 5 km wide) is cut into the Sierra de los Órganos and scattered with precipitous *mogotes* the height of skyscrapers towering over a plain of impossibly deep green. Between the *mogotes* are *hoyos,* small depressions filled with deep deposits of rich red soil. Thanks to a very special microclimate of moist nights and cool mornings, tobacco grows well here, dominating the valley economy. One of the special memories you'll take home is the image of farmers in straw hats, machetes at their sides, plowing their fields with ox-drawn plows. Farmers will be delighted to take you out into their *vegas* and curing sheds to demonstrate the skill of raising tobacco, much of which lies under acres of cheesecloth stretched over the plants to protect against insects and an excess of sun.

Other, lesser-known vales offer similar scenery and this area lends itself to scenic day excursions by car, scooter, or bicycle.

◖ PARQUE NACIONAL DE VIÑALES

The Valle de Viñales is enshrined within Viñales National Park. Dominating the valley are the dramatic *mogotes* in whose shadows *guajiros* lovingly tend their plots of tobacco and maize. The setting resembles a Vietnamese or Chinese painting, particularly in the early morning, when mists settle above the valley. At its heart is the eponymous village, **Viñales** (pop. 10,000), whose sleepy yesteryear charm is a draw unto itself. Viñales is 26 kilometers north of Pinar del Río and 212 kilometers west of Havana, and was founded in 1875.

Calle Salvador Cisneros

Viñales's wide main street is lined with turn-of-the-century, red tile–roofed cottages shaded by rows of stately pine trees. The handsome main square is shaded by palms and has a

PINAR DEL RÍO

Parque Nacional de Viñales

SIERRA DE
LOS ÓRGANOS

To Bahía Honda, Havana,
San Cayetano and Dimas

● HOTEL HORIZONTES
RANCHO SAN
VICENTE

▼ EL RANCHÓN

LAS
MAGNOLIAS ●   ★ RESTAURANTE CUEVAS DEL INDIO

CUEVAS DEL
INDIO

★ CUEVAS DE
VIÑALES

▼ EL PALENQUE DE
LOS CIMARRONES

Valle de San Vicente

Valle de Ancón

Sierra la Guasasa

Viñales

de

Valle de la Guasasa

Vegas de Tabaco

▲ Mogote de Robustiano

Río

Río Palmarito

Valle el Silencio

Sierra

COMUNIDAD DE
AQUÁTICOS

MURAL DE LA
PREHISTORIA ★   ● CAMPISMO
DOS HERMANOS

RESTAURANTE
DOS HERMANOS ▼   Mogote   del   Valle

▲ Mogote Dos
Hermanos

Viñales

▲ Mogote Coco Sol

SEE "VIÑALES" MAP

de

Viñales

HOTEL LA
ERMITA

← To Caverna de Santo
Tomás and Pons

Sierra   de   los   Órganos

Valle

● CASA DE
VEQUERO

▲ Mogote la Feita

VIEWPOINT ★

HOTEL
HORIZONTES
LAS JASMINES

To Pinar del Río

0   1 mi
0   1 km

© AVALON TRAVEL PUBLISHING, INC.

bust of José Martí at its center. To one side is a pretty 19th-century church. On the north side, a beautiful arcaded colonial building houses the **Casa de Cultura.**

Museo Municipal Adela Azcuy (Salvador Cisneros #115, tel. 08/79-3395; Tues.–Sat. 9 A.M.–10 P.M., Sun. 9 A.M.–noon; CUC1) has motley displays telling the history of the region. Outside stands a bronze bust of Adela Azcuy Labrador (1861–1914), a local captain in the War of Independence.

The other local treasure is the **Casa de Don Tomás** (Salvador Cisneros #140, tel. 08/79-6300), dating to 1822 and now an atmospheric restaurant (see *Food*).

Two widows, Carmen and Caridad Miranda, maintain the **Jardín Botánico de Viñales** (8 A.M.–7 P.M.; entry by contribution), a garden full of fruit trees, medicinal plants, and orchids. The garden is festooned with plastic teddy bears, decapitated doll's heads, and desiccated fruits, giving it airs of shamanic intrigue.

MOGOTES

Making up as much as one third of the island's surface, dramatic limestone mountain formations called *mogotes* ("haystacks") stud the landscape of Cuba. The isolated, sheer-sloped, round-topped mounds are the remnants of a great limestone plateau that rose from the sea during the Jurassic era, about 160 million years ago. Over the ensuing eons, rain and rivers dissolved and eroded the porous limestone mass, leaving hummocks as high as 1,000 feet. The terrain is also found in Jamaica, Puerto Rico, China's Guangxi Province, and the eponymous Karst region of the Dalmatian coast.

Rainwater interacts with limestone to produce a mild carbonic acid (the chemical reactions are speeded along by high tropical temperatures), which assists the erosive action of underground streams, so that structural joints are further weakened. The erosive agents carve a system of underground caverns that become so huge that eventually their roofs collapse, forming sheer-sided valleys. Many caverns can be reached by traipsing through natural tunnels to follow rivers that suddenly disappear down holes in their own valley floors. Pre-Columbian Indians inhabited the caves.

Many species of flora and fauna are found only atop the strange mesas, such as unique varieties of snails. Fauna is so highly endemic that certain mollusks are found only on one or a few *mogotes*. Although the surface soil is thin, and water scarce (it percolates rapidly into the rock), the formations are luxuriantly festooned with epiphytes, ferns, and the rare and ancient cork palm (*Mycrocycas calocoma*), a botanical relic that grows only here.

Cuevas del Indio

The Caves of the Indian (tel. 08/79-6280; daily 9 A.M.–5 P.M.; CUC5), five kilometers north of Viñales, is named for the Indian remains found inside. The large grotto is entered via a slit at the foot of a *mogote*. You can explore the cave with or without a guide. The cave is four kilometers long, although you only explore the first kilometer by foot. A flight of steps leads to the main entrance, where you follow a well-lit path (slippery in parts) through the mesmerizing catacomb, which in places soars to a height of 135 meters. Eventually you reach an underground pier where a motorized boat takes you on a trip up the subterranean, milky green river that runs deep beneath the mountain and is a habitat for opaque fish and blind crustaceans. The cave is also inhabited by small bats. It is like a crossing of the Styx, setting your imagination racing in the Stygian gloom. Try to avoid it when the numerous tour groups are in.

A bird-watching trail begins at the El Ranchón restaurant, outside the cave.

Cueva de Viñales (CUC1 with a guide), one kilometer south of Cuevas del Indio, is mostly a curiosity. The cave entrance has been converted into a discotheque replete with laser lights. Bats and swallows nest in nooks and swoop in and out, disturbed by the flashing fandango of the lights and the discordant beat of the disco (see *Entertainment*).

Mural de la Prehistoria

The much-touted Prehistoric Mural (tel. 08/79-6260; 8 A.M.–7 P.M. daily; CUC1), five kilometers west of Viñales, is painted onto the exposed cliff face of Mogote Dos Hermanos. The mural illustrates evolution in the Sierra de los Órganos, from mollusk and dinosaur to club-wielding Guanajay Indian, the first human inhabitants of the region. The mural, which measures 200 feet high and 300 feet long, was commissioned by Castro and painted by 25 campesinos in 1961 while the artist, Leovigilda González, directed from below with a megaphone. The cliff face has been repainted in gaudy colors—a red brontosaurus, a yellow tyrannosaurus, and a blood-red *homo sapiens!* What was formerly a modestly appealing curiosity is now a testament to bad taste splotched on the wall of what is otherwise a splendidly beautiful valley. A curiosity in the restaurant is the *órgano pinareño*, an antique hand-driven

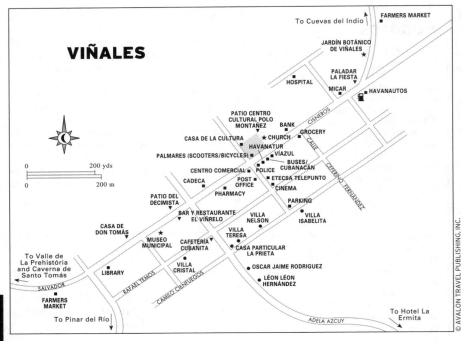

VIÑALES

To Cuevas del Indio

FARMERS MARKET

JARDÍN BOTÁNICO DE VIÑALES

PALADAR LA FIESTA

HOSPITAL

MICAR

HAVANAUTOS

PATIO CENTRO CULTURAL POLO MONTAÑEZ

BANK

CISNEROS

CASA DE LA CULTURA

CHURCH

GROCERY

CALLE

HAVANATUR

PALMARES (SCOOTERS/BICYCLES)

VÍAZUL

BUSES/ CUBANACÁN

CEFERINO FERNÁNDEZ

CENTRO COMERCIAL

POLICE

CADECA

POST OFFICE

ETECSA TELEPUNTO

PHARMACY

CINEMA

PATIO DEL DECIMISTA

PARKING

BAR Y RESTAURANTE EL VIÑRELO

VILLA NELSON

VILLA ISABELITA

CASA DE DON TOMÁS

VILLA TERESA

MUSEO MUNICIPAL

CAFETERÍA CUBANITA

CASA PARTICULAR LA PRIETA

To Valle de La Prehistória and Caverna de Santo Tomás

LIBRARY

VILLA CRISTAL

OSCAR JAIME RODRIGUEZ

RAFAEL TEMOS

CAMILO CIENFUEGOS

LÉON LÉON HERNÁNDEZ

SALVADOR

FARMERS MARKET

To Pinar del Río

ADELA AZCUY

To Hotel La Ermita

0   200 yds

0   200 m

© AVALON TRAVEL PUBLISHING, INC.

organ fed, like a Jacquard loom, with a belt of cards punched with the musical score.

Horseback rides are offered (CUC5 per hour).

A small **Museo de Prehistoria** in the Campismo Dos Hermanos displays pre-Columbian artifacts, natural history specimens, and more.

Comunidad Los Acuáticos

The Comunidad Los Acuáticos comprises 12 families who live midway up the east-facing slope of Sierra de Viñales and rarely descend into the valley. The community, which believes in the healing power of water, was founded in 1943 by Antoñica Izqui>erdo, who Cuban authorities later judged insane (she was institutionalized and died in an insane asylum). Her followers continued their ritual practice, which included three daily baths and drying off in the wind. The tradition is virtually dead

in the community, following the death of the village patriarch in 2002.

The trailhead to the community is about three kilometers along a dirt road that begins at Campismo Dos Hermanos. A more direct trail begins on the Viñales– Pons road, about 500 meters west of the turn for Mogote Dos Hermanos; the actual trailhead begins about one kilometer from the main road. You can make a complete loop.

Tour agencies are not allowed to offer services to Los Acuáticos, but you can hire "illegal" freelance guides in town. Better yet is to rent a horse (about CUC10) for the journey.

Entertainment

You can't beat **Bar y Restaurant El Viñelo** for a place to sup and play dominoes with locals.

A disco is hosted in the **Cueva de Viñales** (tel. 08/79-6290; Tues.–Sat. at 10:30 P.M.; CUC5 including a cocktail), four kilometers north of Viñales. A *cabaret espectáculo* precedes the disco on Saturday.

ARTex's **Palacio del Decimista** (Salvador Cisneros #102, tel. 08/79-6014; CUC1) has live music nightly at 10 P.M. The happening scene at last visit, however, was the **Centro Cultural Polo Montañez,** on the patio of the Casa de la Cultura on the main plaza, with entertainment nightly, including *noches campesinas* ("peasant nights") on Thursday and disco Friday–Saturday (CUC2).

There's a **cinema** at Calle Ceferino Fernández, esq. Rafael Temos.

Recreation

Caving and Climbing: The area is evolving as a mecca for caving and climbing. At least 100 climbing routes have been mapped up the *mogotes.* The unofficial base camp is the Viñales home of Oscar Jaime Rodríguez (Adela Azcuy #43, tel. 08/79-3381), who is also a good source of information. Local climbers José Millo (Calle Rafael Trejo #108) and Abel Fleitas (Calle Joaquín Pérez #1, tel. 08/79-3231) also act as guides. For further information, visit www.cubaclimbing.com.

Hikes: The **Museo Municipal Adela Azcuy** (Salvador Cisneros #115, tel. 08/79-3395) offers five specialist hiking excursions for CUC5 per person, available 9 A.M.–3 P.M. The "Nature & Campesina" trip (four hours) is a stiff hike to traditional farmsteads; there's also an easier three-hour hike. "In the Heart of the Valley" is good for learning about tobacco production. There's also a three-hour coffee tour, and a "Paseo Artístico" that visits artists' studios.

Hotel La Ermita offers guided hiking excursions, plus horseback riding (CUC per hour).

Accommodations

Casas Particulares: There are dozens of private house rentals to choose from. All charge CUC15 (or CUC20 with a/c) and offer meals (usually CUC3 for breakfast, CUC5–10 for dinner). Contrary to some reports, foreigners are now permitted to have Cuban girlfriends and boyfriends as registered guests.

Villa Isabelita (Camilo Cienfuegos #1B, tel. 08/79-3267), close to the plaza, is nicely kept and has an air-conditioned bedroom with two double beds plus fan and a private bathroom with hot water. The delightful hosts prepare filling breakfasts.

One block west, **Villa Nelson** (Camilo Cienfuegos #4, tel. 08/79-3268) is recommended for its simply furnished independent apartment with hot water. Meals are served in a delightful *ranchón* in the rear patio, and taxi service is offered.

Villa Teresa (Camilo Cienfuegos #10, e/ Adela Azcuy y Seferino Fernández, tel. 08/79-3267 c/o a neighbor) has one well-lit, cross-ventilated, air-conditioned room, and a private hot-water bathroom. Adjoining, and owned by a family member, is **Casa Particular La Prieta** (Adela Azcuy #21), an almost identical offering—one room with a tiled modern hot-water bathroom.

Casa de Oscar Jaime Rodríguez (Adela Azcuy #43, tel. 08/79-3381) has a room downstairs and a smaller, newer room upstairs with a nice bathroom, with meals served on a rustic patio. The place is popular with climbers. Next door, **Casa de León León Hernández** (tel. 08/79-6380) has a clean, attractive room for three people with air-conditioning, large closet, fans, and cross-ventilation, and a lounge with TV and CD player.

Casa Claudina Álvarez (Cienfuegos #26, tel. 08/79-6034) has one air-conditioned room. Claudina is a multilingual guide with the museum.

Hotels: Budget hounds might like **Campismo Dos Hermanos** (tel. 08/79-2223; CUC15 s/d), a pleasing camp resort opposite the entrance to the Mural de la Prehistoria. It has 54 basic cabins with private bathrooms, plus a swimming pool, game room, and a pleasant restaurant. It's used primarily by Cubans—a good chance to mingle—although music is usually cranked up full bore. (Cubamar Viajes.)

Las Magnolias (tel. 08/79-6280; CUC20 s/d rooms, CUC5 per person tents), opposite Cuevas del Indio, is a converted home with three air-conditioned rooms for rent. Each is clean and adequate, with radio, two single

© CHRISTOPHER P. BAKER

The *mogotes* of Valle de Viñales form a fantastic backdrop from the sundeck of the Hotel Las Jazmines.

beds, utility furniture, and private bathroom with cold water only. You can camp in tree-shaded nylon tents. (Palmares.)

The recently renovated **Rancho Horizontes San Vicente** (tel. 08/79-6201, fax 08/79-6265, reserva@vinales.hor.tur.cu; CUC40 s, CUC52 d low season; CUC45 s, CUC60 d high season, including breakfast), 200 meters north of Cuevas del Indio, has a delightful woodsy ambience. There are 34 basic air-conditioned *cabinas* spread among forested lawns surrounding a pool. Each has modest furnishings, small satellite TVs, phones, and private hot-water bathrooms. Twenty newer and spacious cabins are more appealing. Therapeutic thermal water and hot mud treatments are offered, and there's Internet service and a delightful restaurant. (Cubanacán.)

The **Hotel La Ermita** (Carretera de la Ermita Km 2, Viñales, tel. 08/79-6071 or 08/79-6121, fax 08/79-6091, laermita@laermita.co.cu; CUC47 s, CUC60 d low season; CUC50 s, CUC64 d high season), one kilometer south of

town, is magnificently nestled atop the southern scarp of the valley. The gracious contemporary property on a classical theme wraps around a sundeck and swimming pool with poolside bar where you may settle beneath palms to drink in the heavenly views. The 62 air-conditioned rooms are nicely decorated. Make sure you get a room with a balcony facing the valley. The restaurant serves reasonable cuisine and musicians entertain. (Cubanacán.)

Also appealing, the **Hotel Las Jazmines** (Carretera de Viñales Km 25, tel. 08/79-6205, fax 08/79-6215, jaz @vinales.hor.tur.cu; CUC49 s, CUC61 d low season; CUC57 s, CUC71 d high season) is an older but recently restored Spanish hacienda–style hotel, with fancy wrought-iron grillwork and fabulous vistas. The 16 air-conditioned *cabinas* stairstep the hillside and are preferred over the 62 rooms in modern blocks. All have radios and satellite TVs, are pleasantly furnished, and have balconies facing an Olympic-size swimming pool. Forty-eight newer rooms are in a separate block. There's an elegant second-floor restaurant and bar. (Cubanacán.)

Food

Most owners of *casas particulares* will prepare filling and tasty breakfasts and *criollo* dinners. For a little variety, the restaurants at both Hotel La Ermita and Las Jasmines are good bets (CUC5–12). Even better is the **Restaurant Las Arcadas** (tel. 08/79-6201; 7:15–10 A.M. and noon–10 P.M. daily), at Rancho Horizontes San Vicente, serving spaghettis, seafoods, and *criollo* staples. You can dine inside, or outside on the delightful patio.

For traditional ambience, try **Casa de Don Tomás** (Salvador Cisneros #141, tel. 08/79-6300; 10 A.M.–9:30 P.M. daily), a historic wooden structure festooned with climbing plants. This is a favorite of tour groups, although the meals are meager and mediocre. The menu includes *delicias de Don Tomás* (a rice dish with pork, sausage, and lobster, US$10), and *criollo* staples such as pork steak (CUC5.50) and lobster enchiladas (CUC12.50). Troubadours serenade while you eat on the airy rear patio.

The traditional, thatched **Casa del Vequero** (tel. 08/79-6080; 9 A.M.–5 P.M. daily), on a tobacco farm 600 meters southwest of the village, also has heaps of ambience plus *trovadores.* It offers complete lunches for CUC10. Before or after your meal, you can visit the thatched *secadero* (curing shed) for a course in Tobacco 101.

Equally rustic, **Ranchón San Vicente Restaurant** (tel. 08/79-6110; 8 A.M.–midnight daily), adjoining the hotel Rancho Horizontes San Vicente, is recommended for its *ajiaco* (meat and vegetable stew) and charcoal-grilled chicken. However, the grilled fare is even better at the thatched restaurant at Mural de la Prehistoria (tel. 08/79-6260; 11:30 A.M.–7 P.M. daily), where the specialty is succulent grilled pork (CUC15); musicians entertain.

Despite doing a reasonable job of a *criollo* menu, **El Palenque de los Cimarrones** (tel. 08/79-6290; noon –4 P.M.), accessible via a tunnel through the Cueva de Viñales, is a bit of a cheesy joke, as the wait staff are dressed as *cimarrones* (runaway slaves).

The glass-enclosed **Restaurante Cueva del Indio** (tel. 08/79-6280; 9 A.M.–5 P.M.), outside the entrance to Cuevo del Indio, specializes in freshwater prawns. It also has *criollo* staples, plus inclusive meals for CUC8.

For snacks, head to **Cafetería Cubanitas** (Azcuy, esq. Rafael Temos; daily 9:30 A.M.–10 P.M.), an open-air eatery serving pizzas, hot-dogs, *bocaditos,* beers, and sodas.

There's a grocery on Cisneros, 50 meters east of the square.

Services

The hospital is two blocks east of the plaza. There's a 24-hour **pharmacy** (tel. 08/79-3169) one block west of the plaza. **Etecsa** (Calle Ceferino Fernández; daily 8:30 A.M.–7 P.M.), one block south of the plaza, has telephone and Internet service. The post office is across the street.

Bandec (Cisneros #57; Mon.–Fri. 8 A.M.–noon and 1:30–3 P.M.) is immediately east of the plaza.

The **police station** is opposite the plaza on Cisneros.

Getting There and Away

By Bus: Buses arrive and depart Viñales opposite the plaza from outside the Astro ticket office (Cisneros #63A, tel. 08/79-3195; daily 8 A.M.–noon and 1–3 P.M.). Astro buses leave Havana for Viñales at 9 A.M.; and depart Viñales for Havana at 2:30 P.M. (CUC8). However, Astro was not selling tickets to/from Viñales to foreigners at last visit. **Víazul** (tel. 08/75-2572) buses depart Havana for Viñales at 9 A.M. and 2 P.M.; and Viñales for Havana at 2 P.M. and 8 P.M. (CUC12).

Havanatur (tel. 08/79-6262) has a bus to Viñales from the Víazul bus station in Havana at 1:30 P.M. and from Viñales to Havana at 8 A.M. (CUC12), with drop-offs permitted.

By Taxi: A licensed taxi from Havana costs at least CUC100 round-trip. Taxis are available on the plaza in Viñales.

By Car: The following agencies have car rental outlets in Viñales: **Havanautos** (tel. 08/79-6390, vinales@cimex.com.cu), next to the Cupet gas station at the east end of the village; **Transtur** (tel. 08/79-6060), on the southwest corner of the plaza; and **Micar** (Salvador Cisneros, tel. 08/79-1454).

Organized Tours: Tour agencies offer excursions from Havana. In Viñales, **Cubanacán** (tel. 08/79-6393) offers excursions.

Getting Around

Cubataxi offers service from the plaza. A three-hour tour of the valley costs CUC20.

Cubanacán (tel. 08/79-6393) rents scooters, as does **Palmares** (tel. 08/77-8203), on the south side of the plaza and outside Casa Don Tomás (CUC14 first hour, CUC23 per day). Palmares also has mountain bicycles (CUC0.75 per hour, CUC6 per day).

WEST OF VIÑALES

West of Viñales the Sierra de los Órganos provides for a fulfilling day's excursion. Passing the turnoff for the Mural de la Prehistória, the road continues to Pons. It's a very beautiful drive for the first few miles, with serrated *mogotes* to the north. Farther west, tobacco gives way to coffee bushes as you rise to El Moncada and the saddle separating the Valle de Viñales and Valle de Santo Tomás, a scrub-covered, uncultivated valley.

At Pons, about 20 kilometers west of Viñales, the road to the right leads via **Matahabre** to Santa Lucía, on the north coast. Once known for its copper mines, the mines are now derelict, but the industry is honored in a tiny and basic museum (Tues.–Thurs. 8 A.M.–5 P.M., Fri.–Sat. 8 A.M.–

10 P.M.) on the west side of the town plaza, with its pretty hilltop church.

If you turn south at Pons, the deteriorated road leads through the Valle de Quemado and beyond Cabezas, the stupendously beautiful **Valle San Carlos,** hidden off the tourist beaten path yet offering perhaps the most superlative scenery in western Cuba. The valley runs through the heart of the Cordillera de Guaniguanico, with *mogotes* soaring to each side, and the valley bottom intensely farmed in tobacco. All the elements of the Valle de Viñales are here, condensed into a long, tight-knit vale that will have you stopping every few minutes for yet one more photo or to negotiate a pothole—the road is badly deteriorated.

Traveling southwest via sleepy **Sumidero,** you'll arrive on the southwest plains at the town of **Guane.**

You can turn southeast from Cabezas to reach Pinar del Río.

Caverna de Santo Tomás

At El Moncada, 15 kilometers west of Viñales, a turnoff leads through coffee fields to the orderly community of Santo Tomás, in the cusp of *mogotes* pitted with caves. This is the setting for Cuba's largest cave system, the Caverna de Santo Tomás (daily 9 A.M.–4 P.M.), which has more than 45 kilometers of galleries on eight levels, making it one of the largest underground systems in the New World. Guided 90-minute tours cost CUC8 and involve some tricky scrambling up and down ladders, and the caves are unlit. Helmets with lamps are provided.

There's a small museum (10 A.M.–4 P.M.; CUC1), and the Centro Nacional de Espeleología (National Center of Speleology, tel. 08/79-3145) is here.

South and Southwestern Pinar del Río

The south-central province is flatland given to agriculture, but much of the shore is swampy and mangrove and marsh lagoons extend inland for miles. Other than the fishing and hunting grounds of Maspotón, there is nothing of touristic interest. West of the town of Pinar del Río, the climate becomes increasingly dry and the vegetation correspondingly stunted and harsh. Fish-filled lakes lure anglers. María la Gorda, in the Bay of Corrientes, offers great diving, and the Península de Guanahacabibes, Cuba's slender westernmost point, is being developed for ecotourism.

MASPOTÓN

Maspotón, 62 kilometers east of the town of Pinar del Río, is a hunting and fishing club with 134 square kilometers of lowland marshes and woodlands dotted with lakes and canals bordered by mangroves. The lagoons teem with feisty snook and tarpon. The air is almost always full of birds settling and taking off. Blue-winged teal, shoveler ducks, pheasants, guinea fowl, snipes, and mourning doves abound. The still lagoons of black water are negotiated in flat-bottomed fiberglass boats.

Accommodations and Food

The lodge, **Horizontes Club Maspotón** (Granja Arrocera La Cubana, Los Palacios, tel. 08/9-6104; CUC50 per person including all meals), that Carlo Gebler accurately described in *Driving Through Cuba* as "like a dismal holiday camp," has 34 air-conditioned rooms in 16 soulless concrete *cabinas* built around a swimming pool and equipped with refrigerators, radios, and private baths. Take plenty of insect repellent. There's a restaurant and bar, game room, and TV. (Cubanacán.)

Getting There

Finding Maspotón is half the fun—or frustration. The turnoff from the Autopista is at the sign for **Los Palacios.** Go to the east end of town, cross the railroad tracks to the right,

bear immediately left, and take the first right for Maspotón. There are no signs. Follow the zigzagging, muddy red track about 12 kilometers until you reach a sign that reads *Club de caza y pesca* pointing to the right. Maspotón is about eight kilometers farther. Just when you're ready to pack it all in, you arrive.

VUELTA ABAJO

The Vuelto Abajo area, centered on the town of San Juan y Martínez, about 15 kilometers southwest of Pinar del Río city, has none of the dramatic beauty of Viñales, but due to a unique combination of climate and soil, the tobacco grown here is considered the finest in the world, better even than that of the Valle de Viñales. The choicest leaves of all are grown in about 6,500 hectares around San Juan y Martínez and San Luis, where the premier *vegas* are given over exclusively to production of wrapper leaves for the world's preeminent cigars.

In Vuelta Abajo the traditional *bohío* shed has been replaced by ungainly wooden cubes on stilts, with tin roofs and chimneys, where humidity and temperature can be more strictly controlled.

San Juan y Martínez, 23 kilometers west of Pinar del Río, has a pretty main avenue lined with colorful columned streets.

Finca El Pinar San Luis

If you want a thorough immersion in Tobacco 101 and want to learn from the master, then be sure to visit this 16-hectare private farm of Alejandro Robaina (tel. 08/79-7470; Mon.–Sat. 10 A.M.–5 P.M.), the unofficial "official" ambassador for Cuba's cigar industry. For six generations, the Robaina family has been renowned for the excellence of their tobacco (the family has farmed their *vegas* since 1845). So renowned is Alejandro Robaina that the Cuban government even granted him his own cigar label (Robaina cigars come in five different strengths). There's even a postage stamp with his visage.

PINAR DEL RÍO

Forty-minute tours (CUC2) are given. December and January are the best times to visit. Guests are received in a reception room full of photos of Robaina with various heads of state, fashion models, and other celebs on his various world tours. Cigars are not sold on the *finca* (local workers will sell you genuine Robaina cigars, but be prepared to negotiate hard on the quoted price, which is about the same as in stores).

To get there, turn south 12 kilometers west of Pinar del Río; San Luis is 3.3 kilometers south of the highway; turn left onto a dirt road. Ask if you need to! There are several turns along the country lanes.

ISABEL RUBIO AND VICINITY

The landscape grows increasingly spartan as you exit the Vuelta Abajo region heading west, with the road arcing close to the coast.

About 15 kilometers southwest of San Juan y Martínez, a turnoff leads south three kilometers to **Playa Boca de Galafre**, a somewhat muddy beach. Five kilometers further west, near Sábalo, another turnoff leads south eight kilometers to **Playa Bailén**. Both beaches are popular on weekends with Cubans, but they are unappealing, as are the two basic accommodation options (open occasionally): Villa Boca de Galafre (tel. 082/98592) and Villa Playa Bailén (tel. 082/96145). Locals offer to make lobster meals.

Midway between the highway and Playa Bailén you pass **Estación Biológica Zoocriadero** (daily 8 A.M.–5 P.M.; CUC2 entrance, CUC3 for photos), a crocodile farm that at last visit was temporarily closed for restoration following Hurricane Wilma.

Twelve kilometers west of Sábalo you pass through Isabel Rubio, a small yet relatively prosperous agricultural town that thrives on the harvest of citrus groves; and, beyond, the small town of **Sandino**, which has an airport that at last visit was scheduled to be expanded for international traffic. The area is famous for its lagoons stocked with tilapia and largemouth bass. The most popular are **Laguna Pesquero**, 10 kilometers south of Isabel Rubio, and **Laguna Grande**, northwest of Sandino and

reached via a turnoff from the main highway about five kilometers east of town.

North of Isabel Rubio lies **Guane**, at the base of the Cordillera de Guaniguanico, popular with Cubans for hiking and exploring caves.

Two trains daily runs between Pinar del Río and Guane (two hours) via Sábalo and Isabel Rubio. *Camiones* connect Sandino and other towns. If continuing to María la Gorda, tank up on gas at Isabel Rubio or Sandino, as there are no gas stations further west.

Accommodations
Campismo Salto Los Portales (tel. 084/49-7347; CUC5 per person), beside the Río Los Portales, five kilometers north of Guane, has 46 basic four-bunk cabins with private cold-water baths. You'll need to be self-sufficient for food. There's a disco in a nearby cave. It makes a good base for hiking. Make reservations at the Campismo Popular (Isabel Rubio Norte #22, tel. 08/75-5316) in Pinar del Río.

Motel Alexis Aragón (tel. 08/3282; CUC20), off the main road in Sandino, is a *casa particular* with two rooms with air-conditioning, private bath, and private entrances.

Anglers should check into **Villa Laguna Grande** (tel. 084/2430; CUC18 s, CUC26 d low season; CUC20 s, CUC29 d high season), 18 kilometers northwest of Sandino. This hotel has 12 simple thatched cabins with private bath and fridge. Occasionally it has fishing tackle and guides, but it's best to check with Islazul (Martí Oeste #127A, tel. 082/75-5662) in Pinar del Río before arriving. (Islazul.)

RESERVA DE LA BIOSFERA PENÍNSULA DE GUANAHACABIBES

This willowy peninsula (90 km long and 30 km wide) juts out into the Strait of Yucatán and narrows down to the tip at Cabo San Antonio. The geologically young peninsula is composed of limestone topped by scrubby woodland. The entire peninsula (nowhere higher than 25 meters above sea level) is encompassed within the 121,572-hectare Guanahacabibes Peninsula Biosphere Reserve,

TOBACCO

It is generally acknowledged that the world's best tobacco comes from Cuba (the plant is indigenous to the island), and in particular from the 41,000-hectare Vuelta Abajo area of Pinar del Río Province, where the climate and rich reddish-brown sandy loams are ideal. Rainfall is about 165 centimeters per year, but, significantly, only 20 centimeters or so fall during the main growing months of November-February, when temperatures average a perfect 27°C and the area receives around eight hours of sunshine daily.

Most tobacco is grown on small holdings – many privately owned but selling tobacco to the government at a fixed rate. *Vegueros* (tobacco growers) can own up to 60 hectares, although most cultivate less than 4 hectares.

RAISING TOBACCO

Tobacco growing is labor intensive. Cultivation, picking, curing, handling, and rolling tobacco into cigars all require great delicacy.

The seeds are planted around the end of October in well-irrigated and fertilized channels in flat fields – maize is often grown on the same land outside the tobacco season. It is planted in patches at different stages to allow for progressive harvesting when every tobacco plant is at its peak. Straw is laid down for shade, then removed as the seeds germinate. After one month the seeds are transplanted to the *vegas*. Buds have to be picked to prevent them from stunting growth. About 120 days after planting, they are ready for harvesting in March and April.

There is a range of leaf choices, from *libra de pie*, at the base, to the *corona*, at the top. The art of making a good cigar is to blend these in such proportions as to give the eventual cigar a mild, medium, or full flavor and to ensure that it burns well. The binder leaf that holds the cigar together is taken from the coarse, sun-grown leaves on the upper part of the plant, chosen for their tensile strength. Dark and oily, they have a very strong flavor and have to be matured for up to three years before they can be used. The finest leaves from the lower part of the plant are used as wrappers; these must be soft and pliable and free of protruding veins. Plants designated to produce wrappers for the finest cigars are grown under fine muslin sheets (*tapados*) to prevent the leaves from becoming too oily in a protective response to sunlight. Generally, the darker the color, the sweeter the taste.

At harvest, leaves are bundled in a *plancha*, or hand, of five leaves and taken to a barn where they are hung like smoked kippers and cured for about 40 days on poles or *cujes*. Modern barns are temperature and humidity controlled. Traditional thatched barns face west so that the sun heats one end in the morning and the other in the late afternoon, and temperature and humidity are controlled by opening and closing the doors. Gradually the green chlorophyll in the leaves turns to brown carotene. After 45–60 days, they are taken down and stacked into bundles, then taken in wooden cases to the *escogida* – sorting house – where they are shaken to separate them, then dampened and aired before being flattened and tied in bunches of 50. These are then fermented in large piles like compost heaps for anywhere up to three months (the wrapper leaves are fermented least). Ammonia and impurities are released. When the temperature reaches 44°C, the pile is "turned" so that fermentation takes place evenly.

The leaves are then graded for different use according to color, size, and quality. They are stripped of their mid-ribs and flattened, then sprayed with water to add moisture. Finally they are covered with burlap, fermented again, reclassified, and sent to the factories in *tercios* – square bales wrapped in palm bark to help keep the tobacco at a constant humidity. After maturing for up to two years, they are ready to be rolled into cigars.

created by UNESCO in 1987 to protect the semi-deciduous woodland, mangroves, and wildlife that live here. The reserve is split into the El Veral and Cabo de Corrientes nature reserves. At least 14 of the more than 600 woody species are found only on the peninsula. More than 170 bird species have been identified here; endemic birds include the tiny *torcaza* and *zunzuncito* hummingbirds. *Jutías* are abundant, as are wild pigs, deer, iguanas, and various species of lizards, and land crabs that cross the road en masse in springtime.

Several archaeological sites have been uncovered (the region became the final refuge for Cuba's aboriginal population as they were driven west by the more advanced and aggressive Taíno). The few people who live here today eke out a meager living from fishing and farming.

The peninsula encusps the Bahía de Corrientes, enclosing sparkling waters famed for their cut-glass transparency and fabulous diving.

The access road reaches the shore at the hamlet of **La Bajada,** where there's a military barrier and checkpoint at the T junction; you must present your passport for inspection here and at the official park entrance near the community of Manuel Lazo. The road to the left swings around the bay and leads 14 kilometers to María la Gorda and, beyond, Cabo de Corrientes. The road to the right leads 61 kilometers to Cabo San Antonio—the western tip of Cuba. A permit (CUC10) and guide are required to access the reserve and Cabo San Antonio (no permit is required to visit María la Gorda), arranged at the **Estación Ecológico** (tel. 084/75-0366, www.ecovida.pinar.cu), about 500 meters before La Bajada. The station has information on the local ecology. You can climb the adjoining meteorological tower for a view over the park (CUC1).

For most of the way, the road to Cabo San Antonio is rough *pista,* blazing white, underlain by sharp coral (called *diente de perro—* dog's tooth). Stunning beaches lie hidden a stone's throw away. After 40 kilometers or so, beyond Punta Holandés, the road opens onto a cactus-studded coral platform, with fabulous views across the Caribbean. Eventually you reach Cabo San Antonio, the westernmost point of Cuba, dominated by a military post and **lighthouse** (Faro Roncali). The cape hooks around to **Playa Las Tumbas,** a fabulous white-sand beach slated for tourist development (a marina was being built at last visit); and, beyond, **Punta Cajón.** The tarpon fishing is said to be good right off the dock here, and scuba divers might take a look at the sunken wreck just north of the cape.

The road to María la Gorda is easier going, despite being deeply eroded by Hurricane Wilma in October 2005. The mediocre beach here is named, according to legend, for a buxom barmaid, María la Gorda (Fat Mary), who turned to leasing her body to passing sailors. She prospered on the proceeds of her ample flesh, and her venue became known as *Casa de las Tetas de María la Gorda* (House of Fat Mary's Breasts). The *tetas* in question may actually refer to the two protuberances jutting from the cliffs of nearby Punta Caíman.

In springtime, *cangrejos* (crabs) swarm across the road en masse in fulfillment of the mating urge. And stay clear of the beaches around sundown, when tiny no-see-ums (*jejenes*) emerge to feast on unsuspecting humans.

Hiking and Bird-Watching

The 1.5-kilometer-long **Sendero Bosque al Mar** (CUC6 per person including guide) leads from the ecological station to the ocean, where a cave with a *cenote* is good for swimming; much of the "trail" is along the blazing white road. The **Sendero Cuevas Las Perlas** (three hours round-trip, CUC8 per person) leads 1.5 kilometers to the namesake cave system, where about 400 meters is accessible. The **Sendero El Tesoro de María** (four hours round-trip, CUC10 per person) leads from María la Gorda along the shore and is particularly good for bird-watching; *tocororos* and tiny *zununito* are common.

◖ Diving at María la Gorda

Experienced divers rave about the diving, ranging from vertical walls to coral canyons, tunnels, and caves, and even the remains of Spanish galleons. El Valle de Coral Negro

(Black Coral Valley) has 100-meter-long coral walls. Huge whale sharks are commonly seen, as are packs of dolphin and tuna.

Many dive sites are just 200 meters from Playa María la Gorda, where the **Centro Internacional de Buceo María la Gorda** (tel. 082/77-1306) offers dives at 8:30 and 10:30 A.M. and 3:30 P.M. Resort-course (initiation) dives cost CUC30. Single dives cost CUC35, night dives cost CUC40, and a four-day certification course costs CUC365. Use of equipment costs CUC7 extra. Divers must be accompanied by a dive guide.

A diving facility was also planned for the marina at Punta Cajón.

Snorkeling costs CUC12; you can join the divers aboard the dive boat.

In 2001, explorers using a miniature submarine discovered strange stone formations on the seabed that resembled a "lost city." The formations (2,100 ft. down) resemble pyramids, buildings, and roadways, causing some imaginative folks to speculate that they'd found a real-life Atlantis.

Accommodations and Food

Locals rent rooms illegally in La Bajada for CUC5–10 per person—they'll approach you as you drive by. Most make meals, including lobster (CUC6–10).

El Radar Meteorológica (tel. 082/75-1007), the meteorological station opposite the Estación Ecológico, occasionally offers four very basic air-conditioned guest rooms with cold-water showers (CUC9 per person), but at last visit no foreigners were being accepted until long-touted upgrades are made. Camping is permitted (CUC10 per tent), and showers and bathrooms are available.

Hotel María la Gorda (tel. 082/778131, fax 082/77-8077, www.gaviota-grupo.com; CUC38 s, CUC56 d year-round, including breakfast)

is a dive resort with 55 air-conditioned rooms with TVs, minibars, and private baths. There are three types of accommodations: older, simple and rundown cabins with basic bathrooms; newer, better, but still modest rooms in two-story units (each with fridge and private bath, but common TV areas); and 20 newer wooden cabins set back from the beach. It has a small bar, gift store, and the Restaurante El Carajuelo, serving mediocre à la carte buffet lunches and dinners (CUC15) plus somewhat better seafoods. Car rentals can be arranged with 24 hours' notice. The place was full with divers and young backpackers at last visit. You're a long way from the nearest alternate accommodation if the resort is full, so reserve in advance. Credit cards are not accepted. (Gaviota.)

At last visit, Gaviota was building 16 cabins at Playa Las Tumbas.

Thatched, open-air **Cafetería/Bar Restaurante La Bajada** (daily 9 A.M.–10 P.M.), next to the meteorological station, serves sandwiches, simple snacks, and ice cream.

Getting There and Away

A tourist taxi from Pinar del Río costs about CUC60 one-way. **Via Rent-a-Car** offers transfers to/from Pinar del Río for CUC50, and offers scooter and car rentals at Hotel María la Gorda.

A jeep-taxi from María la Gorda to Cabo San Antonio costs CUC50 for up to four people.

Transtur has a minibus from Viñales at 7 A.M. (CUC15) and Pinar del Río (CUC12), departing María la Gorda at 5 P.M. **Gaviota** has a bus transfer from Havana at 8 A.M. on request (CUC50 one-way, CUC80 round-trip).

You can book a "seafari" (CUC10) at the Estación Ecológico.

Yachters can moor alongside a wharf or in the shallows offshore. Immigration and Customs services are available, as are gas and water.

PINAR DEL RÍO

ISLA DE LA JUVENTUD SPECIAL MUNICIPALITY

Slung below the underbelly of Havana Province in the shallow Gulfo de Batabanó is Isla de la Juventud, by far the largest of Cuba's many offshore islands and one with an intriguing history and individuality. Scattered across the ocean to the east are 350 or so isles and cays that make up the Archipiélago de los Canarreos. Together they comprise the special municipality of Isla de la Juventud.

Isla de la Juventud (Isle of Youth, so named for the erstwhile socialist experiment of International Youth Brigades), about 100 kilometers south of the mainland, is hardly an island paradise, for which reason it receives relatively few visitors. The island is sparsely populated and there are no striking physical features and no lush tropical vegetation—the island was once smothered with native pine and became known at an early stage as the Isle of Pines. The island's appeal lies in some of the finest diving in the Caribbean, several historical sites of importance, and untapped nature reserves. The entire southern half of Isla de la Juventud comprises brush and marsh that harbor wild boar, deer, *jutías,* and *Crocodilus rhombifer,* the endemic Cuban crocodile that is aggressive from the moment it emerges from its egg.

Most of the islands of the 160-kilometer-long Archipiélago de los Canarreos necklace are girt by beaches of purest white and haloed by barrier reefs guarding bathtub-warm waters. For now, tourism development is limited to Cayo Largo, the easternmost island and the only one accessible from the mainland.

Besides their spectacular beaches, the cays

HIGHLIGHTS

◖ Presidio Modelo: Fidel Castro and other revolutionaries who survived the attack on the Moncada barracks were imprisoned in this prison turned museum (page 267).

◖ Refugio Ecológico Los Indios: Swampy and scrubby wilderness area offering fabulous bird-watching. Home to the Cuban sandbill crane (page 269).

◖ Scuba Diving off Punta Francés: Just off the coast scuba divers will find fan-

tastic coral formations, sponges, and both Spanish galleons and Soviet military vessels to explore (page 269).

◖ Criadero de Cocodrilos: Get up close and personal with Cuba's endemic crocodile at this breeding farm (page 270).

◖ Cayo Largo: Secluded from the mainland, the gorgeous beaches and turquoise waters of Cayo Largo provide the perfect spot to get that all-over tan (page 271).

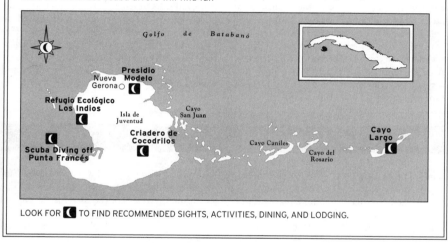

LOOK FOR ◖ TO FIND RECOMMENDED SIGHTS, ACTIVITIES, DINING, AND LODGING.

are a scuba diver's delight. In addition to astounding coral formations, some 200 shipwrecks have been reported in the Canarreos. The Nueva España treasure fleet, for example, foundered in 1563 on the reefs between Cayo Rosarío and Cayo Largo. One of the best sites is Cabeza Sambo, 70 kilometers west of Cayo Largo. The large shallow is strewn with cannons and coral-encrusted Spanish doubloons. And over 800 species of fish gambol among the exquisite coral.

The cays shelter tens of thousands of seabirds, including crab-eating sparrow hawks; fishing orioles, cormorants, and pelicans that

prey on the schools of fish; and egrets, majestic white and black herons, and other stilt-legged waders. Marine turtles are always in the water, particularly during the nesting seasons, when big males hang off the edge of the reef, waiting for the females to return from laying their eggs in coral sand above the high-water mark.

PLANNING YOUR TIME

Unless you're keen on bird-watching or diving, or are an aficionado of revolutionary history, you can safely skip Isla de la Juventud. Nonetheless, it is popular with backpackers and budget travelers keen to sample an offbeat part of Cuba. Two days is sufficient for exploring the island, although scuba divers will want to pack in a few more days for exploring the waters of the Bahía de Siguanea and off Punta Francés, where the diving rivals anywhere in the Caribbean.

Nueva Gerona, the capital city, can be explored in mere hours, its colonnaded main street and ceramic workshops being the only sights of any appeal. Outside town, however, be sure to visit the **Presidio Modelo,** formerly Cuba's main prison, where Fidel Castro and other participants of the attack on the Moncada barracks were held; and El Abra, a historic farmstead where national hero José Martí once labored under sentence of sedition.

An entire day is needed for a visit to the Área Protegida Sur de la Isla de la Juventud, a swampy wilderness area offering fabulous bird-watching and wildlife-viewing. Guided excursions (easily arranged locally) are compulsory, including to the glorious white-sand beach of Playa Punta del Este, where the Cueva del Punta del Este is adorned with pre-Columbian paintings; and to the **Criadero de Cocodrilos,** where you can learn the ecology of the pugnacious Cuban crocodile; and to the **Refugio Ecológico Los Indios,** where Cuba's endemic crane and endangered parrots (*cotorras*) can be seen.

Cayo Largo is reserved exclusively for foreigners, many of whom arrive from abroad on package tours and never feel the need to leave this island. Its beaches shelving into warm turquoise waters are superb. It can be visited on day-long and overnight excursions from Havana and a visit here makes a splendidly relaxing end to any visit to Cuba.

Traveling between Isla de la Juventud and Cayo Largo is impossible. You need to backtrack to Havana.

Isla de la Juventud

Isla de la Juventud (pop. 70,000), or "La Isla," as it is known throughout Cuba, is shaped like an inverted comma. At 3,050 square kilometers, it is about the same size as Greater London. Most of the island is flat, with a hilly central core that reaches 310 meters in elevation. Marmoreal hills—the **Sierra de Caballo** and **Sierra del Casas**—flank the city of Nueva Gerona and are the source of most of the gray marble found in buildings throughout Cuba.

The north is predominantly flat or rolling lowland, perfect for raising cattle in the east and citrus (especially grapefruit) in the west, where the fertile flatlands are irrigated by streams dammed to create reservoirs. The sweet smell of jasmine floats over the island January–March, when the citrus groves are in bloom.

Most of the south is composed of scrubland and the marshy **Lanier Swamp,** which extends the full width of the island and is a habitat for crocodiles, wild pigs, and waterfowl. Beautiful white-sand beaches rim the south shore. The entire southern half of the island is a protected area and ecotourism to the region is nascent. It is accessed by a single dirt road; an official guide is compulsory for visitors.

The people are called *pineros* and *pineras*. Many make their living as ceramists (the world-famous artist Kcho hails from *la isla*). The local drink—a mix of grapefruit juice, white rum, and ice—is named a *pinerito*. It is consumed in the late afternoon as a remedy for the heat, but local lore says it's an aphrodisiac.

History

The island was inhabited in pre-Columbian days by the Ciboney, whose legacy can be seen in cave paintings at Punta del Este on the south coast. The early Indians knew the island as Siguanea—the first of a dozen or so names given the island over the years. Columbus named it La Evangelista. Pirates, who used the isle as a base from which to plunder Spanish treasure ships and raid mainland cities, named it the Isle of Parrots for the many endemic *cotorras*. The southwestern shore is known as the Pirate Coast. And the island claims, unconvincingly, to be the setting for Robert Louis Stevenson's *Treasure Island*. The English pirate Henry Morgan even gave his name to one of the island's small towns.

Although the Spanish established a fort to protect the passing treasure fleets, it remained a neglected backwater and the first colony wasn't established until 1826, on the banks of the Río Las Casas. Throughout the century, the Spanish used the island they had renamed Isla de los Pinos (Isle of Pines) as a prison, while the Spanish military billeted recruits on the isle to escape the tropical diseases that plagued them on the mainland; those already ill were sent here to regain their health at the mineral springs in Santa Fe. After the Santa Rita hotel was built in 1860, tourists from North America began to arrive.

Following the War of Independence, the Treaty of Paris (signed in 1898) left the island in legal limbo. Although the Platt Amendment in 1902 recognized Cuba's claim on the island, only in 1925 did the island officially became part of the national territory. In consequence, Yankee real estate speculators bought much of the land and sold it for huge profits to gullible Midwestern farmers, who arrived expecting to find an agricultural paradise. The 300 or so immigrants established small communities and planted the first citrus groves, from which they eked out a meager living. Settlers of English and Scottish descent from the Cayman Islands also arrived in the 19th century and founded a turtle-hunting community called Jacksonville (now called Cocodrilo) on the south coast. Many U.S. citizens stayed; their legacy can still be seen in the cemetery and the ruins of their settlement at Columbia, near the Presidio Modelo, the prison that President Gerardo Machado built in 1931 and in which Fidel Castro and 25 followers were later imprisoned following their abortive attack on the Moncada barracks.

The U.S. Navy established a naval base here during World War II and turned the Presidio Modelo into a prisoner-of-war camp for Axis captives. In the post-war years, wealthy Cubans sold land to another generation of U.S. citizens, who used it for vacation homes. By the 1950s, the island had become a favored vacation spot (at its peak, 10 flights a day touched down from Miami), and gambling and prostitution were staples.

Following the Revolution, the Castro government launched a settlement campaign and planted citrus, which today extends over 25,000 hectares. Thousands of young Cubans went to work as "voluntary laborers" in the citrus groves. In 1971, the first of over 60 schools was established for foreign students—primarily from Africa, Nicaragua, Yemen, and North Korea—who formed what were called International Work Brigades and came to learn the Cuban method of work-study. The Cuban government paid the bill, and, in exchange, the foreign students joined Cuban students in the citrus plantations. To honor them, in 1978 the Isle of Pines was formally renamed the Isle of Youth. At the height of Cuba's internationalist phase, more than 150,000 foreign students were studying on the island.

The Special Period dealt the international schools a deathblow. The schools (and many of the citrus groves) have since been abandoned; in 2005, the government began converting many into hospitals-cum-hotels for Latin American medical patients (the airport is scheduled to be expanded to accommodate them). Meanwhile, local youth work the fields, beginning as young as 11 years old (most schools are deplorably deteriorated—some lack running water—and the children often have only meager nourishment, according to local parents).

NUEVA GERONA AND VICINITY

Nueva Gerona (pop. 36,000) lies a few kilometers inland from the north coast along the west bank of the Río Las Casas. It's a port town and exports primarily marble and citrus.

Calle 39 (Calle Martí), the main street, is lined with recently restored colonial buildings; it's pedestrian-only between Calles 20 and 30. The node is **Parque Guerrillero Heróico** (between Calles 28 and 30), a wide-open plaza facing a pretty, ocher-colored colonial church, **Iglesia Nuestra Señora de los Dolores** (tel. 046/32-3791), erected in 1929 in Mexican colonial style with a simple marble altar. Note the side altar dedicated to the Virgen de la Caridad. Masses are offered Sunday at 9 A.M., Wednesday at 7 P.M., and Friday at 9 A.M.

Also of interest is the **Galería de Arte Marta Machado** (daily 9 A.M.–10 P.M.), in a pretty colonial house on Calle 39. The adjacent *plazuela* features a beautiful ceramic mural and intriguing ceramic seats of a pointillist design.

The **Museo de Ciencias Naturales y Planetario** (Calle 41 y 46, tel. 046/32-3143; Tues.–Sat. 9:30 A.M.–noon and 1–5 P.M., Sun. 8 A.M.–noon; CUC1 museum, CUC1 planetarium), about 0.8 kilometer south of town, has displays of endemic flora and fauna in recreations of native habitats, plus stuffed (and somewhat moth-eaten) exotics, including a tiger and apes. There's even a small re-creation of the Cueva Punta del Este. The adjoining planetarium hosts occasional demonstrations explaining the heavens.

The **Museo Municipal** (Calle 30, e/ 37 y 39, tel. 061/32-3791; Tues.–Sat. 9 A.M.– 10 P.M., Sun. 9 A.M.–1 P.M.; CUC1), in the Casa de Gobierno (the former town hall), built in 1853, gives the lowdown on local history, including the era of piracy and how, in 1957, Guillermo Sardiñas became the only priest in Cuba to join Fidel Castro's army in the Sierra Maestra, rising to the rank of *comandante.*

The tale of local involvement in the Revolution is told at the **Museo de la Lucha Clandestina** (Calle 24, e/ 43 y 45, tel. 046/32-4582; Tues.–Sat. 9 A.M.–5 P.M., Sun. 8 A.M.–noon; CUC1). *El Pinero* (Calle 33, e/ 26 y 28) is the large ferry that carried Fidel and his fellow revolutionaries to freedom following their release from prison on the Isle of Pines. Alas, it was trashed by Hurricane Michele and only the hull remains.

ISLA DE LA JUVENTUD

★ LOS INDIOS WALL (DIVE SITE)

Cayo Los Indios

Playa Buenavista

Mina de Oro

★ WRECKS OF THE JIBACOA AND SPARTA (DIVE SITES)

REFUGIO ECOLÓGICO LOS INDIOS

Rio

Punta Los Indios

SCUBA DIVING OFF PUNTA FRANCÉS

Parque Nacional Punta Francés

Punta Francés

Punta de Piedra

Bahía de

★ DIVE SITE

Siguanea

Punta Pedernales

★ DIVE SITE

Caleta Grande

MARINE SCIENCE STATION AND TURTLE BREEDING CENTER

Cocodrilo

Cabo Pepe

To Surgidero de Batabanó (Ferry/Jet-Cat)

Golfo   de   Batabanó

SEE "ARCHIPIÉLAGO DE
LOS CANARREOS" MAP

◖ CAYO LARGO

Punta El
Lindero

Ensenada de
Los Barcos

Las Casas

Playa
Paraíso

CAMPISO
ARENAS NEGRAS

Playa
Bibijagua

Cayo de
El Navio

Embalse del
Medio-Las
Cuevas

Nueva
Gerona

EL ABRA ★

◖ PRESIDIO MODELO

Archipiélago

★ VILLA ISLA DE LA JUVENTUD
★ VILLA RANCHO EL TESORO

de los

Sierra de
Siguanea

Canarreos

Las Nuevas

✕ RAFAEL
CABRERA
AIRPORT

Júcaro

Atanagildo
Cagigal

Embalse
Mal País
Uno

Embalse
Viet-Nam
Heróica

Embalse
La Fe

Cayo San
Juan

La Melvis

La
Victoria

★ LA JUNGLA
DE JONES

La Fe

Los Indios

Argelia
Libre

ISLA   DE   LA   JUVENTUD

La
Reforma

To Cayo Largo

SIGUANEA
AIRSPIRT
(NOT IN USE)

Río San Pedro

◖ CRIADERO DE
COCODRILOS

★

Punta
Rancho
Viejo

Playa
Rojas

● HOTEL COLONY

MARINA
SIGUANEA

MILITARY
CHECKPOINT

Cayo
Piedra

ESTACIÓN
METEROLÓGICO

Punta del
Este

★ CUEVA PUNTA
DEL ESTE

Playa Punta
del Este

Área Protegida Sur de la
Isla de la Juventud

Playa Blanca

Punta del
Maracayero

Sea

LIGHTHOUSE ■

Playa
Larga

Punta Rincón
del Guanal

Caribbean

0   5 mi

0   5 km

Museo Finca El Abra

This farm-cum-museum (Carretera Siguanea Km 2, no tel.; Tues.–Sat. 9 A.M.–4 P.M., Sun. 9 A.M.–1 P.M.; CUC1), nestled in the lee of the Sierra del Casas, one kilometer south of Nueva Gerona, is associated with José Martí, who lived here under house arrest in 1870 after being sentenced to six years' imprisonment for sedition at the age of 18. After a brief spell in prison on the mainland, Martí was released into the custody of José Sardá (a family friend and respected Catalonian landowner) at El Abra. Martí remained for only three months before departing for exile in Spain.

The museum is reached off the main highway by a long driveway shaded by Cuban oak trees. At the end is the farmhouse, still a family home, with a large bronze bust of Martí outside. The exhibits include personal belongings, documents, and other artifacts of Martí's life.

Entertainment and Events

The **Festival de la Toronja** (Grapefruit Festival), held in February or March, depending on the harvest, features a carnival.

Watch for performances by Mongo Rivas and his relatives, who form **La Tumbita Criolla,** masters of the compelling dance rhythm *sucusuco,* born here early in the 19th century and deeply rooted in the island's culture. The word comes from the onomatopoeic sound of feet moving to its infectious rhythm. They and other exponents of traditional music perform at the **Casa de la Cultura** (Calle 24, esq. 37, tel. 046/32-3591), which has a rumba on Saturday at 3 P.M.

Cabaret El Patio (Calle 24, e/ Martí y 37, tel. 046/32-2346) offers a basic *cabaret espectáculo* Friday–Sunday at 11 P.M. (CUC3 per pair), plus disco only on other nights (CUC1 per pair). Doors open at 9 P.M.; ostensibly entry is for couples only.

The other dance spot of choice is **Super Disco** (no tel.), outside town at Villa Club la Juventud. Locals pack in to shake some booty Thursday–Sunday from 10 P.M. onwards. And **Restaurante El Dragón** (tel. 046/32-4479) hosts a disco Tuesday–Sunday evenings at 10 P.M. in its rear courtyard.

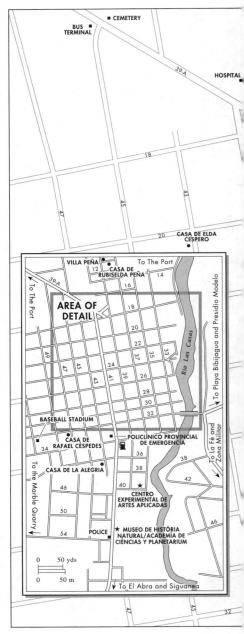

NUEVA GERONA

CUBANA AIRLINES OFFICE

BUS TO CRIADERO COCODRILO

BANK

POST OFFICE/ INTERNET

CASA DEL VINO

CADECA

TRANSTUR

Río Las Casas

JET-CAT/FERRY TICKET OFFICE/TERMINAL

POST OFFICE/DHL

CADENA DE PAN

CAMPISMO POPULAR

ECOTUR

Plaza el Viajero

DISCO NUEVO CAFÉ VIRGINIA

CASA DE CULTURA

CABARET EL PATIO

FARMERS MARKET

RESTAURANTE EL COCHINITO

BAR DIA Y NOCHE

FONDO DE BIENES CULTURALES

GALERÍA DE ARTE MARTA MACHADO

BANK

RESTAURANTE DRAGON

TALLER DE CERÁMICA ARTISTICA

EL PINERO FERRY

TIENDA PANAMERICANOS/ WESTERN UNION

IGLESIA DE NUESTRA SEÑORA DE LOS DOLORES

CINE CARIBE

Parque

BUS TO AIRPORT

PIZZERIA ISOLA

ETECSA

Guerrillero

Heróico

SHOPPING CENTER

COPPELIA

MUSEO MUNICIPAL

HAVANAUTOS

VILLA NIÑITA

0   25 yds

0   25 m

IMMIGRATION

JOSÉ MARTÍ   CALLE

For a quiet tipple, try **Casa del Vino** (Calle 20, esq. 41, no tel.; Mon.–Wed. 1–10 P.M., Fri.–Sun. 1–10 P.M.), a rustic wooden home with nautical windows and festooned with fishermen's nets, sells locally brewed, flavored wines—Vino de Anís, Vino de Coco, Vino de Rosa—for pesos.

Cine Caribe (Calle 37, tel. 046/32-2416), on the east side of the main square, charges two pesos and might satisfy your movie craving.

Baseball games are played October–April at the newly renovated **Estadio Cristóbal Labra** (Calle 32, e/ 49 y 51, tel. 046/32-1044).

Recreation

Hiking: The Sierra del Casas, immediately southwest of town, is good for hiking. By following Calle 22 westward you can ascend via a dirt track to the summit—**Loma de Cañada** (1,020 feet)—with good views over the island. At the base are three caves—**Cueva del Agua, Cueva del Indio,** and **Cueva del Hondón.** They're worth a peek for their stalagmites, stalactites, and petroglyphs. Steps lead down into Cueva del Agua and a natural pool good for bathing.

By following Calle 54 west you'll loop around to where gray *mármol* (marble) is quarried—the island has Cuba's largest reserves of marble.

Paragliding: The **Club de Parapente** (c/o Reynaldo Prendes Montes, Calle 49 #1615, e/ 16 y 18, tel. 046/32-3552) arranges paragliding from atop the Sierra de Las Casas for CUC30 for 30 minutes or CUC1 per minute.

Accommodations

All the state-run hotels are a considerable distance outside town. Owners of *casas particulares* in town meet arriving ferries.

Casas Particulares: One of the best private rentals is **Casa Particular Rafael Céspedes** (Calle 32 #4701-A, e/ 47 y 49, tel. 046/32-3167; CUC15–20), with two modestly furnished yet clean and adequate rooms with private hot-water bathrooms and firm mattresses. There's a TV lounge and an upstairs patio with rockers. The hosts are a delight. You can rent the entire house long-term at a reduced rate.

Casa de la Alegría (Calle 43 #3602, e/ 36 y 38, tel. 046/32-3664; CUC15–20) offers two modestly furnished, air-conditioned rooms. The first is large, has fans and a small but clean, modern hot-water bathroom. The second is cross-ventilated, well lit, and more elegantly furnished, and has a fridge, a larger modern bathroom with a bath/shower, and an independent entrance. The home has parking plus a nice patio with fountain and *ranchón.* Meals are offered.

Villa Niñita (Calle 32 #4110, e/ 41 y 43, tel. 046/32-1255, zerep@web.correosdecuba.cu; CUC15–20), in a peaceful part of town, is a handsome home with two air-conditioned rooms, each with private hot-water bathroom; one has a kitchen and fridge. There's a TV lounge (with artificial fireplace!), and meals are offered.

Nearby, **Villa Peña** (Calle 10 #3710, e/ 37 y 39, tel. 046/32-2345; CUC10 year-round) is a pleasant home with a two-room air-conditioned unit with telephone, double and single bed, plus private hot-water bath. Meals (including vegetarian) are offered. It has secure parking. In the same family, **Casa de Rubiselda Peña** (Calle 10 #3707, e/ 37 y 39, tel. 046/32-2345; CUC10) is run by a gracious hostess who rents two well-lit air-conditioned rooms upstairs with fans and a small shared hot-water bathroom. There's a TV lounge with rockers, and private bathrooms and a rooftop terrace.

Hotels: Gran Caribe's **Complejo Hotelero Rancho Villa** combines two hotels. The **Villa Isla de la Juventud** (Carretera La Fe Km 1.5, tel. 046/32-3290, ranchoij@enet.cu; CUC23 s, CUC32 d low season; CUC25 s, CUC36 d high season, including breakfast), known locally as Villa Gaviota, is a mediocre property that was recently taken over by Gran Caribe and was slated for a much-needed renovation at last visit. The 20 air-conditioned rooms have marble floors, local TV, telephones, refrigerators, and clean, modern hot-water bathrooms. There's a pool to which Cubans flock on weekends. A better bet is **Hotel Rancho El Tesoro** (Carretera La Fe Km 2.5, tel. 046/32-3035, fax 046/32-3657, ranchoik@enet.cu;

same prices as Villa Isla), a handsome property with 34 air-conditioned rooms and two suites (one for guests with disabilities), each with telephone, satellite TV, radio, minibar, and terrace, plus modern bathrooms. There's a restaurant and bar.

The **Campismo Popular** (Calle 37 #2208, e/ 22 y 24, tel. 046/32-4367) office handles reservations for cabins at Playa Bibijagua.

Food

If you rent a *casa particular,* your host will usually feed you, which is generally a much better option than the mediocre state restaurants.

Albeit out of town, the best option is **Restaurante El Cofre** (Carretera La Fe Km 2.5, tel. 046/32-3035; daily 7–9:45 A.M., noon–2:30 P.M., and 7–9 P.M.), a modestly elegant eatery in the Hotel Rancho El Tesoro.

Restaurante Dragón (Calle 39, esq. 26, tel. 046/32-4479; daily noon–10 P.M.), one block north of the church, has a strong Chinese flavor and a menu featuring a chop suey special (CUC5.30) and other quasi-Chinese dishes; **Restaurante El Cochinito** (Calle 39, esq. 24, tel. 046/32-2809; noon–10 P.M. daily) specializes in pork dishes, especially roast suckling pig. Shorts and tank tops are not permitted.

Basic pizza costs five pesos per slice at **Pizzeria Isola** (Calle 30, esq. 35). If the restaurant appears closed, nip into the back courtyard where take-out is sold.

Coppelia (Calle 32, esq. 37, tel. 046/32-2225; Tues.–Sun. noon–10 P.M.) sells ice cream for pesos.

You can buy fresh produce from the **mercado agropecuario** at Calles 24 and 35, and on Calle 41 at the south end of town; and Western groceries at the dollars-only **Cubalse** supermarket (Calle 30, e/ 35 y 37; Mon.–Sat. 9:30 A.M.–6 P.M.).

Shopping

Fondo de Bienes Culturales (Calle 39, e/ Calles 24 y 26, tel. 046/32-3151) sells leather shoes, wood carvings, and beautiful ceramics. Next door, the **Galería de Arte Marta Machado** sells quality art.

You can watch ceramics being made at the **Taller de Cerámica Artistica** (Calles 37, esq. 26, tel. 061/32-2634; Mon.–Fri. 8 A.M.–5 P.M.), and at the **Centro Experimental de Artes Aplicadas** (Calle 40, e/ 37 y 39; Mon.–Fri. 8 A.M.–4 P.M., Sat. 8 A.M.–noon).

Information and Services

There's a **Bandec** (Calle 39, esq. 18, tel. 046/32-4805) and **Banco Popular** (Calle Martí, esq. 26, tel. 046/32-2742). You can obtain pesos at **Cadeca** (Calle 39 y 20, tel. 046/32-3462; Mon.–Sat. 8:30 A.M.–6 P.M., Sun. 8:30 A.M.–1 P.M.).

The **post office** (Calle 39, esq. Calle 18, tel. 046/32-2600; Mon.–Sat. 8:30 A.M.–10 P.M.) has Internet service, as does **Etecsa** (Calles 41 y 28; daily 9 A.M.–9:30 P.M.).

The **Hospital Héroes de Baire** (Calles 18 y 41, tel. 046/32-3012) has a recompression chamber. Foreigners are also treated at the **Policlínico Provincial de Emergencia** (Calle 41, e/ 32 y 34, tel. 046/32-2236). The **pharmacy** (Calle 39, esq. 24, tel. 046/32-6084; Mon.–Sat. 8 A.M.–11 P.M.) is meagerly stocked.

The **police station** (Calle 41, esq. 54) is one kilometer south of town. **Inmigración** (Calle 35, esq. 34; Mon.–Thurs. 8:30 A.M.–noon) can issue *prórrogas* (visa extensions).

The **Cupet gas station** is at Calles 39 y 30.

Getting There and Away

A passport is compulsory for travel to Isla de la Juventud.

By Air: The **Aeropuerto Rafael Cabrera** (tel. 046/32-2690) is 15 kilometers south of Nueva Gerona. **Cubana** (Calle 39 #1415, esq. 18, Nueva Gerona, tel. 046/32-4259; Mon.–Fri. 8:30 A.M.–noon and 1:30 P.M.–4:30 P.M.) operates three flights daily from Havana, but only two on Tuesday and Thursday (CUC64 round-trip). Book your flight as far in advance as possible. Arrive early for check-in. Demand always outstrips supply, and if you're late, your seat will be given to someone else. For the same reason, it's best to book a round-trip ticket.

A bus marked *Servicio Aereo* connects flights with downtown Nueva Gerona (one peso). The

High-speed catamarans offer daily service between Batabanó and Nueva Gerona.

bus to the airport departs from Calle 53 and passes by Cine Caribe (Calle 37, e/28 y 30); it is usually packed to the gills. A taxi into town costs CUC5.

By Ferry: Two high-speed catamarans serve Nueva Gerona from Surgidero de Batabanó, in Havana Province 70 kilometers south of Havana. Departures from Surgidero are listed as daily at noon and 7 P.M., but the actual departure times depend on the number of passengers (sometimes only one cat departs). The 350-passenger cat has 20 seats reserved for foreigners; the 240-passenger cat has 10 seats for foreigners. The journey takes 135 minutes (CUC11). (See *Batabanó* in the *Greater Havana and Havana Province* chapter for details on buses between Havana and Surgidero.)

In Surgidero, you can buy your ticket at the wharfside **Viamar** (tel. 062/58-5355, viajeroij@transnet.cu) ticket office, or in advance from **Astro** (tel. 07/878-1841) in the main bus terminal in Havana; it's best to buy your ticket the day before departure, especially on weekends when the vessels are guaranteed to be full. You'll need to show your passport when buying

a ticket and when boarding. I recommend buying return (*regreso*) tickets when you purchase your outbound (*ida*) tickets. There's a 20-kilogram baggage limit. Your baggage is searched before boarding. No bicycles are permitted.

On board, you're served a *bocadito* and a *refresco*. There's also a small bar selling *bocaditos* wharfside in Surgidero.

In Nueva Gerona vessels berth at the **Naviera Cubana Caribeña** (Calles 31 y 24, tel. 046/32-4406) ferry terminal.

The catamarans depart Nueva Gerona for Surgidero daily more predictably at 8 A.M. and noon. The vessels' arrivals in Surgidero de Batabanó are timed to link with a connecting bus to Havana; you should buy tickets (CUC2.10) at the terminal in Nueva Gerona when you buy your catamaran passage. *Camiones* are also available for the journey to Havana (10 pesos).

Taking a Vehicle: You can ship your car or motorbike aboard a *transitaria* (flatbed barge) towed by a tug. You, however, will have to take a catamaran and meet the barge in Nueva Gerona. The barge departs daily at

11 P.M. The loading dock is next to the ferry terminal in Surgidero (tel. 062/58-4455, ask for Jorge). You'll need to register your vehicle at least two hours in advance at the tiny office at the beginning of the pier in Surgidero de Batabanó. Cars cost CUC40 each way, motorbikes CUC15. The barge arrives in Nueva Gerona at 7 A.M. the following day, docking two kilometers north of the ferry terminal. The return barge departs Nueva Gerona at noon, arriving in Batabanó next day at 7 P.M.; make your reservations in advance at the *transitaria* office (tel. 062/32-3240; Mon.–Fri. 8 A.M.–11 P.M.).

By Private Vessel: Private vessels can berth upstream of the ferry terminal.

By Bus: Bus #431 to La Fe (35 centavos) and bus #441 to Siguanea depart from Calles 39A and 45. Bus #38 for the Presidio Modelo and Playa Bibijagua departs five times daily beginning at 7:45 A.M. from the bus station at Calles 39A and 45.

By Taxi: A taxi tour of the island will cost about CUC44.50.

Excursions: Recently established **Eco-Tur** (Calle 13 final, Sierra Caballos, tel./fax 046/32-7101, ecoturisla@enpa.gerona.inf.cu; Mon.–Fri. 8 A.M.–5 P.M., Sat. 8 A.M.–noon) offers ecotourism excursions (CUC8–12, including guide; you'll need to provide your own transport).

Getting Around

Nueva Gerona is small enough that you can walk most places comfortably. Bus service in town is limited. Horse-drawn buggies congregate around the main square, and by the ferry terminal when boats arrive. Two pesos (or CUC2) will take you anywhere you want to go. Licensed taxis congregate at the corner of Calles 32 and 39.

Havanautos (Calles 39 y 32, tel. 046/32-4432; 7 A.M.–7 P.M. daily) and **Transtur** (Calle 37, e/ 20 y 22, tel. 046/32-6666) also rent sedans and jeeps (CUC40 per day including insurance), plus scooters (CUC20 per day with full tank). Both agencies provide cars with a half tank of gas (CUC19; Transtur says you get your money back for any gas you don't consume; Havanautos does not).

EAST OF NUEVA GERONA
◖ Presidio Modelo

The island's most interesting attraction—the Model Prison—is five kilometers east of Nueva Gerona. It was built 1926–31 during President Machado's repressive regime and was designed—based on the model of the penitentiary at Joliet, Illinois—in a "panopticon" plan that called for circular buildings that put prisoners under constant surveillance. The prison was designed to house 6,000 inmates in four five-story circular buildings. At the center of each rondel was a watchtower. A fifth circular building, in the center, housed the mess hall, dubbed "The Place of 3,000 Silences" because talking was prohibited. Prisoners were woken at 5 A.M.; *silencio* was at 9 P.M. The last prisoner went home in 1967, and only the shells remain.

You approach an impressive neocolonial facade with a stairway of local marble that leads up to the old administrative building (now a hobby center and school for UJotaCe, the Young Communists). The rondels and museum are reached by following the perimeter road to the left.

The two oblong buildings that now house the **Museo Presidio Modelo** (tel. 046/32-5112; Mon.–Sat. 8 A.M.–4 P.M., Sun. 8 A.M.–noon; entrance CUC2, cameras CUC3, videos CUC25) were used during World War II to intern Japanese-Cubans and Germans captured in Cuban waters. The first wing of the museum contains black-and-white photos and memorabilia from the Machado era. Another wing was the hospital, which in 1953 housed Fidel Castro and 25 other revolutionaries sentenced to imprisonment here following the attack on the Moncada barracks. They lived apart from the other prisoners and were privileged. Their beds are still in place, with a black-and-white photo of each prisoner on the wall. Fidel's bed is next to last, to the left, facing the door. Castro used his time here to good effect. Batista foolishly allowed him to set up a school where the group

ISLA DE LA JUVENTUD

© CHRISTOPHER P. BAKER

Fidel Castro and other participants of the attack on the Moncada barracks were imprisoned in the former Presidio Modelo, outside Nueva Gerona.

studied economics, revolutionary theory, and guerrilla tactics. On May 15, 1955, the revolutionaries were released to much fanfare. The Academía Ideológica Abel Santamaría is cordoned off; it amounts to three long tables and a blackboard. Immediately to the left of the museum entrance is the room where Fidel—prisoner RN3859—was later kept in solitary confinement (ostensibly for heckling dictator Fulgencio Batista during a visit). It's surprisingly large (about 400 square feet), with a lofty ceiling, marble seat, and a spacious bathroom with shower of gleaming white tiles. A glass case contains some of his favorite books.

A taxi from Nueva Gerona will cost about CUC6 round-trip.

Playas Paraíso and Bibijagua

Playa Paraíso, five kilometers east of Nueva Gerona and three kilometers north from the main road, has an attractive white-sand beach. Three kilometers beyond the turn-off for Presidio Modelo is Playa Bibijagua, a narrow sliver of gray sand fringed by a row of palms. The

French pirate Latrobe reportedly buried his treasure here. Buses serve the beaches from Nueva Gerona.

Accommodations and Food

Campismo Arenas Negras (tel. 046/32-5323; CUC5 per person), about 0.5 kilometer beyond the community of Bibijagua, is set amid palm-shaded lawns, although the beach is only a sliver. It has basic cabins, a small eatery, video room, and a kid's playground. It's frequently closed, so inquire and make advance bookings through **Campismo Popular** (Calle 37 #2208, e/ 22 y 24, tel. 046/32-4517; Mon.–Fri. 8 A.M.–4 P.M., Sat. 8 A.M.–noon) in Nueva Gerona. Community members in Bibijagua may be willing to make meals.

LA FE

A four-lane freeway runs south from Nueva Gerona to La Fe, an agricultural town that was founded by U.S. citizens and originally called Santa Fe. Some of their plantation-style houses still stand around the main square. The ruins of the **Manantial Agua La Cotorra** mineral springs are touted as an attraction, but aren't worth the drive.

La Jungla de Jones

This 30-hectare botanical reserve (no tel.), about three kilometers west of La Fe, was founded in 1902 by a U.S. couple, Harry and Helen Jones, who introduced exotic tree species for study in cooperation with the U.S. Department of Agriculture. It was abandoned in 1976. Today the woodsy reserve boasts about 72 species, including 10 bamboo species and 20 mangrove species, plus dozens of bird species that include parrots, woodpeckers, and owls. The highlight is the "Bamboo Cathedral," a 100-meter-long vaulted glade. A guide provides an interesting spiel as he leads you along the trail (30 minutes; CUC1,80). Group visitors receive a *criollo* lunch with musicians. Horseback rides are offered (CUC5).

The turn-off from the main highway is one kilometer north of La Fe; follow the road west for two kilometers, then turn south and follow the dirt road for one kilometer.

Ecotur (Calle 13 final, Sierra Caballos, tel./fax 046/32-7101, ecoturisla@enpa.gerona.inf. cu; Mon.–Fri. 8 A.M.–5 P.M., Sat. 8 A.M.–noon) includes La Jungla de Jones on its excursions.

BAY OF SIGUEANEA

This bay, to the southwest of the island, is the site of Columbus's landing on June 13, 1494. Later, it was a favored harbor for pirates. There are beaches hemmed in by mangroves; few are accessible by road. The Hotel Colony (see *Accommodations*), 30 kilometers southwest of Nueva Gerona, began life in the 1950s as a Hilton and backs a mediocre beach whose shallows have sea grasses and urchins; day visitors pay CUC1 to use the hotel facilities (you'll need your passport).

◖ Refugio Ecológico Los Indios

Much of the bayshore is a 4,000-hectare reserve protecting a fragile environment that includes mangroves, savanna, and endemic pines and palms. There are at least 60 native floral species, 15 of them limited to this particular spot (14 are endangered, including a species of carnivorous plant). The 153 species of birds include the endemic Cuban sandbill crane (called *la grulla*) and the *cotorra*—the equally threatened Cuban parrot (*Amazona leucocephala*), which you may recognize from pirate movies, sitting on the shoulders of corsairs. There are also at least six species of endemic reptiles, plus an endemic bullfrog and tiny frog species.

Rough trails lead into the reserve from Siguanea. A guide is compulsory and can be arranged through the hotel or Ecotur (Calle 13 final, Sierra Caballos, tel./fax 046/32-7101, ecoturisla@enpa.gerona.inf.cu; Mon.–Fri. 8 A.M.–5 P.M., Sat. 8 A.M.–noon).

Parque Nacional Punta Francés

Covering 6,079 hectares, of which 4,313 are ocean terrain, this national park is at the southwesterly tip of the island, some 120 kilometers from Nueva Gerona. Its semi-deciduous forest distinguishes it from the Lanier swamp. Blind shrimp inhabit the many *cenotes* that stud the shore, which is lined with mangroves and beaches. Offshore, gorgonias, corals, and marine turtles abound.

◖ Scuba Diving off Punta Francés

The bay offers spectacular diving. There are 56 dive sites concentrated along **La Costa de los Piratas** (the Pirate Coast), whose tranquil waters are protected from the Gulf Stream currents. The sites extend along a 15-kilometer-long axis offshore between Punta Pedernales and Punta Francés. Off Punta Francés, the basin's wall begins at depths of 20 to 30 meters and plummets into the depths of the Gulf of Mexico. The wall is laced with canyons, caves, and grottoes. Huge coral parapets loom out over the cobalt abyss below. Site 39 is renowned for the **Caribbean Cathedral,** said to be the tallest coral column in the world. Two other sites of interest are **Black Coral Wall** and **Stingray Paradise,** where you may stroke these friendly fish. Marine turtles are profuse.

A naval battle between Thomas Baskerville's pirate ships and a Spanish fleet resulted in many ships being sunk near Siguanea. Northeast of Punta Francés, between the cape and Cayo Los Indios, are three well-preserved Spanish galleons close together. A cluster of freighters was scuttled several decades ago to provide bombing and naval gunnery targets for the Cuban armed forces.

The **Centro Internacional del Buceo** (International Scuba Diving Center, tel. 046/39-8181), 1.5 kilometers south of the Hotel Colony, offers dives for CUC30, CUC45 for a night dive. A full certification course costs US$365. The facility has a large decompression chamber, plus a scuba shop that sells and rents gear. It generally takes well over one hour to reach the dive spots—a tedious journey in basic launches. Drop-in visitors hoping for a day's diving may find that the staff will usually take you to the nearest sites, rather than the most interesting. Diving with a guide is compulsory, as the bay lies within the marine reserve. You get a 20 percent discount if you book your dive through Ecotur (Calle 13 final, Sierra Caballos, tel./fax 046/32-7101, ecoturisla@enpa.gerona.inf.cu; Mon.–Fri. 8 A.M.–5 P.M., Sat. 8 A.M.–noon).

Yachting and Sportfishing

The **Marina El Colony** (tel. 046/39-8181) offers fishing for bonefish and tarpon in inner waters from a *lancha* (small boat, CUC200).

Accommodations

The **Hotel Colony** (Carretera de Siguanea Km 41, tel. 046/39-8181, fax 046/39-8420, reservas@colony.co.cu; CUC26 s, CUC48 d low season; CUC30 s, CUC56 d high season) is a deteriorated 1950s hotel with 24 modestly decorated, air-conditioned bungalows (plus 77 rooms in restoration at last visit) with telephones, radios, TVs, and private baths. It offers water sports. A narrow pier leads out to the Mojito Bar. Excursions are offered. (Gran Caribe.)

Getting There and Away

A taxi from Nueva Gerona will cost about CUC30 round-trip.

You can rent cars, bicycles, or scooters at the Hotel Colony, but there's nothing to drive to for miles.

Marina El Colony (tel. 046/39-8181) has 15 berths with electricity, water, gas, and diesel. Berthing fees are about CUC0.45 per foot per day. If this is your first port of arrival, you'll have a long wait for the officials to travel down from Nueva Gerona.

ÁREA PROTEGIDA SUR DEL ISLA DE LA JUVENTUD

The entire Isla de la Juventud south of Cayo Piedra along its east–west parallel lies within the South of the Isle of Youth Protected Area, a wilderness region covered in bush and swamp and populated by such wildlife as wild pig, deer, and crocodiles. The coast is lined with glorious beaches whose sugar-white sands slope down to calm turquoise waters protected by an offshore reef.

Visits are permitted only with an official guide arranged through Ecotur in Nueva Gerona. There's a military checkpoint just south of Cayo Piedra, so don't try sneaking in on your own.

A resort is planned for Playa Punta del Este, but for now there's not even a crude *ranchita* restaurant or snack bar. Take food and drink.

◀ Criadero de Cocodrilos

This crocodile breeding farm, 30 kilometers south of Nueva Gerona, has over 500 crocodiles of varying ages. The reptiles are separated by age, as older crocs are cannibalistic. A trail leads to natural lagoons where mature beasts swim freely amid the water hyacinths. You'll hear them plopping into the water as you approach. Others stick their ground and eye you leerily. The oldest and biggest male is a mean-looking sexagenarian giant who guards his harem jealously. The juveniles feast upon the remains of sardines and lobster, while the full-grown monsters are fed hacked-up cattle. Feeding time is usually between 9 and 10 A.M.

Cueva Punta del Este

From Cayo Piedra, a dirt road leads east 20 kilometers through the Ciénaga de Lanier to Punta del Este. There's a beautiful beach here—**Playa Punta del Este**—but the main attraction is the group of caves containing important aboriginal petroglyphs on the roofs and walls. The caves are considered Cuba's "Sistine Chapel" of Caribbean pre-Columbian art, with 238 pictographs in perfect condition. The paintings date from about A.D. 800 and are among the most important aboriginal petroglyphs in the Antilles.

The petroglyphs, which display a high level of "geometric abstraction," seem to form a celestial plan thought to represent the passage of days and nights in the cult calendar. Among them are 28 concentric circles of red and black, pierced by a red arrow of two parallel lines and thought to represent the lunar month. Each day the sun's rays enter through the portal of the most important cave. As the sun follows its astral route, it illuminates different sections of the mural. On March 22, when spring begins, the sun appears in the very center of the cave entrance, revealing a red phallus penetrating a group of concentric circles on the back wall, an obvious allusion to procreation.

A side trip from the Cayo Piedra–Punta del Este road leads south to **Playa Blanca.**

Cayo Piedra to Punta Francés

The road south from Cayo Piedra leads directly to **Playa Larga,** a real stunner of a beach. Five kilometers before the beach is a turnoff to the right that leads west 28 kilometers to Punta Francés. The badly deteriorated road runs inland of the shore the whole way, and there is no view of the beautiful shoreline until you reach the tiny seaside community of **Cocodrilo,** formerly Jacksonville, named for Atkin Jackson, who founded the hamlet in 1904. The isolated villagers eke a living as fishermen or as workers in the eco-reserve. Many are descendants of immigrants who arrived from the Cayman Islands over a century ago; a lilting Caribbean English is still spoken.

One kilometer beyond Cocodrilo there's a **Marine Science Station and Turtle Breeding Center** at Caleta Grande. The center has about 6,000 green and hawksbill turtles in a series of pools.

There's a *faro* at the very southernmost tip near Punta Rincón del Guanal, midway to Cocodrilo.

Farther west you'll find perfectly lonesome beaches such as **Playa El Francés,** where Spanish galleons and coral formations await scuba divers a short distance from shore. You need to give 72 hours' notice to travel beyond Caleta Grande, a military zone.

Cruise ships berth offshore of Punta Francé and tender passengers ashore for day visits.

Getting There: It's a full-day drive from Nueva Gerona and back. The journey is not worth the cost involved unless you are absolutely keen to see Cuevas del Este or the turtle farm, or to spend the day on a beach. Bus #704 leaves from Calle 37, esq. 18, in Nueva Gerona for Cocodrilo at 4 P.M. and returns at 6 A.M. (2.30 pesos).

Archipiélago de los Canarreos

C CAYO LARGO

Cayo Largo, 177 kilometers south of Havana and 120 kilometers east of Isla de la Juventud, is a three-kilometer-wide, 25-kilometer-long, boomerang-shaped sliver of land fringed by an unbroken 20-kilometer stretch of beaches with sand as blindingly white as Cuban sugar. The beaches merge gently into waters that run from lightest green through turquoise and jade to deep cobalt far out. There are water sports and a top-class hotel (plus several less impressive options). Cayo Largo is favored by Canadians and Europeans escaping the snows and also makes for a fabulous getaway on an excursion from Havana. If all you want to do is laze in the sun, this is the place to be. Uniquely, the Cuban government tolerates

ISLA DE LA JUVENTUD

nude sunbathing here, and many people on the beach are in the buff.

You won't learn a thing about Cuban life, however, as everything here is a tourist contrivance, you are totally cut off from the mainland, and Cayo Largo is off-limits to Cubans (despite the Cuban models in the promotional literature). The only Cubans on the island are hotel staff who live in their community—El Pueblo—north of the airport; less fortunate construction workers live in virtual hovels.

The English privateer Henry Morgan careened his ship here for repairs three centuries ago. Other pirates used Cayo Largo, and there are several galleons and corsairs on the seabed.

In recent years several hurricanes have swept over the cay, stripping several of the beaches of sand.

A single road links the airport, at the northwest end of Cayo Largo, with the resort (3 km south), the marina, and continues east, unpaved as far as Playa Los Cocos (14 km). The workers' community of **El Pueblo** features a bank, marina, medical clinic, and the **Granja de las Tortugas** (9 A.M.–noon and 1–5 P.M. daily; CUC1), where you can see marine turtles in pools at a small turtle farm. Nearby, the **Casa Museo** (9 A.M.–noon and 2–6 P.M. daily; CUC1) has motley exhibits relating to Cayo Largo's history and natural history.

Entertainment and Events

Each September, Cayo Largo hosts the **International Marlin Tournament.**

Most hotels have their own discos and bars.

The Cuban hotel workers have an open-air bar—**La Carpa**—in El Pueblo that gets lively with dancing. Nearby, the waterfront **El Pirata Taberna** (tel. 045/24-8213) is a good spot to imbibe.

Recreation

Beaches and Water Sports: Cayo Largo has 27 kilometers of serene beaches, which run the entire length of the seaward side (the leeward side is composed of mangroves and salty lagoons). Occasionally swimming is forbidden due to strong currents or when the sea gets too rough; red warning flags are posted.

The loveliest beach is 2.3-kilometer-long **Playa Sirena,** on the west side of Punta Sirena, the western end of the island. Facilities include a souvenir kiosk, toilets, game room, and restaurant, and sailboards and catamarans can be rented. Playa Sirena slopes steeply below the waterline—wading is not recommended for children. The beach is reached by dirt road. A tractor-pulled shuttle operates to **Playa Paraíso,** immediately west of Playa Sirena (you can walk the one kilometer to Playa Sirena from here), at 9, 10:30, and 11:30 A.M. (CUC2). The shuttle departs from Paraíso at 1, 3, and 5 P.M. A free bus runs to the marina at 9 and 10:30 A.M. (returning at 1:15 and 3:15 P.M.), from where you can catch a boat to Playa Sirena (CUC4), departing the marina at 9:30 and 11 A.M. Boats depart Playa Sirena at 3 and 5 P.M. Day excursions to Playa Sirena are offered from the hotels (CUC25).

Playa Lindamar, setting for the Sol Club

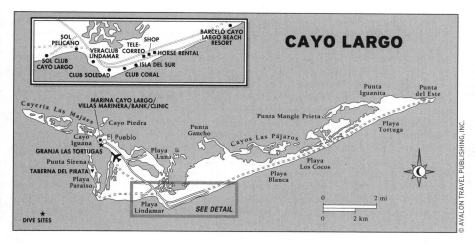

Cayo Largo and Sol Pelícano hotels, is a scimitar-shaped beach extending east about one kilometer, where a rocky point divides it from seven-kilometer-long **Playa Blanca** (which was entirely stripped of sand by Hurricane Wilma in 2005). Immediately east are **Playa Los Cocos** and then **Playa Tortuga**, where giant sea turtles come ashore May–October to lay their eggs in the warm sands (eggs are collected to be incubated at the turtle farm).

All the hotels offer water sports; the Sol hotels even rent Hobie Cats.

Horseback Riding: You can rent horses (CUC6 per hour) from outside the Hotel Isla del Sur.

Fishing: The offshore waters teem with game fish, including white and blue marlin. Bonefish (*macabí*) and tarpon (*sábalo*) are abundant. **Casa Batida Fishing Club,** in El Pueblo, offers fly-fishing trips (from CUC120 per person half-day, two people; or CUC360 daily for one person with guide) and supplies all equipment. Bookings are handled by **Planet Fly Fishing** (www.planetflyfishing.com).

Snorkeling and Scuba Diving: A barrier reef lies about one kilometer offshore, protecting Cayo Largo from rough seas. There's an absence of currents, and the water never falls below 25°C. Dives are available from the marina for CUC31–35 (single dive) or CUC60–70

(two dives). A 10-dive package costs CUC284. You can rent snorkeling gear from CUC8.

Accommodations and Food

Most guests arrive on an all-inclusive basis. There are no eateries outside the resort hotels, most of which serve mediocre fare.

Villas Marinera (tel. 045/24-8385, fax 045/24-8212, carpeta-marina@repgc.cls.tur .cu; CUC38 s, CUC64 d low season; CUC56 s, CUC84 d high season, including breakfast), at El Pueblo, operates primarily as a fishing lodge and has 16 air-conditioned log cabins overlooking the mangrove-lined shallows. They're nicely furnished with wrought-iron and hardwoods, soft-cushion seats, satellite TV, telephones, and spacious modern bathrooms. French doors open to balconies with lounge chairs. Rooms adjoin to form family units.

All other hotels are operated on an all-inclusive basis by Cuba's Gran Caribe chain. All have air-conditioning, satellite TV, refrigerators, and safes in guest rooms, plus water sports, volleyball, tennis, entertainment, and other activities.

Club Isla del Sur (tel. 045/24-8111, fax 045/24-2201, reserva@isla.cls.tur.cu) comprises the following four entities, used almost exclusively by Italy's Eden Viaggi and colloquially

ISLA DE LA JUVENTUD

known as Eden Village, but other tourists are accepted. **Club Isla del Sur** (CUC103 s, CUC147 d low season; CUC109 s, CUC155 d high season) has 59 air-conditioned rooms in a twin-level hotel block with a circular swimming pool. The rather plain resort has a buffet restaurant, a poolside bar, two grills, tourist bureau, and hairdresser, nightly poolside entertainment, plus water sports. The adjacent **Club Coral** (same rates as Isla del Sur) has 24 rooms in two-story duplex units surrounding a half-moon pool with swim-up bar atop a coral ledge above the beach. Rooms are done up in a lively Caribbean color scheme and have king-size beds. The facility also includes the rather plain 43 single-story *cabinas* of **Club Soledad** (same rates as Isla del Sur), and the 63 slightly more upscale thatched bungalows of **Club Lindamar** (CU107 s, CUC158 d low season; CUC134 s, CUC192 d high season), which has its own Italian restaurant and is used primarily by clients of Italy's VeraClub.

Sol Pelícano Hotel (tel. 045/24-8333, fax 045/24-8116, www.solmeliacuba.com; CUC160 s, CUC200 d standard, CUC210 s, CUC260 d junior suite low season; CUC240 s, CUC300 d standard, CUC300 s, CUC360 d junior suite high season), managed by the Meliá chain, is a mediocre and overpriced low-rise hotel built haphazardly in vaguely Spanish-colonial style around a freeform pool amid unkempt grounds. It has 324 rooms, including two suites and 110 *cabinas,* all with modest yet appealing decor. The buffet restaurant is ho-hum; the open-air beachfront restaurant (reservations only) offers commendable fare. There's a nightclub and small gym.

A far better bet is the more upscale yet inexplicably lower-priced **(Sol Cayo Largo** (tel. 045/24-8260, fax 045/24-8265, www.solmeliacuba.com; CUC157 s, CUC194 d standard, CUC204 s, CUC260 d junior suite low season; CUC231 s, CUC292 d standard, CUC301 s, CUC370 d junior suite high season), a deluxe all-inclusive with 301 spacious rooms in four-plex units graced by sponge-washed walls, lively ice-cream colors, and pleasingly understated furnishings. A splendid beach restaurant serves an impressive buffet luncheon; there's a 24-hour snack bar, plus specialist restaurant, game room, choice of bars, and Internet service.

Barceló Cayo Largo Beach Resort (tel. 045/24-8080, fax 045/24-8088, reservabarcelo@caylargo.co.cu; CUC85 s, CUC150 d low season; CUC140 s, CUC250 d high season; suites cost CUC30 additional) opened in 2005 just in time to see its beach washed away by Hurricane Wilma. Its contemporary design won't suit all tastes, the grounds are poorly laid out, and construction standards are clearly questionable. Still, if the other hotels are full, it has 306 rooms in two-story bungalows and the three-story main building, plus most of the facilities you could wish for. (Gran Caribe.)

Information and Services

The **Clínica Internacional** (tel. 045/24-8238; 24 hours) is next to the marina in El Pueblo and has a dentist. The **bank** (tel. 045/24-8225; 9 A.M.–noon and 1–3:30 P.M.) is opposite the marina; you'll need to bring your passport for credit card withdrawals.

The **post office** (8 A.M.–7:30 P.M. Mon.–Fri.) opposite the Isla del Sur Hotel has telephone and fax service.

Inmigración (tel. 045/24-8250) and **Customs** (tel. 045/24-8244) are at the airport.

A store (9:30 A.M.–9:30 P.M.) opposite the Club Isla del Sur sells fashion wear, beachwear, duty-free items, and souvenirs.

Getting There and Away

International travelers can arrive without a visa if they have no intention of visiting the Cuban mainland. This is true of sailors arriving by private yacht. You can obtain a visa to visit the mainland upon arrival in Cayo Largo.

By Air: Charter flights operate directly from Canada, Europe, Mexico, and Grand Cayman to **Vilo Acuña International Airport** (tel. 045/24-8141).

Cubana (www.cubana.cu) serves Cayo Largo from Havana and Varadero. **AeroGaviota** (tel 045/24-8364) flies from the Baracoa airstrip, about 15 kilometers west of Havana.

At press time, Ecotur and WestPoint Air International were planning to introduce seaplane service linking Cayo Largo with Havana and Varadero.

Excursions: If you're already in Cuba, you can book your own flight and hotel reservations if you wish, but it is far more expensive than a package deal through a Cuban tour agency. Most excursions from Havana begin with an early-morning hotel pickup and departure. A typical one-day package costs from CUC175. Two-day excursions include an overnight at your choice of hotel (typical cost is around CUC200, including the flight and overnight at Sol Cayo Largo; with late afternoon return the following day).

Tour agencies in the hotels offer excursions to Isla de la Juventud, Trinidad, and Havana.

By Sea: Private yachters can berth at **Cayo Largo del Sur Marina** (tel. 045/24-8213, fax 045/24-8212, VHF channel 16). It has 90 berths with 110- and 220-volt electricity, water hook-ups, and gas and diesel available (CUC0.45 per foot). There's a ship's chandler, laundry, and repair service.

Getting Around
The best way to get around is by bicycle or scooter (CUC8 one hour, CUC11 two hours, CUC22 per day), available at all the hotels. Car and jeep rental (CUC33 for three hours, CUC40 for six hours, CUC52 per day) are offered at hotels, but there are only 20 kilometers of road.

OTHER CAYS
West of Cayo Largo, uninhabited cays extend all the way to the shores of Isla de la Juventud. Sprinkled like diamonds across a sapphire sea, they are a yachting and diving paradise, although as yet there are no facilities whatsoever.

The Archipiélago de los Canarreos deserves a reputation for some of the best wildlife-viewing in Cuba, from a small population of monkeys on **Cayo Cantiles** (the only monkeys in Cuba) to the flamingos inhabiting the salty lagoons of **Cayo Pasaje. Cayo Iguana,** a nature reserve immediately north of Cayo Largo, is noted for its large population of endemic iguanas, as baked and lifeless as the ground they walk on. Access, however, is another matter!

Cruise excursions are offered from Cayo Largo to Cayo Iguana and neighboring cays, with snorkeling and lobster lunch on board (CUC69–73). You can book at the **Cubatur** and **Havanatur** tour desks in the hotels on Cayo Largo.

ISLA DE LA JUVENTUD

MATANZAS

Matanzas Province is a triptych of diverse appeal. Its north shore boasts some of the island's finest beaches. The lodestone is Varadero, Cuba's biggest beach resort. The resort, occupying the slender 20-kilometer-long Península de Hicacos, is a mini-Cancún with almost three-quarters of all hotel rooms on the island and most of the services beach vacationers would want. Betwixt Havana and Varadero is the namesake city of Matanzas, a once-wealthy sugar- and slave-trading port known as the Athens of Cuba for its literary and artistic vitality. Today, it is recognized as a center for Afro-Cuban culture, although the predominant impression when passing through is that of modern port industries, not least petrochemicals—oil is pumped from the shore hereabouts.

A range of hills separate the coastal strip from central Matanzas, which is smothered in a vast plain (the Llanura Roja) where red soils support sugarcane fields and vast citrus orchards that extend east into Villa Clara Province, providing the orange and grapefruit for boxed juices.

The southern part of Matanzas Province is taken up by the low-lying Península de Zapata, the Caribbean's largest marshland system harboring fantastic bird life and a large population of Cuban crocodiles. In April 1961 the Zapata region was launched from obscurity to fame as the setting for the Bay of Pigs invasion. Today the region is enshrined within Parque Natural Ciénaga de Zapata, luring travelers keen on bird-watching, fishing, and a sampling of revolutionary history. There are pleasant beaches

HIGHLIGHTS

◖ Castillito de San Severino: The restored fortress houses the Museo de la Ruta del Esclavo, an intriguing museum on slavery and Afro-Cuban religions (page 284).

◖ Cuevas de Bellamar: Visitors will find dripstones galore in this cool underground cavern system (page 285).

◖ Las Américas: An exorbitant mansion built by industrial magnate Irénée Du Pont overhangs the crashing Atlantic in Varadero (page 294).

◖ Scuba Diving off Varadero: While divers might look elsewhere for superlative corals, the superb wreck diving revolves around a Russian frigate, patrol boat, and airplane (page 298).

◖ Museo Oscar María de Roja: This superb regional museum covers everything from natural history to numismatics and the Wars of Independence (page 311).

◖ Parque Nacional Ciénaga de Zapata: The Caribbean's preeminent wetland area is chock-full of birdlife, crocodiles, and game fish. It's nirvana to bird-watchers and anglers (page 319).

◖ Museo Playa Girón: Featuring warplanes and U.S. and Soviet military hardware, this excellent museum recalls the failed CIA-sponsored Bay of Pigs invasion (page 322).

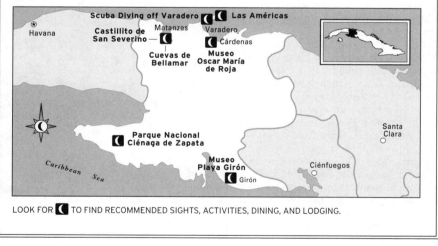

LOOK FOR ◖ TO FIND RECOMMENDED SIGHTS, ACTIVITIES, DINING, AND LODGING.

at Playa Larga and Playa Girón, both major landing sites for the CIA-inspired invasion by Cuban exiles. Memories of the fiasco—and Cuba's proud moment (Cubans refer to it not as the "invasion" but rather as *la victoria*)—are kept alive at a museum. The area even offers good scuba diving.

Note for Boaters: Private skippers should note that the entire coastline from the Bay of Pigs (21° 45') to Cienfuegos harbor (21° 50') is strictly off-limits.

PLANNING YOUR TIME

The Vía Blanca, or Circuito Norte, runs along the coast between Havana and Matanzas (102 km), and thence to Varadero, 34 kilometers farther east. Many visitors make Varadero their main center for a vacation in Cuba. I recommend against it: There are better beach resorts, if sun and sand are your main interests. Two or even three days relaxing on the beach here should suffice anyone. That said, the scuba diving is excellent, boat excursions are fun, and organized excursions to the timeworn historic city of Cárdenas—with its fabulous and must-see **Museo Oscar María de Roja**—and further afield provide an adequate sampling of Cuba's broader pleasures.

The city of Matanzas appeals for its still vital heritage of Afro-Cuban music and dance; for its faded colonial architecture highlighted by the recently restored **Castillito de San Severino** with an important museum recalling the era of slavery; and for the **Cuevas de Bellamar** caverns, full of fabulous dripstone formations. One day is more than adequate to explore the city. Day trips to Matanzas are offered from Varadero; even more popular—and worthwhile—is a nocturnal excursion to the Tropicana nightclub.

Between Havana and Matanzas sits the Valle de Yumurí, a huge basin lushly cultivated with sugarcane. It is enfolded by a crescent of low mountains famed for their mineral springs, most notably at San Miguel de los Baños, whose once-fine mansions are now in tragic decay.

The Zapata region deserves at least a day's visit. At Boca de Guama, Cuba's most important crocodile farm is open for visits. Birdwatchers and wildlife enthusiasts are in their element. Laguna del Tesoro and Las Salinas set a world standard for tarpon and bonefish angling (anglers might plan on two or three days casting). Scuba divers have a unique opportunity to dive a *cenote,* while snorkelers can enjoy Caleta Buena. The **Museo Playa Girón** is well worth the visit for Cuba's take on the Bay of Pigs story.

When traveling east–west or vice versa, take your pick of the super-fast Autopista, which skips all towns and runs through flat agricultural lands from Havana to Santa Clara; or the winding Carretera Central, which runs north of and parallel to the Autopista, linking the city of Matanzas with Santa Clara and passing through dusty old country towns.

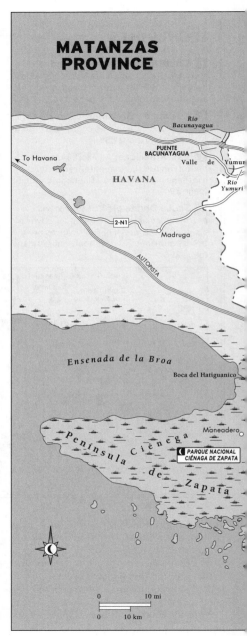

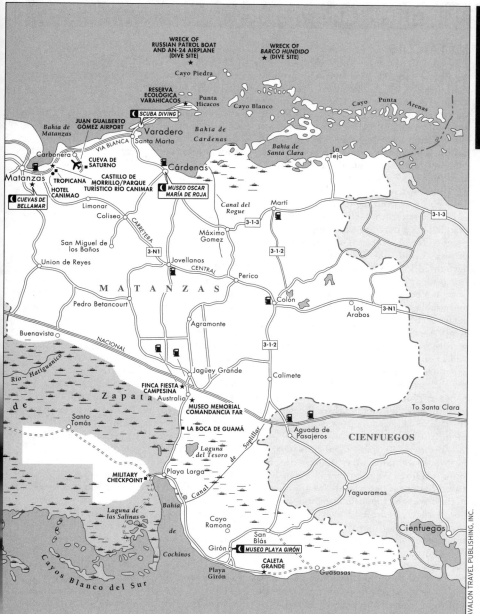

WRECK OF
RUSSIAN PATROL BOAT
AND AN-24 AIRPLANE
(DIVE SITE)
★

WRECK OF
BARCO HUNDIDO
★ (DIVE SITE)

Cayo Piedra

RESERVA
ECOLÓGICA
VARAHICACOS   Punta
               Hicacos   Cayo Blanco   Cayo   Punta   Arenas
[SCUBA DIVING

JUAN GUALBERTO   Varadero   *Bahía de*
GÓMEZ AIRPORT   Santa Marta   *Cárdenas*
Bahía de   *Bahía de*
Matanzas   *Santa Clara*   La
Carbonera   VIA BLANCA   Teja
CUEVA DE
✈   SATURNO   Cárdenas
Matanzas   ▪   CASTILLO DE
TROPICANA   MORRILLO/PARQUE
HOTEL   TURÍSTICO RÍO CANIMAR   [MUSEO OSCAR
CANIMAO   MARÍA DE ROJA
[CUEVAS DE   Limonar   *Canal del*
BELLAMAR   *Rogue*   Martí
            Coliseo   ▪
                                      Máximo   3-1-3   3-1-3
San Miguel de   Gomez
los Baños   3-1-2
           3-N1   Jovellanos
Union de Reyes   CENTRAL
                                      Perico
M A T A N Z A S
                                                     ▪ Colón   Los
Pedro Betancourt   Arabos   3-N1

                 Agramonte

Buenavista ○   3-1-2
            NACIONAL
Río   ▪ ▪
Hatiguanico   Jagüey Grande   Calimete

d e   Z a p a t a   Australia ★   FINCA FIESTA ★
CAMPESINA
                                                              To Santa Clara
            Santo   MUSEO MEMORIAL
            Tomás   COMANDANCIA FAR
                          ▪ LA BOCA DE GUAMÁ   Aguada de   CIENFUEGOS
                                               Pasajeros
                          *Laguna
                          del Tesoro*
            MILITARY   Playa Larga
            CHECKPOINT ▪   Cienfuegos
                         Bahía
Laguna de   Yaguaramas
las Salinas   *de*   Cayo
                         Ramona
                                    San   Cienfuegos
                         Cochinos Blás
                         Girón   [MUSEO PLAYA GIRÓN
C a y o s   CALETA
Blanco del Sur   Playa   GRANDE
                          Girón   ★   Guasasas

© AVALON TRAVEL PUBLISHING, INC.

Matanzas and Vicinity

MATANZAS

The city of Matanzas (pop. 142,000) lies within the deep, 11-kilometer-long, five-kilometer-wide Bahía de Matanzas. The city was founded at the end of the 17th century on the site of an Indian village, Yacayo. The Spanish wrought havoc on the Indians and renamed the site San Carlos y San Severino de Matanzas. In 1694 a castle—Castillo de San Severino—was initiated to guard the bay. A decade later the land between the Ríos Yumurí and San Juan was surveyed and lots distributed among settlers from the Canary Islands.

During the 18th century, Matanzas grew gradually as a port city exporting beef, salted pork, coffee, and tobacco. During the heyday of sugar in the mid-19th century, the region accounted for more than 50 percent of national sugar production. The city was as important a center for the importation of slaves and established itself as Cuba's most important center of cult religions such as Regla Iyessá and Regla Arará. Many white citizens grew immensely wealthy on the sugar and slave trades, and a fashionable café society evolved. Matanzas sponsored the arts and sciences. In 1828 the citizens began printing Cuba's first newspaper. A philharmonic society and a library were formed, followed by three theaters, and the city quickly acquired its Athens of Cuba moniker.

More than 20 Spanish galleons lie at the bottom of Matanzas Bay (Cuba's deepest), sunk by Dutch Admiral Piet Heyn in 1628. Later, Matanzas became a battleground during the Wars of Independence and was even bombarded by the USS *New York.* Today the wide bay is filled with oil tankers and freighters waiting to be loaded with sugar. Tall chimney stacks rise to the north above the bayfront. They belong to a thermoelectricity plant fueled by hot underground waters, a chemical factory (pouring out insipid, sulfurous fumes), and a paper mill that uses *bagazo* (crushed cane fiber). Nonetheless, the town's setting is pleasing—Matanzas rises above the Ríos Yumurí and San Juan, which cut through the center of town, in the cusp of gently rising hills.

East of the city, the Vía Blanca (also called the Matanzas–Varadero Expressway) hugs the coast, winds past sisal plantations, and cuts inland through scrub-covered hills, with the turquoise sea teasingly appearing between the casuarina trees. Oil derricks by the water's edge suck forth black gold from atop coral platforms.

Today, Matanzas remains Cuba's most potent center for *santería* and other African-derived religions, and for Afro-Cuban music and dance.

Orientation

Matanzas lies on the western and southern shore of the sausage-shaped bay. The town is divided by the Ríos Yumurí and San Juan into three distinct sections. To the north is **Reparto Versalles,** a late colonial addition climbing the gentle slopes. The predominantly 19th-century **Pueblo Nuevo** extends south of the Río San Juan along flatlands. The historic city center—**Reparto Matanzas**—lies between them and rises gradually to the west. **Reparto Playa** and its eastward extensions front the bay for several miles.

The Vía Blanca from Havana descends into town from the north and skirts the Reparto Playa bayshore as Calle General Betancourt (Calle 129) en route to Varadero.

The town is laid out in a near-perfect grid. Odd-numbered streets run east–west, even-numbered streets north–south. Many streets have both a name *and* a number; most also have *two* names, one pre- and one post-Revolution. For example, Calle 79 is also called Calle Contreras, though locals still refer to it as Calle Bonifacio Byrne. Contreras and Calle 83 (Milanés) run west from the Vía Blanca six blocks to the main square, Plaza de la Libertad. Calle Santa Teresita (Calle 290) runs

© CHRISTOPHER P. BAKER

statue of the Indian maiden breaking free of her chains, with the Ayuntamiento (town hall) behind, Plaza de la Libertad

perpendicular to the west, and Calle Ayuntamiento (Calle 288) to the east.

The first three digits of a house number refer to the nearest cross street.

For a fabulous view over town, follow Calle Contreras uphill westward from Plaza de la Libertad to **Parque René Fraga,** which contains a bronze bust of Bonifacio Byrne, National Poet (1861–1936). En route, turn right (north) onto Calle 306 and follow it to **Ermita de Monserrate** (Monserrate Hermitage), a *mirador* offering spectacular views over both Matanzas and the Valle de Yumurí. The hermitage itself is but a shell and has no inherent interest.

Plaza de la Libertad

The old parade ground (once known as Plaza de Armas) is a pleasant place to sit under the shade trees and watch the world go by. At its heart is a granite edifice topped by the **Monumento a José Martí** with life-size bronze figures of Martí and the Indian maiden breaking free of her chains. No buildings of architectural note stand out at first sight, but closer scrutiny reveals several much-deteriorated historic gems, notably the **Casa de la Cultura** in the former Lyceum Club, and the **Biblioteca** in the former Casino Club, both on the north side. The former city hall on Calle Ayuntamiento today houses the **Poder Popular,** on the east side.

On the south side, the **Museo Farmacéutico** (Pharmaceutical Museum, Calle 83 #49501, tel. 045/24-3179; daily 10 A.M.– 5 P.M.; CUC2) is a wood-paneled pharmacy dating from 1882, when a pharmacy—La Botica Francesa—was opened by a French pharmacist, Trilet. It functioned as a family-owned pharmacy until 1964, when it metamorphosed into a museum preserving the store just as it was the day it closed, with salves, dried herbs, pharmaceutical instruments, and original porcelain jars neatly arranged on the exquisite carved hardwood shelves. Out back a laboratory contains copper distilleries. Note the bright red and orange *vitrales*. Originally they were red, white, and blue—the colors of

MATANZAS

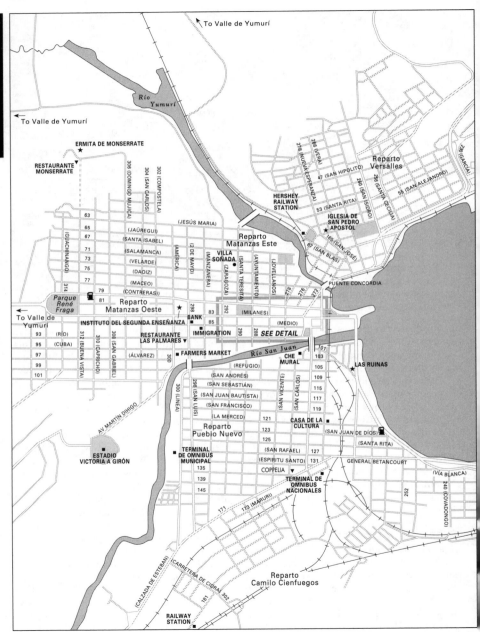

To Valle de Yumurí

To Valle de Yumurí

Río Yumurí

To Valle de Yumurí

ERMITA DE MONSERRATE ★

RESTAURANTE MONSERRATE

306 (DOMINGO MUJICA)
304 (SAN CARLOS)
302 (COMPOSTELA)

HERSHEY RAILWAY STATION

278 (VERA)
286 (VERA)
218 (NUEVA ESPERANZA)
47 (SAN HIPOLITO)
260 (SANTA RITA)
256 (SANTA CECILIA)
59 (SAN ALEJANDRO)
59 (GARCIA)

Reparto Versalles

53 (SANTA RITA)

IGLESIA DE SAN PEDRO APOSTOL ★

165 (SAN JOSE)
67 (SAN BLAS)

(JESÚS MARIA)

63
65 (JAÚREGUI)
67 (SANTA ISABEL)
71 (SALAMANCA)
73 (VELARDE)
75 (DAOIZ)
77 (MACEO)
79 (CONTRERAS))
81

12 (AMERICA)
12 DE MAYO)
(MANZANERA)
(ZARAGOZA)
(SANTA TERESITA)
(AYUNTAMIENTO)
(JOVELLANOS)

Reparto Matanzas Este

VILLA SOÑADA

278
276
272

PUENTE CONCORDIA

(GUACHINANGO)
314

Parque René Fraga

Reparto Matanzas Oeste ★

INSTITUTO DEL SEGUNDA ENSEÑANZA

83
85

298
292
290
288

(MILANES)
(MEDIO)

BANK
IMMIGRATION

SEE DETAIL

To Valle de Yumurí ←

93 (RÍO)
95 (CUBA)
97
99
101

312 (BUENA VISTA)
310 (SAN GABRIEL)
308 (SAN GABRIEL)
300
300 (LINEA)
298 (SAN LUIS)

(ÁLVAREZ)

RESTAURANTE LAS PALMARES ▼

FARMERS MARKET

Río San Juan

CHE MURAL

101
103
105
109
115
117
119

701

LAS RUINAS ★

(REFUGIO)
(SAN ANDRÉS)
(SAN SEBASTIÁN)
(SAN JUAN BAUTISTA)
(SAN FRANCISCO)
(LA MERCED)

(SAN VICENTE)
(SAN CARLOS)

121
123
125
127
131

CASA DE LA CULTURA

(SAN JUAN DE DIOS)
(SANTA RITA)

Reparto Pueblo Nuevo

AV MARTÍN DIHIGO

ESTADIO VICTORIA A GIRÓN

TERMINAL DE OMNIBUS MUNICIPAL

135
139
145

(SAN RAFAEL)
(ESPIRITU SANTO)

COPPELIA ▼

TERMINAL DE OMNIBUS NACIONALES

GENERAL BETANCOURT

(VÍA BLANCA)

252
240 (COVADONGO)

171
173 (MARURI)

(CALZADA DE ESTEBAN)
(CARRETERA DE CIDRA) 302
151

Reparto Camilo Cienfuegos

RAILWAY STATION

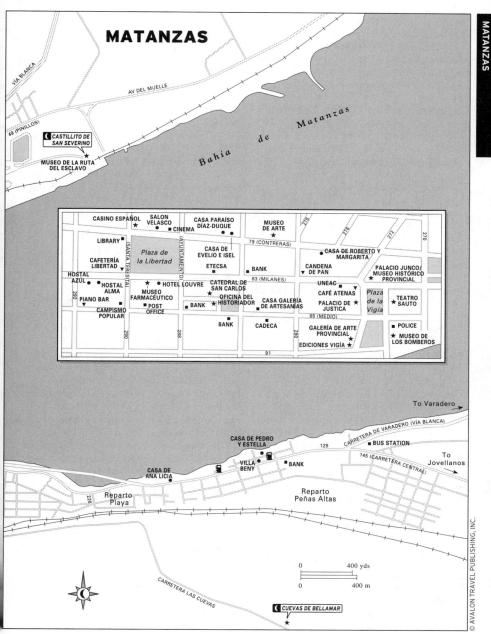

MATANZAS

France—but Spanish authorities insisted that they be replaced with Spain's national colors.

One block east, the **Museo de Arte** (Calle 9 #28007, e/ 280 y 282, tel. 045/29-0735; Tues.–Sat. 10 A.M.–5 P.M., Sun. 8 A.M.–noon) displays a modest collection of art and antiques.

Catedral de San Carlos Borromeo

This recently restored cathedral (Calle 282, e/ 83 y 85; Mon.–Fri. 8 A.M.–noon and 3–5 P.M., Sun. 9 A.M.–noon), one block southeast of Plaza de la Libertad, was built in 1878. Today the opulently frescoed ceiling gleams. The curator has an office at the side of the church; she is usually available in the afternoons (except Monday).

The tiny **Plaza de la Iglesia** fronting the church has a bronze statue of local poet José Jacinto Milanés (1814–63), whose former home is now the **Archivo Histórico** (Calle 83 #28013, e/ 280 y 282, tel. 045/24-4212). One block east, the **Asociación de Artesanas y Artistas** (Calle 85 #26, e/ 280 y 282, tel. 045/25-3657; Mon.–Sat. 8 A.M.–5 P.M.) displays fabulous artwork.

Plaza de la Vigía

The city's other plaza of note is four blocks east of Plaza de la Libertad, at the junction of Milanés and Calle 270, immediately north of the **Puente Calixto García** over the Río San Juan. This, the original town plaza, has at its heart a marble statue of an unnamed freedom fighter during the Wars of Independence. It also boasts the **Teatro Sauto** (tel. 045/24-2721), considered one of Cuba's preeminent neoclassical buildings. It was built in 1863 at the height of the city's prosperity, and in its heyday it attracted the likes of Sarah Bernhardt, Enrico Caruso, and Anna Pavlova. It is easy, staring up at the carved wood and delicate frescoes—representing the muses of comedy, dance, music, theater, and tragedy—to believe you hear the swish of crinoline ball gowns on the marble stairs. The auditorium boasts three tiers with circular balconies supported by thin bronze columns, and the original theater curtain painted to represent the Puente de la Con-

cordia. The much-deteriorated theater still hosts performances on weekend evenings. It was not open for guided tours at last visit.

South of the theater is the tiny, neoclassical fire station, still functioning but also containing the **Museo de los Bomberos** (Mon.–Fri. 10 A.M.–5 P.M., Sat. 1–5 P.M.), worth a visit to marvel at the antique fire engines on display—the oldest, from London, dates from 1864.

Facing the fire station is the **Galería de Arte Provincial** (Calle 272, Calles 85 y 91; Mon.–Fri. 10 A.M.–5 P.M., CUC1); and next door, the **Ediciones Vigía** (Mon.–Fri. 9 A.M.–6 P.M.; CUC1), which produces handmade books in limited editions.

On the north side is the Palacio de Junco, a sky-blue 1840 mansion housing the city's **Museo Histórico Provincial** (Calles 83 y 91, tel. 045/24-3195; Tues.–Sat. 10 A.M.–noon and 1–5 P.M., Sun. 9 A.M.–noon; CUC2), which traces the city's development.

◖ Castillito de San Severino

This partially restored fortress, completed in 1745 on the west side of the bay, is the most intriguing site in town. A cannon dating from 1775 stands by the entrance gate, and a brace of cannon still point across the harbor. Slaves were landed here and held in dungeons, awaiting sale and transfer to sugar plantations. During the 19th century, Cuban nationalists were imprisoned here; according to a plaque, 61 patriots were executed here, and you can see the bullet holes in the moat on the south side of the castle. Today, the fortress houses the excellent little **Museo de la Ruta del Esclavo** (tel. 045/28-3259; Tues.–Sun. 9 A.M.–4 P.M., Sun. 9 A.M.–noon; CUC2). One exhibition room regales local pre-Columbian and colonial history. The *Sala de Orishas* is dedicated to Afro-Cuban religions and, not least, displays life-size figures of the major *orishas* in their colorful garb. Eventually a third exhibit will be dedicated to the legacy of slavery.

The castle stands at the east end of Reparto Versalles, accessed from downtown via the **Puente de la Concordia,** built in 1878 over the Río Yumurí with decorative Babylonian-style

© CHRISTOPHER P. BAKER

Museo de la Ruta del Esclavo, Castillito de San Severino

columns at each end. The region was settled last century by French-Haitian refugees and is pinned by the twin-towered **Iglesia de San Pedro Apóstol** (Calles 57 and 270).

(Cuevas de Bellamar

These caves (tel. 045/25-3538 or 045/25-3190; Tues.–Sun. 9:30 A.M.–5 P.M.; CUC5 for one-hour guided tour, cameras and videos CUC5), in the hills about three kilometers southeast of downtown Matanzas, form one of Cuba's largest cave systems. There are more than 3,000 meters of galleries full of stalactites and stalagmites, including the 80-meter-long, 26-meter-high Gothic Temple, plus gurgling streams and shimmering flower-like crystal formations known as dahlias, many shaped like crystal goblets without stems. "It seemed the coolest, most magical place on the island," thought Lourdes, a character in Cristina García's novel *Dreaming in Cuban.* The air is thin and temperate. A small museum describes the geological formations. Tours depart at 9:30 A.M., 10:30 A.M., 11:30 A.M., 1:15 P.M.,

2:15 P.M., and 4:15 P.M. There's a pleasant thatched restaurant with live music.

Bus #16 departs Calle 300, esq. 83, and will drop you at Calle 226 from where it's a 30-minute uphill hike along the road to the caves (cars will need to take Calle 252, as Calle 226 is closed to cars).

Entertainment and Events

The **Festival del Danzón** (tel. 045/24-3512) is a biennial held in November, with workshops and competitions of *danzón* and folk dance. In mid-October, the Teatro Sauto hosts the **Festival del Bailador Rumbero,** with performances by Cuba's finest Afro-Cuban rumba bands, including the homegrown Los Muñequitos and AfroCuba de Matanzas.

Afro-Cuban musicians also play the **Casa de la Cultura Bonifacio Byrne** (Calle 272 #11916, e/ 119 y 121, tel. 045/29-2709), with programs most evenings.

Teatro Sauto (Plaza de la Vigía, tel. 045/24-2721; CUC5) also hosts classical and folkloric performances Friday–Sunday evenings plus

Sunday at 3 P.M.; the Conjunto Folklórico Nacional and Ballet Nacional de Cuba also perform here.

The **Tropicana Matanzas** (Autopista Varadero Km 4.5, tel./fax 045/26-5555, reservas@trpivar.co.cu; Tues.–Sat. 10 P.M.; CUC40, or CUC49 excursion from Varadero, including cocktail) offers a spectacular Las Vegas–style cabaret. A disco follows.

Las Ruinas (Vía Blanca y Calle 101, tel. 045/25-3387; 24 hours) has live music and disco Friday–Sunday at 9 P.M. and recorded music on other nights in this converted 19th-century warehouse.

You can learn to dance Cuban style in the rear of the **Café Velasco** (tel. 045/28-7793), on the north side of Plaza de la Libertad; dance classes are offered Monday, Wednesday, and Friday 8–10 P.M.

Matanzas's baseball team—the Matanzas—play at the 30,000-seat **Estadio Victoria a Girón** (Avenida Martín Dihigo), one kilometer west of town, October–May (one peso).

Recreation

Scuba divers and snorkelers can explore portions of **Cueva de Saturno** (tel. 045/25-3272; daily 8 A.M.–6 P.M.; CUC3 entrance, CUC5 extra for snorkeling), a 17-kilometer-long cave system with a lagoon and dramatic stalagmites and stalactites. The caves, one kilometer south of the Vía Blanca on the road to Varadero airport about 10 kilometers east of Matanzas, are also touted for sightseers but they're nowhere near as impressive as Cuevas de Bellamar and the scene is less than placid when tour groups arrive. A small museum explains the geology.

Accommodations

Casas Particulares: There are more than 100 *casas particulares* to choose from. One block from Plaza Independencia, **Hostal Alma** (Calle 83 #29008 altos, e/ 290 y 292, tel. 045/24-2449; CUC20) is run by a pleasant couple. Two air-conditioned rooms have high ceilings, fans, radio-cassette players, fridges stocked with beer and water, and modern private bathrooms with hairdryers and hot

water. The vast upstairs lounge has a balcony. Next door, and owned by the same family, is **Hostal Azul** (Calle 83 #29012, e/ 290 y 292, no tel., quena.cb@atenas.int.cu; CUC20), a huge colonial home with two simply furnished air-conditioned rooms with modern ceilings, refrigerators, fans, and small modern bathrooms with hot water. They open to a sparse patio.

The most pleasing downtown option is **Casa de Roberto y Margarita** (Calle 79 #27608, e/ 276 y 280, tel. 045/24-2577; CUC20), a colonial home with two spacious rooms with floor-to-ceiling windows opening to a delightful courtyard. They share a hot-water bathroom.

Casa Soñada (Santa Teresa #6701, esq. Santa Isabel, tel. 045/24-2761, mandy_rent_habitaciones@yahoo.com; CUC25) is a colonial home with a spacious, airy lounge. The owners offer a small air-conditioned apartment to the rear with a mezzanine bedroom with radio and two single beds, a kitchenette, and clean tub-shower.

Casa de Evelio e Isel (Calle 79 #28201, e/ 282 y 288, tel. 045/24-3090, www.cubacasas .net; CUC20) is a pleasant place to rest your head. The owners offer one simply furnished air-conditioned room with refrigerator, fan, TV, radio, and private hot-water bathroom. Guests get use of a TV lounge with leather sofa set and stereo system. This building has several other *casas particulares*. Nearby, **Casa Paraíso Díaz-Duque** (Calle 79 #28205, e/ 282 y 288, tel. 045/24-3397; CUC20) has two cross-ventilated, air-conditioned rooms that share a modern bathroom.

In the Reparto Playa district, east of the center, **Casa de Ana Lilia** (Calle General Betancourt 129/#21603, e/ 216 y 218, tel. 045/26-1576; CUC25) is a bayfront 1940s home with two air-conditioned rooms, each clean and spacious, with TV, its own independent entrance, and modern hot-water bathroom. A rear garden gets the breezes.

Nearby, **Villa Beny** (Calle 129 #20813, e/ Abra y San Miguel, tel. 045/29-3800; CUC20) is a similar option, with one air-conditioned room with fridge, independent entrance, private hot-water bath, plus a terrace and secure parking.

The most spectacular room rental in town is **[** **Casa de Pedro y Estella** (Calle 127 #20807, e/ 208 y 210, tel. 045/26-1260; CUC25), a beautiful, well-kept 1950s home in modernist style with a skylit atrium and walled rear garden overhanging the ocean. It has one spacious, well-lit air-conditioned room with fans, fridge, and a clean, period-themed tiled bathroom.

Campismos: Budget travelers might check into **Campismo Canimar Abajo** (tel. 045/26-1516; CUC5 per person), on the north bank of the Río Canimar. It has 17 basic cabins with cold water only in private bathrooms. Similarly, there's **Campismo Faro de Maya** (tel. 045/26-3129; CUC5 per person), beside the lighthouse on the eastern side of the Bahía de Matanzas, about 16 kilometers east of town (turn left in Carbonera and follow the road to Playa Coral). It, too, has ascetic cabins with private bath (cold water) but no restaurant. You can book either *campismo* at the **Campismo Popular** (Calle 290, e/ 83 y 85, tel. 045/24-3951) office in Matanzas.

Hotels: The historic **Hotel Louvre,** on the south side of Parque de la Libertad, was being restored at last visit.

Food

Matanzas is a culinary disaster, pitifully served by eateries and with no legal *paladares.*

The best option in town is the hilltop **Restaurante Monserrate** (no tel.; daily noon–10:30 P.M.), at the end of Calle 306 on the northwest side of town. This modestly elegant open-air eatery serves a limited *criollo* menu (all dishes CUC5 and under)and has a bar. You come for the views, but you'll need wheels to get here.

The air-conditioned **Café Atenas** (Calle 82, esq. 272, tel. 045/25-3493; daily 10 A.M.–midnight), on Plaza de la Vigía, has an outdoor patio with shady arbor, and serves simple pizzas, sandwiches, and snacks. I asked for, and received, an excellent shrimp enchilada, not on the menu. All menu items are CUC5 and under.

There are several peso restaurants, but the only one worth recommending is **Restaurante En Familia** (Calle 288, esq. 93), serving seafoods, pizzas, and *criollo* fare.

Cafetería Casa Grande (Calle 83 #29010, e/ 290 y 292; daily 10 A.M.–8 P.M.) makes simple boxed meals (*cajitas*).

For ice cream, try **Coppelia** (Calle 272, esq. 127; Tues.–Sun. 10 A.M.–10 P.M.).

You can buy groceries at **Mercado San Luis** (Calles 298 y 291); breads and baked goods at **Cadena de Pan** (Calle 83, e/ 278 y 280; 24 hours); and produce at the **Mercado La Plaza** (Calles 97 y 298) farmers market, where peso stalls sell fried foods and *batidos.*

Information and Services

The **post office** (Calles 85 and 290; Mon.–Sat. 7 A.M.–8 P.M.) is one block south of the main square. **Etecsa** (Calle 83, esq. 282; daily 9 A.M.–9:30 P.M.) has Internet and international telephones.

Bandec (Calle 85, e/ 282 y 288, tel. 045/24-2781) and **Banco Financiero Internacional** (Calles 85 y 298, tel. 045/25-3400; Mon.–Fri. 8 A.M.–3 P.M.) have branches. And you can change foreign currency at **Cadeca** (Calle 286, e/ 83 y 85; Mon.–Sat. 8 A.M.–6 P.M., Sun. 8 A.M.–noon).

Hospital Faustino Pérez (tel. 045/25-3426), on the Carretera Central about two kilometers southwest of town, has a clinic for foreigners.

Inmigración (Calle 85 #29408; Mon.–Thurs. 8:30 A.M.–noon) can issue *prórrogas.*

Getting There and Away

By Air: International flights arrive and depart the **Juan Gualberto Gómez International Airport,** 20 kilometers east of Matanzas. (See *Getting There and Away* in the *Varadero* section of this chapter for details.)

By Bus: Astro and Víazul buses operate to and from the **Terminal de Ómnibus Nacional** (Calles 131 and 272, tel. 045/29-1473) on the south side of town. **Víazul** (tel. 045/29-1473) has Havana–Varadero buses that drop off in Matanzas (CUC7). Buses depart for Havana at

A SUGAR OF A JOURNEY

Rail journeys hold a particular magic, none more so in Cuba than the Hershey Train, which runs lazily between Casablanca and Matanzas year-round, four times a day.

Before the Revolution, the Hershey estates belonging to the Pennsylvania-based chocolate company occupied 69 square miles of lush canefields around a modern sugar-factory town (now called Camilo Cienfuegos), with a baseball field, movie theater, and amusements, and a hotel and *cabinas* for rent next to the mill.

At its peak, the estate had 19 steam locomotives. Their sparks, however, constituted a serious fire hazard, so they were replaced with seven 60-ton electric locomotives built especially for the Hershey-Cuban Railroad. Milton Hershey also introduced a three-car passenger train service between Havana and Matanzas every hour, stopping at Hershey. Alas, the diminutive vermilion MU-train locomotive that looked like it could have fallen from the pages of a story about Thomas, the little "live" engine, was replaced in 1998 with a spiffy fleet of more comfortable, antique Spanish cars.

The train departs the Estación de Casablanca (Carretera de los Cocos, tel. 07/862-4888), on the north side of Havana harbor. The train winds in and out among the palm-studded hills, speeds along the coast within sight of the Atlantic, then slips between palms, past broad swathes of sugarcane, and through the Yumurí Valley. Two hours into the journey, you'll arrive at a blue station still bearing the Hershey sign. You are now in the heart of the old Hershey sugar factory (now closed), where the train pauses sufficiently for you to get down and capture the scene for posterity. After a mesmerizing four-hour journey, you finally arrive at the Matanzas station.

The train – which makes about 40 stops en route – departs Casablanca at 4:43 and 8:35 A.M. and 12:30, 5:21, and 9:17 P.M., arriving Matanzas 3.5 hours later (the 8:35 A.M. departure is an express and takes only about 2.5 hours). Return trains depart Matanzas at 7:28 and 11:28 A.M., 3:23 and 8:16 P.M., and 12:10 A.M. Tickets cost CUC2.80 to Matanzas and go on sale one hour in advance. Kids ride half-price. Passengers are assigned seat numbers.

You can order a 60-minute VHS video, *Hershey Electric: Adios to the Brills,* from Canadian Caboose Press (Box 844, Skookumchuck, BC V0B 2E0, Canada; CAN/US$29.95).

8:55 A.M., 12:10 P.M., 4:55 P.M., and 6:55 P.M.; and for Varadero at 10:15 A.M., 2:10 P.M., 6:15 P.M., and 8:15 P.M.

Astro buses depart Matanzas for Camagüey at 9 A.M. on alternate days (CUC19), Cienfuegos at 8 A.M. (CUC7), Havana at 5:35 A.M. and 1:30 P.M. (CUC5), Santa Clara at 4:45 P.M. (CUC8), and Santiago de Cuba at 10:40 A.M. on alternate days (CUC32). Only two seats per bus are reserved for foreigners; you must buy your tickets one hour prior to departure.

The **Terminal de Ómnibus Municipal** (Calles 298 y 127, tel. 045/29-2701) serves destinations throughout Matanzas Province, including Cárdenas at 1:40 P.M. (CUC2), Jagüey Grande at 1:30 P.M. Tuesday and Thursday (CUC2.85), and Varadero at 9 A.M., 10 A.M., noon, and 2 P.M. (CUC2).

By Train: The rail station (Calle 181, tel. 045/29-9590) is on the south side of town. All trains between Havana and Santiago de Cuba stop here, calling at provincial capitals en route: Camagüey (CUC22), Santa Clara (CUC6.50), Sancti Spíritus (CUC11), Ciego de Ávila (CUC14), Las Tunas (CUC20), and Holguín (CUC24). Eight trains serve Havana (CUC4) daily beginning at 3:21 A.M. Santiago de Cuba–bound (CUC32) trains ostensibly depart Matanzas at 4:41, 6:51, and 7:30 P.M. Additional trains depart for Cienfuegos at 5:30 A.M. (CUC6), Bayamo at 10:03 A.M. (CUC23), Manzanillo at 7:48 A.M. (CUC25), and Holguín at 8:38 P.M.

The Hershey Train leaves from **Terminal Hershey** (Calles 55 y 67, tel. 045/24-4805), in Reparto Versalles, three blocks northeast of the Río Yumurí bridge. (See the sidebar *A Sugar of a Journey*.)

Other: A licensed taxi costs about CUC80 one-way between Matanzas and Havana and about CUC40 between Matanzas and Varadero. *Colectivo* taxis operate from the rail and bus terminals but it is illegal for drivers to give rides to foreigners.

Getting Around

Bus service within town is very limited. Bus #16 runs to the Terminal de Ómnibus Municipal from Calle 79, one block west of the main square. Most people get around by *coches* (horse-drawn cabs) and *bici-taxis*.

There are three gas stations on the Vía Blanca, east of downtown. You can rent cars from **Havanautos** (Calle 129, esq. 208, tel. 045/25-3294), next to the Cupet gas station, and **Micar** (Calle 129, esq. 210), one block west, at the Oro Negro gas station.

VALLE DE YUMURÍ

Humboldt called it "the loveliest valley in the world." The Cubans call it "the Valley of Delight." The eight-kilometers-wide Yumurí Valley is held in the cusp of 150-meter-high limestone cliffs—the Cuchillas de Habana–Matanzas—immediately west of Matanzas, from which it is separated by a high ridge. The hills form a natural amphitheater hidden from the modern world. Two rivers, the Yumurí and Bacunayagua, thread their silvered way to the sea through a landscape as archetypically Cuban as any you will find on the island.

The Hershey Train (see the sidebar *A Sugar of a Journey*) passes through the valley. Get off at Mena; it's a two-kilometer walk from here.

Accommodations

The **Horizontes Casa del Valle Motel** (Carretera de Chirno Km 2, Valle del Yumurí, tel. 045/25-3584, fax 045/25-3300) was closed to tourists at last visit.

RÍO CANIMAR

Four kilometers east of Matanzas, immediately beyond the bridge over the Río Canimar, a road to the left loops downhill into **Parque Turístico Río Canimar** (tel./fax 045/26-1516), where there's a tiny beach and a pleasant restaurant. A 45-minute boat trip upriver (CUC10, or CUC20 with snorkeling, plus horseback riding and lunch) includes a visit to Cueva La Eloísa, a flooded cave where you may swim in the pellucid waters. Motorized inflatable boats can be rented (CUC15 for 15 minutes, CUC45 one hour, CUC140 six hours). This excursion—the "Challenge Tour"—can be booked through tour agencies in Havana and Varadero.

A small fort, **Castillo El Morrillo** (Tues.–Sun. 9 A.M.–4 P.M.; CUC1), stands over the west bank of the rivermouth. Built in 1720, it is now a museum dedicated to revolutionary leaders Antonio Guiteras Holmes (1906–35), founder in 1934 of the radical student group Joven Cuba (Young Cuba), and Venezuela revolutionary Carlos Aponte Hernández (1901–35), who were executed nearby by General Machado's henchmen while trying to flee into exile. They are buried beneath a marble mausoleum inside the fort. Prehistoric artifacts and Indian remains are displayed upstairs. Guides give a full spiel.

Bus #16 departs Calle 300, esq. 83, in Matanzas and will drop you here.

Accommodations

Hotel Canimao (tel./fax 045/25-3429, director@canimao.co.cu; CUC24 s, CUC32 d low season; CUC28 s, CUC36 d high season), off the Vía Blanca about eight kilometers east of Matanzas, is a pleasant no-frills bargain. The 158 air-conditioned rooms are modestly furnished, with satellite TV, safes, and hairdryers in modern bathrooms. The hotel sits above the Río Canimar adjacent to the Tropicana nightclub, and offers excursions to the Cuevas de Bellamar and Río Canimar. (Islazul.)

MATANZAS

Varadero

"In all the beaches in Cuba the sand was made of grated silver," says a character in Robert Fernández's *Raining Backwards,* "though in Varadero it was also mixed with diamond dust." Varadero, 34 kilometers east of Matanzas and 140 kilometers east of Havana, is Cuba's tourist mecca, the artificial Cuba frequented by budget-minded Canadian and European charter groups. On certain mid-winter days, more than 50 international flights service Varadero, which receives more than one-third of all tourists to Cuba.

The Cuban government is hell-bent on developing Varadero as Cuba's Cancún. There are already more than 60 hotels, and the gaps are being filled in. All-inclusive resorts dominate the scene, so that independent state-run restaurants and services receive little business. No private restaurants or room rentals are permitted. Varadero lacks vitality, especially at night. And at night, when the breeze blows offshore, occasional fumes from the petrochemical works and oil rigs across Bahía de Cárdenas drift to town, bringing a stink of rotten eggs. More importantly, it bears no relation to Cuban reality. In many ways, it's designed as a Potemkin village: the best-maintained road in the nation is that from the airport into town; the fully stocked stores (notably the bou-tiques and supermarket in Plaza América) belie the shortages affecting ordinary Cubans; few tourists know that the Cuban service staff in hotels are paid less than US$1 per day in near-worthless pesos. And although the resort spans a Cuban village (pop. 15,000), visitation by Cubans from outside the area is strictly regulated, social interactions between Cubans and foreigners are closely monitored (plainclothes secret police are present, as everywhere else in Cuba, including in hotels), and the local residents pretty much keep to themselves.

Strictly speaking, Varadero is the name of the *beach* area. It lies on the ocean-facing side of an 20-kilometer-long peninsula called Península de Hicacos, which encloses Bahía de Cárdenas and is separated from the mainland by the Laguna de Paso Malo. The peninsula is only 1.2 kilometers at its widest point. It slants to the northeast, where its tip—Punta Hicacos—is the northernmost point in Cuba. The scrub-covered eastern half is broken by a series of flat-topped mesas and low-lying raised coral platforms pitted with sinkholes and caves full of marine fossils.

The main beach, Playa Mayor, is a virtually unbroken 11.5-kilometer-long swath that widens eastward (where facilities are more upscale), then breaks up into smaller beaches

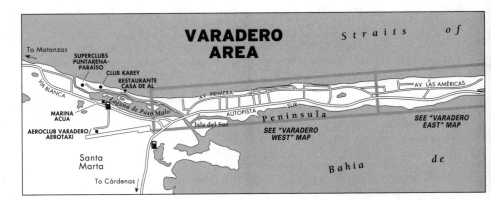

divided by rocky headlands, where most of the deluxe hotels sit over their own "private" beaches. The beaches shelve gently into waters the color of a Maxfield Parrish painting. A coral reef lies offshore. Red flags are posted when seas are rough.

Varadero offers snorkeling and scuba diving (principally wreck-diving), although these are somewhat overrated if its corals you're seeking, in which case you'll do better elsewhere in Cuba. Water sports abound. And there are heaps of excursions for those who want to explore farther afield.

HISTORY

The Spanish settled the region around 1587, when Don Pedro Camacho developed charcoal and salt-pork enterprises on salt flats and began supplying Spanish fleets. A small community of fisherfolk later sprouted on the south shore, in the village today known as Las Moralas. In the 1870s, families from Cárdenas built wooden summer homes and developed the beach with boardinghouses for summer vacationers. Rowing regattas developed (the prize was the Cuban Cup), necessitating more lodging, and the first hotel—the Varadero Hotel—opened in 1915.

In 1926, U.S. industrialist Irénée Du Pont bought much of the peninsula and built himself a large estate, complete with golf course. Other wealthy *norteamericanos* followed, albeit in less grandiose style (Du Pont, who had paid four centavos a square meter, sold them the land for 120 pesos a square meter). Al Capone bought a house here. So did the dictator Fulgencio Batista. Soon, Varadero was a budding Miami in miniature, with exclusive neighborhoods patrolled by private police.

By the 1950s, Varadero had a casino and was a favored hangout of Hollywood stars, high-class prostitutes, and mobsters. On the eve of the Revolution, much of the peninsula was in private hands. The Castro government likes to claim that Cubans were banned from the beach, but in reality this was only on privately owned sectors, and villagers had access to the long swath in front of the village. Ironically, during the 1990s only Cubans who lived in the village were permitted access to Varadero. Today, access remains restricted, so things have come full circle.

ORIENTATION

There is only one way onto the island-peninsula: the bridge over Laguna de Paso Malo, at the extreme west end of the Hicacos Peninsula and from where two roads run east along the peninsula. The fast Autopista Sur runs along the bayfront all the way to the end of the peninsula. Avenida Primera (1ra)—the main street—runs along the oceanfront from Calle 8 in the west to Calle L and the Hotel Internacional in the east. West of Calle 8,

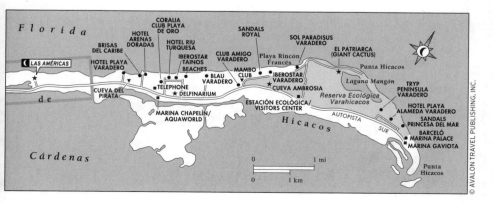

© AVALON TRAVEL PUBLISHING, INC.

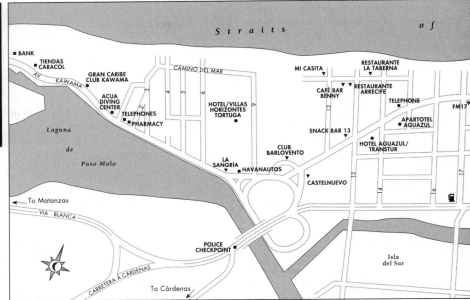

S t r a i t s   o f

BANK
TIENDAS CARACOL
GRAN CARIBE CLUB KAWAMA
AV KAWAMA
CAMINO DEL MAR
ACUA DIVING CENTER
TELEPHONES
PHARMACY
HOTEL/VILLAS HORIZONTES TORTUGA
MI CASITA
RESTAURANTE LA TABERNA
CAFÉ BAR BENNY
RESTAURANTE ARRECIFE
TELEPHONE
FM17
APARTOTEL AGUAZUL
SNACK BAR 13
HOTEL AGUAZUL/ TRANSTUR
CLUB BARLOVENTO
LA SANGRÍA
HAVANAUTOS
CASTELNUEVO
Laguna
de
Paso Malo
To Matanzas
VIA BLANCA
POLICE CHECKPOINT
Isla del Sur
CARRETERA A CARDENAS
To Cárdenas

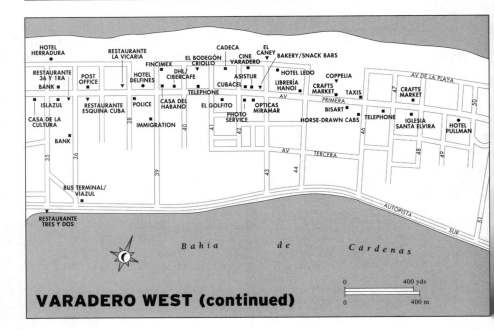

HOTEL HERRADURA
RESTAURANTE LA VICARIA
CADECA
EL CANEY
BAKERY/SNACK BARS
FINCIMEX
EL BODEGÓN CRIOLLO
CINE VARADERO
RESTAURANTE 36 Y 1RA
POST OFFICE
HOTEL DELFINES
DHL/ CIBERCAFE
HOTEL LEDO
COPPELIA
AV DE LA PLAYA
BANK
ASISTUR
LIBRERÍA HANOI
CRAFTS MARKET
CRAFTS MARKET
CUBACEL
TELEPHONE
TAXIS
ISLAZUL
RESTAURANTE ESQUINA CUBA
POLICE
CASA DEL HABANO
EL GOLFITO
OPTICAS MIRAMAR
BISART
PRIMERA
CASA DE LA CULTURA
PHOTO SERVICE
IMMIGRATION
HORSE-DRAWN CABS
TELEPHONE
IGLESIA SANTA ELVIRA
HOTEL PULLMAN
BANK
AV
TERCERA
BUS TERMINAL/ VÍAZUL
RESTAURANTE TRES Y DOS
AUTOPISTA
SUR

B a h í a   d e   C á r d e n a s

VARADERO WEST (continued)

0		400 yds
0		400 m

MATANZAS

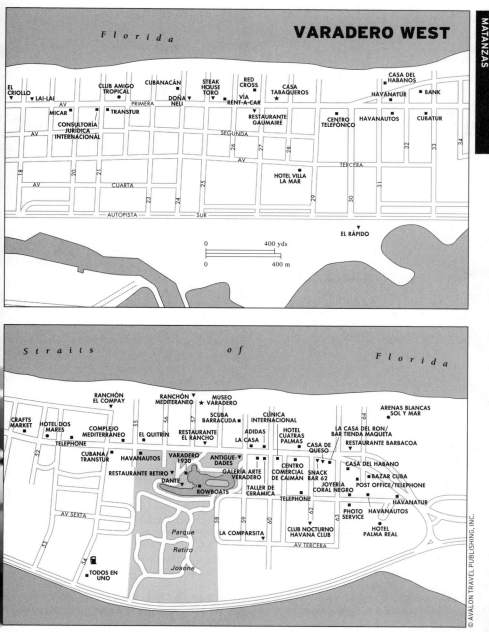

VARADERO WEST

Florida

EL CRIOLLO
LAI-LAI
CLUB AMIGO TROPICAL
CUBANACÁN
STEAK HOUSE TORO
RED CROSS
CASA TABAQUEROS
CASA DEL HABANOS
HAVANATUR
BANK
MICAR
TRANSTUR
DOÑA NELI
VÍA RENT-A-CAR
CONSULTORÍA JURÍDICA INTERNACIONAL
PRIMERA
RESTAURANTE GAUMAIRÉ
CENTRO TELEFÓNICO
HAVANAUTOS
CUBATUR
SEGUNDA
AV
26
27
28
32
33
34
AV
18
20
21
25
TERCERA
HOTEL VILLA LA MAR
29
30
31
AV
CUARTA
23
24
AUTOPISTA
SUR
EL RÁPIDO

0   400 yds
0   400 m

Straits   of   Florida

RANCHÓN EL COMPAY
RANCHÓN MEDITERANEO
MUSEO VARADERO
ARENAS BLANCAS SOL Y MAR
CRAFTS MARKET
HOTEL DOS MARES
COMPLEJO MEDITERRANEO
SCUBA BARRACUDA
CLÍNICA INTERNACIONAL
TELEPHONE
EL QUITRÍN
RESTAURANTE EL RANCHO
ADIDAS
LA CASA
HOTEL CUATRAS PALMAS
LA CASA DEL RON/ BAR TIENDA MAQUETA
RESTAURANTE BARBACOA
55
56
57
64
CUBANA/ TRANSTUR
HAVANAUTOS
VARADERO 1920
ANTIGUE-DADES
CASA DE QUESO
CASA DEL HABANO
RESTAURANTE RETIRO
GALERÍA ARTE VERADERO
CENTRO COMERCIAL DE CAIMÁN
SNACK BAR 62
BAZAR CUBA
DANTE
ROWBOATS
TALLER DE CERÁMICA
JOYERÍA CORAL NEGRO
POST OFFICE/TELEPHONE
AV SEXTA
58
59
60
TELEPHONE
62
63
PHOTO SERVICE
HAVANATUR
HAVANAUTOS
Parque
LA COMPARSITA
CLUB NOCTURNO HAVANA CLUB
HOTEL PALMA REAL
53
Retiro
54
Josone
AV TERCERA
TODOS EN UNO

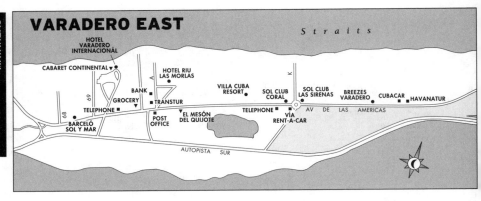

Avenida 1ra becomes Avenida Kawama, which runs through the Kawama district to the westernmost tip of the island.

Cross streets begin at Calle 1, in the Kawama suburb, and run eastward consecutively to Calle 69, in the La Torre area. Farther east, they are lettered, from Calle A to L. The luxury hotel zone begins east of Calle 69, where Avenida 1ra becomes Avenida las Américas. The old village of funky wooden houses occupies the central section of town, roughly between Calles 23 and 54.

SIGHTS

A castellated water tower next to the Mesón del Quijote restaurant, atop a rise on Avenida las Américas, looks like an old fortress tower but was, in fact, built in the 1930s. A quaint touch is added by a modernist sculpture of Don Quixote on his trusty steed, galloping across the hillcrest.

The small **Museo de Varadero** (Calle 57 y 1ra, tel. 045/61-3189; 10 A.M.–7 P.M. daily; CUC1), in a turn-of-the-century house—Casa Villa Abreu—has separate sections dedicated to the local flora and fauna, aboriginal culture, Irénée Du Pont, and Castro and his achievements. There's also a reproduction period lounge. Upstairs is dedicated to sports in Cuba, notably the historic rowing regattas for which the town was once famous.

(Las Américas

The most interesting attraction is Las Américas (tel. 045/66-7750; restaurant and bar daily 10 A.M.–11:30 P.M.; closed to sightseers), munitions magnate Irénée Du Pont's Spanish-style mansion at the far eastern end of Avenida las Américas. The green tile–roofed mansion, which Du Pont named Xanadu, was built in 1926 as a sumptuous winter hideaway (complete with nine-hole golf course). The Du Pont family lived here until 1959. He fitted his house with a Carrara marble floor, great dark wooden eaves and precious timbers, original hardwood antiques, an organ, and a massive wine cellar and wine bar beneath the house. Light pours into the library, where the vast array of volumes went unread. On the top floor is a bar (once a ballroom) decorated in Italian rococo.

A faded tapestry in the dining room transcribes the lines of Samuel Coleridge's poem:

In Xanadu did Kubla Khan
A stately pleasure dome decree

The six marble-floored bedrooms can be rented (see *Accommodations*).

Parque Retiro Josone

Varadero's well-kept landscaped park (Av. 1ra, e/ 54 y 59; daily 9 A.M.–midnight; free) is centered

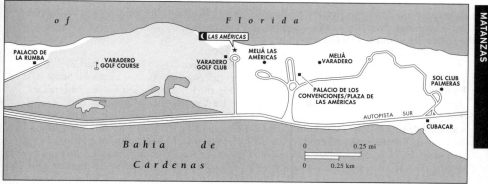

© AVALON TRAVEL PUBLISHING, INC.

on an old mansion furnished with colonial-era antiques. Businessman José Fermín Iturrioz and his wife, Onelia, lived here in the 1950s. After departing Cuba following the Revolution, Sr. Fermín had to give his property up to the Castro regime in exchange for safe passage from the country for the rest of his extended family. It was then used as a protocol house for foreign dignitaries. Today the romantic park is favored for photo shoots by girls in frilly dresses celebrating their *quinceañeras.*

Facilities include a lake with geese, and there are peacocks and ostriches, a swimming pool (CUC3 entrance, including CUC2 credit towards food and drink) on the south side of the park, several outdoor bars, four restaurants, and a *guarapería.* You can rent rowboats (CUC0.50 per person 30 minutes, CUC1 per hour) and bicycles (CUC5 per hour), and even ride a camel (CUC5 adults, CUC2.50 children) or kiddie train (CUC1).

Reserva Ecológica Varahicacos

This 450-hectare reserve (tel. 045/61-3594; 9 A.M.–4:30 P.M. daily; CUC3) of scrub and woodland at the eastern tip of the peninsula is riddled with limestone caves, many of which contain aboriginal pictographs. The most important is **Cueva Ambrosia,** in a cliff called Loma La Caseta, on the inner (south) side of the peninsula and accessed by trail from the park entry. The cave has pre-Columbian petro-glyphs. A second trail leads to **Cueva de los Musulmanes** (Cave of Muslims), once used as an aboriginal tomb (replete with a replica of a cadaver). Near the shoreline is a huge cactus— **El Patriarca** (the Patriarch)—thought to be at least 500 years old. The access road leads to **Playa Calaveras** and **Laguna Mágon,** a lake good for bird-watching.

A separate 17-hectare section of the reserve surrounds **Cueva de la Pirata,** which is closed to the public by day (at night it hosts a cabaret).

The entrance fee includes a guided walk to Cueva Ambrosia and is payable at Cueva Ambrosia or the **Centro Visitantes** (also called **Estación Ecológico**), at the junction on the Autopista Sur.

Delfinario

Dolphins are the star performers at the Delfinario (Autopista Km 11, tel. 045/66-8031; 9 A.M.–5 P.M. daily), in a coral-rimmed lagoon 400 meters east of Marina Chapelín. Shows are offered at 11 A.M. and 3:30 P.M. (CUC15, cameras CUC5). You can even swim with the dolphins at 9:30 A.M., 11:30 A.M., and 2:30 P.M. (CUC87). Children under five enter free.

ENTERTAINMENT AND EVENTS

Varadero is relatively dead at night. The majority of guests stay in the all-inclusive hotels, which feature their own bars, cabarets, and entertainment. Although Cubans are permitted in most entertainment venues, secret police work the scene and any Cuban female getting too friendly with tourists faces the likelihood of arrest.

Festivals and Events

Varadero's homegrown **Carnaval** is held in mid-July, but it isn't held every year. The **Varadero International Marathon** is held in November. **Festival de Invierno,** held each second week in December, attracts artists from throughout Latin America, with fashion shows, music, and a classic-auto parade.

Varadero has a full-blown **Centro de Convenciones** (Autopista Sur Km 11, tel. 045/66-8181, fax 045/66-7012, comercial@plamer.var.cyt.cu) at Plaza América.

Traditional Music and Dance

Many of the hotels provide Afro-Cuban shows. The rundown **Casa de la Cultura** (Av. 1ra y Calle 34, tel. 045/61-2562; CUC5) has folkloric music and dance shows on Thursdays at 10 P.M.

A "Noche de Santería" folkloric show is hosted in Parque Retiro Josone Friday and Saturday at 9 P.M. (CUC3).

Bars

There are very few bars, other than in the hotels, though you'll find several unremarkable open-air bars along Avenida 1ra. **Café Bar Benny** (Camino del Mar, e/ 12 y 13; 24 hours) is lent ambience by the silky jazz riffs of Benny Moré on the sound system. Occasional live music.

The genteel **Bar Mirador Casablanca** (10 A.M.–11:45 P.M.), in Mansion Xanadu, has live jazz each afternoon at 4 P.M.

If you're serious about sampling rums, head to **Bar Tienda Maqueta** (Av. 1ra, esq. 63, tel. 045/66-9833; 9 A.M.–9 P.M. daily), in La Casa del Ron. It serves 96 types of rum and offers sample shots, and there's a scale model reproduction of Distilería Santa Elena rum factory (1906–38) with a working railway. The **Varadero 1920** (daily 9 A.M.–10 P.M.)

bar in Parque Retiro Josone specializes in piña coladas (CUC3).

Discos

Most hotels have their own bars and discos (nonguests are welcome at some). Some bars keep the fire exits locked for security reasons.

La Comparsita (Calle 60, esq. 3ra, tel. 045/66-7415; Sun.–Fri. 10:30 P.M.–2:30 A.M., Sat. 10:30 P.M.–3 A.M.; CUC7 including all drinks) was the happening spot for tourists at last visit. The open-air venue downstairs hosts a *cabaret espectáculo* and/or live music nightly at 11:30 P.M., with disco to follow. There's a karaoke bar upstairs. The place gets packed.

Cubans from out-of-town flock on weekends to the **Palacio de la Rumba** (tel. 045/66-8210; 11 P.M.–3 A.M. daily; CUC10 including all drinks), a Western-style disco. A dress code applies. The main competition is **Club Nocturno Havana Club** (Calle 62 final, tel. 045/66-7500; 10:30 P.M.–3 A.M. daily; CUC10 including all drinks), in Centro Comercial Copey; and the more upscale **Mambo Club** (tel. 045/66-8565; Tues.–Sun. 11 P.M.–3 A.M.; CUC10 including all drinks), outside the Club Amigo Varadero at the east end of the peninsula, and featuring a cabaret before the disco.

The once-kicking **Disco La Bamba,** in the defunct Hotel Tuxpan, and **Habana Café** were closed indefinitely at last visit.

Cabarets Espectáculos

Hotel tour desks sell excursions to the Tropicana Varadero, which happens to be in Matanzas (see *Entertainment and Events* in the *Matanzas* section earlier in this chapter).

Cabaret Continental (tel. 045/66-7038; Tues.–Sun. at 10 P.M. and midnight; CUC25, or CUC40 with lobster dinner), at Hotel Varadero International, is the best emporium of exotica in town, with kaleidoscopes of stiletto-heeled showgirls teasingly swirling their boas while musicians beat out sambas and salsa. It's followed by the New Age disco (CUC10 for disco entrance only). There's a teens' disco on Sunday afternoon.

At **Cueva del Pirata** (Autopista Sur, Km 11,

© CHRISTOPHER P. BAKER

A smiling Bacchus welcomes visitors to the Bar Tienda Maqueta.

tel. 045/66-7751; Mon.–Sat. at 11 P.M.; CUC8 including all drinks), a swashbuckling cabaret—think eye-patches and cutlasses with g-strings and high heels—takes place in a natural cave. It's followed by a disco.

You can book the above cabarets at any hotel tour desk.

A free open-air mini-cabaret is hosted nightly at 9:30 P.M. at **FM-17** (Av. 1ra y Calle 17, tel. 045/61-4831).

The **Cabaret Eco-Disco** (Av. 1ra, e/ 34 y 35, tel. 045/61-2460; CUC5) in a basic open-air patio has cabaret nightly at 8:30 P.M., followed by a disco.

Other

Snack Bar 62 (Av. 1ra, esq. 62; 24 hours) hosts free live music nightly 9:30 P.M.–midnight. The **Cine Varadero** (Av. de la Playa y Calle 42; CUC2) shows films nightly at 6:30 P.M. **Restaurante Estrella** (tel. 045/66-2649), in Parque Retiro Josone, has pool tables and a bowling alley (CUC2). **Todo En Uno** (Autopista Sur y Calle 54; Tues.–Thurs. 6–11 P.M., Fri.–Sun. 11 A.M.–11 P.M.; CUC1 per ride)

also has a 24-hour *bolera* (bowling alley, CUC2.50 per game), plus *carros locos* (bumper cars) and a small roller coaster called Russian Mountain.

SPORTS AND RECREATION

Most resort hotels have tennis courts (non-guests pay a court fee) and most upscale all-inclusives include water sports in their room rates. Several outlets along the beach offer snorkeling (CUC3 per hour), sea-kayaks and Aquabikes (CUC5 per hour), sailboards (CUC10), and banana-boat rides (CUC5 for 10 minutes).

Golf

You can practice your swing at **Varadero Golf Club** (tel. 045/66-7788, fax 045/66-8481, www.varaderogolfclub.com; 7 A.M.–7 P.M. daily) at Las Américas. The 18-hole, par-72 course has a well-stocked pro shop (8 A.M.–5 P.M. daily), electric carts, and caddie house, plus restaurant and snack bar. Greens fees are CUC70; club rental CUC30; golf cart CUC30. Golf classes are offered. Bring your own golf balls: The club has a shortage and sells them for CUC5 each!

Fans of mini-golf can putt around a crude "crazy golf" course at **El Golfito** (CUC3; 24 hours), with a snack bar.

Paragliding and Skydiving

Fancy seeing Varadero as the frigate birds see it? The **Centro Internacional de Paracaidismo** (International Parachuting Center, tel. 045/66-7256, fax 045/66-7260, skygators@cubairsports.itgo.com), at the airstrip off the Vía Blanca, Km 1.5, offers initiation courses, technical training, and jumps including a tandem jump in a two-harness parachute with a professional trainer (CUC180 including transfers and an eight-minute fall from 3,000 meters; CUC50 additional for a video of your fall). The fall is made from a Russian biplane. You can also take an Ultralight flight (CUC30 for 10 minutes, or CUC150 per hour).

◖ Scuba Diving and Snorkeling

There are more than 30 dive sites off Varadero, several with old wrecks. However, the diving for corals here is not as good as elsewhere in Cuba. Most sites are in **Parque Marino Cayo Piedras del Norte,** northeast of Varadero, and require a one-hour boat ride to reach. Thrillingly the park features several wrecks including an AN-24 aircraft, a 102-meter frigate, and even a gunboat with missiles. A scuba center is on-site, and excursions are offered from Varadero's marinas. Another good site is the Blue Hole—*Ojo de Mégano*—an underwater cave 70 meters deep in the reefs east of Varadero. Forests of black coral are prevalent, especially at deeper levels. Hawksbill turtles are commonly seen.

When seas are too rough for diving, divers are transferred to the Playa Girón (Bay of Pigs, a three-hour ride), where seas are generally calmer.

Marlin S.A. operates three dive outlets. All charges CUC40–50 per dive and have certification courses (CUC365) and multi-dive pack-

the beach at Varadero

© CHRISTOPHER P. BAKER

ages. **Barracuda Scuba Cuba** (Av. 1ra, e/ 58 y 59, tel. 045/61-3481, fax 045/66-7072, www.aquaworldvaradero.com; daily 8 A.M.–7 P.M.) is the main outlet. It has a seafood restaurant and a decompression chamber. **Diving Center Coral** (Av. Kawama y Calle 1, tel. 045/66-8063; daily 8 A.M.–5 P.M.), at the Hotel Coral, has Nitrox. **Diving Center Marina Chapelín** (tel. 045/66-8871; daily 9 A.M.–4 P.M.), at Marina Chapelín, is solely for certified divers.

Many upscale all-inclusive hotels also have dive facilities. All scuba outfitters rent snorkeling gear (CUC5) and most offer snorkeling trips (typically CUC25).

Centro Médico Sub Acuático (Sub-Aquatic Medical Center, tel. 045/62-2114) at Cárdenas, 10 kilometers east of Varadero, has a decompression chamber.

Sportfishing

Sportfishing trips are offered at the three marinas: **Marina Dársena** (tel. 045/66-8060, fax 045/66-7773), on the Vía Blanca, one kilometer west of Varadero; **Marina Chapelín** (tel. 045/66-7550, fax 045/66-7093), toward the east end of the Autopista Sur; and **Marina Varadero** (tel. 045/66-7755), at the far east end of the Autopista. Typical prices are CUC250 for four people for four hours.

Varadero hosts the **Gregorio Fuentes White Marlin Fishing Tournament** in June.

Boat Excursions

A 90-minute underwater journey is offered by **Varasub** (Av. de la Playa, e/ 36 y 37, tel. 045/66-7203, fax 045/66-7026; CUC35 adults, CUC20 children), a semi-submersible that travels out to El Cayuelo where you view the underwater world from large windows, with a TV monitor for alternate viewing angles; it departs six times daily; however, I found the views disappointing. Book at hotel tour desks or any tour agency.

Aquaworld Varadero (tel. 045/66-8886), at Marina Chapelín, offers a boat trip—"Seafari Cayo Blanco"—to Cayo Blanco (CUC75, including lunch on the cay); plus a nocturnal "Noche Marinera" cruise with lobster dinner at the marina (CUC45).

A guided two-hour personal watercraft **"Jungle Tour"** (tel. 045/66-8440, jungle@ip.etecsa.cu; CUC39) is offered hourly 9 A.M.– 4 P.M. from Marina Chapelín.

ACCOMMODATIONS

There are scores of accommodations to choose from, with something for every budget, although true "budget" offerings are few. Dozens of charter flights daily disgorge package tourists and in high season properties often sell out. Reservations are highly recommended. An air-hotel package from abroad offers considerable discounts.

Accommodations become more upscale as you move east, with the so-called luxury resorts clustered east of Las Américas mansion and along Playa Los Taínos. The vast majority of hotels are run on an all-inclusive basis, signifying that meals, alcoholic beverages, entertainment (including *animaciones*—the Cuban phrase for audience-participation entertainment), and, usually, water sports are included in the quoted room rate. In the all-inclusives you're entirely divorced from any interaction with Cubans (who are barred from entry) other than hotel staff. Guests must wear colored plastic bands, not least so that security guards can keep all others out. If you're familiar with the high standards of many all-inclusives elsewhere in the Caribbean, you may be disappointed in most hotels. Even the best hotels here have niggly problems such as ho-hum buffet fare, questionable service and, often, outrageous prices by international comparison. Standards are generally higher in foreign-managed hotels than in purely Cuban-managed properties. Properties offering the best value for the money include the Hotel Internacional, the Barceló and Meliá properties (www.solmelia-cuba.com), and the Sandals Royal Hicacos Resort & Spa; while the Barceló Marina Palace, Blau Varadero Hotel, and Iberostar Varadero, all of which opened in 2005, are stunners that compete with the best of abroad.

The deluxe, easterly properties are far from the action, which concentrates between Calles 11 and 64, and constantly getting to and from downtown Varadero can rack up a hefty taxi bill. At last visit, no hotel was able to accept credit card payments due to some temporary quirk in the system, so come prepared with a cash backup!

Some have 110-volt outlets, while others have 220 volts; some have both, so check before plugging in any appliances.

In 1998 the government banned *casas particulares* in Varadero and adjacent towns. Many locals still rent rooms illegally (owners often approach budget travelers at the bus station; going rate is CUC20). Ask around discreetly, as owners are fined CUC1,500 if caught and could even have their houses seized.

Hotels below are categorized according to high-season rates for twin occupancy, and arranged west to east. There are more hotels in actuality than listed here, but these are the pick of the litter.

Under CUC50

Villa La Mar (3ra Av., e/ 28 y 30, tel. 045/61-3910, fax 045/61-2508, vlamar@enet.cu;

CUC26 s, CUC32 d low season; CUC33 s, CUC42 d high season) has 264 simply furnished air-conditioned rooms with private baths, satellite TV, video, and telephone, plus restaurant, grill, pool with thatched umbrellas, disco, and parking. (Islazul.)

Seeking a self-catering apartment? **Aparthotel Islazul Mar del Sur** (3ra Av. y Calle 30, tel. 045/61-2246, fax 045/66-7481) has modestly furnished, air-conditioned units.

Hotel Ledo (Av. de la Playa, e/ 43 y 44, tel. 045/61-3206, ledo@varade2.var.cyt.cu; CUC26 s, CUC34 d) is a simple, older property with 20 air-conditioned rooms with local TV and hot water. It has a small restaurant. (Islazul.)

CUC50-100

Hotel Aguazul (Av. 1ra y Calle 13, tel. 045/66-7132, fax 045/66-7245; CUC35 s, CUC48 d low season; CUC45 s, CUC60 d high season) is an uninspired one-star property (the Cubans give it three stars, but the price is right) with 240 air-conditioned rose-pink rooms with modest rattan furnishings, satellite TV, safe, and balcony. In the same complex, **Aparthotel Varazul** has 69 one-bedroom air-conditioned apartments with kitchens, bathrooms, living rooms, satellite TVs, and telephones. (Islazul.)

A favorite of budget travelers, the **Hotel Pullman** (Av. 1ra y Calle 49, tel. 045/66-2702, fax 045/66-7499; CUC37 s, CUC47 d low season; CUC44 s, CUC57 d high season, including a meager breakfast) is a down-to-earth hotel in a colonial mansion. The 15 air-conditioned rooms have satellite TVs, telephones, safes, colonial furniture, and modern bathrooms; however, some were clearly in need of restoration at last visit. It has a small, airy restaurant and a patio bar. One block away, and operated jointly with the Pullman, is the slightly better **Hotel Dos Mares** (Av. 1ra and Calle 53, tel. 045/61-2702 or 045/66-7510, fax 045/66-7499; same rates as the Hotel Pullman), with a certain bed-and-breakfast charm. It has 34 large, modestly furnished, no-frills air-conditioned rooms with satellite TV and 24-hour room service. It has a restaurant and bar. (Islazul.)

Hotel Islazul Herradura (Av. de la Playa, e/ 35 y 36, tel. 045/61-3703, fax 045/66-7496; CUC42 s, CUC58 d low season; CUC50 s, CUC67 d high season, including breakfast) is a favorite of Germans. This small, intimate option has 75 air-conditioned rooms in apartments with satellite TVs, telephones, and safes. There's a restaurant and two bars, plus a store and a tourism bureau. The hotel was in need of refurbishing at last visit. (Islazul.)

One of the few resort hotels offering a non-all-inclusive option, the **Hotel Arenas Doradas** (tel. 045/66-8150, fax 045/66-8158, reserva@arenas.gca.tur.cu; CUC50 s, CUC80 d low season; CUC60 s, CUC90 d high season) has 316 rooms set amid 20 acres of landscaped grounds surrounding a freeform pool with sunken pool bar and open-air whirlpool tub. Interior decor is attractive, and the prices are fair, though this is no Ritz. It has water sports and entertainment, plus an all-inclusive option. (Gran Caribe.)

CUC100-150

Hotel & Villas Tortuga (Calle 7, e/ Camino del Mar y Bulevar, tel. 045/61-4747, fax 045/66-7845; villas CUC74 s, CUC108 d low season, CUC84 s, CUC128 d high season; superior rooms CUC79 s, CUC120 d low season, CUC86 s, CUC132 d high season) is a modern, 280-room, two-story complex centered on a pool. The rooms have heaps of light but no TVs or telephones. You can also rent villas. It has a tourist bureau. Credit cards are not accepted. (Gran Caribe.)

Club Amigo Tropical (Av. 1ra, e/ 21 y 22, tel. 045/61-3915, fax 045/61-4676; CUC57 s, CUC100 d low season; CUC69 s, CUC112 d high season) is an all-inclusive property with 173 rooms with lively fabrics. Its pleasant lobby bar and elegant restaurant appeal. (Cubanacán.)

Hotel Los Delfines (Av. 1ra, e/ 38 y 39, tel. 045/66-77270, fax 045/66-7727; CUC50 s, CUC60 d low season; CUC75 s, CUC85 d high season.) caters primarily to Italian package tourists but is open to all comers. The 89 rooms here have a lively contemporary decor, plus satellite TVs, safety deposit boxes, and minibars. It has four suites and nine junior suites. (Islazul.)

The popular all-inclusive **Mercure Cuatro Palmas** (Av. 1ra, e/ 61 y 62, tel. 045/66-8101, fax 045/66-7208, www.mercure.com; CUC90 s, CUC120 d year-round) boasts attractive colonial-era architecture and a preferred location. The hotel, run by the French Accor chain, is built on the grounds of Fulgencio Batista's summer house and is centered on an attractive swimming pool. It has 282 rooms, all with air-conditioning, satellite TV, hairdryers, radios, and telephones; some have king beds. (Gran Caribe.)

CUC150-250

The all-inclusive **Gran Hotel Club Kawama** (Av. 1ra, esq. 1, Rpto. Kawama, tel. 045/66-4416, fax 045/66-7254, www.grancaribe.cu; CUC104 s, CUC149 d low season; CUC124 s, CUC189 d high season) dominates the Kawama peninsula on seven hectares and has 235 nicely albeit modestly furnished rooms with satellite TV. The resort has several bars and restaurants, plus water sports, bike, scooter, and car rentals. Its clientele are mostly German. (Gran Caribe.)

Club Karey (Av. Kawama, tel. 045/66-7296, fax 045/66-7254), adjacent to Club Kawama, rents out villas with maid service. (Gran Caribe.)

Nearby, **Club Barlovento** (Av. 1ra, e/ 10 y 12, tel. 045/66-7140, fax 045/66-7218; CUC105 s, CUC150 d low season; CUC133 s, CUC190 d high season) is a handsome modern all-inclusive hotel done up in a contemporary interpretation of Spanish-colonial style, with 269 rooms and three suites, all attractively appointed and with satellite TVs, balconies, telephones, and safe deposit boxes. The complex surrounds a large swimming pool and offers water sports and entertainment. (Gran Caribe.)

The contemporary aesthetic of the all-inclusive **Hotel Palma Real** (Av. 2da y 64, tel. 045/61-4555, fax 045/61-4550, jrecep.palmreal@hotetur.com; CUC90 s, CUC150

d low season; CUC110 s, CUC180 d high season) appeals, although this hotel faces over the bay not the sea. It has 297 rooms, all with satellite TV and lively decor. It has two restaurants and three bars, plus entertainment.

Often sold out to tour groups, the 1950s-era **Hotel Varadero Internacional** (Carretera las Américas, tel. 045/66-7038, fax 045/66-7246, reserva@gcinter.gca.tur.cu; from CUC86 s, CUC123 d, CUC140 s/d suite low season, CUC110 s, CUC157 d, CUC165 s/d suite high season) is a venerable all-inclusive that successfully combines period decor with an elegant contemporary look following a recent remake. There the good points end. This Cuban-run property has too many issues with awful food, poor upkeep, and lousy management to be anything but a last resort when all other hotels in this price range are full. (Gran Caribe.)

Villa Cuba Resort (tel. 045/66-8280, fax 045/66-8282, director@vcuba.gca.cma.net; CUC97 s, CUC139 d, CUC249 s/d suite, CUC127–339 bungalows low season; CUC132 s, CUC189 d, CUC350 s/d suite, CUC234–596 bungalows high season) is an all-inclusive, 245-room hotel centered on a beautiful pool complex and offering a range of accommodations, including 23 beachfront chalets with valet service (seven villas have their own pools). All have balconies and are furnished in contemporary vogue, including satellite TV and safes. Facilities include a beauty salon, boutiques, scuba diving classes, and cabaret. (Gran Caribe.)

For a unique experience, check into **❶ Mansion Xanadu** (Carretera Las Morlas, tel. 045/66-7750, fax 045/66-8481, www.varaderogolfclub.com; CUC120 s, CUC150 d low season; CUC160 s, CUC210 d high season, including breakfast and green fees) at the Varadero Golf Club. This mansion's six rooms are perhaps the most gracious rooms in Varadero. Imagine marble floors, wrought-iron beds, throw rugs, lofty ceilings with wainscoting, and all-marble bathrooms with vast walk-in showers. There's a splendid restaurant.

Hotel RIU Turquesa (Carretera las Américas, tel. 045/66-8471, fax 045/66-8495, www.riu.com; CUC145 s, CUC190 d low season; CUC190 s, CUC240 d high season) is a 268-room all-inclusive with all modern-contemporary bedrooms featuring satellite TV, in-room safes, hairdryers, and balconies. Facilities run the gamut from Internet service, massage, shops, and entertainment to motorized and non-motorized water sports.

Iberostar Taínos (Carretera Los Taínos, tel. 045/66-8656, fax 045/68-8657, comercial@ibstain.gca.tur.cu; CUC130 s, CUC180 d low season; CUC190 s, CUC240 d high season) has a gracious aesthetic. The 300 air-conditioned rooms, in two-story units, are pleasantly furnished in pastels. It offers the usual range of facilities, from specialty restaurants to shops, entertainment, and water sports.

To consider if the other hotels are full are Cubanacán's 227-room **Brisas del Caribe** (Carretera Las Morlas Km 22.5, tel. 045/66-8030, fax 045/66-8120, gerencia@bricar.var.cyt.cu), the ungainly **Club Amigo Varadero Hotel** (Carretera Las Morlas Km 11.5, tel. 045/66-8243, fax 045/66-8202, gerencia@granhot.var.cyt.cu), and ho-hum **Hotel Riu Las Morlas** (Av. las Américas, tel. 045/66-7230, fax 045/66-7215, carpeta@morlas.gca.tur.cu); Gaviota's **Hotel Playa Alameda Varadero** (tel. 045/66-8822, fax 045/66-8833) and **Hotel Playa Varadero 1920** (tel. 045/66-8288, fax 045/66-8414), until 2003 operated by Club Med but now managed by Spain's Piñero group; and Gran Caribe's **Coralia Club Playa de Oro** (Carretera Las Morlas Km 12.5, tel. 045/61-4872, fax 045/66-8555, comercial@poro.gca.tur.cu), run by the French Accor chain, and the venerable twin-block, high-rise Puntarena-Paraíso (formerly run by Jamaica's SuperClubs chain), which was being remodeled at last visit and will reopen as the **C Playa Caleta Hotel** (Av. Kawama y Final, tel. 045/66-7120, fax 045/66-7779, reserva@playacaleta.gca.tur.cu).

CUC250 and Up

I like the all-inclusive **C Barceló Solymar Beach Resort** (Carretera Las Américas y Calle 69, tel. 045/61-4499, fax 045/61-1086, www.barcelo.com; CUC107 s, CUC174 d low season; CUC170 s, CUC300 d high season), a modern resort with a dynamic contemporary vogue. Its 525 air-conditioned rooms and 193 bungalows each have satellite TV, fridge, safe, hairdryer, and exquisite marble-top bathroom. The resort enfolds a vast pool complex and offers upscale shops and two restaurants, six bars, tennis courts, water sports, and miniature golf. (Gran Caribe.)

Managed by Spain's Sol Meliá, **Meliá Las Américas Suites & Golf Resort** (tel. 045/66-7600, fax 045/66-7625, www.solmeliacuba.com; from CUC155 s, CUC220 d standard, CUC200 s, CUC300 d suite low season; CUC170 s, CUC265 d standard, CUC280 s, CUC380 d suite high season), another all-inclusive, boasts a stunning lobby. Arched terraces support a beautiful pool and sundeck overlooking its own private beach. Its 335 air-conditioned rooms and 25 suites feature kitchenettes and small lounges below mezzanine bedrooms with pleasing bamboo and wicker furniture. It has a full compliment of facilities, from five restaurants and five bars to boutiques, water sports, and disco. It was being remodeled and expanded at last visit.

Meliá's **Sol Sirenas Coral Resort** (Av. las Américas y Calle K, tel. 045/66-8070, fax 045/66-8076, www.solmeliacuba.com; CUC170 s, CUC230 d standard, CUC210 s, CUC270 d junior suite, CUC240 s, CUC320 d suite low season; CUC200 s, CUC270 d standard, CUC240 s, CUC310 d junior suite, CUC270 s, CUC360 d suite high season) is an elegant 650-room all-inclusive complex centered on a mammoth pool. The gracious air-conditioned apartments and rooms in four-story blocks feature satellite TVs, direct dial telephones, safes, and lively tropical colors. Suites have whirlpool tubs. It has salons and boutiques, two swimming pools, six restaurants, eight bars, and a panoply of recreational facilities.

I like **Breezes Varadero** (Carretera Las Américas Km 3, tel. 045/66-7030, fax 045/66-7005, www.superclubscuba.net; in

North America 800/467-8737; in the U.K., 01/749-677200; CUC174 s, CUC226 d standard, CUC192 s, CUC250 d suite low season; CUC273 s, CUC352 d standard, CUC291 s, CUC378 d suite high season), a 270-suite all-inclusive property managed by Jamaica's SuperClubs chain. Spacious air-conditioned rooms and suites feature king or twin beds, telephone, satellite TV, safes, plus private terraces overlooking the ocean and 26 acres of grounds. Facilities include specialty restaurants, an room and gym, and every sport in, on, or under water.

The all-inclusive **Meliá Varadero** (tel. 045/66-7013, fax 045/66-7012, reservas@solmeliacuba.com; CUC175 s, CUC260 d standard, CUC200 s, CUC300 d superior, CUC290 s CUC400 d suite low season; CUC195 s, CUC305 d standard, CUC202 s, CUC340 d superior, CUC310 s, CUC445 d suite high season), adjoining Plaza Las Américas, has 483 rooms and seven suites in six arms that fan out from a soaring circular atrium with a curtain of vines cascading down from the balconies. The effect is fabulous—made more so by the chattering of parrots. Facilities include seven restaurants, five bars, sauna, gym, beauty salon, and water sports.

Similarly priced, the adjoining **Sol Palmeras** (tel. 045/66-7009, fax 045/66-7209, www.solmeliacuba.com), immediately east, is a sprawling and gracious property entered through a lobby with lush foliage, fountains, and caged birds. It has 375 air-conditioned rooms, 32 suites, and 200 *cabinas* arrayed around a huge pool with a thatched bar. All rooms have satellite TVs, telephones, and safes. Facilities include five restaurants, five bars, a kid's club, three pools, two tennis courts, and water sports.

Better still is the sibling ◖ **Sol Meliá Paradisus Varadero** (Carretera Las Morlas, tel. 045/66-8700, fax 045/66-8705, www.sol-meliacuba.com; CUC260 s, CUC340 d junior suite, CUC330 s, CUC440 d suite low season; CUC290 s, CUC380 d junior suite, CUC360 s, CUC480 d suite high season), a

beautiful all-inclusive with a quasi-Thai motif. Centered on a huge freeform pool, it has 408 air-conditioned junior suites, 12 suites, and one garden villa (with butler service) exquisitely appointed with sponge-washed walls, canopy beds, wrought-iron and rattan furniture, satellite TV, direct-dial telephones, minibars, safes, hairdryers, and exquisite bathrooms with telephones. Facilities include five restaurants, several bars, plus football court, water polo, archery, volleyball, tennis courts, a boutique, gym, sauna, whirlpool tub, a kid's club, and plentiful water sports. (Gaviota.)

One of the outstanding options is the new ◖ **Blau Varadero Hotel** (Carretera Las Morlas Km 15, tel. O45/66-7545, fax 045/66-7494, www.blauhotels.com; CUC105 s, CUC150 d standard, CUC175 s, CUC230 d suite low season, standard CUC155 s, CUC250 d, suite CUC245 s, CUC370 d high season), a dramatic take on a Mayan pyramid. The sparsely furnished lobby opens to a dramatic soaring atrium with blue-tinted skylight. A contemporary vogue infuses the guest rooms, with their sophisticated ocher, gold, and brown color scheme, rattan pieces, marble-clad bathrooms, and spacious balconies with brushed steel and glass rails. A hip buffet restaurant, an alfresco poolside restaurant, beach grill, a bi-level pool, large kid's club, and state-of-the-art theater and gym are among the amenities.

◖ **Sandals Royal Hicacos Resort & Spa** (Carretera Las Morlas Km 14, tel. 045/66-8844, fax 045/66-8851, www.sandalshicacos .com; per person rates CUC140 garden view suites, CUC165 premium suites, CUC185 concierge suites low season; CUC250 garden view, CUC275 premium, CUC295 concierge high season) is a couples-only, all-suite resort and one of the most resplendent and impressive hotels in Varadero. The entrance is a dramatic play on a Polynesian theme, with thatched walkways over landscaped water courses. Lively Caribbean colors meld with rich ocher. It has 404 rooms (all junior suites) in three-story units, with terra-cotta floors, lively color schemes, calming blue fabrics, dark hardwoods, and a lovely contemporary feel. Facilities include

MATANZAS

five restaurants, six bars, plus a squash court, scuba, and spa.

Iberostar Varadero (tel. 045/66-999, fax 045/66-8842; CUC155 s, CUC220 d low season; CUC185 s, CUC280 d high season; CUC45 more for junior suites) also gets two thumbs up for its calming mood and creative design subtly infused with Mughal influences. At its heart is a vast freeform pool. Rooms, in tri-level blocks, are pleasantly decorated in orange, rose, and robin's-egg-blue pastels, with gracious bathrooms and modern appointments. Dining options include Japanese and Mediterranean.

Hotel Tryp Península Varadero (tel. 045/66-8783, fax 045/66-8805, www.solmeliacuba.com; standard CUC220 s, CUC280 d low season, CUC330 s, CUC410 d high season; suite CUC270 s, CUC340 d low season, CUC380 s, CUC475 d high season), at the far eastern extreme of the peninsula, follows the standard format, with a beautiful freeform pool at its heart. It has 591 rooms in 20 three-story units in pastel ice-cream color, with rattan, minibar, satellite TV, safe deposit box, hairdryer, and gracious bathroom. Facilities include four restaurants, five bars, a kid's club, gym, beauty center, sauna, game room, jogging trail, and water sports.

Despite its ho-hum aesthetic, the liveliest place in town at last visit was the 434-room **Sandals Princesa del Mar** (tel. 045/66-7200, fax 045/66-7201, sales@princesadelmar .co.cu; per person from CUC138 junior suite, CUC170 suite low season; CUC165 junior suite, CUC198 suite high season). The couples-only, all-inclusive resort has 360 junior suites, 72 one-bedroom suites, and two presidential suites, plus eight restaurants, 10 full-service bars, and a cigar lounge, plus spa, seven whirlpool tubs, and a business center. (Gaviota.)

Perhaps the finest hotel in Varadero, the **Barceló Marina Palace Resort** (Punta Hicacos Final, tel. 045/66-9966, fax 045/66-7022, www.barcelo.com; from CUC115 s, CUC190 d low season; CUC235 s, CUC430 d high season), which opened in December 2005 at the very tip of the peninsula, demonstrates

that the best is often saved for last. Sprawling along the shore betwixt road and sand dunes, its pleasing architecture, subtle pastels, contemporary vogue, and all mod-cons combine to raise the ante for competitors. Its 296 junior suites and four suites are furnished in bold style with blue-and-white color themes. All the required facilities are here, including a waterslide augering down to a huge pool. (Gaviota.)

To consider as a last resort in this price range is the ho-hum **Beaches Varadero** (Carretera Las Morlas Km 15, tel. 045/66-8470, fax 045/66-8554, www.beachescuba.ca; from CUC133 s, CUC240 d low season, CUC166 s, CUC270 d high season), operated by Jamaica's Sandals chain.

FOOD

Varadero has the largest choice of eateries outside Havana. Don't set your hopes too high, as standards in most state-run restaurants are mediocre, as are the buffet meals in most all-inclusive hotels, and the menus in most restaurants are identical. Deluxe hotels managed by international hotel groups usually offer fare approaching international quality (some allow nonguests to eat in their restaurants and poolside grills for a day-pass fee that permits use of other facilities). Private restaurants—*paladares*—aren't permitted in Varadero, but some locals will prepare lobster and other meals for you on the sly.

Fast Food and Snacks

The **Complejo Mediterráneo** (Av. 1ra, e/ 54 y 55, tel. 045/62460) has three eateries in one: the air-conditioned **Restaurant El Vesuvio** has Romanesque decor and serves continental snacks noon–10 P.M.; **Café Aladdin** offers sandwiches 24 hours; and **D'Prisa Mediterráneo** is a 24-hour open-air grill serving *criollo* fare and pizzas.

Criollo

One of the best options is **Restaurante Guamairé** (Av. 1ra, esq. 27, tel. 045/61-1893; daily noon–midnight), an old wooden home with plenty of ambience. I enjoyed a piquant crocodile with pineapple (CUC10), although it often isn't available. Despite its modern, rather soulless ambience, **Chez Plaza** (Plaza América, tel. 045/66-8181, ext. 270; daily 10 A.M.–9 P.M.) offers creative dishes such as shrimp in rum (CUC6).

Shrimp in rum is also on the menu at **La Casa del Tabaco** (Av. 1ra y 31, tel. 045/61-1431; daily 10 A.M.–11 P.M.), where the atmospheric restaurant also has grilled lobster with rum (CUC20 including cigar) and chicken supreme with mustard (CUC7).

Lobster in pepper sauce (CUC6) and beef filet stuffed with bacon (CUC7) feature at **Restaurante El Criollo** (Av. 1ra y 18, tel. 045/61-4794; daily noon–midnight), a rustic colonial home-turned-restaurant whose menu also includes bean soup (CUC1.50).

Restaurante La Vicaria (Av. 1ra y 38, tel. 045/67-4721; daily noon–10:45 P.M.) offers alfresco dining under thatch, with the usual *pollo asado* (roast chicken) and fish dishes for CUC5–8.

Live music and a 1914 Ford and 1955 Oldsmobile as decor add ambience to the **Restaurante Esquina Cuba** (Av. 1ra y 38, tel. 045/61-4019; daily 10 A.M.–midnight), an open-sided restaurant offering a ho-hum roast chicken (CUC12) and lobster (CUC24). I recommend the *ropa vieja* (CUC8).

El Bodegón Criollo (Av. de la Playa y Calle 40, tel. 045/66-7784; noon–11 P.M. daily) attempts to replicate the famous Bodeguita de Medio in Havana with its graffiti. You can dine outside on a shady veranda or inside in a rustic setting with eaves and ships' wheels turned lamps hanging from the ceiling. Typical dishes include roast leg of pork (CUC7) and grilled pork steak (CUC6).

One of my favorite places is the hilltop **El Mesón del Quijote** (Av. las Américas, tel. 045/66-7796; noon to midnight, daily), boasting romantic rustic decor: beamed ceiling, metal lamps, brass plaques, and potted plants and climbing ivy on a solarium dining terrace. It specializes in lobster dishes (CUC10–30).

At the west end of town, **Mi Casita** (Camino del Mar, e/ 11 y 12, tel. 045/63787; 3–11 P.M. daily) boasts a beautiful beachfront setting and an elegant air-conditioned dining room with period antiques. A set meal of chicken (CUC12), shrimp (CUC18), or lobster (CUC25) includes soup, salad, dessert, and coffee.

Continental

The romantic and upscale **Restaurante Antigüedades** (Av. 1ra y 59, tel. 045/66-7329; noon–11 P.M. daily), outside Parque Retiro Josone, has antiques, walls decorated with posters and photos of Hollywood stars, and genuine silverware and porcelain place settings. It offers set dinners, including filet mignon (CUC14) and lobster (CUC22–38).

Also chic, **Restaurante La Fondue** (Av. 1ra, esq. 62, tel. 045/66-7747; daily noon–10 P.M. daily) offers elegant decor combined with classical music. The menu lists a large range of fondues using Cuban cheeses (CUC7–18). Special cheeses such as Gruyere, Sbrinz, and Gouda cost extra, per gram. You can also order filet mignon (CUC10), squid in tomato sauce (CUC3), and the like. It has a good selection of wines.

The **Restaurante Las Américas** (tel. 045/66-7750; noon–4 P.M. and 7–11 P.M. daily), on the ground floor of Mansion Xanadu, specializes in French-style seafood and meats, such as lobster (CUC39), fish sautéed with capers (CUC13), seafood casserole (CUC19), and chateaubriand tenderloin (CUC32).

For Italian fare the best option is **Dante** (tel. 045/66-7738, noon–midnight, daily), in Parque Retiro Josone, with views over the lake. It offers a pleasant contemporary ambience and has both air-conditioned and open-air options. The menu features pastas (from CUC6), pizzas (from CUC4.50), and tiramisu, plus a large wine list.

I like **36 y 1ra** (Av. 1ra, esq. 36; Mon.–Sat. 10 A.M.–10 P.M.) for its contemporary elegance. This former home has walls of glass and offers buffet meals, café-style.

Restaurante Castelnuevo (Av. 1ra y 11, tel. 045/66-7786; noon–11 P.M.) has an appropriately Italianate motif and serves spaghetti, pastas, and pizzas (CUC5–10). The best pizza around, however, is at **Pizza Nova** (11 A.M.–10 P.M.), a fast-food style pizzeria upstairs in Plaza Las Américas.

Al Capone's former home (built in 1934 on the Kawama Peninsula) is today the atmospheric **Casa de Al** (tel. 045/66-7090). It was closed for restoration at last visit.

Seafood

Several beach grills overhang the sands. I like **Ranchón Mediteráneo** (Calle 57; 24 hours), serving grilled seafoods (CUC6–14), and **Ranchón El Compay** (Calle 54; 24 hours), a rustic open-air thatched restaurant with a grill; I enjoyed an excellent dish of grilled shrimp (CUC7.55).

El Rancho (tel. 045/61-4760; 11 A.M.–10 P.M. daily), opposite the entrance to Parque Retiro Josone, also serves grilled seafoods (CUC6–14), in a handsome thatched roadside setting with live musicians.

The antique-filled, classically elegant **Restaurante El Retiro** (tel. 045/66-7316; noon–11:30 P.M. daily), in Parque Retiro Josone, specializes in lobster dishes, including garlic lobster (CUC15).

At the west end, the simple **Restaurante Arrecife** (Calle 13, esq. Camino del Mar, tel. 045/61-2407; noon–11 P.M. daily) serves seafood specials, including grilled fish and lobster (CUC7–17). A complete special for CUC10 includes soup, grilled fish, dessert, and beer.

Meats

Steak House Toro (Av. 1ra y 25, tel. 045/66-7145; noon–11 P.M. daily) is an atmospheric colonial house where you may dine alfresco on a shady terrace, or inside, where the modestly elegant decor attempts a steakhouse ambience. The overpriced menu runs from veal chops (CUC14) to chateaubriand (CUC38).

Asian

Two restaurants take a stab at oriental fare. **Restaurant Chang Kwok** (Av. 1ra, esq. 55, tel. 045/61-3526; noon–10 P.M. daily) is a lit-

tle charmer with genuine oriental decor plus a large menu featuring fried wontons, soups, chicken chop suey, and sweet-and-sour lobster (CUC10.50). **Lai-Lai** (Av. 1ra, e/ 18 y 19, tel. 045/66-7793; noon–11 P.M.), also with a strong Chinese ambience, features spring rolls, fried rice with shrimp or lobster, lobster chop suey, and Tin Pan chicken (CUC5–15).

Ice Cream, Desserts, and Coffee

Alas, **Coppelia** (Av. 1ra, e/ 44 y 46, tel. 045/62866; daily 9 A.M.–6 P.M.) sells ice cream at the rip-off price of CUC0.95 per tiny scoop.

The **Casa del Habano** (Av. 1ra, esq. 29, 9 A.M.–9 P.M. daily) has a pleasant espresso bar.

Self-Catering

Panadería Doña Neli (Av. 1ra y 43) is a 24-hour bakery selling croissants, pastries, and breads. You can buy Western foodstuffs in the **El Cacique Shopping Center** (Av. 1ra y 62); at **Grocery Caracol** (Calle 15 e/ 1ra y 3ra); and **Grocery La Trovatta** (Av. 1ra y A).

Plaza América has a fully stocked supermarket (8:30 A.M.–8 P.M. daily); as does **Todo en Uno** (Autopista Sur y 54).

SHOPPING

Some stores sell clothing and other items without price tags—a sure sign that you're about to get ripped off. Move on to the next store.

Arts and Crafts

There are numerous crafts markets along Avenida 1ra. The largest is at Calle 44. **Casa de las Artesanías Latinoamericanas** (Av. 1ra y 63; daily 9 A.M.–7 P.M.) has a superb range of goods from Latin America including jewelry, jackets, shawls, and belts. For world-class ceramics head to **Taller de Cerámica Artística** (Av. 1ra y 59, tel. 045/66-7554; daily 8 A.M.–7 P.M.). Look for dining sets and individual plates by renowned artists such as Osmany Betancourt, Alfredo Sosabravo, and Sergio Roque. Next door is Varadero's **Galería de Arte** (tel. 045/66-8260; daily 8:30 A.M.–7 P.M.), with wooden statues, paintings, and

© CHRISTOPHER P. BAKER

La Casa del Ron stocks more than 100 different rum labels.

other artwork, plus genuine antiques (much of it confiscated by the state from rightful owners). Items are sold with export permits.

Cigars and Rum

The two locations of **Casa del Habano** (Av. 1ra y 39, tel. 045/61-4719; and Calle 63, e/ 1ra y 3ra, tel. 045/66-7843; daily 9 A.M.– 9 P.M.) are the best-stocked shops in town. Each has a bar and smokers' lounge. **Casa de Tabaco** (Av. Playa y 31, tel. 045/61-1431; daily 9 A.M.–9 P.M.; and in Plaza América, tel. 045/66-8181, ext. 251; daily 9:30 A.M.–7 P.M.) is also well stocked.

La Casa del Ron (Av. 1ra, esq. 63, tel. 045/66-9833; 9 A.M.–9 P.M. daily) stocks more than 100 different rum labels.

Books and Music

The best outlet is **La Casa** (Av. 1ra, e/ 59 y 60, tel. 045/61-3033; 9 A.M.–7 P.M. daily), with a bookstore and music store.

Librería Hanoi (Av. 1ra, esq. 44, tel. 045/61-2694; daily 9 A.M.–9 P.M.) is meagerly stocked with social, historical, and political

works on a leftist theme. There's also a bookstore in Plaza América.

Boutiques

Centro Comercial de Caimán (Av. 1ra, e/ 61 y 62) has boutiques and cosmetic stores. **Plaza América** has designer boutiques, plus a duty-free jewelry store. **Joyeria Coral Negro** (Calle 64 y 3ra, tel. 045/61-4870) sells duty-free name-brand watches plus perfumes and quality Cuban jewelry.

El Quitrín (Av. 1ra, e/ 55 y 56, tel. 045/61-2580) sells hand-made *guayaberas,* lace skirts, and blouses.

SERVICES
Banks and Money

Most hotels can change small amounts of foreign currency. Euros are accepted as direct payment in Varadero without the need to change to CUC. Banks include **Banco Financiero Internacional** (Av. Playa y 32; and in Plaza América; Mon.–Fri. 8 A.M.–12:30 P.M. and 1:30–7 P.M.); **Bandec** (Av. 1ra y 36; Mon.–Fri. 8 A.M.–3 P.M.); and **Banco Popular**

(Av. 1ra y 36; Mon.– Fri. 8 A.M.–noon and 1:30–4:30 P.M.).

Fincimex (Av. Playa, e/ 39 y 40, tel. 045/66-8046) handles Tran$card transactions and represents foreign credit card companies.

Post and Telecommunications

Varadero has two post offices: one at Avenida 1ra and Calle 36 (Mon.–Sat. 8 A.M.–7 P.M., Sun. 8 A.M.–5:30 P.M.), and another in the gate house at Avenida las Américas and Calle A (tel. 045/61-4551; 8 A.M.–8 P.M.). **DHL** (Av. 1ra #3903, e/ 39 y 40, tel./fax 045/66-7730; Mon.–Fri. 8 A.M.–noon and 1–5 P.M., Sat. 8 A.M.–noon) offers international courier service.

Etecsa (Av. 1ra, esq. 30; daily 8:30 A.M.–8:30 P.M.) has international phone and Internet service, as does the Etecsa outlet upstairs in Plaza Las Américas (daily 8:30 A.M.–7:30 P.M.). The **Cibercafe** (Av. 1ra, esq. 39, tel. 045/61-4451; Mon.–Sat. 9 A.M.–6 P.M., Sun. 9 A.M.–4 P.M.) also has Internet service.

You can rent cellular telephones from **Cubacel** (Edificio Marbella, Av. 1ra, e/ 42 y 43, tel./fax 045/80-9222; Mon.–Fri. 8 A.M.–5 P.M., Sat. 8 A.M.–noon).

Medical Services

Clínica Internacional (Av. 1ra y 61, tel. 045/66-7710 or 045/66-8611; 24 hours) charges CUC25 per consultation (CUC30 after 4 P.M., but CUC60 after 11 P.M.; CUC50 for hotel visits) and has an ambulance and pharmacy. There are two other international pharmacies (Plaza América, tel. 045/66-8181, ext. 239; and Avenida Kawama, e/ 3 y 4, tel. 045/61-4470; both 9 A.M.–7:30 P.M. daily).

Ópticas Miramar (Av. 1ra, esq. 43, tel. 045/66-7525) has optician service.

The **Red Cross** (Calle 27, tel. 045/61-2950), 50 meters north of Avenida 1ra, has ambulance service.

Legal Aid and Safety

Petty theft is common on the beaches; never leave your possessions unguarded while you swim. Red flags are flown when undertows and waves make swimming dangerous. In winter and spring, small Portuguese man-o'-war jellyfish are common; their long trailers can't easily be seen and can give a very nasty sting, and they're easy to step on once washed up on the beach.

Asistur (Edificio Marbella, Apto. 6, Av. 1ra, e/ 42 y 43, tel./fax 045/66-7277, asisturvaradero@enet.cu; Mon.–Fri. 9 A.M.–noon and 1:30–4:30 P.M., Sat. 9 A.M.–noon) can provide medical, legal, and financial assistance in an emergency. Likewise, the **Consultoría Jurídica Internacional** (Av. 1ra #2008, esq. 21, tel. 045/66-7077, cjivaradero@enet.cu; 8:30 A.M.–noon and 1:30–5:30 P.M. Mon.–Fri.) offers legal services for foreigners.

Other Services

The **police** station is at Avenida 1ra, e/ 38 y 39. **Inmigración** (Calle 39 y 1ra, tel. 045/61-3494; Mon.–Fri. 8 A.M.–noon and 1–3:30 P.M.) issues *prórrogas*.

The **Canadian Consulate** (Calle 13 #422, e/ 1ra y Camino del Mar, tel. 045/61-2078, vra.honcon@enet.cu) also represents Australia.

GETTING THERE AND AWAY
By Air

The **Aeropuerto Juan Gualberto Gómez** (tel. 045/61-2133 or 045/61-3036) is 16 kilometers west of Varadero. A tourist taxi ride will cost about CUC25.

Aerocaribbean (Av. 1ra, e/ 54 y 55, tel. 045/66-3016) normally offers flights from Havana and Santiago de Cuba but was temporarily out of service at last visit. **Cubana** (Av. 1ra, e/ 54 y 55, tel. 045/61-3010) was not offering flights to Varadero at press time, but has done so in the past.

At press time, EcoTur and WestPoint Air International were planning to introduce seaplane service linking Varadero with Havana, Cayo Largo, Cienfuegos, and Trinidad.

Air France (Av. 1ra, esq. 30, tel. 045/66-8285) and **Air Transat** (Calle 30, esq. 3ra, tel. 045/66-7595) have offices in town.

By Sea

Marina Marlin Dársena (Vía Blanca Km 31,

tel. 045/66-8060, fax 045/66-7456, www.puertosol.net, HF-2790 or VHF-1668) has berths for 60 vessels (CUC.45 per foot per day), plus electricity, water, diesel, and gas. **Marina Chapelín** (tel. 045/66-7550, fax 045/66-7093, channel 72 on VHF), eight kilometers east of downtown Varadero on Carretera Las Morlas, was not accepting foreign yachts at last visit. **Marina Varadero** (Carretera Las Morlas Km 21, tel. 045/66-7755, fax 045/66-7756) has dry-dock facilities and pleasure craft can be rented, but foreign visitors are usually steered to the other marinas.

By Bus

Astro and Víazul buses arrive and depart the **Terminal de Ómnibus Interprovinciales** (Calle 36 y Autopista Sur, tel. 045/61-2626).

Astro's bus #323 departs daily from Havana's main bus terminal at 8 A.M., 8:30 A.M., and 4 P.M. (three hours, CUC8). Buses depart Varadero for Havana at 8:20 A.M., 4 P.M., and 6 P.M. Buses run between Matanzas and Varadero hourly (CUC2); no reservations are needed.

Víazul (tel. 045/61-4886; daily 7 A.M.–6 P.M.) buses for Varadero depart Havana at 8 A.M., noon, 4 P.M., and 6 P.M. (CUC10); Santiago de Cuba (stopping at cities in between) at 8:30 P.M. (CUC49); and Trinidad (stopping in Santa Clara and Cienfuegos) at 2:25 P.M. (CUC20). Buses depart Varadero for Havana at 8 A.M., 11:40 A.M., 4 P.M., and 6 P.M.; for Trinidad at 7:30 A.M.; and for Santiago de Cuba at 8:55 P.M.

Bus #236 departs hourly for Cárdenas from the **Terminal Ómnibus de Cárdenas,** next to the main bus station, and from Avenida 1ra y Calle 13 (CUC1). A hotel workers' bus (signed Omnibus Bellamar) linking Varadero and Cárdenas (CUC1) and Matanzas (CUC2) may accept foreigners; you can catch it in front of Bandec (Av. 1ra y Calle 36).

You can also travel by excursion tour buses operated by Cuba's tour agencies for about CUC25 each way. Hotel tour desks can make reservations; the buses pick you up at your hotel.

By Taxi

A **tourist taxi** from Havana costs about CUC90 one-way.

By Car

Most hotels have car rental outlets and there is no shortage of offices along Avenida 1ra. Main offices include **Havanautos** (Av. 1ra y Calle 31, tel. 045/61-733); **Micar** (Av. 1ra y 20, tel. 045/66-2218); **Transtur** (Av. 1ra y 21; and Av. 1ra, e/ 54 y 55, tel. 045/61-1875; and Av. las Américas y A, tel. 045/61-4444); and **Vía Rent-a-Car** (Av. 1ra, e/ 25 y 26, tel. 045/61-4391). **Rex,** which rents Audis and Volvos (and accepts payment with U.S. MasterCard), has outlets at the Hotel Meliá Las Américas (tel. 045/66-7739) and at the airport (tel. 045/66-7539).

Foreign drivers pay a CUC2 toll on the Vía Blanca, about two kilometers west of Varadero.

There are gas stations on the Autopista Sur, esq. 17; on the Autopista, esq. 54; next to Marina Aqua on the Vía Blanca west of town; and in Santa Marta.

Organized Excursions

You can book excursions at tour desks in all the major tourist hotels. Typical excursions include a full-day tour of Havana (from CUC69, CUC129 including the Tropicana cabaret); Matanzas and the Cuevas de Bellamar (CUC25); Boca Guama and the Bay of Pigs, known as Playa Girón (CUC51); and Trinidad (CUC60), and to **Cayos Blancos,** a series of small beach-rimmed cays about eight kilometers due east of the peninsula. The "Discover Tour" includes a jeep and boat safari plus horseback ride (CUC73).

Tour agencies include **Cubanacán** (Calle 24 y Playa, tel. 045/33-7061); **Cubatur** (Av. 1ra y 33, tel. 045/66-7217); **Gaviotatours** (Av. 1ra y 25, tel. 045/66-7325, vartour@gavvara.gav.cma.net); **Havanatur** (Av. 3ra, e/ 33 y 34, tel. 045/66-7027), with four other branches in Varadero; and **Paradiso** (tel. 045/61-4759, fax 045/61-4758).

EcoTur (Av. 3ra, e/ 33 y 34, tel. 045/66-8612, ecoturvar@enet.cu) offers ecotourism excursions.

GETTING AROUND
By Bus

Transtur offers the **Varadero Beach Tour** (daily 9:30 A.M.–5 P.M.; CUC5) aboard a double-decker bus that hourly runs up and down Avenida 1ra and the length of the peninsula. It stops at all the major hotels and you can hop on or off at any stop. Your ticket can be purchased at hotels and tour outlets and is valid all day.

Trenes Turísticos (artificial trains with Jeep engines and shaded open-air carriages) run along Avenida 1ra 9 A.M.–7 P.M. (CUC2 for any part of a journey; CUC4 complete round-trip).

With pesos you can also hop aboard public buses #47 and 48 (20 centavos), which run along Avenida 1ra between Calle 64 and the Santa Marta district, west of the access bridge; and #220, which runs from Santa Marta the full length of the Autopista Sur.

By Taxi and *Coche*

Cubataxi (tel. 045/52-3168) and **Taxi OK** (tel. 045/61-4444) taxis hang around outside the major tourist hotels. No journey between Calle 1 and Calle 64 should cost more than CUC5.

Coco-taxis, hollow egg-shaped three-wheel vehicles known as *huevitos* ("little eggs") locally, cost CUC3 minimum and rent for CUC20 hourly. A journey the length of Avenida 1ra costs CUC8.

Horse-drawn *coches* ply Avenida 1ra. You can ride the full length of Avenida 1ra for CUC5. An "all-Varadero" tour costs CUC10.

Bicycles and Scooters

Scooters and mountain bikes can be rented at most hotels as well as booths along Avenida 1ra (typically CUC9 first hour, CUC3 each additional hour, CUC25 per day). Most outlets issue helmets. No motorcycle license is required.

Bicycles cost CUC2 for one hour and CUC10 per day. There are outlets up and down Avenida 1ra, including outside Parque Retiro Josone.

Central Matanzas

From Havana the Autopista runs ruler-straight east to west through south-central Matanzas Province. There are no diversions to distract you until you reach Km 142 and the turnoff for Jagüey Grande, Australia, and the Zapata Peninsula. Dozens of people hitch rides at this major crossroads. There's a Cupet gas station in Jagüey Grande.

Alternately you can follow the Carretera Central (route 3-N-1) through a string of dusty old towns; or the Circuito Norte coast road, an unremarkable route whose only town of interest is Cárdenas, serving as a dormitory town for Varadero's workers.

CÁRDENAS

The Península de Hicacos forms a natural breakwater protecting the large Bahía de Cárdenas, whose southern shore is fringed with oil derricks amid a desolate landscape covered with *marabú* scrub, stunted trees and henequen plantations. In their midst is the town of Cárdenas (pop. 82,000), a world away from the commercialism of Varadero, 10 kilometers to the northwest.

The city was founded in 1828. Swampland was drained and canals and streets laid out like a chessboard. The town developed rapidly as a port serving the prosperous sugar-producing hinterland. Otherwise, Cárdenas has a lackluster history, punctuated by a singular event in 1850, when the Cuban flag was first flown here. That year, a Venezuelan adventurer called Narciso López came ashore with an invasion army to free the locals from Spanish rule and annex Cuba himself. Many of the 600 men that left New Orleans on May 13, 1850, were mercenaries from the state of Kentucky. Only six were Cubans. Although López's ragtag army captured the town, his meager force failed to rally local support and the invaders beat a hasty retreat. Cárdenas has forever since been called the Flag City.

Cárdenas is hyped for its architectural interest and, being close to Varadero, is favored for excursions. Most of the town is dilapidated, despite being spruced up for news photographers after hometown boy Elián González was rescued in November 1999 after his mother and 10 others drowned at sea in a bid to flee Cuba for the United States. However, Cárdenas boasts a splendid colonial cathedral and a delightful plaza with one of the nation's most impressive museums.

Orientation

Streets running northeast–southwest are called *avenidas* and streets running northwest–southeast are *calles*. Those *avenidas* northwest of Avenida Céspedes—the main boulevard—are suffixed with *oeste* (west); those to the southeast are *este* (east). *Calles* run consecutively from the bay. From Varadero, you enter town along Calle 13 (Calzada), but exit eastward along Calle 14.

Parque Echevarría

This charming tree-shaded plaza, one block east of Avenida Céspedes, is the cultural heart of town and is surrounded by government buildings and museums. On its east side stands a life-size bronze bust of José Antonio Echevarría, the leader of the anti-Batista Directorio Revolucionario Estudantil (Students Revolutionary Directorate). Echevarría planned and led the student's assault on Batista's palace in March 1957; from a captured radio station he announced that Batista had been killed and called for a general strike, but the plug had been pulled and his words never made the air. He was killed later that day in a shoot-out with police.

Museo Casa Natal de José Antonio Echevarría

Museo Casa Natal de José Antonio Echevarría (Av. 4 Este #560, esq. 12, tel. 045/52-4145; Tues.–Sat. 10 A.M.–6 P.M., Sun. 9 A.M.–1 A.M.;

CUC1 entrance, CUC5 per photo), on the west side of Parque Echevarría, is a two-story house built in 1873. The namesake hero was born in this house in 1932. Now a museum, downstairs features memorabilia relating to the Wars of Independence; upstairs is accessed by a beautiful, hand-carved spiral wooden staircase and honors Echevarría and other Cardenians martyred for the Revolution.

◖ Museo Oscar María de Roja

This not-to-be-missed museum (Av. 4 Este, e/ Echevarría y Martí, tel. 045/52-2417; Tues.–Sat. 10 A.M.–6 P.M., Sun. 9 A.M.–1 P.M.; CUC5 entrance including guide, cameras CUC5, videos CUC25), on the south side of Parque Echevarría, is housed in a beautiful restored colonial building that was the former home of the Lieutenant Governor (1861–78) then the town hall (1878–1966). It's one of Cuba's oldest (founded in 1900), finest, and most expansive museums. Fourteen rooms are arrayed by theme, ranging from pre-Columbian culture to a Sala de Armas (full of armaments), coins, the Wars of Independence, José Martí, and so on. The pièce de résistance, however, is a baroque ornate 19th-century horse-drawn hearse that stands in the foyer.

Museo de Batalla de Ideas

The Museum of the Battle of Ideas (Av. 6, e/ 11 y 12; Tues.–Sun. 9 A.M.–5 P.M.; CUC2), in the old yellow-painted firehouse, is better known as the Elián Museum, as it is dedicated to the fight with Miami's Cuban-American extremists and is filled with mementos of the battle and victory: photographs of the boy at Disneyland wearing Mickey Mouse ears, a statue showing Elián walking on water (the waves are actually a sea of human hands), even the T-shirt worn by Donato Dalrymple, the fisherman who plucked the plucky Elián from the sea.

Elián González's school, **Escuela Marcelo Salado** (Calle 13 #165), has been turned into a newly repainted shrine, and even his school desk was repaired for the propaganda parade, reports Ann Louise Bardach. The boy

© CHRISTOPHER P. BAKER

statue of Christopher Columbus in front of the Catedral de la Concepción Inmaculada

lives with his father Juan Miguel at Avenida Céspedes #275 in a one-story house behind a chain-link fence; it is guarded day and night by police.

Avenida Céspedes

Tiny **Parque Colón** (Céspedes, e/ 8 y 9), or Columbus Park, is dominated by the **Catedral de la Concepción Inmaculada,** a beautiful old cathedral fronted by an impressive statue of Columbus with a globe at his feet (it dates from 1858). The church, built in 1846, has notable stained-glass windows.

The former mayor's mansion, now the near-derelict **Hotel Dominica,** is a national monument—it was here that Narciso López first raised the Cuban flag. Avenida Céspedes continues northeast to a **flagpole** and monument commemorating the events of 1850.

At the southwest end of Céspedes, a small fortress named for Oscar María de Roja stands in the central median (Elián González's home

faces the fortress on the east side of the street). There's a similar fortress at the west end of town, on Avenida 13 (Calzada).

Plaza Molokoff

Occupying an entire city block (Av. 3 Oeste, e/ 12 y 13), this two-story plaza is almost entirely taken up by the *mercado agropecuario.* The historic market building was built of iron in 1856 in the shape of a cross, with a lofty metallic domed roof in Islamic style. Its wrought-iron balustrades are held aloft by colonnades. Molokoff refers to the "dome-like" crinoline skirts fashionable in the mid-19th century.

Entertainment and Events

Cárdenas holds a **culture week** in early March to honor the founding of the city. The **Casa de la Cultura** (Av. Céspedes #706, e/ 15 y 16, tel. 045/52-1292), in a faded but charming colonial building, offers traditional music and dance, plus other cultural events from readings to rap.

Accommodations and Food

Casas particulares are illegal in Cárdenas, although numerous people break the law and rent out rooms. Nor are there any hotels, the historic and decrepit Hotel Dominica having finally reached the point of collapse.

You'll be equally hard-pressed to find anywhere exciting to eat. The best place is **Café Espriu** (Calle 12, e/ Av. 4 y 6, tel. 045/51-3273; 24 hours), on the north side of Parque Echevarría. The menu includes tuna salad (CUC1.60), garlic chicken (CUC1.95), and grilled steak (CUC3.50).

Restaurante Las Palmas (Céspedes, esq. 16, tel. 045/52-4762; 8 A.M.–2 P.M. daily), in a colonial mansion, offers ho-hum *criollo* fare plus draft Cristal beer. It has a cabaret Friday–Sunday at 10:30 P.M.

Services

There's a **post office** (Céspedes y Calle 8; Mon.–Sat. 8 A.M.–6 P.M.); an **Etecsa** *telepunto* (Céspedes y Calle 13; 7 A.M.–11 P.M. daily); **Bandec** (Céspedes #252, esq. 11); and

© CHRISTOPHER P. BAKER

Plaza Molokoff

a **Cadeca** (Av. 3 Oeste, e/ 12 y 13), where you change dollars for pesos.

Hospital José M. Aristegui (Calle 13), one kilometer west of town, has the **Centro Médico Sub Acuática** (tel. 045/52-2114; Mon.–Sat. 8 A.M.–4 P.M.), with a decompression chamber (CUC80 per hour).

Getting There and Away

Astro buses depart the **Terminal de Ómnibus Provincial** (Céspedes, e/ 21 y 22, tel. 045/52-1214). A bus to Havana departs daily at 1:45 A.M. (CUC7); a bus to Santa Clara departs daily at 2:40 A.M. (CUC7.50).

Bus #376 runs between Varadero and Cárdenas (30 minutes; CUC1), arriving and departing from Calle 14 and Avenida 8. Also serving Varadero, bus #236 arrives and departs Calle 13 and Avenida 13 Oeste.

A taxi from Varadero costs about CUC15. There are few taxis in Cárdenas, so if you plan on returning to Varadero, it is best to arrange a pick-up time with your driver. *Máquinas* (private jalopy taxis) depart from Céspedes, e/ 21 y 22, but they're not allowed to take foreigners.

Trains connect Cárdenas with Jovellanos and Colón, departing and arriving **Estación San Martín** (Av. 8 Este y Calle 5, tel. 045/52-1362).

Getting Around

Horse-drawn *coches* ply Avenida Céspedes and are the main means of transport. They gather by Parque Colón. For a taxi call **Cubataxi** (tel. 045/52-3160).

There's a Cupet gas station at the west end of Calle 13, on the road to Varadero.

SAN MIGUEL DE LOS BAÑOS

San Miguel de los Baños is a little spa town hidden deep amid rolling hills. It's reached via a turnoff from the Carretera Central at Coliseo, 37 kilometers east of Matanzas, at the junction with Route 3-1-1 to Cárdenas. The town's lofty setting makes it cool and airy. This, combined with the healing properties of its mineral waters, fostered the town's growth last century as a popular health spa. The gentry built villas here in neoclassical and French provincial style, with filigreed balconies and gingerbread woodwork. Most are in tumble-down condition.

As you enter town, you'll pass the ornate but near-derelict **Balneario San Miguel** on your left, topped by Islamic-style turrets. Pathways lead down the garden to disused *baños,* resembling Roman or Turkish baths. Sulfurous water still runs into a small sink at which locals fill their pails.

JOVELLANOS TO COLÓN

The Carretera Central continues east past fields of sugarcane. Sixteen kilometers east of Coliseo, you reach the small agricultural town of Jovellanos, with a predominantly black population and known as a center of Afro-Cuban music and dance (influenced by the Arara tribe from Benin, who arrived in the late 18th century via Haiti). There's a Cupet gas station on the Carretera Central at the east end of town, with a dollars-only café.

South of Jovellanos, the 3-182 cuts south-west to **Pedro Betancourt,** a pleasant colonial town with a beautiful church at its core. Pedro Betancourt is the gateway to mile upon mile of citrus groves criss-crossed by ruler-straight roads and extending all the way south to the Autopista.

Colón

Colón, 33 kilometers east of Jovellanos, is worth a quick browse. Its colonnaded streets are lined with tumbledown neoclassical structures centered on **Parque de Libertad,** two blocks south of the main street, Máximo Gómez. The park is fronted by some attractive buildings and surrounded by shade trees and a wide promenade. At its heart is a life-size, patinated bronze statue of the town's namesake, Christopher Columbus (Cristóbal Colón).

There's a Cupet gas station on Máximo Gómez and another outside town on the road (Rt. 3-1-2) that leads south to Calimete and the Autopista.

JAGÜEY GRANDE AND VICINITY

Jagüey Grande, one kilometer north of the Autopista at Km 142, is an agricultural

an old steam train and 1953 Chevrolet outside the sugar-processing factory in Pedro Betancourt town encircled to the northwest by a vast citrus complex and to the northeast by sugarcane fields. Farther east along the Autopista, Route 3-1-2 links **Aguada del Pasajeros** with Colón, on the Carretera Central via Calimete. It's a 22-kilometer beeline past sugarcane and banana plantations shaded by thick stands of palms. The land is as flat as a billiard table. Five miles east of Jagüey Grande, an ungated railway track crosses the Autopista. *Slow down!*

Finca Fiesta Campesina

This contrived "peasant's farm" (tel. 045/92045; daily 9 A.M.–5 P.M.; free, parking CUC1) is an appealing tourist stop about 200 yards south of the junction at Km 142. It offers a small zoo inhabited by deer, agoutis, snakes, crocodiles, and birds. You can sample fruits, Cuban coffee, and *guarapo* (sugarcane juice) crushed in a traditional *trapiche*. A restaurant serves *criollo* cuisine. Horseback rides cost CUC1, and you can even ride a bull!

Museo Memorial Comandancia FAR

An abandoned sugar factory—Central Australia—looms over the sugarcane fields two kilometer south of Jagüey Grande and one kilometer south of the Km 142 junction, on the road to Playa Girón. Fidel Castro set up his military headquarters here on the afternoon of April 15, 1961, during the Bay of Pigs invasion. Castro, who knew that the sugar factory had the only telephone for miles around, directed his troops from the *central* before dashing off to lead *un barraje infernal* (an infernal barrage) of howitzers against the invaders attempting to break out of Playa Larga.

Remains of aircraft shot up in the fighting lie outside the small Revolutionary Armed Forces Command Center Memorial Museum (tel. 045/91-2504; Tues.–Sat. 9 A.M.–5 P.M., Sun. 8 A.M.–noon; entrance CUC1, guide CUC1,

cameras CUC1), which has photographs from the invasion, the desk and telephone used by Fidel, plus an anti-aircraft gun, uniforms, and parachutes.

Accommodations and Food

In Jagüey Grande, **Casa de Lázaro Alayón** (Calle 17 #7402, e/ 74C y 76, tel. 045/91-2668; CUC15–20) has two air-conditioned rooms with private hot-water bathrooms, plus secure parking.

Motel Batey Don Pedro (tel. 045/91-2825, sistema@cienaga.var.cyt.cu; CUC CUC25 s/d, CUC38 t/q), adjoining Finca Fiesta Campesina, has eight rustic yet pleasant and roomy thatched, log cottages with terra-cotta tile floors, large bathrooms, satellite TVs, ceiling fans, and small kitchenettes. Some cabins have loft bedrooms and sleep four people. *Criollo* meals are served in a thatched restaurant.

Pío Cua (tel. 045/91-2371; CUC25 s/d, CUC38 t/q), about two kilometers south of Australia, has three simply furnished, air-conditioned cabins; one for two people, two each for four people. All have local TV and modern bathrooms with hot water. The two larger concrete ones are musty; the smaller is of wood but gets hot. It has an atmospheric restaurant and bar (restaurant noon–5 P.M.; bar 8 A.M.–10 P.M.) popular with tour groups and offering simple *criollo* dishes. It hosts a disco on weekends.

Services

Parador de Carretera (Autopista Km 142, tel. 045/91-3224, sistema@cienaga.var.cyt.cu; 8 A.M.–8 P.M. daily) is a tourist information center that arrange guides, sells excursions, and handles bookings for Motel Batey Don Pedro and Pío Cua.

There are gas stations 100 meters west of Parador de Carretera, and at the junction of Calles 13 and 70, at the south end of Jagüey Grande.

MATANZAS

Península de Zapata and Vicinity

South of Australia, the sugarcane fields and dark-soiled miles of agro-industry abruptly end, and the sawgrass, reed, and *marabú* brush begins. This swampland (the Ciénega de Zapata) sweeps south to the Caribbean Sea, smothering the Zapata Peninsula, a great shoe-shaped extension jutting west into the Golfo de Batabanó. The 4,230-square-kilometer landmass is a region of limestone with flooded faults called *cenotes*. Much of the peninsula comprises Parque Nacional Ciénaga de Zapata, a wildlife reserve within the larger Reserva Biosfera Ciénaga de Zapata.

Zapata extends west of a deep, finger-like bay, the 20-kilometer-long Bahía de Cochinos—Bay of Pigs, named for the local *cochinos cimarrones,* wild pigs, which once formed a staple diet for local Indians. The name is known to every U.S. citizen for the Bay of Pigs invasion, when about 1,300 heavily armed, CIA-trained Cuban exiles came ashore to topple the Castro regime.

Route 3-1-18 runs like a plumb line from Australia to Playa Larga, a small fishing village tucked into the head of the bay. Concrete monuments rise along the coast road, each one representing a Cuban soldier (161 in all) who fell during the three-day battle in April 1961.

History

The region was inhabited by pre-Columbian Indians. The Spanish conquistadores managed to destroy the Taíno population before abandoning the region. It has remained a virtual no-man's-land ever since. The sparse population (about 8,000 souls inhabited the area on the eve of the Revolution) remained cut off from the rest of Cuba. Before the Revolution (the *cenagueros*—swamp people—refer to the Revolution as a milestone, as if it separated B.C. from A.D.) there had been no roads, no schools, no electricity. Charcoal-making was the major occupation of the impoverished population (charcoal is prized as a fuel for cooking).

The *cenagueros* were among the first benefi-

ciaries of the Revolution. The youthful Castro government built highways of hard-packed limestone into the swamps. It also established schools, and more than 200 teachers from the national literacy campaign arrived. The indigent community of Cayo Ramón even got a hospital. Tourist *cabinas* went up at Girón, and an airstrip was built. Today *carboneros* still build their ovens, but their charcoal now goes to town on trucks.

RESERVA DE LA BIOSFERA CIÉNAGA DE ZAPATA

This 628,171-hectare UNESCO Biosphere Reserve enshrines the entire Península de Zapata and surrounding wilderness area. The park entrance (no fee) is midway along Route 3-1-18. The entrance to the actual wildlife reserve is at Buena Ventura, two kilometers west of Playa Larga, 32 kilometers south of Australia; a fee applies and a guide is obligatory.

Two **Estaciones de Reproducción de Fauna Silvestre e Ictofauna,** study and breeding centers for local wildlife, weren't open to the public at last visit. The first, set off the road about four kilometers south of Australia, raises *jutías* (large guinea pig–like rodents) and other mammal species. The second, on the right, about eight kilometers south of Australia, breeds indigenous fish, including the endangered *manjuarí* (garfish), looking like a cross between a fish and a crocodile and tracing its ancestry back to the antediluvian dawn. Wading birds strut atop the water lilies.

For a perspective on the reserve, call in at the **Centro Ecológico** (tel. 045/91-5539; 8 A.M.–4 P.M.; CUC2 including an interpretive trail walk), a visitors ecological center five kilometers south of La Boca. It features an exhibition on the region. A live *manjuarí* swims in a fish tank. Leaf-cutter ants go about their business farming fungi in a glass case, and a separate exhibit details the Indian heritage locally.

Mosquitoes are ferocious here; bring repellent!

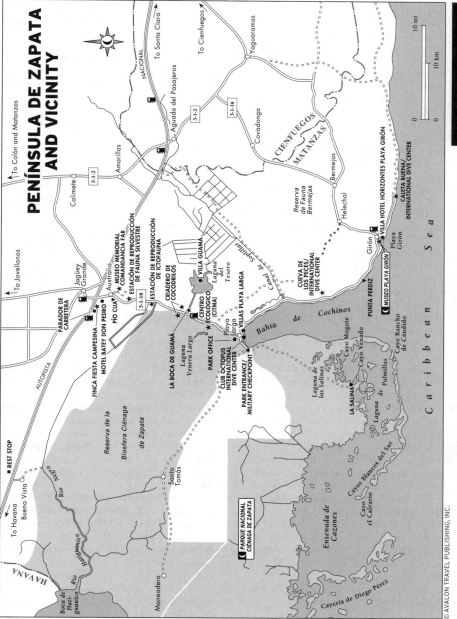

PENÍNSULA DE ZAPATA AND VICINITY

MATANZAS

To Colón and Matanzas

To Santa Clara

To Cienfuegos

NACIONAL

Yaguaromas

Aguada del Pasajeros

3-1-2

3-1-16

Amarillas

Covadonga

Calimete

3-1-2

CIENFUEGOS

MATANZAS

To Jovellanos

Reserva de Fauna Bermejas

Bermejas

Helechal

Jagüey Grande

MUSEO MEMORIAL COMANDANCIA FAR

Australia

ESTACIÓN DE REPRODUCCIÓN DE FAUNA SILVESTRE

ESTACIÓN DE REPRODUCCIÓN DE ICTOFAUNA

VILLA GUAMA

VILLA GUAMA

Laguna del Tesoro

VILLA HOTEL HORIZONTES PLAYA GIRÓN

CALETA BUENA/ INTERNATIONAL DIVE CENTER

PARADOR DE CARRETERA

PÍO CUA

3-1-18

3-1-18

CRIADERO DE COCODRILOS

CENTRO ECOLÓGICO (CITMA)

VILLAS PLAYA LARGA

Playa Larga

Girón

Playa Girón

FINCA FIESTA CAMPESINA

MOTEL BATEY DON PEDRO

LA BOCA DE GUAMA

Laguna Venera Largo

PARK OFFICE

CLUB OCTOPUS INTERNATIONAL DIVE CENTER

PARK ENTRANCE/ MILITARY CHECKPOINT

Canal de Soplillar

CUEVA DE LOS PECES/ INTERNATIONAL DIVE CENTER

PUNTA PERDIZ

MUSEO PLAYA GIRÓN

Bahía de Cochinos

Canal

AUTOPISTA

■ REST STOP

Reserva de la Biosfera Ciénaga de Zapata

Santo Tomás

Laguna de las Salinas

Cayo Mogote

Cayo Venado

Cayo Rancho de Candido

LA SALINA

Laguna de Palmillas

Caribbean Sea

To Havana

Buena Vista

Río Negro

Río Hatiguanico

PARQUE NACIONAL CIÉNAGA DE ZAPATA

Maneadero

Cayos Blancos del Sur

Cayo el Calvario

Ensenada de Cazones

HAVANA

Boca de Hati- guanico

Cayería de Diego Pérez

10 mi

10 km

0

0

© AVALON TRAVEL PUBLISHING, INC.

La Boca de Guamá

La Boca (tel. 045/91-2458), 16 kilometers south of Australia, is an important roadside stop and a staple of tour groups. It comprises thatched *bohíos* with numerous attractions and services, including an atmospheric bar and restaurant, a well-stocked souvenir shop that sells crafts, a crocodile farm, and a gas station. No credit cards are accepted.

The **Criadero de Cocodrilos** (tel. 045/91-5666; 7 A.M.–7 P.M. daily; CUC5 adults, CUC3 children) is Cuba's most important crocodile farm, with more than 3,000 crocodiles, which laze in the sun amid swampy lagoons surrounded by large, circular pens. On the east side of the road, raised wooden platforms provide vantage points to admire the awesome beasts lying still as death, jaws agape, hoping obviously for a careless visitor to stumble and fall into a pit. The crocs are born and raised at a separate facility (the actual "farm") across the road, where you can learn about the entire breeding cycle and ecology. When they're seven years old, some are transferred to the larger facility; others are killed for meat and leather.

The **Laguna del Tesoro** (Treasure Lagoon) is a 16-square-kilometer lake stocked with largemouth bass, plus trout, haddock, carp, native *biajacas,* tarpon, tilapia, and meterlong *manjuarí.* The lake, reached via a five-kilometer-long canal from La Boca, is named for the religious objects that the Taíno supposedly threw into the water to hide them from the Spanish conquistadores. Indian artifacts have been raised from the lake and are now exhibited in the **Museo Guamá,** on an island in the middle of the lake. It features a mock Indian village and 32 life-size sculptures depicting the Taíno engaged in daily activities.

Tours of the lake are offered aboard a cruise boat from La Boca, where rowboats can be hired (CUC2 per hour). Four-hour fishing trips are also offered (tel. 045/91-3224, CUC85 for two people).

An open-air tour boat leaves La Boca for Villa Guamá at 10 A.M. and noon (CUC10 adults, CUC5 children), returning 30 min-utes later. Speedboats can be hired for the journey (CUC10 per person; two passenger minimum).

Playa Larga and Bahía de los Cochinos (Bay of Pigs)

Playa Larga, a beach community at the head of the Bahía de los Cochinos, was one of the two main landing sites during the Bay of Pigs fiasco. The village comprises a few fishermen's huts, military buildings, the International Bird-Watching Center, and a hotel facing a small cream-colored beach. The park office is here.

A road leads west from Playa Larga two kilometers to the ramshackle hamlet of **Buena Ventura.** There's a guard post here, at the entrance to the Parque Nacional Ciénaga de Zapata.

East of Playa Larga, white beaches extend around the bay. At **Caleta del Rosario,** about three kilometers from Playa Larga, is a splendid little cove with good swimming. The route is also lined with *cenotes,* limestone sinkholes. Columbus discovered them and recorded that they contained subterranean streams with waters "so cold, and of such goodness and so sweet that no better could be found in the world."

Cueva de los Peces (Cave of Fishes; 9 A.M.–5 P.M. daily; CUC1), 15 kilometers from Playa Larga, is one of the largest *cenotes.* The huge cave is 70 meters deep and a superb spot for scuba diving. Gaily colored tropical fish swim in the dark water. You can rent scuba and snorkeling gear; the beach in front of the *cenote* also offers good snorkeling in jade-colored waters.

A little way east is **Bar/Restaurante Punta Perdiz** (9 A.M.–4 P.M. daily), a small recreation area with a bird-watching trail, **Sendero El Tocororo.**

Scuba Diving and Snorkeling: Marlin S.A. operates the **Club Octopus International Dive Center** (tel. 045/91-7294, pedro@cristal.hlg .old.cu) at the Villas Horizontes Playa Larga. It offers scuba dives daily at 8 A.M. and 5 P.M.; CUC25 one dive, CUC35 cave dive and Nitrox dives, CUC365 certification. There are 12 dive sites. Marlin has outlets at the Cueva de los Peces (10 A.M.–6 P.M. daily) and Caleta Buena (see *Playa Girón).*

Snorkeling at Cueva de los Peces costs CUC3.

◀ Parque Nacional Ciénaga de Zapata

The 490,417-hectare Zapata is encompassed within a national park protecting Cuba's most important wetland area. As yet, it is little utilized by ecotourists, though a handful of bird-watchers and fisherfolk are savvy to its allure. The complex ecosystems include marsh grass, mangrove thickets, and thickly wooded swamp forest of dense *marabú* bushes with their inch-long thorns. It is a biological mirror of the Everglades of Florida—there are even beautifully banded *liguus* snails, a kind of tree snail common in the Everglades. Vegetation includes the button tree, so small that it looks like a bonsai.

Zapata harbors more than 900 species of flora (including poisonous *guao* plants), 171 species of birds, 31 of reptiles, and 12 of mammals, including the pygmy *jutía* native to the Zapata swamp. The Río Hatiguanico harbors manatees. There are freshwater turtles, many of which end up as fricassee, a popular dish among the marsh people. Iguanas will come up to you, totally fearless. The alligator gar (*manjuarí*), the most primitive of Cuban fish, is found in lagoons, as are crocodiles and caimans, a diminutive species of alligator.

Refugio de Fauna Bermejas, accessed from north of Playa Girón, is a separate section of the park (the entrance fee is payable in the Hotel Playa Larga) with an overgrown bird-watching trail. Guided bird-watching tours cost CUC19.

Bird-Watching: Of Cuba's 22 endemic bird species, 18 inhabit the marshes. Zapata protects the bee hummingbird (the world's smallest bird) as well as an endemic tanager and *gallinuela de Santo Tomás,* the Zapata sparrow, Zapata rail, and Zapata wren. Cuba's national bird, the Cuban trogon or *tocororo,* is also found here, as is the long-tailed sparrow hawk, plus a significant population of Cuban parrots.

Zapata is also a favorite stop for tens of thousands of migratory birds. The best time is

FLAMINGOS

There are six species of flamingos worldwide (four in the New World, and two in Africa). Standing over 1.2 meters tall, the roseate West Indian flamingo (*Phoenicopterus ruber*) is the largest of the New World species. The ungainly yet beautiful bird can be seen feeding in large congregations in the shallow lagoons of Zapata, the Jardines del Rey, and Jardines de la Reina, where evaporation keeps salinity much higher than in the open sea. The supersalty soup teems with larval brine flies and diatoms (blue-green algae) – favorite foods of flamingos. Their food supply contains canthaxanthin, a substance that gives the birds their soft pink color.

Flamingos breed en masse. The mating instinct, once sparked, gathers steam until hundreds or even thousands of birds may be displaying in a tumult, parading up and down, marching stiff-necked in great columns. Occasionally an individual will break step, stand bolt upright, and shoot out its wings, while others fluff up their feathers and drop their heads as surely as if their necks had been broken.

The birds build nests by ladling wet mud into miniature volcanoes, which the sun then hardens. Soon the forest of legs conceals tiny youngsters swaddled in gray fluffy plumage.

October to April, when overwhelming numbers of birds flock in, among them sandhill cranes, great blue herons, tricolored herons, and wood ibis. Even flamingos wade in the soupy lagoons.

The best spots for bird-watching are **Laguna de la Salina,** a 36,400 hectare expanse of flats, watercourses, and islets on the southern shores of Zapata and where flamingos flock in their thousands; and also around **Santo Tomás,** about 30 kilometers west of Playa Larga (CUC10 per person by jeep, including guide). The areas around Soplillar and Bermejes are splendid for upland bird-watching, including the *tocororo.*

CRABS!

Mid-March through April, giant land crabs (*cangrejos*) emerge from the vegetation and swarm, legion upon legion, to meeting grounds where they gather for vast orgies and egg-laying parties. They move in such numbers that the main coast road, and those along much of the southern and eastern coasts of Cuba, becomes a veritable carpet of crushed crabs, like giant M&Ms crushed underfoot.

In *Mi Moto Fidel: Motorcycling Through Castro's Cuba*, I write: "The air stank of fetid crabmeat. Vultures hopped about, drawn greedily to the prodigal banquet. I passed my first live crab scurrying toward the sea. Bright orange. A newborn. Then a large black crab with terrifying red pincers ran across my path, the forerunner of a lethal invasion heading the other way. Suddenly I was surrounded by a battalion of armored, surly crustaceans that turned to snap at my tires. I slalomed between them as they rose in the road with menacing claws held high. Then I hit one square on. POOF! It sounded like bubble wrap exploding."

Early morning is best for bird-watching, and springtime is the best time of year.

Fishing: Zapata has been isolated from fishing pressure since 1959, making this huge reserve as close to a virgin fishery as one can find in today's world. There are said to be places where you can catch the fish with your bare hands, the way the indigenous Indians did. Tarpon and bonefish are the species of choice. Bonefishing is most productive late fall through June; tarpon fishing peaks late February/early March through June.

There are two distinct areas for fishing—the 200-meter-wide Río Hatiguanico and its tributaries, and La Salina, which is world-famous for bonefish; several well-traveled anglers consider La Salina the standard by which all other locations should be judged worldwide. Being shallow and firm-bottomed, it is ideal for wading and spotting bonefish. Other species include *palometa* (permit), which can reach 20 pounds.

Underpowered skiffs mean long periods getting to the best lagoons.

Permits and Guides: Access is by permit only (CUC12 per person, including an obligatory guide), obtained from the **Oficina Parque Nacional** (tel. 045/98-7249; Mon.–Sat. 8 A.M.–4:30 P.M.), beside the highway in Playa Larga. You can also hire a guide and arrange nature hikes, jeep trips, bird-watching, fishing, and crocodile tours through **Parador de Carretera** (see *Jagüey Grande*). You'll need your own vehicle, with a spare seat for the guide.

Just beyond the guard post, a rough dirt road leads southwest to Laguna de las Salinas, and another leads west, to Santo Tomás and Maneadero (51 km).

Accommodations and Food

Laguna Tesoro was one of Castro's favorite fishing spots. The Cuban leader spent many weekends in a *cabina* that became known as "Fidel's Key." One day, lounging on his bed, he supposedly announced, "We're going to build a Tahitian village here!" And they did. The revolutionary government dredged a canal network and created a series of islands featuring a replica Taíno village, **Villa Guamá,** with 13 tiny islands connected by hanging bridges. At last visit, the 50 thatched bungalows on stilts were being rebuilt after being trashed by Hurricane Ivan in 2005.

Several homeowners in Playa Larga rent rooms. My favorite is ◖ **Villa Juana** (tel. 045/98-7308, caribesolpz@yahoo.es), a pleasant home with modern amenities. The single air-conditioned room with its own refrigerator, fan, and modern bathroom, opens to a charming garden patio where meals are served. The family are a delight. Privately guided scuba dives are offered, as are horseback rides, plus free laundry and coffee.

Casa de Enrique Rivas (tel. 045/98-7178; CUC25 per person including breakfast and dinner), at Caletón, one kilometer west of Playa Larga, offers one spacious, clean air-conditioned room with private hot-water bathroom.

The lifeless beachfront **Villas Playa Larga** (tel./fax 045/98-7294; CUC32 s, CUC40 d low season; CUC38 s, CUC44 d high season, including breakfast) has 57 spacious, albeit modestly furnished, air-conditioned rooms in *cabinas,* each with private bath, radio, small beds, tiny TV, and basic kitchenette. There's an uninspiring restaurant, bar, cafeteria, beach volleyball, and water sports. It rents bicycles, scooters, and cars. (Cubanacán.)

Campismo Victoria de Girón, seven kilometers southeast of Playa Larga, was not taking foreigners at last visit.

At La Boca, the modestly elegant, air-conditioned **Colibrí Restaurant** (noon–5 P.M. daily) serves *criollo* fare, including crocodile (CUC10) and lobster (CUC11). The open-air **Bar y Restaurante La Rionda** (9:30 A.M.–5 P.M. daily), adjacent, is nicer on cooler days. Thatched **La Boca Restaurant** (noon–4:30 P.M. daily) overlooks a lagoon full of water hyacinths; it was closed for repair at last visit.

Cueva de los Peces has a bar and thatched restaurant serving *criollo* fare, including lobster (CUC15).

Getting There

Bus #818 links Jagüey Grande and Playa Girón via Playa Larga. Service is inconsistent, as is the bus service to and from Havana on Friday, Saturday, and Sunday.

Tour agencies in Havana and Varadero offer excursions.

PLAYA GIRÓN

Finally you arrive at the spot where socialism and capitalism slugged it out, and what do you find? Vacationers from cool climates, lathered with suntan oil, splashing in the shallows where 30-odd years before blood and bullets mingled with the sand on the surf. You are welcomed by a huge billboard that reads, Playa Girón—The First Rout of Imperialism in Latin America.

Playa Girón is a small *pueblo* of a few hundred people. It was named in honor of Gilbert Girón, a French pirate captured here. The community lies inland of the tourist facility and beach, which has been off-limits to Cubans since 1998 and at last visit was being used exclusively for Venezuelans receiving medical

a Soviet T-34 tank and British-made Sea Fury at Museo Playa Girón

BAY OF PIGS

The Bay of Pigs invasion – Cubans call it the Battle of Girón or La Victoria (the victory) – was the brainchild of Richard Bissell, Deputy Director of the CIA. The plan was to infiltrate anti-Castro guerrillas onto the island so that they could link up with domestic opponents. The "Program of Covert Action Against the Castro Regime" called for creation of a Cuban government in exile, covert action in Cuba, and "a paramilitary force outside of Cuba for future guerrilla action." In August 1959 President Eisenhower approved a US$13 million budget with the proviso that "no U.S. military personnel were to be used in a combat status."

Under a flexible mandate, Bissell radically expanded the original concept. The CIA borrowed officers from the armed services and created an air force that eventually numbered 80 U.S. pilots. By the time President Kennedy was briefed, in November 1960, the plan had grown to include 1,500 men backed by a rebel air force of B-26s.

THE UNITED STATES PREPARES TO INVADE

The CIA recruited Cuban exiles for the invasion force and used an abandoned naval base at Opa-Locka, outside Miami, to train the brigade. They were later moved to U.S. military locations in Guatemala and Puerto Rico (in violation of U.S. law). Meanwhile, a "government in exile" was chosen from within a loose, feud-riven group of political exiles, many of them corrupt right-wing politicians nostalgic for Batista days. The group was to be transformed into a provisional government once it had gained a foothold in Cuba.

The plan called for the invasion force to link up with guerrillas operating out of the Sierra Escambray, more than 100 kilometers east of the Bay of Pigs, where the brigade would land at three beaches 25 kilometers apart and surrounded by swamps. In photos taken by U-2 spy planes, the CIA's photo interpreter identified what he claimed was seaweed offshore. "They are coral heads," said Dr. Juan Sordo, a brigade member: "I know them. I have seen them." Another brigade member agreed. The water would be too shallow for the landing craft, he said. But the CIA wouldn't listen.

The invasion plan relied on eliminating the Cuban air force. The CIA wanted U.S. air support; the State Department wanted it kept to a minimum so that the planes could later be claimed to have originated in Cuba (U.S. involvement was supposed to be deniable). On April 15, two days before the invasion, B-26 bombers painted in Cuban air force colors struck Cuba's three military air bases.

Thus Castro was fully forewarned. Worse, only five aircraft were destroyed, and Cuba still had at least three T-33 jet fighters and four British-made Sea Fury light-attack bombers.

THE INVASION

The U.S. Navy aircraft carrier Essex and five destroyers escorted six freighters carrying

treatment (see *Into the New Millennium* in the *History* section of the *Background* chapter). The beautiful white-sand beach is enclosed within a concrete barrier (*rompeola*), which protects against any future wave of CIA-backed anti-Castroites foolish enough to come ashore. Nonetheless, it's a carbuncle on the coast and made worse by the military watchtower to the east end, where soldiers with high-powered binoculars have a vantage for spying on topless bathers.

The paved coastal highway (Route 3-1-16) turns inland at Playa Girón and runs 39 kilometers through scrubland to Yaguaramas (forsake the road from Covavango; it's terribly deteriorated). Here, it connects with Route 3-1-2, which runs north to Aguada de Pasajeros and the Autopista and east to Cienfuegos.

◖ Museo Playa Girón

This small museum (tel. 045/98-4122; daily 8 A.M.–5 P.M.; entrance CUC2, guide CUC1,

the Cuban fighters and their supplies. They moved in radio silence.

The landings began about 1:15 A.M. on April 17 at Playa Girón and Playa Larga. Landing craft (LCVPs) came roaring in. About 140 meters offshore, they hit the coral reefs the CIA had dismissed as seaweed. The brigade had to wade ashore. Meanwhile, the fiberglass boats used by the Second and Fifth Battalions capsized. The Cubans had installed tall, extremely bright lights right on the beach. "It looked like Coney Island," recalls Gray Lynch, the CIA point man who ended up directing the invasion. The brigade had also been told that "no communications existed within 20 miles of the beach." In fact, there was a radio station only 100 meters inland. By the time the brigade stormed it, Castro had been alerted.

Kennedy had approved taking the Cubans to the beaches; beyond that, they were on their own. Worried about repercussions at the United Nations, Kennedy ordered cancellation of a second strike designed to give the invasion force cover. With that decision, the operation was lost.

Castro set up headquarters in the Central Australia sugar mill and from there directed the Cuban defense. As the exiles landed, Cuba's aircraft swooped down. Two supply ships containing ammunition and communications equipment were sunk. Two other ammunition vessels fled and had to be turned back by the USS *Eaton*. The brigade did, however, manage to unload WWII-era Sherman tanks. They fought the "battle of the rotunda" against Cuba's equally outdated T-34 and Stalin tanks.

Despite the CIA's predictions, the local people ("armed only with M-52 Czech rifles," writes Peter Wyden in *Bay of Pigs*) defended their homeland until the first Cuban battalion of 900 student soldiers arrived in buses (half the cadet troops were killed when the convoy was strafed by the brigade's B-26s). Reinforcements poured in and encircled the invasion forces, and the fight became a simple matter of whittling away at the exiles.

A U.S. jet-fighter squadron flew reconnaissance over the invasion but was forbidden to engage in combat. As the situation deteriorated, Kennedy came under increasing pressure to order U.S. air strikes. He refused. Nonetheless, six U.S. pilots flew combat missions under CIA orders without President Kennedy's knowledge. Four were shot down and killed. The Cubans recovered the body of one of the pilots – Thomas Ray – and found his dog tags (his corpse remained in a Havana morgue unclaimed by the U.S. government; Ray's daughter brought his body home for burial in 1979).

ABANDONING THE *BRIGADISTAS*

On the third day of the battle, the U.S. destroyers advanced on the shore. Castro instinctively knew they were sailing in for an evacuation and ordered Cuban artillery not to fire. The destroyers picked up those *brigadistas* who had made it back to sea, then sailed away, leaving the survivors to fend for themselves. The brigade had lost 114 men (the Cubans lost 161), but a further 1,189 were captured. Eventually, 1,091 prisoners were returned to the United States in exchange for US$53 million in food and medical supplies.

cameras CUC1, videos CUC5) gives an accurate portrayal of the drama of the Bay of Pigs invasion. Black-and-white photographs confirm the appalling poverty of the local peasantry before the Revolution. Others profile the events preceding the invasion: the Agrarian Reform Law, the literacy campaign, and sabotage and other counterrevolutionary activity culminating in the act to which the museum is dedicated—the invasion of April 15, 1961, by 1,297 CIA-trained Cubans.

The story of the invasion is shown on maps that trace the evolution of the 72-hour battle. There are photographs, including gory pictures of civilians caught in the midst of explosions, and of all the martyrs—the "Heroes de Girón"—killed in the fighting (the youngest, Nelson Fernández Estevez, was only 16 years old; the oldest, Juan Ruíz Serna, was 60). Note the photo of a young militiaman, Eduardo García Delgado, who wrote "Fidel" on a wall with his own blood before dying, face-down, with his hand on the L. And, of course, Fidel is there, leaping from a T-34 tank. Other displays include weapons and a Sea Fury fighter-aircraft, complete with rockets, which sits on the forecourt alongside Soviet T-34 and SAU-100 tanks.

Guides give you a blow-by-blow account.

Caleta Buena

This exquisite cove (daily 10 A.M.–6 P.M.; CUC12), eight kilometers east of Playa Girón, contains a natural pool good for swimming. There are pocket-size beaches atop the coral platform, with red-tiled *ranchitas* for shade and lounge chairs for sunning. The seabed is a multicolored garden of coral and sponges, ideal for snorkeling (CUC3 for equipment rental) and diving (CUC25). Lunch is served noon–3 P.M. (the bar is open until 5 P.M.).

East of Caleta Buena, the road deteriorates rapidly. The area is uninhabited. Eventually you'll reach a sharp curve with a small cove to the right. The "main" route veers left and eventually leads to Yaguaramas.

Accommodations

There are more than two dozen *casas particulares,* most being similar in style—many have walls inset with shells—and price (CUC20). Try **Casa de Gelasió y Lourde** (tel. 045/98-4146), whose handsome house offers one simply but adequately furnished room with fan, fridge, and a clean, modern hot-water bathroom. Meals are made, and there's parking.

Hostal Silvia Acosta Lima (tel. 045/98-4249) has two rooms that appeal for their cleanliness and decor. They're well-lit, cross-ventilated, and have fans and private bathrooms with large hot-water showers. A TV lounge boasts leather sofas. Meals are offered.

Also try **Hostal Tito** (tel. 045/98-4179).

Hotel Playa Girón (tel. 045/98-4110), once popular with budget-minded Europeans, was being used for Operación Milagro at last visit.

Services

There's a coin laundry, pharmacy, dollars-only shop, plus a post office opposite the museum.

Getting There, Away, and Around

Bus #818 operates from Jagüey Grande; it ostensibly departs Playa Girón for Jagüey Grande at 7:30 A.M. *Camiones* also operate from Cienfuegos daily at 12:30 P.M., and from Playa Girón for Cienfuegos at 5 A.M. Service is unreliable.

Most tour agencies in Havana and Varadero offer excursions.

Transauto (tel. 045/98-4144), at Hotel Playa Girón, has taxi service and rental cars.

CIENFUEGOS AND VILLA CLARA

Villa Clara and Cienfuegos Provinces lie due east of Matanzas Province, with Villa Clara north of Cienfuegos. Together they share some of the prettiest scenery in Cuba, much of it rarely visited by travelers despite its easy accessibility. The region is skipped by most tourists, who whiz by along the Autopista or Carretera Central bound for Oriente or the colonial city of Trinidad, in Sancti Spíritus Province. Such haste is a pity, for you are likely to miss one of my favorite regions in Cuba.

The southern and eastern portions of Villa Clara Province, for example, are dominated by beautiful rolling uplands called the Alturas de Santa Clara. The Alturas rise gradually to the steep, pine-clad Sierra Escambray, whose reservoirs supply towns for miles around. Today cool forests tantalize bird-watchers and hik-ers, with man-made lakes good for fishing, a famous health spa, and a cool, invigorating climate to lure you away from the coast. The mountains extend south and west into Cienfuegos Province, which, despite being Cuba's second smallest, surpasses even Havana in industrial output.

Industry is centered on the city of Cienfuegos, a major port town that also boasts some splendid colonial architecture and, nearby, a fine botanical garden, while the city of Santa Clara (also an important industrial and university city) should be on every traveler's itinerary for the fascinating Museo de Che (Guevara). Nearby, the historic town of Remedios is a tiny charmer caught in its own delightful time warp from which the modern-day visitor may find it very hard to escape.

HIGHLIGHTS

◖ **Parque Martí:** Cienfuegos's expansive central plaza is surrounded by impressive neoclassical structures and a marble-clad cathedral (page 330).

◖ **Palacio del Valle:** This Mogul-inspired confection in stone is a one-of-a-kind mansion turned restaurant; sure, the food and service win no awards, but the memorable setting is enhanced at night by Carmen Iznaga at the piano (page 332).

◖ **Jardín Botánico Soledad:** This vast botanical garden on the outskirts of Cienfuegos has separate sections for cactus, rubber trees, and other plants, including 307 varieties of palm (page 338).

◖ **El Nicho:** The placid Sierra Escambray setting of this recreational site features beau-

tiful waterfalls and horseback riding, hiking, and other activities (page 341).

◖ **Monumento Ernesto Che Guevara:** A small but splendid museum sits beneath the imposing Che Guevara monument in Santa Clara. A reverential mausoleum contains the revolutionary hero's remains (page 345).

◖ **Remedios:** Time your visit to this beautiful colonial town, good for serendipitous discoveries, for year's end to catch the *parranda* – a fireworks battle like no other (page 353).

◖ **Cayo Santa María:** A 50-kilometer-long land bridge provides access to stunning white-sand beaches and jade waters on a remote cay with great fishing and scuba diving and top-class resorts (page 357).

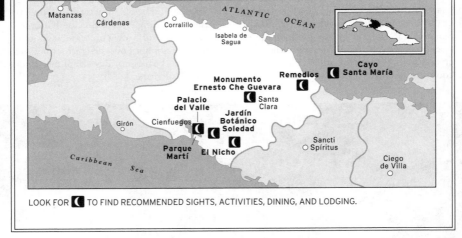

LOOK FOR ◖ TO FIND RECOMMENDED SIGHTS, ACTIVITIES, DINING, AND LODGING.

Villa Clara is second only to Pinar del Río as a center of tobacco production, centered on the scenic Vuelta Arriba region, east of the provincial capital. Here, Remedios and neighboring villages are renowned for their *parrandas,* unique year-end carnival-style revelries that border on mayhem. Nearby, gorgeous beaches lie at hand at Cayo Santa María.

PLANNING YOUR TIME

All the main highways merge into (or radiate out from) the city of Santa Clara, which boasts the must-see **Monumento Ernesto Che Guevara.** A full day is sufficient for this city, which has several good *casas particulares.*

Northwest of Santa Clara, the Circuito Norte linking Villa Clara with Matanzas

Province skirts the north coast and offers little of visual appeal. You can enjoy a massage and steep in mud at Baños de Elguea, where more serious treatments are also offered. Northeast of Santa Clara, the route passes through Vuelta Abajo and is superbly scenic. I recommend overnighting in the town of **Remedios** to savor its historic charm. If possible, time your visit for Christmas week, when the entire town explodes in revelry; accommodation is in short supply at year's end, so book well in advance. When the dust settles, head out to **Cayo Santa María** for sunning, swimming, and to reel in some game fish from the placid jade waters.

The Carretera Central through central Villa Clara and will take you through aged provincial towns, although there are no sites or sights of significance. Similarly, the Autopista runs through northern Cienfuegos and southern Villa Clara Province and should be used for rapid transit through the region. (East of Santa Clara city, the scenery takes a dramatic turn as the Autopista cuts through the beautiful hills of the Alturas de Santa Clara and passes into Sancti Spíritus Province.) The main turnoff for the city of Cienfuegos is at Aguada de los Pasajeros, where there's a gas station alongside an appealing bar and restaurant, with an antique steam engine on display. Just east of Ranchuelo, an ungated railway track runs across the Autopista. Use caution, and avoid the freeway entirely at night!

The city of Cienfuegos is a popular destination with an intriguing historic city core. Nearby, the ho-hum beach at Rancho Faro has a Delfinario with dolphin shows, and anyone with a love of flora will find fascination in the **Jardín Botánico Soledad.** The city has two excellent hotels (by Cuban standards), plus many excellent *casas particulares.* By following the scenic southern coast road, you can use Cienfuegos as a gateway for exploring the Sierra Escambray, although Trinidad, in Sancti Spíritus Province, is the best base.

You'll need at least a week to see all the highlights, with two days for Cienfuegos, a day in the Sierra Escambray, one night in Santa Clara, at least one night in Remedios, and one or two days in Cayo Santa María. Santa Clara is well situated as home base, especially for forays into the Sierra Escambray, although Cienfuegos is the more interesting city.

Santa Clara and Cienfuegos are served by Víazul buses, and Santa Clara is a main stop for the Havana–Santiago de Cuba train service.

Cienfuegos and Vicinity

CIENFUEGOS

Cienfuegos (pop. 105,000), 340 kilometers east of Havana and 69 kilometers southwest of Santa Clara, lies on the east side of the Bahía de Cienfuegos, a deep, 88-square-kilometer bay with an umbilically narrow entrance. It's Cuba's third-largest port and shelters a large fishing and shrimping fleet. International influences (especially French) have made themselves felt. Cienfuegos even had its own Chinatown (now long since devoid of Chinese people), west of Parque Martí on the edge of the port.

Cienfuegos means "100 fires" and is sometimes written "100 fuegos." Citizens call their town La Perla del Sur (the pearl of the south). The city's appeal lies partly in the European flavor of its colonial hub, with a wide Parisian-style boulevard and elegant colonnades. Nonetheless, Cienfuegos has neither the grace of Trinidad nor the flair of Havana. Still, there is an ambience that inspired Benny Moré, the celebrated Cuban *sonoro,* to sing, "Cienfuegos is the city I like best."

Orientation

Approaching from the Autopista, the two-lane highway enters the city from the north and widens into a broad boulevard, the Paseo del Prado (Calle 37), the city's main thoroughfare

CIENFUEGOS / VILLA CLARA

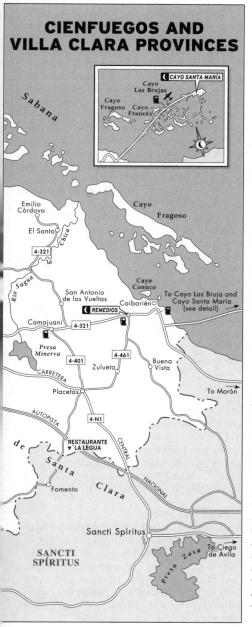

CIENFUEGOS AND VILLA CLARA PROVINCES

CAYO SANTA MARÍA

Cayo Las Brujas

Cayo Fragoso   Cayo Francés

Sabana

Emilio Córdova

El Santo

4-321

la Chica

Rio Sagua

Cayo Fragoso

Cayo Conuco

San Antonio de las Vueltas

REMEDIOS

Caibarién   To Cayo Las Bruja and Cayo Santa Maria (see detail)

Camajuani   4-321

Presa Minerva   4-401   4-461   Buena Vista

Zulueta

CARRETERA

Placetas   To Morón

AUTOPISTA   4-N1

de   RESTAURANTE ▼ LA LEGUA

Santa   CENTRAL

Fomento   Clara   NACIONAL

Sancti Spíritus

SANCTI SPÍRITUS   Zasa   To Ciego de Ávila

Presa

CIENFUEGOS / VILLA CLARA

leading to the historic core, called Pueblo Nuevo. Parque Martí, the main plaza, is four blocks west of the Prado and reached via Avenidas 54 and 56. Avenida 54 (El Bulevar), the principal shopping street, is pedestrian-only.

At Avenida 46, the Prado becomes the Malecón, a wide seafront boulevard stretching south one kilometer along a narrow peninsula ending at Punta Gorda, a once-exclusive residential district that recalls 1950s North American suburbia, with Detroit classics still parked in the driveways of mid-20th-century homes. Beyond Punta Gorda is a short, slender isthmus lined with old French-style plantation homes.

The city is laid out in a perfect grid, with even-numbered *calles* running north–south, crossing odd-numbered *avenidas* running east–west.

A six-lane highway, the *circunvalación,* bypasses the city to the north.

History

Columbus supposedly discovered the bay in 1494. Shortly after the Spanish settled Cuba and established their trade restrictions, the bay developed a thriving smuggling trade. Sir Francis Drake and Henry Morgan were among privateers who called for plunder.

Construction of a fortress—Castillo de Jagua—was begun in 1738 to protect the bay and to police smuggling through the straits. It wasn't until 1817 that Louis D'Clouet, a French émigré from Louisiana, devised a settlement scheme that he presented to Don José Cienfuego, the Spanish captain-general. The Spanish government would pay for the transportation of white colonists from Europe, and every male would receive a *caballería,* a 13-hectare plot of land. The Spanish Parliament approved. By April 1819, the first 137 French settlers arrived. That hamlet was destroyed by a hurricane six years later, was rebuilt in 1831 and renamed Cienfuegos, and rapidly grew to wealth thanks to the deep-water harbor. Merchants and plantation owners graced the city with a surfeit of stucco.

The city continued to prosper during the

early 20th century and had an unremarkable history—until September 5, 1957, when young naval officers and sailors (supported by the CIA) at the Cienfuegos Naval Base rebelled against the Batista regime and took control of the city's military and electrical installations. Members of Castro's revolutionary 26th of July Movement and students joined them. Batista's troops managed to recapture the city by nightfall.

Since the Revolution, the city's hinterland has grown significantly, mostly to the west in Reparto O'Bourke, where a new port and industrial and residential complex was initiated in the 1980s.

Cienfuegos has its fair share of poverty-stricken slums that are best avoided after dark; stick to the main streets by night.

◖ Parque Martí

Most of Cienfuegos's buildings of note surround Parque Martí, on the ground where the founding of the first settlement was proclaimed on April 22, 1819. The *majagua* tree that once stood at the center has long since died and been replaced by a bandstand and gazebo. The city's most prominent and illustrious sons are commemorated in bronze or stone, including a statue to José Martí, guarded by two marble lions. Note the triumphal arch on the west side, unveiled in 1902 on the day the Cuban Republic was constituted.

The **Catedral de la Purísima Concepción** (tel. 043/52-5297; daily 7 A.M.–noon), on the east side of the square, dates from 1870. It has a splendid interior, with marble floors and a pristine gilt Corinthian altar beneath a Gothic vaulted ceiling. The stained-glass windows of the 12 apostles were brought from France following the revolution of 1789.

On the north side is the **Colegio San Lorenzo,** a handsome neoclassical building. Adjoining it is **Teatro Tomás Terry** (tel. 043/51-3361; daily 9 A.M.–6 P.M.; CUC1 including guide), completed in 1895 and named for a local sugar baron, a Venezuelan who had arrived penniless in Cuba in the mid-1800s. The proscenium is sumptuously decorated with laurel wreaths, lyres, trumpets, and a bas-relief centerpiece of Dionysius. Allegorical figures cling to the arch over the stage, and naked nymphs cavort across the ceiling. The auditorium, with its three-tiered balconies, is made entirely of Cuban hardwoods and can accommodate 900 people in old-fashioned, fold-down wooden seats. The theater floor can be raised to stage level to create a grand ballroom. Enrico Caruso, Sarah Bernhardt, and the Bolshoi Ballet have performed here. The Nacional Ballet and Ópera de Cuba still perform, bringing the bats from their hiding places to swoop harmlessly over the heads of the audience.

On the west side, the **Casa de la Cultura** (Calle 25 #5403, tel. 043/51-6584; 8:30 A.M.–midnight; free) occupies the much-dilapidated Palacio Ferrer, an eclectically styled former mansion of sugar baron José Ferrer Sirés. It has a *mirador* tower with fine views across the bay (CUC0.50). At night, music and dance spill into the square.

The former Spanish Club (the initials CE, inset in the pavement, stand for Club Español), on the south side, dates from 1898 and now houses the **Museo Histórico Provincial** (Av. 54 #2702, esq. Calle 27, tel. 043/51-9722; Tues.–Sat. 10 A.M.–6 P.M., Sun. 9 A.M.–noon; CUC2). It displays a modest assortment of antiques, plus an archaeological room honoring the Indians of the Americas. Fifty meters east is the **Primer Palacio,** now the Poder Popular, the local government headquarters.

Cater-corner to the Poder Popular is the **Casa del Fundador** (Av. 54, esq. 29, tel. 043/55-2144; Mon.–Sat. 9 A.M.–5:30 P.M., Sun. 9 A.M.–12:30 P.M.; CUC1), where lived city founder Don Luis Declouet.

Paseo del Prado

Calle 37—the Prado—is lined its full length with a central median with plaques and busts honoring illustrious citizens, including a life-size bronze figure of Benny Moré (esq. Av. 54). The Prado remains a social center and in the cool evenings bustles with gossipy life, when citizens promenade and bootblacks still shine shoes beneath the pink colonnades.

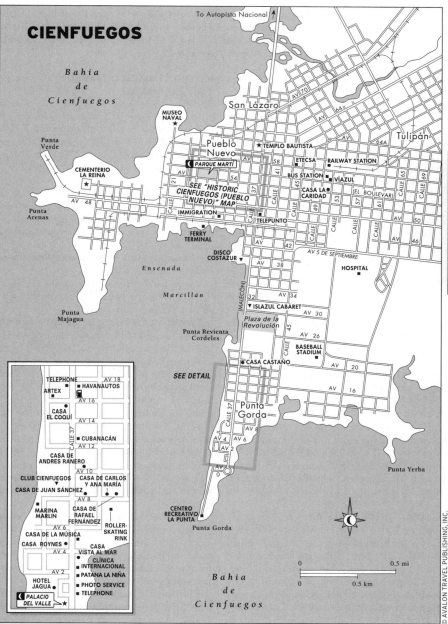

CIENFUEGOS

Bahía
de
Cienfuegos

To Autopista Nacional

Punta
Verde

CEMENTERIO
LA REINA

Punta
Arenas

AV 48

MUSEO
NAVAL

San Lázaro

Tulipán

Pueblo
Nuevo

PARQUE MARTÍ

TEMPLO BAUTISTA

ETECSA   RAILWAY STATION

BUS STATION   VIAZUL

CASA LA
CARIDAD

SEE "HISTORIC
CIENFUEGOS (PUEBLO
NUEVO)" MAP

IMMIGRATION

TELEPUNTO

FERRY
TERMINAL

DISCO
COSTAZUR

AV 5 DE SEPTIEMBRE

HOSPITAL

Ensenada

Marcillán

ISLAZUL CABARET

Plaza de la
Revolución

Punta
Majagua

Punta Revienta
Cordeles

BASEBALL
STADIUM

CASA CASTAÑO

SEE DETAIL

Punta
Gorda

Punta Yerba

TELEPHONE   AV 18
ARTEX   HAVANAUTOS

AV 16

CASA
EL COQUÍ   AV 14

CUBANACÁN

AV 12

CASA DE
ANDRÉS RANERO

AV 10

CLUB CIENFUEGOS   CASA DE CARLOS
CASA DE JUAN SÁNCHEZ   Y ANA MARÍA

AV 8

MARINA   CASA DE
MARLIN   RAFAEL
FERNÁNDEZ
AV 6   ROLLER-
CASA DE LA MÚSICA   SKATING
CASA ROYNES   RINK
AV 4

CASA
VISTA AL MAR
CLÍNICA
INTERNACIONAL
AV 2   PATANA LA NIÑA

HOTEL   PHOTO SERVICE
JAGUA
TELEPHONE

PALACIO
DEL VALLE

CENTRO
RECREATIVO
LA PUNTA

Punta Gorda

Bahía
de
Cienfuegos

0   0.5 mi

0   0.5 km

CIENFUEGOS / VILLA CLARA

© AVALON TRAVEL PUBLISHING, INC.

Note the **Templo Bautista** (esq. Av. 62), a simple Baptist Temple in art nouveau style; and the **Casa de los Leones** (e/ 58 y 60), an old mansion guarded by two life-size bronze lions.

❰ Palacio del Valle

Cienfuegos's architectural pride and joy is a palace (Calle 37, esq. Av. 2, tel. 043/51-1226; daily 10 A.M.–11 P.M.; CUC1) at the tip of Punta Gorda. This architectural stunner—now a restaurant—originated as a modest home for a trader, Celestino Caceres. It passed out of his hands and was given as a wedding present to a member of the local Valle family, who added to it in virile Mogul style, with carved floral motifs, cupped arches, bulbous cupolas, and delicate arabesques. The entire edifice drips with ornate carvings in Venetian alabaster. Note the mural of the Magi on the Carrara marble staircase. A spiral cast-iron staircase deposits you at a rooftop bar and *mirador*.

Three blocks north is the **Club Cienfuegos** (Calle 37, e/ Av. 8 y 12, tel. 043/52-6510), in a gleaming white baroque building erected in 1920 and which served for decades as the yacht club. The lobby exhibits antique silver trophies and other yachting memorabilia.

Necrópolis Tomás Acea

This cemetery (Av. 5 de Septiembre, tel. 043/52-5257; daily 8 A.M.–5 P.M.; CUC1), two kilometers east of town on the road to Rancho Luna, is worth a browse for its impressive neoclassical structures and tombs. It is entered via a gate (erected in 1926) that is a scaled-down replica of the Parthenon, supported by 64 columns. The cemetery overlooks the bay from atop a bluff.

Cementerio La Reina

Anyone with a morbid fascination for graveyards, or a love of baroque architecture, might find this evocative cemetery (Avenida 50 y Calle 7) appealing. The cemetery is entirely of Carrara marble. The walls contain tombs with the bodies of soldiers from the War of Independence. Many of the tombs are caved in, with the skeletons open to view. A *custodio*

is usually available to open the gates and act as a guide. It's reached via the decrepit old Barrio Chino, or Chinatown (from downtown, take Avenida 48, then turn right).

Museo Histórico Naval

This museum (Calle 21, e/ 60 y 62, tel. 043/51-9143; Tues.–Fri. 9 A.M.–5 P.M., Sat.–Sun. 9 A.M.–noon; CUC1), in the former navy headquarters, has motley nautical miscellany, although exhibits range to archaeology and revolutionary history. It was here in 1957 that naval officers rebelled against the Batista regime.

Entertainment and Events

Cienfuegos hosts the week-long *Festival Naútica* in mid-July, featuring a parade of fishermen, water sports, rowing and sailing regattas.

The **Benny Moré International Festival of Popular Music** is held each alternate August.

Locals flock on weekends to the Malecón, between Calles 32 and 36, where simple open-air bars pump out free music.

Traditional Music: The **Casa de la Cultura** (Calle 37 #5615, esq. Av. 58, tel. 043/51-6584; 8:30 A.M.–midnight, daily; free) hosts traditional music and dance and other cultural events, as does the down-to-earth **Café Cantante Benny Moré** (Prado y Av. 54; Sun.–Fri. 9 A.M.–9 P.M., Sat. 9 A.M.–6 P.M.), where the dancing is hot enough to roast the pork. **UNEAC** (Calle 25 #5425, tel. 043/51-6117, www.uneac.com), on the west side of Parque Martí, also has cultural events in an open-air patio, ranging from Afro-Cuban folkloric events to *bolero*. Nearby, the **Café Teatro Terry** hosts rumbas and other live entertainment nightly.

Cabaret and Disco: The **Club Benny Moré** (Av. 54 #2907, e/ 29 y 31, tel. 043/55-1105; Thurs.–Sun. 10 P.M.–3 A.M., CUC8 per pair including bottle of rum and a Coke) is an elegant cabaret theater with live music, comedians, and cabaret acts followed by disco.

The laser-lit **Cabaret Guanaroca** (tel. 043/55-1003) in the Hotel Jagua offers a mediocre *cabaret espectáculo* Wednesday–Monday

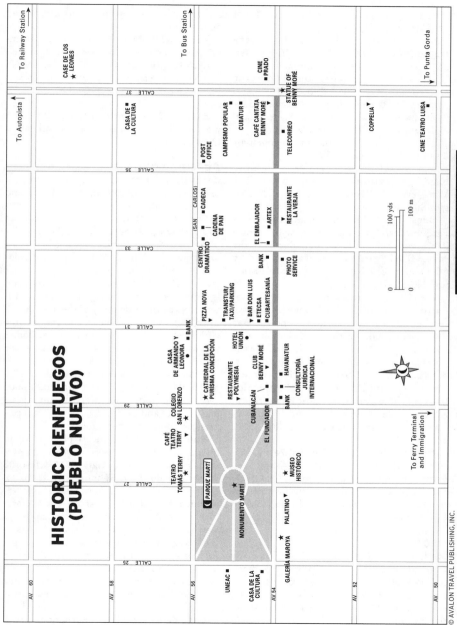

HISTORIC CIENFUEGOS (PUEBLO NUEVO)

To Railway Station

To Autopista

CASE DE LOS LEONES ★

CALLE 37

CASA DE LA CULTURA ■

CALLE 35

To Bus Station

CINE ■ PRADO

■ POST OFFICE

CAMPISMO POPULAR ■

CUBATUR ■

CAFÉ CANTATA BENNY MORÉ ■

STATUE OF ★ BENNY MORÉ

TELECORREO ■

To Punta Gorda

■ CADECA (SAN   CARLOS)

CADENA DE PAN ■

EL EMBAJADOR ■

ARTEX ▼

RESTAURANTE LA VERJA ■

COPPELIA ▼

CINE TEATRO LUISA ■

CALLE 33

CENTRO ■ DRAMATICO

PIZZA NOVA ▼

TRANSTUR/ ■ TAXI/PARKING

▼ BAR DON LUIS

■ ETECSA

■ CUBARTESANÍA

BANK ■

PHOTO SERVICE ■

100 yds
100 m
0
0

CALLE 31

BANK ■

CASA DE ARMANDO Y LEONORA ●

★ CATHEDRAL DE LA PURÍSIMA CONCEPCIÓN

RESTAURANTE ▼ POLYNESIA

HOTEL UNIÓN ●

CLUB ■ BENNY MORÉ

■ HAVANATUR

CONSULTORIA JURIDICA INTERNACIONAL

CALLE 29

COLEGIO SAN LORENZO ★

CUBANACÁN ■

BANK ■

EL FUNDADOR ■

CAFÉ TEATRO TERRY ▼

To Ferry Terminal and Immigration

CALLE 27

TEATRO TOMAS TERRY ★

MUSEO HISTÓRICO ★

《 PARQUE MARTÍ 》

MONUMENTO MARTÍ ★

PALATINO ▼

CALLE 25

GALERÍA MAROYA ★

UNEAC ■

CASA DE LA CULTURA ■

AV   60
AV   58
AV   56
AV   54
AV   52
AV   50

CIENFUEGOS / VILLA CLARA

© AVALON TRAVEL PUBLISHING, INC.

at 11 P.M. (CUC5), followed by disco. Watch for scams by the wait staff!

Locals also catch *son* and *salsa* riffs at **Centro Cultural Artex** (Calle 35, e/ 16 y 18, tel. 043/55-1255), with outdoor music and dancing, including Sundays 2–4 P.M.; **Disco Costazur** (Av. 40, esq. Calle 35; Wed.–Sun. 9 P.M.– 2 A.M.; CUC3); and at **Centro Recreativo La Punta** (no tel.; 10 A.M.–6 P.M. and 8 P.M.–1 A.M. daily) at the tip of the peninsula.

The hot spot at last visit was the open-air **Casa de la Música** (Calle 37, e/ Av. 4 y 6, tel. 043/55-2320; CUC5 per pair), with live bands—everything from rap to Los Van Van—every Friday and Saturday at 10 P.M. plus Sunday at 5 P.M.

Bars: The **Palatino,** on the west side of Parque Martí, is a pleasant spot to savor a drink while being serenaded. Nearby, the smoke-filled **Bar Don Luis** (Calle 31, e/ 54 y 56; noon–midnight) is a popular hole-in-the-wall bar good for cheap rum.

For elegance, check out the contempo waterfront bar in the **Hotel Jagua** (24 hours), serving international cocktails; and the **Bar Terrazas** upstairs in the Hotel Unión, with live music nightly at 10 P.M. I also like the terrace bar of **Club Cienfuegos** (Calle 37, e/ Av. 8 y 12, tel. 043/52-6510; Sun.–Fri. 10 P.M.– 1 A.M., Sat. until 2 A.M.; CUC3–5), which has views across the bay; musicians perform. A dress code applies. A second bar downstairs has pool and billiards tables (Sat.–Sun. 10 A.M.–8 A.M.).

Other: The **Teatro Tomás Terry** (tel. 043/55-5361, box office 11 A.M.–3 P.M. and 90 minutes prior to performances; CUC1) on the north side of Parque Martí, hosts performances ranging from classical symphony to live salsa music.

Recreation

Marina Marlin Cienfuegos (Calle 35, e/ 6 y 8, tel. 043/55-1241, fax 043/55-1275, marinacfg@nautica.cfg.cyt.cu) offers deep-sea fishing (from CUC150 for up to four people) and scuba diving (CUC30 one dive, with instructor) from Hotel Rancho Luna. You can rent

sailcraft (CUC16 per hour) plus kayaks and pedal-boats.

The **Hotel Unión** has a gym, aerobics, swimming pool, and sauna, all open to the public.

Club Cienfuegos (Calle 37, e/ Av. 8 y 12; Sun.–Fri. 10 P.M.–1 A.M., Sat. until 2 A.M.), has crazy cars (*carros locos,* CUC1), go-karts, and tennis.

Estadio 5 de Septiembre (Av. 20, e/ 45 y 55, tel. 043/51-3644) hosts baseball games October–May.

Accommodations

Casas Particulares: Cienfuegos has scores of *casas particulares,* notably in Punta Gorda and along Calle 50.

Pueblo Nuevo: An excellent option is **Casa de Armando y Leonora** (Av. 56 #2927, e/ 29 y 31, tel. 043/51-6143; CUC20), one block east of Parque Martí, in a much dilapidated colonial home. The three rooms are basic, as are the dour shared bathrooms. However, the place is highly recommended by past guests and I, too, enjoyed the hospitality of the hosts, dedicated socialists who make all comers welcome with lively conversation. Leonora welcomes you with her "Coctel Leonora" and gets rave reviews for her special chicken dish.

Casa La Caridad (Av. 54 #4923, e/ 49 y 51, tel. 043/51-9056) has two air-conditioned rooms in an independent apartment with a patio terrace and garden. Each room has a private bathroom with hot water.

Punta Gorda: The nicest places—all in middle-class 1950s homes—are between Avenidas 6 and 14, east of Calle 37. My favorite is ◖ **Casa de Juan Sánchez** (Av. 8 #3703, e/ 37 y 39, tel. 043/51-7986; CUC25 including breakfast), a striking architectural statement built in 1959, with original furnishings and heaps of plate glass and stained glass in the lounge, which runs through to a beautiful rear garden with shade trees. It offers one clean, spacious air-conditioned room, well-lit and cross-ventilated, with a large handsome bathroom in splendid condition. The host is a delight.

Casa de Rafael "Pipe" Fernández (Av. 8

#3903, e/ 39 y 41, tel. 043/52-5274; CUC20–25) is a nicely furnished, cross-ventilated home with a single room full of antiques and private hot-water bathroom. It has front and rear gardens. **Casa de Carlos y Ana María** (Av. 8 #3901, tel. 043/51-6624; CUC20–25), next door, is virtually identical but has two air-conditioned rooms with private bathrooms.

I also like **Casa El Coquí** (Calle 37 #1407, e/ 14 y 16, tel. 043/52-5460; CUC20–25), a spacious 1950s bungalow with three air-conditioned rooms, each with fans and private hot-water bath. Decor is uninspired, but there's a large garden and secure parking.

Vista al Mar (Calle 37 #210, e/ 2 y 4, tel. 043/51-8378, gertrudisternotea@yahoo.es; CUC20) has one room with a separate lounge, independent entrance, and clean, modern hot-water bathroom, plus a rear terrace and tiny beach overlooking the bay.

Casa de Andrés Ranero (Av. 10 #3707, e/ 37 y 39, tel. 043/51-7993, josera@jagua.cfg.sld.cu; CUC20–25) is a great option and has two well-lit air-conditioned rooms, each with fridges, pleasant furnishings, and clean, handsome hot-water bathrooms. Guests have their own small lounge. Meals are served on an outside patio with fish pond and parrots (a small swimming pool was planned). There's secure parking.

Casa Castaño (Calle 37 #1824, esq. 20, tel. 043/52-5251; CUC20) has two rooms furnished with antiques, fans, air-conditioning, and a large shared hot-water bathroom. There's a large lounge with TV and music system, and meals are served in a cozy atrium patio or a handsome rear patio with a grill. It has secure parking.

Hotels: The **Hostal Palacio Azul** (Calle 37 #1201, e/ 12 y 14, tel. 043/55-5828, comercial@union.cfg.cyt.cu; CUC35 s, CUC38 d year-round, including breakfast) offers seven huge rooms in a restored mansion on the Malecón. They're attractive, with high ceilings and colonial tile floors. Each has satellite TV, refrigerator, and safe. It has a small but charming bar and restaurant.

The **Hotel Jagua** (Calle 37, e/ 0 y 2, tel. 043/55-1003, fax 043/55-1245, reservas@jagua.co.cu; CUC60 s, CUC85 d low season; CUC74 s, CUC105 d high season) boasts contemporary furnishings and lively color schemes in its gracious lobby and 149 large, air-conditioned rooms plus 13 poolside *cabinas*. All rooms have satellite TVs, safes, and attractive bathrooms with marble countertops. Fifth-floor rooms offer views over Palacio Valle and the bay. Facilities include a tour desk, 24-hour lobby bar with Internet service, a splendid bayside bar, swimming pool, shopping gallery, rental cars and scooters, and a cabaret. The buffet restaurant, however, fails miserably. (Gran Caribe.)

⟪ Hotel Unión (Av. 54 y Calle 31, tel. 043/55-1020, fax 043/55-1685, comercial@union.cfg.cyt.cu; CUC80 s, CUC90 d, CUC100 junior suite, CUC130 suite, CUC170 signature suite, year-round), one block east of Parque Martí, is a beautifully restored neoclassical re-creation of a 19th-century hotel. It has 49 air-conditioned rooms (11 are junior suites, two are suites, one is a signature suite) arrayed around a courtyard with fountain. Rooms have satellite TVs, telephones, radios, mini-fridges, and safes. Facilities include an open-air pool in a Romanesque setting, plus a sauna, whirlpool tub, gym, pharmacy, shop, tour desk, business center, car rental, and commendable restaurant. (Gran Caribe.)

Food

Legal *paladares* had all been forced to close at last visit.

Budget hounds might try **Café Cantante Benny Moré** (Prado y Av. 54; Sun.–Fri. 9 A.M.–9 P.M., Sat. 9 A.M.–6 P.M.), serving simple *criollo* fare for pesos. No tank tops are allowed.

Nearby, **Pizza Nova** (Calle 31, e/ 54 y 56, tel. 043/55-2020; noon–11 P.M. daily) has a modestly elegant Mediterranean feel suitable to its menu of basic pizzas and pastas (from CUC5).

On the south side of Parque Martí, the **Palatino** (tel. 043/55-1244; 9 A.M.–11 P.M.) serves sandwiches and snacks. For more substantive fare, try **Restaurante Polinesia** (tel. 043/51-5723; daily noon–3 P.M. and 3–11 P.M.), on the east side of the plaza. It has a Tahitian motif and hints of the South Seas (think pineapple) find their way onto the *criollo* menu (CUC5 and under). For colonial atmosphere, opt for **Restaurante La Verja** (Av. 54, e/ 33 y 35, tel. 043/51-6311; daily noon–3 P.M. and 6–10 P.M.), which serves *criollo* staples (lobster CUC10) in a colonial home full of antiques.

Despite the filthy tablecloths, plan on dining at **Palacio de Valle** (tel. 043/55-1226; 10 A.M.–10 P.M. daily) for the remarkable ambience (see *Sights,* earlier in this section). It has a large seafood menu, including lobster prepared six ways (but overpriced at CUC25), though the dishes are merely average. Carmen Iznaga tickles the ivories of an out-of-tune grand piano.

The nicest place in town by far is the overly air-conditioned **Restaurante 1869** (Av. 54 y Calle 31, tel. 043/55-1020; 7–9:45 A.M., noon–2:45 P.M., and 7–9:45 P.M. daily) in the Hotel Unión, with elegant period decor. The menu features paella (CUC12), skewered shrimp (CUC15.50), and an excellent calamari in tomato sauce (CUC10).

Coppelia (Calle 37, esq. 52; 11 A.M.–11 P.M. Tues.–Sun.) is good for ice cream (pesos only). For an espresso or cappuccino head to the **Café Teatro Terry** on the north side of Parque Martí, with an arbor-shaded patio.

Shopping

Galería Maroya (Av. 54 #2506, tel. 043/55-1208; Mon.–Sat. 8 A.M.– 6 P.M.), on the west side of Parque Martí, has a splendid collection of arts and crafts: leatherwork, batiks, carvings, and paintings. Check out Fidel López's incredible wooden galleons.

Casa El Embajador (Av. 54, esq. 29, tel. 043/55-2144; Mon.–Sat. 9 A.M.–5:30 P.M., Sun. 9 A.M.–12:30 P.M.) is a fully stocked rum and cigar store in the Casa del Fundador.

Information and Services

The following *burós de turismo* are geared to selling excursions: **Cubanacán** (Av. 54, e/ 29 y 31, tel. 043/55-1680; Mon.–Fri. 8 A.M.–5 P.M., Sat. 8 A.M.–1 P.M.) and **Havanatur**

Fidel López had been at work six months on this galleon, for sale at Galería Maroya.

© CHRISTOPHER P. BAKER

(Av. 54 #2906, e/ 29 y 31, tel. 043/51-1370; daily 8:30 A.M.–4:30 P.M.).

The **post office** (Av. 56 and Calle 35, tel. 043 /55-1686) is one block west of the Prado.

Etecsa (Av. 54, e/ 35 y 37; daily 8:30 A.M.–6:30 P.M.), opposite the Hotel Union, has international phone and Internet service. Etecsa also has an Internet café upstairs in the bus station.

Banks include **Banco Financiero Internacional** (Av. 54 y Calle 29; Mon.–Fri. 8 A.M.–3 P.M.), on the southeast corner of Parque Martí, and **Bandec** (Av. 56 y Calle 31). **Cadeca** (Av. 56, e/ 33 y 35) also converts foreign currency for pesos.

The **Clínica Internacional** (Calle 37, e/ 2 y 4, tel. 043/55-1622), opposite the Hotel Jagua, has a doctor and nurse on 24-hour call, and a small pharmacy (consultations cost CUC25).

Inmigración (Av. 48, e/ 29 y 31, tel 043/52-4437; Mon.–Thurs. 8 A.M.–noon and 1–3 P.M.) office can issue *prórrogas*. **Asistur** (Calle 52 #3111, e/ 32 y 34, tel./fax 043/55-1624, asisturcfg@cfg.intermar.cu) can provide emergency assistance. The **Consultoría Jurídica Internacional** (Calle 54 #2904, e/ 29 y 31, tel. 043/55-1572, fax 043/55-1323) provides legal services.

Getting There and Away

By Air: The **Aeropuerto Internacional Jaime Gonzalez** (tel. 043/55-2047) is five kilometers northeast of town. It was not functioning at last visit.

By Bus: The interprovincial bus terminal (Calle 49 e/ Av. 56 y 58) is six blocks east of the Prado. **Víazul** (tel. 043/51-5720) buses serve Cienfuegos daily en route between Havana and Trinidad, departing Havana at 8:15 A.M. and 1 P.M. (CUC25). Buses depart Cienfuegos for Havana at 9:25 A.M. and 4:50 P.M.; for Trinidad at 12:20 P.M. and 5 A.M. (CUC6); and for Varadero at 4 A.M. (CUC16).

Astro (tel. 043/52-3604) buses depart Cienfuegos for Havana at 6 A.M., 10 A.M., 12:30 P.M., 3 P.M., and 11:50 P.M. (five hours via the Autopista; CUC17 *especial*, CUC14 *regular*); Aguada Pasajeros (CUC5) and Jagüey Grande (CUC3)

eight times daily; Camagüey at 8 A.M. (alternate days; CUC13); Matanzas at 2:30 P.M.; Santa Clara at 9 A.M. and 2 P.M. (CUC13); and Santiago at 4 P.M. (alternate days; CUC31 *especial*, CUC25 *regular*); and Trinidad at 6:30 A.M. (CUC3).

By Train: The train station (Calle 49, e/ Av. 58 y 60, tel. 043/52-5495) is one block north of the bus station. Trains depart for Cienfuegos from Havana at 7 A.M. and 6 P.M. (CUC11); and from Santa Clara at 5:20 P.M. (CUC2.10, second-class only). You can also catch an *especial* from Havana to Santa Clara and then connect to Cienfuegos, which lies at the end of a branch line off the main Havana–Santiago railroad. Trains depart Cienfuegos for Havana at 7 A.M. and 2 A.M.; and from Santa Clara at 4:10 P.M.

By Private Yacht: Arriving yachters must report for clearance at the **Guardía Frontera** post, one kilometer south of the Jagua fortress on the western shores of the entrance to Bahía de Cienfuegos. **Marina Marlin Cienfuegos** (Calle 35, e/ 6 y 8, tel. 043/55-1241, fax 043/55-1275, marinacfg@nautica.cfg.cyt.cu) has moorings for 30 yachts (from CUC0.45 per foot), with water, electricity, and diesel.

Getting Around

Bus #9 runs the length of Calle 37 (10 centavos), but service is unpredictable.

Horse-drawn taxis (*coches*) are the main means of getting around; they ply Calle 37 and the major thoroughfares; one peso (foreigners are usually charged CUC1).

Cubataxi (Av. 50 #3508, esq. 37, tel. 043/55-9145) charges CUC1.80 between the Hotel Jagua and downtown, as does **Transtur** (Av. 52, e/ 29 y 31, tel. 043/55-2014).

You can rent cars from **Cubacar** (tel. 043/55-1700), in the Hotel La Unión; **Havanautos** (Calle 37 y Av. 18, tel. 043/55-1211); **Transtur** (tel. 043/55-2166), at the Hotel Jagua; **Micar** (Calle 37 y Av. 28, tel. 043/55-1605); and **Rex** (tel. 043/55-6059).

Marina Marlin Cienfuegos (Calle 35, e/ 6 y 8, tel. 043/55-1241) offers bay excursions aboard the *Flipper* catamaran for two or more

CIENFUEGOS / VILLA CLARA

passengers (CUC16 per person). Excursions are also offered aboard the older *Jagua*.

There are gas stations at Calle 37, e/ Av. 18; about 10 kilometers east of town just beyond the turnoff for Trinidad, on the road to Rancho Luna; and at the north end of Calle 37, at the entrance to town.

◖ JARDÍN BOTÁNICO SOLEDAD

This splendid garden (tel. 043/54-5115; daily 8 A.M.–4:30 P.M.; CUC2.50), is about 10 kilometers east of Cienfuegos, on the main coast road to Trinidad, between the communities of San Antón and Guaos. It was begun in 1899 by a New Englander, Edward Atkins, who owned vast sugar estates in the area and brought in Harvard botanists to develop hardier and more productive sugarcane strains. Later, Harvard University assumed control under a 99-year lease, and a general collection making up one of the tropical world's finest botanical gardens—the Harvard Biological Laboratory—was amassed. Since the Revolution, the garden has been maintained by the Cuban Academy of Science's Institute of Botany.

Pathways lead through the 94-hectare garden, reached along an avenue of royal palms. It harbors a collection of some 2,000 species, 70 percent of which are exotics, including rare tropical plants with important medicinal uses. A bamboo collection has 23 species. Of rubber trees, there are 89 species; of cactus, 400. The prize collection is the 307 varieties of palms. The facility includes a laboratory (in Harvard House) and library. A basic café serves drinks.

The bus from Cienfuegos to Cumanayagua passes the garden. A taxi will cost about CUC40 round-trip.

PLAYA RANCHO LUNA AND PASACABALLO

A turnoff at San Antón leads southwest to the coast and the entrance to the Bahía de Cienfuegos at Pasacaballo. En route there's a pleasant beach, Playa Rancho Luna, with calm turquoise waters. The road then swings west past the **Faro**

Luna and follows the rocky coast eight kilometers to Pasacaballo, facing the Castillo de Jagua across the 400-meter-wide mouth of Cienfuegos Bay, 22 kilometers from Cienfuegos.

Delfinario

This delphinarium (tel. 043/54-8120; Thurs.–Tues. 9:30 A.M.–4 P.M.; CUC10 adults, CUC6 children; cameras CUC1, videos CUC2), in an enclosed lagoon at Rancho Luna, offers sea lion and dolphin shows at 10 A.M. and sea lion–only shows at 2 P.M. You can kiss the dolphins for CUC5, and even swim with them (10:30 A.M.–4:30 P.M.; CUC50 adults, CUC33 children). There's a snack bar.

Recreation and Entertainment

Water sports outlets on Playa Rancho Luna offer catamarans and pedal-boats. Scuba diving is offered at the **Faro Luna Dive Center** (tel. 043/54-8040, dcfluna@acuc.cfg.cyt.cu) betwixt the Hotel Faro Luna and the Delfinario. Prices range from CUC25 for one dive to CUC380 for 20 dives. At least eight ships lie amid the coral reefs. Diving is also offered at Hotel Carrusel Faro Luna (tel. 043/54-8012).

Villa Rancho Luna (10 A.M.–9 P.M.) is a beachfront restaurant hosting the **Discoteca Delfín Azúl** on Saturday 9 P.M.–2 A.M.

Accommodations

Casas Particulares: There are several private rentals to choose from near the Hotel Faro Luna, including **Casa de Julio Cortizo Hernández** (tel. 043/51-5744; CUC25), with one simply appointed air-conditioned room with fan, fridge, and a clean modern bathroom.

◖ **Finca los Colorados B&B** (Carretera de Pasacaballo Km 18, Playa Rancho Luna, tel. 043/54-8044, fax 043/51-3265, fincaloscolorados@casapineiro.com; CUC30) is a remarkable *casa particular* enjoying a breeze-swept position on the cliffs 100 meters east of the lighthouse. This whitewashed contemporary charmer is the European-style home of English-speaking José Piñeiro, a catering professional who prepares classical Cuban cuisine in a kitchen boasting all modern facilities. The home abounds in antiques and modern furnishings, with walls painted in Roman-style motifs. Two modestly furnished, cross-ventilated rooms have metal-frame antique beds, fans, and private hot-water bathrooms. You can dine on an outside patio beneath an arbor, with a barbecue pit and bar. There's even a kids' playground.

Hotels: The **Hotel Pasacaballo** was being used exclusively for Venezuelan medical clients at last visit.

The recently restored Soviet-era **Hotel Rancho Luna** (Carretera de Rancho Luna Km 18, tel. 043/55-1484; CUC55 s, CUC70 d low season; CUC65 s, CUC80 d high season) is a staple of Canadian and European tour groups. Now boasting lively tropical pastels and rattan furnishings, it is a pleasant option with 225 rooms, all nicely furnished, with yellow, blue, and ocher color schemes, tile floors, satellite TVs, telephones, and delightful modern bathrooms of gleaming white and Atlantic-blue tiles. Two rooms are for guests with disabilities. Facilities include two restaurants, massage, tour and car rental desks, water sports, games room, and a large swimming pool.

Identically furnished as the Hotel Rancho Luna, the **Hotel Carrusel Faro Luna** (Carretera de Pasacaballos Km 18, Playa Rancho Luna, tel. 043/54-8030, fax 043/54-8062, carpeta@fluna.cfg.cyt.cu; CUC44 s, CUC55 d low season; CUC52 s, CUC66 d high season, including breakfast) has 46 spacious, air-conditioned rooms, with satellite TVs and balconies. It has a small swimming pool, shop, and restaurant and offers scuba diving. (Cubanacán.)

Getting There

Buses ostensibly depart Cienfuegos three times daily (50 centavos; 45 minutes). A taxi will cost you about CUC12. Ferries leave for Rancho Luna on a regular basis from the terminal on Avenida 46 and Calle 25 (CUC1).

CASTILLO DE JAGUA

Across the bay from Pasacaballo sits a 17th-century Spanish fort, Castillo de Jagua, guard-ing the entrance to the Bahía de Cienfuegos. The original fortress was expanded in the 18th century to defend against the English Royal Navy. A ghost—the Blue Lady—is thought to haunt the small fortress that overlooks a fishing village perched above the water.

Up on the hill behind Jagua is **Ciudad Nuclear** (Nuclear City), a modern city built in the 1980s to house workers constructing Cuba's first nuclear power station nearby at Juragua. The half-completed reactor, about two kilometers west of town, stands idle. Construction began in 1983, when Soviet aid flowed freely. The initial project called for four reactors, but that was downsized to two 417,000 kilowatt reactors, either of which could save around two million tons of oil a year. Construction was mothballed in September 1992 after Cuba announced it could not meet the financial terms set by the new Russian government. When construction ceased, assembly on one of the reactors was about 90 percent complete (the second reactor was about 20 percent complete). Meanwhile, maintenance crews attempt to keep the reactors rust-free while awaiting the day when construction resumes.

Getting There

A ferry departs the wharf on Avenida 46 and Calle 25 in Cienfuegos at 8 A.M., 1 P.M. and 5 P.M. (30 minutes; one peso or CUC1, depending on your luck). A ferry also operates between Pasacaballo, across the bay.

You can also get there by road. Exit Cienfuegos on Calle 37 past the industrial complexes. Keep the bay on your left.

MUSEO DEL VAPOR

Central Maltiempo, near the town of Cruces, 30 kilometers northeast of Cienfuegos, is Cuba's only sugar mill producing refined sugar. The *central* is five kilometers southwest of Cruces, on the road to San Fernando de Camarones. It is best known for its steam engine museum and more than 20 kilometers of winding narrow-gauge track. The term "museum" is a stretch. Six old steam trains have been abandoned inside a near-derelict shed. There is no

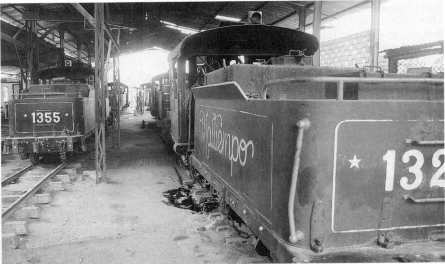

© CHRISTOPHER P. BAKER

steam trains at the Museo del Vapor, Maltiempo

information whatsoever, nor a guide, but serious railway buffs might get a thrill. An annual **Festival Internacional del Vapor** (International Steam Festival) is held here each November, when as many as 25 working steam locomotives are displayed.

If diverting from the Autopista to see the museum, turn south at Ranchuelo. It's 16 kilometers to Cruces from there.

THE CIRCUITO SUR

The Circuito Sur coast road dips and rises eastward of Cienfuegos with the Sierra Escambray to the north. A series of beaches lie hidden in coves at the mouths of rivers that wash down from the hills, as at the mouth of the **Río La Jutía,** 42 kilometers from Cienfuegos, and eight kilometers farther east, at **Playa Inglés,** where you are deposited beside a beautiful and lonesome beach with fishing boats and a rustic hut that serves *refrescos* and snacks to local fishermen.

Hacienda La Vega (tel. 043/55-1126; 9 A.M.–6 P.M. daily), about three kilometers west of Playa Inglés, is a cattle farm—*vaquería*—where horseback riding is offered (CUC4 per hour) and demonstrations of traditional farm life are

given. A roadside restaurant serves snacks and *criollo* fare. Lather up with insect repellent!

Three kilometers east of the turnoff for Playa Ingles, you'll cross the **Río Yaguanabo** and pass into Sancti Spíritus Province.

Cueva Martín Infierno

This stupendous cavern, 27 kilometers east of Cienfuegos, is reached by following the Río Yaguanabo through the Valle de Yaguanabo. It's a stunningly scenic drive as you cut into the foothills of the ragged Escambray. The cave boasts Latin America's largest stalagmite—67 meters tall—as well as mineralogical rarities such as gypsum flowers (*flores de yeso*). At last visit it was closed to the public, but speleologists can visit with advance notice; contact the **Sociedad Espeleológica de Cuba** (tel. 07/209-2885, angel@fanj.cutlcu) in Havana.

Accommodations and Food

Villa Guajimico (tel. 043/55-1206, www .cubamarviajes.com; CUC28 s, CUC30 d low season; CUC35 s, CUC40 d high season) sits at the mouth of the Río La Jutía. Some of the 51 air-conditioned brick cabins line a pretty little white-sand beach in the river estuary. Others stair-step a steep hill where a swimming pool and restaurant offer views. All cabins are modestly yet pleasantly furnished, with satellite TVs, private bathrooms, and hot water. Services include a medical facility, car rental, scuba diving, and catamarans. (Cubamar.)

SIERRA ESCAMBRAY

The Sierra Escambray, Cuba's second-highest mountain range, lies mostly within Cienfuegos Province, descending gradually into Villa Clara Province to the north, edging into Sancti Spíritus Province to the east, and dropping steeply to the southern coast. The Escambray's highest peaks and densest forests are protected in Parque Nacional Topes de Collantes, in the chain's southeast corner (see *Gran Parque Natural Topes de Collantes* in the *Sancti Spíritus* chapter). The mountains reach 1,140 meters atop Pico San Juan.

In the late 1950s, these mountains were the site of a revolutionary front against Fulgencio Batista, led by Che Guevara. After the revolutionaries triumphed in 1959, the Escambray hid another band of olive green–clad rebels, this time counterrevolutionaries who opposed Castro. The CIA helped finance and arm these resistance fighters, whom the Castro regime tagged "bandits." They were split into various rival groups, however, and had no philosophical program other than to resist Castro. Castro formed counterinsurgency units called Battal-ions of Struggle Against Bandits, and forcibly evacuated campesinos to deny the anti-Castroites local support. The *bandidos* weren't eradicated until 1966. A museum in Trinidad tells the Communist government's version of *la lucha contra los bandidos.*

Access from Cienfuegos is from the Circuito Sur, via the valley of the Río Mataguá and the community of La Sierrita, about 30 kilometers east of Cienfuegos (the road continues to Topes de Collantes, but was badly washed out at last visit and was suitable for 4WD only). It's a stupendously scenic route that rises past sheer-walled, cave-riddled limestone *mogotes,* at their most impressive near the town of **San Blas,** eight kilometers east of La Sierrita. San Blas sits in the lee of great cliffs where huge stalactites and stalagmites are exposed in an open cave high atop the mountains.

🄲 El Nicho

This recreational site (no tel.; daily 8:30 A.M.–6:30 P.M.; CUC5), seven kilometers north of La Sierrita, is popular with locals for its spectacular waterfalls and chilly pools good for swimming. The mountain vistas are superb. Simple meals are served at a *ranchón,* where horseback riding is also offered (CUC2 per hour).

If driving, you'll need a four-wheel drive, as the access road is in terrible shape. You can take a *colectivo* to Cumanayagua from either Cienfuegos or Santa Clara; another *colectivo* runs from Cumanayagua at 5:30 A.M. and 5 P.M. Excursions are offered from Santa Clara.

Santa Clara and Vicinity

SANTA CLARA

Santa Clara (pop. 175,000), 300 kilometers east of Havana, is the provincial capital of Villa Clara. Straddling the Carretera Central and within five minutes of the Autopista, it is strategically located at the center of Cuba. The city was established within the confluence of the Ríos Bélico and Cubanicay in 1689, when residents of Remedios grew tired of constant pirate raids, pulled up stakes, and moved inland. Much later it functioned as a plum in Cuba's Wars of Independence, and again during the battle to topple Batista. On December 31, 1958, Che Guevara's Rebel Army attacked the town and derailed a troop train carrying reinforcements and U.S. armaments bound for Oriente. Two days later, the Rebel Army captured the city, which became known as *el último reducto de la tiranía batistiana* (the last fortress of Batista's tyranny). Within 24 hours, the dictator fled the island.

As Minister of Industry, Che Guevara developed a soft spot for the city. Today Santa Clara is an important industrial town. The suburbs contain many factories. It is also home to the University de las Villas. A full-scale zoo covering five hectares was being prepared at last visit and will include monkeys, lions, ostriches, and leopards.

One day's sightseeing will suffice.

Orientation

Santa Clara is a large city, and although laid out roughly in a rectilinear grid of one-way streets, it's complicated to get around. The city is encircled by a ring road (*circunvalación*). The Carretera Central enters from the west and arcs south around the town center, accessed from the west by Rafael Tristá and from the south by Calle Cuba, which run to Parque Vidal, the main square (Calle Marta Abreu runs west from the square and connects with the Carretera Central). The Carretera Central continues east to Placetas.

Independencia, one block north of Parque Vidal, runs parallel to Marta Abreu, and (eastward) crosses the Río Cubanicay and (as Avenida de Liberación) leads to Remedios. (Independencia between Zayas to the west and Maceo to the east is a pedestrian precinct known as El Bulevar—The Boulevard.)

Máximo Gómez (Calle Cuba) and Luis Estévez (Calle Colón) run perpendicular to Abreu, on the west and east side of the park. Maceo (one block east of Estévez) runs north seven blocks to the railway station and becomes Avenida Sagua, which leads to Sagua la Grande and the north coast. Enrique Villanueva (one block west of Máximo Gómez) runs south to Manicaragua.

Parque Vidal

This large paved square is named for the revolutionary hero Leoncio Vidal, who—according to a monument—was killed at this exact spot. A curiosity of the square is its double-wide

SANTA CLARA

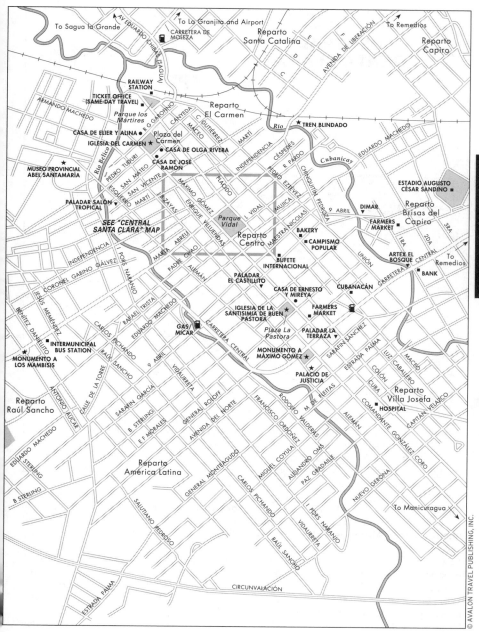

To Sagua la Grande

To La Granjita and Airport

AV. EDUARDO CHIBÁS (SAGUA)

CARRETERA DE MOLEZA

Reparto Santa Catalina

To Remedios

Reparto Capiro

AVENIDA DE LIBERACIÓN

ARMANDO MACHEDO

RAILWAY STATION

TICKET OFFICE (SAME-DAY TRAVEL)

Parque los Mártires

R.G. GASOFINO

CANYEDA

C. GUTIÉRREZ

MACEO

MARTÍ

Reparto El Carmen

Río

TREN BLINDADO

Cubanicay

EDUARDO MACHEDO

CASA DE ELIER Y ALINA

IGLESIA DEL CARMEN

Plaza del Carmen

CASA DE OLGA RIVERA

Río Belico

PEDRO TUDURI

SAN MATEO

SAN VICENTE

CASA DE JOSÉ RAMÓN

MUSEO PROVINCIAL ABEL SANTAMARÍA

ESQUERRA

SAN MARTÍ

ZAYAS

MÁXIMO GÓMEZ

ENRIQUE VILLUENDAS

PLÁCIDO

INDEPENDENCIA

CÉSPEDES

R. PARDO

PEDRO ESTÉVEZ

CHINGUITIN PEDROZA

ESTADIO AUGUSTO CÉSAR SANDINO

PALADAR SALÓN TROPICAL

SEE "CENTRAL SANTA CLARA" MAP

Parque Vidal

VIDAL

MUJICA

MAESTRA NICOLÁS

9 ABRIL

DIMAR

FARMERS MARKET

Reparto Brisas del Capiro

1RA

2DA

3RA

MARÍA

ABREU

Reparto Centro

BAKERY

CAMPISMO POPULAR

UNIÓN

ARTEX EL BOSQUE

CARRETERA CENTRAL

To Remedios

INDEPENDENCIA

CORONEL GABINO GÁLVEZ

I. PORS NARANJO

PADRE CHAO

ALEMÁN

BUFETE INTERNACIONAL

BANK

JESÚS MENÉNDEZ

BENÍTEZ DANIELITO

RAFAEL TRISTÁ

EDUARDO MACHEDO

PALADAR EL CASTILLITO

CASA DE ERNESTO Y MIREYA

CUBANACÁN

INTERMUNICIPAL BUS STATION

CARLOS PICHANDO

RAÚL SANCHO

GAS MICAR

IGLESIA DE LA SANTISIMIA DE BUEN PASTORA

FARMERS MARKET

MONUMENTO A LOS MAMBISIS

9 ABRIL

VIDAURRETA

CARRETERA CENTRAL

Plaza La Pastora

PALADAR LA TERRAZA

SARAFÍN SÁNCHEZ

ESTRADA PALMA

LUZ CABALLERO

MACEO

Reparto Raúl Sancho

ANTONIO AUCAR

CALLE DE LA TORRE

SARAFÍN GARCÍA

B. STERLING

E.F MORALES

MONUMENTO A MÁXIMO GÓMEZ

GENERAL ROLOFF

AVENIDA DEL NORTE

FRANCISCO ORDÓÑEZ

RODOLFO VALDERAS

M. DE FLEITAS

PALACIO DE JUSTICIA

COLÓN

CUBA

COMANDANTE GONZÁLEZ CORO

CAPITÁN VELAZCO

Reparto Villa Josefa

HOSPITAL

EDUARDO MACHEDO

STERLING

B. STERLING

Reparto América Latina

SALUTIANO PEDROSO

GENERAL MONTEAGUDO

CARLOS PICHANDO

MIGUEL COYULA

ALEJANDRO OMS

PAZ GRADAILE

I. PORS NARANJO

VIDAURRETA

RAÚL SANCHO

NUEVO GERONA

ALEMÁN

To Manicuragua

ESTRADA PALMA

CIRCUNVALACIÓN

CIENFUEGOS / VILLA CLARA

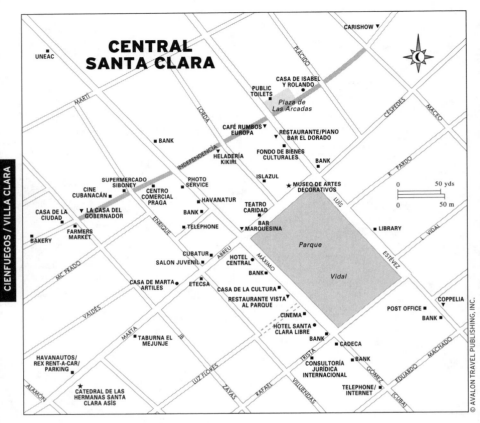

sidewalk. In colonial days, this was divided by an iron fence, and whites perambulated on the inner half while blacks kept to the outside. In springtime, the park blazes with pink blossoms of *guasíma* trees and poinciana, full of noisy Cuban blackbirds. The bandstand at its center is used for concerts on weekends.

Keeping her eye on things is a bronze **Monumento Marta Abreu de Estévez.** Abreu (1845–1904) was a local heroine and philanthropist who funded construction of the **Teatro la Caridad** (Marta Abreu, e/ Máximo Gómez y Lorda, tel. 0422/20-5548; daily 9 A.M.– 5 P.M.; CUC1), built in 1885 on the north side of the square. Albeit tragically deteriorated due to water damage, the spectacular four-

story, horseshoe-shaped theater, which Enrico Caruso considered a fitting venue, boasts its original cast-iron seats plus stunning murals representing the works of Shakespeare and Spanish writers.

Fifty meters east of the theater is the **Museo de Artes Decorativos** (e/ Luis Estévez y Lorda, tel. 0422/20-5368; Mon., Wed., and Thurs. 9 A.M.–6 P.M., Fri.–Sat. 1–10 P.M., Sun. 6–10 P.M.; CUC2 entrance, CUC1 guide, CUC1 per photo), featuring an eclectic array of stunning colonial antiques and furniture. Note the beautiful *ventrales* above the inner courtyard, and the so-called Empire Hall, with its delicate parquetry.

On the square's east side is the old **Palacio**

© CHRISTOPHER P. BAKER

A massive bronze statue of Che looms over Plaza de la Revolución.

Provincial, now housing the city *biblioteca.* The imposing neoclassical frontage is supported by Ionic columns. The building dates to 1922 and occupies the site of the original city hall.

While here, the ecclesiastically inclined might stroll west along Marta Abreu three blocks to the **Catedral de las Hermanas Santa Clara Asís** (9 A.M.–noon daily), with a statue of the Virgin Mary in the entrance.

◖ Monumento Ernesto Che Guevara

Looming over this wide hilltop Plaza de la Revolución on the west side of the city, at the west end of Rafael Tristá, the monument comprises a massive bronze statue of Che bearing his rifle. Beneath the monument, on the north side, is the excellent **Museo de Che** (tel. 0422/20-5878; Tues.–Sat. 8 A.M.–9 P.M., Sun. 8 A.M.–5 P.M.; free), which worships the Argentinian revolutionary and has a detailed account of the capture of Santa Clara in December 1958. Che Guevara's history is traced

from childhood, with many photos from his youthful journey through Latin America. Exhibits include his pistol from the Sierra Maestra, letters to and from Fidel, his green PVC jacket with brown corduroy elasticized sides, and his black beret with the five-pointed star made memorable by the photo by Alberto "Korda" Díaz Gutiérrez. Surveillance cameras watch your every move. No cameras or bags (not even fanny packs) are allowed.

Che's remains (recently discovered in Bolivia) were laid to rest here in October 1997 in an adjacent mausoleum that has empty space for the 37 other guerrillas who lost their lives in Guevara's last campaign. The mausoleum has walls of granite inset with the 3-D motifs of the revolutionaries, including Che's, with a small five-point star illumined top-right from a light beam inset in the ceiling. Che actually inspires indifference among ordinary Cubans and there is an eerie absence of Cuban pilgrims to this vast Stalinist shrine with, wrote Mark Ottaway, "its edgy staff and enough manouevering space outside for a regiment of tanks."

CHE GUEVARA

Ernesto "Che" Guevara was born into a leftist middle-class family in Rosario, Argentina, in 1928. He received a medical degree from the University of Buenos Aires in 1953, then set out on an eight-month motorcycle odyssey through South America that had a profound influence on his radical thinking (as regaled in Brazilian director Walter Salle's 2004 movie, *The Motorcycle Diaries,* which canonizes Che and his awakening).

In 1954, he spent a brief period working as a volunteer doctor in Guatemala and was on hand when the Arbénz government was overthrown by a CIA-engineered coup (his experience left him intensely hostile to the United States). He fled Guatemala and went to Mexico where, in November 1955, he met Fidel Castro and, seeing in him the characteristics of a "great leader," joined the revolutionary cause.

The two had much in common. Guevara was a restless soul who, like Castro, was also daring and courted danger. They were both brilliant intellectuals (Guevara wrote poetry and philosophy and was probably the only true intellectual in Cuba's revolutionary leadership). Each had a relentless work ethic, total devotion, and an incorruptible character. Although the handsome, pipe-smoking rebel was a severe asthmatic, Che also turned out to be Castro's best field commander, eventually writing two books on guerrilla warfare that would become standard texts for revolutionaries in developing nations. He commanded the Third Front in the Sierra Escambray and led the attack that on December 28, 1958, captured Santa Clara and finally toppled the Batista regime. It was Che Guevara who took command of Havana's main military posts on New Year's Day, 1959.

SHAPING THE REVOLUTION

The revolutionary regime declared Guevara a native Cuban citizen, rendering him legally entitled to hold office in Cuba. Che (the word is an affectionate Argentinian appellation meaning "pal" or "buddy") became head of the National Bank of Cuba and Minister of Finance and, in 1961, Minister of Industry. He also led the tribu-

nals that dispensed with scores of Batista supporters – Guevara never flinched from pulling the trigger himself – and was instrumental in the general repression that was meant to crush "counterrevolutionaries." To U.S. officials, says biographer Jon Lee Anderson, he was "the fearsome Rasputin of the regime." His mystical influence on others attracted to him a crowd of fanatically loyal disciples, *los hombres del Che.* Nonetheless, Guevara narrowly escaped an assassination attempt on February 24, 1961, outside his home on Calle 18 in Miramar.

Guevara supervised the radical economic reforms that swept through Cuba and embraced the Soviet Union with innocent fervor as a bulwark for the coming break with the United States. He negotiated the trade deals with the Soviet Union and COMECON countries (Soviet representative Alexandr Alexiev said, "Che was practically the architect of our relations with Cuba").

Though born into a bourgeois family, he developed an obsessive hatred of bourgeois democracy, the profit motive, and U.S. interests. He believed that the individualistic motivations that determine behavior in a capitalist system would become obsolete when collective social welfare became the stated goal. Che believed that liberty eroded moral values: Individualism was selfish and divisive and essentially detrimental to social development.

Guevara's grand ambition was to export peasant revolution around the world: Che "had become the high priest of international revolution," says Anderson. "Stealthily, Che was setting up the chessboard for his game of continental guerrilla warfare, the ultimate prize being his homeland." He worked ceaselessly to goad a conflict between the Soviet Union and United States. The forces he helped set in motion in Latin America created a dark period of revolutionary violence and vicious counter-repression throughout the continent.

FALL FROM GRACE

However, Guevara was greatly at odds with Castro on fundamental issues. Castro's scheme to institutionalize the Revolution hand-in-hand with the Soviets, for example, ran counter to Guevara's beliefs (Guevara considered the Soviet Union as rapacious as the capitalists).

Although they were intellectual equals, in many ways Che Guevara and Fidel Castro were unmatched. Where Castro was pragmatic, Guevara was ideological. And Guevara was fair-minded toward Cubans critical of the Castro regime, unlike Castro. Guevara gradually lost his usefulness to Fidel's revolution. His frankness eventually disqualified him, forcing him into suicidal exile.

Guevara left Cuba in early 1965. He renounced all his positions in the Cuban government, as well as his honorary Cuban citizenship. Guevara apparently severed his ties with Cuba voluntarily, although the reasons have never been adequately explained.

DEATH AND ETERNAL GLORY

Che fought briefly in the Congo with the Kinshasa rebels before returning into secret to Cuba. He reemerged in 1966 in Bolivia, where he unsuccessfully attempted to rouse the Bolivian peasantry and "to create another Vietnam in the Americas" as a prelude to what he hoped would be a definitive world war in which socialism would be triumphant. Che was betrayed to the Bolivian Army Rangers by the peasants he had hoped to set free. He died on October 9, 1967, ambushed and executed along with several loyal members of the Cuban Communist Party.

Critics claim that he was abandoned by Castro, who may have foreseen the benefits that would derive from Che as martyr. Castro has since built an entire cult of worship around Che. He has become an icon, exploited as a "symbol of the purest revolutionary virtue." Che became the official role model of the *hombre nuevo*, the "New Man." The motto *seremos como Che* ("We will be like Che") is the official slogan of the Young Pioneers, the nation's youth organization. His image is everywhere. The photographer Korda shot the famous image – "The Heroic Guerrilla" ("Fidel's gift to the T-shirt industry," thought writer Tom Carson) – showing Guevara wearing a windbreaker zippered to the neck, in his trademark black beret with five-point revolutionary star, his head tilted slightly, "his eyes burning just beyond the foreseeable future," wrote Tom Miller.

Che has been turned into a modern myth the world over. He became a hero to the New Left radicals of the 1960s. The ultimate, and most absurd, tribute perhaps came from the French philosopher Jean-Paul Sartre, who honored Guevara as "the most complete man of our age."

In 1997 Che's remains were delivered to Cuba and interred in Santa Clara.

Museo Provincial Abel Santamaría

Housed in the Escuela Abel Santamaría (tel. 0422/20-3041; Mon.–Fri. 8:30 A.M.–5 P.M., Sat. 9 A.M.–1 P.M.; CUC1), at the north end of Calle Esquerra in the Reparto Osvaldo Herrera neighborhood, this museum is brimful of colonial furniture but is dedicated to the province's role in the Wars of Independence and the fight against Batista. It features a large collection of weaponry, plus a natural-history exhibit downstairs. The school was formerly a military barracks, fulfilling Castro's dictum to turn all Batista's barracks into centers of learning.

Plaza del Carmen

This exquisite little plaza, at the north end of Máximo Gómez, five blocks north of Parque Vidal, is dominated by the **Iglesia Nuestra Señora del Carmen,** a national monument dating to 1748. It is fronted by a granite monument that arcs around a tamarind tree where the first Mass was held to celebrate the founding of Santa Clara on July 15, 1689. The monument features 18 columns carved with the names of the original founding families. The church, which was used as a women's prison during the Wars of Independence, is riddled with bullet holes fired from the police station—now named El Vaquerito—across the street during the battle of December 29, 1958. On the north side of the church is a life-size figure of revolutionary hero Roberto Rodríquez Fernández—*el vaquerito*—of whose death Che Guevara said, "We have lost one hundred men."

Plaza la Pastora and Vicinity

This small plaza, on Calle Cuba, five blocks south of Parque Vidal, has at its heart the **Iglesia de la Santísima de Buen Pastora** (tel. 0422/20-6554; daily 10 A.M.–4 P.M.), restored in contemporary vogue with an ungainly tin roof, and featuring original statuary and a beautiful stained-glass window in the shape of the cross. On its northeast corner is **Monumento a Miguel Gerónimo Gutiérrez**, honoring a local patriot.

If you walk two blocks south and cross the Carretera Central, you'll come upon the **Monumento General Máximo Gómez**, with bas-reliefs. It stands in front of the neoclassical **Palacio de Justicia**, the local courthouse.

Tren Blindado

This site (tel. 0422/22758; Mon.–Sat. 9 A.M.–5:30 P.M.; CUC1), at the east end of Independencia beyond the railway crossing, was the setting where on December 29, 1958, rebel troops led by Che Guevara derailed one of Batista's troop trains, setting in rapid motion the train of events that toppled Batista. Four rust-colored carriages are preserved higgledy-piggledy in suspended animation as they came to rest after the train was run off the rails. There is an exhibit inside one of the carriages, with armaments and the like.

Entertainment and Events

Troubadours play most evenings and weekend afternoons at the **Casa de la Cultura** (Máximo Gómez, tel. 0422/20-7181), on the west side of Parque Vidal); **UNEAC** (National Union of Cuban Writers and Artists, Cuba #107, www .uneac.com) has cultural events and *peñas;* and the no-frills, overly air-conditioned **Piano Bar** (Luis Estevez #13, e/ Independencia y Parque

Vidal, tel. 0422/21-5215; 9 P.M.–1 A.M. daily) hosts *boleros, instrumental,* and *trova.*

Casa de la Ciudad (Independencia #102, esq. Juan Bruno Zayas, tel. 0422/20-5593; Tues.–Thurs. 8 A.M.–noon and 1–5 P.M.; Fri. 8 A.M.–noon, 1–5 P.M., and 5–8 P.M.; Sat. 1–5 P.M. and 8–10 P.M.; Sun. 5–8 P.M.; CUC1) has art galleries and hosts cultural activities.

Everything from comedy and drag to live music is featured at **Carishow** (Independencia #225, e/ Unión y Maceo, tel. 0422/21-6236; Tues.–Sun. 10 P.M.–2 A.M.; CUC2), a hip space where performances are followed by disco. Get the ball rolling with a shot of rum at **Bar Marquesina** (nightly 9:30 P.M.–1 A.M.), on the northwest corner of Plaza Vidal.

Taberna El Mejunje (Marta Abreu #107, e/ Zayas y Alemán; Tues.–Fri. 10 P.M.–4 A.M., Sat. 5 P.M.–4 A.M., Sun. 10 A.M.–4 P.M.), an open-air space amid brick ruins, hosts a varying program that ranges from rap and rock to traditional *trova;* plus a *cabaret espectáculo* on Friday. A less spectacular cabaret is hosted on weekends at the former governor's house, **La Casa del Gobernador** (Independencia, esq. Zayas, tel. 0422/20-2273; Fri.–Sun. 9 P.M.–2 A.M.; CUC5). **Artex El Bosque** (Carretera Central, tel. 0422/20-4444; Wed.–Sun. 10 P.M.–2 A.M.; CUC1), overhanging the Río Cubanicay, also has a 24-hour bar with open-air cabaret and disco.

Hotel Los Caneyes hosts a nightly poolside fashion show at 9:30 P.M. (free to guests; outsiders pay CUC5, including CUC3 drinks).

There's a **cinema** on the west side of the main square, and another, **Cine Cubanacán**, on the Boulevard. Classical and other performances are hosted at **Teatro la Caridad.**

Baseball is hosted October–May at **Estadio Sandino** (Avenida 9 de Abril), about one mile east of Parque Vidal.

Accommodations

No *campismos* in Santa Clara Province were taking foreigners at last visit. Check with **Campismo Popular** (Maceo Sur #315, e/ San Miguel y Nazareno, tel. 0422/20-4905; Mon.–Fri. 8 A.M.–noon and 1–4:30 P.M.).

Casas Particulares: I always enjoy staying at **Casa de Elier y Alina** (Calle San Pablo #19, e/ Carolina y Máximo Gómez, tel. 0422/27-4293, cell 05-283-7053; CUC20), facing Plaza del Carmen. The friendly hosts have a spacious lounge with color TV, nicely decorated in 1950s style. Two spacious air-conditioned bedrooms have private bathrooms with beautiful tile work and hot water. Filling meals are made.

Casa de Olga Rivera (Yanes #20, e/ Máximo Gómez y Callejón del Carmen, tel. 0422/21-1711; CUC20–25), on the south side of the plaza, is a well-kept colonial home with two air-conditioned rooms that open to a lounge graced by plush sofas (one has tall windows opening onto Plaza del Carmen; the second is smaller and indoors). Each room has TV, fridge, a mix of antiques and modern furnishings, and a private hot-water bathroom. There's parking, and meals are served in a pleasant dining room or in an exquisite rear tiled patio.

Casa de José Ramón (Máximo Gómez #208 altos, e/ Berenguer y Yanes, tel. 0422/20-7239, joseleys7@webcorreo.co.cu; CUC15–20) is a historic house with an independent apartment upstairs. It's a super place: modern, with air-conditioning, TV, antique furnishings, a full kitchen, and private hot-water bathroom). It has a rooftop terrace.

Hospedaje Consuelo Ramos (Independencia Este #265, Apto. 1, e/ Unión y San Isidro, tel. 0422/20-2064, marielatra@yahoo.es; CUC15–20) is a spacious and well-kept home with two air-conditioned rooms (one with two double beds) with large private hot-water bathrooms. Consuelo speaks English and French and is a great cook. Meals are served on a rear patio.

Casa Isabel y Rolando (Independencia #107, e/ Estévez y Plácido, tel. 0422/20-7073; CUC15) is a well-kept colonial home with stone walls and a pleasing ambience. The single room has a private hot-water bathroom. There's a patio for relaxing.

Casa de Hospedaje Marta Artíles Alemán (Marta Abreu #56 altos, e/ Villuendas y Zayas, tel. 0422/20-5008, martaartiles@yahoo .es; CUC15–20) is a spacious old home with plush leather sofas and wicker rockers. It has two simply furnished air-conditioned rooms with fans and private hot-water bathrooms. It has parking, and the hosts are friendly.

Casa de Ernesto y Mireya (Calle Cuba #227 altos, e/ Sindico y Pastora, tel. 0422/27-3501, ernesto_tama@yahoo.com; CUC15) is an appealing bargain. This independent upstairs apartment has a handsome lounge with balcony overlooking Plaza la Pastora, plus a TV, stereo system, and heaps of light. The spacious, simply appointed air-conditioned bedroom has a ceiling fan, TV, radio, refrigerator, and attractive hot-water bathroom. There's parking.

Hotels: The only downtown option is **Hotel Santa Clara Libre** (tel. 0422/20-7548, fax 0422/20-5171; CUC22 s, CUC29 d low season; CUC27 s, CUC37 d high season), overlooking Parque Vidal. This high-rise has 132 dowdy air-conditioned rooms with local TV and telephone, desperately in need of renovation at press time. There's a mediocre restaurant on the 10th floor and a rooftop bar above. Water supply is never guaranteed and noise from the basement disco is a problem. (Islazul.)

A better bet is **Hotel Los Caneyes** (Av. de los Eucaliptos y Circunvalación de Santa Clara, tel./fax 0422/21-8140, reservas@caneyes .hor.tur.cu; CUC38 s, CUC50 d low season; CUC42 s, CUC55 d high season), two kilometers west of town and favored by tour groups. It has 96 appealing air-conditioned rooms in thatched, wooden octagonal *cabinas* spread amid landscaped grounds and featuring terra-cotta tile floors, refrigerators, satellite TVs, and modern bathrooms. Facilities include an attractive restaurant, snack bar, disco, swimming pool, hairdresser, car rental, Internet service, massage, and a tourism bureau. (Cubanacán.)

Carrusel La Granjita (Carretera Malez Km 2.5, Santa Clara, tel. 0422/28190, fax 0422/28192, reserva@granjita.vcl.cyt.cu; CUC38 s, CUC50 d, CUC75 suite year-round) is a similar concept—thatched cabins in a landscaped setting—built around a handsome pool and sundeck where a cabaret is hosted. The 75 rooms in *cabinas* and two-story

CIENFUEGOS / VILLA CLARA

octagonal cabins are pretty and feature air-conditioning, satellite TV, radio, telephone, and marble bathroom. There's a tennis court, restaurant, and shop. (Cubanacán.)

Food

The only *paladar* still open at last visit was **Paladar Sabor Tropical** (Esquerra #157, e/ Julio Jover y Berenguer, tel. 0422/20-6539; noon–midnight daily), a clean, modern private restaurant serving *criollo* dishes for below CUC8. It's a better bet than any of the state restaurants.

The top-floor restaurant in the **Hotel Santa Clara Libre** (tel. 0422/20-7548; 7:15–9:30 A.M., noon–2:30 P.M., and 7:15–9:30 P.M. daily) has views over the square but meager *criollo* fare; try the roast loin of pork (CUC9.65).

The Boulevard has several snack bars, including **Café Europa** (tel. 0422/21-6350; 7 A.M.–2 A.M. daily) facing Plaza de las Arcadas. It's a favored hangout for tourists, not least for its draft Cristal beer; it also serves pizzas and sandwiches.

For seafoods, head to the clean, air-conditioned **Dimar** (9 Abril, esq. 1ra, tel. 0422/20-1375; daily 10 A.M.–10 P.M. daily). I recommend the garlic shrimp (CUC2.50) and lobster enchiladas (CUC6.25).

Coppelia (Calle Colón, esq. Mujica, tel. 0422/20-6426; Tues.–Sun. 10 A.M.–11:30 P.M.), one block south of the main square, sells ice cream for pesos. **Heladería Kikiri** (Independencia, esq. Luis Estéves; daily 10 A.M.–10 P.M.) also serves ice cream, but you'll pay in CUC.

There are lots of peso food stalls around the *mercado agropecuario* (1ra, e/ Morales y General Roloff), where you can buy fresh produce; and baked goods at **Panadería Doña Neli** (Maceo Sur, esq. Av. 9 de Abril; 6:30 A.M.–6 P.M.).

Information and Services

The **post office** (Colón #10, e/ Parque Vidal y Machado, tel. 0422/20-3862; Mon.–Fri. 9 A.M.–6 P.M., Sat. 8:30 A.M.–noon) also offers DHL service.

Etecsa (Marta Abreu, esq. Villuendas; daily 9:30 A.M.–9:30 P.M.) has international telephone and Internet service. There's also a telephone kiosk at Cuba y Machado.

Bandec (Marta Abreu y Luis Estéves, and Máximo Gómez y Rafael Tristá); plus a **Banco Financiero Internacional** (Cuba #6, e/ Triste y Machado, tel. 0422/20-7450) have branches on Parque Vidal. You can change foreign exchange at **Cadeca** (Máximo Gómez, esq. Rafael Tristá). **Western Union** (Independencia, e/ Máximo Gómez y Enrique Villuendas) is in the Praga department store.

The **Policlínico Docente** (Serafín García Oeste #167, e/ Alemán y Carretera Central, tel. 0422/20-2244) offers basic medical service. **Farmacia Campa** (Independencia Este y Luis Estévez; daily 8 A.M.–8:30 P.M.) is poorly stocked.

The **Bufete Internacional** (Luis Estévez #119, e/ San Miguel y 9 de Abril, tel. 0422/20-8458) and **Consultoría Jurídica Internacional** (Trista #5, e/ Villuendas y Cuba, tel./fax 0422/21-8114, cjivillaclara@enet.cu) offer legal assistance.

Inmigración (Av. Sandino, esq. Sextra; Mon.–Thurs. 8 A.M.–noon and 1–3 P.M.), three blocks east of Estadio Sandino, can issue *prórrogas*.

Getting There and Away

By Air: Flights arrive at **Aeropuerto Internacional Abel Santamaría** (tel. 0422/20-9138), about 10 kilometers northeast of the city.

By Bus: The **Terminal de Ómnibus Nacionales** (Av. Cincuentenario, Independencia y Oquendo, tel. 0422/29-2214) is on the Carretera Central about 2.5 kilometers west of the city center. **Víazul** (tel. 0422/22-2523) buses that stop in Santa Clara depart Havana at 9:30 A.M., 5 P.M., and 10 P.M.; Santiago de Cuba at 9 A.M., 3:15 P.M., 10 P.M., and 10:30 P.M.; Trinidad at 5:25 P.M.; and Varadero at 7:30 A.M. and 8:55 P.M. Buses depart Santa Clara for Cienfuegos and Trinidad at 10:50 A.M.; for Havana at 3:40 A.M., 9:45 A.M., and 10 P.M.; for Santiago at 1 A.M., 1:50 A.M., 1:55 A.M., and 7:30 P.M. (stopping at provincial capitals en route); and for Varadero at 8:15 A.M. and 5:25 P.M.

Astro buses depart Santa Clara for Havana thrice daily (CUC15 *especial,* CUC12 *regular*); for Cienfuegos at 7:10 A.M. and 9:10 P.M. (CUC5 *especial,* CUC2.50 *regular*); for Sancti Spíritus at 8:32 A.M. and 2 P.M. (CUC5 *especial,* CUC3.50 *regular*); for Trinidad at 1:20 P.M. and 5:15 A.M. (CUC7 *especial,* CUC6 *regular*); for Holguín at 6 A.M. and 3:25 P.M. (CUC22 *especial,* CUC18 *regular*); and for Santiago de Cuba at 7 A.M. and 4 A.M. (CUC27 *especial,* CUC22.50 *regular*).

Veracuba, Gaviota, and Transtur offer city transfers by bus (Havana, CUC19; Varadero, CUC13; Cienfuegos, CUC6; Trinidad, CUC9; Camagüey, CUC16) and microbus or taxi (Havana, CUC46; Varadero, CUC28; Cienfuegos, CUC16; Trinidad, CUC28; Camagüey, CUC38).

By Train: Most trains traveling between Havana and Santiago de Cuba stop in Santa Clara. The **Estación de Ferrocarriles** (tel. 0422/20-2895) is at the northern end of Luis Estévez, seven blocks from Parque Vidal. Same-day tickets are sold at the ticket office (tel. 0422/20-0854) on the *south* side of the square. Seats on the *regular* are sold up to 24 hours in advance; seats on the *especial* can be bought only one hour in advance of departure.

Train #46 departs Santiago for Santa Clara at 4:35 A.M., arriving at 5:20 P.M. Train #47 departs Santa Clara for Santiago at 7:45 A.M. Westbound trains depart Santa Clara for Havana at 4:01 A.M., 4:22 A.M., 5:18 A.M., 7:38 A.M., 8:30 P.M., 10 A.M., 10:13 A.M., 9:18 P.M., and 11:55 P.M. Eastbound trains depart Santa Clara for Sancti Spíritus at 3:07 A.M.; for Camagüey at 5:37 P.M.; for Holguín at 11:38 P.M.; for Bayamo at 1 A.M.; and for Santiago de Cuba at 7:17 P.M., 9:15 P.M., 11:19 A.M., and 10:51 P.M. Trains also depart for Morón at 8:28 P.M.

In addition, provincial trains to Santa Clara depart Caibarién at 4:21 A.M.; Sagua at 4:42 A.M.; and Cienfuegos at 4:10 A.M. Trains depart Santa Clara for Caibarién at 5:30 A.M.; Sagua at 4:30 P.M.; and Cienfuegos at 5:20 P.M.

By Car: You can rent cars from **Transtur** (Tristá, esq. Amparo, tel. 0422/20-2040; and in the Hotel Santa Clara Libre, tel. 0422/20-

4512); **Havanautos** (Marta Abreu #130, tel. 0422/20-9118); **Micar** (Servicentro Oro Negro, Carretera Central y San Miguel, tel. 0422/20-4570); and **Rex** (Marta Abreu #130, tel. 042/22-2244).

By Organized Excursion: Tour agencies include **Cubanacán** (Maceo #453, e/ Carretera Central y Caridad, tel. 0422/20-5189), **Havanatur** (Máximo Gómez #13, e/ Independencia y Barreras, tel. 0422/20-4001), and **Cubatur** (Martha Abreu #10, e/ Máximo Gómez y Villuendas, tel. 0422/20-8980, cubaturvc@enet.cu).

Getting Around

Local buses depart the **Terminal de Ómnibus Intermunicipal** (Marta Abreu, tel. 0422/20-3470), 10 blocks west of Parque Vidal. Bus #11 runs between Parque Vidal and the Hotel Los Caneyes between 7 A.M. and 7 P.M.

Tourist taxis can be hailed from outside the stations and by phoning **Cubataxi** (tel. 0422/22-2691).

There are gas stations on the Carretera Central, esq. General Roloff; and two blocks north at Carretera Central, esq. Avenida 9 de Abril.

ALTURAS DE SANTA CLARA

The Alturas de Santa Clara rise sensually to the south and east of the city and merge gradually into the heights of the Sierra Escambray. The hills and valleys are pocked with quaint timeworn villages and quilted by tobacco fields tilled by oxen and tended by *guajiros* in straw hats and white linen field clothes.

Both the Autopista and Carretera Central pass through the region.

One of the most scenic drives in Cuba is the route directly south from Santa Clara to Manicaragua and into the foothills of the Sierra Escambray along route 4-474 to Topes de Collantes (see *Gran Parque Natural Topes de Collantes,* in the *Sancti Spíritus* chapter). There's a gas station in Manicaragua.

Embalse Hanabanilla

This huge (32 square km) manmade lake fills what was once a deep valley on the northern slopes of the Escambray. The lake, which has an average depth of 35 meters and supplies water to Santa Clara and Cienfuegos, shimmers through every shade from pea-green to cobalt, depending on the mood of the weather, below its backdrop of pine-studded mountains. The lake is stocked with trout and bass. The Hotel Hanabanilla offers fishing trips (CUC20–45 per person; four hours).

The lakeshore curls like a jigsaw puzzle piece, perfect for scenic boat trips from the dock of the hotel. A ferry from the hotel (CUC5) takes passengers across the lake to the **Casa del Campesino,** a small working farm where you can get a taste for the campesino lifestyle. You can also get there by one of three mountain trails from the hotel.

The turnoff for Hanabanilla is midway between Cumanayagua and Manicuraga, on Route 4-206, at La Macagua, just west of Ciro Redondo.

Accommodations and Food

The only hotel for miles, and a place of last resort, is the run-down **Hotel Hanabanilla** (tel. 042/20-2399, fax 042/20-3506, director@ hanabanilla.vcl.cyt.cu; CUC18 s, CUC24 d low season; CUC24 s, CUC30 d high season), a Soviet-style complex that perches over the western shore. It has 125 air-conditioned, modestly furnished rooms, each with satellite TV, telephone, radio, and modern bathroom. Facilities include a restaurant, bar, cafeteria, disco (the music reverberates through the hotel), swimming pool, shop, and tourism bureau. The road to the hotel has been flooded for years; visitors are ferried by wobbly boat (0.50 centavos), or you can walk a 400-yard trail. (Islazul.)

Lunch is served at the **Río Negro Restaurante,** on the southern shores of the lake. Here you're fed *criollo* cuisine such as roast pork or chicken with pineapple (the house specialty) while troubadours entertain. It is accessed by boat (CUC8 low season, CUC10 high season) from the hotel.

THE NORTH COAST

There is little to recommend along the coast northwest of Santa Clara, as beaches are few

and the scenery unimpressive. Still, the well-paved Circuito Norte (Rt. 4-13) runs parallel to the shore, providing an easy, off-the-beaten-path route for travelers heading between Santa Clara and Varadero.

Encrucijada, 25 kilometers due north of Santa Clara, was the birthplace of revolutionary heroes Abel Santamaría and Jesús Menéndez. Their houses are now museums dedicated to their memory. East of Encrucijada, Route 4-13 runs through **San Antonio de las Vueltas,** a sleepy town that wakes up for the year-end *parranda.* The highway then merges with Route 4-321, which runs west to Santa Clara and east to Remedios and Caibarién.

Beach-fringed cays lie scattered in the jade-colored waters offshore. The white-sand beaches are untapped for tourism. The cays' landward shores are fringed by mangroves—havens for herons, flamingos, roseate spoonbills and other stilt-legged waders, as well as manatees, while hawksbill, green, and loggerhead turtles come ashore to lay eggs. At last visit the **Área Protegida Las Picuas-Cayo del Cristo** (tel. 042/69-0141) was being developed for tourism. The office is in the fishing community of Carahatas, 14 kilometers north of the Circuito Norte.

Baños de Elguea

The Elguea Thermal Center, about five kilometers northwest of Corralillo and 135 kilometers northwest of Santa Clara, is supplied by hyperthermal (up to 50°C) springs containing bromine, sodium, radium, and sulfur. The waters are good for treating rheumatism, skin ailments, and respiratory problems. It has swimming pools, a marching tank, mud baths, gym, solarium, massage rooms, and more, although facilities are a bit crude by Western standards. Still, the prices are fair (massage CUC10, mud wrap CUC5, thermal bath CUC10).

Accommodations

Horizontes Elguea Hotel & Spa (tel. 042/68-6298, fax 042/68-6442, elguea@islazulvc.vcl .cyt.cu; UC30 s, UC40 d low season; CUC36 s, CUC48 d high season) is promoted as a spa resort but receives few guests. It has 135 pleasant, albeit modest air-conditioned rooms (four are suites), with bamboo furnishings, satellite TVs, phones, safes, refrigerators, and modern bathrooms. One room serves travelers with disabilities. Facilities include volleyball, basketball, and tennis courts and a large swimming pool. The modestly elegant restaurant is the only eatery for miles. (Islazul.)

Eastern Villa Clara

VUELTA ABAJO

East of Santa Clara, the Carretera Central and Route 4-321 run through the Vuelta Abajo region (not to be confused with the similarly named tobacco region in Pinar del Río Province), one of Cuba's premier tobacco-growing regions. The scenery is marvelous and you sense that you're in an *Alice in Wonderland* time-warp as you pass fields tilled by ox-drawn ploughs and stir up the dust in small agricultural towns lent a Wild West feel by horses tethered to sagging arcades that line the main streets.

The district is unique within Cuba for the year-end *parrandas,* festivals in which rockets whiz through the streets and hand-held fireworks and "mortars" explode with a military boom as the townsfolk of each community divide into two historic camps and vie with each other to see who can produce the best parade float and the loudest din (see the sidebar *Fireworks Fever*). In all, 14 local communities hold *parrandas,* most notably Placetas, Remedios, Zulueta, and San Antonio de las Vueltas, which uniquely holds its *parranda* in August.

Route 4-231 links Santa Clara to Remedios, dipping and rising through photogenic tobacco country.

◖ REMEDIOS

This time-warp town (pop. 18,000), 45 kilometers northeast of Santa Clara, is one of the most beautiful little towns in Cuba, full of Spanish colonial charm. It is in a good state of preservation, with a graceful symmetry and charisma. The entire city was justifiably named a national monument in 1979.

Remedios was founded in 1514 when a land grant was given to a conquistador named

cowboy at rodeo, Villa Clara

© CHRISTOPHER P. BAKER

CIENFUEGOS / VILLA CLARA

Vasco Porcallo de Figueroa. A city hall wasn't built, however, and supposedly for that reason the town was never acknowledged as one of the first seven cities, despite its antiquity. It was originally situated closer to the shore. In 1544, it was moved a short distance inland to escape pirates. The town continued to come under constant attack and in 1578, the townsfolk uprooted again and founded a new settlement, which they renamed San Juan de los Remedios del Cayo. In 1682, a group of citizens uprooted and founded Santa Clara, which in time grew

FIREWORKS FEVER

The villages and towns due east of Santa Clara are renowned islandwide for *parrandas*, the noisy year-end revels that date back more than a century. The festival apparently began in Remedios on Christmas Eve in 1822, when a zealous priest went through the streets making frightening noises meant to rouse the townspeople and scare them into attending midnight Mass. The villagers took the fiesta-like din to heart and gradually evolved a classic Mardi Gras-type carnival celebrated during the days around Christmas and New Year's.

Eventually the *parrandas* spread to the neighboring villages (14 communities now have *parrandas*). Fireworks were introduced and the revels developed into competitions – really, massive fireworks battles – to see who could make the loudest noise. Each of the villages divides into two rival camps represented by mascots: the Carmelitas of Remedios, for example, are represented by a *gavilán* (hawk), and the Sansacrices (from San Salvador) by a *gallo* (rooster).

The villagers invest ludicrous emotional value in their wars and spend months preparing in secret. Warehouses are stocked full of explosives and sawhorses studded with fireworks, and the final touches are put on the floats (*trabajos de plaza*) that will be pulled by field tractors around 3 A.M. Spies infiltrate the enemy camp. Even sabotage is not unknown.

The rivals take turns parading all through the night. Rum flows. The beating drums, singing, and dancing gather pace. Conga lines weave through town. Huge banners are waved, to be met by cheers or shouts of derision. *¡Viva la Loma! ¡Viva Guanijibes!* The excitement builds as each neighborhood stages fireworks displays. The opposing sides alternately present their pyrotechnics. The streets are filled with deafening explosions from stovepipe mortars, rockets and whirling explosives whizzing overhead and sometimes into the panicked crowd, and the smoke is so thick that you can barely see your way through the streets.

Finally, the wildest fireworks are unleashed and the fiesta culminates in an orgy of insane firepower. Pretty fireworks don't earn points. The most relentless, voluminous bombast determines who wins.

When it is over, the triumphant neighborhood dances through the streets, accompanied by the losing team. Next day both sides fittingly proclaim victory. Thus sibling solidarity is overnight reaffirmed, proving once again in Cuba's exemplary fashion that what counts is the *spirit* of competition and conciliation.

to become the provincial capital. Apparently, in 1691, the clique returned to Remedios, determined to raze it to the ground. They were rebuffed in a pitched battle.

Much of the pleasure today is to be had in roaming the back streets, especially in late afternoon and early evening, when the low sun glows richly against the pastel walls and the church bells ring through town, tolling the hour.

Plaza Martí

The town's main square is shaded by tall royal palms beneath which you can sit on marble and wrought-iron benches. Dominating the square is the venerable **Parroquia de San Juan Batista** (Camilo Cienfuegos #20; Mon.–Sat. 9–11 A.M.), dating from 1692. Its pious exterior belies the splendor within, not least a carved cedar altar that glimmers with 24-carat gold leaf, a statue of the Immaculate Virgin heavy with child, and—the pièce de résistance—a Moorish-style ceiling of carved mahogany, splendidly gabled and fluted. The church has an impressive bell tower with three stories (a bell in each). It was badly damaged by an earthquake in 1939 and restored over the ensuing 15 years at the behest of a local benefactor, who also donated European paintings.

The **Museo de la Música Alejandro García Caturla** (Camilo Cienfuegos #5, tel. 042/39-6851; Tues.–Sat. 9 A.M.–noon and 1–5 P.M., Sun. 9 A.M.–5 P.M.; CUC1), on the north side

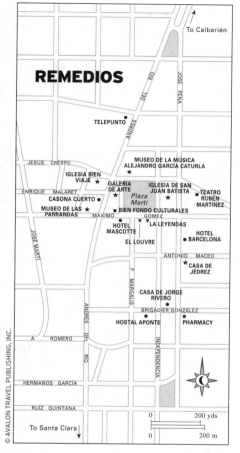

On the park's northwest corner stands the **Iglesia Buen Viaje** (Alejandro del Río #66), a prim little church with a three-tiered bell-tower with a life-size figure of the Virgin Mary and Jesus in the "dove-hole." It is fronted by a marble statue of the Liberty-like Indian maiden hewn from marble.

Museo de las Parrandas

This museum (Calle Máximo Gómez #71, no tel.; Tues.–Sat. 9 A.M.–noon and 1–6 P.M., Sun. 9 A.M.–1 P.M.; CUC1) celebrates the festivals unique to the region and contains costumes, flags, and banners, examples of homemade fireworks, and floats. Given the spectacular ostentation of the actual *parrandas,* the museum is almost boring.

Entertainment and Events

Any time is a good time to visit, but if possible time your visit for Christmas week for the annual *parranda.* By December, the townsfolk are feverishly preparing for their *parranda,* which culminates on the last Saturday of the year. Bring your earplugs and camera for a wild and racket-filled revelry you'll never forget. Be warned, it's a dangerous business, as rockets whiz into the crowd and every year several people are injured. Don't wear flammable nylon clothing. Be sure to check out the midnight Mass in the cathedral. The crowd drinks through the night and into next day, when the streets are littered with spent drunks and fireworks. Pickpockets abound.

On December 26 those citizens still sober enough to participate celebrate the city's "liberation" by Che Guevara's Rebel Army.

Traditional music and dance is performed at the **Casa de la Cultura** (Gómez, esq. José de Pena, tel. 042/39-5581; Tues.–Sun. 9 A.M.–11 P.M.) one block east of the main square. **Las Leyendas** (tel. 042/39-6264; 9 A.M.–2 A.M. daily), on the south side of the main square, has a pleasant open-air bar in the form of a faux cave with *parranda* elements; it hosts a *cabaret espectáculo* Wednesday–Sunday at 10 P.M. (CUC0.50).

The **Teatro Ruben Mártinez** (Cienfuegos

CIENFUEGOS / VILLA CLARA

of Plaza Martí, honors one of Cuba's foremost avant-garde composers. The house features beautiful green-tinted *mamparas,* period furniture, and many of Caturla's original manuscripts. The musical prodigy began writing music in 1920, when he was only 14. He was heavily influenced by the rhythms and sounds of Africa and fell under the sway of Stravinsky. The iconoclastic composer (for example, he married a black woman; when she died, he married her sister) was a noted liberal and an incorruptible lawyer who rose to become judge for the city. He was assassinated in 1940.

#30; Mon.–Fri. 8 A.M.–5 P.M.), built in the late 19th century with a triple-tiered horseshoe-shaped auditorium, hosts classical and other performances.

Accommodations

At last visit, more than 20 homes were licensed as *casas particulares.* During the end of year *parrandas,* when visitors flood town, restrictions on rentals are lifted and many nonregistered households rent rooms. Calle José Peña has lots.

For colonial ambience, check into ❰ **Casona Cuerto** (Alejandro del Río #72, e/ Enrique Malaret, tel. 042/39-5350, amarelys@capiro.vcl.sld.cu; CUC20–25), a delightful 18th-century home full of antiques and with an exquisite tile floor. The owners rent two air-conditioned rooms; one, in the attic, is reached via a wooden spiral staircase. Both have fans and modern private bathrooms. A beautiful courtyard with caged birds and a landscaped rooftop terrace are to the rear.

❰ **Casa de Jorge Rivero** (Brigadier González #29, tel. 042/39-6310; CUC15–25), two blocks west of the main plaza, is an exquisite room rental. Jorge has two rooms in his well-furnished 1950s-style home with a gracious dining room and lounge. One room (with an independent entrance) is reached via spiral stairs and has its own sunny lounge and patio, fridge, spacious cross-lit bedroom, two double beds, and a modern hot-water bathroom. The second (entered via the house) has fans, a double and single bed, and a small modern bathroom. There's a rooftop patio for sunbathing, and secure parking.

Hostal Aponte (Brigadier González #32 altos, e/ Independencia y P. Magalis, tel. 042/39-5398; CUC20–25) is upstairs in a spacious colonial home. Eccentric owner Gladys Rojas is a *santera,* so a stay here is a great way of learning something about the religion. She has two air-conditioned rooms. The smaller has two single beds, fans, and a hot-water bathroom down the hall. The second is huge, cross-ventilated, well-lit and has fans, two double beds, city views, and a private hot-water bathroom.

The **Hotel Mascotte** (Calle Máximo Gómez, tel. 042/39-5467 and 042/39-5144, fax 042/39-5327, mascote@centro.vcl.cyt.cu; CUC36 s, CUC46 d year-round including breakfast) is a nicely restored 19th-century hotel. It has 14 pleasantly furnished air-conditioned rooms with lofty ceilings and modern amenities, including satellite TV, and marble and ceramics and hot water in bathrooms. A plaque on the outside wall records that here on February 1, 1899, Máximo Gómez met with Robert P. Porter, the special commissioner of U.S. President William McKinley, to negotiate the terms of the Mambí fighters' honorable discharge at the end of the Spanish-Cuban-American War. (Islazul.)

Food

The modern **Restaurante Las Arcadas** (7 A.M.–10 P.M. daily), in the Hotel Mascotte, serves undistinguished *criollo* cuisine (CUC1–5) but is the best place in town. Dine early during the *parranda,* as the place gets packed and it's an hour-long scrum to get served.

The atmospheric **El Louvre** (tel. 042/39-5639; Mon.–Fri. 8 A.M.–midnight, Sat.–Sun. 8 A.M.–2 A.M.), one block south, is a touristy café serving sandwiches, snacks, and coffee.

Getting There and Away

The bus station (tel. 042/39-5185) is on the west side of town, on the road to Santa Clara. Buses for Remedios depart from Havana daily and from Santa Clara four times daily (CUC4.25).

The railway station (tel. 042/39-5129) is eight blocks west of the main square.

Transtur Rent-a-Car has an outlet in the Hotel Mascotte.

Cubanacán in Santa Clara has excursions to the *parranda* for CUC25 (see *Getting There and Away* in the *Santa Clara* section of this chapter).

There's a Cupet gas station on the west side of town, on the road to Santa Clara; and an Oro Negro gas station on the north side of town, on the road to Caibarién.

CAIBARIÉN

This sprawling down-at-the-heels coastal town (pop. 39,000), eight kilometers east of Remedios, has some intriguing albeit much-deteriorated colonial structures. Entering town from Santa Clara, you pass a huge stone crab in the road divide (there's a gas station here). The main street—Máximo Gómez—leads to **Parque de la Libertad,** surrounded by period edifices. Avenida 5, one block west of Máximo Gómez, is a broad boulevard pinned by the **Monumento José Martí.** On the east side of town, a palm-lined shorefront **Malecón** leads east to a funky fishing fleet.

Caibarién has a year-end *parranda.*

C CAYO SANTA MARÍA

About five kilometers east of Caibarién, a fabulously scenic, 50-kilometer-long causeway departs the coast road and leaps from tiny cay to tiny cay, ending at Cayo Santa María, 45 kilometers from the mainland. Eleven kilometers of beaches run along its north shore, shelving into a coruscating lagoon with a coral reef beyond. The cay is in the midst of major development, with several hotels plus shops, a 30-berth marina, nightclub, and other ancillary services slated, all under the umbrella of Cubanacán. The long-term plan calls for 10,000 hotel rooms on Cayo Santa María and neighboring **Cayo Las Brujas.**

There's a *faro* at the end of the road, about three kilometers beyond Sol Cayo Santa María resort. Most of the beaches are the private reserve of the hotels, but day visitors can gain access for a fee. The nearest beach—and a fine option—is that at Villas Las Brujas. Here you can snorkel in turquoise waters as warm as bedtime milk; colorful tropical fish abound.

There's a toll booth checkpoint to enter and exit (CUC2 each way). You'll need your passport. No Cubans are permitted.

Recreation

Fishing here is top-notch, notably for tarpon, sea bass, and snapper. Fishing excursions are offered from all the hotels.

Scuba diving is spectacular also: The best site is the wreck of the **San Pascual,** a tanker that ran aground off the west of Cayo Francés; scuba dives (CUC35 one dive) and boat transfers (CUC6) are offered from **Marina Gaviota** (tel. 042/35-0013), adjoining Villa Las Brujas. The marina also offers Jet Skis, and excursions by catamaran (CUC36 half-day, CUC72 full-day, CUC49 sunset cruise with dinner).

Accommodations and Food

Villas Las Brujas (tel. 042/35-0024, fax 042/20-7599, gaviota@gaviota.gav.tur.cu; CUC56 s, CUC72 d low season; CUC64 s, CUC80 d high season) has 24 wood-and-stone *cabinas* atop Punta Periquillo, on Cayo Las Brujas. The simple facilities feature wooden walls, rattan furniture, and modest appointments. Sailboarding and fishing are offered. The thatched **Restaurante El Farallón** (7:30–10 A.M., noon–3 P.M., and 7–10 P.M. daily) overlooks the beach and is a fabulous breeze-swept location for enjoying fresh seafoods. (Gaviota.)

Sol Cayo Santa María (tel. 042/35-1500, fax 042/35-1505, www.solmeliacuba.com; CUC170 s, CUC210 d standard, CUC220 s, CUC280 d suite low season; CUC252 s, CUC315 d standard, CUC325 s, CUC385 d suite high season) is a deluxe 300-room all-inclusive property run by the Spanish Sol Meliá chain. Its *cabinas* are built on piles and separated by small bridges. Rooms are done up in Meliá's lively trademark pastels and have two twins or a king-size bed, safe deposit boxes, satellite TVs, and air-conditioning. Two suites have whirlpool tubs. Facilities include four restaurants, five bars, tennis courts, gym, game room, water sports, kid's club, and live entertainment. (Cubanacán.)

A tad more upscale, C **Meliá Cayo Santa María** (tel. 042/35-0200, fax 042/35-0550, www.solmeliacuba.com; CUC190 s, CUC250 d standard, CUC280 s, CUC350 d suite low season; CUC290 s, CUC360 d standard, CUC390 s, CUC490 d suite high season) has 360 beautifully decorated rooms and a classy elegance to the public areas, which include three swimming pools, four restaurants, four

CIENFUEGOS / VILLA CLARA

bars, game arcade, beauty parlor, and all the water sports you could wish for. (Gaviota.)

The **Royal Hideaway Ensenachos** was under construction at last visit. When completed it will have 440 rooms, including 10 bungalows, 50 honeymoon rooms, and 10 suites in English-colonial style.

Getting There and Around

International flights arrive at the airport on Cayo Las Brujas.

There's a gas station adjacent to the airport, where **Via Rent-a-Car** has an office.

SANCTI SPÍRITUS

Sancti Spíritus Province is on virtually every visitor's list. Justifiably so, for its southwest corner is uniquely endowed. Trinidad—Cuba's best-preserved colonial city—counts among the triumvirate of preeminent destinations in Cuba, along with Habana Vieja and Valle de Viñales. In fact, many a visitor follows an itinerary that triangulates these three places. No visit to Cuba is complete without a visit to Trinidad, a mellow charmer whose unique combination of quintessentially 18th-century architecture, breeze-swept hillside setting, and pickled-in-aspic way of life are irresistibly charming. In addition, this UNESCO World Heritage Site lies both in the lee of the Sierra Escambray *and* within a 10-minute drive of Playa Ancón—the most beautiful beach along the entire southern shore. Although the Sierra

Escambray lies mainly within the provinces of Cienfuegos and Santa Clara, most of the trails and accessible sites of interest lies on the eastern side, within Sancti Spíritus's Gran Parque Natural Topes de Collantes, most easily accessed from Trinidad. As if that weren't enough, the town also boasts the broadest range of *casas particulares* in Cuba and happens to be a leading center of *santería* and Afro-Cuban culture, with a tremendous nightlife. Trinidad grew to colonial wealth from sugar, and the nearby and scenic Valle de los Ingenios (Valley of the Sugar Mills) recalls that era.

The eponymous provincial capital city struggles to compete. In fact, as provincial capital cities go, it's poorly endowed with sites of interest. To the north, rolling hills flow down towards the coastal plains, farmed in sugarcane

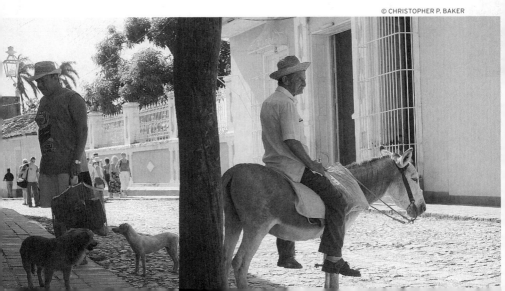

HIGHLIGHTS

Trinidad's Plaza Mayor: This plaza is at the heart of the most complete colonial town center outside Havana, with a fabulous yesteryear ambience and lively Afro-Cuban traditions. There's also a fine choice of *casas particulare* (page 376).

Playa Ancón: Close to Trinidad, this beach offers scintillating sands and excellent scuba diving close to shore (page 385).

Valle de los Ingenios: Planted in sugarcane, this valley is noted for its ruined colonial sugar mills and is best explored on an antique steam train excursion. Stop at Torre de Manaca-Iznaga, a former sugar estate with a fine restaurant, charming setting, and a 43.5-meter-tall tower that can be climbed for the magnificent views (page 386).

Gran Parque Natural Topes de Collantes: This national park hosts magnificent mountain hiking that is great for bird-watching. There are horseback-riding excursions and waterfalls and natural pools good for bathing (page 388).

LOOK FOR ◖ TO FIND RECOMMENDED SIGHTS, ACTIVITIES, DINING, AND LODGING.

and without beaches of noted appeal. The southern coastal plains are mostly inhospitably marshy, with few villages or roads, although bird-watchers, anglers, and nature lovers are served by a number of wetland reserves.

PLANNING YOUR TIME

A full week will barely suffice to enjoy this region, with the bulk of your time centered on Trinidad, a perfect base for forays farther afield. The town itself needs two full days for exploring the colonial sites. However, the Trinidad experience is more about slowing down and immersing oneself in the local life, so a full week here should not be considered too much. Budget one day for an excur-

sion to **Topes de Collantes,** where you can hike mountain trails to waterfalls and even go horseback riding. Bird-watchers will be enthralled, too. Gaviota offers well-thought-out excursions. You'll want beach time, too, so plan one day for sunning, snorkeling, and perhaps even scuba diving at **Playa Ancón,** which is served by two resort hotels. If you prefer the company of Cubans, head to La Boca, where locals flock on weekends. The beach here isn't as large nor as beautiful, but the atmosphere is more lively, and there are *casas particulares.* A steam-train ride from Trinidad to the **Valle de los Ingenios** is de rigueur.

Trinidad is sufficiently popular that Víazul tourist buses operate daily from Havana and

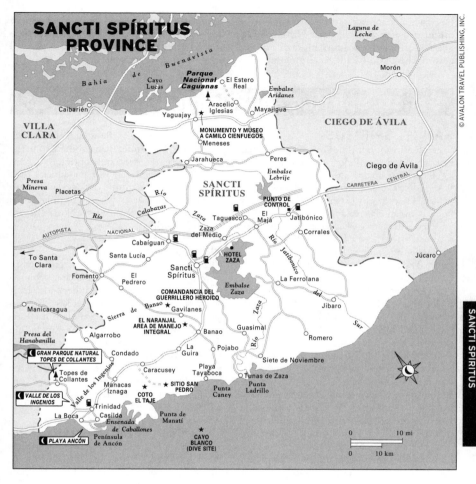

SANCTI SPÍRITUS PROVINCE

© AVALON TRAVEL PUBLISHING, INC.

Varadero. And organized excursions are offered from almost every other tourist destination in Cuba. Fortunately, you don't need your own wheels to get there nor to explore the surrounding region.

The city of Sancti Spíritus, which is well served by buses (but not trains), deserves at least half a day's exploration; you'll be hard-pressed to find more than a full day's worth of things to see and do. Bird-watchers might consider a visit to nearby Zaza, a vast wetland where the fishing for bass and tarpon is world-class. However, Sancti Spíritus sits astride the Carretera Central and makes a well-positioned overnight stop when traveling between Havana and the Oriente. The Autopista runs 15 kilometers north of the city and continues east for 20 kilometers before ending abruptly in the middle of nowhere, near the city of Jatibónico.

The Circuito Norte cuts across the northern province inland of the coast, which has no beaches of appeal. Nature lovers, however, might get a thrill at Parque Nacional Gaguanes, although there are no facilities and getting there is difficult. Interested in revolutionary history? The Monumento y Museo Camilo Cienfuegos, nearby at Yaguajay, is one of the better provincial museums, and well worth the stop in passing.

Sancti Spíritus and Vicinity

SANCTI SPÍRITUS

Sancti Spíritus (pop. 100,000), 390 kilometers east of Havana, is a modern city laid out around a colonial core on a rise above the Río Yayabo. It straddles the Carretera Central, which has helped boost the city's standing as the midway point between Havana and Santiago.

The settlement of Espíritu Santo was co-founded in 1514 by Diego Velázquez and Fernández de Cordoba, who conquered the Yucatán. The city began life about six kilometers from its current position, but was moved eight years later when the original site was plagued by biting ants. The city prospered from cattle ranching and sugar. Its prominence attracted pirates, and during the late 16th and early 17th centuries it was twice ransacked and razed.

In 1895, Winston Churchill arrived in Sancti Spíritus. He loved the cigars but thought the city "a very second-rate place, and a most unhealthy place" (an epidemic of yellow fever and smallpox was raging). By first impressions, it hasn't improved vastly since Churchill passed through: Most of the old town appears forlorn. But quaint cobbled streets and venerable houses with iron filigree and wide doors for carriages attest to the city's antiquity, aided by a restoration of much of the central core.

Orientation

The Carretera Central enters town from the north as Bartolomé Masó (connecting the city to the Autopista) and passes down the town's eastern side before arcing east for Ciego de Ávila.

Streets are laid out in a grid, running northwest–southeast and northeast–southwest. The most important east–west thoroughfare, Avenida de los Mártires, runs west from Bartolomé Masó to Plaza Serafín Sánchez (also called Plaza Central), the main square. Avenida Jesús Menéndez runs south from the plaza, crosses the river, and continues to Trinidad. The main street, Independencia, runs south from the square and divides the city into Este (east) and Oeste (west). Avenida de los Mártires divides the city into Norte (north) and Sur (south).

Plaza Serafín Sánchez

The town's modest square was laid out in 1522 and named for Serafín Sánchez, a homegrown general in the War of Independence. It has none of the charm or grandeur of main plazas elsewhere in Cuba, although it is surrounded by neoclassical buildings, including the impressive *biblioteca* on the west side and the **Teatro Principal** on the south side. The **Museo Provincial General** (tel. 041/27435; Mon.–Thurs. and Sat. 9 A.M.–5 P.M., Sun. 8 A.M.–noon; CUC1), next to the library, is full of antiques and has exhibits on local history, sport, music, and more.

The **Museo de História Natural** (Máximo Gómez Sur #2, tel. 041/26365; Mon.–Wed. 8:30 A.M.– 5 P.M., Fri.–Sat. 2–10 P.M., Sun. 8 A.M.–noon; free), half a block south of the square, has a motley collection of stuffed beasts, plus insects, seashells, and more.

To the northeast, the plaza extends one block along Independencia and opens into a tiny square with a statue of local hero Judas Martínez Moles (1861–1915). South of the park, Independencia is pedestrian-only for two blocks and is lined with shops plus the **Galería Oscar Moresa** (Independencia #55, tel. 41/27106) art gallery, and the **Fondo de Bienes Culturales** (Independencia Sur #55, tel. 0041/27106), selling souvenirs.

statue of Judas Martínez Moles, in a tiny square near Plaza Serafín Sánchez

SANCTI SPÍRITUS

Plaza Honorato del Castillo

This diminutive plaza, at the junction of Calle Jesús Menéndez and Honorato, honors a local general in the War of Independence, but is pinned by a statue of Rudesindo Antonio García Rojo, an eminent citizen in medicine and sciences.

On the plaza's south side is the **Parroquial Mayor del Espíritu Santo** (Agramonte Oeste #58; Tues.–Sat. 9–11 A.M. and 2–5 P.M.), a splendidly preserved church dating to 1680. The triple-tiered tower wasn't completed until 1764, and its cupola not until the middle of the 19th century. The relatively austere church has minimal gilt work and an unimpressive altar, although the ornately carved roof beams are splendid, with dropped gables carved and fitted in cross patterns and supporting a circular center.

The **Farmacia de Medicinas Verdes** (Máximo Gómez #38, tel. 041/24101; Mon.–Fri. 8 A.M.–noon and 1–5 P.M., Sat. 8 A.M.–noon), on the west side of the plaza, is full of old apothecary jars.

One block southwest of the cathedral is the ornate Palacio del Valle, which belonged to one of the wealthiest families in Cuba. The beautiful home now houses the **Museo de Arte Colonial** (Plácido Sur #64, esq. Jesús Menéndez, tel. 041/25455; Tues.–Fri. 9 A.M.–5 P.M., Sat. 2–8 P.M., Sun. 8 A.M.–noon; CUC1), furnished with period decor.

Calle Llano

The quarter immediately south of the cathedral and east of Jesús Menéndez is the city's oldest and quaintest. Here, Calle Llano and adjacent cobbled streets are closed to traffic and lined with quaint houses painted pastel pink, canary, and blue. Lending added grace are fancy wrought-iron balconies, hanging lanterns, and wooden *rejas*. Calle Llano slopes down to the river, overlooked by **La Quinta Santa Elena,** a colonial mansion that is now a restaurant.

Jesús Menéndez crosses the Río Yayabo via **Puente Río Yayabo,** a triple-arched bridge built in 1817 of cut stone in medieval style.

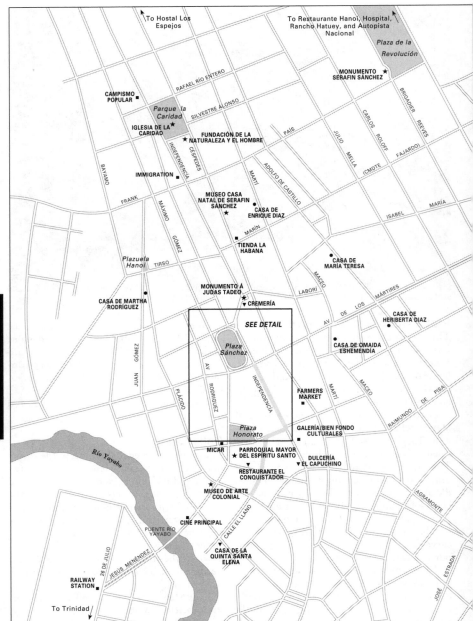

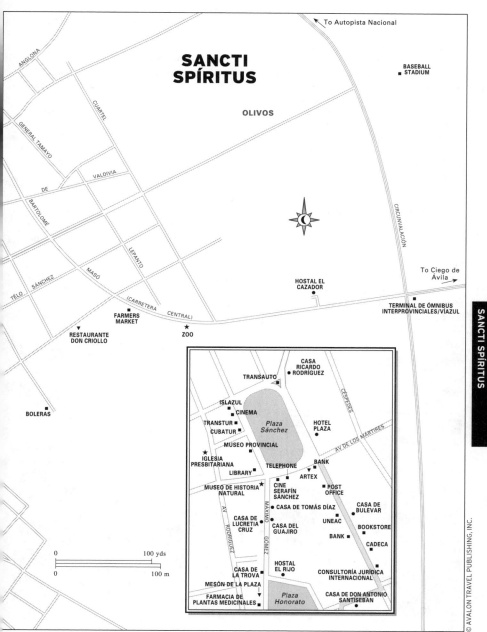

SANCTI
SPÍRITUS

OLIVOS

To Autopista Nacional

BASEBALL
STADIUM

CIRCUNVALACIÓN

To Ciego de
Ávila

TERMINAL DE ÓMNIBUS
INTERPROVINCIALES/VÍAZUL

HOSTAL EL
CAZADOR

ANGLONA
CUARTEL
GENERAL TAMAYO
VALDIVIA
DE
BARTOLOMÉ
LEPANTO
MASÓ
SÁNCHEZ
TELO
(CARRETERA CENTRAL)

FARMERS
MARKET

RESTAURANTE
DON CRIOLLO

ZOO

BOLERAS

CASA
RICARDO
RODRÍGUEZ

TRANSAUTO

CÉSPEDES

ISLAZUL
CINEMA

TRANSTUR
CUBATUR

Plaza
Sánchez

HOTEL
PLAZA

AV. DE LOS MÁRTIRES

MUSEO PROVINCIAL

IGLESIA
PRESBITARIANA

LIBRARY

TELEPHONE

BANK

ARTEX

MUSEO DE HISTORIA
NATURAL

CINE
SERAFÍN
SÁNCHEZ

POST
OFFICE

CASA DE TOMÁS DÍAZ

CASA DE
BULEVAR

CASA DE
LUCRETIA
CRUZ

CASA DEL
GUAJIRO

UNEAC

BOOKSTORE

BANK

CADECA

CASA DE
LA TROVA

HOSTAL
EL RIJO

CONSULTORÍA JURÍDICA
INTERNACIONAL

MESÓN DE LA PLAZA

FARMACIA DE
PLANTAS MEDICINALES

Plaza
Honorato

CASA DE DON ANTONIO
SANTISEBAN

AV. RODRÍGUEZ
MÁXIMO GÓMEZ

0   100 yds
0   100 m

Parque de la Caridad

This small plaza, three blocks north of Plaza Serafín Sánchez, is graced by a simple church, the **Iglesia de Nuestra Señora de la Caridad.** On the southeast corner, the **Fundación de la Naturaleza y el Hombre** (Calle Cruz Pérez #1, tel. 041/28342, funatss@ssp.desoft.cu; Mon.–Fri. 9 A.M.–3 P.M.; CUC0.50) is a museum that honors the 10,889-mile journey by a team of Cubans that paddled from the source of the Amazon to the Bahamas in dugout canoes in 1996. The eclectic miscellany displayed range from the dugout canoe to models of hominids in various stages of evolution, and a copy of Hernán Cortés's medieval suit of armor.

The **Museo Casa Natal Serafín Sánchez** (Céspedes Norte #112, e/ Frank País y Tirso Marín, tel. 041/27791; Tues.–Sat. 8:30 A.M.–5 P.M., Sun. 8 A.M.–noon; CUC0.50), one block south of the plaza, is where the patriot-hero was born. It has exhibits on his life. More interesting is the **Monumento Serafín Sánchez,** a bronze bas-relief wall with plaques showing events in the Wars of Independence; it's on the west side of the **Plaza de la Revolu-**ción on Bartolomé Masó, esq. Frank País, five blocks east of the museum.

Entertainment

The **Casa de la Trova** (Máximo Gómez Sur #26, tel. 041/26802), on Plaza Honorato, features traditional performances Tuesday–Sunday 9 P.M.–midnight, and a *peña* Sunday 10 A.M.–2 P.M.

Artex (Tues.–Sun. 10 P.M.–2 A.M.; CUC1), above the Banco Financiero Internacional on the main plaza, draws youth for karaoke, music, and videos.

Cabaret Los Laureles (Carretera Central Km 383, tel. 041/27016), in the namesake hotel, offers an alfresco *cabaret espectáculo* followed by disco stars (Fri.–Sun. at 10 P.M.; CUC5 entrance, including five beers or a bottle of rum plus two Cokes). The cabaret is preceded by a great jazz group, and includes transvestite acts. Karaoke is hosted Tuesday–Thursday. **Restaurante Don Criollo** hosts a small cabaret on Saturday at 10 P.M.

Cine Serafín Sánchez, on the west side of Parque Central, and **Cine Príncipe,** 50 me-

Bolera has six bowling lanes and is open 24 hours.

© CHRISTOPHER P. BAKER

ters east of the old bridge on Jesús Menéndez, show movies.

Bolera (tel. 041/22339; 24 hours), on Roloff, three blocks south of Avenida de los Mártires, has six bowling lanes (CUC1 for 22 "bowls") and three pool tables (CUC1.80 per hour).

Baseball is played October–May at **Estadio Victoria del Girón**, in Reparto Olivos.

A **zoo** (Tues.–Sun. 9:30 A.M.–3:30 P.M.; CUC0.30) on Bartolomé Masó, 100 meters south of Avenida de los Mártires, features lions, monkeys, hyenas, antelopes, and water buffalo.

Accommodations

You can make reservations for *campismos* throughout Sancti Spíritus Province at the **Campismo Popular** (Independencia Norte #201, off Parque Maceo, tel. 041/26631).

Casas Particulares: The **Casa de Martha Rodríguez** (Plácido Norte #69, e/ Calderon y Tirso Marin, tel. 041/23556; CUC15–20) has two upstairs rooms, simply albeit nicely furnished, with air-conditioning, fans, and clean, modern hot-water bathrooms. It gets street noise. Meals are served on an upstairs terrace with rockers.

Hostal Los Espejos (Socorro #56, e/ Céspedes y Martí, tel. 041/26261; CUC15–20) is a beautifully kept colonial home with polished hardwoods and *vitrales* that open to a beautiful rear patio with rockers. The two rooms each have air-conditioning, TV, fridge and private hot-water bathroom. There's secure parking.

Casa de Don Antonio Santisteban (Honorato #7 sur, e/ Llano y Independencia, tel. 041/24185; CUC15–20) is a simple charmer with two rooms: One is huge, with a high-beamed ceiling and colonial tiled floor plus two double beds, and an old hot-water bathroom; the other is smaller, with two single beds and a modern hot-water bathroom.

Casa de María Teresa Lorenzo (Adolfo del Castillo #33 altos, e/ Av. de los Mártires y Valdina, tel. 041/24733; CUC15–20) offers two pleasing upstairs air-conditioned rooms with fans, fridges, and modern hot-water bath-

rooms. Meals are served on a shaded terrace. There's a nice TV lounge.

Casa de Ricardo Rodríguez (Independencia #28 altos, tel. 041/23029; CUC20) is a centenarian house on the northeast corner of the main plaza, entered via a marble staircase like a fortress dungeon. It has a large lounge with columns, rockers, and rattan furniture, plus a balcony overlooking the plaza. Two spacious upstairs air-conditioned rooms are simply but adequately furnished and have clean private hot-water bathrooms. One room, to the rear, is well-lit and breeze-swept and has its own thatched *ranchón*.

Casa de Enrique Díaz (Martí #111, e/ Sobral y San Cristóbal, tel. 041/27553; CUC20–25) is a spacious colonial home, minimally furnished, but breeze-swept, opening to a rear patio with secure parking. It has two pleasant, albeit simply furnished, rooms with shuttered windows opening to the patio, with small private hot-water bathrooms.

I like **Casa El Guajiro** (Máximo Gómez #9 altos, e/ Cervantes y Honorato, tel. 041/27626; CUC15–20), a colonial home with an airy, cross-ventilated lounge with antique furnishings. It has two slightly dark but spacious air-conditioned rooms with fans and small private bathrooms with hot water. The larger of the two has a balcony overlooking the street.

Casa Bulevar (Independencia #17, tel. 041/26745, CUC15–20) offers an independent colonial-era apartment with huge but minimally furnished lounge with rockers, a separate TV lounge with stereo, and two spacious bedrooms with a modern bathroom with hot water.

Other *casas particulares* to consider include **Hostal El Cazador** (Carretera Central #209 sur, e/ Terminal de Omnibus 7 Fería Agropercuario, tel. 041/27594); **Casa de Lucrecia Cruz** (Máximo Gómez #8, e/ Cervantes y Honorato, c/o tel. 041/27626; CUC20); and **Casa de Tomás Diaz** (Máximo Gómez #9; tel. 041/27626, CUC20–25).

Hotels: The **Hotel Plaza** (tel. 041/27102 and 27168, comercial@hostalesss.co.cu; CUC46 s/d year-round including breakfast),

SANCTI SPÍRITUS

on the east side of Parque Central, is a restored colonial building. Its 27 rooms are small but lofty and pleasantly furnished with wrought-iron furnishings, air-conditioning, satellite TV, and modern bathrooms. The small lobby bar has appeal, but the restaurant usually can muster little on the menu. It offers Internet service. (Cubanacán.)

Of greater appeal, **【 Hostal del Rijo** (Calle Honorato del Castillo #12, tel. 041/28588, fax 041/28577, aloja@hostalesss.co.cur; CUC45 s/d year-round including breakfast) is an 1818 neoclassical structure entered through soaring carriage doors. It has 16 large air-conditioned rooms (including a suite) centered on a patio and boasting lofty beamed ceilings, wrought-iron lamps, terra-cotta tiles, sea-blue and yellow decor, and period-themed art, plus satellite TV and modern marble bathrooms. Facilities include a breakfast room, bar, and humidor. (Cubanacán.)

Villa Los Laureles (Carretera Central Km 383, tel. 041/27016, fax 041/23913, loslaureles@esiss.colombus.cu; CUC26 s, CUC34 d low season; CUC30 s, CUC38 d high season) on Bartolomé Masó, about four kilometers north of town, offers 78 handsome air-conditioned *cabinas* sprinkled throughout meagerly landscaped grounds. All have satellite TV, telephones, refrigerators, telephones, and modern bathrooms. There's a swimming pool, elegant restaurant, and cabaret. (Islazul.)

Villa Rancho Hatuey (Carretera Central Km 383, tel. 041/28315, fax 041/28830, comercial@rhatuey.co.cu; CUC32 s year-round; CUC40 d low season, CUC45 d high season), about three kilometers north of town, has 74 air-conditioned rooms with satellite TVs and telephones in two-story *cabinas* in contemporary Mediterranean style. There's a squash court and swimming pool. (Cubanacán.)

Food
【 Mesón de la Plaza (Máximo Gómez #34, tel. 041/28546; daily 9 A.M.–8:30 P.M.) is the only notable eatery in town. Styled as a Spanish *bodega,* this atmospheric charmer has rough-hewn tables and cowhide chairs. Start-

ers include a *garbanzo mesonero* (garbanzo with bacon, pork, and sausage) or *ensalada de garbanzo* (baked chickpea, green peas, onions, and peppers, CUC1.50). Main dishes include grilled fish (CUC6.50) and baked chicken in orange (CUC4.45). Wash it down with sangria.

The simple restaurant in the **Hostal del Rijo** (tel. 041/28588; daily 7 A.M.–10 P.M.), facing Mesón de la Plaza, offers garlic shrimp (CUC7.50) and roast chicken (CUC5.50), and has a pleasant cocktail bar.

La Quinta Santa Elena (Calle Llano, tel. 041/28167; daily 10 A.M.–10 P.M.) has a fairly large *criollo* menu, but rarely are more than two or three items available. Go for the stately surrounds: lofty beamed ceilings, tasteful art on the walls, and breezes wafting through tall carriage doors.

The thatched **Restaurante Don Criollo** (Raimundo de Pisa, e/ Reeves y Carretera Central, tel. 041/20755; daily 8 A.M.–10 P.M.) is a rustic eatery with farm-themed decor. It serves the usual *criollo* fare and has a fixed meal for CUC5, plus paella (CUC1.85).

Penny-pinchers might try **Restaurante El Conquistador** (Agramonte Oeste, no tel.; noon–2 P.M. and 6–9 P.M. daily), which serves tortillas (from 3 pesos) and roast pork (12 pesos), and offers set meals for five pesos.

You can buy produce at the **mercado agropecuario** (Independencia, esq. Honorato), although hygiene standards are wanting. The charming little **Dulcería el Capuchino,** one block south, sells pastries, and there's a bakery at Máximo Gómez and Frank País.

A **guarapería** (Céspedes, esq. Fajardo) sells delicious fresh-squeezed cane juice.

Information and Services
The **post office** (Independencia Sur #8; 8 A.M.–5 P.M. Mon.–Sat.) is one block south of the main plaza. **Etecsa** (Bartolomé Masó; daily 8:30 A.M.–8 P.M.), 100 meters north of the Plaza de la Revolución, has international telephone plus Internet service.

Banco Financiero Internacional (Independencia Sur #2) is on the southeast corner of Plaza Sánchez; **Banco Popular** is one block south. You can also change foreign currency at **Cadeca** (Independencia Sur #31).

Hospital Provincial Camilo Cienfuegos (tel. 041/24017) is on Bartolomé Masó, opposite the Plaza de la Revolución. There's a **Farmacia** (Independencia #123, tel. 041/24660; 24 hours) on Parque la Caridad, and **Farmacia de Plantas Medicinales** (Máximo Gómez Sur #40, tel. 041/24101; Mon.–Fri. 8 A.M.–noon and 1–5 P.M., Sat. 8 A.M.–noon) on Plaza Honorato.

Inmigración (Independencia Norte #107; Mon.–Tues. and Thurs.–Fri. 8:15 A.M.–noon and 1:30–4 P.M.) can issue *prórrogas*. The **Consultoría Jurídica Internacional** (Independencia #39 Altos Sur, e/ Ernesto Valdés Muñoz y Cervantes, tel. 041/28448; Mon.–Fri. 8:30 A.M.–12:30 P.M. and 1:30–5:30 P.M.) provides legal assistance.

Getting There and Away

The **Terminal Provincial de Ómnibus** (tel. 041/24142) is at the junction of Bartolomé Masó and the *circunvalación,* east of town.

All **Víazul** (tel. 041/22-4142) buses traveling Havana, Varadero, and Trinidad to/from Santiago de Cuba stop in Sancti Spíritus. Buses depart Sancti Spíritus for Havana at 2:20 A.M., 3:05 A.M., 8:15 A.M., and 8:40 P.M.; for Holguín at 10:05 A.M.; for Santiago at 2 A.M., 3:10 A.M., 9:30 A.M., 3:15 P.M., and 8:50 P.M.; for Trinidad at 5:35 A.M.; and for Varadero at 6:25 A.M.

Astro buses depart Sancti Spíritus for Havana at 7:20 A.M. and 9:35 P.M.; for Santa Clara at 6 A.M. (CUC5 *especial,* CUC3.50 *regular*); and for Camagüey at 7 A.M. (CUC8 *especial,* CUC7 *regular*).

Local buses serve nearby towns from the **Terminal Municipal** (Calle Sánchez and Carlos Roloff, tel. 041/22162), one block south of Avenida de los Mártires. *Camiones* (trucks) also run between towns, but foreigners may be denied.

The **train station** (Av. Jesús Menéndez, esq. 26 de Julio, tel. 041/29228, or 27914 express trains) is 400 yards southwest of Puente Yayabo; the ticket office is open daily 8 A.M.–

4 P.M. (until 9 P.M. when there are departures). There is service from Havana every second day at 9:45 P.M. (CUC13.50); and to Havana from Sancti Spíritus at 9 P.M., stopping in Santa Clara (CUC3.50). A train departs Cienfuegos for Sancti Spíritus on Mondays at 1:35 P.M. (CUC5.15) via Santa Clara; return trains depart Sancti Spíritus on Mondays at 4 A.M.

Sancti Spíritus is not on the main Havana–Santiago line, however. Trains traveling between Havana and Santiago de Cuba stop at Guayos, 15 kilometers north of Sancti Spíritus. You should be in the front carriage of the train to alight at Guayos, where taxis are usually available for the run to Sancti Spíritus. If departing Sancti Spíritus to catch the *especial* you should buy your ticket at the rail station before departing for Guayos, as the Guayos ticket office may tell you that all tourist quota tickets are sold out.

Local commuter trains also operate from the **Salón de Ferromozas** (tel. 41/23653), adjacent to the station on Jesús Menéndez.

Getting Around

Most people get around by **horse-drawn taxis,** which ply the main streets. Ten pesos gets you anywhere you want to go, but you may be charged in dollars. Tourist taxis are available on Plaza Serafín Sánchez. *Colectivos* congregate outside the bus terminals.

Excursions are offered by **Havanatur** (Calle Llano, tel. 41/28308), in La Quinta Santa Elena; and **Cubatur** (tel. 041/28518, cubaturss@enet.cu), on the west side of Plaza Serafín Sánchez.

You can rent cars from **Havanautos** (tel. 0141/28403), in Hotel Los Laureles; **Micar** (tel. 041/28257), on Plaza Honorato; and **Transtur** (tel. 041/28181), on Plaza Serafín Sánchez. There's a Cupet gas station on the Carretera Central, about four kilometers north of downtown.

EMBALSE ZAZA

East of Sancti Spíritus, the Carretera Central runs east for Ciego de Ávila Province. Six kilometers east of the city, a side road leads south to

Embalse Zaza, a man-made lake studded with flooded forest and known for extraordinary numbers of trout and world-record-breaking bass. Marsh birds flock in from far and wide. Zaza is a favorite spot for bird-watchers, anglers, and hunters.

Fishing costs from CUC30 per person for four hours; CUC70 for eight hours. Horseback riding is offered. All activities are handled through Hotel Zaza.

Accommodations

Hotel Zaza (tel. 041/27015, fax 041/28359, hzaza@essis.co.cu; CUC27 s, CUC36 d low season; CUC30 s, CUC40 d high season) is a faceless two-story hotel with 124 air-conditioned rooms with private baths, telephones, and satellite TVs. Most rooms enjoy views over the lake and there's a rooftop *mirador*. Facilities include a pleasant lobby bar, a modest restaurant, nightclub, swimming pool, game room, and store. It doubles as a hunting and fishing lodge. (Islazul.)

RESERVA ECOLÓGICO ALTURAS DE BANAO

The road southwest from Sancti Spíritus to Trinidad rises, dips, and swings magnificently along the foothills of the Alturas de Banao, whose sheer, barren crags remind me of the Scottish highlands. Coffee is grown on the upper slopes.

From the village of **Banao,** 20 kilometers west of Sancti Spíritus, you can follow the valley of the Río Banao north into the mountainous heights, where a virtually pristine and beautiful 3,050-hectare swath is protected in the Banao Heights Ecological Reserve, also known as El Naranjal. There are four separate ecosystems: semi-deciduous forest, tropical moist forest, rare cloud forest, and an endemic assembly associated with the dramatic limestone mountain formations called *mogotes.* The region is rich in flora, with more than 700 flowering plants (more than 100 of them endemic), including over 60 orchid species. Banao is a paradise for bird-watchers—parrots are numerous. You can hike to cave systems, waterfalls, and mineral pools at **Las Cortinas.**

There are four biological stations. The visitors center at **La Sabina** offers meals and you can camp. **Flora y Fauna** (Calle 42, esq. 7ima, Havana, tel. 07/203-1433, fax 07/204-9347, ffauna@ceniai.inf.cu) was planning to offer ecotours. It is signed off the main highway.

During the war to oust Batista, Che Guevara established his headquarters—**Comandancia del Guerrillero Heróico**—near the community of Gavilanes, in the heart of the mountains and reached by a dirt trail; the turnoff from the Trinidad road is at the hamlet of Las Brisas, five kilometers east of Banao. It's a stiff hike (about 10 km) from the trailhead, near Campismo Planta Cantú. There's an obelisk at the *comandancia.*

Accommodations

Campismo Planta Cantú (tel. 041/29698; CUC5 per person), tucked into a valley about five kilometers north of Las Brisas, has 32 basic rooms in cabins popular with Cubans on weekends. It has a swimming pool, and a restaurant serves mediocre food when Cubans are in. Horses can be rented. There are electrical outlets for campervans.

NORTH OF SANCTI SPÍRITUS

The Circuito Norte coast road parallels the shore some miles inland, connecting Remedios (in Villa Clara Province) and Morón (in Ciego de Ávila Province).

Monumento y Museo Camilo Cienfuegos

The only site of interest is in the town of Jaguajay, 40 kilometers east of Caibarién, where an impressive five-meter-tall bronze statue of Camilo Cienfuegos stands one kilometer north of town. Within its base is a museum (tel. 0419/52689; Mon.–Sat. 8 A.M.–4 P.M., Sun. 9 A.M.–1 P.M.; CUC1) dedicated to the memory of the revolutionary commander and the battle he led here against Batista's troops in the closing days of December 1958. This excellent museum displays maps, armaments, models,

On the monument:
"CAMILO ES UN HOMBRE DEL PUEBLO
QUE SALIÓ DEL PUEBLO
Y EL CONSUELO QUE DEBE TENER
NUESTRO PUEBLO ES QUE EN EL PUEBLO
HAY MUCHOS CAMILO
Y CAMILO SEGUIRÁ VIVIENDO
EN HOMBRES COMO EL."
FIDEL

© CHRISTOPHER P. BAKER

© CHRISTOPHER P. BAKER

Monumento Camilo Cienfuegos, at Jaguajay

and even Cienfuegos's stuffed horse! The hospital opposite the monument was formerly an army barracks, captured by Cienfuegos's Rebel Army in 1958. A small tank (converted from a tractor) used in the assault on the barracks stands outside.

Schoolchildren are bussed in each October 28 and parade to the shore to toss "a flower for Camilo" into the sea on the anniversary of his death in a mysterious plane crash in 1959.

Parque Nacional Caguanas

Northeast of Jaguajay the sugarcane fields meld into the swampy coastal flats, now protected within a national park. The park harbors almost 200 species of fauna, including Cuba's largest colony of cranes—an endemic subspecies of the *Graus canadensis nesiotes* crane. A highlight is the park's 35 or so caves with subterranean galleries and pre-Columbian petroglyphs. Iguanas are found on **Cayo Piedra,** where you can explore some of the 18 caves.

The park is part of the 313,503-hectare **Reserva de la Biosfera Buenavista,** enshrining eleven separate protected areas.

Access to the park is via **Mayijagua,** about 15 kilometers east of Jaguajay. *Getting* to the park is another matter: At last visit the dirt road was appalling and fit for four-wheel drive only. **EcoTur** (Carretera Meneses–Yaguajay Km 1.5, tel. 041/52312, ppalma@yag.cu) offers excursions.

Accommodations

Just east of Mayijagua is **Villa San José del Lago** (tel. 041/56108, fax 041/56290, jlagos@enet.cu; CUC25 s, CUC32 d year-round), a pleasant spa resort with cabins beneath palms surrounding a lagoon with flamingos, pedalboats and rowboats, plus three swimming pools (one with thermal water). The 30 simple thatched *cabinas* have air-conditioning and satellite TV, and there's a modest restaurant, bars, video and game room. Massages and mud and herbal treatments are offered. It's a popular spot with Cubans and gets lively on weekends, when the music is cranked up. (Islazul.)

Trinidad and Vicinity

TRINIDAD

Trinidad (pop. 38,000), the crown jewel of Cuba's colonial cities, is 67 kilometers southwest of Sancti Spíritus and 80 kilometers east of Cienfuegos. It was the fourth of the seven cities founded by Diego de Velázquez in 1514. No other city in Cuba is so well preserved or so charming. The entire city is a national monument lent charms by its historical landmarks and its setting of great natural beauty, sitting astride a hill, where it catches the breezes and gazes out over the Caribbean against a backdrop of verdurous Sierra Escambray.

Its narrow, unmarked cobbled streets are paved with stones (*chinas pelonas*) shipped across the Atlantic as ballast or taken from the nearby river. The maze of streets is lined with terra-cotta tile-roofed houses in soft pastel colors. Much of the architecture is neoclassical and baroque, with a Moorish flavor. However, there are no great palaces as in Havana. The exquisite buildings are fronted by mahogany balustrades, fancy *rejas* of wrought iron and turned wooden rods, and massive wooden doors with *postigos* that open to let the breezes flow through cool, tile-floored rooms connected by double-swing half-doors (*mamparas*) topped by *vitrales*.

Mule-drawn carts and cowboys on horseback clip-clop through the cobbled streets. Laughing children chase hoops through the plazas. Old folks rock gently beneath shady verandas, serenaded by twittering songbirds in bamboo cages—a Trinidad tradition. At night the town is eerily still. Then the cool air flows downhill, the narrow alleys become refreshing channels, and it is a special joy to stroll the traffic-free streets that make the town feel even more adrift from the 20th century.

Trinidad is steeped in religiosity, both *santería* and Catholicism, and there is no shortage of Afro-Cuban religious practitioners and Catholic processions. Easter and Christmas are good times to visit.

Keeping caged songbirds outside one's home is a Trinidad tradition that is still kept alive.

© CHRISTOPHER P. BAKER

SANCTI SPÍRITUS

TRINIDAD AND VICINITY

Tourists are plentiful, and so are petty thieves and *jiniteros* hoping to separate you from your dollars. Child beggars work you for coins or *chicle* (chewing gum).

History

The initial settlement, named Villa de la Santísima Trinidad, was founded in 1514 by Diego de Velázquez on a site settled by the Taíno. The Spanish conquistadores found the native Indians panning for gold in the nearby rivers. The Spanish established a lucrative (but short-lived) gold mine that lent vigor to the young township and the wharves of nearby Casilda. Hernán Cortés set up base here in 1518 to provision his expedition to conquer the Aztec empire. Soon fleets bearing the spoils of Mexico gathered in Casilda, bringing new prosperity and eclipsing Trinidad's meager mines.

Trinidad was just far enough from the reach of Spanish authorities in Havana to develop a

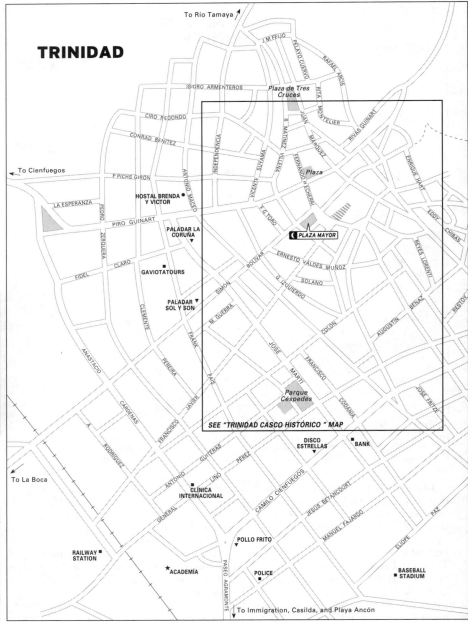

TRINIDAD

To Río Tamaya

To Cienfuegos

To La Boca

To Immigration, Casilda, and Playa Ancón

Plaza de Tres Cruces

HOSTAL BRENDA Y VICTOR

PALADAR LA CORUÑA

GAVIOTATOURS

PALADAR SOL Y SON

Plaza

PLAZA MAYOR

Parque Céspedes

SEE "TRINIDAD CASCO HISTÓRICO " MAP

DISCO ESTRELLAS

BANK

CLÍNICA INTERNACIONAL

POLLO FRITO

RAILWAY STATION

ACADÉMIA

POLICE

BASEBALL STADIUM

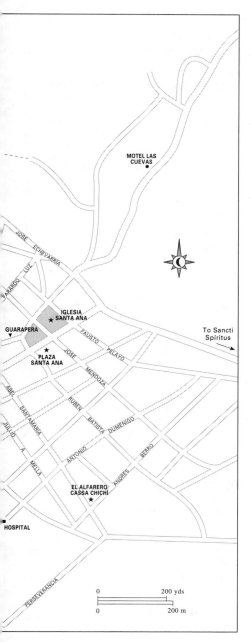

bustling commerce smuggling contraband to circumvent trade restrictions imposed by the Spanish Crown. Its position on Cuba's underbelly was also perfect for trade with Jamaica, the epicenter of the Caribbean slave trade. Trinidad grew prosperous importing slaves, many of whom were put to work locally, stimulating the sugar trade. A mild climate, fertile soil, and easy access to the Caribbean favored Trinidad's agricultural and commercial growth. Money poured in from the proceeds of sugar grown in the Valle de los Ingenios. When the English occupied Cuba, in 1762–3, Trinidad became a free port and prospered even further, entering its golden age.

Wealthy citizens built their sumptuous homes around the main square—Plaza Mayor—and along the adjoining streets. Pianos from Berlin, sumptuous furniture from France, linens, lattices, and silverware from Colombia were unloaded here. Language schools and academies were even set up to prepare the children of the wealthy to complete their studies in Europe. The city's wealth drew pirates. At first, the city created its own fleet to guard against pirates, but later decided to take the pirates to its bosom; many citizens prospered as victualers to the sea-roving vagabonds, while some pirates bought property and settled.

By the early 19th century, Cienfuegos, with its vastly superior harbor, began to surpass Casilda, which had begun silting up. Trinidad began a steady decline, hastened by tumult in the slave trade and new competition from more advanced estates elsewhere in Cuba. Isolated from the Cuban mainstream, Trinidad foundered. By the turn of the 20th century, it was a down-at-the-heels little town. Only the faded beauty remained.

In the 1950s, Batista declared Trinidad a "jewel of colonial architecture." A preservation law was passed—a boon for latter-day tourism but regarded as a bane for the past 40 years, as development was prohibited and the city continued to stagnate in its own beauty. The construction of the Carretera Central on the north side of the Sierra Escambray had already stolen the through traffic, ensuring that Trinidad would be preserved in its past. The town was named a national monument in 1965. A Restoration Committee was established, and the historic core around Plaza Mayor has been completely restored. In 1988 UNESCO named Trinidad a World Heritage Site.

Hurricane Dennis swept through in July 2005, doing considerable damage.

Orientation

Trinidad slopes uphill, to the northeast. The cobbled historical core (*casco histórico*) with most sites of interest takes up the upper quarter bounded to the south by Calle Antonio Maceo and to the east by Calle Lino Pérez. At its heart is Plaza Mayor, at the top of Calle Simón Bolívar. It's a warren—some streets end at T junctions, while others curl or bifurcate, one leading uphill while another drops sharply to another Y fork or right-angled bend. All this was meant to fool marauding pirates, but it does a pretty good job on visitors, too. The streets are each sloped in a slight V, with gutters in the center (according to legend, the city's first governor had a right leg shorter than the other and could thereby be level when walking the streets by staying on the right-hand side). Many streets are closed to traffic by stone pillars and cannons stuck nose-first in the ground—the cannons served in colonial days to protect pedestrians as carriages turned the corners.

Below the touristed core, the streets are paved and laid out on a rough grid with Parque Céspedes at its center. The main street is Calle José Martí, which runs northwest–southeast and is lined with shops and bars. Calle Bolívar runs perpendicular, and leads northeast to Plaza Mayor. Calle Camilo Cienfuegos, one block southeast of Parque Céspedes, is the major northeast–southwest thoroughfare.

The Circuito Sur road from Cienfuegos bifurcates as it enters Trinidad: Calle Piro Guinart (to the left) leads to the historic core; Anastacio Cárdenas (to the right) skirts the southern end of town and connects with Camilo Cienfuegos

TRINIDAD STREET NAMES

COLONIAL NAME	NEW NAME
Alameda	Jesús Menéndez
Amargura	Juan Márquez
Angarilla	Fidel Claro
Boca	Piro Guinart
Carmén	Frank País
Colón	Colón
Cristo	Fernando H. Echerrí
Desengaño	Simón Bolívar
Encarnación	Vicente Suyama
Gloria	Gustavo Izquierdo
Guaurabo	Pablo Pichs Girón
Gutiérrez	Antonio Maceo
Jesús María	José Martí
Lirio	Abel Santamaría
Media Luna	Ernesto Valdés Muñoz
Olvido	Santiago Escobar
Peña	Francisco Gómez Toro
Real	Ruben Martínez Villena
Reforma	Anastasio Cárdenas
Rosario	Francisco Javier Zerquera
San Procopio	Lino Pérez
Santa Ana	José Mendoza
Santo Domingo	Camilo Cienfuegos

(for Sancti Spíritus) and Paseo Agramonte (to Casilda and Playa Ancón).

Most streets have two names: a colonial name and a postrevolutionary name. Locals prefer to use the older names. (See the sidebar *Trinidad Street Names.*)

Plaza Mayor

The graceful plaza lies at the heart of the original settlement. The park at its core is ringed with silver trellises, with shiny white wrought-iron benches beneath the shade of palms and hibiscus bowers. The plaza is adorned with small neoclassical statues, including two bronze greyhounds that would be at home in a Landseer painting.

On the plaza's northeast corner is the modest **Iglesia Parroquial de la Santísima Trinidad** (Mon.–Sat. 11 A.M.–12:30 P.M.). The cathedral

WALKING TOUR OF OLD TRINIDAD

Trinidad has so many sites of interest that it pays to plan your sightseeing. The following tour takes in virtually every site of note. Refer to the main sightseeing text for sights not described here.

Begin at the northest corner of **Plaza Mayor** and perambulate the square counterclockwise, taking in all the sites of interest. Back at the northeast corner, immediately east of the cathedral, cobbled Calle Fernando Hernández (Cristo) leads past a wide staircase. At the base of the steps is a handsome ocher-colored house – the **Mansión de los Conspiradores** – with an ornately woodworked balcony. The house is so named because La Rosa Blanca (the secret organization against Spanish colonial rule) met here.

One block east on Cristo brings you to the triangular **Plazuela de Segarta,** and Calle Jesús Menéndez, containing some of the oldest homes in the city, among them the **Casa de la Trova,** decorated with murals and dating to 1777. Off the northeast corner of the plazuela is Calle Juan Manuel Márquez, featuring a trio of houses with wonderfully photogenic elevated galleries.

Turn left on Márquez and walk west one block to Simón Bolívar. To your right, atop the hill, you'll see the near-derelict **Iglesia de la Virgen de la Candelaria de la Popa.** It was built in 1726 and is named for the *popa* (stern) of a ship called the *Virgen de la Candelaria* that sank off Cartagena. The stern washed ashore near Casilda and a chapel was built. Three patinated bells hang over the door. The only reason to ascend is for the splendid views over the city. The steep ascent is via a path lined with hovels; you'll be hit up for alms.

Three blocks further along Márquez delivers you at **Plaza de Tres Cruces,** a bare-earth area pinned by three wooden crosses that for several centuries have formed the terminus of Trinidad's annual Easter procession. Note the houses with metal crosses on their exterior walls: They're way-stops on the procession.

Return along Márquez to Ciro Redondo; turn right. The house at #261 dates to 1754 and was built for Carlos Merlin, a French pirate. Turn left onto Fernando Hernández Echarrí. On your right, at the end of the block, is the **Antiguo Convento de San Francisco de Asís.** After visiting, turn right onto Piro Guinart and walk one block to **Plaza Jigüe.**

After viewing the **Ayuntamiento y Carcel** and **Casa Templo de Santería Yemaya,** walk southeast one block to Playa Mayor and turn right onto Simón Bolívar. The cobbled street leads downhill past the **Museo Histórico.** At Maceo (three blocks), turn right and follow this wide cobbled street for three blocks. Turn right on Lino Pérez, which leads you two blocks downhill to **Parque Céspedes** at Martí. On the southwest side is the **Iglesia de Paula,** containing impressive statuary.

End your walking tour here. Alternately, anyone with an interest in art might follow Lino Pérez south five blocks to the former Antigua Cuartel de Dragones (Dragoon's barracks), built in 1844 and now the **Academía de Artes Plásticas** (tel. 0419/4350; Mon.-Fri. 8 A.M.-5 P.M.), with a free art gallery.

was rebuilt in 1894 on the spot where once stood the original parish church. Restored in 1996, it is more English than Spanish inside, with a Victorian-Gothic vaulted ceiling and altar carved from mahogany; there's no baroque extravagance, although the carved statuary is intriguing, as is the 18th-century Cristo de la Vera Cruz (Christ of the True Cross).

On the northwest corner is Palacio Brunet, a beautifully preserved, two-story mansion dating from 1741 and housing the **Museo Romántico** (Calle Fernando Hernández Echerrí #52, esq. Calle Bolívar, tel. 0419/4363; Tues.–Sun. 9 A.M.–5 P.M.; entrance CUC2, cameras CUC2, videos CUC5). The dozen rooms are filled with intriguing artwork and fabulous antiques. Note the solid carved-cedar ceiling, dating from 1770, and the *mediopunto* arches. Upstairs, step out onto the balcony to admire the view down over the square. The stunning

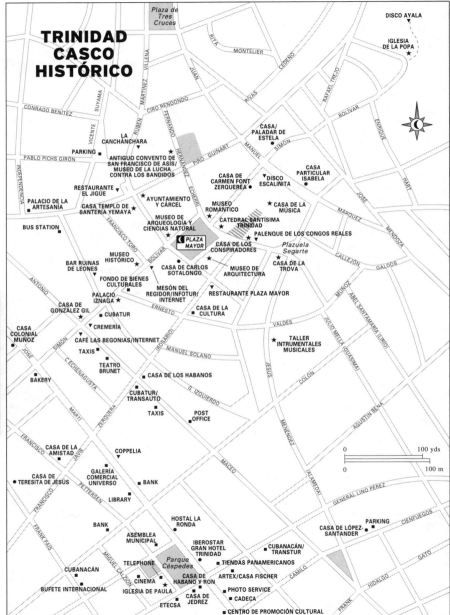

TRINIDAD CASCO HISTÓRICO

Plaza de Tres Cruces

DISCO AYALA

IGLESIA DE LA POPA ★

CONRADO BENITEZ

RITA

MONTELIER

RIVAS

CEDEÑO

RAFAEL TREJO

BOLIVAR

ENRIQUE

HART

MARQUEZ

MENDOZA

GALDOS

PABLO PICHS GIRON

INDEPENDENCIA

PARKING ■

LA CANCHÁNCHARA ▼

ANTIGUO CONVENTO DE SAN FRANCISCO DE ASÍS/ MUSEO DE LA LUCHA CONTRA LOS BANDIDOS ★

RESTAURANTE ▼ EL JIGÜE

PALACIO DE LA ■ ARTESANÍA

BUS STATION ■

CASA TEMPLO DE SANTERÍA YEMAYÁ ★

AYUNTAMIENTO Y CÁRCEL ★

MUSEO ROMÁNTICO ★

CASA DE CARMEN FONT ★ ZERQUERA

CASA/ PALADAR DE ESTELA ▼

SIMON

MANUEL

DISCO ★ ESCALINITA ●

CASA PARTICULAR ISABELA ■

JOSE

CASA DE LA MÚSICA ★

CATEDRAL SANTÍSIMA TRINIDAD ★

MUSEO DE ARQUEOLOGÍA Y CIENCIAS NATURAL ★

FRANCISCO TORO

BAR RUINAS ▼ DE LEONES

MUSEO HISTÓRICO ★

ANTONIO

CASA DE ★ GONZÁLEZ GIL

FONDO DE BIENES CULTURALES ■

PALACIO ★ IZNAGA

■ CUBATUR

▼ CREMERÍA

BOLIVAR

CASA DE CARLOS SOTALONGO ★

MESÓN DEL REGIDOR/INFOTUR/ INTERNET ▼

ERNESTO

PLAZA MAYOR

CASA DE LOS ★ CONSPIRADORES

MUSEO DE ARQUITECTURA ★

RESTAURANTE PLAZA MAYOR ▼

CASA DE LA ★ CULTURA

PALENQUE DE LOS CONGOS REALES ★

Plazuela Segarte

CASA DE LA ★ TROVA

MUÑOZ

VALDES

JULIO MELLA (GUASIMA)

ABEL SANTAMARIA (LIRIO)

CALLEJÓN

CASA COLONIAL ● MUÑOZ

JOSE

SIMON

CAFÉ LAS BEGONIAS/INTERNET ■

TAXIS ■

C. ECHENAGUSTA

TEATRO BRUNET ■

BAKERY ■

MARTI

ROSARIO)

MANUEL SOLANO

CASA DE LOS HABANOS ■

ZERQUERA

CUBATUR/ ■ TRANSAUTO

TAXIS ■

G. IZQUIERDO

POST ■ OFFICE

JESUS

COLON

TALLER INTRUMENTALES MUSICALES ★

MENENDEZ

AGUSTIN BENA

FRANCISCO

JAVIE

CASA DE LA AMISTAD ▼

COPPELIA ●

GALERÍA COMERCIAL UNIVERSO ●

LIBRARY ■

MACEO

ALMEDA)

FRANCISCO

CASA DE ● TERESITA DE JESÚS

PETTERSEN

■ BANK

GENERAL LINO PÉREZ

CIENFUEGOS

FRANK PAIS

BANK ■

ASAMBLEA MUNICIPAL ■

HOSTAL LA RONDA ●

IBEROSTAR GRAN HOTEL TRINIDAD ■

CASA DE LÓPEZ- ● SANTANDER

PARKING ■

CAMILO

GATO

HIDALGO

MIGUEL CALZÓN

CUBANACÁN ■

BUFETE INTERNACIONAL ■

TELEPHONE ■

CINEMA ■

Parque Céspedes ●

IGLESIA DE PAULA ★

CUBANACÁN/ ■ TRANSTUR

TIENDAS PANAMERICANOS ■

CASA DE ★ HABANO Y RON

CASA DE ■ JEDREZ

ARTEX/CASA FISCHER ■

PHOTO SERVICE ■

CADECA ■

FRANK

ETECSA ■

CENTRO DE PROMOCIÓN CULTURAL ■

0   100 yds

0   100 m

wrought-iron bed is the only heirloom of the Brunet family that originates from the house.

Another impressive mansion, the Casa Padrón, on the southwest corner of the plaza, at the corner of Bolívar and Mártinez, hosts the small **Museo de Arqueología y Ciencias Naturales** (Calle Bolívar #457, tel. 0419/3420; Fri.–Wed. 10 A.M.–6 P.M.; CUC1), exhibiting Cuban fauna and flora in glass cases filled with stuffed birds and animals. A portion of the museum is devoted to the region's pre-Columbian peoples. German explorer Alexander von Humboldt stayed here during his investigative sojourn in Cuba in 1801.

On the east side of the square, in the Casa de los Sánchez Iznaga, is the **Museo de Arquitectura Colonial** (tel. 0419/3208; Sat.–Thurs. 9 A.M.–5 P.M.; CUC1) with displays and models relating to Trinidad's architectural development.

Museo de la Lucha Contra Los Bandidos

Rising northwest of the plaza is the much-photographed campanile of the **Antiguo Convento de San Francisco de Asís.** The *torre* (tower) and church are all that remain of the original convent. The church was taken over by the government, and the convent was replaced by a baroque structure now housing the Museum of the Fight Against Outlaws (Calle Echerrí #59, esq. Pino Guinart, tel. 0419/4121; Tues.–Sun. 9 A.M.–5 P.M.; CUC1), which traces the campaign against the counterrevolutionary guerrillas (called "bandits" by the Castro government) in the Sierra Escambray in the years following the Revolution. There are maps, black-and-white photographs, clothing and personal belongings of hero-soldiers, a CIA radio transmitter, a small gunboat the CIA donated to the counter-Castro cause, plus parts of the U-2 spy plane shot down during the Cuban Missile Crisis. You can ascend to the top of the bell tower for a view over the city.

Plazuela Real del Jigüe

This charming triangular plaza (Piro Guinart y Villena), one block west of Plaza Mayor, has a calabash tree in the center. The tree, planted in 1929, is the youngest in a succession of trees kept alive since 1514, the year the Spanish celebrated their first Mass here. The colonial home (now Restaurante El Jigüe) fronting the plaza has a beautiful ceramic fascia. Cater-corner to El Jigüe is the **Ayuntamiento y Cárcel** (Piro Guinart #302), the old town hall and jail, with a portion of the original stone-and-lime masonry exposed for view.

Immediately east, the **Casa Templo de Santería Yemayá** (Villena #59) features *santería* altars and hosts occasional religious ceremonies.

Museo Histórico

This museum (Simón Bolívar #423, esq. Francisco Toro, tel. 0419/4460; Sat.–Thurs. 9 A.M.–5 P.M.; entrance CUC2, cameras CUC1, videos CUC5), one block south of Plaza Mayor, occupies the Palacio Cantero. Once the home of the Borrell family, it featured Roman-style baths that amused 19th-century travelers with a fountain that spouted *eau de cologne* for the ladies and gin for gents. The history of the city is revealed as you move through rooms furnished with rocking chairs, alabaster amphorae, marble-topped tables, and other antiques. Other intriguing exhibits include an antique bell, stocks for holding slaves, banknotes, and a magnificent scale model of the *Andrei Vishinsky,* which entered Trinidad harbor on April 17, 1960—the first Soviet ship to visit Cuba after the Revolution. Stairs lead up to a watchtower with a fine view over the city.

Entertainment and Events

Festivals: Trinidad has a tradition for *madrugadas,* early-morning performances of regional songs sung in the streets. Though rarely heard today, *madrugadas* highlight the town's weeklong **Semana de la Cultura** in early January.

Every Easter, a religious celebration—**El Recorrido del Vía Crucis** (the way of the cross)—is held; the devout follow a route through the old city, stopping at 14 sites marked with crosses. The weeklong **Festival de Semana Santa** (Holy Week celebrations) features Masses plus street processions.

For nine days during Christmas, *trinitarios* enact **Fiestas Navideñas,** a street re-creation of Mary and Joseph's journey by donkey. Each night the procession ends at a different house, with a fiesta for children.

Traditional Music and Dance: Watch for performances by **Conjunto Folklórico de Trinidad** and **Cocoró y su Aché,** which present traditional Afro-Cuban dance routines at the **Palenque de los Congos Reales** (Echerrí #146, esq. Jesús Menéndez; free), which has an *espectáculo afrocubano* nightly 10–11 P.M.

Traditional music performances are hosted at the **Casa de la Trova** (Echerrí #29, tel. 0419/6445; daily 9 A.M.–2 A.M.; CUC1 after 8 P.M.), one block east of Plaza Mayor, where musicians drift in to jam and locals whisk tourists onto the dance floor.

The **Casa de la Cultura** (Zerquera, esq. Ernest Valdes, tel. 0419/4308; daily 8 A.M.–10 P.M.; free) also hosts traditional music, as do **Casa Fischer** (Lino Pérez #312, e/ Codatia y Martí, tel. 0419/6486; CUC0.50), which has *boleros* on Wednesdays; and the ruins of **Teatro Brunet** (Maceo #461, e/ Bolívar y Zerquera; CUC2).

The **Museo Romántico,** on Plaza Mayor, has a *noche romántica* (romantic evening) once a month, with traditional music and dance.

Bars: The atmospheric **Taberna La Canchánchara** (Rubén Martínez, esq. Girón, tel. 0419/6231; 8 A.M.–9 P.M. daily) features traditional live music and is known for its house drink, made from *aguardiente* (raw rum), mineral water, honey, and lime (CUC2).

The lobby bar in the **Plaza Santa Ana** (Camilo Cienfuegos, esq. Rúben Batista, tel. 0419/6423; 9 A.M.–10 P.M. daily) is a pleasing spot for a cool beer or shot of rum.

Cabarets and Discos: Local youth get in their salsa moves in the rear patio disco of **Casa de la Música** (Juan Manuel Marquéz, e/ Bolívar y Menéndez, tel. 0419/3414; CUC2), while everything from folkloric music to *cabaret espectáculo* is hosted in the Casa's front courtyard, off the steps on the northeast side of Plaza Mayor (free).

The **Disco Ayala** (nightly 10:30 P.M.–2 A.M.;

CUC3 including one drink), in the caves immediately west of the Hotel Las Cuevas, offers flashing lights amid the stalagmites and stalactites. Awesome! There are several rooms, including one hosting a *cabaret espectáculo.*

The **Hotel Las Cuevas** features free cabaret nightly at 9:30 P.M.

Several roofless ruins host live music and open-air discos playing world beat and modern pop music; unfortunately the techno beat makes a miserable time of things for neighbors who want to sleep.

Other Entertainment: The **Cine Romelio Cornelio,** on Parque Céspedes, screens movies Tuesday–Sunday at 8 P.M.

The local chess club—**Casa de Jedrez** (Lino Pérez #292)—is on the east side of the square.

Recreation

Horseback riding is offered at **Rancho El Cubano** (tel. 0419/6611; daily 8 A.M.–5 P.M.; CUC6.50 entrance including a drink), one kilometer west of Trinidad (CUC2.50 for one hour; CUC6.50 for longer rides). The rides lead to cascades and natural pools good for swimming. You can rent boats and go fishing. A rustic restaurant serves catfish (CUC6.50).

You can also go horseback riding (CUC5 per hour) at **Finca Dolores** (tel. 0419/6395, fax 0419/6198), a rustic farm turned tourist attraction on the banks of the Río Guaurabo, two kilometers west of Trinidad. A representation of a traditional farm features an aviary, cockfights, milking, and other farm activities. Folkloric shows (CUC5) feature a *guateque*—a good ol' country hoedown (CUC8 including meal).

Accommodations

Casas Particulares: Trinidad has about 300 *casas particulares.* Competition keeps prices low. It's best to compare several before making a choice. Owners will call around to help you find a place if you don't have a reservation. Most offer meals.

My favorite place by far is ◖ **Casa Colonial Muñoz** (Calle Martí #401, esq. Santiago Escobar, tel./fax 419/3673, www.casa.trinidadphoto.com; CUC30), a venerable home built in

1800 and featured in *National Geographic* (Oct. 1999, p. 102). The timeworn house features period furnishings, including swords, old clocks, and centenary prints. It offers two lofty-ceilinged bedrooms, each simply furnished with two double beds, air-conditioning and fans, and modern, private bathrooms with hot water. "You could cook a lobster in the sink," says Julio Muñoz, the English-speaking owner and a professional photographer. His wife, Rosa Orbea Cerrillo, makes the best meals in town. There's secure parking, and a stable with horse (rides are offered). Some other *casa particular* owners pretend to be Julio Muñoz to steal his business, and *jiniteros* are known to steer you to such houses for a commission.

C Casa de Carlos Sotalongo (Calle Ruben Mártinez Villena #33, tel. 0419/4169; CUC20), on the southeast corner of Plaza Mayor, is another atmospheric winner. Vast front doors open to a cavernous lounge with antiques, modern art, and a colonial tile floor. Local art critic Carlos Sotalongo rents two rooms with terra-cotta floors, metal-frame beds and private hot-water bathrooms.

Casa de Isabela Irarragorri (Juan Manuel Márquez #32B, tel. 0419/3918; CUC20), one block north of the main plaza, is another good option. Isabela's large colonial home has a self-contained air-conditioned room to the rear, with fans, its own kitchen and hot-water bathroom, plus washing machine, fridge, and patio.

I also like **C Casa Sara Sanjua Álvarez** (Simón Bolívar #266, e/ Frank País y Martí, tel. 0419/3997; CUC20–25), a well-kept colonial home beautifully furnished with antiques. It opens to an exquisite rose garden with rockers. Two air-conditioned rooms have fans, refrigerators, and modern bathrooms with hot water. There's secure parking.

Hostal Sandra y Víctor (Antonio Maceo #613, e/ Piro Guinart y Pablo Pichs, tel. 0419/2216, fax 0419/3673, www.sandra.trinidadphoto.com; CUC20), just 100 meters from the bus station, has three upstairs air-conditioned rooms with private bathrooms and hot water. A spacious lounge has rockers and a de-lightful rooftop terrace features artistic ceramic walls and a bar. The owners are gracious and accommodating.

Casa López-Santander (Camilo Cienfuegos #313, e/ Jesús Menendez y Camilo Cienfuegos, tel. 0419/3541; CUC15–25) has two adequately furnished rooms along a patio arcade with rockers. One is colonial, the other is smaller but modern. Each has a private bathroom. The TV lounge is a pleasing spot to relax. It has secure parking.

I enjoyed my stay at **Casa de Nelson y Marilú** (Santiago Escobar #172, e/ Frank País y Martí, tel. 0419/2899, hostalmarilu@yahoo.es, CUC25), with a pleasant cross-ventilated rooftop chamber with a small but modern bathroom with hot water. Meals are served alfresco on the rooftop terrace with rockers and hammock.

Hospedaje Estela (Simón Bolívar #555, tel. 0419/4329; CUC20), one block north of Plaza Mayor, is a beautiful colonial home full of period furnishings and modern paintings. It has one simply furnished upstairs room with private hot-water bathroom, and a balcony overlooking a tree-shaded patio that doubles as Paladar Estela. Note the life-size statues of Christ and Mary in the lounge!

Hotels: The Instituto Cubano de la Amistad runs the **Casa de la Amistad** (Zerquera, esq. Frank País, tel. 0419/3824, amistur@ceniai.inf.cu; CUC15 s/d), which offers modestly furnished rooms with private bath. Normally, it hosts "solidarity" groups, but you might try your luck.

Hotel La Ronda (Calle Martí #239, tel. 0419/4011, reservas@hotelronda.co.cu; CUC30 s, CUC38 d year-round, including breakfast), 50 meters west of Parque Céspedes, is a recently renovated colonial-era hotel with 17 meagerly furnished air-conditioned rooms around a charming atrium courtyard; each has a lofty ceiling, satellite TV, telephone, fridge, and safe deposit box. It has a restaurant. (Cubanacán.)

Mesón del Regidor (Simón Bolívar #20, tel. 0419/6572; CUC48 s, CUC58 d), one block southwest of Plaza Mayor, in atmospheric

Spanish *parador* style, has four attractive rooms with beamed ceilings, antique reproductions, and private hot-water bathrooms. There's a pleasant restaurant.

Hotel Horizontes Las Cuevas (Calle General Lino Pérez final, tel. 0419/6133, fax 0419/6161, reservas@cuevas.co.cu; CUC50 s, CUC65 d low season; CUC59 s, CUC79 d high season, including breakfast), on the hillside above town, has 109 modestly furnished air-conditioned rooms with phones and radios. The restaurant and bar are in a thatched *bohío* (the food is mediocre). A swimming pool with snack bar, plus shop, are farther up the hill. It has car rental, Internet service, tour desk, game room, and nightly cabaret. (Cubanacán.)

Finca María Dolores (tel. 0419/6395, fax 0419/6198; CUC40 s, CUC48 d rooms, CUC46 s, CUC56 d cabins, year-round including breakfast), two kilometers west of Trinidad, enjoys an appealing rustic setting and offers 19 air-conditioned rooms each with satellite TV and hot-water showers, plus 26 cabins with kitchen, minibar, and TV. They're pleasantly furnished with rattan. *Criollo* meals are served in an open-sided thatched restaurant. It has a disco, shop, and swimming pool.

At last visit, the old Hotel Canada, on Parque Céspedes, was being restored to become the 45-room **Iberostar Gran Hotel Trinidad.**

Food

Most *casas particulares* provide meals.

Paladares: Only three *paladares* existed at last visit. The best meals in town by far are served at ◖ **Paladar Estela** (Bolívar #557, tel. 0419/4329; 7–10:30 P.M. daily, and until midnight in winter), one block north of Plaza Mayor, which offers *criollo* meals served on a delightful tree-shaded patio. I recommend the lamb (CUC8) or roast pork (CUC8).

The antique-filled **Paladar Sol y Son** (Simón Bolívar #238, e/ Frank País y José Martí, tel. 0419/2926; 7–11 P.M. daily) also has courtyard dining and offers a roast chicken special (CUC7).

The lesser option is **Paladar La Coruna** (Martí #428, esq. Fidel Claro, tel. 0419/3838;

7 A.M.–midnight daily), which serves *criollo* dinners under an arbor on a patio.

Restaurants: Of state-run restaurants, my favorite is ◖ **Restaurante Vía Real** (tel. 0419/6476; 10:30 A.M.–10:30 P.M. daily), facing Plazuela Real del Jigüe, in an atmospheric colonial home with black-and-white checkered floor and antique chandeliers. The wide menu features a filling *pollo el jigüe* (CUC5.05), with spaghetti and cheese served in an earthenware dish (CUC12). It also has lobster for a ridiculous CUC22.50. Wash your dish down with a delicious homemade lemonade (CUC0.65).

Similarly appealing, the **Restaurante Plaza Mayor** (Zerquera, esq. Villena, tel. 0419/6470; noon–10 P.M. daily) offers the option of patio dining or within the colonial mansion, with ceiling fans and bamboo seating. It has an accomplished buffet—the best lunch option in town.

The equally atmospheric **Restaurant Santa Ana** (Camilo Cienfuegos, esq. Rúben Batista, tel. 0419/6423; 9 A.M.–10 P.M. daily), in Plaza Santa Ana (it was originally the Cárcel Real, or Royal Prison), has a large *criollo* menu with the usual staples. Live musicians entertain.

Mesón del Regidor (Simón Bolívar #20, tel. 0419/6572; 7:30 A.M.–10 P.M. daily) specializes in grilled meats and has bargain-priced set meals served with salad, dessert, wine, and coffee, including an excellent fish fillet (CUC8) and lobster enchilada (CUC11).

Snacks: For ice cream, head to the **Cremería** (Antonio Maceo, e/ Bolívar y Zerquera; daily 9 A.M.–10 P.M.); or **Coppelia** (Martí, e/ Zerquera y Colón; Tues.–Sun. 8 A.M.–10 P.M.).

A *guarapería* on Pérez, esq. Callejón Consero, sells fresh-squeezed sugarcane juice.

Self-Catering: The best-stocked supermarket is **Galería Comercial Universo** (Martí, e/ Zerquera y Colón). You can buy produce at the *mercado agropecuario* (Pedro Zerquera, esq. Manuel Fajardo; Mon.–Sat. 8 A.M.–6 P.M.; Sun. 8 A.M.–noon).

Shopping

All manner of arts and crafts are sold at the **artisan's markets** held in Plazuela Segarte, and east and south of Plaza Mayor.

© CHRISTOPHER P. BAKER

Many of the ceramics around town are made at El Alfarero Casa Chichí.

SANCTI SPÍRITUS

The widest option of arts and crafts under one roof is offered by **Fondo de Bienes Culturales** (Bolívar #418, tel. 0419/3590; Mon.–Sat. 9 A.M.–5 P.M., Sun. 9 A.M.–noon), one block south of Plaza Mayor. Another good bet is **Palacio de la Artesanía** (Piro Guitart #221, esq. Independencia).

For cigars and rum, head to **Casa del Habano** (Maceo, esq. Zerquera, tel. 0419/6256; daily 9 A.M.–7 P.M.) or **Casa del Habano y Ron** (Martí, esq. Lino Pérez).

The **Casa de la Música** (Juan Manuel Márquez, e/ Bolívar y Menéndez, tel. 0419/3414) has a wide selection of CDs. Musical instruments can be bought at the **Taller de Instrumentales Musicales** (Menéndez #127-A, e/ Ernesto Valdés y Colón, tel. 0419/4348), where bongos, *timbales,* and other instruments are made.

Much of the ceramic work sold locally is made at **El Alfarero Casa Chichí** (Andres Berro Macias #51, e/ Pepito Tey y Abel Santamaría, tel. 0419/3053; Mon.–Sat. 7 A.M.–7 P.M.), a home-cum-ceramic workshop where the Santander family carries on a tradition of pottery-making.

Information and Services

The **Centro de Promoción Cultural** (Martí, esq. Camilo Cienfuegos) has a tourist information bureau.

Banks include **Bandec** (Martí #264, e/ Colón y Zequera); **Banco Popular** (Colón y Miguel Calzada); and **Banco Financiero Internacional** (Cienfuegos, esq. Martí). You can also exchange foreign currency at **Cadeca** (Martí #164, e/ Lino Pérez y Céspedes; Mon.–Fri. 8 A.M.–3 P.M.).

The **post office** is at Maceo #418, e/ Zerquera y Colón. **Etecsa** (Lino Pérez y Francisco Pettersen, tel. 0419/6020; Mon.–Fri. 8 A.M.–7 P.M., Sat. 8 A.M.–10 P.M.) has international phone plus Internet service.

Café Las Begonias (Maceo #473, esq. Bolívar; daily 9 A.M.–9 P.M.) has Internet service (CUC6 per hour). You need to present your ID.

The **Clínica Internacional** (Lino Pérez #103, esq. Cárdenas, tel. 0419/6492; 24 hours) has a pharmacy as well as a doctor and nurse on hand; it charges CUC25 per consultation, but CUC30 4–7 P.M. and CUC50 after 7 P.M. and for house calls. The **hospital** (Maceo #6, tel. 0419/3201) is five blocks east of Cienfuegos.

Inmigración (Perseverancia, off Paseo Agramonte; Tues.–Thurs. 8 A.M.–4 P.M.), 400 yards south of the train station, can issue *prórrogas.* You'll need to buy a CUC25 stamp (*cello*) in advance from Bandec. The **police station** (Manuel Fajardo, esq. Cárdenas) is two blocks to the northeast.

The **Bufete Internacional** (Frank País, esq. Colón, tel. 0419/6489, fax 0419/6374, notario@bufete.tdad.cyt.cu; Mon.–Fri. 8:30 A.M.–5 P.M.) can assist with legal matters.

Getting There and Away

By Air: The **Aeropuerto Alberto Delgado** (tel. 0419/6393) is one kilometer south of town, off Paseo Agramonte. No scheduled air service was offered at last visit.

By Bus: Buses arrive and depart the **Terminal de Ómnibus** (Izquierda, esq. Piro Guinart, tel. 0419/6676). The ticket office for Astro and Víazul buses is open daily 7 A.M.–7 P.M.

Astro buses depart Havana for Trinidad at 5:45 A.M. (CUC17 *regular,* CUC21 *especial*), and Trinidad for Havana at 1:30 P.M. Buses also operate to Cienfuegos at 9 A.M. and 2:35 P.M. (CUC3) and Santa Clara four times weekly at 10:15 P.M. (CUC6).

Víazul (tel. 0419/4448) buses to Trinidad depart Havana at 8:15 A.M. and 1 P.M. (CUC25), and Varadero at 7:30 A.M. (CUC20). Buses depart Trinidad for Havana at 7:45 A.M. and 3:15 P.M., and for Varadero at 2:25 P.M.

Local buses (tel. 0419/2404) leave irregularly for Sancti Spíritus (CUC2.10) and Topes de Collantes (CUC1). Eight *camiones* daily also serve Sancti Spíritus.

By Train: The train station (tel. 0419/3348) is at the bottom of Lino Pérez; the ticket booth is open daily 8 A.M.–4 P.M. The only service at last visit was a daily train from Trinidad to Meyer (see the *Valle de los Ingenios* section later in this chapter).

By Car: Car rental agencies also offer taxi service, including **Transauto** (Lino Pérez, e/ Martí y Francisco Cadalia, tel. 0419/6633) and **Gaviota** (tel. 0419/6235), which offers a house-to-house taxi service between Havana and Trinidad (about CUC110). Other car rental agencies include **Vía Rent-a-Car** (tel. 0419/6388), at the airport; and **Micar** (tel. 0419/6192), at the **Oro Negro gas station** northeast of town on Fausto Pelayo. Another gas station is three kilometers southeast of Trinidad on the road to Casilda.

You can park at **Casa López-Santander** (CUC2 per night) and at the public parking on Vicente Suyama, esq. Girón.

Excursions: Cubatur (Maceo y Zerquera, tel. 0419/6314; daily 9 A.M.–9 P.M.) and **Cubanacán** (Martí, e/ Lino Pérez y Codahia, tel. 0419/4753) offer excursions. **Gaviotatours** (Frank País, e/ Piro Guinart y Bolívar, tel. 0419/6236) specializes in nature trips in the Sierra Escambray.

Getting Around

Coches (horse-drawn taxis) operate through the new town. **Taxi Transtur** (tel. 0419/5314) and **Cubataxi** (tel. 0419/2340) provide taxi service. *Coco-taxis* (tel. 0419/2214) cruise the streets. A CUC1 minimum applies. Expect to pay about CUC5 one-way to Playa Ancón.

The **Centro de Promoción Cultural** (Martí, esq. Cienfuegos, tel. 0419/6316; Mon.–Sat. 9 A.M.–7 P.M., Sun. 9 A.M.–noon) has guides and offers city tours (CUC2) and tours of the Valle de los Ingenios. It sells a superb, detailed full-color guide to the city for anyone interested in a complete architectural profile of Trinidad. **Paradiso** (Lino Pérez, e/ Codania y Martí, tel. 0419/6486, paradiso@sctd.artex .cu), in the Casa Fischer, specializes in cultural tours. A guided city tour costs CUC10.

LA BOCA AND PENÍNSULA DE ANCÓN

La Boca, five kilometers west of Trinidad, is a quaint fishing village with traditional tile-

© CHRISTOPHER P. BAKER

steam train used for daily excursions

roofed *bohíos*. It appeals for its pocket-scale beaches amid coral coves favored by *trinitarios* on weekends, and is a great place to mingle with locals.

Casa Museo Alberto Delgado (no tel., no set hours; free), two kilometers east of La Boca, honors a Castroite killed during the counterrevolutionary war. Eduardo Soler Ruiz, a campesino who lives adjacent, acts as *custodio* and will open the museum on demand. Tip him.

The coast extends south of La Boca to a small point, **Punta María Aguilar,** beyond which the long narrow Península de Ancón curls east, limned by touristy Playa Ancón. Behind lies a mangrove-lined lagoon, the Ensenada de Casilda.

☾ Playa Ancón

The four-kilometer-long beach is fabulous, with sugary white sand and pavonine waters fringed with pines and palms offering shade. Choose your section carefully as parts of the beach shelve into rocky waters with sea grasses. Cuban couples and families come to picnic, but for the most part this beach is the preserve

of tourists at the two all-inclusive hotels (you can buy day passes to use the facilities). Topless bathing is tolerated. The sea is perfect for snorkeling, though during certain times of year a microscopic sea lice (*agua mala* or *caribe*) can cause all manner of nasty infections.

Recreation

Ancón's offshore coral reefs have more than 30 dive spots and the added attraction of sunken vessels. **Cayo Blanco,** nine kilometers southeast of Ancón, is famous for its kaleidoscopic variety of corals and sponges.

Scuba diving is offered by the three hotels, and at **Marina Marlin** (tel./fax 0419/6205, marinastdad@ip.etecsa.cu), which charges CUC30 per dive, CUC35 for night dives, and CUC230 for a 10-dive package. Snorkeling costs CUC10.

The marina also offers "seafari" excursions to Cayo Blanco (CUC40), including snorkeling and lunch; plus a sunset cruise (CUC10, CUC15 with dinner); fly-fishing (CUC200 for up to four people); and deep-sea fishing (CUC30 per person).

SANCTI SPÍRITUS

Accommodations and Food

There are several *casas particulares* in La Boca. My favorite is **Hostal Vista al Mar** (Calle Real #47, tel. 0419/3716; CUC20–25), a simply furnished home overlooking the beach and rivermouth. Manolo, the owner, is a gracious and fun host. He offers two rooms with fans (one, smallish, faces the ocean and is cross-ventilated; the second has air-conditioning). They share a small hot-water bathroom. It has parking. Guests get the whole house.

Hostal El Capitán (Playa La Boca #82, tel. 0419/3055; CUC20), 400 meters south of the village, boasts a mix of antiques and modern furnishings. The single air-conditioned room is cross-ventilated, well-lit with louvered windows, and has a fan and private hot-water bathroom. Meals are served on a raised patio over the rocky shore. It has parking. The owner speaks English and Italian.

Hotel Ancón (tel. 0419/6120, reserva@ancon.co.cu; CUC70 s, CUC110 d low season; CU84 s, CUC150 d high season) has 279 rooms, all with air-conditioning, private baths, telephones, and radios. The Soviet-style structure has been nicely upgraded and is a favorite of Canadian and European charter groups. Facilities include a game room, cabaret, a huge swimming pool, a tourism bureau, an atmospheric restaurant, seven bars, car rental, scuba diving, plus excursions. It now operates as an all-inclusive resort. (Gran Caribe.)

Hotel Costa Sur (tel. 0419/6174 or 6173, rpublicas@costasurhor.co.cu), one kilometer west, is a less-appealing 131-room hotel popular with German tour groups. It was closed for restoration at last visit.

Brisas Trinidad del Mar (tel. 0419/6500, fax 0419/6565, reservas@brisastdad.co.cu; standard CUC75 s, CUC130 d low season, CUC103 s, CUC160 d high season; junior suite CUC85 s, CUC150 d low season, CUC115 s, CUC180 d high season), adjacent to the Hotel Ancón, is a more luxe, low-rise property in a neocolonial style, with units arrayed around a large freeform pool. The 241 air-conditioned rooms (including nine junior suites) are spacious, with modern (albeit drab) furnishings

and decor, plus satellite TV, telephone, radio, and safe deposit box, plus appealing bathrooms. Facilities include three restaurants, piano bar, live entertainment, water sports, plus tennis court, game room, and gym with sauna. (Cubanacán.)

The **Grill Caribe** (no tel.; 9 A.M.–10 P.M. daily), above the coral shore between La Boca and Ancón, is a seafood grill.

Getting There, Away, and Around

A motorized faux steam train offers shuttle service from Trinidad (CUC2 each way). You can catch it at Plaza Santa Ana and along Paseo Agramonte.

Buses to La Boca leave Trinidad four times daily. A **taxi** between Trinidad and Ancón costs about CUC10 one-way.

The three hotels offer car rental, and Hotel Ancón and Las Brisas rent **bicycles.** The ride to Trinidad is flat but it's hot and windy, and the last stretch is a gradual climb.

Marina Marlin (tel./fax 0419/6205, marinastdad@ip.etecsa.cu) has moorings with water, electricity, and diesel. Before berthing, you must clear customs (tel. 0419/5312) and immigration at the wharf of Casilda.

Bare-boat yachts and catamarans can be chartered from **Sunsail** (tel./fax 0419/6290, fedecassiopea@hotmail.com) at Marina Marlin. No reservations are accepted at the marina, nor within Cuba; reservations must be made prior to arrival in Cuba through the company's head office (The Port House, Port Solent, Portsmouth, Hampshire, PO6 4TH, U.K., tel. 0870/112-8612, www.sunsail.com) or regional offices in North America (tel. 410/280-2553 or 888/350-3568, sunsailusa@sunsail.com) or Australia and New Zealand (tel. 7/4948-9509, sunsail@sunsail.com.au).

◖ VALLE DE LOS INGENIOS

East of Trinidad, the Carretera de Sancti Spíritus drops spectacularly into the Valley of the Sugar Mills, known more correctly as the Valle de San Luis and declared a UNESCO Cultural Heritage Site. It is named for the many sugar mills, or *ingenios* (43 at its peak), that sprang up over the centuries to grind the cane produced by the valley's remarkably fertile soil. The valley was the most important sugar-producing region into the 19th century, when the development of the *central* plantation system elsewhere in Cuba sounded a death knell for the valley's relatively primitive factories.

Many of the mills and estate houses remain, albeit mostly in ruin. Several historic sites are signed from the main highway. Most notable is **Sitio Histórico Guaímaro,** which boasts fabulous but much-deteriorated wall murals. It is slated to become a museum on sugarcane; restoration was underway at last visit. Guaímaro is about 600 meters off the highway (you'll need to ask directions) via a dirt road that continues for another five kilometers (to be attempted in dry season only) to **Sitio Histórico San Isidro,** which is hidden behind trees at a 90-degree bend, beyond which you find yourself amid the canefields. The ruins of San Isidro feature a three-story campanile.

Sitio Histórico San Pedro is a rural village of tumbledown wattle-and-daub huts with a couple of restored colonial homes. It's not worth the 11-kilometer drive via badly potholed road.

You gain a good vantage over the valley from the **Mirador del Valle de los Ingenios,** about five kilometers east of Trinidad. There's a snack bar and bar.

Torre de Manaca-Iznaga

The quaint village of Iznaga is a picture-perfect gem with a prim little railway station. The village, 14 kilometers east of Trinidad, is most famous for **Hacienda Iznaga** (tel. 0419/7241; daily 9 A.M.–5 P.M.; CUC1), built 1835–45 by Alejo María del Carmen e Iznaga, once one of the wealthiest sugar planters in Cuba. The hacienda features a 43.5-meter-tall tower that according to legend was built as a wager. Alejo was to build a tower while his brother Pedro dug a well. The winner would be whoever went highest or deepest (no well has been found). It has seven levels, each smaller than the one beneath. You can ascend the 136 steps with the *custodio* (a tip is appreciated).

© CHRISTOPHER P. BAKER

Sitio Histórico Guaímaro

SANCTI SPÍRITUS

The restored hacienda is now a restaurant with a terrace overlooking the valley. A traditional *guarapería* at the rear serves fresh-squeezed cane juice.

Lacework is a local specialty sold at the base of the tower.

Horseback Riding

You can go horseback riding at **Casa Guachinango** (no tel.; daily 9 A.M.–5 P.M.), three kilometers north of Iznaga; a one-hour ride leads to mineral springs good for bathing. This 200-year-old hacienda-turned-restaurant boasts a beautiful setting above the Río Ay. You can also milk cows and be shown how to extract honey from beehives. Lunches using home-grown organic vegetables are served.

Getting There

A local commuter train departs Trinidad for Meyer via the Valle de los Ingenios at 5 A.M., 9 A.M., 1 P.M., and 5:20 P.M. (CUC10). It stops at Iznaga and Guachinango. Trains depart Meyer for Trinidad at 6:30 A.M., 10:30 A.M., 2:40 P.M., and 6:40 P.M.

A 1907 steam train also runs an excursion from Trinidad to Guachinango daily at 9:30 A.M., with a lunch stop at Iznaga (CUC10; you pay for lunch separately). Tour agencies in Trinidad make reservations.

◖ GRAN PARQUE NATURAL TOPES DE COLLANTES

Five kilometers west of Trinidad, a turnoff from the coast road leads north and begins to climb into the southeastern Sierra Escambray, whose slopes swathed in Caribbean pines and an abundance of ancient tree ferns, bamboo, and eucalyptus are protected within this national park. The area is tremendous for hiking; there are plenty of trails, and the rich bird life includes an abundance of parrots. Bring raingear and waterproof footwear.

At its heart, at a refreshingly cool 790 meters, is **Topes de Collantes,** a spa-hotel complex 21 kilometers from Trinidad and dominated by a massive concrete structure—the Kurhotel—designed in 1936, when it served as a sanato-

lace embroidery for sale

© CHRISTOPHER P. BAKER

rium for victims of tuberculosis. Following the Revolution, the disease was finally eradicated in Cuba. The structure was then sanitized and turned into a teacher-training facility. The complex, which includes smaller hotels, was developed as a resort area in the late 1970s and now focuses on nature and health tourism.

The complex is mainly used by Latin Americans and Cubans seeking post-operative rehabilitation or specialized therapies. You can take simple treatments such as massages.

The park is divided into sections accessed by trails. A guide is compulsory.

The most popular trail leads from Topes de Collantes northeast four kilometers to **Salto de Caburní,** a 75-meter-high waterfall at the heart of **Parque Caburní** (CUC6.50, payable at the entry gate at Villa Caburní, east of the Kurhotel). The trail begins beside the Aparthotel, and zigzags steeply downhill; the trail can be slippery. In dry season, the falls can dry up. Allow 90 minutes for the round-trip.

STILL PUFFING AWAY

Cuba maintains about 200 operating steam trains, projecting yet another surreal image of an island lost in time – what railroad expert Adolf Hungry Wolf calls a "twilight zone in the world of railroading." Most of these puffing treasures date from the 1920s (the first Cuban railway was built by the British in 1837) and are still capable of thundering down the slim tracks with a full load of sugarcane. Almost all are of U.S. progeny and operate on sugar estates, with a concentration around Guardalavaca. The oldest train in operation is a coal-burning Baldwin 0-4-2T at the Villena sugar mill built by Baldwin in 1878 (the oldest train in Cuba is La Junta, from 1843, displayed in the lobby of the Museo de Ferrocarril in Havana). The trains are kept going because the sugar mills operate only four to five months a year, providing plenty of time to overhaul the engines and keep them in good repair so as to extract a few more thousand miles of hard labor.

However, the drastic closures of sugar mills initiated in 2002 threaten to deliver many clunky old steam engines to the grave... as does the recent arrival of diesel locomotives imported from Canada, Mexico, and Europe. Nonetheless, Cuba has been actively restoring many of its jaded jewels and sprucing them up for passenger and tourist endeavors. Tourist steam trains currently operate at Rafael Freyre (see the *Las Tunas and Holguín* chapter) and from Trinidad.

Annual steam train festivals are held at Maltiempo in November, and at Morón in December (see the *Ciego de Ávila and Camagüey* chapter).

Canadian Caboose Press (Box 844, Skookumchuck, BC V0B 2E0, Canada, tel. 250/342-1421) sells videos of Cuban steam train plus *Trains of Cuba*, a guidebook with maps, rosters, and details on individual steam trains islandwide. I also recommend Adolf Hungry Wolf's *Letters from Cuba*, regaling tales of his time chasing steam trains in Cuba.

STEAM TRAIN TOURS

Belgian-run **Transnico Train Tours** (Lonja del Comercio, Piso 6, Plaza San Francisco de Asís, Habana Vieja, tel. 07/66-9954, fax 07/66-9908, www.transnico.com) ostensibly offers 7-day luxury train trips on the "Cuba & Caribe Express" between Havana and Santiago de Cuba.

Steam in Paradise (3a Leamington Place, Hayes, Middlesex UB4 8QZ, England, tel. 020/8561-5981, http://home.btclick.com/cubasteam) also offers train tours to Cuba.

Trains Unlimited Tours (1105 Terminal Way, Suite 111, Reno, NV 89502, 775/852-4448 or 800/359-4870, www.trainsunlimitedtours.com) has offered Cuban rail tours in prior years.

About 400 yards south of the Kurhotel, the **Sendero La Batata** leads to a cave system (with underground river and pools good for swimming) within **Parque La Represa,** a park with profuse forest growth (CUC3.50). This park can also be accessed from Hotel Los Helechos. About 100 meters east of the Parque La Represa entrance, another trail leads east to the **Salto Vega Grande** cascade, in **Parque Vegas Grandes** (CUC5).

Another trail leads south seven kilometers to **Parque Codina** (CUC3), centered on Finca Codina, an erstwhile coffee estate that serves as a post for bird-watchers and hikers. Special luncheons are laid on for tour groups, with roast suckling pig and a house cocktail made from rum, honey, and ginger. After a couple of toddies, you may feel brave enough to wallow in a pool of medicinal mud. Codina has an orchid garden with trails that lead to waterfalls and caves.

Parque Guanayara (CUC5) is the most developed site. Its highlight is the Sendero Centinelas del Río Melidioso, which follows the rivercourse to the **Cascada El Rocío** waterfall, where you can swim in a chilly pool. By road, it is accessible only by four-wheel drive or by Gaviota excursion.

Other trails lead to **Parque El Nicho** (CUC5) and **Parque El Cubano** (CUC6.50).

For information, contact the **Complejo**

Turístico Topes de Collantes (tel. 042/54-0330 or 042/54-0117, fax 042/54-0272, www.gaviota-grupo.com; daily 7:30 A.M.–7:30 P.M.) at the entrance to Topes de Collantes.

See the *Sierra Escambray* section of the *Cienfuegos and Villa Clara* chapter for more information on the Sierra Escambray.

Accommodations and Food

The massive **Kurhotel Escambray** (tel. 042/54-0117; CUC27 s, CUC34 d standard, CUC35 s, CUC44 d suite low season; CUC37 s, CUC44 d standard, CUC47 s, CUC64 d suite high season) has a Stalinist aesthetic and is reached via a stone staircase on a Siberian scale. The 210 air-conditioned rooms and 16 suites are satisfactory, and have TV, refrigerator, safe deposit box, telephone, rattan furniture, and attractive bathrooms. The hotel features its own TV station (Tele Caburní), a modest restaurant, five gyms, a beauty salon, movie theater, cabaret acts, and a thermal swimming pool where massage and therapeutic treatments are offered. (Gaviota.)

Villa Caburní (CUC29 s, CUC34 d low season; CUC37 s, CUC44 d high season), adjoining the Kurhotel, has apartment *cabinas* for up to four people.

Hotel Los Helechos (tel. 042/54-0330, fax 042/54-0272; CUC29 s, CUC34 d low season; CUC37 s, CUC44 d high season) hides in a cool valley below the Kurhotel. The shocking pink-and-green exterior belies a pleasing restoration inside, with bamboo decor in spacious air-conditioned rooms with satellite TVs, telephones, and modern bathrooms. Take a room in the front; the rest are poorly lit. There's a pleasant swimming pool and restaurant, plus bowling alley.

Restaurante Mi Retiro (no tel.; daily 7 A.M.–5 P.M.) is a marvelous modern eatery built in traditional style on a hilltop overlooking deep vales about three kilometers south of Topes, on the road to Trinidad.

Getting There

A *camión* runs between Topes and Trinidad, but service is unreliable.

The road from Trinidad rises in a steep, potholed switchback. Drive with utmost caution! A second road rises more gradually from Santa Clara via Manicaragua.

If coming from Cienfuegos, you can turn left at La Sierrita and follow the valley of the Río Mataguá; however, at last visit this road was badly deteriorated and suitable for four-wheel drive only.

Gaviotatours offers excursions by truck to Topes and Finca Codina from Trinidad (CUC55).

CIEGO DE ÁVILA AND CAMAGÜEY

These contiguous and geographically similar provinces together form Cuba's central plains, dominated inland by rolling savannas and, off the north coast, by the Cayería del Norte, low-lying, sandy coral islands limned by Cuba's most spectacular beaches with sand as soft and scintillatingly white as confectioner's sugar dissolving into waters of mesmerizing peacock blue hues.

Officially called the Archipiélago de Sabana-Camagüey, but known to all Cubans as the Jardines del Rey (King's Garden), this seagirt wilderness of coral reefs, cays, islands, and sheltered seas extends for some 470 kilometers in a great line parallel to the coast, between 10 and 18 kilometers from shore. Tourism development is progressing at a steady pace, concentrated on Cayo Coco and Cayo Guill-

ermo—there is no better beach experience to be had in all Cuba.

The otherwise uninhabited islands are mostly covered with low scrub, which forms a perfect habitat for wild pigs and iguanas and birds such as mockingbirds, nightingales, and woodpeckers. The briny lagoons are favored by pelicans, ibis, various duck species, and—the stars of the show—as many as 20,000 flamingos. Running along the northern edge of the cays are endless miles of coral reef. Scuba divers will be in heaven!

Ernest Hemingway actively pursued German submarines in these seas in the 1940s, immortalizing his adventures in his novel *Islands in the Stream*. It is possible to follow the route of the novel's protagonists as they pursued the Nazis east–west along the cays,

HIGHLIGHTS

《 Parque Nacional Jardines de la Reina: World-class sportfishing and diving await at this park's way-off-the-beaten-track offshore cays (page 400).

《 Cayo Coco and Cayo Guillermo: Beaches don't get any more gorgeous than these, with warm waters and top-class all-inclusive resort hotels to match (pages 405, 409).

《 Plaza San Juan de Díos: This square is the most impressive of several atmospheric colonial plazas in the large provincial capital of Camagüey (page 415).

《 Finca La Belén: There's good hiking and bird-watching at this farm with exotic wildlife and noteworthy accommodation (page 421).

《 Cayo Sabinal: Coral fringes this lonesome cay with scintillating white sand and peacock blue waters. Its rustic dining and accommodations make for the perfect me-and-only-me getaway (page 422).

《 Scuba Diving at Playa Santa Lucía: Though the Playa Santa Lucía beach resort is otherwise a dud, the diving is superb (page 424)!

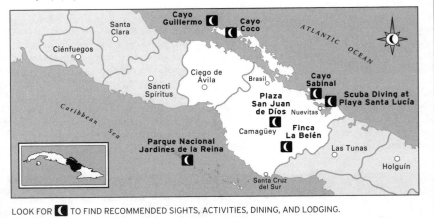

LOOK FOR **《** TO FIND RECOMMENDED SIGHTS, ACTIVITIES, DINING, AND LODGING.

passing Confites, Paredón Grande, Coco, Guillermo, and on to Santa María. Hemingway was meticulous in his descriptions of landmarks, although he sometimes shifted their position.

Much of the coastal plain is covered with barren deciduous scrubland grazed by swampy marshland, perfect for bird-watching; and by lagoons, perfect for fishing. Further inland, the flatlands are drowned by vast undulating seas of green sugarcane. Nonetheless, much of the region comprises cattle country dominated by ranches—*ganaderías*—worked by *vaqueros* with lassoes and machetes lashed to the flanks of their horses.

Pancake-flat Ciego de Ávila (the average elevation of the land is less than 50 meters above sea level) is Cuba's least-populous province and though the nation's leading pineapple producer, almost three-fourths of the province is devoted to cattle. The wedge-shaped province (6,910 square km) forms Cuba's waist, stretching only 50 kilometers from coast to coast. There are few rivers and no distinguishing features, and few sights of historical interest, even in Ciego de Ávila and Morón, the only two towns of importance. By contrast, the city of Camagüey, capital of the nation's largest province, offers plenty of colonial charm. The surrounding honey-colored rolling plains are reminiscent of Montana, parched in summer by a scowling wind that bows down the long flaxen grasses. These upland plains are bounded to the north by a line of low mountains, the Sierra de Cubitas.

The sparsely populated southern plains are covered almost entirely by marshland and swamps that attract migratory ducks, doves, snipes, quail, and guinea fowl. Bird-watchers will get a thrill, but as yet there are no facilities to accommodate them.

A slender archipelago—the Jardines de la Reina—lies off the southern coast, sprinkled east–west in a straight line across the Gulf of Santa Ana María. This necklace of coral isles boasts fabulous beaches and bird life, coral formations perfect for scuba diving, and shallow waters that offer angling delights.

PLANNING YOUR TIME

Travel through the provinces is easy. Running through the center of the provinces is the Carretera Central, which connects Ciego de Ávila and Camagüey cities with Havana and Santiago de Cuba. One lane in each direction, this fast central highway requires caution when driving. There's plenty of traffic, plenty of traffic police, and plenty of bicyclists, free-roaming cattle and other dangerous obstacles. Astro and Víazul buses link both capital cities with destinations islandwide. The cities are also major stops on the main east–west railway.

The paved and less-trafficked Circuito Norte highway parallels the north coast at an average distance of five kilometers inland. It is mostly in good condition. Feeder roads connect it with the Carretera Central.

The 400 or so cays of the Jardines del Rey are separated from one another by narrow channels and from the coast by shallow lagoons in which flamingos tiptoe around in hot pink. However, only three are currently accessible by *pedraplenes* that link Cayo Coco, Cayo Romano, and Cayo Sabinal to the mainland.

Two days is barely sufficient for relaxing on **Cayo Coco** and neighboring **Cayo Guillermo** (connected by another *pedraplén*), the most developed and beautiful of the keys. Think gorgeous beaches and jade-blue seas. Visitors can select from half a dozen world-class all-inclusive resort hotels, although they can be pricey. If all you want is to relax with a rum cocktail on fine white sand, with breaks for windsurfing and other water sports, then this could be for you. No Cubans are allowed, so don't expect interactions with locals nor to glean even an inkling of Cuban life. You can rent cars (skip the scooters for long-haul excursions) for forays farther afield.

Gateway to these two cays is Morón, a small-scale town that boasts the excellent Museo Caonabo and the Museo de Azucar (Sugar Museum), where a steam-train ride is offered. Anglers can cast for tarpon, snook, and other game fish in nearby Lago La Redonda. Morón makes a good base for day trips to Cayo Coco and has several *casas particulares*. It is also well

CIEGO DE ÁVILA / CAMAGÜEY

CIEGO DE ÁVILA AND CAMAGÜEY PROVINCES

served by trains, with direct connection to both Havana and Ciego de Ávila, the provincial capital. The city's sites are few, but it is well-served by *casas particulares* and even a few restaurants of note.

More interesting by far is Camagüey. You could easily justify three days in this colonial city, which boasts several historic plazas. Pity about the *jiniteros,* who are more numerous and aggressive here than in other cities. The choice of accommodations includes scores of *casas particulares* and even two fine historic hotels.

Camagüey is a gateway to Playa Santa Lucía. This second-rate beach resort is touted in tourist literature, but appeals mostly to budget-minded Canadians and Europeans, with second-rate hotels and a desultory nightlife to suit. Sure, the diving is exceptional, but that's about it (even the beach pales in comparison to Cayo Coco). To make matters worse, the hinterland is physically unappealing, although a worthwhile excursion is to Rancho King, a cattle ranch where rodeos are hosted; and to **Cayo Sabinal,** with spectacular beaches and waters touted for future development. Consider Santa Lucía a place to lay your head while traveling the Circuito Norte, which otherwise has few hotels.

Opportunities abound for bird-watchers, not least on the cays, but also at **Finca La Belén,** a wilderness area southeast of Camagüey city. Set amid scenic terrain, it provides a rare opportunity for hiking in this region, and is served by its own delightful hotel.

Divers and anglers should set their sights on the **Parque Nacional Jardines de la Reina.** This necklace of cays off the southern coast is accessed solely from the funky fishing village of Júcaro, south of Ciego de Ávila. This is pristine terrain for divers, and for yachters. Visitation is controlled exclusively through a single agency, based in Júcaro.

Ciego de Ávila and Vicinity

CIEGO DE ÁVILA

The provincial capital city (pop. 85,000), 460 kilometers east of Havana, is the least inspirational of Cuba's provincial capitals and at times is infested with mosquitoes from a swamp immediately north of town.

The derivation of the town's name is intriguing. The first land grants locally were given in the mid-16th century, when the region was almost entirely forested. Gradually cattle ranches were established. Local lore says that one of the earliest hacienda owners was named Jacomé de Ávila. His property, established in 1538, occupied a large clearing, or *ciego,* and was used as a way station for travelers. A small settlement grew around it, known locally as Ciego de Ávila. The city is also known as *ciudad de las piñas* ("pineapple town") for the local fields of pineapples processed locally at Empresa Piña.

The streets are laid out in a perfect grid. The Carretera Central (called Calle Chicho Valdés) runs east–west through the center of the city. The main street is Independencia, running east–west two blocks north of Chicho Valdés. Independencia divides the city into Norte (north) and Sur (south) sections; Marcial Gómez is the main north–south street, dividing the city into Este (east) and Oeste (west).

Parque Martí

The town's central plaza, between Independencia and Libertad, and Marcial Gómez and Honorate del Castillo, has a bust of the hero at its center. Shade trees and Victorian-era lampposts surround the square. On the south side is the **Poder Popular,** the old town hall, built in 1911.

On the southeast corner, the **Museo de Artes Decorativos** (Marcial Gómez #2, esq. Independencia, tel. 033/20-1661; Mon.–Tues. 8 A.M.–4:30 P.M., Wed.–Sat. 8:30 A.M.–10:30 P.M., Sun. 8 A.M.–noon and 6–10 P.M.; entrance CUC1, cameras CUC1, videos

Monumento Máximo Gómez

CUC3) is housed in a restored colonial mansion replete with priceless antiques, with rooms set out as if the occupants were still there.

The **Teatro Principal** (Joaquín Agüera, esq. Honorario del Castillo, tel. 033/22-2086), one block south of Martí, was built at the whim of a local society figure, Ángela Hernández Vida de Jiménez. Its enormous hand-carved wooden doors open onto an elaborately decorated interior, a mix of imperial, baroque, and renaissance styles, with allegorical statuary, an oval grand marble staircase, and bronze chandeliers.

Plaza Máximo Gómez

This small plaza, four blocks west of Parque Martí, is worth a visit to view the life-size bronze statue of the hero-general, sword raised, on his charger.

An old Spanish fort—**Fortín de la Trocha**—stands on the park's east side. It is the only one still standing of seven military towers built during the Ten Years War (1868–78),

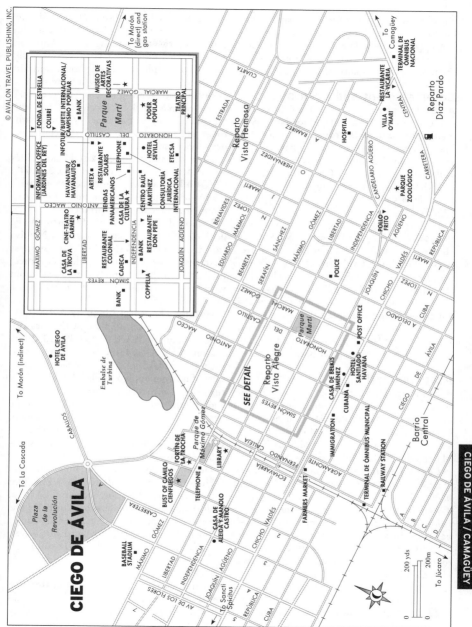

CIEGO DE ÁVILA

To Morón (indirect)

To La Cascada

Plaza de la Revolución

Embalse de Turbina

HOTEL CIEGO DE ÁVILA

BASEBALL STADIUM

BUST OF CAMILO CIENFUEGOS

FORTÍN DE LA TROCHA

Parque de Máximo Gómez

LIBRARY

TELEPHONE

CASA DE ALEIDA Y MANOLO CASTRO

FARMERS MARKET

IMMIGRATION

TERMINAL DE ÓMNIBUS MUNICIPAL

RAILWAY STATION

CASA DE BEKIS JIMÉNEZ

CUBANA

HOTEL SANTIAGO-HAVANA

POST OFFICE

Parque Martí

Reparto Vista Alegre

SEE DETAIL

Barrio Central

POLICE

HOSPITAL

POLLO FRITO

PARQUE ZOOLÓGICO

Reparto Vista Hermosa

Reparto Diaz Pardo

VILLA O'MARI

RESTAURANTE LA VICARIA

TERMINAL DE ÓMNIBUS NACIONAL

To Camagüey

To Morón (direct) and gas station

To Jócaro

To Sancti Spíritus

Detail inset:

FONDA DE ESTRELLA

COLIBRI

BANK

INFOTUR/BUFETE INTERNACIONAL/CAMPISMO POPULAR

MUSEO DE ARTES DECORATIVAS

Parque Martí

PODER POPULAR

TEATRO PRINCIPAL

HOTEL SEVILLA

ETECSA

INFORMATION OFFICE (JARDINES DEL REY)

HAVANATUR/HAVANAUTOS

ARTEX

RESTAURANTE SOLARIS

TELEPHONE

CENTRO RAÚL MARTÍNEZ

CONSULTORÍA JURÍDICA INTERNACIONAL

CASA DE LA TROVA

CINE-TEATRO CARMEN

TIENDAS PANAMERICANOS

CASA DE LA CULTURA

BANK

RESTAURANTE DON PEPE

RESTAURANTE COLONIAL

CADECA

COPPELIA

BANK

Street names: MARCIAL GÓMEZ, HONORATO DEL CASTILLO, ANTONIO MACEO, MÁXIMO GÓMEZ, LIBERTAD, INDEPENDENCIA, JOAQUÍN AGÜERO, SIMÓN REYES, CUARTA, ESTRADA, RAMIREZ, HERNÁNDEZ, MARTÍ, BENAVIDES, MÁRMOL, SÁNCHEZ, MÁXIMO GÓMEZ, LÓPEZ, EDUARDO, BEMBETA, SERAFÍN, GÓMEZ, JOAQUÍN, CHICHO, VALDÉS, CUBA, REPÚBLICA, MARTÍ, CANDELARIO AGÜERO, CARRETERA, CENTRAL, DELGADO, ÁVILA, CIEGO, AGRAMONTE, ECHAVARRÍA, FERNANDO, CABALLOS, CARRETERA, AV DE LOS FLORES

200 yds
200m

© AVALON TRAVEL PUBLISHING, INC.

when a wooden barricade—*la trocha*—was built by the Spanish to thwart a westward advance by the rebels. The line, which extended from coast to coast, featured 43 forts. Today the fort houses a restaurant.

Entertainment and Events

Artex El Patio (Libertad #162) hosts live music on its patio Wednesday–Monday 9 P.M.–3 A.M. The **Casa de la Trova** (Libertad #130; Tues.–Thurs. noon–6 P.M. and 9 P.M.–1 A.M., Fri.–Sat. until 2 A.M., Sun. 10 A.M.–2 P.M. and 9 P.M.–2 A.M.; CUC3 including one drink) hosts traditional music; as does the **Casa de la Cultura** (Independencia #76, tel. 033/23974).

The happening dance spot at last visit was the **Colibrí** (Tues.–Sat. 9 P.M.–3 A.M., Sun. 4–10 P.M.; CUC1 Tues.–Fri. but CUC5 per pair on Sat. including CUC4 of drinks, Sun. CUC3 per pair including CUC2 of drinks), which has a tiny *cabaret espectáculo* followed by disco. No singles are allowed. It's a scrum to get in without a reservation! You need ID to enter.

To sup some suds, head to the pirate-themed **Taberna Bucanero** (República #420, tel. 033/25-3413; 24 hours), serving draft Bucanero.

Accommodations

Accommodations can make reservations for *campismos* throughout Ciego de Ávila Province at the **Campismo Popular** (Chicho Valdés Oeste #111, tel. 033/22-2501; Mon.–Fri. 8 A.M.–4 P.M.) and also on the west side of Parque Martí (tel. 033/22-2501, 8 A.M.–4 P.M.).

Casas Particulares: The **Villa O'Mari** (Máximo Gómez #352, e/ 4ta y 5ta Este, tel. 033/22-3267; CUC20) is a marvelous option. This two-story house, hidden at the end of a cul-de-sac, is smothered in bougainvillea and has a garden patio with rockers, a lounge with TV and stereo system, plus two air-conditioned rooms with safe deposit boxes. One room has a kitchen, fridge, TV, and its own entrance via a spiral staircase; the other is spacious and has a terrace. Both have modern bathrooms.

☾ Casa de Aleida Castro (Calle 3 #16, e/ Independencia y Joaquín de Agüero, tel.

033/22-8355; CUC20–30) is a fabulously preserved 1959 middle-class home with a double garage and two rooms: The spacious upstairs wood-paneled room has stylish retro furnishings, two double beds, telephone, and air-conditioning (not functioning at last visit), and opens to a vast rooftop terrace with rockers; a second room is small, but nicely furnished with air-conditioning and a modern en-suite bathroom. Huge meals are made, and there's laundry service plus a sumptuous TV lounge.

Casa de Bilkis Jiménez (Chicho Valdés #76, e/ Maceo y H. Castillo, tel. 033/22-4609; CUC15) has two air-conditioned rooms with telephones, fridges, private hot-water bathrooms, and independent entrances.

I enjoyed a stay at **Casa de Carmen** (Fé del Valle #64, e/ Abraham Delgado y Narciso López, tel. 033/20-5467), with two spotless upstairs rooms with independent entrance, modern furnishings, and a shared bathroom with hot water. The larger of the two has a lounge with rockers and a balcony.

Hotels: The **Hotel Ciego de Ávila** (Carretera Ceballos, tel. 033/22-8013, islazul@ ciego.cav.cyt.cu; CUC22 s, CUC30 d low season; CUC27 s, CUC36 d high season, including breakfast), two kilometers northwest of downtown, is a faceless but pleasantly furnished four-story building with 144 air-conditioned rooms with telephones and private baths. There's a beauty parlor and barbershop, nightclub, tourism bureau, and rent-a-car service. The local populace flocks to the swimming pool on weekends. (Islazul.)

Hotel Santiago-Havana (Independencia y Honorario del Castillo, tel. 033/22-5703; CUC22 s, CUC30 d low season; CUC27 s, CUC36 d high season) dates back to 1957. The modest hotel has 76 air-conditioned, dourly furnished rooms with TVs and hot water. There's a bar and cabaret disco. (Islazul.)

Food

The most elegant spot in town is the **Restaurante Solaris** (tel. 033/22-2156; 12:30 P.M.–10 P.M. daily), atop the Doce Plantas building on the west side of Parque Martí; the elevator is to the rear of the building. No shorts are allowed. Slide into a red leather banquette for *criollo* dishes (below CUC10) while a pianist entertains.

For historic colonial ambience check out **Fonda La Estrella** (Máximo Gómez, esq. Honorato Castillo, tel. 033/26-6186; daily 11:30 A.M.–midnight), with a wooden bar, murals, wrought-iron seating, and live music. I recommend the *ropa vieja* (CUC3.25) or paella (CUC3.50).

Alternately, try **Restaurante Don Pepe** (Independencia Oeste #113, e/ Maceo y Simón Reyes, tel. 033/22-3713; Wed.–Mon. noon–3 P.M. and 8–10 P.M.), another atmospheric option serving the usual *criollo* fare for about CUC2. It has live music.

The **Restaurante Colonial** (Independencia Oeste #110, tel. 033/22-3595; daily 6 P.M.–midnight) replicates a Spanish *bodega* and is lent character by its contemporary statues of flamenco dancers, a bull's head over the bar, and cowhide chairs. Alas, the menu offers the usual *criollo* staples such as fried chicken or pork.

Stalls outside the train station sell pizzas and other snacks, *resfrescos,* and *batidos.*

Coppelia (Independencia Oeste, esq. Simón Reyes; 10 A.M.–10 P.M.) sells ice cream.

You can buy produce at the *mercado agropecuario,* beneath the overpass at Chicho Valdés and Fernando Calleja; groceries at **Supermercado Cruz Verde** (Independencia and Máximo Gómez); and baked goods at **Panadería Doña Neli,** on the northwest corner of Parque Martí.

Information and Services

Infotur (Honorato del Castillo, e/ Libertad y Independencia, tel. 033/20-9109; Mon.–Fri. 9 A.M.–6 P.M., Sat. 8:30 A.M.–noon) provides tourist information.

The **post office** (Marcial Gómez, esq. Chico Valdés) is two blocks south of Parque Martí. **Etecsa** (Joaquín Agüera, e/ Honorato y Maceo; daily 8:30 A.M.–7 P.M.) has international phone and Internet service.

Bandec (Independencia Oeste, esq. Simón Reyes, and Independencia Oeste, esq. Antonio Maceo) and **Banco Popular** (Independencia, e/ Simón Reyes y Maceo) have branches, and you can also change foreign currency at **Cadeca** (Independencia Oeste #118, e/ Maceo y Simón Reyes).

The **hospital** (Máximo Gómez, tel. 033/22-2429) is at the east end of town.

Inmigración (Independencia Este #14, tel. 033/22-3625; Mon.–Tues. 8 A.M.–noon and 1:30–3:30 P.M., and Wed. and Fri. 8 A.M.–noon) can issue *prórrogas.* The **Consultoría Jurídica Internacional** (Independencia, e/ Honorato y Maceo, tel. 033/26-6238; Mon.–Fri. 8:30 A.M.–5 P.M.) offers legal aid; the **police station** is one block east of the main square, on Delgado.

Getting There and Away

By Air: The **Aeropuerto Máximo Gómez** (tel. 033/22-5717) is 22 kilometers north of town. **Cubana** (Chicho Valdés #83, e/ Maceo y Honorario, tel. 033/22-1117; Mon.–Fri. 8:30 A.M.–3 P.M.) flies once weekly from Havana (CUC74 one-way). Some charter flights to Cayo Coco land here.

By Bus: The **Terminal de Ómnibus Nacional** (tel. 033/22-2407) is on the Carretera Central, 1.5 kilometers east of town.

Astro public buses link Ciego de Ávila with Havana (CUC22 *especial,* CUC18.50 *regular*), Sancti Spíritus (CUC5 *especial,* CUC3 *regular*), Camagüey (CUC5 *especial,* CUC4 *regular*), and other provincial capitals, but they're usually full when they pass through. Buses depart Ciego de Ávila for Havana daily at 8:25 P.M.

Víazul (tel. 031/25109) buses connecting Havana, Trinidad, and Varadero with Holguín and Santiago de Cuba stop here. Eastbound buses depart Ciego de Ávila for Santiago at 3:15, 4:30, and 10:50 A.M. and 4:35 and 10:10 P.M., and for Holguín only at 2:20 A.M. Westbound buses depart Ciego de Ávila for Havana at 1, 1:55, and 6:55 A.M. and 6:35 P.M.; for Trinidad at 4:15 A.M., and for Varadero at 5:10 A.M.

The **Terminal de Ómnibus Municipal** (tel. 033/22-3076), next to the railway station, serves towns within the province.

By Train: The **Estación Ferrocarril** (tel. 033/223-313) is at the base of Agramonte, three blocks west and six blocks south of Parque Martí. Ciego de Ávila is on the main railroad between Havana and Santiago and all trains stop here (often in the middle of the night).

Westbound trains depart Ciego de Ávila for Havana (CUC22 *especial,* CUC16 *regular*) at 1:21 A.M., 2:31 A.M., 4 A.M., 5:34 A.M., 8:01 A.M., 11:40 A.M., 6:15 P.M., and 6:25 P.M.; and for Santa Clara at 2:10 P.M. Eastbound trains depart Ciego de Ávila for Bayamo (CUC12) at 3:25 A.M.; for Camagüey (CUC3) at 7:29 P.M.; for Holguín (CUC11) at 2:30 A.M.; and for Santiago de Cuba (CUC21 *especial,* CUC14.50 *regular*) at 10:45 A.M., 12:14 P.M., 1:36 P.M., 9:56 P.M., and 11:16 P.M. Trains also depart for Morón (CUC1) at 8:30 A.M., and 2:05, 6:10, and 11:30 P.M. (CUC1).

By Car: You can rent cars through **Havanautos** (tel. 033/26-6345) and **Transtur** (tel. 033/26-6228), at the Hotel Ciego de Ávila; and **Micar** (tel. 033/22-2530, Carretera Central y Independencia).

There are gas stations at the junction of the *circunvalación* y Carretera Morón (northeast of town); on Chicho Valdés, esq. Martí; and two blocks east at Chicho Valdés y Independencia.

For Morón, take Carretera a Caballo (Carretera de Morón), on the west side of town.

Excursions: You can book excursions through **Havanatur** (Libertad, e/ Maceo y Honorato, tel. 033/26-6342).

Getting Around

Horse-drawn cabs line up outside the train station. No ride should cost more than two or three pesos, although you may be charged in dollars.

For a taxi, call **Cubataxi** (tel. 033/22-7636) or **Transtur** (tel. 033/22-2997).

█ PARQUE NACIONAL JARDINES DE LA REINA

The Garden of the Queens archipelago comprises around 660 of deserted coral cays in a long chain that extends east–west for some 350 kilometers off the southern coast of Ciego

de Ávila and Camagüey Provinces. Flamingos wade in the briny shallows of the Golfo de Ana María. An extensive coral reef runs along the chain's southern shore, which is lined by white-sand beaches. Iguanas are common, and marine turtles consider these pristine beaches perfect for laying the seeds of tomorrow's turtles.

There's a **visitor center** on **Cayo Anclitas,** which also has a turtle farm, and there's a fishing lodge on **Cayo Bartolo.** Otherwise this is virgin terrain. Development for tourism (limited to catch-and-release fishing and scuba diving) is nascent, overseen by the **Centro de Investigaciones Medio Ambientales de Camagüey** (Céspedes y Carretera Central, Camagüey, tel. 032/29-8268, bombino@cimac.cmw.inf.cu). At last visit, an office was being planned for Santa Cruz del Sur, 75 kilometers south of Camagüey.

Recreation

The cays are nirvana for sportfishing and diving. Reservations are handled by an Italian company, **Avalon Dive Center/Press Tours** (tel. 33/98104, VHF 19A, Júcaro; tel. 0335/814-9111 in Italy, 928/222-1631 in the United States; www.avalons.net), which has been granted exclusive permits to the Jardines de la Reina.

There are 26 dive sites. Diving is permitted only with a guide provided by Avalon, even if you arrive on your own yacht. Professional scuba instructors even stage shark-riding—yes, riding sharks like cowboys do horses! Six-day/seven-night diving packages cost from CUC1,180 double occupancy. One-day dives are also available; one dive costs CUC30 (CUC40 for night dives).

Prices for fishing packages are given on request.

Accommodations

Participants on fishing and scuba diving packages are accommodated aboard the **La Tortuga Lodge,** a former barge turned permanently moored hotel that can accommodate 22 people in seven air-conditioned cabins, each with toilet and shower; the **Halcyon Cruiser,** a 75-foot cruise yacht with six cabins sharing three hot-water showers; and the older **Explorador Cruiser,** a 69-foot cruise vessel with four cabins with hot water showers. The latter has a compressor. Non-divers and non-fishers are given rates upon request.

Getting There

All visits to the cays are handled through **Avalon Dive Center/Press Tours,** in the brow-beaten fishing village of Júcaro, 20 kilometers south of Ciego de Ávila (trains depart Ciego for Júcaro at 11:10 A.M. and 4:35 P.M.).

Boats leave from **Marina Júcaro.** Private vessels arriving in the cays must report to Avalon, who has exclusive use of the marina, which has six moorings with electricity, diesel, and water. Yachts can moor at the cays with prior permission.

MORÓN

Morón (pop. 50,000), 37 kilometers due north of Ciego de Ávila, is the main gateway to Cayo Coco and Cayo Guillermo and is perfectly positioned for day excursions if you don't want to pay the exorbitant hotel rates on the cays. It is known as the City of the Rooster, a name bequeathed in the 18th century by settlers from Morón de la Frontera, in Andalusia, Spain. In the 1950s, Morón's city fathers erected a rooster at the entrance to town. Fulgencio Batista was present for the unveiling. After the Revolution, an officer in the rebel army ordered the monument's destruction. In 1981, the city government decided to erect another cockerel in bronze at the foot of a clock tower fitted with an amplifier so that citizens could hear the rooster crow daily at dawn and dusk. It stands outside the entrance to the Hotel Morón.

Morón featured prominently during the Wars of Independence. The area around Morón was the scene of heavy fighting, and the town itself was captured by rebel troops in 1876. The Spanish colonial army built the 50-kilometer-long wooden barricade—La Trocha—from Morón to Júcaro, on the south coast.

The city is enclosed to the north and east by a vast quagmire of sedges, reeds, and water. Yes, there are crocodiles in the water, although you'll have a better chance of seeing them at the **Zoocriadero Cocodrilo** (daily 9 A.M.– 7 P.M.; CUC2) about five kilometers east of Morón; and at **Área Protegida de Cunagua** (daily 6 A.M.– 6 P.M.; CUC1) about 10 kilometers east of town. The latter has hiking trails and a mountaintop restaurant, and horses can be rented.

Museo de Azucar

The now-closed Central Patria o Muerte sugar mill at Patria, five kilometers southeast of town, has been turned into the Sugar Museum (tel. 0335/50-3309; Mon.–Fri. 7:30 A.M.– 4:30 P.M., Sat. 7:30 A.M.–1 P.M.; CUC3) describing sugarcane cultivation and refining. Visitors are welcomed with a *canchanchara* (a rum and honey drink) preceding a six-minute video on sugar production (alas, purely visual without any explanations). There's a model of the *central,* where much of the original machinery is in place within the near derelict building. There are no descriptions, however, and you may come away knowing nothing about the process of sugar production. To the rear of the facility are three steam trains. Rides are offered on a 1917 Baldwin steam train (daily at 10:30 A.M.).

Museo Caonabo

This museum (Martí #115, tel. 0335/50-4501; Tues.–Sat. 10 A.M.–6 P.M., Sun. 8 A.M.–noon) is one of Cuba's more interesting regional museums and well worth a peek. Occupying a three-storey neoclassical former bank, the museum is on two levels. Downstairs is dedicated to pre-Columbian culture. Upstairs the historical artifacts range from Spanish swords and *mantillas* to Revolutionary icons, all thoughtfully displayed and labeled.

Laguna de la Leche

This 66.5-square-kilometer lake, five kilometers due north of Morón, is named for its milky complexion, which derives from deposits of gypsum and calcium carbonate stirred up from

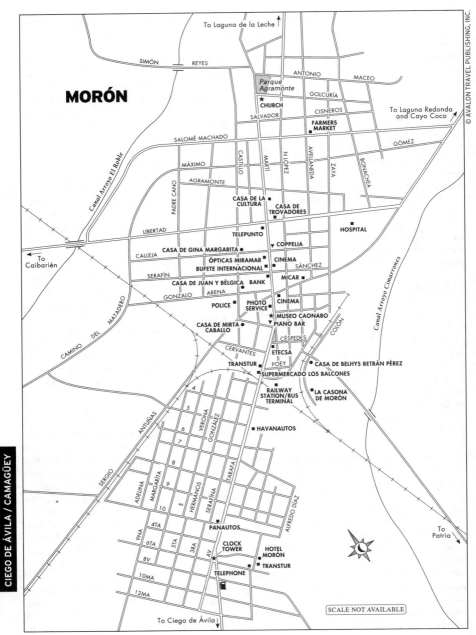

the lakebed by breezes. The lake is chock-full of tilapia, carp, snook, and tarpon. Bird life is abundant, including flamingos. You can take a boat tour (daily 10 A.M.–5:30 P.M.; CUC2) from La Cueva, on the west shore.

Lago La Redonda

This lake, northeast of Morón on the road to Cayo Coco, claims the largest concentrations of bass in Cuba. Fourteen kilometers north of Morón, you'll pass a turnoff for **Centro Turístico La Redonda** (tel. 0335/30-2489; daily 9 A.M.–7 P.M.), a basic angling center. Fishing programs (CUC35 for four hours) are handled through the Hotel Carrusel Morón and La Casona de Morón. Jet skis (CUC1 per minute) are rented, and boat trips (CUC4) offered. There's a restaurant and a bar. Private boaters can berth here.

Entertainment and Events

Each July, the **Carnival Acuático** (Water Carnival) takes place in a canal leading to Laguna de la Leche. Musicians serenade the crowd while the city's prettiest young maidens row boats decorated with garlands of flowers. The annual **Festival de Vapor** (Steam Train Festival), when steam trains from around the nation gather, takes place each December at Central Patria o Muerte.

The **Casa de la Trova** (Libertad #74, e/ Martí y Narciso López) hosts traditional music, as does the **Casa de la Cultura** (Martí #224, tel. 0335/50-4309).

La Casona de Morón (Cristóbal Colón #41, Ciego de Ávila, tel. 0335/50-2236) has pool tables and hosts an outdoor disco Thursday–Sunday (CUC4 per pair). **Disco La Cueva,** three kilometers north of town on the road to Laguna de la Leche, offers karaoke, *cabaret espectáculo,* and disco (CUC1).

The **Piano Bar** (Martí #111, tel. 0335/50-2045; daily 10 A.M.–midnight) has live music nightly, but the garish lighting kills whatever romantic ambience might otherwise exist.

Accommodations

Casa de Belhys Beltrán Pérez (Colón #38, e/ Carretera de Patria y Ferrocarril, tel. 0335/50-5763; CUC20) has one high-ceilinged air-conditioned room in a spacious albeit dowdy colonial home; it has two double beds and a basic hot-water bathroom across the hallway. Meals are served in a rear patio.

Casa de Gina Margarita (Callejas #89, e/ Martí y Castillo, tel. 0335/50-3798; CUC20) is an attractive 1950s home full of antiques and kitsch, with rockers and piano in the TV lounge. It has two modestly furnished, cross-ventilated air-conditioned rooms with small private hot-water bathrooms and independent entrance. There's parking and a delightful patio.

Casa de Mirta Caballo (Dimas Daniel #19, e/ Castillo y Serafina, tel. 0335/50-3036; CUC20) is a smallish, simply furnished home that rents two rooms off the rear patio with rockers. Each has a fridge and private hot-water bathroom, plus independent entrance and parking.

Casa de Juan y Bélgica (Castillo #189, e/ San José y Serafín Sánchez, tel. 0335/50-3823; CUC20) is a well-kept home with two air-conditioned rooms with fans and modern hot-water bathrooms. Meals are served on a nice patio with planters.

Hotel Carrusel Morón (Av. Tarafa, tel. 0335/50-2230, fax 0335/50-2133, www.cubanacan.cu; CUC26 s, CUC34 d low season; CUC29 s, CUC38 d high season) is a modest concrete two-story hotel with 144 rooms, eight of which are junior suites, all with satellite TV. Facilities include a tourism desk, massage salon, barber shop, swimming pool, bar, coffee shop, and disco. (Cubanacán.)

La Casona de Morón (Cristóbal Colón #41, Ciego de Ávila, tel. 0335/50-2236; CUC20 s, CUC26 d year-round) is a colonial mansion immediately east of the railroad station. It has seven air-conditioned rooms reached by a marble staircase. Each of the mammoth but musty and dowdy rooms has a handsome tiled bathroom, ceiling fan, satellite TV, telephone, safe deposit box, minibar, and antique lamps. There's a meager bar, grill, elegant restaurant, and a swimming pool plus small disco. (Palmares.)

Food

Pickings are slim. The best bet is the nautically themed (think ship's wheels for ceiling lamps, and waitresses in naval costume) **(Restaurante La Atarralla** (tel. 0335/50-5351; Tues.– Sun. 2:30–6 P.M.), on a pier overhanging Laguna de la Leche. Choose the breeze-swept balcony or the elegant and airy interior cooled by ceiling fans. It serves paella (CUC5), oyster cocktail (CUC2.50), and grilled lobster (CUC7.30). However, get here early as the restaurant closes at dusk before the mosquitoes settle in.

Restaurante Las Fuentes (Calle Martí, e/ Libertad y Agramonte, tel. 0335/50-5758; daily 11 A.M.–11 P.M.) is clean and modern and has a *criollo* menu for CUC2–6.

Coppelia (Martí y Calleja; 10 A.M.– midnight) serves ice cream. You can buy bread at **Panadería Doña Neli** (Serafín Sánchez #86, e/ Narciso López y Martí); produce at the *mercado agropecuario* (Machado, esq. Avellaneda); and groceries at **Supermercado Los Balcones** (Avenida Tarafa y Calle 3).

Services

Etecsa (Céspedes, esq. Martí; daily 8:30 A.M.– 6:30 P.M.) offers international phone and Internet service. **Bandec** (Martí, esq. Serafín Sánchez) has a branch. The **hospital** (tel. 0335/50-3530) is at the east end of Libertad.

The **Bufete Internacional** (Martí, e/ Serafín Sánchez y Calleja, tel. 0335/50-2215) offers legal services.

Getting There and Away

For air travel, see *Getting There and Away* in the *Ciego de Ávila* section in this chapter.

The **bus station** (tel. 0335/50-3398) and **railway station** (tel. 0335/50-3683) are next to each other on Avenida Tarafa. Eight buses daily connect Morón with Ciego de Ávila.

Trains depart for Morón from Havana daily at 4:45 P.M. (CUC24); from Camagüey at 1:35 and 6:15 P.M. (CUC4.50); and from Ciego de Ávila at 8:30 A.M. and 2:05, 6:10, and 11:30 P.M. (CUC1). Trains depart Morón for Havana at 5:40 A.M.; for Camagüey at 3:15 A.M. and 12:55 P.M.; and for Ciego at 6:10 and 11:45 A.M. and 4 and 8:10 P.M.

Getting Around

Horse-drawn carriages congregate outside the railway station. They also ply the main streets.

You can rent cars with **Havanautos** (tel. 0335/50-2115) at the Hotel Carrusel Morón; **Transtur** (Avenida Tarafa, tel. 0335/50-2222), outside the railway station; and **Rex** (tel. 0335/50-2385).

The Cupet gas station is one block south of the Hotel Morón.

COMUNIDAD CELIA SÁNCHEZ

Known locally as the Pueblo Holandés, this eye-catching "Dutch village" atop a hillock rising above Isla de Turiguanó, 28 kilometers north of Morón, makes you do a double take. The clique of 59 gable-roofed houses supported by timber-beam facades transports you lyrically back to Holland. The village is named for Fidel Castro's secretary and revolutionary alter ego, who apparently conceived the village. Turiguanó was a U.S.-owned private cattle estate before the Revolution. In 1960–61, the land was expropriated and modern houses in Dutch style built for the 30 or so families who live here and raise the island's high-yield native beef breed, the Santa Gertrudis.

Horseback riding (CUC5 per hour) is available at nearby **Agroturístico Rodeo.** It has rodeo on alternate Saturdays and Sundays at 2 and 9 P.M. (CUC1).

Cayo Coco and Cayo Guillermo

These two contiguous islands, separated from the mainland by the Bahía de Perros (Bay of Dogs) and joined to it by a man-made *pedraplén*, are the third-largest tourist destination in Cuba, after Havana and Varadero. Boasting the finest beaches in Cuba, and some of the most beautiful jade-colored waters, these cays offer the finest beach experience for serious sand, sea, and sun hounds who enjoy hotels with a little luxe. Two small facilities cater to budget travelers. However, all the resort hotels operate on an all-inclusive basis and cater almost exclusively to package tours. Long-term plans call for 22,000 rooms for the twin islands, with heaven knows what ecological consequences. (The 27-kilometer *pedraplén* is made of solid landfill and cuts the Bahía de Perros in two. There are only two sluices, preventing sufficient flow of currents, resulting in significant damage to the mangrove systems and, consequently, the wildlife.) Soupy mangroves line the southern shores—breeding grounds for hordes of mosquitoes.

MININT (Ministry of the Interior) has a security checkpoint at the entrance to the bridge, where there's a toll booth (CUC2 each way). You must present your passport. No unauthorized Cubans are allowed.

Drive carefully; there are no barriers on the sides of the narrow road, which is deeply potholed in places, so one mistake and you'll be in the drink. Eventually, you reach a traffic circle. The road straight ahead leads to the hotel complex and main beaches of Cayo Coco. The road to the right leads to leads to the marina and, beyond, **Cayo Romano** and **Cayo Paredón,** where a lighthouse—**Faro Diego Velázquez**—built in 1859 pins the cay's northern tip; there's a military barrier on Cayo Romano and access is subject to the official whim.

◖ CAYO COCO

This 364-square-kilometer cay is a stunner on account of its 21 kilometers of superlative beaches divided into five sections, westward: Playa Colorada, Playa Larga, Playa Prohibida, Playa Los Flamencos, and, most importantly, Playa Palma Real (Royal Palm Beach).

Cayo Coco, which is named for a bird—the roseate ibis, or *coco*—was immortalized by Ernest Hemingway. In *Islands in the Stream,* his protagonist, Thomas Hudson, sets foot on the beach at Puerto Coco seeking traces of Nazi

ERNEST HEMINGWAY, NAZI HUNTER

In May 1942, Ernest Hemingway showed up at the U.S. embassy in Havana with a proposal to fit the *Pilar* out as a Q-boat, with .50-caliber machine guns, other armaments, and a trained crew with himself at the helm. The boat would navigate the cays off the north coast of Cuba, ostensibly collecting specimens on behalf of the American Museum of Natural History, but in fact on the lookout for Nazi U-boats, which Hemingway intended to engage and disable.

Hemingway's friend Col. John W. Thomason Jr. was Chief of Naval Intelligence for Central America and pulled strings to get the plan approved. The vessel was "camouflaged" and duly set out for the cays. Gregorio Fuentes – who from 1938 until the writer's death was in charge of the *Pilar* – went along and served as the model for Antonio in *Islands in the Stream,* Hemingway's novel based on his real-life adventures.

They patrolled for two years. Several times they located and reported the presence of Nazi submarines that the U.S. Navy or Air Force were later able to sink. Only once, off Cayo Mégano, did Hemingway come close to his dream: A U-boat suddenly surfaced while the *Pilar* was at anchor. Unfortunately, it dipped back below the surface and disappeared before Hemingway could get close.

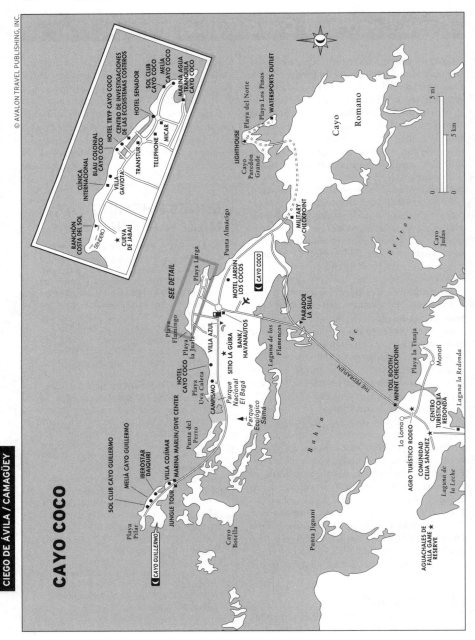

CAYO COCO

RANCHÓN COSTA DEL SOL

CLÍNICA INTERNACIONAL

BLAU COLONIAL CAYO COCO

HOTEL TRYP CAYO COCO

CENTRO DE INVESTIGACIONES DE LAS ECOSISTEMAS COSTEROS

HOTEL SENADOR

SOL CLUB CAYO COCO

MELIÁ CAYO COCO

MARINA AGUA TRANQUILA CAYO COCO

VILLA GAVIOTA

TRANSTUR

TELEPHONE

MICAR

SENDERO

CUEVA DE JABALÍ

SEE DETAIL

Playa Larga

Punta Almácigo

LIGHTHOUSE

Playa del Norte

Playa Los Pinos

WATERSPORTS OUTLET

Cayo Romano

Cayo Paredón Grande

MILITARY CHECKPOINT

los Perros

Cayo Judas

HOTEL JARDÍN LOS COCOS

CAYO COCO

PARADOR LA SILLA

Playa Flamingo

VILLA AZUL

SITIO LA GÜIRA

BANK/ HAVANAUTOS

Laguna de los Flamencos

de

Playa la Jaula

HOTEL CAYO COCO

CAMPISMO

Playa Uva Caleta

Parque Nacional El Bagá

THE PEDRAPLÉN

TOLL BOOTH/ MININT CHECKPOINT

Playa la Tinaja

Manatí

Laguna la Redonda

SOL CLUB CAYO GUILLERMO

MELIÁ CAYO GUILLERMO

IBEROSTAR DAIGUIRÍ

VILLA COJÍMAR

JUNGLE TOUR

MARINA MARLIN/DIVE CENTER

Punta del Perro

Parque Ecológico Sámá

Bahía

La Loma

AGRO TURÍSTICO RODEO

COMUNIDAD CELIA SÁNCHEZ

CENTRO TURÍSTICO LA REDONDA

Laguna de la Leche

Playa Pilar

CAYO GUILLERMO

Cayo Botella

Punta Jiguaní

AGUACHALES DE FALLA GAME RESERVE

5 mi

5 km

0

0

soldiers. Wandering farther inland, he discovers the lagoon where flamingos come to feed at high tide.

Cayo Coco has one of Cuba's largest flamingo colonies, concentrated between Punta Almácigo and Punta del Perro. The rose-pink birds seem to float atop the water, like mirages. Every day, they fly over the north end of the *tombolo* shortly after sunrise and again at dusk. Flamingos are one of 158 bird species here, including the miniature hummingbird, Cuban cuckoo, ibis, herons, egrets, and sea swallows. Migratory birds flock here, too, in vast numbers, and ducks and other waterfowl are common in the shallows. The most prominent animals are *jabelis*—wild pigs—and endemic iguanas. There are even deer. Much of the island (90 percent of which is covered by scrub vegetation) is supposedly a protected reserve, though Jet Ski tours through the mangroves harass the bird and fish colonies, and dynamiting for hotel development does the same.

The **Centro de Investigaciones de las Ecosistemas Costeros** (tel./fax 033/30-1151, ciec@ciec.fica.inf.cu), immediately east of the Tryp resort complex, is responsible for protecting the local ecology.

Parque Nacional El Bagá

This 769-hectare national park (tel. 033/30-1063; 9:30 A.M.–5:30 P.M. daily), protecting the west end of Cayo Coco, features a cultural center, a recreation of a native Taíno village, a crocodile farm, butterfly reservation, bird-watching areas, and nature trails. A three-hour guided tour of the park costs CUC18. Guided 90-minute bird-watching (CUC18) and nature and cultural tours (CUC10) are also offered, as is a "Flamingos and Crocodiles" tour (CUC5).

Entertainment

All the hotels offer theme parties, cabarets, and discos. A *cabaret espectáculo* is offered at the **Cueva del Jabalí** (tel. 033/30-1206; Tues.–Sat. at 10 P.M.; CUC5). Excursions are available from the hotels. Bring repellent.

To jive with Cubans, head to the disco at

Villa Azul (Tues.–Sun.; free), the hotel workers' complex one kilometer west of the roundabout.

Recreation

The hotels all have water sports. Nonguests can pay for banana-boat rides and water skiing, snorkeling, and catamaran and personal watercraft rental. You can rent an Ultralight from outside Meliá Sol Club for flights over Cayo Coco (CUC3 per minute).

Diving is available at the Hotel Tryp Cayo Coco and Blau Colonial Cayo Coco, and through **Blue Diving** (tel. 033/30-8179, www.bluediving.com), between the Sol Cayo Coco and Meliá Cayo Coco. Single dives cost CUC40.

Horseback riding is offered at **Sitio La Güira** (tel. 033/30-1208; CUC7 per hour), a rather hokey facility inland, about six kilometers west of the roundabout. You can even ride a water buffalo, and there's an animal show with trained acrobatic dogs.

Sportfishing trips are offered from **Marina Marlin Aguas Tranquilas** (tel. 033/30-1328; from CUC250 for four hours), east of the main roundabout.

Accommodations

Campismo Cayo Coco (tel. 033/30-1039; CUC13 s/d), at Playa Uva Caleta, 15 kilometers west of the Cupet gas station, serves Cubans—mostly top-producing workers—with basic cabins, but foreigners are permitted in 15 upgraded four-person cabins with private bathrooms. It has a simple restaurant and a swimming pool. The place gets lively in summer, when the Cubans are in. Book in advance through the Campismo Popular (Chicho Valdés Oeste #111, tel. 033/22-2501) in Ciego de Ávila. If the *campismo* is full, budget travelers might try **Sitio La Güira** (tel. 033/30-1208; CUC20 s/d), about six kilometers west of the roundabout, which has three very rustic huts with private baths, plus a thatched restaurant.

Motel Jardín Los Cocos (tel. 033/30-9121; CUC30 s/d year-round), about four kilometers from the beach, serves Cubanacán staff but is open to tourists. It offers 24 air-conditioned no-frills yet adequately furnished rooms with satellite TVs, minibars, and modern hot-water bathrooms. It has a café-bar with pool table, and a swimming pool. (Cubanacán.)

Villa Gaviota (tel. 033/302180, fax 033/302190, carpeta@villagaviota.co.cu; CUC70 s, CUC130 d low season; CUC75 s, CUC150 d high season) has 48 air-conditioned rooms in two-story blocks arrayed around a handsome pool with bar; plus eight seafront *cabinas*. All are nicely furnished with tropical color schemes, rattan, satellite TVs, modems, fridges, and safes. Facilities include a buffet restaurant, snack bar, and traditional *criollo* restaurant, plus water sports club, pool room, tennis, TV lounge, and a gym and sauna.

The **Hotel Tryp Cayo Coco** (tel. 033/30-1300, fax 033/30-1386, www.solmeliacuba.com; CUC160 s, CUC200 d, CUC230–280 suites, standard low season; CUC252 s, CUC315 d, CUC325–400 suites, standard high season), a Sol Meliá property, is a sprawling all-inclusive resort. A stunning contemporary lobby with shopping arcade opens to an elevated lobby bar with views down over a serpentine swimming pool—one of four on-site. The resort has 508 nicely furnished air-conditioned rooms in two- and three-story villa units. All have, satellite TV, radio, minibar, and cavernous marble bathrooms.

Adjacent to the Tryp, the **Hotel Blau Colonial Cayo Coco** (tel. 033/30-1311, www.blau-hotels.com; from CUC94 s, CUC170 d) is a conversion of the former Tryp Colonial Village, with 485 rooms and full resort amenities, including complete watersports, entertainment, and a wide choice of eateries.

Sol Cayo Coco (tel. 033/30-1280, fax 033/30-1285, www.solmeliacuba.com; CUC150 s, CUC200 d standard, CUC210 s, CUC280 d suite low season; CUC180 s, CUC240 d standard, CUC240 s, CUC20 d suite high season), also managed by Sol Meliá, is a compact and handsome all-inclusive with 266 handsome rooms and four suites in condo-style units around a long, sinuous swimming pool. Rooms are equipped to inter-

national standard, and the hotel is brim-full with facilities.

Meliá Cayo Coco (tel. 033/30-1180, fax 033/30-1381, www.solmeliacuba.com; CUC145 s, CUC220 d standard, CUC185 s, CUC285 d junior suite, CUC230 s, CUC360 d suite low season; CUC230 s, CUC345 d standard, CUC265 s, CUC410 d junior suite, CUC315 s, CUC485 d suite high season), adjoining Sol Club, is a more gracious all-inclusive property nestled between the beach and a lagoon, with lush landscaping. The 250 spacious rooms are done up in a subdued contemporary take on traditional Spain. A specialty seafood restaurant is suspended over the lagoon, as are two-story villas. Two other restaurants, several bars, water sports, a beauty salon, boutique, and car and scooter rental round out the facilities.

The Cuban-run **Hotel El Senador** (tel. 033/30-1498, fax 033/30-1490, www.el-senador.com; CUC85 s, CUC170 d club room, CUC135 s, CUC210 d junior suite, CUC125 s, CUC250 d suite low season; CUC170 s, CUC250 d club room, CUC190 s, CUC290 d junior suite, CUC210 s, CUC330 d suite high season) is a three-star all-inclusive resort that aims at families. It is divided into two sections, the Senador and El Empredador, and has 690 spacious albeit modestly furnished rooms, with satellite TV, safe deposit boxes, and modern bathrooms. You get a choice of restaurants, plus there's a cigar lounge, disco, kid's club, and roller-skating rink.

Gaviota runs the similarly priced **Hotel Playa Coco** (tel. 033/30-2250, fax 033/30-2255, www.gaviota-grupo.com), a two-star hotel billed as a four-star, at Playas Las Jaulas. It has 306 air-conditioned rooms and 18 suites, including three for guests with disabilities.

Food

Nonguests can purchase a day or night pass to eat in hotel restaurants. If you wish to escape the resorts, your choices are limited to **Parador La Silla** (tel. 033/30-2137), a simple thatched café on one of the cays that precede Cayo Coco; the simple **Ranchón Puesta del**

Sol beach grill at Playa Flamingo; and **Cueva del Jabalí** (tel. 033/30-1206), a cave behind Playa Los Flamencos, with restaurant and bar open for dinner only; bring insect repellent.

Information and Services

Infotur (tel. 033/30-9109, aeroinfotjr@enet.cu) has a desk in the airport.

Etecsa (daily 8:30 A.M.–5:30 P.M.) has a telephone center west of Hotel El Senador. It's far cheaper to call from here than from the hotels.

The **Clínica Internacional** (tel. 033/30-2158; 24 hours), adjacent to Villa Gaviota, offers medical service to foreigners. This extensive facility has it all: dental clinic, clinical lab, high-pressure oxygen chamber, and appears like a case of overkill meant to impress. It has massage and hydrotherapy.

Asistur (tel. 033/30-8173 or 033/30-8150, asisturcayococo@enet.cu) can assist travelers with problems.

Most area hotels can change foreign currency.

Getting There and Away

International flights serve **Cayo Coco International Airport** (tel. 033/30-9165). Some flights still arrive at Máximo Gómez International Airport in Ciego de Ávila, from where arrivals are bussed to Cayo Coco. **Cubana** (tel. 033/30-1300) operates service from Havana and Santiago. At last visit, EcoTur and West-Point Air International were planning to introduce seaplane service linking Cayo Coco with Havana.

There is no bus service to Cayo Coco.

Cubataxi (tel. 0335/50-3290) charges CUC50 round-trip from Morón in a classic car (higher rates apply for newer cars).

Marina Marlin Aguas Tranquilas (tel. 033/30-1328; from CUC250 for four hours), at the eastern half of the cay, has electricity, water, and gas for private yachters.

Getting Around

Cubataxi (tel. 033/27636) charges CUC25–30 for an island tour in a classic car. A tour by *coche* (horse and buggy) costs CUC5 per per-

son. And *tren* shuttles (open-sided faux trains) run between the hotels (CUC2).

You can hire bicycles, mopeds, and cars at all the hotels. You don't need a car if you're only interested in exploring the cays; a bicycle or moped is a fun and simple way to go. You can also rent cars from **Havanautos** (tel. 033/30-1371), at the airport and at the Cupet gas station; **Rex** (tel. 033/30-2244), at the airport; and **Transtur** (tel. 033/30-1175), with outlets in most hotels.

A guided two-hour **Jungle Tour** (tel. 033/30-1515, www.jungletour-cuba.com; CUC39) is offered aboard Jet Skis departing Cayo Guillermo at 9 A.M., 11 A.M., 1 P.M., and 3 P.M. Alas, you tear through the supposedly protected mangroves.

CAYO GUILLERMO

This 18-square-kilometer cay lies three kilometers west of Cayo Coco, to which it is joined by an umbilical *pedraplén* elevated over the iridescent waters. Egrets and herons pick in the shallows, which are also favored by flamingos.

The star attraction is chalky, five-kilometer-long **Playa El Paso.** There are other beaches, including **Playa del Medio, Playa Pilar,** and **Playa Larga,** at the far western end, where sand dunes pile up 15 meters high (the road is a potholed piste). At low tide, you can wade out for 400 meters or more on the sandbars. The inshore fishing is excellent: Snapper, grouper, mackerel, and bonefish are the species of choice. Farther out, beaked marlin and swordfish run through the Old Bahama Channel—Hemingway's "great blue river." One of the first people to discover the charms of Cayo Guillermo was, in fact, the great fisherman and novelist. ("On the inner side, gentlemen, is Guillermo. See how green she is and full of promise?" says Hemingway's alter ego and main character, Thomas Hudson, in *Islands in the Stream.*)

There's a **Banco Financiero Internacional** outside the entrance to the Iberostar Daiquirí.

Recreation

Scuba diving is available at the Meliá Cayo Guillermo (tel. 033/30-1738). Sportfishing is offered from **Marina Marlin** (tel. 033/30-1718; from CUC250 four hours), at the east end of Cayo Guillermo.

Accommodations

Villa Cojímar (tel. 033/30-1712, fax 033/33-1727, ventas@cojimar.gca.tur.cu; CUC81 s, CUC115 d low season; CUC117 s, CUC175 d high season), on Playa El Paso, is a beautiful low-rise all-inclusive property with spacious lawns, 211 rooms and one suite in small one- and two-story air-conditioned *cabinas,* each with satellite TV, international phone, hairdryer, and safe. Facilities include tennis, soccer court, plus car rental. (Gran Caribe.)

Iberostar Daiquirí (tel. 033/30-1560, fax 033/30-1645, ventas@ibsdaiq.gca.tur.cu; CUC110 s, CUC160 d low season; CUC130 s, CUC200 d high season) is an all-inclusive property in contemporary Spanish vogue. The high point is the lush landscaping. Its 312 air-conditioned rooms in three-story buildings are simply furnished, feature telephones, satellite TVs, fridges, safes, plus beautiful bathrooms, and are much in need of refurbishing. It has a panoply of water sports and land activities, plus entertainment nightly. Excellent children's facilities draw families.

Sol Cayo Guillermo (tel. 033/30-1760, fax 033/30-1748, www.solmeliacuba.com; CUC150 s, CUC200 d low season; CUC180 s, CUC240 d high season), managed by Spain's Sol Meliá, is another beautiful 264-room all-inclusive property in a lively tropical motif. Accommodation is in two-story units and *cabinas,* all with air-conditioning, satellite TVs, direct-dial telephones, mini-fridges, safes, and terraces.

(Meliá Cayo Guillermo (tel. 033/30-1680, fax 033/30-1685, www.solmeliacuba.com; CUC190 s, CUC250 d standard, CUC220 s, CUC290 d junior suite, CUC260 s, CUC350 d suite low season; CUC220 s, CUC290 d standard, CUC330 s, CUC240 junior suite, CUC290 s, CUC390 d suite high season), adjacent, is a slightly more upscale all-inclusive with 314 air-conditioned rooms in the company's trademark turquoise and Caribbean pastels. Each has satellite TV, direct-dial telephone, minibar, and nicely appointed bathrooms. Facilities include three restaurants, five bars, plus a gym, activity center, kid's club, and a full compliment of entertainment and water sports.

Getting There

Transtur operates a shuttle between Cayo Coco and Cayo Guillermo five times daily, calling at all the hotels (CUC5).

Camagüey and Vicinity

CAMAGÜEY

Camagüey (pop. 270,000), 570 kilometers east of Havana and 110 kilometers east of Ciego de Ávila, sits in the center of the namesake province on a bluff above the vast plains. Cuba's third-largest city is full of beautifully restored plazas that lend the city its nicknames, "City of Squares" and "Corinth of the Caribbean." Much of the city has justifiably been declared a national monument.

Camagüey lacks the heavy baroque architecture of Havana. Its style is simpler, more discreet. Even the homes of the wealthiest Camagüeyans were built without palatial adornments: the bourgeoisie built their homes around a courtyard patio surrounded by arches and galleries, or, in more modest abodes, with eaves supported by unembellished wooden columns. Always there was a *tinajón,* the big earthenware jars unique to the city and which lent it a third nickname: "City of the *Tinajones.*"

It's a pleasure to walk the colonial streets, especially in late afternoon, when the sun gilds the facades like burnished copper; and at night, too, when light silvers the Spanish grills and facades of the poorly lit streets, full of impending intrigue. In the dark, full of shadows, it is easy to imagine yourself cast back 200 years.

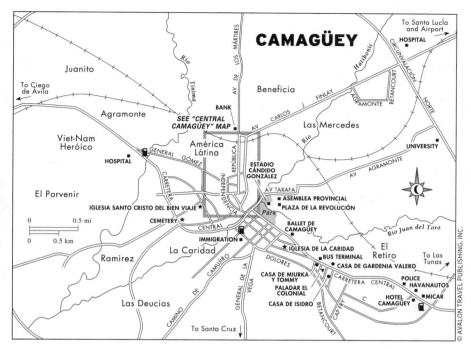

Camagüey can be explored in one day but is fully deserving of two. There's no shortage of *jiniteros* waiting to part you from your dollar. When not accosting you on their bicycles as you enter the city by car, they congregate at Plazuelita de las Cubanitas (locally referred to as Plazuelita de los Jiniteros), at the north end of Calle Independencia.

History

Camagüey was one of the original seven settlements founded by Diego Velázquez, though the first buildings were erected in 1515 miles to the north, on the shores of Bahía de Nuevitas. The site lacked fresh water and came under constant attack from local Indians. It was finally moved to its present location, where it was built on the site of an Indian settlement. In 1903, the city was renamed for the local chieftain, Camaguei.

The early settlers were beset with water shortages. The town's Catalonian potters therefore made giant earthenware amphorae called *tinajones* to collect and store rainfall. Soon the large red jars (up to 2.5 meters tall and 1.5 meters wide) were a standard item outside every home, partly buried in the earth or standing in the shade to keep them cool, but always under the gutters that channeled the rain from the eaves. Citizens began to compete with each other to boast the most *tinajones* and demonstrate their wealth. According to local legend, an outsider offered water from a *tinajón* will fall in love and never leave.

The city prospered from cattle raising and, later, sugar, which fostered a local slave-plantation economy. Descendants of the first Spanish settlers evolved into a modestly wealthy bourgeoisie that played a vital role in the national culture. The wealth attracted pirates. The unfortunate city was sacked and almost destroyed twice during the 17th century—in 1688 and

CIEGO DE ÁVILA / CAMAGÜEY

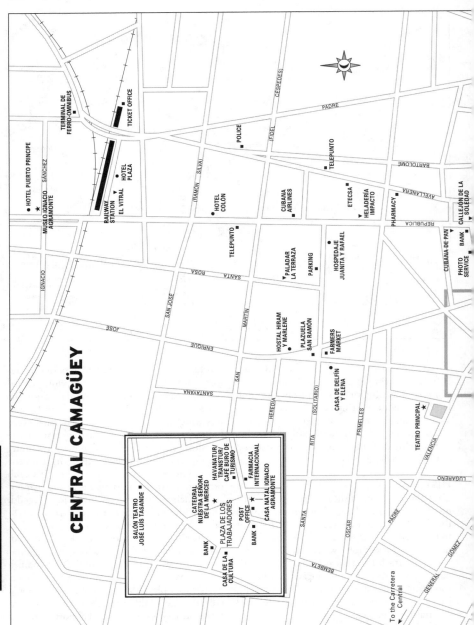

CENTRAL CAMAGÜEY

- HOTEL PUERTO PRINCIPE
- MUSEO IGNACIO AGRAMONTE
- TERMINAL DE FERRO-OMNIBUS
- TICKET OFFICE
- RAILWAY STATION
- HOTEL PLAZA
- EL VITRAL
- POLICE
- TELEPUNTO
- HOTEL COLÓN
- CUBANA AIRLINES
- ETECSA
- HELADERÍA IMPACTO
- PHARMACY
- TELEPUNTO
- PALADAR LA TERRAZA
- PARKING
- HOSPEDAJE JUANITA Y RAFAEL
- CUBANA DE PAN
- BANK
- PHOTO SERVICE
- HOSTAL HIRAM Y MARLENE
- PLAZUELA SAN RAMÓN
- FARMERS MARKET
- CASA DE DELFÍN Y ELENA
- TEATRO PRINCIPAL

Streets: PADRE, CESPEDES, (FIDEL), BARTOLOME, AVELLANERA, CALLEJÓN DE LA SOLEDAD, REPUBLICA, (RAMON SILVA), SANTA ROSA, SAN JOSE, JOSE, ENRIQUE, SANTAYANA, SAN, MARTIN, HEREDIA, (SOLITARIO), RITA, PRIMELLES, VALENCIA, LUGAREÑO, SANCHEZ, IGNACIO

Inset: CENTRAL CAMAGÜEY

- SALÓN TEATRO JOSÉ LUIS TASANDE
- CATEDRAL NUESTRA SEÑORA DE LA MERCED
- HAVANATUR/ TRASTUR/ CAFÉ BURÓ DE TURISMO
- FARMACIA INTERNACIONAL
- CASA DE LA CULTURA
- BANK
- PLAZA DE LOS TRABAJADORES
- POST OFFICE
- BANK
- CASA NATAL IGNACIO AGRAMONTE
- SANTA
- OSCAR
- PADRE
- BEMBETA
- GOMEZ
- GENERAL
- LUGAREÑO

To the Carretera Central

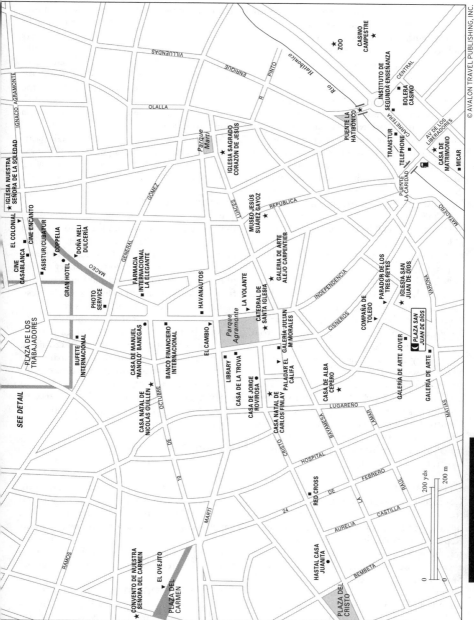

© AVALON TRAVEL PUBLISHING, INC.

CIEGO DE ÁVILA / CAMAGÜEY

ZOO

CASINO CAMPESTRE

INSTITUTO DE SEGUNDA ENSEÑANZA

BOLERA CASINO

CARRETERA CENTRAL

PUENTE LA HATIBÓNICO

Río Hatibónico

TRANSTUR

TELEPHONE

PUENTE LA CARIDAD

CASA DE MATRIMONIO

MICAR

AV. DE LOS LIBERTADORES

MATADERO

VILLUENDAS

ENRIQUE

PINTO

OLALLA

IGNACIO AGRAMONTE

Parque Martí

IGLESIA SAGRADO CORAZÓN DE JESÚS

GÓMEZ

LUACES

REPÚBLICA

MUSEO JESÚS SUÁREZ GAYOZ

GENERAL

VERONA

IGLESIA NUESTRA SEÑORA DE LA SOLEDAD

EL COLONIAL

CINE ENCANTO

CINE CASABLANCA

ASISTUR/CUBATUR

COPPELIA

DOÑA NELI DULCERÍA

FARMACIA INTERNACIONAL LA ELEGANTE

MACEO

GRAN HOTEL

PHOTO SERVICE

HAVANAUTOS

GALERÍA DE ARTE ALEJO CARPENTIER

INDEPENDENCIA

PARADOR DE LOS TRES REYES

IGLESIA SAN JUAN DE DIOS

LA VOLANTE

CATEDRAL DE SANTA IGLESIA

Parque Agramonte

EL CAMBIO

COMPAÑÍA DE TOLEDO

CISNEROS

PLAZA DE LOS TRABAJADORES

SEE DETAIL

BUFETE INTERNACIONAL

CASA DE MANUEL "MANOLO" BANEGAS

BANCO FINANCIERO INTERNACIONAL

LIBRARY

CASA DE LA TROVA

CASA DE JORGE ROVIROSA

GALERÍA JULIÁN M MORALES

PALADAR EL CALIFA

CASA DE ALBA CEPERO

PLAZA SAN JUAN DE DIOS

GALERÍA DE ARTE JOVER

GALERÍA DE ARTE

OCTUBRE

CASA NATAL DE NICOLÁS GUILLÉN

CASA NATAL DE CARLOS FINLAY

CRISTO

LUGAREÑO

LAMAR

MATÍAS

DE

10

HOSPITAL

BAYAMESA

RED CROSS

DE

24

FEBRERO

RAÚL

AURELIA

CÁSTILA

LA

MARTÍ

RAMOS

CONVENTO DE NUESTRA SEÑORA DEL CARMEN

EL OVEJITO

PLAZA DEL CARMEN

HASTAL CASA JUANITA

BEMBETA

PLAZA DEL CRISTO

200 yds

200 m

0

0

1679. Many Camagüeyans were themselves notorious smugglers who went against the grain of Spanish authority. "This town has always been looked upon with suspicion by the authorities on account of the strong proclivities its people had for insurrection," wrote Samuel Hazard in 1871. U.S. Marines even occupied the city in 1917–23 to quell antigovernment unrest.

The Camagüeyans' notoriety for insurrection did not translate to strong support for Communism, however. True enough, its citizens vigorously opposed the Machado and Batista regimes, when student and worker strikes often crippled the city. They supported the armies of Che Guevara and Camilo Cienfuegos when they entered the city in September 1958. But the province had been one of the most developed before the Revolution, and Fidel's turn to Communism received little support from the independent-minded people of Camagüey.

Following the Revolution, the town and its hinterlands were administered by Huber Matos, the popular Camagüeyan military commander who challenged Castro's increasingly Communist turn. He accused Castro of "burying the revolution." Situated as he was in the wealthy and conservative Cuban heartland, Matos posed a real threat. He was arrested for treason and sentenced to 20 years in prison in a sedition trial, in which other anti-Communists were sent to the firing squads. (Camilo Cienfuegos, whom Fidel sent to arrest Matos and reorganize the military command, mysteriously died when his plane disappeared on the return trip to Havana).

Orientation

Camagüey is bisected by the Carretera Central, which arcs around the southern side of the historic city core, north of the Río Hatibónico. República runs north from the Carretera Central through the heart of the historic quarter and eventually becomes Avenida de los Mártires. South of the river, Avenida de la Libertad links with the Carretera Central Este (one-way westbound), linking Camagüey with Las Tunas.

The historic core is irregular. Fear of pirate attacks prompted the early founders to build the streets in a meandering labyrinth, with some bearing off at odd angles and others meeting at a single point where invaders could be ambushed. Calle Martí bisects the city east–west, linking Parque Agramonte—the main square, two blocks west of República—to the Carretera Central westward.

The city is encircled by a *circunvalación,* a wide four-lane freeway.

Many streets have a modern (official) name and an original (now colloquial) name. For example, Bartolomé Masó is colloquially called San Fernando.

Casino Campestre

This leafy urban park, on the south side of the river and accessed from the historic center via the stone-and-metal **Puente Hatibónico** bridge dating from 1773, draws locals to gossip and flirt. It has several prerevolutionary statues plus a small **zoo** (free), with animals ranging from lions and monkeys to hyenas. On its west, across the Carretera Central, rises the imposing neoclassical **Instituto de Segunda Enseñanza** (Institute of Secondary Education).

To the east of the park is the **Plaza de la Revolución** with an impressive marble and granite **Monumento Ignacio Agramonte** inscribed with 3-D sculptures of Fidel, Che, and other revolutionaries. The pink-faced **Asemblea Provincial,** or town hall, occupies the north side.

Museo Provincial Ignacio Agramonte

This museum (Av. de los Mártires #2, tel. 032/28-2425; Tues.–Sat. 10 A.M.–5 P.M., Sun. 10 A.M.–1 P.M.; CUC2), in a huge colonial structure dating from 1884, was formerly a garrison for Spanish cavalry. Today it exhibits an eclectic array of Cubana, from artwork, archaeology exhibits, and stuffed flora and fauna to historical records up to the Revolution.

Parque Agramonte

This attractive plaza—a parade ground in colonial days—is bounded by Cisneros (west), In-

Fidel, Che Guevara, and other figures in the revolutionary pantheon look out over Plaza de la Revolución from the Monumento Ignacio Agramonte.

one of Latin America's foremost poets, Guillén served as chairman of the National Union of Cuban Writers and Artists (UNEAC), which he helped found. The house, which contains some of his personal possessions and a library of his works, hosts the **Instituto Superior de Arte,** where music is taught.

The **Casa Natal de Carlos Finlay** (Cristo #5, tel. 032/29-6745; Mon.–Sat. 9 A.M.–5 P.M.; CUC1), 50 meters west of the plaza, is the birthplace of the scientist who discovered the vector for yellow fever. It has apothecary jars and basic exhibits in Spanish only.

One block east of the plaza, the seemingly dilapidated red-brick **Iglesia Nuestra Señora de la Soledad** (República, esq. Agramonte) dates from 1755 and has interior frescos, an elaborate gilt altar, and beautifully restored wood-beam ceiling.

Parque Martí

Pinned by a small statue of José Martí, this small plaza four blocks east of Parque Agramonte, is worth the visit to admire the neo-Gothic **Iglesia Sagrado Corazón de Jesús.** Dating from 1920, it was in the final stages of restoration at last visit. Its beautiful interior gleams with marble and gold. It features tromp l'oeils and beautiful stained-glass windows.

dependencia (east), Martí (north), and Luaces (south). At its center is a life-size bronze **Monumento Major General Ignacio Agramonte** (see *Plaza de los Trabajadores* later in this section), mounted atop his steed and brandishing his machete. The square has Victorian lamps, and its trees are ablaze with pink and yellow blossoms in spring.

The **Catedral de Nuestra Señora de Candelaria Santa Iglesia** (tel. 032/29-4965) stands on the south side. The cathedral was built in 1864 atop a predecessor established in 1530. Somewhat simple within, it's worth a peek for its statuary and beamed roof. In 1688, the pirate Henry Morgan locked the city fathers in the church and starved them until they coughed up the location of their treasures.

Afro-Cuban poet Nicolás Guillén (1902–89) was born in the house now called **Casa Natal de Nicolás Guillén** (Hermano Agüiro #57, e/ Cisneros y Principe, tel. 032/29-3706; Mon.–Fri. 8 A.M.–4:30 P.M.; free), one block north of the plaza. A loyal nationalist and revolutionary and

Plaza del Carmen

This intimate cobbled square (Martí and 10 de Octubre), six blocks west of Parque Agramonte, features life-size ceramics figures: an old man pushing a cart, three women sipping *tazas* of coffee, two elderly lovers sharing gossip. Marvelous! The tiny plaza is surrounded by venerable houses in bright pastels. On the west side, the former **Convento de Nuestra Señora del Carmen,** built in 1825 and recently restored to former grandeur, today houses the **Galería de Arte Fidelio Ponce de León** (tel. 032/29-5603; Tues.–Sat. 9 A.M.–5 P.M. Sun. 9 A.M.–noon; CUC1).

◖ Plaza San Juan de Díos

The most impressive square is hidden away two blocks south of Parque Agramonte and

CIEGO DE ÁVILA / CAMAGÜEY

© CHRISTOPHER P. BAKER

one block west of Cisneros. The plaza is today a national monument and has been magnificently restored. The bright pastel buildings have huge doorways and beautifully turned *rejas.* They date from the 18th century and reflect how the city must have looked at its prime, 200 years ago.

On the west side is a beautiful blue-and-white house, still privately owned, where once lived poet and songwriter Antón Silvio Rodríguez. A bronze plaque on the wall has the words of his famous "El Mayor," which celebrates Agramonte in song.

On the east side is the **Antiguo Hospital de San Juan de Dios,** a former military hospital dating from 1728, with arcaded cloisters added in 1840 and a Moorish facade and courtyards. Today it houses the **Museo de Arquitectura Colonial** (tel. 032/29-1388; Tues.–Sat. 9 A.M.– 5 P.M., Sun. 9 A.M.–1 P.M.; CUC1). Adjoining it is the **Iglesia de San Juan de Dios** (open Monday) featuring a splendid mahogany ceiling and commanding bell tower.

Plaza de los Trabajadores

The Workers' Plaza, on Calle Ignacio Agramonte, three blocks north of Parque Agramonte and two blocks west of República, is a triangular piazza with a venerable ceiba tree at its heart.

On the east side is the deteriorated **Catedral Nuestra Señora de la Merced** (tel. 032/29-2740), dating to 1748 and boasting an elaborate gilt altar beneath a barrel vaulted ceiling with faded murals. The devout gather to request favors at a silver coffin, the Santa Sepulcro, in a separate chapel. Check out the catacombs, with skeletons in situ.

Casa Natal Ignacio Agramonte (Agramonte #459, esq. Candelaria, tel. 032/29-7116; Tues.–Sat. 9 A.M.–5 P.M.; CUC2) faces La Merced on the west side of the square. Ignacio Agramonte was born here on September 23, 1841. He rose to become a sugar estate owner and head of the Camagüeyan rebel forces during the first War of Independence. He was killed in May 1873 at the Battle of Las Guasimas. The house was the Spanish con-

sulate during the early Republic. Beautifully restored, it is now a museum containing an important art collection, plus mementos and colonial furniture.

Entertainment and Events

Events: In early February, the **Jornadas de la Cultura Camagüeyana** celebrates the city's founding. The **Theater Festival of Camagüey** is a September biennial. A religious festival is held on September 8 to honor Nuestra Señora de la Caridad, the city's patron saint.

On Saturday nights, República is closed to traffic for a general fiesta.

Folk Music: The **Casa de la Trova** (Cisneros #171, tel. 032/29-1357; Tues.–Sun. 10 A.M.– 1 P.M.; CUC3), on the west side of Parque Agramonte, hosts traditional music, as does **Galería UNEAC** (Cisneros #159, Sat. 5–9 P.M.).

Discos and Cabarets: The **Hotel Colón** (República #472, e/ San José y San Martín, tel. 302/28-3346) has a disco and cabaret Friday and Saturday at 10 P.M. (CUC1). The **Centro Nocturno El Colonial** (Agramonte, esq. República, Fri. and Sun. 10 P.M.–2 A.M., Sat. 10 P.M.–2 A.M.; CUC5 including two drinks, CUC7 Sat.) has a small open-air cabaret followed by disco nightly and is the most popular place in town.

The **Gran Hotel** (Calle Maceo #67, tel. 032/29-2314 and 92094) hosts a *ballet acuático* at 9 P.M. when there are sufficient guests (free).

Bars: The moody, dark piano bar (4 P.M.– 2 A.M. daily; CUC5 per couple including one drink; free to hotel guests) in the **Gran Hotel** has a slightly salacious feel—you half expect the Rat Pack to show up. **El Cambio** (10 A.M.– 2 A.M. daily), on the northeast corner of Parque Agramonte, offers moody decor and attracts a young crowd, including *jiniteros* and *jiniteras* on the scrounge. And the **Hotel Colón** has a gracious tourists-only bar.

Classical Music and Theater: The world-acclaimed Ballet de Camagüey perform at the recently restored **Teatro Principal** (Padre Valencia #64, tel. 32/29-3048), dating to 1850 and where notables such as Enrico Caruso once sung.

Other: The **Bolera Casino** (Carretera

© CHRISTOPHER P. BAKER

Dating to 1850, the Teatro Principal is still used for events and hosts the Ballet de Camagüey.

Central Este, esq. San Joaquín; 24 hours) has two bowling alleys (CUC1) and pool tables (CUC0.50).

Baseball games are held at the **Estadio Cándido González** October–May.

Accommodations

You can make reservations for *campismos* throughout the province at the **Campismo Popular** (Av. de la Libertad #208, e/ Pancha y Agramonte, tel. 032/29-6855).

Casas Particulares: I like **Casa de Manuel "Manolo" Banegas** (Independencia #251 altos, e/ Hermanos Agüero y Gómez, tel. 032/29-4606; CUC15–20) for its location overlooking Plazuela Maceo. The cavernous upstairs home has a wraparound veranda and rockers in the cross-ventilated lounge. My lofty-ceiling bedroom had a comfy bed; a second room is huge, with two double beds and French doors that open to a balcony. They share a bathroom off the hallway.

Hospedaje Juanita y Rafael (Santa Rita #13, e/ República y Santa Rosa, tel. 032/28-

1995; CUC15–20) is beautifully kept and offers a sunlit, breezy lounge filled with contemporary art. The owners rent two rooms, each spacious, modestly furnished, and with modern, private hot-water bathrooms.

◖ Hostal Hiram y Marlene (San Ramón #216, e/ Santa Rita y San Martín tel. 032/29-8309; CUC20) is a charming colonial home with a nicely furnished lounge with modern sofa set and TV, and that opens to a handsome garden with *tinajones*. Two spacious air-conditioned rooms face the garden and have colonial tiles, double and single beds, fans, and clean, modern hot-water bathrooms. It has parking.

Casa de Jorge Rovírosa (Cristo #2C, e/ Cisneros y Lugareño, tel. 032/229-8305; CUC15) is entered by tall carriage doors. The corroded hallway is off-putting, but persevere: upstairs is a pleasant colonial home that offers a bargain. It has two air-conditioned rooms, each well-lit, spacious, and attractive; one has an en-suite bathroom with a deep tub. Meals are served on a spacious rooftop with views. There's a pleasant TV lounge.

CIEGO DE ÁVILA / CAMAGÜEY

Hostal Casa Juanita (Cristo #186, e/ Bembeta y Santa Catalina, tel. 032/28-5620, yokivis@terra.es; CUC20), one block east of Plaza Cristo, is a spacious colonial home with a lounge filled with rockers, a TV and VCR, and stereo system. The single, simply furnished air-conditioned room with hot water bathroom opens to a pleasant palm-shaded patio where meals are served.

I enjoyed a stay at **Casa de Delfin y Elena** (San Ramón #171, e/ Primelles y Solitario, tel. 032/29-7262, delfingb@medscape.com; CUC15–20), with two spacious and attractive rooms with antiques, fan, a double and single bed, plus modern hot-water bathroom. The owner speaks English and Italian; ask Elena to make her delicious *arroz dulce* (sweet rice dessert).

Casa de Alba Cepero (San Juan de Díos #63, e/ ángel y San Domingo, tel. 032/29-2572, albita_cepero@yahoo.es; CUC15–20) is a colonial home with a lofty ceiling and traditional tile floor in the TV lounge. It has one airy, cross-ventilated, air-conditioned upstairs room with independent entrance, fan, and a 1950s-era bathroom with hot water.

Hospedaje Niurka y Tommy (Calle la Paz #2, e/ Carretera Central y General Reeve, tel. 032/27-1031; CUC20), 100 meters from the bus station, rents two air-conditioned rooms in a pleasant middle-class home with modern furnishings. Nearby, **Casa de Gardenia Valero** (Carretera Central #515, e/ Argentina y 2da, tel. 032/27-1203; CUC20) is another splendid middle-class home with two air-conditioned rooms with fans and private hot-water bathrooms; one bathroom is a stunner. There's a TV lounge and secure parking. Similarly, **Casa de Isidro** (Calle Victoria #6, e/ Carretera Central Este y General Reeve, tel. 032/27-1614; CUC20–25) is a spacious 1950s home with period furniture. Its two air-conditioned rental rooms have fans, refrigerators, and private bathrooms with hot water. The family has a third room in an adjoining home: This upstairs apartment has a basic kitchen and a delightful period bathroom.

Hotels: The bargain-priced ◖ **Hotel Colón**

(República #472, e/ San José y San Martín, tel. 032/28-3368, fax 032/28-3346, cbercolon@yahoo.es; CUC28 s, CUC34 d low season; CUC32 s, CUC40 d high season including breakfast), has served as a hotel since 1927. Splendidly restored, it offers gleaming hardwoods, colonial tiles, lofty ceilings, and elegant furnishings. The 48 air-conditioned rooms have satellite TVs, minibars and telephones, and sparkling modern bathrooms. It has three mini-suites and a room for travelers with disabilities, plus an atmospheric lobby bar and fine restaurant, Internet service, a tour desk, and shop. (Islazul.)

Hotel Plaza (Van Horne #1, e/ República y Avellaneda, tel. 032/28-2413, reservas@hplaza .camaguey.cu; CUC21 s, CUC26 d low season; CUC23 s, CUC32 d high season), opposite the rail station, is another atmospheric hotel with 67 pleasantly furnished air-conditioned rooms with satellite TVs. It has a cafeteria and restaurant, plus car rental and shops. (Islazul.)

The **Gran Hotel** (Calle Maceo #64, e/ Gómez y Agramonte, tel. 032/29-2314, fax 032/29-9333, reserva@hgh.camaguey.cu; CUC29 s, CUC38 d low season; CUC38 s, CUC48 d high season, including breakfast) is a beautifully restored 18th-century building whose pleasing ambience is enhanced by dark antiques. It has 72 lofty-ceilinged air-conditioned rooms with handsome furnishings, telephone, satellite TV, safes, and modern bathrooms. A swimming pool, lively café, elegant rooftop restaurant, and piano bar highlight the facilities. (Gran Caribe).

Islazul's **Hotel Camagüey** (Carretera Central Este Km 4.5, tel. 032/28-7267, fax 032/28-7181) and Cubanacán's **Hotel Managuan** (Camino de Guanabaquilla, tel. 032/27-2017, fax 032/36-5247) were being used exclusively for Latin American medical patients at last visit.

Food

The atmospheric **Paladar La Terraza** (Santa Rosa #8, e/ San Estebán y San Martín, tel. 032/29-8705; 11 A.M.–midnight daily) has a wood-paneled bar and, upstairs, a breeze-kissed open-sided eatery serving *criollo* fare with a flourish.

The **🅒 Restaurante Santa María** (República #472, tel. 032/28-3346; 7–9:45 A.M., noon–2:45 P.M., and 7–9:45 P.M. daily), in the Hotel Colón, is the best eatery in town. The menu includes soups, spaghetti, roast chicken or pork, and the like, plus there's a buffet (CUC6.50).

Another good bet is the elegant rooftop restaurant of the **Gran Hotel** (Calle Maceo #64, e/ Gómez y Agramonte, tel. 032/29-2314; 7 A.M.–9:30 P.M.), where a lobster enchilada costs CUC6 and a buffet dinner costs CUC10.

More historic, albeit touristy, options include **Campaña de Toledo** (Plaza San Juan de Díos, tel. 032/29-5888; daily 10 A.M.–10 P.M.), full of ambience, with terra-cotta tile floors and rustic furniture, although now serving only sandwiches, spaghettis, tortillas. It hosts flamenco dancing Saturday 6–8 P.M.

Equally atmospheric is **El Ovejito** (Hermano Aguero #280, tel. 032/29-2524; Wed.–Sun. noon–9:30 P.M.), with lamb and pork dishes (CUC7–15).

For snacks, try **Café Buro de Turismo** (Agramonte, tel. 032/29-8947; 24 hours), 50 meters east of Plaza de los Trabajadores, and serving pizzas and sandwiches; or **Callejón de la Soledad** (tel. 032/29-1961; noon–11 P.M. daily), a Parisian-style café with shaded tables set on the cobbled street and serving omelettes, spaghetti, and pizzas (all less than CUC3).

Penny pinching? **La Volante** (Independencia, tel. 032/29-1974; noon–midnight daily), on Parque Agramonte, offers views over the square; it serves basic *criollo* fare for pesos with dinner seatings at 6, 8, and 10 P.M.

Coppelia (Independencia, e/ Agramonte y Gómez; Tues.–Sun. 3–10 P.M.) serves delicious ice cream for pesos. **Heladería Impacto** (República, e/ Oscar Primelles y Santa Rita; 10 A.M.–midnight daily) sells ice cream for dollars.

Self-Catering: You can buy baked goods for dollars at **Panadería Doña Neli** (Maceo; 7 A.M.–10 P.M. daily), opposite the Gran Hotel. You can buy produce from the *mercado agropecuario* (Matadero; daily 7 A.M.–6 P.M.).

Information and Services

The **post office** (Agramonte #461, esq. Cisneros, 8 P.M.–5 P.M.) is on the south side of Plaza de los Trabajadores; it has **DHL** (tel. 032/29-3985) service. **Etecsa** (Avellada, e/ San Martín y Primelles; daily 8:30 A.M.–6:30 P.M.) has international telephone and Internet service. The Hotel Colón has a **CyberCafé** (República #472, e/ San José y San Martín; 9 A.M.–10 P.M. daily).

Banks include **Bandec** (Plaza de los Trabajadores; and República, one block north of Ignacio Agramonte) and **Banco Financiero Internacional** (Independencia, on Parque Maceo). You can also change foreign currency at **Cadeca** (República #353, e/ Primelles y Solitario; Mon.–Sat. 8:30 A.M.–6 P.M., Sun. 8:30 A.M.–1 P.M.).

Hospital Provincial (Carretera Central Km 4.5, tel. 032/28-2012) is west of town. **Farmacia Internacional** (Agramonte, 20 meters east of Plaza de los Trabajadores; and Maceo, e/ Gómez y Parque Maceo; Mon.–Sat. 9 A.M.–5 P.M.) stocks imported medicines.

Consultoría Jurídica Internacional (Joaquín de Agüero #166, e/ Tomás Betancourt y Julio Sanguily, Rpto. La Vigía, tel. 032/28-3159) and the **Bufete Internacional** (Cisneros, e/ Gómez y Plaza de los Trabajadores, tel. 032/28-7289) offer legal assistance. **Asistur** (Agramonte #449, e/ López Recio e Independencia, tel. 032/28-6317, asisturcmg@enet.cu) assists travelers in distress.

Inmigración (Calle 3ra #156, e/ 8 y 10, Rpto. Vista Hermosa; Mon.–Tues. and Thurs.–Fri. 8–11:30 A.M. and 1–3 P.M.) can issue *prórrogas*.

Universitur (Avellanda #281, e/ Primelles y Solitario, tel. 032/29-2561, omarihe@yahoo .com) arranges Spanish-language study programs at the local university.

Getting There and Away

By Air: The **Ignacio Agramonte Airport**, tel. 032/26-1000 and 032/26-7154) is 14 kilometers northeast of the city on the road to Morón (bus #22 runs to the airport from Parque Finlay, opposite the Terminal de Ferro-Ómnibus). A taxi costs about CUC8. **Cubana** (República

#400, esq. Correa, Camagüey, tel. 032/29-2156; Mon.–Fri. 8:15 A.M.–4 P.M.) flies from Havana and Santiago.

By Bus: The **Terminal de Ómnibuses Intermunicipales** (Carretera Central Oeste, esq. Perú, tel. 032/27-2480) is two kilometers southeast of town and is served by local buses (#2, 14, and 72).

Astro buses depart Camagüey for Havana daily at 10 A.M. and 9:40 P.M. There is also daily Astro service to and from Bayamo (CUC9), Ciego de Ávila (CUC5), Cienfuegos (CUC16), Holguín (CUC9), Las Tunas (CUC7), Manzanillo (CUC10), Santa Clara (CUC12), Sancti Spíritus (CUC9), and Santiago de Cuba (CUC15).

Víazul (tel. 032/27-1668) buses between Havana and Santiago de Cuba stop at Camagüey. Eastbound buses depart Camagüey for Holguín at 4 P.M. and for Santiago de Cuba at 12:10 A.M., 2:05 A.M., 5:15 A.M., 6:30 A.M., 1:35 P.M., and 6:35 P.M. Westbound buses depart Camagüey for Havana at 12:10 A.M., 4:55 A.M., 4:50 P.M., 11:10 P.M., and 11:35 P.M.; for Trinidad at 2:25 A.M.; and for Varadero at 3:20 A.M.

Buses and *camiones* to provincial destinations depart from the **Terminal de Municipales** (tel. 0322/28-1525), adjoining the train station.

By Train: The railway station is at the north end of Avellaneda (tel. 032/29-2633); the ticket office (tel. 032/28-3214) is at the east end of the station. All trains on the Havana–Santiago de Cuba route stop in Camagüey. In addition, train #33 departs Havana for Camagüey at 2 P.M., arriving at 8:50 P.M. Other trains with Camagüey as their final destination depart Bayamo at 5:20 A.M.; Morón at 3:15 A.M. and 12:55 P.M.; and Las Tunas at 6:25 A.M.

Westbound trains depart Camagüey for Havana (CUC32 *especial,* CUC19 *regular*) at 12:25 A.M., 3:55 A.M., 5:25 A.M., 6:35 A.M., 4:34 P.M., 11 P.M., and 11:47 P.M.; and for Morón at 4:20 P.M. and 6:15 P.M. Eastbound trains depart Camagüey for Las Tunas (CUC10 *especial,* CUC4 *regular*) at 1:50 P.M.; for Holguín (CUC8) at 5:11 A.M.; for Bayamo

at 5:40 A.M. and 12:10 P.M. (CUC7); and for Santiago de Cuba (CUC16 *especial,* CUC11 *regular*) at 12:06 P.M., 2:58 P.M., 1:22 P.M., and 3:27 P.M.

The **Terminal de Ferro-Ómnibus** (tel. 0322/28-7525), adjacent to the main station, serves local destinations. Trains depart for Santa Cruz del Sur (CUC3) at 5:30 A.M. and 1 P.M.; and for Nuevitas (CUC2.15) at 6 A.M. and 2 P.M.

Getting Around

Bus #10 runs between the Terminal de Ómnibus Municipales and the historic quarter. You'll find *coches* outside the rail station, and near the Iglesia de Nuestra Señora de la Soledad, on República (most rides cost one to two pesos); and **bici-taxis** hang out on the main squares.

For a taxi, call **Cubataxi** (tel. 0322/28-1245).

You can rent cars from **Havanautos** (tel. 032/27-2239), at the airport and on Independencia, esq. Martí; **Transtur** (tel. 032/28-5327), in the Café Buro de Turismo and on the Carretera Central, esq. Av. de los Libertadores; and **Rex** (tel. 032/26-2444), at the airport.

There's a secure 24-hour parking lot at Santa Rita #22, two blocks west of República (CUC2).

There are two gas stations within 100 yards of each other on the Carretera Central, just west of Puente La Caridad; as well as outside town, on the road to Nuevitas; and at Carretera Central, esq. General Gómez.

Excursions: Both **Cubatur** (Agramonte #421, e. Independencia y República, tel. 032/25-4785) and **Havanatur** (tel. 0322/28-8604) offer excursions. **EcoTur** (Calle Céspedes, e/ C y Carretera Central, tel. 032/27-4994, ecotur@cmg.colombus.cu) offers ecotourism excursions.

ÁREA PROTEGIDA DE RECURSOS MANEJADOS SIERRA DEL CHORRILLO

Southeast of Camagüey is an upland area—the Sierra Chorrillo—marked by *mogotes.* The formations lie within the 4,115-hectare Sierra

a zebra at Finca La Belén

del Chorrillo Managed Resources Protected Area, about 13 kilometers south of the community of Najasa, 43 kilometers southeast of Camagüey. The reserve has two distinct regions: undulating plains with scrub and semi-deciduous woodland, and tropical montane forest. It protects 110 species of higher plants (six are endangered), a rare cactus called *mamilaria* (found only here), large numbers of *jutías,* and at least 80 bird species, including parrots and *tocororos.*

◖ Finca La Belén

From the entrance, on the south side of the community of El Pilar, a dirt track winds two kilometers uphill to this working farm, where zebu and other exotic cattle species are raised. There's even a zebra and various species of antelope (previously raised for the hunting pleasure of Communist bigwigs). Hiking trails lead to mineral springs with cool pools. Horseback riding (two hours CUC5) and guided bird-watching (two hours CUC10) are offered.

Accommodations: The reserve has a sur-prisingly modern hotel, ◖ **Motel La Belén** (tel. 032/34249; CUC10 per person), with a large swimming pool, a pleasant TV lounge with leather sofas, and five modern and spacious air-conditioned rooms with modern bathrooms with intermittent hot water. Its rustic restaurant has chandeliers of antelope horns and specializes in meals of buffalo!

Tours: Tours and reservations are handled through **Ecotur** (Calle Céspedes, e/ C y Carretera Central, Rpto. Jayama, Camagüey, tel. 0322/27-4994, ecotur@cmg.colombus.cu).

GUÁIMARO

This small town, straddling the Carretera Central 65 kilometers east of Camagüey, has an intriguing granite column in the town square, **Parque Constitución.** The monument—with bronze bas-reliefs of Ignacio Agramonte, Carlos Manuel de Céspedes, and other heroes of the Wars of Independence—commemorates the opening in April 1869 of the Constitutional Assembly, where the first Cuban constitution was drafted, Céspedes elected President of the Free Republic of Cuba, and the abolition of slavery decreed. The building where the 1869 Assembly was held today houses the **Museo Histórico de Guáimaro.**

Between Camagüey and Guáimaro, **Sitio Histórico Ingenio El Rebelde,** an old sugar mill where General Ignacio Agramonte launched his first attack of the War of Independence in 1868, is promoted along the Carretera Central. Beginning two kilometers east of Sibanicú and eight kilometers west of Guáimaro, it's a 14-kilometer drive along a dirt track to the community of Oriente Rebelde, but the site is of interest only to serious historians.

Hotel Guáimaro (tel. 032/82102) is a no-frills Islazul hotel on the east side of town. And **Campismo Monte Oscuro** (tel. 032/8062), 20 kilometers north of town, has basic lakeside cabins and horseback riding; book through **Campismo Popular** (Av. de la Libertad #208, e/ Pancha y Agramonte, tel. 032/29-6855) in Camagüey.

There's a Cupet gas station on the Carretera Central in Guáimaro.

CIEGO DE ÁVILA / CAMAGÜEY

MINAS

Travelers en route between Camagüey and Playa Santa Lucía will pass through the small town of Minas, 37 kilometers northeast of Camagüey. The town is known for its violin factory, **Fábrica de Instrumentos Musicales** (tel. 032/96232; Mon.–Fri. 7–11 A.M. and 1–5 P.M., Sat. 7–11 A.M.; free), at the south end of town. Workers turn native hardwoods into elegantly curved violins, violas, cellos, and guitars. The quality isn't the best, but it's a fascinating visit. Miniature trinket instruments are for sale. You can't buy full-size instruments here, but factory workers will sell privately made guitars (from about CUC50) at their homes.

There's a **criadero de cocodrilos** (daily 7 A.M.–4 P.M.; CUC2), or crocodile farm, outside the village of Senado, about 10 kilometers northwest of Minas, on the road to Sola. This farm raises the American crocodile (it has no endemic crocs) for leather.

Ingenio de Santa Isabel, roadside about 15 kilometers east of Minas on the road to Santa Lucía, is the ruins of a historic sugar mill; it has a pleasant café under shade trees.

The Camagüey–Nuevitas train stops at Minas.

The Fábrica de Instrumentos Musicales manufactures violins and other instruments.

© CHRISTOPHER P. BAKER

North Coast of Camagüey

The Circuito Norte coast road runs west–east about 10 kilometers inland of and parallel to the coast.

CAYO ROMANO

Cayo Romano is the largest of the cays in the Archipiélago de Camagüey. The cay actually comprises *two* huge cays (the westernmost abuts Cayo Coco), and more than a score of sandbars and tiny cays sprinkled like stardust offshore. They are all deserted and virtually unexplored, despite translucent waters and reefs that provide some of the best snorkeling and diving in the hemisphere. The government's tourism master plan contemplates a maximum of 4,700 hotel rooms on these cays. Cayo Romano is all man-groves (take repellent!), brine pools, and pristine beaches. At press time, there were no facilities whatsoever.

Cayo Romano is accessed via the town of Brasil, from where a road leads north five kilometers to a 12-kilometer-long *pedraplén,* which leapfrogs over the Bahía de Jiguey to Cayo Romano. There's a military checkpoint at the beginning of the pedraplen. You'll need your passport. However, permission to access the cay is fickle and never guaranteed.

CAYO SABINAL

Cayo Sabinal is the easternmost cay in the archipelago and one of my favorites. It is attached to the north coast of Camagüey by a hair's-breadth isthmus and encloses the flask-shaped Bahía de Nuevitas. Sabinal has 33 kilometers of beaches protected by coral reefs. The entire island is virgin marshland, brush, and small pines, dotted with saucer-like pools filled with an unappetizing broth.

In all your explorations, you will pass only a couple of military posts (these cays are favored as a drop-off and pickup point by international drug smugglers; visitors to these lonesome cays are liable to receive a thorough search by the Guardia Frontera) and no more than a half-dozen humble *bohíos* belonging to impoverished charcoal-burners and fishermen. There are plenty of birds and iguanas, *venado* (small deer), and wild pigs called *jabalí,* a relative of the peccary. While crossing the isthmus, you'll see snowy white egrets, cranes, and flamingos wading in the soupy shallows of **Laguna de los Flamencos.**

At the far eastern end of Cayo Sabinal is a lighthouse—**Faro Colón**—built in 1850; and an even older fortress—**Fuerte San Hilario**—built to protect the entrance to Bahía de Nuevitas.

There are three main beaches: **Playa Brava** to the west, **Playa Los Pinos** in the center, and **Playa Bonita** to the east (rugged going by 4WD). You can walk for two hours in either direction and leave your footprints the whole way in white sand. The reef lies within one kilometer of shore.

The best place to spend your time is the fantastically lonesome Playa Los Pinos, with sand as white as Cuban sugar, and sea shading from the shore through an ever-deepening palette of greens. Occasionally a small group of tourists may arrive for a day visit from Santa Lucía, but it's more likely you will have the place to yourself.

Bring insect repellent.

Accommodations and Food

The Cuban government reckons Sabinal has a potential capacity for 12,000 hotel rooms. Ouch! For now, the only place to stay is ◖ **Restaurante Playas Los Pinos** (tel. 032/42201 or 44754; CUC25 per person, including breakfast and dinner), with five rustic yet handsome *cabinas* made of palm trunks and mangrove roots, with thatch for a roof, set amid sand dunes. The cabins have simple bathrooms with cold-water showers. There's a bucolic open-air restaurant. Simple seafood dishes are made to order. It appeals for its very rusticity!

If the cabins are full, you can stay at the no-frills **Hotel Caonaba** (tel. 032/44803; CUC14 s, CUC19 d low season; CUC19 s, CUC24 d high season), 100 meters east of the gas station at the entrance to Nuevitas. (Islazul.)

Getting There

Cayo Sabinal is reached via a bridge over the Ensenada de Sabinal, where there's a military checkpoint (you'll need your passport). The gate is usually locked; honk your horn to summon the guard, or retreat 200 yards and drive down to the guard post visible on the flat. Your car will be thoroughly searched coming and going. A CUC5 entrance charge is collected about 600 meters beyond the gate. After a few miles you reach a crossroad. Playa Brava is straight ahead; Playa Los Pinos is about six kilometers to the right (alternately, drive straight to the shore and turn right for Playa Los Pinos). In places, the narrow tracks are smothered in sand. The going can be challenging after heavy rains, when a four-wheel drive would be wise.

Finding the turnoff from the Circuito Norte is the hard part. If coming from the east, your best route is through the port town of Nuevitas, 12 kilometers north of the Circuito Norte and 65 kilometers northeast of Camagüey. Nuevitas is linked to Sabinal via a road of hard-packed dirt and rock that runs along the western shore of the Bahía de Nuevitas. If you're coming from the west, however, the turnoff from the Circuito Norte is about 11 kilometers west of the junction for Nuevitas. It's entirely unmarked—look for the blindingly white dirt road at an unsigned four-way junction. The dirt road leads eight kilometers to the guard post.

Trains depart Camagüey for Nuevitas (CUC2.15) at 6 A.M. and 2 P.M.

PLAYA SANTA LUCÍA

Popular with budget-oriented German, Italian, and Canadian charter groups, Playa Santa Lucía, 110 kilometers east of Camagüey, 85 kilometers north of Las Tunas, and 20 kilometers north of the Circuito Norte (the turnoff is just north and west of **Camalote,** about 30 km east of Nuevitas), has been touted for years as a top-class destination. Forget the promotional hype. Santa Lucía is an embryonic ugly duckling with minimal infrastructure and zero pizzazz. The meager facilities spread out over several kilometers, with stretches of grassy nothingness between them. What Santa Lucía *does* have is an astounding 20 kilometers of beach protected by an offshore coral reef. Diving is superb just offshore.

The shorefront road extends west of Santa Lucía to a funky fishing hamlet—**La Boca**—with its own beach, **Playa Los Cocos,** with atmospheric restaurants, plus toilets and showers. This is by far the best place to hang by day, as the mood is far superior to that of Santa Lucía. The dirt road to La Boca is full of deep pools and mud; a four-wheel drive is recommended although not essential.

Mangrove-lined **Laguna Daniel** and **Laguna El Real** form a swampy morass parallel and inland of the shore. Flamingos occasionally flock to wallow by day, then take off in a flash of bright pink at dusk. The ecosystem harbors diverse birdlife.

Rancho King

This cattle ranch, on the Circuito Norte about seven kilometers west of the junction for Santa Lucía, was once owned by the owners of the famous King Ranch in Texas. The Castro regime expropriated the property, which today receives tourists. You can watch *vaqueros* herding cattle and getting coated with dust and manure. A rodeo provides entertainment, and horseback riding is offered. Excursions are offered from Santa Lucía (CUC31 including lunch and rodeo).

Entertainment and Events

Major hotels have theme night *animaciones* (entertainment). You can buy a night pass for most hotels (about CUC25). To shake some booty, head to **La Jungla** (daily 11:30 P.M. until the last guest leaves; CUC5), a little thatched beachside disco at Hotel Brisas Santa Lucía; or to **Mar Verde** (10:30 P.M.–2 A.M. daily; CUC1), where you can mingle and dance with Cubans.

There's a video game room with pool tables adjacent to the Cupet gas station.

Scuba Diving

Scuba diving is superb. The warm waters support dozens of coral species and an infinity of fishes. And the mouth of the entrance to the Bahía de Nuevitas is a graveyard of shipwrecks, including the steamship *Mortera,* which sank in 1898, its prow resting at a depth of 20 feet. Diving (including resort, certification, and specialized courses) is offered at the hotels and from **Shark's Friend Dive Center** (tel./fax 032/36-5182, shark_friend@nautica.stl .cyt.cu), between Brisas and Hotel Club Santa Lucía, with dive trips daily at 9 A.M. and 1 P.M. (CUC30, CUC40 night dive). It has a "shark show" in which you can witness sharks being hand fed (CUC65); plus snorkeling trips (CUC20).

Other Recreation

Marlin Náutico (tel. 032/33-6404), at the west end of the beach, offers fishing (three hours, CUC204 for four people), catamaran and Jet Ski rentals, plus waterskiing.

Horseback rides are offered at Playa Los Cocos.

Hotel tour desks can arrange **Ultralight** flights (CUC30 per 10 minutes; CUC150 for one hour).

Accommodations

Hotels can sell out during Christmas and New Year's, when a reservation is advisable. Locals rent barebones apartment rooms illegally (CUC15–20); penalties are severe, so be discreet.

Campismo Popular Punta de Ganado (tel. 032/36289), about three kilometers east of the roundabout at the entrance to Santa Lucía, is a basic facility for Cubans. It is often closed. Inquire through the **Campismo Popular** (Av. e. de la Libertad #208, e/ Pancha y Agramonte, tel. 032/29-6855) in Camagüey.

Hotel Escuela Santa Lucía (tel. 032/33-6310, fax 032/36-5166, www.ehtstl.co.cu; CUC25 s, CUC35 d year-round) is a motel-style property that functions as a training hotel. It has 31 spacious air-conditioned rooms modestly furnished with rattan and bamboo, and with telephones, radios, satellite TVs, safes, and small modern bathrooms. Facilities include a bar and small store. (Formatur.)

The ho-hum, all-inclusive **Club Amigo Mayanabo** (tel. 032/36-5168, fax 032/36-5176, aloja@mayanabo.stl.cyt.cu; CUC58 s, CUC80 d standard, CUC62 s, CUC90 suite low season; CUC65 s, CUC100 d standard, CUC75 s, CUC110 d high season) is a Soviet-style building with 213 air-conditioned rooms and 12 suites, with balconies (first floor only) and king-size or twin beds, telephones, and satellite TVs. There's a restaurant, a piano bar, tennis court, attractive swimming pool, water sports, plus a nightclub, tour desk, and car and scooter rental. (Cubanacán.)

Club Amigo Caracol (tel. 032/36-5158; CUC55 s, CUC80 d low season; CUC65 s, CUC100 d high season), a less appealing sibling to the Mayanabo, with 150 air-conditioned junior suites, was being used exclusively for Venezuelan medical patients at last visit. (Cubanacán.)

Gran Club Santa Lucía (tel. 032/33-6109, fax 032/36-5153, aloja@clubst.stl.cyt .cu; CUC45 s, CUC90 d standard, CUC55 s, CUC100 d suite low season; CUC65 s, CUC115 d standard, CUC85 s, CUC140 d suite high season) has 252 drab and minimally furnished air-conditioned rooms spread around unkempt grounds. The raised pool with thatched bar is attractive, however, and the elegant buffet restaurant has reasonable fare. It has 24-hour Internet service, entertainment, shop, water sports, and car and scooter rental. (Cubanacán.)

The classiest option, albeit still only two-star in my book, is **Hotel Brisas Santa Lucía** (tel. 032/33-6317, fax 032/36-5142, aloja@brisas .stl.cyt.cu; CUC60 s, CUC100 d low season; CUC75 s, CUC120 d high season), a modern, 214-room all-inclusive low-rise combining a contemporary design with traditional thatch. All rooms have a satellite TV, radio, telephone, and minibar. At its heart is a magnificent swimming pool with swim-up bar. It offers entertainment and has water sports, tour desk, and car and scooter rental. (Cubanacán.)

Food

The hotels all have restaurants; there are few other options. The best bet is **Alfonsia,** a rustic seafood restaurant at the end of the pier at Gran Club Santa Lucía. And the beachfront **Restaurante Luna Mar,** in the Centro Comercial Villa Vientos, has an Italianate motif and serves spaghetti and pizzas (CUC4–9) plus seafoods in the air-conditioned restaurant or alfresco.

At Playa Los Cocos, Rumbos' thatched **Bar y Restaurante Bucanero** (daily 9 A.M.– 6 P.M.) plays on a pirate theme and serves seafood and *criollo* fare, including lobster (from CUC15).

Information and Services

Etecsa (tel. 032/33-6126; daily 8:30 A.M.– 7 P.M.), next to the Cupet gas station at the east end of Santa Lucía, has international telephone and Internet service.

Bandec has a branch on the coast road, 1.5 kilometers east of the tourist center. A **Clínica Internacional** (tel. 032/33-6370; 24 hours) is 200 meters farther east. The police station is 400 meters west of the bank.

Getting There and Away

International charter flights for Santa Lucía arrive at the Camagüey and Las Tunas airports. A taxi from Camagüey will cost about CUC50 one-way.

Buses operate from Las Tunas and Camagüey (CUC10).

You can rent cars at the hotels and from **Transtur** (tel. 032/36368), immediately west of Hotel Brisas Santa Lucía.

CIEGO DE ÁVILA / CAMAGÜEY

All the hotels have tour desks. **Cubatur** (tel. 032/33-5383) and **Cubanacán** (tel. 032/33-6404) offer excursions, including to Rancho King (CUC31 with lunch and rodeo), "Discover Santa Lucía" (CUC12), a "Seafari" (CUC25), and "Flamingo Tour" (CUC53).

Getting Around

Coches ply the shorefront strip (CUC2 between points, or CUC5 one hour), as does a **Shuttle-Tren** (CUC2 minimum, CUC5 for an tour), a faux train with open-sided carriages.

You can rent **bicycles and scooters** at the major hotels.

LAS TUNAS AND HOLGUÍN

Rich in history, physically diverse, and on the cusp of major tourist development, this region is as interesting as any in the nation. Holguín, rather than Las Tunas, steals the show.

Las Tunas Province forms a flat, narrow band across the island, broadening to the northeast. The capital city occupies a low-lying ridge (the Cuchilla Holguín) in the center of the province, on the eastern edge of the great plains that dominate central Cuba. It is dull, unvarying terrain, mostly farmed for sugar and cattle. The scenery begins to grow more lush and interesting eastward. The province has few beaches (at last visit, only Playa Covarrubias had a hotel), and there are few sites of interest other than a modicum of historic buildings in the eponymous provincial capital.

Holguín, by contrast, is far more diverse and chock-full of things to see and do. The capital city itself boasts several colonial plazas and an active nightlife, and the hinterlands have several unique sites, foremost among them Fidel Castro's birthplace. Holguín's north-central shore is in the throes of touristic development, centered on Playas Guardalavaca, Pesquero, Esmeralda, and Costa Verde. Several quality all-inclusive resort hotels have opened, and long-term plans call for a golf course, cruise port, and even a theme park. Inland, the dramatic formations of the Grupo de Maniabon will have you reaching for your camera, and there are pre-Columbian museums and archaeological sites to explore.

East of Holguín city, the coastal plain narrows down to a panhandle extending along the shore. Inland, pine-clad mountains—the Sierra

HIGHLIGHTS

Plaza Calixto García: The largest of Holguín's three plazas, this one is home to a monument and two museums of note (page 439).

Mirador de Mayabe: Magnificent valley vistas soothe you while you relax by the pool. There's a fine restaurant, and a beer-swilling donkey to boot (page 446)!

Gibara: This laid-back fishing town with fine colonial architecture makes a cool place to steep in Cuban culture (page 447).

Guardalavaca: The scorching beaches and magnificent teal-blue waters, fabulous diving offshore, and hotels ranging from budget to deluxe all-inclusives could keep you plenty happy, but be sure to make time for Museo Aborigen Chorro de Maísa, an excellent small museum and archaeological site recording pre-Columbian culture (page 450).

Museo Indocubano: Banes is home to Cuba's largest display of pre-Columbian relics, including gold and ceramic pieces (page 455).

Sitio Histórico Birán: Fidel's birthplace and childhood home provides fascinating insight into the boyhood background of Cuba's enigmatic leader (page 456).

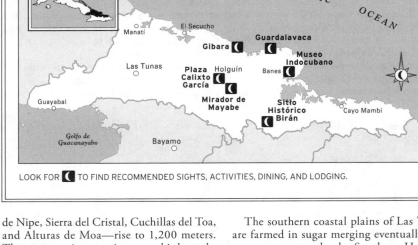

LOOK FOR [C TO FIND RECOMMENDED SIGHTS, ACTIVITIES, DINING, AND LODGING.

de Nipe, Sierra del Cristal, Cuchillas del Toa, and Alturas de Moa—rise to 1,200 meters. These mountains are nirvana to bird-watchers and hikers. The color of heated chrome, the mountains are also rich in precious minerals, notably cobalt, manganese, and nickel. The ores are processed locally, most notably at the coastal town of Moa, in the far east of Holguín Province; the immediate area is blighted by the mineral extraction industry, which may be the main reason for the prohibition on photography hereabouts.

The southern coastal plains of Las Tunas are farmed in sugar merging eventually into mangrove swamplands. Southern Holguín Province is flat as a lake, with savanna and sugar sharing the landscape. The Sierra Maestra hovers in the distance.

PLANNING YOUR TIME

Basically, Las Tunas is a place to pass through en route to Holguín and Oriente. That said, the city of Las Tunas is worth a quick browse, although one day is more than sufficient. All routes through the province pass through the capital, which has several decent *casas particulares* if you choose or need to stay the night.

The larger city of Holguín offers considerably more to see, including three plazas of note, a natural history museum, some colonial structures of interest, and, outside town, the **Mirador de Mayabe,** where you can buy a beer for a suds-supping donkey. Holguín also has a well-developed cultural scene, with everything from an excellent Casa de la Cultura to bargain-priced cabarets. For these reasons, I recommend a two-day minimum stay. The city is also perfectly situated as a base for daytime forays farther afield.

The seafront town of **Gibara** is popular with budget travelers but will appeal to all types for its marvelous setting, laid-back lifestyle, and bracing ocean airs. It has a marvelous natural history museum and an excellent choice of well-kept colonial-era *casas particulares.*

The Parque Monumento Nacional Bariay, where Christopher Columbus supposedly first set foot on Cuban soil in 1492, is strongly touted for a half-day visit, with most participants buying into package excursions from the nearby beach resorts. I consider it a waste of money. Far more rewarding are the nearby town of Gibara, with some intriguing historical buildings and a fabulous seafront setting; the Museo Chorro de Maísa, an archaeological site where you can learn about pre-Columbian culture; and the similarly focused **Museo Indocubano,** in Banes. And how about **Sitio Histórico Birán,** Fidel Castro's birthplace and childhood home, recently opened to view? Make this a must-see, but call ahead to make sure it's open.

The beach resort of **Guardalavaca** and nearby Playa Pesquero are imbued with all-inclusive resorts plus plenty of facilities for trippers on day visits from Holguín. Scuba diving, a dolphin show, and bird-watching, hiking, horseback riding, kayaking, and similar activities in Bioparque Rocazul are among the things to do here. Railway buffs should put the fancifully named Museo de Industria Azucar y de Locomotora de Vapor on their to-do list, and you can even take a ride into the Grupo de Maniabon in a 1920 Baldwin steam train. To make the most of Guardalavaca, you should plan on overnighting at a state-run hotel (there are no *casas particulares* in the region).

Nature lovers, particularly bird-watchers, might head for Pinares de Mayarí, in the Sierra de Nipe (4WD is essential to get there); or to Cayo Saetía, where the wildlife-viewing is somewhat surreal (think zebra and African antelope).

The swampy southern plains are of minimal tourist interest, although bonefish and tarpon provide challenging fishing in the coastal lagoons.

The Carretera Central cuts through the center of the provinces. At Holguín, the Carretera turns southwest for Bayamo, in Granma Province. If heading from Camagüey direct to Granma Province and Santiago, you can bypass Holguín via a paved road that leads southeast from Las Tunas to Bayamo and cuts across the Río Cauto plains via the town of Jobabo.

In Italy all roads lead to Rome. In Oriente, they lead to Holguín. The Circuito Norte runs inland of the Las Tunas coast road and, east of Jesús Menéndez, turns inland for Holguín, beyond which it continues east along the coast for Baracoa and Guantánamo Province. Other roads radiate out from Holguín to Gibara, Guardalavaca, and Banes. Note, however, that an 18-kilometer-long section of the Circuito Norte between Manatí and Marañon was so badly deteriorated at last visit that it is impassable to all but the most rugged of four-wheel drives, forcing a detour via the city of Las Tunas.

Havana–Santiago trains call at Las Tunas and Holguín (service to Holguín is complicated by the fact that its train station is a considerable distance out of town), as do Víazul and Astro buses. If traveling the Circuito Norte you'll need your own wheels; otherwise, you'll need to rely on local buses.

Las Tunas and Vicinity

LAS TUNAS

Las Tunas (pop. 80,000) is a small-time capital of a small-time province. The town is officially known as La Victoria de las Tunas, a name bequeathed by the Spanish governor in 1869 to celebrate a victory over Cuban patriot forces in the War of Independence. Patriots under General Vicente García recaptured the town in 1895. Two years later, the town was put to the torch by rebel forces as Spanish forces attempted to retake it. Alas, the fire destroyed many of the original buildings, and the town today lacks edifices of architectural note.

Las Tunas (nicknamed "City of Sculptures") is famed for its terra-cotta ceramics, expressed in contemporary art scattered all over the city. Look for works by some of Cuba's leading art-ists, such as *Liberation of the People* by Manuel Chong, opposite the Provincial Assembly building.

Orientation

The town sits astride the Carretera Central, which enters from the west along Avenida 1ro de Enero, becomes Avenida Vicente García and slopes up to the central square—Parque Vicente García—where it turns 90 degrees and runs southeast for Holguín as Calle Francisco Verona. A *circunvalación* bypasses the town to the south.

The historic core is laid out in a grid, aligned northeast–southwest and centered on Parque García, at the top of Vicente García, between Calles Francisco Varona and Francisco Vega.

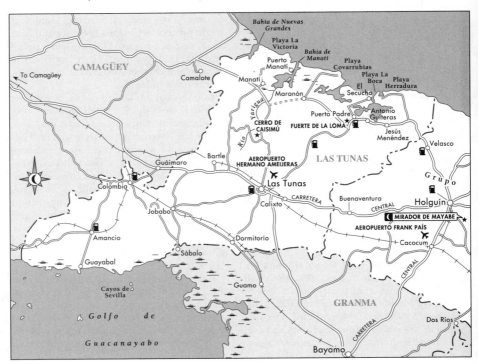

Ángel de la Guardia runs northeast to the railway station, where it forks for the airport and Puerto Padre, on the north coast.

Casa del Vicente García González

This restored colonial house (Vicente García #5, tel. 031/45164; Mon. 3–7 P.M., Tues.–Sat. 11 A.M.–7 P.M.; CUC1) is where, on September 26, 1876, General Vicente García purportedly began the fire that burned the city. The building, which miraculously survived, is now a museum commemorating the Wars of Independence and, particularly, the story of García and the battles for Las Tunas.

Museo de Mártires de Barbados

The Museum to the Martyrs of Bardados (Luca Ortíz #344, tel. 031/47213; Tues.–Sun. 11 A.M.–7 P.M.; CUC0.50), at the base of Vicente García, occupies a small wooden house where lived Carlos Leyva González, Cuba's champion *florete* (fencer). Leyva died, along with his brother and the entire Cuban fencing team, when Cubana flight CUT-1201 was destroyed by a bomb en route to Georgetown, Barbados, on October 6, 1976. In all, 73 people died, including 57 Cubans, 5 Koreans, and 11 Guyanese. Right-wing Cuban-American exiles have been implicated in the terrorist act; Otto Bosch was convicted, but he was pardoned by President Bush and is hailed as a hero by extremist Cuban-Americans.

Outside the museum is a dramatic piece of contemporary art showing an arm and clenched fist (like a fencer's clutching a foil) made from wreckage of the doomed aircraft.

Parque Vicente García

The town's main square, at the top of Avenida Vicente García, features a marble statue of

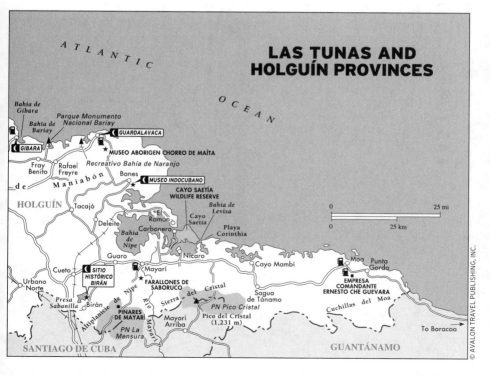

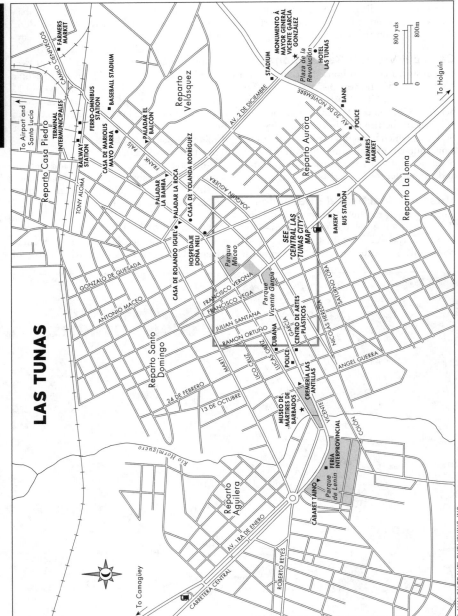

LAS TUNAS

To Camagüey

To Holguín

To Airport and Santa Lucía

Reparto Casa Piedra

Reparto Velázquez

Reparto Aurora

Reparto La Loma

Reparto Santo Domingo

Reparto Aguilera

MONUMENTO Á MAYOR GENERAL VICENTE GARCÍA GONZÁLEZ

Plaza de la Revolución

HOTEL LAS TUNAS

STADIUM

BANK

POLICE

FARMERS MARKET

BUS STATION

BAKERY

"SEE CENTRAL LAS TUNAS CITY MAP"

FARMERS MARKET

TERMINAL INTERMUNICIPALES

FERRO-OMNIBUS STATION

BASEBALL STADIUM

RAILWAY STATION

CASA DE MARIOLIS MAYO PARRA

PALADAR EL BALCÓN

PALADAR LA BAMBA

PALADAR LA ROCA

CASA DE YOLANDA RODRÍGUEZ

CASA DE ROLANDO IGUEL

HOSPEDAJE DOÑA NELI

Parque Maceo

Parque Vicente García

CENTRO DE ARTES PLÁSTICOS

POLICE

CREMERÍA LAS ANTILLAS

MUSEO DE MÁRTIRES DE BARBADOS

CABARET TAÍNO

Parque de Lenin

FERIA INTERPROVINCIAL

CAMILO CIENFUEGOS

TONY ALOMÁ

PAIS

FRANK PAIS

JOAQUÍN AGÜERA

GONZALO DE QUESADA

ANTONIO MACEO

MARTÍ

LICO CRUZ

LUCAS ORTIZ

24 DE FEBRERO

13 DE OCTUBRE

VICENTE

COLÓN

NICOLÁS HEREDIA

SATURNO LORA

ANGEL GUERRA

GARCÍA

CUBANA

RAMON ORTUÑO

JULIÁN SANTANA

FRANCISCO VEGA

FRANCISCO VERONA

AV. 2 DE DICIEMBRE

AV. 30 DE NOVIEMBRE

AV. 1RA DE ENERO

CARRETERA CENTRAL

ROBERTO REYES

Río Hormiguero

800 yds

800 m

© AVALON TRAVEL PUBLISHING, INC.

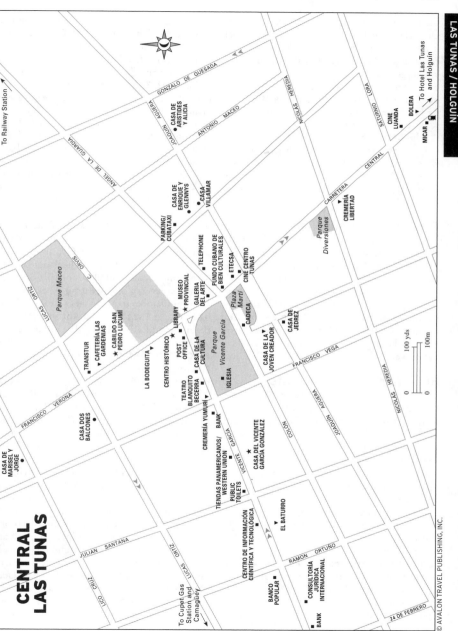

CENTRAL LAS TUNAS

To Railway Station

GONZALO DE QUESADA

CASA DE ARISTIDES Y ALICIA

ANTONIO MACEO

ANGEL DE LA GUARDIA

JOAQUIN AGUERA

NICOLAS HEREDIA

SATURNIO LORA

CINE LUANDA

BOLERA

To Hotel Las Tunas and Holguín

MICAR

CASA DE ENRIQUE Y GLENNYS

CASA VILLAMAR

PARKING/ CUBATAXI

TELEPHONE

FUNDO CUBANO DE BIEN CULTURALES

ETECSA

CINE CENTRO TUNAS

CARRETERA

CENTRAL

CREMERIA LIBERTAD

Parque Diversiones

LUCAS ORTIZ

Parque Maceo

SIMON C

MUSEO PROVINCIAL

GALERIA DEL ARTE

Plaza Martí

CADECA

Parque Vicente García

CASA DE LA JOVEN CREADOR

CASA DE JEDREZ

FRANCISCO VEGA

NICOLAS HEREDIA

TRANSTUR

CAFETERIA LAS GARDENIAS

CABILDO SAN PEDRO LUCUMI

CENTRO HISTÓRICO

POST OFFICE

LIBRARY

CASA DE LA CULTURA

IGLESIA

LA BODEGUITA

TEATRO BLANQUITO BECERRA

CREMERIA YUMURÍ

TIENDAS PANAMERICANOS/ WESTERN UNION

PUBLIC TOILETS

BANK

VICENTE GARCIA

CASA DEL VICENTE GARCÍA GONZALEZ

COLON

JOAQUIN AGUERA

FRANCISCO VERONA

CASA DOS BALCONES

CASA DE MARISEL Y JORGE

JULIAN SANTANA

LICO CRUZ

LUCAS ORTIZ

To Cupet Gas Station and Camagüey

CENTRO DE INFORMACION CIENTIFICA Y TECNOLOGICA

EL BATURRO

RAMON ORTUÑO

CONSULTORIA JURIDICA INTERNACIONAL

BANCO POPULAR

BANK

24 DE FEBRERO

0   100 yds

0   100m

© AVALON TRAVEL PUBLISHING, INC.

the local hero, Major General Vicente García González, who burned the city rather than let it fall into Spanish hands. On the southwest corner is an aged church, very small and simple yet in good condition.

On the park's northeast corner, separated by Calle Colón, is the petite **Plaza Martiana de las Tunas,** which features a contemporary sculpture and a bust of José Martí.

The **Centro Histórico** (Francisco Verona, esq. Vicente García, tel. 031/48201), 20 meters west of the main park, features meager exhibits on local history but is more noteworthy for the bas-relief ceramic map of the historic city on its outside wall.

Plaza de la Revolución

The otherwise ungainly Revolution Plaza, on the northeast side of town, is graced by the huge **Monumento a Mayor General Vicente García González,** hewn in pink concrete with 3-D motifs showing the local hero of the Wars of Independence with his sword held high. Beneath the monument, the **Salón de los Generales** (tel. 031/47751) features bronze busts of other homegrown generals in the independence wars.

Entertainment and Events

Las Tunas hosts the **Jornada Cucalambeana** (Cucalambé Folkloric Festival, tel. 031/47770), when songsters from all parts of Cuba honor Juan Cristóbal Nápoles Fajardo (1829–62), nicknamed "El Cucalambé," a 19th-century poet known for his 10-syllable rhyming songs called *décimas.* It takes place at Motel El Cornito (tel. 031/45015), ten kilometers west of town, each June or July. The Museo Provincial (Francisco Varona, esq. Vicente García, tel. 031/48201; Tues.–Sat. 1– 9 P.M., Sun. 8 A.M.–noon) has an exhibition about Nápoles Fajardo.

The **Feria Interprovincial** in mid-February features rodeos and horse and cattle fairs; it's held at Parque de Lenin, at the base of Vicente García.

The **Casa de la Cultura** (Vicente García #8, tel. 031/43501), on the west side of Parque

Vicente García, offers poetry readings and musical recitals. The **Cabildo San Pedro Lucumí** (Francisco Verona, e/ Angel Guardia y Lucas Ortíz; free) celebrates Afro-Cuban tradition with music and dance on Sunday at 9 P.M.

Cabaret Taíno (tel. 031/43823), at the base of Vicente García, hosts a *cabaret espectáculo* with crooners and plenty of boas and behinds Friday–Sunday at 9 P.M. (CUC10, including bottle of rum and can of cola). It's followed by a disco, also offered without cabaret Tuesday–Thursday 9 P.M.–2 A.M.

The hottest salsa scene is **Bolera** (Carretera Central, esq. Saturno Lora, tel. 031/48671; nightly 11 P.M.–2 A.M.; CUC5 Mon.–Thurs. including CUC3 of drinks, CUC10 Fri.–Sun. including CUC5 of drinks), a Western-style disco featuring laser lights. It also has two bowling lanes (2–5 P.M.; CUC1).

To sup suds with Cubans check out **Unidad Don Pancho** (24 hours), a no-frills open-air *cervecería* serving draft beer for 6 pesos.

From October to May you can catch a baseball game at **Estadio Julio Antonio Mella,** at the north end of Avenida 2 de Diciembre.

Accommodations

Casas Particulares: Near the center, **Hospedaje Doña Nelly** (Lucas Ortíz #111, e/ Gonzalo de Quesada y Coronel Fonseca, tel. 031/42526; CUC15–20) is a large colonial home with a piano in the lounge, plus an air-conditioned room with a private hot-water bathroom. Laundry service is offered, and there's a patio.

Next door, **Casa de Yolanda Rodríguez** (Lucas Ortíz #101, tel. 031/43641; CUC20), with a pleasant hostess, is an admirable home furnished in 1950s style. It has two rooms facing the breeze-kissed patio (with an arbor), with air-conditioning, fridge, and private hot-water bathroom. Her daughter Marianela Santiago also rents a room above her mother's home. And nearby **Casa Dos Balcones** (Lucas Ortíz #210 altos, e/ Francisco Vega y Francisco Varona, tel. 031/45280; CUC20) has a nicely furnished air-conditioned room that shares a hot-water bathroom.

Casa de Rolando Miguel (Villalón #13, e/ Lucas Ortíz y Lico Cruz, tel. 031/42264; CUC15–20) is a pleasant middle-class home with two upstairs air-conditioned rooms, each with fridge and private hot-water bathroom.

Casa de Enrique y Glennys (Villamar #30A altos, e/ Agüero y Guardia, tel. 031/45596; CUC15–25), accessed by a spiral staircase, has a lounge with TV and stereo system, plus a pleasing cross-lit air-conditioned room with 1950s hardwood furnishings, radio, fridge, and a modern hot-water bathroom. Meals are offered, and there's parking adjacent. If full, try **Casa Villamar** (Villamar #30, tel. 031/47245; CUC20), with two rooms next door.

Casa de Marisel y Jorge (Lico Cruz #188, e/ Francisco Varona y Francisco Vegas, tel. 031/45533; CUC20) has a single well-lit, air-conditioned, yellow-themed room with a modern bathroom with hot water.

Conveniently located near the train station and *paladares,* **Casa de Mariolis Mayo Parra** (Frank País, Edif. 11, Apt. B1, e/ Máximo Gómez y Camilo Cienfuegos, tel. 031/44311; CUC20–25) offers a simply appointed air-conditioned room in an apartment building with fan, refrigerator, private hot-water bathroom, and secure parking.

Casa de Aristides y Alicia (Joaquín Agüero #17 alto, e/ Gonzalo de Quesada y Maceo, tel. 031/34-0301; CUC25) has one simply appointed room with a nice private bathroom with hot water. The elderly couple are the local *vanguardia,* and sit in their rockers out on the porch until 1 A.M.

Hotels: The **Hotel Las Tunas** (tel. 031/45014, fax 031/43336; CUC18 s, CUC24 d low season; CUC23 s, CUC30 d high season), one kilometer east of town on Avenida de 2 Diciembre, is a five-story neo-Stalinist prefab hotel atop a hillock. The 142 no-frills air-conditioned rooms have TVs, telephones, and refrigerators. It has a restaurant, bar, and car rental.

The **Hotel Caribe** (Lorenzo Ortíz, e/ Agüera y Heredia, tel. 031/44262), run by Universitur, S.A., was not taking foreigners at last visit.

Food

There are lots of flies!

The best private dining option is **Paladar El Balcón** (Calle Fernando Suárez #14, tel. 031/49312; daily 8 A.M.–midnight; CUC5), with huge portions served on a shaded patio or in charmless rooms. Nearby, **Paladar La Bamba** (Ángel de la Guardia y 2 de Diciembre, no tel.; 8 A.M.–10 P.M. daily) has dining under thatch. I recommend the rabbit enchilada (CUC3.50). The **Paladar La Roca** (Lucas Ortíz #108, no tel.; noon–midnight daily) is an also-ran if the two other *paladares* are closed.

I recommend the Spanish-themed **Restaurante El Baturro** (Vicente García, e/ Santana y Ortuño, tel. 031/46270, ext. 108; daily 11 A.M.–11 P.M.) for its cozy ambience and excellent shrimp enchilada (CUC5). It also offers paella (CUC4), grilled fish (CUC5.70), and *criollo* staples. For open-air dining, head to **Ranchón La Rotonda** (tel. 031/46926; daily 8 A.M.–2 A.M.), on the Carretera Central, about two kilometers east of town. This

El Baturro... *the* place to eat!

open-air thatched restaurant is popular with locals, but don't get your hopes up that the shrimp (CUC6) or lobster (CUC14.50) on the menu will actually be available.

The popular and modestly elegant **La Bodeguita** (Francisco Varona #295, no tel.; daily 11 A.M.–11 P.M.) features salads, spaghettis, and paella for CUC2, plus *criollo* dishes. The noise from the bar next door can intrude.

For snacks, try **Café Las Gardenias** (8 A.M.–11 P.M. daily), selling coffee, tortillas, pastries, and juices.

You can buy ice cream for pesos at **Cremería Yumurí** (10 A.M.–10 P.M. daily) on the west side of Parque Vicente García, and **Cremería Las Antillas** (Vicente García, esq. Ángel Guerra (10 A.M.–10 P.M. daily).

For baked goods, head to **Panadería Doña Neli** (Carretera Central; daily 7 A.M.–10 P.M.), next to the Oro Negro gas station. The *mercado agropecuario* on Camilo Cienfuegos, 200 meters north of the railway station, sells produce.

Information and Services

Bandec (Av. 30 de Noviembre; and Vicente García #69), **Banco Financiero Internacional** (Vicente García, esq. 24 de Octubre), and **Banco Popular** (Vicente García, esq. Francisco Vega) have branches.

The **post office** (Vicente García #6) is on the west side of Parque García.

Etecsa (Francisco Varona, esq. Joaquín Agüera; daily 8 A.M.–8:30 P.M.) has international telephone and Internet service. The **Centro de Información Científica y Tecnológica** (Francisco Varona, e/ Santana y Ortuño, tel. 031/46198; Mon.–Fri. 8 A.M.–5 P.M., Sat. 8 A.M.–3 P.M.) also has Internet service.

Hospital Che Guevara (Av. Carlos J. Finlay, esq. Av. 2 de Diciembre, tel. 031/45012) is 400 meters east of Plaza de la Revolución.

Inmigración (Av. Camilo Cienfuegos), about one kilometer north of the railway station, can issue *prórrogas*. The **Consultoría Jurídica Internacional** (Vicente García, e/ 24 de Febrero y Ramón Ortuño, tel./fax 031/46845; Mon.–Fri. 8:30 A.M.–noon and 1:30–5:30 P.M.) offers legal assistance.

Getting There and Away

By Air: The **Aeropuerto Hermano Ameijeras** (tel. 031/42484) is on Carretera Rafael Martínez about three kilometers north of town. **Cubana** (Lucas Ortíz, esq. 24 de Febrero, tel. 031/46872; Mon., Wed., and Fri. 7:30 A.M.–2 P.M.) serves Las Tunas from Havana twice weekly (CUC94).

By Bus: The **Terminal de Ómnibus** (tel. 031/43060 interprovincial buses; tel. 031/42117 intermunicipal buses) is on the Carretera Central about 800 meters east of Parque Vicente García.

Most **Astro** buses traveling along the Carretera Central to whatever destination stop in Las Tunas. Buses depart Las Tunas for Camagüey at 6:15 A.M., for Havana at 7:30 P.M., for Holguín at 1 P.M., and Santiago de Cuba at 5:15 A.M. **Víazul** (tel. 031/43060) buses depart Las Tunas for Holguín at 4 A.M.; and for Santiago de Cuba at 2:10 A.M., 7:25 A.M., 8:30 A.M., 3:35 P.M., and 8:35 P.M. Westbound Víazul buses depart Las Tunas for Havana at 2:45 A.M., 2:40 P.M., 9:05 P.M., and 10:15 P.M.; for Trinidad at 12:15 A.M.; and for Varadero at 1:15 A.M.

Camiones depart for destinations within Las Tunas and Holguín from outside the railway station.

By Train: The train station is at Terry Alomá (e/ Lucas Ortíz y Ángel de la Guardia, tel. 031/48140). All trains between Havana and Santiago de Cuba stop in Las Tunas (CUC23 to/from Havana; CUC7 to/from Santiago). Trains for Las Tunas depart Camagüey at 1:50 P.M.; and Holguín at 11 A.M. Trains depart Las Tunas for Camagüey at 6:25 A.M.; and for Holguín at 12:45 P.M. In addition, westbound trains depart Las Tunas for Havana at 12:02 A.M. and 8:30 P.M.; and for Santa Clara at 8:54 A.M. Eastbound trains depart Las Tunas for Holguín at 7:26 A.M.; and for Santiago de Cuba at 1:45 A.M. and 3:47 A.M.

Major towns throughout the province are linked to Las Tunas by a two-car commuter train—*ferro-ómnibus*. Reservations are recommended; there's a specific time to make reservations, usually the day before; check the schedule outside the station.

By Car: You can rent cars from **Havanautos** (tel. 031/46228), in the Hotel Las Tunas; and **Transtur** (Francisco Verona, esq. Lucas Ortíz, tel. 031/37-1505; and in the Hotel Las Tunas, tel. 031/46899).

There are gas stations on the Carretera Central: about 400 meters west of Parque Lenin, and four blocks east of Parque Vicente García.

Getting Around

Taxis are available outside the Hotel Las Tunas (CUC2 to downtown), or call **Cubataxi** (tel. 031/42036), which offers secure parking (CUC1). *Coches* gather outside the railway station. You can hop aboard anywhere in the city (one peso for locals; CUC1 for foreigners).

PUERTO PADRE

This pleasant port town, about 30 kilometers northeast of Las Tunas, is one of Cuba's oldest. Locals claim that Christopher Columbus made his first landfall in Cuba in the bay on October 28, 1492, and the settlement first appeared, as Portus Patris, on early 16th-century maps of the New World. During the 19th century, Puerto Padre grew to become Cuba's most important port for sugar export and was known as the City of Mills. It featured prominently in the Wars of Independence, when the Spanish built a fortress, **Fuerte de la Loma,** to protect the southern entrance to town. Well-preserved, and today a national monument, it still stands atop the hill at the end of Puerto Padre's handsome central boulevard, pinned by the **Monumento Máximo Gómez.**

Playa Covarrubias

Las Tunas's north coast is lined with beautiful beaches, although the only one with a resort hotel is Playa Covarrubias, a four-kilometer-long strip of silky white sands with turquoise waters protected by a coral reef. The beach is 22 kilometers north of the rural community of Marañón, 15 kilometers west of Puerto Padre;

it's virtually all scrub and briny pools to each side the whole way. (West of Marañon, the Circuito Norte linking Puerto Padre with Manatí was abysmal at last visit and impassable to all but tractors and trucks.)

You can buy a day pass (CUC25) to utilize the hotel facilities. Alternately, you can access the beach immediately west of the hotel, but you'll need to be self-sufficient; the turn off is on the left, beside the *mirador*.

Playas La Herradura and Las Bocas

About 10 kilometers east of Puerto Padre, you pass through Jesús Menéndez and Loma, where a road leads north eight kilometers to **Playa La Herradura** and, eight kilometers further west, **Playa Las Bocas.** Both are glorious and popular with locals on weekends. A boat for Las Bocas (one peso) leaves from the wharf at El Secucho, 16 kilometers north of town by dirt road.

Accommodations

Casas Particulares: Puerto Padre has several private room rentals. Options include **Casa de Leonardo Silva Gómez** (Mártires de la Herradura #98, tel. 031/53446; CUC15), with two rooms: The ground floor room has a private bath; the upstairs room shares a bathroom. Nearby, **Villa María** (Mártires de la Herradura #90, e/ Vicente García y Antonio Maceo, tel. 031/53366; CUC15) also has two air-conditioned rooms, with shared bath on the ground floor. And **Casa de Luis González** (Cuba #28, 3/ Martí y 24 de Febrero, tel. 031/52548; CUC20, CUC35 for the entire house) offers two rooms with private bath.

At Playa Las Bocas, the beachfront **Hospedaje Familiar** (Calle 2 #46, La Playa, tel. 031/53243; CUC20) has two simply furnished rooms. There are other rentals in Las Bocas and at Playa La Herradura.

Hotels: The **Villa Covarrubias** (tel. 031/55530, fax 031/55352, valentin@villacovarrubias.co.cu; CUC81 s, CUC115 d standard, CUC116 s, CUC186 d suite low season; CUC102 s, CUC145 d standard, CUC134 s, CUC210 d high season) is a tranquil property facing onto the exquisite beach. Its 180 spacious air-conditioned rooms in low-rise units have contempo furnishings and large showers; some have king-size beds. A suite has a whirl-pool tub for two. A huge freeform pool has a thatched bar and theater, plus there's a kid's playground, disco, small gym, plus water sports including scuba diving. (Gran Caribe.)

Holguín and Vicinity

HOLGUÍN

Holguín (pop. 195,000), 775 kilometers east of Havana and 200 kilometers northwest of Santiago de Cuba, is the fourth-largest city in Cuba. When Columbus landed nearby in 1492, believing he had arrived in Asia, he sent an expedition inland to carry salutations to the Japanese emperor's court. The explorers came across a large Indian village called Cubanacán. Three decades later, a land grant was made to Capitán García Holguín, who built a settlement on the site of the Indian village and immodestly named the site San Isidoro de Holguín.

The center of town contains many fine houses of Spanish origin. Despite the historic core's colonial charm, Holguín is an industrial city that has expanded rapidly since the Revolution; Cuba's major brewery and a sugarcane-harvester factory are here. The city is surrounded by steep hills that offer fine views over the city.

Orientation

Holguín's road system is convoluted and city center roads are narrow and congested. The Carretera Central enters from the west and swings south for Granma Province, skirting the city center. Aguilera (eastbound) and Frexes (westbound) link the Carretera Central to the city center. At its heart is Parque Calixto García, bounded by Calles Frexes (north), Martí (south), Libertad (also known as Manduley; east), and Maceo (west).

Martí runs east from the square and merges to the east with Avenida de los Libertadores, which leads through the modern Plaza de la Revolución district and continues to Moa and Baracoa. The city is bypassed to the south by a *circunvalación* linking the Carretera Central with the road to Moa.

Avenida XX Aniversario leads north from Avenida de los Libertadores for Guardalavaca.

Libertad runs north from Parque Calixto García to Avenida Capitán Urbino, which leads northeast to Gibara.

Avenida de los Libertadores

This broad boulevard is lined with statues and monuments to South American "liberators" and revolutionary heroes: Benito Juárez (esq. Aricoches), Simón Bolívar (esq. Cables), Máximo Gómez (esq. San Carlos), and Antonio Maceo (400 meters west of Av. de los Internacionalistas). The most notable monument is a bas-relief of Che Guevara (esq. Av. de los Internacionalistas).

Fábrica de Órganos

Still manufacturing mechanized organs in traditional manner, this organ factory (Carretera de Gibara #301, tel. 024/42-6616; Mon.–Fri. 8 A.M.–3:30 P.M.; free), on the Gibara road about one kilometer east of General Marrero, provides a fascinating peek at age-old Cuban craftsmanship as workers fashion traditional organs, plus guitars and other musical instruments in rather Dickensian conditions. A mechanical organ is played in Plaza San José each Sunday evening.

Loma de la Cruz

Looming over Holguín to the north is the Hill of the Cross, named for the cross that has stood here since 1790. From here you can look across the dry, barren plains towards the strange mountain formations of the Grupo de Maniabon. There's an excellent restaurant.

© CHRISTOPHER P. BAKER

Traditional Linotype is still used at the Instituto Cubano de Libros.

To get there, climb the 450 or so steps that begin at the north end of Calle Maceo, 10 blocks north of Plaza San José, or drive via Avenida Capitán Urbino.

Plaza Calixto García

The city's main square is an expansive plaza with, at its heart, a marble **Monumento General Calixto García**. Holguín's most famous son was born in the simple **Casa Natal de Calixto García** (Miró #147, tel. 024/42-5610; Tues.–Sat. 9 A.M.–9 P.M.; CUC1), one block east of the square. Some of his personal effects are on view inside the museum.

On the north side, the **Museo Provincial de História** (Frexes #198, tel. 024/46-3395; Wed.–Mon. 8:30 A.M.–9:30 P.M.; entrance CUC1, cameras CUC2), with an eclectic range of historical artifacts. It was built in 1860–68 as the Casino Español, where Spanish gentry caroused. It is colloquially known as La Periquera—the Parrot's Cage—supposedly after Spanish troops in their garish yellow, blue, and green uniforms were trapped inside the build-

ing, with its cage-like barred windows, when the town was besieged in 1868 by General Calixto García's troops. The museum's pride and joy is a 35-centimeter-long pre-Columbian axe (the *hacha de Holguín*) carved in the figurine shape of a human. The axe has become the provincial symbol.

The **Museo de la História Natural Carlos de la Torre** (Maceo #129, tel. 024/42-3935; Tues.–Sat. 9 A.M.–10 P.M., Sun. 9 A.M.–9 P.M.; CUC1), one block south of the square, is housed in an impressive neoclassical building with beautiful ceramic tile work. The museum features an eclectic array of dead animals and birds, including a stuffed manatee and a leatherback turtle, plus a dazzling collection of over 4,000 colorful polymite (snail) shells.

Plaza Julio Graves de Peralta

This small square, four blocks south of Parque Calixto García, is anchored by a marble statue of its namesake, General Graves de Peralta (1834–72), who led the rebel assault on October 30, 1868, that captured Holguín from the Spanish.

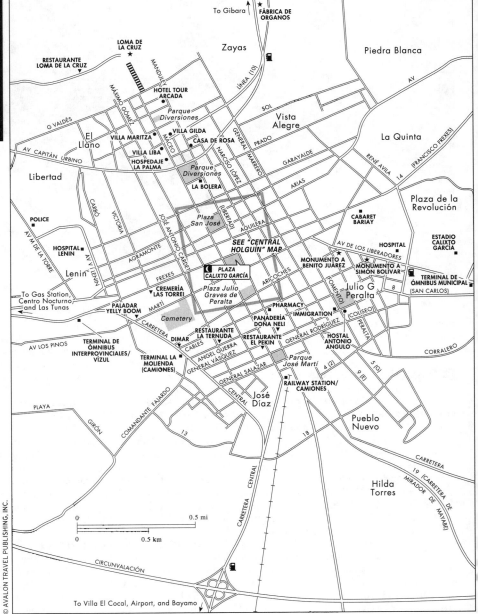

To Gibara

★ FÁBRICA DE ÓRGANOS

Zayas

Piedra Blanca

LOMA DE LA CRUZ ★

RESTAURANTE LOMA DE LA CRUZ ■

HOTEL TOUR ARCADA ■

Parque Diversiones

VILLA GILDA ■

CASA DE ROSA ■

Vista Alegre

La Quinta

El Llano

VILLA MARITZA ■

VILLA LIBA ■

HOSPEDAJE LA PALMA ■

Parque Diversiones

LA BOLERA ■

Libertad

Plaza San José

SEE "CENTRAL HOLGUÍN" MAP

Plaza de la Revolución

POLICE ■

CABARET BARIAY ■

HOSPITAL LENIN ■

HOSPITAL ■

ESTADIO CALIXTO GARCÍA ■

Lenin

PLAZA CALIXTO GARCÍA ■

MONUMENTO A BENITO JUÁREZ ★

MONUMENTO A SIMÓN BOLÍVAR ■

TERMINAL DE ÓMNIBUS MUNICIPAL (SAN CARLOS) ■

CREMERÍA LAS TORREI ▼

Plaza Julio Graves de Peralta

Julio G Peralta

To Gas Station, Centro Nocturno, and Las Tunas

PALADAR YELLY BOOM ▼

PHARMACY ■

IMMIGRATION ■

Cemetery

RESTAURANTE LA TERNUDA ▼

PANADERÍA DOÑA NELI ▼

HOSTAL ANTONIO ANGULO ■

TERMINAL DE ÓMNIBUS INTERPROVINCIALES/ VÍZUL ■

DIMAR ▼

RESTAURANTE EL PEKIN ▼

CORRALERO

AV LOS PINOS

TERMINAL LA MOLIENDA (CAMIONES) ■

Parque José Martí

José Díaz

RAILWAY STATION/ CAMIONES

Pueblo Nuevo

PLAYA

Hilda Torres

0   0.5 mi

0   0.5 km

CIRCUNVALACIÓN

To Villa El Cocal, Airport, and Bayamo

To Guardalavaca

GARCÍA

NICIO

AV XX ANIVERSARIO

HOLGUÍN

MONUMENTO A
★ CALIXTO GARCÍA

Plaza de la
Revolución

HOTEL PERNIK   TABERNA
▼ PANCHO

VILLA
EL BOSQUE

BANK   To Cuerto and
Pinares de
Mayarí →

MONUMENTO A
MÁXIMO GÓMEZ

(CARRETERA DE MAYARÍ)

■ TELECORREO

MONUMENTO A   MONUMENTO A
ANTONIO MACEO   CHE GUEVARA

La Aduana

AV   DE   LOS   INTERNACIONALISTAS

AL

VALLE

DE

MAYABE

■
HOSPITAL

CIRCUNVALACIÓN

↓ To Mirador de Mayabe

On the east side is the **Iglesia San Isidro,** dating from 1720, but restored in 1996 and named for the town's patron saint. The wooden ceiling is noteworthy. A bronze statue of Pope John Paul II stands on the grounds.

Plaza de la Marqueta

This tiny plaza (tel. 024/461187), between Máximo Gómez and Mártires, and Martí and Luz Caballero, occupies the site of a former market and former candle factory (*marqueta* refers to the moulds). At its heart, the erstwhile derelict market has been restored as a concert hall and café. The surrounding buildings have been brought back to life, and life-size bronze figures of local personalities shown in everyday activities dot the square.

The **Instituto Cubano de Libros** (Callejón de Mercado #2, tel. 024/42-2874), also known as Imprenta Lugones, on the south side, is worth a peek; this print shop still makes books using Linotype. The **Casa del Habano,** on the plaza's north side, is stocked with good smokes.

Plaza San José

This antique cobbled square (aka Parque Céspedes), two blocks north of Parque Calixto García, is surrounded by colonial buildings and has a statue to local patriots executed during the Wars of Independence. It is dominated on its east side by the beautiful **Iglesia de San José,** topped by a domed neoclassical clock tower. The church dates from 1820 and features baroque innards.

The **Museo de História** (tel. 024/46-2121; Mon.–Fri. 8 a.m.–noon and 1–4:30 p.m.; free), on the north side, has a motley display relating to the city's past.

Plaza de la Revolución

This huge modern plaza, on Avenida XX Aniversario, to the northeast of the city, is dominated by a huge frieze depicting important events in Cuba's history. Calixto García's mausoleum is here. His mother (also a patriot) is buried behind the plaza beneath a copse of shade trees, where a bronze monument features

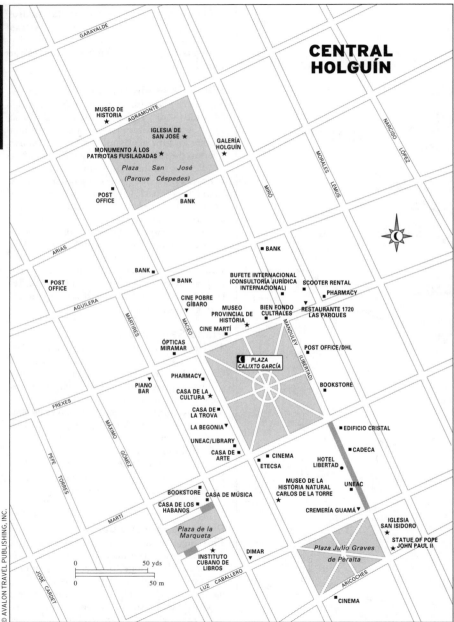

CENTRAL HOLGUÍN

GARAVALDE

MUSEO DE HISTORIA ★

AGRAMONTE

IGLESIA DE SAN JOSÉ ★

GALERÍA HOLGUÍN ■

MONUMENTO Á LOS PATRIOTAS FUSILADADAS ★

Plaza San José (Parque Céspedes)

MORALES

LEMUS

MIRÓ

NARCISO LÓPEZ

POST OFFICE ■

BANK ■

ARIAS

BANK ■

POST OFFICE ■

BANK ■

BANK ■

BUFETE INTERNACIONAL (CONSULTORÍA JURÍDICA INTERNACIONAL) ■

SCOOTER RENTAL ■

PHARMACY ■

AGUILERA

CINE POBRE GÍBARO ▼

MACEO

MÁRTIRES

BIEN FONDO CULTRALES ■

RESTAURANTE 1720 LAS PARQUES ■

MUSEO PROVINCIAL DE HISTÓRIA ★

CINE MARTÍ ■

ÓPTICAS MIRAMAR ■

MANDULEY

POST OFFICE/DHL ■

PLAZA CALIXTO GARCÍA

LIBERTAD

PHARMACY ▼

PIANO BAR ▼

CASA DE LA CULTURA ★

BOOKSTORE ■

FREXES

MÁXIMO GÓMEZ

CASA DE LA TROVA ■

LA BEGONIA ▼

EDIFICIO CRISTAL ■

UNEAC/LIBRARY ■

CADECA ■

PEPE TORRES

CASA DE ARTE ■

CINEMA ■

ETECSA ■

HOTEL LIBERTAD ■

MARTI

BOOKSTORE ■

CASA DE MÚSICA ■

MUSEO DE LA HISTÓRIA NATURAL CARLOS DE LA TORRE ★

UNEAC ■

CASA DE LOS HABANOS ■

CREMERÍA GUAMÁ ▼

Plaza de la Marqueta

IGLESIA SAN ISIDORO ★

STATUE OF POPE JOHN PAUL II ★

INSTITUTO CUBANO DE LIBROS ★

DIMAR ▼

Plaza Julio Graves de Peralta

JOSÉ CARDET

ARICOCHES

LUZ CABALLERO

CINEMA ■

0   50 yds

0   50 m

a faux Cuban flag draped in the shape of Holguín Province.

The **Estadio Calixto García** baseball and sports stadium, 200 meters south of the plaza, contains the **Museo del Estadio Calixto García** (tel. 024/46-2606), a baseball museum featuring sports memorabilia.

Entertainment and Events

Events: Mid-January welcomes **Semana de Cultura Holguinera**, when the town is bursting with cultural events. Every May 3, a religious procession—**Romería de Mayo**—ascends to the top of Loma de la Cruz, where a Mass is held. The **Festival Internacional de Ballet** is held in November every even-numbered year; and the **Fiesta Iberoamericana de la Cultura** in October celebrates the Spanish heritage in music, dance, and theater.

Traditional Music: Be sure to check out the **Casa de la Trova "El Guayabero"** (Maceo #174, no tel.; Tues.–Sun.; CUC1), on the west side of Parque Calixto García, where Faustino Oramas "El Guayabero" Osorio—born in 1911—was still performing traditional *guayaberos* (although he fell asleep between numbers) during my last visit. It has music programs at 3:30 P.M. and 10:30 P.M.

Cabarets and Discos: The best *cabaret espectáculo* is Islazul's **Cabaret Nocturno** (tel. 024/42-5185; Wed.–Mon. at 10 P.M.; CUC10 including one drink), on the Carretera Central two kilometers west of town. It's open-air; no performances during rains. You need your passport or ID to get in. The open-air **Cabaret Bariay** (Frexes), has a less impressive *espectáculo* Friday–Sunday at 8 P.M. followed by disco until 2:30 A.M. (CUC1).

The **Hotel Pernik** (Av. Dimitrov, tel. 024/48-1011; Wed.–Mon. 9 P.M.–2 A.M.; CUC6 per pair including CUC5 of drinks) has a cabaret featuring a magician, comedian, and singers. It's followed by the town's hottest disco.

Bars: To hear silky *música filín* head to the overly air-conditioned **Piano Bar** (Frexes, esq. Mártires, tel. 024/42-4322; daily noon–2 A.M.), with live music nightly.

Serious sudsters should check out **Taberna Pancho** (Av. Dimitrov, tel. 024/48-1868; noon–2 P.M., 2:15–4:15 P.M., 6–8 P.M., and 8:15–10:15 P.M. daily), next to the Hotel Pernik. This German-style beer hall serves Mayabe beer on tap served in ceramic mugs honoring Pancho, the famous beer-swilling mule.

Salon 1720 (Frexes #190, e/ Manduley y Miró, tel. 024/45-8150) has an elegant bar, with comedy (Friday) and magic shows (Saturday) at 10:30 P.M.

You can schmooze with local artists and intellectuals at **UNEAC** (National Union of Cuban Writers and Artists, Libertad #148, tel. 024/46-4066; daily 8 A.M.–midnight, www.uneac.com), with a lively patio bar hosting cultural events.

Karaoke anyone? Try **Club Karaoke** (tel. 024/42-5855; 9 P.M.–2 A.M. daily), on the third floor of the Edificio Pico Cristal.

Other: For ten-pin bowling, head to **La Bolera** (Habana, esq. Libertad, tel. 024/46-8812; daily 10 A.M.–2 A.M.; CUC1).

Teatro Comandante Eddy Suñol (Martí #111, tel. 024/46-3111), on Parque Calixto García, hosts ballet, classical, and theatrical performances.

Cine Martí, on the north side of Parque Calixto García, shows movies.

You can catch a baseball game October–May at **Estadio Calixto García** (Avenida XX Aniversario).

Accommodations

Casas Particulares: My favorite place is **Ⓒ Villa Liba** (Maceo #46, esq. 18, Rpto. El Llano, tel. 024/42-3823, villaliba@yahoo.es; CUC25). This beautiful 1950s home is replete with period furnishings in the spacious lounge. Two air-conditioned rooms are rented, each well lit, cross-ventilated, and with period furnishings. Each has a clean, tiled private hot-water bathroom. Erudite and gracious owners Jorge and Liba Mezerene make wholesome meals served on a rear patio with a vine arbor. There's secure parking.

Next door, **Ⓒ Hospedaje La Palma** (Maceo #52, tel. 024/42-4683; CUC25–30) is another marvelous 1950s home in Southern California style. It offers two large air-conditioned rooms. One has a soaring beamed ceiling, double and single beds, contemporary hardwood furniture, and a marvelous tiled bathroom with piping hot water. The second room has more classical furniture and a larger albeit less appealing bathroom. It has a huge back garden.

Villa Maritza (Maceo #22, tel. 024/42-3228; CUC25) has a handsome lounge with wicker antique rockers, plus two rooms, each with a double and single bed. The first is an independent apartment with its own entrance, fridge, and private hot-water bathroom. A second room is large and has a lovely oversize pink-tiled bathroom. The house has parking.

Villa Gilda (Línea #148, e/ Libertad y Maceo, cell 5-889-8967, gildaluz2005@ yahoo.es; CUC25) has an appealing, modern, independent upstairs apartment with two well-lit albeit simply furnished air-conditioned rooms with private bathrooms and hot water. A kitchen and dining area opens to a small balcony.

Casa de Rosa (Libertad #35, esq. 24, tel. 024/42-4630, rosama@aldia.cu; CUC25) is a beautifully maintained, cross-ventilated 1940s home with tiled floor and pleasant furnishings, with spirited artwork. It has two large air-conditioned rooms with double and single beds, and clinically clean hot-water bathrooms. There's parking.

Hostal Antonio Angulo (Peralejo #15, esq. Fomento, tel. 024/46-1730, awangulo52@ yahoo.com; CUC20–25) has two modestly furnished rooms in a 1950s bungalow. Each has a fridge and modern private hot-water bathroom, plus independent entrance.

Hotels: The **Hotel Tour Arcada** (Manduley, e/ 8 y 10, tel. 024/46-2823) is run by Universitur and offers nine air-conditioned rooms for academics, students, and tourists. It was closed at last visit.

Hotel Pernik (Av. Dimitrov, tel. 024/48-1011, fax 024/48-1667, www.hotelpernik.cu; CUC29 s, CUC40 d low season; CUC36 s, CUC48 d high season), near the Plaza de la Revolución, is a Soviet-style hotel. The 202

air-conditioned rooms are pleasantly decorated with local art pieces and have satellite TVs and telephones; some have Internet access. It has a swimming pool, tennis court, Internet service, and car rental. The restaurant is better than at most urban hotels of this type. (Islazul.)

Villa El Bosque (tel. 024/48-1012, fax 024/48-1140; CUC29 s, CUC38 d low season; CUC36 s, CUC48 d high season), about 400 meters farther east, is a more intimate option despite uninspired grounds with a dowdy sundeck and pool. It has 69 air-conditioned cabins, each with satellite TV and refrigerator. Facilities include an elegant restaurant, car rental, shop, and a disco. (Islazul.)

Food

The best private dining in town is the air-conditioned **(Restaurante La Ternuda** (José Cardet #293; 6–11 A.M. daily), hidden upstairs off a narrow street, with a charming and elegant ambience. The menu features soups (CUC1), lamb (CUC5), and *criollo* staples. When full, it has a terrible habit of telling potential patrons that it's closed. Lunch is sometimes served by reservation.

Paladar Yelly Boom (Martí, #180 e/ Carretera Central y Antonio Guiteras, tel. 024/42-4096; 11 A.M.–11 P.M. daily) serves *criollo* fare, including an enjoyable chicken in herbs and orange sauce (CUC5), in a converted garage of this modern home. Pity about the awful service and dirty tablecloths.

(Restaurante 1720 Las Parques (Frexes #190, e/ Manduley y Miró, tel. 024/45-8150; noon–10:30 A.M. daily) offers classical elegance in a restored colonial mansion full of antiques. The menu includes onion soup (CUC2.15), smoked salmon (CUC6), creole shrimp in brandy (CUC13), and paella (CUC5). Reservations recommended. A dress code applies.

For views over town, ascend the Loma de la Cruz to the atmospheric **(Restaurante Loma de la Cruz** (no tel.; daily noon–9:30 P.M.), a delightful open-air space in traditional Spanish style. I recommend the lamb in tropical sauce (CUC6.55).

Taberna Pancho (Av. Dimitrov, tel. 024/48-

1868; noon–10 P.M.) serves set meals, including decent shrimp and pork dishes (CUC2.50–5, including two beers).

Alternately, try the modestly elegant **Restaurant Isla Cristal** (Manduley, esq. Martí, tel. 024/42-5855; daily noon–2:45 P.M. and 6:30–10 P.M.), on the third floor of the Edifico Cristal. It has simple spaghetti dishes, grilled seafoods, and more.

For seafoods, I recommend **Dimar** (Carretera Central, esq. Cables, no tel.; daily 10 A.M.–10 P.M.), a small overly air-conditioned, glass-enclosed restaurant serving dishes such as ceviche (CUC2) and grilled shrimp (CUC4.65).

The 24-hour **La Begonia** snack bar with a pleasant little courtyard and an arbor for shade, is on the west side of Parque Calixto García. **Cremería Guamá** (daily 10 A.M.–10:45 P.M.), on Plaza Julio Graves, serves ice cream for pesos.

For baked goods head to **Panadería Doña Neli** (Manduley #285; 6 A.M.–11 P.M.), two blocks south of Plaza Julio Graves, a clean, air-conditioned bakery. You can buy fresh produce at the *mercado agropecuario* at the east end of Coliseo.

Information and Services

The **post office** (Máximo Gómez, e/ Aguilera y Arias) is on the east side of Parque Calixto García. **DHL** (Manduley, esq. Frexes, tel. 024/46-8254; Mon.–Fri. 9 A.M.–6 P.M., Sat. 8:30 A.M.–noon) has an office in the Edificio Cristal.

Etecsa (Martí, esq. Maceo; daily 9 A.M.–7 P.M.) has international telephone and Internet service.

Banks include **Bandec** (on the south side of Plaza San José; and Maceo, esq. Aguilera); **Banco Financiero Internacional** (Aguilera, esq. Maceo); and **Banco Popular** (Maceo, e/ Aguilera y Arias; and one block south of the Villa El Bosque).

Hospital Lenin (Av. Lenin, tel. 024/42-5302) is on the west side of town. The Hotel Pernik and Hotel Bosque have nurses. **Ópticas Miramar** (Frexes #212, e/ Maceo y Mártires, tel. 024/42-1176; Mon.–Fri. 9 A.M.–5 P.M.) has optical service. **Farmacia Turno Especial** (Maceo #170; Mon.–Sat. 8 A.M.–10 P.M.), on

the west side of Parque Calixto García, is meagerly stocked.

Consultoría Jurídica Internacional (Peralta #46, e/ Coliseo y Segunda, Rpto. Peralta, tel. 024/46-8299) and **Bufete Internacional** (Manduely, e/ Frexes y Aguilera, tel. 024/46-8133; Mon.–Fri. 8:30 A.M.–5:30 P.M.) provide legal services.

Inmigración (Peralejo y Fomento; Mon.–Wed. and Fri. 8 A.M.–noon and 2–4 P.M.) can issue visa extensions.

Getting There and Away

By Air: The **Aeropuerto Frank País** (tel. 024/46-2512) is 10 kilometers south of town, on the Carretera Central. The international and domestic terminals are 400 meters apart, with separate exits off the highway. The domestic terminal is served by a bus from Calle Rodríguez, near the train station six blocks south of Parque Calixto García. A taxi from downtown costs about CUC10.

Cubana (Edificio Cristal, tel. 024/46-8111 or 024/42-5707) flies between Havana and Holguín daily.

By Bus: The **Terminal de Ómnibus Interprovinciales** (Carretera Central #19, e/ 20 de Mayo e Independencia, tel. 024/46-1036) is on the west side of town. **Víazul** (tel. 024/42-2111) buses depart Havana for Holguín at 10:30 P.M. (CUC44). The bus for Havana departs Holguín at 9 P.M. Eastbound buses depart Holguín for Santiago de Cuba at 3:20 A.M., 8:35 A.M., 9:55 A.M., 4:45 P.M., and 10:45 P.M. Westbound buses depart Holguín for Havana at 1:30 A.M., 1:25 P.M., 7:50 P.M., and 9 P.M.; for Trinidad at 11 A.M.; and for Varadero at midnight.

Astro buses depart Holguín for Havana at 7 P.M. (CUC36 *especial,* CUC30 regular), and at 7 A.M. on alternate days; for Las Tunas at 9:40 A.M. (CUC5 *especial,* CUC3 regular); and for Santiago on alternate days at 7:45 A.M. (CUC9 *especial,* CUC7.50 regular).

Buses to/from Guardalavaca, Moa, Baracoa, and other towns east of Holguín arrive and depart the **Terminal de Ómnibus Municipales** (Av. de los Libertadores, tel. 024/48-1170), opposite the baseball stadium. *Camiones* to the same destinations also leave from this terminal; west- and southbound trucks leave from **Terminal La Molienda** (Carretera Central y Comandante Fajardo, tel. 024/42-2322), on the west side of town.

By Train: Cuba's main railway line serves Cacocum, 15 kilometers south of town, and from where a branch line serves Holguín's **Estación de Ferrocarriles** (Calle Pita, tel. 024/42-2331), eight blocks south of Plaza Calixto García.

The #9 Havana–Santiago de Cuba express arrives Cacocum at 3:26 P.M.; train #10 from Santiago to Havana arrives Cacocum at 1:23 A.M. Train #46 from Santa Clara to Santiago arrives Cacocum at 7:17 A.M.; train #47 from Santiago to Santa Clara arrives Cacocum at 5:06 P.M. All trains depart Cacocum 10 minutes later.

Train #15 from Havana arrives Holguín at 9:30 A.M. (CUC26.50); train no. #departs Holguín for Havana at 6:15 P.M. Train #86 leaves Holguín for Las Tunas at 8:25 A.M.; train #87 from Las Tunas arrives Holguín at 3:50 P.M. Train #610 from Santiago arrives Holguín at 10:50 A.M.; train #611 departs Holguín for Santiago at 2:40 P.M.

By Car: You can rent cars through **Transtur** (tel. 024/48-1011, in Café Las Begonias on Parque Calixto García; tel. 24/42-8196, Hotel Pernik); **Havanautos** (tel. 024/46-8412, domestic terminal); and **Rex** (tel. 024/46-4644, international terminal) at Aeropuerto Frank País.

There are gas stations on Carretera a Gibara; on Avenida de los Libertadores; Avenida de los Internacionalistas; and at the junction of the Carretera Central and *circunvalación.*

Getting Around

Buses run through most areas of the city (10 centavos *regular,* 40 centavos *especial*). Bus #16 connects the Hotel Pernik with downtown. Bus #3 runs from the terminal to the foot of Loma de la Cruz.

The favored mode of transport in town is the *coche* or, failing that, a *bici-taxi.* You should be able to get anywhere downtown for 10 pesos or CUC1.

Cubataxi (tel. 024/42-3290) and **Transtur** (tel. 024/42-4187) offer taxi service.

Palmares (tel. 024/46-8150), on the west side of Plaza Calixto García, rents scooters for CUC12 first hour or CUC24 daily.

◖ MIRADOR DE MAYABE

The Mayabe Lookout (10 A.M.–6 P.M. daily; CUC3 entrance including two beers) is high above the Mayabe Valley, eight kilometers southeast of town. The facility includes a fine restaurant, a swimming pool, and sundeck with fine views over the valley. The place draws the locals on weekends and is popular with *quinceañeras* for photo shoots.

You can also visit Finca Mayabe, a "typical" campesino farmstead. The ersatz farm raises two dozen species of fruit trees. Enclosures hold turkeys, geese, and other farm animals. It even has a *gallería*—a cock pit—where you can watch cockfights. Horseback riding is also available.

The Mirador's claim to fame was a beer-loving burro called Pancho (1960–2002), who consumed over 45,000 bottles of beer before his recent passing (probably of cirrhosis). Pancho's equally thirsty young sidekick Panchito keeps the tradition alive. He is given Monday off, presumably to sleep off his weekend hangover. Panchito lives in a stall next to the bar, appropriately named Bar Burro. You'll need to buy the donkey a beer for photos.

Accommodations and Food

◖ **Villa Mirador de Mayabe** (tel. 024/42-2160, mayabe@islazul.hlg.tur.cu; CUC26 s, CUC32 d low season; CUC33 s, CUC42 d high season) has 20 hilltop air-conditioned *cabinas* nicely furnished with hardwood pieces, ceramic floors, satellite TV, telephones, refrigerators, and modern bathrooms with marble countertops. The lobby is inspiring, with its swing seats of polished hardwoods. There's also a fully staffed house—**Casa de Pancho** (tel. 024/42-2160)—with four air-conditioned double rooms. The facility includes a pleasant thatched restaurant and bar (daily noon–3 P.M. and 6–9 P.M.). A folkloric cabaret is featured.

COCKFIGHTING

Whatever you think about cockfighting – undoubtedly a cruel and vicious "sport" – it is an integral part of macho Cuban culture, particularly in the countryside.

Though gambling is generally prohibited, and cockfighting thereby illegal, the authorities tolerate the sport, which takes place at *vallas* (rings) throughout the country. Hundreds of dollars are bet during matches, when the all-male crowd gets excited to the point of hysteria.

Gaming cocks are trained to fight beginning when they are about eight months. They are exercised to strengthen their wings, legs, and claws, and to build up stamina. Before combat, their wattles, ears, and crests are removed, as they bleed and could otherwise be seized by their opponents. Their feathers are also plucked from the lower body and the birds are shaved. Owners rub their birds down with rum, like seconds massaging prize-fighters.

The cocks, which fight in weight categories, are fitted with artificial metal spurs. Fights are to the death.

A state-run enterprise, Alcona, S.A., organizes fairs, runs breeding farms (including a center outside Santiago de las Vegas, in Havana Province, dedicated to genetic improvement), and is in charge of export of gaming cocks (primarily to other Latin American countries).

North of Holguín

◖ GIBARA

Gibara (pop. 20,000), 28 kilometers north of Holguín, is a dusty, time-encrusted fishing port that overlooks the Bahía de Gibara. It was a major sugar-trading port in colonial days, when it was known as Villa Blanca and colloquially as La Perla del Oriente (Pearl of the Orient). It has no shortage of intriguing colonial structures, though only remnants remain of the original 18th-century city walls. It has a delightful mood, made more so by its seafront promenade, the **Malecón,** that fronts the Atlantic shoreline and boasts a patinated **statue of Camilo Cienfuegos.**

The streets rise steeply south and west of the main plaza. If you follow Independencia west, uphill past charming little **Plaza Colón,** then turn right at Calle Cabada, you'll reach the paltry ruins of **Fuerte del Cuartelón,** a 30-minute hike. Go for the fabulous view.

You can hire a boat to **Playa Blanca,** a beach on the east side of the bay (CUC5 round-trip); or drive the 15 kilometers northwest to **Playa Caletones.**

Rising over the flatlands southeast of Gibara is a flat-topped mountain, the **Silla de Gibara** (Saddle of Gibara), considered to be the hill described by Christopher Columbus in his journal when he first landed in Cuba with his three caravels from Hispaniola on October 28, 1492. The landing site and its extensive hinterland is protected within **Parque Natural Cristóbal Colón** (Christopher Columbus National Park), a somewhat amorphous area that at last visit extended from Bahía de Gibara eastward to Bahía de Bariay, and will eventually extend from Gibara to Baracoa, in Guantánamo Province.

Parque Calixto García

The pretty main plaza is framed by African oaks (*robles africanos*) and is pinned by a **Monumento a Los Libertadores de la Patria** (Liberators of the Fatherland), commemorating those who fought in the Wars of Independence. Here, too, is the recently restored **Iglesia de San Fulgencio** church, with Byzantine-style cupolas, dating from 1850.

The excellent **Museo de Historia Natural** (Luz Caballero #23, no tel.; Tues.–Sat.

Parque Calixto García, Gibara

© CHRISTOPHER P. BAKER

9 A.M.–noon and 1–5 P.M., Sun. 9 A.M.–noon; entrance CUC1, cameras CUC1, videos CUC5) displays a broad-ranging miscellany of stuffed animals and other exhibits on a natural history theme.

The **Museo de Arte Decorativo** (Independencia #19, tel. 024/34687; Tues.–Sat. 9 A.M.–noon and 1–5 P.M., Sun. 8 A.M.–noon; entrance CUC2, cameras CUC1, videos CUC5), in a restored neoclassical mansion 50 meters southwest of the square, boasts a modest collection of period furniture and paintings upstairs.

Entertainment

The open-air **Centro Cultural El Colonial** (Peralta, esq. Sartorio; CUC2) has live music Tuesday–Sunday nights.

Accommodations and Food

There are several excellent *casas particulares* from which to choose. One of my favorites is **Villa Caney** (Sartorio #36, e/ Peralta y Luz Caballero, tel. 024/34552; CUC20–25), a superb option. This large colonial home is well maintained and has a huge lounge with rock-

ers and antiques and opens to a garden terrace with hammocks, palms, and a thatched restaurant—a delightful space! The owners rent two air-conditioned rooms with fans and private bathrooms with hot water.

Equally gracious is impeccably clean **La Casa de los Hermanos** (Céspedes #13, e/ Peralta y Luz Caballero, tel. 024/34542; CUC20), another colonial gem full of period pieces, including antique wicker rockers. It has two large and exquisitely appointed rooms with fans, antique wardrobes, and modern hot-water bathrooms. The lovely rear patio has an arcade with rockers beneath ceiling fans.

Hostal La Mina (Joaquín Agüero #13, tel. 024/34493; CUC15), facing the bus station, rents two upstairs air-conditioned rooms with fans, double beds, and a shared hot-water bathroom. You can dine on a breeze-swept terrace.

The seafront **Villa Boquerón** (Av. Rabi #53, e/ Peralta y Luz Caballero, tel. 024/34559; CUC15) is a modest seafront home on the Malecón, with one nice albeit simply furnished air-conditioned room with hot water shower.

Eateries are few. I recommend **Paladar La Bombilla** (Céspedes #7, e/ Luz Caballero y Peralta, tel. 024/34535), serving seafoods and *criollo* staples under thatch in the back garden.

Services
Banks include **Bandec** (Independencia, esq. Peralta) and **Banco Popular** (Cuba, esq. Independencia).

Getting There and Away
The bus station (tel. 024/34215) is at the entrance to town. Buses depart Holguín for Gibara at 6 A.M. and 5:40 P.M.; and Gibara for Holguín at 5 A.M. and 4 P.M. *Camiones* also make the journey.

There's a gas station at the entrance to town.

RAFAEL FREYRE AND VICINITY
This small town, about 35 kilometers northeast of Holguín, is dominated by the now-defunct Central Rafael Freyre sugar mill. The area around Rafael Freyre is punctuated by *mogotes.* The photogenic setting was until 2002 made more so by the 1882 30-inch gauge Baldwin steam locomotive that worked the Central Rafael Freyre and by larger antique steam trains that hauled cane through this stupendous mountain terrain, drawing steam-train enthusiasts from around the world.

The town, also known as Santa Lucía (not to be confused with the resort of that name), lies a few kilometers inland of Bahía de Bariay. If you zigzag through Rafael Freyre and go past the *central,* the road north will take you to the bay and **Playa Blanca,** a gorgeous beach with a commemorative plaque to Columbus that declares this the "site of the first landing of Christopher Columbus in Cuba."

Museo de Industria Azucar y de Locomotora de Vapor
The former *central* is the setting for what is touted in local tourist literature as the Sugar Industry and Steam Train Museum (tel. 024/20493; Mon.–Fri. 7:30 A.M.–4:30 P.M., Sat. 7:30–11 A.M.). Despite years of promise,

the museum has yet to emerge. What visitors find are six engines (five still running, albeit barely) in derelict sheds. You can witness mechanics working to magically keep the engines running. Entry is solely by either of two steam-train excursions—"Choo Choo Train" (CUC10) and "Cuba Inside" (CUC7)—offered by Cubatur and Gaviota in Guardalavaca (see the *Guardalavaca and Vicinity* section in this chapter); advance purchase is compulsory.

Parque Monumento Nacional Bariay
Created in 2002 to honor Columbus's landing, this 206-hectare park (daily 8:40 A.M.–4:30 P.M.; CUC8 entrance including cocktail, cameras CUC1, videos CUC2) features a re-created Indian village—**Aldea Aborigen**—where rather strained reenactments of Taíno life take place, with Cubans in Indian garb; an archaeological site with a small museum of Indian artifacts; and the uninspired **Monumento al Medio Milenio** commemorating Columbus's landing.

The park is touted heavily as an excursion from the nearby tourist resorts at Guardalavaca, but it's a meager facility and ludicrously overpriced! Most visitors probably wished they'd spent the day at the beach. Alternatively, a horse-drawn shuttle takes you on a tour from the parking lot, although you may be allowed to drive your car. There's a restaurant.

To get there, turn north at Frey Benito, four kilometers west of Rafael Freyre. (The Rafael Freyre–Frey Benito road continues west to Gibara but is deplorably deteriorated, though the scenery is spectacular.)

Accommodations
Campismo Silla de Gibara (tel. 024/42-1586; CUC5–7 per person), at the base of a *mogote* about four kilometers west of Frey Benito, is a simple holiday camp with 42 basic cabins sleeping four (including a bunk), with fans and private bathrooms; there are two categories. It has a swimming pool, café, plus volleyball, horseback rides, and hiking trails. (Cubamar Viajes.)

At Playa Blanca, the **Hotel Don Lino** (tel. 024/30259) looks over its own small beach. It was closed for restoration at last visit. (Cubanacán.)

☪ GUARDALAVACA AND VICINITY

Guardalavaca (the name means "Guard the Cow") is a small but fast-developing resort about 55 kilometers northeast of Holguín. The beaches are gorgeous. Scuba diving and snorkeling are excellent. You can whiz around on a Jet Ski or Hobie Cat. And most hotels are well managed (they're also all-inclusive and cater almost exclusively to package charter groups).

Still, although every year sees new amenities, it's small fry compared to Varadero or Cayo Coco and a stay here may come as a disappointment to sun-sea-and-sand-loving tourists who are expecting, say, the variety and scope of Cancún. Guardalavaca is also a tourists-only affair, virtually off-limits to Cubans.

The original resort, where most facilities are concentrated, is at the twin-beach strip of **Playa Mayor** and **Playa Las Brisas.** More recent development has focused further west, at sugar-fine **Playa Esmeralda,** on the east side of Bahía de Naranjo three kilometers west of Guardalavaca; and **Playa Pesquero** and **Playa Yuraguanal,** on the west side of

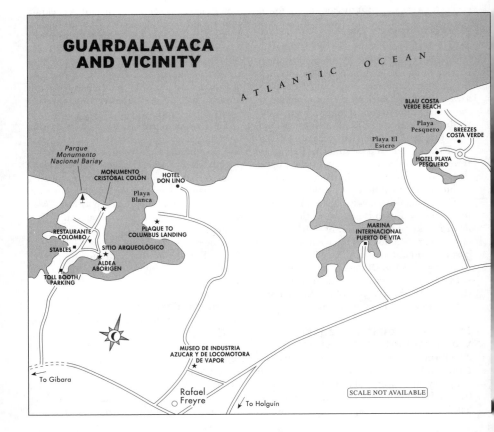

Bahía de Naranjo, midway between Guardalavaca and Rafael Freyre. (Many of the new hotels have been built on the former Santa Lucía sugar plantation, owned since 1857 by the Sánchez-Hill family, who fled Cuba following the Revolution. Under U.S. law, foreign hotel management companies operating these hotels are considered to be "trafficking" in expropriated property. Jamaica's SuperClubs pulled out in 2004 under threat of sanctions by the United States.)

Museo Aborigen Chorro de Maíta

This aboriginal museum (tel. 024/30421; Mon.–Sat. 9 A.M.–5 P.M., Sun. 9 A.M.–1 P.M.; entrance

CUC2, cameras CUC1, videos CUC5), on a hilltop seven kilometers east of Guardalavaca and two kilometers south from the main highway, is on part of the largest aboriginal burial site thus far discovered in the Caribbean (almost 200 skeletons have been unearthed). It is thought that a large Indian village called Bani occupied the site, today a national monument. A gallery surrounds the burial ground within a building where the skeletons lie in peaceful repose. Pre-Columbian artifacts are displayed. A life-size model Indian village—**Aldea Taína**—has been re-created across the road (CUC2 additional) with an ensemble of locals hired to dress and act like Taíno Indians.

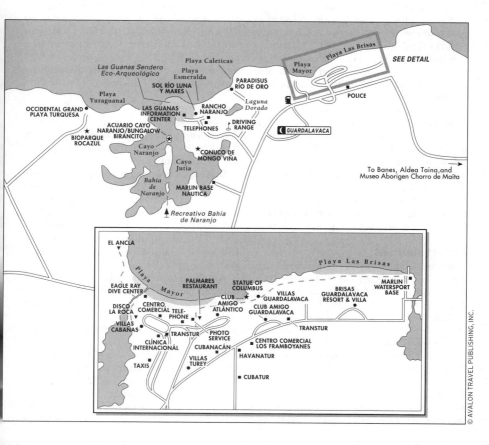

Recreativo Bahía de Naranjo

This huge flask-shaped bay, about four kilometers west of Guardalavaca, is a 400-hectare *estero* (estuary) fringed by mangroves and dry forest. The bay's eastern headland is accessible via the overpriced **Las Guanas Sendero Eco-Arqueológico** (8:30 A.M.–5 P.M. daily; CUC6), where trails lead to archaeological sites and the Cueva Ciboney, a funerary cave with petroglyphs. *Miradores* (lookout towers) provide a bird's-eye view over the park. An interpretive center at the entrance offers introductions to the flora and fauna.

Acuario Cayo Naranjo (tel. 024/30132) occupies a natural lagoon on the tiny island in the middle of the bay. Sea lions and dolphins perform acrobatics at noon (CUC25 including boat tour and dolphin show, CUC2 cameras, CUC5 videos). Visitors can even swim with the dolphins (CUC30 extra). A restaurant serves seafood. All the hotels in Guardalavaca offer excursions. Boats leave for the aquarium from Marlin Base Náutica.

To learn more about local ecology, head to **Bioparque Rocazul** (daily 9 A.M.–5 P.M.; entrance CUC8, cameras CUC1, videos CUC2), a 1,487-hectare recreational facility on the west side of the bay. Its information center has excellent maps and descriptive profiles on flora, fauna, pre-Columbian culture, and geology. Trails lead from the visitors center through the scrub and mangroves, and to **Finca Monte Bello** (CUC16), a slightly hokey typical Cuban farm.

Entertainment

The hotels all have nightly *animaciones* (cabarets). *The* place to be, however, is the canopied, open-air **Disco La Roca** (tel. 024/30167; Tues.–Sun. 10 P.M.–3 A.M.; CUC6), overlooking the beach at the west end of Guardalavaca. A *cabaret espectáculo* precedes the disco Wednesday–Sunday.

The **Arcada de Juegos** in the Centro Comercial Los Flamboyanes has electronic games.

Recreation

Horseback riding is offered at **Centro Hípico Rancho Naranjo**, at Playa Esmeralda; and

Bioparque Rocazul (CUC15–19), which also offers mountain biking (CUC12–14), guided hiking (CUC11–13), and boat excursions focusing on nature viewing and snorkeling (CUC11).

You can practice your golf swing at a **driving range** (daily 8 P.M.–7 A.M.; from CUC4) on the Playa Esmeralda road; and your tennis swing on the night-lit courts at **Tennis Club Las Brisas** (CUC5).

Marlin Watersport Base (tel. 024/3774), at the east end of Playa Las Brisas, and **Marlin Eagle Ray Dive Center** (tel. 024/33-6702), at the west end of Playa Mayor, offer banana-boat rides, waterskiing, and kayak and Hobie Cat rental. They also offer scuba diving trips at 9 A.M. (CUC35 one dive), and at 2 P.M. on demand; plus snorkeling trips (CUC25). Gear rental costs CUC5 extra. Certification courses are offered (CUC350). There are more than 30 dive sites, including wrecks, with the coral reef a mere 200 meters offshore.

Accommodations

Private room rentals are banned. You can secure lower rates than the rack rates quoted here by booking in advance through tour agencies anywhere in Cuba.

Guardalavaca: At the budget end, **Villas Cabañas** (tel. 024/30314; CUC26 s, CU36 d low season; CUC33 s, CUC45 d high season), at the west end of Guardalavaca, offers simple air-conditioned three-person *cabinas* with satellite TVs, radios, kitchenettes, and modern bathrooms (cold water only and no toilet seats when I visited). (Islazul.)

All the following hotels are run by Cubanacán (www.cubanacan.cu). All rooms are air-conditioned and feature satellite TVs and telephones.

Club Amigo (tel. 024/30180, fax 024/30200, reserva@guard.gcv.cyt.cu) incorporates four properties run on an all-inclusive basis. **Club Amigo Guardalavaca** (from CUC65 s, CUC100 d low season; CUC72 s, CUC114 d high season), 100 yards inland from the beach, has 234 pleasantly appointed, recently refurbished rooms. Activity revolves around a huge swimming pool with a water slide, and there's tennis, volleyball, a game room, and entertainment. **Club Amigo Atlántico** (CUC69 s, CUC108 d low season; CUC76 s, CUC124 d high season), with 232 rooms and one suite, is similar, though a tad more upscale, with the advantage of a beachfront setting, though not all rooms have ocean views. The hotel has large swimming pool, game room, boutique, water sports. **Villas Guardalavaca** (CUC75 s, CUC116 d low season; CUC84 s, CUC130 d high season) has 144 beachside *cabinas* including four mini-suites, a junior suite, and four rooms for the physically challenged. The strikingly contemporary **Villas Turey** (CUC79 s, CUC124 d low season; CUC88 s, CUC138 d high season) has 136 air-conditioned rooms in gracious two-story villas around a swimming pool set in landscaped grounds.

The nicest place is **Brisas Guardalavaca Resort & Villa** (tel. 024/30218, fax 024/30418, www.brisasguardalavaca.com; CUC95 s, CUC140 d low season; CUC115 s, CUC180 d high season standard; CUC110 s, CUC160 d low season, CUC130 s, CUC200 d high season mini-suite; CUC180 s/d low season, CUC220 s/d high season junior suite), on Playa Las Brisas. This four-star all-inclusive resort has 357 pleasantly furnished rooms, 80 mini-suites, and four junior suites and is divided into villa and hotel complexes with two large pools. There's a Kid's Kamp, a choice of restaurants, plus water sports, volleyball, and tennis courts.

Bahía de Naranjo: Marlin Base Náutica rents the charming two-room **Bungalow Birancito** (tel. 024/30132, fax 024/30433, bahiaup@bahiaueh.co.cu; CUC75 including breakfast) on Cayo Naranjo, adjacent to the dolphinarium. It sleeps four people. Meals can be arranged.

All the following hotels are run by Gaviota (www.grupo-gaviota.cu) and include a full range of facilities, plus entertainment and water sports. All rooms are air-conditioned and feature satellite TVs, telephones, minibar, and safes.

Playa Esmeralda: The **Sol Río de Luna y Mares** (tel. 024/30030, fax 024/30035, www

.solmeliacuba.com; from CUC150 s, CUC200 d standard, CUC210 s, CUC280 d suite low season; from CUC180 s, CUC d standard, CUC240 s, CUC320 d suite high season), operated by Spain's Sol Meliá and comprising two adjacent hotels, is a 564-room all-inclusive done up in eye-pleasing Caribbean pastels and set in beautifully landscaped grounds. Facilities include a sailing school and scuba diving.

Paradisus Río de Oro (tel. 024/30090, fax 024/30095, www.solmeliacuba.com; CUC240 s, CUC300 d standard, CUC260 s, CUC330 d superior, CUC310 s, CUC400 d suite low season; CUC270 s, CUC340 d standard, CUC290 s, CUC370 d superior, CUC340 s, CUC440 d suite high season), also managed by Sol Meliá, is a more upscale all-inclusive property with similarly lively tropical decor and an exquisite contemporary vogue. It has 300 standards, superior rooms, and suites. A highlight is its Japanese restaurant.

Playas Pesquero and Yuraguanal: The **Blau Costa Verde Beach** (tel. 24/30510, fax 24/30515, www.blau-hotels.com; CUC85 s, CUC130 d low season; CUC130 s, CUC180 d high season) is a four-star all-inclusive property with 307 rooms and two suites. Despite its ungainly exterior, its interior is strikingly handsome, and the vast freeform pool with swim-up bar is a nice feature.

Hotel Playa Pesquero (tel. 024/30530, fax 024/30535; CUC138 s, CUC220 d junior suite, CUC200 s, CUC320 d suite low season; CUC175 s, CUC280 d junior suite, CUC238 s, CUC380 d suite high season) is an exquisite all-inclusive property with a vast Asian-style lobby with fish ponds. The 928 junior suites (eight equipped for guests with disabilities) and 16 suites feature lively Caribbean colors and a contemporary neoclassical chic. The complex has a vast freeform pool.

Also exuding a pleasing contemporary aesthetic, the **Hotel Playa Costa Verde** (tel. 024/30520, fax 024/30525, sales@plyacostaverde.co.cu; CUC119 s, CUC190 d standard, CUC154 s, CUC246 d suite low season; CUC169 s, CUC270 d standard, CUC298 s, CUC404 d suite high season) is a four-star all-inclusive with 464 standard rooms and 16 suites and all the amenities you could want of a beach resort.

Raising the bar is the classy **⬤ Occidental Grand Playa Turquesa** (tel. 024/30540, fax 024/30545, www.occidental-hoteles.com; CUC150 s, CUC200 d all-inclusive) at Playa Yaraguanal. Opened in 2005, it features seven pools connected by cascading waterfalls. It has 520 tastefully furnished rooms. Choose from six restaurants, including Italian and Chinese.

Food

⬤ El Ancla (tel. 024/30381; daily 11 A.M.–10:30 P.M.), atop a coral outcrop at the west end of Playa Mayor, specializes in seafood; it serves fish dishes for CUC6 and up (lobster costs a ludicrous CUC30). The *bodega*-style **Palmares Restaurant** (noon–midnight daily), overlooking Playa Mayor, serves seafoods and *criollo* dishes from CUC5.

Conuco de Mongo Viña (tel. 024/30771; daily 8:30 A.M.–3:30 P.M.; under CUC5), on the east shore of Bahía de Naranjo, serves *criollo* meals in its thatched restaurant. It has a small zoo, cactus and medicinal gardens, and caged birds.

Most hotels sell day and evening passes (CUC35–50), which include all-inclusive use of their restaurants and other facilities.

You can buy groceries in the three *centros comerciales* in Guardalavaca.

Information and Services

The post office and DHL service are in the Las Brisas resort. International calls from any hotel will break the bank. Better to use the *minipuntos* (telephone kiosks) roadside at Playa Mayor and Playa Esmeralda.

There's a **bank** at Club Amigo Guardalavaca and a *Clínica Internacional* (tel. 024/30312; 24 hours) at the west end of Guardalavaca.

Asistur (tel. 024/30148; Mon.–Fri. 8:30 A.M.–5 P.M.), in the Centro Comercial Guardalavaca, offers legal, financial, and other emergency assistance.

The **Canadian Consulate** (tel./fax 024/30320) is in Club Amigo Atlántico.

Getting There and Away

Guardalavaca has no airport. Vacationers arriving from abroad on package tours land at Holguín.

Buses ostensibly operate from Holguín and Banes and drop off and depart opposite Villas Turey, but service is unreliable. A taxi from Holguín will cost about CUC40 one-way.

You can rent cars from **Transtur** (tel. 024/30134), at the west end of Guardalavaca; and **Cubacar** (tel. 024/30490), adjacent to Club Amigo Guardalavaca. All the resort hotels have car rental desks.

All the hotels have tour desks. You can also book direct with **Cubatur** (tel. 024/30170), 50 meters south of Centro Comercial Los Framboyantes; **Havanatur** (tel. 024/30406), at the west end of Guardalvaca; or **Gaviota** (tel. 024/30903, fax 024/30908, dircon .hog@gaviotatours.co.cu). **EcoTur** (Villa Cabaña, tel. 024/30155, ecotur.guardalavaca@enet.cu) offers ecotourism excursions.

Marina Internacional Puerto de Vita (tel. 024/30909, fax 024/30446, marvita@enete .cu), one kilometer west of Playa Pesquero, has 38 slips.

Getting Around

Coches run between Guardalavaca and the various beaches. A shuttle—**Tuti-Tren**—runs between the Acuario and Museo Aldea Taina via Guardalavaca. Bicycles and scooters (CUC7 one hour, CUC12 two hours, CUC25 per day, CUC100 per week) can be rented at most hotels.

Taxis await custom west of Villa Turey, or call **Cubataxi** (tel. 024/42-3290) or **Taxi OK** (tel. 024/30124).

The gas station is one kilometer west of town.

BANES

Banes (pop. 84,000), about 34 kilometers southeast of Guardalavaca and 70 kilometers northeast of Holguín, is a sleepy provincial sugar town with a colonial core of mostly wooden houses. This is the real Cuba, with all the sundry life that Guardalavaca lacks.

For much of the past century, the town

BIG FRUIT

After the Wars of Independence, the vast sugarcane fields of Holguín gradually fell into the hands of U.S. corporations, especially the United Fruit Company (UFC), which bought the land for a pittance and came to dominate economic and political life in the region. While the UFC was also a philanthropic agent of good deeds locally, paying, for example, for a sewer system for the town of Banes, Tad Szulc explains that it was "emblematic of almost everything that was wrong in Cuba's relationship with the United States: the powerlessness, the degree to which the mill constituted a world unto itself in which Cubans had no rights except those conceded by the company." One of the few Cubans who benefited economically from the UFC arrangement was Fidel Castro's father, Ángel Castro, who leased lands from UFC and grew to be both prosperous and powerful. The pitiful existence of many among the Cuban peasantry was not lost on the young Fidel, who, it is claimed, first agitated on workers' behalf as a boy – and on his father's estate.

was run by the United Fruit Company, which owned virtually all the land hereabouts and had a massive sugar mill called Boston (since renamed Nicaragua) five kilometers south of town. (The mill was recently closed and "El Panchito," a 1888 steam locomotive built by the Porter Locomotive Works, of Pittsburgh, Pennsylvania, and which for more than a century hauled sugarcane, now stands idle on Calle Tráfico in the center of town.)

Fulgencio Batista was born here in 1901. His future archenemies, Fidel and Raúl Castro, were born nearby at Birán. As youths the brothers would come into town in a red convertible to party at the American Club. On October 12, 1948, Fidel married Mirta Diaz-Balart, daughter of the wealthy mayor of Banes, in the art deco **Iglesia de Nuestra Señora de la Caridad,** on Parque Martí (the marriage dissolved five years later but produced a son, Fidelito).

Mirta's brother, Rafael, headed Batista's youth organization and would later be named Batista's Minister of the Interior, in charge of the secret police (he fled Cuba after the Revolution; his son keeps the right-wing flame burning as a U.S. congressman from Florida).

The drive between Banes and Guardalavaca is one of the most beautiful in the country as the road rises and falls between the *mogotes* and Royal palms of the Grupo de Maniabon uplands.

◖ Museo Indocubano

The Museum of Indian Civilization (General Marrero #305, tel. 024/82487; Tues.–Sat. 9 A.M.–5 P.M., Sun. 8 A.M.–noon and 7–9 P.M.; CUC1) exhibits a collection of more than 20,000 pre-Columbian relics and artifacts, most importantly a small gold fertility idol wearing a feather headdress, thought to date from the 13th century and the first gold piece ever discovered in Cuba.

Entertainment

On Sundays it all happens at **Café Cantante** (General Marrero #320, no tel.), with afternoon *trova* (2–7 P.M.; free) and evening music and dancing, from Buena Vista Social Club–style *son* to salsa. The **Casa de la Cultura** (tel. 024/82111; CUC1), next door, competes with its own Sunday-afternoon *trova,* and broad-ranging evening sessions from *boleor* to reggaeton.

Accommodations and Food

Casas particulares include **Casa Evelyn Feria Diesquez** (Bruno Merino #3401-A, e/ Delfín Pepo y Heredia, tel. 024/82270; CUC15), with two upstairs rooms opening to a terrace. Each has private bathroom. The hostess is a delight. There's secure parking across the street.

I also recommend **Casa de Alfredo Serrano** (Delfin Pupo #1105, e/ Bruno Meri y Máximo Gómez, tel. 024/82464; CUC20), a delightful home run by the friendly Alfredo and his wife Esther, who offer two air-conditioned rooms with private bathrooms. No meals are made, but there's a *paladar* close by.

A good alternative is **Casa de Marcia Pupo**

Zaldipar (Thelmo Esperance #1119, e/ Bayamo y Máximo Gómez, tel. 024/83329; CUC15–25), with one air-conditioned room with fridge and private bathroom with hot water.

The only state-run option is **Motel El Oasis** (tel. 024/83425; CUC10 s, CUC14 d), at the entrance to Banes. It has 28 no-frills *cabinas* with cold water only. They're set in nice grounds with a restaurant and bar popular with locals.

The best dining is at **Paladar Las Delicias** (Augusto Blanco #1107, tel. 024/82638; noon–midnight daily), offering creole dishes with beer for less than CUC10.

Getting There and Away

Buses operate between Holguín and Banes, where the bus terminal is at the east end of Calle Los Angeles. You can also take a six-times-daily *camión*.

Holguín to Guantánamo Province

◖ SITIO HISTÓRICO BIRÁN

Fidel Castro was born on August 13, 1926, at Finca Manacas, at Birán, below the western foothills of the Altiplanici de Nipe, 60 kilometers southeast of Holguín. The two-story house on wooden pilings—with a cattle barn underneath is a replica—the original apparently burned to the ground in 1954. The property also contained a slaughterhouse, repair shop, store, bakery, and other facilities. The handsome *finca* looks out over a large lake.

Castro's father, Ángel, began leasing land from the United Fruit Company in 1910, farmed sugarcane to sell to the mills, hired labor, and grew wealthy on the proceeds of his 26,000-acre domain. Eventually, Fidel's father acquired forests and a sawmill in Pinares as well as a small nickel mine. He even owned the village store and was the most important man in the region. Fidel, however, has worked to downplay his social privilege and prefers to exaggerate the simplicity of his background. "The house was made of wood. No mortar, cement or bricks," he told Brazilian theologian Frey Beto in *Fidel: My Early Years*. In truth it's a substantial house—clearly the home of a well-to-do man.

In late 2002 the *finca* (tel. 024/28-7116; Tues.–Sat. 8 A.M.–4 P.M., Sun. 8 A.M.–noon; entrance CUC10, cameras CUC5, videos CUC10) opened to the public as a National Historic Site run by the Consejo de Estado

(Council of State). Security is heavy, and an armed soldier and guard will accompany you as you're shown the graves of Castro's parents, Ángel and Lina (the family housemaid); the simple schoolhouse that Fidel attended (his desk is front row, center, of course); and the local post office and telegraph office. The huge main house has many original furnishings, including a still-functional Crosley TV, Fidel's personal effects (including his baseball glove and basketball), and the bed in which it is claimed he was born. (In *After Fidel,* author and former CIA analyst Brian Latell cites convincing evidence that Fidel, who was born illegitimate and not legally acknowledged by his father until he was 17, lived his first few years with his mother and apart from his father and his formal wife.) The former guest house now bears invaluable gifts to Fidel.

From Holguín, take the Cueto road (6-123). Turn south five kilometers west of Cueto to Loynaz Echevarría. Turn east (left) just beyond the *central*. The community of Birán is seven kilometers farther, and Finca Las Manacas is two kilometers to the north. The abysmally potholed roads were scheduled to be relaid for the visit of Fidel Castro and Hugo Chávez in August 2006.

MAYARÍ ABAJO AND VICINITY

This medium-size town is 80 kilometers east of Holguín, on the banks of the Río Mayarí, six kilometers inland of the Bahía de Nipes. Other than to top up on gas, there's no reason to stop here. However, nearby, nature lovers might divert to the following two sites.

Cayo Saetía

This 42-square-kilometer cay (CUC10 entrance), 18 kilometers north of the coast highway, is separated from the mainland by a hair's-breadth waterway and forms the easternmost side of the Bahía de Nipes. Its ecosystems range from mangrove swamps to evergreen forests harboring many endangered species, including *jabalí* (wild boar), plus exotic animals—ostrich, zebra, two types of antelope, and water buffalo—originally imported for the hunting pleasure of top Communist officials, for whom Cayo Saetía was until recent years a private vacation spot. Antelope are commonly seen as you drive the unpaved road to the hotel.

One-hour jeep safaris (CUC9) and horseback riding (CUC6 per hour) are available, as is a one-hour boat excursion (CUC15). There are beaches for sunning.

If driving, note that many maps show a non-existent road direct from the Carretera Costa Norte to Cayo Saetía. The real road leads to Felton, a T junction with an unmarked turnoff to the right for Cayo Saetía.

Gaviota (tel. 024/30903, fax 024/30908, dircon.hog@gaviotatours.co.cu) offers helicopter excursions from Guardalavaca.

Pinares de Mayarí

South of Mayarí, the Sierra Cristal climbs sharply. Montane rainforest thrives adjacent to pine forest at these cool heights, where mists drift languidly through the branches. Much of the region is enshrined in the recently formed **Parque Nacional La Mensura.** En route, you'll pass a turnoff to the south for the **Farallones de Seboruco,** a cavern system where indigenous Indian artifacts dating back 5,000 years have been found.

The Cuban Academy of Sciences has a biological research station overlooking **Lago La Presa,** a scenic lake at Pinares de Mayarí,

20 kilometers south of Mayarí. Nearby is a horticultural garden—**La Planca**—adding bright colors to the lushly green landscape. Horseback rides are available, and you can hire guides for hikes to **Salto el Guayabo,** a 280-foot waterfall.

Tour companies in Guardalavaca offer day excursions to Pinares, accessed from Mayarí Abajo by a rough dirt road that will stump all but the sturdiest four-wheel drive; until the road is improved, a visit is not worth the hardship of getting there unless you're a dedicated bird-watcher or hiker.

Further east, and as yet closed to the public, is 18,537-hectare **Parque Nacional Pico Cristal,** created in 1930 as the first national park in Cuba (the park was much bigger originally, and was reduced to permit mining after precious minerals were discovered). It rises to 1,214 meters atop sharp-peaked Pico de Cristal. There are plans to establish trails and tourist facilities.

Accommodations and Food

Casa de Elin y Ilsïa (Calle Moncada #89, tel. 024/53315, jesusenrique@cristal.hld.sld.cu; CUC20 downstairs, CUC25 upstairs, including breakfast), 200 meters south of the Cupet gas station in Mayarí, is the only *casa particular* for miles. Stone walls enhance the pleasing effect in the two air-conditioned guest rooms (one upstairs), each with TV, refrigerator, and private hot-water bathroom. Meals are served in a thatched *rancho* in the delightful rear garden. There is secure parking.

Villa Pinares de Mayarí (tel. 024/53308, fax 024/30126, gaviota@gaviota.gav.tur.cu; CUC25 s, CUC36 d low season; CUC30 s, CUC40 d high season) is a mountain eco-resort operated by Gaviota. It has 36 rooms in rustic, wooden, red tile–roofed one-, two- and three-bedroom cottages, all with satellite TV, minifridge, safe, and private bathrooms (some with hot water). There's an exercise room, steam baths, swimming pool, basketball, tennis, mountain bikes, and even a baseball diamond.

Villa Cayo Saetía (tel. 024/96900,

vsaetia@ip.etecsa.cu; CUC30–70 s, CUC35–80 d low season; CUC35–80 s, CUC40–95 d high season), on Cayo Saetía, has 12 handsome yet rustic *cabinas* and suites amid handsome grounds. Rooms have telephones, TVs, and refrigerators. The eyes of animals that wandered between crosshairs glower eerily as you pass by. There's a handsome bar and restaurant.

MOA

East of Mayarí, the Circuito Norte coast road leads past a series of port towns that rely on the nickel and mineral ore industries. Tall chimneys belching out smoke announce your arrival at the coastal town of Moa, the center of Cuba's metal ore industry. The town is smothered with red dust from the nearby processing plants. It has been claimed (probably in jest) that Cuban engineers would rather sacrifice their careers than work here. Nonetheless, Moa has the only accommodations in the many lonesome miles between Mayarí and Baracoa.

A few miles east of Moa you'll pass a huge smelting plant (one of two alongside the road) called Empresa Comandante Ernesto Che Guevara, guarded by a statue of the namesake hero towering astride the gates, cast in concrete on the scale of the Colossus of Rhodes. The environment has been hammered and sickled into a grotesque gangue pitted with pestilential lagoons. Gnarled, splintered trees add to the dramatic effect, like the aftermath of a World War I bombardment. Try not to notice the children swimming in the sickly soup that passes for the sea.

After the mining operations were nationalized in 1960, Soviet money financed future expansion. In the 1990s, Canadian mining ventures took the lead; in 2004 China also made huge investments.

Photography hereabouts is prohibited—one suspects more because the government is embarrassed by the horrendous blight than for any strategic reason!

Accommodations

Hotel Miraflores (Av. Amistad, tel. 024/66103, fax 024/66332, hmiraflores@moa.minbas.cu; CUC18 s, CUC24 d year-round) has 139 modestly furnished rooms, plus a swimming pool, restaurant, and disco, and Transtur car rental. (Islazul.)

Getting There and Away

Cubana (tel. 024/67916) flies from Havana twice weekly (US$80 one-way) to Moa's **Orestes Acosta Airport** (tel. 024/67012), three kilometers east of town.

A bus departs Holguín for Moa daily, but at last visit no bus was operating between Moa and Baracoa (70 km further east), although *camiones* make the journey.

There's a gas station one kilometer west of town and another at the entrance to Empresa Comandante Ernesto Che Guevara, about three kilometers east of town.

GRANMA

Granma, Cuba's southwesternmost province, abounds with sites of historical importance. Throughout Cuba's history, the region has been a hotbed of rebellion, beginning in 1512, when Hatuey, the local Indian chieftain, rebelled against Spain. The citizens of Bayamo were from the outset at the forefront of the drive for independence, and the city, which became the capital of the provisional republic, is brimful of sites associated with the heady days when Cuba's *criollo* population fought to oust Spain. Nearby, at La Demajagua, Carlos Céspedes freed his slaves and proclaimed Cuba's independence. And Dos Ríos, in the northeast of the province, is the site where José Martí chose martyrdom in battle in 1895.

The region also became the first battleground in the revolutionary efforts to topple the Batista regime, initiated on July 26, 1953, when two dozen of Castro's rebels attacked the Bayamo garrison in concert with an attack on the Moncada barracks in Santiago. In 1956, Castro, Che Guevara, and 80 fellow revolutionaries came ashore at Las Colorados to set up their rebel army. The province is named for the vessel—the *Granma*—in which the revolutionaries traveled from Mexico; prior to 1976, when the province was created, the region was part of Oriente.

Several sites recall those revolutionary days, not least La Comandancia de la Plata (Fidel Castro's guerrilla headquarters), deep in the Sierra Maestra. Steep trails lead to these forested mountains, where an enormous swath is protected within Gran Parque Nacional Sierra Maestra, fabulous for bird-watching and hiking.

© CHRISTOPHER P. BAKER

HIGHLIGHTS

◖ **Parque Céspedes:** Setting of important events in Cuban history, and recently restored to its colonial splendor, Bayamo's main plaza has two fine museums and other buildings of import (page 465).

◖ **Plaza del Himno:** This intimate cobbled square in Bayamo boasts one of the nation's finest and most important churches (page 466).

◖ **La Comandancia de la Plata:** The ridgetop trail to Castro's former guerrilla headquarters is a splendid hike that is far less demanding than the hike to Pico Turquino (page 471).

◖ **Hiking to Pico Turquino:** For the ultimate high, this overnight guided hike to the summit of Cuba's highest peak is strenuous but richly rewarding (page 471).

◖ **Parque Nacional Desembarco del Granma:** Trails through tropical dry forest provide ample opportunities for spotting rare birds. Caves with dripstone formations, and fabulous views from higher up, are bonuses (page 479).

◖ **Marea del Portillo to Santiago de Cuba Province:** The ultimate scenic drive is also an adventure. It's driving for driving's sake, but break out the camera (page 481)!

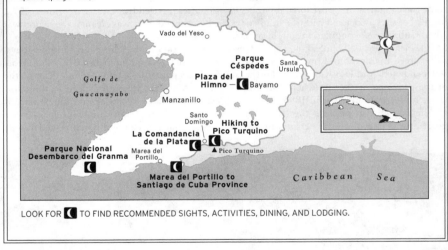

LOOK FOR ◖ TO FIND RECOMMENDED SIGHTS, ACTIVITIES, DINING, AND LODGING.

You can even ascend the trail to Pico Turquino, where there are staggering views south over the coast and north across the plains.

For physical drama, Granma Province is hard to beat. Whereas the north side of the Sierra Maestra has a moist microclimate and is lushly foliated, the south side lies in a rain shadow. Greenery yields to cacti-studded semi-desert. The narrow coastal plain provides a superb scenic drive past rocky bays and deserted beaches, with the mountains escalat-

ing to cloud-draped crescendos that will have you reaching for your camera post-haste. The Río Cauto—Cuba's longest river—runs out of these mountains and feeds the rich farmland of the northern plains. The river delta is a vast mangrove swampland.

PLANNING YOUR TIME

The province is neatly divided into plains (to the north) and mountains (to the south). Most sites of interest can be discovered by following

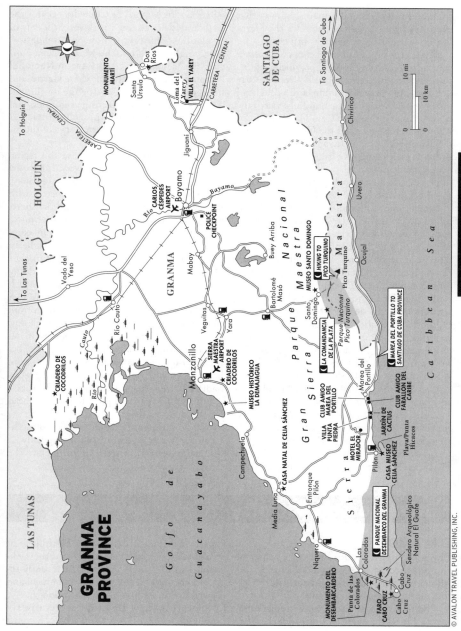

GRANMA

GRANMA PROVINCE

LAS TUNAS

HOLGUÍN

To Holguín

To Las Tunas

CARRETERA CENTRAL

MONUMENTO MARTÍ

Dos Ríos

Santa Ursula

Loma del Yarey / VILLA EL YAREY

Jiguaní

CARRETERA CENTRAL

SANTIAGO DE CUBA

To Santiago de Cuba

Chivirico

10 mi

10 km

GRANMA

RÍO CARLOS CÉSPEDES AIRPORT

Bayamo

Río

POLICE CHECKPOINT

GRANMA

Maboy

Vado del Yeso

Río Cauto

Cauto

Veguitas

Yara

Bartolomé Masó

Buey Arriba

MUSEO SANTO DOMINGO

Santo Domingo

HIKING TO PICO TURQUINO

Pico Turquino

Uvero

Ocujal

Parque Nacional Pico Turquino

Maestra

Sierra

Caribbean Sea

CRIADERO DE COCODRILOS

Río

Cauto

Manzanillo

SIERRA MAESTRA AIRPORT

CRIADERO DE COCODRILOS

MUSEO HISTÓRICO LA DEMAJAGUA

Parque Maestra Nacional

Gran Sierra

LA COMANDANCIA DE LA PLATA

MAREA DEL PORTILLO TO SANTIAGO DE CUBA PROVINCE

Golfo de Guacanayabo

Campechuela

Media Luna

CASA NATAL DE CELIA SÁNCHEZ

CLUB AMIGO MAREA DEL PORTILLO

VILLA PUNTA PIEDRA

Marea del Portillo

CLUB AMIGO FARALLÓN DEL CARIBE

JARDÍN DE CACTUS

MOTEL EL MIRADOR

Pilón

CASA MUSEO CELIA SÁNCHEZ

Playa/Punta Hicacos

Entronque Pilón

Niquero

Las Colorados

PARQUE NACIONAL DESEMBARCO DEL GRANMA

Sendero Arqueológico Natural El Guafe

MONUMENTO DEL DESEMBARCADERO

Punta de las Colorados

FARO CABO CRUZ

Cabo Cruz

© AVALON TRAVEL PUBLISHING, INC.

a circular route along the main highway that runs west from Bayamo, encircles the Sierra Maestra, and runs along the south coast.

If you're into the urban scene, concentrate your time around Bayamo, the provincial capital. Its recently restored central plaza—**Parque Céspedes**—and **Plaza del Himno** have a delightful quality and several historic buildings worth the browse, among them the Casa Natal de Carlos Manuel de Céspedes and the Iglesia Parroquial del Santísima Salvador. If you're in a rush to get to Santiago de Cuba, it's a straight shot along the Carretera Central, perhaps with a short detour to Dos Ríos (with a monument commemorating José Martí's martyrdom here in 1895).

Fancy some mountain hiking? Then the Sierra Maestra calls. This vast mountain chain runs about 140 kilometers west–east from the southwest tip of the island (Cabo Cruz) to the city of Santiago de Cuba. Although laced with campesino trails, the only area developed for ecotourism is at Santo Domingo, gateway to the trailhead to Pico Turquino (overnight hike) and **La Comandancia de la Plata** (same-day hike). A guide is compulsory. You'll need to bring appropriate cold-weather clothes and raingear at any time of year. The access road to Santo Domingo is not for the faint of heart (think hill grades that appear like sheer drops).

Consider the town of Manzanillo a place to rest your head, as it has few sites of touristic interest. The coast road south of Manzanillo, however, has several intriguing sites sufficient for a day's browsing. My favorites are the Criadero de Cocodrilos (croc farm) and Museo Histórico La Demajagua, the former farm

where Carlos Manuel de Céspedes became the first landowner to free his slaves. Students of revolutionary history, or those on a "solidarity" tour, might check out the Museo Celia Sánchez (in Media Luna) and **Parque Nacional Desembarco del Granma**, where Castro and his guerrillas landed to pursue the revolution. The latter makes for a fleeting visit unless you care to hike the trails that provide spectacular bird-watching on the western slopes of the Sierra Maestra.

For me, a singular reason to visit this region is for the spectacular drive between Marea del Portillo and Santiago de Cuba. Running along the coastline for more than 100 kilometers, with the Sierra Maestra rising sheer from the shore, this roller-coaster ride turns a scenic drive into a fantastic adventure. There are virtually no communities en route. You'll need your own wheels; public transport is extremely limited. Hurricane Dennis roared ashore here in July 2005 doing considerable damage to the coastal zones. Much of the coast road was washed out, and at last visit had still to be repaired. You can push on from Manzanillo to Santiago de Cuba in a single day, although be prepared to arrive after dark if you plan on visiting all the sites en route. A better bet is to overnight at Marea del Portillo, a ho-hum beach resort with three hotels (many budget Canadian charter groups use it as a base; I say, give it a miss other than as a place to rest your head for the night as there are very few sites to see hereabouts and the mediocre beach and modicum of activities here wear thin very quickly).

Accommodations are limited outside the two main towns.

Bayamo and Vicinity

BAYAMO

Bayamo (pop. 130,000) lies at the center of the province, on the Carretera Central, 130 kilometers northwest of Santiago and 95 kilometers southwest of Holguín.

The town was the setting for remarkable events during the quest for independence from

Spain. The city is called the "Birthplace of Cuban Nationality" and has earned the nickname "La Heróica." Much of the recently restored historic core is a national monument and is well worth a stop of a half day or longer.

Unfortunately, Bayamo is literally fly infested.

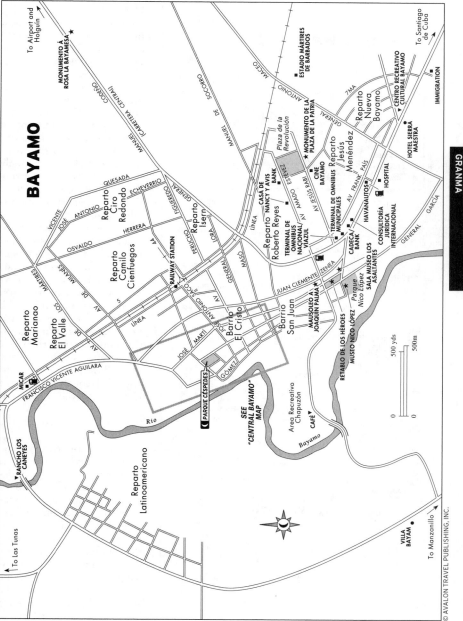

GRANMA

© AVALON TRAVEL PUBLISHING, INC.

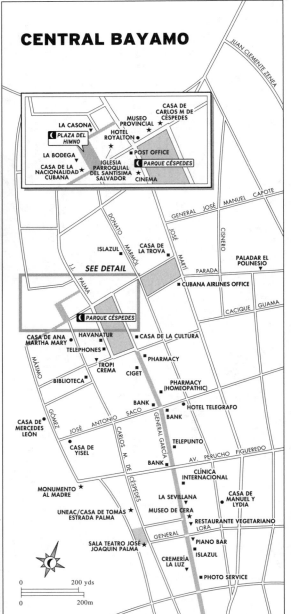

CENTRAL BAYAMO

CASA DE CARLOS M DE CÉSPEDES
MUSEO PROVINCIAL
LA CASONA
PLAZA DEL HIMNO
HOTEL ROYALTON
LA BODEGA
POST OFFICE
IGLESIA PARROQUIAL DEL SANTISIMA SALVADOR
CASA DE LA NACIONALIDAD CUBANA
PARQUE CÉSPEDES
CINEMA

JUAN CLEMENTE ZENEA

GENERAL JOSÉ MANUEL CAPOTE

DONATO

JOSÉ

CISNERO

ISLAZUL
CASA DE LA TROVA
MÁRMOL
MARTI
PARADA
PALADAR EL POLINESIO

SEE DETAIL
J.J. PALMA
CUBANA AIRLINES OFFICE

CACIQUE   GUAMA

PARQUE CÉSPEDES

CASA DE ANA MARTHA MARY
HAVANATUR
TELEPHONES
CASA DE LA CULTURA

MÁXIMO
TROPI CREMA
CIGET
PHARMACY

BIBLIOTECA
PHARMACY (HOMEOPATHIC)

GÓMEZ
BANK
SACO
HOTEL TELEGRAFO
BANK
CASA DE MERCEDES LEÓN
JOSÉ   ANTONIO

CARLOS   M.

GENERAL GARCÍA

TELEPUNTO
CASA DE YISEL
BANK
AV. PERUCHO FIGUEREDO

CLÍNICA INTERNACIONAL
MONUMENTO AL MADRE
DE CÉSPEDES
LA SEVILLANA
CASA DE MANUEL Y LYDIA
UNEAC/CASA DE TOMÁS ESTRADA PALMA
MUSEO DE CERA
GENERAL   LORA
RESTAURANTE VEGETARIANO
SALA TEATRO JOSÉ JOAQUIN PALMA
PIANO BAR
ISLAZUL
CREMERÍA LA LUZ
PHOTO SERVICE

0   200 yds
0   200m

History

Bayamo, the second settlement in Cuba, was founded in 1513 as Villa de San Salvador de Bayamo by Diego Velázquez on a site near contemporary Yara. It was later moved to its present site. Almost immediately Diego Velázquez set to enslaving the aboriginal Indian population with cross and cutlass. Black slaves began to arrive from Africa, increasingly so as sugar was planted, giving rise to a flourishing slave trade through the port of Manzanillo. Spain's monopolistic restrictions on trade also led to a flourishing illicit trade, and Bayameses from all walks of life were active in contraband.

In 1604, a force led by French pirate Gilbert Girón raided Bayamo and took hostage the Bishop of Cuba, Fray Juan de las Cabezas Altimirano. Rather than pay the ransom, the citizen-army stormed the pirate camp, killing the bishop in the process. However, they also managed to kill Girón. His head was proudly displayed in the main square.

By the 19th century, Bayamo's bourgeoisie were at the forefront of a swelling independence movement influenced by the American War of Independence and the revolutionary fervor then sweeping Europe. In 1867, following the coup that toppled Spain's Queen Isabella, Carlos Manuel de Céspedes and the elite of Bayamo rose in revolt. The action sparked the Ten Years War that swept the Oriente and central Cuba. Other nationalists rallied to the cause, formed a revolutionary junta, and in open defiance of Spanish authority, played in the parochial church the martial hymn that would eventually become the Cuban national anthem, "To the battle, Bayameses!" With a small force of about 150 men, Céspedes seized Bayamo from Spanish forces on October 20.

In January 1869, as Céspedes's army of mulattos, freed slaves, and poor whites was attacking Holguín, Spanish troops were at Bayamo's doorstep. The rebellious citizens burned their beloved Bayamo to the ground rather than cede it to Spanish troops. Alas, internal dissent arose among the revolutionary leadership and the Ten Years War fizzled. Spanish troops left Bayamo for a final time on April 28, 1898, when the city was captured by rebel leader General Calixto García during the War of Independence.

Orientation

Bayamo is laid out atop the eastern bluff of the Río Bayamo, which flows in a deep ravine. The historic core sits immediately above the gorge.

The Carretera Central (Carretera Manuel Cedeño) from Holguín enters Bayamo from the northeast and skirts the historic core as it sweeps southeast for Santiago. Avenida Perucho Figueredo leads off the Carretera Central and runs due west to Parque Céspedes. Calle General García—the main commercial street and a pedestrian precinct—leads south from Parque Céspedes, paralleled by Calles José Martí and Juan Clemente Zeneo to the east. To the south they merge with the Carretera Central. To the north they merge into Avenida Francisco Vicente Aguilera, which begins one block north of Parque Céspedes, swings west over the ravine of the lily-choked Río Bayamo, and leads to Las Tunas.

Museo de Cera CerArte

This mini Madame Toussaud's in the tropics (Calixto García #173, e/ Perucho Figueredo y General Lora, no tel.; Mon.–Fri. 9:30 A.M.– 1 P.M. and 2–4:30 P.M., Sat. 10:30 A.M.–2 P.M.;

free) is Cuba's only wax museum. It features some 70 waxworks, including life-size figures of world-renowned Cuban musicians Compay Segundo (real name Francisco Repilado) and Polo Montañez (real name Fernando Borrego), as well as foreigners ranging from Albert Einstein to Fabio di Celmo, the Italian tourist killed by a terrorist bomb in a Havana hotel in 1997. The figures are the work of self-taught artists Rafael Barrios Madrigal and his son Leander Barrios Milan (their wax portrait of Nat King Cole is on display at the Hotel Nacional in Havana).

Parque Céspedes

This beautiful square is surrounded by important buildings. At its center is a granite column topped by a larger-than-life bronze statue of the "Father of Our Country" (Céspedes). There's also a bust of the local patriot Perucho Figueredo (1819–70), inscribed with the words (in Spanish) he wrote for the *himno nacional*, "La Bayamesa":

To the battle, run, Bayamases
Let the fatherland proudly observe you
Do not fear a glorious death
To die for the fatherland is to live.

Céspedes was born on April 18, 1819, in a handsome two-story dwelling on the north side of the square. The house, **Casa Natal de Carlos Manuel de Céspedes** (Maceo #57, tel. 023/42-3864; Tues.–Fri. 9:30 A.M.–5 P.M., Sat. 9:30 A.M.–2 P.M. and 8–10 P.M., Sun. 10:30 A.M.–1 P.M.; CUC1) was one of only a fistful of houses to survive the fire of January 1869. Downstairs are letters, photographs, and maps, plus Céspedes's gleaming ceremonial sword. The ornately decorated upstairs bedrooms are full of his mahogany furniture. The law books that filled his study are still there, as is the printing press on which Céspedes published his *Cubana Libre*, the first independent newspaper in Cuba.

Next door is the **Museo Provincial** (Maceo #58, tel. 023/42-4125; Wed.–Mon. 9 A.M.–noon and 1–5 P.M., Sat.–Sun. noon–5 P.M.; CUC1), in the house where Manuel Muñoz Cedeño, composer of the *himno nacional,* was born.

On the east side is the house (now the Poder Popular) where, as president of the newly founded republic, Céspedes announced the abolition of slavery.

Parque Ñico López

Also known as Plaza de la Patria, this small plaza is named for a revolutionary hero who, along with 24 other members of Fidel Castro's rebels, suicidally attacked Batista's army barracks here on July 26, 1953. López survived and fled to Mexico, where he met Che Guevara and first introduced him to Fidel. He was killed shortly after landing in Cuba in 1956 aboard the *Granma.*

López is honored on the **Retablo de los Héroes** (Calles Martí and Amado Éstevez), a bas-relief in the center of the square; in the **Museo Ñico López** (Abihail Gonzaléz; Tues.–Sat. 8 a.m.–noon and 2–5 p.m., Sun. 9 a.m.–noon; CUC1), in the former barracks 100 meters southwest of the square; the tiny **Sala Museo Los Asaltantes** (Agusto Marquéz, tel. 023/42-3181; Tues.–Fri. 9 a.m.–5 p.m., Sat. noon–8 p.m., Sun. 8 a.m.–noon; CUC0.50), 50 meters east of the square; and on the **Plaza de la Revolución** (Avenida Jesús Rabi, east of the Carretera Central), where the **Monumento de la Plaza de la Patria** features a bas-relief of López, Fidel, and other heroes of the *Granma* landing.

◖ Plaza del Himno

Parque Céspedes opens to the northwest onto this charming plaza, dominated by the beautifully restored **Iglesia Parroquial del Santísima Salvador** (tel. 023/42-2514; Mon.–Fri. 9 a.m.–noon and 3–5 p.m., Sat. 9 a.m.–noon), a national monument also known as the Parroquial Mayor. The revolutionary national anthem was sung for the first time in the cathedral (by a choir of 12 women—the Bayamesas) during Corpus Christi celebrations on June 11, 1868, with the dumbfounded colonial governor in attendance. Its most admirable feature is the beautiful mural of Céspedes

Iglesia Parroquial del Santísima Salvador

and the Bayamesas above the altar. The church occupies the site of the original church, built in 1516, rebuilt in 1733, and rebuilt again following the fire of 1869. On the north side of the cathedral is a small chapel—**Capilla de la Dolorosa**—that dates back to 1630 and miraculously survived the fire. It has a Mudejar ceiling, a figure of Christ (now in a glass case), and a baroque altarpiece of gilt and laminated wood dedicated to the Virgen de Dolores. The original flag, sewn by Céspedes's wife, is preserved here.

The quaint **Casa de la Nacionalidad Cubana** (tel. 023/42-4833; Mon.–Fri. 8 a.m.–noon and 1–5 p.m., Sat. 8 a.m.–noon), on the west side, houses the town historian's office and displays period furniture.

Entertainment and Events

Fireworks and candles are lit each January 12 on Parque Céspedes to commemorate the burning of the town in 1869, and a procession of horses symbolizes the abandonment of Bayamo by its residents.

The lively **Casa de la Trova** (Martí, esq.

Maceo, tel. 023/42-5673; 9 A.M.–6 P.M. and 9 P.M.–2 A.M.; free by day, CUC1 at night) is fabulous for hearing traditional music.

Bolero is performed each Saturday at 4 P.M. at **UNEAC** (Céspedes #158, tel. 023/42-3670, www.uneac.com; free), in the Casa de Tomás Estrada Palma, where in 1835 Tomás Estrada Palma was born (he became the first president of Cuba following independence). Nearby, the **Sala Teatro José Joaquín Palma** (Céspedes, tel. 023/42-4423) hosts drama, children's theater, and folkloric performances. And the **Casa de la Cultura** (tel. 023/42-5917; daily 8:30 A.M.–5 P.M.), on the east side of Parque Céspedes, hosts cultural programs.

The elegant **Piano Bar** (General García, esq. Lora, tel. 023/42-4027; daily 2 P.M.–2 A.M.) has live music nightly; bring a sweater; it has a dress code. For charm, check out **La Bodega** (Plaza del Himno, tel. 023/42-7911; daily 10:30 A.M.–1 P.M. and 9 P.M.–1 A.M.), a Spanish-style *bodega* with seats made of barrels and cart wheels. It has live music in a rear patio overhanging the river canyon. A less lively but similar alternative is the nearby **La Casona** (Plaza del Himno; daily 8–10 A.M., noon–4 P.M., and 6 P.M.–midnight).

You can get your kicks at **Centro Recreativo Cultural Bayamo** (tel. 023/48-6918), opposite the Hotel Sierra Maestra, with a *cabaret espectáculo* Saturday–Sunday at 10:30 P.M. (CUC5 per pair). It has a children's show at 10 A.M.

Accommodations

Casas Particulares: Among the better town-center options is **Casa de Ana Martí Vázquez** (Céspedes #4, e/ Maceo y Canducha, tel. 023/42-4218; CUC15–25), a gracious home beautifully furnished throughout with antiques and chandeliers. The lounge opens to a shady stone patio. Ana hosts two rooms: One is like a honeymoon suite, with wooden pillars and a bed with canopy drape; the second room, entered by steep metal stairs, is gloomy yet still appealing.

Casa de Manuel y Lydia (Donato Mármol #323, e/ Figueredo y Lora, tel. 023/42-3175, nene19432001@yahoo.es; CUC15–20) offers a simply furnished, air-conditioned room with fan, double and single bed, and shared hot-water bathroom. A second air-conditioned room in an adjacent house opens to a spacious patio with a hammock and rockers and has an older private bathroom. It has parking.

Casa de "Yisel" (Saco #16, e/ Céspedes y Máximo Gómez, tel. 023/42-4973; CUC20) is a colonial home with an airy lounge with rockers, TV, and stereo system. The owners rent one air-conditioned room with fan and private hot-water bathroom off a patio arcaded with planters. It has parking.

I enjoyed my stay at **Casa de Nancy y Avis** (Calle Amado ésteves #67, e/ 8 y 9, Rpto. Jesús Menéndez, tel. 023/42-4726), a short walk from downtown. The delightful owners offer one small but pleasing air-conditioned room with fan and private bathroom with hot water; the mattress is soft, however. It has secure parking in a garden patio.

Hotels: The **Hotel Royalton** (Maceo #53, tel. 023/42-2290, fax 023/42-4792; CUC21 s, CUC27 d, CUC30 junior suite low season; CUC26 s, CUC33 d, CUC36 junior suite high season), on the west side of Parque Céspedes, is a pleasant bargain. An all-marble staircase leads to 33 small air-conditioned rooms with satellite TVs, telephones, firm mattresses, and small but modern private bathrooms. One room is for travelers with disabilities. (Islazul.)

Hotel Telígrafo (Saco #108, e/ García y Marmól, tel. 023/42-5510, fax 023/42-7389, www.ehtgr.co.cu; CUC15 s, CUC20 d, CUC30 suite year-round) functions as a hotel school. It has 12 air-conditioned rooms with lofty ceilings, contemporary furnishings, patios, and modern bathrooms. It has a diminutive bar and restaurant open to the street. (Formatur.)

If the above lodgings are full, try **Villa Bayamo** (Carretera de Manzanillo, tel. 023/42-3102; CUC14 s/d, CUC27 s/d cabins, CUC32 s/d suite), two kilometers west of Bayamo. It has 34 uninspired air-conditioned rooms and cabins with phones, TVs, radios, and refrigerators. It has a swimming pool and small nightclub. (Islazul.)

GRANMA

The Soviet-style **Hotel Carrusel Sierra Maestra** (Carretera Central Km 7.5, tel. 023/42-7970), three kilometers southeast of the city center, was being used exclusively for Latin American medical patients at last visit. (Cubanacán.)

Food

The nicest place by far is ⬤ **La Sevillana** (Calixto García #171, e/ Perucho Figueredo y General Lora, tel. 023/42-1462; noon–2 P.M. and 6–10 P.M. daily), an upscale Spanish-themed bar and restaurant serving garbanzo (CUC6), chicken in wine (CUC14), plus Cuban staples. The bar offers sangria, wines, and rum cocktails and is a nice place to tipple. The restaurant has separate dinner sittings 6–8 P.M. and 8–10 P.M.

Paladar El Polinesio (Parada #125, e/ Cisnero y Pío Rosaro, tel. 023/42-3860; noon–11 P.M.) has alfresco dining beneath the stars on an upstairs patio. It does a great salad for CUC2, and shrimp enchilada (CUC8).

Otherwise your best bet is the restaurant in the **Hotel Royalton,** serving snacks and simple *criollo* dishes for CUC2.70–8.90.

Vegans are offered relief at **Restaurante Vegetariano** (General García, esq. General Lora; Mon.–Fri. 7–9 A.M., noon–2:40 P.M., and 6–9:30 P.M.; Sat. noon–midnight; and Sun. 6–10:30 P.M.), which offers salads and dishes like stuffed eggplant.

Tropi Crema (8:40 A.M.–11 P.M.), on Parque Céspedes; and **Cremería La Luz** (General García, e/ Lora y Masó; Mon.–Fri. 10 A.M.–9:40 P.M., Sat.–Sun. 11 A.M.–11 P.M.) serve ice cream for pesos.

Information and Services

The **post office** (tel. 023/42-3305; Mon.–Sat. 9 A.M.–6 P.M.), on the west side of Parque Céspedes, has **DHL** service. **Etecsa** (daily 8:30 A.M.–9 P.M.), on the west side of Parque Céspedes, has international telephone service, but not Internet. The **Centro de Información Gestión y Tecnológica** (CIGET, tel. 023/42-5547; Mon.–Fri. 8:30 A.M.–8 P.M., Sat. 8:30 A.M.–noon), on General García 50 meters

south of Parque Céspedes, has Internet service (CUC5 per hour).

Banks include **Bandec** (General García, esq. Saco; and García, esq. Figueredo) and **Banco Popular** (General García, esq. Saco). You can also change foreign currency at **Cadeca,** on the Carretera Central, next to the bus station.

Hospital Carlos Manuel de Céspedes (Carretera Central Km 1.5, tel. 023/42-5012) is near the Hotel Sierra Maestra. There's a **Farmacia Internacional** (General García, e/ Figueredo y Lora, tel. 023/42-9596; Mon.–Fri. 8:30 A.M.–noon and 1–5 P.M., Sat. 8:30 A.M.–noon).

The **Consultoría Jurídica Internacional** (Carretera Central, e/ Av. Figueredo y Calle Segunda, tel. 023/42-7379; Mon.–Fri. 8:30 A.M.–noon and 1:30–5:30 P.M.) provides legal services.

Inmigración (Carretera Central y 7ma; Mon.–Tues. and Thurs.–Fri. 9 A.M.–noon and 1:30–4 P.M.) can issue *prórrogas.*

Getting There and Away

By Air: The **Aeropuerto Carlos Céspedes** (tel. 023/42-7506) is four kilometers northeast of town. A bus operates between the airport and the Terminal de Ómnibus. **Cubana** (Martí, esq. Parada, tel. 023/42-7507, or 023/42-3695 airport) flies between Havana and Bayamo twice weekly (CUC98).

By Bus: Buses arrive and depart the **Terminal de Ómnibus** (Carretera Central, esq. Augusta Márquez, tel. 023/42-4036). All the buses to and from Santiago and major cities throughout Cuba stop in Bayamo.

Astro buses depart Bayamo for Havana at 8 P.M. (CUC36 *especial,* CUC30 *regular*); and for Santiago at 6 A.M., 7:20 A.M., and 2:10 P.M. (CUC6). *Camiones* leave from an adjoining terminal; others leave from opposite the rail station.

Víazul buses depart Bayamo for Santiago de Cuba at 12:10 A.M., 4:45 A.M., 10 A.M., 11:20 A.M., and 6:10 P.M.; and westbound for Havana at 12:10 A.M., 11:10 A.M., and 5:25 P.M.; for Trinidad at 9:40 P.M.; and for Varadero at 10:40 P.M.

By Train: The **railway station** (Saco, esq. Línea, tel. 023/42-4955) is one kilometer west of the Carretera Central. Trains depart Bayamo for Havana at 7:40 P.M.; for Guantánamo at 4:25 A.M. and 3:25 P.M.; for Manzanillo at 9:55 A.M., 10:52 A.M., and 1:10 P.M.; and for Camagüey at 5:20 A.M. Train #13 departs Havana for Bayamo daily at 8:25 P.M. (14 hours, CUC25.40) and continues to Manzanillo at 9:55 A.M. Other trains for Bayamo depart Guantánamo at 7 A.M. and 5:55 P.M.; Manzanillo at 8:50 A.M., 2:15 P.M., and 5:20 P.M.; Santiago de Cuba at 6:25 A.M. and 8:30 A.M.; and Camagüey at 2:20 P.M.

By Car: You can rent cars from **Havana-utos** (Carretera Central, esq. José Menendez, tel. 023/42-7375), in the gas station; **Transtur** in the Hotel Royalton; and **Micar** (Aguilera #418), in the gas station two kilometers north of Parque Céspedes.

Getting Around

Coches and *bici-taxis* are everywhere, especially outside the rail and bus terminals. For a taxi, call **Cubataxi** (tel. 023/42-4313).

Julio César Aguilera (Cisnero #35, tel. 023/42-2553) is a multilingual Cubanacán tour guide who also freelances.

DOS RÍOS

The Carretera Central runs east from Bayamo across the Río Cauto floodplain. At Jiguaní, a nondescript town 26 kilometers east of Bayamo, a road leads north to Dos Ríos (Two Rivers), the holy site where José Martí, apostle of independence, national poet, indefatigable freedom fighter, and national hero, gave his life for the cause of independence.

On April 11, 1895, Martí had returned to Cuba from exile in the United States. On May 19, General Máximo Gómez's troops exchanged shots with a small Spanish column. Martí, as nationalist leader, was a civilian among soldiers. Gómez halted and ordered Martí and his bodyguard to place themselves to the rear. Martí, however, took off down the riverbank towards the Spanish column. His bodyguard took off after him—but too late.

obelisk at Dos Ríos, site of José Martí's martyrdom

Martí was hit in the neck by a bullet and fell from his horse without ever having drawn his gun. Revolutionary literature describes Martí as a hero who died fighting the enemy on the battlefield. In fact, he may have committed suicide for the sake of martyrdom.

Monumento Martí is a simple 10-meter-tall obelisk of whitewashed concrete in a trim garden of lawns and royal palms. White roses surround the obelisk, an allusion to his famous poem, *Versos Sencillos:* "*Cultivo una rosa blanca en julio como enero...*"A stone wall bears a 3-D bronze visage of Martí and the words, "When my fall comes, all the sorrow of life will seem like sun and honey." A plaque on the monument says simply, "He died in this place on May 19, 1895."

A tribute is held each May 19, when Cubans gather to pay their respects.

Accommodations and Food

Villa el Yarey (Jiguaní, tel. 042/7684; CUC35 s, CUC45 d) enjoys a breezy location atop Loma el Yarey, a massif offering

© CHRISTOPHER P. BAKER

GRANMA

360-degree views over the plains and towards the Sierra Maestra. This lodge has 14 thatched, wood-paneled cabins with soaring ceilings, terra-cotta floors, small single beds, satellite TV, and large modern bathrooms. The cabins are set amid cactus and trees full of old man's beard dangling like fishermen's nets. Birdsong is everywhere. The lobby hints of an African game lodge, and the swimming pool with swim-up bar is set amid a natural rock garden. To get here, take the road that leads north from the Carretera Central, seven kilometers east of Jiguaní. (Cubanacán.)

The Sierra Maestra

The Sierra Maestra hangs against the sky along the entire southern coast of Oriente, from the western foothills near Cabo Cruz eastward 130 kilometers to Santiago de Cuba. At its broadest, it is 50 kilometers north–south. The towering massif gathers in serried ranges that precede one another in an immense chain rising to Pico Turquino. It is forbidding terrain creased with steep ravines and boulder-strewn valleys. These mountains were the setting for the most ferocious battles in the fight to topple Batista (see the sidebar *The War in the Mountains* in this chapter).

Cut off from civilization down on the plains, the hardy mountain folk continue to eke out a subsistence living, supplemented by a meager income from coffee, carried on mules laden with wicker baskets. Small schools, rural clinics, and farm cooperatives have been built over the past four decades, but the majority of local peasants live together in thatched huts without running water.

PARQUE NACIONAL PICO TURQUINO

This 17,450-hectare national park is named for Pico Turquino, Cuba's highest mountain (1,974 meters). Hiking to the summit is popular with Cubans, almost like a pilgrimage. Fidel Castro had his guerrilla headquarters amid these serried slopes; the hike to La Comandancia is richly rewarding, as well as shorter and far less challenging than the hike up Pico Turquino.

These mountains are also important for their diversity of flora and fauna. At least 100 species of plants are found nowhere else, and an additional 26 are peculiar to tiny enclaves within the park. Antediluvian tree ferns and wispy bamboo are common. Orchids cover the trunks of semi-deciduous montane forest and centenarian conifers. Higher up is cloud forest, festooned with old man's beard, bromeliads, ferns, and vines, fed by mists that swirl through the forest primeval. Pico Turquino is even tipped by sub-*páramo* (marshy grassland) above 1,900 meters, with wind-sculpted, contorted dwarf species on exposed ridges.

The calls of birds—including the *tocororo* (the national bird)—explode like gunshots in the green silence of the jungle. Wild pigs and *jutías* exist in small numbers, but there are especially large numbers of reptiles and amphibians, including three species of frog found only on Pico Turquino.

Pico Turquino looms over, and is accessed via, the tiny community of **Santo Domingo,** on the east bank of the Río Yara (the village is accessed via a rickety log pedestrian-only bridge); Santo Domingo is 20 kilometers south of the sugarcane processing town of Bartolomé Masó (60 km southwest of Bayamo).

Santo Domingo was the setting for fierce fighting June–July 1958. The small **Museo Santo Domingo** (open by request; CUC1) features a 3-D model of the Sierra Maestra with a plan of the various battles and movements of Castro's and Batista's forces. Small arms and mortars are displayed.

From Santo Domingo the corrugated cement road climbs at an ever-increasing gradient: the last hundred meters is a breathtakingly steep climb with hairpin bends. After five kilometers the road ends at Alto del Naranjo (950 meters elevation), the trailhead to Pico Turquino and La Comandancia de la Plata. The drive back down is not for the fainthearted!

Entry to the park is permitted 7:30 A.M.–2:30 P.M. only. A guide is compulsory, arranged through the **Centro de Visitantes** (Visitors Center; daily 7 A.M.–5 P.M.), beside the road barrier—and entry point to the park—at Santo Domingo.

La Comandancia de la Plata

Fidel named his rebel army headquarters in the Sierra Maestra after the river whose headwaters were near his camp on a western spur ridge of Pico Turquino. The camp occupied a large forest clearing atop the crest, reached only by a single tortuous narrow track—a tough climb over rocks and mud. The wooden structures were well hidden at the edge of the clearing and covered with branches to conceal them from air attacks. Castro's house was built against the side of a ravine, with an escape route into the creek. It consisted of a bedroom with double bed for Fidel and Celia Sánchez, plus an office, a kitchen, and a deck, where Castro received visitors. In time, a small hospital (run by Che Guevara, who was a qualified doctor), a guest house, and a dental office were added. La Plata was also linked by field telephone to outlying rebel units and by radio to the rest of Cuba (a transmitter for Radio Rebelde loomed above the clearing).

Preserved as a museum, La Plata is reached by a ridgetop trail from Alto de Naranjo (3 km). Visits cost CUC11 per person (CUC10 per person for groups, CUC2 cameras, CUC5 videos), arranged at the Centro de Visitantes. No photographs are permitted between Campamento Medina (Km 1.5, where you must leave your camera with the ranger) and the Comandancia.

Hiking to Pico Turquino

From Alto de Naranjo it's 13 kilometers to the summit, from where the views are staggering. Even here you cannot escape the Revolution.

In 1952 soon-to-be revolutionary heroine Celia Sánchez and her liberal-minded father, Manuel Sánchez Silveira, hiked up Turquino carrying a bronze bust of José Martí, which they installed at the summit. In 1957 Sánchez made the same trek with a CBS news crew for an interview with Fidel beside the bust. It was Castro's first ascent of "El Pico." Che Guevara recorded how El Jefe checked his pocket altimeter to assure himself that Turquino was as high as the maps said it was.

The **Sendero Pico Turquino** begins at Alto de Naranjo, from where it's a rugged uphill hike. En route you'll pass through several remote communities, including Palma Mocha and Lima (which have campsites) and Aguada de Joaquín and El Cojo (which have shelters). Hikers normally overnight at Aguada de Joaquín, then set off before dawn for the five-kilometer climb to the peak before the clouds set in (usually by midmorning). It's possible to attain the peak and hike back in one day, but it is extremely arduous; most trekkers return to Aguada de Joaquín, then continue down the next day.

From the summit, you can also continue down the south side of the mountain to Las Cuevas by prearrangement, in which case a second guide will meet you at the summit. There are also two camps on the south side of the mountain, Pico Cuba and La Majagua (see *Hiking to Pico Turquino* in the *Santiago de Cuba* chapter). All campsites are at biological stations.

Hikers need to take their own food and plenty of water. You can buy packaged meals (CUC9) at Villa Santo Domingo. If you want to bring your own food, don't leave buying until the last minute, as there are no stores hereabouts! Warm clothing and waterproof gear are essential (heavy rains are frequent; the mountain weather is fickle and can change from sunshine to heavy clouds within minutes), as are a flashlight and bed roll.

Permits cost CUC33 per person, including guide and use of dormitory (there was no limit to the number of nights for this price at last visit). Tip the guides!

Accommodations and Food

Serving Cubans and backpackers, the riverside

THE WAR IN THE MOUNTAINS

Between 1956 and 1959, the Sierra Maestra was the headquarters for Castro's rebel army. Fidel and Raúl Castro, Che Guevara, and a ragged band of survivors from the ill-fated *Granma* landing stumbled into the Sierra Maestra in December 1956. Here Fidel intended to establish and fashion a revolutionary army drawn from the peasantry and deal blows to Batista's army. "The story of how Castro was able to recover from a terrible initial defeat, regroup, fight, start winning against Batista units, and form an ultimately victorious rebel army is the story of the extraordinary support he received from Sierra Maestra peasants," writes Tad Szulc in *Fidel: A Critical Portrait*. It wasn't difficult: Batista's troops tortured destitute peasants, who rallied to the cause, providing shelter and serving as conduits for supplies.

GAINING GROUND

The initial year in the mountains was difficult. The tiny rebel band won small skirmishes with Batista's troops, but gained their major coup on February 16, 1957, when Herbert L. Matthews of the *New York Times* was led into the mountains to meet the next day with Castro. Matthews' report hit the newsstands on February 24. It began, "Fidel Castro, the rebel leader of Cuba's youth, is alive and fighting hard and successfully in the rugged, almost impenetrable vastness of the Sierra Maestra." Batista had lifted censorship the week before, and Matthews's story ran as lead headlines in Cuba, creating a sensation that Castro milked by releasing his *Appeal to the People of Cuba*, a manifesto calling for violent uprising against the regime.

Castro had established a base at La Plata, on the northwest slope of Pico Turquino. The rebel army consolidated its control of the mountains throughout 1957. The first real battle occurred on May 28, when Castro and a force of 80 men came down from the mountains and attacked a garrison at El Uvero, on the coast. They lost six men but gained two machine guns and 46 rifles.

In early 1958, the rebel army split into four separate units. Castro continued to lead from La Plata, Che Guevara held the northern slopes, Camilo Cienfuegos led a group on the plains near Bayamo, and Raúl Castro opened a

Campismo La Sierrita (tel. 023/52326; CUC16 up to four people), about six kilometers south of Bartolomé Masó, has 27 simple four-person cabins with bunks. There's a basic restaurant but I recommend bringing your own food. It often fills up on weekends. You can make reservations c/o **Campismo Popular** (General García #112, tel. 023/42-4200) in Bayamo.

Villa Balcón de la Sierra (tel. 023/56-5535; CUC24 s/d room, CUC31 s/d suite low season; CUC28 s/d room, CUC35 s/d suite high season), on a windswept hillock 800 meters south of Bartolomé Masó, is a basic facility with 20 air-conditioned *cabinas* with meager and jaded furniture, and sagging, stained mattresses. However, the so-called "suite" (merely a large room) above the restaurant is nicely furnished and has a modern bathroom; a balcony offers spectacular views. The elegant **Restaurant Los Pinos** (7 A.M.–10 P.M. daily) overlooks a swimming pool. It serves basic criollo fare for less than CUC5.

Villa Santo Domingo (tel. 059/56-5613, vstdomingo@islazul.grm.tur.cu; CUC29 s, CUC34 d low season; CUC32 s, CUC37 d high season including breakfast), on the banks of the river beside the visitors center in Santo Domingo, has 20 modestly decorated air-conditioned cabins, each with two single beds and a refrigerator. It also has 10 two-person tents pitched on a canopied deck (CUC3 per person). There's a bar, game room, video room, and an open-air riverside restaurant serving *criollo* staples. (Islazul.)

You can also book Villa Balcón and Villa Santo Domingo c/o **Islazul** (General García #207, e/ Masó y Lora, tel. 023/42-3273, comercial@islazul.grm.tur.cu) in Bayamo.

new front in the mountains near Santiago. By spring the rebel army had control of most of the mountain regions of Oriente. The enemy was being denied more and more territory. And a radio station – Radio Rebelde – was set up to broadcast revolutionary messages to the nation. All the while, Castro was kept abreast of rival groups in Havana and worked assiduously to maintain control of the opposition.

VICTORY

In May 1958 Batista launched an all-out attack – Operation FF (*Fin de Fidel*) – using air strikes, naval bombardments, and 10,000 troops. However, Fidel's peasant-based rebel army knew "every path in the forest, every turn in the road, and every peasant's house in the immensely complicated terrain." To Fidel, "Every entrance to the Sierra Maestra is like the pass at Thermopylae, and every narrow passage becomes a death trap."

For three months they skirmished. By June 19, Castro's troops were virtually surrounded atop their mountain retreat. The rebels rained mortars down into the valley, along with a psychological barrage of patriotic songs and exhortations blasted over loudspeakers to demoralize Batista's tired troops, many of whom switched sides (some were spies; when caught, they were summarily executed). Then at the battle of Jigue, which lasted 10 days, Castro's rebels defeated a battalion whose commander, Major José Quevedo, joined the rebels. Batista's army collapsed and began to retreat in disarray.

By the time Batista's offensive collapsed, Castro and his meager force of peasant soldiers had captured tanks, along with hundreds of modern weapons. Radio Rebelde broadcast details of the victories to anxious Cubans. Castro then launched his counteroffensive. In August 1958 Castro's troops came down out of the mountains to seize, in swift order, Baire, Jiguaní, Maffo, Contramaestre, and Palma Soriano. On January 2, 1959, the rebel army entered Santiago de Cuba. Castro walked up the stairs of the Moncada barracks to accept the surrender of Batista's army in Oriente at the very site where he had initiated his armed insurrection six years before.

GRANMA

Getting There

A bus departs Masó for Santo Domingo on Tuesday at 6 A.M. and departs Santo Domingo for Masó at 4 A.M.

A taxi from Bayamo costs about CUC25 each way (save paying until you arrive, otherwise the driver might let you off too soon to avoid the daunting hills that precede Santo Domingo).

South of Masó, the concrete road climbs steadily, getting steeper and steeper as it ascends to Providencia, a little village in the lee of a river valley. Turn left at the T junction for Santo Domingo (8 km) and Parque Nacional Pico Turquino (the village of Providencia is hidden off to the right). In places the road descends precipitously into river valleys. Good brakes are essential!

Manzanillo to Cabo Cruz

MANZANILLO

Manzanillo (pop. 105,000) extends along three kilometers of shorefront on the Gulf of Guacanayabo. In colonial days, it was a smuggling port and a center of slave trading. Later the city became the main underground base for Castro's rebel army in the late 1950s (Celia Sánchez coordinated the secret supply routes and information network from here, under the noses of Batista's troops and spies). Today the weatherworn town functions as a fishing port where shrimp and lobster are landed. Many

GRANMA

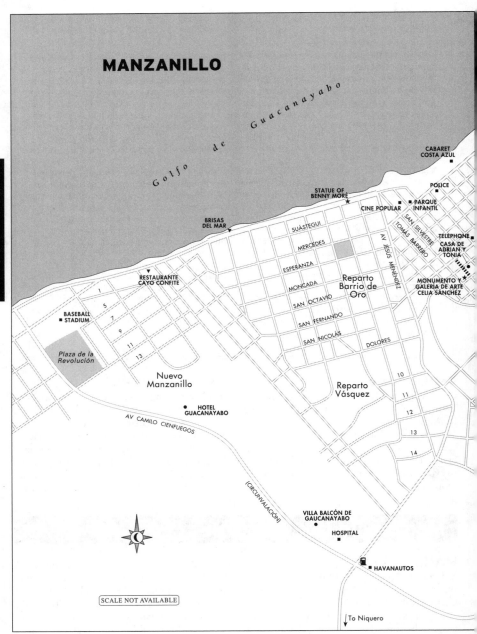

MANZANILLO

Golfo de Guacanayabo

CABARET
COSTA AZUL

POLICE

STATUE OF
BENNY MORÉ
CINE POPULAR
PARQUE
INFANTIL

SAN SILVESTRE

TOMÁS BARRERO

BRISAS
DEL MAR

SUÁSTEGUI

MERCEDES

TELEPHONE

CASA DE
ADRIAN Y
TONIA

ESPERANZA

AV JESÚS MENÉNDEZ

RESTAURANTE
CAYO CONFITE

Reparto
Barrio de
Oro

MONCADA

MONUMENTO Y
GALERÍA DE ARTE
CELIA SÁNCHEZ

SAN OCTAVIO

BASEBALL
STADIUM

1

5

7

9

11

13

SAN FERNANDO

SAN NICOLÁS

DOLORES

Plaza de la
Revolución

10

Nuevo
Manzanillo

Reparto
Vásquez

11

12

HOTEL
GUACANAYABO

13

AV CAMILO CIENFUEGOS

14

(CIRCUNVALACIÓN)

VILLA BALCÓN DE
GAUCANAYABO

HOSPITAL

HAVANAUTOS

SCALE NOT AVAILABLE

To Niquero

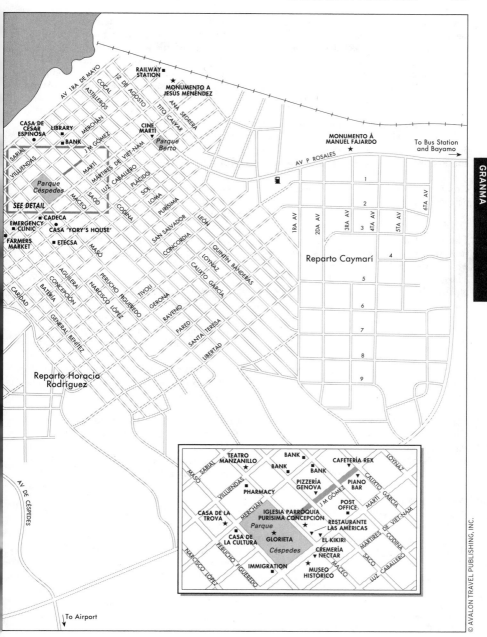

GRANMA

RAILWAY STATION ■

★ MONUMENTO A JESÚS MENÉNDEZ

AV 1RA DE MAYO
CORAL
ASTILLEROS
12 DE AGOSTO
TITO CALVAR
ANA SEGRERA

CASA DE CÉSAR ESPINOSA ●
LIBRARY ■
MERCHÁN
J M GÓMEZ
■ BANK

CINE MARTÍ
Parque Berto

SARIAL
VILLUENDAS
MÁRTIRES DE VIET-NAM
MARTÍ
LUZ CABALLERO
PLÁCIDO
SOL

Parque Céspedes

MACEO
SACO
CODINA
LOMA
PURÍSIMA

SEE DETAIL

■ CADECA
EMERGENCY ■ CLINIC
CASA 'YORY'S HOUSE'
SAN SALVADOR
CONCORDIA
LEÓN

FARMERS MARKET ■
■ ETECSA
MASÓ
QUINTÍN BANDERAS
LOYNÁZ

CARIDAD
AGUILERA
CONCEPCIÓN
BATERÍA
NARCISO LÓPEZ
PERUCHO FIGUEREDO
TÍVOLI
GERONA
RAVENO
PARED
SANTA TERESA
LIBERTAD
CALIXTO GARCÍA

GENERAL BENÍTEZ

Reparto Horacio Rodríguez

MONUMENTO A MANUEL FAJARDO ★

To Bus Station and Bayamo →

AV P ROSALES

1
2
3
4
5
6
7
8
9

1RA AV
2DA AV
3RA AV
4TA AV
5TA AV
6TA AV

Reparto Caymarí

AV DE CÉSPEDES

↓ To Airport

TEATRO MANZANILLO ★
BANK ■
BANK ■
CAFETERÍA REX ▼

BANK ■

MASÓ
SARIAL
VILLUENDAS
MERCHÁN

PHARMACY ■

PIZZERÍA GENOVA ▼
PIANO BAR ▼

J M GÓMEZ
CALIXTO GARCÍA
LOYNÁZ
MARTÍ

CASA DE LA TROVA ★

IGLESIA PARROQUIA PURÍSIMA CONCEPCIÓN ★
Parque

POST OFFICE ■

RESTAURANTE LAS AMÉRICAS ▼

MÁRTIRES DE VIET-NAM
CODINA

NARCISO LÓPEZ
PERUCHO FIGUEREDO

CASA DE LA CULTURA ★
GLORIETA ★
Céspedes

EL KIKIRI ▼
CREMERÍA NECTAR ▼

SACO
MACEO
LUZ CABALLERO

IMMIGRATION ■

MUSEO HISTÓRICO ★

buildings have been influenced by Moorish design. In Barrio de Oro, the cobbled streets are lined with rickety wooden houses where elders play dominoes or rock beneath sagging eaves with cactus growing between the faded roof tiles. Don't be surprised to chance upon a street organ being played—the tradition is strong here.

The **Malecón** seafront boulevard, to the northwest of the town, features a life-size bronze statue of Cuban crooner Benny Moré and a seawall lined with life-size figures of women in various poses. Offshore, the easternmost cays of the Jardines de la Reina archipelago float on the horizon.

Orientation

The road from Bayamo enters Manzanillo from the east as Avenida Rosales, which runs west to the shore, fronted by Avenida 1 de Mayo and the Malecón and paralleled five blocks inland by Avenida Martí. These roads run west to Avenida Jesús Menéndez, which climbs southward and continues to Cabo Cruz and Marea del Portillo. The old city lies within this quadrangle.

To the east the city Avenida Camilo Cienfuegos (the *circunvalación*) runs south from Avenida Rosales, intersects Avenida Jesús Menéndez, and drops to the Malecón.

Parque Céspedes

City life revolves around this handsome square bounded by Martí, Maceo, Marchen, and Masó. Music is piped into the square, which has little stone sphinxes at each corner and is ringed by royal palms and Victorian-era lampposts. The most notable feature is an Islamic-style *glorieta* (bandstand) inlaid with cloisonné.

The **Iglesia Parróquia Purísima Concepción** (Mass Tues. at 4 P.M., Wed. and Fri. at 7 A.M., Thurs. and Sat. at 8:15 P.M., and Sun. at 7:30 A.M. and 9 A.M.), on Maceo, is a 19th-century church with beautiful barrel-vaulted ceiling and elaborate gilt altar. It was being restored at last visit.

The **Casa de la Cultura** (Masó #82, tel.

023/54210; 8 A.M.–6 P.M. daily; free), on the south side in an impressive colonial building with stunning tile work. Inside the latter is a roofless courtyard with mosaics of Columbus's landing and Don Quixote tilting at windmills.

On the east side, the **Museo Histórico** (Martí #226, tel. 023/52053; Tues.–Fri. 9 A.M.–noon and 2–6 P.M., Sat.–Sun. 8 A.M.–noon and 6–10 P.M.; free) displays cannon and antiques.

Monumento Celia Sánchez

Manzanillo's main attraction takes up two entire blocks along Caridad (e/ Martí y Luz Caballero), where a terra-cotta tile staircase is graced to each side with ceramic murals and ceramic sunflowers inset in the walkway. At the top is the striking ceramic monument to Celia Manduley Sánchez. Fresh-cut flowers are kept at its base. To one side is a tiny room with a few portraits and personal effects (Mon.–Fri. 8 A.M.–noon and 2–6 P.M., Sat. 8 A.M.–noon; free) dedicated to the memory of *"La más hermosa y autóctona flor de la Revolución"* (the most beautiful native flower of the Revolution). (See the sidebar *Revolutionary Heroes* in the *Essentials* chapter.)

The **Plaza de la Revolución** (Av. Camilo Cienfuegos) has a bas-relief mural of Celia Sánchez and other revolutionary heroes.

Entertainment and Events

The **Casa de la Cultura** (tel. 023/54210; 8 A.M.–6 P.M.; free), on the main square, holds music performances and cultural events, as does the **Casa de la Trova** (Merchan #213, esq. Masó, tel. 023/55423; Tues.– Sun. nights; free).

Piano Bar Mi Manzanillo (J. M. Gómez, esq. Calixto García, tel. 023/55312; Tues.–Sun. 2 P.M.–2 A.M.; free) is surprisingly elegant; a dress code applies. A quartet plays jazz, *música filín*, and even salsa.

The open-air **Costa Azul** (Av. 1ra de Mayo, esq. Narciso López, tel. 023/53158) has a *cabaret espectáculo* Friday–Sunday at 10 P.M. (CUC1), followed by a disco. The bar is in a ship hauled ashore!

Teatro Manzanillo (Villuendas, esq. Maceo, tel. 023/52973; 5 pesos), dating to 1856 and lovingly restored, hosts ballet, drama, and other cultural programs, including matinees.

Baseball games are hosted October–May at **Estadio Wilfredo Pages,** off Avenida Céspedes.

Accommodations

There were four *casas particulares* in town at last visit. My favorite is ◖ **Casa de Adrian y Tonia** (Mártires de Viet Nam #49, esq. Caridad, tel. 023/53028; CUC20–25), a delightful house with a nice TV lounge with rockers and a balcony overlooking the stairs to the Monumento Celia Sánchez. The owners rent a splendid independent cross-ventilated, air-conditioned apartment upstairs with fans, huge arcing closet, and a modern bathroom plus roof terrace with an arbor of vines and a tiny inflatable pool for cooling off on hot days.

Casa "Yory's House" (Pedro Figueredo #121, e/ Luz Caballero y Mártires de Viet Nam, tel. 023/52127; CUC25) offers two spacious, air-conditioned rooms with fans and firm mattresses. They share a bathroom with hot water. The family is pleasant. Guests get use of the TV lounge.

An also-ran is **Casa de César y Blanca** (Sariol #245, e/ Saco y Dr. Codina, c/o tel. 023/57-8218; CUC20–25), a colonial house with a TV lounge and one spacious upstairs room with meager furnishings and private hot-water bathroom.

The uninspired **Hotel Guacanayabo** (Av. Camilo Cienfuegos, tel. 023/54012) and adjoining **Villa Balcón de Guacanayabo** were being used exclusively for Operación Milagro at last visit.

Food

Manzanillo is a culinary wasteland and lacks legal *paladares.*

The simple but pleasant **Pizzería Genova** (Gómez, e/ Saco y Codina; daily 7 A.M.–9:30 P.M.) offers simple spaghettis and pizzas for pesos.

Several no-frills eateries around Parque Céspedes include **Restaurante Las Américas** (tel. 023/53043; 6:45 A.M.–10 P.M. daily) on the northeast corner. It offers basic *criollo* dishes for CUC3 or less.

Cafetería El Kikiri (Martí, e/ Maceo y Masó; 10 A.M.–10 P.M. daily) is a snack bar selling ice creams.

You can buy fresh produce at the *mercado agropecuario* (Martí, e/ Batería y Concepción).

Information and Services

The **post office** is on Martí (e/ Saco y Codina). **Etecsa** (Narciso López seq. Luz Caballero) has international phone service, as does the *minimpunto* (Benitez esq. Martí).

Banks include **Bandec** (Marchan, esq. Codina) and **Banco Popular** (Marchan, esq. Codina; Machan, esq. Calixto). You can also change foreign currency at **Cadeca** (Martí #184, e/ Figueredo y Narciso López).

Hospital Celia Sánchez (Circunvalación y Av. Jesús Menéndez, tel. 023/54011) is on the west side of town. There's a 24-hour **Policlínico de Urgencia** (Aguilera, esq. Martí, tel. 023/57538) for emergencies.

The **police station** is on Villimedas (e/ Aguilera y Concepción). **Inmigración** (Martí, esq. Masó) can issue *prórrogas.*

Getting There and Away

The **Aeropuerto Sierra Maestra** (tel. 023/53019) is 10 kilometers southeast of town on the road to Cayo Espino. **Cubana** (tel. 023/54984 airport) flies to Manzanillo from Havana twice weekly (CUC98).

The **bus terminal** (Av. Rosales, tel. 023/53404) is two kilometers east of town. **Astro** buses depart Manzanillo for Bayamo twice daily (CUC1.80) and daily for Havana (CUC29) and Pilón (CUC3). *Camiones* depart from the bus station, and from the junction of Camilo Cienfuegos and Avenida Jesús Menéndez (southbound only).

The **railway station** (tel. 023/52195) is at the far north end of Avenida Marchan. Trains depart Manzanillo daily for Bayamo at 5:20 P.M. (CUC1.70), and for Havana (CUC28) and Santiago (CUC5.75).

GRANMA

Getting Around

You can rent a car from **Havanautos** (Camilo Cienfuegos and Av. Jesús Menéndez, tel. 023/57204) next to the gas station. There's another gas station on Avenida Rosales (esq. Av. 1ra).

Cubataxi (tel. 023/54922) offers taxi service.

MANZANILLO TO NIQUERO

The coastal plains south of Manzanillo are awash in lime-green sugarcane rippling in the breeze like sheets of silk.

Entronque Pilón, about 60 kilometers southwest of Manzanillo, is an important junction where a road leads east to Pilón, Marea del Portillo, and Santiago de Cuba. Continue straight, however, and you'll arrive at **Niquero,** unique for its ramshackle buildings in French-colonial style, lending it a similarity to parts of New Orleans and Key West. Note the **Communist Party headquarters,** one block from the main square, in a fabulous art nouveau building. Niquero has a gas station (selling *regular* gas only), two banks, and a *telepunto,* all on the main street south of the Hotel Niquero.

Hurricane Dennis did considerable damage along this shore in July 2005.

Criadero de Cocodrilos

This crocodile farm (Mon.–Fri. 7 A.M.–4 P.M.; CUC1), about five kilometers south of Manzanillo, has about 1,200 American crocodiles in algae-filled ponds. They're separated by age. A guide will lead you around, but you'll need to ask probing questions to learn about the reptile's fascinating ecology. Tip the guide.

Museo Celia Sánchez

This museum (Av. Podio #11, tel. 023/59-3466; Tues.–Sun. 9 A.M.–5 P.M.; CUC1), in the sugar-processing town of Media Luna, 50 kilometers southwest of Manzanillo, occupies a simple green-and-white gingerbread wooden house where Celia Sánchez was born on May 9, 1920. It is dedicated to the revolutionary heroine's life.

FOR WHOM THE BELL TOLLS

Since independence, the La Demajagua bell had been entrusted to Manzanillo as a national shrine. In November 1947, a politically ambitious law student named Fidel Castro thought the bell would toll well for him. He arranged for the venerable 300-pound bell to be brought to Havana to be pealed in an anti-government demonstration. Castro accompanied the bell from Manzanillo to Havana, to great popular fanfare. The bell was placed in the Gallery of Martyrs in the university, but disappeared overnight, presumably at the hands of President Grau's police. Castro, who may have set up the theft himself, took to the airwaves denouncing the corrupt Grau government.

Several days later, the bell was delivered "anonymously" to President Grau and was immediately sent back to Manzanillo. The incident was over, but young Castro had achieved new fame as Cuba's most promising rising political star.

Media Luna's town park has a fountain with a **statue of Celia Sánchez** sitting atop rocks with her shoeless feet in the trickling water.

Museo Histórico La Demajagua

La Demajagua (Mon.–Sat. 8 A.M.–noon and 1–5 P.M., Sun. 8 A.M.–noon; CUC1), 13 kilometers south of Manzanillo, was the sugar estate owned by Carlos Manuel de Céspedes, the nationalist revolutionary who on October 10, 1868, unilaterally freed his slaves and called for rebellion against Spain (see the sidebar *Heroes of the Wars of Independence* in the *Background* chapter). His house (of which only the original floor remains) is now a museum (closed for restoration at last visit). The eclectic displays include the revolutionary Flag of Céspedes, and period weaponry.

A path leads to a monument of fieldstone in a walled amphitheater encircling two venerable trees and remnants of the original sugar

The land stair-steps 507 meters up toward the Sierra Maestra in a series of marine terraces left high and dry over the eons by receding sea levels. More than 80 percent of the park is covered by virgin woodland. Floral and faunal species are distinct. Drier areas preserve cacti more than 400 years old. Two endemic species of note are the blue-headed quail dove and the Cuban Amazon butterfly. Even endangered manatees are occasionally seen in the swampy coastal lagoons. It was recently named a UNESCO World Heritage Site and is fabulous for hiking and bird-watching.

Two trails are signed on the road. The **Sendero Morlotte-Fustete** leads to cavern systems. The more popular **Sendero Arqueológico Natural El Guafe,** about eight kilometers south of the entrance, also leads through mangroves and scrub to caverns containing dripstone formations. One—the Idolo del Agua—is thought to have been shaped by pre-Columbian Taínos.

The park is named for the spot where Fidel and Raúl Castro, Che Guevara, and 79 other revolutionaries came ashore at the southern end of Playa las Coloradas on December 2, 1956. The exact spot where the *Granma* ran aground is one kilometer south of the hamlet of Las Colorados. Here, the **Monumento de Desembarcadero** consists of a replica of the *Granma* (the original is in the Museo de la Revolución in Havana), a plaza, and a tiny museum (entrance CUC1, cameras CUC2, videos CUC5) with a few photos, rifle, and a map showing the route of the *desembarcaderos* into the Sierra Maestra.

A concrete pathway leads 1.8 kilometers through the mangroves to the exact spot where the *Granma* bogged down. Bring insect repellent!

the "Liberty Bell" at La Demajagua

© CHRISTOPHER P. BAKER

mill. Here a plaque bears inspirational words of Céspedes, José Martí, and Fidel Castro. Inset in the wall is La Demajagua bell, the Cuban equivalent of the American Liberty Bell, which Céspedes rang at his estate to mark the opening of the 1868 War of Independence.

Accommodations

The pleasant ◖ **Hotel Niquero** (tel. 023/59-2367; CUC16 s, CUC20 d low season; CUC22 s, CUC28 d high season), on the main street of Niquero, offers 26 rooms with colonial tile floors, elegant furnishings, and large, modern bathrooms. It has an appealing restaurant, and a rooftop bar. (Islazul.)

◖ PARQUE NACIONAL DESEMBARCO DEL GRANMA

This park (CUC3 entrance, payable at a checkpoint 1 km south of the hamlet of Las Colorados, about 20 km south of Niquero; passport required) protects the southwestern most tip of Cuba, from Cabo Cruz to Punta Hicacos, 40 kilometers farther east.

Cabo Cruz

The lonesome, badly potholed road south from Las Colorados dips and rises through dense scrubland; twists around **Laguna Guafes,** where wading birds jab for crustaceous food; and ends at the ramshackle fishing village of Cabo Cruz, the southwesterly tip of Cuba. Here, the **Faro Cabo Cruz,** built of limestone in 1871, rises 33 meters and contains a few exhibits. The lighthouse keeper in the adjoining building will open up on demand and let you clamber to the top for stupendous 360-degree vistas over the park and the teal-blue Caribbean.

A plaque inset in a rock atop the cliff states that Christopher Columbus arrived here in May 1494.

Accommodations

Campismo Villas Las Colorados, at Playa Las Colorados, was destroyed by Hurricane Dennis and was being rebuilt at last visit. (Cubamar.)

The South Coast

From Entronque Pilón, a scenic road cuts through the western foothills of the Sierra Maestra and drops down through a narrow pass to emerge on the coastal plains near Pilón, where a gas station is the last gas station before Santiago de Cuba, about 200 kilometers to the east.

PILÓN

The flyblown fishing (and, until recently, sugar-processing) town of Pilón sits in a bowl ringed on three sides by mountains and on the fourth by the Caribbean Sea. The land west of Pilón is smothered in now-dying sugarcane. This is the last greenery you'll see for a while; east of Pilón, the land lies in the rain shadow of the Sierra Maestra and is virtually desert. Tall cacti appear, and goats and white zebu cattle graze hungrily amid stony pastures.

Casa Museo Celia Sánchez

This clapboard house (Conrado Benitez #20, tel. 023/59-4507; Mon.–Fri. 8 A.M.–noon and 1–5 P.M., Sat. 8 A.M.–noon; CUC1) in gaily painted Caribbean vernacular style was used by Celia Sánchez as a base for her underground supply network for Castro's rebel army. Exhibits deal with the area's aboriginal history and revolutionary literacy campaign, as well as the revolutionary heroine's life.

Accommodations

Motel El Mirador (tel. 023/59-4365; CUC10 s, CUC15 d), about five kilometers east of Pilón, sits on the mountainside and offers fabulous views from its four simple cabins and thatch-roofed restaurant.

MAREA DEL PORTILLO

Fifteen kilometers east of Pilón the mountains shelve gently to a wide scimitar bay rimmed by a deep two-kilometer-wide beach of pebbly gray-brown sand. A small down-at-the-heels fishing village is hidden within a cove at the northeast end of the bay, where mountains clamber down to the sea. Marea del Portillo is favored by budget-minded Canadian and European charter groups, but the beach isn't the prettiest and facilities are limited to the two resorts.

Activities

Water sports and scuba diving are offered at **Marlin Albacora Dive Center** (tel. 023/59-7034), between the Club Amigo resorts. Dive sites include the wreck of the *Cristóbal Colón,* a Spanish warship sunk in the war of 1898 and lying just 20 meters from shore. Dives cost CUC30.

Horseback rides cost CUC5 one hour, CUC3 each additional hour, and CUC35 for a half-day excursion to a waterfall.

Accommodations

Cubanacán operates three hotels, including the humble **Villa Punta Piedra** (tel. 023/59-7032; CUC17.50 s, CUC25 d year-round), five kilometers west of Marea. It has 13 spacious air-conditioned villas with views over a tiny beach. There are a restaurant and bar and café, and a disco draws Cubans. At last visit, it was in bad shape following Hurricane Dennis and is a place to rest overnight rather than to vacation.

The all-inclusive beachfront **Club Amigo Marea del Portillo** (tel. 023/59-7103, fax 023/59-7080, recepcion@marea.co.cu; per person CUC30 low season, CUC40 high season) has 70 air-conditioned rooms and four suites plus 56 *cabinas,* all pleasantly furnished and with satellite TVs plus patios or balconies onto the beach. There's a restaurant, bar, shop, car rental, swimming pool, and simple cabaret.

The fancier hillside **Club Amigo Farallon del Caribe** (same contact information; per person CUC35 low season, CUC45 high season) looks down literally and figuratively upon its smaller sibling. The 140 air-conditioned rooms, enfolding a swimming pool with swim-up bar, have satellite TV and splendid vistas. Facilities include disco and cabaret, car rental, shop, and entertainment.

Getting There, Away, and Around

A crowded *camión* runs between Pilón and Santiago de Cuba on alternate days.

You can rent cars at the Club Amigo properties, and through **Cubacar** (tel. 023/59-7185, fax 023/59-7027). **Palmares** rents scooters (CUC8 one hour, CUC3 each extra hour, CUC26 all day). *Coches* charge CUC3 for a tour of the nearby fishing village.

Excursions are offered at Club Amigo.

If driving from Bayamo, you can reach Marea via a road that crosses the Sierra Maestra, beginning in Bartolomé Masó and passing through the mountain communities of San Lorenzo and La Habanita. It's a rugged and challenging but magnificent drive best tackled by four-wheel drive and in dry season.

MAREA DEL PORTILLO TO SANTIAGO DE CUBA PROVINCE

The rugged coast that links Marea del Portillo and Santiago de Cuba is a stunner—to my mind the most exhilarating drive in all Cuba. The journey begins in earnest east of Marea del Portillo, 40 kilometers east of Entronque Pilón. The paved road hugs the coast the whole way, climbing over steep headlands and dropping through river valleys. The teal blue sea is your constant companion, with the Sierra Maestra pushing up close on the other side. There are no villages or habitations for miles, and no services whatsoever. Landslides occasionally block the long, lonesome road. In late 2005, much of the road had been washed away and the makeshift road ran along the beach in places. It may be impassable at high tide and in storms. Check ahead.

In springtime, giant land crabs march across the road in fulfillment of the mating urge. Amazingly, the battalions even scale vertical cliffs. The bases of the steepest cliffs become graveyards that are a veritable potlatch of crabmeat for vultures. Drive with care, for the broken shells can damage tires. This is no place for a puncture.

The bridge over the Río Macio, 15 kilometers from Marea, marks the border with Santiago de Cuba Province. See *Santiago to Chivirico* in the *Santiago de Cuba* chapter for more information.

GRANMA

SANTIAGO DE CUBA

Santiago de Cuba Province is one of the most interesting and historically important regions in the country. In fact, the province claims to be the Cradle of the Revolution. The first charge of machete-wielding *Mambí* was at Baire in 1868. And in 1953 Fidel Castro's attack on Batista's barracks took place at Moncada, in the city of Santiago, initiating the Revolution that six years later brought him to power.

The namesake capital city, second only to Havana in size, is distinctive in mood and teems with sites of historical and cultural interest, from a castle and the 16th-century house where Diego Velázquez governed Cuba to a notable cathedral and the Moncada barracks. Nearby there are beaches and such attractions as Parque Bacanao, featuring a cactus garden, an aquarium, a crocodile farm, and the pre-historic world of Valle de la Prehistoria; and Parque Nacional Gran Piedra, reached by a circuitous road that leads through cool pine forest to a splendid garden perched atop a peak at over 1,200 meters. Another well-known haunt is the holy shrine of El Cobre.

The Santiagüeros carry themselves here with a certain lassitude and speak in a lilting tongue with a musical tone. French and African words appear, a legacy of the many French and Haitian families that settled here in the late 18th century. Santiago (and adjacent Guantánamo Province) has the highest percentage of African blood in Cuba. Though the traditional architecture is mostly Spanish, the faces are mostly black. Such musical forms as *son* were birthed here, and the city remains Cuba's most vital center of Afro-Cuban culture.

© CHRISTOPHER P. BAKER

HIGHLIGHTS

(Casa de Don Diego Velázquez: The house where Diego Velásquez ruled Cuba is the island's oldest house. In superb condition, it houses a fine museum (page 492).

(Museo Municipal Emilio Bacardí Moreau: The museum begun by a member of the famous rum family holds his eclectic and fascinating collection inside a beautiful neoclassical edifice (page 492).

(Cuartel Moncada: This is where it all began: The scene of the attack by Castro & Co. that launched the revolution is now a school with a gory Museum of the Revolution (page 494).

(Parque Histórico El Morro: An enormous restored 17th-century castle with a dramatic clifftop setting holds a nightly cannon-firing ceremony (page 496).

(Cementerio de Santa Ifigenia: A who's who of important figures in Cuban history, not least José Martí, are buried in this cemetery (page 497).

(Basílica de Nuestra Señora del Cobre: A pilgrimage here is de rigueur to see the Cubans praying and making offerings to the Black Virgin (page 507).

(El Saltón: Lace up those boots and head to the hills for hiking and a breath of fresh air (page 508).

(Museo de la Guerra Hispano-Americano: This small yet excellently arranged museum displays maps, artillery pieces, and other articles relating to the Spanish-American War (page 513).

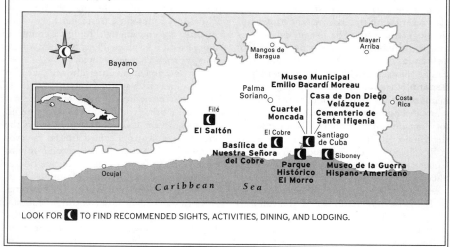

LOOK FOR **(** TO FIND RECOMMENDED SIGHTS, ACTIVITIES, DINING, AND LODGING.

Most of the province is mountainous. The Sierra Maestra rises west of Santiago, extending along the coast as far as the westernmost tip of Granma Province. East of the city, an elevated plateau extends for miles, slanting gradually to the sea, with a great serrated whaleback of mountains—the tall Cordillera de la Gran Piedra—behind. Behind these rise the Sierra de Baracoa and Sierra Cristal, extending into Holguín and Guantánamo Provinces. Together, they lure hikers and bird-watchers, as well as anyone interested in revolutionary history.

PLANNING YOUR TIME

Many visitors make the city of Santiago de Cuba their first, and sometimes their only, stop in Cuba. I don't rate it *that* highly, but it *does* have enough to keep you intrigued and engaged for three or four days or even longer. Sights are spread throughout the city and beyond. Downtown is pedestrian friendly, so plan on walking the narrow, sometimes traffic-clogged streets. The list of must-sees is long and includes the **Casa de Don Diego Velázquez** (reputedly the oldest building in Cuba); the excellent **Museo Municipal Emilio Bacardí Moreau,** which while honoring this member of the famous rum factory is actually a broad-ranging museum spanning arts, history, and culture; the **Cuartel Moncada,** now the Museo de la Revolución; and the Plaza de la Revolución, with its humongous statue of General Antonio Maceo. A walk through the once-wealthy Reparto Vista Alegre district is rewarding. Here, the highlight is the Museo de las Religiones Populares, where you can learn about Afro-Cuban religions.

After exploring the central sites accessible on foot, you'll want wheels to reach sites of interest on the outskirts. These include the **Cementerio de Santa Ifigenia,** where José Martí heads a long list of illustrious figures buried here; and the **Parque Histórico El Morro,** the castle guarding the entrance to Santiago de Cuba bay. Time your arrival for the nightly *cañonazo.*

Use the city as a base for excursions to sites elsewhere in the province. I recommend renting a car rather than relying on the spotty and iffy public transport. A visit to the basilica and pilgrimage site of El Cobre is de rigueur and might be combined with the rugged drive to **El Saltón.** This mountain resort, with acceptable accommodations, is an excellent base for bird-watching and hiking. For a scenic drive, head west from Santiago to Chivirico, beyond which lies the trailhead to Pico Turquino, Cuba's highest mountains (a guided overnight hike is easily arranged). Better yet is to head all the way to Marea del Portillo, in Granma Province, where the coastal highway and scenery are most dramatic.

The misleadingly named Reserva de la Biosfera Baconao, beginning a short distance east of Santiago de Cuba, is an eco-reserve only in name. Still, it's worth a full-day's excursion. Here, the highlight not to miss is the **Museo de la Guerra Hispano-Americano,** with superb displays recalling the Spanish-American War. Most other sites are rather hokey, but the drive is scenic enough. Budget a couple of hours for beachtime at Playa Siboney, where *casas particulares* can be rented.

Santiago de Cuba's entertainment scene is robust. The city's world-famous Casa de la Trova is still the heartbeat of *son* in the nation, and a visit is compulsory by day or night. The yang to the Casa de la Trova's yin is the open-air Tropicana. Themed around the evolution of Cuban culture, it is second only to Havana's Tropicana as a sexy, scantily-clad Las Vegas–style cabaret. If you're planning a mid-year visit, consider July, when the city erupts for Carnaval, Cuba's most colorful street fiesta. Though a far cry from those in Trinidad or Rio de Janeiro, this colorful festival is a marvelous expression of Afro-Cuban rhythms and of Santiagüerans let-loose sense of fun. Students of Afro-Cuban rhythms often settle in here to study music and dance with one of several *comparsas* (troupes), such as Tumba Francesa.

Santiago de Cuba is well served by trains and buses from Havana and elsewhere in Cuba. Dozens of *casas particulares* offer an excellent range of accommodations beyond the state-run hotels, which here include some of the best

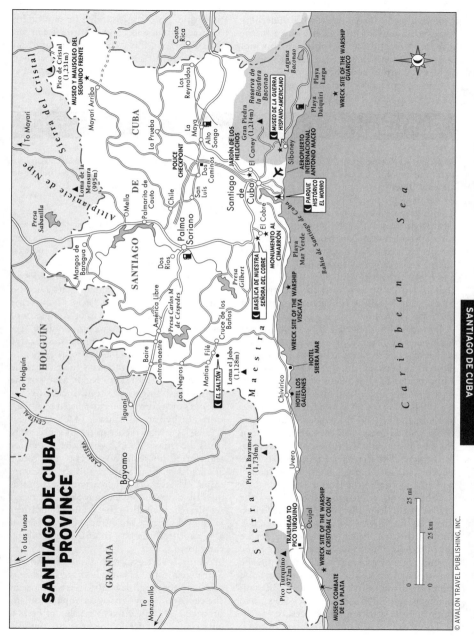

SANTIAGO DE CUBA PROVINCE

Pico de Cristal (1,231m)
MUSEO Y MAUSOLEO DEL SEGUNDO FRENTE
Costa Rica
Los Reynaldos

Sierra del Cristal
Altiplanicie de Nipe
Mayarí Arriba
Loma de la Mensura (995m)
CUBA
La Prueba
La Maya
Alto Songo
JARDÍN DE LOS HELECHOS
Gran Piedra
Reserva de la Biosfera Baconao
MUSEO DE LA GUERRA HISPANO-AMERICANO
Laguna Baconao
Playa Larga
Playa Daiquirí
WRECK SITE OF THE WARSHIP GUARICO

To Mayarí
Presa Sabanilla
Mella
Palmarito de Couto
Chile
San Luis
Dos Caminos
POLICE CHECKPOINT
El Caney (1,214m)
Siboney
AEROPUERTO INTERNACIONAL ANTONIO MACEO

DE
SANTIAGO
Mongos de Baragua
Dos Ríos
Palma Soriano
El Cobre
Santiago de Cuba
PARQUE HISTÓRICO EL MORRO

HOLGUÍN
Presa Carlos M de Céspedes
América Libre
Presa Gilbert
MONUMENTO AL CIMARRÓN
BASÍLICA DE NUESTRA SEÑORA DEL COBRE
Playa Mar Verde
Bahía de Santiago de Cuba

To Holguín
Baire
Contramaestre
Los Negros
Matías Filé
Cruce de los Baños
EL SALTÓN
Loma el Jobo (1,128m)
WRECK SITE OF THE WARSHIP VISCAYA
HOTEL SIERRA MAR
HOTEL LOS GALEONES
Chivirico

CARRETERA CENTRAL
To Las Tunas
Bayamo
Jiguaní
GRANMA
Pico la Bayamese (1,730m)
Uvero

To Manzanillo
Pico Turquino (1,972m)
Ocujal
TRAILHEAD TO PICO TURQUINO
WRECK SITE OF THE WARSHIP EL CRISTÓBAL COLÓN
MUSEO COMBATE DE LA PLATA

Sierra Maestra

Caribbean Sea

0   25 mi
0   25 km

SANTIAGO DE CUBA

© AVALON TRAVEL PUBLISHING, INC.

regional digs in the country, with something for every budget. Options elsewhere in the province are limited, for which reason, not least, you should make Santiago a base for sightseeing throughout the province.

Come prepared for heat! Santiago de Cuba sits within a bowl surrounded by mountains that form windbreaks and at times it can feel like an oven, and witheringly so in midsummer. The rainiest season is May–October. Relief may be found in the mountains and at beaches where breezes ease the heat.

Santiago de Cuba

Santiago de Cuba (pop. 375,000), home of rum and revolution, has a unique, enigmatic appeal. Older even than Havana, the historic center is a potpourri of rustic, tile-roofed dwellings graced by fancy forged-iron railings, weathered timbers, shady hanging balconies, turned wooden *rejas,* Moorish balustrades, and facades painted in faded pastels. Adding to the charm are cacti growing profusely from red-tile roofs, fulfilling an Oriente superstition that a cactus will keep away the evil eye. If a Santiagüero lets his or her cactus die, a year of bad luck will follow.

It is sometimes referred to as "Cuba's most Caribbean city." Santiago's east-facing position and proximity to Jamaica and Haiti fostered close links between the city and the two Caribbean islands. The majority of the 30,000 or so French planters and merchants who fled Haiti following the revolution in 1791 chose to settle in and around Santiago, stitching their habits and customs onto the cultural quilt of the city. Eventually black Haitians came also, as workers. The rich racial mixture has produced some of the most exciting music, art, and architecture in the Caribbean.

Proud Santiagüeros tout their city as the "Hero of the Republic of Cuba," the "Hero City," or the *capital moral de la Revolución,* though this is belied by the extreme degree of *jiniterismo* and begging. *Jiniteros* are more openly aggressive here than elsewhere on the island. Many approach quite shamelessly and simply demand, "Give me one dollar!" Fortunately, in late 2005 a police crack-down had improved the situation immeasurably.

The port city is a major industrial center: the distilleries of the original Bacardi rum are here, as are a chemical factory, oil refinery, and electricity generating plant.

HISTORY

Diego Velázquez founded the city in 1514 and named it for the King of Spain's patron saint, St. Jago. The city, built on hills on the east side of the Bahía de Santiago de Cuba, was named the Cuban capital and grew rapidly on the strength of trade inspired by its splendid harbor. Its first *capitán-general* was none other than Hernán Cortés, soon to be conqueror of Mexico. Other famous conquistadores resided here, too, including Francisco Pizarro (conqueror of Peru), Don Pedro de Alvarado (founder of Guatemala), and Juan Ponce de León (colonizer of Puerto Rico). Many of the original buildings still stand, including Velázquez's own sturdy home, financed by wealth from nearby copper mines at El Cobre.

Santiago remained capital of Cuba only until February 1553, when the governor transferred his residence to Havana. Santiago had lost its advantage and the El Cobre mines closed shortly thereafter. It was subsequently damaged by earthquakes and razed by pirates, including the French buccaneer Jacques de Sores. The pirate Henry Morgan also captured the city in 1662 after taking the Morro Castle.

Spanish settlers from Jamaica boosted Santiago's numbers when that island was seized by the English in 1655. At the close of the century, when Santiago's population approached 10,000, a massive influx of French émigrés from Haiti doubled the city population and added new vitality. Another boost in fortunes came in 1793, when Spanish authorities granted Santiago an *asamiento* (unlimited license) to import slaves to be sold to sugar plantations elsewhere on the island. Countless West African slaves gained their first look at the New World as they stepped shackled and confused into the harsh light on Santiago's wharves.

The Heroes' City

Santiago has had a reputation as a liberal city dating to 1836, when city fathers proclaimed local elections in defiance of the governor in Havana. Governor Tacón won the battle, but Santiago had asserted an autonomy that propelled it to the forefront in the evolving quest for independence. During the Wars of Independence, the city became a concentration camp held by Spanish troops and enclosed by barbed wire. On July 1, 1898, after the United States entered the fray, U.S. troops reached the outskirts of Santiago and the defenses atop San Juan Hill that protected the city. Throughout the morning, the U.S. artillery softened up the Spanish defenders before about 3,000 U.S. and Cuban troops (including Teddy Roosevelt and his Rough Riders) stormed the hill under cover of punishing fire from Gatling guns. Though Roosevelt's part has been vastly overblown by U.S. history texts, the victory (at a cost of 223 U.S. soldiers and 102 Spanish troops) sealed the war. The Spanish navy, meanwhile, had sheltered in Santiago harbor. On July 3, it attempted to escape. A battle ensued and the Spanish fleet was destroyed.

The Spanish surrender was signed on San Juan Hill on July 17. The Spanish flag came down and up went the Stars and Stripes.

Hotbed of Revolution

During the 20th century the city evolved as a major industrial and intellectual center and became a hotbed of revolutionary activity during the decades before 1950. The opening shots in Castro's revolution were fired here on July 26, 1953, when the 26-year-old lawyer and his followers attacked the Moncada barracks at dawn in an attempt to seize arms and inspire a general uprising. (See the sidebar *The Attack on Moncada* in this chapter.)

Assassinations and summary executions were common. The terror and turmoil reached a crescendo on November 30, 1956, when a 22-year-old Santiago teacher named Frank País led a group of Castro's 26th of July Movement (M-26-7) rebels in a daring attack on the police headquarters in Santiago, timed to coincide with the landing of the *Granma* bringing Castro and other revolutionaries from exile in Mexico. País's attack was ill-fated, and after the fiasco, Batista's henchmen initiated a campaign of indiscriminate murders. Frank País was shot on the street on July 30, 1958. His funeral erupted into a massive protest led by Santiago's mothers while the city workers went on strike, inspiring similar protests throughout Cuba.

On January 2, 1959, two days after Batista fled the island, Fidel Castro and his Rebel Army arrived in Santiago to accept the surrender of Batista's general. Castro gave his victory speech in Parque Céspedes before setting of on a victory parade for Havana.

The postrevolutionary years have seen massive construction. An oil refinery was built north of the city, along with a power-generating plant, a huge textile mill, a cement factory, and port expansion.

ORIENTATION

The Carretera Central from Bayamo enters Santiago from the north, descends to Plaza de la Revolución, and runs into the heart of the city as Avenida de los Libertadores. The coast road from Marea del Portillo enters the city from the west as Paseo de Martí, which rises to Avenida de los Libertadores. The road from Guantánamo enters the city from the east as Avenida Raúl Pujol.

The historic core (*casco histórico*) is roughly arranged in a grid. At its heart is Parque Céspedes, bounded by Félix Pena and Lacret (north–south) and Aguilera and Heredia (east–west). Most sites of interest are within

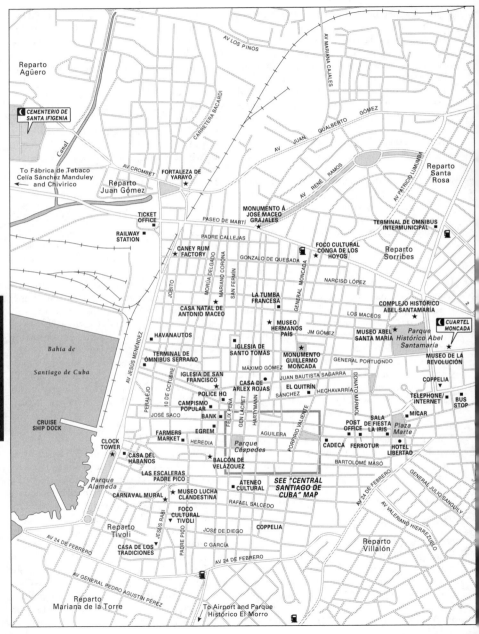

Reparto Agüero

CEMENTERIO DE SANTA IFIGENIA

To Fábrica de Tabaco Celía Sánchez Manduley and Chivirico

Reparto Juan Gómez

AV LOS PINOS

AV MARIANA CAJALES

CARRETERA BACARDI

Canal

AV CROMBET

FORTALEZA DE YARAYÓ

AV JUAN GUALBERTO GOMEZ

AV RENÉ RAMOS

AV PATRICIO LUMUMBA

Reparto Santa Rosa

MONUMENTO A JOSÉ MACEO GRAJALES

PASEO DE MARTI

TICKET OFFICE

RAILWAY STATION

PADRE CALLEJAS

CANEY RUM FACTORY

MARIANO CORONA

MORÚA DELGADO

GONZALO DE QUESADA

SAN FERMÍN

JOBITO

CASA NATAL DE ANTONIO MACEO

FOCO CULTURAL CONGA DE LOS HOYOS

NARCISO LÓPEZ

LA TUMBA FRANCESA

GENERAL MONCADA

LOS MACEOS

TERMINAL DE OMNIBUS INTERMUNICIPAL

Reparto Sorribes

COMPLEJO HISTÓRICO ABEL SANTAMARÍA

MUSEO HERMANOS PAÍS

JM GÓMEZ

MUSEO ABEL SANTA MARÍA

Parque Histórico Abel Santamaría

CUARTEL MONCADA

HAVANAUTOS

Bahía de

Santiago de Cuba

AV JESÚS MENÉNDEZ

TERMINAL DE OMNIBUS SERRANO

IGLESIA DE SANTO TOMÁS

MONUMENTO GUILLERMO MONCADA

GENERAL PORTUONDO

MUSEO DE LA REVOLUCIÓN

10 DE OCTUBRE

PERALEJO

IGLESIA DE SAN FRANCISCO

POLICE HQ

CAMPISMO POPULAR

MÁXIMO GÓMEZ

CASA DE ARLEX ROJAS

FELIX PEÑA

GEN LACRET

HARTMANN

JUAN BAUTISTA SAGARRA

EL QUITRÍN

SÁNCHEZ

HECHAVARRÍA

DONATO MÁRMOL

COPPELIA

TELEPHONE/ INTERNET

BUS STOP

MICAR

CRUISE SHIP DOCK

JOSÉ SACO

BANK

EGREM

FARMERS MARKET

HEREDIA

CLOCK TOWER

CASA DEL HABANOS

LAS ESCALERAS PADRE PICO

AGUILERA

Parque Céspedes

BALCÓN DE VELÁZQUEZ

PORFIRIO VALIENTE

POST OFFICE

SALA DE FIESTA LA IRIS

CADECA FERROTUR

Plaza Marte

HOTEL LIBERTAD

BARTOLOMÉ MASÓ

Parque Alameda

CARNAVAL MURAL

MUSEO LUCHA CLANDESTINA

ATENEO CULTURAL

SEE "CENTRAL SANTIAGO DE CUBA" MAP

AV 24 DE FEBRERO

GENERAL JULIO SANGUILY

AV VALERIANO HIERREZUELO

Reparto Tivoli

JESÚS RABÍ

FOCO CULTURAL TIVOLI

PADRE PICO

RAFAEL SALCEDO

JOSÉ DE DIEGO

C GARCÍA

COPPELIA

CASA DE LOS TRADICIONES

AV 24 DE FEBRERO

Reparto Villalón

AV GENERAL PEDRO AGUSTÍN PÉREZ

Reparto Mariana de la Torre

To Airport and Parque Histórico El Morro

SANTIAGO DE CUBA

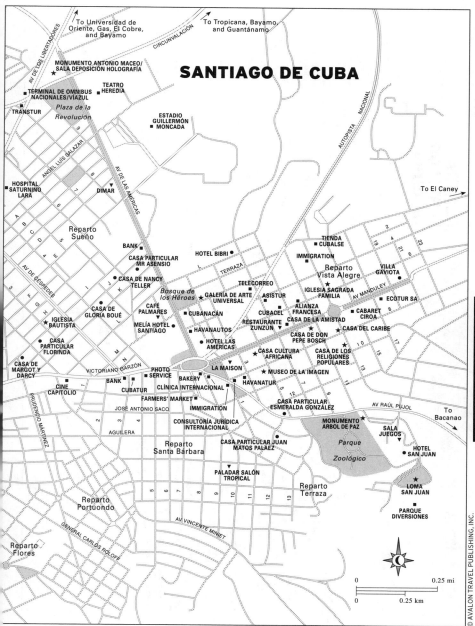

SANTIAGO DE CUBA

To Universidad de Oriente, Gas, El Cobre, and Bayamo

To Tropicana, Bayamo, and Guantánamo

CIRCUNVALACIÓN

AV. DE LOS LIBERTADORES

MONUMENTO ANTONIO MACEO/ SALA DEPOSICIÓN HOLOGRAFÍA ★

AUTOPISTA NACIONAL

TERMINAL DE OMNIBUS NACIONALES/VIAZUL ■
TEATRO HEREDIA ■

TRANSTUR ■

Plaza de la Revolución

ESTADIO GUILLERMÓN MONCADA ■

ANGEL LUIS SALAZAR

AV. DE LAS AMÉRICAS

HOSPITAL SATURNINO LARA ■

DIMAR ■

To El Caney

Reparto Sueño

TIENDA CUBALSE ■

BANK ■

HOTEL BIBRI ●

IMMIGRATION ■

CASA PARTICULAR MR ASENSIO ●

TERRAZA

Reparto Vista Alegre

VILLA GAVIOTA ■

AV. DE CÉSPEDES

CASA DE NANCY TELLER ●

TELECORREO ■

ASISTUR ■

IGLESIA SAGRADA FAMILIA ■

AV. MANDULEY

ECOTUR SA ■

Bosque de los Héroes ★

GALERÍA DE ARTE UNIVERSAL ★

CASA DE GLORIA BOUÉ ●

CAFÉ PALMARES ●

CUBANACÁN ■

ALIANZA FRANCESA ■

CABARET CIROA ■

IGLESIA BAUTISTA ★

MELÍA HOTEL SANTIAGO ●

HAVANAUTOS ■

RESTAURANTE ZUNZUN ▼

CUBACEL ■

CASA DE LA AMISTAD ★

CASA DEL CARIBE ★

CASA PARTICULAR FLORINDA ●

HOTEL LAS AMÉRICAS ●

CASA DE DON PEPE BOSCH ★

CASA DE MARGOT Y DARCY ●

VICTORIANO GARZÓN

LA MAISON ▼

CASA CULTURA AFRICANA ★

CASA DE LOS RELIGIONES POPULARES ★

CINE CAPITOLIO ■

BANK ■

PHOTO SERVICE ■

BAKERY ■

HAVANATUR ■

MUSEO DE LA IMAGEN ★

FRAUDENCIO MARTINEZ

CUBATUR ■

CLÍNICA INTERNACIONAL ■

FARMERS' MARKET ■

IMMIGRATION ■

CASA PARTICULAR ESMERALDA GONZÁLEZ ●

AV. RAÚL PUJOL

To Bacanao

JOSE ANTONIO SACO

CONSULTORÍA JURÍDICA INTERNACIONAL ■

MONUMENTO ARBOL DE PAZ ★

SALA JUEGOS ■

AGUILERA

Reparto Santa Bárbara

CASA PARTICULAR JUAN MATOS PALÁEZ ●

Parque Zoológico

HOTEL SAN JUAN ●

PALADAR SALÓN TROPICAL ▼

Reparto Terraza

LOMA SAN JUAN ★

Reparto Portuondo

AV. VINCENTE MINIET

PARQUE DIVERSIONES

GENERAL CARLOS ROLOFF

Reparto Flores

0   0.25 mi

0   0.25 km

SANTIAGO DE CUBA

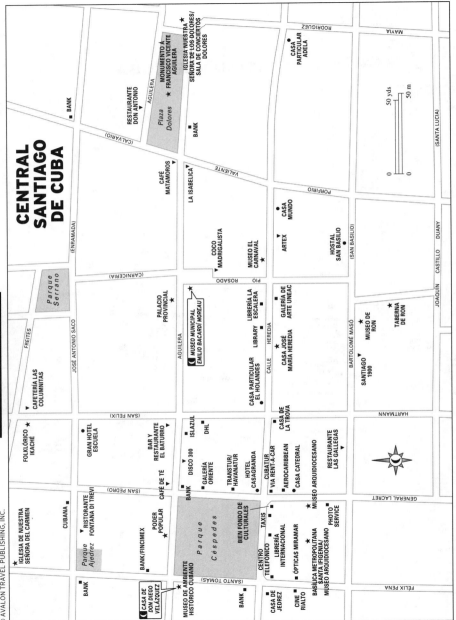

CENTRAL SANTIAGO DE CUBA

- IGLESIA DE NUESTRA SEÑORA DEL CARMEN
- CUBANA
- RISTORANTE FONTANA DI TREVI
- PODER POPULAR
- BANK/FINCIMEX
- FOLKLÓRICO IKACHE
- CAFETERÍA LAS COLUMNITAS
- GRAN HOTEL ESCUELA
- BAR Y RESTAURANTE EL BATURRO
- CAFÉ DE TÉ
- PALACIO PROVINCIAL
- CAFÉ MATAMOROS
- RESTAURANTE DON ANTONIO
- MONUMENTO A FRANCISCO VICENTE AGUILERA
- IGLESIA NUESTRA SEÑORA DE LOS DOLORES/ SALA DE CONCIERTOS DOLORES
- CASA PARTICULAR ADELA
- LA ISABELICA
- COCO MADRIGALISTA
- MUSEO EL CARNAVAL
- CASA MUNDO
- ARTEX
- HOSTAL SAN BASILIO
- MUSEO MUNICIPAL EMILIO BACARDÍ MOREAU
- LIBRERÍA LA ESCALERA
- LIBRARY
- GALERÍA DE ARTE UNEAC
- CASA JOSÉ MARÍA HEREDIA
- CASA PARTICULAR EL HOLANDÉS
- MUSEO DE RON
- TABERNA DE RON
- SANTIAGO 1900
- CASA DE LA TROVA
- DISCO 300
- ISLAZUL
- DHL
- GALERÍA ORIENTE
- TRANSTUR/ HAVANATUR
- HOTEL CASAGRANDA
- CUBATUR
- VÍA RENT-A-CAR
- AEROCARIBBEAN
- CASA CATEDRAL
- MUSEO ARQUIDIOCESANO
- RESTAURANTE LAS GALLEGAS
- TAXIS
- BIEN FONDO DE CULTURALES
- CENTRO TELEFÓNICO
- LIBRERÍA INTERNACIONAL
- ÓPTICAS MIRAMAR
- BASÍLICA METROPOLITANA SANTA IFIGENIA/ MUSEO ARQUIDIOCESANO
- PHOTO SERVICE
- CASA DE JEDREZ
- CINE RIALTO
- MUSEO DE AMBIENTE HISTÓRICO CUBANO
- CASA DE DON DIEGO VELÁZQUEZ
- BANK

Parque Serrano

Parque Ajedrez

Parque Céspedes

Plaza Dolores

0   50 yds

0   50 m

(ENRAMADA)
(CALVARIO)
AGUILERA
VALIENTE
PORFIRIO
(SANTA LUCIA)
RODRIGUEZ
MAYIA
DUANY
(SAN BASILIO)
(SANTO TOMÁS)
(SAN PEDRO)
(SAN FÉLIX)
(CARNICERÍA)
FREITES
JOSÉ ANTONIO SACO
AGUILERA
CALLE HEREDIA
PÍO ROSADO
BARTOLOMÉ MASÓ
HARTMANN
GENERAL LACRET
FELIX PEÑA
JOAQUÍN
CASTILLO
SANTIAGO DE CUBA

a few blocks of the park. Aguilera leads east from Parque Céspedes uphill to Plaza de Marte, a major hub on the eastern edge of the historic quarter. Avenida 12 de Agosto leads south from Plaza de Marte to the airport and Parque Histórico El Morro. Avenida Victoriano Garzón leads east from Plaza de Marte to the residential Reparto Sueño and Vista Alegre districts, also accessed from Plaza de la Revolución via Avenida de las Américas and where many of the best *casas particulares* and hotels are located.

The Autopista Nacional begins in Vista Alegre and extends only 45 kilometers before petering out in the middle of nowhere near Palma Soriano. Driving it is a dangerous business. *Avoid the Autopista entirely at night!*

A *circunvalación* circles the east and south sides of the city.

Most historic streets have both modern and older names (see the sidebar *Santiago Street Names*).

PARQUE CÉSPEDES AND VICINITY

Formerly known as Plaza de Armas, this compact square at the heart of Santiago de Cuba is ringed with gas lamps, metal grills, and tall shade trees. It is crowded by important buildings and has at its center a stone statue of the square's namesake hero, who is buried in Santiago.

Ayuntamiento

The beautiful white colonial building on the north side is the town hall (Aguilera, e/ Genera Lacret y Felix Peña; not open to the public), former headquarters of the Spanish colonial governor. The original building was first occupied by Hernán Cortés; the current structure dates from the 1950s and is based on a design from 1783. Its antecedent, built in 1855, was toppled by an earthquake and had housed the U.S. military during its occupation of Cuba. It was from the overhanging balcony that Fidel Castro gave the victory speech on January 2, 1959, after he entered town following Batista's flight from Cuba.

SANTIAGO STREET NAMES

OLD NAME	NEW NAME
Alameda	Jesús Menéndez
Calvario	Porfirio Valiente
Carnicería	Pío Rosado
Clarín	Padre Quiroga
Corona	Mariano
Enramada	José Antonio Saco
Marina	Aguilera
Reloj	Mayía Rodríguez
San Agustín	Donato Marmól
San Basilio	Bartolomé Masó
San Félix	Hartmann
San Pedro	General Lacret
Santa Lucía	Joaquín Castillo Duany
Santo Tomás	Féliz Peña
Trinidad	General Portuondo
Trocha	24 de Febrero

Basílica Metropolitana Santa Ifigenia

Raised on a pedestal on the southern side of the plaza, which it dominates, is the cathedral (open for mass Mon. and Wed.–Fri. 6:30 P.M., Sat. 5 P.M., Sun. 9 A.M. and 6:30 P.M.), otherwise known as the Catedral de Nuestra Señora de la Asunción. The cathedral is the fourth building to occupy the site (the original was begun in 1528). The current edifice dates to 1922, although its nave is held aloft by walls erected in 1810. Part of the interior has been restored, including choir stalls exquisitely hand-carved in precious hardwoods. The remains of Diego Velázquez are entombed within. Between the church's twin towers is a statue of the Angel of the Annunciation holding a trumpet. The entrance is on Felix Peña.

WALKING TOUR ALONG CALLE HEREDIA TO PLAZA DOLORES

Calle Heredia leads east from Parque Céspedes and is full of sights of interest. The street has traditionally been closed to traffic on weekend evenings, when it hosts a cultural fair.

Your first stop should be the **Casa de la Trova** (Heredia #208, tel. 022/62-3943), one block east of Parque Céspedes, formerly the home of revered composer Rafael Salcedo (1844-1917). Most afternoons and evenings the haunting melodies and plaintive *boleros* of the *trova* reverberate down the street.

One block east, you'll pass **Casa José María Heredia** (Heredia #260, tel. 022/62-5350; Tues.-Sat. 9 A.M.-7 P.M., Sun. 9 A.M.-2 P.M.; CUC1), birthplace of the 19th-century poet José María Heredia (1803-39), the first Cuban poet to champion independence. José Martí acclaimed him as the "first poet in Latin America." The house is furnished in colonial fashion.

Break out your camera at **La Librería La Escalera** (Heredia #265), a picture-perfect bookstore festooned with intriguing bric-a-brac and photos taken by visitors through the

years. Across the street, the **Galería de Arte UNEAC** (Heredia, e/ Hartmann y Pio Rosada, tel. 022/65-3465, ext. 106, www.uneac.com) is worth a peek for its superb art. Cater-corner, follow the stairs to the **Museo El Carnaval** (Heredia #304, tel. 022/62-6955; Tues.-Sun. 9:30 A.M.-5 P.M.; entrance CUC1, cameras CUC1, videos CUC5), which tells the history of Santiago's colorful carnival. Some of the outlandish costumes are on display. Try to time your visit for the folkloric shows daily at 4 P.M. or "*Domingo de la Rumba*" on Sunday at 11 A.M.

At the next junction (Valiente), turn left and walk one block into **Plaza Dolores,** a delightful little plaza with wrought-iron seats surrounding a larger-than-life bronze statue of Francisco Vicente Aguilera (1821-77), a revolutionary leader in the Ten Years War. The **Iglesia Nuestra Señora de los Dolores,** on the east side, is now a concert hall (musicians congregate outside to practice) and adjoins the **Colegio Jesuita Dolores,** the college where Fidel Castro was educated as a youth.

The east side of the cathedral contains the **Museo Arquidiocesano** (tel. 022/65-4586; Mon.–Sat. 9:30 A.M.–5:30 P.M.; entrance CUC1, cameras CUC1, videos CUC3), a cramped space brim-full of religious art and antiques.

◖ Casa de Don Diego Velázquez

On the park's west side is the former home of Cuba's first colonizer. It dates from 1516 and is supposedly the oldest house in Cuba. The somber Spanish mansion is fronted by dark wooden Moorish window grills and shutters. Velázquez lived upstairs. A gold foundry was maintained downstairs (it is still there, in the rear). The house today contains the **Museo de Ambiente Histórico Cubano** (Felix Peña #602, tel. 022/65-2652; Mon.–Thurs. and Sat. 9 A.M.–12:45 P.M. and 2–4:45 P.M., Fri. 2–4:45 P.M., Sun. 9 A.M.–12:45 P.M.;

entrance CUC2, cameras CUC1, videos CUC5), with separate rooms full of period furniture, tapestries, crystal ware, and artwork. Magnificent!

◖ Museo Municipal Emilio Bacardí Moreau

This museum (Pío Rosado, e/ Aguilera and Heredia, tel. 022/62-8402; Tues.–Sat. 9 A.M.–9 P.M., Sun. 9 A.M.–1 P.M.; CUC2) was founded by Emilio Bacardí Moreau (1844–1922) in 1899 and contains his astounding collection. A member of the expatriate and anti-Castroite Bacardí rum family, Emilio, patriot writer and mayor of Santiago, is in good graces; he was imprisoned in the Morro Castle for his revolutionary activities. The museum is housed in a huge neoclassical edifice with Corinthian columns in the heart of Santiago's oldest quarter.

WALKING TOUR FOR REVOLUTIONARIES

The hilly streets west and north of Parque Céspedes are brimful of sites associated with figures in the nationalist and revolutionary pantheon.

Beginning at the park's southwest corner, follow Felix Peña south one block to Masó. Turn left. One block along, at the corner of Calle Corona, you'll pass the **Balcón de Velázquez** (9 A.M.-5 P.M. daily; CUC1), a small plaza atop an old Spanish fort. Continue west 100 meters to Calle Padre Pico. Turn left. The broad steps ahead are known as **La Escalanita.** Here, three members of the 26th of July Movement were killed on November 30, 1956, while attacking a nearby police station. To learn more, ascend the steps to the former station, now the **Museo Lucha Clandestina** (Museum of the Underground Fight, Jesús Rabi #1, tel. 022/62-4689; Tues.-Sun. 9:30 A.M.-5 P.M.; CUC1), which tells the tale of Castro's 26th of July Movement (M-26-7). Fidel Castro lived across the street (Jesús Rabi #6) as a youth. The museum, in the 17th-century Tivoli district, offers superb views over the bay. While here, walk south to the end of the block to admire the **murals of Carnaval.**

Retrace your steps along Padre Pico to Aguilera. On the corner stands the **Antiguo Carcel Provincial** (Aguilera #131), where Fidel was imprisoned following the attack on Moncada. Turn right for Parque Céspedes (two blocks), then follow Félix Peña north three short blocks to Avenida Sánchez Hechavarría. Turn right. The street is lined with houses used by revolutionaries during the effort to topple Batista; concentrated between Hartmann and Valiente, they are marked by bronze plaques. Your destination is the former home of Vilma Espin, a M-26-7 member who later married Raúl Castro and who today heads the Women's Federation of Cuba; today it is **El Quitrín** (Hechavarría #473, e/ Porfirio Valiente y Pio Rosada, tel. 022/62-2528), a bar and Cuban store where fashion and folkloric shows are hosted.

After imbibing a pick-me-up, turn left onto Valiente. After three blocks turn left onto Calle Miguel Gómez. At Banderas (three blocks) turn right. Ahead, with a black-and-red flag of the M-26-7 fluttering outside, is the **Museo Hermanos País** (Banderas #266, e/ General Portuondo y Habana, tel. 022/65-2710; Mon.-Sat. 9 A.M.-5 P.M.; CUC1) the birthplace of brothers Frank and José País, who headed the Santiago M-26-7 organization and were killed by Batista's police (see the sidebar *Revolutionary Heroes* in the *Background* chapter). Continuing, at the end of the block, turn left onto Maceo, named for Antonio Maceo Grajales, a mulatto who rose to become second in command of the Liberation Army during the Wars of Independence (see the sidebar *Heroes of the Wars of Independence* in the *Background* chapter). The house where he was born is now the **Museo Casa Natal de Antonio Maceo** (Maceo #207, e/ Corona y Rastro, tel. 022/62-3550; Mon.-Sat. 9 A.M.-5 P.M.; CUC1).

Four blocks west brings you to the waterfront Avenida Jesús Menéndez, walled by a 656-foot-long fresco with panels that chart key events in Cuban history. Follow the boulevard north to the railway crossing, where the road divides, with Menéndez forking left. Cross the tracks and walk one block to the railway station, keeping to the left (west) side of the road to better admire the west-facing wall across the street. Painted with a colorful revolutionary mural depicting Fidel leading the Revolution, this is the warehouse of **Fábrica de Ron Caney** (Av. Peralejo, e/ Gonzalo de Quesada y Padre Callejas), one block east. The oldest rum factory in Cuba, it was built in 1868 by the Bacardí family and nationalized in 1959, after which the Cuban government continued to make rum while Bacardí set up shop in Puerto Rico. It is not open to view, but you can sample the goods in the tasting room (Av. Peralejo #103, tel. 022/62-5575; Mon.-Sat. 9 A.M.-5 P.M., Sun. 9 A.M.-noon).

The Cementerio de Santa Ifigenia (see main text) is a short walk away, passing by the **Fuerte de Yarayó** (Carretera Bacardí, esq. Paseo de Martí), a small fort built in the late 19th century.

FOR THE SAINT WITHIN

The Los Hoyos district north of Parque Céspedes is known for its 18th-century churches. Clerics on a busman's holiday might visit the **Iglesia de Nuestra Señora del Carmen** (Félix Peña #505, esq. Tamayo Freites), known for its statuary; **Iglesia de San Francisco** (Sagarra #121, esq. Mariana Corona), with its triple nave; **Iglesia de Santo Tomás** (Félix Peña #308, esq. General Portoundo); and **Iglesia de la Santísima Trinidad** (General Portoundo, esq. General Moncada), overlooking a tiny plaza dedicated to Guillermo Moncada (1840-95), the black nationalist and Liberation Army general who was born hereabouts.

The first floor contains a miscellany of colonial artifacts, from slave shackles and stocks to a huge array of antique weapons. The second floor art gallery includes 19th-century and contemporary works by leading figures. Also here: a small but impressive display of pre-Columbian artifacts from throughout the Americas, including colorful feather headdresses, a shrunken head (*cabeza reducida*), pottery shards, and Peruvian mummies.

The museum fronts a tiny plaza on whose north side rises the 1920s neoclassical **Palacio Provincial,** seat of local government.

REPARTO SUEÑO

This 19th-century, triangular district lies northeast of the old city and **Plaza de Marte,** a small plaza built in 1860 as the Spanish parade ground and execution spot for Cuban patriots. Baseball fans gather here to argue over their passion under the gaze of Cuban patriots, whose busts speckle the square.

The district is framed by Avenida Victoriano Garzón, Avenida de las Américas, and **Avenida de los Libertadores,** a broad boulevard lined with bronze busts of revolutionary heroes.

Complejo Histórico Abel Santamaría

Pinned by a Mount Rushmore in miniature, this site (General Portuondo, esq. Av. de los Libertadores) features a huge granite cube carved with the faces of Abel Santamaría and José Martí. A fountain seems to hold the cube aloft. To its north, the **Museo Abel Santamaría** (tel. 022/62-4119; Mon.–Sat. 9:30 A.M.– noon and 2–5 P.M.; CUC0.50) occupies the former hospital where Abel Santamaría and 22 fellow rebels fired at the Moncada barracks and where they were later captured, tortured, and killed. Here, too, Fidel Castro gave his famous "History Will Absolve Me" speech while being judged by an emergency tribunal. Seven rooms house exhibits relating to the event and to the life of Abel Santamaría.

◖ Cuartel Moncada

This former military barracks (General Portuondo, e/ Av. de los Libertadores y Carlos Aponte), with castellated walls and turrets, is renowned for the fateful day on July 26, 1953, when Fidel Castro and his poorly armed cohorts stormed the barracks. After the Revolution, Moncada was turned into a school, the Ciudad Escolar 26 de Julio. A portion of the main building near the entrance gate is riddled with bullet holes. They're not the originals, however; Batista's troops filled those in. Castro apparently had the holes redone using photographs. This section today houses the **Museo Histórico 26 de Julio** (also known as the Museo de la Revolución, tel. 022/62-0157; Tues.–Sat. 9:30 A.M.– 6 P.M., Sun. 9:30 A.M.–1 P.M.; entrance CUC2, cameras CUC1, videos CUC5), which tells the tale of the attack and subsequent revolutionary history. Prolific weaponry includes Castro's personal sharpshooter rifle. A separate room is dedicated to José Martí.

Plaza de la Revolución

This huge plaza at the junction of Avenida de las Américas and Avenida de los Libertadores is dominated by the massive **Monumento Antonio Maceo** dedicated to the homegrown son of a local merchant who rose to become the hero-

THE ATTACK ON MONCADA

At 5 A.M. on Sunday, July 26, Fidel Castro and 122 young followers sang the national anthem. Then, dressed in brown Cuban Army uniforms, they set out from Granjita Siboney crammed inside 16 cars, with Castro in the fifth car – a brand-new 1953 Buick sedan. The third car, containing Raúl (leading a second unit), took a wrong turn and arrived at his target – the Palace of Justice – after the fighting had begun. Another car had a flat tire and yet another car took a wrong turn, which reduced the fighting force to 105 men, who attacked Moncada with a few Winchester rifles, hunting shotguns, a single M-1 rifle, a single Browning submachine gun, and assorted sporting rifles.

Castro had studied the plans of the Moncada barracks for months and concluded that the fort could be rushed through the southeastern gate. The commandos would then fan out through the barracks with newly seized weapons. At first, the attack went according to plan. The sentinels were taken by surprise and disarmed. As the commandos rushed into the barracks, an Army patrol appeared. Gunfire erupted. The alarm bells were sounded. Then a volley of machine-gun fire sprayed the rebels, who were forced to retreat. The battle lasted less than 30 minutes. Only eight rebels were killed in combat, but 61 others were caught and tortured to death.

Batista's army, which lost 19 soldiers, claimed that Moncada was attacked by "between 400 and 500 men, equipped with the most modern instruments of war," and that Castro's men had been gunned down at Moncada. A photographer, however, managed to get photos of the tortured *fidelistas*. The gruesome photos were printed five days later, exposing Batista's lie and unleashing a wave of disgust.

general of the War of Independence as second-in-command of the rebel forces. Maceo was nicknamed the Bronze Titan—the mammoth statue of the general on a rearing horse is appropriately cast in bronze. On the north side, an eternal flame flickers in a marble-lined bowl cut into the base by the entrance to the **Sala Deposición Holográfia** (Mon.–Sat. 8 A.M.–4 P.M.; free) with holograms telling of Maceo's life and of the War of Independence.

REPARTO VISTA ALEGRE

This leafy residential district is bounded on the west by Avenida de las Américas and on the south by Avenida Pujol (Carretera Siboney). Avenida Manduley runs east–west through the center of Vista Alegre and is lined with once-upscale villas. Many were confiscated after the Revolution and turned into government offices, clinics, and schools.

Museo de la Imagen

This museum (Calle 8 #106, esq. 5, tel. 022/64-2234; Mon.–Sat. 9 A.M.–5 P.M.; CUC1) was established by cameraman Bernabá Muñiz, who gained his first screen credit when he captured on film a man who decided to play Tarzan—naked—down Avenida de los Misiones in Havana. He went on to film Fulgencio Batista's coup d'état in 1952, the surrender of the Moncada barracks to the revolutionaries in 1959, and Fidel's victory parade from Santiago to Havana. The Museum of Images features almost 500 photographic, film, and TV cameras—from CIA espionage cameras to a stereoscopic viewfinder from 1872—plus a library of over 200 feature films and documentaries dating back to 1926.

Parque Histórico Loma de San Juan

San Juan Hill rises on the south side of Avenida Pujol to a pleasant park shaded by palms. Every U.S. schoolchild knows that Teddy Roosevelt and his Rough Riders defeated the Spanish here. The landscaped park contains a replica fort, plus monuments and cannons, including a Tomb of the Unknown *Mambí*, Cuba's

SANTIAGO DE CUBA

A WALK THROUGH VISTA ALEGRE

Leafy Vista Alegre makes for a shaded walking tour and will appeal strongly to those with an interest in Afro-Cuban culture.

Begin at the Hotel Meliá Santiago de Cuba, on Avenida de las Américas. Cater-corner to the hotel, on the east side of the boulevard, the **Bosque de los Mártires de Bolivia** (esq. Calle 2) features marble tableaux engraved with the bas-reliefs of Che Guevara and his band of revolutionaries who died in Bolivia. The **Galería de Arte Universal** (Calle 1, esq. M, tel. 022/64-1198; Mon.-Sat. 9 A.M.-5:30 P.M.), on the east side of the park, is worth a peek before continuing south along Calle 1 three blocks to Avenida Manduley, where facing you is **La Maison** (Manduley #52, esq. Calle 1, tel. 022/64-3449; Mon.-Sat. at 10:30 P.M.), a resplendent mansion hosting high-class boutiques and a nightly cabaret. Call in to admire the antiques.

Eastward, on the next block, call in at the **Casa Cultura Africana Fernando Ortiz** (Manduley, esq. Calle 5, tel. 22/64-2487; Mon.-Sat. 9 A.M.-5 P.M.; CUC1), which hosts Afro-Cuban music and dance and displays African masks, carvings, and musical instruments.

Three blocks farther along Manduley brings you to **Casa de Don Pepe Bosch** (esq. Calle 11), a grand neo-baroque mansion once owned by a Mambí general. It is now a Young Pioneer's School and has a Soviet MiG fighter jet in the playground. If you're into churches, cross Manduley and walk uphill one block to **Iglesia Sagrado Familia** (Calle 11, e/ 4 y 6; open for mass only, Mon. and Fri. at 5 P.M. and Sun. at 10:30 A.M.), a Gothic-style Catholic church built in 1898 and beautifully maintained, with fine stained-glass windows.

Continuing along Manduley to Calle 11; turn right. One block away, at the corner of Calle 8, awaits the **Casa del Caribe** (Calle 13 #154, tel. 022/64-2285, caribe@cultstgo.cult.cu), with exhibits honoring Caribbean cultures; it also organizes the annual Festival of the Caribbean Culture. The highlight of your walk lies one block south at the **Museo de las Religiones Populares** (Calle 13 #206, e/ 8 y 10, tel. 022/64-2285, ext. 114; daily 9 A.M.-5:30 P.M.; CUC1 entrance, CUC1 guide). Dedicated to the *santería* religion and related Afro-Cuban sects, its *altares* (shrines) include a typical Palo Monte layout, with owls, an alligator, and various animal skins.

---

independence fighters. One memorial is dedicated to "the generous American soldiers who sealed a covenant of liberty and fraternity between the two nations." There is no monument, however, to Roosevelt and his Rough Riders, because the Cuban liberationists who helped storm the hill weren't even invited to the surrender ceremony on July 16, 1898, beneath a huge ceiba tree. The **Monumento Arbol de Paz**, in its own little park off Avenida Pujol 100 yards west of San Juan Hill, occupies the site of the original tree. Various cannon and howitzers surround giant bronze plaques (shaped as open books) inscribed with the names of all the U.S. soldiers killed in the war.

SOUTHERN SUBURBS
◖ Parque Histórico El Morro
The **Castillo de San Pedro del Morro** (tel.

022/69-1569; 9 A.M.–7:30 P.M.; entrance CUC4, cameras/videos CUC1) is an enormous piece of military architecture begun in 1638 and poised ominously atop the cliffs at the narrow entrance to Santiago Bay, about 14 kilometers south of Santiago. The Morro was rebuilt and strengthened in 1664 after the English pirate Henry Morgan reduced it to rubble. It was recently restored using coral chunks and red brick alongside the much-worn original limestone blocks. The effect is not lost, however, and you still gain a full sense of the power of the Morro. Cannons are everywhere, and the views from the battlements are spectacular! Exhibits include old blunderbusses, muskets, cutlasses, and more. A *cañonazo* ceremony is held at sunset, when soldiers in period costume load and put a torch to a cannon in a time-honored tradition that once announced the nightly sealing of the harbor.

© CHRISTOPHER P. BAKER

a cannon in the entrance to El Morro castle

The clifftops are pinned by the **Faro del Morro,** a lighthouse built in 1920 and still using the original hand-wound Fresnel lens floating in mercury. It's part of a military complex and thereby off-limits.

Bus #212 runs from downtown to Embarcadero Cayo Granma, from where you can hike up to the castle. If driving, the Morro is signed from Santiago. Follow Avenida 12 de Agosto south from Plaza de Marte; this leads to Carretera del Morro. Alternately, you can drive the Carretera Turística, which begins at the southern end of Avenida Jesús Menéndez, following the bayshore to emerge atop the cliffs immediately east of the castle. En route, you'll pass **Punta Gorda,** a slender peninsula once fashionable with Santiago's upper class. A large statue of revolutionary hero Frank País looms over the point in **Parque Frank País.**

Cayo Granma

This small island sits in the bay less than one kilometer offshore of El Morro. The small fishermen's colony looks as if it has been magically transferred from the Mediterranean, with its rowboats berthed beneath the eaves of quaint red-tiled waterfront houses. Narrow streets lead up to a hilltop church, **Iglesia de San Rafael.**

The **Restaurante El Cayo** (tel. 022/69-0109; noon–5 P.M. daily), on the northeast side of the cay, sits over the bay and serves seafood and *criollo* dishes.

A passenger ferry (20 centavos) serves Cayo Granma from Embarcadero Cayo Granma and continues to **Playa Socapa,** a beach with cannon battery on the headland facing El Morro.

NORTHERN SUBURBS
❰ Cementerio de Santa Ifigenia

This cemetery (Calzada Crombet, tel. 022/63-2723; 8 A.M.–6 P.M.; entrance CUC1, cameras CUC1, videos CUC5) is the final resting place of several key figures in Cuban history. The grand gateway is dedicated to Cuban soldiers who died fighting in Angola. Just beyond is the **Mausoleo de Martí,** the tomb of José Martí, beneath a crenellated hexagonal tower (each side represents one of the six original provinces of Cuba). Marble steps lead down to a circular mausoleum, designed so that the sun would always shine on his coffin, which is draped with the Cuban flag. The cemetery also contains the graves of Carlos Manuel Céspedes, Emilio Bacardí, Tomás Estrada Palma (Cuba's first president), heroes of the attack on the Moncada barracks (look for the red and black flags on their graves), and heroes of the War of Independence, who are entombed in a tiny castle.

Fábrica de Tabaco Celia Sánchez Manduley

You can watch men and women rolling, snipping, and pressing fine Cuban cigars at this cigar factory (tel. 022/63-0872; Mon.–Fri. 8 A.M.–3 P.M.), locally called Fábrica Textilera (the factory made textiles until 2005, when the cigar factory moved in). Guided tours are offered. Visits are permitted only with a voucher (CUC3) sold at **Cubatur** on Parque Céspedes.

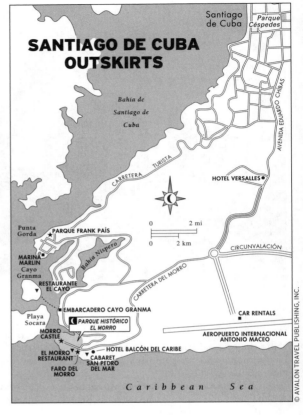

Jardín de los Helechos

For an escape from the sometimes frenetic bustle of downtown, head to this peaceful Orchid Garden (Carretera de la Caney #129, tel. 022/64-8335; Mon.–Sat. 9 A.M.–5 P.M.; CUC1), where more than 350 fern species also grow. A guide will lead you through the well-tended gardens, best visited in winter, when the orchid blooms are profuse. You can take bus #15 from Plaza Marte.

ENTERTAINMENT AND EVENTS
Festivals and Events

Noche Santiaguera (also called the Festival de Rumba) is held on January 12, featuring a mini-carnival centered on Calle Heredia. The Big Enchilada, however, is **Carnaval** (officially called the Fiesta del Caribe), in late July, when everyone in town downs shots of *aguardiente* and gets caught up in the street rumbas and conga lines. The center of carnival activities is at the southern end of Avenida Jesús Menéndez, around Avenida 24 de Febrero. It traditionally runs July 22–28.

In August, people converge in Parque Céspedes for the **Festival de Pregón,** arriving in carriages smothered with flowers and dressed in traditional costume to compete in the improvisation of traditional verse and song.

CARNAVAL!

Carnaval in Santiago de Cuba has been performed since the 19th century, when it was an Easter celebration. Originally it was called the Fiesta de las Mamarrachos (Festival of the Nincompoops), when slaves were given time to release their pent-up energies and frustrations in a celebration full of sexual content. The celebration was bound irrevocably to the secret societies of ancient Africa, transformed in Cuba into neighborhood societies called *carabalí* that vied with one another to produce the most colorful and elaborate processions (*comparsas*). Since each *comparsa* comes from a different neighborhood, each dance and tune varies.

The hourglass drums of the ancestors pound out their *tun q'tu q'tu q'tun* rhythm. The wail of Chinese cornets adds to the racket. And young and old alike rush to join the conga lines full of clowns and celebrants in colonial period dress, finding a release from the melancholy of everyday life. The conga lines are followed by floats graced by girls (*luceros* – morning stars) in riotous feathers and sequined bikinis or outrageous dresses. Huge papier-mâché heads supported by dancing Cubans bash into each other. There are representations of the *orishas* in the *comparsas*, and characters representing the various gods lead the way.

Every year there's a different theme, and contestants are judged on originality and popularity.

The main procession takes place on Avenida Jesús Menéndez.

Traditional Music and Dance

Santiago's **Casa de la Trova** (Heredia #208, tel. 022/62-3943; 11 A.M.–1 A.M.; CUC1 by day, CUC3 at night) is the island's most famous "house of trova." The *trova* tradition of romantic ballads was born here, and many famous Cuban musicians perform daily. *Son* (the saucy music of the Buena Vista Social Club) is particularly favored. Wednesday and Saturday evenings are usually the best times to go.

Coco Madrigalista (Pío Rosada #555, esq. Aguilera; CUC1) is a similar, simpler venue with *son* and *bolero* nightly at 9 P.M.

Patio de Artex (Heredia #304, tel. 022/65-4814; 9:30 P.M.–2 A.M.; CUC2), nearby, packs in a younger crowd and is a hip spot favored for boy-meets-girl.

In Vista Alegre, **Casa del Caribe** (Calle 13 #154, tel. 022/64-2285) hosts a rumba every Sunday afternoon; the nearby **Casa Cultura Africana Fernando Ortiz** (Manduley, esq. 5, tel. 22/64-2487) has rumba Friday–Sunday at 6 P.M.

The following Afro-Cuban *comparsas* (folkloric associations) have workshops where you can watch, and even participate in, practice sessions: **La Tumba Francesa** (Calle Los Maceos #501, esq. General Bandera, no tel.; Tues. and Fri. at 9 P.M.); **Folklórico Ikaché** (Hartmann, esq. Tamayo Fleites); **Foco Cultural Conga de los Hoyos** (Paseo, esq. General Moncada); **Foco Cultural El Tivoli** (Desiderio Mesnier #208, Mon.–Fri. 8 A.M.); and **Ballet Folklórico Cutumba** (Saco, e/ Corona y Padre Pico, tel. 022/62-5860, Tues.–Sun.), which performs *cumbia, tumba francesa,* and other dance styles at Teatro Oriente (Calle Enramadas #115, tel. 022/62-2441) each Saturday at 9:30 P.M. and Sunday at 10:30 A.M. (CUC3).

Cabarets and Discos

The **Tropicana** (Autopista Nacional Km 1.5, tel. 022/68-7020, fax 022/68-7090; Thurs.–Sat. at 10 P.M.; CUC30 including one drink), four kilometers northeast of town, hosts a colorful theme show tracing Caribbean history and culture. This is saucy Las Vegas–style *cabaret espectáculo* at its best. Colored floodlights reveal feathered showgirls high amid the palm trees, quivering and cooing like denizens of an exotic harem. The post-show disco is the hottest dance spot in town.

Cabaret San Pedro del Mar (Carretera del Morro km 7.5, tel. 022/69-1287; Wed.–Sun.

SANTIAGO DE CUBA

A crooner woos the crowd at the Tropicana cabaret.

10 P.M.–2 A.M.; CUC10), near El Morro castle, eight kilometers south of town, offers a smaller *espectáculo*. A disco follows.

The colonial-themed **Santiago Café** (nightly 10 P.M.–2 A.M.; CUC5 Mon.–Thurs., CUC10 Fri.–Sun.), in the Hotel Meliá Santiago, features a small cabaret followed by disco. It has a dress code. The **Hotel San Juan** and **Hotel Las Américas** also have cabarets.

The ritzy **Pico Real Bar** (CUC6 including one drink; hotel guests free) atop the Hotel Santiago hosts live music and disco nightly at 10:30 P.M.

Local youth head to **Sala de Fiestas La Iris** (Aguilera #617, e/ Plácido y Monseñor Bernada, tel. 022/65-4910; 10 P.M.–3 A.M. Wed.–Mon.; CUC3).

Classical Performances

The **Teatro Heredia** (Av. de las Américas, esq. Av. de los Desfiles, tel. 022/64-3134), by the Plaza de la Revolución, hosts classical performances, as does **Sala de Conciertos**

Dolores (Aguilera, esq. Mayía Rodríguez, tel. 022/65-3857).

Bars

Club 300 (Aguilera, e/ Hartmann y General Lacret, tel. 022/65-3532; nightly 8:30 P.M.–2 A.M.; CUC2) is a dark and moody bar in a colonial home. The clientele is mostly Cuban women and foreign males. It's a free-for-all to enter, but a tip usually does the trick.

El Baturro (Aguilera, esq. Hartmann; daily 10 A.M.–10:45 P.M.) is an atmospheric Spanish tavern with bull heads on the wall. It serves rum and beer and has live music.

A shot of quality rum costs a mere CUC1 at the **Taberna del Ron** (Pío Rosado, esq. Bartolomé Masó, no tel.; daily 9 A.M.–9 P.M.), a simple *bodega*-style bar beneath the Museo de Ron (Bartolomé Masó #358, esq. Carnecería), which is not worth two bucks' entry.

Other Entertainment

Cine Rialto (Félix Peña, e/ Heredia y Bartolomé Masó, tel. 022/62-3035) is the city's main movie house.

The **Ateneo Cultural** (Félix Peña, e/ Castillo Duany y Diego Palacios, tel. 022/65-1969; CUC2) offers cultural activities from poetry readings to live rap.

La Maison (Manduley #52, tel. 022/41117; Mon.–Sat. at 10:30 P.M.; CUC5 including one drink) offers an alfresco fashion show followed by a cabaret. Diners get free entry. Watch out for the raffle swindle: When selling tickets, the model holds up a bottle of Havana Club *añejo,* but when the drawing is held the winner gets a bottle of cheap wine.

El Quitrín (Hechavarría #473, e/ Porfirio Valiente y Pio Rosada, tel. 022/62-2528) hosts live traditional music nightly, plus a fashion show on Friday and Saturday, in a delightful patio space with a bar and an arbor of plumeria.

Estadio Guillermo Moncada (Av. de las Américas y Calle E, tel. 022/64-2640) hosts baseball games October–March, each Tuesday–Thursday evening and Saturday and Sunday at 1:30 P.M.

SPORTS AND RECREATION

Marina Marlin (tel. 022/69-1446, fax 022/68-6108; 10 A.M.–10 P.M. Tues.–Sun.), at Punta Gorda, offers water sports, including sportfishing charters. You can rent watercraft. It also has a modern bowling alley, plus pool. The **Sala Juegos,** at Hotel San Juan, has two mini bowling lanes plus pool tables.

Kids will probably enjoy the **Parque Zoológico** (Av. Pujol; Tues.–Fri. 10 A.M.–5 P.M., Sat.–Sun. 9 A.M.–5 P.M.; CUC1 adults, CUC0.40 children), immediately west of Hotel San Juan. Animals from most continents are represented, including mandrills, baboons, and other monkeys.

ACCOMMODATIONS

You can book *campismos* at the **Campismo Popular** (Cornelio Robén #163, e/ Mariano Corona y Padre Pico, tel. 022/62-9000).

Casas Particulares

There are more than 400 *casas particulares* in Santiago de Cuba.

Downtown: There are numerous private room rentals along Calle Heredia, a noisy street; ideally you'll want a room to the rear. The **Casa Particular El Holandés** (Heredia #251, esq. Hartmann, tel. 022/62-4878; CUC20) is a delightful old home with three spacious, simply furnished air-conditioned rooms upstairs plus an antique-filled lounge (there's even an antique dentist's chair). The rooms are clean and share a hot-water bathroom. Nearby, **Casa Particular Adela** (Heredia #374, esq. Reloj, tel. 022/65-3696; CUC20) is a spacious old home with one simple but appealing and well-lit room with air-conditioning, fan, and a clean, private hot-water bathroom. And **Casa Mundo** (Heredia #308, e/ Pío Rosado y Porfirio Valiente, tel. 022/62-4097, co8kz@yahoo.es; CUC15–20) is a pleasant colonial home extending to a small patio. It has two simply furnished air-conditioned rooms, each with double and single bed, fan, and private hot-water bathroom.

Casa Catedral (San Pedro #703 altos, e/ Heredia y San Basilio, tel. 022/65-3169; CUC20)

has views over the plaza from a breeze-swept, marble-floored lounge that opens onto a balcony. The owners rent two rooms. One, with a huge, tiled colonial bathroom that is a feature in itself, is simply furnished and has a fan plus a separate sitting room. The second room has air-conditioning plus a small, modern bathroom, kitchenette, and private entrance.

Casa de Abel y Milagros (Jagüey #164, e/ Padre Pico y Corona, tel. 022/65-9320, www.realcubaonline.com; CUC25), on a steep street, is a neocolonial home with massive doors, wide verandas with railings, a high ceiling, period furniture, and a patio plus roof terrace with a fabulous view. The house has four large air-conditioned bedrooms with five bathrooms, although only two rooms are rented. Meals include vegetarian and non-observant kosher.

Casa de Arlex Rojas (San Francisco #303, e/ Hartmann y San Bartolomé, tel. 022/62-2517, arlexjorge@yahoo.com; CUC15–20) is a beautiful colonial house filled with antiques and ceramics. The gay owners have two air-conditioned rooms with private hot-water bathrooms that open to an exquisite rear patio with planters. One room is meagerly furnished, but features colonial tiles and ceiling fan; the other has more furnishings, including a metal-frame bed.

Reparto Sueño: One of the nicest houses in town is ◖ **Casa de Florinda Chaviano Martínez** (Calle I #58, e/ 2da y 3ra, tel. 022/65-3660; CUC25) with a modern lounge and a single, well-lit, nicely furnished room with air-conditioning, radio, fridge, and modern hot-water bathroom. A handsome patio with grapevine arbor proves perfect for enjoying breakfast. The hosts are liberal and attentive.

Casa de Margot y Darcy (Calle I #12, e/ 1ra y 2da, tel. 022/65-2407; CUC25) is run by a friendly hostess who rents a large, air-conditioned upstairs room that is well-ventilated, well-lit, and has a large closet, plus a clean modern hot-water bathroom and a fridge in a meagerly appointed lounge.

Casa de Gloria Boué (Calle J #212, e/ 5ta y 4ta, tel. 22/62-3837; CUC25) has two nicely furnished air-conditioned rooms with

TV, radio, fridge, and large, clean modern hot-water bathrooms. The TV lounge boasts leather sofas.

Casa Particular Nancy Téllez (Calle J #265, e/ 6ta y 5ta, tel. 022/62-5109; CUC20) is a well-furnished, breeze-swept home with a TV lounge plus two air-conditioned rooms. One, though dark, has a large handsome bathroom. A dining room opens to a charming patio, and there's secure parking.

For a self-contained option try **Casa de Mr. Asensio** (Calle J #306, e/ Av. de las Américas y 6ta, tel. 022/62-4606, manuel@sierra.scu.sld.cu; in Italy, tel. 019/692-067; CUC20–25). The upstairs air-conditioned apartment is splendid, with lively 1950s decor, cross-ventilation, fans, and even an ironing board and burglar alarm. There's a small kitchen, plus a rooftop patio and private garage.

Repartos Vista Alegre and Terraza: These leafy residential suburbs offers some of the nicest houses in town. **Casa Particular Esmeralda González** (Av. Pujol #107, esq. 5ta, tel. 022/64-6341, rachelbarreiro@yahoo.es; CUC20) is a nice middle-class home with 1960s furnishings. Esmeralda rents a spacious, well-lit, cross-ventilated air-conditioned room with fans, kitchenette, and refrigerator, an independent entrance, and a marvelous period hot-water bathroom. It has secure parking.

Casa Particular Juan Matos Palaez (Calle Bitirí #102, esq. Taíno, tel. 022/64-1427, cmatos@eccs.ciges.inf.cu; CUC25–30) is a beautiful 1950s-style home with two nicely furnished rooms with air-conditioning, ceiling fans, and exquisite tiled hot-water bathrooms. There are huge patios to the front and rear.

Hotels

Under CUC50: The impecunious might try **Hotel Bitiri** (Calles L y 7, tel. 022/64-2047, fax 022/64-3186; CUC8 s, CUC10 d), in Reparto Vista Alegre. Run by Universitur, it offers basic air-conditioned rooms with TV and shared bathrooms with cold water only.

Hotel Escuela Gran Hotel (Saco, esq. Hartmann, tel. 022/65-3020, fax 022/68-7123, www.granhotelstgo.cu; CUC26 s, CUC32 d year-round) is a training hotel with 30 large, functional air-conditioned rooms, with satellite TVs, safes, and simple hot-water bathrooms. It has a bar, café, and restaurant.

Hotel Libertad (Aguilera #658, tel. 022/62-8360; CUC26 s, CUC32 d low season; CUC32 s, CUC38 d high season, including breakfast), on the south side of Plaza de Marte, has a classical motif and exquisite tilework and hardwoods throughout. It offers 42 smallish but amply furnished rooms with satellite TVs, radios, and small modern bathrooms. It has a lobby bar, elegant restaurant, disco, and Internet service.

The recently opened **Hostal San Basilio** (San Basilio #403, e/ Calvario y Carnicería, tel. 022/65-1702, hostalsb@stgo.scu.cyt.cu; CUC34 s, CUC48 d year-round) has turned a former colonial mansion into a delightful eight-room hotel. Rooms are nicely decorated in 19th-century style and have satellite TVs, phones, safes, refrigerators, and beautiful modern bathrooms with hot water. It has a small restaurant and 24-hour lobby bar. (Islazul.)

Hotel Balcón del Caribe (Carretera del Morro Km 7.5, tel. 022/69-1506, fax 022/69-2398, balcon@islazul.scu.tur.cu), atop the cliffs near the Morro Castle; and **Hotel Rancho Club** (Carretera Central Km 4.5, tel. 022/63-33202, fax 022/62-2049), on the hillside four kilometers north of town, were being used exclusively to host Venezuelan medical patients at last visit. (Islazul.)

CUC50–100: The **Hotel San Juan** (Av. Siboney y Calle 13, tel. 022/68-7200, fax 022/68-7017, jcarpeta@sanjuan.co.cu; CUC44 s, CUC58 d low season; CUC53 s, CUC69 d high season, including breakfast), on San Juan Hill, has 110 air-conditioned rooms in villa-style blocks—take an upstairs room with a lofty ceiling to help dissipate the heat. Each has satellite TV, modest furniture, safe, and large bathroom (12 have tubs only). Facilities include a swimming pool, boutique, tour desk, Internet, car rental, and restaurant and nightclub. (Islazul.)

Hotel Versalles (Alturas de Versalles Km 1, Carretera del Morro, tel. 022/69-1016, fax

022/68-6039, comercial@hotelversalles.co.cu), on the southern outskirts of town, was being used exclusively to host Venezuelan medical patients at last visit. (Cubanacán.)

Hotel Las Américas (Av. de las Américas y General Cebreco, tel. 022/64-2011, fax 022/68-7075, jcarpeta@hamerica.hor.tur.cu; CUC44 s, CUC58 d low season; CUC53 s, CUC69 d high season, including breakfast) is an uninspired property with 68 air-conditioned rooms, all with satellite TVs, phones, radios, and in-room safes. It offers two restaurants, a bar, entertainment, Internet service, tour desk, and car rental. (Islazul.)

Villa Gaviota (Manduley #502, e/ 19 y 21, tel. 022/64-1370, fax 022/68-7166, reservas@gaviota.co.cu; CUC40 s, CUC50 d standard, CUC53 s, CUC63 junior suite low season; CUC49 s, CUC59 d standard, CUC59 s, CUC69 d junior suite high season), in Vista Alegre, features 46 air-conditioned rooms with modestly handsome furnishings, telephone and satellite TV. There's a swimming pool, store, and a restaurant and disco. (Gaviota.)

CUC100-150: The ◖ **Hotel Casagranda** (Heredia #201, e/ Lacret y Hartman, tel. 022/68-6600, fax 022/68-6035, reserva@casagran.gca.tur.cu; CUC67 s, CUC96 d, CUC88–115 suite low season; CUC73 s, CUC112 d, CUC100–135 suite high season, including breakfast), on Parque Céspedes, is the place to be. It was recently restored and has 58 rooms, including three junior suites (one for guests with disabilities), all with air-conditioning, telephone, and satellite TV. Many rooms have splendid antique reproductions in walnut. Suites even have gold silk fabrics. It has an upscale restaurant, and you can sit on its first-floor veranda and sip a Cuba libre, smoke a *puro,* and watch the flood of life through the colonial plaza. (Gran Caribe.)

The ritziest place in town is the ◖ **Meliá Santiago de Cuba** (Av. de las Américas, esq. M, tel. 022/68-7070, fax 022/68-7170, www .meliasantiagodecuba.solmelia.com; CUC115 s/d standard, CUC145 s/d junior suite, CUC165 s/d suite year-round), a 15-story modernist structure with 270 rooms, 30 junior suites, and three suites. The spacious air-conditioned rooms are done up in lively fabrics with contemporary furniture, satellite TVs, telephones, and huge bathrooms. Facilities include a spa tub, sauna and massage, small gym, large swimming pool, cigar shop, beauty parlor, barber shop, business center, tour and rental desks, and nightclub. (Cubanacán.)

FOOD
Paladares

At last visit, of the 115 *paladares* in existence in 1996, only two survived. The best is **Paladar Salón Tropical** (Fernández Marcané #310, e/ 9 y 10, tel. 022/64-1161; Mon.–Fri. 6 P.M.–midnight, Sat. noon–midnight), offering rooftop dining beneath an arbor or a romantic cross-ventilated room with stained-glass windows. The large menu ranges from barbecue chicken (CUC6) and garbanzo stew (CUC4) to fricasséed lamb (CUC8). Scams are frequent here; check your bill carefully!

Downtown, and much the lesser option, **Paladar Las Gallegas** (Bartolomé Masó #305 altos, e/ Hartman y General Lacret, tel. 022/62-4700; daily noon–midnight; CUC3–5) offers goat fricassée, pork chops, and fried or roast chicken served in an upstairs room with balcony.

Criollo

On Plaza Dolores, **Restaurante Don Antonio** (Aguilera, e/ Calvario y Reloj, tel. 022/65-2205; noon–midnight daily) is housed in a beautiful colonial building, although the *criollo* dishes (CUC3–8) are uninspired. Here I prefer the modestly elegant **Café Matamoros** (Valientes, esq. Aguilera, tel. 022/62-2675; daily 11 A.M.–11 P.M.), serving *criollo* fare for less than CUC4; it has live music.

For colonial ambience, try **Santiago 1900** (Bartolomé Masó #354, e/ Pío Rosado y Hartmann, tel. 022/62-3507). This former home of the Bacardí family has an outdoor patio beneath an arbor around a fountain where you may dine on overpriced *criollo* food (CUC6 and up).

The best *criollo* fare is served at ◖ **Restaurante El Morro** (tel. 022/69-1576; noon–10 P.M. daily), at Parque Histórico El Morro. Set atop the cliffs with fabulous views, you dine on a terra-cotta–tiled terrace shaded by a gazebo covered by trumpet vine. Goat-hide chairs (the one hanging on the wall is there because Paul McCartney sat on it when he dined here), and serenades by troubadours add to the ambience. I recommend the bean soup (CUC1.50) and baked fish stuffed with shrimp (CUC15).

Continental

For cheap and basic Italian, head to **Ristorante Fontana di Tresi** (Saco, e/ General Lacret y Felix Peña; noon–5 P.M. and 6–11 P.M.), a no-frills air-conditioned diner serving pizzas and spaghetti.

The elegant **La Isabelica** (tel. 022/68-7070; 7–11 P.M. daily), in the Hotel Santiago, serves quality continental cuisine, but expect to pay CUC20 or more.

Some of the best cuisine in town is served at the stylish **Restaurante Casa Grande** (7–10 A.M., noon–3 P.M., and 7:30–10 P.M.), in the Hotel Casa Grande on Parque Céspedes; cuisine is *criollo* with a hint of the Continent (set meals from CUC15, à la carte dishes, such as grilled fish, about CUC10).

Seafood

My favorite restaurant in town is the **Restaurant Zunzún** (Av. Manduley #159, tel. 022/64-1528; noon–10 P.M. daily), in Vista Alegre. The old mansion has a more varied menu than most restaurants, ranging from *tapas* (CUC2) to lobster enchiladas (CUC24.50) and garlic shrimp (CUC14).

Dimar (Av. de las Américas, esq. D, tel. 022/69-1889; daily 10 A.M.–1 A.M.) is a clean café-style restaurant serving seafoods, including lobster, for below CUC10.

Cafés and Desserts

To relax after exploring the frenetic streets, head to the **Café de Té** (Aguilera, esq. General Lacret; Tues.–Sun. 9 A.M.–9 P.M.), which sells herbal and flavored teas; or **La Isabelica** (Aguilera, esq. Valientes, no tel.; 7 A.M.–10:45 P.M.), a 300-year-old tavern and coffeehouse favored by locals and where troubadours entertain.

For ice cream, head to **Coppelia** (Av. de los Libertadores, esq. Av. Garzón, tel. 022/62-0435; Tues.–Sun. 10 A.M.– 11:30 P.M.), selling scoops for pesos.

Self-Catering

You can buy fresh produce and meats at the **mercado agropecuario** at Aguilera and Padre Pico; and Western goods at supermarkets along Aguilera or in the stores of the Hotel Santiago.

SHOPPING

Calle Heredia, east of Parque Céspedes, is lined with arts and crafts stalls. For fine art head to **Galería de Arte UNEAC** (Heredia, e/ Hartmann y Pio Rosada, tel. 022/65-3465, ext. 106, www.uneac.com).

Fábrica de Instrumentos Musicales (Patricio Lumumba #55, tel. 022/62-5256) is a workshop where guitars, drums, and other musical instruments are made and sold. For recorded music, check out **Egrem** (Corona #564, e/ Saco y Aguilera, tel. 022/65-2227), with a large CD selection.

The tasting room adjoining **Fábrica de Ron Caney** (Av. Peralejo #103, tel. 022/62-5575) sells a wide range of national rums, including rare 25-year-old Ron Paticruzado in special porcelain bottles. It is also well-stocked with cigars, as is the **Casa del Habano** (Aguilera, esq. Jesús Menéndez, tel. 022/65-4207; Mon.– Fri. 8 A.M.–4 P.M.), with a small smokers' lounge and bar upstairs. The **Casa del Tabaco** (daily 8 A.M.–8 P.M.) in the Hotel Santiago is also recommended.

For a genuine *guayabera*, head to **El Quitrín** (Hechavarría #473, e/ Porfirio Valiente y Pio Rosada, tel. 022/62-2528; Mon.–Fri. 8 A.M.–4 P.M.), where hand-embroidered shirts, blouses, and skirts are sold.

INFORMATION AND SERVICES

Money: There are branches of **Banco Financiero Internacional** on Félix Pena one block north of Parque Céspedes, and on Saco, esq. Porfirio Valiente; **Bandec** on both east and west sides of Parque Céspedes, and on Saco, esq. Mariano Corona; and **Banco Popular** on the south side of Plaza Dolores, and on Saco, esq. Mariano Corona. You can also exchange foreign currency at **Cadeca** (Aguilera #508, tel. 022/65-1383).

Communications: The **post office** (Aguilera #310, esq. Padre Quiroga) adjoins **DHL** (tel. 202/68-6323 or 65-4750).

Etecsa (Heredia, e/ Félix Pena y General Lacret, tel. 022/62-4784; daily 8:30 A.M.– 9 P.M.), on the south side of Parque Céspedes, has international telephone and Internet service. All the tourist hotels have Internet service, with pricing in proportion to room rate: for example, the Hotel Meliá Santiago de Cuba charges CUC9 hourly, the Hotel San Juan charges CUC5.

Cubacel (Calle 6, e/ 7 y 9, tel. 022/588-5022; Mon.–Fri. 8 A.M.–1 P.M. and 1:30–4:30 P.M., Sat. 8 A.M.–noon) rents cellular phones and will hook up your personal cellular.

Medical: The **Clínica Internacional** (Av. Raúl Pujol, esq. Calle 8, tel. 022/68-2589 or 68-7071; 24 hours) charges CUC25 per consultation, or CUC30 between 4 P.M. and 7 A.M. and for hotel visits. The clinic has a modestly stocked pharmacy, and an **Ópticas Miramar** (tel. 022/62-5259) for optical services.

Emergency, Legal, and Immigration Services: In trouble? **Asistur** (Calle 4, e/ 7 y 9, tel. 022/68-6128, asisturstago@enet.cu; Mon.–Sat. 8 A.M.–5 P.M.), on Parque Céspedes, provides travelers' emergency assistance. The **Consultoría Jurídica Internacional** (Calle 8 #54, e/ 1 y 3, Rpto. Vista Alegre, tel. 022/68-7236) provides legal services.

Immigration (Calle 13, e/ Carretera de Carey y 14, tel. 022/64-1983; Mon., Tues., Thurs., and Fri. 8:30 A.M.–noon and 1–4 P.M.) issues *prórrogas*. You'll need your passport, tourist card, and airline ticket, but first you must go to Bandec on the west side of Parque Céspedes to buy a *sello* (official stamp; CUC25).

GETTING THERE AND AWAY
By Air
Aeropuerto Internacional Antonio Maceo (tel. 022/69-1014), off Carretera del Morro, is eight kilometers south of Santiago. Buses #212 and 213 (via Punta Gorda) operate between the airport and opposite the hospital on Avenida de los Libertadores, downtown. A taxi costs about CUC6 one-way.

Cubana (Enramada, esq. San Pedro, tel. 022/65-1577; at the airport, tel. 022/69-8614) serves Santiago de Cuba with direct flights from Europe. Cubana also has three flights daily from Havana to Santiago on Monday, and two flights on other days; as well as service between Santiago and Varadero, Camagüey, and Baracoa. **Aero Caribbean** (San Pedro, e/ Heredia y San Basilio, tel. 022/68-7255; at the airport, tel. 022/69-1014) also flies daily from Havana.

By Bus
Buses arrive and depart the **Terminal de Ómnibus Nacional** (Av. de los Libertadores, esq. Av. Juan Gualberto Gómez, tel. 022/62-3050) **Víazul** (tel. 022/62-8484) buses for Santiago de Cuba depart daily from Havana at 9:30 A.M., 3 P.M., 6:15 P.M. (express), and 10 P.M.; from Baracoa at 2:15 P.M.; from Trinidad at 8 A.M.; and from Varadero at 8:55 P.M. Buses depart Santiago de Cuba for Havana at 9 A.M. (express), 3:15 P.M., 6 P.M., and 10 P.M.; for Baracoa at 7:45 A.M.; for Trinidad at 7:30 P.M.; and for Varadero at 8:30 P.M.

Astro (tel. 022/62-6091) public buses depart for Havana (CUC42) daily at 2:30 P.M. and 7:30 P.M.; for Baracoa (CUC9) at 8 A.M.; for Bayamo (CUC5) at 9:40 A.M. and 10:40 A.M.; for Camagüey (CUC12.50) at 6 P.M.; for Cienfuegos (CUC25.50) at 4 P.M. on alternate days; for Holguín (CUC7.50) at 12:20 P.M.; for Matanzas (CUC30.50) at 3:20 P.M.; for Niquero (CUC10) at 7 A.M. on alternate days; for Pilón (CUC10.50) at 7:20 A.M. on alternate days; and for Santa Clara (CUC22.50) at 4 P.M.

Local buses and *camiones* operate to outlying destinations, including El Cobre and Baconao, from the **Terminal de Ómnibus Municipales** (Av. de los Libertadores y Calle 4, tel. 022/62-4329).

Camiones for Bayamo and Guantánamo

leave from the **Terminal de Ómnibus Inter-municipales Serrano** (Av. Jesús Menéndez, e/ Máximo Gómez y Juan Bautista Sagarra, tel. 022/62-4325).

By Train

Trains arrive and depart the railway station (Av. Jesús Menéndez y Martí, tel. 022/62-2836). Buy your tickets at the ticket office (*espendido de boletas,* tel. 022/65-3978) on the north side of the station, or at the **Centro Único de Reservaciones** (Aguilera #165, tel. 022/65-2143; Mon.–Fri. 8:30 A.M.–3:30 P.M.).

See the sidebar *Train Schedule and Fares* chart in the *Essentials* chapter for details of train service.

By Sea

Ships berth at the cruise terminal (Av. Jesús Menéndez, tel. 022/65-1763).

Marina Marlin (tel. 022/69-1446, fax 022/68-6108), at Punta Gorda, has moorings for 60 yachts (CUC0.40 per foot per day, including water and electricity).

Heave-Ho Charters (180 Main St., Ocho Rios, Jamaica, tel. 876/974-5367, fax 876/974-5461, www.heave-ho.net) offers passage between Ocho Rios and Santiago de Cuba aboard a catamaran.

By Car

All tourist hotels have rental car agencies, but there's a shortage of cars and advance reservations are a must. **Havanautos** (Hotel Las Américas, tel. 022/68-7160), **Transtur** (Hotel San Juan, tel. 022/68-7206; Av. de los Libertadores, esq. Av. Juan Gualberto Gómez, tel. 022/62-3884; and beneath the Hotel Casa Grande on Parque Céspede, tel. 022/68-6170),

Vía (on the southeast corner of Parque Céspedes), and **Rex** (tel. 022/68-6445 downtown; tel. 022/68-6446 airport) all have offices at the airport.

There are gas stations at Avenida de Céspedes, esq. Avenida de los Libertadores; on Paseo; on Avenida 24 de Febrero; and, two kilometers farther north, on the road to Bayamo.

GETTING AROUND

Buses serve most of the city (fare is 20 centavos), but they are horrendously crowded. Bus #1 runs between Parque Céspedes and both the interprovincial and intermunicipal bus terminals. Bus #213 runs from Avenida de los Libertadores to Punta Gorda. Most people get around on *camiones,* penned in shoulder-to-shoulder like cattle! One leaves from the south side of Parque Céspedes for Cuartel Moncada and Vista Alegre; others run along the main boulevards.

Taxis hang out on the south side of Parque Céspedes and outside the tourist hotels. A taxi between the Vista Alegre district and Parque Céspedes should cost about CUC3. **Cubataxi** (tel. 226/65-1038) has taxis on call and is cheaper than tourist taxis outside hotels.

You can rent **scooters** at the Hotel San Juan (Av. de las Américas, esq. M).

All the tourist hotels offer excursions. City tours are offered by **Cubatur** (Heredia, esq. General Lacret, tel. 022/65-2560); **Cubanacán** (Av. de las Américas y M, tel. 022/64-2202); and **Paradiso** (tel. 022/62-7037, cuesta@artexsc.esisc.colombus.cu), which specializes in cultural tours. **EcoTur** (Carlos Duboi #309, e/ Princesa y San Fernando, tel. 026/65-3859) offers ecotourism excursions.

North and West of Santiago

EL COBRE

The small town of El Cobre, on the Carretera Central, 20 kilometers northwest of Santiago, takes its name from the copper mine that the Spanish established in the mid-1500s, run by German engineers. By the end of the century the mine was providing Havana's artillery works' entire supply of copper. In 1630, it was abandoned, and the African slave-miners were unilaterally freed. A century later it was reopened by Colonel Don Pedro Jiménez, governor of Santiago, who put the slaves' descendants back to work. The slaves were officially declared free in 1782, a century before their brethren in the cane fields. Although the mine closed in 2000, the pit (filled with a turquoise lagoon) can be seen from the **Monumento al Cimarrón,** beyond the village. This monument, reached by steep stairs, is dedicated to the slaves who rebelled.

◖ Basílica de Nuestra Señora del Cobre

Dominating the town from atop a small hillock is the ocher-colored, red-domed, triple-towered Basílica del Cobre (tel. 022/36118; daily 6:30 A.M.–6 P.M.). The church—Cuba's only basilica—was erected in 1927 (a hermitage has occupied the site since 1608, however) and is a national shrine. Once a year, thousands of devoted Cubans make their way along the winding road, many crawling painfully uphill to fulfill a promise made to the saint at some difficult moment in their lives. The unlucky fisherman in Ernest Hemingway's *Old Man and the Sea* promises to "make a pilgrimage to the Virgin de Cobre" if he wins his battle with the massive marlin. In 1952, Hemingway dedicated his Nobel Prize for Literature to the Virgin, placing it in her shrine.

The front entrance is reached via a steep staircase. More usual is to enter at the rear, from the parking lot. Touts will rush forward to sell you iron pyrite (fool's gold) culled from the residue of the nearby mine. *"Es real!"* they

interior of the Basílica de Nuestra Señora del Cobre

say, attempting to put a small piece in your hand. Here, the church lobby—the Sala de Milagros (Salon of Miracles)—contains a small chapel with a silver altar crowded with votive candles and flowers. To left and right are tables with miscellaneous objects placed in offering. On the walls hang scores of silver adornment and little *milagros* of limbs and other body parts. The two centuries of ex-votos include a small gold figure left by Castro's mother, Lina Ruz, to protect her two sons, Fidel and Raúl, during the war in the Sierra Maestra. Incredibly, here too are bequests for the freedom of Cuban political prisoners.

The church nave has a large marble altarpiece and stained-glass windows. The **Virgen de la Caridad del Cobre** (Virgin of Charity), the patron saint of Cuba to whom miraculous powers are ascribed, resides in effigy in an air-conditioned glass case in a separate altar above the main altar. You can view her

THE LEGEND OF THE BLACK VIRGIN

All Cubans know the legend of the Virgen de la Caridad (colloquially known as the Virgen del Cobre), the most revered religious figure in Cuba. According to folklore, in 1608, two mulatto brothers, Rodrigo and Juan de Hoyos, and a young black boy, Juan Moreno, were fishing in the Bay of Nipes, off the north coast of Cuba, when they were caught in a storm. As their boat was about to capsize, a small raft appeared bearing a statue of a black Virgin Mary holding a black baby Jesus and a cross. The statue was inscribed with the words *Yo soy la Virgen de la Caridad* (I am the Virgin of Charity). At that moment the seas calmed.

The story gained popularity and miracles were ascribed to the virgin. In time a shrine was built near the copper mine at El Cobre. Pope Benedicto XV declared her the Patron Saint of Cuba on May 10, 1916.

Today, the black Virgin is associated with Ochún, the *santería* goddess of love and water. She is usually depicted in a yellow gown, standing atop the waves with the three fishermen in their little boat at her feet.

up close by taking a staircase marked *subida* from the lobby. The virgin's figure, clad in a golden cloak and crown, is surrounded by a sea of flowers, and the entire shrine is suffused with narcotic scents.

Masses (*misas*) are offered Monday–Saturday (except Wed.) at 8 A.M., on the eighth day and the first Thursday of each month at 8 P.M., and Sunday at 8 and 10 A.M. and 4:30 P.M.

Accommodations and Food

The **Hospedaje El Cobre** (tel. 022/36246), behind the church, serves pilgrims and has 16 basic rooms where foreigners are welcome when space allows; each room has three single beds and a private bathroom (eight pesos per person per night). You can also bunk in a dormitory (five pesos per person). Married couples must show ID with the same address. A refectory serves basic fare at 7:30 A.M., 11:30 A.M., and 6 P.M. For reservations, write Hermana Elsa Aranda, Hospedaje El Cobre, El Cobre, Santiago de Cuba.

Getting There

Bus #202 operates four times daily to El Cobre from Santiago's Terminal de Ómnibus Intermunicipales, and several *camiones* run daily from Avenida de las Américas, esq. Calle M, and from Avenida de los Libertadores y Calle 4. A taxi from Santiago will cost about CUC25 round-trip. Tour operators in Santiago offer excursions.

◖ EL SALTÓN

The easternmost spurs of the Sierra Maestra rise west of Santiago de Cuba. El Saltón is touted as a mountain health resort, with a natural pool and picture-perfect cascades nestled in a valley high in the mountains. Few roads penetrate the mountains, making your arrival at El Saltón all the more breathtaking. The lodge offers massage, sauna, and whirlpool, as well as horseback rides (CUC2 per hour). It is excellent for bird-watching, and guided hikes lead to a cocoa plantation.

Accommodations

Hotel Horizontes El Saltón (Carretera Puerto Rico a Filé, III Frente, tel. 0225/6326, fax 0225/6492; CUC33 s, CUC35 d low season; CUC35 s, CUC48 d high season) is an eco-lodge built in the 1970s as an anti-stress center for the Cuban elite. Accommodations are in 22 modestly appointed double rooms in four separate buildings, with satellite TV. There's an open-sided, thatched restaurant overlooking the river. The hotel was planning on adding tents on its lawns. (Cubanacán.)

Getting There

El Saltón is reached from Contramaestre, on the Carretera Central about 70 kilometers northwest of Santiago de Cuba; then 27 kilometers south to the village of Cruce de los Baños, where the paved road gives out. El

Saltón is eight kilometers west of Cruce via the community of Filé. (An alternate route from Santiago via Dos Palmas, 15 km northwest of El Cobre and appearing more direct on maps, is badly deteriorated. With a four-wheel drive vehicle, you may be able to tackle the steep and rugged dirt road that crosses the Sierra Maestra from Río Seco, on the south coast, but this is purely a dry-weather drive for those who like a challenge.)

Buses operate into the Sierras from Terminal de Ómnibus Intermunicipales Serrano in Santiago.

SANTIAGO TO CHIVIRICO

The drive west along the coast from Santiago is magnificent, with the Sierra Maestra plummeting to a crashing sea. The road becomes gradually more lonesome as you pass rustic fishing villages and pocket-size beaches tucked along paradisiacal bays. In late 2005, much of the road had been washed away; a temporary makeshift road ran along the beach in parts and may be impassable at high tide and in storms.

The only settlement of note is Chivirico, about 80 kilometers west of Santiago. This small, dusty fishing village is protected within a cove in the lee of a steep peninsula. Here you'll find two foreign-operated hotels with knockout views. To the west of town is a long brown-sand beach that gets thronged by locals. Nearby **Las Cuevas de Murciélagos** is full of harmless bats, while about 22 kilometers further west of Chivirico, at **Uvero** and reached via a glade of palms, is a monument marking the site where Castro's Rebel Army won its first major victory against Batista's troops on May 28, 1957.

Museo Combate de la Plata

About 12 kilometers west of Ocujal (48 km west of Chivirico), you cross the mouth of the Río La Plata. It was here, on January 17, 1957, that Castro's rebel army first came down from the Sierra Maestra to attack a small garrison of Batista's Rural Guard. The small museum (Tues.–Sat. 9 A.M.–noon and 2–6 P.M., Sun. 9 A.M.–noon; CUC1) is 400 meters off the

road, beside the river, on the west side of the bridge. It comprises three thatched huts amid trim lawns with roses, and exhibits uniforms, maps, small arms, and more. There's no sign when traveling eastbound. In wet season, you may need to hike from the main road.

Hiking to Pico Turquino

Just as Edmund Hillary climbed Everest "because it was there," so Pico Turquino lures the intrepid who seek the satisfaction of reaching the summit of Cuba's highest peak, heart of the 17,450-hectare Parque Nacional Pico Turquino (see *Parque Nacional Pico Turquino* in the *Granma* chapter). The 13-kilometer trail begins at Las Cuevas (55 km west of Chivirico), where the **Estación Biológica Las Cuevas del Turquino** has a **Centro de Informaciones.** Wooden signs point the way to the summit, from where the views are spectacular.

It's best to set off before dawn to attain the summit before clouds set in. No departures are permitted after 7 A.M. A guide is compulsory (CUC15 per person, plus CUC3 for cameras), arranged through the Centro de Informaciones at Las Cuevas; the Centro de Visitantes on the north side in Santo Domingo; or **Empresa Flora y Fauna** (tel. 059/56-5349), in Bartolomé Masó. Don't forget to tip the guide! You normally ascend and return in one day, an eight- to 10-hour feat, although there are shelters at 1,650 meters on the flanks of Pico Cuba, and at 600 meters at La Esmajagua, midway between Pico Cuba and Las Cuevas. A crude map posted beside the road and trailhead shows the campsites, which also include a basic facility at Gumajacua, about 600 meters from Las Cuevas, where you can camp at Estación Las Cuevas or sleep in a basic dormitory with three beds (CUC5 per person).

If you want to cross the Sierra, you can hike all the way from Las Cuevas to Alto del Naranjo, on the north side of the mountain, a two- or three-day journey. You'll need two sets of guides; one for each side of the mountain. The north side is longer, but slightly easier; the southern route from Las Cuevas is dauntingly steep.

You'll need to be self-sufficient (bring all the food and water you need). The weather is unpredictable; dress accordingly. Cold winds often kick up near the summit; the humidity and wind-chill factor can drop temperatures to near freezing. Rain is always a possibility, and short downpours are common in mid-afternoon. Fog is almost a daily occurrence at higher elevations, often forming in mid-morning.

Recreation

Fishing and horseback riding are available at the Brisas hotels, as is a jeep safari (CUC35).

The Brisas Sierra Mar offers **scuba diving** (CUC30, or CUC60 for a wreck-dive; CUC365 for a certification course). The most popular dive site is the wreck of the Spanish ironclad cruiser *Colón,* sunk on July 3, 1898, by the U.S. Navy when the Spanish navy attempted to break out of Santiago harbor. It rests on a submarine shelf just 20 meters below the surface, 35 meters from shore just east of Ocujal. Two other wrecks can be seen by snorkelers or divers: offshore at Km 24.7 is the wreck of the Spanish-American warship *Juan González;* and off Asseredero, at Km 32, lies the wreck of the cruiser *Viscaya.*

Accommodations

Campismo La Mula (reservations: Campismo Popular, Cornelio Robén #163, e/ Mariano Corona y Padre Pico, Santiago de Cuba, tel. 022/62-9000; CUC5 per person) at the mouth of the Río La Mula, five kilometers east of Ocujal and 12 kilometers from Las Cuevas, is a simple holiday camp where you can mingle with Cubans (many of whom will probably be hiking to Pico Turquino). Ten of its 50 basically appointed cabins with cold showers are reserved for foreigners and a thatched restaurant serves simple fare. Mosquitoes abound. (Cubamar.)

Brisas Sierra Mar (Carretera de Chivirico Km 60, tel. 022/62-9110, fax 022/62-9007, galeones@smar.scu.cyt.cu; CUC46 s, CUC84 d low season; CUC55 s, CUC94 d high season) is a beautiful 200-room oceanfront all-inclusive property 10 kilometers east of Chivirico.

A spacious lobby opens onto a wide terrace and swimming pool high above the beach, with fine coast and mountain views. Air-conditioned rooms are nicely furnished and have modern accoutrements. It has two restaurants, five bars, a boutique, fitness room, a whirlpool tub, a huge pool with water slide, plus tennis and water sports. (Cubanacán.)

The smaller **Brisas Los Galeones** (Carretera de Chivirico Km 60, tel. 022/62-6160, fax 022/62-9116, galeones@smar.scu.cyt.cu; same rates as Brisas Sierra Mar) is a more intimate 34-room all-inclusive perched atop a headland with views. The spacious air-conditioned rooms have king-size beds, hardwood ceilings, tile floors, and balconies. A pleasing restaurant overlooks the pool. Facilities include a game room, basic fitness center, sauna, and dive shop. A 296-step staircase leads to a beach with bar. Guests can also use the facilities of the Sierra Mar, to which a shuttle operates. (Cubanacán.)

Food

Nonguests can buy day passes to the **Sierra Mar** and **Los Galeones** hotels (CUC15 per person 9 A.M.–6 P.M.; CUC20 7–11 P.M., CUC25 9 A.M.–11 P.M., including all meals and drinks).

MAYARÍ ARRIBA

The rugged, mineral-rich Sierra del Cristal rise over northeast Santiago de Cuba Province. French coffee planters established estates here in the 19th century, though the region remained remote and sparsely inhabited until the Revolution, when a paved road was built. The road leads via the crossroads village of Alto Songo, 23 kilometers northeast of Santiago, to the town of Mayarí Arriba, 35 kilometers northeast of Alto Songo. Carlos Manuel de Céspedes established his revolutionary government here in the 1860s, and Raúl Castro established his military headquarters here when he opened the Second Front in 1958.

The **Museo Comandancia del Segundo Frente** (Museum of the Second Front, Av. de los Mártires, tel. 022/25249, Tues.–Sun. 7:30 A.M.–

noon and 1–5:30 P.M.; CUC1) displays photos, maps, and military hardware, including a helicopter in the grounds.

Continuing uphill past the museum, a palm-lined boulevard delivers you at the **Mauso-leo del Segundo Frente,** a dramatic marble mausoleum set in an arc of Royal palms, surrounded by red *califo rojo* plants (they represent the blood of revolutionary martyrs). A ceremony is held here each March 11.

Reserva de la Biosfera Baconao

The 32,400-hectare Baconao Biosphere Reserve extends 40 kilometers from the eastern suburbs of Santiago to Laguna Baconao and the border with Guantánamo Province. The park is mostly mountainous and was named a biosphere reserve by UNESCO for its biodiversity, including more than 6,000 species of higher plants, more than 800 insect species, plus 29 reptile species, 60 bird species, and 19 mammal species, many endemic to the region.

The area boasts no end of other attractions, from beaches and artist communities to museums and revolutionary shrines. A full day is barely sufficient. It is reached from Santiago via the Carretera Siboney, lined with 26 **monuments** to the heroes of the Moncada attack.

Much of the region is a coastal plain with several rocky gold-sand beaches popular with locals on weekends. They're not particularly inspiring (except Playa Siboney and Playa Daiquirí, which is exclusively for the use of members of the Cuban military and their families) and despite the availability of tourist hotels, they're more suited to a day visit than a vacation base.

© CHRISTOPHER P. BAKER

SANTIAGO DE CUBA

The dolphins at Acuario Baconao are friendly critters.

Getting There and Away

Bus #214 operates from Santiago de Cuba's Terminal de Ómnibus Municipales (Av. de los Libertadores, esq. Calle 4) and travels to Playa Siboney, which is also served by *camiones*. Bus #401 departs the same terminal at 6 A.M. and 6:30 P.M. and travels to the end of the road at the hamlet of Baconao (return buses depart two hours later). Bus #407 travels as far as Playa Juragua thrice daily.

A taxi from Santiago will cost about CUC35 round-trip to Siboney. If you take a taxi to Baconao, be sure to pre-arrange a pick-up for the return.

If driving, be sure to slow for the *punto de control* (police checkpoint) two kilometers east of Sevilla. The only gas station (24 hours) is 26 kilometers east of Santiago, at the entrance to the auto museum.

Legions of large crabs scurry across the road in springtime causing many a puncture (and quite a stench) when they're crushed by passing vehicles.

PARQUE NACIONAL GRAN PIEDRA

This park encompasses the Cordillera de la Gran Piedra, a splendidly cool lush environment for bird-watching and hiking. Access is from a T junction at Las Guasimas, 13 kilometers from Santiago, where the **Prado de las Esculturas** (8 A.M.–4 P.M. daily; CUC1) is a sculpture garden with about 20 uninspired contemporary works lining a trail.

The much deteriorated road winds up through ravines, growing ever steeper and more serpentine until it deposits you at the top of **Pico Gran Piedra** (1,234 meters), a distance of 14 kilometers. You pass through several ecosystems. Below is lush and thick with forest. As you climb, the vegetation opens out, becoming scrubbier, and the views grow more dramatic. Suddenly you emerge on a ridge with a view down the mountains to the north. It's noticeably crisper and cooler up here, where clouds hover, swirling through the ancient tree ferns, tall pines, and bamboo. The road follows the ridgeline, giving views of the Atlantic to the north and the Caribbean below.

A restaurant and hotel sit at 1,150 meters elevation, where guides can be hired to hike the four trails (CUC2 per person). From here a 454-step stairway leads up to the **Gran Piedra** (Great Rock), where you can climb a steel ladder onto the massive boulder for a spectacular view down the mountainside. On a clear day you can see the Blue Mountains in Jamaica; and by night, the lights of Port-au-Spain, Haiti.

A bus from Santiago de Cuba runs only once weekly.

Jardín Ave de Paraíso

This 45-hectare garden (7 A.M.–4 P.M. daily; CUC1), 800 meters west of Villa Gran Piedra, was created in 1960 on a former coffee plantation to raise flowers. The garden is a riot of color and scents, difficult to dampen in even the wettest of weather. The guides will gladly show you around a series of interlocking, juxtaposed gardens, each with its own color scheme, surrounded by neatly clipped topiary hedges. Amaryllis grow with carnations, *salvia roja* spring up beside daisies, blood-red dahlias thrive beside the garden's namesake "bird of paradise," almost overwhelming with their vivid oranges, blues, and purples. There are potting sheds, too, full of begonias and anthuriums, and a prim little courtyard with a small café and *florería* where you can buy floral displays.

in a sheltered bay with a modestly appealing beach, **Playa Siboney,** encusped by coral rocks. Being the closest beach to the city, it's popular with Cubans who flock from Santiago to relax. A war memorial recalls the landing of U.S. troops on June 24, 1898.

Granjita Siboney

This red-and-white, red-tile-roofed farmhouse, about one kilometer inland of Siboney, is the site from which Fidel and his loyal cohorts gathered for their attack on the Moncada barracks: They sang the national anthem in whispers, and at five o'clock on the morning of Sunday, July 26, 1953, Castro and 123 fellow rebels set out in a convoy of 26 cars. Today it is a museum (tel. 022/39168; 9 A.M.–5 P.M.; entrance CUC1, cameras CUC1, videos CUC5) displaying weapons and bloodstained uniforms, along with a map of the Moncada attack. Newspaper clippings tell the tale of horrific torture. (Six of the attackers died in the attack; 61 others died in captivity. Batista's henchmen then took the already-dead revolutionaries to Granjita Siboney, laid them on the porch and inside the house, then blasted them with gunfire to give the impression that they had been caught plotting and were shot in a battle.)

◖ Museo de la Guerra Hispano-Americano

This excellent little museum (tel. 022/39119; Mon.–Sat. 9 A.M.–5 P.M.; entrance CUC1, cameras CUC1, videos CUC5), 100 meters west of Granjita Siboney, is dedicated to the Spanish-American War. It displays photos and original cannons and other weaponry, including shells and two Spanish torpedoes (one unexploded; the second the remains of a torpedo that struck the USS *Merrimac*), plus miscellaneous parts from both the U.S. and Spanish vessels.

Accommodations

About two dozen *casas particulares* cater to foreigners.

Casa de Ovidio González Sabaldo (Av. Serrano y Calle del Barco, tel. 022/39340;

Visits are permitted only with a voucher sold by **Cubanacán** (Av. de las Américas y M, tel. 022/64-2202; CUC5) in Santiago.

Cafetal La Isabelica

Two kilometers east of Gran Piedra via a rutted dirt road are the remains of a coffee plantation and manor built by Victor Constantin Couson, a French immigrant fleeing Haiti during the slave rebellion of 1792. Now a museum (8 A.M.–4 P.M. daily; CUC1), the ruins of the two-story *finca* exhibit farming implements and furniture. The coffee-crushing wheel can still be seen. Trails lead through the now-overgrown estate and forests.

Accommodations

Villa Gran Piedra (Carretera de la Gran Piedra, Km 14, tel. 022/68-6147, villa@gpiedra.scu.cyt.cu) has 22 rustic, modestly furnished red-brick cottages atop the ridge crest—a spectacular setting! They were temporarily closed at last visit. A restaurant and bar sit atop the ridge. (Islazul.)

SIBONEY

The little village of Siboney, replete with wooden French-style Caribbean homes, lies

CUC20–50) is a splendid three-story wooden home with two modestly furnished rooms with private hot-water bathrooms. Upstairs a separate two-bedroom, cross-ventilated apartment is beautiful with its tropical colors. **Casa de María Elena González** (Obelisco #10, tel. 022/39200; CUC20) is a clean, cross-ventilated modern three-story house with a swimming pool in the stone patio and a preferred position above the shore. It has two rooms: One opens to a breeze-swept terrace with rockers and fabulous views; the second, atop the roof, has floor-to-ceiling louvered glass windows.

Food

The breeze-swept **Restaurante La Rueda** (tel. 022/39325; Mon.–Tues. 9 A.M.–6 P.M., Thurs.–Sun. 9 A.M.–midnight), at the junction of the main street and Calle del Barco, serves *criollo* fare for less than CUC5.

SIBONEY TO PLAYA VERRACO

From a T junction at Granjita Siboney, a spur road south leads to and dead-ends in Siboney while the main road leads east to other sights.

Comunidad Artística Oasis and Vicinity

First up is this pretty little hamlet of field-stone cottages, about three kilometers from the T junction. This entire community, comprising 10 families, works as artists and has open studios. Horseback rides are offered at **Finca Guajira Rodeo,** where rodeos are held on Tuesday, Thursday, Saturday, and Sunday at 2:30 P.M. (CUC5).

The side road through the hamlet continues to **Playa Arroyo,** a small beach, and then **Playa Bucanero,** a magnificent golden-sand beach that is the private reserve of the Hotel Bucanero. About three kilometers east of El Oasis, another side road leads south to **Playa Jaragua,** a beige-colored beach popular with Cubans from Santiago.

Valle de la Prehistoria

It's a shock to find a *Tyrannosaurus rex* prowling the Prehistoric Valley (Carretera de Baconao; 8 A.M.–4:45 P.M. daily; entrance CUC1, cameras CUC1, videos CUC5) of the Río Arenas, about six kilometers east of El Oasis. The ferocious-looking dinosaur is one of dozens of life-size reptiles that lurk in a lush, natural setting. *Apatosaurus* (the erstwhile brontosaurus) is there, wallowing in a pool that dries out in the dry season. There are even woolly mammoths and a pterodactyl, wings outspread atop a nearby hillock. Real-life goats nibble contentedly amid the fearsome make-believe beasts made of concrete.

A **Museo de Ciencias Naturales** (tel. 022/39-239; 8 A.M.–4:45 P.M. daily; CUC1) displays butterflies, polymite snails, and recreations of various environments replete with stuffed animals and birds.

Museo Nacional de Transporte Terreste

Dowagers from the heyday of Detroit and Coventry are on view at this auto museum (tel. 022/39197; 8 A.M.–5 P.M. daily; entrance CUC1, cameras CUC1, videos CUC2), behind the Cupet gas station, two kilometers east of the Valle de la Prehistoria. Custodians put the spit and polish to about three dozen cars, from a 1912 Model-T Ford to a 1960 Lincoln Continental, a 1958 Thunderbird, a 1954 MG sports car, and singer Benny Moré's Cadillac. Here, too, the **Museo de Autos Miniaturas** (Miniature Car Museum) contains more than 2,500 tiny toy cars, from the earliest models to modern-day productions. Separate cases are dedicated to fire trucks, ambulances, racing cars, and others.

Playa Daiquirí

A side road at the gas station leads to Playa Daiquirí, which lent its name to the famous drink. It was here that Teddy Roosevelt and his Rough Riders disembarked in 1898 during the Spanish-American War; and that U.S. Marines landed in 1912 and 1917 to quell a series of strikes in Santiago and Guantánamo. Playa Daiquirí and nearby Playa Bacajagua are off-limits to all but the privileged members of FAR (the Armed Forces) and their families.

Playa Verraco

About eight kilometers east of the gas station, you'll come to a bend in the road with a huge, brightly colored mosaic of a *tocororo,* the national bird of Cuba, inlaid in the hillside. A few kilometers beyond is **Comunidad Artística Los Mamoncillas,** at Playa Verraco. Here, the entire community is engaged in arts, particularly pottery and sculpture. You're welcome to browse the open studios.

Accommodations and Food

✿ Casa de Enrique y Rosa (Carretera de Baconao Km 17.5, Comunidad Artística Los Mamoncillas, Playa Verraco, tel. 022/35-6205; CUC20) is the home of a wonderful family of ceramists who rent one lofty, cool and spacious air-conditioned room with fan, refrigerator, lots of closet space, and a delightful tiled bathroom with hot water. The incredible oval kitchen table of wood and clay is their own priceless creation! Walls are festooned with ceramics. They have their own generator, secure parking, and a peaceful courtyard sculpture garden.

Villas Los Mamoncillos (tel. 022/39233; CUC15 up to four people), about 400 meters inland of Playa Verraco, has basic stone *cabañas* utilized by Cuban workers on holiday. Foreigners can rent air-conditioned units with fans, refrigerators, and private bathrooms with cold water. A basic restaurant serves unappetizing fare. It's open May–August only.

Nearby, **Campismo Playa Larga** (tel. 022/35-6280), also with simple cabins, was closed at last visit, while **Coralia Club Bucanero** (Carretera de Baconao Km 4, Arroyo La Costa, tel. 022/68-6363, fax 022/68-6070), a 200-room all-inclusive resort, was trashed by Hurricane Dennis and was scheduled to be rebuilt. (Gran Caribe.)

EAST OF VERRACO

Beyond Verraco, a massive limestone plateau shoulders up against the coast, with the road running between them. The Carretera Baconao ends just beyond the hamlet of Baconao, where there's a military barrier.

Acuario Baconao

It's quite a surprise to come across this dolphinarium and aquatic park (tel. 022/36-5156; Tues.–Sun. 9 A.M.–5 P.M.; CUC5 adults, CUC3 children) in the middle of nowhere, about 50 kilometers east of Santiago de Cuba. The rather dismal exhibits include moray eels, marine turtles, and a shark tank with walk-through glass tunnel. The highlight is the 15-meter-wide dolphin pool into which you may plop to swim with Floppy, Jupey, and Junca (CUC39 adults, CUC25 children). Two sea lions perform tricks alongside the dolphins at 10:30 A.M. and 3 P.M.

Complejo Turístico Laguna Baconao

The large Laguna Baconao, immediately west of the hamlet of Baconao, is encusped by mountains at the far east end of Bacanao reserve. There are a few dolphins (and crocodiles, apparently) in the lake. Boat excursions are offered (CUC3) and pedal-boats can be hired (CUC5) at the Baconao Lagoon Tourist Complex (Carretera Baconao Km 53; 8 A.M.–5 P.M. daily), where crocs are bred as a tourist attraction.

Jardín de Cactos

The land hereabouts is covered with cacti, most spectacularly featured in the small but impressive Cactus Garden (daily 8 A.M.–3 P.M.; CUC5), set into the hillside just beyond the modestly appealing Playa Sigua. Some 200 species from around the world are displayed. **Expo Mesoamérica** is another cactus garden containing Mesoamerican sculptures at the base of cliffs opposite the Club Amigo Los Corales.

Accommodations and Food

The **Hotel Costa Marena** (Playa Larga, Carretera de Baconao, Km 38.5, tel. 022/35-6126, fax 022/35-6155), plus Cubanacán's **Club Amigo Carisol** (tel. 022/35-6115, fax 022/35-6106, reserva@carisol-corales.co.cu) and nearby **Club Amigo Los Corales** (tel. 022/35-6122, fax 022/35-6116, reserva@carisol-corales.co.cu), were being used exclusively for Venezuelan medical patients at last visit.

The Costa Marena's **Restaurante El Curujey,** a thatch-and-stone eatery overhanging the ocean adjoining the hotel, remains open to the public. (Islazul.) The thatched **La Casa Rolando** (tel. 022/35-6156; daily 8 A.M.–5 P.M.; CUC2–5), at Complejo Turístico Laguna Baconao, serves *criollo* dishes. And the colorful **Restaurante Los Corales,** on a hillside above Playa Colorados, has a terrace where cocktails and seafood dishes are served.

GUANTÁNAMO

Guantánamo. The name reverberates around the world. Everyone knows it as a U.S. naval base and a humiliating thorn in the side of Castro's Cuba. In fact, Guantánamo is also both a city and province, which tapers eastward to Punta de Maisí, the easternmost point of the island. The province is almost wholly mountainous. Except for a great scalloped bowl surrounding the town of Guantánamo, the lushly forested uplands push up against a thread-thin coastal plain.

If Cuba has an untamed, undiscovered quarter, it is here. The wild eastern shore and secluded mountains of Guantánamo Province offer fantastic but as yet untapped opportunities for hiking and ecotourism. Uniquely, traces of indigenous culture linger, notably around Baracoa, Cuba's oldest city, near where a ball court similar to those of the Mayan culture has been discovered recently. Baracoans unnecessarily attempt to boost their city's image by claiming that Columbus first set foot in Cuba here and left a wooden cross (now on view in the town's cathedral) as a memento. Whatever the truth, it's undisputed that the Spanish conquistadores who came on Columbus's heels established the first town in Cuba at Baracoa. The town retains an aged colonial feel in a setting that any other city would die for. Surrounded by lushly carpeted mountains and steeped in antiquity, it is one of the most popular places in Cuba for independent-minded travelers seeking somewhere just a little bit different.

Today a great part of the mountain region is protected within a system of reserves slowly

HIGHLIGHTS

◖ Mirador de Malones: While Uncle Sam detains terrorist suspects in the U.S. naval base, the Cuban military offers you a cocktail and let's you use their look-out point to spy in on the goings-on (page 526).

◖ Zoológica de Piedra: There's no question that a mountainside zoo where the life-size critters are hewn from boulders is one of a kind (page 528).

◖ La Farola: A steep mountain road snaking into the pine-clad Sierra Cristal offers fabulous vistas, but watch those bends (page 529)!

◖ Museo Arqueológico Cueva del Paraíso: This fascinating albeit simple mu-

seum of Taíno culture is set in hillside funerary caverns with pre-Columbian skeletons still in situ (page 531).

◖ Parque Natural Duaba and El Yunque: Rugged mountain terrain provides a challenging but rewarding hike to the top of the famous rock formation El Yunque, with incredible views as an added bonus (page 537).

◖ Parque Nacional Alejandro de Humboldt: Wilderness supreme! This park provides great opportunities for bird-watching and hiking into the mountains, and manatees can be spotted along the shore (page 538).

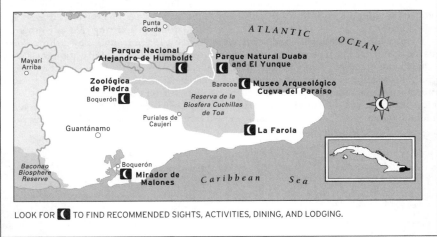

LOOK FOR ◖ TO FIND RECOMMENDED SIGHTS, ACTIVITIES, DINING, AND LODGING.

being developed for ecotourism. Few foreign travelers ever make the journey into these wildlife-rich mountains harboring rare plant and bird species and polymites (snails that haul fabulously colored shells on their backs). There are plenty of beaches, too.

The northeast coast and north-facing mountains around Baracoa make up the rainiest region in Cuba, with annual precipitation ranging from 200 centimeters in the coastal

zone to 360 centimeters in the upper Toa river valley and majestic heights of the Sierra Sagua-Baracoa. By contrast, valleys along the southern coast are pockets of aridity, and cacti grow in the lee of Cuba's wettest slopes.

PLANNING YOUR TIME

A single main road hugs the coast, providing a direct link between Holguín and Santiago de Cuba via Baracoa and Guantánamo city.

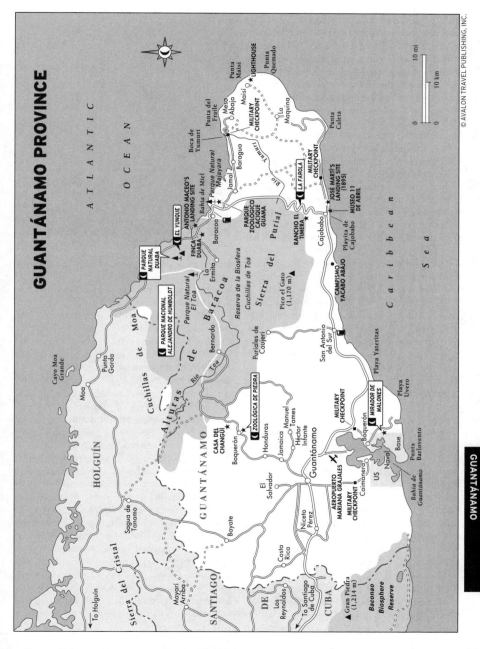

GUANTÁNAMO PROVINCE

ATLANTIC OCEAN

Caribbean Sea

LIGHTHOUSE

Punta Maisí
Punta Quemado
Mesa Abajo
Maisí
MILITARY CHECKPOINT
Isla Maquina
Punta Caleta
Punta del Fraile

Baragua

JOSÉ MARTÍ'S LANDING SITE (1895)
LA FAROLA
MILITARY CHECKPOINT
MUSEO 11 DE ABRIL

Boca de Yumurí
Jamal
Parque Natural Majayara
Bahía de Miel
ANTONIO MACEO'S LANDING SITE
EL YUNQUE
Baracoa
FINCA DUABA
PARQUE NATURAL DUABA

RANCHO EL TIMERA
PARQUE ZOOLÓGICO CACIQUE GUAMA
Cajobabo
Playita de Cajobabo

La Ermita

PARQUE NACIONAL ALEJANDRO DE HUMBOLDT
Parque Natural El Toa
Reserva de la Biosfera
Cuchillas de Toa
Sierra del Purial

Bernardo

CAMPISMO YACABO ABAJO
Pico el Gato (1,170 m)

Cayo Moa Grande
Punta Gorda
Moa

HOLGUÍN

Cuchillas de Moa

Alturas de Baracoa

Río Toa

Río Moa

Purieles de Caujerí

San Antonio del Sur
Playa Yateritas

Sierra del Cristal

Sagua de Tánamo

Mayarí Arriba

To Holguín

SANTIAGO DE CUBA

Bayate

Los Reynaldos

To Santiago de Cuba

Costa Rica

Niceto Pérez

El Salvador

Boquerón

CASA DEL CHANGÜÍ
ZOOLÓGICA DE PIEDRA
Jamaica
Manuel Tames
Héctor Infante
Honduras

GUANTÁNAMO

Guantánamo
AEROPUERTO MARIANA GRAJALES
MILITARY CHECKPOINT
Caimanera
US Naval Base
Bahía de Guantánamo

MILITARY CHECKPOINT
MIRADOR DE MALONES
Playa Uvero
Boquerón
Punta Barlovento

Gran Piedra (1,214 m)
Baconao Biosphere Reserve

10 mi
10 km
0

© AVALON TRAVEL PUBLISHING, INC.

GUANTÁNAMO

Hence, you don't need to backtrack if you have your own car. For scenery, you should definitely plan on the Guantánamo city to Baracoa route via **La Farola,** a wheezing mountain switchback that has some nerve-wracking bends and slingshots you over the Sierra Cristal. Trains connect Guantánamo city to Santiago de Cuba and Havana. Víazul also offers daily bus service from Santiago de Cuba to Guantánamo and Baracoa, but demand is tight and advance reservations are recommended. If you're driving, be forewarned that the north coast road linking Holguín to Baracoa is very badly deteriorated with no sign of being improved any time soon. And public transport along this route is infrequent.

The town of Guantánamo is more a place to overnight in passing, unless you're into Afro-Cuban music and dance. Despite its size it has very little in the way of sightseeing. The music scene, however, is another matter. Guantánamo has more traditional Afro-Cuban cultural centers than you can shake a stick at.

The hinterlands of Guantánamo township boast two sites of unique appeal. First, the U.S. naval base holds a fascination that many travelers can't resist. While the chances of visiting the base are actually less than you winning the lottery, you *can* get to see it from the most unlikely place imaginable: a Cuban military lookout at **Mirador de Malones,** where foreign visitors are treated almost like VIPs. You'll need to set things up in advance, but the Cubans make it easy by offering pre-arranged tours handled through the Gaviota tour agency (though the wheres and hows of booking tours keep changing—check with Gaviota in advance). The second place not to miss is the **Zoológica de Piedra.** Within a one-hour drive of the city, this "stone zoo" features more than 200 life-size animals hewn from rock. And its mountainside setting offers spectacular views. Plan a half-day visit, timed to coincide with a music performance at the nearby Casa de Changuí.

History buffs on the trail of José Martí should make a pilgrimage to Cajobabo, with its Museo Municipal 11 de Abril honoring Martí's landing at nearby Playitas, where a clamber over beach boulders reveals a marble monu-

lobstermen returning home at Yumurí

© CHRISTOPHER P. BAKER

ment at the exact spot where the nationalist hero stepped ashore. You can take in both the stone zoo and Cajobabo in one day's leisurely drive between Guantánamo and Baracoa.

Baracoa deserves two days minimum. One day is more than sufficient for sightseeing, with the highlights being the Catedral Nuestra Señora de la Asunción and the not-to-miss **Museo Arqueológico Cueva del Paraíso.** The second day you'll want to hike to the top of **El Yunque,** perhaps combined with horseback riding nearby or kayaking in search of manatees in **Parque Nacional Alejandro de Humboldt.** Day three is for a drive to Yumurí for a boat trip upriver and, if the road is open again, to land's end at Punta Maisí (at last visit, military checkpoints immediately east of both Cajobabo and the Río Yumurí sealed the way for foreigners wishing to visit Maisí, which is off-limits). Many visitors choose to linger to simply kick back and steep in the sense of having been transported to Gabriel García Marquez's Macondo (the surrealistic village in *One Hundred Years of Solitude*).

State-run hotels are few throughout the province. Fortunately, Guantánamo city has some worthy *casas particulares,* while Baracoa has even more (more than 100, in fact). Outside these two towns, accommodations are few and far between.

Guantánamo and Vicinity

GUANTÁNAMO

Guantánamo, 82 kilometers east of Santiago de Cuba, is a large city (pop. 180,000) at the head of a deep bay of the same name and some 25 kilometers inland of the U.S. naval base, which lies at the mouth of the bay. Guantánamo is not the most appealing of towns. The colonial heart of the city, however, has several buildings of interest, and the people are warm and lively. Much of the population is descended from Jamaican and Haitian immigrants who arrived in the 1920s to work in the sugar fields. Others arrived from Barbados, St. Kitts, and other islands. The connections are strong: A British West Indian Welfare Center (an association for English-speaking descen-

dants, locally called *ingleses*—Englishmen) and a Haitian cultural center, Tumba Francesa, work to keep alive the traditions and anomalous culture (Haitians are called *franceses*—Frenchmen).

It's a somnolent place, except when serious friction occurs between Cuba and the United States and the city gears up for a worst-case scenario. Given the proximity of the U.S. naval base, there's a strong Cuban military presence. U.S. marines first arrived here in June 1898 during the Spanish-Cuban-American War, following which the town developed a near-total economic dependency on the base, which soon employed hundreds of Cuban workers and eventually paid out US$4 million in wages each year. It is claimed that prostitution was the major

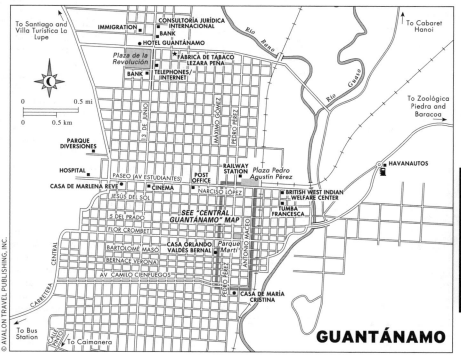

GUANTÁNAMO

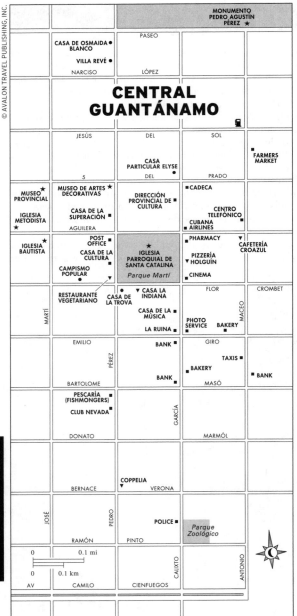

CENTRAL
GUANTÁNAMO

industry. Says an early guide-book, "The flourishing prostitution business passed from generation to generation like titles to land, and it was not unusual to find three generations of women in service to the base."

Orientation

Guantánamo is laid out in a near-perfect grid. It is approached from Santiago de Cuba by a four-lane highway that enters town from the northwest. The historic district is accessed by Paseo (Avenida Estudiantes), and further south by Avenida Camilo Cienfuegos, a wide boulevard that runs along the southern edge of downtown. North of Paseo is Reparto Caribe, where the Hotel Guantánamo and modern high-rise apartments are concentrated near Plaza de la Revolución. The center of town is Parque Martí, six blocks north of Camilo Cienfuegos and four blocks south of Paseo.

Calle 5 de Prado (one block north of Parque Martí) leads east across the Río Bano for Baracoa. A *circunvalación* runs north of the city.

Parque Martí and Vicinity

Most of what little there is to see surrounds this attractive and cozy little square with its beautifully-restored church—**Iglesia Parroquial de Santa Catalina**—on the north side; note its impressive *alfarje* ceiling. A **monument of José Martí,** shown seated, is on the west side of the church.

Built in Parisian fashion and topped by a cupola—*La Fama*—bearing a herald with trumpet, the exquisite turn-of-the-century building one block northwest of the square houses the **Museo de Artes Decorativos** (Pedro Pérez #804, esq. Prado, tel. 021/32-4407; Tues.–Thurs. 8:30 A.M.–noon and 2:30–5 P.M., Fri. 8:30 A.M.– noon and 5–9 P.M.; free), displaying period furniture, vases, and more.

One block west, the small but impressive **Museo Provincial** (Martí #804, tel. 021/32-5872; Mon.–Fri. 8 A.M.–noon AND 2–6 P.M.; CUC1) dates from 1862 and was once a prison. The museum features an exhibit on pre-Columbian culture, plus a natural history exhibit; a *sala* showing cigar bands; and a numismatic collection. A bas-relief map of the U.S. naval base and Cuban defense system is accompanied by exhibits demonstrating the "inhumane conditions" applied by U.S. occupants on Cuban civilians. A 1940s-era Harley-Davidson in the lobby belonged to a revolutionary messenger, Capitán Asdrúbal.

The pink neoclassical **Plaza del Mercado** (Antonio Maceo, esq. Prado), two blocks northeast of the square, was built last century to house the original agricultural market and is still used for that purpose.

Plaza de la Revolución Marian Grajales Coello

This huge, barren square is enlivened by the **Monumento a los Héroes,** a huge concrete structure with the faces of heroes from the War of Independence. The bones of Los Mártires de Angola (Cuban military personnel who died fighting in Angola) are interred here. Military ceremonies are often held.

Entertainment and Events

Festivals: Every Saturday evening, Pedro Pérez is cordoned off and the locals bring their tables and chairs onto the street; roasted suckling pig, pizzas, and other food and drink are served; and musicians play on every block. Often two or more bands perform on the same block, drowning each other out and vying against the radios or CD players that add to the general cacophony. Beware aggressive drunks.

Fiesta a la Guantanamera, in early December, highlights traditional music and dance. The **Festival Nacional de Changüí** is held in mid-December.

Traditional Music and Dance: The **Casa de la Trova** (Pedro Pérez, esq. Flor Crombet, no tel.; daily 3 P.M.–1 A.M.; CUC3 entrance) is a pleasant spot to hear traditional music performed live nightly.

The **British West Indian Welfare Center** (Serafín Sánchez #663, e/ Paseo y Narciso López, tel. 021/32-5297) hosts music and dance sessions featuring Caribbean forms such as *changüí* (an antecedent of *son*). One block south, **Tumba Francesa** (Serafín Sánchez #715) is a great place to hear the music and dance styles evolved by Haitians. And the **Casa de Changüí** (under construction at last visit across the street) will host traditional music.

The **Casa de la Música** (Calixto García, e/ Crombet y Gulo, tel. 021/32-7266; Tues.–Sun.; CUC1–3) has an open-air amphitheater for music and cabaret, including weekend matinees. Next door, **La Ruina** (daily 9 A.M.–1 A.M.; free), an atmospheric colonial structure run *bodega*-style, hosts karaoke, traditional dance, and more and is a great spot to bend an elbow at wooden benches.

The **Dirección Provincial de Cultura de Guantánamo** (Calixto García #806, e/ Aguilera y Prado, tel. 021/33-3210, milene@gtmo. cult.cu) arranges music and dance events. Watch for performances by Orquestra Revé, a local (and world-famous) exponent of *son-changüí*.

Cabarets and Discos: If titillating boas and bums is your thing, head to **Cabaret Hanoi** (tel. 021/38-2901; CUC1), four kilometers northeast of town, where there's a *cabaret espectáculo* followed by disco on Saturday–Sunday at 10 P.M.

The dance spot of choice is the air-conditioned **Club Nevada** (Bartolomé Masó, esq. Pedro Pérez; daily 6 P.M.–2 A.M.; CUC5), with nightly karaoke followed by a disco. The **Hotel Guantánamo** (Calle 13, e/ Ahogado y Oeste,

GUANTÁNAMO

GUANTANAMERA... GUAJIRA GUANTANAMERA!

Every where you go, you'll hear "Guajira Guantanamera" played by troubadours. It's become a kind of signature tune in Cuba. The melody was written in 1928 by Joseito Fernández (1908-1979), who at the time was in love with a woman from Guantánamo. When the song was first played on the radio in 1934, it became an overnight hit. In 1962, Cuban classical composer Julian Orbon (1925-91) added the words of José Martí's *Versos Sencillos* (simple verses) to Fernández's melody and played it to friends and family, including Hector Angulo, one of his students. In the early 1960s, Angulo taught the song to folk singer Pete Seeger, who transcribed it for guitar. Angulo and Seeger launched it to international fame.

tel. 021/38-1015; CUC5) also has disco nightly 8 P.M.–1 A.M.

Guantánamo is a rough city, and discos can be violent places.

Accommodations

You can make reservations for *campismos* throughout the province at the **Campismo Popular** (Flor Crombet #410, tel. 021/32-7356; Mon.–Fri. 8 A.M.–noon and 2–4 P.M.).

Casas Particulares: The **Villa Reve** (Pedro Pérez #670A, e/ Paseo y Narciso López, tel. 021/32-2159, reve@infosol.gtm.sld.cu; CUC15–20) offers a choice of eight rooms in a colonial home. Interior rooms downstairs are gloomy. Upstairs rooms are well lit and cross-ventilated, and have TVs and modern hot-water bathrooms. Meals are served in an airy patio.

Casa de Osmaida Blanca (Pedro Pérez #664, e/ Paseo y Narciso López, tel. 021/32-5193; CUC15–20) has two air-conditioned rooms in a rear courtyard, each with modern hot-water bathrooms. Osmaida has laid out a splendid rooftop terrace with bar.

Casa de Elsye Castillo Osoria (Calixto García #766, e/ Prado y Jesús del Sol, tel. 021/32-3787; CUC20) is a pleasant colonial home with 1950s decor in the TV lounge (noise can be a disturbance). The owners rent two air-conditioned rooms with fan, and private bathroom with hot water. Opt for the modern upstairs room. Meals are served in a patio with arbor and swing seat.

West of downtown, **Casa de Marlena Reve Duran** (1 Oeste #652, esq. Paseo, tel. 021/32-6646, elsoftweriano@yahoo.es; CUC15–20) is a 1950s bungalow with a nice TV lounge plus two large air-conditioned rooms with fans and large hot-water bathrooms; one room has a fridge and TV.

Casa Orlando Valdés Bernal (Máximo Gómez #959 altos, e/ Giro y Masó, tel. 021/32-7876; CUC20) has two spacious, cross-ventilated air-conditioned rooms with fans and private hot-water bathrooms.

Casa de María Cristina (2 Sur #402, e/ Pedro Pérez y Martí, tel. 021/32-4386, mileydis05@yahoo.es; CUC20) has one room with ceiling fan and a small bathroom with cold water only.

Hotels: The **Villa Turística La Lupe** (tel. 021/38-2602; CUC20 s, CUC24 d low season; CUC24 s, CUC30 d high season), four kilometers north of town on the banks of the Río Bano, is a tranquil option but for the noise from the lively poolside bar that draws Cubans on weekends. It has 50 modestly appointed rooms in two-story units; upstairs rooms have lofty ceilings. All have air-conditioning, TVs, and refrigerators. There's a small restaurant.

The functional **Hotel Guantánamo** (Calle 13, e/ Ahogado y Oeste, tel. 021/38-1015, fax 021/38-2406) was reserved exclusively for Venezuelan medical patients at last visit. (Islazul.)

Food

The dire dining in Guantánamo is reason enough to head out of town, and the sole *paladar* (Restaurante La Cubanita) is a dirty fly-infested dive that could barely scrape together a meal when I dined there.

Your best bet is **Restaurante Vegetariano** (Pedro Pérez, esq. Flor Crombet; daily noon–2:30 P.M. and 5–10:30 P.M.), a clean, modern, air-conditioned eatery serving paella and soy and maize dishes for pesos.

Islazul's 24-hour **Café Croazul** (Aguilera, esq. Antonio Maceo) can manage only spaghetti and ham-and-cheese sandwiches.

Five pesos will buy you a slice of what passes for pizza at **Pizzería Holguín** (daily 10:30 A.M.–3 P.M. and 5:30–10 P.M.), on the east side of Parque Martí.

At least the coffee is good at **Casa La Indiana** (daily 7 A.M.–2 P.M. and 3–10:30 P.M.), on the south side of Parque Martí. And **Coppelia** (Pérez, esq. Bernace Verona; daily 10 A.M.–10 P.M.) serves delicious ice cream for 2.50 pesos a bowl.

You can buy produce at the *mercado agropecuario* (Antonio Maceo, esq. Prado; Mon.–Sat. 8 A.M.–6 P.M., Sun. 8 A.M.–2 P.M.).

Information and Services

Bandec has a branch at Calixto García y Bartolomé Masó; **Banco Popular** is one block east. The **post office** is at Pérez y Aguilera. **Etecsa** (13 de Mayo, esq. Ahogados; Mon.–Sat. 9 A.M.–6:30 P.M., Sat. 9 A.M.–12:30 P.M.), on the east side of Plaza de la Revolución; and also at Aguilera, esq. Maceo (tel. 021/32-7878; daily 9 A.M.–6:30 P.M.) has international phone and Internet service.

Hospital Agostinho Neto (Carretera El Salvador Km 1, tel. 021/35-5450) is half a kilometer south of town. You'll find basic **pharmacies** on Pérez and Bartolomé Masó, on the northeast corner of Parque Martí, and on Paseo.

The **Consultoría Jurídica Internacional** (Ahogados #6501, esq. a 15 Norte, Rpto. Caribe, tel. 021/38-3543, fax 021/35-52370) offers legal services.

Imigración (Calle 1 Oeste, e/ 14 y 15 Norte; Mon.–Thurs. 8:30 A.M.–noon and 2–4 P.M.), one block north of the Hotel Guantánamo, can issue *prórrogas*. First you need to buy a *cello* (stamp; CUC25) from Bandec (Calixto García, esq. Masó).

Getting There and Away

The **Aeropuerto Mariana Grajales** (tel. 021/32-3564) is 12 kilometers east of town, but is not served by international flights. **Cubana** (Calixto García #817, e/ Prado y Aguilera, tel. 21/32-4533) flies between Havana and Guantánamo daily.

The **bus terminal** (tel. 021/32-5588) is two kilometers south of town, on the road to Niceto Pérez. **Víazul** (tel. 021/80121) buses for Guantánamo depart Santiago de Cuba at 7:45 A.M. (CUC6), and Baracoa at 2:15 P.M. (CUC9). Buses depart Guantánamo for Santiago de Cuba at 5:25 P.M., and Baracoa at 9:30 A.M. **Astro** buses depart Guantánamo for Havana at 7:30 P.M.; for Holguín at 5 A.M.; Camagüey at 5 P.M.; and Santiago de Cuba at 7:40 A.M. and 3:40 P.M.

The **train station** (tel. 021/32-5518) is on Pedro Pérez, one block east of Paseo. Trains depart Havana for Guantánamo at 4:38 A.M. and 6:50 A.M.; and from Guantánamo for Havana at 6:50 P.M. and 9:07 P.M. (CUC43 *especial*, CUC32 *regular*). The regular train stops in Cacocum (CUC6.50), Las Tunas (CUC8.50), Camagüey (CUC13), Ciego de Ávila (CUC16.50), Santa Clara (CUC22), and Matanzas (CUC28.50).

There are gas stations at Jesús del Sol, esq. Maceo; 200 meters east of the bridge over the Río Bano, on the road to Baracoa; and on the road to El Salvador.

Getting Around

There are plenty of *coches* (no more than 10 pesos anywhere in town). Bus #9 runs past the Hotel Guantánamo from Paseo.

Cubataxi (tel. 021/32-3636) offers taxi service.

Havanautos (tel. 021/35-5405) has a car rental office beside the Cupet gas station on the east side of town. **Transtur** (tel. 021/35-5515) is in the Hotel Guantánamo.

U.S. NAVAL BASE AND VICINITY

The U.S. naval base (colloquially referred to as Gitmo, for the official airport code, GTMO;

GUANTÁNAMO NAVAL BASE

Guantánamo (Gitmo) is the oldest U.S. overseas military base. It's also the only one located in a Communist country – and a constant thorn in the side of Cuban-U.S. relations. Since 1903 the United States has held an indefinite lease on the property, which it claimed as a prize at the end of the Cuban-Spanish-American War. The Platt Amendment to the Cuban Constitution stated that "to enable the United States to maintain the independence of Cuba, and to protect the people thereof... the Cuban Government will sell or lease to the United States the lands necessary for coaling or naval stations." The 45 square miles of land and water were formally handed over to the United States in ceremonies aboard the USS *Kearsarge*, anchored in the bay, on December 10, 1903.

The Platt Amendment was dropped in 1934, and a new treaty was signed. Although it confirmed Cuba's "ultimate sovereignty," the treaty stipulated that the lease would be indefinite and could be terminated only by agreement of both parties (or if the United States decides to pull out). "As a result," writes Tom Miller, "the United States is in the enviable position of an imperious tenant who establishes the rent, controls the lease, and ignores the landlord." In the original lease, the United States agreed to pay Cuba the sum of US$2,000 in gold per year. In 1934, when gold coins were discontinued, the rent was upped to US$4,085, payable by U.S. Treasury check. The first rent check that Uncle Sam paid to Castro's regime, in 1959, was cashed. Since then, Fidel has kept the uncashed checks in a drawer in his office desk.

The gates between the base and Cuba were closed on January 1, 1959, and have not been reopened.

LIFE ON THE BASE

Today, 7,000 U.S. servicemen and their dependents live here amid all the comforts

www.nsgtmo.navy.mil) occupies both sides of the entrance to Guantánamo Bay, which is inhabited by endangered manatees and marine turtles (iguanas, the unofficial Gitmo mascot, roam on land). The Naval Air Station (NAS), on the western side of the bay, is separated by four kilometers of water from the naval station, on the east side. Hence, the bay is crisscrossed by helicopters, boats, and an hourly ferry, while Cuban vessels also pass to and fro (the treaty guarantees free access to the waters to Cuban vessels and those of Cuba's trading partners heading in and out of the Cuban port of Boquerón; an Anti-Air Warfare Center monitors Cuban traffic).

The bay is ringed by several Cuban military bases, two Cuban naval facilities—Glorieta and Boquerón—and the "Cactus Curtain" planted in the 1960s to form a natural barrier (as much to stop Cubans from defecting as to stop U.S. troops from attacking).

The main gate (which has been permanently closed since 1959) is at **Caimanera,** 22 kilometers south of Guantánamo. This small Cuban town is surrounded by salt flats and its economy is based on salt, fishing, and a Frontera Brigada military complex. Before the Revolution, many *caimaneros* worked on the U.S. naval base, while *caimaneras* worked in the strip joints and the more than 50 brothels that were the town's staple industry.

Caimanera is a restricted military zone and has been off-limits to visitors in past years. The situation is fluid and depends on the state of international relations. If you visit, from the three-story observation tower of the Hotel Caimanera you can look out past Cuban watchtowers to the naval base that Castro has called "a dagger plunged in the heart of Cuban soil," and that blazes brightly at night like a mini–Las Vegas.

◖ Mirador de Malones

The Cuban military has a command center buried deep beneath the mountain on the east

of a small Midwestern town. There are five swimming pools, four outdoor movie houses, 400 miles of paved road, and a golf course. McDonald's even has a concession – the only one in Cuba. Another 7,000 civilians also work here, including 800 Jamaican laborers and a small number of Cubans who chose to remain following the Revolution (they receive rent-free housing and have their own community center). A dwindling number of Cubans also "commute" to work daily through the base's Northeast Gate.

In 1964 the Cuban government cut off the base's water supply. It was replaced with a seawater desalinization plant that today provides 3,000,000 gallons of fresh water daily, along with electrical power.

The facility was until recently ringed by the largest U.S. minefield in the world, laid down during the Cuban Missile Crisis of 1962 but dug up and disarmed in 1999. The Cuban mines remain and are clearly marked with red triangular warning signs in English and Spanish. Nonetheless, each year many young Cuban "fence-jumpers" risk death to reach a "paradise" promised by radio and television stations broadcasting from the base. The United States accuses Cuba of using weapons to stop people from swimming to the base. Cuba denies the charges and says that U.S. troops routinely provoke "clashes." One such incident, in the summer of 1986, led to the death of a private who snitched on a marine firing over the fence and was beaten to death by fellow marines (the episode was portrayed in the movie *A Few Good Men*, starring Demi Moore, Tom Cruise, and Jack Nicholson).

Since 2002, the base has been used to house suspected Taliban and Al Qaeda terrorists.

Castro has proposed to make the base a regional medical center for all of the Caribbean if Uncle Sam relinquishes his hold.

---

side of the bay. The major lookout point—Mirador de Malones (U.S. marines call it "Castro's Bunker")—is here, on the south side of a hill called Loma Malones. It is open to tourists, making it one of the world's most unlikely tourist destinations!

Visitors are shown the bunker, which contains a diorama of the base, while the camouflaged *mirador* has a restaurant from where you can look right down on the U.S. base, about two miles away. There's even a U.S.-made telescope for a better view over Camp Delta, where Taliban and Al Qaeda prisoners are held.

Access is from the military post and barrier on the Carretera Central, just east of Glorieta, at the turnoff for Boquerón (also called Mártires de la Frontera), 26 kilometers southeast of Guantánamo. It's 14 kilometers from here through scrubland and cacti to Mirador de Malones. You can't go alone or arrive unannounced, but must book a guided excursion at least 24 hours in advance with Gaviota in Santiago (CUC15).

Accommodations

Hotel Caimanera (Loma Norte, Caimanera, tel. 021/99414) sits atop a low hillock in the center of town and, as far as foreigners are concerned, is open only to groups pre-arranged through Gaviota in Santiago de Cuba. It has 17 air-conditioned rooms with TVs plus a restaurant, café, bar, nightclub, and a swimming pool with a water slide. (Islazul.)

Getting There

Prior permission to visit Gitmo is required from the U.S. military and isn't granted to your average Joe. Military flights depart the Norfolk Naval Air Station and Jacksonville, Florida, on Tuesdays and Fridays. **Air Sunshine** (tel. 954/434-8900 or 800/327-8900, http://airsunshine.com) flies between Kingston, Jamaica, and Gitmo on Fridays and Sundays (US$129 one way, US$189 round-trip).

Commuter trains depart Guantánamo for Caimanera five times daily (50 minutes).

Believe it or not, U.S. (and other) skippers can sail right past the U.S. naval base and into the Cuban-controlled harbor and port of Caimanera. Private yachters are not made welcome by either Cuban or U.S. authorities, either of which will most likely search your vessel.

NORTH OF GUANTÁNAMO

North of the city, sugarcane fields merge into mountains.

▌ Zoológica de Piedra

The "stone zoo" (no tel.; daily 8 A.M.–5 P.M.; entrance CUC1, cameras CUC1, videos CUC5), near the village of Boquerón (not to be mistaken for the port on the east side of Guantánamo Bay), 25 kilometers northeast of Guantánamo, features a menagerie of wild animals from around the world—lions, tapirs, hippopotamuses, elephants, and other species—hewn from huge calcareous rocks

with hammer and chisel by a coffee farmer, Ángel Iñigo. Iñigo has carved more than 426 animals that he had seen only in photographs in books, representing more than 26 years of work. Over a kilometer of stone pathways lead through the thick foliage, revealing such carved scenes as a buffalo being attacked by mountain lions, two monkeys picking fleas from each other, and Stone Age figures killing a wild boar. The zoo is a work in progress.

The **Restaurante Mirador La Piedra** (Tues.–Sun. 7:30 A.M.–11 P.M.), at the zoo, is a pleasant thatched eatery offering only fried chicken but with fantastic views down the mountain. Live musicians sometimes perform.

Casa del Changüí

The family of Eduardo "Pipi" Goul (tel. 021/95188) keep alive *changüí,* the authentic music of Guantánamo, at this small *finca* in

The Zoológica de Piedra is named for the animals hewn from rocks in situ and is a highlight of any visit to Guantánamo

the hamlet of **Güirita,** about three kilometers above the Zoológico de Piedra. Pipi's The Estrellas Campesinos (Country Stars), a group founded in 1952 and led by the indefatigable Pipi, perform the country music that evolved here last century and forms the basis of later Cuban sounds, such as *son.* The group performs *changüí* in its original form beneath thatch, where a rum drink is served and you are encouraged to dance. Performances are on demand.

Visits are by appointment only, and can be arranged through the Dirección Provincial de Cultura de Guantánamo (Calixto García #806, e/ Aguilera y Prado, tel. 021/33-3210, milene@gtmo.cult.cu).

Guantánamo to Baracoa

About 20 kilometers east of Guantánamo city, the coast road rises up a two-kilometer-long hill where you have your views back down over the milky bay. Beyond the crest, the road drops to the coast and you emerge at **Playa Yateritas,** a golden beach popular with residents of Guantánamo on weekends. For the next few miles, you'll pass little coves cut into the raised coral shore, with pellucid waters and tiny beaches as private as your innermost thoughts. The coast grows more dramatic, with mountains rising ahead. Beyond the pleasant little village of **Imias,** the terrain turns to semi-desert, with scrub-covered hills and valley bottoms filled with orchards and oases of palms. Playa Imias is a broad, gray-sand beach fronted by shallow turquoise waters.

Accommodations

Campismo Yacabo Abajo (tel. 021/80289; CUC6 per person), about five kilometers west of Imias, has basic albeit large modern cabins in two-story stone units fronting the beach. There's a café, video room, volleyball, and horseback rides (CUC3). It's often closed, so check ahead with the *campismo popular* offices in Baracoa or Guantánamo.

CAJOBABO

The community of Cajobabo, 45 kilometers east of Guantánamo, is hallowed ground. Here, at **Playitas,** two kilometers further east, José Martí, Máximo Gómez, and four other prominent patriots put ashore in a small rowboat on April 11, 1895, after years of exile. The tiny beachfront **Museo Municipal 11 de Abril** (daily 8:30 A.M.–noon and 1–5:30 P.M.; CUC1) honors Martí. A replica of the boat sits outside the museum and is used each April 11, when the landing is reenacted and cultural activities are hosted. Visitors receive a complimentary glass of *té de tebenque,* made with honey. A guide will lead you along a three-kilometer trail via Playitas (CUC1), reached via a steep headland. If you clamber over the rocks at the far east end of the beach you'll discover a tiny cove with a **marble monument** inset into the cliff face, laid in 1947 with a base resembling the prow of a boat.

The shorefront road continues east to Punta Maisí at the eastern tip of Cuba. It is one of the most dramatic drives in all Cuba. Alas, it is off-limits to foreigners: A military checkpoint bars the way.

◖ LA FAROLA

Immediately beyond Cajobabo, the highway turns north and climbs into the Sierra del Purial along La Farola, initiated during the Batista era (it was called the Vía Mulata) and completed since the Revolution to link Baracoa with the rest of Cuba. This scenic highway spirals over precipitous peaks and through deep ravines, twisting and curling uphill through the valley of the Ríos Yumurí and Ojo, carpeted with palms like Moroccan oases. The road narrows with the ascent, the bends growing tighter, the views more dramatic and wide-ranging. Soon you are climbing through pine forests amid the most non-Cuban landscapes in Cuba.

The summit (Alto de Coltillo) houses a tiny café, beyond which the road drops through a moist valley brimful of banana trees until you emerge by the sea at Baracoa.

The unlit road is subject to landslides. *Drive with care!*

Baracoa and Vicinity

BARACOA

Baracoa (pop. 65,000) lies 200 kilometers east of Santiago, 120 kilometers east of Guantánamo, and is really miles from anywhere. The somnolent town is nestled hard up against the ocean beneath rugged mountains, most notably the great hulking mass of El Yunque, a huge, flat-topped mesa. Baracoa curves around the wide Bahía de Miel (Honey Bay), lined with black-sand beaches.

Isolation breeds individuality, and Baracoa is both isolated and individual, so much so that the town has been likened to Macondo in Gabriel García Márquez's surrealistic novel *One Hundred Years of Solitude.* The town looks and feels antique, with its little fortresses and streets lined with venerable wooden edifices, rickety and humbled with age, with red-tiled eaves supported on ancient timber frames.

Baracoans have a good deal of Indian blood, identified by their short stature, olive-brown skins, and squared-off faces.

History

On October 27, 1492, approaching Cuban shores for the first time, Christopher Columbus saw "a high, square-shaped mountain, which looked like an island." For centuries, it was widely accepted that the mountain he saw was El Yunque. It is now thought, however, that Columbus was actually describing a similar flat-topped mountain near Gibara, many miles to the west (don't argue the case with a Baracoan, however; they're staunchly partisan on the subject).

In 1510, Don Diego Velázquez de Cuellar arrived fresh from Spain with 300 men and founded La Villa de Nuestra Señora de la Asunción, the first of the original seven cities founded by Velázquez. As such, it is the oldest colonial city in the Americas. The indigenous Taíno population resisted the strange cutthroat proselytizers who came dressed in leathers, metal helmets, and breast-plates. A Dominican-born chief named Hatuey rallied the Indians in a rebellion against Spanish enslavement, and the city was besieged. The Spanish managed to hold out for three months before repelling the Indians and capturing Hatuey. The noble "savage" was burned at the stake. (Before putting flame to the pyre, the Spaniards offered Hatuey an option—redemption in Heaven by renouncing his pagan practices and accepting a Christian God, or a life in Hell. He replied that if all Christians were as wicked as Velázquez's men, he would rather not go to Heaven. To hell with him!)

The city was remote and surrounded by mountains. Baracoa's inauspicious geographical circumstance did little to favor the settlement. After five years, Santiago de Cuba, with its vastly superior harbor, was proclaimed the new capital. Baracoa limped along based on a limited agricultural economy that produced yucca, coffee, cocoa, and maize. The town languished in limbo for the next two centuries, without road or rail link to the rest of Cuba until La Farola was completed in the early 1960s.

Orientation

The road from Guantánamo (via La Farola) enters town from the east as Calle José Martí. The town is only a few blocks wide, with narrow roads running parallel to the shore. The wind-swept Malecón runs along the seafront, two blocks north of Martí.

Baracoa and the Bahía de Miel

From Holguín, the town is accessed via Avenida Primero de Abril, which curls around the western harbor.

El Castillo

This fortress is built atop the rocky marine terrace that looms 40 meters above the city, offering a bird's-eye view. It was constructed during the War of Jenkins' Ear (1739–41) between Spain and Britain, when the two nations' navies battled it out over the issue of trading rights in the new world. The fort—known as Castillo Seboruco—subsequently became a prison. It has metamorphosed as the Hotel El Castillo and is accessed by a steep staircase at the southern end of Frank País.

Fuerte Matachín

This tiny fortress, at the east end of Martí and the Malecón, dates to 1802 and guards the eastern entrance to the old town. A bronze bust of General Antonio Maceo stands outside the fortress, with its thick walls topped with cannons in embrasures. The storehouse houses the **Museo Matachín** (tel. 021/42122; daily 8 A.M.–noon and 2–6 P.M.; CUC1), tracing the history of the region since pre-Columbian days. It also displays polymites (the local polychromatic snails).

The round tower—**Torreón de Toa**—immediately south of the fort served as a Spanish customs checkpoint to quash the contraband trade. (The **Fortaleza de la Punta,** at the far west end of Martí, is a small semicircular fort built in 1803 to guard the harbor entrance. It is of only modest interest and has no cannons.)

Plaza Independencia

This triangular plaza (Antonio Maceo, e/ Frank País y Ciro Frias) is the town hub and is pinned by a **bust of Hatuey,** the Indian chief.

The plaza is dominated by the near-derelict **Catedral Nuestra Señora de la Asunción** (tel. 021/43352; open by request, and for mass daily at 6 P.M. plus Sun. at 9 A.M.), dating from 1805 on the site of an earlier church destroyed by pirates in 1652. The church is famous for the "Cruz de la Parra," a dark, well-worn, meter-tall cross (supposedly the oldest European relic in the Americas) on display inside a glass case. Baracoans love to tell the tale of how Columbus supposedly left the cross upright amid stones at the harbor entrance in 1492. Carbon-dating analysis confirms that it is indeed about 500 years old, although perusal by experts from the Royal Museum for Central Africa determined that the cross hadn't traveled from the Old World, but was instead made of *Coccoloba diversifolia,* a native hardwood of the sea grape family that grows abundantly around Baracoa. Perhaps Columbus whittled the cross himself in Cuba! To view the church, you'll need to search out the priest in the beautifully restored house at Calle Antonio Maceo, esq. Ciro Frias.

◖ Museo Arqueológico Cueva del Paraíso

The highlight of Baracoa is this archaeological museum (no tel.; Mon.–Fri. 8 A.M.–5 P.M., Sat.–Sun. 8 A.M.–noon; CUC2), inside a cave

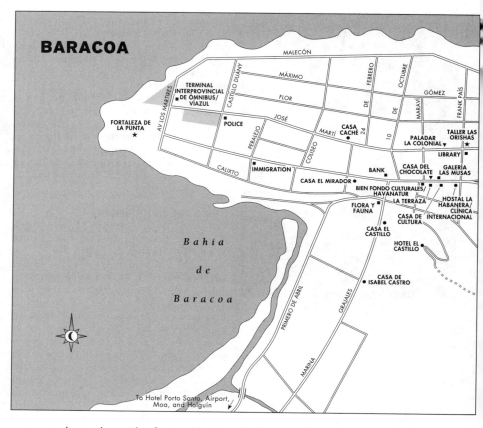

system on the southern side of town. Aboriginal artifacts, carvings, and jewelry, plus skeletons (one possibly being the Cacique Guamá, who rebelled against Spain) are displayed within floodlit glass cases ensconced within crevices between the dripstone formations. A stiff clamber leads to a funerary cave with several skeletons in situ. Access is via makeshift wooden scaffolding; you clamber at your own risk! To get there, follow Calle Moncada uphill to a tiny traffic circle; the museum is signed from here. The entrance is hidden amid a banana grove.

Parque Natural Majayara
The forest-covered headland that rises over

the bar east of town is protected within an archaeological park and features caves with dripstone formations and Taíno petroglyphs, one of which local archaeologists purport represents Columbus's three caravels shown at anchor. Trails also lead to a broad pre-Columbian pathway paved with flat stones. It was closed to visitors at last visit.

Parque Zoológico Cacique Guama
This small zoo (tel. 021/43409; Tues.–Sun. 9 A.M.–5 P.M.; 20 centavos), seven kilometers east of Baracoa, contains monkeys, a hippo, a lion, birds, crocodiles, rodent-like *jutías,* and a near-extinct relative, the *almique,* indigenous to eastern Cuba.

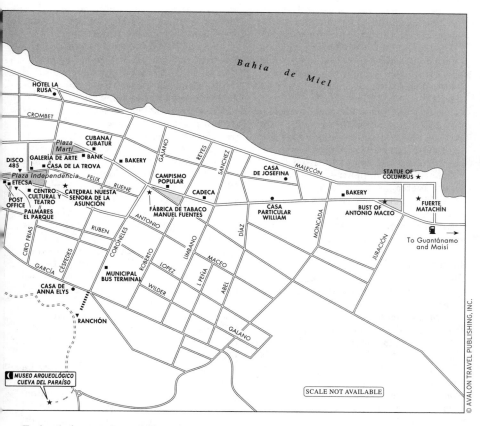

Map labels:
Bahía de Miel
HOTEL LA RUSA
CROMBET
Plaza Martí
CUBANA/CUBATUR
DISCO 485
GALERÍA DE ARTE
BANK
CASA DE LA TROVA
BAKERY
GALIANO
REYES
SANCHEZ
CASA DE JOSEFINA
MALECÓN
STATUE OF COLUMBUS
ETECSA
Plaza Independencia
FELIX
RUENE
CAMPISMO POPULAR
CADECA
POST OFFICE
CENTRO CULTURAL Y TEATRO
CATEDRAL NUESTA SEÑORA DE LA ASUNCIÓN
FÁBRICA DE TABACO MANUEL FUENTES
CASA PARTICULAR WILLIAM
BAKERY
BUST OF ANTONIO MACEO
FUERTE MATACHÍN
PALMARES EL PARQUE
ANTONIO
DÍAZ
MONCADA
JURACIÓN
To Guantánamo and Maisí
CIRO FRIAS
RUBEN
CORONELES
ROBERTO
LIMBANO
MACEO
CÉSPEDES
GARCÍA
MUNICIPAL BUS TERMINAL
LOPEZ
L PEÑA
ABEL
WILDER
CASA DE ANNA ELYS
RANCHÓN
GALANO
MUSEO ARQUEOLÓGICO CUEVA DEL PARAÍSO
SCALE NOT AVAILABLE
© AVALON TRAVEL PUBLISHING, INC.

Entertainment and Events

At night, the lively social scene concentrates at Plaza Hatuey, which is packed with young adults and adults on the make. Locals also gather in Plaza Martí at 7 P.M. most nights to watch the TV that by day is locked inside its case atop a stand in the plaza. Saturday nights are best, when the movie double bill lasts until 2 A.M.

Festivals and Events: The **Semana de la Cultura** is a week-long cultural festival kicked off on April 1 to celebrate Antonio Maceo's landing at nearby Duaba in 1895.

Every Saturday night, an open-air disco—*fiesta callejera*—is set up on Calle Maceo (bring your own drinks), which is cordoned off and lit with Christmas lights, while the boom-box music reverberates until well past midnight, and only the dead can sleep.

Traditional Music and Dance: The **Casa de la Trova** (Maceo #149, e/ Ciro Frías y Pelayo Cuervo; daily 10 P.M.–2 A.M.; CUC1) is a great place to sample traditional music. Likewise, **Casa de la Cultura** (Maceo, e/ Frank País y Maraví, tel. 021/42349), where locals perform adaptations of Cuban *son* known as *el nengen* and *el kiriba;* and **Fondo de Bienes Culturales** (9 P.M.–midnight; 50 centavos), 50 meters west.

Bars and Discos: For a quiet sip, try the peaceful open-air bar in the **Hotel El Castillo.** For boy-meets-girl, it has to be open-air **Palmares El Parque** (24 hours; Tues.–Thurs. free,

Fri.–Sun. CUC0.50) on the south side of Plaza Independencia, where live music is offered.

The rooftop **La Terraza** (Maceo, e/ Maraví y Frank País) has a middling *cabaret espectáculo* featuring scantily clad showgirls in stiletto heels Tuesday–Sunday at 11 P.M. (CUC1).

The thatched hilltop **Ranchón,** overlooking town 800 meters east of the Hotel El Castillo (you can also ascend the dark staircase at the south end of Coroneles Gajano), is a breeze-swept bar with occasional disco at 9 P.M. (CUC1).

Other Entertainment: The **Centro Cultural y Teatro** (tel. 021/42340), on the south side of Plaza Independencia, shows films most evenings.

Estadio Manuel Fuentes Borges, east of town, hosts baseball game October–May.

Accommodations

You can book basic cabins at local *campismos* through **Campismo Popular** (Martí #225, e/ Galano y Reyes, tel. 021/42776).

Casas Particulares: There are scores of private rooms for rent. Most serve meals.

Casa de William Montoya (Martí #287, e/ Abel Díaz y Glicerio Blanco, tel. 021/42798, williamsbaracoa@yahoo.com; CUC15–20) is a lofty-ceilinged colonial home with tile floors, a pleasant lounge, and two air-conditioned rooms with private hot-water bathrooms. It has secure parking.

【 Casa Particular El Mirador (Maceo #86, e/ 24 de Febrero y 10 de Octubre, tel. 021/42647, jodn@toa.gtm.sld.cu; CUC15–20) is one of the best room rentals in town. Hostess Iliana Sotorongo Rodríguez's attractive wooden colonial home is well kept and has two spacious upstairs rooms with air-conditioning, fans, and lofty ceilings that open to an airy balcony with rockers and views. They have private bathrooms and hot water.

Casa El Castillito (Marian Grajales #9-A, e/ Calixto García y Julia Mella, tel. 021/43625; CUC20) is a good bet for a self-contained apartment. This upstairs unit has a large kitchen with open dining room attached, plus a modestly furnished bedroom and clean,

modern hot-water bathroom. There's a laundry. César, the owner, lives next door.

I really like **【 Casa de Isabel Castro** (Marian Grajales #35, tel. 021/42217; CUC 15–20). This colonial wooden home in fine repair, with 1950s decor, rents two air-conditioned rooms with small, clean private hot-water bathrooms. The patio to the rear gets the sun and opens to a large garden with fruit trees. It has secure parking.

Another great option is **Casa Caché** (Martí #71, e/ Coliseo y 24 de Febrero, tel. 021/42489; CUC20–25), with a vast lounge with *vitrales,* 1950s leather sofa set, and a bar. It has one simply furnished air-conditioned room with fridge, double and single beds, and a large private hot-water bathroom. The delightful rear patio has a fountain and arbor.

I enjoyed my stay at **Casa de Josefina** (Flor Crombet #269, c/o tel. 021/42798; CUC15–20), where the pleasant hosts offer two air-conditioned rooms with firm mattresses, fans, and private hot water-bathrooms. Their daughter also has two rooms in a nearby colonial home: **Casa de Yancy y Noel** (Calle Martí #304, tel. 021/42133, casayancynoel@hotmail.com; CUC15–20).

Hotels: Opened in 2004, **【 Hostal La Habanera** (Maceo #68, esq. Frank País, tel. 021/45273; CUC 35 s, CUC47 d low season; CUC39 s, CUC50 d high season) is a splendid restoration of a colonial-era hotel. It has 10 air-conditioned rooms on two levels around a central breeze-swept atrium patio with rattan seating. Rooms have high ceilings, satellite TVs, refrigerators, and pleasant rattan furniture, and modern bathrooms. There's a small bar and restaurant.

Hotel La Rusa (Máximo Gómez #161, tel. 021/43011, fax 021/42337; CUC27 s, CUC18 d low season; CUC30 s, CUC36 d high season) is an endearing little place facing the Malecón. It once belonged to a Russian woman, Mima Rubenskaya, who fled the Soviet Union in 1917 and settled in Baracoa long before it turned Communist (if you want to know more about her, check out the museum in the Fuerte Matechín). After her death in 1979 the property was converted into a hotel

(Fidel Castro and Che Guevara both stayed here, apparently, as did Errol Flynn). It has 12 simply appointed and recently refurbished air-conditioned rooms with louvered windows overlooking the ocean and small modern bathrooms. There's a small bar and open-air restaurant with seafront views. (Islazul.)

(Hotel El Castillo (tel. 021/45165, fax 021/35-5223, dtorca@gavbcoa.co.cu; CUC40 s, CUC54 d low season; CUC42 s, CUC58 d high season), built atop the foundations of El Castillo, overlooks the town and has 34 air-conditioned rooms furnished colonial style, with terra-cotta-tiled floors, carved cedar furniture, plus telephones and private baths. There's a TV lounge. The balconies and sundeck offer El Yunque views, and the restaurant is the best in town. (Gaviota.)

If El Castillo is full, consider **Hotel Porto Santo** (Carretera del Aeropuerto, tel. 021/45106; CUC40 s, CUC54 d low season; CUC42 s, CUC58 d high season) on the west side of the bay. It has 36 air-conditioned rooms and 24 *cabinas* centered on an amoeba-shaped pool. The ho-hum facilities include a restaurant, two bars, a shop, tennis court, and car rental. (Gaviota.)

Food

The only *paladar* is **(La Colonial** (Martí #123, e/ Maraví y Frank País, tel. 021/45391; daily 11 A.M.–10 P.M.), with heaps of cozy colonial charm. It even serves swordfish and shark and *dorado* in huge portions, but avoid the turtle— a protected species! Most dinners cost CUC8.

I highly recommend the **(Restaurant Duaba** (tel. 021/45165; daily 7–9:45 A.M., noon–3 P.M., and 7–10 P.M.), in the Hotel El Castillo. The menu favors local dishes, including lobster (CUC25), but has such adventurous fare as gouda aubergine (eggplant, CUC2.75), plus seafoods prepared in coconut sauce with herbs, and a delicious rice in sweet coconut sauce dessert (CUC1.50).

Another winner is **Restaurante La Habanera** (Maceo #68, esq. Frank País, tel. 021/45273; daily 7 A.M.–10 P.M.), in the Hostal La Habanera. Modestly elegant, it opens to

THE LOCAL FLAVOR

Baracoa is acclaimed for its original cuisine based on the coconut, which finds its way into such local delicacies as *calalú*, a spinach-like vegetable simmered in coconut milk; *bacán*, a tortilla made of baked plantain paste mixed with coconut milk, wrapped in banana leaves, and filled with spiced pork; *cucurucho*, an ambrosial pudding made of shredded coconut mixed with papaya, orange, nuts, and sugar or honey and wrapped in palm leaves; and *frangollo*, a dish of green bananas toasted and mashed. (You're hard-pressed, however, to find these local dishes.)

For drinks, try *chorote*, a tasty chocolate drink thickened with cornstarch; *sacoco*, a concoction of rum and coconut milk served in green coconuts; *sambumbia*, made of honey, lemon, and water; and the less appetizing *pru*, a drink made from pine needles and sugar syrup introduced from Haiti by French planters in the mid-19th century.

Local fishermen also net a local oddity, *tetí*, a tiny red fish that migrates like salmon up the Río Toa. The fish arrive at the mouth of the river enveloped in a gelatinous cocoon that splits apart on contact with fresh water. *Tetí* is eaten raw with cocktail sauce, like shrimp.

the street and offers a house special of *pescado a la Baraquesa* (filet of fish with malanga marinade, garlic and herbs, CUC6).

You can buy a chocolate drink (30 centavos), *natilla* (a kind of chocolate mousse, 45 centavos), and chocolate bars (2 and 10 pesos) at the **Casa del Chocolate** (Antonio Maceo #121, esq. Maraví; daily 7:30 A.M.–9:45 P.M.).

Bakeries include **Panadería La Mia** (Martí #335) and **Panadería El Triunfo,** both on Martí one and two blocks west of Fuerte Matachín, respectively. Try delicious *pudín de boniato* (made from sugar, coconut milk, and sweet potato), spongy biscuits called *panquecitos,* or deep-fried pastry called *buñuelos.* Look for *yemitas,* sweet balls made with chocolate, coconut, and sugar;

and delicious *turrón de coco,* a baked bar of grated coconut mixed with milk and sugar.

The **Fábrica de Cucurucho** (Carretera Mabuajibo, tel. 021/42646), near the Hotel Porto Santo, makes a sweet sugar-and-coconut candy called *cucurucho.*

You can buy produce at the *mercado agropecuario* (24 de Febrero y Malecón).

Shopping

Galería Pelay Alvarez López (Félix Ruenes #25), on the north side of Plaza Independencia, sells paintings, carvings, and furniture inlaid with mother-of-pearl by the town's best-known artist. Also try **Taller la Musa** (Calle Maceo #124, e/ Maraví y Frank País), where noted artists Roel Caboverde and Orlando Piedra sell original paintings; and **Taller las Orishas** (Ciro Frías #48, e/ Ruber López y Calixto García), which makes dolls.

Information and Services

There are tour information desks in the Hotel El Castillo and Hotel Porto Santo. **Flora y Fauna** (Calixto García, esq. Marina Grajales, tel. 021/43665; Mon.–Fri. 8 A.M.–noon and 2–5 P.M.) provides information on national parks.

The post office is on the south side of Plaza Independencia. Next door, **Etecsa** (Maceo #134, tel. 021/42543; daily 9 A.M.–6:30 P.M.) has international telephone and Internet service.

Bandec (Maceo, esq. Marina Grajales; and on Plaza Martí) has two branches.

Hospital General Docente (tel. 021/43014, 021/42568 for emergencies) is two kilometers east of town. The **Clínica Internacional** (Mon.–Fri. 8 A.M.–5 P.M., Sat. 8 A.M.–noon) is in Hostal La Habanera.

The police station is on Calle Antonio Maceo. **Inmigración** (Maceo, esq. Peralejo; Mon.–Thurs. 8:30 A.M.–noon and 2–4 P.M.) can issue *prórrogas.*

Getting There and Away

Aeropuerto Gustavo Rizo (tel. 021/42216) is on the west side of the bay. **Cubana** (Martí #181, tel. 021/45374; Mon.–Sat. 8 A.M.–6 P.M., Sun. 8 A.M.–noon) connects Baracoa with Havana twice weekly (CUC128) and with Santiago de Cuba once weekly (CUC30).

Buses arrive and depart the **Terminal Interprovincial** (Los Mártires, esq. Martí, tel. 021/43880). A **Víazul** bus for Baracoa departs Santiago de Cuba at 7:45 A.M. (CUC15), and Guantánamo at 9:30 P.M. (CUC9). The bus departs Baracoa for Guantánamo and Santiago de Cuba at 2:15 P.M. **Astro** buses for Baracoa depart Havana on alternate days (CUC43.50 *regular,* CUC53 *especial;* 20 hours); and Santiago de Cuba at 6:40 A.M. (CUC9 *regular,* CUC11 *especial*). Buses depart Baracoa for Havana every second day at 7:30 P.M. (24-hour advance reservation usually required), and for Santiago every second day at 1:50 P.M.; and for Guantánamo at 1 P.M. (CUC5.50 *regular,* CUC7 *especial*).

Camiones serve both Moa (5 pesos) and Guantánamo (10 pesos) from the **Terminal Municipal** (Coroneles Galano, esq. Rubio López).

An express bus (*Expreso Ferrocarril*) to the Guantánamo rail station departs at 11 A.M. (CUC7.50).

You can rent cars from **Havanautos** (tel. 021/4-5343) at the airport; **Transtur** in Hotel La Habanera; and **Vía** (tel. 021/45135) at the Hotel Porto Santo and Hotel El Castillo.

If driving to Holguín, the coast is deeply rutted and potholed much of the way, with frequent and long sections of dirt and mud.

Getting Around

Coches plod the main streets and follow fixed routes (one peso), and *bici-taxis* are everywhere (expect to pay from five pesos). For a taxi, call **Cubataxi** (tel. 021/43737).

You can rent **scooters** at the Hotel El Castillo (CUC6 first hour, CUC13 three hours, CUC26 per day).

Cubatur (Martí #181, tel. 021/45306) and **Gaviotatours** (tel. 021/45165), in the Hotel Castillo, offer excursions.

The gas station is east of Fuerte Matachín.

RESERVA DE LA BIOSFERA CUCHILLAS DE TOA

West of Baracoa, the 208,305-hectare Cuchillas de Toa Biosphere Reserve encompasses most of the Alturas de Sagua-Baracoa, Cuchillas de Toa, and Cuchillas de Moa mountain ranges, and rises from sea level to 1,139 meters in elevation. The reserve has a great diversity of climate types and corresponding ecosystems—acclaimed by UNESCO as "the most important and significant natural habitats for in-situ conservation of terrestrial biological diversity in the entire insular Caribbean." It protects the richest fauna in Cuba, including more endemic species of flora (928 thus far identified) than anywhere else on the island, not least several types of palms and the colorful *ocujé,* or Santa María tree, plus the polymite (a colorful snail species), parrots, and even manatees.

Much of the area is composed of Cuban pine, a perfect habitat for the ivory-billed woodpecker and its cousin, the endemic and endangered royal woodpecker. The large ivory-billed woodpecker was once common throughout the American South, but logging has since devastated their habitat, and they have not been seen in the United States since the 1940s. The bird was considered extinct until the mid-1980s, when it was identified in these mountains. The sightings resulted in the Cuban government's establishing a 220-square-kilometer protection area. However, no sightings have since been made.

The reserve, which is under the aegis of the **Unidad de Servicios Ambientales Alejandro de Humboldt** (Calle 15 N, e/ Ahogados y 1 Oeste, Rpto. Caribe, Guantánamo, alicia@ upsa.gtmo.inf.cu), is divided into several national parks. Tourism facilities are as yet minimal. Visits are coordinated through **Flora y Fauna** (Calixto García, esq. Marina Grajales, tel. 021/43665) and **Gaviota** (tel. 021/45165), at the Hotel Castillo in Baracoa.

🄲 Parque Natural Duaba and El Yunque

At the mouth of the Río Duaba, five kilometers west of Baracoa, is **Playa Duaba,** a long black-sand beach where the mulatto general Anto-

---

POLYMITES

Polymita pictas is a species of tiny snail unique to the Baracoa region. This diminutive critter is much sought by collectors for its Joseph's coat of many colors, which are as unique to each individual polymite as fingerprints are to humans.

According to an Indian legend, the snails' shells were originally colorless. One snail, while slowly roaming the region, was taken by the area's lush beauty and asked the mountains for some of their green. Then he admired the sky and asked for some blue. When he saw the golden sands, he asked for a splash of yellow, and for jade and turquoise from the sea.

---

nio Maceo and 22 compatriots landed in April 1895 to fight the War of Independence. Immediately beyond is the site where he fought his first battle. He is honored by a roadside bust.

You can turn inland here and follow a dirt road one kilometer to **Finca Duaba** (no tel.), a fruit farm with a thatched restaurant serving *criollo* meals beneath the palms. Guided tours are offered (CUC1), as are boat trips to the rivermouth (CUC2). Reservations should be made through Gaviota (tel. 021/45165), in the Hotel Castillo, in Baracoa; it offers an excursion with lunch for CUC12.

The park also enfolds El Yunque ("the anvil"), the spectacular table-top mountain (575 meters) that dominates the landscape west of Baracoa and seems to float above the surrounding hills. This sheer-sided giant—the remains of a mighty plateau that once extended across the entire area—was hallowed by the Taíno Indians. Mists flow down from the summit in the dawn hours, and it glows like hot coals at dusk, when the setting sun pours over the red rocky walls like molten lava. Waterfalls pour from its summit, washing away soil and mineral nutrients. The soils are thin, and the oases of orchids, lichen, mosses, and forest seem to survive on water and air alone.

You can hike (four hours round-trip; CUC15

from the *campismo* or CUC20 from Baracoa, with compulsory guide) to the summit via **Sendero El Yunque** from Campismo El Yunque; to get there, take the turn off for Finca Duaba, then keep left at the Y fork (the *campismo* is to the left; Finca Duaba is to the right). **Sendero El Jutiero** from the *campismo* leads to cascades (CUC8 from the *campismo* or CUC12 from Baracoa, with compulsory guide); you can hike or take a Jeep. You can also arrange excursions and guides at the park office four kilometers beyond Finca Duaba; at the Flora y Fuana office in Baracoa; or with Gaviotatours.

Parque Natural el Toa

This park, immediately west of Parque Natural Duaba, extends into the interior mountains. The river has the largest flow of any in the country and lots of rapids, with the potential for whitewater rafting. You can even hike across the mountains, following the river valley (farmed in cocoa and coconut palms) via the lonesome village of **Palenque** and drop down to Guantánamo—an arduous haul across wild terrain. Again, all visits need to be coordinated with Flora y Fauna or Gaviota in Baracoa.

◖ Parque Nacional Alejandro de Humboldt

This 70,835-hectare park extends west from the Río Nibujón and into Holguín Province, and is the one most visited on excursions. There's a two-meter-tall statue of the German explorer roadside near the **park office** (tel. 021/38-1431) on the east side of the community of Recreo, five kilometers west of the Río Nibujón. There are three trails. The invigorating five-kilometer-long **Sendero Balcón de Iberia** leads inland to waterfalls and natural swimming pools; a guide is compulsory (CUC8, or CUC25 with transport provided from Baracoa). The shorter **Sendero El Recreo** hugs the shore of **Parque Natural Bahía de Taco,** incorporated within Parque Nacional Alejandro de Humboldt, and protecting 2,263 hectares of marine ecosystems, including mangroves, an offshore cay, and white-sand beaches shelving to a coral reef. Manatees inhabit these waters and can be seen

on boat excursions. Gaviota offers daily excursions from Baracoa to **Playa Maguana.**

Accommodations and Food

Campismo El Yunque (tel. 021/45262), midway between Finca Duaba and the summit of El Yunque, has 16 basic huts, each sleeping up to six people. It was not open to foreigners at last visit.

The reclusive and charming four-room ◖ **Villa Maguana** (c/o tel. 021/45165; CUC37 s, CUC51 d low season; CUC42 s, CUC57 d high season, including meals), just east of Bahía de Taco, about 28 kilometers west of Baracoa, nestles in its own little cove with a scintillating white beach with shade trees. It was being expanded at last visit and when complete will have 16 new rooms in two-story wooden structures, with satellite TVs and telephones. A seafood restaurant was being added. Hopefully the expansion won't spoil it, but I fear it will. (Gaviota.)

BARACOA TO PUNTA MAISÍ

The coast road east from Baracoa follows a winding course inland via the hamlet of Jamal, touching the coast again 20 kilometers east of Baracoa at **Playa Baragua,** famous for its long, ruler-straight silver-sand beach backed by palms, with a fabulous view towards El Yunque. Break out the camera!

Boca de Yumurí

Beyond Baragua, the road eventually passes through a cleft in the vertical cliffs spanned by a natural arch called Túnel de los Alemanes (Germans' Tunnel). A stone's throw beyond, you emerge at the mouth of the Río Yumurí, which cuts through a deep canyon to meet the hissing breakers of the Atlantic. *Jiniteros* are thick as flies along this section of road and you will be accosted as soon as you step from your car as they attempt to lasso you into a boat ride upriver (CUC2 round-trip) or a lobster lunch (CUC10) at illegal *paladares.*

Punta Maisí

Immediately east of the Río Yumurí, the road begins a daunting first-gear switchback ascent and beyond Mesa Abajo deteriorates to a rutted dirt road that leads to **La Máquina,** the center of a coffee growing region on the cooler eastern slope of the Meseta de Maisí, 22 kilometers beyond the rivermouth.

Access to La Máquina was closed to foreigners at last visit; military checkpoints on the east side of the Río Yumurí and east of Cajobabo bar the way.

La Máquina looks down over a vast fan-shaped plain studded with cacti. Far below, a *faro* built in 1862 at Punta Maisí pins the easternmost tip of Cuba, where day breaks 40 minutes before it occurs in Havana. A rugged, much eroded track of red earth descends from La Máquina onto the plain. The distance is deceptive: The lighthouse is actually 12 kilometers away. Eventually you reach land's end, 1,280 kilometers from Havana.

GUANTÁNAMO

BACKGROUND

The Land

Cuba lies at the western end of the Greater Antilles group of Caribbean islands, which began to heave from the sea about 150 million years ago. Curling east and south like a shepherd's crook are the much younger and smaller Lesser Antilles, a cluster of mostly volcanic islands that bear little resemblance to their larger neighbor.

Cuba is by far the largest of the Caribbean islands at 114,524 square kilometers. It is only slightly smaller than the state of Louisiana, half the size of the United Kingdom, and three times the size of the Netherlands. It sits just south of the Tropic of Cancer at the eastern perimeter of the Gulf of Mexico, 150 kilometers south of Key West, Florida, 140 kilometers north of Jamaica, and 210 kilometers east of Mexico's Yucatán Peninsula. It is separated from Hispaniola to the east by the narrow, 77-kilometer-wide Windward Passage, or Old Bahamas Channel.

Cuba is actually an archipelago with some 4,000-plus islands, islets, and cays dominated by the main island (104,945 square km), which is 1,250 kilometers long—from Cabo de San Antonio in the west to Punta Maisí in the east—and between 31 and 193 kilometers wide. Cuba is a crescent, convex to the north.

Slung beneath the mainland's underbelly is the Isla de la Juventud (2,200 square km), the

© CHRISTOPHER P. BAKER

CUBA'S VITAL STATISTICS

Area: 114,478 square kilometers (42,804 square mi)

Population: 11,346,670 (July 2005 est.)

Annual Population Growth: 0.33 percent

Urbanization: 75.9 percent

Capital: Havana, pop. 2,200,000

Principal Cities: Camagüey, 740,000; Ciego de Ávila, 365,000; Cienfuegos, 370,000; Guantánamo, 495,000; Holguín, 985,000; Las Tunas, 420,000; Matanzas, 610,000; Pinar del Río 695,000; Sancti Spíritus, 435,000; Santa Clara, 810,000; Santiago de Cuba, 990,000

Religion: secular; most of those who practice religion are Roman Catholic, but traditional Afro-Cuban paganism has a large following; 4 percent Protestant

Language: Spanish

Climate: subtropical, with a wet season from May to October and a dry season from November to April. Average annual temperature is 24°C, with little variation. January and February are the coolest months.

Time: GMT -5. Daylight saving time operates April-October.

Currency: peso (for nationals only); convertible peso (official rate of exchange floats, but was 0.89 peso to US$1 in January 2006)

Business Hours: government offices: Monday-Friday 8:30 A.M.-12:30 P.M. and 1:30-5:30 P.M., alternate Saturday 8 A.M.-5 P.M.; national banks: Monday-Friday 8:30 A.M.-noon and 1:30-3 P.M., Saturday 8:30-10:30 A.M.

Literacy: 99.8 percent

Life Expectancy: 77.23 years

Annual Birth Rate: 12.03 per 1,000

Mortality Rate: 7.19 per 1,000

Infant Mortality Rate: 6.33 per 1,000

---

westernmost of a chain of smaller islands—the Archipiélago de los Canarreos—which extends eastward for 110 kilometers across the Golfo de Batabanó. Farther east, beneath east-central Cuba, is a shoal group of tiny coral cays—the Archipiélago de los Jardines de la Reina—sprinkled with beaches like powdered diamonds poking up a mere four or five meters from the sapphire sea.

The central north coast, too, is rimmed by a necklace of coral jewels limned by sand like crushed sugar shelving into bright turquoise shallows, with surf pounding on the reef edge. It's enough to bring out the Robinson Crusoe in anyone, with the trail of a tiny lizard leading up toward the scrubby pines as perhaps the only sign that any living creature has been here before.

TOPOGRAPHY

Cuban landscapes are soft and calming, epitomized by sensual waves of lime-green sugarcane undulating like a great swelling sea. Emerald greens flow into burning golds; soft, faded pastels and warm ochers are relieved by brilliant tropical colors, flower petals as red as lipstick, pavonine waters shading through dazzling jade, and, always, the chartreuse of the cane fields.

Plains cover almost two-thirds of the island. Indeed, Cuba is the *least* mountainous of the Greater Antilles, with a median elevation of less than 100 meters above sea level.

Cuban Highs

The fecund flatlands are disjoined by three mountain zones, where the air is cool and inviting and the roads dip and rise through very untropical-looking countryside. Each of the three *alturas* offers its own compelling beauty, with cool pine forests and sparkling lakes.

The westernmost is the slender, low-slung Sierra del Rosario and Sierra de los Órganos that together constitute the Cordillera de Guaniguanico, forming a backbone along the length of northern Pinar del Río Province. In their midst is the striking Valle de Viñales, a classic karst landscape of limestone formations called *mogotes* that rise abruptly from the plain.

CUBA'S CLIMATE

Average temperatures are listed in degrees Celsius.

	Jan.	Feb.	Mar.	April	May	June	July	Aug.	Sept.	Oct.	Nov.	Dec.
National Average	26	26	27	29	30	31	32	32	31	29	27	26
Havana	22	22.5	23	25	26	27	28	28	27.5	26	24	22.5
DAYS WITH RAINFALL												
Havana	6	4	4	4	7	10	9	10	11	11	7	6

The compact Sierra Escambray rises steeply from the coast of west-central Cuba, dominating eastern Cienfuegos and southern Villa Clara Provinces.

A third mountain zone, incorporating several adjacent ranges, overshadows the provinces of Granma, Santiago de Cuba, and Guantánamo and spills over into Holguín Province. To the west, the precipitous ranges of the Sierra Maestra rise steeply from the sea, culminating atop Pico Turquino at 1,974 meters. To the east, the Cuchillas de Toa, Sierra de Puriscal, and Sierra de Cristal are separated from the Sierra Maestra by the Nipe Plateau.

Down by the Shore

Cuba has more than 400 beaches in shades of oyster white, chocolate brown, golden, and taupe. The most beautiful line the ocean side of the innumerable coral cays beaded like pearls off the north coast. Most beaches along the south coast can't compare; notable exceptions include Playa Girón, Playa Ancón, and Cayo Largo.

The north coast is indented by dozens of huge bays shaped like deep flasks with narrow inlets. They are havens for shipping today as they were for pirates and Spanish galleons years ago. Not least of these is Bahía de Habana, on whose western shores grew Havana.

Rivers

Cuba has over 500 rivers, most of them short, shallow, and unnavigable. The principal river, the 370-kilometer-long Río Cauto, which originates in the Sierra Maestra and flows northwest, is navigable by boat for about 80 kilometers. On the flatlands, especially those of the southern plains, the rivers loop lazily to the sea through a morass of mangroves.

Most rivers dwindle to trickles in the dry season, then often swell to rushing torrents, flooding extensive areas on the plains when the rains come (80 percent falls in summer). To assuage the deluge, Cuba is now studded with huge man-made reservoirs that help control water flow.

CLIMATE

Cuba lies within the tropics, though its climate—generally hot and moist—is more properly semi- or subtropical. There are only two seasons: wet (May to November) and dry (December to April), with regional variations.

The island is influenced by the warm Gulf Stream currents and by the North Atlantic high-pressure zone that lies northeast of Cuba and gives rise to the near-constant *brisa,* the local name for the prevailing northeast trade winds that caress Cuba year-round. Indeed, despite its more southerly latitude, Havana, wrote Ernest

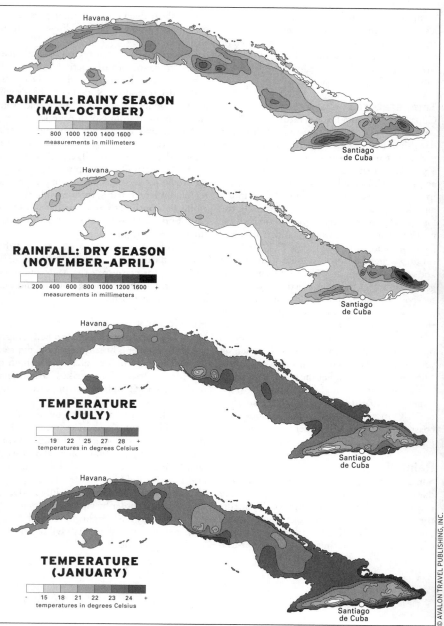

**RAINFALL: RAINY SEASON
(MAY–OCTOBER)**

800 1000 1200 1400 1600 +
measurements in millimeters

**RAINFALL: DRY SEASON
(NOVEMBER–APRIL)**

200 400 600 800 1000 1200 1600 +
measurements in millimeters

**TEMPERATURE
(JULY)**

19 22 25 27 28 +
temperatures in degrees Celsius

**TEMPERATURE
(JANUARY)**

15 18 21 22 23 24 +
temperatures in degrees Celsius

Havana

Santiago
de Cuba

© AVALON TRAVEL PUBLISHING, INC.

Hemingway, "is cooler than most northern cities in those months [July and August], because the northern trades get up about ten o'clock in the morning and blow until about five o'clock the next morning." Summer months, however, can be insufferably hot and humid.

Temperatures

Cuba's mean annual temperature is 25.2°C, with an average of eight hours of sunshine per day throughout the year. There is little seasonal variation, with an average temperature in January of 22°C, rising (along with humidity) to an average of 27.2°C in July. Nonetheless, in summer the temperature can rise to 32°C or more, and far higher in the Oriente, especially the lowlands of Guantánamo Province (the hottest part of the country), where the thermometer rises inexorably until you may, like one 19th-century writer, be "forced to take off your flesh and sit in your bones." The southern coast is generally hotter than the north coast, which receives the trades. Hot winds sometimes rip across the central plains in summer, drawn by the rise of hot air off the land.

Midwinter temperatures can take a sharp dip, infrequently falling below 10°C, when severe cold fronts sweep down into the Gulf of Mexico. Atop the higher mountains temperatures may plunge at night to 5°C.

Sea temperature rises from 26°C in winter to 28°C in summer, although the northern coastal waters are often cooler due to the varying influence of the Gulf Stream.

Rainfall

Some rain falls on Cuba an average of 85–100 days a year, totaling an annual average of 132 centimeters. Almost two-thirds falls during the May–October wet season, which can be astoundingly humid. Summer rain is most often a series of intermittent showers (or dra-matic, short-lived deluges) interspersed with sunshine, but downpours and lingering storms are common.

Central and western regions experience a three- to five-month dry period known as La Seca. February through April and December are the driest months. Nonetheless, heavy winter downpours are associated with cold fronts sweeping south from North America.

The Atlantic coast tends to be slightly rainier than the southern coast. The mountains receive the highest rainfall, especially the uplands of eastern Oriente (up to 400 cm fall in the Cuchillas de Toa). The mountains produce regional microclimates, forming rain shadows along the southeast coast, so that pockets of cacti and parched scrub grow in the lee of thick-forested slopes.

Years of relative drought are common. When it rains hard, pools of water collect in the streets, waves crash over the Malecón, power snaps off, telephone lines go down, and taxis are impossible to find.

Hurricanes

Cuba lies within the hurricane belt. August through October is hurricane season, but freak tropical storms can hit Cuba in other months, too. Most hurricanes that strike Cuba originate in the western Caribbean during October and move north over the island.

Cuba has been hard-struck by several hurricanes in recent years. Most recently, Hurricane Charles swept north through Havana Province in August 2004, followed only weeks later by Ivan, which pummeled Pinar del Río; and Hurricane Dennis killed 16 people and caused devastating damage in July 2005, followed in swift order by two more *ciclones*.

The country has a highly developed disaster preparedness and exemplary civil defense network for evacuations.

Flora

Cuba's ecosystems tout the most impressive species diversity of any Caribbean island. Despite four centuries of devastating deforestation, extensive tracts remain cloaked in a dozen shades of tropical green. Coastal mangrove and wetland preserves, dry forest, scrubby pine forest, pockets of rainforest and even montane cloud forest, almost desert-dry terrain supporting cacti, and other wild places are strewn like isles within an isle.

Cuba boasts more than 6,700 higher-plant species, of which some 3,180 are endemic and about 950 are endangered. The Sierra Maestra, for example, is one huge botanical garden, profusely smothered in everything from delicate orchids to prehistoric ferns. Above 2,000 meters, the vegetation changes abruptly to cloud forest. Some wind-battered elfin woods on exposed ridges are dwarfed, whereas more protected areas have majestically tall trees festooned with bromeliads, lichens, mosses, yellow-flowering *palo de cruz* vines, and all manner of lianas and creepers.

TREES

Indigenous tree species include mahogany, cedar, pine, rosewood, ebony, lignum vitae, cottonwood, logwood, *majagua,* and the deciduous, silvery *yagruma,* which shimmers as if frosted and bursts forth with huge lily-like blooms. Cuban craftsmen highly prize these timbers, many of which are now in short supply following centuries of logging to supply the furniture makers of Europe and to clear the land for King Sugar. The mountain ranges still have ecosystems typical of original Antillean vegetation. Many woody species are exotics, imports from far-off lands. Two examples are the eucalyptus from Australia and the cola nut from Africa.

Other archetypal species include the swollen baobab, which looks as if it has its roots in the air (for which it is sometimes called the "upside-down tree"), and the silver-trunked *kapok,* or silk-cotton, better known in Cuba as the revered *ceiba* (*Ceiba pentandra*), with broad trunk and wide-spreading boughs. It is considered sacred by adherents of *santería.*

The bully of trees is the *jagüey,* a species of strangler fig. It sprouts from the tops of trees from seeds dropped by birds or bats. It then sends roots to the ground, where they dig into the soil and provide a boost of sustenance. Slowly—it may take a full century—the roots grow and envelop the host tree, choking it until it dies and rots away, leaving the hollow, freestanding fig tree.

There are fruit trees, too, such as the alligator pear tree; the big, dark green *aguacates;* and the *zapote,* whose pulpy red fruit is the queen of Cuban fruits. One of Sierra del Rosario's endemic species, *Psidium guayabita,* produces a berry from which sweet *licor de guayabita* and dry *guayabita seca* brandy are made. Sea grape trims the island's shores, as does the coastal manchineel, whose poisonous sap and tiny apple-like fruits should be avoided.

On higher ground, palms and large-leafed undergrowth such as the "everlasting plant," whose large leaves form habitats for other plants, give way to ferns, bracken, pine trees, feathery-leafed *palo de cotorra* (parrot tree), and parasitic *conde de pino* (Count of the Pine) vine, whose bright red berries add color to the trunks of its pine tree hosts.

Many trees play hosts to epiphytes, arboreal nesters ("epiphyte" comes from the Greek, "upon plants") that attach themselves to tree trunks or branches. The epiphytic environment is a kind of nutrient desert. Thus bromeliads—brilliantly flowering, spiky leafed "air plants" up to 120 centimeters across—have developed tanks or cisterns that hold great quantities of rainwater and decaying detritus in the whorled bases of their stiff, tightly overlapping leaves. The plants gain nourishment from dissolved nutrients in the cisterns. Known as "tank epiphytes," they provide trysting places and homes for tiny aquatic animals high above the ground.

Palms

Visually, the predominant species are the palms, of which Cuba has more than 30 types, including the rare cork palm, found in the western part of Cuba (see the sidebar *The Cork Palm* in the *Pinar del Río* chapter). Those palms with the swollen *lower* trunks are not mutations but *barrigonas,* or belly palms, so named because of their remarkable ability to store water. The coconut palm is severely outnumbered, although it holds its own in northeast Cuba around Baracoa, where an entire local cuisine has evolved from the nut.

The king of palms is the silver-sheathed *Roystonea regia,* the royal palm, which grows singly or in great elegant clumps. Its smooth gray trunk, which can tower 25 meters, resembles a great marble column with a curious bulge near the top. Long leaves droop sinuously from the explosive top, blossoming afresh with each new moon. The ubiquitous royal palm is as useful as it is stately. Its fronds (*pencas*) make good thatch, and the thick green base—the *yagua*—of the *penca,* being waterproof, also makes an excellent roof or siding material. The trunk itself makes good timber. Bees favor palm honey. The seeds are used for pig feed. Humans devour the delicious, succulent palm-heart (*palmito* from the center of the trunk. And birds love its black fruit and carry the seeds (*palmiche*) all over the country. As part of the national emblem, it is protected by law, despite its ability to thrive almost anywhere.

Mangroves

Cuba's shorelines are home to five species of mangrove. These pioneer land builders thrive at the interface of land and sea, forming a stabilizing tangle that fights tidal erosion and reclaims land from the water. The irrepressible, reddish-barked, shrubby mangroves rise from the dark water on interlocking stilt roots. Small brackish streams and labyrinthine creeks wind among them like snakes, sometimes connecting, sometimes petering out in narrow cul-de-sacs, sometimes opening suddenly into broad lagoons.

Mangroves—most wonderfully seen in Zapata or the northern cays—are halophytes, plants that thrive in salty conditions. Although they do not require salt (in fact they grow better in fresh water), they thrive where no other tree can. Cuba's rivers carry silt out of the mountains onto the coastal alluvial plains, where it is trapped by mangroves. The nutrient-rich mud generates algae and other small organisms that form the base of the marine food chain. Food is delivered to the estuaries every day from both the sea and the land so those few plants—and creatures—that can survive here flourish in immense numbers. Their sustained health is vital to the health of other marine ecosystems.

A look down into the water reveals luxuriant life: oysters and sponges attached to the roots, small stingrays flapping slowly over the bottom, and tiny fish in schools of tens of thousands. Baby black-tipped sharks—and other juvenile fish too—spend much of their early lives among mangrove roots, out of the heavy surf, shielded by the root maze that keeps out large predators. High tide brings larger diners—big mangrove snappers and young barracudas hang motionless in the water. Mangrove swamps are esteemed as nurseries of marine life and havens for water birds—cormorants, frigate birds, pelicans, herons, and egrets—which feed and nest here by the thousands, producing guano that makes the mangroves grow faster.

Mangroves build up the soil until they strand themselves high and dry. In the end they die on the land they have created.

FLOWERS AND GARDENS
Monet Colors

The forests and grasslands flare with color. Begonias, anthuriums, "Indian laburnum," oleander, and poinsettia are common, as are mimosa, hibiscus, blossoming hydrangea, bright-pink morning glory, and bougainvillea in its rainbow assortment of riotous colors. Trees such as the vermilion flame-of-the-forest, purple jacaranda, blue rosewood, and almost fluorescent yellow *corteza amarilla* all add their seasonal bouquet to the landscape.

Cuba's national flower is the brilliant white, heady-scented *mariposa*, a native species of jasmine that became a symbol of rebellion and purity at the time of the Wars of Independence.

African golden trumpet is found everywhere. Water hyacinths, with their white and purple blooms, crowd the freshwater lakes. The brilliant scarlet Cupid's tears (*Lágrimas de Cupido*) speckle green meadows. Congea clambers up over houses. Fence posts cut from the piñon tree grow from a stick in the ground and burst into bright-pink efflorescent blossom. And jasmine, orange *jubia d'oro*, and azalea flank major thoroughfares and run down the central divides.

Many herbs also grow wild in Cuba, though surprisingly few find their way into local stores and, hence, into cooking. An exception is mint (*yerba buena*), cultivated on the island since at least 1535 and a key ingredient in *mojitos*. Pimento is an important cash crop that finds its way into local hot sauce. And locally produced vanilla flavors Coppelia ice cream.

Orchids

Cuba has several hundred known species of orchids, and countless others await discovery. In 1990, the purple Ames orchid (thought to be extinct) was discovered, as was another variety, *Marathrum cubanum,* which has no common name. At any time of year dozens of species are in bloom, from sea level to the highest reaches of the Sierra Maestra.

Not only are orchids the largest family of flowering plants, they're also the most diverse: Poke around with magnifying glass in hand and you'll come across species with flowers less than one millimeter across. Others have pendulous petals that can reach more than half a meter. Some flower for only one day. Others will last several weeks. The greatest diversity exists in humid mid-elevation environments, where they are abundant as tropical epiphytes. While not all orchids lead epiphytic lives—the Spanish called them *parásitos*—those that do are the most exotic of epiphytes.

Fauna

No one is quite sure how many species of fauna Cuba possesses. The vast majority are invertebrates (mostly insects), with a great many species endemic to specific regions. Unique species and subspecies include the world's smallest frog (*Sminthillus limbatus*) and smallest bird (the bee hummingbird, also called the *pájaro mosco*—fly bird—for its diminutive size, or *zunzuncito* for the swish of its wings); an endemic crocodile species; and unique, beautifully colored snails of the genus *Polymita*.

BIRDS

Cuba has 354 recorded species of birds, of which 149 species breed on the island, and 21 are native to Cuba. Birds that have all but disappeared in other areas still find tenuous safety in protected pockets of Cuba, although some 37 species are listed as threatened due to habitat destruction, pesticide pollution, and hunting (a popular Cuban pastime).

Cuba is a major stopover for migratory waterfowl, and more than a score of species of dove, duck, quail, mallard, snipe, and pigeon flock seasonally to the country's lakes and coastal lagoons. Spoonbills and flamingos are also common on the cays and among marshy lagoons. White egrets (*coco blanco*) are found around cane fields and water flats, and their cousins the *coco negro,* or ibis, and blue heron (*garza*) can be seen picking at a buffet of fresh delicacies that extends for miles. Black frigate birds, with their long scimitar wings and forked tails, hang like sinister kites in the wind. *Gaviotas,* or gulls, needless to say, also prefer maritime regions, as does the *gincho* (the sea osprey). The *codorniz,* or diver, lives beside freshwater lakes, where it is frequently found alongside the *yagauza,* a cross between a goose and a duck. The shimmering kingfisher prefers moving water.

Of terrestrial species, the wood stork can be

seen in scrub areas, also favored by the *cararia*, a goose-stepping relative of the Senegalese snakebird. Tanagers and woodpeckers brighten the forests. Listen at night for the hoot of the barn owl. Pygmy owls, with their old women's voices, perch in sapodilla trees. The *tocororo* (a member of the trogon family) is the national bird, perhaps because its brilliant blue, white, and red plumage copies the colors of the national flag. It wears a scarlet sash across its breast. Listen for its tell-tale call: *có, co, có, co, có, có.*

Other birds you might expect to see include pelicans, the yellow-necked green finch, the wedge-tailed *chuchinguaco*, the aura vulture wheeling and sliding on thermals, Everglade kites soaring in hunt of carrion, and common house sparrows and blackbirds.

There were so many parrots and macaws in the New World 500 years ago that the Americas were shown on maps as *Terra Psittacorum*, land of the free parrot. Even Columbus took home as a pet a Cuban parrot. These are now on the road to extinction; the Cuban macaw became extinct in the 19th century. The best place to spot parrots is the Los Indios forest reserve on Isla de la Juventud, inhabited by 153 species of birds, including the Cuban *grulla* or sandbill crane, but most notably by the Cuban parrot.

Cuba also has three species of hummingbirds, whose magnificent emerald and purple liveries shimmer iridescent in the sunlight as they sip nectar from the blooms and twirl in midair, their wings a filmy blur. Hummers earned a place in the mythology of the Taíno, who called them *colibrí*, meaning "god bird." They symbolized rebirth, since the Indians believed that the creature died when the weather turned dry and was born again when the rains came. They worshiped the bird as a *zemi*, a fetish idol representing the path of the sun across the sky. Legend lives on in folklore—some Cubans still believe that the most effective love potion is one made from dead hummers that have been dried and ground up.

Good resources include *Field Guide to the Birds of Cuba,* by Orlando H. Garrido and Arturo Kirkconnell (Comstock Publish-

THE WORLD'S SMALLEST BIRD

Imagine a bird that tips the scales at a mere two grams – less weight than a penny! It is easy to be fooled into thinking of *Mellisuga helenae* as an insect. In fact, it's the world's smallest bird, about the size of a large bee (hence its colloquial name: the bee hummingbird). This tiny jewel is endemic to Cuba.

At 2.5 centimeters (about 1 inch) long, the male hummer is shorter than the female by about 6 millimeters (0.25 inches). The female's cotton-soft nest is barely bigger than a doll's teacup.

The solitary hummer guards its territory with a ferocity remarkable for its diminutive size. One scientist records having seen a bee hummer "explode with rage" when a vulture had the nerve to perch too close. "The furious hummer attacked it so relentlessly that within minutes the chastened vulture flew off."

It forages on tiny spiders, flies, and other insects, but also takes nourishment from the nectar of plants such as trumpetvines, which depend symbiotically on the bird for pollination.

The bird's range has been gradually depleted, and it is now considered endangered.

ing, 2000), and *Aves de Cuba,* edited by Dr. Hiram Alonso González (Instituto de Ecológia y Sistemática, Havana, 2002), a large-format illustrated guide to the birds of Cuba.

AMPHIBIANS AND REPTILES

The most common reptiles you'll see are any of 46 lizard species, especially the bright green Lagartija lizard with its vermilion wattle, the comical curly-tailed lizard, chameleons, and quaint mosquito-eating geckos. Dragonlike iguanas, which can grow to two meters in length, can be seen in coastal areas (particularly on Cayo Largo and other offshore cays) crawling through moist deciduous forest leaf litter or basking on branches that hang over water—its preferred route of escape when threatened. Its head is crested with a frightening wig of leathery spines, its heavy body encased in a scaly hide, deeply wrinkled around the sockets of its muscular legs. Despite its menacing *One Million Years B.C.* appearance, it is a nonbelligerent vegetarian.

Aquatic turtles (terrapins) are also common, particularly in the Zapata Peninsula, where you can see them basking in rows on logs.

The amphibians are primarily represented by the frogs and toads, most of which you're probably more likely to hear than to see—especially the horny bullfrogs, croaking their lusty two-tone serenade through the night. Spelunkers might spot the axolotl, a blind, albino cave-dwelling newt.

Cuba is also home to 14 species of Neotropical snakes. None is venomous. Among the more common snake species are the wide-ranging boas. The *majá,* or Cuban boa, can grow to four meters in length and proves adept at slithering up trees. Its converse is the 20-centimeter-long pygmy boa, found solely in the caves of the Valle de Viñales.

Anfibios y Reptiles de Cuba, a large-format illustrated guide edited by Lourdes Rodríguez (Instituto de Ecológia y Sistemática, Havana, 2003) is widely available in Cuba.

Crocodiles and Caimans

The speckled caiman is relatively common in parts of Cuba's wet lowland. It is no more than two meters long. Another species, the nonnative caiman or *babilla,* is found on the Isla de la Juventud. Its scales take on the blue-green color of the water it slithers through. Their nests are heavily disturbed by dogs, foxes, lizards, and humans, who turn their skins into stuffed frog ashtrays and the like.

An endemic crocodile species, the yellow and black *Crocodylus rhombifer,* is found only in the Zapata Peninsula but is being reintroduced to the Lanier swamps, Río Cuato estuary, and other native areas. The crocodile, with a lineage going back 250 million years, was hunted to near extinction during colonial days and today has the most restricted geographi-

cal range of any crocodile species in the world. *Lagarto criollo* (as the Cuban croc is colloquially known) is much more aggressive than its cousin, the placid American crocodile, which inhabits many of the estuaries and coastal mangroves around the island and which interbred with the Cuban crocodile. Since the Revolution, Cuba has had an active and highly successful breeding program to save the indigenous species. Today the population is abundant and healthy (about 6,000 exist in the wild). In 1995, the Cuban government was authorized by the Convention of International Trade in Endangered Species to market the skins of the rare animals worldwide to be turned into shoes and handbags, with the money to be plowed back into conservation—only crocs in the captive-breeding program are culled.

The creatures, which can live 80 years or more, spend much of their days basking on mud banks. At night, they sink down into the warm waters of the river for the hunt. While the American species is a fish eater, the omnivorous Cuban crocodile occasionally likes meat—wild boars, deer, unsuspecting fishermen. Crocs cannot chew. They simply snap, tear, and swallow. Powerful stomach acids dissolve everything, including bones. A horrible way to go!

Mating season begins in February. The polygamous males (who form harems) will defend their breeding turf from rival suitors with bare-toothed gusto. When estrous females approach, the ardent male gets very excited and goes through a nuptial dance, roaring intensely and even kicking up clouds of spray with his lashing tail. A curtsey by the damsel and the male clasps her ardently with his jaws, their tails intertwine, and the mating begins (the couple can remain intertwined for more than an hour).

For all their beastly behavior, crocodiles are devoted parents. A female crocodile selects a spot above the high-water mark and exposed to both sunlight and shade, then makes a large nest mound out of sticks, soft vegetation, and mud, which she hollows out to make room for her eggs (usually between 30 and 70). She will guard the nest and keep it moist for several months after laying. The rotting vegetation creates heat, which incubates the eggs. When they are ready to hatch, the hatchlings pipe squeakily and she uncovers the eggs and takes the babies into a special pouch inside her mouth. She then swims away with the youngsters peering out between a palisade of teeth. The male assists, and soon the young crocs are feeding and playing in a special nursery, guarded by the two watchful parents. Only 10 percent of newborn hatchlings survive in the wild.

Crocs have an amazing immune system that can even defeat gangrene. Cuba is looking at the commercial potential, including extraction and development of potential medicines and, purportedly, aphrodisiacs.

Marine Turtles

Marine turtles, notably the hawksbill and, to a lesser degree, the green, nest on Cuban beaches, mostly on Isla de la Juventud and southern cays. Most of the important nesting sites in Cuba are now protected, and access to some is restricted. Despite legislation outlawing the taking of turtle eggs or disturbance of nesting turtles, however, adult turtles continue to be captured for meat by Cuban fishermen. Hawksbills are also hunted illegally in Cuba for the tourist trade—one often sees stuffed turtle specimens for sale, and shells are used in jewelry and ornaments.

Of the hundreds of eggs laid by a female in one season, only a handful survive to maturity.

FISH AND SHELLFISH

The warm waters off Cuba's coast are populated by more than 900 species of fish and crustaceans—from octopus, crabs, turtles, and spiny lobsters the size of house cats to sharks, tuna, and their cousins the billfish, which aerodynamically approach swimming perfection with their long pointed snouts, tapered bodies, and crescent-shaped tails. Some billfish grow as long as 3.6 meters and weigh as much as 650 kilograms, with eyes contoured so as not to bulge and interrupt the smooth streamlined head. These creatures breathe not with

gills but by taking in huge amounts of water through wide-open mouths. Thus they swim at high speed in order to breathe. The sailfish (a type of billfish) has been timed swimming over short distances at 110 kilometers per hour, which is faster than the cheetah, the fastest land mammal. Unlike other fish, they are also warm-blooded, with temperatures considerably higher than those of the water around them.

The lucky diver may also spot whale sharks (the largest fish in the world) and manta rays, which swim close to the surface and whose wings can be up to seven meters across.

Fish to avoid include the fatally toxic and heavily camouflaged stonefish and the beautiful orange-and-white-striped lion fish, whose long spines can inflict a killer sting. The bulbous Jimenea and the puffer fish, which can blow itself up to the size of a baseball, are also poisonous. Jellyfish are common, too, including the lethal Portuguese man-o'-war. And don't go probing around inside coral, where moray eels make their home—their bite can take your fingers off.

Inland, Lago de Tesoro harbors the rare *manjuarí,* the Cuban "alligator gar" (*Atractosteus tristoechus*), a living fossil that seems part fish, part reptile.

Cuba's food shortages have led to wholesale overfishing. Large fish are becoming rarer, and even illegal culling of juvenile fish in the mangrove nurseries isn't unknown. Collecting shells—and coral—is against both Cuban and international law; the Cuban government mandates that only 600 kilograms of black coral can be harvested annually, but much, much more is taken illegally to end up in *coral negro* jewelry.

Coral Reefs

Coral reefs—the most complex and variable community of organisms in the world—rim much of Cuba at a distance of usually no more than one kilometer offshore. The reefs are an aquatic version of the Hanging Gardens of Babylon. On the sea floor sit the massive brain corals and the delicate, branching sea fans and feathers; nearer the surface are elkhorn corals, frond-like gorgonians spreading their fingers upward toward the light, lacy outcrops of tubipora like delicately woven Spanish mantillas, and soft flowering corals swaying to the rhythms of the ocean currents.

Coral cays are prodigal places. Here, amid sprawling thickets of bright yellow staghorn, great rosettes of pale mauve brain coral, and dazzling blue tubastras almost luminescent in the bright sunlight, a multicolored extravaganza of polka-dotted, piebald, zebra-striped fish protect their diminutive plots of liquid real estate among the reef's crowded condominiums.

Corals are animals that secrete calcium carbonate. Each individual soft-bodied coral polyp resembles a small sea anemone and is surrounded by an intricately structured calyx of calcium carbonate, an external skeleton that is built upon and multiplied over thousands of generations to form fabulous and massive reef structures. Though stinging cells protect it against some predators, coral is perennially gnawed away by certain snails and fish (such as the colorful parrot fish), surviving by its ability to repair itself and at the same time provide both habitat and food for other fauna. Alas, the disappearance of inshore fish stocks, which by grazing on coral algae help maintain corals' health, has resulted in an increase in coral diseases caused by overproliferation of nuisance algae.

MAMMALS

Given the diversity of Cuba's ecosystems, it may come as a surprise that only a few dozen mammal species live here, half of them bats. Wild boar (*jabalí*) are common in many wild regions, including the cays of Jardines de la Rey, the Lanier swamps of Isla de la Juventud, and the Peninsula de Guanahicabibes, all areas where a small species of deer is also found.

Much of the wildlife is glimpsed only as shadows, such as the *jutía* (*Capromyys*), a large forest rodent related to the guinea pig and coypu of South America. It is edible and has been hunted for meat since indigenous times. Today it is endangered though found islandwide. A well-known indigenous animal that

you are *not* likely to see is the solenodon, a rare and primitive insectivorous mammal. The solenodon was thought to have become extinct early this century, but a sole female was spotted in the 1970s, prompting creation of a protected reserve in the Cuchillas de Toa mountains. This ratlike mammal (also called the *almiqué*) has large padded feet and claws and a long proboscis good for sucking up ants.

Bats are by far the most numerous mammals: Cuba has 27 species. You may come across them slumbering by day halfway up a tree or roosting in a shed and at night swooping between treetops or urban nests to take mosquitoes and other insects on the wing. Most species—like the Cuban flower bat and the giant Jamaican fruit bat, with a wingspan of more than 51 centimeters—are frutivores or insectivores. Weighing in as the smallest bat in the world is Cuba's butterfly bat, also known as the moth bat. There are no vampire bats in Cuba.

Marine Mammals

Cuba, like most Neotropical countries, has few marine mammals, though several species of dolphins are common and seven species of whales are occasionally seen in Cuban waters, and the West Indian manatee inhabits parts of the southern swamps. This herbivorous, heavily wrinkled beast looks like a tuskless walrus, with small beady eyes, fleshy lips that hang over the sides of its mouth, and no hind limbs—just a large, flat, spatulate tail. The creatures, distant cousins of elephants, can weigh up to 900 kilograms and reach 4.3 meters in length. Now endangered, only a few remain in the most southerly waters of the United States and isolated pockets of the Caribbean. Zapata, where the animals are legally protected, has one of the few significant populations, and they are often seen off the northeast coast near Baracoa.

INSECTS

Cuba's long isolation has enabled countless butterflies, moths, ants, termites, wasps, bees, and other tropical insects to evolve in profusion. With almost 200 identified species of butterflies and moths (at least 28 endemic), Cuba is a lepidopterist's paradise. You can barely stand still for one minute without checking off a dozen dazzling species: the transparent Cuban clear-wing butterfly, metallic gold monarchs, delicate black-winged heliconius splashed with bright red and yellow, the scintillating yellow orange-barred sulphur, and huge swallowtails fluttering and diving in a ballet of stupendous color.

Many insect species are too small to see. The hummingbird flower mite, for example, barely half a millimeter long, is so small it can hitch rides from flower to flower inside the nostrils of hummingbirds. At dusk the air trills with the sound of cicadas (*cigarras*), while fireflies flit by all atwinkle with phosphorescence.

Of course, a host of unfriendly bugs also exists: chiggers, wasps and bees, mosquitoes, and the famous "no-see-ums" (*jejenes*). All of these insects can inflict irritating bites on humans.

Conservation

Cuba is likened by socialists to the setting of Ernest Callenbach's novel *Ecotopia*, about an egalitarian and environmental utopia where the streets are clean, everything is recycled, and nothing is wasted; where there are few cars and lots of bicycles; where electricity is generated from methane from dung; where free health and education services reach the farthest rural outpost; and where city dwellers tend agricultural plots designed to make the island self-sufficient in food and break its traditional dependence on cash crops for export.

Though simplistic, there's truth in this vision. The Cubans are ahead of the times in coping with ecological problems the entire world will eventually face. Indeed, during the Rio Earth Summit in Brazil in 1993, Cuba was one of only two countries worldwide to receive an A+ rating for implementation of sustainable development practices.

Cuba: Red or Green?

One of the first proposals of Cuba's revolutionary government in the early 1960s was to create a greenbelt around Havana. Volunteers spent weekends planting trees, flowers, and ornamental shrubs before the plan died on the vine. In 1978 the government established the National Committee for the Protection and Conservation of Natural Resources and Environment, with responsibility to manage natural resources and wildlife and control air and water pollution. It has done a poor job, and much of the self-congratulatory hype is propagandist rhetoric.

Much of Cuba's advances are recent, necessitated by the collapse of the Soviet bloc. The fuel shortage caused Cubans to relinquish their cars in favor of a more environmentally sound mode of transportation—the bicycle. Everything from solar power (neglected, despite the perfect climate) to windmills (encouraged since the mid-1970s) are now being vaunted as alternatives to fossil fuels. For example, a majority of Cuba's sugar mills are now powered by *bagazo* (waste from cane processing); almost 35 percent of Cuba's energy supply comes from biomass conversion.

By necessity, in the 1980s, Cuba began to edge away from debilitating farming systems based on massive inputs of pesticides and fertilizers. It initiated sustainable organic farming techniques and soil conservation program, while experiments were undertaken to determine which plants had medicinal value. Herbal medicine—known as "green" medicine in Cuba—is today a linchpin in the nation's besieged health system.

Nonetheless, there is a lack of public education about ecological issues and few qualified personnel to handle them. And despite much-touted environmental laws, Cuba suffers from horrific waste and pollution. Industrial chimneys cast deathly palls over parts of Havana, Moa, and other nickel-processing towns of Holguín Province. The cement works at Mariel smother the town in a thick coat of dust. And heaven knows what cancer statistics can be culled among the workers at the asbestos works at Jatibónico. Then there are the decades-old Yankee automobiles and the Hungarian-made buses that, in Castro's words, "fill the city with exhaust smoke, poisoning everybody. We could draw up statistics on how many people the Hungarian buses kill." Havana Harbor is indisputably one of the most polluted bodies of water in the world (although it *is* being cleaned up and the shipping gradually moved to Mariel). And in townships nationwide, rivers and streams are polluted like pestilential sewers which, in many cities, are often broken.

Deforestation and Conservation

When Christopher Columbus arrived in Cuba, more than 90 percent of the island was covered in forest. Some 467 years later, on the eve of the Revolution, only 14 percent of the land was forested. Seven million hectares had been felled for sugar and cattle, most within this century. During 1945–60, indiscriminate logging reduced forested areas from more than 40 percent to less than 10 percent of Cuba's land area.

The revolutionary government undertook a reforestation program in the mid-1960s; by the late 1970s, the program had increased the total wooded area to almost 20 percent. Since the collapse of the Soviet bloc, however, Cuba has had to replace more than 300,000 cubic meters of imported timber by felling its own trees. Castro called for a reinvigorated reforestation program. The government announced the Manatí Plan, named for the eastern province where the program was initiated. Since its inception, about 697,000 hectares have been planted. Virtually the entire reforestation program, however, is in firs, not diverse species. There is little effort to regenerate primary forest.

Recent engineering projects to promote tourism in the northern cays have been ecological disasters. Construction of the *pedraplén* linking Cayo Coco to mainland Ciego de Ávila Province has cut off the flow of tidal waters, to the severe detriment of local ecology. Dynamiting for hotel construction has scared away flocks of flamingos, while that same construction—and that of an international airport on ecologically sensitive Cayo Coco—have had further debilitating effects. Meanwhile, coral reefs have suffered from turbidity from land-generated sediments and by agricultural runoff of poisonous pesticides used in the sugarcane fields, and fertilizers that are ideal for the proliferation of seabed grasses and algae that starve coral of vital oxygen.

Although Cuba has had notable success in bringing the Cuban crocodile back from the dead, the Cuban government has shown little concern for international conservation laws. Hawksbill turtle shells and severed turtle heads are sold openly at market, and turtle meat can still be found on restaurant menus, although the various species are close to extinction. Endangered black coral is the staple of Cuba's jewel industry. And lobsters, conch, and shrimp are becoming endangered in Cuban waters to cater to the tourist market and for export.

National Parks and Nature Reserves

Cuba officially claims 13 national parks, 23 ecological reserves, 5 nature reserves, 11 fauna refuges, 9 flora reserves, and 17 other protected areas. In addition, UNESCO has declared six regions to be biosphere reserves: Reserva de la Biosfera Sierra del Rosario and Reserva de la Biosfera Península de Guanahacabibes in western Pinar del Río; Reserva de la Biosfera Ciénaga de Zapata in Matanzas; Reserva de la Biosfera Buenavista, in north-central Cuba; and Reserva de la Biosfera Cuchillas del Toa and Reserva de la Biosfera Baconao in eastern Cuba. The **Centro Nacional de Áreas Protegidas** (CNAP, Calle 18A #1414, e/ 43 y 47, Miramar, Havana, tel. 07/202-7970, fax 07/204-0798, www.snap.cu) administers Cuba's burgeoning system of parks and reserves.

Cuba recently has begun to promote and develop the reserves as ecotourism destinations. As yet, no uniform management standards apply, however, and the government has thus far been slow in establishing a coherent plan (hunting is also allowed in some reserves and hunting tours are promoted by the state-run Ecotur tour agency).

History

Cuba has a sunny geography shadowed by a dark, brooding history. The Castroite Revolution, which replaced the Batista regime with another brand of authoritarianism, is part of a continuum in the struggle for freedom from oppression and tyranny that began with the Indian chief Hatuey's revolt in 1513. A sound knowledge of the island's history is integral to understanding Cuba today. To gloss over the nuance of detail is to easily misread the march of events. It is as fascinating a tale of pathos as that of any nation on earth—perhaps keener, suggests Frank Tannebaum, "because nature has been kind to the island."

PRE-COLUMBIAN HISTORY

The aborigines numbered no fewer than 100,000 when Christopher Columbus chanced upon the island in 1492. The Spaniards who claimed the island lent the name *Arahuacos,* or Arawaks, to the indigenous peoples, but there were several distinct groups that had left the Orinoco basin of South America and island-hopped their way up Caribbean islands over the course of many centuries.

The earliest to arrive were the Gauanajatabeys, hunter-gatherers who lived in the west, in what is now Pinar del Río Province. They were followed by the Ciboneys, who settled along the south coast, where they established themselves as farmers and fishermen. Mostly, it appears, they lived in caves. Little is known of these pre-Ceramic peoples (3500 B.C.–A.D. 1200). The pre-Ceramic tribes were displaced by the Taíno, who first arrived from Hispaniola around A.D. 1100 and, in a second wave, in the mid-15th century, when they were driven from their homeland on Hispaniola by the barbarous, cannibalistic Caribs, who leap-frogged northward through the island chain with the ferocity of a forest fire.

A Peaceable Culture

The Taíno lived in *bohíos,* thatched circular huts. Villages, which allied with one another, consisted of 15 or so families who shared property and were governed by a *cacique,* or clan leader. Since the land produced everything, the indigenous peoples were able to live well and peaceably, dedicated to the production of children. The parents put pressure on the soft skulls of newborn infants to induce broad, flat foreheads, esteemed as a mark of beauty in adults. The indigenous peoples culled fish from the rivers (often using *guaicán,* or sucker fish, tethered on lines to bait larger fish) and birds from the trees, which also produced tropical fruits and nuts in abundance. The Taíno also used advanced farming techniques to maximize yields of yucca (also called manioc) and corn, which they called *mahis* (maize), as well as yams and peppers.

Although they went naked, the Taíno were skilled weavers who slept in tightly woven cotton nets (a precursor to today's hammocks) strung from poles—the Spaniards would later use native labor to weave sailcloth. They were also skilled potters and boat builders who hewed canoes from huge tree trunks. It seems they had evolved at least basic astronomical charts, which can be seen painted on the walls of caves islandwide.

Columbus "Discovers" Cuba

After making landfall in the Bahamas in 1492 during his first voyage to the New World, Columbus took on indigenous guides and threaded the maze of islets and shallows that lay to the southwest. On the evening of October 27, 1492, Columbus first set eyes on the hazy mass of Cuba. The explorer voyaged along the north coast for four weeks, and finally dropped anchor on November 27, 1492, near today's Gibara, in Holguín Province. According to legend, he left a wooden cross that today can be seen in Baracoa.

"They are the best people in the world," Columbus recorded of the Indians, "without knowledge of what is evil; nor do they murder or steal. ... All the people show the most singular loving behavior... and are gentle and always laughing." The Spaniards would change that forever.

THE SPANISH TAKE OVER

In 1509 King Ferdinand gave Christopher Columbus's son, Diego, the title of Governor of the Indies with the duty to organize an expedition to explore Cuba. To lead the expedition, he chose Diego Velázquez de Cuellar (1465–1524). In 1511 four ships from Spain arrived carrying 300 settlers under Diego Columbus and his wife, María de Toledo (grandniece of King Ferdinand). Also on board was tall, portly, blond Velázquez, the new governor of Cuba, and—very dashing in a great plumed hat and a short velvet cloak tufted with gold—his secretary, young Hernán Cortés (1485–1547), who later set sail from Havana for Mexico to subdue the Aztecs.

Velázquez founded the first town at Baracoa in 1512, followed within the next few years by six other crude *villas*—Bayamo, Puerto Príncipe (today's Camagüey), San Cristóbal de la Habana, Sancti Spíritus, Santiago de Cuba, and Trinidad—whose mud streets would eventually be paved with cobblestones shipped from Europe as ballast aboard the armada of vessels now bound for the Americas.

A Sordid Beginning

The Spaniards were not on a holy mission. Medieval Spain had a penchant for foreshortening its cultural lessons with the sword and musket ball. The Spaniards had set out in quest of spices, gold, and rich civilizations. Thus the

bust of the Indian chief Hatuey in Baracoa's Plaza Independencia

indigenous island cultures—considered by the Spaniards to be a backward, godless race—were subjected to the Spaniards' ruthless and mostly fruitless quest for silver and gold.

A priest named Bartolomé de las Casas (1474–1566) accompanied Velázquez and recorded in his *History of the Indies:*

The Indians came to meete us, and to receive us with victuals, and delicate cheere ... the Devill put himselfe into the Spaniards, to put them all to the edge of the sword in my presence, without any cause whatsoever, more than three thousand soules, which were set before us, men, women and children. I saw there so great cruelties, that never any man living either have or shall see the like.

Slavery was forbidden by papal edict, but the ingenious Spaniards immediately found a way around the prohibition. Spain parceled its new conquests—Hispaniola and Cuba—among the conquistadores. The Indians were turned into *peones*—serfs. Each landowner was allotted from 40 to 200 Indian laborers under a system known as the *encomienda,* from the verb to entrust. Those Indians not marched off to work in mineral mines were rounded up and placed on plantations, where they were forced to labor under the guise of being taught Christianity. Since the Indians were supposed to be freed once converted, they were literally worked to death to extract the maximum labor.

The Indian resistance was led by Hatuey, an Indian chieftain who had fought the Spanish on the island of Hispaniola and fled to Cuba after his people were defeated. Hatuey was the first in a long line of Cuban rebels—down to Fidel Castro—who learned how to use the mountains for guerrilla warfare. Eventually the Spaniards captured the heroic Indian chief and burned him at the stake on February 2, 1512. As the flames crackled around Hatuey's feet, Father Juan de Tesín offered to baptize him, promising the chieftain that he would then go to heaven. Hatuey asked the priest whether the Spaniards also went to heaven when they died. When Tesín replied, "Yes," Hatuey scornfully replied that he did not want to go where there were "such cruel and wicked people as the Christians." Thus the Spaniards, in their inimically cruel fashion, provided Cuba with its first martyr to independence.

The 16th century witnessed the extinction of a race. Those Taíno not put to the sword or worked to death fell victim to exotic diseases. Measles, smallpox, and tuberculosis also reaped the Taínos like a scythe, for the Indians had no natural resistance to European diseases. Within 100 years of Columbus's landfall, virtually the entire indigenous Cuban population had perished.

The Key to the New World

The Spanish found little silver and gold in Cuba. They had greater luck in Mexico and Peru, whose indigenous cultures flaunted vast quantities of precious metals and jewels. Cuba was set to become a vital stopover for Spanish galleons and traders carrying the wealth of the Americas back to Europe.

In 1564 a Spanish expedition reached the Philippines. The next year it discovered the northern Pacific trade winds that for the next 250 years propelled ships laden with Chinese treasure to Acapulco, from where the booty was carried overland to Veracruz, on the Gulf of Mexico, and loaded onto ships bound for Havana and Europe. Oriental perfumes, pearls, silks, and ivories passed through Havana. To these shipments were added silver from Bolivia, alpaca from Peru, and rare woods from Central America, plus Cuban tobacco, leather, fruit, and its own precious woods. To supply the fleets, the forests were felled, making room for cattle and tobacco (and, later, sugar) for sale in Europe. Meats, hides, and precious hardwoods were shipped to Europe alongside gold and silver.

With the Indian population devastated, the Spanish turned to West Africa to supply its labor. By the turn of the century, an incredibly lucrative slave trade had developed. Landowners, slave traders, merchants, and smugglers were in their heyday—the Spanish Crown heavily taxed exports, which fostered smuggling on a remarkable scale. The Spaniards tried to regulate the slave trade, but it was so profitable that it resisted control. Daring foreigners—such as John Hawkins (1532–95) and his nephew Francis Drake (1540–96)—cut in on the trade.

The Period of Piracy

Lured by Cuba's vast wealth, pirates followed in the Spaniards' wake. As early as 1526, a royal decree declared that ships had to travel in convoy to Spain. En route, they gathered in Havana harbor. The crown had a vested interest in protecting the wealth from pirates; it received one-fifth of the treasure. In 1537, Havana itself was raided. One year later, Jacques de Sores sacked the capital and demanded a ransom. When a bid by the Spaniards to retake the city faltered, de Sores put men, women, and children to the sword before razing the city. French corsairs preyed mercilessly on smaller cities and plantations across the island.

Soon, pirates were encouraged (and eventu-

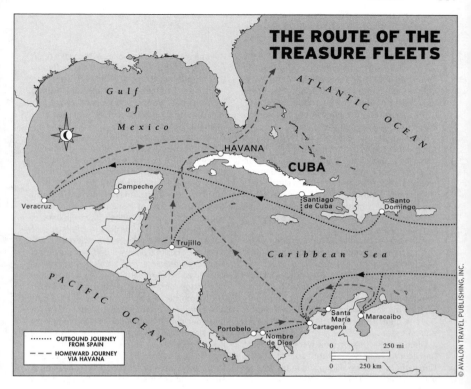

THE ROUTE OF THE TREASURE FLEETS

Gulf of Mexico

ATLANTIC OCEAN

HAVANA

CUBA

Campeche

Veracruz

Santiago de Cuba

Santo Domingo

Trujillo

Caribbean Sea

PACIFIC OCEAN

Portobelo

Nombre de Dios

Santa María

Maracaibo

Cartagena

- - - - - OUTBOUND JOURNEY FROM SPAIN

— — — HOMEWARD JOURNEY VIA HAVANA

0 _____ 250 mi

0 _____ 250 km

© AVALON TRAVEL PUBLISHING, INC.

ally licensed) by the governments of France, Holland, and England to prey upon Spanish shipping. In 1587 King Philip of Spain determined to end the growing sea power of England and amassed a great armada to invade her. Francis Drake, Hastings, and Sir Walter Raleigh assembled a fleet and destroyed the armada, breaking the power of Spain in the Old World.

Now, no city was safe. There were hundreds of raids every year, severely disrupting the economy. Spain was impotent. In 1662, Henry Morgan, a stocky Welshman and leader of the Buccaneers, a motley yet disciplined group of pirates that would later operate under British license from Port Royal in Jamaica, ransacked Havana, pilfered the cathedral bells, and left with a taunt that

the Spanish weren't equal to the stone walls that Spain had built: "I could have defended Morro Castle with a dog and a gun." Only when the pirate attacks began to ease up towards the end of the 17th century were the Spanish colonizers able to settle down to raise cattle, tobacco, and sugar.

The Spanish Crown treated Cuba as a cash cow to milk dry as it pleased. For example, it had monopolized tobacco trading by 1717. The restriction so affected farmers' incomes that the *vegueros* (tobacco growers) marched on Havana. The rebellion, the first against Spain, was brutally crushed. In 1740, Spain created the Real Compañía, with a monopoly on all trade between Cuba and Spain. It bought Cuban products cheaply and sold necessities from Europe at inflated prices.

SLAVE SOCIETY

Black slavery in Cuba began in 1513 with the arrival of slaves from Hispaniola, and it wasn't abolished until 1886. At the peak of the trade, in the 1840s, slaves formed about 45 percent of Cuba's population. Only about one-third, however, worked the plantations. Most were domestics who lived in the cities.

The majority of slaves who were shipped to Cuba came from highly developed West African tribes such as the Fulani, Hausa, and Yoruba. They came mostly from Senegal, Gambia, and Guinea at first, and later from Nigeria and the Congo. Distinct ethnic groups were kept together, unlike in North America. As a result, their traditions and languages have been retained and passed down.

After being rounded up and herded to African ports, slaves were loaded onto ships where they were scientifically packed like sardines. Space meant profit. Chained together body-to-body in the airless, dark, rancid hold, they wallowed in their own excrement and vomit on the nightmare voyage across the Atlantic. Dozens died. They arrived in Cuba diseased and half-starved.

Once ashore, the Africans were herded into *barracoons* to be stored until sold to plantation owners or to work in grand mansions. No attention was paid to family relationships. Parents, children, and siblings were torn asunder forever. After being sold, they were worked as beasts of burden.

Understandably, rebellion was always around the corner. The first slave revolt occurred in 1532 in Oriente. A few years later,

Havana was sacked by slaves in the wake of an attack by French pirates. Other slaves fled to the mountains. To track down runaways, the authorities used posses with specially trained hunting dogs. When a slave was caught, it was standard procedure to cut off one ear as a warning to other slaves.

Nonetheless, slaves had the legal right to buy their own and their relatives' freedom. Slaves could keep a percentage of whatever fee their masters charged for hiring them out as labor and apply it towards buying their manumission. Free blacks formed a significant part of Havana's populace: "In no part of the world, where slavery exists, is manumission so frequent as in the island of Cuba," noted Alexander von Humboldt. Once free, they could even own and sell property. Many free blacks set up small businesses or worked as artisans, while women hired out as domestics. Some rose to positions of wealth and prominence, and there evolved a significant slave-owning black middle class. An overseer called the *síndico* existed to ensure that slave's rights were enjoyed: For example, if a slave wished to change his master, the *síndico* could force an owner to grant a slave three days absence to look for one, and a slave could set his own price; he could also ask the owner to value the price of a slave's freedom, after which that sum could not legally be raised.

All in all, slaves fared better in Cuba than on neighboring islands, and far better than in the United States. Anthony Trollope, compar-

England Takes Over

On January 4, 1762, George III of England declared war on Spain. Some years before, the British governor of Jamaica, Charles Knowles, had been hosted on an official visit to Havana, where he spent much of his time reconnoitering the city's defenses. Knowles was consulted, and a plan drawn up for an attack on Havana.

On June 7, a British fleet of 200 warships carrying 11,000 troops put ashore and Havana erupted in panic. The Spanish scut-

tled three ships in the harbor mouth, ineptly trapping their own warships inside the harbor. That night, when Spanish guards atop the Cabaña began firing at British scouts, the Spanish warships began blasting the ridge, causing their own troops to flee. The British took the ridge and laid siege to Havana. On July 29 sappers blew an enormous hole in the Castillo de Morro, and the flag of St. George was raised over the city.

The English immediately lifted Spain's trade

ing Cuba to Jamaica, wrote that "a present healthy condition is cared for, but long life is not regarded." The estates in Cuba were "on a much larger scale, in much better order, overlooked by a larger proportion of white men, with a greater amount of skilled labor. The evidences of capital were very plain in Cuba; whereas, the want of it was frequently equally plain in our own island."

Slaves were rarely allowed to marry and raise families. Certain slave owners bred slaves like cattle for sale. Strong males were picked out to mate with the healthiest women, who were expected to produce healthy babies every year. Wet nurses looked after the *criollitos*, who sometimes never saw their parents again.

It was common for white men to take a black mistress, and their offspring usually received their freedom. Occasionally, a black mistress would be particularly favored and treated well, although there were limits to their upward mobility. Any mulatta who had ideas of rising above her station usually ended up caught short, as with Cecilia Valdés, the beautiful heroine of the marvelous, tragic, and eponymous novel by Cirilo Villaverde about a mulatta who cherishes the idea of rising to become accepted by Havana's upper social stratum, but whose ambition ends in a violent denouement.

PLANTATION LIFE

Plantation slaves lived in *barracoons*, where they were laid out in rows. They had only mud floors and little ventilation. The huts swarmed with fleas and ticks. A hole in the ground served as a communal toilet.

The slaves were awakened at 4:30 A.M. By 6 A.M. they were marching in file to the fields, where they worked until sunset, with only brief pauses for rest. At 8:30 P.M., the silence bell was rung, and everyone had to go to sleep. Slaves stopped working when they reached 60 years of age. Sunday was rest day.

Men were issued sturdy, coarse linen clothes, and the women blouses, skirts, and petticoats. The women also wore gold jewelry and earrings bought from Moorish tinkers who traveled between plantations. Chinese peddlers also made the rounds, selling sesame seed cakes and other items. Small private plots were the slaves' salvation. Here, they could grow sweet potatoes, gourds, beans, yucca, and peanuts and raise pigs and chickens, which they often sold to whites who came out from the villages. Some plantation owners even allowed slaves to visit nearby taverns, where they were able to trade, drink rum, and play wager games.

House slaves, while treated poorly, experienced better conditions than slaves in the country. Even so, urban slaves were not spared harsh punishment, which was carried out in public by trained experts.

The most comprehensive account of plantation life is *Autobiography of a Runaway Slave*, by Estefan Montejo, who related his life as a slave and runaway (*cimarron*) in 1963 at the age of 105.

restrictions. Foreign merchant vessels flocked, and Cuba witnessed surging prosperity. Jamaican sugar planters, however, pressured England to cede back to Spain what would otherwise become a formidable rival for the English sugar market. On February 10, 1763, England exchanged Cuba for Florida in the Treaty of Paris, which ended the war. In the interim, Spain had acquired a more enlightened king, Charles III, who continued the free-trade policy. The boom continued, encouraged a de-

cade later when the newly independent United States began trading directly with Cuba.

KING SUGAR RULES

The North Americans' collective sweet tooth fostered the rapid expansion of sugar plantations in Cuba. Wealthy Cuban and U.S. slave merchants funded planting of new lands in sugar by granting loans for capital improvements, all meant to foster an increasing need for slaves. Land planted in sugar multiplied

HEROES OF THE WARS OF INDEPENDENCE

CARLOS MANUEL DE CÉSPEDES

Céspedes (1819-74), known as "Father of Our Country," was a sugar planter in Oriente. As a young and ardent nationalist, he published *Cubana Libre*, the first independent newspaper in Cuba, and was arrested for revolutionary activity. On October 10, 1868, he freed his slaves, enrolled them in an army, and, in an oration known as the *Grito de Yara* (Shout of Yara), declared an open revolt against Spain. Céspedes was named head of the Revolutionary government. When Spanish troops captured Céspedes's son Oscar and offered to spare his life in exchange for the father's surrender, the father claimed that all Cubans were his sons and that he could not trade their freedom for that of one person. His son was promptly shot. In 1873 Céspedes was removed from his position as President of the Republic in a meeting to which no one had bothered to invite him. He was cut down in a hail of bullets a year later – ambushed by the Spanish at San Lorenzo, where he had retreated to await a ship to take him to a life as a revolutionary in exile.

CALIXTO GARCÍA

Calixto García Iñiguez (1840-98) was born in Holguín of a Spanish noble family and rose to become top commander of the rebel army in the Oriente in the Ten Years War, during which he was captured by the Spanish. García attempted suicide rather than be captured, but the bullet miraculously exited his forehead without killing him. He was held under supervision in Spain, where he lived for 15 years. In March 1896, García escaped from Spain and returned to Cuba. As second-in-command of the rebel Mambí army during the War of Independence (1895-98) he led a brilliant campaign in which his army liberated many Spanish-held cities. His troops participated alongside U.S. troops in the assault on Santiago de Cuba that sealed Cuba's independence from Spain. When García and fellow Mambí leaders were barred from the victory ceremony, García composed a letter of protest to the U.S. commander. Nonetheless, García, who died of pneumonia, was buried with full U.S. military honors in Arlington National Cemetery.

more than tenfold by the turn of the 18th century. The massive expansion was significantly boosted with the Saint Domingue (Haiti) rebellion in 1791 and subsequent demise of the sugar industry. About 30,000 French planters washed up in Cuba, bringing their superior knowledge of sugar production.

These events sent the slave trade soaring. In 1713, the Treaty of Utrecht, which ended the War of the Spanish Succession, had granted the British sole rights to the Spanish-American slave trade, with Britain agreeing to supply 144,000 slaves to the Spanish West Indies over a period of 30 years. The trade grew throughout the century: as many as 200 slaving ships called into Havana annually during the 1830s. Between 1791 and 1810, over 100,000 slaves arrived, and countless more undocumented slaves were brought in illegally. Although in 1817 Spain signed a treaty with England to abolish the slave trade, Cuban officials were

so enriched by bribes from slave traders that the industry continued unabated for most of the century. Only in 1888 was slavery in Cuba abolished, and then only because of a crisis in the sugar industry.

The prosperity encouraged development of the island. By 1760 Havana was already larger than New York or Boston. The first University of Havana had been established in 1728, the first newspaper in 1763, and the postal service in 1764. Cuba's citizenry were growing vastly wealthy on trade with North America, with the difference that now much of the prosperity flowed back to Cuba, changing the face of Havana, Santiago de Cuba, and other cities. Spanish ships unloaded builders and craftsmen, hired to help citizens display their earnings in an outpouring of architectural sophistication. They brought with them a Moorish aesthetic, which they translated into what Juliet Barclay calls a unique "tropical synthesis of column,

MÁXIMO GÓMEZ

Máximo Gómez y Baez (1836-1905) was born in Santo Domingo, Dominican Republic. He joined the Spanish Army in 1856 and commanded Spanish reserve troops in Cuba before switching sides. He was immediately named a general at the outbreak of the Ten Years War and rose to become commander-in-chief of the liberation army before retiring to his plantation in the Dominican Republic. He returned to Cuba alongside José Martí on April 11, 1895, as supreme commander of the Army of Liberation. His brilliant guerrilla tactics were instrumental in weakening the Spanish forces that eventually surrendered to U.S. forces in 1898. Prominent Cuban leaders invited Gómez to run for the presidency of the newly independent republic, but he declined. He died in Havana.

ANTONIO MACEO GRAJALES

Maceo (1845-96), a mulatto of mixed African and Spanish descent, hailed from Santiago and rose from the rank of private to that of a general in the rebel army in the Ten Years War (1868-78). Considered a brilliant guerrilla strategist, Maceo was known for his whirlwind strikes against superior forces. He fought in over 900 battles and was wounded 24 times, earning the nickname the "Bronze Titan." Maceo also survived a slander campaign by white commanders, who charged him with seeking a "Black Republic." His father died in battle in Maceo's presence, as did two of his brothers, one of whom died in his arms. The fearless leader refused to accept the treaty ending the war in 1878 and fought on for several months until fleeing into exile – his act is known as the Protest of Baraguá. He returned on March 30, 1895, to help lead the War of Independence and as a commander of the Army of Liberation led an army all the way to Pinar del Río before being killed in battle near Havana on December 7, 1896.

JOSÉ MARTÍ

José Martí is the single most important person in colonial Cuban history (see the sidebar *José Martí* in the *Havana* chapter).

courtyard, and chiaroscuro." Monuments and parks were erected, along with public libraries and theaters. Streets were paved, and beautiful colonial homes were erected. In 1790 street lamps went up in Havana.

While the British went out to their colonies to grow rich and return, the Spanish went to grow rich and stay. They brought a permanence of design and planning to their New World cities that other colonial powers never achieved. "The Spanish built cities where they settled, but the English just let cities grow. The poorest street of Havana had dignity compared to the shanty towns of Kingston," wrote Graham Greene.

THE REVOLUTIONARY ERA

Spain, however, continued to rule Cuba badly. Spain's colonial policy, applied throughout its empire, was based on exploitation, with power centralized in Madrid, and politics practiced only for the spoils of office and to the benefit solely of *peninsulares*—native-born Spaniards. "The Spanish officials taxed thrift right out of the island; they took industry by the neck and throttled it," thought Frederic Remington on his visit in 1899. Spain's monopoly laws encouraged the migration to Cuba of a kind of Spanish carpetbagger, many drawn from the poorer lower classes. Cuban-born *criollos* resented the corrupt *peninsulares* who denied them self-determination. No Cuban could occupy a public post, set up an industry or business, bring legal action against a Spaniard, or travel without military permission. Onerous taxation on income and property imposed in 1867 added further salt to the wound.

Following the Napoleonic Wars in Europe, Spain's new royal family—the Bourbons—took over a weakened country. Spain's New World territories were wracked by wars of independence led by Simón Bolívar. By 1835 only Cuba and Puerto Rico had not gained independence from Spain. Meanwhile, a new generation of young Cuban intellectuals and patriots began to make their voices heard. The American Revolution had a profound affect on the *criollos*. The French Revolution added to the liberation zeal, as did the slave revolution on neighboring Saint Domingue.

In 1843, Miguel Tacón became governor. Tacón would brook no sentiments for independence. He suppressed patriotic sentiment and exiled leading nationalists. Many *criollos* were shot for treason. Others suspected of self-rule sentiments were lashed in public squares, often until they died. Meanwhile, the island, says historian Louis A. Pérez Jr., "had achieved a level of modernity that far surpassed Spain's, emphasizing the gap between the Cuban potential and Spanish limitations. Spain could not provide Cuba with what it did not itself possess." Spain clung to its colony with despairing strength and the support of wealthy *criollos* (concentrated in western Cuba), who feared that abolitionist sentiments in Europe would lead to abolition of slavery in Cuba. They looked to the United States, where slavery was thriving, for support.

Uncle Sam Stirs

Annexation sentiment in the United States had been spawned by the Louisiana Purchase of 1803. The Mississippi River became the main artery of trade and Cuba's position at the mouth of the Gulf of Mexico took on added strategic importance. Thus in 1809 Thomas Jefferson wrote, "I candidly confess that I have ever looked upon Cuba as the most interesting addition that can be made to our system of States, the possession of which would give us control over the Gulf of Mexico and the countries and isthmus bordering upon it." Jefferson had attempted to purchase Cuba from Spain in 1808 (he was the first of four presidents to do so). John Quincy Adams thought Cuba a fruit that would ripen until it fell into the lap of the United States.

Sentiment didn't come into it. By 1848, 40 percent of Cuba's sugar was sold to the U.S.

market; manufactures began flowing the other way. Yankees yearned for expanded trade. Thus President James Polk (1845–49) offered Spain US$100 million for Cuba. President Franklin Pierce (1853–57) upped the ante to US$130 million. His successor, James Buchanan, tried twice to purchase Cuba for the same price. But Spain wasn't selling.

The American Civil War changed the equation. With slavery in the United States ended, it became impossible for Spain to keep the lid on Cuba. In 1868 the pot boiled over.

The Ten Years War

The planters of western Cuba were determined to forestall the abolition of slavery in Cuba. But the relatively poor, backward, and *criollo* eastern planters had little to lose. Their estates were going bankrupt and falling into the hands of rapacious Havana moneylenders.

On October 10, 1868, a lawyer, poet, and planter named Carlos Manuel de Céspedes freed the slaves on his plantation at La Demajagua, near Manzanillo, in Oriente. Fellow planters rushed to join him, and as the dawn broke over the dewy plantations of Oriente, they raised the *Grito de Yara* (Shout of Yara), the cry of liberty heard throughout the island. Within a week, 1,500 men had flocked to Céspedes's calling (he was eventually elected president; after later being deposed in an internal feud, he was killed in battle in 1873). The group called themselves the *Mambí*, after a freedom fighter in Santo Domingo. The Mambí quickly captured the town of Bayamo. When Spanish forces arrived to retake the town, the rebels razed it. For the next 10 years Cuba would be roiled by the bitter First War of Independence (the Ten Years War, 1868–78), in which white and black *criollos* fought side by side against 100,000 troops shipped from Spain. Once arrived, the Spanish Volunteers were given a virtual carte blanche to terrorize the people of Cuba.

Guerrilla warfare seized the island. Led by two brilliant generals—one a white, General Máximo Gómez, and the other a mulatto, Antonio Macéo—the rebels liberated much of the island and seemed on the verge of victory. However, the movement collapsed, and in 1878 the forces signed the Pact of Zanjón. The rebels were given a general amnesty—slaves who had fought with the rebels were also given freedom—in exchange for surrender.

The Cuban economy had been devastated by the war, and huge tracts of land lay abandoned. Amid the chaos, North American investors stepped in and bought up ravaged sugar plantations and many of the sugar mills at ludicrously low rates. Meanwhile, the Spanish reverted to the same old recipe of tyranny. Independence, the one dignified solution refused the *criollos,* was the cause which united the population of Cuba.

The long, bloody war claimed the lives of 250,000 Cubans and 80,000 Spaniards. At least 100,000 Cubans were forced to flee; their lands were expropriated and given to loyalists. Among those arrested was a teenager named José Martí y Pérez. After a brief imprisonment, the young gifted orator, intellectual, poet, and political leader was exiled to Spain.

Martí's Martyrdom

José Martí had been born in Havana in 1853. As a lad of 15 he had startled his mother, reportedly, with the words "To many generations of slaves must succeed one generation of martyrs." Somewhere in his boyish brain he tucked away that foreboding notion. Following his exile to Spain, the journalist and political thinker traveled to the United States, where he settled and through his writings and indefatigable spirit became the acknowledged "apostle" and "intellectual author" of independence. In 1892 he formed the Cuban Revolutionary Party, and led the swelling movement for independence.

In 1895 Martí joined General Máximo Gómez in the Dominican Republic. Together they sailed to Cuba. On April 11, they pulled away from their steamer and rowed ashore, landing amid a storm at a beach called Playitas at the eastern end of the island. Martí kissed the Cuban soil he had not seen for 16 years. From here, they linked up with the great Cuban general Antonio Maceo and his ragtag army. Together they launched the War of Independence (1895–98).

Barely one month after returning from exile, Martí martyred himself on May 19, 1895, at the age of 42. His motto was, "To die for the fatherland is to live." Martí's death left Cuba without a spiritual leader. But the Cubans were determined to seize their freedom. Generals Gómez and Maceo led an army of 60,000 the full length of Cuba, smashing Spanish forces en route. Maceo's brilliant tactics earned worldwide acclaim until he was finally killed in battle in December 1896—his father and 10 of his brothers also died for the cause.

After Maceo's death, the struggle degenerated into a destructive guerrilla war of attrition. In a desperate bid to forestall independence, the ruthless Spanish governor, Valeriano Weyler began a rural pacification program in which virtually the entire campesino population was either slaughtered or herded into concentration camps called protectorates, where thousands starved to death. The *reconcentración* campaign claimed the lives of 10 percent of Cuba's population. In turn, the rebels torched the sugarcane fields and kept them burning until the conflagration licked at the suburbs of Havana.

THE SPANISH-CUBAN-AMERICAN WAR

The ideal of *¡Cuba libre!* (Free Cuba!) had genuine support among the U.S. populace, which saw echoes of its own struggle for independence a century earlier. The public hungered for information about the war, feeding sales of newspapers throughout North America. The *New York World* and *New York Journal,* owned by Joseph Pulitzer and William Randolph Hearst respectively, started a race to see which newspaper could first reach one million subscribers. The press took on the job of inflaming Yankee patriotism and fanning war fever. While Hearst's hacks made up stories from Cuba, the magnate himself worked behind the scenes to orchestrate dramatic events. He sent the photographer Frederic Remington to Cuba in anticipation of the United States entering the war. At one point Remington wired Hearst: "There will be no war. I wish to return." Hearst hastily replied: "Please remain. You furnish the pictures and I'll furnish the war."

Remember the *Maine!*

McKinley desperately wanted to avoid a war with Spain but was powerless to do so. Responding to public pressure, he sent a warship—the USS *Maine*—to Havana to protect U.S. citizens living there. On February 5, 1898, the ship mysteriously exploded and sank in Havana Harbor, killing 258 people. Evidence suggests this was an accident, but Hearst had his coup and rushed the news out in great red headlines, beating the *World* to the one million mark. He blamed the Spanish, and so did the public. His *New York Journal* coined the phrase "Remember the Maine, to hell with Spain." The paper belabored the jingoistic phrase. Theodore Roosevelt, then Assistant Secretary of the Navy, also fanned the flames, seeing the venture as "good for the navy."

On April 25, 1898, Congress declared war against Spain. U.S. forces also invaded Guam, Puerto Rico, and the Philippines, which they captured in one day.

The Cavalry Arrives

The Cuban general, Máximo Gómez, did not want U.S. troops, however. He wanted arms and ammunition. His guerrilla army— the Mambi—was on the verge of victory and would have undoubtedly won their independence before the close of the century. However, Cuba's freedom fighters soon found themselves forced into the back seat away from the brief fighting, which was restricted to Oriente.

The Yanks thought the Cubans a dirty and decrepit lot—most of whom weren't even *white!* "A collection of real tropic savages," reported Hearst journalist Stephen Crane. Where the Mambi did fight, heroically, their part was dismissed, as at the pivotal engagement at San Juan Hill in Santiago de Cuba, where, on July 1, 1898, a cavalry charge ostensibly led by Theodore Roosevelt supposedly sealed the war. In

a decisive naval battle on July 3, the U.S. Navy decimated the Spanish fleet as it attempted to escape Santiago Harbor. On July 17, Spain surrendered. The Spanish flag was lowered and the Stars and Stripes raised, ending one of the most foolishly run empires in the world. Cuba ended the century as it had begun—under foreign rule.

Uncle Sam Takes Over

Washington "granted" Cuba "independence"— at the end of a short leash. The U.S. military occupation formally began on January 1, 1899, when 15 infantry regiments, one of engineers, and four of artillery arrived to "pacify" Cuba. They would remain for four years. Washington dictated the peace terms embodied in the Treaty of Paris, signed on April 11, 1899. Even the Cuban Constitution was written by Washington in 1901, ushering in a period known as the Pseudo-Republic. Rubbing salt in the wound of Cuban sensibilities was a clause called the Platt Amendment, named for Senator Orville H. Platt of Connecticut but written by Elihu Root, Secretary of War. Through it, Uncle Sam acquired the Guantánamo naval base and the right to intervene whenever the United States deemed it necessary. Even the governor-general, U.S. Army General Leonard Wood, wrote President McKinley that "there is, of course, little or no independence left in Cuba under the Platt Amendment."

On Ascension Day (May 20) 1902, the Stars and Stripes was lowered and the lone-star flag of Cuba rose into the sunny sky. Havana broke out in a three-day spree of rejoicing. "It's not the republic we dreamed of," said Máximo Gómez.

THE ERA OF "INDEPENDENCE"

The Pseudo-Republic was an era of Yankee colonization and domestic acquiescence. Economically, North America held sway over the lives of Cubans through its control of the sugar plantations. Politically, Washington called the shots—and maintained a revolving door to the increasingly corrupt Cuban presidency.

United States officers who spoke no Spanish, had never lived in a hot country, and had no notion of Spanish or Cuban history and ideals found themselves in charge of a tired, starving people and a devastated land wrecked by war. As Hugh Thomas suggests: "This continuous U.S. presence, benevolent though it often set out to be, paternalistic though it usually was in practice, fatally delayed the achievement of political stability in Cuba."

Nonetheless, the United States pumped millions of dollars into reconstruction. Under General Wood, the U.S. authorities set up schools, started a postal system, established a judiciary and civil service, organized finances, paved roads in cities throughout the nation, and managed within a few years to eradicate yellow fever in a campaign based on the discovery by a Cuban physician, Dr. Carlos Finlay, that the fever was spread by mosquitoes.

The United States installed its first president, Tomás Estrada Palma, who received his salary, as well as instructions, directly from Washington. Palma, though reelected in 1905, was too honest and weak to hold greedy politicians in check. Each Cuban president forged new frauds of their own and handed out sinecures (which the Cubans called *botellas*—milk bottles given to babies) to cronies. Through successive administrations, Cuban politics sank deeper into iniquity.

Washington's intentions were mostly honorable: It firmly wanted to establish a stable, democratic government in the U.S. tradition. Unfortunately, centuries of corruption and graft could not be eradicated overnight. The U.S. government was constantly influenced to support this or that Cuban who had given, or would give, opportunities to U.S. investors or had borrowed from North American banks. When U.S. economic interests were threatened, Uncle Sam sent in troops—"dollar diplomacy" it was called, a phrase coined by President Howard Taft. The United States landed Marines in 1906 to "restore order" when an armed rebellion attempted to topple the reelected Estrada regime; in 1912, when black rage exploded into open revolt; and again in 1917, when workers called a general strike. Dollar diplomacy was blind to the corruption, state violence, and poverty plaguing the country.

A U.S. Colony

The opening years of the Cuban republic were a time of great opportunity for everyone except Cubans—whose economy was in shambles. Agriculture was devastated; industry had been destroyed. Everything was up for grabs. Cuba witnessed a great influx of capital as U.S. companies invested in every major industry—tobacco, railroads, utilities, mining, and, above all, sugar. Several thousand U.S. citizens settled, bringing their North American style and sensibilities to the city. In short order, every major industry was U.S. owned. U.S. interests in the sugar industry increased almost overnight from 15 percent to 75 percent. Cuba had become a giant Monopoly board controlled by Uncle Sam.

Thanks to billions of dollars of investment, the Cuban economy bounced back with vigor, though the mass of rural families struggled to survive. Although the sugar workers had no other way of earning a living, the sugar companies paid them wages for only half a year. Employment lasted only as long as the dry season, when the downtime began. Most workers and their families lived in squalor and suffered miserably for half the year. Not all estates were of this model. For example, the Hershey company built modern homes for its Cuban employees and provided clinics, schools, and social services, and, noted writer Herbert Lang: "Whereas in other towns and villages there are always a number of ill-kempt street urchins begging for money, here all are well dressed, playing together in an orderly manner."

Profits from sugar were so great that Cubans sold out their other properties and poured their money into the industry, deriving dividends from sweetening the desserts of the world. The peak of the sugar boom—the "dance of the millions"—lasted from 1915 to 1920, when the price of sugar climbed to US$0.22 a pound. Then came the crash. In 1924, Cuba produced more than 4.5 million tons of sugar. The next year it produced a million tons more—but the sugar sold for less than US$0.01 a pound.

Sugar money paid for massive civic constructions and public utilities and for the plush mansions in Beaux-Arts and art deco style then blossoming in cities all over Cuba. Havana—jewel of the Caribbean—wore a new luster. Cuba of the 1920s was far and away the richest tropical country anywhere, with a per capita income equivalent to that of Ireland, two-thirds that of Britain, and half that of the United States. As Prohibition and a wave of morality swept through the United States, Yankees flocked to Havana where those who chose to could wallow up to their noses in cocaine and sex. Havana, wrote Juliet Barclay, was filled with "milkshakes and mafiosi, hot dogs and whores. Yanqui Doodle had come to town and was having martini-drinking competitions in the Sevilla Bar."

The Machado Epoch

In 1924, President Alfredo Zayas, having made his millions, declined to run for reelection. General Gerardo Machado y Morales (1871–1939), who had cut his teeth as a cattle rustler, stepped into the breach. Machado acted on his promises to construct schools, highways, and a health care system, and initiated the most ambitious development plan for Cuba since that of colonial governor Miguel Tacón in the 1830s. However, he was also a uniquely corrupt man susceptible to la mordida (literally, "the bite"—bribes), which undercut law and order. Machado's promise to keep his fingers out of the till seemed plausible: He had lost three fingers while working as a butcher. In 1928 Machado manipulated a phony election and became a tropical Mussolini, supported by a personal police force of 15,000. His politics were to make himself rich and to protect U.S. investments. His method was to assassinate anyone who opposed his government.

When the Great Depression hit, Cuba's one-crop economy was dealt a deathblow, bringing misery throughout the country. Meanwhile, the United States had raised its import tariffs on sugar, exacerbating Cuba's plight. The Cuban economy collapsed, and the nation soon disintegrated into violent mayhem. Havana and other cities were swept by random bombings and assassinations. Machado responded to a growing number of hunger marches, strikes, and antigovernment demonstrations with greater repression. President Calvin Coolidge, of course, thought that "under Machado, Cuba is a sovereign state. … her people are free, independent, in peace, and enjoying the advantages of democracy." Finally, in the summer of 1933, a general strike brought the whole country to a halt. On August 11, Machado fled the country carrying a suitcase full of gold.

Batista Days

Diplomat Sumner Welles, sent to Cuba earlier that summer by Franklin D. Roosevelt, appointed Carlos Manuel de Céspedes (son of the hero of the Ten Years War) as Cuba's provisional president. Within the month he had been overthrown by an amalgam of students (a potent political force) and army officers, including a pivotal 32-year old sergeant named Fulgencio Batista y Zaldivar (1901–73). Batista was at Camp Columbia in Havana on September 4, the day he led other noncommissioned officers in a golpe called the Sergeant's Revolt, which ousted the senior officers. They handed power to a five-man civilian commission that named a leftist university professor, Dr. Ramón Grau San Martín, president.

Grau lasted only four months. His proposed worker's compensation law and regulation of utility rates were far too reformist for Washington. Batista, self-promoted to colonel and chief of the army, was under no illusions as to the intentions of the United States, which sent 30 warships to Cuba as a warning. On January 14, 1934, Batista ousted Grau and seized the reins of power. Batista would have center stage until driven from power in 1959. Impressed by Batista's fealty to Washington, in 1934 the United States agreed to annul the Platt Amendment—with the exception of the clause regarding the Guantánamo naval base. In exchange, the United States established the Reciprocal Trade Agreement, which gave the United States total control over Cuba's market. Following promulgation of a new and progressive constitution in 1940, Batista ran for the presidency himself on a liberal platform. Cuban voters gave him a four-year term (1940–44) in what was perhaps the nation's first clean election.

Despite his personal ambitions, Batista at first displayed relative benevolence and good sense—with U.S. blessing, Batista suppressed the far right as well as extreme leftist elements. He maintained enlightened attitudes on elections, civil liberties, public welfare, and workers' rights, enacted progressive social reforms and a new, liberal constitution. For pragmatic reasons, Batista legalized the *Partido Comunista de Cuba,* and two leading Communists—Juan Marinello and Carlos Rafael Rodríguez—became ministers in his 1940–44 government. The influence of the Communist Party ebbed and flowed during the next two decades; intriguingly, it opposed Fidel Castro's revolution, and Castro was never associated with the party until he usurped it following the Revolution.

In the 1944 election, Batista's hand-picked successor lost to Ramón Grau San Martín, the president Batista had deposed. Batista retired to Florida having accumulated US$20 million during his 11-year tenure, and leaving his country in the hands of men who permitted their administrations to again sink into chaos. Assassinations and bombings were once again daily events on the streets of Cuba. Two rival gangster groups—the Socialist Revolutionary Movement (MSR) and Insurrectional Revolutionary Union (UIR)—ruled the streets. Street demonstrations erupted, organized on behalf of the opposition *Ortodoxo* party led by Senator "Eddy" Chibás, revered for his rare honesty. His public suicide on August 5, 1951, brought together a broad spectrum of Cubans fed up with corruption and student gangsterism.

In 1952 Batista again put himself up as a presidential candidate in the forthcoming elections. It soon became clear that he wouldn't win. On March 10, only three months before the election, he upended the process with a bloodless pre-dawn *golpe.* Batista dissolved the

GENERAL FULGENCIO BATISTA

Fulgencio (he was christened Rubén) Batista y Zaldívar was born out of wedlock and into dire poverty in 1901 at Veguitas, near Banes, a backyard region of Oriente. His father was a sugarfield worker and the son of an indentured Chinese laborer; his mother was black. Batista enlisted and became a professional soldier and, after learning stenography, was promoted to sergeant.

Batista – who one commentator thought was an insecure, "fiery little bantam of a fella" – rose to the top during a *golpe* in 1934, when Fidel Castro was only seven. He became chief of staff of the army and, as such, took over the government. Though he controlled Cuban politics for more than two decades, he was blackballed by the social elite for being mulatto (members of the Havana Yacht Club famously once turned out the lights when he entered).

After fleeing Cuba at midnight on New Year's Eve 1958, Batista settled in Spain, where he lived a princely life until his death in 1973. The poor cane cutter died as one of the world's wealthiest men – he had milked Cuba of almost US$300 million.

congress and canceled the election. One of the reform-minded candidates for congress whose political ambitions were thwarted by Batista's coup was a dashing young lawyer with a predilection for stylish suits and the limelight. His name was Fidel Castro. (In 1952, the 25-year-old had risen to great prominence as the most outspoken critic of corrupt government and was being hailed as a future president.) Harry Truman immediately recognized the infant regime. Had Truman acted with greater rectitude there may never have been a revolution in 1959. Batista's rule was so widely hated that it unified the Cuban people. Batista had forsaken his interest in the Cuban people. He had lingered too long in Miami with *mafiosi.* The general had come back to power to commit grand larceny hand in hand with the Mob.

Batista initiated another round of progressive acts and massive civic construction work that conjured a tourist boom, spurring economic growth and fueling a period of prosperity. As the Batista epoch progressed, however, gangsters began to take over the hotels and casinos with Batista's blessing—for a cut of the proceeds, of course. It wasn't until the mid-1950s that an infusion of foreign capital built Havana's mobster-run Las Vegas–style hotel-casinos with which prerevolutionary Cuba will always be associated. "A few years of profitable frivolity ensured its lasting reputation as the premier pleasure island of the time and offered a rallying cry and a focal point for anti-government rebels," notes historian Rosalie Schwartz. North Americans arrived by plane or aboard the *City of Havana* ferry from Key West to indulge in a few days of sun and sin. They went home happy, unaware that behind the scenes chaos and corruption were rife.

In November 1954, Batista won the national presidential election. Though the elections were rigged, Washington quickly embraced the "constitutional" regime. But it made no difference. Batista maintained his cynical rule with a brutal police force. Many Cubans were disgusted by the depth of repression and depravity into which Havana had sunk, made more wretched by the poverty and destitution endemic in the slums of Havana and by the illiteracy and malnourishment that were still part of the rural condition.

Throughout this sordid period, the United States reluctantly supported Batista. Neither Washington nor Batista understood the revolutionary forces at work. In the towns, Batista's secret police tortured suspected opposition members and hung them from trees while, says Schwartz, "militants of Castro's Twenty-Sixth of July Movement placed phosphorous bombs in movie houses, buses, nightclubs, theaters, and parks." In the countryside, night fell with a blackness made creepier by the awareness of mysterious forces. "The President's regime was creaking dangerously towards its end," wrote Graham Greene in *Our Man in Havana*.

THE GATHERING STORM

Almost immediately following Batista's *golpe*, Fidel Castro began to plot Batista's downfall. Castro possessed a vision of his place in Cuba's future that seemed preordained. He was also ruthlessly focused. His plan: street protests and legal challenges to the Batista regime and a secret conspiracy simmering underneath.

The secret police came to arrest Castro within 24 hours of Batista's coup, forcing him underground. He organized the Movement and ran it with military discipline. Washington's support of Batista ostensibly revolved around the issue of Communism—an entirely irrelevant question with regard to Cuba at the time. Castro had shunned the Communist Party, whose members were automatically excluded from the Movement. Even Castro's Communist brother, Raúl, was kept out for a time. Instead, political instruction centered on the nationalist philosophy of José Martí.

The Attack on the Moncada Barracks

Castro, then 26 years old, launched his revolution on July 26, 1953, with an attack on the Moncada barracks in Santiago de Cuba. Unfortunately, everything conspired to go wrong the moment the attack began. It quickly collapsed in a hail of bullets. Batista declared a state of emergency. His propaganda machine went to work to convince the nation that the rebels had committed all kinds of atrocities. Unknown to Batista, however, the torture and assassination of 64 rebels who had been captured had been photographed. When the gruesome photos were published, a wave of revulsion swept the land—thousands of Cubans attended a Mass for the dead martyrs. The Catholic hierarchy stepped in and negotiated a guarantee of the lives of any future captives.

Castro was eventually captured by an army detachment whose commander—tall, 53-year-old, black Lieutenant Pedro Sarría—disobeyed orders to kill Castro on sight. Batista later jailed Sarría, but Sarría would go on to become a captain in Fidel's Revolutionary Army and a hero of the Revolution. Once in Santiago jail,

the flag of Castro's M-26-7 movement

reporters were even allowed to interview Castro, who told them in detail of the rationale for the Moncada attack—a public relations coup that sowed the seeds of future victory. Amazingly, Fidel was allowed to broadcast his story over the national radio to demonstrate to the Cubans how subversive he was. "Imagine the imbecility of these people!" Fidel later said, "At that minute, the second phase of the revolution began."

History Will Absolve Me

Castro, who acted as his own attorney, was sentenced in a sealed court that opened on September 21, 1953. Castro never attempted to defend against the charges leveled at him and his fellow conspirators. He relied solely on attacking Batista's regime, and proudly defended his own actions in a mesmerizing oratory in which he devastatingly denounced the Batista regime, citing history's precedents for taking up arms against tyrants, and ending with the words, "Condemn me, it does not matter. History will absolve me!" (The Moncada attack

parallels in many ways Hitler's failed Rathaus Putsch in 1924, suggests biographer Georgie Ann Geyer. Indeed, Castro had studied and memorized *Mein Kampf,* and his "History Will Absolve Me" speech was closely modeled on the words of Adolf Hitler at the end of his Putsch trial, which ended with the words, "You may pronounce us guilty, [but] history will smile. … For she acquits us!")

Castro was cheered as he was led away in handcuffs to serve 15 years in jail on the Isle of Pines (now Isla de la Juventud). José Martí had also been imprisoned on the Isle of Pines, adding to Castro's symbolic association with the original revolutionary hero. Fidel was imprisoned with 25 other companions of the July 26 attack. The media gave wide coverage to Castro, whose stature increased with each day in jail. A nationwide campaign to free Castro added to his now lustrous sheen. In May 1955 Batista bowed to mounting public pressure and signed an amnesty bill passed by congress. Castro and the Moncada prisoners were free. Nonetheless, Castro was forced to move constantly for his own safety. On July 7, 1955, he boarded a flight to Mexico. "From trips such as this, one does not return or one returns with the tyranny beheaded at one's feet," he stated in a message printed in the *Bohemia* newspaper.

Castro's Exile

Castro's goal in exile was to prepare a guerrilla army to invade Cuba. Fidel's enthusiasm and optimism were so great that he managed to talk aged revolutionaries such as Alberto Bayo, a hero of the Spanish Civil War, into giving up their careers and businesses to train his nascent army—now known as M-26-7 (*Movimiento Revolucionario 26 Julio*)—in guerrilla warfare. (One of the foreigners who signed up was Ernesto "Che" Guevara, an Argentinean doctor, intellectual, and revolutionary.)

In a brilliant coup, Fidel sent a powerful message to the congress of the *Ortodoxo* party, in which he called for the 500 delegates to reject working with Batista through congressional elections and to take the high road of revolution. The delegates jumped to their feet chanting "Revolution! Revolution!" The Communists continued to shun him—the "objective conditions" defined by Karl Marx didn't exist.

Castro also authored the Movement's "Manifesto No. 1 to the People of Cuba," laying out the revolutionary program in detail: "The outlawing of the *latifundia,* distribution of the land among peasant families. ... The right of the worker to broad participation in profits. ... Drastic decrease in all rents. ... Construction by the state of decent housing to shelter the 400,000 families crowded into filthy single rooms, huts, shacks, and tenements. ... Extension of electricity to the 2,800,000 persons in our rural and suburban sectors who have none. ... Confiscation of all the assets of embezzlers acquired under all past governments. ..." It was a long list.

Castro's plan called for a long-term war in both countryside and urban areas, although he eschewed random violence against the public. To raise money for the endeavor, he toured the United States, speechmaking to thousands of Cuban exiles and Yankees alike, inspiring them by invoking Martí's legend.

The *Granma* Landing

Shortly after midnight on November 25, 1956, Castro and his revolutionaries set off from Tuxpán, Mexico, sailing without lights for Cuba aboard a 38-foot-long wooden luxury cruiser. The *Granma* had been designed to carry 25 passengers. Battered by heavy seas and with a burden of 82 heavily armed men and supplies, the vessel lurched laboriously toward Cuba, which Castro had planned to reach in five days. However, one engine failed and the boat slowed, falling two days behind schedule.

At dawn on December 2, the ship ran aground at low tide, two kilometers south of the planned landing site at Playa Las Coloradas. The men had to abandon their heavy armaments and supplies and wade ashore through dense mangroves. Two hours later, just after dawn, Fidel Castro stood on *terra firma* alongside 81 men, with minimal equipment, no food, and no contact with the Movement

ashore. "This wasn't a landing, it was a shipwreck," Che Guevara later recalled.

The motley group set out towards the safety of the Sierra Maestra none too soon. Within two hours of landing, *Granma* had been sighted and a bombardment of the mangroves began. On December 5, the exhausted column was ambushed. Only 16 men survived, including, remarkably, Castro, Che Guevara, Raúl Castro, Camilo Cienfuegos, and other key leaders. "There was a moment when I was Commander in Chief of myself and two others," Castro later recalled.

On December 13, Castro's meager force finally made contact with a peasant member of the 26th of July Movement, and with that, word was out that Fidel had survived. Aided by an efficient communications network and intense loyalty from the Sierra peasants, the rebel unit was passed from homestead to homestead as they moved deeper into the mountains, and safety.

THE CUBAN REVOLUTION

Soon men began joining the Rebel Army, mostly idealists keen to help oust a corrupt regime, but many of them, claims Jon Lee Anderson, "former rustlers, fugitive murderers, juvenile delinquents, and marijuana traffickers." On January 16, Castro's modestly armed force struck an army post for the first time since the attack on Moncada. Batista responded with a ruthless campaign against the local populace, while B-26 bombers and P-47 fighter planes supplied by the United States strafed the Sierra Maestra. Batista managed to alienate the peasantry upon whom Castro's forces relied, while the Rebel Army cemented the *guajiros'* support by assisting with the coffee harvest in May 1957.

Washington, meanwhile, continued to supply arms and full support to Batista.

War in the Cities and Countryside

While the Rebel Army nibbled away at its foes in the mountains, a war of attrition spread throughout the countryside and cities. Sugarcane fields were razed; army posts, police

© CHRISTOPHER P. BAKER

José Antonio Echevarría, leader of the Students' Revolutionary Directorate, led an ill-fated attack on Batista's presidential palace.

stations, and public utilities were destroyed. On March 13, an attack on the presidential palace in Havana by the Students' Revolutionary Directorate—acting independently of Castro—failed, and 35 students died in the attack. Castro, far off in the mountains of Oriente, increasingly found himself in a battle for revolutionary leadership with the Movement's urban wings and on July 12 committed himself to "free, democratic elections"—the central point of his Sierra Maestra Manifesto, designed to assuage the growing leadership crisis.

Casto also issued a manifesto affirming the Movement's choice of a respected liberal judge, Manuel Urrutia Lleó, to head a provisional government after Batista's fall. Urrutia promptly left for exile in the United States, where he was instrumental in Eisenhower's pledge to stop arming Batista. However, Washington kept shipping arms secretly (including napalm, which was used to bomb peasant villages) and even re-armed Batista's warplanes at Guantánamo naval base. Meanwhile, the CIA

was channeling funds—at least US$50,000 was delivered between November 1957 and mid-1958—to Castro's Movement (the top-secret operation still remains classified by the U.S. government).

Batista met the increasing storm with brutal violence. Finally he decided to launch an all-out offensive in the Sierra Maestra with 14 battalions and 10,000 men—Operation FF (*Fin de Fidel*). The *fidelistas,* however, beat back the 76-day offensive and even captured two tanks and huge quantities of modern weapons. Radio Rebelde broadcast the victories to the rest of the nation from La Plata, Castro's secret headquarters.

In July Castro and eight leading opposition groups—excluding the Communists; Castro decided to co-opt the Communists separately—signed the Caracas Pact, an agreement to create a civic coalition. The writing now on the wall, Washington began negotiations with Castro while maneuvering to keep him from power. In September, Castro—fueled by massive contributions of finances and arms from the Venezuelan government—led an offensive to take Santiago de Cuba. On December 30, Che Guevara captured Santa Clara. The scent of victory was in the air.

The Revolution Triumphs

Washington persuaded Batista to hand over power to a civilian-military junta led by General Eulogio Cantillo. At midnight on New Year's Eve 1958, Batista and his closest supporters boarded a plane for the Dominican Republic. On January 2, the same day that the rebel armies of Camilo Cienfuegos and Che Guevara entered Havana, Castro's army took over Santiago de Cuba. That night he delivered a televised victory speech and the following day the triumphant guerrilla army began a five-day Romanesque victory march to Havana, with crowds cheering Castro atop a tank, all of it televised to the nation.

Castro—now the "Maximum Leader"—was intent from day one on turning the old social order upside down. Fidel moved cautiously but vigorously to solidify his power under the guise

REVOLUTIONARY HEROES

CAMILO CIENFUEGOS

Camilo Cienfuegos Gorriarán (1932–59) was born to Spanish anarchists and became a radical student activist against the Batista regime. In 1956 he joined Castro's guerrilla army in Mexico and was a participant in the *Granma* landing. He was named Chief of Staff under Castro, and established himself as a brilliant and capable commander in Castro's guerrilla army. Cienfuegos's column occupied Havana immediately following the toppling of Batista. Although not considered a Communist, Cienfuegos was, along with Che Guevara, the most influential and popular figure in the early Castro regime. In October 1959, Castro sent Cienfuegos to arrest the Camagüeyan rebel commander, Hubert Matos. While returning to Havana on October 28, Cienfuegos's Cessna disappeared under mysterious circumstances.

CHE GUEVARA

Ernesto "Che" Guevara is promoted as Cuba's most important contemporary hero (see the sidebar *Che Guevara* in the *Cienfuegos and Villa Clara* chapter).

JULIO ANTONIO MELLA

Julio Antonio Mella (1903–29) was born in Havana and was educated in the United States and, later, at the University of Havana, where he led Communist-inspired demonstrations that included a student takeover of the university demanding the expulsion of professors. He founded the University Student's Federation and the periodical *Juventud*. Mella also initiated actions against the corrupt Machado regime. In August 1925, Mella co-founded the Cuban Communist Party and the Anti-Imperialist League of the Americas. He was expelled from the university and later imprisoned. In 1926 he was exiled to Mexico, where he wrote works denouncing imperialism. He became embroiled in in-fighting within the Mexican Communist party and was assassinated in 1929.

FRANK PAÍS

Frank País (1935–58) was born in Santiago de Cuba and became a student activist at the University of Santiago, where he founded the anti-Batista Movimiento Nacional Revolucionario. Later he became a teacher, and merged his MNR with Castro's M-26-7 movement, becoming the movement's principal leader in Oriente and head of the urban underground. País was named head of Cuban-based revolutionary activities during Castro's absence in Mexico. He led the ill-fated attack on the police headquarters in Santiago on November

---

of establishing a pluralist democracy, but his aim was clear. Although Manuel Urrutia had been named president and an unusually gifted coalition cabinet had been formed (Urrutia genuinely attempted to establish a democratic government, which the U.S. government recognized on January 4, 1959), Castro—the real power-holder—immediately set up a "parallel" government behind the scenes. In public, however, he stressed that he had no political ambitions. He began secretly negotiating with the Communists to co-opt them and build a Marxist-Leninist edifice.

Castro recognized that the Cuban people were not yet ready for Communism; first he had to prepare public opinion (many of his wartime *compadres* who resigned over this issue were jailed for treason). He also had to avoid antagonizing the United States into intervention. Castro began to manipulate Urrutia, first by getting himself named prime minister with power to direct government policy. He also manipulated the public: Speaking before large crowds, he molded and radicalized the public mood, using this as a tool to pressure the Urrutia government, which he repeated must obey "the will of the people." Meanwhile, the old walls of the *cabaña* fortress echoed with the fusillades of firing squads as hundreds of Batista supporters and "enemies of the revolution"

30, 1956, timed to coincide with the *Granma* landing. País provided logistical support to the rebel army in the mountains, while leading the reprisal assassinations of Batista henchmen. His young brother José was shot and killed by Batista's police in June 1957, and Frank was assassinated by police agents one month later.

CELIA SÁNCHEZ

Celia Sánchez Manduley (1920–80) was born in Media Luna, Oriente, and at an early age became a dedicated anti-Batista revolutionary. Later, as a leader in Castro's 26th of July Movement, she set up and ran the urban and peasant-based networks that smuggled men and munitions to Castro's Rebel Army in the mountains under the noses of Batista's spies. She also saw combat at the Battle of Uvero. Sánchez was 36 years old when she met Fidel for the first time, on February 16, 1957 – the beginning of a 33-year association with the Cuban leader. She became his secretary, his "eyes and ears," and, some say, his lover. For many years she was the most important person in Fidel Castro's life and held various important positions in the Castro government. Celia was his compass and kept Fidel in touch with the people; she helped balance and minimize Fidel's absolutist side and was one

of only a handful of people who could give him news and opinions he didn't want to hear. Her death from cancer in January 1980 profoundly shook Castro and removed from his life the only person with whom he could truly relax and be himself.

ABEL AND HAYDEE SANTAMARÍA

Brother and sister Abel (1925–53) and Haydee (1931–80) Santamaría were born in Havana and were early participants in the efforts to oust Batista. A confidante of Fidel Castro and his designated successor in the revolutionary movement, Abel Santamaría helped organize the attack on the Moncada barracks. He led a contingent that captured the hospital across the street. Santamaría and his men continued to snipe at the barracks, unaware that the attack had failed. Batista's troops stormed the hospital, where Santamaría and his 23 men had taken to bed, pretending to be patients (Haydee was also one of the attackers and pretended to be a nurse). They were betrayed and ruthlessly tortured: Haydee's fiancé, Boris Luis, was beaten to death on the spot with rifle butts, and Abel died later that day. Following the Revolution, Haydee became an influential figure in the Castro government, including as head of the Casa de las Américas. She committed suicide in 1980.

---

were dispatched following summary trials. The executions, presided over by Che Guevara, were halted after international protests.

Uncle Sam Decides to Oust Castro

Castro—determined to assert Cuba's total independence—feared the possibility that U.S. Marines would steal his revolution as they had stolen independence at the end of the Spanish-Cuban-American War in 1898. Just as Washington became obsessed with the Communist issue without understanding or taking into account Cuban nationalism, Castro allowed himself to become obsessed with the United

States and its Plattist mentality. An antagonistic relationship between a Castroite Cuba and the United States was inevitable. History ordained it. The Revolution was born when the east–west struggle for power was at its zenith. There was no way Uncle Sam could tolerate a left-leaning revolution beyond its control only 90 miles from Florida, especially one that was aligning itself with America's principal enemy and presented ominous potential for U.S. national interests.

Cuban sovereignty was no longer an issue in which Uncle Sam had a say—a theme that underlay Castro's visit to the United States in March 1959. Vice President Nixon met with

THE U.S. EMBARGO

For four decades, Washington has clamped a strict trade embargo on Cuba in the expectation that economic distress would oust Castro or at least moderate his behavior. Since 1996 the U.S. embargo has been embodied in law (heretofore it was an executive order). Here's what Uncle Sam says the failed embargo, enacted by President Kennedy in 1961, is all about:

The fundamental goal of U.S. policy toward Cuba is to promote a peaceful transition to a stable, democratic form of government and respect for human rights. Our policy has two fundamental components: maintaining pressure on the Cuban Government for change through the embargo and the Libertad Act while providing humanitarian assistance to the Cuban people, and working to aid the development of civil society in the country.

Noble sentiments perhaps, but critics call it a violation of international law, including the International Human Rights Law and Conventions, that injures and threatens the welfare of Cuban people. The United Nations General Assembly routinely votes to condemn it (the 2005 vote was 182-4, with only the Marshall Islands, Palau, and Israel – which trades with Cuba – joining the United States in voting against the resolution). Even Cuba's leading dissidents have unanimously denounced the U.S. embargo and the transition program outlined in current U.S. law.

The effects of the embargo (which Castro calls *el bloqueo*, or blockade) are much debated. In 1999, Cuba filed a claim for US$181 billion in reparations. However, in 2000, the International Trade Commission (ITC) determined that the embargo has had a minimal impact on the Cuban economy, citing domestic policies as the main cause of Cuba's economic woes (for three decades, the effects of the embargo were almost entirely offset by massive subsidies from the Soviet Union). As President

Carter noted during his visit to Havana in May 2002: "These restraints are not the source of Cuba's economic problems. Cuba can trade with more than 100 countries, and buy medicines, for example, more cheaply in Mexico than in the United States." Although export of medicines to Cuba has been permitted since 2000, the licensing requirements are a minefield. In 2004, for example, Chiron Corp. was fined US$168,500 because a European subsidiary had shipped two vaccines for infants to Cuba between 1992 and 2002. And the Bush administration's strategy of tightening restrictions, using hunger as a weapon, "dramatically reduces the funds average Cubans have to put food on their tables," notes the Center for International Policy. Nor can Cuba sell any goods to the United States. After 40 failed years, the embargo's sole accomplishment has been to make Cubans poorer, not freer.

In short, U.S. sanctions are intended to starve Cubans and stir them into righteous anger against Castro. The paradox is that the policy achieves the opposite effect to its stated goals: It provides a wonderful excuse for the Communist system's economic failings, and a rationale to suppress dissidents and civil liberties under the aegis of national security for an island under siege (it also permits Fidel Castro to perform the role of Cuba's anti-imperialistic savior that he has cast for himself – as the giant-killer in the tradition of José Martí).

Although State Department officials privately admit that the embargo is the fundamental source of Fidel's hold on power, no U.S. president has had the intelligence or guts to call Fidel's bluff. Instead, they are wed to what Ann Louise Bardach calls a "transparently disastrous policy, trading off sensible and enduring solutions for short-term electoral gains" (see the sidebar *The Cuban-Americans* in this chapter). The Bush administration's anti-Castroite passion is so intense that dozens of Cuban artists, musicians (even those invited to receive Grammy awards), and academics have been denied visas to visit the United States, while U.S. scientists and other academics have been denied permits to visit Cuba.

Every few years the United States does something immoral or unjust against Cuba, feeding new oxygen onto the anti-U.S. sentiment stoked by Fidel.

The embargo is increasingly under attack, and not just from the left. The groundswell in Congress has been toward lifting the embargo and for engagement with Cuba. In recent years, numerous bills have passed to stop enforcement of travel restrictions, and to permit expanded trade with Cuba, although Republican House representatives have sabotaged the efforts. As Bardach commented: "With enemies like us, Castro really doesn't need any friends."

WHAT U.S. CITIZENS CAN DO TO HELP END THE EMBARGO AND TRAVEL BAN

U.S. citizens who oppose the embargo and restrictions on U.S. citizens' constitutional right to travel can make their views known to representatives in Washington.

Contact Your Senator or Representative in Congress (U.S. Congress, Washington, DC 20510, 202/224-3121 or 800/839-5276). Write a simple, moderate, straightforward letter to your representative that makes the argument for ending the travel ban and embargo and requests he/she cosponsor a bill

to that effect. The **Latin America Working Group** (424 C St. NE, Washington, DC 20002, 202/546-7010, www.lawg.org), which campaigns to lift the travel restrictions and U.S. embargo, monitors legislators and can advise on how representatives have voted on Cuba-related issues.

Write or Call the President (The President, The White House, Washington, DC 20500, 202/456-1414, president@whitehouse.gov). Also call or fax the **White House Comment Line** (202/456-1111, fax 202/456-2461, www.whitehouse.gov); **National Security Advisor** (202/456-2255, fax 202/456-2883), and the **Secretary of State** (202/647-5291 or 202/647-6575, fax 202/647-7120).

Publicize Your Concern. Write a simple, moderate, straightforward letter to the editor of your local newspaper as well as any national newspapers or magazines and make the argument for ending the embargo.

Support the Freedom to Travel Campaign. Contact the **Center for International Policy** (1717 Massachusetts Ave. NW, Suite 801, Washington, DC 20036, 202/232-3317, www.ciponline.org), which organizes the "Freedom to Travel Campaign" dedicated to changing U.S. policy by lifting the prohibition on travel.

Also see the sidebar *Key Organizations to Know* in the *Essentials* chapter.

Castro and badly misread the Cuban leader—he considered Castro to be controlled by the Communists—with profound implications. Castro disingenuously promised not to expropriate foreign-owned property and repeated the mantra, "We are not Communists." He also affirmed that elections would *follow* "democracy," which he publicly defined as when all Cubans were employed, well fed, well educated, and healthy. "Real democracy is not possible for hungry people," he said.

Let the Reforms Begin!

On March 6, 1959, all rents in Cuba were reduced by 50 percent. Two months later, Cuba enacted an Agrarian Reform Law acclaimed, at the time, by the U.N. as "an example to follow." The large sugar estates and cattle ranches were seized without compensation in violation of Cuba's 1940 constitution and the reform law itself. To achieve it, Castro created the National Institute of Agrarian Reform, or INRA, which became an immensely powerful political tool headed by the Rebel Army. The agrarian reform significantly upped the ante in the tensions between Cuba and Washington and established a still unresolved grievance: nonpayment for illegally seized land. (The interests of Spanish, British, French, Canadian, and Dutch citizens were all affected. Over time, all claims with those governments except the United States were settled through bilateral agreements.)

Understandably, however, Miami received a flood of unhappy exiles. At first, these were composed of corrupt elements escaping prosecution—pimps, politicos, thugs, assassins, henchmen, political hacks and their accomplices, *mafiosi,* and the thousands of underlings that support a corrupt regime. As the reforms extended to affect the upper and middle classes, they, too, began to make the 90-mile journey to Florida. The trickle turned into a flood. About 250,000 Cubans left by 1963, most of them white, urban professionals—doctors, teachers, engineers, technicians, businesspeople, and others with entrepreneurial skills. As Castro's Revolution turned blatantly Communist and authoritarian, many of his revolutionary cohorts also began to desert him. Later, intellectuals and homosexuals were persecuted, and they, too, joined the flood. (Those who were forced to leave Cuba had to leave their possessions behind. Their houses were confiscated and divvied up to loyal *fidelistas* and citizens in need of housing, while others became schools, medical facilities, and social centers for the elderly and disadvantaged. "Donated to the Revolution" is the official verbiage.)

On July 13, 1959, President Urrutia denounced the growing Communist trend. Castro resigned as prime minister, then played a typically brilliant gambit. At the time of his resignation, Castro had arranged for peasants to be brought to Havana from all over Cuba to celebrate the anniversary of the attack on Moncada. Castro then appeared on television and denounced Urrutia, manipulating public sentiment through direct appeals to the masses. The streets of Havana erupted in calls for the president's resignation and pleas for Castro's return. Urrutia resigned. Castro had carried out the world's first coup d'état by TV! On May 1, 1960, Castro defaulted on his promise to hold elections within a year. The "people," he proclaimed, had declared them unnecessary, rationalizing the suspension of the Constitution and refusal to seek a popular mandate.

Into Soviet Orbit

Castro had decided on a profound new relationship. He knew, wrote Lee Anderson, "if he was ever to govern as he saw fit and achieve a genuine national liberation for Cuba, he was going to have to sever [U.S. relations] completely." The Kremlin had shared the Cuban Communists' views that Castro was his own man and too unreliable. By 1960, however, Cuba seemed like a perfect strategic asset. So Castro and Khrushchev signed a pact.

The emerging Havana–Moscow axis chilled Washington. Ever fearful of a U.S. invasion and unsure as yet of the depth of Soviet assistance, Castro initiated a massive militia training program, while emissaries began to purchase arms overseas. The first shipment arrived from Belgium on March 4, 1960, aboard the French ship *Le Coubre.* One week later, the steamship exploded in Havana Harbor with 700 tons of arms and munitions still in the hold. More than 80 Cubans were killed. One school supports Castro's contention that the CIA was responsible; another school believes Castro may have arranged the bombing. Whatever the truth, the event managed to rally the Cuban people around Castro at a time when he was facing increasing opposition at home.

During the funeral ceremony for the victims, Castro uttered the rallying cry that would later become the Revolution's supreme motto: *¡Patria o muerte!* ("patriotism or death!"). Recalls Nobel Laureate Gabriel García Márquez:

The level of social saturation was so great that there was not a place or a moment when you did not come across that rallying cry of anger, written on everything from the cloth shades on the sugar mills to the bottom margin of official documents. And it was repeated endlessly for days and months on radio and television stations until it was incorporated into the very essence of Cuban life.

When Soviet oil began to arrive in May 1960, U.S.-owned refineries refused to refine it. In response, the Cuban government took over the refineries. The dramatic occasion seems to have been carefully plotted by Che Guevara. The U.S.- and British-owned Shell refineries had been supplying Cuba with oil on credit and were owed US$50 million by the Castro government; Che, claims Jon Lee Anderson, "informed the American oil firms that in order for him to pay off the debt owed them, they each had to buy 300,000 barrels of the Soviet oil and process it. In one fell swoop, Cuba had freed itself of a fifty-million-dollar debt and gained an oil-refining industry." The United States then hit Cuba where it hurt most: In July, President Eisenhower refused to honor a purchase agreement for Cuban sugar. Cuba's biggest market for virtually its entire source of income had slammed the door. Washington couldn't have played more perfectly into the hands of Castro and the Soviet Union, which happily announced that it would purchase the entire Cuban sugar stock.

Hit with Eisenhower's right cross, Castro replied with a left hook: he nationalized *all* Yankee property, including 36 sugar mills, two utility companies, and two nickel mines. In October the Eisenhower administration banned exports to Cuba. In January 1961 the Kennedy administration broke diplomatic ties with Cuba; in March Kennedy extended the embargo to include Cuban imports—the beginning of a trade embargo that is still in effect. Kennedy pressured Latin American governments to follow suit through the Alliance for Progress. Every Latin American country except Mexico fell in line.

By slamming the door to Cuban sugar and American goods, the United States had severed Cuba's umbilical cord. The island faced economic collapse. During that period of intense Cold War, there were only two routes for underdeveloped nations. One way led West, the other East. Lock one door and there ceases to be a choice. "That's stupid, and it's a result of the howls of zealous anti-Communists in the United States," said Khrushchev. "Castro will have to gravitate to us like an iron filing to a magnet." But Castro was ahead of the game.

The Bay of Pigs Fiasco

Meanwhile, internal opposition to Castro was growing as government repression increased. Bands of counterrevolutionary guerrillas had set up a front in the Sierra Escambray, supported by the CIA. Many former Castroite supporters fought against him when they realized that he had turned Communist *caudillo* and that a personality cult was being erected. Alas, the anti-Fidelistas didn't have a Fidel. Nonetheless, the *Lucha Contra Bandidos* (Struggle Against Bandits) lasted until 1966 before finally being eradicated.

Castro, with his highly efficient intelligence operation, knew that the CIA was plotting an invasion of Cuba by Cuban exiles. In mid-1960 Castro began to suppress the independent press. He also established the Committees for the Defense of the Revolution (CDRs)—a countrywide information network for "collective vigilance." On December 31, 1960, Castro ordered a general mobilization to defend Cuba against military attack, while Cuba's State Security began a nationwide sweep against suspected "counterrevolutionaries" and suspected opponents.

On April 15, 1961, Cuban exiles strafed Cuban airfields as a prelude to a CIA-sponsored invasion. Castro turned the funeral for the seven persons killed into a stirring call for revolutionary defiance: "What the imperialists cannot forgive us for... is that we have made a socialist revolution under the nose of the United States." It was his first public characterization of the Revolution as socialist. The debacle thus created the conditions by which socialism became acceptable to a nation on the brink of invasion.

President Kennedy was assured that the Cuban people would rise up in arms. They did, and within 72 hours they had defeated the CIA-backed invasion at the Bay of Pigs on April 17, 1961 (see the sidebar *Bay of Pigs* in the *Matanzas* chapter). The Bay of Pigs, or Playa Girón as Cubans call it, brought a new sense of unity to Cuba. United States ambassador Bonsal declared that the Bay of Pigs "consolidated Castro's regime and was a determining factor

THE CUBAN MISSILE CRISIS

The Cuban Missile Crisis, which Cubans refer to as the October 1962 Crisis or Caribbean Crisis, was the result of the escalating tensions of the deepening Cold War. The Soviet Union felt severely threatened by the American deployment of intermediate-range ballistic missiles on the Turkish border with the USSR. To the Soviets, the Bay of Pigs fiasco provided an opening for them to establish bases at equally close range to the United States, which could then be used as bargaining chips for a reduction of U.S. bases in Turkey.

The Soviets told Castro that the United States was planning to invade Cuba. Fidel accordingly requested "strategic defensive weapons." The Soviets began their military build-up in Cuba in early 1962, then pressured the Cuban government to formally request that the Soviet Union install nuclear missiles. Cuban ports were closed and a curfew enacted while the missiles were brought in.

On October 14, a U-2 spy plane over western Cuba discovered missile sites. President Kennedy demanded that they be removed. Khrushchev refused. On October 22, Kennedy went on national TV and announced, "I have directed... initial steps to be taken immediately for a strict quarantine on all offensive military equipment. ... It shall be the policy of this nation to regard any nuclear missile launched from Cuba as an attack by the Soviet Union on the United States, requiring full retaliatory response on the Soviet Union." As he began speaking, 54 Strategic Air Command (SAC) bombers took to the air, Polaris submarines put to sea, and a U.S. naval task force set out to intercept Soviet vessels and blockade Cuba. That day, *Revolución* published the banner headline "U.S. Prepares Invasion of Cuba."

A volatile exchange of messages between Kennedy and Khrushchev followed. Tensions mounted. On October 24 the U.S. military went to DefCon (Defense Condition) 2 – for the first and only time in history. In the middle of the escalating tensions, the destroyer USS *Beale* dropped depth charges on Soviet submarine B-59, not knowing that the sub had nuclear-tipped torpedoes on board. The two superpowers verged on full-scale nuclear war.

ROGUE ELEPHANTS

While Kennedy was looking at the regional implications, Thomas Powers, commander of SAC, and Curtis LeMay, U.S. Air Force Chief of Staff, were thinking of – and apparently hoping for – a preemptive war. Powers and LeMay knew that the United States and USSR had been moving toward a policy of mutual deterrence based on a pact of "no first-strike," a policy the two figures publicly abhorred. Their missiles would then be a "wasting asset." They pushed Kennedy to bomb Cuba and take out the missiles, believing the Soviets wouldn't dare to respond – at the time, the USSR had only 44 ICBMs (Intercontinental Ballistic Missiles) and 155 heavy bombers, compared to the United States' 156 ICBMs, 144 Polaris submarine-launched missiles, and 1,300 strategic bombers.

At the height of the crisis, on October 26, Powers ordered a launch of an ICBM from Vandenberg Air Force Base. Although it was launched across the Pacific and hit the missile test range in Kwajalein atoll in the Marshall Islands, it was still a deliberate provocation. After Khrushchev complained that U-2 spy planes flying over Siberia "could be easily taken for a nuclear bomber, which might push us to a fateful step," Powers ordered SAC bombers to deliberately fly past their turnaround points into Soviet airspace. They were recalled at the eleventh hour when Khrushchev relented and ordered missiles removed.

ROGUE COMANDANTE

Fidel – always the gambler – was equally reckless. According to Carlos Franquí, editor of *Revolución* at the time, Fidel "drove to one of the Russian rocket bases, where the Soviet generals took him on a tour [the missile sites were Russian territory]. ... At that moment, an American U-2 appeared on a radar screen, flying low over the island. ... The Russians showed him the ground-to-air missiles and said that with a push of a button, the plane would be blown out of the sky.

"Which button?" Fidel reportedly asked.

"This one," a general replied.

At that, says Franquí, "Fidel pushed it and the rocket brought down the U-2. Anderson, the American pilot, was the only casualty in that war. The Russians were flabbergasted, but Fidel simply said, 'Well, now we'll see if there's a war or not.'"

Castro has vigorously denied that he (or any Cuban) had shot down the U-2 on October 27. "It is still a mystery how it happened," he claims. However, Soviet ambassador Alexeev had cabled Moscow on October 25 warning that Castro wanted "to shoot down one or two piratic American planes over Cuban territory." He had not only created a potential world catastrophe, he had wanted to pursue it to its most horrific consequences: In another cable sent to Moscow on October 26, claiming that a U.S. invasion was imminent, he had urged the Soviets to make a preemptive nuclear strike at the United States: "However difficult and horrifying this decision may be, there is, I believe no other recourse," he wrote.

Castro learned of Khrushchev's decision to back down over the radio, along with the rest of the world. He was livid. When United Nations Secretary-General U Thant met Castro immediately after the crisis to arrange for verification that the missiles had been removed, Castro refused all cooperation.

WHAT IF...?

The majority of Cubans remained on combat alert for a month, prepared to face down the atomic bomb with rifles. Maurice Halperin, in *Return to Havana*, recalls living in Havana in October 1962: "Unbelievably, the popular mood was defiance. *'iPatria o Muerte!'* Fidel shouted, and the masses seemed almost eager to take on the Yankees. There was an air of celebration in the city. ... Havana was throbbing."

A conference sponsored by the Center for Foreign Policy Development at Brown University and held in Havana in January 1992 revealed that the Soviets had 45 nuclear missiles readily deployable in Cuba, including nine tactical missiles to be used at the discretion of Soviet field commanders in the event of a U.S. invasion of the island. The United States was by then fully mobilized for invasion. Once the invasion began, Soviet generals would have repelled it with the nine tactical missiles, which in turn would have spurred a U.S. nuclear strike against the Soviet Union. Or maybe not; Franquí, writing in 1984, made the remarkable claim that the Russians never tried to run the nuclear warheads through the U.S. blockade and therefore the missiles were entirely harmless.

in giving it the long life it has enjoyed." As Castro admitted: "Our Marxist-Leninist party was really born at Girón; from that date on, socialism became cemented forever with the blood of our workers, peasants, and students."

The debacle not only solidified Castro's tenure but also provoked a repressive housecleaning of anyone thought to be too independent or deviant. As Castro saw it, you were either for the Revolution or against it. By 1965, at least 20,000 political prisoners—including homosexuals, practicing Catholics, and other "social deviants"—toiled in labor camps or languished in jails.

The Cuban Missile Crisis

On December 1, 1961, Castro informed Cuba and the world that Cuba was officially a Marxist-Leninist state. The news was a bombshell to the Kennedy administration, which in March 1962 launched Operation Mongoose—a six-phase program to oust Castro. Four hundred CIA agents were assigned full-time to the operation, which was led by Bobby Kennedy. Plans included a full-scale U.S. military invasion (eventually postponed) set for October 20, 1962, which Castro was aware of.

Kennedy's threat to do away with socialist Cuba virtually obliged Fidel to ask the Soviets for rockets to defend Cuba in the event of a U.S. invasion. The Soviets were pleased to assist. In August, Soviet personnel and MiG fighter-bombers began to arrive. Kennedy had warned the Soviets that the United States would not tolerate the installation of missiles. Khrushchev promised Kennedy that no "offensive weapons" were being supplied to Cuba. His deceit had near-calamitous consequences. No direct contact was made with Castro during the crisis, and the Kennedy tapes show that no one in the administration attempted to consider what Castro's part in the game of Russian roulette might have been (see Ernest May and Philip Zeilkow's *The Kennedy Tapes*).

Castro may have correctly calculated that the threat of nuclear conflict could save him from a non-nuclear attack. The crisis had ended with a guarantee from Kennedy that the United States would not invade Cuba (though there is no public record of an *explicit* commitment), and the no-invasion pledge was withdrawn after Castro refused to permit verification. Nonetheless, the Kennedys had initiated another invasion plan for 1964—OPLAN 380-63. Before it could be implemented, the president was dead, shot by Lee Harvey Oswald.

Castro was now free to move forward with his socialist revolution.

MAKING THE REVOLUTION

Cuba in 1959 was comparatively advanced in socioeconomic terms. It had a huge middle class constituting between one-quarter and one-third of the population. Shops were full of produce cheap enough for mass consumption. And the island's per capita rankings for automobiles, telephones, televisions, literacy, and infant mortality (32 per 1,000 live births) were among the highest in the Western hemisphere. But hundreds of thousands of Cubans also lived without light, water, or sewage. Poverty was endemic, and thousands of citizens lived by begging and prostitution.

Castro's government poured its heart and soul into improving the lot of the Cuban poor. First came health and education, where instant gains could be seen. Castro, for example,

dubbed 1961 the Year of Education. On the eve of the Revolution, 43 percent of the population was illiterate according to government statistics and half a million Cuban children went without school (U.N. sources, however, suggest that as many as 80 percent of the population were literate). In 1960, "literacy brigades" were formed of university students and high school seniors, who left the cities and fanned out over the countryside with the goal of teaching every single Cuban to read and write. Within two years, the regime had added 10,000 classrooms. By the end of its first decade, the number of elementary schools had nearly doubled and the number of teachers had more than tripled. Castro also set up special schools for the indigent, the blind, deaf, and mute, and ex-prostitutes. Electricity, gas, and public transport fees were dramatically lowered, as were rents and other fees. Price controls were instituted on goods sold on the free market. The government poured money into health care. And the Revolution brought unparalleled gains in terms of racism and social relations.

However, Castro's reforms came at the cost of politicizing all private choices and the totalitarian insistence that doctrinal projects took precedence over individual liberties. Havana and other cities were neglected and left to deteriorate. (Says Claudia Lightfoot: "Fidel was never really enamored of Havana, as his support base came overwhelmingly from the peasant classes mainly in the east of the island. He was distrustful of the capital. He had inherited a largely Americanized cityscape representing sophistication, corruption, intellectuals, and possible dissent.") And the free-thinking entrepreneurial middle class was effaced. Cuba's far-reaching social programs also had a price tag that the national economy could not support. Cuba's infant socialism was living off the wealth accumulated by Cuban capitalism.

Mismanaging the Economy

The young revolutionaries badly mismanaged the Cuban economy, swinging this way and that as Castro capriciously tacked between Soviet dictate and misguided personal whim.

WHAT A JOKE!

After the Revolution Che Guevara was named president of the bank and Minister of Finance. He loved to regale the joke of how he'd gotten the job, according to author Jon Lee Anderson. Supposedly at a cabinet meeting to decide on a replacement of bank president Felipe Pazos, Castro asked who among them was a "good *economista.*" Che raised his hand and was sworn in as Minister of Finance and head of the National Bank. Castro said: "Che, I didn't know you were an economist." Che replied, "I'm not!" Castro asked, "Then why did you raise your hand when I said I needed an economist?" To which Guevara replied, "Economist! I thought you asked for a Communist."

In 1960 Castro had created JUCEPLAN, a central planning agency modeled on the Soviet's GOSPLAN. Few of its concepts were given a chance to mature. Fidel kept jumping in. In confusedly searching for "truly original socialism," Castro committed economic errors that were worsened by bureaucratic mismanagement and abrupt reversals in direction. Sound economic decisions were sacrificed to revolutionary principles intended to advance the power of the state over private initiative. Che Guevara, president of the National Bank of Cuba and Minister of Finance and Industry, sought to replace trained managers with Communist cadres and market forces with "moral incentives."

The awesome brain drain, a lack of foreign exchange, CIA sabotage, bad administration, lack of economic incentives, and naive policy all conspired to reduce production. Gradually, inventories of imported goods and cash at hand were exhausted. As machinery wore down or broke down, no replacements could be ordered from the United States because of the trade ban enacted in 1961. Raw materials could not be bought. Soon the economy was in appalling shape. In 1962 rationing was introduced. The black market began to blossom.

Sugar monoculture was held to blame for many of Cuba's ills. Castro and Che Guevara decided to abandon a sugar-based economy and industrialize. When the attempt to diversify away from sugar failed, Castro switched tack and mobilized the entire workforce to achieve a record sugar harvest: 10 million tons a year by 1970 (the all-time previous record was only 6.7 million tons). To achieve the goal, the country went onto a war footing. Tens of thousands of inexperienced "voluntary" workers left their jobs in the cities and headed to the countryside. Holidays were abolished. Every inch of arable land was turned over to sugar. Nonetheless, only 8.5 million tons were harvested and the economy, which everywhere had been severely disrupted, was left in chaos. (Castro blamed technical reasons for the mammoth failure. Unable to accept his blunder, he repeated the same mistake with other products, notably milk.)

By 1968 the Cuban economy was coming apart at the seams. To make matters worse, that year Castro nationalized the entire retail trade still in private hands. More than 58,000 businesses—from corner cafés and ice-cream vendors to auto mechanics—were eliminated in the "Great Revolutionary Offensive." As a result, even the most basic items disappeared from the shelves. (Says journalist Wendy Gimbel: "Most Cubans will tell you that Havana actually died in March 1968, when Fidel Castro closed the small businesses that lent their color and texture to the life of the city: the cafés, the pawnshops, the laundries and hardware stores, the shops where people gathered to tell their stories, and the bars where they had a beer or a Bacardi rum.")

The Soviets saved the day. Bit by bit, Castro was forced to follow Soviet dictates. Castro's zealous experimentations gave way to a period of enforced pragmatism. In 1976, Cuba joined COMECON, the Soviet bloc's economic community. Cuba would henceforth supply sugar to the European socialist nations in exchange for whatever the island needed; sugar was even rationed in Cuba to meet obligations. Meanwhile, that year the First Communist Party

Congress initialed a new constitution that recognized Marxist-Leninism as the state's official ideology and the party as the sole representative of the people. Fidel Castro's tenure as head of state was written into the Constitution.

Adventurism Abroad

Kept afloat by Soviet largesse, Castro turned his attention to world affairs. He was committed to exporting his Revolution abroad (he had been complicit in armed plots against several neighboring countries from the moment the Revolution succeeded, including support for a failed invasion of the Dominican Republic in June 1959). In 1962 Guevara launched a wave of Cuban-backed guerrilla activity throughout Latin America that was endorsed by Castro in his "Second Declaration of Havana"—a tacit declaration of war on Latin American governments. This adventurism rankled the more cautious Soviet leadership, which tried to bring Castro to heel. Nonetheless, at the Organization of Latin American Solidarity conference in Havana in August 1967, Castro launched his Fifth International, to "create as many Vietnams as possible" in defiance of the Soviet Union's policy of coexistence with the United States. Said Castro: "The duty of every revolutionary is to make the Revolution."

Cuban troops had already been sent to countries as far afield as Algeria and Zaire. Soon revolutionary fighters from Angola, Mozambique, and elsewhere were being trained at secret camps on Isla de la Juventud. By the 1970s Castro, aspiring to leadership of developing nations, was shipping his politico-military mercenaries abroad. In Ethiopia and Angola, Cuban troops fought alongside Marxist troops in the civil wars against "racist imperialism," while in Ethiopia they shored up a ruthless regime. In Nicaragua, Cubans trained, armed, and supported the Sandinista guerrillas that toppled the Somoza regime. More than 377,000 Cuban troops were rotated through Angola during the 15-year war (the last troops came home in May 1991), proportionally far greater than the U.S. troop commitment in Vietnam. Tens of thousands of Cuban doctors and technical specialists were also sent to more than two dozen developing nations to assist in development (more than 50,000 were rotated through Angola alone). Meanwhile Castro was welcoming fugitives from U.S. law, such as convicted members of the Black Panther organization.

El Jefe launched his international initiatives at a time when Washington was looking at rapprochement with Cuba, beginning with the Ford administration, which worked out several agreements with the Castro government—a gradual lifting of the embargo was approved. Castro's adventurism cooled Uncle Sam's enthusiasm.

The Mariel Boatlift

In 1980, 12 Cubans walked through the gates of the Peruvian embassy in Havana and asked for asylum. The Peruvians agreed and refused to hand them over to the Cuban police. Carter announced that the United States would welcome Cuban political refugees with "open arms." In a fit of pique, Castro removed the embassy guards, and 11,000 Cubans rushed into the embassy. When the foreign press gave the case prominence, Castro decided to allow them to leave, along with dissidents and other disaffected Cubans. Many were coerced to leave, while Castro added to the swelling numbers by emptying his prisons of criminals and homosexuals and other "antisocial elements." Thus Castro disposed of more than 120,000 critics and disaffected. The Carter administration was forced to accept the *Marielitos*. (In November 1987, Cuba agreed to take back about 2,500 *Marielitos* with histories of mental illness or criminal records, plus almost 4,000 Cubans convicted of crimes since their arrival in the United States.)

In the 1980s President Ronald Reagan took a much harder line. Castro's adventurism received its first bloody nose in 1983, when President Reagan ordered U.S. Marines to storm the Caribbean island of Grenada to topple Maurice Bishop's Cuban-backed socialist regime. The Reagan administration also spawned the

Cuban-American National Foundation to give clout to the right-wing Cuban-American voice. In 1985 it established Radio Martí to broadcast anti-Castro propaganda into Cuba.

THE BUBBLE BURSTS

You know, when the Soviet Union was paying, it was kind of a party here. The problem is, the party's over.
– A character in Martin Cruz Smith's
Havana Bay

Meanwhile, Mikhail Gorbachev had become leader of the Soviet Union and was initiating fateful reforms—just as Castro turned more sharply toward Communist orthodoxy. Castro's program of Rectification of Errors and Struggles Against Negative Tendencies, initiated in 1986, resulted not least in the closure of free farmers markets, a brief fling that had led to an increase in the food supply and placed unobtainable items such as garlic back on kitchen tables. Castro, however, was alarmed at the success of the free-market experiment and railed against "millionaire garlic growers." The basic structure of Soviet-style planning and management would not be altered. It was Castro's first warnings that *glasnost* and *perestroika,* Gorbachev's "heresies," would not be tolerated in Cuba, where the achievements of North Korea's Kim Il Sung were suddenly praised in the media.

In 1989 the Berlin Wall collapsed and the Communist dominoes came tumbling down. However, the news in Cuba was dominated by a political show trial that made it clear that reform was not in the cards. General Arnaldo Sánchez Ochoa, a powerful and charismatic national hero with impeccable credentials going back to the Sierra Maestra, was accused of colluding with the Colombian drug cartel to smuggle drugs to the United States via Cuba. After a closed trial, Ochoa and 13 other high-ranking officers were convicted of treason and corruption. Ochoa and three others were executed. A massive purge followed, notably of the Ministry of the Interior (MININT), but

also of dissidents and private entrepreneurs. Rumors swept the island that Ochoa, who had been espousing reformist discontent, had been conspiring to oust Castro.

The "Special Period"

With the Eastern bloc umbilical cord severed, Cuba's economy collapsed. In January 1990, Castro declared that Cuba had entered a Special Period in a Time of Peace. He also announced a draconian, warlike austerity plan. A new slogan appeared throughout Cuba: *¡Socialismo o muerte!* (Socialism or death!). Inevitably, rising political discontent boiled over on April 21, 1991, when clashes erupted against the police—the first act of spontaneous rebellion since 1959. Then on August 18, 1991, on the last day of the highly successful Pan-American Games in Havana (which Cuba won with 140 gold medals), the Soviet Union began its dizzying unraveling. Reformer Boris Yeltsin took power. Subsidies and supplies to Cuba virtually ceased. The same year, General Noriega was ousted in Panama—Cuba's main source for Western goods. Cuba was cast adrift, a lone socialist island in a capitalist sea.

After the last Soviet tanker departed in June 1992, the government began electricity blackouts that soon became daily, for up to 18 hours. There were no fans, no air-conditioning, no refrigeration, no lights. Nor was there fuel for transportation. Buses and taxis gave way to horse-drawn carts. Human and animal labor replaced oil-consuming machinery. Without oil or electricity to run machines, or raw materials to process, or spare parts to repair machinery, factories closed down and state bureaucracies began transferring laid-off workers to jobs in the countryside. Gaiety on the streets was replaced with a forlorn melancholy.

What began as inconveniences turned into real hardships as domestic purchasing power plummeted. Meanwhile, harvests simply rotted in the fields for want of distribution. People accustomed to a government-subsidized food basket guaranteeing every person at least two high-protein, high-calorie meals a day were stunned to suddenly be confronting shortages of almost every staple. When East German powdered milk ceased to arrive, Cuba eliminated butter; when Czechoslovakian malt no longer arrived, Cuban beer disappeared. Soaps, detergents, deodorants, toilet paper, clothing, everything vanished. Cubans had to resort to making hamburger meat from banana peels and steaks from grapefruit rinds. Many Cubans began rearing *jutías,* ratlike native rodents—and the most desperate resorted to rats. Crime rose swiftly and envy and anomie filled the vacuum left by the collapse of the egalitarian promise. Cuba, the only country in Latin America to have eliminated hunger, began to suffer malnutrition and debilitating diseases. Thousands of people starved to death, while many more committed suicide.

Believing that Cuba was on the verge of collapse, Uncle Sam tightened the screws by passing the Cuban Democracy Act, which reduced economic assistance to countries trading with Cuba; increased punitive action against individuals breaking the embargo; and prohibited U.S. subsidiary companies abroad from trading with Cuba.

While Fidel Castro dashed hopes of reform by announcing a "sacred" duty to save the Revolution, the reformist movement found an unexpected ally in Raúl Castro, who argued for deregulating key sectors of the economy. Market-savvy reformers were elevated to positions of power and scrambled to nail together a long-term economic recovery plan led by tourism. The Revolution's ideological principles were turned on their head. Possession of the dollar was legalized. Private enterprise was permitted. And major investments were made to promote tourism.

By 1994 a cautious sense of optimism began to emerge as things slowly began to improve. The awful *apagones* (blackouts) were trimmed. Food crops no longer rotted in the fields. And the legal availability of dollars eased life for those Cubans who had access to greenbacks, while farmers markets eased life for those without. Nonetheless, the economic situation had deteriorated so much that a growing human tide had begun washing across the Straits of Florida.

The Balsero Crisis

On August 5, 1994, crowds gathered along the Malecón in response to a rumor that a major exodus was to be permitted and that a flotilla of boats was en route from Florida. When police attempted to clear the boulevard, a riot ensued. Passions were running dangerously high, and two police officers were killed. Castro saw a chance to defuse a dangerous situation and benefit. He declared that Cuba would no longer police the U.S. borders: if the United States would not honor its agreement to allow people to migrate legally, then Cuba would no longer try to prevent anyone from going illegally. (Leaving Cuba without an exit permit is illegal; Cubans are rarely granted such visas. Meanwhile, the United States' 1966 Cuban Adjustment Act *guaranteed* residency to Cubans who stepped foot on U.S. soil. The United States had agreed to accept an annual quota of 20,000-plus Cuban immigrants, but most Cubans who petitioned the United States for a visa were rejected. The more difficult the economic circumstances became in Cuba, the fewer legal immigrants were accepted, while the greater the number of *illegals* who were taken in.)

The United States was hoisted on its own petard as thousands of *balseros* (rafters) fled Cuba on makeshift rafts. During the next three weeks, at least 20,300 Cubans had been rescued at sea and shipped to Guantánamo naval base, which was expanded to eventually house up to 65,000 refugees. President Clinton's major goal was to avoid a replay of the 1980 Mariel boatlift. By September 9, when the two countries agreed to measures "to ensure that migration between the two countries is safe, legal, and orderly," another 11,060 Cubans had been rescued. Henceforth the Coast Guard would intercept Cubans heading for the United States and return them to Cuba.

Meanwhile, a Miami-based volunteer group called Brothers to the Rescue had been operating rescue missions. When the flood of *bal-*

seros stopped, pilots of the organization began buzzing Havana and dropping "leaflets of a subversive nature." On February 24, 1996, three Brothers to the Rescue Cessnas took off from Opalocka airfield near Miami, Florida. The planes were cleared to fly to the Bahamas. Once airborne, they diverted to Cuba. Cuban jet fighters shot two Cessnas down, killing both pilots. (The Cuban government claimed that the aircraft came down in Cuban territorial waters, but an investigation by the independent International Civil Aviation Organization confirmed that the two Cessnas were downed 10.3 and 11.5 miles *north* of Cuban airspace.) Cuban-American exiles and Republican presidential candidates campaigning for the mid-March Florida primary erupted in fury. The incident scuttled the Clinton administration's carefully calibrated policy on Cuba of promoting democratic change as a prelude to easing the embargo.

The Helms-Burton Legislation

In 1995 Sen. Jesse Helms and Rep. Dan Burton had introduced the Cuban Liberty and Democratic Solidarity Act, aimed at significantly tightening the embargo. Following the Brothers to the Rescue incident, Helms rode the wave of anti-Castro sentiment in Miami and Washington and steered the legislation through Congress. Clinton signed the bill, which significantly limited presidential powers to change U.S. policy toward Cuba in the future. (U.S. presidents must now seek congressional approval if they seek to modify or lift the embargo.)

The law codified all executive orders in effect relevant to the embargo, which will remain in place until a "transition government" is in place in Cuba that meets U.S. criteria. The bill also withdraws funding from any international institution providing humanitarian aid to Cuba; provides for a $50,000 civil fine for any U.S. citizen who travels to and "trades with" Cuba; denies entry into the U.S. territory to anyone who has "trafficked" in or done business with people or businesses that have trafficked in property confiscated from U.S. nationals; and bars U.S. banks from lending to these companies. Finally, Helms-Burton will allow any U.S. citizen whose property was confiscated after the Revolution to sue any foreign corporation that has "benefited" from the property or from its use. (Behind the bluster about toppling Castro, the law really represents the interests of very wealthy Cuban-Americans, such as the Bacardi Corporation and the Fanjul family. In fact, the legislation was drafted with the help of lawyers representing Bacardi, the National Association of Sugar Mill Owners of Cuba, and the Cuban Association for the Tobacco Industry, who clearly benefit while Cuban products are banned.)

The law has earned the wrath of the United States' leading allies; Canada even enacted retaliatory legislation. The law has been condemned by everyone from the Pope to the Organization of American States and clearly violates international law, including the General Agreements on Tariffs and Trade (GATT). Plus, the law helped unite Cubans behind the Castro government as nothing had done in years, allowing *el comandante* to revive flagging anti-Yankeeism and jail dissidents in the face of a new threat from U.S. imperialism.

Holy Smoke

In January 1998, Pope John Paul II made a highly publicized four-day visit to Cuba. For the occasion, Castro made Christmas an official holiday and festive lights went up in the streets for the first time in decades. Castro had invited the pope in the hope that a papal embrace magnified by television exposure might diffuse much of the internal opposition and give the regime new legitimacy. Castro had been counting on air-play from the 4,000 journalists who descended on Havana to cover the event, including the major U.S. media, who promptly turned heel and fled when the Monica Lewinsky scandal broke as the pope touched Cuban soil.

Meanwhile, in 1997, Miami-based Cuban exiles launched a short-lived bombing campaign against the Cuban tourist industry, killing an Italian tourist (Miami-based

Cuban-American terrorist groups, some spawned by the CIA, have operated with impunity for two decades). But the real enemy lay within. Serious crime had returned to the streets of Cuba. An armored van was even robbed by armed youths (an unprecedented occurrence). Cocaine was being sold on the street and at discos. Thousands of young Cuban women had turned to quasi-prostitution. And corruption among police and government officials was becoming entrenched. When two Cuban women died of cocaine overdoses in December 1998, Havana's discos and bars were closed down, and thousands of young men and women were arrested on the streets.

Reasserting State Control

On January 1, 1999, Cubans celebrated the 40th anniversary of the Cuban Revolution. Commented *The Economist:* "There does not seem much to celebrate. ... The grand promises of the past 40 years are in tatters. In some ways, Cuba seems worse off in 1999 than it was in 1959." Nonetheless, economically things were much improved: the economy was bouncing back, driven by dollars from tourism and was given a boost in January when President Clinton eased the trade embargo, permitting U.S. citizens to send up to US$1,200 annually to Cuban individuals and non-government organizations. Castro called the move a "fraud" and announced draconian legislation—the Law for the Protection of Cuba's National Independence and Economy—while thousands of Special Brigade police were deployed on street corners throughout Havana and major cities (the police remain around-the-clock, checking IDs at random).

The policy was officially "a battle against disorder, crime, disrespect for authority, illegal business, and lack of social control." But the new law was also designed to chill relations between Cubans and foreigners by creating a new counterrevolutionary felony: "supporting" hostile U.S. policies. Outlawed were the "supply, search or gathering of information" for and the "collaboration" with foreign media. To get the point across, in March 1999 four prominent dissidents—the Group of Four—were labeled "counterrevolutionary criminals" and received harsh sentences for sedition. The sentences signaled a harsh crackdown, resulting in the United Nations Commission on Human Rights condemning Cuba as a "significant violator." In June 1999 dozens of high officials within the tourism and business sectors were fired and arrested for corruption. In 2001, a new anti-corruption ministry was created. The state was also reasserting control throughout the private economy.

INTO THE NEW MILLENNIUM

Cuba saw the millennium in with a new battle with Uncle Sam, this one over a five-year-old boy, Elián González, saved by the U.S. Coast Guard after his mother and 10 other people drowned when their boat sank en route from Cuba to Florida during Thanksgiving 1999. Elián, plucked from his inner tube, launched a continuing soap opera. Miami's

Cubans demonstrate their demand that Elián González be returned to Cuba.

© CHRISTOPHER P. BAKER

THE "CUBAN FIVE"

Every few years the entire nation of Cuba is mobilized against a grand injustice perpetrated by the United States. The Helms-Burton Law. The cause of Elián González. And, most recently, the campaign to free the "Cuban Five." The faces of these five Cuban men have for the past few years been ubiquitous throughout Cuba, from billboards and daily news items to T-shirts and every website, while massive demonstrations for their cause continue to be held nationwide.

Accused by the U.S. government of "espionage," the five Cubans – Fernando González, René González, Antonio Guerrero, Gerardo Hernández, and Ramón Labañino – were convicted in U.S. federal court on June 8, 2001, and sentenced to from 15 years to life terms.

The five "innocents," as they are called in Cuba, were indeed spies. However, the agents of Cuban intelligence weren't spying against the U.S. government. Instead, they had infiltrated extreme right-wing Cuban-American groups, such as Omega 7 and Alpha 66, that continue to plan and perpetrate terrorist acts (including bombings and assassinations) against moderate Cuban-Americans espousing dialogue with Cuba; against Cuba-bound travelers and Cuba-travel suppliers; and

against Cuba, including machine gun raids on Varadero and, in 1997, a bombing campaign in Havana that killed an innocent Italian tourist.

Such groups have acted with impunity for decades, and the U.S. government has basically turned a blind eye to their terrorist acts. (For example, anti-Castroite, CIA-trained Bay of Pigs operative Orlando Bosch was convicted of conspiring in the bombing of a Cubana airliner on October 6, 1976, that killed 73 passengers, but he was granted a pardon by President Bush. His co-conspirator, Luis Posada, was convicted of the bombing in Venezuela but escaped from jail and returned to Miami, where he has never been prosecuted, despite bragging about his terrorist exploits.) Because the U.S. government refuses to prosecute Cuban-American terrorists, Cuban agents have infiltrated such groups to monitor them and identify future threats. However, in 2001, when Cuban authorities contacted U.S. authorities and reported a plot to bomb a Cuban-bound airliner, the FBI uncovered and arrested the "five."

An effort to free the "five" has garnered the support of leading international figures. For more information, contact **Free the Five** (415/821-6545, www.freethefive.org).

anti-Castroite Cubans and right-wing politicians turned the child into a poster boy for the American Way of Life—a "new Dalai Lama," thought Wayne Smith—and demanded that the boy remain in the United States against the Cuban father's wishes. Castro (who routinely denies permission for the children of Cuban exiles to join their parents abroad) responded by demanding that the "kidnapped" boy be returned and turned the issue into an anti-American crusade by organizing "Free Elián" protests and summoning Cubans to attend the nationwide rallies.

In January 2000, Castro vowed that protests would last "10 years, if necessary," while the case wound through the Florida courts. Elián's custodians refused to hand him over

to his loving father when the latter arrived in the United States in April 2000 to collect his son. In a dawn raid, the INS grabbed Elián and reunited him with his father, who is happily reconciled with life in Cuba. In late June Elián and his father returned to Cuba after the U.S. Supreme Court affirmed the father's right to custody of his son. To Fidel Castro, the battle for Elián was personal, recalling with astonishing parallels an incident that occurred forty-odd years ago when a Cuban father discovered that his estranged wife had left for the United States and taken their five-year-old son with her. The courts awarded custody of the son to the mother. But the father, who was enraged by the thought of his son being raised in Miami by relatives who were his sworn political enemies, refused to acknowledge his loss: "One day I'll get my son and my honor back—even if the earth should be destroyed in the process. ... I am prepared to reenact the Hundred Years War. And I'll win it," he wrote to his sister. The man later talked the mother into letting the boy visit him in Mexico on his word "as a gentleman" that the boy would be returned in two weeks. Instead the boy was secreted away, so that the wife had to enlist the Mexican police to get her son back. They did so at gunpoint, seizing him from the father's henchmen while he was being taken for a drive near Mexico City's Chapultepec Park. The mother remarried and returned with the boy to her new home in Havana. But Cuba turned Communist and in 1964 she fled the island for Spain. The father, however, wouldn't let the woman take her son with her. The mother was Mirta Diaz-Balart, whose nephew, Lincoln Diaz-Balart, is a Republican Congressman for Florida, an arch anti-Castroite and champion of the crusade to keep Elián González in the United States. The boy's name was Fidelito. His father is Fidel Castro.

Meanwhile, Castro launched the "Battle of Ideas," an ongoing ideological campaign to shore up flagging support for socialism.

New Battles

In 2001, the George W. Bush administration initiated an increasingly hard-line approach to Cuba, halting the partial thaw in relations during the Clinton era. In July, Fidel fainted at the podium while giving a televised speech, raising speculation as to his health. Meanwhile, 2001 was officially "The Year of the Victorious Revolution in the New Millennium," and witnessed increased belligerence against the United States and European allies and a tightening of government controls, led by installation of military figures throughout the economy.

The following spring, George W. Bush denounced Cuba as a sponsor of terrorism on the eve of a five-day visit by President Jimmy Carter to Havana—the first visit by a U.S. president to Cuba since Calvin Coolidge in

FÉLIX VARELA

Félix Varela Morales (1788-1852) was born in Havana and, after being orphaned at an early age, was raised by his maternal grandfather – a Spanish army colonel and Counselor to the Governor of Florida – in St. Augustine, Florida, which was then a Spanish territory. Varela graduated from Havana's Seminario de San Carlos y San Ambrosio, where he later taught philosophy, chemistry, physics, theology, and music. He rose to become the leading Cuban intellectual and patriot of the early 19th century.

Elected in 1821 to the Spanish legislature, he lobbied for the abolition of slavery and for Cuban independence and in 1823 was forced to flee Cuba for New York. Varela was assigned a New York parish and tended the predominantly Irish diocese throughout the famous cholera epidemic. He eventually became Vicar General of the New York diocese and dedicated the rest of his life to humanitarian causes while continuing to write and lobby on behalf of Cuba's nationalist cause. His *El Habanero* was the first journal dedicated to Cuban independence. Varela died in St. Augustine, Florida.

He is considered the forefather of José Martí, who called Varela "Cuba's Saint." In 2002, his name was lent to the Varela Project, in which Cuban dissidents gathered 11,000 signatures demanding reforms.

1928. Just days before Carter's arrival, dissidents delivered to the National Assembly a petition presented by a dissident group, Proyecto Varela (Varela Project), containing 11,020 signatures demanding sweeping reforms in Cuba. Amazingly, Fidel permitted Carter to address the nation live on TV. Carter denounced the U.S. embargo, as Fidel no doubt had wished, but focused primarily on the call for greater freedoms in Cuba and mentioned Proyecto Varela by name—the first time most Cubans learned of the organization.

Three weeks later, with Carter safely off the island, Castro sought to stamp out the

Varela germ. Fidel led several hundred thousand *cubanos* on a march past the US Interests Section to affirm the Cuban peoples' unwavering commitment to socialism. The Castro regime then pulled out of its hat a petition of more than 8 million signatures, it claimed, calling for a resolution to make the existing constitution "eternal" and "untouchable." (Signing wasn't voluntary, however; the government had knocked on everyone's door and confronted individuals face to face, and the names of those who failed to vote was recorded.) With the world media's attention focused on the war in Iraq, in March 2003 Castro initiated a harsh crackdown on dissidents, independent journalists, and librarians. Meanwhile, two Cuban planes were successfully hijacked to the United States, and an attempt to hijack a ferry failed when it ran out of fuel 30 miles from Havana. The Cuban military towed the vessel back to Havana and in a swift trial, three of the hijackers were sentenced to death and immediately executed by firing squad. When European nations protested, the Cuban government imposed a freeze on relations (it even organized demonstrations against the Spanish and Italian Embassies).

The Past Few Years

The following year was notable for power cuts that have plagued the nation, for the worst drought in more than a century, and for more hurricanes (Ivan and Charlie), which struck Havana, Isla de la Juventud, and Pinar del Río. Meanwhile, the Bush administration implemented new restrictions aimed at stopping all travel to Cuba (including by Cuban-Americans) as part of a broader attempt to cut the flow of dollars to Cuba. Even foreign banks have been threatened with sanctions for processing Cuban deposits. Meanwhile, responding to the President's Commission for Assistance to a Free Cuba (the brainchild of, and staffed by, ultra-conservative Cuban-Americans), the Bush administration also directed that US$59 million be spent for anti-Castro activities, including beaming TV Martí—a boondoggle that the Cuban government has successfully blocked for years—from a U.S. military plane (the broadcast was seen in Santa Clara on the first day before Cuba successfully jammed the signal). It also outlined colonial era–style plans to set up a counterrevolutionary "transitional government" in Cuba.

In response, Castro warned of a possible attack and launched the Strategic Bastion 2004 Exercise. Cubans awoke to air-raid sirens and put on gas masks and practiced shooting and duck-and-cover drills, to test the nation's defense readiness. Meanwhile, Castro (who in November 2004 tripped and fractured his left knee and right arm in a fall captured live on TV; he swiftly recovered) was buoyed by a major discovery of crude oil offshore of Havana. Having allied himself ever more closely with Venezuela's Hugo Chávez and increasingly with China, Castro stepped up retrenchment of the socialist system. Many foreign companies have been ousted. The U.S. dollar was banned. And harsh new restrictions augered a return to hard-line ways.

In July 2005, Hurricane Dennis struck Cuba, killing 16 people and causing an estimated US$1.5 billion in damage. It was followed weeks later by Hurricane Wilma, which did further damage. That year witnessed increased shortages of electricity and most staples, and an increase in crime. Meanwhile, the first of tens of thousands of poor patients from Latin America arrived for free eye operations bankrolled by Venezuela; Operación Milagro will eventually treat more than 100,000 patients from developing nations.

On July 31, 2006, Fidel Castro was taken seriously ill and underwent intestinal surgery on the eve of his 80th birthday. He handed power (ostensibly temporarily) to his brother Raúl Castro, while other communist figures were appointed to lead key ministries. Cuba remained calm as the apparent permanent transition to a new post-Castro era got underway. Caught unawares, the U.S. promised to respect the sovereignty of the Cuban people and tried to calm fears that Washington planned to interfere directly, while committing to boost efforts to effect a transition to democracy.

Government

Cuba is an independent socialist republic. The Cuban Constitution, adopted in 1975, defines it as a "socialist state of workers and peasants and all other manual and intellectual workers." Dr. Fidel Castro Ruz is head of both state and government (in Latin America, "Doctor" is an honorific given to anyone with a Bachelor's degree). He is normally referred to as Comandante-en-Jefe (Commander in Chief).

Total power is legally vested in Castro as first secretary of the Communist Party, president of the Republic, chairman of the State Council, chairman of the Council of Ministers, and commander in chief of the armed forces. His younger brother, Raúl, is first vice president of both the Council of State and the Council of Ministers, the second secretary of the Communist Party, defense minister, and General of the Army. (Raúl—who in August 2006 was provisionally named president following his brother's illness—is a little-understood figure. Though exacting in work, he is said to be a good-humored family man. Raúl has four children by Vilma Espín, head of the Cuban Women's Federation and from whom he has been amicably divorced for two decades.)

There are no legally recognized political organizations independent of the Communist Party, which controls the labyrinthine state apparatus and which the Constitution recognizes as "the highest leading force of the society and of the state."

The Constitution, copied largely from the Soviet Constitution of 1936, guarantees the "freedom and inviolability of the individual" as well as freedom of speech, press, and religion—as long as these conform to the "goals of socialist society." In reality, no dissent is permitted.

The government has a website: www.cubagob.cu.

STATE STRUCTURE
The Central Government
The highest-ranking executive body is the Consejo de Ministros (Council of Ministers),

headed by Fidel Castro and comprising several vice presidents and ministers. The council is empowered to conduct affairs of the state and draw up bills for submission to the Assembly. The Executive Committee of the Council of Ministers administers Cuba on a day-to-day basis. The council is accountable to the National Assembly of People's Power, which "elects" the members at the initiative of the head of state. The council has jurisdiction over all ministries and central organizations and effectively runs the country under the direction of Fidel Castro.

The Asemblea Nacional (National Assembly) is invested with legislative authority but exercises little legislative initiative. Discussion is usually restricted to subjects introduced from the leadership. It is mostly a rubber-stamp legislature, headed since 1993 by Ricardo Alarcón, tipped as a potential successor to Fidel. The Assembly is elected for a five-year term but meets only twice annually. Members are part-timers, not full-time legislators. There were 589 deputies in the 1993–98 *quinquenio* (five-year term). Deputies are elected directly by voters, although candidacies must first be approved by the Communist Party and run unopposed, and voters are carefully monitored. Most deputies are drawn from the party bureaucracy and are predominantly male and white. The Assembly elects high government officials and ratifies executive appointments.

The Consejo del Estado (Council of State) is modeled on the Presidium of the former Soviet Union, and functions as the Executive Committee of the National Assembly when the latter is not in session. It, too, is presided over by Fidel Castro.

The Cuban Communist Party
The sole political party is the Partido Comunista de Cuba (PCC), of which Fidel Castro is head and his brother Raúl vice secretary. The party's goal is "to guide common efforts

HUMAN RIGHTS

Disobedience is the capital sin under Cuba's subtly repressive regime. "It is fair to say that under Castro, Cubans have lost even the tenuous civil and political liberties they had under the old regime," claims Professor Wayne Smith, former head of the U.S. Interests Section in Havana. "Woe to anyone who gets on a soap box in downtown Havana and questions the wisdom of the Castro government." The Cuban penal code states that disrespect for authorities is good for one to seven years in prison. Castro is careful not to crack down too hard, but free speech is tightly controlled. As a result, Cubans talk in whispers when discussing the government, are fearful of mentioning Fidel by name, and live generally in a state of fear about police informers, known as *emboris* and a score of other terms.

The regime is not above jailing even its most loyal supporters if they renege on the Revolution. Elizardo Sánchez, a former revolutionary leader and, later, president of the dissident Cuban Commission of Human Rights and National Reconciliation, has spent years in jail. Carlos Franquí, leading revolutionary, founder of Radio Rebelde, and editor-in-chief of *Revolución*, was even expunged from photos (airbrushed into nonexistence) and made a nonperson until he was forced to flee surreptitiously to France.

FREEZE AND THAW

Contemporary Cuba, however, is a far cry from the 1960s, when crushing sentences were imposed en masse following secret, often puppet, trials. In 1965 when the CIA was doing its best to overthrow the Cuban government, Castro admitted that there were 20,000 "counterrevolutionary criminals" in Cuban jails, including cultural and political dissidents. The true numbers were unquestionably higher. Today, the number of political prisoners hovers somewhere around 300 in jail for strictly political offenses. The repression runs hot and cold. The past few years has seen a new round of repression that resulted in the United Nations Human Rights Commission placing Cuba on its list of worst offenders, while Amnesty International has named Cuba and Colombia the worst offenders in Latin America.

Plantados (dissidents who remain firm) are often taken to Villa Marista, the state security headquarters, where psychological abuse is said to be common. The unlucky ones are said to end up at either the Combinado del Este penitentiary, south of Havana, or the Carbó Serviá ward at the Mazorra, the Havana Provincial Psychiatric Hospital, where dissidents have reported electric-shock treatment and other physical abuses. Cuba is one of the few countries that does not allow the Red Cross or other international organizations to inspect its prisons.

In 2002, dissidents led by Oswaldo Payá Sardiña (winner of the 2002 Sakharov Prize for Freedom of Thought) formed Proyecto Varela, which represented the most significant political challenge to Castro in four decades. Although enough signatures to make a draft law were presented to the National Assembly, they were ignored by the Cuban government. Instead, while the world's attention was focused on the war on Iraq in early 2003, dissident leaders were rounded up, charged with trumped-up charges of sedition, and brutally sentenced in the harshest crackdown in memory. (The mock trials also exposed that the dissident movement is riddled with government spies, even among the leaders of dissident organizations.)

In 2004, a group of Cuban political, social, labor, cultural, intellectual, religious, and human rights organizations formed Consenso Cubano (www.consensocubano.org), committed to reconciliation and non-violent transition to a democratic system in Cuba.

The government refers to dissident organizations as *grupúsculos*, "tiny little groups," and most recently, "mercenaries," after the U.S. Interests Section began offering radios (to tune in to Radio Martí) and financial support, effectively turning dissidents – most of whom decry the U.S. efforts – into paid agents of a foreign government.

toward the construction of socialism." The PCC occupies the central role in all government bodies and institutions. It is led by the Buró Político (Politburo). Steering the party is the Comité Central (Central Committee) of the PCC, whose members are selected by Castro, who—surprise!—is its chairman. The Comité elects members of the Politburo. It meets every six months and is the principal forum through which the party leadership disseminates party policy to lower echelons.

At the base of the PCC chain is the party cell of 10 members organized at work and educational centers. The cells recruit new members, who go through a six-month scrutiny as to their ideological purity. The youth organizations are the most common avenue for passage into the PCC. Current membership is about 600,000 (about five percent of the population).

Castro has drawn from "the elite of the elite" of the party to maintain his government. Loyalty to Castro takes precedence over all other considerations. Policy emanates from Castro, who has used his own charismatic qualities and inordinate tactical skills to consolidate almost hegemonic authority. Although the Council of State and Council of Ministers ostensibly make the decisions, Castro shapes those decisions. The PCC has no program—Castro defines the flavor of the day.

Local Government

The country is divided into 14 provinces and 169 municipalities (*municipios*), dominated by the city of Havana, a separate province. Each province and municipality is governed by an Assembly of Delegates of People's Power, representing state bodies at the local level. Traditionally the councils elected members of the Provincial Assemblies; members are elected by popular ballot and serve two-and-a-half-year terms.

The organs of *poder popular* (popular power) also serve as forums for citizens' grievances and deal with problems such as garbage collection, housing improvement, and running day-care centers. They are not autonomous; the Communist Party closely monitors their performance.

The country is also unofficially divided into three areas that are sometimes still referred to colloquially by their colonial titles: Occidente (the western region), Las Villas (the center), and Oriente (the east).

Committees for the Defense of the Revolution

The linchpins in maintaining the loyalty of the masses and spreading the Revolution at the grassroots level are the neighborhood Comités para la Defensa de la Revolución. There are 15,000 CDRs in Havana, and 100,000 throughout the island. Almost every block has one.

On one hand, the CDRs perform wonderful work: They collect blood for hospitals, take retired people on vacations, discourage kids from playing hooky, organize graduation parties, and so on. But they are also the vanguard in keeping an eye on the local population, watching and snitching on neighbors (the CDRs are under the direction of MININT, the Ministry of the Interior). Above the voluntary CDR head is the *jefe del sector,* the sector boss and government snoop in charge of four CDRs and who specifically looks for revolutionary delinquency; anyone nay-saying the Revolution, mocking Castro, or dealing on the black market is likely to be reported.

People face harsh retribution if they cross the line into political activism. In 1991, Rapid Response Detachments were formed, ostensibly made up of volunteers from local CDRs but under the purview of MININT, to deal with public expressions of dissent. This they do through distasteful pogroms called *actos de repudios,* beating up dissidents, much as did Hitler's Blockwarts.

Other Mass Organizations

Citizen participation in building socialism is manifested through a number of mass organizations controlled by the PCC. Prominent among them are the Federation of Cuban Women, the Confederation of Cuban Workers, and the Union of Communist Youth. Although ostensibly representing the interests of their members, the bodies subordinate these to state goals. No independent labor organizations are permitted.

Membership in various mass organizations is a virtual prerequisite for getting on in Cuban society. Promotions, access to university, even to vacations and material incentives for the average citizen, rely upon being a "good revolutionary" through participation in an organization. Those who are not members become social outcasts.

The Judiciary

Courts are a fourth branch of government and are not independent. The individual in Cuba enjoys few legal guarantees. The judiciary is not charged with protecting individual rights, as in democratic societies, but rather, according to Article 121 of the Constitution, with "maintaining and strengthening socialist legality." Thus it is subject to interference by the political leadership. The Council of State, for example, can overturn judicial decisions, and Castro frequently does so in political trials. Interpretation of the Constitution is the prerogative of the National Assembly, not the courts. Cuba's legal system is modeled on *Alice in Wonderland's* topsy-turvy world in which defendants are required to prove their innocence, rather than for prosecutors to prove the defendants' guilt. For this reason, thousands of Cubans languish in jails or are fined for crimes the State assumes they committed, or for which it finds it convenient to convict them. (Due process is systematically flouted in political cases according to the apolitical Washington-based human-rights group American Watch.)

The highest court in the land is the People's Supreme Court in Havana. Its president and vice president are appointed by Fidel Castro; other judges are elected by the National Assembly.

Private practice of law is permitted, and the accused are denied recourse to defense counsel other than state-appointed officials. The penal code accepts a defendant's confession as sufficient proof of his guilt, and there are many cases of individuals pressured into confessing to crimes they did not commit.

Cuba, however, has a policy of criminal rehabilitation for all but political crimes. In meting out punishment, the penal system allows for amends and guarantees an individual's job upon release from prison. People considered a menace to society receive harsh sentences. Capital punishment by firing squad remains for 112 offenses (79 for violations of state security).

The Military and Security Apparatus

Cuba once boasted a formidable military under the aegis of the Fuerzas Armadas Revolucionarias (Revolutionary Armed Forces) (FAR; www.cubagob.cu/otras_info/minfar), commanded by Raúl Castro. Its military and militia are replete with battle-tested soldiers—as many as 350,000 Cuban troops served on active duty in Angola and Ethiopia during the 1970s and '80s. However, the number of men and women on active duty has shrunk from over 180,000 in 1993 to about 58,000 in 2004, according to the International Institute for Strategic Studies. In addition, Cuba has more than 100,000 reservists supplemented by about 100,000 in the "youth labor army," 50,000 in the civil defense force, and 1.3 million in the territorial militias. (All males between the ages of 16 and 45 are subject to conscription—conscripts complete a basic training program and are assigned to one of the regular armed forces. Women between 17 and 35 may volunteer for military service.)

In 1991 the military was re-engineered to help the economy and now earns its way by virtue of what it produces from its investments in tourism, agriculture, and industry. In recent years, high-ranking military figures have been promoted to key positions throughout the economy, and the military budget has begun to expand again.

The key to defense is the "Guerra de Todo el Pueblo" (War of All the People). In the event of an attack, the *entire* population of Cuba will be called into action. All Cuban citizens undergo compulsory military training one Sunday each month—called "Día de la Defensa"—though this, too, has been scaled back.

HOW CUBANS FEEL ABOUT THE REVOLUTION

The disintegration of the Soviet Bloc brought expectations of a Ceausescu-like ending for Castro. Why, then, have Cuba's internal and external crises not produced Castro's downfall? The U.S. State Department sows the field with stories of a "one-party monopoly," "40 years of brainwashing," and the "grip of fear" imposed on Cubans by "the police state." True enough. However, these assessments don't take into account the unifying power of national pride, the very real achievements of the Revolution, and above all, Castro's unique charisma and the way he is able to shape *cubanos'* minds like a hypnotist.

Many of the same Cubans who complain about harrowing privation and the ubiquitous and oppressive presence of the state will, in almost the same breath, profess loyalty to Castro, who still retains a substantial base of popular support among the Cuban public. Those with a hate-hate relationship are resigned to sullen silence, prison, or exile. Most Cubans, however, have a love-hate relationship with *el máximo*, although no one in his or her right mind would dare express their negative feelings openly for fear of the consequences.

TANGIBLE GAINS

While it is easy to compare themselves – and to be compared by Westerners – to North America, loyal revolutionaries prefer to compare Cuba to Haiti and other countries beset by true poverty. Cuba has invested 40 years of resources to become one of the few underdeveloped nations that protects virtually all members of society from illiteracy and ill health. This, plus tremendous advances in racial and sexual equality and the fact that Cuba's vital culture is nourished and protected have produced mammoth goodwill, especially in the countryside, where support for the Revolution is strongest. Even in hardship, loyalists see the glass as half full. They appreciate life for what it offers, not for what it lacks; for what it has given the people, not for what it has taken away or can no longer provide.

Many among the Party faithful, of course, espouse support because they're the beneficiaries of the system, which nurtures its own social elite with access to cars and other privileges. For loyalists, defending the system is a knee-jerk reaction. The party faithful are so defensive of their system that, says Isadora

State security is the responsibility of the Ministry of the Interior, which operates a number of intelligence-related services, plus the National Revolutionary Police (PNR), with paramilitary and military units under its umbrella. Other intelligence units—most notoriously, the much-feared Seguridad del Estado or G-2—are operated by the Department of State Security and the General Directorate of Intelligence. There are more security-linked officials than meet the eye—as many as 1 in 27 Cubans, including informers, according to Guillermo Cabrera Infante, the former editor of *Revolución*.

GOVERNMENT BY PERSONAL WHIM

Cuba is really a *fidelista* state, one in which Marxist-Leninism has been loosely grafted onto Cuban nationalism, then tended and shaped by one man. The Cuban leader likes to leave his development choices wide open, allowing a flexible interpretation of the correct path to socialism. Ideological dogma is subordinated to tactical considerations. Castro's emotions, what Castro biographer Tad Szulc calls his *caudillo* temperament (that of a modernizing but megalomanical political strongman), are powerful factors in his decision-making, which involve the minutest aspects of government. Fidel even chooses Miss Cuba every year, and it was he who decided that nurses should wear trousers, not skirts, because a nurse in a skirt leaning over a patient, he suggested impishly, might cause a man lying in a bed behind her to have a heart attack.

Government officials must study Castro's speeches intently to stay tuned with his

Tattlin, "if you mention material hardship, they will launch right into education and health care, as if no other country in the world offered free education and health care."

WHOLESALE DISCONTENT

Despite the gains, the majority of urbanites long ago lost faith in *el jefe*. They usually speak of Castro with the anger a son feels for an overbearing father who can't get with the times. Urbanites, especially, are anxious for a return to the market economy and a chance to control and improve their own lives. Most Cubans are tired of the inefficiencies, the endless hardships, the inequalities, the endless sacrifices to satisfy Castro's pathological battle with Uncle Sam. How, for example, can the government explain the US$60,000 Mercedes tourist taxis (or the fully stocked pharmacies for foreigners) when local pharmacies lack medicines?

Forty-odd years of Communism has created palpable discontent. The mood on the streets is one of frustration. Most Cubans are pained by their own poverty and the political posturing to disguise it. They are tired of being answerable to the state for their every move. They feel like they are on a yo-yo; any brief liberalization is always followed by a yank on the string. They hate being forced to break the law constantly to survive; of living under the stress of being caught for the slightest transgression; and of having to look over their shoulder for the government spies, informers, and secret police in the shadows. Says Catherine Moses: "Because of the resentment Cubans harbor toward these individuals, the choice for them truly may be socialism or death, as Fidel's downfall could lead to violent retribution against them."

Most Cubans say that things cannot go on as they are: "We must have change!" But when you ask them how change will come, most roll their eyes and shrug. Silence, congruity, and complicity – pretending to be satisfied and happy with the system – are cultural reflexes that have been called indicative of cultural decay. As James Michener wrote of Havana, perhaps "Only the kindness of the climate prevents the smoldering of revolt that might accompany the same conditions in a cold and relentless climate."

forever-changing views. The fear of repercussions from on high is so great that the bureaucracy—Cubans call it a "*burro*cracy"—has evolved as a "mutually protective society." Says Gabriel García Márquez: "Beside the enormous achievements that sustain the revolution—the political, scientific, sports, cultural achievements—there is a colossal bureaucratic incompetence affecting nearly every order of daily life, and most particularly domestic happiness." The result—besides an "endless labyrinth of errors committed and about to be committed" (in a speech in early 1987, Castro said, "We must correct the errors we made in correcting our errors")—is minimal accountability. Castro has been quick to admit the shortcomings of the system, which he blames on irresponsible managers, lack of discipline, and greed and corruption in high places—making, suggests Maurice Halperin, "the noticeable exception of his own performance."

"The fundamental problem," says Tad Szulc, "remains Fidel Castro's psychological inability, rather than conscious refusal, to let go of any power... a state of affairs that paralyzes all initiative at lower levels." Nonetheless, the past decade has seen the rise of a new generation with greater decision-making powers in the upper echelons of Cuba's newly established, self-supporting state enterprises.

"Direct Democracy"

Fidel Castro runs Cuba as much by charismatic as through institutional leadership: *personalismo* is central in *fidelismo*. Castro has called Western democracies "complete garbage." He prefers what he calls "direct democracy"— his appeals ("popular consultations") to the people, relying on his ability to whip up the crowds at mass rallies. Castro uses persuasive arguments to keep revolutionary ardor alive. Images of destitution in neighboring countries are standard fare, as is the threat from the United States.

For the first years, Fidel bounced around the countryside in his jeep to learn firsthand what the people felt, identifying their problems and working to resolve them. Gradually, however, it is claimed, Fidel lost touch with what the average Cuban feels and became caught in his own delusions, while apparatchiks and technocrats, who form the loyal crowds at speeches, seek to protect or further their careers by telling Castro what he wants to hear.

A State of Acquiescence

Castro has engineered a state where an individual's personal survival requires a display of loyalty and adherence to the Revolution. Castro maintains control through intimidation and repressive laws: the state is a domineering entity in every aspect of Cubans' lives. According to Wayne Smith, "A margin of public criticism is allowed, to vent political pressure. The headiest steam is periodically allowed to leave for Florida on rafts and inflated inner tubes."

The government maintains a file on *every* worker, a labor dossier that follows him or her from job to job. Cubans have to voice—or fake—their loyalty. To become *integrado* (integrated) is essential to get by. Transgressions are reported in one's dossier. Complaints are relatively few, to avoid inviting trouble. If "antisocial" comments or behavior are noted, the worker may be kicked out of his or her job, or blackballed, or one's child might be put on the slow track in education. The government keeps close tabs on anyone "guilty" of antisocial behavior. Such individuals are barred from government employment and face perpetual harassment from government agents.

Most Cubans have accommodated themselves to the parameters of permissible behavior set out years ago. The hardcore opponents left for Miami long ago. Most of the rest go along. The fear of the unknown, of losing one's benefits, of vengeance from the disaffected, are powerful factors in the inertia that pervades the country.

FIDEL CASTRO

Born and dispatched into this world with the engine of an athlete, Castro has the discipline of a warrior, the intellect of a chess master, the obsessive mania of a paranoiac and the willfulness of an infant.
– Ann Louise Bardach

Whatever you think of his politics, Fidel Castro is unquestionably one of the most remarkable and enigmatic figures of this century, thriving on contradiction and paradox like a romantic character from the fiction of his Colombian novelist friend Gabriel García Márquez.

Fidel Castro Ruz, child prodigy, was born on August 13, 1926, at Manacas *finca* near Birán in northern Oriente, the fifth of nine children of Ángel Castro y Argiz. Fidel's father was an émigré to Cuba from Galicia in Spain as a destitute 13-year-old. In Cuba, he made money from the presence of the American-owned United Fruit Company and became a wealthy landowner who employed 300 workers on a 26,000-acre domain; he owned 1,920 acres and leased the rest from the United Fruit Company, to whom he sold cane. Fidel's mother was the family housemaid, Lina Ruz González, whom Ángel married after divorcing his wife. Fidel weighed 10 pounds at birth—the first hint that he would always be larger than life. The early records of his family are sketchy, and Castro, who seems to have had a happy childhood, likes to keep it that way, much as he attempts to suppress the notion that he comes from a well-to-do family.

As a boy Fidel was extremely assertive, rebellious, and combative. He was a natural athlete and grew especially accomplished at track events and baseball. He was no sportsman, however; if his team was losing, he would often leave the field and go home.

AFTER FIDEL?

Fidel Castro turned 80 in August 2006. He celebrated his birthday in the hospital, where he was recuperating from an operation for an undisclosed life-threatening disease. He may last another decade, but he can't live forever. The groundwork for his succession has already been laid and well-rehearsed. The phase-in began on July 31, 2006, when Fidel temporarily ceded power to his four-years-younger brother, Raúl Castro, the armed forces minister and number two in the Communist Party. Fidel has called Raúl his *relevo* – relief pitcher.

Although an immensely capable manager, Raúl has none of his brother's charisma and is far less popular than Fidel (at least with the average Cuban on the street), from whom he derives his political strength; he enjoys the absolute loyalty of the army, however, which he has led with skill and savvy for four decades. Most likely, Raúl will top a Soviet or Chinese model of "collective leadership" with Raúl heading an executive council, with authority exercised collegially (although pragmatic, Raúl is absolutely devoted to preserving the socialist Revolution) among a youthful clique of savvy ministers. Indeed, Fidel named other key communist figures to head various ministries during his incapacitation. For a while, no doubt, this elite group will band together, stepping up the pace of economic reform while keeping a tight lid on political dissent.

But key differences exist among the most prominent young politicians, led by Ricardo Alarcón, the ambitious, relatively moderate National Assembly president and top emissary in dealings with the United States; and Carlos Lage, the economics czar and vice president of the Council of State, the economic guru in charge of day-to-day government responsibilities.

The real test will come with Raúl's passing, when the true power struggle begins and the role of the military and the people in the street, not to mention the Cuban-Americans in Miami (and, by extension, the White House), could be decisive.

The Army will be key, as will the transitional leadership's need to move ahead rapidly with the reforms that the Cuban people demand. Says Wayne Smith: "This transitional leadership would probably be included to have a constructive relationship with the U.S. Unfortunately the attitude of the Bush administration precludes that." President Bush loathes the Cuban government and what it stands for. On the other hand, he's very fond of the Cuban-American vote in a state that was very close to the 2000 election. Support for the internal opposition is an integral part of U.S. policy – a clear violation of the Charter of the Organization of American States. Bush, who has stated that he "will not accept a successor regime," even sent 10,000 short-wave radios to the U.S. Interests Section for distribution in Cuba, and has plans to appoint a U.S. "Transition Coordinator," as it did in Iraq.

While the Bush administration called for people to take their future in their own hands after Fidel turned power over to Raúl (the U.S. Secretary of State, Condoleeza Rice, also promised to respect the sovereignty of the Cuban people and assuaged fears of a U.S. invasion), the predicted popular unrest that Washington expected and hoped for didn't happen. Cubans remained calm. Within the Cuban government, the transition appeared smooth.

Gabriel García Márquez has said, "I do not think anyone in this world could be a worse loser." This trend has continued into adulthood (in December 1999, Castro withdrew the Cuban boxing squad from the world amateur boxing championship in Houston because he disagreed with some of the referees' decisions). It became a matter of principle to excel at everything (to this day, Fidel enjoys nothing so much as winning for winning's sake). His Jesuit teachers identified what Richard Nixon later saw in Castro: "that indefinable quality which, for good or evil, makes a leader of men." His school yearbook recorded that he was *excelencia* and predicted that "he will fill with brilliant pages the book of his life."

Star Rising

In October 1945 Fidel enrolled in Havana University's law school, where he immediately plunged into politics and gained the limelight as a student leader. Castro earned his first front-page newspaper appearance following his first public speech, denouncing President Grau, on November 27, 1946. In 1947, when the foremost political opposition figure, Edward Chibás, formed the Ortodoxo party, Castro, at the age of 21, was sufficiently well known to be invited to help organize it. He stopped attending law school and rose rapidly to prominence as the most outspoken critic of the Grau government, including as head of his own revolutionary group, Orthodox Radical Action.

The period was exceedingly violent: armed gangs roamed the campus, and Fidel never went anywhere without a gun. As organizer of the street demonstrations calling for Grau's ouster, Castro was soon on the police hit list, and several attempts were made on his life. In February 1949, Fidel was accused of assassinating a political rival. (According to biographer Georgie Ann Geyer, Castro appeared at the home of his brother-in-law, Rafael Díaz-Balart, and blurted out, "Rafael, let me in. I just killed Leonel Gómez," referring to a rival gang member.) After being arrested and subsequently released on "conditional liberty," he went into hiding.

He remained determined to stay in the limelight, however. In March, he flew to Bogotá to attend the Ninth Inter-American Conference, where foreign ministers were destined to sign the charter of the Organization of American States. Soon enough, Castro was in the thick of student demonstrations opposing the organization as a scheme for U.S. domination of the hemisphere. One week later, while he was on his way to meet Jorge Eliécer Gaitán (the popular leader of the opposition Progressive Liberal Party), Gaitán was assassinated. Bogotá erupted in spontaneous riots—the Bogotazo. Castro was irresistibly drawn in and, arming himself with a tear-gas shotgun and police uniform stolen from a police station, found himself at the vanguard of the revolution. Inevitably, Castro again made headline news.

On October 12, 1949, Castro married a pretty philosophy student named Mirta Díaz-Balart, and they honeymooned extravagantly—even staying in the Waldorf-Astoria—for several weeks in the United States. Castro, the consummate opportunist, may have married for political gain: Mirta's father was mayor of Banes, a Cuban congressman, and a close friend of Fulgencio Batista, who gave the couple US$1,000 for their honeymoon. Back home, Castro was once again in the thick of political violence. Gangsterism had soared under President Prío. In November, Fidel gave a suicidal speech in which he denounced the gangster process, admitted his past associations with gangsterism, then named all the gangsters, politicians, and student leaders profiting from the "gangs' pact." Again in fear for his life, Fidel left Cuba for the United States.

He returned four months later to cram for a multiple degree. In September 1950, Castro graduated with the title of Doctor of Law. He then began a law practice, concentrating on "lost causes" on behalf of the poor—most of his legal work was offered pro bono.

Congressional Candidate

By 1951, Castro was preparing for national office. Fulgencio Batista, who had returned from retirement in Florida to run for president, even asked to receive Castro to get the measure of the young man who in January 1952 shook Cuba's political foundation by releasing a detailed indictment of President Prío. According to Ann Louise Bardach, Castro perused Batista's library. "'You have many books here but you don't have a very important book, Curzio Malaparte's *The Technique of the Coup d'État*. I'll send you a copy,'" he apparently said. Castro's campaign was far ahead of its time. The imaginative 25-year-old utilized mass mailings and stump speeches with a foresight and veracity theretofore unknown. His personal magnetism, his brilliant speeches, and his apparent honesty aroused the crowds, who cheered him deliriously.

Castro was certain to be elected to the Chamber of Deputies. It was also clear that Batista was going to be trounced in the presidential contest, so at dawn on March 10, 1952, he effected a *golpe* and, next day, moved back into the presidential palace he had vacated eight years before. Says Tad Szulc: "Many Cubans think that without a coup, Castro would have served as a congressman for four years until 1956, then run for the Senate, and made his pitch for the presidency in 1960 or 1964. Given the fact that Cuba was wholly bereft of serious political leadership and given Castro's rising popularity... it would appear that he was fated to govern Cuba—no matter how he arrived at the top job."

The rest, as they say, is history.

A Communist *Caudillo*

At 30 years old, Castro was fighting in the Sierra Maestra, a disgruntled lawyer turned revolutionary who craved Batista's job. At 32, he had it. He was determined not to let go. When he came down from the mountains, he was considered a "younger, bearded version of Magwitch: a tall outlaw emerging from the fog of history to make Pips of us all," wrote Guillermo Cabrera Infante, a brilliant novelist who, like thousands, supported Castro but later soured on him: "The outlaw became a law unto himself." Fidel used the Revolution to carry out a personal *caudillista* coup. "Communist or not, what was being built in Cuba was an old-fashioned personality cult," wrote Jon Lee Anderson.

Castro has since outlasted nine U.S. presidents, each of whom predicted his imminent demise and plotted to hasten it by fair means or foul. He shows no sign of relinquishing power and has said he will never do so while Washington remains hostile—a condition he thrives on and works hard to maintain. Castro—who knew he could never carry out his revolution in an elective system—is consummately Machiavellian: masking truth to maintain power. Says Infante, "Castro's real genius lies in the arts of deception and while the world plays bridge by the book, he plays poker, bluffing and holding his cards close to his olive-green chest." "He has lied all his life, although he does not see his 'lies' as lies," suggests biographer Georgie Ann Geyer. "Often the first person he deceived was himself," added historian Hugh Thomas.

A Heart of Gold or Cold Steel?

Castro genuinely believes that disease, malnutrition, illiteracy, economic inadequacy, and dependence on the West are criminal shames and that a better social order can be created through the perfection of good values. "Political ideas are worthless if they aren't inspired by noble, selfless sentiments," he has said. Says Gabriel García Márquez: "He has the nearly mystical conviction that the greatest achievement of the human being is the proper formation of conscience and that moral incentives, rather than material ones, are capable of changing the world and moving history forward."

Despite the turn of events, Castro clings to the thread of his dream: "I have no choice but to continue being a Communist, like the early Christians remained Christian. ... If I'm told 98 percent of the people no longer believe in the Revolution, I'll continue to fight. If I'm told I'm the only one who believes in it, I'll continue."

Nonetheless, he is far from the saint his ardent admirers portray.

A Hatred of Uncle Sam

Castro turned to Communism mostly for strategic, not ideological, reasons—Graham Greene determined that Castro was "an empirical Marxist, who plays Communism by ear and not by the book"—but his bitterness towards the United States undoubtedly also shaped his decision. He has been less committed to Marxism than to anti-imperialism, in which he is unwavering. He has cast himself in the role of David versus Goliath, in the tradition of José Martí, who wrote "my sling is the sling of David." Castro sees himself as Martí's heir, representing the same combination of New World nationalism, Spanish romanticism, and philosophical radicalism. His trump card is Cuban nationalist sentiment.

His boyhood impressions of destitution in Holguín Province under the thumb of the United Fruit Company and, later, the 1954 overthrow of the reformist Arbenz government in Guatemala by a military force organized by the CIA and underwritten by "Big Fruit," had a profound impact on Castro's thinking. Ever since, Castro has viewed world politics through the prism of anti-Americanism. During the war in the Sierra Maestra, Castro stated, "When this war has ended, a much bigger and greater war will start for me, a war I shall launch against them. I realize this will be my true destiny."

He brilliantly used the Cold War to enlist the Soviet Union to move Cuba out of the U.S. orbit, and was thus able—with Soviet funds—to bolster his stature as a nationalist redeemer by guaranteeing the Cuban masses substantial social and economic gains while exerting constant energy and creativity to keep the United States at a distance. Castro, however, has no animosities towards North Americans. His many close personal contacts have ranged from media maverick Ted Turner to the late actor Jack Lemmon and even the Rockefeller clan.

Many Talents

Castro has a gargantuan hunger for information, a huge trove of knowledge (Fidel is an avid speed-reader), and an equally prodigious memory. He never forgets facts and figures, a remarkable asset he nourished at law school, where he forced himself to depend on his memory by destroying the materials he had learned by heart. He is a micromanager and is most alert late at night.

There is a sense of perfection in everything he does, applied through a superbly methodical mind and laser-clear focus. He has astounding political instincts, notably an uncanny ability to predict the future moves of his adversaries (Castro is a masterly chess player). Castro's "rarest virtue," says his intimate friend Gabriel García Márquez, "is the ability to foresee the evolution of an event to its farthest-reaching consequences."

Castro is also a gambler of unsurpassed self-confidence. His daring and chutzpah are attributed by some observers to his stubborn Galician temperament—that of an anarchist and born *guerrillero* (guerrilla fighter). He has stood at the threshold of death several times and loves to court danger. For example, in 1981, he chose to run to the Mexican port of Cozumel in a high-speed launch just to see whether the U.S. Navy—then patrolling the Gulf of Mexico to stop Cuban arms shipments to Nicaragua—could catch him. "Fidel has to manufacture the danger that lets him feel alive," notes journalist Eugene Robinson.

Above all, Castro has an insatiable appetite for the limelight, and a narcissistic focus on his theatrical role: The one thing that infuriates Fidel is to be ignored. Says Mead: "Castro needs international celebrity the way a fire needs oxygen." His vanity is so monumental that on one of his rare visits to see his illegitimate and ignored daughter, Alina, he asked if she wanted to see a movie. She wanted to see *The Godfather,* but instead her father treated her to a screening of a film about his triumphal tour of Eastern Europe. His beard is also more than a trademark; he likes to hide his double chin; likewise, he wears false teeth, and his long fingernails are lacquered and filed. He never laughs at himself unless he makes the joke. And he assiduously avoids singing or dancing—he is perhaps the only male in Cuba who has never been seen to dance.

A pathological genius, Castro nurtures his image with exquisite care, feigning modesty to hide his immense ego. "I am not here because I assigned myself to this job. ... I am here because this job has been thrust upon me," Castro told journalist Ann Louise Bardach in 1994. He sees himself as a leader of vast international significance, and the "absolute patriarch" of his country, suggests Bardach. He also claims that his place in history does not bother him: "All the glory in the world can fit into a kernel of corn." Yet in the same breath he likens himself to Jesus Christ, one of his favorite allusions. Castro has carefully cultivated the myth of Fidel the Christlike redeemer figure.

Castro's revolutionary concept has been built on communicating with the masses, and he conducts much of his domestic government through his frequent public speeches, usually televised in entirety. He understood at an early stage that he and television were made for each other. Castro—a consummate television actor—is masterfully persuasive, an amazingly gifted speaker who holds Cubans spellbound with his oratory textured in rich, gilded layers, using his trademark combination of flattery and enigmatic language to obfuscate and arouse. Says the *Wall Street Journal:* "Say this for Fidel: the man knows spin."

His speeches often last for hours. Fidel's loquaciousness is legendary. When he and Raúl were imprisoned together on the Isle of Pines in 1954, Raúl complained that his elder brother "didn't let me sleep for weeks... he just talked day and night, day and night." He is not, however, a man of small talk; he is deadly serious whenever he opens his mouth. His digressive repertoire is immense: "Castro, the former lawyer, can argue anything from any side at any time," writes Bardach. He also listens intently when the subject interests him; he is a great questioner, homing immediately to the heart of the matter.

Adored or Hated?

A large segment of Cubans see Castro as a ruthless dictator who cynically betrayed the democratic ideals that he used to rally millions to his banner. To Miami exiles especially, *el líder* is just a common tyrant. Nonetheless, Castro retains the admiration of many among the Cuban people to whom he was and remains a hero. There persists an adulation for *el máximo* or *el caballo* (the horse—an allusion to the Chinese belief that dreaming of certain figures represents numbers to place bets on, and that the horse is number one). Traveling through Cuba you'll come across families who keep a framed photograph of him, though many do so to keep in Fidel's good books.

Cubans' bawdy street wisdom says that Castro has various domiciles—a sane precaution in view of the CIA's numerous attempts on his life—so that he can attend to his lovers. "Like many Cuban men, he is a dedicated womanizer but he does not take any chances," says Bardach. "Any woman who captures his fancy is first checked out by security to ensure that she is not a CIA or hostile plant." Unbeknownst to the woman, a third party usually extends an invite for a seemingly innocent rendezvous in which Fidel makes his move. (Castro is an avid consumer of Cuba's anti-cholesterol drug, PPG, renowned for its Viagra-like side effects. He has admitted to having at least 12 children, but acknowledges there may be others; "almost a tribe," he stated.)

Many highly intelligent and beautiful women have dedicated themselves to Castro and his cause. But Fidel saves his most ardent passions for the Revolution, and the women (and children) in his life have been badly treated, as revealed in *Havana Dreams,* Wendy Gimbel's biography of his former lover, Naty Revuelta. Meanwhile, Delia Soto del Valle, Castro's wife of 30-odd years and with whom he has five sons, is rarely seen in public, and *never* with her husband. The average Cuban in the street knows virtually nothing of the private life of their secretive leader. The Cuban media are prohibited from reporting on Castro's personal life, and photos of Soto del Valle—a former schoolteacher from Trinidad—and their children have only recently been published in Cuba.

Castro is a "dilettante extraordinaire" in esoteric pursuits, notably gourmet dining (but not cigars; Fidel quit smoking in 1985). His second love is deep-sea fishing. He is also a good diver and used to frequently fly down to spearfish at his tiny retreat on Cayo Piedra.

Castro retains the loyalty of millions of Cubans, but he is only loyal to those who are loyal to him. His capacity for Homeric rage is renowned, and it is said that no official in his right mind dares criticize him. Paradoxically, he can be extremely gentle and courteous, especially towards women, in whose company he is slightly abashed. Cubans fear the consequences of saying anything against him, discreetly stroking their chins—an allusion to his beard—rather than uttering his name. He feels that to survive he must be "absolutely and undeviatingly uncompromising." In 1996 his biographer Tad Szulc wrote, "He is determined not to tolerate any challenge to his authority, whatever the consequences." You are either for the Revolution or against it. Castro does not forget, or pardon—he never apologizes as a matter of policy. Beneath the gold foil lies a heart of cold steel. Castro's former mentor at the Colegio de Belén, Father Armando Llorente, noted that he "had the cruelty of the Gallego… The Spaniard of the north is cruel, hard." Thus, while he has always shown solicitude for those who have served him or the Revolution, he is prepared to eliminate anyone, no matter who, if it serves him, and he demands that loyalists sever personal ties with family members who have turned their backs on Cuba. His policies have divided countless families, and Castro's family is no exception. His sister, Juanita, left for Miami in 1964 and is an outspoken critic of her brother's policies. His tormented daughter, Alina Fernández Revuelta, fled in disguise in 1993 and vilifies her father from her home in Miami. Castro's long-suffering former wife, Mirta Díaz-Balart—they divorced in 1954—lives in Spain but is reconciled with Castro and makes regular visits (it is Raúl Castro, however, who tends to her).

Castro denies that a personality cult exists. Yet Castro lives, suggests Szulc, "bathed in the absolute adulation orchestrated by the propaganda organs of the regime." Everywhere monuments, posters, and billboards are adorned with his quotations and face. His visage is the banner of the daily newspaper, *Granma,* while the front page of newspapers and television news are dominated by Castro's public acts or speeches. And at school gatherings and public rallies around the country, stooges work the crowds with chants of "Fee-del! Fee-del!"

Rumors of ill health have been touted for years, despite his doctors' assurances that Fidel is as fit as a fiddle (he has maintained a mostly vegetarian diet and worked out every day on an exercise bicycle). Nonetheless, Castro fainted in public in 2001 and fell in November 2004, fracturing his kneecap and elbow. At times he has seemed gaunt and pale, and his speech incoherent and faltering; when I last met him in 2003, he walked with aides supporting his arms (in 2005, Castro was walking more briskly, suggesting the possibility that he received knee replacements). More dramatically, the indefatigable Cuban leader, who turned 80 in 2006 and has outlasted all other leaders of his time, was taken life-threateningly ill in mid-2006 and underwent emergency surgery. The exact illness is a state secret, and his recovery far from certain.

The Economy

One may wait fifteen minutes to buy a pound of rice, or thirty minutes for a bus that never shows. Another may wait four days in a provincial terminal for an airplane that's sitting in a hangar in some other province waiting for repairs from a mechanic who happens to be waiting in line at the doctor's office, but the doctor is late, still waiting for a permission slip from a government functionary who's behind schedule because she, too, had to wait in line all morning trying to reschedule her daughter for an eye exam *that was delayed because the optometric lens was waiting to be repaired by the technician who was busy waiting at the train station for his relatives to arrive.*
    – Ben Corbett, This Is Cuba

THE PREREVOLUTIONARY ECONOMY

For several decades prior to the Revolution, U.S. corporations virtually owned the island. Most of the cattle ranches, more than 50 percent of the railways, 40 percent of sugar production, 90 percent of mining and oil production, and almost 100 percent of telephone and utility services were owned by U.S. companies. Every year, beginning in 1934, the U.S. Congress established a preferential quota for Cuban sugar. In exchange for a guaranteed price that was US$0.02 above the world market price, Cuba had to guarantee tariff concessions on U.S. goods sold to Cuba. The island's manufacturers thereby found it impossible to compete with U.S. imports, and the agreement kept Cuba tied to the U.S. as a one-commodity economy. It also bound Cuba to U.S. goods. In 1958 the U.S. imported more than 75 percent of all Cuban exports (mostly sugar) and supplied the island with more than 80 percent of its imports.

Nonetheless, Cuba had a vibrant economy and despite immense poverty throughout the country, its national income in 1957 of US$2.3 billion was topped only by that of the much larger countries of Argentina, Mexico, and Venezuela. Cuba had a large middle class and a mature market economy and banking sector.

COMMUNISM ON STEROIDS

Castro and Che Guevara, who became the Minister of Industry, might have been great revolutionaries, but they didn't have the sharply different set of skills and understanding necessary to run an efficient economy, which they had swiftly nationalized. There were few coherent economic plans in the 1960s—just grandiose schemes that almost always ended in near ruin. The revolutionaries had zero experience in marketing, financing, and so on. They replaced monetary work incentives with "moral" incentives, set artificially low prices, and got diminishing supplies in return.

The minimum wage allowed Cubans to buy all available necessities, but there was nothing else to purchase. Therefore there was no incentive to earn more. Rationing inhibited the work incentive that would in turn permit the elimination of rationing. Socialism had nationalized wealth but, says Guillermo Cabrera Infante, in a "Hegelian capriole" it "socialized poverty" too. Forty-odd years of *fidelismo*, reports *The Economist*, "has left Cubans with a ruined economy."

Dependency on Comrade Joe

"As early as 1981, it was calculated that since Castro took over Cuba it had experienced an annual average per-capita-growth-rate of minus 1.2 percent. By 1990 the minus growth-rate had increased to an average of over two percent," records historian Paul Johnson. Fortunately the Soviet Union acted as Cuba's benefactor, providing aid estimated at around US$11 million per day—the greatest per capita aid program in world history. Says P. J. O'Rourke, "The Cubans got the luxury of running their economy along the lines of a Berkeley commune, and like California hippies wheedling their parents for cash, someone else paid the tab." The Soviet Union also sustained the Cuban economy by buying 85 percent of its foreign exports "at reasonable market prices." On the eve of the collapse of the Soviet Union, 84 percent of Cuba's trade was with the Soviet Union and Eastern Europe.

The End of Subsidies

After the fall of the Berlin Wall and collapse of the Soviet Union, Cuba's "rust-bucket" economy was cut adrift. Between 1990 and 1994, the economy shrank 34 percent according to the Cuban government—the U.S.–Cuba Trade and Economic Council claims that the fall was as much as 70 percent. By the end of 1994, half the country's industrial factories had closed, as had 70 percent of its public transport network. Sugar mills were shut down and cannibalized for parts to keep more efficient mills operating. Power outages further disrupted industrial production. The work force was left idle.

To compound the problem, the world market price of sugar, which in the 1980s accounted for 80 percent of Cuba's export earnings, also plummeted. In 1989, one ton of sugar bought seven tons of oil; in 1993, a time when Cuba desperately needed oil, it would buy just 1.3 tons. Meanwhile, the sugar harvest plummeted from 8.1 million tons in 1989–90 to only 3.3 million tons in 1993. It was an unmitigated disaster.

A FAREWELL TO MARXISM

In October 1991 the Cuban Communist Party Congress adopted a resolution establishing profit-maximizing state-owned Cuban corporations that operate independently of the central state apparatus. In September 1995 the Cuban National Assembly passed a law allowing foreigners to have wholly owned businesses in all sectors of the economy except defense, national security, education, and public health. Foreign corporations (but not individuals) could even buy buildings (but not land). Duty-free zones were also created with special incentives for foreign corporations. As of 2003, about 800 foreign companies were doing business with Cuba.

The result was dubbed "market dictatorship" (or *capitalismo frío,* cold capitalism) in which the state owns and runs the show.

Reinventing Capitalism

Cuba sends its best and brightest abroad for crash courses in capitalist business techniques. The University of Havana now features courses on capitalism. And an International Business Center of Havana opened in June 1993 to teach marketing and management seminars. Havana has even handed over large chunks of the economy to the military, which began sweeping experiments, including Western-style management techniques. Today generals in civilian clothes run quasi-private corporations such as Gaviota, whose resort hotels are built by the army's construction company, Unión de Empresas Constructoras. TRD Caribe, a subsidiary of Gaviota, even runs the nationwide chain of stores selling Western goods.

In 1993, to get hold of foreign currency floating freely in the black market and coming into the country as aid from relatives abroad (estimated in 2003 at about US$1 billion per year) or as tips from foreign tourists, the Cuban government legalized possession of the U.S. dollar, possession of which had heretofore been illegal. To soak up the dollars, the government opened up "foreign exchange recovery stores" (shops) selling every imported item imaginable, from toothpaste to Japanese TVs.

In the summer of 1993, Castro also opened up the service sector and agriculture by converting state farms to cooperatives run on the basis of profitability. The government also legalized self-employment for plumbers, electricians, tailors, cobblers, barbers, photographers, and dozens of others who could—upon registration—ply their trades freely. By mid-1995, 210,000 Cubans (about five percent of Cuba's labor force) had officially registered as self-employed individuals, or *cuentapropistas.* Personal foreign exchange income and various "profitable activities" became subject to taxation at rates from 10 percent to 50 percent which, says *The Economist,* "seem designed not to raise revenue from such businesses but to wipe them out."

Back from the Brink

Cuban authorities have hesitated about wholesale economic reforms and soon began back-pedaling. Hence, in 1995 the Cuban government began muscling its way into joint-venture businesses and putting inappropriate pressures on foreign partners. In 1999 Castro warned: "We want the minimum of foreign ownership and capital in this little island." Orthodox hard-liners who held their noses over the reforms are back in the saddle again. In early 2005, Castro asserted that the economy had finally come out of its post-Soviet abyss (although international experts calculated that the GDP, estimated by the CIA as being US$32.13 billion in 2004, remained 12 to 15 percent below 1989 levels). With the economy stabilized, and bolstered by growing economic ties to China and Venezuela (now Cuba's chief trading partner), the Communist government began rolling back reforms. By the end of 2005, only a handful of key foreign investors remained while state enterprises have lost much of their autonomy.

Cuba's self-employed, who typically earn far more than the average monthly salary of 350 pesos (equivalent to US$14), have also found Cuban-style capitalism bruising in the face of growing government regulation meant to force them back out of business ("Mr. Castro understands that when you are free economically, you are free politically," wrote *The Economist*).

Cash remittances (*remesas*)—from families in Miami, which topped US$1.194 billion in 2003—account for most of the increase in standard of living for Cuban individuals. (Restrictions since imposed by the Bush administration reduced the amount sent to US$460 million in 2005. Since 2000, when U.S. law was altered to allow shipments of food and medicine, U.S. companies have also sold more than US$800 million of goods to Cuba, making the United States Cuba's seventh-largest trade partner.) Most of the money eventually ends up in state hands, absorbed through state stores, where the markup is now an average of 240 percent.

Then, in 2004, Castro banned the dollar, forcing millions of locals to exchange hoarded greenbacks—or *fula,* as Cubans call it in a reference to the green-gray gunpowder used in *santería* to invoke the spirits—for convertible pesos, resulting in an instant injection of US$1.5 billion into the Cuban economy. Next, Castro revalued the convertible peso 8 percent against all other currencies, making the country that much more expensive for foreign visitors and Cubans with foreign exchange (Cubans now receive only 83 convertible pesos for every US$100 sent from Florida after the Cuban government skims off commissions and following revaluation of the convertible peso).

Meanwhile Cuba is running a massive trade deficit, now averaging more than US$3 billion a year. (The Cuban government claims to have had a positive balance of payments of US$176 million in 2004.)

AGRICULTURE

"There must be much hunger," says one of Ernest Hemingway's characters in *Islands in the Stream.* "You cannot realize it," comes the reply. "No I can't," Thomas Hudson thought. "I can't realize it at all. I can't realize why there should ever be any hunger in this country ever." Traveling through Cuba, you'll also sense the vast potential that caused René Dumont, the outstanding French agronomist, to say that "with proper management, Cuba could adequately feed five times its current population."

Before the Revolution, Cuba certainly couldn't feed itself: The best arable lands were planted in sugarcane for export. Alas, since the revolution management of agriculture has been dumbfoundingly inept. First, Castro organized land in a system of centralized, inefficient state farms dedicated to sugarcane monoculture to satisfy the Soviet sweet tooth. Food distribution was also centralized and highly inefficient—"for every peso of fruits and vegetables on the stand, US$0.23 are lost to spoilage," reported journalist Gail Reed. Cuba is the only country in Latin America whose production of rice, for example, hasn't risen since 1958, remaining static with a yield of 2,400 kilograms per hectare; by contrast, Cuba's Caribbean neighbor, the Dominican Republic, has increased its rice production fourfold.

Agricultural production in the early 1990s collapsed due to a combination of factors, including lack of machinery, fertilizers, and labor incentives, plus a series of alternating droughts and torrential storms that conspired with a series of pest plagues to devastate crop harvests. Deteriorating living conditions also induced farmers and agricultural workers to put down their hoes to move in with better-off city cousins.

In September 1993 Cuba made dramatic changes and established autonomous cooperatives that farm government land but own the crop they harvest (although they are still obliged to follow state directives and sell all their crops to the state at prices fixed by the latter). In addition the law authorized the transfer of idle land to private owners, who currently utilize about 20 percent of Cuba's cultivable land. They, too, are obliged to sell 80 percent of their produce to the state at fixed prices.

The Cubans also began experimenting with alternative farming in the early 1980s. The demise of the Soviet Union forced them to plunge in headlong, assisted by the U.N. Food and Agricultural Organization. Cuba has rediscovered traditional peasant methods and invented its own alternative technologies. A small worm-eating fly now guards the yucca crop; zillions of wasps are being bred to attack the sugarcane borer; and ants have been unleashed in the banana and sweet potato crops. Meanwhile, several thousand community-operated gardens have also eased the shortfalls. Alongside private farms, the gardens, or *agropónicos,* account for about half the vegetables grown in Cuba.

Despite these changes, production remains insufficient to meet domestic needs. Only 1.5 million hectares—a mere 12 percent of the land under cultivation—is planted in food crops; the rest is dedicated to pasture and export crops (more than 60 percent of Cuba's rice, grains, and other staples are imported, normally through food-for-sugar barter deals as, for example, with France, which provides 70 percent of Cuba's wheat and flour needs).

Cattle

Cuba has always had a strong cattle industry, particularly in the provinces around Camagüey, which has been famous for beef and dairy production since before the Revolution.

There were 6.5 million head of cattle on the eve of the Revolution, when milk production was 9.6 million liters a year. Following the Revolution, the herds were slaughtered to compensate for falling production of other foods; by 1963, there were only 2 million head. That year, Castro took a lively interest, especially in the importation of foreign breeds and development of new strains intended to make animal husbandry a national priority. The central uplands are a focus for genetic breeding of cattle, such as Cuba's homegrown Charolais, Santa Gertrudis, and F1 strains. Zebu from India, for example, have been crossed with Canadian Holstein, producing offspring adapted to the tropics. By 1980, Cuba had replenished its herds. Thereafter the industry again declined.

In 1990 Cuba could no longer afford to import feed for domestic livestock. Herds of delicate imported cattle, particularly Holsteins and Swiss Brown, died en masse. Consequently, milk production has plummeted. Private farmers are now again permitted to raise cattle, but they are severely restricted.

© CHRISTOPHER P. BAKER

Oxen are a staple in the fields of Cuba, working as beasts of burden.

THE *ZAFRA*

With the onset of the dry season, Cuba prepares for the *zafra*, the sugar harvest, which runs from November through June. Then the temperatures soar and the *macheteros* are in the fields from dawn until dusk, wielding their short, wide, blunt-nosed machetes after first burning the cane stalks to soften them for the cut. The *macheteros* grab the three-meter-tall stalks, which they slash close to the ground (where the sweetness concentrates). Then they cut off the top and strip the dry leaves from the stalk.

Before the introduction of mechanical cane cutters in the 1970s, 350,000 laborers were required for the harvest, and workers used to come by the tens of thousands from Haiti and Jamaica just for the season. Today, three-quarters of the crop is harvested mechanically. The Cuban-designed combine-harvester can cut a truckload of cane (close to seven metric tons) in 10 minutes, three times more than the most skilled *machetero* can cut by hand in a day.

The cut cane is delivered to one of the approximately 70 sugar mills in Cuba (recently reduced from about 150), which operate 24 hours a day, pouring bilious black smoke into the air. Here the sugarcane is fed to the huge steel crushers that squeeze out the sugary pulp called *guarapo*, which is boiled, clarified, evaporated, and separated into molasses and sugar crystals. The molasses makes rum, yeast, and cattle feed. *Bagazo*, the fiber left after squeezing, fuels boilers or is shipped off to mills to be turned into paper and wallboard. The sugar is shipped by rail to bulk shipping terminals for transport to refineries abroad.

(Killing cattle for private consumption or sale of meat is illegal and farmers are fined for each head of cattle they lose.)

Citrus

In 2001, Cuba produced about 900,000 tons of citrus, about the same as the 1989–90 harvest, when Cuba was the world's biggest citrus exporter. Most citrus goes to produce juices and extracts, much of it for export to Europe. Effort has been made in recent years to upgrade with investments from Chile and Israel. A 20,000 hectare citrus operation at Jagüey Grande is the world's largest under one management (it is operated by an Israeli company) and accounts for more than 60 percent of domestic production, equivalent to about one percent of total U.S. production.

Coffee

Cuba produces excellent coffee. The finest quality is grown in the Sierra Escambray, although most coffee is grown in the mountains of eastern Cuba on small plots worked by hand in quasi-cooperatives that must sell their entire crop to the government at fixed prices.

In the 19th century, Cuba was one of the world's leading coffee producers. Most *cafetales* (coffee plantations), however, were destroyed during the 10-year War of Independence. The introduction of a tariff to protect Cuban coffee in 1927 prompted a revival, and Cuba enjoyed modest exports on the eve of the Revolution. Production has since declined markedly. A plan—*Plan Turquino*—was therefore conceived to motivate farmers and their families to remain in the mountains and train young people in coffee cultivation—these days the government uses thousands of unskilled high school students to bring in the harvest. More than 20,000 acres of poorly used or vacant state lands have been transformed into more than 10,000 privately managed coffee farms and given to families in search of a home and work. And much of the 300,000 acres devoted to coffee production is being upgraded.

Japan and France account for almost 80 percent of Cuba's coffee exports, buying at fixed below-world-market prices. Cuba today imports low-grade coffee beans to meet domestic demand; domestic coffee is adulterated with roasted wheat and peas.

Sugar

¡Azúcar! The whole country reeks of sweet, pungent sugar, Cuba's curse and her blessing. The Cuban landscape is one of endless cane fields, lorded over by the towering chimneys of great sugar mills. Due to Cuba's soil and climate, sugar thrives here as nowhere else in the world. The unusual depth (up to seven meters) and fertility of Cuba's limestone soils are unparalleled in the world for producing sugar— sugar plants can be raised without replanting for up to 20 years, a longer period than anywhere else in the world. And the sucrose content of Cuban sugar is higher, too.

The nation's bittersweet bondsman has been responsible for curses like slavery and the country's almost total dependence on not only the one product, but, as history as proven, on single imperial nations: first Spain, then the United States, and most recently the Soviet Union. Cuba's traditional dependence on sugar exports changed little during three decades of socialism. Production rose gradually from about five million tons a year in the early 1970s to 7.5 million tons on average in the late 1980s. Three-quarters went to feed the Soviet bear; the rest to capitalist markets to earn hard currency. The collapse of the Soviet bloc rendered a triple whammy to Cuba's obsolete sugar industry. Not only did its main market collapse, but preferential prices guaranteed by the Soviet Union also vanished, forcing Cuba to sell its sugar at depressed world market prices. Cuba's sugar-dependent economy has

THE LIFE CYCLE OF CIGARS

THE PRODUCTION PROCESS: FROM LEAF TO CIGAR

The tobacco leaves, which arrive from the fields in dry sheets, are first moistened and stripped. The leaves are then graded by color and strength (each type of cigar has a recipe). A blender mixes the various grades of leaves, which then go to the production room, where each *tabaquero* and *tabaquera* receives enough tobacco to roll approximately 100 cigars for the day.

While they work in large rooms, where they sit at rows of *galeras* (workbenches) with piles of loose tobacco leaves at their sides. The rollers' indispensable tool is a *chaveta*, a rounded, all-purpose knife for smoothing and cutting leaves, tamping loose tobacco, circumcising the tips, and sometimes banging a welcome to factory visitors.

While they work, a *lector* (reader) reads aloud from a strategically positioned platform or high chair. Morning excerpts are read from the *Granma* newspaper; in the afternoon, the *lector* reads from historical or political books, or short stories and novels. Alexandre Dumas, Agatha Christie, and Ernest Hemingway are favorites; Dumas's novel *The Count of Monte Cristo* was such a hit in the 19th century that it lent its name to the famous Montecristo cigar. In Cuba before the Revolution, men who were completely illiterate knew the classics, the plays of Shakespeare, and modern novels, and were well versed in current political issues. Such is still the case.

ROLLING THE CIGAR

The *torcedor* (cigar roller) fingers his or her leaves and, according to texture and color, chooses two to four filler leaves, which are laid end to end and gently yet firmly rolled into a tube, then enveloped by the binder leaves to make a "bunch." The rough-looking "bunch" is then placed with nine others in a small wooden mold that is screwed down to press each cigar into a solid cylinder. Next, the *tabaquera* selects a wrapper leaf, which she trims to size. The "bunch" is then laid at an angle across the wrapper, which is stretched and rolled around the "bunch," overlapping with each turn. A tiny quantity of flavorless tragapanth gum (made from Swiss pine trees) is used to glue the *copa* down. Now the *torcedor* rolls the cigar, applying pressure with the flat of the *chaveta*. Finally, a piece of wrapper leaf the size and shape of a quarter

had to produce more and more sugar to generate the same income. Moreover, Cuba has faced growing competition from Brazil and new producers such as India and the increasingly more efficient sugar beet producers. Attempts in the early 1990s to reorganize the industry and make it more efficient failed. Although the government spent vast sums to raise productivity, the fields were being overtaxed. From seven million tons in 1991, the harvest plummeted to a paltry 2.5 million tons in 2004.

In 2002, the government announced a dramatic overhaul of the industry. More than 3.1 million acres of canefields will be converted to grow food crops (pineapple has been planted in all 14 provinces, for example). Meanwhile, all but 71 of the nation's 156 sugar mills have been permanently closed and 100,000 sugar workers have been made redundant.

Tobacco

Tobacco has traditionally been Cuba's second most important agricultural earner of foreign exchange. About 50,000 hectares are given to tobacco, which is grown in rich valleys and slopes throughout Cuba, but predominantly in a 90-mile-long, 10-mile-wide valley—Vuelta Abajo—in Pinar del Río. Cuban tobacco is grown on small properties, many privately owned by the farmers—the average holding is only 10 hectares (about 25 acres).

Production reached about 40,000 tons in 1990—enough for 90 million cigars, worth about US$100 million. Cuba thereafter

---

is cut to form the cap; it is glued and twirled into place, and the excess is trimmed.

The whole process takes about five minutes. Hence, a good cigar maker can roll about 100 medium-sized cigars a day; the average for the largest cigars is far less.

Cigar rollers serve a nine-month apprenticeship, and each factory has its own school. Those who succeed graduate slowly from making petit corona cigars to the larger and specialized sizes. Rollers are paid piece rates based on the number of cigars they produce. They can puff as much as they wish on the fruits of their labor while working.

The majority of rollers are women. Prior to the Revolution, only men rolled cigars; the leaves were selected by women, who often sorted them on their thighs, giving rise to the famous myth about cigars being "rolled on the dusky thighs of Cuban maidens."

AND SO TO MARKET

The roller ties cigars of the same size and brand into bundles – media ruedas (half-wheels) – of 50 using a colored ribbon. These are then fumigated in a vacuum chamber. Quality is determined by a revisador (inspector), according to eight criteria, such as length, weight, firmness, smoothness of wrappers, and whether the ends are cleanly cut. Catadores (professional smokers) then blind test the cigars for aroma, draw, and burn, the relative importance of each varying according to whether the cigar is a slim panatela (draw is paramount) or a fat robusto (flavor being more important). The catadores taste only in the morning and rejuvenate their taste buds with sugarless tea.

Once fumigated, cigars are placed in cool cabinets for three weeks to settle fermentation and remove any excess moisture. The cigars are then graded according to color and then shade within a particular color category. A trademark paper band is then put on by an anillado. Finally, the cigars are laid in pinewood boxes, with the lightest cigar on the right and the darkest on the left (cigars range from the very mild, greenish-brown doble claro to the very strong, almost black oscuro). The boxes are then inspected for alignment and uniformity. A thin leaf of cedar wood is laid on top to maintain freshness, and the box is sealed with a green-and-white label guaranteeing the cigars are genuine Havanas, or puros habanos (today the terms puro and habano are synonyms for cigar).

experienced a series of disastrous harvests. Production plummeted before recovering with the financial aid of European importers. Although cigar exports again plunged in 2000, in 2001 they reached 170 million, valued at US$240 million. Domestic sales to tourists adds about US$150 million. However, the tobacco industry was devastated in 2002 and 2004 by hurricanes, causing massive devastation and losses within the industry.

INDUSTRY

The Castro regime has invested considerable money in metal processing, spare parts industries, and factories turning out domestic appliances, albeit often of shoddy quality. Cement, rubber, and tobacco products, processed foods, textiles, clothing, footwear, chemicals, and fertilizers are the staple industries. It also has steel mills, bottling plants, paper-producing factories, and animal feed factories, plus electronics assembly plants. Even Cuban-designed computers are assembled from foreign parts, as are Sony TVs using parts imported from Panama.

Cuba's biggest problem is gross mismanagement and the fact that many factories date from the antediluvian dawn. An exception is in pharmaceuticals, where its investments in biotechnology generate substantial export earnings.

Mining

Cuba boasts large mineral resources, particularly of chromite, cobalt, and iron (up to 3.5 billion tons of ore), gold and silver (up to 600,000 tons), plus copper, manganese, lead, and zinc, all concentrated in northeastern Cuba.

Cuba is also the world's sixth-largest producer of nickel (which accounted for 46 percent of Cuba's total exports in 2004) and has about 37 percent of the world's estimated reserves (about 19 million tons). Exports have quadrupled since 1990, mostly to Europe, India, Canada, and China. Mining has attracted 30 percent of all foreign business ventures on the island, although European and Canadian investors have cooled their heels in recent years, replaced in 2005 (when revenues

from nickel were expected to exceed US$700 million) by a US$500 million investment for a new nickel processing plant by China, which will own 49 percent.

Oil

In April 1960 the Soviet ship *Chernovci* arrived with a 70,000-barrel load of oil—the beginning of a 10,000-kilometer petroleum pipeline that was maintained for three decades. Cuba traded nickel, citrus, and sugar to the Soviet Union in return for 10–12 million tons of crude oil and petroleum per year. As much as half of this was re-exported for hard currency to purchase necessities on the world market (by the mid-1980s, oil surpassed sugar as the island's major money-maker). Russia's decision to halt supplies of subsidized oil in 1991 triggered Cuba's desperate crisis. Today, Cuba meets the bulk of its needs with some 90,000 barrels a day of Venezuelan oil imported at preferential rate; Cuba's unpaid debt to Venezuela exceeded US$750 million in 2004, and is being paid in part in medical and other services.

Cuba *does* have oil, and crude is currently being pumped from 20 oil fields. The five main producers are along the north coast concentrated near Varadero, which has estimated reserves of one billion barrels. Production, initiated in 1988, had risen to 75,000 barrels per day in 2004—enough to cover almost 50 percent of the island's power generation needs. However, Cuba's crude oil is heavy, with a high sulfur content that makes it hard to process. Seeking higher-quality oil, the Cuban government has opened up a 112,000-square-kilometer zone of the Gulf of Mexico for deep-water exploration by foreign companies. In December 2004, Castro announced discovery of a crude oil deposit containing up to 100 million barrels.

TOURISM

Before 1959 Cuba was one of the world's hottest tourist destinations. When Batista was ousted, most foreigners stayed home. Havana's former hot spots gathered dust. Apart from a handful of Russians, the beaches belonged to the Cubans throughout the 1960s, '70s, and '80s, when tourism contributed virtually nothing to the nation's coffers. Havana's view of tourism, however, profoundly shifted with the demise of the Soviet Union, and Cuba is already well on the way to recapturing its 30 percent pre-Castro share of the Caribbean market: Cuba posted a 19.8 percent *average* annual growth in the 1990s, compared to 4.7 percent for the Caribbean as a whole. In 2005, Cuba received 2.3 million visitors. The U.N. Economic Commission for Latin America & the Caribbean reckons that tourism earns Cuba about US$3 billion a year (41 percent of all Cuba's foreign exchange earnings, according to the Cuban government).

Canada is the island's chief tourism provider (accounting for 40 percent of tourism revenues, almost all of it at all-inclusive beach resorts), followed by Italy and Great Britain, then Spain. Even tourists from China are now arriving in significant numbers, with direct flights planned at press time. In 2002, U.S. citizens constituted the third-largest source of tourists to Cuba. However, the number of U.S. visitors has since plummeted after the Bush administration enacted new restrictions (200,859 U.S. citizens visited Cuba in 2003 according to official Cuban statistics, of which 115,050 were Cuban-Americans; in 2004, the numbers fell to 108,172 and 57,145, respectively).

The government had set itself an ambitious long-term goal of five million tourists annually by 2010. Cuba's Tourism Development Master Plan focuses on eight regions: the city of Havana (number one in tourist visits), Varadero (number two), Cayo Largo, Cayo Coco, Santiago de Cuba, Trinidad, Santa Lucía, and northern Holguín. Having upgraded most of its hotel infrastructure to international standards, the Ministry of Tourism is now positioning Cuba as a destination for higher-income travelers, ecotourism, and incentive travel.

Still, Cuba has failed to establish a significant level of repeat business because of poor service, lousy food, state-sponsored rip-offs, and outrageous prices.

Cuba's Tourism Structure

The Ministry of Tourism (3ra Av. y F, Vedado, Havana, tel. 07/832-7535, www.cubatravel. cu) oversees tourism development and acts as watchdog over the operations of state-owned tourism agencies that operate autonomously with the authority to form joint-management agreements with foreign hotel corporations and tourism entities. Since 2005 it has been run by a military figure, Manuel Marero Cruz, charged with bringing discipline to the sector; the ministry has fired dozens of managers, restructured hotel groups, and directly taken over car rental services, restaurants, nightclubs, and extra-hotel businesses, which it has centralized under its own direction.

Cuban Society

I was at that hallucinatory early stage in my encounter with this new country, the stage at which a perfect descriptive framework emerges, distinct and complete, and all that seems left to do is fill in a few blanks and add a bit of ornament. From that golden and illusion-filled moment, ignorance always increased geometrically. For the next week or month or decade, each day adds a bit of understanding about the place. But if you're paying attention, *each day also takes a bit of understanding away."*
– Eugene Robinson, *Last Dance in Havana*

It is a rare visitor to Cuba who, exploring beyond the tourist circuit, does not at some time break down in tears. Everyone, everything, touches your heart. It is the way the Cubans embrace you with global innocence, how their disarming charm and irrepressible gaiety amid the heartrending pathos of their situation moves you to examine the meaning of your own life. "It is not easy to describe the strength and enthusiasm of the Cubans," wrote Angela Davis after attending the 1962 World Youth Peace Festival in Helsinki, when the Revolution was only three years old. The cultural presentation given by the Cuban delegation illustrated for Davis the "infectious dynamism" that moves so many visitors.

DEMOGRAPHY

Cuba's population in July 2005 was estimated at 11,346,670, of which 75.9 percent were classified as urban; 19.9 percent live in the city of Havana, with a population of about 2,200,000. Santiago de Cuba, the second-largest city, has about 350,000 people. The annual average growth rate is 0.33 percent, down from 2.3 percent from 1953 to 1970 and 1.1 percent in the 1980s. More than two million Cubans have left the island since 1959.

Cuba's family planning policies have helped the country reduce its birth rate from 4.2 percent in 1960 to 1.9 percent today—about the same as in the United States. Cuba is in the company of the world's developed nations in respect to its aging population and low birth rates. Fertility rates are 1.9 children per woman, compared to 1.8 in both the United States and Great Britain. The declining birth rates are due to the population's cultural development, the high percentage of women engaged full-time as workers, and access to health care, including abortion services. The low birth and mortality rates and high life expectancy also mean a rapidly aging population. About 10.4 percent of the population is 65 years or older—an enormous social security burden for the beleaguered government. The number of elderly will triple by 2030, when the nonworking population will equal the working population.

The United Nations Development Programme ranks Cuba fifth in Latin America in its "Human Development Index," behind Argentina, Chile, Uruguay, and Costa Rica.

The Ethnic Mix

Officially about 37 percent of the population is "white," mainly of Spanish origin. About 11 percent is black, and 53 percent is mulatto of mixed white-black ethnicity—Cuban lore claims there is some African in every Cuban's blood. Chinese constitute about 0.1 percent. While there are no pure-blooded native Indians left in Cuba, in the east—especially around Baracoa—genetic traces recall the indigenous culture.

The population has grown markedly darker since the Revolution. Of the roughly two million Cubans who have emigrated since 1959, the vast majority were white.

Race Relations

Slavery has burdened many countries of the Americas with racial and social problems. But Cuba has gone as far as any other to untangle the Gordian knot. Cuban society is as intermixed as any other on earth. Racial harmony is everywhere evident.

Despite slavery, by Caribbean norms Cuba historically has been a "white" society whose numbers were constantly fed by a steady in-pouring of immigrants from Spain. After emancipation in 1888, the island was spared the brutal segregation of the American South, and a black middle class evolved alongside a black underclass, with its own social clubs, restaurants, and literature. "Cuba's color line is much more flexible than that of the United States," recorded black author Langston Hughes during a visit in 1930: "There are no Jim Crow cars in Cuba, and at official state gatherings and less official carnivals and celebrations, citizens of all colors meet and mingle." Havana society of the time, wrote Hugh Thomas, was "one in which relations between black and white were of an extreme, if tolerant complexity... The prejudices which kept blacks from the new luxury hotels of the late 1950s were still things of the future." Gradually, U.S. visitors began to import Southern racial prejudice to their winter playground. To court their approval, hotels that were formerly lax in their application of color lines began to discourage even mulatto Cubans. Cuba on the eve of the revolution had adopted "whites only" clubs, restaurants, schools, hotels, beaches, recreation centers, housing areas, and, of course, discrimination in job hiring. When dictator Fulgencio Batista—who was a mixture of white, black, and Chinese—arrived at the exclusive Havana Yacht Club, they turned the lights out to let him know that although he was president, as a mulatto he was not welcome.

Cuba's revolutionary government swiftly outlawed institutionalized discrimination and vigorously enforced laws to bring about racial equality. The social advantages that opened up after the Revolution have resulted in the abolition of lily-white scenes. Mixed marriages raise no eyebrows in Cuba. Everyone shares a Cubanness. Black novelist Alice Walker, who knows Cuba well, has written, "Unlike black Americans, who have never felt at ease with being American, black Cubans raised in the Revolution take no special pride in being black. They take great pride in being Cuban. Nor do they appear able to feel, viscerally, what racism is." (A negative perspective is offered by Carlos Moore, an Afro-Cuban writer who left Cuba in 1963, in his *Castro, the Blacks, and Africa,* Center for Afro-American Studies, University of California, Los Angeles, 1988.) As a whole, Afro-Cubans are far healthier, better educated, and more skilled and confident than blacks in Brazil, Colombia, Panama, Jamaica, Haiti, or even the urban underclass of the United States. They enjoy the lowest rate of infant mortality in Latin America, the Caribbean, and that of black ghettoes in the United States. Hence, blacks are, on the whole, more loyal to Castro than whites.

There are still cultural barriers, however. The most marginal neighborhoods still have a heavy preponderance of blacks. Most Cuban blacks still work at menial jobs and earn, on average, less than whites. Blacks are notoriously absent from the upper echelons of government. And blacks were, until recently, nowhere to be seen in the tourist industry. (Since 1994,

when Havana witnessed what were essentially race riots, the government has been promoting black officials and elevating blacks to more prominent positions in tourism.) Nor has the Revolution totally overcome stereotypical racial thinking and prejudice. Black youths, for example, claim to be disproportionately harassed by police (though, ironically, blacks are well represented among the uniformed police). They're also far more likely to come up against tourist apartheid, such as being prevented from entering hotel lobbies. And you still hear racist comments. Still, most racial references—and Cuba is full of them—are well-meaning (see *Cuban Spanish* in the *Resources* section).

AfroCuba Web (www.afrocubaweb.com) offers information on all things related to Afro-Cuban affairs.

CHARACTER, CONDUCT, AND CUSTOMS

Although a clear Cuban identity has emerged, Cuban society is not easy to fathom. Cubans "adore mystery and continually do their damnedest to render everything more intriguing. Conventional rules do not apply," thought author Juliet Barclay. "When it came to ambiguity, Cuba was the leader of the pack," added author Pico Iyer. "An ironist can have a field day." The Cubans value context and philosophical approach to life differs markedly from North America or northern Europe. Therefore, attempts to analyze Cuba through the North American value system are bound to be wide of the mark.

The Cubans are somewhat schizoid. In the four decades since the Revolution, most Cubans have learned to live double lives. One side is spirited, inventive, irrepressibly argumentative and critical, inclined to keep private shrines at home to both Christian saints and African gods, and profit however possible from the failings and inefficiencies of the state. The other side commits them to be good revolutionaries and to cling to the state and the man who runs it. When loyalists (those faithful to Fidel) speak of the "Revolution,"

SPANISH SURNAMES

Spanish surnames are combinations of the first surname of the person's father, which comes first, and the mother's first surname, which comes second. Thus, the son of Ángel Castro Argiz and Lina Ruz González is Fidel Castro Ruz.

After marriage, women do not take their husbands' surnames; they retain their maiden names.

A single woman is addressed as *señorita* if less than 40 years old, and *señora* if above 40.

they don't mean the toppling of Batista's regime, or Castro's seizure of power, or even his and the country's conversion to Communism. They mean the ongoing process of building a society where everyone supposedly benefits. Most Cubans, regardless of their feelings for Castro, take varying degrees of pride in the "Revolution." Despite a pandemic of disaffection, many Cubans seem happy to accept the sacrifice of individual liberties for the abstract notion of improving equality. The incredible value system that has infused Cuban society and individuals with gracious and noble virtues has prerevolutionary antecedents: As early as 1929 T. Phillip Terry wrote of how the Cubans' "altruistic helpfulness for which no financial gain is expected is one of the most pleasing of the national characteristics."

The Cuban people are committed to social justice, and the idea that democracy includes every person's right to guaranteed health care and education is deeply ingrained in their consciousness. True, city folk crave the opportunity to better their lives materially, but few Cubans are concerned with the *accumulation* of material wealth. Instead, they find gratification in developing their strengths and, in rising to the challenges of love, restraint, and raising children. Most Cubans are more interested in sharing something with you than getting

something from you. They are unmoved by talk of your material accomplishments.

It is more important to enjoy life. Indeed, four decades of socialism has not changed the hedonistic culture of Cubans: The traditional Afro-Cuban tropical culture has proved resistant to puritanical revolutionary doctrine. They are sensualists of the first degree. Judging by the ease with which couples neck openly and spontaneously slip into bed, the dictatorship of the proletariat that transformed Eastern Europe into a perpetual Sunday school has made little headway in Cuba. The state may promote the family, but Cubans have a notoriously indulgent attitude towards casual sex. Infidelity is "as Cuban as sugarcane," suggests Ann Louise Bardach (see the *Sexual Mores* section, and the sidebar *Prostitution, or Merely Permissive?*, both in this chapter).

Cubans are also notoriously toilet- and fashion-conscious. Even the poorest Cuban manages to keep fastidiously clean and well dressed. It has been said that "to take away their soap would be Castro's greatest folly. Almost anything else can be tolerated, but take away their soap and the regime would fall!"

The struggles of the past four decades have fostered a remarkable sense of confidence and maturity. As such, there's no reserve, no emotional distance, no holding back. Cubans are self-assured and engage you in a very intimate way. They're not afraid of physical contact; they touch a lot. They also look you in the eye: They don't blink or flinch but are direct and assured. And free of social pretension. They're alive and full of emotional intensity, and chock-full of *chispas* (sparks).

Social Divisions

The Revolution destroyed the social stratification inherited from Spanish colonial rule. Distinct delineations among the classes withered away. Not that prerevolutionary Cuba was entirely rigid—it was unusual in Latin America for its high degree of "social mobility." Castro's father, for example, was a poor farm laborer when he emigrated from Spain but rose to become a wealthy landowner. Prerevolutionary life was not simply black and white, rich and poor. There was a huge middle class.

As an agrarian-populist movement pitted against Havana-based middle-sector interests, *fidelismo* warred against the middle class and destroyed it, eradicating the hard-earned wealth of hundreds of thousands and tearing families asunder. The "privileged" classes were replaced by a new class of senior Communist Party members and army officials who control everything and enjoy benefits unavailable to other Cubans (who call them *chupadores,* bloodsuckers).

Cubans lack the social caste system that makes so many Europeans walk on eggshells. There is absolutely no deference, no subservience. Cubans accept people at face value and are slow to judge others negatively. They are instantly at ease, and greet each other with hearty handshakes or kisses. Women meeting for the first time will embrace like sisters. A complete stranger is sure to give you a warm *abrazo,* or hug. Cubans call each other *compañero* or *compañera,* which Martha Gellhorn described as having a "cozy sound of companionship." Even the most fleeting acquaintances will offer you a meal, or go out of their way to help you however they can. As a foreigner, you'll meet with the warmest courtesies wherever you go. Every Cuban wants to open his or her home and is eager to please, uncommonly generous, extremely courteous and gracious, and self-sacrificing to a fault. Cubans can't understand why foreigners are always saying, "Thank you!" Doing things for others is the expected norm. There is a profound spirituality to the Cubans, who give love because they have little else to give.

In the current crisis, however, society is unraveling, a stratified society is emerging, and the values and ethics are becoming strained. Prostitution is once again rampant. An economic elite of *masetas* (rich Cubans) has become visible, as has a class of desperately impoverished, along with class resentments and tensions. And low-level corruption, long a necessity for getting around Cuba's socialist inefficiencies, has blossomed into more insidious high-level graft and racketeering. Many people are alternately sad and high-spirited, and Cuba has the world's thirteenth-highest suicide rate (18.2 per 100,000 Cubans, almost double that of the United States), the greatest cause of death between the ages of 15 and 45. The *jiniteras,* the petty thieves on the streets, the children who now resort to begging: all these things are the result of Cuba's poverty. The principles of the New Man are being eroded (see the sidebar The *"New Man"*). "The world is poorer for the loss of that intangible, optimistic, altruistic spirit," says Saul Landau. Indeed it is.

Cuban Curiosity

A sense of isolation and a high level of cultural development have filled Cubans with intense curiosity. In the country, few Cubans have ever traveled beyond a 50-mile radius of their homes. One reason why so many Cubans ask foreigners *"¿Qué hora es?"* is to strike up a conversation. Another reason is that they really do need to know the time in a country where time stopped years ago. They will guess at your nationality and quiz you about the most prosaic matters of Western life, as well as the most profound. Issues of income and costs are areas of deep interest, and you may be questioned in intimate detail. Sexual relations arouse equally keen interest, and Cubans of both genders are often excited to volunteer their services to help guide Cupid's arrow.

On one hand, the average Cuban is far more educated and worldly than the average U.S. citizen. Yet Cubans are also starved of much information. In private, they pepper you with questions. They watch Hollywood movies and often converse with a surprising mix of worldly erudition and astounding naïveté. If you tell them you are a *yanqui,* most Cubans light up. They are genuinely fond of U.S. citizens. However, although Cubans thrive on debate, they are hesitant to discuss politics openly except behind closed doors. Only in private, and once you have earned their trust, will you be able to gauge how they really feel about Cuba and Castro.

THE CUBAN-AMERICANS

There are more than one million Cuban-born people in the United States, half of them naturalized citizens, according to the U.S. Census Bureau. They are concentrated in Dade County, Florida, and New Jersey. Their capital is Miami, just 140 miles from Havana – a distance protracted by a generation of despair, hubris, and bile. Even Fidel has family in exile, and not just his errant daughter Alina, who has called her father a "tyrant" and "mediocrity," and his granddaughter, but also his sister Juanita, who fled to Miami in the early 1960s and speaks out against the pain and turmoil her brother has caused.

The "old guard" (*destierros*, or *"gusanos"* – worms, as Castro called them) were forced to flee Cuba, where they formed the wealthy and middle classes, shortly after the Revolution. Many were corrupt *batistianos* who have grown inordinately powerful, infusing Miami politics and business with their repressive, anti-democratic, illicit, and profane ways. Many of these Cuban-Americans have grown militant with distance and time, cultivating delusion "like hothouse orchids," in the words of Cristina García (their leaders have even bankrolled terrorists such as Luis Posada Carriles, who took credit for bombing a Cuban commercial airliner, killing all 73 aboard; see the sidebar *The "Cuban Five"* in this chapter). They can't get over their bitterness, not least because Fidel Castro won't let them. Says Walter Russell Mead: "Castro destroyed the world the exiles knew and loved... over the decades, he has showered them with infamy and filth and done his best to offend every patriotic, religious, and personal sensibility they have. Miami is furious, and Castro knows how to twist the knife to keep the wounds always fresh."

The Cuban-American National Foundation (CANF, www.canf.org), the largest and by far the richest and most powerful of the exile groups, for long considered itself the Cuban government in exile and has been more or less treated as such by U.S. administrations. The CANF's powerful founder and former chairman, Jorge Mas Canosa, made no secret of his desire to be president of post-Castro Cuba. His death in 1997 left the old anti-Castro faction in disarray, boosting the moderate voice. Florida's Cuban community is now divided between the hard-line old guard and those who arrived in the past two decades (mainly for economic reasons) who now form more than 50 percent of Cuban-Americans, maintain closer ties with their families in Cuba, and hold less passionate anti-Castro political views. Similarly, younger American-born second-generation Cuban-Americans display less hard-line attitudes toward Castro.

Moderates, such as Cambio Cubano (Cubans for Change), the Cuban Committee for Democracy, and the Cuban-American Alliance Education Fund, want to see a measured policy, including direct negotiations with Castro to encourage phased-in democracy and avoid a period of anarchy and civil war. These centrist groups have limited influence however; they can't get Washington's ear because the right wing has out-organized and outspent them. However, the moderate voice is getting stronger and was undoubtedly assisted by the Elian González debacle (see *Into the New Millennium* in the *History* section of this chapter), and in 2004 when the Bush administration imposed travel restrictions to Cuba by Cuban-Americans, creating a new groundswell of anti-embargo sentiment within the community.

HARDBALL POLITICS

Contemporary U.S. policy toward Cuba is largely shaped by the hard-nosed constituency, which has pumped millions of dollars into the U.S. political system. Democrats attempt to win their votes by appearing more anti-Castro than the Republicans. The powerful right-wing Cuban-American lobby is dead-set against any wide-ranging U.S.-Cuba talks and works hard to keep Washington from cutting a deal. Its fanaticism is so unyielding that U.S. Congressman Lincoln Díaz-Balart (R-Florida), first cousin to Castro's son Fidelito (his father was Castro's brother-in-law and head of Batista's much-feared security services), and fellow Cuban-American Republican Congresswoman Ileana Ros-Lehtinen (whose campaign manager was Jeb Bush) even blocked a contribution of food aid to the U.N. World Food Program intended to stem critical food shortages caused by two years of severe drought in Cuba. (Díaz-Balart has made no secret of the fact that he hopes to replace his former uncle by marriage.)

Like King Lear, the extremist Cuban-American lobby is so caught up in desire for vengeance that it has been blinded by its own rage, unable to see itself as the unwitting fulcrum upon which Castro levers Washington's policy. Thus whenever Washington has showed signs of seeking rapprochement with Castro, the Cuban leader (who has displayed little desire to see the embargo lifted) creates a crisis to which the CANF reacts like Pavlov's dog. Says columnist Walter Mead: "Time after time, [Castro] plays them like a violin. He can provoke them into paroxysms of gibbering rage, he can lock them into self-destructive political opinions, he can even turn their greatest strength – their ability to monopolize the American political debate over Cuba policy – into a pillar propping up his regime."

Many powerful Cuban-Americans don't want to see a change for reasons of personal gain. Says Saul Landau: "A small group of rich and extreme right-wing Cubans – some of whom have clear connections to terrorism – use anti-Castroism to control U.S. policy and thereby increase their own power and for-

tunes." The embargo has become a linchpin of their domestic clout, including control over the financially lucrative Radio and TV Martí transmissions into Cuba. Cuban-American companies also lobby hard to maintain the embargo: the exiled Fanjul family has become Florida's largest sugar producer; Bacardi is the world's largest rum producer (lawyers for both companies were instrumental in writing the Helms-Burton Bill). It is hardly conceivable that they would wish to see Cuban sugar and rum enter the U.S. market!

THE VIEW FROM CUBA

The Cuban government portrays the rightist exiles (which it calls the "Miami Mafia") as the top rung of a class structure that left a racist society and carried their prejudice with them – "had Elián González been black, they would have tossed him back into the sea," suggests Ann Louise Bardach. No Cubans see the CANF leadership defending free health or education or the interests of the elderly and poor. They also fear that their homes and land will be sold from under them if the ultraconservative exiles ever return to power. It's a well-founded fear. Many Cuban-Americans are determined to gain back what they left behind, while others seem eager to make money from selling off Cuban assets.

The best primer on the subject is Ann Louise Bardach's *Cuba Confidential* (see *Suggested Reading* in *Resources*).

Many families are torn by divided feelings towards the Revolution and Castro and don't even talk with one another. The worst divisions, fired by true hatred, are found among family split between those who departed for Miami and those who stayed. *Se fue* (he/she left) and *se quedó* (he/she stayed) carry profound meaning. Every year tens of thousands plot their escapes to Miami, often without telling their relatives, and sometimes not even the spouse. Cubans thus tend to evolve speedy relationships and/or grasp at opportunity. "All the Cubans' experience tells them that there is no

time to go slow, that pleasures and love must be taken fast when they present themselves because tomorrow... *se fue*," wrote Lightfoot.

Humor

Despite their hardships, Cubans have not lost the ability to laugh. Their renowned humor is called the "yeast for their buoyant optimism about the future." Stand-up comedy is a tradition in Cuban nightclubs. *Chistes*—jokes—race around the country. Cubans turn everything into a *chiste,* most of which are aimed at themselves. Theirs is a penetrating black humor that spares no one—the insufferable bureaucrat, *jiniteras,* the Special Period. There are no sacred cows. Not even Fidel—perhaps especially not El Jefe—is spared the barbs, although his name is never used (the silent reference is usually communicated by the gesture of a hand stroking a beard), and no one in his right mind would tell such a joke in public.

Cubans also boast a great wit. They lace their conversations with double entendres and often risqué innuendo. The Spanish-speaking foreigner is left behind by subtle inflections and Cuban idioms.

The Nationalist Spirit

Cubans are an intensely passionate and patriotic people united by nationalist spirit and love of country. They are by culture and tradition politically conscious. The revolutionary government has engaged in consciousness-raising on a national scale, instilling in Cubans that they can have pride as a nation. Primary school children not only lisp loyalty to the flag daily at school, they recite their willingness to *die* for it.

Cubans are nationalists before they are socialists or even incipient capitalists. Cubans had not expected socialism from the Revolution, but those who could accept it did so not simply because so many benefited from the social mobility the Revolution had brought but because, as Maurice Halperin suggests, "it came with nationalism; that is, an assertion of economic and political independence from the United States, the goal of Cuban patriots for a half century." This reality provides Cubans with a different perspective and viewpoint on history.

Labor and the Work Ethic

Cubans combine their southern joy of living with a northern work ethic that makes them unique achievers. Through the centuries, Cuba has received a constant infusion of the most energetic people in the Caribbean, what author James Michener calls "a unique group, one of the strongest cultural stocks in the New World": the wealthier, better-educated, and most motivated colonizers fleeing rebellion

and invasion on Haiti, Santo Domingo, and Jamaica. The entrepreneurial spirit isn't dead, as attested by the success of the self-employed that sprang up in 1993 before being quashed by crippling taxation and state harassment. The Cuban government likes to present the self-employed as a parasitic *nouveau riche* (in actuality, says Catherine Moses, "this class of conspicuous consumers is usually thought of by peso-earning Cubans as being comprised of the privileged children of high-level Party officials," known derisively to Cubans as *los hijos de Papá,* which roughly translates as the "brat pack").

The vast majority of Cubans work for the state, which with few exceptions dictates where an individual will work. However, a huge proportion of the adult population is unemployed or has no productive work, despite official figures that 98 percent of adults are employed. Thus the degree of anomie is great. Many Cubans ask their doctor friends to issue *certificados* (medical excuses) so that they can take a "vacation" from the boredom of employment that offers little financial reward and little hope of promotion. *Socio* is the buddy network, used to shield you from the demands of the state. *Pinche* and *mayimbe* are your high-level contacts, those who help you get around the bureaucracy, such as the doctor who writes a false note to relieve you of "voluntary" work in the countryside. Meanwhile, so many teachers have left their profession to work in tourism, where they can earn tips and put food on the table, that tourism companies are now forbidden from hiring teachers.

The improvements in the living standards among rural families in the early decades of the Revolution have not been enough to keep the younger generation on the land. There has been a steady transfer of workers from agricultural to industrial and service-oriented jobs. Following the onset of the Special Period, migration from the *campos* accelerated—the government has since banned such freedom of movement. To make up for the labor shortfall, Castro invented "volunteer" brigades. Urban workers, university students, and even school-

THE "NEW MAN"

A key goal of the Revolution has been the elimination of individualism, as laid out by Che Guevara in his essay "Man and Socialism in Cuba." By removing market forces and profit or personal gain, replacing these with production for the social good and planning instead of market "anarchy," a new individual would emerge committed to a selfless motivation for the communal good. Castro agreed with Guevara – though probably for practical, not philosophical, motives – and a revolution to create the New Man was launched. It called for collective spartanism.

The government moved to censure work for personal benefit. Bonuses and other financial incentives were replaced with "moral incentives"; consumerism was replaced by the notion of "collective and individual satisfaction" from work. Private enterprise and trade were banned. Ideological debate was quelled. Apathy was frowned upon. And psychological and other pressures bore down on anyone who refused to go along with the new values imposed from above.

For many Cubans, the idea of the New Man struck a resonant chord (unless, of course, you were one of the unfortunates whose business or property were being seized). There was nothing the believers wouldn't do. The state didn't even need to ask. "No one worked from eight to five," a 59-year-old woman told reporter Lynn Darling. "You worked around the clock. The horizons were open. We had a world to conquer, a world to give to our grandchildren."

Over time, an intrinsic sense of egalitarianism and dignity was nourished and seeped into the Cuban persona as many individuals strove to embody the New Man ideal. Of course, not everyone agreed: more than a million Cubans opted to leave rather than suffer the crushing suppression of individual freedoms that the effort to create the New Man required.

---

children are shipped to the countryside to toil in the fields as *microbrigadistas*. Although the legal minimum working age is 17, the Labor Code exempts 15- and 16-year-olds to allow them to fill labor shortages. Volunteer workers get an *estímulo*, a reward, such as priority listing for apartments. There are moral rewards and material rewards—perhaps a week at Varadero, or the right to buy a refrigerator—for other workers.

Wages are according to a salary scale of 22 levels, with the top level getting six times that of the lowest. Highly trained professionals share the same struggles as unskilled workers. Life is little different for those who earn 225 pesos (US$10, the official minimum wage as of May 2005) a month and those who earn 850 (US$34). Pensioners get between 110 and 200 pesos monthly, depending on whether they live with family or alone, and are the most impoverished sector of society. Many workers receive no salary; instead they are paid in kind. Moreover, workers such as waiters in tourist restaurants have to pay for broken crockery, missing cutlery, or if a client walks out without paying; they're also obliged to "donate" half their earnings to state-controlled "humanitarian funds"—advertised in hotel lobbies to impress tourists—without any accountability whatsoever. (And though the government receives US$450 monthly per Cuban worker from foreign hotel partners, the government pockets the money and workers are paid a normal salary in near-worthless pesos; this policy is the source of a lawsuit filed in June 1999 on behalf of the Cuban Committee for Human Rights.)

Such wages don't go far in contemporary Cuba. The system is set up so that no matter how hard a Cuban works, he or she can't really get ahead. Denied the means of self-advancement, most Cubans are left treading water, unable to accumulate resources by which to improve their lot (the Communist elite is a clear exception, and many have aggrandized themselves). Tens of thousands are trapped in

PROSTITUTION, OR MERELY PERMISSIVE?

"What effect is dollarization having on families and society?" asked one of [the journalists]. Said Maruetti [a Cuban economist], looking bureaucratically oblivious, "Number One: foreign investment. Two: intensive development of tourism. Three: opening to foreign trade." Sis had been out hitchhiking and someone made a foreign investment in her. It's all part of Cuba's intensive development of tourism. And, boy, is she open to foreign trade.

– P. J. O'Rourke

Before the Revolution, Batista's Babylon offered a tropical buffet of sin: Castro declared that there were 100,000 prostitutes in Havana, about ten times the true figure. In 1959, the revolutionary government closed down the sex shows and porn palaces and sent the prostitutes to rehabilitative trade schools, thereby ostensibly eliminating the world's oldest trade. Prostitution reappeared, however, within a few years. Fred Ward recorded in 1977 how "a few girls have been appearing once again in the evenings, looking for dates, and willing to trade their favors for goods rather than money."

Jiniteras – the word comes from *jineta*, horsewoman, or jockey – have always been part of the postrevolutionary landscape, especially at embassy functions (the Cuban government, claimed Guillermo Cabrera Infante, has always made "state mulattas" available to foreign dignitaries, for whom it even maintains a "discreet house of select prostitutes" in Jaimanitas, according to journalist Pedro Alfonso). Critics even claim that in the early 1990s, the Cuban government sponsored the island's image as a cheap sex paradise to kick-start tourism. The situation reached its nadir when Rumbos, a Cuban tourism company, was stung by allegations of exporting "dancing girls" to Latin America, while in 1999 a Mexican company, Cubamor, was accused of operating organized sex tours with official connivance.

THE GOVERNMENT'S RESPONSE

"The state tries to prevent it as much as possible. It is not legal in our country to practice prostitution, nor are we going to legalize it. Nor are we thinking in terms of turning it into a freelance occupation to solve unemployment problems. We are not going to repress it either," Castro told *Time* magazine, while boasting that Cuba had the healthiest and best-educated prostitutes in the world.

However, the Cuban government was clearly stung by foreign media reports on the subject. In 1996, Cuban women were barred from tourist hotels, and the police initiated a crackdown. A mandatory two-year jail term (since increased to four years) was imposed for any female the government considers a "prostitute." Thousands of young women (many of them innocent females) were picked up on the streets and jailed, while anyone without an official Havana address was returned to her home in the countryside. Several provinces temporarily banned sexual relations between Cubans and tourists entirely.

Nonetheless, sexual relations between tourists and Cubans continue. Foreigners may legally bed with Cubans in *casas particulares* (see *Cuban Guests* in the *Accommodations* section of the *Essentials* chapter). Many cabaret showgirls operate a kind of unofficial prostitutes' guild. And *jiniteras* continue to work the major tourist discos and bars with the complicity of the staff (and often of local police). Cuban males, too, tout themselves as gigolos and are often warmly received by foreign females seeking Cuban lovers.

Like everything in Cuba, the situation is complex and needs some explaining.

A CHANCE TO GET AHEAD – AND GET AWAY

The women who form intimate relationships with tourists are a far cry from the uneducated prostitutes of Batista days. Most are ordinary Cubans who would laugh to be called *jiniteras*. A recent study by the Federation of Cuban Women (FMC) declared that even among *jiniteras*, "Most have the benefit of extensive educational opportunity compared to the lot of their sisters before the Revolution. Most are not ashamed [and] few have low self-esteem.

... Instead, what motivates these women... is the desire to go out, to enjoy themselves, go places where Cubans are not allowed to go." They're seeking a *papiriqui con guaniquiqui* (a sugar daddy) as a replacement for a paternalistic government that can no longer provide even the basics. Says writer Coco Fusco, "on the street these women are seen as heroic providers whose sexual power is showing up the failures of an ailing macho regime."

A pretty *cubana* attached to a generous suitor can be wined and dined and get her entrance paid into the discos, drinks included, to which she otherwise wouldn't have access. Many women hook up with a man for the duration of his visit in the hope that a future relationship may develop. No small number succeed in snagging foreign husbands. Their dream is to live abroad — to find a foreign boyfriend who will marry them and take them away.

It happens all the time, especially for good-looking *negras de pelo* (black women with straight hair). "Italian and German men are *locos* for *negras y mulatas de pelo*," says Lety, in Isadora Tattlin's *Cuban Diaries*. "'Ay, being *una negra de pelo* in Cuba is as good as having a visa to Canada or western Europe, guaranteed. And being *una negra* with blue eyes' — Lety shakes her fingers again, like they have been scalded — 'when the girl turns fourteen, people say, '*el norteño* is coming, *chica*, pack your bags!'"

In a society where promiscuity is rampant and sex on a first date is a given, any financial transaction — assuredly, more in one night in *fula* (dollars) than she can otherwise earn in a month's salary in worthless pesos — is reduced to a charitable afterthought to a romantic evening out. Thus, educated and morally upright Cuban women — doctors, teachers, accountants — smile at tourists passing by on the street or hang out by the disco doorways, seeking affairs and invitations, however briefly, to enjoy a part of the high life.

Sex is legal at the age of 16 in Cuba, but under Cuban and international law foreigners can be prosecuted for sex with anyone under 18 (*menores de edad*). Foreign males intending to have sexual relations with a Cuban female should always be sure to check her *carnet* to determine her age; note that discos permit entry to anyone 15 years of age or older, and many "women" in discos are *menores de edad*.

If you know of anyone who is traveling to Cuba with the intent of sexually abusing minors, contact **Interpol** (France tel. 33/4-72-44-71-63, www.interpol.int); the **Task Force for the Protection of Children from Sexual Exploitation in Tourism** (World Tourism Organization, Haya 42, 28020 Madrid, Spain, tel. 91/567-81-72, fax 91/571-82-19, www.world-tourism.org); or the **U.S. Customs Service** (International Child Pornography Investigation and Coordination Center, 45365 Vintage Park Rd., Suite 250, Sterling, VA 20166, 703/709-9700, icpicc@customs.sprint.co).

a poverty from which there is no escape. There are few safety nets for injured or unemployed workers, no avenues to sue for safety violations, and no independent labor unions in Cuba to challenge blatant exploitation or to fight for workers' rights.

Cuban Passivity

Politically the majority of Cubans—those not firmly committed to the political apparatus—are weighed down with passivity. Open demonstrations against the government are extremely rare. Those who touch the third rail of government displeasure are swiftly dealt with. Few dare take such a step. Silence, congruity, and complicity—pretending to be satisfied and happy with the system—are cultural reflexes that have been called indicative of cultural decay. Jacobo Timerman's *Cuba: A Journey* provides a baneful look at this passivity.

Sexual Mores

Cuba is a sexually permissive society. As journalist Jacobo Timerman wrote, "Eros is amply gratified in Cuba and needs no stimulation." A joyous eroticism pervades Cuban men and women alike, transcending the hang-ups of essentially puritanical Europe or North America. Seduction is a national pastime pursued by both sexes—the free expression of a high-spirited people confined in an authoritarian world. After all, Cubans joke, sex is the only thing Castro can't ration.

Cubans had elevated eroticism into "national genius" long before 1959, but Cubans' overt sexuality owes much to the revolution. Che Guevara's widow, Aleida March, told biographer Jon Lee Anderson that women were "throwing themselves" at the *barbudos* after the Triumph of the Revolution and that, "Well—with a big smile as if to indicate it was quite a scene—there had been a lot of 'lovemaking' going on." Thus the tone was set early, noted Lois Smith and Alfredo Padula, by a "bacchanal in which the triumphant revolutionaries and euphoric nation celebrated between the sheets." Cuban sexuality has ever since defied the efforts of the Revolution to tame and control it.

Promiscuity is rampant. So are extramarital affairs ("infidelity is the national sport," says Ann Louise Bardach). Love is not associated with sex. Both genders are unusually bold. Men and women let their eyes run slowly over strangers they find attractive. Long glances—*ojitos*—often accompanied by uninhibited comments, betray envisioned improprieties. Even the women murmur *piropos* (catcalls or courtly overtures) and sometimes comic declarations of love.

In a country where consumer pleasures are few and far between, casual sex has become the most desirable and available leisure activity among youth. Teenagers become sexually active at an average age of 14, according to Cuba's National Center for Sex Education, which dispenses sex counseling to youths, along with condoms and birth control pills. Regardless of age, one is *expected* to enjoy sex, and as much of it as one can handle, regardless of gender orientation.

Nonetheless, pornography is expressly forbidden (though an underground video market exists), as are sex parties, adult stores, and the like.

Homosexuality

Cuban homosexuals must find it ironic that the heart of the homosexual world is Castro Street in San Francisco. It is assuredly not named in El Jefe's honor, as gays—called *maricones* (queens), *mariposas* (butterflies), *pájaros* (birds), *patos* (ducks), or *gansos* (geese) in the Cuban vernacular (and *tortillas* for "dykes")—were persecuted following the Revolution. Castro (who denies the comment) supposedly told journalist Lee Lockwood that a homosexual could never "embody the conditions and requirements of a true revolutionary." Before 1959, the most visible expression of homosexuality was in prostitution, which led to support for the Stalinist notion that homosexuality was a product of capitalist decadence. Thus, homosexuals were among the groups identified as "undesirable."

Castro says that such prejudices were a product not of the Revolution but of the existing social milieu. "We inherited male chauvinism—and many other bad habits—from the conquistadores," he told Tomás Borge in *Face to Face with Fidel Castro* (Ocean Press, 1992). "That historical legacy... influenced our attitude toward homosexuality." At the time, the gay rights movement had not yet been born in the United States and the same prejudices that the revolutionaries inherited about homosexuals were prevalent elsewhere in the world, too.

Thus gays and lesbians met with "homophobic repression and rejection" in Cuba, just as they did in the United States. In Cuba, however, it was more systematic and brutal. The pogrom began in earnest in 1965; homosexuals were arrested and sent to agricultural work and reeducation camps—UMAP (Units for Military Help to Agricultural Production). Echoing Auschwitz, over the gate of one such camp in Camagüey was the admonition: "Work Makes You Men." Many brilliant intellectuals lost their jobs because they were gay or accused of being gay through anonymous denunciation. Homosexuality was also considered an aberration of nature that could weaken the family structure. Hence homosexuals were not allowed to teach, become doctors, or occupy positions from which they could "pervert" Cuban youth.

Although UMAP camps closed in 1968 and those who had lost their jobs were reinstated and given back pay, periodic purges occurred throughout the 1970s and early '80s. Julian Schnabel's acclaimed 1999 movie *Before Night Falls,* based on the life of the gay writer Reinaldo Arenas, chronicles the brutality of the period. Understandably, many homosexuals left—or were forced to leave—on the Mariel boatlift. However, by the mid-1980s, Cuba began to respond to the gay rights movement that had already gained momentum worldwide. Officially the new position is that homosexuality and bisexuality are no less natural or healthy than heterosexuality. In 1987, a directive was issued to police to stop harassment. And an official atonement was made through the release at the 1993 Havana Film Festival of *Vidas paralelas* (Parallel Lives) and *La bella de Alhambra* (The Beauty at the Alhambra), and the hit movie *Fresa y chocolate* (Strawberry and Chocolate).

However, persecution and discrimination continue. Gay organizations, magazines, and clubs are banned.

Not Because Fidel Castro Says So (1988) by Graciela Sanchez, and *Gay Cuba* (1995) by Sonja de Vries, are documentary films that look candidly at the treatment of gays in Cuba since the Revolution, while *Gladys, A Cuban Mother* (2001) by Xavier-Daniel documents the life of a lesbian mother living in a society driven by machismo. You can order copies from Frameline (145 9th St. #300, San Francisco, CA 94103, tel. 415/703-8650, www.frameline.org).

LIFE IN CUBA

On the eve of the Revolution, Cuba was a semi-developed country with more millionaires than anywhere south of Texas, a rapidly evolving capitalist infrastructure, and an urban labor force that had achieved "the eight-hour day, double pay for overtime, one month's paid vacation, nine days' sick leave, and the right to strike." On the other hand, in 1950, a World Bank study

team reported that 40 percent of urban dwellers and 60 percent of rural dwellers were undernourished, while over 40 percent of Cuban people had never gone to school and only 60 percent had regular full-time employment.

The Revolution immeasurably improved the material and spiritual condition of millions of Cubans, eliminating the most abject poverty while destroying the middle and wealthy urban classes, emasculating individualism, and imposing a general paucity, if not poverty, on millions of others. But at least everyone had the essentials and enjoyed two two-week vacations a year at the beach. And the government provided five crates of beer as a wedding present and birthday cakes for kids under 10. (The state still issues a nightgown to a bride and also to pregnant women, "causing some irreverent wags to note that these were exactly the two times when a woman least needed one," says Georgie Ann Geyer.)

The 1990s were devastating for a population accustomed to a higher standard of living. The worst year, 1993, was "so hard, so difficult, so terrible," said Castro. Only in 1995 did things begin to improve in the cities. In the countryside, however, things threaten to come full circle as the government drastically cuts back its investments in sugar. Campesinos whose families have depended for centuries on sugarcane are now unemployed, and entire communities now face the possibility of rural depression.

The Bare Essentials

Row upon row of citrus trees grow just 30 miles from Havana, but it is near impossible to find an orange for sale. Vast acres of state farms and cooperatives go unfarmed, while cultivated land goes virtually untended. What happens to the food produced is a mystery. Hospitals, schools, and work canteens get priority, but almost nothing reaches the state groceries—almost 40 percent of produce is stolen as it passes through the distribution system known as *acopio.* The campesinos do okay. But many urban dwellers go without. The *libreta*—the ration book meant to supply every Cuban citizen with the basic essentials—provides, at best, supplies

Every Cuban is entitled to a monthly ration of basic necessities. This youth is picking up his family's allowance at the local *bodega*.

for perhaps 10 days per month. Cubans must pick up their rations from the *bodega* on the first of the month, because by next day there may not be anything left.

So much is allowed per person from the state grocery store per month—six pounds of rice, eleven ounces of beans, five pounds of sugar, four ounces of lard, eight eggs (that's four omelettes)—although the items aren't always available. Candles, kerosene, and matches also appear in the ration books but are hardly ever in stock. Nor are cooking oil, household detergent, or soap. The average Cuban faces absences of everything you've probably taken for granted in life. Daily necessities such as toilet paper and luxury goods such as TVs are available to those with access to convertible pesos, although the government made a symbolic improvement in Cubans' lives in spring 2005 when Castro announced that every household would receive a free pressure cooker and electric rice steamer.

The U.S. embargo—*el bloqueo*—worsens the situation by denying the export of U.S.-made goods to Cuba. Nonetheless, Cuba has no problem importing whatever it needs from other countries, and there's no shortage of U.S. products in Havana, from Marlboro cigarettes, Nikes, and Coca-Cola to computers and Mack trucks, imported through Mexico or other countries. Thousands of cars (including US$60,000 Mercedes taxis, and Audi, BMW, and Volvo rental cars) and buses are imported each year from Europe and Asia, and there's no shortage of computers for offices, nor of all the necessary imported furnishings to stock tourist hotels. And the pharmacies serving foreigners only are full of foreign-made medicines.

The real problem is that Cubans are paid virtual slave-labor wages in pesos but anything worth buying—including basic necessities—are sold by Cuban state enterprises for "convertible pesos" (obtainable only in exchange for foreign currency) at extortionate prices.

The Black Market and *Resolviendo*

The black market, known as the *bolsa* (the exchange), resolves the failings of the state-controlled economy. Most Cubans rely on the underground economy—*los bisneros*—doing business illegally; on theft or fortuitous employment; or, for the exceedingly fortunate, a wealthy relative or a lover abroad. The black market touches all walks of life. Gas station attendants sell gasoline "stretched" with kerosene (the good stuff is siphoned off and sold on the black market), while store managers routinely steal part of the state-supplied stock to sell on the *bolsa*. Illegal vendors surreptitiously knock on neighborhood doors selling everyday essentials, carrying out their trade *sotto voce* for fear of being caught. Even otherwise loyal Revolutionaries are forced to break the law to survive. (In October 2005, after disclosing that half the gasoline in the country was being stolen, Castro fired gas station attendants en masse and replaced them with thousands of university students and young Communist Party supporters.)

Cubans have always survived by *resolviendo*—the Cuban art of barter, the cut corner, the gray market where much of Cuba's economy operates. What the black market can't provide, the Cubans often take for themselves. During the early 1990s, when things were dire, offices were plundered for light bulbs, and restaurants had to chain the tableware to the table to stop it from walking off. In 1993 the government had no option but to legalize both farmers markets (*mercados agropecuarios*) and the dollar. As a result, black market prices tumbled in response to the law of supply and demand, but market prices remain high and a typical Cuban salary buys little. The average monthly wage in spring 2005 was 312 pesos (about US$14 at market exchange rates), yet meat in the farmers market can cost 25 pesos a pound, and black beans nine pesos. Fortunately, rent, food (at least that which is available on the rations), and utilities are so heavily subsidized that they are virtually free.

A few years ago a peso income had some value. Today it is virtually worthless. Life has become organized around a mad scramble for foreign currency and *pesos convertibles*. The lucky ones have access to family cash, known as *fula*, sent from Miami. Cubans joke about getting by on *fé*, Spanish for faith, but today an acronym for *familia extranjera*—family abroad. Cuban economists reckon that about 60 percent of the population now has some form of access to dollars. The rest must rely on their wits. Very little money from tourism, however, trickles down to the Cuban people, so that the majority of Cubans have to simply *buscar la forma*, find a way. Those with a few dollars might buy scarce products and then barter them to other Cubans who have no link to the dollar economy. One neighbor might bring another canned goods in exchange for fish. A third can get his car engine fixed in exchange for peanut butter.

Every morning people prepare to cobble together some kind of normalcy out of whatever the situation allows them. Cubans are masters at making the best of a bad situation. *Resolver* (to resolve, to overcome obstacles with ingenuity, spontaneity, and humor) and *conseguir* (to get or obtain) are two of the most commonly used verbs on the island. The very elderly with no access to foreign currency, however, fare extremely badly, and thousands are malnourished, existing in abject poverty at a level barely above *sobrevivencia;* mere survival.

For all the training and education of its population, Cuban technology is virtually nonexistent. Everything is a hand-me-down from the Soviet bloc or North America—mummified American cars, taped-together Russian biplanes, and 45-pound Chinese bicycles that resemble armor-plated tanks. Almost everything is broken, canceled, or closed. The staple of transport in cities is the horse-drawn cart. The staple for inter-city travel is the open-topped truck, often with jerry-rigged seating, but often without seats altogether. Cubans are moved about like cattle.

Having sacrificed for the Revolution for four decades, many Cubans are exhausted. It's a remarkable testament to the spirit of the people, and to the efficiency of the State Security apparatus and the power the system holds over people's lives, that they have been able to withstand the upheavals without grave social and political consequences. But then, there's always *la yuma*—the United States (from the 1957 film *3:10 to Yuma* starring Glenn Ford and Van Heflin)—beckoning just 90 miles away (in 1996, when the U.S. Interests Section held a lottery to issue 20,000 visas, it received 541,500 applications by the cut-off date). Cubans lucky enough to receive visas to emigrate to the United States are bilked by the Cuban government, which requires an official medical exam, US$400 for adults and US$200 for each child; and *carta blanca* or "letter of exit parole," US$150; in addition to a passport, US$50; airport tax, US$20; and, of course, the airline ticket. Meanwhile, the families' possessions are seized by the government; a state inspector takes an inventory immediately the lucky Cubans are notified of being granted a U.S. visa, and if anything is missing on the day of departure, the *carta blanca* is revoked and with it any chance of leaving.

Simple Pleasures

Invited to Moscow in the 1960s, archivist of the Cuban Revolution Carlos Franqui tried gamely to define its essence for jaded Soviet apparatchiks. Finally he exclaimed, "Look, we Cubans try to have fun with everything—cyclones, demonstrations, hunger, even war!" Knitted brows. Fun with war? Well, when they were fighting Batista's men in the Sierra Maestra, he explained, there was a three-hour truce so they could all have a dance.

Cuba has no *fiesta* tradition. The Cubans are too industrious for that—too busy playing volleyball or baseball or practicing martial arts while the other half whittles away the long, hot afternoons in the cool shade of arcaded balconies, playing dominoes, or making love. In rural areas pleasures are simple: cockfights, rodeos, fiestas, cigars, cheap rum, and sex. Urban life is more urbane, offering movies, discos, theater, cigars, cheap rum, and sex.

Cuban social life revolves around the family and friends and neighbors. Cubans are a gregarious people, and foreigners are often amazed by the degree to which Cubans exist in the public eye, carrying on their everyday lives behind wide-open windows open to the streets as if no one were looking. Cubans are also noisy folks. It is almost impossible to find peace and quiet in towns.

Nonetheless, for all its musical gaiety and pockets of passionate pleasure, life for the average Cuban is dreary, even melancholy. Socialist equality looks dismal as you contemplate the aged and impoverished walking around inconsolably as if they'd been castrated—*jaca* is the local term—and at a loss over their lives, ruminating over what has gone terribly wrong with a Revolution that held greater promise. Thousands of Cubans live, to greater or lesser degree, like Pedro Juan, the protagonist in the brilliant novel *Dirty Havana Trilogy,* who is forced to become a gigolo, a pimp, and a black marketeer, picking up incremental income wherever he can and finding relief from the repetitiveness of daily life in elemental hedonism. "Rum, women, marijuana, a little rumba whenever possible."

Living Conditions

Half an hour in Havana is enough to cure you of a taste for that distressed look so popular in Crate & Barrel stores.
— P. J. O'Rourke

Until the Revolution, government expenditures were concentrated mostly in and around Havana and the provincial cities. The countryside was neglected and had few sewers or plumbing, few paved roads or electricity. Rural housing was basic. According to the 1953 census, only 15 percent of rural houses had piped water, 54 percent had no toilet whatsoever, and 43 percent had no electricity. Since the Revolution, the government has concentrated its energies on developing the countryside. Most housing built since the Revolution (in both town and country) is concrete apartment block units of a standard Bulgarian design—the ugly Bauhaus vision of uniform, starkly functional workers' housing, which had the advantage of being cheap to build and, in theory, easy and cheap to maintain. Most were built by unskilled volunteer labor

Much housing is delapidated to the point of endangering the occupants.

and have not been maintained, adding salt to the wound of the aesthetic shortfall.

The typical country house, or *bohío,* is a time-honored low, one-story structure with thick walls to keep out the heat, built of adobe or porous brick covered with stucco painted blue, pink, green, or buff, and roofed with red tiles. It's often whitewashed within and has high ceilings; tall, barred, glassless windows; and cool stone or tile floors. But tens of thousands of rural dwellers still live in slum shacks of scrap tin and wood, woven bamboo, with dirt floors, and, if they're lucky, a thick thatched roof to keep out the rains. Most have a crude outhouse toilet, an open-air kitchen, and perhaps a well or a hand-pump for water. However, virtually every house on the island today has electricity (payments are made directly to state authorities), although everyone is subject to occasional blackouts (*apagones*), which come and go without warning, blowing precious fuses whenever the power surges.

Most cities ache with penury and pathos. Havana, sultry seductress of prerevolutionary days, has been a city in lamentable decline for more than a century, but policies since the Revolution have only hastened the tragic decay. Today she needs a million gallons of paint. Most prerevolutionary housing is deteriorated to a point of dilapidation (a 1999 report by the Havana municipal authorities admitted that 100,000 houses are officially considered unsafe, and 20 percent of the population live in housing considered to be in "precarious condition"—"a little shake, say five on the Richter scale, would bring 75 percent of Havana down in seconds flat," suggests Ben Corbett). Still, there *are* many fine, well-kept houses, and every city has a section that resembles its middle-class American counterpart. A large percentage of houses do not have hot water—it is normal for certain areas to have their water supply cut off for much of the day because demand outstrips supply—and even after four decades of socialist triumphalist rhetoric, many houses still have no water at all, including 8.7 percent that have no toilets whatsoever, according to the 2002 census.

In certain areas, conditions are now truly sordid. Many Cubans cling tenaciously to family life behind crumbling facades festooned with makeshift wiring and inside tottering buildings that should have faced the bulldozer's maw long ago. Many buildings have fallen masonry and piles of plaster on the floor, unpainted walls mildewed by the tropical climate, and stairs so dilapidated one is afraid to step onto them. The worst examples are hidden behind more substantial housing and often surrounded by garbage and leaking sewage. Everywhere the housing shortage is so critical that many Cubans live in a *barbecue,* a room divided in two. Due to lack of space, the high-ceilinged rooms of many old colonial buildings have been turned into two stories by adding new ceilings and wooden staircases. Several generations are often crowded together unwillingly; there is simply nowhere for the offspring to go—many adult "children" are forced to share the same bed as their parents.

By law, no renter can pay more than 10 percent of his or her salary in rent, and almost 80 percent of Cubans own their own homes. Martha Gellhorn noted: "Rents pile up like down payments year after year, until the sale price of the flat is reached, whereupon bingo, you become an old-fashioned capitalist owner." Those who owned houses before the Revolution have been allowed to keep them; those who fled Cuba had their property seized by the state. Cubans can swap their houses without state approval but cannot buy or sell them. Cash transactions involving houses are illegal, and for those that are approved, the government has the right to acquire the property at a sharp discount. Nice houses in good neighborhoods are often taken by the government for the political elite or for government offices. The laws are full of quicksand. For example, only houses of similar sizes may be swapped. And some neighborhoods have had their populations "frozen" by law, so that if a family of four wants to move out, no more than four may move in. Since there's no such thing as classified ads or websites for real estate, Cubans hang signs outside their homes announc-

ing *se permuta* ("For swap"). A swap can take years to arrange, after which the government must approve it—another year or so. Cubans can have their property seized for any number of seemingly minor infractions while others, after being moved out because the government claims their homes are no longer safe, are powerless when the government then refurbishes the building for its own ends.

Interiors often belie the dour impression received on the street. Rooms everywhere are kept spick-and-span and furnished with family photos, kitschy ceramic animals, plastic flowers, bisque doll babies, erotic posters, and other effusive knickknackery—and frequently a photo of Fidel, Che, or Camilo Cienfuegos, often as a safeguard to keep in good standing. Virtually every home in Cuba retains its original, tattered prerevolutionary furniture. Always there is a large refrigerator (Russian or prerevolutionary Yankee) and at least one TV, and the lucky ones with access to *fula* (dollars) usually have a VCR and perhaps some other electronics—though only a few trusted loyalists are permitted to own a computer. And usually there's a *perrito* (a small dog), as Cubans are animal lovers.

Most houses haven't seen a pot of paint in four decades and feature grimy walls and chipped tiles and often near-derelict bathrooms. Supplies for repairs are virtually impossible to find. Nails? Paint? Forget it. Everything has to be foraged. Why is there no paint? Because the centralized planning process is intent on meeting production quotas, not on allocating scarce resources for maintenance and repair, which are not foreseen in their plans. Spare parts aren't ordered to maintain sewers or electrical boxes, so over time everything is jerry-rigged and/or deteriorates without hope of repair.

Anyone who wants to repair or remodel a home must prove that all building materials were purchased from the state. (What little there is for sale in state stores is sold at vastly inflated prices: Black-market cement and other items—most of it stolen from government sources—sell at a fraction of official prices; the equivalent of Home Depot or Ace Hardware doesn't exist.) Hence, merely to fix a falling-down wall can lead to a home being confiscated. Meanwhile, municipal administration is a disaster. When telegraph poles fall down, no one moves them; when sidewalks collapse, no repairs are made; when pavements buckle, they go unattended.

Squatting is common, and homelessness is a growing problem.

CHILDREN AND YOUTH

One of the simplest pleasures for the foreign traveler is to see smiling children in school uniforms so colorful that they reminded novelist James Michener of "a meadow of flowers. Well nourished, well shod and clothed, they were the permanent face of the land." And well behaved, too! You almost never hear a child crying in Cuba, nor even a parent scolding their children.

Children are treated with as much indulgence by the state as by family members. The government has made magnificent strides to improve the lot of poor children—though, to be sure, many are still so poor they go without shoes. And it teaches youngsters magnificent values. Children are sworn in at the age of six to become Pioneros—Communist Pioneers— where they learn the virtues of public service doing duty, such as collecting litter.

After high school has ended, all Cuban males must perform two years of military service while most girls serve two years as *trabajadores sociales* doing social work; in late 2005, many girls were assigned to pump gas at service stations.

Youth are served by their own newspapers, such as *Pionero* and *Juventud Rebelde* (Rebel Youth).

The "I" Generation

More than 65 percent of the Cuban population was born after the Revolution. The older generation had attempted to make the Revolution, had faced down the threat of U.S. invasion, and had witnessed astounding social achievements—all through collective endeavor. Where their parents use "we," Cuba's youth use "I"—I

TURNING SWEET FIFTEEN

Four decades of socialism have killed off many traditional celebrations – but not *las fiestas de quince*, the birthday parties celebrating a girl's fifteenth birthday and her coming of age. There is nothing like a *quince* party (a direct legacy of a more conservative Spanish era) for a young *cubana*.

Parents will save money from the day the girl is born to do her right with a memorable fifteenth. A whole arsenal might be involved, from the hairdresser and dressmaker (a special dress resembling a wedding gown or a knock-'em-dead Scarlett O'Hara outfit is de rigueur) to the photographer and the classic American car with chauffeur to take the young woman and her friends to the party, usually featuring a feast of not-so-adult ice cream, sponge cake, and soft drinks.

want to do so and so. The majority are bored by the constant calls for greater sacrifice and tired of being treated as if they were stupid. They want to enjoy life like kids the world over, and in much the same way.

As the quest for U.S. dollars tightens its grip, an increasing number of Cuban youth are asking, "What's the point in studying?" A worrisome number of students are dropping out of class or playing truant. Many youths realize they can get further through their own work and savvy and are going into business for themselves as *jiniteros* and *cuenta propistas* (freelancers), making a buck driving taxis, while their sisters turn to dating foreign tourists. In recent studies to ascertain high school students' goals, almost every student stated a desire to work as a *cuenta propista* or with tourists.

The government worries that the increased association with foreign tourists helps foster nonconformism, such as the growing number of rap fans, Rastafarians, and long-haired youths—

Cuban youth learn the dance moves at an early age, and dance competitions are standard fare on the matinee scene.

roqueros and *frikis*—who sport ripped jeans and would look at home at a Metallica concert.

Cuban youth are expressing their individuality—they want to be themselves, which today means showing a marked preference for anything North American, especially in clothing. They wouldn't be caught dead in a *guayabera,* the traditional tropical shirt favored by older men (and considered a sure sign of someone who works for the government). Young women dress in the latest fashion—tight jeans, halter tops, mini-skirts, short shorts, diaphanous blouses, flared pants, and trendy platform shoes. Young men follow suit, though more conservatively, as well as their budgets allow. "Egotism" is flourishing (a cell phone is now de rigueur for those with the means to afford one). Consumerism is capturing the imagination of Cuban youth, spawned by the notion that the only way to advance is by making money.

FEMINISM AND MACHISMO

The country has an impressive record in women's rights. A United Nations survey ranks Cuba among the top 20 nations in which women have the highest participation in politics and business. Women make up 50 percent of university students and 60 percent of doctors, although they are still poorly represented in the highest echelons of government. A review of the University of Havana yearbooks shows that women were well represented *before* the Revolution also.

Law 1263, passed in 1974, guarantees women the same salaries as men. Women receive 18 weeks of paid maternity leave—six before the birth and the remainder after. Working mothers have the right to one day off with pay each month, or the option of staying home and receiving 60 percent of their full salary until the child reaches the age of six months. And every woman and girl can get free birth control assistance, regardless of marital status. The Cuban Family Code codifies that the male must share household duties.

Despite this, prejudices born of the patriarchal Spanish heritage still exist. Male machismo continues, and women walking down the street are often bombarded with comments ranging from *piropos* to forthright invitations to sex. And though the sexes may have been equalized, the Revolution has not been able to get the Cubanness out of Cuban women who, regardless of age, still adore coquetry.

RELIGION

Cuba was officially atheist from the early 1960s until 1992 (it has since officially been a secular state). Nonetheless, a recent government survey found that more than half of all Cubans are *creyentes,* believers of one sort or another.

Christianity

Cubans have always been relatively lukewarm about Christianity, and the church has never been strong in Cuba. In colonial times, there were few churches in rural districts, where it was usual for a traveling priest to call only once a year to perform baptisms and marriages. Moreover, the Catholic Church sided with the Spanish against the patriots during the colonial era and was seen by *criollos* as representing illiberalness and authoritarianism hand-in-hand with the Spanish crown.

Later, the Catholic Church had a quid pro quo with the corrupt Machado, Grau, and Batista regimes. When the Revolution triumphed, many of the clergy left for Miami along with the rich to whom they had ministered. The Catholic Church grew concerned as the Revolution moved left; when Fidel nationalized the church's lands, it became a focus of opposition. In August 1960, the Catholic bishops issued a pastoral letter formally denouncing the Castro government. Many priests were expelled and persecution began. Church attendance came to be considered antisocial. Practicing Catholics were banned from the Communist Party. Practitioners were harassed. Religious education was eliminated from the school curriculum, and a scientific understanding of the world was promoted.

In 1986 Fidel Castro performed an about face: Religion was no longer the opiate of the masses. In 1990, he admitted that "believers" had been unjustly treated. That year, radio and

television stations began transmitting religious music and songs. The following year, the Communist Party opened its doors to believers, and security agents disappeared from churches. It was a timely move, co-opting the shifting mood. The collapse of the Soviet Union and onset of the Special Period left a spiritual vacuum that has fed church attendance, while the number of seminarians has also skyrocketed. Castro has attempted to go with the rising tide, while recognizing, too, that the church has a valuable role to play in upholding ethical values in the face of flagging enthusiasm and growing doubt.

In November 1996, Castro met with Pope John Paul II in Rome. The pontiff's emotionally charged visit to Cuba in January 1998 was an extraordinary event that boosted the influence of the Catholic Church in Cuba and reignited an expression of faith among the Cuban people. As a goodwill gesture to the pope, Castro declared Christmas a holiday three decades after it was canceled. The pope's visit prompted a tidal flood of Protestant missionaries, notably Baptists and Methodists, who seem more fearful of the spread of "papism" than Communism. (Castro has preferred the Protestant church, with which he initiated a dialogue aimed at finding a strategy to unite atheists and believers. Though Protestantism was only introduced at the turn of the century, prerevolutionary Cuba evolved the highest percentage—almost 15 percent—of Protestants of any Latin American nation. Protestants are estimated to number about 300,000, with about 23 distinct churches represented.)

Skirmishes continue, however. The Catholic Church hierarchy has continued to be highly critical of the Castro government. Despite increased tolerance of the church, harassment continues. In December 1999 the pope, disappointed with the meager progress since his visit, urged Castro to respect human rights and display "a more generous opening."

A huge percentage of Cubans remain atheistic, or at least agnostic. A far larger percentage, however, are superstitious and believe to lesser or greater degree in *santería.* Even devout

Catholics will have a *limpieza* (ritual *santería* cleansing) performed to hedge their bets in times of need.

Santería

Santería, or saint worship, has been deeply entrenched in Cuban culture for 300 years. The cult is a fusion of Catholicism with the *Lucumí* religion of the African Yoruba tribes of modern-day Nigeria and Benin. Since slave masters had banned African religious practice, the slaves cloaked their gods in Catholic garb and continued to pray to them in disguise. Thus, in *santería,* Catholic figures are avatars of the Yoruban *orishas* (divine beings, or guardian spirits, of African animism worshiped in secretive and complex rituals that may feature animal sacrifices along with chanting, dancing, and music). Metaphorically *orishas* change their identity—even their gender—at midnight. By day, adherents may pray in front of a figure of Santa Barbara and at night worship the same figure as Changó. There are about 400 guardian spirits in the pantheon, but only about 20 are honored in daily life.

It is thought that the *orishas* control an individual's life, performing all kinds of miracles on a person's behalf. They are thus consulted and besought. A string of bad luck will be blamed on an *orisha* and must therefore be placated. They're too supreme for mere mortals to communicate with directly: *santeros* or *babalawos* (priests) act as go-betweens to interpret their commands for a fee. *Babalawos* use divination to interpret the *obi* and *ifá*—oracles—and solve everyday problems, notably those related to health, using pieces of dried coconut shells and seashells.

Many a home has a statue of a *santería* god and a glass of water to appease the spirits of the dead. Even Fidel Castro, a highly superstitious person, is said to be a believer. He had triumphed on January 1, a holy day for the *orishas.* The red and black flag of the revolutionaries was that of Eleguá, god of destiny. Then, on January 8, 1959, as Fidel delivered his victory speech before the nation, two doves flew over the audience and circled the brightly

---

SANTERÍA TERMS

Abakuá: Secret all-male society in Cuba

Babalawo: High priest of Lucumi

Batá: Set of three drums of Yoruba origin – *iya, itotele,* and *okonkolo* – used in *santería*

Cajón: Crate or box having a predominantly bass tone, which is sat on and played during a rumba

Changó: The mighty *orisha* of fire, thunder, and lightning

Elegguá: Messenger of all *orishas;* guardian of the crossroads and god of destiny

Fundamento: A strict set repertoire of rhythms for each *orisha* and/or the essence of playing traditional *batá*

Iyawó: *Santería* initiate; or "bride" of the *orishas*

Obatalá: *Orisha* king of the white cloth; symbol of peace and purity

Obi and Ifá: Oracles

Ochún: The sensuous black goddess that many Cuban women identify as the *orisha* of love; syncretistically, the Virgen de la Caridad

Ogún: *Orisha* represented as an iron worker or warrior

Orishas: Deities of the Lucumi religion; most are symbolic of human qualities and aspects of nature

Toque: Specific rhythm attributed to an *orisha*

---

lit podium; miraculously, one of the doves alighted on Fidel's shoulder, touching off an explosion from the ecstatic onlookers: *"Fee-del! Fee-del! Fee-del!"* In *santería,* doves are symbols of Obatalá, the Son of God. To Cubans—and perhaps Fidel himself—the event was a supreme symbol that the gods had chosen Fidel to guide Cuba. It was "one of those rare, magical moments when cynics are transformed into romantics and romantics into fanatics," wrote photojournalist Lee Lockwood.

Nonetheless, following the Revolution, the government stigmatized *santería* as *brujería* (witchcraft). Over ensuing years, Castro's dogma of scientific Communism attempted to convert *santería* into a folkloric movement. Religious rites were restricted. As Marxism lost its appeal in the late 1980s, *santería* bounced back. The desperate conditions of the Special Period have caused millions to visit their *babalawos*. In 1990 the Castro government began to co-opt support for the faith—it is said that Castro also encourages *santería* as a counterpoint to the rising power of the Catholic Church. Reportedly, many *babalawos* have been recruited as agents by MININT, for they above all know people's secrets.

Throughout Cuba, you'll see believers clad all in white, having just gone through their initiation rites as *santeros* or *santeras*. A follower of *santería* may choose at any stage in life to undertake an elaborate initiation that will tear the follower away from his or her old life and set their feet on *La Regla de Ocha*—the Way of the *Orishas*. During this time, the *iyawó*—an initiate or "bride" of the *orishas*—will be possessed by, and under the care of, a specific *orisha* who will guide the initiate to a deeper, richer life for the rest of his or her time in this world. Initiations are highly secret and involve animal sacrifice (usually pigeons and roosters). The rites are complex. They include having to dress solely in white and stay indoors at night for a year, though exceptions are made for employment. And an *iyawó* may not touch anyone or permit him- or herself to be touched, except by the most intimate family members or, this being Cuba, by lovers.

Santería is a sensuous religion. It lacks the arbitrary moral prescriptions of Catholicism—the *orishas* let adherents have a good time. The gods themselves are fallible and hedonistic philanderers, such as the much feared and respected Changó (or Santa Barbara), god of war, fire, thunder, and lightning, whose many mistresses include Oyá (or Santa Teresa, patron saint of the ill and dead, and guardian of cemeteries) and Ochún (the Virgen de la Caridad), the sensuous black goddess that many Cuban women identify as the *orisha* of love.

Each saint has specific attributes. Changó, for example, dresses in red and white and car-ries a scepter with double-headed axe. Followers of Changó wear collars decorated with red and white plastic beads. Ochún wears yellows; thus her followers wear yellow and white beads. Eleguá (Saint Anthony), the guardian of highways and the crossroads to the future, wears red and black. Obbatalá (the Virgen de la Merced), goddess of peace and creation, dresses in white. Yemayá (the Virgen de Regla), goddess of the sea and of motherhood, wears blue and white. Each saint also has his or her own dance, as well as an "altar" where offerings (fruits, rum-soaked cakes, pastries, and coins) are placed. Devout *santeros* even keep a collection of vases in their bedrooms in which one's personal *orisha*, plus Obbatalá, Yemayá, Ochún, and Changó live, in that hierarchical order.

Homage is paid to *orishas* on specific saints' days. For example, Ochún is honored on September 18.

African Cult Religions

Other spiritualist cults exist in Cuba. The most important is the all-male Abakuá secret mutual protection society that originated in Nigeria, appearing in Cuba in the early 19th century. It still functions among the most marginalized black communities, where it is known as *ña-ñiguismo*. The first duty of an adherent is to protect a fellow member. Membership is restricted to "brave, virile, dignified, moral men" who contribute positively to their communities. Nonetheless, it is extreme and involves worship of ancestral devil figures, called *dia-blitos* or *iremes,* where dancers appear dressed from head to toe in hooded woven hessian costumes. Members use a system of writing called *anaforuana* with symbols employed for religious powers.

Palo Monte (known also as *reglas congas*) also derives from west-central Africa and is a spirit religion that harnesses the power of the deceased to control supernatural forces. Adherents (called *paleros*) use ritual sticks and plants to perform magic. Initiates receive small incisions in their body into which magical substances are inserted. A three-legged cauldron called a *nganga* is used as a form of altar, containing all the natural elements of the world, plus the dead person's spirit.

EDUCATION

Despite its onerous restrictions on individual liberty, Cuba's education system is justifiably a source of national pride. The country enjoys one of the greatest proportions of university graduates in the world, and it is a joy to hear everywhere the intelligent voices of an educated and philosophical people. In general, Cubans display an astonishing level of intellectual development and erudition. Their conversations are spiced with literary allusions and historical references. Even in the most remote Cuban backwater, you'll come across bright-eyed children laden with satchels, making their way to and from school in pin-neat uniforms colored according to their grades (younger ones wear short-sleeved white shirts, light-blue neckerchiefs, and maroon shorts or mini-skirts; secondary school children wear white shirts, red neckerchiefs, and ocher-yellow long pants or mini-skirts; the neckerchiefs show that they are Pioneers, *pioneros,* similar to Cub and Boy and Girl Scouts).

During Spanish colonial times, no country in Latin America spent less on education and more on its army. Better education was one of the prime motivations for the revolution that overthrew General Machado in 1933; much was achieved, but education in the rural areas made moderate progress in the post-war decades while educational funds became a huge source of graft. Official statistics are contradictory. The Cuban government claims that on the eve of the Revolution, 43 percent of the population was illiterate and half a million Cuban children went without school; however, the U.N. Statistical Yearbook suggests that as much as 80 percent of the population was literate, behind only Argentina, Chile, and Costa Rica for the time.

Private and religious schools are forbidden.

Remarkable Accomplishments

In December 1960 the government announced a war on illiteracy. On April 10, 1961, 120,000 literacy workers—*brigadis-*tas—spread throughout the island to teach reading and writing to one million illiterates. The government followed up by establishing about 10,000 new classrooms in rural areas and introducing traveling libraries. Today literacy is about 99.8 percent, according to UNESCO, exceeding all other Latin American nations (compared to 96 percent for the United States and 99 percent for the United Kingdom). The statistics also show that the average Cuban child receives about 11.3 years of schooling—the U.S. equivalent is 15.9; that of the U.K. is 16.6. At age 15 (ninth grade), children are evaluated and graded to determine their future: At 16 they begin two years of pre-university study (called *pre*) or technical school to train them for trades.

In 2002, Castro announced a comprehensive new effort to raise education, with the goal of having one teacher per 20 students in all elementary classes; installation of computer labs; and a crash course to train "emergency teachers." In 2004, it claimed to have achieved only 12 students per teacher, less than half the number of students per teacher than in the United States.

Cuban children display inordinate literary and mathematical abilities; a UNESCO study of language and mathematics skills throughout Latin America found that Cuba was way ahead of all other nations (the World Bank's *World Development Indicators* shows Cuba as topping virtually all other poor countries in education statistics, despite which since 1960 Cuba is the *only* developing country to have never received any assistance from the World Bank). One in every 15 people is a college graduate. Children with special talents may opt to attend specialist schools that foster particular skills in art, music, or sports. The best pupils go to highly prized vocational schools—assuming, of course, that they display the correct behavioral attitudes (children of dissidents and "counter-revolutionaries" are often punished along with their parents). And children of the Communist party and military elite get special treatment.

Cuba has four universities. In addition, although the government severely restricts Cubans' access to computers and the Internet, in 2002 it opened the **Universidad de las Ciencias Informáticas** (Carretera a San Antonio de los Baños Km 2.5, Torrens, Municipio Boyeros, Havana, tel. 07/835-8799, beatriz@uci.cu), with 10,000 students and a multigigabite fiber-optic service to computers in every student room. Students are arranged into teams to develop commercial software.

The Downside

As the Brazilian economist Roberto Campos said, statistics are like bikinis: They show what's important but hide what's essential. For one, the hyper-educated population is hard pressed to find books and other educational materials. Few schools have a library or gym or laboratory. The entire literary panorama is severely proscribed: Only politically acceptable works are allowed. Many senior students have little choice of university study; the state often dictates what they'll study. Schoolchildren are constantly monitored for their "political soundness," and their ability to move up into institutions of higher education depends on their accumulating points by attending political rallies, demonstrating their support for the revolution, and favorably answering politically pointed questions. And options for adult education are virtually nonexistent.

Work-Study

The Cuban education system combines learning with work. Cuban children are expected to be *estudiantes hoy, trabajadores mañana, soldados de la patria siempre*—students today, workers tomorrow, soldiers always—fulfilling José Martí's dictum: "In the morning, the pen—but in the afternoon, the plow."

Most secondary students spend their two final years at a PRE (for *pre-universitario*), or *escuela del campo,* in the country. Here they live in boarding schools attached to 500-hectare plots of arable land. Time is equally divided between study and labor, the latter most often in citrus plantations, where the kids bring in the harvest. Often, very little work gets done in the fields and youth spend much of their time in carnal dalliance.

HEALTH

According to the Castro government, in prerevolutionary Cuba only the monied class could afford good medical care; it also has claimed that there were only 6,250 physicians in all of Cuba on the eve of the Revolution. Of these, 70 percent were in Havana (as were 60 percent of all hospital beds). Many people in rural areas went without medical services of any kind. According to the United Nations Statistical Yearbook, however, in 1958 Cuba had an advanced medical system that ranked third in Latin America, behind only Uruguay and Argentina, in numbers of physicians and dentists per capita, with 128 physicians and dentists per 100,000 people—the same as the Netherlands, and ahead of the United Kingdom, with 122 per 100,000 people—and one hospital bed for every 190 inhabitants. And Cuba's infant mortality rate of 32 per 1,000 live births in 1957 was the lowest in Latin America and the 13th lowest in the world (today it is 39th lowest).

From the beginning, health care has assumed an inordinately prominent place in revolutionary government policies (the government spends about 12 percent of its budget on health care). Today some 20 medical schools churn out 4,000 doctors each year. In 1978, Castro predicted that Cuba would become the bulwark of Third World medicine, put a doctor on every block, become a world medical power, and surpass the United States in certain health indices. In all four, he has been vindicated. Moreover, Cuban doctors are inspired by a genuine concern for the Hippocratic oath, without concern for money.

Cuba's life expectancy of 77.23 years is the highest in Latin America and compares favorably with 77.71 for the United States and 78.38 for the United Kingdom. In 2004 Cuban authorities reported an infant mortality rate of 6.45 per 1,000 births—on a par with the United States (6.5) and almost as good as Great Britain (5.16). The Revolution's accomplishment is due to its emphasis on preventive medicine and community-based doctors. A near 100 percent immunization rate has ensured the total eradication of several preventable

CUBA'S FLYING DOCTORS

Since 1963 when Cuba sent 56 doctors to newly independent Algeria, the country has provided medical assistance to developing countries regardless of its own economic straits. In 1985 the *New York Times* dubbed Cuba's international medical aid program "the largest Peace Corps-style program of civilian aid in the world." That year Cuba had 16,000 doctors, teachers, agronomists, and other technical specialists serving in 22 developing nations, including more doctors than the World Health Organization. Cuba regularly deploys medical brigades to regions struck by disasters, while thousands of other medical personnel continue to serve on a rotating basis in scores of countries around the world. (In 2005, some 26,000 Cuban doctors were serving abroad; more than half were in Venezuela in exchange for oil on favorable credit terms.) Cuba has donated entire hospitals to developing countries. It even offered 27 tons of medical aid plus 1,600 doctors for New Orleans after Hurricane Katrina in 2005, but the Bush administration declined, putting politics ahead of the needs of the victims.

Cuba has also offered free medical care in Cuba for patients from abroad, most famously for child victims of the Chernobyl nuclear disaster in the Soviet Union. In addition, prior to the Special Period, Cuba offered more than 20,000 international scholarships a year to medical students from developing countries – many times the number offered by the United States. And in November 1999 it converted a naval academy into the Latin American School for Medical Sciences, offering free medical education to students from Latin America, the Caribbean, Africa, and including full scholarships for 250 students from disadvantaged communities in the United States (see the sidebar *Studying in Cuba* in the *Essentials* chapter). More than 1,800 students entered the school that year for six-year courses; in 2005, it had more than 7,200 students enrolled from 23 countries. The only stipulation is that upon graduation, the new doctors return to their home countries to practice medicine.

contagious diseases. The Pan American Health Organization declared Cuba the first polio-free country in the Americas. Cuba has the highest rate of immunization against measles in the world, says UNICEF, which uses the measles immunization rate as the most reliable barometer of a country's commitment to bringing basic medical advances to its people. Cuba has also eradicated malaria and diphtheria.

Family Doctor Program

Castro set out to train doctors en masse. In 2004, Cuba claimed to have 5.3 doctors per 1,000 people—the highest in the world, and three times as many per capita as the United States. (Dental care lags behind, however, with one dentist for about every 1,280 inhabitants.) The idea is for every Cuban to have his or her own doctor trained in comprehensive general medicine close by, living and working in the neighborhood, combining the duties of a family doctor

and public health advocate. Every community has a *casa del médico* (family doctor's home), with a clinic on the ground floor, living quarters for the doctor's family on the second floor, and quarters for the nurse's family above. Every town also has a hospital, plus a maternity home and a day-care center for the elderly. Fifteen mobile laboratories travel the country performing pre-clinical diagnostics for breast cancer. Virtually the entire population has been screened for AIDS. And local clinics even provide sex education for youngsters and exercise classes for elderly persons. All medical services are free.

Beyond Primary Care

Cuba also commands the kind of technology that most poor countries can only dream about: ultrasound for obstetricians, CAT scans for radiologists, stacks of high-tech monitors in the suites for intensive care. Cuba has performed heart transplants since 1985, heart-lung transplants since 1987, coronary bypasses, pacemaker implantations, microsurgery, and a host of other advanced surgical procedures. A 1988 Pan-American Health Organization assessment of Cuba's foremost hospital, the Hospital Hermanos Almeijeiras, concluded that it "conducts research and uses technology at the international cutting edge in the 38 specialties in which services are rendered." In 1992 *Science* magazine rated the Ibero-Latin American Center for Nervous System Transplants and Regeneration as the world's best for the treatment of Parkinson's disease.

In addition, prior to the Special Period, the homegrown pharmaceutical industry supplied 80 percent of Cuba's needs. Cuba has made notable leaps in advancing the field of molecular immunology. It even manufactures interferons for AIDS treatment; a meningitis vaccine first "discovered" at the Finlay Institute; even a cure for the skin disease vitiligo. Cuba continues to share its stupendous commitment with the rest of the world (see the sidebar *Cuba's Flying Doctors*).

Cuba's Medical Crisis

Why, then, are so many Cubans so obviously malnourished and sickly?

Cuba's admirable health system has suffered a catastrophic setback since the collapse of the Soviet bloc. Cubans' average caloric intake has fallen and for many Cubans is still below the World Health Organization recommended minimum (in 2002, the UN noted that malnutrition affects 19 percent of the Cuban populace). The incidence of babies born with low birth weights and of anemia among expectant mothers has risen. And beriberi, scurvy, typhoid, and tuberculosis—all eradicated since the Revolution—reappeared. Foreign public health experts say that the impact of the Special Period could have been catastrophic had Cuba not had such a superb health system nationwide.

Even before the Special Period, Cuba's health system faced severe shortages and long waiting lists for operations. Since 1991 services have been vastly curtailed. Priority is given to those in most urgent need. Dissemination of medicines has plummeted. Local pharmacies

---

HUMANITARIAN COURIERS

You can make tax-deductible donations to the following relief organizations, which are licensed by OFAC to run food, medicine, and other humanitarian aid to Cuba using ordinary U.S. citizens as volunteer couriers. (The Bush administration has denied a renewal of humanitarian licenses to many organizations, and it is worth checking the current status.)

Caribbean Medical Transport (1393 Cold Hill Rd., Lyndonville, VT 05851, www.cuba-caribe.com).

Cuba AIDS Project (500 West Leota St., Suite 200, P.O. Box 1289, North Platte, NE 69103-1289, 308/532-4700, www.cubaaidsproject.com).

Operation USA: Cuba Medical Relief Project (8320 Melrose Ave., Suite 200, Los Angeles, CA 90069, 323/658-8876, fax 323/653-7846, www.opusa.org).

U.S.-Cuba Medical Project (c/o MADRE, 121 West 27th St. #301, New York, NY 10001, 212/627-0444, www.madre.org).

The **U.S.-Latin American Medical Aid Foundation** (1215A Castle Hill, Austin, TX 78703, 512/477-2438, www.medaid.org).

---

are meagerly stocked; Cuban pharmaceuticals are exported to obtain foreign funds. And resources have increasingly been shifted from primary care toward turning Cuba's medical system into a profit-making enterprise catering to foreigners, notably in the surgical and advanced medicines fields. Dr. Hilda Molina, founder of Havana's International Center for Neurological Restoration (and a former member of the Cuban National Assembly), claims that "foreigners are assigned the highest priority, followed by government functionaries and their families, followed by athletes with good records of performance, then dancers, and lastly, ordinary Cuban patients."

Everywhere, hospital equipment is broken. Critical medicines are in such short supply that doctors have turned to herbal remedies.

Doctors even use acupuncture to anesthetize patients. Faced with a severe shortage of X-ray film, radiologists have turned to more dangerous fluoroscopy. Hospitals even tell their patients to bring their own towels and bed sheets. The absence of sulfa drugs, antibiotics, antibacterial medicines, and disinfectants has turned routine health problems into serious illnesses. Shortages of soap, toilet paper, chlorine, and other water-treatment chemicals have made many drinking-water supplies unsafe and brought a rise in diarrhea and hepatitis in health facilities and countrywide.

The situation was worsened in 1992, when the U.S. Congress passed the Torricelli Act, which banned all shipments of foods and medicines to Cuba except humanitarian aid. In addition, all medical equipment and supplies manufactured in the United States or under U.S. patent could not be exported to Cuba by third-country companies without a license from the U.S. Commerce Department. The restrictions have since been rescinded. (Nonetheless, in September 1998 when Washington committed US$7 million to the U.N. World Food Program's relief campaign for Cuba, Castro refused to accept it; in December 1999, he also turned away 55,000 pounds of desperately needed U.S. medical supplies meant for pediatric hospitals.) In 2001, Cuba began purchasing millions of dollars of U.S. medical products.

Arts

Since the Revolution, the government's sponsorship of the arts has yielded a rich harvest in every field. Cuba is one of the few tropical countries to have produced a modern culture of its own. The Centro Nacional de Escuelas de Arte (National Center of Schools of Art), created in 1960, has 41 schools under its umbrella, including the national Escuela de la Música, a national folkloric school, two ballet schools, two fine-arts schools, and a school of modern dance, plus schools at the provincial level. The graduates are superbly trained, despite great shortages of instruments and other materials.

Cuba's Ministry of Culture works to expose every Cuban to a range of cultural offerings. Visit a cigar factory and you'll hear the *lector* reading from the works of Ernest Hemingway, Nicolas Guillén, or Gabriel García Márquez. Nor is it unusual to hear of ballet being performed in factories or for a traveling puppet theater group to perform in a mountain village.

During the first two years of the Revolution, Castro enjoyed being the "bohemian intellectual," and artists and writers enjoyed relative freedom. As the romantic phase of the Revolution passed into an era of more dogmatic ideology, the Culture Council took a hard line.

In 1961 the government invited intellectuals to a debate on the meaning of cultural liberty at which Castro offered his "Words to the Intellectuals," which he summed up with a credo: "Within the Revolution, everything. Outside the Revolution, nothing!" The government acquired full control of the mass media. Many talented intellectuals, writers, and artists were intimidated into ideological straitjackets. Thousands chose to leave Cuba. Many talented individuals stayed, of course, and produced rich and lively works. But these were dark years of a relative spiritual vacuum. Ever since, no politically incorrect works have been allowed.

MUSIC AND DANCE

Author Norman Mailer scolded President Kennedy for the Bay of Pigs defeat by asking, "Wasn't there anyone around to give you the lecture on Cuba? Don't you sense the enormity of your mistake—you invade a country without understanding its music." These days it's Cuba that's invading the United States and the rest of the world. Says *Rhythm Music* magazine: "From Babalu to Bamboleo, a wealth of musicians is pouring out from under the Mango Curtain." The rhythm juggernaut is typified by

FOR LOVERS OF MUSIC AND DANCE

A good percentage of travelers to Cuba visit primarily to savor the music and dance. Whether your interests are primarily in son (the old-time music form brought to world fame by the Buena Vista Social Club), sizzling salsa, or even classical music and ballet, few destinations in the world quite so satisfy the soul. You can stitch your own tour program together, although far better might be to sign up for a specialized music and dance tour offered by organizations in North America or Europe, with additional time to strike out on your own. Here are the key venues to know; see the destination chapters for more information.

GENERAL

The crème de la crème of youthful musicians train at the **Instituto Superior de Arte**, located in Havana's Cubanacán district. Visits by appointment.

AFRO-CUBAN MUSIC

An Afro-Cuban rumba is held every Sunday at noon on **Callejón de Hamel**, in Havana's Centro district.

Asociación Cultural Yoruba de Cuba, in Habana Vieja, hosts traditional Afro-Cuban music and dance every Sunday evening.

Conjunto Folklórico Nacional (National Folklore Dance Group), in Havana's Miramar district, has a Saturday afternoon rumba year-round.

The city of **Matanzas** is a center for Afro-Cuban music (Cuba's premier rumba band, Los Muñequitos, hails from here). The city's two casas de las trovas are the principal venues.

Santiago de Cuba has its own music and dance forms (such as columbia and tumba francesa) that have formed an inspiration for the rest of the isle. Several Afro-Cuban dance troupes have studios which you can visit, including Ballet Folklórico Cutumba and La Tumba Francesa, which hosts a traditional rumba nightly. ·

CLASSICAL MUSIC AND BALLET

Havana's **Escuela Nacional de Ballet** (National School of Ballet), in Habana Vieja. Visits by appointment.

Gran Teatro, in Habana Vieja, is Havana's premier venue for ballet and classical concerts.

Iglesia de San Francisco de Asís, in Habana Vieja, hosts classical concerts nightly in the nave of this former basilica.

On Fridays evenings, the delightful little **Iglesia de San Francisco de Paula,** in Habana Vieja, is the place to come for ecclesiastical and baroque chamber music.

Teatro Amadeo Roldán, in Havana's Miramar district, features classical concerts year-round.

JAZZ

La Zorra y el Cuervo is a dedicated jazz club on La Rampa in Havana's Vedado.

Jazz Café, in Vedado, regularly features Cuban jazz maestro Chucho Valdés.

Gato Tuerto nightclub, also in Vedado, has jazz, bolero, and filin music.

SIZZLING SALSA (AKA TIMBA)

One of the best places to cook the pork is **Casa de la Música**, in Havana's Miramar district. Cuba's top bands regularly perform here, but don't think of arriving before midnight.

Attracting a vast yet mostly impecunious crowd of Cubans, the **Salón Rosado Benny Moré** (colloquially called "El Tropical") also features top salsa bands.

SON

On Monday nights in Habana Vieja, **"Encounter with Cuban Music"** is hosted atop a private rooftop.

The **Afrocuban Allstars** perform weekly at several venues throughout Havana, including the Copa Room (in the Hotel Havana Riviera) and Habana Café (in the Meliá Cohiba).

Son was birthed in **Santiago de Cuba,** where the casa de la trova is still the island's foremost house of son.

the explosive 1999 success of the Grammy-winning *Buena Vista Social Club* and four-set album *Cuba: I Am Time* (Blue Jacket Records). Music—the pulsing undercurrent of Cuban life—is everywhere. Dance, from the earliest *guaguancó* to the mambo craze, has always been a potent expression of an enshrined national tradition: Cuban sensualism. Girls are whisked onto the dance floor and whirled through a flurry of complicated steps and sensuous undulations just a little closer than cheek to cheek. It's a wonder the birth rate isn't higher.

The development of Cuban music styles since 1800—from *contradanza, danzón, habanera,* mambo, and *son* to *nueva trova*—is the story, writes Erroll McDonald, "of a swinging dialectic between West African choral and percussive genius and European melodic and harmonic sophistication."

Folkloric Music and Dance

In Cuba, folkloric music (*música folklórica*) usually refers to Afro-Cuban music. The earliest influence was Spanish. The colonists brought the melodies (such as the *bolero*), guitars, and violins from which evolved folk music, or *guajira,* influenced through contact with black culture. The fusion gave rise to *punto campesino* (peasant dances), including the all-important *danzón* (the first dance in Cuba in which couples actually touched each other), the *zapateo,* the slow and sensual *yambú* and the *colombia,* a solo men's dance performed blindfolded with machetes—all popular in past centuries among white country people and accompanied by small accordions, kettledrums, gourds, and calabashes. The melancholic love song *Guantanamera* is undoubtedly the most famous of Cuban *guajiras.*

From Europe, too, came the *trovas,* poetic songs (*canciones*) concerned with great historical events and, above all, with love. *Trovas,* which were descended from the medieval ballad, were sung in Cuba throughout the colonial period. Later they lent themselves perfectly to the Revolutionary cause in "protest songs." *Trovadores* performed for free, as they still do at *casas de la trova* islandwide. The duty of the *casas* is to nurture the music of the provinces, and their

success is one reason why Cuba is today a powerhouse on the international music scene.

This century has seen the evolution of the romantic, melancholic, and sultry *bolero* (a fusion of traditional *trovas* with Afro-Cuban rhythms), and more recently *trovas nuevas,* which often includes subtle criticism of governmental dogma and the contemporary state of affairs, as echoed by the works of Pablo Milanés and Silvio Rodríguez.

The African Influence

Almost from the beginning, the Spanish guitar (from the tiny *requinto* to the *tres,* a small guitar with three sets of double strings) joined the hourglass-shaped African *bata* and bongo drum, claves (two short hardwood sticks clapped together), and *chequerí* (seed-filled gourds) to give Cuban music its distinctive form. Slaves played at speakeasies in huts in the slaves' quarters. Their jam sessions gave birth to the *guaguancó,* a mix of flamenco guitar and African rhythm that is the mother of Cuban dance music. *Guaguancó* is an erotic rumba—"a vertical suggestion of a horizontal intention," it has been called—in which the man tries to make contact with the woman's genitals with whatever part of his body he can, and the woman dances defensively, with handfuls of skirt in front of her groin. Later, slaves would take the *guaguancó* a few steps farther to create the sensuous rumba, a sinuous dance from the hips from which tumbled most other forms of Cuban music. Typically playing on makeshift instruments and bottles hit with spoons, performers sang of everyday life using African phrases while dancers mimed an overtly sexual act. Rumba remains deliriously popular among Cuba's blacks. The *tumba francesa,* a dance of French-African fusion, also derived from the *guaguancó.*

From *guaguancó* also came *son,* traditionally performed by *sextetos*—six-person groups using the bongo, clave, double bass, *güiro* (or scraper, usually made of a hollowed gourd), plus guitar, and the *tres* as its defining instrument. *Son,* which originated in the eastern provinces of Oriente, derived as a campesino-based form combining African call-and-response verse to

© CHRISTOPHER P. BAKER

A trumpet player practices in Plaza Dolores, Santiago de Cuba.

Spanish folk tunes using *décima* verses (octosyllable ten-line stanzas). In turn, *son* birthed *danzón* and was eventually adopted in the cities where it became massively popular and was actually banned by authorities. Popularized on radio by the 1920s artists such as Rita Montaner and Ignacio Piñero's Septeto Nacional orchestra, *son* became the national music form.

By the 1930s, *son* was adopted and melded with U.S. jazz influences by large band orchestras (*orquestras típicas*) with percussion and horn sections and tall conga drums called *tumbadores,* epitomized by the roaring success of Benny Moré (born Bartolomé Maximiliano Moré, 1919–63), the flamboyant *bárbaro del ritmo*—the wild man of rhythm—who became a national idol and had his own big band, the Banda Gigante. The success of big band paved the way for the eventual evolution of salsa. Such contemporary salsa groups as Los Van Van have incorporated the *son,* which has its own variants, such as the fast, infectious, overtly sexual *son changüí* from Guantánamo Province, typified by the music of Orquestra Revé. Meanwhile, the runaway success of the

Buena Vista Social Club has helped revive an appreciation of traditional *son* abroad.

The mambo, like the cha-cha, which evolved from *son,* is a derivative of the *danzón* jazzed up with rhythmic innovations. Mambo is a passé but still revered dance, like the jitterbug in the United States, danced usually only by older people. Created in Cuba by Orestes López in 1938, mambo stormed the United States in the 1950s, when Cuban performers were the hottest ticket in town. Though the craze died, mambo left its mark on everything from American jazz to the old Walt Disney cartoons where the salt and pepper shakers get up and dance. People were titillated by the aggressive sexual overtures required of women in the elegant but provocative dance.

The mix of Cuban and North American sounds created blends such as *filin* music, a simple, honest derivative of the *bolero,* as sung by Rita Montaner and Nat "King" Cole, who performed regularly in Havana; and *Cu-bop,* which fused bebop with Afro-Cuban rhythms, epitomized by Moré, who was considered the top artist of Cuban popular music.

THE BUENA VISTA SOCIAL CLUB

In 1996, Cuban music promoter Juan de Marcos rounded up a clique of legendary but largely forgotten veteran musicians to make a comeback album. Eclectic U.S. slide guitarist Ry Cooder happened to make a musical pilgrimage to Cuba around the same time, struck a deal with Marcos, and gifted the world the Buena Vista Social Club, named for a Havana venue where many of the artists performed in the 1950s. German film director Wim Wenders tagged along with his Beta steadicam to chronicle how Cooder ushered the half-forgotten relics of prerevolutionary Cuba into recording studios, cut an album of sepia-toned tunes, and dispatched them on a world tour and runaway success. The documentary celebrates the elderly musicians' performance on the world stage and offers a portrait of their life back in an impoverished Cuba.

The tender heart of the movie is crooner Ibrahim Ferrer, a soft-spoken septuagenarian who had been a singer with the legendary Benny Moré band in the 1950s, but who was shining shoes at the time Cooder's team rediscovered him for the Buena Vista album. His weathered yet still nimble voice is supported by the arthritic fingers of 76-year-old pianist Ruben González, creator in the early 1940s of the modern Cuban piano sound, flying into action after long retirement (his piano had been reduced to dust by termites when Cooder brought him back from obscurity); the slick guitar work of Francisco Repalido, known as "Compay Segundo," the grandfather of *son* music, who plays in his trademark Panama hat; guitarist Eliades Ochoa, a maestro of the *guajira* (country lament), easily recognized in his trademark cowboy hat; and the dulcet voice of Omara Portuono, who was once one of the leading *bolero* singers in Cuba.

This suave old bunch of codgers wowed the world when the documentary movie, produced by Cooder, was released in 1999, swept the United States, and introduced it to the richness of *son*, *danzón*, and *bolero* in a style untouched by contemporary trends. The result was a runaway success. The CD won the Grammy for Tropical Music and topped the charts among Latin albums, taking Cuban music international for the first time, selling several million copies worldwide, and creating international nostalgia for the old Havana whose charmingly dilapidated streets are the setting for Wenders's wonderful movie.

Alas, all the main stars except Ochoa and Portuondo have since passed away.

Modern Sounds

Salsa (a sensual fast-paced derivative of *son*) has flourished since the 1980s. It is the heartbeat of most Cuban nightlife and a musical form so hot it can cook the pork. Los Van Van—one of Cuba's hottest big, brassy salsa-style bands—and Irakere have come up with innovative and explosive mixtures of jazz, classical, rock, and traditional Cuban music that have caused a commotion in music. They regularly tour Europe and Latin America, earning the country scarce hard currency. And Bamboleo is a leader in *timba* (high-speed new-wave salsa); their bald-headed female singers also started a new craze in hairstyles.

For a long time, the playing of jazz in Cuba was completely discouraged as "representative of Yankee imperialism." Cuban musicians missed out on the Latin Jazz effervescence of the 1960s. Paquito D'Rivera, for example, was discouraged from playing jazz when he became director of the Orquestra Cubana de Música Moderna in 1970. The government began to lighten up in the 1980s, by which time D'Rivera had left Cuba for New York. (His music was pulled from the shelves in Cuba, and for nine years Castro refused to let D'Rivera's son join him.) Today, Cuba boasts wonderful jazz players. The undisputed king of contemporary jazz is pianist Chucho Valdés, winner of five Grammy awards for his scorching-hot compositions.

More recently, rap has come to Cuba. Although the rhythms, gestures, and posturing take their cues from U.S. urban ghettoes, Cuban hip-hop is gentler, less dependent on guttural, driving aggression and more based on melodic fusion, and it is heavily influenced by reggae. At last visit, rap-based, reggae-influenced *reggaeton* was the most universally popular and ubiquitous sound on the island, performed by such groups as Sintesis and Obsesión. Alamar, in Habana del Este, is the acknowledged center of rap. The Festival de Rap de Alamar has been held every year since 1991. There's even a hip-hop radio show. Beginning in 2002, however, the government responded to increasingly critical hip-hop content with a severe yank on the leash, ironically by lending it official support (there's even a Minister of Hip-Hop), permitting the government to usurp and control it. Certain songs were "suspended" and hip-hop performers on the "outs" have found it impossible to se-

cure venues or radio air time (to a large degree, the state decides what music can be played, and when and where). Playing unofficial venues can get performers arrested and it is not unknown for officials to literally pull the plug on unofficial rehearsals and concerts.

The same holds true for rock, which has been lassoed by the Unión Juventud de Cuba (the Young Communists) to corral disaffected youth. Rock was once officially banned. Cuba's *roqueros* (rockers) and *friquis* (freaks, known for their torn clothes and punkish scruffy hair) faced a hard time of things for many years, as the government considered them social deviants and, hence, harassed and suppressed them. These days, the government tolerates domestic rock groups, whose fans wear the same stereotypical uniforms—long hair, tattered Led

TUNING WITH THE ENEMY

When Benjamin Treuhaft first visited Cuba, he marveled at the ability of young musicians to raise beautiful sounds from decrepit pianos – Wurlitzer short uprights from the turn of the century, unpromising 1970s Russian Tchaikas, and pre-1959 U.S. instruments eaten by salt air and termites.

Treuhaft, a piano tuner who has tuned on behalf of Steinway, vowed to collect pianos and ship them to Cuba. He sent letters to piano dealers across the nation soliciting parts and soon had pledges for dozens of pianos. His mission of musical mercy, however, struck a dissonant note with the U.S. Commerce Department, which declared that pianos are not humanitarian aid and were therefore barred. When Treuhauft replied in jest that the Cubans might use the pianos for military purposes, the case was shifted to the department's Office of Missile and Nuclear Technology! Due considerations were presumably given to piano throw weights and trajectories before official permission was given to ship his pianos, providing that they were not "used for the purpose of torture or human rights abuse" – proof that U.S. policy toward Cuba is overdue for its own major tuning.

The first 22 pianos (plus an organ and half a ton of spare parts) reached Havana in December 1995, to be dispersed to deserving students and teachers by the Instituto Cubano de la Música (Cuban Institute of Music). Several hundred pianos have since been shipped.

In 2003, the U.S. government denied Treuhaft's export license application and revoked his license to tune in Cuba. Treuhaft, however, continued to defy the Bush administration, which eventually renewed his license to ship pianos and his permit to travel and tune.

Treuhaft has even installed a German wire-spinning machine in Havana and established a year-round workshop where experts train Cubans in modern rebuilding techniques. Volunteers are needed to visit Havana to teach students and fix up pianos. Treuhaft needs piano wire, tuning pins, and tools, but most of all that old piano (in rebuildable condition) languishing in your basement. Monetary donations are also requested.

Contact **Send a Piana to Havana** (39 E. 7th St., Apt. 3, New York, NY 10003, 212/505-3173, www.sendapiana.com).

Zeppelin and Metallica T-shirts—as do those beyond Cuban shores. Foremost groups include Combat Noise, Zeus, and Garage Hall.

Classical Music and Ballet

"In the realm of classical music Cuba has been an inspirational locale rather than a breeding ground for great composers and instrumentalists," says noted pianist Daniel Fenmore. An exception would be composer-pianist Ernesto Lecuona (1896–1963), whose acclaimed compositions were infused with Afro-Cuban rhythms. Nonetheless, it is astounding how many contemporary Cubans are accomplished classical musicians. Everywhere you go, you will come across violinists, pianists, and cellists serenading you for tips while you eat. Cuba also boasts several classical orchestras, notably the Orquestra Sinfónica Nacional. It first performed in November 1960 and has a repertoire ranging from 17th-century works to contemporary creations by Cuban composers such as Amadeo Roldán and Alejandro García Caturla. Watch, too, for performances by Frank Fernández, Cuba's finest classical pianist.

Cubans love ballet, which is associated in Cuba with one name above all: Alicia Alonso. Havana got its own ballet company—the Sociedad Pro-Arte Música—in 1931, with a conservatory that produced many outstanding ballet dancers, including Alonso, born to an aristocratic family in Havana on December 21, 1921. Alonso was a prima ballerina with the American Ballet Theater since its inception in the 1940s. She returned to Cuba and, sponsored by Batista (who hated ballet but considered her star status a propaganda bonus), founded the Ballet Alicia Alonso, which in 1955 became the Ballet de Cuba. Alonso was outspoken in her criticism of the "Sordid Era," and she went into exile in 1956 when Batista withdrew his patronage. The Revolution later adopted her (Alonso is a favorite of Fidel), and her ballet company was re-formed and renamed the Ballet Nacional de Cuba, which became a showpiece for the Cuban Revolution, making regular forays abroad. Her company is renowned worldwide for its original choreography and talent.

The Camagüey Ballet—founded since the Revolution by Alicia's husband, Fernando Alonso—is also renowned for its innovative streak, as is the Santiago-based Ballet Folklórico de Oriente, which lends contemporary interpretations to traditional themes.

ART

Artists followed classical European prescriptions (not least religious themes) throughout the early colonial period, and only in the 19th century did a distinctly national school arise, with mulatto artists José Nicolás de la Escalera (1734–1804) and Vincente Escobar (1762–1834) at the fore. Their *costumbrista* movement presented an idealized vision of *criollo* culture from a classical, romantic perspective. Meanwhile, Francisco Javier Báez helped launch xylography (wood-cut drawings) in designing drawings for tobacco and cigar brands.

In 1818, Juan Bautiste Vermay opened the Academía Nacional de Bellas Artes, the second national arts school in the Americas, which perpetuated the French allegorical, neoclassical stylistic form of painting, marked by a courtly stiffness.

The coming of independence opened Cuba to a wave of new influence, led by Armando García Menocal and Leopoldo Romanach Guillén. Europe's avant-garde movement swept in as painters such as Eduardo Abela (1889–1965) and Cabrera Moreno (1923–84) adopted international styles to represent emblemic Cuban themes, such as the figure of the *guajiro*. Victor Manuel García (1897–1965) and Marcelo Pogolotti (1902–88) were instrumental in formation of a Cuban post-impressionist school, while Wilfredo Lam (1902–82), perhaps the greatest painter to emerge from Cuba during the 20th century, adopted Afro-Cuban mysticism to his exploration of the surrealist style inspired by Picasso. Lam traveled to Paris and developed close ties with the surrealists and primitivists. Picasso took Lam under his wing and offered the young Cuban his studio to work in. Lam lived briefly in Marseilles before returning to Havana. In 1956, he returned to Europe, where he died in Paris on September

CUBAN POSTER ART

Cuba's strongest claim to artistic fame is surely its unique poster art, created in the service of political revolution and acclaimed as "the single most focused, potent body of political graphics ever produced in this hemisphere."

The three leading poster-producing agencies – the Organization of Solidarity with the Peoples of Africa, Asia and Latin America; the Cuban Film Institute; and the Editora Política, the propaganda arm of the Cuban Communist Party – have produced over 10,000 posters since 1959. Different state bodies create works for different audiences: Artists of the Cuban Film Institute (ICAIC), for example, design posters for movies from Charlie Chaplin comedies to John Wayne westerns; Editora Política produces posters covering everything from AIDS awareness, baseball games, and energy conservation to telling children to do their homework.

Cuba's most talented painters and photographers rejected Soviet realism and developed their own unique graphic style influenced by Latin culture and the country's geography. The vibrant colors and lush imagery are consistent with the physical and psychological makeup of the country, such as the poster urging participation in the harvest, dripping with psychedelic images of fruit and reminiscent of a 1960s Grateful Dead poster.

See ¡Revolución! Cuban Poster Art by Lincoln Cushing.

11, 1982. Lam broke with the traditional rules and created his own style using the myths, rituals, customs, and magic of his background to explore a world of Caribbean negritude, marrying Cubism and Surrealism with Afro-Cuban and Caribbean motifs. The traditions of Afro-Cuban *santería* also influenced the works of René Portacarrero (1912–85).

The artists who grew up *after* the 1959 revolution have been given artistic encouragement (even entire villages, such as Verraco near Santiago, exist as art communities). In the late 1960s, the government tried to compel Cuban artists to shun then-prevalent decadent abstract art and adopt the realistic style of the party's Mexican sympathizers such as Diego Rivera and David Alfaro Siqueiros. In 1980 the Cuban government began to loosen up. The artists began shaking off their clichés and conservatism, and began holding unofficial exhibitions in their homes. By the late 1980s they were overstepping their bounds. Armando Hart, then Minister of Culture, decided that the Cuban artists' enthusiasm should be promoted from afar. Mexico City was selected and a community of deported artists has evolved— quixotically, with official Cuban sponsorship. Contemporary Cuban artists express an in-

tense Afro-Latin Americanism in their passionate, visceral, colorful, socially engaged, and eclectic body of widely interpretive modern and postmodern works. Says *Newsweek*, "Like the German and Italian neoexpressionists who took over the scene in the 1970s and '80s, the Cuban artists may be on the brink of changing the face of contemporary art."

Cuba has 21 art schools, organized regionally with at least one per province. The Instituto Superior de Arte, Cuba's premier art school, remains key as an educational center and gateway to the world of Cuban art. The art-education system is both traditional and modern, with fundamental classical drawing and painting techniques at its core. The Cuban state fosters academic training in still life, landscape, and figure form. On attaining mastery of these skills, artists are encouraged to experiment in personal expression without overstepping Castro's 1961 dictum to think more of the message than the aesthetic. As a result, says critic Tina Spiro, "most Cuban artwork, regardless of its style, is informed by a precision of line and a beautiful technical finish."

Upon matriculation, artists receive the support of the **Fondo Cubano de Bienes Culturales** (Cuban Cultural Fund, Av. 47 #4702, esq. 38,

Rpto. Kohly, Havana, tel. 07/204-8005, www .min.cult.cu/instituciones/fcbc.html). Until recent years, artists were employed by various Cuban state institutions and received a small portion of receipts from the sale of their work. In 1991 the government finally recognized that copyright belongs with the artist. It has created independent profit-making, self-financing agencies to represent individual artists on a contractual basis whereby the agency retains 15 percent of sales receipts. Artists ostensibly retain up to 85 percent of earnings from the sale or licensing of copyrights abroad, making them a hugely privileged group (Cuba's few truly wealth individuals are all world-renowned, royalty-earning artists and musicians).

Eroticism—often highly graphic—is an integral component of contemporary Cuban art, in keeping with the culture's expressive sensuality and as exemplified by the works of Chago Armada, Carlos Alpizar, and Aldo Soler. A new religious element has also taken root. And much of current art subtly criticizes the folly of its socio-political environment, but usually in a politically safe, universal statement about the irony in human existence, expressing the hardships of daily life in a dark, surreal way. Within limits, this artistic dissent is not censored.

Among Cuba's most revered contemporary artists is Alfredo Sosabravo—a painter, draftsman, engraver, and ceramist born in 1930, and the most versatile and complete artist among those making up the plastic-arts movement in Cuba today. You'll come across his works (and influence) everywhere, including a permanent exhibition at Havana's Museo Nacional and the Palacio de Bellas Artes. He is dramatically present in hotel lobbies and other tourist spots. Look, too, for the works (inspired by nature and *santería*) of Manuel Mendive; the flamboyant naive works of José Fuster; and the existential works by Alicia Leal.

A good resource is www.galeriascubanas .com (Spanish language only).

LITERATURE

Cuba's goals and struggles have spawned dozens of literary geniuses whose works are mostly clenched fists that cry out against social injustice. Says writer Errol McDonald, "The confluence of the struggle against Spanish and American imperialism, the impact of the cultivation of sugar and tobacco, a high appreciation of the 'low-down' sublimities of Afro-Cuban and Hispanic peasant life, a deep awareness of European 'high' and American popular culture, and the shock of the revolution has resulted in a literature that is staggering for its profundity and breadth—its richness."

Cuban literature was born in exile. The most talented Cuban writers all produced their best works abroad. Cirilo Villaverde (1812–94) fought with the rebel army and was imprisoned as a nationalist, and his spellbinding novel *Cecilia Valdés,* written in exile in the 1880s, helped establish Villaverde as Cuba's foremost 19th-century novelist. From exile, too, José Martí, the 19th-century nationalist leader and man of letters whose works helped define the school of modern Latin American poetry, produced a long list of brilliant works, including the seminal *Versos Sencillos.* The promiscuous Cuban 19th-century woman of letters, Gertrudis Gómez de Avellaneda y Artega (1814–73), also flourished as a writer in exile, as have a panoply of gifted writers cast into purgatory since the Revolution.

There evolved in the 1930s and '40s a *poesía negra* (black poetry) that drew heavily on the myths and memories of slavery, very socialist in content, as portrayed by the works of mulatto poet Nicolás Guillén (1902–89), which spawned a sentimental fashion still prevalent in the works of contemporary poets. Guillén also spent time in exile during the closing years of the Batista regime, having become a Communist while serving as a journalist covering the Spanish Civil War. Following the Revolution, he helped found the **Unión Nacional de Escritores y Artistas de Cuba** (National Union of Cuban Writers and Artists or UNEAC, Calle 17 #351, esq. H, Vedado, Havana, tel. 07/832-4551, www.uneac.com). His works, in which everything, including love, is colored by suffering and rebellion, earned him a place as revolutionary Cuba's poet laureate.

Similarly, Alejo Carpentier (1904–80), acclaimed as Cuba's greatest latter-day writer, was imprisoned by the dictator Machado but escaped and fled Cuba for Paris on a false passport. He returned to Cuba in 1937 but in 1946, during the violent excesses of the Batista era, fled Cuba for Venezuela, where he wrote his best novels. He was also a gifted musicologist and in 1945 published a seminal work called *Music in Cuba*. When the Castro revolution triumphed, Carpentier returned as an honored spiritual leader and was named head of the state publishing house. He is known for his erudite and verbally explosive works that were seminal in defining the surreal Latin American magic-realist style. Following the Revolution, Carpentier became a bureaucrat and sycophant and in 1966 was appointed ambassador to Paris, where he died in 1980.

Freeze and Thaw

In the first two years of the Revolution, literary magazines such as *Lunes de Revolución* attained an extraordinary dynamism. In 1961, however, Castro dictated that only pro-revolutionary works would be allowed. Ever since, the state has determined who gets published, as well as who speaks on radio or television. The newspaper *Revolución* became a powerful organ that according to its former editor, the late exiled writer Guillermo Cabrera Infante, "literally blasted many writers into submission—or oblivion" (later it was reborn as *Granma*). The ice age lasted for a decade and came to a climax in 1970–76, a period euphemistically called "the gray five years" (*quinquenia gris*). The worst years ended when the Ministry of Culture was founded in 1976, ushering in a period of greater leniency. Most of the boldest and best writers, many of whom had been devoted revolutionaries, left. Among them were Infante, Carlos Franquí, Huberto Padilla, Reinaldo Arenas, and Virgilio Piñera.

Although much of the cream of the crop left Cuba, the country still maintained a productive literary output. Notable examples are Lezama Lima (1912–76), author of *Paraíso*, which was later made into a successful film; Nicolás Guillén; Dulce María Loynaz (1902–97), Director of the Cuban Academy of Language and acclaimed as the leading Cuban poet; and the poet Eliseo Diego.

The 1990s saw a considerable thaw from the 1960s and '70s. The Cuban government began to salvage those artists and writers who, having produced significant works, were never allowed to publish. Many writers previously reduced to nonpersons now see their works dusted off, published, and awarded honorifics. (Ironically, this new openness coincided with the hardships of the Special Period, which caused a severe paper shortage.)

Cuba's political climate, however, runs hot and cold. In spring 1996, writers began to feel a sharp tug on the leash and those who have pushed the boundaries of expression further than ever before face harassment. There are no independent publishing houses. Hence, many splendid writers find it difficult to get their books published because their works are too radical. Some authors have resorted to sending manuscripts with foreigners, such as Pablo Juan Gutiérrez, whose blistering *Dirty Havana Trilogy* is an indictment on the hardships of life in contemporary Cuba. Others become "official writers," producing pabulum that panders to the Castro government's self-congratulatory ego.

The influence of Kafka is abiding, claims J. M. Cohen in *The New Writers in Cuba,* reflecting the tussle between the solid liberalism of the writers' union and Casa de las Américas and the Communist puritanism and petty persecution of nonconforming writers.

Reading matter remains severely proscribed by the government, which decides what may or may not be read. And finding books is a problem: Bookstores are few and meagerly stocked, so that tattered antique editions do the rounds until they crumble to dust. Nonetheless, Cubans are avid readers, and not just of home-country writers. The works of many renowned international authors, such as Ernest Hemingway, Tennessee Williams, Gabriel García Márquez, Günter Grass, Isabel Allende, and Jorge Amado, are widely read—one 21-year-old Cuban told me she enjoyed reading

Agatha Christie, Tennessee Williams, and even Anne Rice.

FILM

In 1959 Cuba established a high-quality cinema institute to produce feature films, documentaries, and newsreels. All movies in Cuba—their production, importation/exportation, and distribution—are under the control of the **Instituto Cubano de Cinematografía** (ICAIC, Calle 23 #1155, e/10 y 12, Vedado, Havana, tel. 07/831-3145 or 55-2864, www.cubacine.cu), the Cuban Film Institute. Much of ICAIC's works are documentary-style movies in support of the Revolution, perfected by Santiago Álvarez (1919–98), as in his *Hasta la Victoria Siempre* (1967) and *Mi Hermano Fidel* (1977). Perhaps the most powerful movies in the documentary-style genre is *Soy Cuba* (I Am Cuba), Soviet director Mikhail Kalatozov's agonizingly serious black-and-white early-1960s Cold War agitprop made when the idealism and the promise of the Cuban Revolution were genuine. (A good resource for documentaries is www.cubacine.cu/caminos.)

Undoubtedly the most respected of Cuba's filmmakers was Tomás Gutiérrez Alea (1928–96), one of the great masters of Cuban cinema, whose works were part of a general questioning of things—part of the New Latin American Cinema. The Film Institute granted a relative laxity to directors such as Gutiérrez, who was instrumental in its formation and whose populist works are of an irreverent picaresque genre. For example, his 1966 *La muerte de un burócrata* (*Death of a Bureaucrat*) was a satire on the stifling bureaucracy imposed after the Revolution; and *Memorias del subdesarrollo* (*Memories of Underdevelopment*), made in 1968, traced the life of a bourgeois intellectual adrift in the new Cuba.

Gutiérrez's finest film is *Fresa y chocolate* (*Strawberries and Chocolate*), released in 1994. The poignant and provocative movie, set in Havana during the repressive heyday of 1979, explores the nettlesome friendship between a fla-

grant homosexual and a macho Party member, reflecting the producer's abiding questioning of the Revolution to which he was nonetheless always loyal. (*Fresa y chocolate* and the subsequent movie, *Guantanamera,* the producer's last, starred his wife, Mirta Ibarra, in a leading role.) The extraordinary subtleties of his films proved too sophisticated for Cold War mentalities to the north; Gutiérrez's work was frequently misinterpreted outside Cuba, and the critical, parodying nature of his films led to the producer being regarded incorrectly as an arch anti-Castroite, much to his own dismay.

Humberto Solas (born 1941) is another leading director within the New Latin American genre. His *Lucía* (1969), which tells the tale of three women of that name living in different epochs, is considered a classic of feminist sensitivity. Most recently, his *Miel para Oshun* (*Honey for Oshun,* 2001) addresses the story of exiled Cubans returning to the island. As a tale of loss, longing, and rediscovery the movie is a visceral, moving examination of the emotional scars created by the Revolution in Cuba.

Another leading Cuban director is Juan Carlos Tabío (b. 1944), who follows in the traditional of Alea, with whom he co-directed *Guantanamera,* a farcical parody on Communist bureaucracy, told through the tale of a cortege attempting to return a body to Havana for burial. Tabío's *Lista de espera* (*The Waiting List,* 2000), another magical-realist whimsy, aims its arrow at the dire state of transportation in Cuba, focusing on a group of disparate Cubans waiting in vain for a bus, eventually transforming the bus station into a kind of socialist utopia in which they themselves find transformation.

The most recent sensation is Fernando Pérez's *Suite Havana,* an affectionate, humanist, almost silent documentary look at 24 hours in the lives of 10 ordinary families.

The annual **International Festival of New Latin American Cinema** (www.habanafilm-festival.com), better known as the Havana Film Festival, is held in December, as it has been since 1978.

ESSENTIALS

U.S. Law and Travel to Cuba

It is a remarkable anomaly that there are political leaders in this government who believe that they contribute to increasing freedom in Cuba by restraining freedom at home.

— William Rogers, former U.S. Secretary of State

Most *yanquis* harbor the false impression that it's illegal for U.S. citizens to visit Cuba; it's not, it's merely illegal to spend money there (the U.S. Supreme Court has affirmed the constitutional right of unrestricted travel; thus the U.S. government invokes the 1916 Trading with the Enemy Act to prohibit travelers from *trading* with Cuba).

To visit Cuba legally you must either spend no money there, or qualify for a license issued by the U.S. Treasury Department in order to buy goods (a meal at a hotel, for example) or services (an airline ticket, tour package, or hotel room). Except as specifically licensed by the Office of Foreign Assets Control (OFAC), payments in connection with travel to Cuba are prohibited, whether travelers go directly or via a third country such as Mexico, Canada, or another Caribbean island. Any person under U.S. jurisdiction is subject to these restrictions, regardless of citizenship.

© CHRISTOPHER P. BAKER

The regulations change frequently and are open to interpretation by the understaffed office.

The Clinton administration eased restrictions on who may visit and spend money in Cuba. President George W. Bush has since backtracked with a vengeance, even going so far as to restrict Cuban-Americans to one visit every three years and then only to visit immediate family members for reasons solely of humanitarian need. The Bush administration has rescinded several previously permitted categories for legal travel (notably cultural exchange licenses, which allowed just about any American to travel to Cuba), has raised the bar of eligibility in all categories for permissible travel (for example, the number of humanitarian organizations issued licenses has fallen from 160 in 2004 to just 20 in 2005), and has adopted a witch-hunt mentality regarding persons who have traveled without a licence (Elizardo Gutiérrez-Menoyo, a leading dissident who in 2004 returned from exile to live in Cuba, was even threatened in absentia with a fine). Just four OFAC officers were assigned to investigate Osama Bin Laden and Saddam Hussein's financial transactions, while almost two dozen have been assigned to Cuban embargo violations!

To determine if you or your organization qualifies for a **general license** (which does not require prior government authorization) or a **specific license** (which does require prior government authorization), contact the Licensing Division, **Office of Foreign Asset Control** (U.S. Department of the Treasury, 1500 Pennsylvania Ave. NW, Washington, DC 20200, tel. 202/622-2480, www.treas.gov/offices/enforcement/ofac/programs/cuba/cuba.shtml).

Who Is an "Individual Subject to United States Law"

An individual subject to U.S. law includes: any individual, wherever located, who is a citizen or resident of the United States; any person who is within the United States (a non-U.S. citizen in transit at an airport, for example); any corporation organized under the laws of the United States or of any state, territory possession, or district of the United States; any corporation, partnership, or association, wherever organized or doing business, that is owned or controlled by an individual or individuals subject to U.S. law.

General Licenses

Persons who are visiting close relatives are no longer permitted to travel under a general license, and fully-hosted travel, formerly allowed, is no longer legal. The following categories of travelers are permitted to spend money for Cuban travel without the need to obtain special permission from OFAC, nor are they required to inform OFAC in advance of their visit to Cuba.

Official Government Travelers: U.S. and foreign government officials, including representatives of international organizations of which the United States is a member, who are traveling on official business.

Journalists: Individuals who are regularly (full-time) employed by a news-gathering organization (television network, television station, television production company, radio station, newspaper, newsletter, magazine, video production company, etc.), and persons regularly employed as supporting broadcast or technical personnel. (Note that if you travel as a journalist, the Cuban government requires that you be issued a journalist's visa, not a tourist card.)

Full-time professionals whose travel transactions are directly related to "noncommercial, academic research" in their professional field and whose research will comprise a full work schedule in Cuba and has a likelihood of public dissemination; plus full-time professionals whose travel transactions are directly related to attendance at professional meetings or conferences that do not promote tourism or other commercial activity involving Cuba or the production of biotechnological products, so long as such meetings are organized by "qualifying international bodies."

Specific Licenses

A specific license requires written government approval. Applicants should write a letter to OFAC stating the date of the planned visit and the length of stay; the specific purpose(s) of the visit; plus the name(s), title(s), and background(s) of the traveler. OFAC is notoriously slow: Allow two or three months.

U.S. universities, colleges, and nongovernmental organizations may apply for one-year travel permits to Cuba that will permit students and academic staff to travel to Cuba (see *Students and Academic Employees* later in this section). Religious and humanitarian organizations can apply for a similar license permitting individuals affiliated with that organization to make such transactions. Special licenses are also issued by OFAC on a case-by-case basis authorizing travel transactions by persons in connection with the following travel categories.

Humanitarian Travel: Persons traveling to Cuba to accompany licensed humanitarian donations (other than gift parcels); or persons traveling in connection with activities of recognized human rights organizations investigating human rights violations.

Persons Visiting Immediate Family: People with parents, children, and siblings in Cuba may visit them in circumstances of humanitarian need for no longer than 14 days. This authorization is valid only once every three years and contains no provision for emergency visits permitting a second visit within three years, even for circumstances of grave illness or death.

Freelance Journalists: Persons with a suitable record of publication who are traveling to do research for a freelance article. Licenses may be issued for multiple trips.

Professional Research and Meetings: Persons engaging in professional research or attending professional meetings that do not meet the general license requirements.

Educational Research: Travel in connection with educational activities that are not related to an academic institution's specific license, including educational exchanges that promote people-to-people contact. For example, graduate students enrolled at non-licensed universities may apply for a specific license as long as research specifically relates to Cuba and so long as that research will be accepted

for credit toward their graduate degree; undergraduate students enrolled in a degree program at a non-licensed college can apply for a specific license to participate in a formal course of study of not less than 10 weeks at a Cuban academic institution.

Travelers affiliated with religious institutions that hold a specific license may engage in travel transactions without seeking OFAC authorization so long as travel is under the auspices of the institution and that a full-time program of religious activity is pursued in Cuba. However, any religious organization that does not fall into the "established church" category is limited to bringing 25 individuals every three months. (The Bush administration has even denied the Presbyterian Church a renewal of its license, stating that it is not a religious body! Only evangelical church bodies with an anti-Castroite position were being approved at time of writing.)

Religous Activities: Travel in connection with religious activities that are not related to a religious institution's specific license.

Students and academic employees affiliated with an academic institution that has been issued a specific license may engage in travel transactions so long as travel is for participation in a structured educational program that is part of a course offered at the U.S. college or university (students must be enrolled in a degree course). Such travelers must carry a letter from the licensed institution stating the institution's license number and students have to show that travel is for course work of not less than 10 weeks at a Cuban academic institution. Graduate students can conduct research in Cuba so long as that research will be accepted for credit toward their graduate degree. Faculty of licensed U.S. academic institutions may conduct academic research or attend professional meetings (see *Full-Time Professionals* under *General Licenses*).

Support for the Cuban People: Travel aimed at promoting "independent activity intended to strengthen civil society in Cuba."

Private Foundations or Research or Educational Institutions: Persons traveling to

Cuba on behalf of such institutions to collect information for noncommercial purposes.

Amateur or semiprofessional athletes traveling to participate in athletic competition held under the auspices of an international sports federation.

Export, Import, or Transmission of Informational Materials: Persons traveling to engage in exportation, importation, or transmission of informational materials.

Licensed Exportation: Individuals traveling to engage in activities directly related to marketing, sales negotiation, delivery, or servicing of exports of health care products or other exports consistent with the export licensing policy of the Department of Commerce.

What You May Spend, Take, and Return Home With

Since 2004, the Bush administration has imposed a limit of US$50 per day for travelers visiting immediate family. Other licensed travelers are authorized to spend up to the State Department Travel *per diem* allowance, which was US$167 per day in Havana and US$125 outside Havana at press time. Journalists may spend more than this allowance (the amount is unspecified) to cover expenses incurred in the reporting of a story, and other licensed travelers may spend additional money "for transactions directly related to the activities for which they received a license."

Money may be spent only for purchases of items directly related to licensed travel such as hotel accommodations, meals, and goods personally used by the traveler in Cuba. Credit cards, including those issued by foreign firms, may *not* be used.

Accompanied baggage is limited to 44 pounds.

Licensed travelers were previously permitted to return from Cuba with up to US$100 worth of Cuban products for their personal use. Such travelers are no longer permitted to return to the United States with any Cuban purchases, other than literature; there is no restriction on the amount that may be spent on informational materials.

Qualified Travel Service Providers

U.S. law states, "U.S. travel service providers, such as travel agents and tour operators, who handle travel arrangements to, from, or within Cuba must hold special authorizations from the U.S. Treasury Department to engage in such activities."

OFAC licenses companies as authorized Travel Service Providers (TSPs), who are legally entitled to make commercial travel arrangements to Cuba. TSPs can only make reservations for individual travel for licensed travelers. You must obtain approval before proceeding with a reservation. Some TSPs are also CSPs (Carrier Service Providers) licensed to operate their own charters to Cuba. See the sidebar *Licensed Carrier Service Providers* for information on individual companies.

OFAC also issues TSP licenses to certain companies and organizations permitting them to offer pre-packaged group tours spanning the spectrum from salsa and music study to Jewish heritage tours. As of March 2003, the Treasury Department began to close what it sees as a "loophole" and no new licenses or renewals of existing ones have been granted.

However, referring to other travel agencies and tour operators (i.e., non-TSPs), "It is possible to provide travel services to U.S. persons legally able to travel to Cuba for family visits, professional research, or news gathering," says Michael Krinsky, a partner in the law firm of Rabinowitz, Boudin, Standard, Krinsky and Lieberman, which represents the Cuban government in the United States.

They may also be able to provide services, such as travel arrangements to Jamaica, from where a traveler makes his or her own arrangements for travel to and within Cuba. Treasury Department regulations do not "show a clear penalty against travel agents who book travel this way." Travel agents should double-check the regulations, however, with OFAC or with Krinsky (740 Broadway, New York, NY 10003, 212/254-1111, fax 212/674-4614, mkrinsky@rbskl.com).

Cuban Visas for Licensed Travelers

All licensed travelers to Cuba must have a visa from the Cuban government prior to reserving their flight. TSPs can assist you in acquiring your visa. TSPs typically charge about US$35 for the visa, and often an additional fee for preparing the documents. Allow at least 30 days for processing.

"Illegal" Travel

In 2003 about 30,000 U.S. citizens slipped into Cuba through Canada, Mexico, the Bahamas, and other third countries to worship at the shrine of 1950s kitsch and savor the frisson of the forbidden. Cubans usually play their part by abstaining from stamping passports (however, several readers report having received a small, almost illegible mark on page 16 of their passports, familiar to U.S. authorities).

Persons subject to U.S. jurisdiction who travel to Cuba without a license bear a "presumption of guilt" and may be required to show documentation that all expenses incurred were paid by a third party not subject to U.S. law. *Individuals who choose to circumvent U.S. law do so at their own risk and the author and publisher accept no responsibility for any consequences that may result from such travel.*

Until recently, the U.S. government basically turned a blind eye to illegal travel to Cuba, but in 2001 the Bush administration began to tighten control of unsanctioned travel. Perceived offenders first receive a questionnaire and, if the Feds believe the law has been broken, a "pre-penalty notice" listing the amount of the proposed fine: In the first quarter of 2005, OFAC sent out 307 such notices for unauthorized travel, almost as many as the 316 in all 2004. (Trading with Cuba illegally is good for up to a US$55,000 fine under provisions of the Helms-Burton Bill, plus up to US$250,000

under the Trading with the Enemy Act, but most demands for fines have been US$7,500.) The US Government never previously brought this regulation to court, and the only fines ever collected were from people who upon receiving the "pre-penalty" notice voluntarily paid up. Anyone receiving a pre-penalty notice could kill the action dead by requesting a hearing. More than a decade after Congress granted the right of a civil hearing for anyone accused of violating the travel ban, no judges had been hired, no hearings had been held, and not a single person had been prosecuted. However, in 2004 the Bush administration appointed three judges to review the backlog of cases.

If issued a penalty notice by OFAC, you have 30 days to appeal. If the case is not settled out of court, the case ostensibly goes before an administrative law judge, who can uphold or dismiss the penalty. At press time, only two such adjudications had been made. In January 2005 a judge slapped the first-ever such fine (for US$5,250) on a Michigan couple who traveled in 2001 on a religious mission; the second penalty was for US$780. If you choose to pay the fine requested in the pre-penalty notice, you can negotiate the amount.

How to Defend the Right to Travel: The **National Lawyers Guild** (132 Nassau St., Suite 922, New York, NY 10038, tel. 212/679-5100, fax 212/679-2811, www.nlg.org) has a Cuba subcommittee that can aid in defending against "these restrictions and enforcement actions" and maintains a database of lawyers willing to provide such representation.

The **Center for Constitutional Rights** (666 Broadway, New York, NY 10012, tel. 212/614-6464, fax 212/614-6499, www.ccr-ny.org) is the primary institutional clearinghouse for legal information about the Cuba travel regulations and represents those who have been accused of violating the ban.

Getting There

BY AIR

About 40 airlines service Cuba (Cuba's Ministry of Tourism website has a not entirely accurate site listing most flights to the island: www.cubatravel.cu/client/get_cuba/airlines.php). The majority of flights arrive at Havana's José Martí International Airport. Cuba has a well-developed air transport network with eight additional international airports: Camagüey (Ignacio Agramonte), Cayo Coco, Cayo Largo del Sur, Cayo Santa María, Holguín (Frank País), Santa Clara (Abel Santamaría), Santiago de Cuba (Antonio Maceo), and Varadero (Juan Gualberto Gómez). See the regional chapters for listings of airlines that service these airports.

Cuba's national airline is **Cubana de Aviación** (www.cubana.cu), which generally offers lower fares than competing airlines. Cubana has DC-10s and Airbus A-320s that serve Europe and Mexico. However, the workhorses in the stable remain uncomfortable and poorly maintained Soviet-made aircraft. The airline is poorly managed, service is charmless, passengers are treated with disdain (although service aboard is fairly good), and its safety record is the worst in the world.

(At press time, all aircraft of Cuba's Aero Caribbean were being used exclusively to airlift patients for Operación Milagro; see *Into the New Millennium* in the *History* section of the *Background* chapter.)

Fares quoted in this book are based on rates advertised at press time. They are subject to change and should be used only as a guideline.

Practicalities

To get the cheapest fares, make your reservations as early as possible, especially during peak season, as flights often sell out. Low-season and mid-week travel is often cheaper, as are stays of more than 30 days. **STA Travel** (www.statravel.com), with offices worldwide, specializes in low fares.

BUYING YOUR TICKET ONLINE

U.S. websites such as www.orbitz.com and www.travelocity.com are barred from making reservations for Cuba flights. However, numerous foreign-based websites, including those of foreign airlines such as COPA and Grupo Taca (but not Air Jamaica), offer reservation services for travel to Cuba. Except as specifically licensed by the Office of Foreign Assets Control (OFAC), it is illegal for any U.S. citizen or resident to make payments in connection with travel to Cuba through such websites.

The Cuban government runs its own interactive site (www.cubasi.cu), although it is dysfunctional and not recommended. Cuba-based **Cubalinda** (www.cubalinda.com) invoices clients by email and issues electronic tickets; payment by U.S. citizens is made by bank transfer to an account in Germany, or direct to Cuba for transactions originating outside the United States.

Most scheduled airlines permit two pieces of checked baggage; most charter airlines permit 20 kilos of baggage, and charge extra for overweight bags. Cubana has a zero-tolerance policy on overweight baggage, for which it charges extortionate rates for each kilo over your 20-kilo limit. Keep any valuable items, such as laptop computers, in your carry-on luggage. Always reconfirm your reservation and return flight within 72 hours of your departure (reservations are frequently cancelled if not reconfirmed, especially during peak season; Cubana is particularly bad in this regard) and arrive at the airport with plenty of time to spare. Reconfirming can be a problem within Cuba for charter ticket holders, as often the local representative is based at a particular resort and may prove elusive. Always keep a photocopy of your ticket separate from your ticket and other documents as a safeguard in the event of loss or theft.

From the United States

Licensed Flights: About two dozen companies—called Carrier Service Providers (CSPs)—are authorized to fly direct charters to Cuba from the United States (see the *Licensed Carrier Service Providers* sidebar). CSPs are only authorized to carry properly documented passengers as permitted by the U.S. Treasury Department. CSPs and licensed TSPs (which can make arrangements for travel to Cuba, but are not licensed to offer their own charter service) may also make reservations for authorized or fully-hosted travelers on flights between third countries and Cuba, including Cuban carriers for authorized travelers.

Licensed charter flights operate to Havana from Miami daily and at press time typically cost US$499 round-trip, US$325 one-way. In addition, scheduled charter flights operated by Grupo Taca depart Los Angeles for Havana (about US$699 round-trip, US$530 one-way); and Continental flies from New York's John F. Kennedy airport (about US$629 round-trip, US$429 one-way). The government fixes prices, which are the same for the first-class section as the back of the plane.

Via Third Countries: At press time, no scheduled commercial flights were permitted between the United States and Cuba. For that reason, thousands of U.S. citizens travel to Cuba via third countries. The most popular routes are through Canada, the Bahamas, Mexico, or Jamaica. However, the Treasury Department issues the following advisory: "The Regulations prohibit all transactions relating to travel-related tourist transactions in Cuba including prepayment in third countries for Cuba-related expenses" for unlicensed travelers (see *"Illegal" Travel* in this chapter).

Under existing U.S. law, citizens showing an airline reservation that includes an onward flight to Cuba will be refused boarding on the flight out of the United States. Hence, travel requires completely separate tickets and reservations for your travel into and out of Cuba from any third country: For example, you can reserve your ticket with a foreign carrier such as Air Jamaica (but not via its website), but you have to pay for the Jamaica-Cuba leg upon arrival in Jamaica.

You can also search online with ticketing agencies such as www.travelocity.com, www.expedia.com, or www.orbitz.com and purchase a ticket to a third country gateway using a secure server to pay by credit card. However, U.S. travel websites such as www.orbitz.com and www.travelocity.com are barred from making reservations for Cuba flights, and except as specifically licensed by the Office of

---

LICENSED CARRIER SERVICE PROVIDERS (CSPs)

The following are recommended CSPs:

ABC Charters (6101 Blue Lagoon Dr., Suite 150, Miami, FL 33126, 305/871-1260 or 866/411-1147, fax 305/447-0965, www.abc-charters.com).

Cuba Travel Services (7300 Corporate Center Dr., Suite 703, Miami, FL 33126, 305/476-9400 or 800/963-2822, www.cubatravelservices.com) offers charter flights from Los Angeles to Havana, and from Miami to Havana and Cienfuegos.

Gulfstream (545 NW 42nd Ave., Miami, FL 33126, 305/428-2822, fax 305/428-2826, www.gulfstreamair.com) operates charters from Miami. It also operates one flight a week to Havana exclusively for staff of the U.S. Interests Section.

Marazul Charters (725 River Rd., Edgewater, NJ 07020, 201/840-6711 or 800/223-5334, fax 201/840-6719, www.marazulcharters.com) operates charters from New York on Saturday, plus charters from Miami and Los Angeles.

Wilson International Services (4919 S.W. 75 Ave., Miami, FL 33152, 305/662-6842).

Foreign Assets Control (OFAC), it is illegal for any U.S. citizen or resident to make payments in connection with any travel to Cuba through such websites (See the sidebar *Buying Your Ticket Online*.)

Travelers should assume a possibility that passenger manifests for flights arriving to Havana are shared with U.S. authorities.

From Canada

There are plenty of flights between Canada and Cuba; most fly to Varadero—a three-and-a-half-hour flight from Toronto—and other beach destinations. You might find cheap airfares—about C$400 round-trip—through **Wholesale Travel** (tel. 416/366-1000 or 888/388-1000, www.wholesaletravel.com) and **Travel Cuts** (tel. 416/614-2887 or 800/592-2887, www.travelcuts.com).

A. Nash Travel Inc. (5865 McLaughlin Rd., Unit 2B, Mississauga, Ontario L5R 1B8, tel. 905/755-0647 or 866/537-7608, fax 905/755-0729, www.nashtravel.com) and **Southwind Travel** (1235 Bay St., Suite 400, Toronto, Ontario M5R 3K4, tel. 416/921-4012, fax 416/969-8916, www.southwindtravel.com) are recommended Cuba specialists.

Scheduled Flights: Cuba's **Cubana** (1240 Bay St., Suite 800, Toronto, tel. 416/967-2822, sales@cubanatours.com) has departures from Montreal to Havana twice daily on Monday and Saturday, to Camagüey on Thursday, to Cayo Largo on Friday, to Cienfuegos on Thursday; and from Toronto to Havana on Friday and Sunday, and to Cienfuegos on Friday.

Air Canada (tel. 800/247-2262, www.aircanada.com) flies from Toronto to Havana four times weekly, to Cayo Coco on Friday, to Holguín on Friday, to Varadero on Friday; from Montreal to Havana three times weekly, to Ciego de Ávila on Sunday, to Santa Clara on Saturday, and to Varadero on Sunday; and from Vancouver to Havana three times weekly.

Air Jamaica (tel. 416/229-6024 or 800/526-5585, www.airjamaica.com) offers connecting flights to Havana through Montego Bay, Jamaica, departing Toronto. However, the airline has a reputation for losing luggage.

Charter Flights: Most charter flights are designed as beach vacation packages, but charter operators will sell "air-only" tickets.

Air Canada Vacations (www.aircanadavacations.com), a division of Air Canada, offers air-hotel packages. Tickets are issued only via travel agencies.

Air Transat (tel. 866/847-1112, www.airtransat.com) flies to Camagüey, Cayo Coco, Holguín, Santa Clara, Santiago de Cuba, and Varadero with departures from Montreal, Quebec, St. Johns, and Toronto.

Skyservice (tel. 416/679-5700, www.skyserviceairlines.com) flies to Camagüey, Cayo Coco, Cayo Largo, Holguín, Manzanillo, Santiago de Cuba, and Varadero, with departures from Calgary, Kitchener, Montreal, Ottawa, Toronto, Vancouver, Windsor, and Winnipeg.

Westjet (tel. 888/937-8538, www.westjet.com) serves Camagüey, Cayo Coco, Cayo Larga, Holguín, Santa Clara, Santiago de Cuba, and Varadero, with departures from Calgary, Edmonton, Halifax, Montreal, Saskatoon, Toronto, Vancouver, and Winnipeg.

From Europe

Direct air service to Cuba is available from most western European countries. You can also find cheap fares via Caribbean destinations, from where you can take a flight to Cuba. Note that if flying aboard a U.S. carrier, you must have your ticket for the Cuban portion issued on a separate ticket stock, and you must make your reservation for the Cuba leg separately.

From France: Havana is served by **Air France** (tel. 0802/80-28-02, www.airfrance.com), four times weekly from Paris's Charles de Gaulle airport (from €629 round-trip). **Air Europa** (www.aireuropa.com) flies between Paris and Havana on Saturday (from about €625). **Cubana** (41 Boulevard du Montparnasse, 75006 Paris, tel. 01/53-63-23-23) flies from Paris Orly airport to Havana via Santiago de Cuba twice weekly using a DC-10.

Good online resources for discount airfares

PRIVATE AIRCRAFT

Private pilots must contact the **Instituto de Aeronáutica Civil de Cuba** (Calle 23 #64, e/ Infanta y P, Vedado, tel. 07/55-1121, fax 07/834-4571) at least 10 days before arrival in Cuba and at least 48 hours before an overflight.

U.S. owners of private aircraft, including air ambulance services, who intend to land in Cuba must obtain a temporary export permit for the aircraft from the U.S. Department of Commerce before departure.

include www.travelprice.fr, www.anyway.fr, and www.wasteels.fr.

From Germany: Charter company **Condor** (tel. 06171/65-3604, www.condor.com) flies between Dusseldorf and Holguín. **LTU** (tel. 0211/941-8333, www.ltu.de) flies to Havana, Holguín, and Varadero from Berlin and Dusseldorf (Nov.–Apr.).

From Italy: Italy's **Air Europe** (tel. 199/414-500, www.aireurope.it) flies from Milan to Havana on Sunday (about €750 round-trip) December–May.

Blue Panorama (tel. 06/6550-8203, www.blue-panorama.com) carries the bulk of Italian tourists to Cuba with 10 flights weekly to Havana, Varadero, Cayo Coco, Cayo Largo, Holguín, and Santiago de Cuba, using new Boeing wide-body aircraft. **Cubana** (Via Appia Nouva 45, Scala B, 00182 Roma, tel. 06/700-0714, fax 06/700-1670, cubana.aviacion@flashnet.it) flies from Milan to Havana via Santiago de Cuba once weekly using a DC-10. **Lauda Air** (Strada Provinciale 52, 21010 Vizzola Ticino, Italy, tel. 0331/759300 or 8000/52832, fax 0331/230-467, www.lauda.it) flies charters from Milan to Havana, Santa Clara, and Holguín.

From the Netherlands: Havana is served by **Martinair** (tel. 20/60-11-767, www.martinair.com) from Amsterdam twice weekly in summer and three times weekly in winter (Oct.–Mar.). It also serves Varadero once weekly in

summer and twice weekly in winter, and Holguín once weekly year-round.

From Russia: Russian carrier **Aeroflot** (tel. 095/753-5555 in Moscow, 812/718-5555 in St. Petersburg, 020/7409-2779 in London, www.aeroflot.ru/eng/) flies from Moscow to Havana on Saturday and Monday using a Boeing 767. **Cubana** (tel. 095/238-4343, www.cubana.ru) operates a DC-10 once a week from Moscow.

From Spain: Havana is served by **Cubana** (tel. 091/758-7751, cubanamad@deico.es) from Madrid on Monday and Thursday using a DC-10 (from €560 round-trip), and from Las Palmas (tel. 0928/272-408, fax 0928/272-429) once weekly using an Ilyushin. Cubana also flies Madrid to Holguín once weekly July through September. **Iberia** (tel. 902/400-500, www.iberia.com), flies to Havana from Madrid daily (from €450 round-trip), as do **Air Europa** (tel. 971/178-0033, www.air-europa.com) and **Iberworld Airlines** (www.iberworld.com), with flights from €805 round-trip.

From Sweden: Cubana (Kungsgatan 50, Box 3410, 103 68 Stockholm, tel. 8/5684-9820, fax 8/210-211, www.cubana.se) flies from Stockholm to Havana via Holguín on Wednesday.

From the United Kingdom: The main carrier is **Virgin Atlantic** (tel. 0870/574-7747, www.virgin-atlantic.com), which flies twice weekly from Gatwick to Havana, with fares as low as £587 round-trip in summer. **Cubana** (Unit 49, Skyline Village, Limeharbour Rd., London E14 9TS, tel. 020/7536-8177, www.cubanacan.cu) flies from Gatwick to Havana via Holguín on Wednesday and Saturday (from £449 roundtrip). **Air Jamaica** (tel. 0207/9629-9349, www.airjamaica.com) flies to Havana from Heathrow on Monday via Kingston.

British Airways (tel. 0870/850-9850, www.britishairways.com) flies to Madrid, connecting to Iberia's Madrid–Havana flight (£669 roundtrip).

Monarch (www.flymonarch.com) has weekly charter flights.

Virgin Holidays (tel. 0871/222-0304, www.virgin.com/holidays) has one- and two-week packages featuring Havana and Varadero.

Captivating Cuba (tel. 0870/887-0123, www.captivating-cuba.co.uk) is the United Kingdom's largest tour agency handling air traffic to Cuba. Also try **Journey Latin America** (tel. 020/8747-3108, fax 020/8742-1312, www.journeylatinamerica.co.uk), or **Cubawelcome** (tel. 020/7584-6092, www.cubaflightswelcome.com).

Good online resources for discount tickets include www.ebookers.com, www.cheapflights.co.uk, and www.travelsupermarket.com; and for charter flights, **Charter Flight Centre** (tel.0845/045-0153, www.charterflights.co.uk).

From the Caribbean

From the Bahamas: Cuban's **Havanatur** (East Bay Shopping Centre, East Bay St., Nassau, tel. 242/393-5281, fax 242/393-5280, havanatur@batelnet.bs) operates a daily **Cubana** charter flight to Havana from Nassau. The flight times change frequently but were as follows at press time: Monday–Saturday 2:30 P.M. and Sunday at 6:15 P.M. (about US$239 round-trip, plus US$20 visa and US$10 ticket tax). Neither Havanatur nor the various tour agencies in Nassau that offer Cuba air-hotel packages using the Cubana flight accept credit card reservations by phone or email, but require you to pay a deposit in advance through a Western Union wire transfer or by certified check, which has to be mailed. You can pick up your ticket in Nassau, but most will also deliver the ticket to the airport for pick-up (usually at the airport liquor store, or similar). You should demand confirmation of your reservation and receipt of payment.

Returning from Cuba, you pass through Bahamian immigration, even in transit. The departure terminal for flights to the United States is to the left of the exit from the arrivals hall. You have to pay US$15 departure tax, despite your brief stay in the Bahamas. You must pass through U.S. Immigration and Customs here. U.S. officials may ask you outright if you've been to Cuba, or where you stayed in the Bahamas and how long, and there is a strong likelihood that all passengers arriving from Havana are monitored.

From the Cayman Islands: Havana is served weekly by **Cubana** (tel. 345/949-4606) from Grand Cayman.

From the Dominican Republic and Haiti: Copa (www.copaair.com) flies twice daily between Santo Domingo and Havana (from US$409 round-trip). **Cubana** (Av. Tiradentes y 27 de Febrero, Santo Domingo, tel. 809/227-2040, fax 809/227-2040, cubana.aviacion@codetel.net.do) serves Havana from Santo Domingo on Thursday (via Santiago de Cuba) and Sunday for US$419 round-trip. **CaribAir** (tel. 809/542-6688, caribair@caribair.com.do) flies from Santiago de los Caballeros, in Dominican Republic, to Santiago de Cuba.

From Jamaica: At press time, troubled **Air Jamaica** (tel. 800/523-5585 in North America, 888/359-2478 in Jamaica, www.airjamaica.com) was set to halt its thrice weekly flights from Montego Bay to Havana, as was affiliate **Air Jamaica Express** (same contact information), which also flies between Montego Bay and Santiago de Cuba. **Cubana** (tel. 876/978-3110, Kingston) has a code-sharing agreement with Air Jamaica, which operates the flights.

Caribic Vacations (tel. 876/952-0293 or 888/462-2822, www.caribicvacations.com) offers Cubana charter flights from Montego Bay to Havana on Friday and Sunday (US$180 one-way, US$299 round-trip, including Cuban visa), utilizing the service of Cuba's Aero Gaviota. It also has hotel packages. **Tropical Tours** (tel. 876/953-9100, www.tropicaltours-ja.com) also offers package tours to Cuba plus flights between Montego Bay and Santiago de Cuba. **Marzouca Marketing & Sales** (tel. 876/971-3859, www.cubaonweb.com) also offers package excursions.

From Central America

Taca (tel. 305/870-7500 or 800/400-8222, www.grupotaca.com) has flights from El Salvador to Havana four times weekly (from US$521 round-trip), with connecting flights from the United States, and from Costa Rica and Guatemala at no extra cost.

Cubana (Edifio Edicol, Sabana Sur, San José, tel. 506/290-5095, fax 506/290-5101, cubanaju@racsa.co.cr) flies from Costa Rica to Havana on Thursday and Sunday (US$499). **Eco Tours** (tel. 506/262-3424, 888/698-9660 in North America, www.ecotourscostarica.co.cr) sells a seven-night Cuba package designed for U.S. citizens, with overnights in Costa Rica the first and last nights. **COPA** (tel. 507/217-2672 or 800/359-2672 in the U.S., www.copaair.com) flies to Havana from Panama City twice daily from US$532 round-trip.

From Mexico: The national carrier **Mexicana** (tel. 55/5448-1050 in Mexico City, 800/509-8960 from elsewhere in Mexico, 800/531-7921 in the U.S., www.mexicana.com) has daily flights to Havana from Cancún (from US$357 round trip), Mexico City (from about US$609 round-trip), and Mérida (from US$402 round-trip). **Cubana** (tel. 5/250-6355 in Mexico City, tel. 98/877-210 in Cancún, reservaciones@cubanamexico.com) also offers from Mexico City twice weekly (from US$450 round-trip) using a DC-10, and flights on Monday–Saturday from Cancún (from US$255 round-trip) using antiquated Soviet planes.

Tourist cards for Mexico are handed out on the flight just before arriving in Mexico. It's a good idea to reconfirm your outbound flight 48 hours before departure.

Cuban-owned **Viajes Divermex** (Av. Cobá #5, Centro Comercial Plaza América, Cancún, Quintana Roo, México CP 77500, tel. 9988/884-5005, www.divermex.com) specializes in Cuba packages.

From South America

Lan Chile (tel. 600/526-2000, 866/435-9526 in the U.S., www.lanchile.com) flies to Havana from Santiago de Chile twice weekly for about US$905 round-trip.

Aeropostal (tel. 0-800/237-6252, 305/592 0827 or 888/912-8466 in the U.S., www.aeropostal.com) flies to Havana from Caracas thrice weekly for about US$370 round-trip.

Cubana flies to Havana from Quito, Ecuador; Buenos Aires, Argentina; Sao Paulo, Brazil; Bogota, Colombia; and Caracas, Venezuela.

From Asia

You can fly to Paris, London, Madrid, Mexico City, Canada, or South America and connect with flights to Cuba. If traveling via the United States, flying nonstop to Los Angeles, then to Mexico City or Cancún, is perhaps the easiest route.

Cuba and China recently discussed plans to begin direct flights from Beijing to Havana.

STA Travel (www.statravel.com) is a good resource for tickets and has branches in Hong Kong, Tokyo, Singapore, Bangkok, and Kuala Lumpur.

From Australia and New Zealand

The best bet is to fly either to Los Angeles or San Francisco and then to Cuba via Mexico, El Salvador, or Panama; or to Canada and on to Havana. **Air New Zealand** (in Australia tel. 02/8235-9999, in New Zealand tel. 0800/737-0000, www.airnewzealand.com), **Qantas** (tel. 131-313; in New Zealand tel. 0800/808-767, www.qantas.com.au), and **United Airlines** (tel. 131-777; in New Zealand tel. 0800/747-400) offer direct service between Australia, New Zealand, and North America.

A route via Buenos Aires or Santiago de Chile and then to Havana is also possible.

Specialists in discount fares include **STA Travel** (in Australia tel. 1300/733-035, www.statravel.com.au; in New Zealand tel. 0508/782-872, www.statravel.co.nz), which has regional offices throughout the region.

A good online resource for discount airfares is **Flight Centre** (tel. 133-133, www.flightcentre.com.au).

BY SEA
By Cruise Ship

The U.S. embargo has restricted the cruise industry's access to Cuba. Nonetheless, several foreign cruise ships feature Cuba on their itineraries. In theory, it's entirely legal for any U.S. citizen to partake of these cruises without breaking the law as the in-transit visa used, which allows up to 48 hours in Cuba, means that no port fees apply (this, of course, assumes that you don't spend a dime ashore nor partake of shore excursions arranged by the ship and involving transfer of funds to Cuban entities). However, a prohibition for U.S. citizens regarding "all transactions relating to travel-related tourist transactions in Cuba" now applies. We recommend you check the latest regulations (also see *"Illegal" Travel* in the *U.S. Law and Travel to Cuba* section in this chapter).

Cruiseserver (www.cruiseserver.net) is a good source and includes passengers' reviews of cruises to Cuba.

Of the several companies that have launched regular scheduled cruises to or from Cuba, none has stood the test of time.

Spain's **Pullmantur** (Calle Orense 16, 1ra planta, Madrid 28020, tel. 91/418-8790, www.pullmanturcruises.com) offers eight-day all-inclusive cruises aboard the 1,047-passenger *Holiday Dream*. The vessel home ports in Havana and makes once-weekly trips to Montego Bay, Cozumel, Cienfuegos, and Punta Francés, on Cuba's Isla de la Juventud. Guests can embark in Cozumel on Monday.

England's **Fred Olsen Cruise Lines** (tel. 01473/746-175, www.fredolsencruises.co.uk) featured Havana and Santiago de Cuba on its 2006 Caribbean cruises using the *Braemar*.

Germany's **Hapag Lloyd** (www.hapag-lloyd.com) occasionally features Havana on its peak-season programs, as does **Aida Cruises** (www.aida.de).

By Freighter

Hamburg-Süd Reiseagentur GMBH (Ost-West 59, 20457 Hamburg, tel. 040/3705-2652 or 01805/322232, fax 040/370-5242, www.freighter-voyages.com) books passage aboard the *Cala Providencia* (with three twin-bed cabins) sailing from Barcelona to Havana on a 35-day journey (from €2,975).

In the United Kingdom, book through **Strand Voyages** (1 Adam St., London WC2N 6AB, tel. 020/7766-8220, fax 020/7766-8225, www.strandtravel.co.uk). U.S. citizens can book through **Freighter World Cruises** (180 S. Lake Ave., #335, Pasadena, CA 91101, tel. 626/449-3106 or 800/531-7774, fax 626/449-9573, www.freighterworld.com).

By Ferry and Excursion Boat

No ferry service currently connects Cuba with any international port.

Heave-Ho Charters (180 Main St., Ocho Rios, Jamaica, tel. 876/974-5367, fax 876/974-5461, www.heaveho.net) offers passage between Ocho Rios and Santiago de Cuba aboard a catamaran.

By Private Vessel

No advance permission is required to arrive by sea. However, it is wise to give at least 72 hours advance warning by faxing complete details of your boat, crew, and passengers to the harbormaster's office at Marina Hemingway (fax 07/204-3104). Anyone planning on sailing to Cuba should obtain a copy of Simon Charles's *Cruising Guide to Cuba* and Nigel Calder's *Cuba: A Cruising Guide* (see *Suggested Reading* in the *Resources*).

The Bush administration requires that U.S. boaters get pre-authorization from the Coast Guard Marine Safety Office (www.uscg.mil/hq/g-o/g-opl/CubaTravel.htm). U.S. boaters are also expressly forbidden to travel to Cuba without an export license from the Commerce Department and a specific license from OFAC. Applications must be made through the Seventh Coast Guard District (tel. 305/415-6920, fax 305/415-6925). All persons subject to U.S. law aboard vessels, including the owner, must be an authorized traveler to engage in travel transactions in Cuba. Vessel owners are prohibited from carrying travelers to Cuba who pay them for passage if the owner does not have a specific license from OFAC authorizing him or her to be a Service Provider to Cuba.

At the present time, the United States and Cuba do not have a Coast Guard agreement. Craft developing difficulties in Cuban territorial waters cannot expect assistance from the U.S. Coast Guard. Cuba's territorial waters extend 12 miles out. Although Cuban authorities have usually proven to be helpful to yachters in distress, there are reports of corruption among Cuban officials involving foreign yachters, some of whom have had their vessels impounded as collateral against the cost of rescue or salvage.

John G. Alden Insurance Special Risks, Inc. (89 Commercial Wharf, Boston, MA 02110, tel. 617/227-7670, fax 617/227-7933, www.johngalden.com) can assist with inquiries regarding supplemental insurance coverage to yachters cruising in Cuban waters.

Maps and Charts: Yachting charts can be ordered from **Bluewater Books & Charts** (1811 Cordova Rd., Ft. Lauderdale, FL 33316, tel. 954/763-6533 or 800/942-2583, fax 954/522-2278, www.bluewaterweb.com).

In Havana, **Tienda el Navegante** (Calle Mercaderes #115, e/ Obispo y Obrapía, Habana Vieja, tel. 07/861-3625, fax 07/33-2869; for boaters, VHF channel 16 CMYP3050; Mon.–Fri. 8 A.M.–5 P.M., Sat. 8 A.M.–1 P.M.) sells nautical charts, including a "Chart Kit" containing maps of the entire Cuban coast.

BY ORGANIZED TOUR

Joining an organized tour offers certain advantages over traveling independently, such as the learning passed along by a knowledgeable guide. The petty bureaucratic hassles and language problems you may otherwise not wish to face are eliminated, too. However, you'll be almost entirely divorced from the local culture as you are hauled off to the next official tourist site.

Check the tour inclusions carefully to identify any hidden costs such as airport taxes, tips, service charges, extra meals, and entertainment. Most tours are priced according to quality of accommodations, from budget to deluxe.

Tours from the United States

U.S. citizens can legally travel to Cuba by qualifying for certain organized tours with nonprofit organizations and other entities that arrange trips with government licenses in hand. However, since 2003, the number of licensed entities has been dramatically curtailed,

---

SPANISH-LANGUAGE COURSES

The **Universidad de la Habana** (Calle J #556 e/ 25 y 27, Vedado, Havana, tel. 07/832-4245 or 870-4667, www.uh.cu/infogral/estudiaruh/postgrado/english.html) offers Spanish-language courses of 20–80 hours (CUC100–300), plus "Spanish and Cuban Culture" courses of 320–480 hours (CUC960–1,392). Courses begin the first Monday of the month, year-round.

The **Centro de Idiomas y Computación José Martí** (José Martí Language and Computer Center, Calle 90 #531, e/ 5ta B y 5ta C, Miramar, Havana, tel. 07822-9338, fax 07/824-4846, www.ain.cubaweb.cu) also offers Spanish language courses of 20–80 hours (CUC130–330).

Universitur (Calle 30 #768, e/ Kohly y 41, Nuevo Vedado, tel. 07/55-5683, fax 07/55-5978, www.universitur.cu), with regional offices in Canada and Europe, arranges Spanish-language courses at the universities of Havana, Cienfuegos, Ciego de Ávila, Granma, Holguín, and Matanzas, plus Havana's Instituto Superior Politécnico José Antonio Echeverría.

See *By Organized Tour* in the *Getting There* section of this chapter for foreign companies that offer language-learning programs to Cuba.

---

and options are now limited to trips that fall within the legal exemptions to the U.S. ban on travel to Cuba (i.e., educational study, newsgathering, professional research, and religious study).

The following organizations offer trips and/or can make arrangements for organized tours:

Center for Cuban Studies (124 W. 23rd St., New York, NY 10011, 212/242-0559, fax 212/242-1937, www.cubaupdate.org).

Global Exchange (2017 Mission St. #303, San Francisco, CA 94110, 415/255-7296, fax 415/255-7498, www.globalexchange.org).

Island Travel & Tours (2111 Wisconsin Ave. NW, Suite 319, Washington, D.C. 20007,

STUDYING IN CUBA

Thousands of people every year choose to study in Cuba, be it for a monthlong dance course or six years of medical training. You'll need a solid grasp of Spanish. Bring any supplies you think you'll need; course materials and academic supplies are scant. Be prepared for basic living conditions if signing up for a long-term residential course.

Under existing U.S. regulations, the only U.S. students currently permitted to study in Cuba are undergraduates enrolled in a degree program and who intend to participate in formal study of not less than 10 weeks at a Cuban academic institution; graduate students whose research specifically relates to Cuba; and those students attending universities and colleges that hold specific licenses permitting students and academic staff to travel to Cuba.

Universitur (Calle 30 #768, e/ Kohly y 41, Nuevo Vedado, tel. 07/55-5683, fax 07/55-5978, www.universitur.cu) arranges study at centers of higher learning, plus working holidays.

See *By Organized Tour* in the *Getting There* section of this chapter for information on organized study tours originating outside Cuba.

STUDENT VISAS

You can no longer study in Cuba using a tourist visa, however short the duration of study, unless you travel via Universitur. All others require a student visa (CUC80), which can be requested in advance from the Director of Graduate Degrees of the relevant university 20 days prior to your intended arrival date. Visas can ostensibly be picked up at the Cuban consulate in your country. Visas are good for 30 days but can be extended upon arrival in Cuba for CU25 (you'll need to buy *sellos* at a Bandec).

You can *arrive* in Cuba with a tourist visa, however. You then have 48 hours to register for your university program and request a change of visa status (CUC65). You'll need six passport photos, your passport and tourist card, plus a license certificate for the *casa particular* where you'll be staying.

For study at the **Universidad de la Habana,** contact the Dirección de Posgrado (Calle J #556, e/ 25 y 27, Vedado, tel. 07/832-4245, www.uh.cu).

ARTS, MUSIC, AND DANCE

The **Cátedra de Danza** (5ta #253, e/ D y E, Vedado, tel. 07/832-4625, fax 07/33-3117, www.balletcuba.cu) offers monthlong ballet courses for intermediate- and advanced-level professionals and students (CUC250 monthly), plus courses in modern dance, and a children's vocational workshop.

202/342-3171 east coast, 619/749-6068 west coast, or 866/488-8687, www.islandtravel-tours.com).

Last Frontier Expeditions (4900 NW Cherry St., Vancouver, WA 98663, tel. 360/597-3455, www.hemingwaytoursandsafaris.com) also offers packages for cigar lovers, classic car enthusiasts, plus sports-related events, and bird-watching, fishing, and cultural tours.

Marazul Tours (8328 SW 40th St., Miami, FL 33155, tel. 305/485-1203 or 800/993-9667, www.marazulcharters.com).

Volunteer Programs: "Solidarity" tours where participants perform voluntary work appeal to anyone wishing to contribute to the human community and learn some invaluable life lessons. However, the Bush administration has rescinded the fully-hosted travel and person-to-person exchange provisions under which such tours operated (U.S. law also prohibits U.S. citizens from receiving remuneration for work in Cuba).

Friendship Force International (34 Peachtree St. NW, Suite 900, Atlanta, GA 3030, 404/965-4357, www.friendshipforce .org) still holds a humanitarian license where program members participate in community restoration projects.

Pastors for Peace (402 W. 145th St., New York, NY 10031, 212/926-5757, fax 212/926-5842, www.ifconews.org) delivers humanitar-

The **Centro Nacional de Conservación, Restauración y Museología** (Calle Cuba #610, e/ Sol y Luz, Habana Vieja, tel. 07/861-2877, fax 07/866-5696, www.cnpc.cult.cu) offers residential courses for urban planners, conservationists, and architects.

The **Instituto Superior de Arte** (Calle 120 #11110, e/ 9na y 13, Cubanacán, tel. 07/208-0288 or 208-8075, fax 07/33-6633, isa@cubarte.cult.cu) offers short-term courses in music, dance, theater, and visual arts. It also accepts foreigners for full-year study beginning in September, for which applicants must take an entrance exam.

The **Unión de Escritores y Artistas de Cuba** (Calle 17 #351, esq. H, Vedado, tel. 07/832-4551, fax 07/33-3158, www.uneac.com) offers courses in the arts and Cuban culture, focusing on music.

The **Taller Experimental de Gráfica** (Callejón del Chorro #6, Plaza de la Catedral, Habana Vieja, tel. 07/862-0979, fax 07/204-0391, tgrafica@cubarte.cult.cu) offers courses in engraving and lithography.

The arts promotion entity **ARTEX** (Av. 5ta #8010, esq. 82, Miramar, tel. 07/833-2710) sponsors courses in the arts and literature. Artex's **Paradiso: Promotora de Viajes Culturales** (Calle 19 #560, esq. C, Vedado, tel. 07/832-6928, fax 07/33-3921, www.soycubano.com/artex/paradiso/index.asp) arranges participation in cultural courses and programs, from children's book publishing to theater criticism, plus festivals such as the International Benny Moré Festival and the International Hemingway Colloquium.

The **Universidad de la Habana** (Calle J #556, e/ 25 y 27, Vedado, Havana, tel. 07/832-4245 or 870-4667, www.uh.cu) has two- to four-week courses in Cuban culture beginning the first Monday of every month.

MEDICAL TRAINING

The Cuban **Ministerio de Salud Pública** (Ministry of Public Health), Calle 23 #201, Vedado, tel. 07/55-5532) offers free scholarships for disadvantaged and minority students from the United States and developing nations to attend the **Escuela Latinoamericana de Medicina** (Latin American School of Medical Sciences, ELACM, Santa Fe, Havana, tel. 07/29-7477, www.elacm.sld.cu). Courses last six years and graduates are full-fledged doctors. Apply through the Cuban Interests Section, 2630 16th St. NW, Washington, DC 20009, 202/797-8518, ext. 109, or at www.afrocubaweb.com/infomed/medscholarships.htm.

---

ian aid to Cuba through the annual U.S.–Cuba Friendship Caravan, which gathers aid in cities across the United States before traveling via Canada or Mexico, where the aid is shipped to Cuba. The U.S. administration has traditionally blocked the caravan, which operates without a license. Similarly, the **Venceremos Brigade** (P.O. Box 5202, Englewood, NJ 07631-5202, 212/560-4360, www.venceremosbridgade.org) organizes solidarity trips and "work-camp" brigades without a license, as it has done yearly since 1967.

Volunteers for Peace (1034 Tiffany Rd., Belmont, VT 05730, 802/259-2759, www.vfp.org) and **Witness for Peace** (707 8th St. SE, Suite 100, Washington, DC 20003, 202/547-6112, www.witnessforpeace.org) have taken participants to Cuba in past years, as has **People to People Ambassadors** (Professional Programs, Dwight D. Eisenhower Bldg., 110 S. Ferrall St., Spokane, WA 99202, 509/534-0430, www.ambassadorprograms.org).

Also see the sidebar *Tuning with the Enemy* in the *Cuban Society* section of the *Background* chapter.

Academic Exchanges: Recent changes in U.S. policy with regard to study have also affected academic exchanges, which in past years have been offered by the **Cuba Exchange Program** (School of Advanced International Studies at Johns Hopkins University, 1740 Massachusetts Ave. NW, Washington, DC

20036, 202/663-5732, fax 202/663-5737), **MacArthur Cuba Scholarly Exchange** (Center for Latin American Studies, University of Chicago, 5848 S. University Ave., Chicago, IL 60637, 773/702-8420, fax 773/702-1755, clas@uchicago.edu), and **Student Exchange between Cuba and America** (SECA, 21 Pinehurst Circle, Madison, WI 53717, 617/869-9080, www.seca.org).

In 2005, the **Cuba Academic Alliance** (Center for Cross-Cultural Study, 446 Main St., Amherst, MA 01002, 413/256-0011) initiated a lawsuit against the federal government to challenge restrictions on academic travel.

Cultural Programs: Most entities that held licenses to operate cultural programs no longer do so except for individuals who are serious about learning and for professionals gathering information and knowledge for use in their field.

Plaza Cuba (P.O. Box 3083, Berkeley, CA 94703, 510/848-0911, www.plazacuba.com) specializes in cultural workshops where tour participants learn music and dance. Chucho Valdés, Juan Formell, Changuito, and legendary flautist Richard Esqúes are among the faculty who provide one-on-one tuition.

Tours from Canada

Active Journeys (4891 Dundas St. W, Suite 4, Toronto, ON M9A 1B2, Canada, tel. 416/236-5011 or 800/597-5594, www.activejourneys.com) has bicycle trips.

CCS&CF Sports & Cultural Festivals (7171 Torbram Rd., Suite 51, Mississauga, ON L4T 3W4, tel. 905/678-0426 or 800/8181-8840, fax 905/678-1421, www.pathcom.com/~cancuba) focuses on sports and cultural exchange programs, including music and dance.

Cuba Education Tours (2278 East 24th Ave., Vancouver BC, V5N 2V2, tel. 877/687-3817, www.cubafriends.ca) offers solidarity and special-interest tours.

Leading Edge Seminars (988 Major St., Toronto ON M5S 2L1, tel. 416/964-1133 or 888/291-1333, fax 416/964-7172, www.leadingedgeseminars.org) has educational programs focusing on Cuba's health and child-care systems.

Quest Nature Tours (1170 Sheppard Ave. W., Suite 45, Toronto, Canada M3K 2A3, tel. 416/633-5666 or 800/387-1483, www.questnaturetours.com) offers bird-watching tours.

Real Cuba (Box 2345, Swan River, Manitoba, R0L 1Z0, tel. 416/656-2061, www.realcubaonline.com) offers special theme trips, including bicycling, cultural programs, walking and bird-watching, and art and photography workshops in Cuba.

Vacation Culture Cuba (5059 Saint-Denis, Montreal H2J 2L9, tel. 514/982-3330 or 800/691-0101, fax 514/982-2438, www.culturecuba.com) specializes in cultural trips, including Spanish-language and salsa courses.

WowCuba (430 Queen St., Charlottestown, Prince Edward Island, Canada CIA 4E8, tel. 902/368-2453 or 800/969-2822, www.wowcuba.com) specializes in bicycle tours of Cuba, but has other programs, including scuba diving.

Several companies offer air-hotel beach packages, including **Signature Vacations** (tel. 866/324-2883, www.signaturevacations.com), **Sunquest Vacations** (tel. 877/485-6060, www.sunquest.ca), and **Transat Holidays** (tel. 866/322-6649, www.transatholidays.com).

Tours from the United Kingdom

Captivating Cuba (tel. 0870/887-0123, www.captivating-cuba.co.uk) specializes in holidays to Cuba and offers a wide range of trips.

Journey Latin America (12 Heathfield Terr., London W4 4JE, tel. 020/8747-3108, fax 020/8742-1312, www.journeylatinamerica.co.uk) offers tours focusing on culture and bicycling.

Regal Holidays (58 Lancaster Way, Ely, Cambs, CB6 3NW, tel. 0870/2201-777, www.regal-diving.co.uk) and **Scuba en Cuba** (7 Maybank Gdns., Pinner, Mddx. HA5 2JW, tel. 01895/624100, fax 01895/624377, www.scuba-en-cuba.com) offer dive packages to Cuba.

Windsor & Neate Travel (9107 Bartholomew St., Newbury, Berkshire, RG14 5ED, tel. 01635/528-355, fax 01635/580-074, www.photographyholidays.co.uk) offers photography tours to Havana.

Virgin Holidays (tel. 0870/220-2788,

www.virginholidays.co.uk) has packages, as does Cuban-owned **San Cristobal UK** (tel. 020/7623-5510, www.scuktravel.com).

Volunteer Programs: The **Cuban Solidarity Campaign** (The Red Rose Club, 129 Seven Sisters Rd., London N7 7QG, tel. 020/7263-6452, www.cuba-solidarity.org) offers "solidarity" work brigades, and **Caledonia Languages Abroad** (The Clockhouse, Bonnington Mill, 72 Newhaven Rd., Edinburgh, EH6 5QG, Scotland, tel. 0131/621-7721, www.caledonialanguages.co.uk) offers volunteer work programs at the Centro Estudiantil youth center.

Spanish-Language Courses: Both **Caledonia Languages Abroad** (The Clockhouse, Bonnington Mill, 72 Newhaven Rd., Edinburgh, EH6 5QG, Scotland, tel. 0131/621-7721, fax 0131/621-7723, www.caledonialanguages.co.uk) and **Cactus Language** (tel. 0845/130-4775, www.cactuslanguage.com) offer language courses in Cuba.

Tours from Europe

In Germany, contact **Kubareisen** (Zschoner Ring 30, 01723 Kesselsdorf, tel. 3/5204-92112, www.kubareisen.com), whose trips include bicycle tours.

In Italy, try **Eden Viaggi** (tel. 0721/4421, www.edenviaggi.it), **Lovely Cuba** (tel. 02/4549-8557, www.lovelycuba.com), **Mappa Mondo** (tel. 06/487-891, www.mappamondo.com), or Cuba's own **Havanatur** (tel. 02/676-0691, www.havanatur.it).

Avalon Dive Center/Press Tours (tel. 33/98104, VHF 19A, Júcaro, Cuba; tel. 0335/814-9111 in Italy; www.avalons.net) offers diving from live-aboards in the Jardines de la Reina.

In Spain, contact **Viajes Cuba** (tel. 902/887-515, www.viajescuba.com).

Tours from Australia and New Zealand

Caribbean Bound (379 Pitt St., Suite 102, Sydney 2000, NSW, tel. 2/9267-2555, www.caribbean.com.au) and **Caribbean Destinations** (291 Auburn Rd., Melbourne, VIC 3122, tel. 03/9813-5258, www.caribbeanislands.com.au).

New Zealand's **Innovative Travel** (P.O. Box 21247, Edgeware, Christchurch, New Zealand, tel. 3/365-3910, www.innovative-travel.com) has packages to Cuba.

Volunteer Programs: The **Australia Cuba Friendship Association** (8 Leicester St., North Balwyn, VIC 3104, tel. 09/311-4611) offers "Southern Cross Brigade" work programs.

Getting Around

BY AIR

Most of Cuba's main cities have an airport, and virtually every major tourism destination is within a two-hour drive of an airport. Cuba's poorly managed, state-owned national airlines have a monopoly. Their safety records do not inspire confidence, and treatment of passengers is appalling. Because of Cubans' attempts to hijack planes, Cuban authorities are known to restrict the amount of fuel on aircraft on internal flights. I recommend against internal air travel if possible.

See the destination chapters for flight details.

Cubana (Calle 23, e/ 0 y P, Havana, tel. 07/834-4449, www.cubana.cu) has service between most major airports using aged and unreliable Soviet junkers. Its fares are 25 percent cheaper if booked in conjunction with an international Cubana flight. You can book at tour desks in most tourist hotels.

Aero Caribbean (Calle 23 #64, Vedado, tel. 07/879-7524, fax 07/336-5016, www.aero-caribbean.com) normally operates charter flights from Havana to Cayo Coco, Holguín, Santiago, Trinidad, and Varadero; between Varadero and Cayo Coco; and between Santiago de Cuba and Baracoa, Holguín, and Varadero.

Aerogaviota (Av. 47 #2814, e/ 28 y 34, Rpto. Kohly, Havana, tel. 07/203-0668, fax 07/204-2621, www.aerogaviota.com) offers charter flights in 39-passenger Soviet Antonov-26s and 45-passenger French-built ATR-42s, as well as "executive" service in 18-seat helicopters.

AeroTaxi (Calle 27 #102, e/ M y N, Vedado, Havana, tel. 07/836-4064, aerotaxi@ ensa.avianet.cu) now flies charters only using a combination of small modern jets, aged DC-3s, and 12-passenger Russian. You have to hire the entire plane.

Reservations

Flights are frequently fully booked weeks in advance, especially in the August–December peak season, when Cubans take their holidays. Foreigners are usually given priority on waiting lists. Tickets are normally nonrefundable. Make your booking *in person* at the airline office or through one of the major tour agencies. If you make your reservations before arriving in Cuba, you'll be given a voucher to exchange for a ticket upon arrival in Cuba.

Be sure to arrive on time for check-in; otherwise your seat will likely be given away. Don't expect a refund or to be able to get a seat on the next flight. Delays, flight cancellations, and changes in schedule are common.

BY BUS
Tourist Buses

Víazul (Av. 26, esq. Zoológico, Nuevo Vedado, Havana, tel. 07/881-1413, fax 07/66-6092, www.viazul.cu; 7 A.M.–9 P.M. daily) operates bus services for foreigners (and Cubans with dollars) to key places on the tourist circuit using modern air-conditioned buses. Take a sweater! Children travel at half price. (See the sidebar *Víazul Bus Schedule* chart in this chapter for details.)

You can also book yourself onto an excursion bus operated by state-run tour agencies. Hotel tour desks offer excursions.

Public Buses

Virtually the entire population relies on the bus system for travel within and between cities.

There are two classes of buses for long-distance travel: *Especiales* are faster, air-conditioned, and more comfortable than *regulares,* which are often noisy and rickety with butt-numbing seats.

Most towns have *two* bus stations for out-of-town service: a Terminal de Ómnibus Intermunicipales (for local and municipal service) and a Terminal de Ómnibus Interprovinciales (for service between provinces). Often they're far apart, so be sure to go to the correct terminal. Terminals are chaotic; buses are asphyxiatingly crowded and interminably slow. Don't rely on published schedules. Beware pickpockets and don't display wads of money when purchasing your ticket.

Interprovincial Services: The state agency **Astro** (Asociación de Transportes por Ómnibus, Av. Independencia #101, Havana, tel. 07/870-3397) operates all interprovincial services linking cities throughout the island. Most inter-city buses move at night. For Cubans, demand so exceeds supply that they sometimes have to wait *weeks* to get a seat. Hence, Cuban bus stations have been called "citadels of desperation." Foreigners pay in dollars and receive reserved seating (only two seats per bus at last visit). Reservations are essential; do *not* expect to show up at the station and simply board a bus. However, you can buy a ticket as late as one hour before departure. Only one-way tickets are available; book any return or ongoing trip as far in advance as possible. On the day of travel, arrive at the terminal at least one hour ahead of departure, otherwise your seat may be issued to people on the waiting list. If you don't have a reservation or miss your departure, you can try getting on the standby list—*lista de espera*—for Cubans (foreigners, however, are normally shooed away to the dollars-only counter).

Passengers are granted a 22-kilogram baggage limit plus one piece of hand luggage, although it seems not to be strictly enforced. *Travel light!*

Conditions can get very cramped and—if the air conditioner isn't working—very hot; the back tends to get the hottest (and often

VÍAZUL BUS SCHEDULE

Route	Departure Times (Duration)	One-Way Fare
Havana-Santiago Santiago-Havana	9:30 A.M., 3 P.M., and 6:15 P.M. (13 hours) 9 A.M., 3:15 P.M., and 10 P.M. Stops are made at Entronque de Jagüey (CUC12), Santa Clara (CUC18), Sancti Spíritus (CUC23), Ciego de Ávila (CUC27), Camagüey (CUC33), Las Tunas (CUC39), Holguín (CUC44), and Bayamo (CUC44).	CUC51
Havana-Trinidad Trinidad-Havana	8:15 A.M. and 1 P.M. (5 hours, 45 mins) 7:45 A.M. and 3 P.M. Stops are made at Entronque de Jagüey (CUC12), Aguada de Pasajeros (CUC13), Yaguarama (CUC14), Rodas (CUC15), and Cienfuegos (CUC20)	CUC25
Havana-Varadero Varadero-Havana	8 A.M., noon, and 6 P.M. (3 hours) 8 A.M., 4 P.M., and 6 P.M. Stops are made at Matanzas (CUC7) and Aeropuerto de Varadero (by request).	CUC10
Havana-Viñales Viñales-Havana	9 A.M. (3 hours, 15 mins) 2 P.M. A stop is made in Pinar del Río (CUC11).	CUC12
Santiago-Baracoa Baracoa-Santiago	7:30 A.M. (5 hours) 2:15 P.M.	CUC15
Trinidad-Santiago Santiago-Trinidad	8:15 A.M. (12 hours) 7:30 P.M.	CUC33
Varadero-Trinidad Trinidad-Varadero	7:30 A.M. (6 hours) 2:30 P.M.	CUC20

smelliest). Long-distance buses make food stops, but often there isn't sufficient food for everyone; bring snacks and water. Toilet stops can be few and far between. Fortunately, in 2005 Cuba began importing modern Chinese-made buses of international standards to replace its aging fleet.

Intermunicipal Services: Usually no reservations are available for the short-distance intermunicipal services (between towns within specific provinces). You'll have to join the queue. At other times, you'll be issued a *tike* (a slip of paper, not a ticket) that records your destination and position in line. You board when your number is called, so don't wander off—and don't dally once it's called. Fares are collected on board. Since buses are often full, try to board the bus at its originating point.

Camiones: The staple of travel between towns in most areas is a truck, or *camión*. Often these are the only option for public transport, especially in the Oriente. Most travel only to the nearest major town, so you'll need to change *camiones* frequently for long-distance travel. Some are open-sided flatbeds featuring basic wooden seats welded to the floor, with a canvas roof. Sometimes it's a truck with a container with makeshift windows cut out of the metal sides, but hot as Hades, with no seats.

Camiones depart from designated transportation hubs (often adjacent to bus or railway stations) in all towns and cities. You pay in pesos: between 1 and 10 pesos, depending on distance. Fares are collected as you board. However, officially, foreigners are now banned from all forms of peso transport, so expect to be turned away by the drivers—officials have even been known to turf foreign travelers off *camiones*.

Within Towns: Most provincial capitals have intracity bus service, which in many towns means makeshift *coches* or *camiónes*. Most buses—*guaguas,* pronounced WAH-wahs—are either secondhand Yankee school buses; horribly uncomfortable Hungarian or Cuban buses; or, in Havana, crude truck-pulled behemoths called *camellos*. They are usually cloyingly overcrowded and cost 10–20 centavos (the standard fare), which you normally drop into a fare box next to the driver.

Expect a long wait in line. Cuban lines (*colas*) are always fluid but tend to re-form when the bus appears, so you should follow the Cubans' example and identify the last person in line ahead of you by asking for *¿el último?* ("last?"). It's like a game of tag. You're now *el último* until the next person arrives. Thus you don't have to stand in line, but can wander off to find some shade and then simply follow the person ahead of you onto the bus. Many Cubans board through the rear door (although technically this is illegal), in which case, if the bus is jam-packed like a sardine can, you can pass your fare to the front via other passengers.

Buses stop frequently, but when full, the driver may stop only when requested to do so. Bus stops—*paradas*—are usually well marked. To stop the bus, shout *¡pare!* (stop!), or bash the box above the door in Cuban fashion. You'll need to elbow your way to the door well in advance (don't stand near the door, however, as you may literally be popped out onto your face; exiting has been compared to being birthed). Don't dally, as the bus driver is likely to hit the gas when you're only halfway out.

BY TRAIN

One main rail axis spans the country connecting all the major cities, with secondary cities linked by branch lines. Commuter trains called *ferro-ómnibus* provide suburban rail service in and between many provincial towns.

Published schedules are subject to frequent change. Also check the arrival time at your destination carefully and plan accordingly, as many trains arrive (and depart) in the wee hours of the morning. Few trains run on time, and departures are frequently cancelled.

Nonsmoking compartments haven't yet made it to Cuba.

Bicycles are allowed in the baggage compartment (*coche de equipaje*). You usually pay (in pesos) at the end of the journey.

Classes

Two services operate between Havana and Santiago de Cuba, connecting major cities en route. The fast *especial* (train #01) takes 12.5 hours for the 860-kilometer journey. It stops at Santa Clara and Camagüey en route but is not particularly good for sightseeing as most of the journey takes place at night. Take your pick of *clase primera* (first class), with comfy recliner seats, or *clase segunda* (second class), with smaller, non-reclining seats. Both classes have bone-chilling air-conditioning and TVs showing movies. The train has a poorly stocked *cafetería* car, plus *ferromoza* (rail hostess) meal service. Regardless, take snacks and drinks.

Slower *regular* trains (colloquially called the *lechero,* or "milkman," because it makes frequent stops) also depart daily and make

TRAIN SCHEDULES AND FARES
FROM HAVANA

Destination	No.	Origin Station	Depart	Arrive
Bayamo	13	Estación Central	8:25 P.M.	10:30 A.M.
Camagüey	33	Estación Central	2 P.M.	8:50 P.M.
Cienfuegos	19	Terminal La Coubre	7:30 A.M.	6:35 P.M.
Cienfuegos	37	Terminal La Coubre	6:45 P.M.	11:45 P.M.
Guantánamo	25	Combinado	4:38 A.M.	6:50 A.M.
Holguín	15	Estación Central	7 P.M.	8:30 A.M.
Matanzas	905	Terminal La Coubre	12:05 P.M.	4:41 P.M.
Matanzas	907	Terminal La Coubre	4:03 P.M.	7:40 P.M.
Morón	35	Estación Central	4:45 P.M.	11:10 P.M.
Pinar del Río	39	Estación Central	5 P.M.	9:10 A.M.
Pinar del Río	21	Estación Central	10:35 P.M.	4:20 A.M.
Sancti Spíritus	17	Estación Central	9:45 P.M.	6 A.M.
Santiago de Cuba	01	(*Especial*) Estación Central	6:05 P.M.	6:35 A.M.
Santiago de Cuba	11	Estación Central	3:15 P.M.	5:15 A.M.
Santiago de Cuba	31	Estación Central	5:25 P.M.	6:10 A.M.

(continued on next page)

TRAIN SCHEDULES AND FARES (continued)

TO HAVANA

Origin	No.	Destination Station	Depart	Arrive
Bayamo	14	Estación Central	7:40 P.M.	9:45 A.M.
Camagüey	34	Estación Central	6:35 A.M.	1:35 P.M.
Cienfuegos	38	Terminal La Coubre	2 A.M.	6:50 P.M.
Cienfuegos	20	Terminal La Coubre	7 A.M.	5:50 P.M.
Guantánamo	26	Combinado	6:50 P.M.	9:07 P.M.
Holguín	16	Estación Central	6:15 P.M.	8:50 A.M.
Matanzas	902	Terminal La Coubre	8:30 A.M.	11:31 A.M.
Matanzas	904	Terminal La Coubre	12:30 P.M.	4:05 P.M.
Morón	36	Estación Central	5:40 A.M.	12 P.M.
Pinar del Río	40	Estación Central	5:10 A.M.	9:20 P.M.
Pinar del Río	22	Estación Central	8:45 A.M.	2:30 P.M.
Sancti Spíritus	18	Estación Central	9 P.M.	5:15 A.M.
Santiago	02	(Especial) Estación Central	5:05 P.M.	6 A.M.
Santiago	12	Estación Central	8:25 P.M.	10:45 P.M.

FARES (REGULAR) FROM/TO HAVANA

Cacocum (Holguín) CUC26.50; Camagüey CUC19; Ciego de Ávila CUC15.50; Cienfuegos CUC11; Colón CUC6; Florida CUC17.50; Guantánamo CUC32; Holguín CUC26.50; Jatibónico CUC14; Jovellanos CUC5; Las Tunas CUC23; Matanzas CUC3; Morón CUC24; Pinar del Río CUC6.50; Placetas CUC11.50; Sancti Spíritus CUC13.50; Santa Clara CUC10; Santiago de Cuba CUC30 regular/CUC62.50 especial

© CHRISTOPHER P. BAKER

Most train stations now have a TV to kill the boredom.

more stops at provincial capitals. Some *regular* services are *clase segunda* (second class) only and best suited to hardy travelers—the trains are typically dirty and overcrowded, with uncushioned wooden seats. *Clase primera* (first class) is marginally better, with padded seats, though still crowded and hardly comfortable. Some routes offer *clase primera especial,* which provides more comfort and, often, basic boxed meals. At local stops, peasants come aboard to sell cheese, *caramelos* (candies), bottle cane juice, and thermoses of hot sweet coffee.

Reservations

The state agency **FerroCuba** (Calle Arsenal, e/ Cienfuegos y Apontes, Habana Vieja, tel. 07/861-4259, ferrotur@ceniai.cuz) handles ticket sales and reservations for all national train service. Foreigners pay in dollars, for which you get a guaranteed seat. In Havana you can normally walk up to the FerroCuba office at the central station, buy your ticket, and take a seat on board within an hour. (At last visit, however, the office was closed, and tick-

ets were being sold at the Terminal La Coubre, 100 meters south of the main railway station.) Buy your ticket as far in advance as possible. You should also buy your ticket for the next leg of your journey upon arrival in each destination. Reservations can sometimes be made through Infotur offices (in Havana) and other regional tour agencies. You'll need to show your passport.

Reservations for local commuter services can't be made. You'll have to join the *cola* (queue) and buy your ticket on the day of departure (sometimes the day before; each station usually lists the allotted time for ticket purchase).

Tourist Trains

Steam-train excursions are offered at several locations, as are multiday tour packages for steam enthusiasts offered by tour companies abroad (see the sidebar *Still Puffing Away* in the *Sancti Spíritus* chapter).

BY TAXI
Tourist Taxis

Most *turistaxis* (those serving tourists for dollars) use modern Japanese or European cars and are radio-dispatched. You can also find them at tourist hotels nationwide. By law, Cuban taxi drivers must use their meters, though not all will do so. *Taxistas* have their own *trampas* or *estafas* (swindles), such as resetting the meter to record a much lower mileage, then charging you the going rate for the journey. Since his dispatcher records the destination, mile for mile, usually a dollar per mile, the taxi driver splits the excess with the dispatcher.

Peso Taxis

Havana and most provincial capitals have state-run peso taxis—deprecatingly called *los incapturables* (the uncatchables)—serving the local population and charging in pesos at ludicrously low rates. You'll normally find them at *piqueras* (taxi stands) around the main squares, although they are also assigned to airports, hotels, and other key sites.

The workhorses of the taxi system for Cubans are the privately owned *colectivos* or

CUBA'S VINTAGE AMERICAN CARS

Automotive sentimentality is reason enough to visit Cuba, the greatest living car museum in the world. American cars flooded into Cuba for 50 years, culminating in the Batista era, when Cuba imported more Cadillacs, Buicks, and DeSotos than any other nation in the world. Then came the Cuban Revolution and the U.S. trade embargo. In terms of American automobiles, time stopped when Castro took power.

Today, Cuba possesses about 450,000 cars, of which perhaps one-sixth are prerevolutionary American autos dating back to the 1920s and '30s. High-finned, big-boned dowagers from Detroit's heyday are everywhere. In certain areas, one rarely sees a vehicle that is *not* a venerable, usually decrepit, classic of yesteryear. Model-T Fords. Chrysler Windsors. Chevy Bel Airs and Impalas. Oldsmobile Golden Rockets. Cadillac Eldorados. Kaisers, Hudsons, and Edsels. They're all there, gleaming in the lyrical Cuban sunlight, inviting for-

eigners to admire the dashboard or run their fingers along a tail fin.

The mechanical dinosaurs are called *cacharros*. Normally, the word means a broken-down jalopy, but in the case of old Yankee classics, the word is "whispered softly, tenderly, like the name of a lost first love," says Cristina García.

Lacking proper tools and replacement parts, Cubans adeptly cajole one more kilometer out of their battered hulks. Their intestinally reconstituted engines are monuments to ingenuity – decades of improvised repairs have melded parts from Detroit and Moscow (Russian Gaz jeeps are favorite targets for cannibalization, since their engines were cloned from a Detroit engine). One occasionally spots a shining example of museum quality. The majority, though, have long ago been touched up with house paint and decorated with flashy mirrors and metallic stars, as if to celebrate a religious holiday.

coches (shared cabs that pick up anyone who flags them down, often until they're packed to the gills), sometimes called *botes* (boats) or simply *máquinas* (machines). They run along fixed routes, much like buses, and charge similar fares. Most are old Yankee jalopies. Look for a Pasaje ("passenger") sign in the window, or even a hand-written Taxi sign.

Some *colectivos* also hang around outside railway and bus terminals and provide service between towns. The drivers yell out the names of destinations. They usually take as many passengers as they can cram in and are not supposed to pick up passengers between their designated departure and return points. Reader Bridget Murphy offers this advice: "To avoid getting scolded [by the *chofer*], 'No tire la puerta'"—don't slam the door! Count on traveling about three kilometers per peso.

Peso-only taxis are not permitted to give rides to foreigners. Nonetheless, many drivers will risk huge fines to pick up foreigners for dollars in the absence of police.

"Gypsy" Cabs

Cubans are banned from taking foreigners under any conditions. Still, in a country desperate for dollars (and where everybody breaks the rules), there are still freelancers who'll take the risk. Illegal "gypsy" cabs driven by freelance chauffeurs are usually beat-up Ladas or American jalopies. Says Cristina García, "Twenty dollars buys gas enough for a decent spin. Seventy dollars gets you a day in a top-of-the-line Cadillac convertible with fins so big they block the rear-view mirror. Forget about renting from Hertz or Avis ever again."

You'll find freelance driver-guides outside the largest tourist hotels and outside discos late at night. Your fare is negotiable. Educate yourself about *turistaxi* fares to your destination beforehand, as many drivers attempt to gouge you and you may end up paying more than you would in a tourist taxi. Agree on the fare *before* getting in. Make sure you know whether it is one-way or round-trip.

Some are adorned with multicolored flags to invoke the protection of Changó or another *santería* deity.

Owners of prerevolutionary cars can sell them freely to anyone with money to buy, but the chance of owning a more modern car are slim. Virtually all cars imported since 1959 – Polish Fiats, Soviet UAZs, Jeep-like Romanian AROs, and more recently Mercedes, Nissans, and Citroëns – are owned by the state. New cars are leased out to high-level workers, and others who work for foreign companies, but the cars must be returned if they lose their jobs. Benighted workers such as sports stars and top artists have been gifted or allowed to buy cars, but permission to buy such a car is usually granted in writing from a vice president or even from Fidel Castro himself. The cars can only be resold back to the government, which pays a pittance – in pesos. The government can seize any car sold illegally.

In *Driving Through Cuba*, author Carlo Gébler drives around the island in quest of a '57 Cadillac Eldorado Brougham; a super-deluxe pillarless sedan with a brushed aluminum roof, two front-end protuberances known as "Dagmar" bumpers (which Cadillac unashamedly advertised as "bosoms"), and "a rear end that would've received an X-rating had it been a movie." Alas, the most sumptuous American car ever made proved elusive – not surprisingly, for only 704 Broughams were produced. But you can bet there's at least one to be found on the island. After all, in the 1950s, Havana bought more Cadillacs than any other city in the world. Reason enough to visit!

My own *Cuba Classics: A Celebration of Vintage American Automobiles* (Interlink Books, 2004, www.cuba-automobiles.com) is an illustrated coffee-table book that offers a paean to the cars and the owners who keep them running with ingenuity, resourcefulness, and indefatigable good humor.

Coco-taxis

Toys "R" Us doesn't yet have an outlet in Cuba, but you'd never know it. These motorized tricycles housed in a bright yellow fiberglass hemisphere look like scooped-out Easter eggs on wheels. You'll find them outside major hotels and cruising the tourist zones. They charge about the same as tourist taxis. However, they have no safety features, and several accidents involving tourists have been reported.

Ciclo-taxis

Ciclo-taxis—the Cuban equivalent of rickshaws—patrol the main streets of most Cuban cities. These tricycles have been cobbled together with welding torches or are conversions of Chinese imports, with car-like seats and shade canopies. They offer a cheap (albeit bumpy) way of sightseeing and getting around if you're in no hurry. Some *ciclo-taxis* are only licensed to take Cubans (who pay pesos). Always negotiate a fare before setting off.

Coches

These horse-drawn cabs are a staple of local transport. In Havana, Varadero, and other beach resorts, elegant antique carriages with leather seats are touted for sightseeing. Elsewhere they're a utility vehicle for the hoi polloi and are often decrepit, with basic bench seats and pulled by scrawny mules. They operate along fixed routes and usually charge one to three pesos, depending on distance.

BY CAR

Cuba is a great place to drive if you don't mind the often perilous conditions. There are no restrictions on where you can go. Cuba has some 31,000 kilometers of roads, of which about 15,500 kilometers are paved, though even the major highways are deteriorated to the point of being dangerous. In more remote areas, access is often by unpaved road that can shake both a car and its occupants until their doors and teeth rattle. In the rainy season, such roads become quagmires or even totally flooded. Tolls apply on the Matanzas–Varadero Expressway and the *pedraplenes* to Cayo Jutía, Cayo Coco, and Cayo Santa María.

The main highway, the Carretera Central (Central Highway), runs along the island's spine for 1,200 kilometers from one end of the country to the other. The ordinary two-laner leads through dozens of sleepy rural towns.

For maximum speed and minimum sightseeing, take the A-1, the country's only freeway—six lanes wide and fast. Construction by the Soviets of this Autopista Nacional (National Expressway; sometimes called the *Ocho Vías*—eight-ways) came to a halt with the Special Period and has not been resumed. About 650 kilometers have been completed, from Pinar del Río to a point just east of Santa Clara, and from Santiago de Cuba about 30 kilometers northwestward. Travel time between Havana and Santa Clara is about four hours. Be cautious: The obstacles and dangers are many.

Traffic Regulations

To drive in Cuba, you must be 21 years or older and hold either an International Drivers' License (IDL) or a valid national driver's license, obtainable through Automobile Association offices worldwide (www.aaa.com, United States; www.caa.ca, Canada; www.theaa.com, U.K.; www.aaa.asn.au, Australia; or www.nzaa .co.nz, New Zealand). However, see *Rental* later in this section for caveats.

Traffic drives on the right, as in the United States. The speed limit is 100 kph (kilometers per hour) on freeways, 90 kph on highways, 60 kph on rural roads, 50 kph on urban roads, and 40 kph in children's zones. Speed limits are vigorously enforced.

Seatbelt use is not mandatory, nor are motorcyclists required to wear helmets. Note that it's illegal to 1) enter an intersection unless you can exit, 2) make a right turn on a red light unless indicated by a white arrow or traffic signal (*derecha con luz roja*), or 3) overtake on the right.

The ubiquitous, over-zealous traffic police (*tránsitos* or *tráficos*) patrol the main highways. Oncoming cars will flash their lights to indicate the presence of police ahead. If you receive a traffic fine, the policeman will note this on your car rental contract, to be deducted from your deposit—there's a space for fines provided on the rental-car papers. The *tráfico* cannot request a fine on the spot. Infrequently, however, some Cuban police attempt to extract a subtle bribe. If you suspect any such irregularity, ask for the policeman's name and where you can fight the ticket (this usually results in you being waved on your way).

Throughout Havana and on major country highways, you'll pass *puntos de control*—control points—manned by police.

You must stop at *all* railway crossings before crossing.

Driving Safety

Keep your speed down. Road conditions often deteriorate without warning, and obstacles are numerous: everything from wayward livestock to mammoth potholes. The main cause of traffic deaths in Cuba is collisions with bicycles and wayward livestock. Farmers driving ox-carts and tractors have a tendency to turn into your path at the moment you decide to pass. Driving at night is perilous—most roads are unlighted, few have side rails or painted markings at the margins, there are always pedestrians, animals, and potholes to contend with, plus vehicles without headlights in the incoming lane (even on the darkest of days, with torrential rains falling, Cubans forego using headlights; headlights by day are illegal except for emergency vehicles, but you should use yours and be seen).

Sticks jutting up in the road usually indicate a dangerous hole in the road.

Accidents and Breakdowns

If your car breaks down, there will be no shortage of Cubans willing to offer advice and consummate fix-it skills. If the problem is minor, fine. However, rental car agencies usually have a clause to protect against likely damage to the car from unwarranted repairs. For major problems, call the rental agency; it will arrange a tow or send a mechanic.

You should also call the agency in the event of an accident. After an accident, *never* move

MAKING SENSE OF ADDRESSES

In most Cuban cities, addresses are given as locations. Thus, the Havanatur office is at Calle 6, e/ 1ra y 3ra, Miramar, Havana, meaning it is on Calle 6 between (e/ for *entre* – between) First and Third avenues (Avenidas 1ra y 3ra).

Street numbers are occasionally used. Thus, the Hotel Inglaterra is at Prado #416, esq. San Rafael, Habana Vieja; at the corner (esq. for *esquina* – corner) of Prado and Calle San Rafael, in Old Havana (Habana Vieja).

Piso refers to the floor level (thus, an office on *Piso 3ro* is on the third floor). *Altos* refers to "upstairs," and *bajos* refers to "downstairs."

Most cities are laid out on a grid pattern centered at a main square or plaza (usually called Plaza Central, Parque Central, Plaza Mayor, or named for a local revolutionary hero), with parallel streets (*calles*) running perpendicular to avenues (*avenidas*). Some towns, however, have even-numbered *calles* (usually north – south) running perpendicular to odd-numbered *calles* (usually east – west).

Many streets have at least two names: one predating the Revolution (and usually the most commonly used colloquially) and the other a postrevolutionary name. For example, in Havana, the Prado is the old (and preferred) term for the Paseo de Martí. On maps, the modern name takes precedence, with the old name often shown in parentheses.

the vehicles until the police arrive, and never abandon them (thieves will probably steal any loose parts). Get the names, license plate numbers, and *cédulas* (legal identification numbers) of any witnesses. Make a sketch of the accident. Then call the **transit police** (tel. 07/882-0116 in Havana; tel. 116 outside Havana). In case of injury, call for an **ambulance** (tel. 114 nationwide). Do *not* offer statements to anyone other than the police. Try not to leave the accident scene, or at least keep an eye on your car; the other party may tamper with the evidence. And don't let honking traffic pressure you into moving the cars. If you suspect the other driver has been drinking, ask the policeman to administer a Breathalyzer test—an *alcolemia*.

Warning: Accidents that result in death or injury are treated like crimes, and the onus is on the driver to prove innocence. The *tráficos* often treat foreigners with disdain and, as you have deep pockets, the blame might be assigned to you in the event that it be proved otherwise. Don't expect much help from locals. Cubans are loath to involve themselves where the police are concerned. Prison sentences can range from one to 10 years. Regardless of the nature of the crime or accident, it can take five months to a year for the case to go to trial. In most cases, you will not be allowed to leave Cuba until the trial has taken place. If you are involved in an accident in which someone is injured or killed, you should immediately contact your embassy for legal assistance.

Gasoline

Gasoline (*petróleo*) and diesel (*gasolina*) are sold at Cupet and Oro Negro stations (*servicentros*) nationwide. Most are open 24 hours. There are no self-service stations. *Regular* and *Especial* grades are available (many stations have only *regular*), but not unleaded. *Especial* typically costs CUC0.83 per liter—about CUC3.15 a gallon. (Local gas stations, *bombas,* serve *regular* to Cubans only.)

Gas stations are supposed to sell only *especial* to tourists in rental cars; it's a matter of pot-luck as to whether any attendant will sell you *regular.*

Occasional electrical blackouts shut the pumps down. If you run out of gas, there's sure to be someone willing to sell from private stock, but it may be watered down.

Insurance

If you have your own vehicle, the state-run organization **ESEN** (5ta Calle #306, e/ C y D, Vedado, Havana, tel. 07/832-2500, www.esen .com.cu) insures automobiles and has special packages for foreigners.

Maps and Directions

Most highways are well signed. However, it's extraordinary how little Cubans know of regions outside their own locale. You may as well ask them directions to the far side of the moon. In the countryside, you'll need to phrase your questions so as not to preempt the answer. For example, rather than asking, "Does this road go to so-and-so?" (which will surely earn you the reply, "¡Sí, señor!"), ask "¿Adónde va esta ruta?" ("Where does this route go?").

There are few accurate road maps available. However, you can buy the *Guía de Carreteras* road atlas in booklet form at tour desks and souvenir outlets.

Rental

You can rent a car at the airport upon arrival. If you're tired or jet-lagged, this is not a good idea; relax for a day or two, then rent your car. Drivers under 25 years of age are assessed a CUC5 fee. Additional drivers are charged CUC15 apiece.

Demand for cars sometimes exceeds supply, particularly for the smaller models or a four-wheel drive jeep. If you're planning on traveling during peak Christmas and New Year's season, you'll absolutely need reservations, which can only be done within 15 days of your arrival, and is no guarantee that your reservation will be honored. If you book from abroad, ask for a copy of the reservation to be faxed to you and take this copy with you to Cuba. In any event, expect all kinds of false promises: "a car will be ready in one hour," or "we'll have a car for you this afternoon," and so on. Yeah… and the moon is made of cheese!

Expect to pay about CUC41–115 per day for a car with an unlimited mileage allowance, depending on the size of the vehicle. A three-day minimum usually applies for unlimited mileage rentals. Added charges apply for one-way rentals. Discounts apply for rentals over seven days, and prices are usually negotiable. The companies accept payment by credit cards (except those issued by U.S. banks; see Rex Limousines for an exception), as well as in cash and travelers checks. You will normally be required to pay a deposit of CUC200–500; the agency will run off a credit card authorization that you will receive back once you return the car, assuming it has no damage. And you'll be required to pay separately in cash (CUC0.90 a liter) for the first tank of gas before you drive away; check the fuel level carefully *before* setting off. If it doesn't look full to the brim, point this out to the rental agent and demand a refund, or that it be topped off (but good luck!). Make sure you clarify any one-way drop-off fees, late return penalties, and other details, and that the time recorded on your contract is that for your *departure with the car,* not the time you entered into negotiations.

Cuban car rental agencies have failed to budget for adequate maintenance and cars go to ruin quickly—often dangerously so! At last visit, many cars were unserviced and unroadworthy. Inspect your car thoroughly for roadworthiness, and for damage and marks before setting off; otherwise, you may be charged for the slightest dent when you return. Don't forget the inside, as well as the radio antenna, spare tire, plus the jack and wrench. Don't assume the car rental agency has taken care of tire pressure or fluids. Check them yourself before you set off. Note the *Aviso Próximo Mantenimiento* column on the rental contract. This indicates the kilometer reading by which you— the renter!—are required to take the car to an agency office for scheduled servicing; you're granted a 100 kilometers leeway. If you fail to honor the clause, you'll be charged CUC50. This scam is a pain in the butt, as often you'll have to wait hours, or even overnight, for the car to be serviced. Often you'll have to drive miles out of your way to an agency office. You are within your rights to refuse to pay (as I have, successfully), but clarify this before signing the contract.

Most agencies offer a chauffeur service (CUC40–90 a day).

Rental Companies: Only state-owned car rental agencies operate in Cuba. The following companies are headquartered in Havana.

Havanautos (tel. 07/835-3142 or 203-9825, fax 07/203-9652, www.havanautos.cu) offers a range of Japanese cars in all categories, from a compact Toyota Yaris (from CUC50 per day with unlimited mileage, low season) to Suzuki Vitara jeep (from CUC56 daily). It has dozens of outlets nationwide.

Micar (Calle 13 #562, Vedado, tel. 07/833-0202, fax 07/833-0301, www.micarrenta.cu) rents Fiats (from CUC50), Peugeots (from CUC65), Toyotas (from CUC80), and Mercedes (from CUC140) and has scores of reservation kiosks.

Rex Limousine Service (tel. 07/683-0303, fax 07/273-9167, www.rex-rentacar.com) rents Audis, VW, and Skoda sedans, plus the Audi TT sports car. Rates at last visit started at CUC70 for the Skoda Fabia hatchback, CUC109 per day (CUC545 per week) for an Audi A4, and CUC150 daily (CUC750 weekly) for an Audi A6. Rates include 150 kilometers daily. Insurance is additional. It also has VW minivans plus chauffeured limousines. The company is a Cuban-Danish joint venture and cars are better maintained and the service more trustworthy than any of the other companies. *It accepts U.S.-issued MasterCard.*

Other car rental agencies include **Transtur** (aka Cubacar, Calle L #456, e/ 25 y 27, Vedado, tel. 07/55-3991 or 835-0000, fax 07/835-3727, www.transtur.cu) and **Vía Rent-a-Car** (Av. del Puerto #102, e/ Obrapía y Justíz, tel. 07/260-4455, fax 07/33-2780, www.gaviota-grupo.com).

Four-Wheel Drive: A four-wheel drive is recommended only for exploring the Sierra Maestra, Sierra Cristal, Sierra del Purial, and Cuchillas de Toa, and the extreme south of Isla de la Juventud, especially in rainy season.

Fly-Drive Packages: A "Flexi Fly & Drive" prepaid package is offered through **WowCuba** (430 Queen St., Charlottestown, Prince Edward Island, Canada CIA 4E8, tel. 902/368-2453 or 800/969-2822, www.wowcuba.com). You simply pick up your Skoda Fabia at any of the international airports in Havana, Varadero, Holguín, or Santiago de Cuba and hit the road armed with vouchers good at any of 60-plus hotels islandwide (from CUC699 double for 7 nights; from CUC1,349 14 nights).

Motorhomes: A joint Italian-Cuban venture, **Cubamar Campertour** (3ra Calle, esq. Malecón, Havana, tel. 07/833-7558, cubacamper@enet.cu) rents Mercedes and Ford campervans sleeping six people. The vehicles contain bathroom with flush toilet and shower, kitchen with fridge and three-burner stove, wardrobes, and even a security box. Low-season prices range from CUC140 daily for up to three days, to CUC115 daily for 15 days or more (plus CUC20 per diem insurance), including cell phone, unlimited miles, and 24-hour assistance; high-season prices are from CUC170 daily for up to three days, to CUC150 daily for 15 days or more. Twenty-five "camp" sites are designated islandwide. The company has offices in Havana, Varadero, and Holguín.

Insurance: If you rent a car you will be responsible for any damage or theft. Hence you should purchase insurance offered by the rental agency. You have two choices: Option A (CUC10–15 daily depending on vehicle; with a deductible of CUC200–500 or so) covers accidents, but not theft. Option B (CUC15–20) offers fully comprehensive coverage, except for the radio and spare tire. The insurance has to be paid in cash. If you decline insurance, you'll be required to put down a huge cash deposit. And if your car is broken into or otherwise damaged, you must get a police statement (a *denuncia*), otherwise you may be charged for the damage.

Warning: If you (or anyone else driving your rented vehicle) are deemed in any way at fault in an accident, rental agencies will nullify coverage and seek damages to cover the cost of repairs. Rental agencies are government controlled and can prevent your departure from the country unless payment is obtained.

Guides: You can request a personal guide from most of the car rental offices nationwide. You can also name any licensed Cuban driver on your rental policy.

Scams: Cuban car rental agencies operate like the Mafia. *Trampas* (swindles) and *estafas* (frauds) include renting cars with partially filled gas tanks, attempts to charge for damage you didn't cause, "not returning the car on

DISTANCES IN CUBA
DISTANCE (KM)

	PR	H	M	SC	C	SS
Pinar del Río (PR)	-	176	267	441	419	527
Soroa	89	86	188	362	329	448
Viñales	28	193	295	469	436	555
Havana (H)	176	-	102	276	243	362
Matanzas (M)	267	102	-	197	193	283
Varadero	309	144	42	196	177	282
Santa Clara (SC)	441	276	197	-	74	88
Cienfuegos (C)	419	243	193	74	-	153
Sancti Spíritus (SS)	527	362	283	86	153	-
Trinidad	497	321	271	89	78	67
Ciego de Ávila (CA)	603	438	359	162	229	78
Camagüey (CG)	711	546	467	270	337	184
Santa Lucía	823	658	579	382	446	296
Las Tunas (LT)	835	670	591	394	461	308
Holguín (HG)	913	748	699	472	539	388
Guardalavaca	967	802	723	526	593	440
Bayamo (B)	984	819	740	543	610	457
Santiago de Cuba (S)	1109	944	865	668	735	582
Guantánamo (G)	1191	1026	825	750	817	664
Baracoa	1331	1168	1087	890	957	804

CA	CG	LT	HG	B	S	G
603	711	835	913	984	1109	1191
524	632	756	834	905	1030	1112
631	739	863	941	1012	1137	1219
438	546	670	748	819	944	1028
359	467	591	669	740	865	947
358	466	590	669	739	864	846
162	270	394	472	543	668	750
229	337	481	539	610	735	817
78	184	308	388	457	582	664
143	251	375	453	524	649	731
-	108	232	310	381	506	588
108	-	124	202	273	388	480
220	112	209	287	358	483	565
232	124	-	78	149	274	356
310	202	78	-	71	196	278
364	256	132	54	125	250	332
380	273	149	71	-	125	207
506	398	274	198	125	-	86
588	480	356	278	207	86	-
728	620	496	418	347	226	140

time," or failing to service the car. Rental agencies charge upfront for a full tank of gas when you sign on for the car; your contract states that you must return the tank empty! Inevitably you return the car with gasoline that you've paid for, but for which you cannot receive a refund. The agency pockets the difference.

Precautions: Theft, including of car parts, is a serious problem. Always park in *parqueos*, designated parking lots with a *custodio* (guard). Alternately, tip the hotel security staff or hire someone to guard your car. Under all circumstances, parking lot *custodios* expect a small tip.

THE BICYCLE REVOLUTION

In 1991, when the first shipment of Flying Pigeon bicycles arrived from China, there were only an estimated 30,000 bicycles in Havana, a city of two million people. The visitor arriving in Havana today could be forgiven for imagining he or she had arrived in Ho Chi Minh City. Bicycles are everywhere, outnumbering cars, trucks, and buses 20 to 1. The story is the same across Cuba.

Cynics have dubbed Cuba's wholesale switch to bicycles since the collapse of the Soviet bloc as a socialist failing, a symbol of the nation's backwardness. Others acclaim it an astounding achievement, a two-wheel triumph over an overnight loss of gasoline and adversity. *Granma*, the Cuban newspaper, christened it the "bicycle revolution."

GOODBYE TO GAS
American cars had flooded the island for half a century. Then came the U.S. trade embargo. The 1960s saw the arrival of the first sober-looking Lada and Moskovitch sedans, imported in the ensuing decades by the tens of thousands from the Soviet Union, along with Hungarian and Czech buses. Professor Maurice Halperin, who taught at the University of Havana, does not "recall seeing a single adult Cuban on a bicycle in Havana during the entire period of my residence in the city, from 1962 to 1968."

The collapse of the Soviet Union severed the nation's gasoline pipeline. Transportation ground to a halt, along with the rest of the Cuban economy. In November 1990 the Cuban government launched sweeping energy-saving measures that called for a "widespread substitution of oxen for farm machinery and hundreds of thousands of bicycles for gasoline-consuming vehicles," launched as a "militant and defensive campaign" embodied on

May 1, 1991, when the armed forces appeared on bicycles in the May Day parade. The government contracted with China to purchase 1.2 million bicycles, and by the end of 1991, 500,000 single-gear Chinese bicycles were in use on the streets of Havana.

BICYCLE CAPITAL OF THE AMERICAS
Overnight, Cuba transformed itself into the bicycle capital of the Americas. "The comprehensiveness and speed of implementation of this program," said a 1994 World Bank report, "is unprecedented in the history of transportation." The report noted that about two million bicycles were in use islandwide. Most were made in Cuba, which established five bicycle factories to supplement the Chinese imports (each factory produces a different model). Cuba imports parts such as small bolts, chains, spindles, and brakes, but makes the frames, forks, and handlebars.

Most *bicis* are cumbersome, hard-to-pump beasts (many with only one gear) weighing as much as an elephant. The bikes are made of poor quality parts and, like more modern Chinese bicycles sold at dollar stores throughout Havana, are basically junk... "after two days, the screws are already falling off," says Linda Nauman, director of **Bicycles Crossing Borders** (tel. 416/364-5329, http://bikestocuba .org), a Canadian cooperative that sends new and used bikes to Cuba.

The bicycles are disbursed through MINCIN (Ministerio de Comercial Interior) to schools, factories, and workers' associations; workers pay 125 pesos – equivalent to about half the average monthly salary – while students pay 65 pesos.

Hitchhikers: Your car rental contract states that picking up hitchhikers is not allowed. It is illegal for Cubans to "beg" rides from foreigners. Picking up hitchhikers is integral to showing your goodwill in a land where on any day, tens of thousands of desperate Cubans stand by the roadside beseeching rides. However, there have been many reports of robberies, and I do not endorse picking up hitchhikers.

Motorcycles and Scooters

At press time, you could not rent motorcycles in Cuba other than at the Hotel Comodoro, in Havana. Scooters can be rented in Havana and at resort hotels nationwide.

Several North American entities have attempted to organize motorcycle tours, without much success. **South Wind Tours** (1235 Bay St., Suite 400, Toronto, Ontario M5R 3K4, tel. 416/921-4012, www.havanaflyingclub .com) was promoting a 16-day "Biker's Tour" for 2006; participants' bikes are shipped to Cuba for the duration.

BY BICYCLE

I recommend you take your own bike, although two companies in Havana rent mountain bikes. One essential item: a sturdy lock. Always take precautions against theft. *Parqueos* (bicycle parking lots) are found all over Cuba; most charge one peso.

For further information, see *Bicycling* in the *Outdoor Recreation* section of this chapter; and *By Bicycle* in the *Getting Around* section of the *Havana* chapter.

HITCHHIKING

Stoics among stoics can travel the Cuban way. Four decades of *fidelismo* have had such a traumatic effect on the transportation system that the populace now relies on anything that moves. The roadways of Cuba are lined with hundreds of thousands of hitchers, many of them so desperate after hours in the sun that they wave peso bills at passing cars.

So many Cubans rely on hitching that the state has set up *botellas* (literally bottles, but colloquially used to signify hitchhiking posts)

CUBAN TOUR OPERATORS

Agencía San Cristóbal: Oficios #110, e/ Lamparilla y Amargura, Habana Vieja, tel. 07/860-9585, fax 07/860-9586, reservas@sancrist.get.tur.cu. Tours and excursions within Habana Vieja.

Cubamar Viajes: 3ra Av., e/ 12 y Malecón, Havana, tel. 07/832-1116 or 833-2523, www.cubamarviajes.cu. Primarily nature and maritime related programs, including scuba diving; it also offers motorhome rentals.

Cubanacán Viajes: Calle 23 #156, e/ O y P, Vedado, Havana, tel. 07/833-4090, www.cubanacan.cu. A major tour operator with excursions nationwide.

Cubatur: Calle 23, esq. L, Vedado, Havana, tel. 07/833-3569, www.cubatur.cu.

EcoTur, S.A.: Av. Independencia #116, esq. Santa Catalina, Cerro, Havana, tel. 07/41-0306, fax 07/53-9909, ecoturhabana@ miramar.co.cu. Focuses on nature and ecotourism.

Gaviota Tours: Av. 49 #3620, Rpto. Kohly, Havana, tel. 07/204-7683, fax 204-9470, www.gaviota-grupo.com.

Havanatur/Tours & Travel: 3ra Av., e/ 33 y 34, Miramar, Havana, tel. 07/66-7027 or 204-0993, fax 07/66-7026 or 204-1760, www.havanatur.cu.

Paradiso: Promotora de Viajes Culturales: Calle 19 #560, esq. C, Vedado, Havana, tel. 07/832-6928, fax 07/33-3921, paradis@paradiso.artex.com.cu. Cuba's premier specialist in cultural programs.

Universitur: Calle 30 #768, e/ Kohly y 41, Nuevo Vedado, tel. 07/55-5683, fax 07/55-5978, www.universitur.cu. Arranges programs and lodgings for foreign students and academics.

---

on the edges of towns. Here officials of the Inspección Estatal, wearing mustard-colored uniforms (and therefore termed *coges amarillas,* or yellow-jackets) are in charge. They wave down virtually anything that comes rolling along, and all state vehicles—those with red license plates, or *chapas*—must stop to pick up hitchers. Early morning is easiest for hitching. A queue system prevails: first come, first served.

It can be excruciatingly slow going, and there are never any guarantees for your safety. Hence, we don't recommend or endorse hitchhiking. If you choose to hitch, sticking out your thumb won't do it. The Cuban way is to wave down any passing vehicle—whether it be a tractor, a truck, or a motorcycle. If it moves, in Cuba it's fair game.

Cubans are officially barred from picking up foreign hitchhikers at the risk of huge fines. If you receive a ride in a private car, politeness dictates that you offer to pay for your ride: "*¿Cuánto le debo?*" after you're safely delivered.

ORGANIZED EXCURSIONS

Cuba has a large and modern fleet of buses and minibuses. You can book excursions at the tour desks in most tourist hotels. See the destination chapters for details.

Getting Away

Travelers exiting Cuba are charged CUC25 departure tax on international flights. No charge applies for travelers leaving by private boat.

The **Cubana** (Calle 23 #64, e/ P y Infanta, Vedado, tel. 07/834-4446, www.cubana.cu; Mon.–Fri. 8:30 A.M.–4 P.M., Sat. 8:30 A.M.–noon) office in Havana is always horrendously crowded. Double-check departure times, which change frequently and at short notice. Reconfirm your flight at least 72 hours before departure, as Cubana is notorious for canceling the reservations of those who don't reconfirm on time.

Warning: Cuban check-in staff have a nasty habit of scamming foreigners by attempting to charge you an excess baggage fee where none should apply. It pays to know your legal allowance (which varies between airlines). Be sure to use a counter where the scale's screen is clearly visible and that it is properly zeroed before your bags are put on.

See the sidebar *International Airline Offices in Havana* for a list of airline offices in Havana.

Customs

Cuba prohibits the export of valuable antiques, and of art without a license.

Returning to the United States: U.S. citizens who have traveled to Cuba are not allowed to bring back any Cuban purchases, regardless of whether or not travel was licensed. The exception is literature, posters, and other informational materials, which are protected under the First Amendment of the Constitu-

tion. All other Cuban goods will be confiscated, wherever acquired and regardless of value. No goods of Cuban origin may be imported to the United States unaccompanied, either directly or through third countries, such as Canada or Mexico. Restrictions on importing Cuban-made goods to the United States apply to citizens of *any* country arriving from any other country, including in-transit passengers.

The **Office of Foreign Assets Controls** (U.S. Department of the Treasury, 1500 Pennsylvania Ave. NW, Washington, DC 20220, 202/622-2480, fax-on-demand 202/622-0077, www.treas.gov/offices/enforcement/ofac) publishes a pamphlet called *What You Need to Know about the U.S. Embargo.* Alternately, contact the **U.S. Customs Service** (1300 Pennsylvania Ave. NW, Washington, DC 20229, 202/354-1000, www.custom.gov).

Returning to Canada: Canadian citizens are allowed an "exemption" of C$300 annually (or C$100 per quarter) for goods purchased abroad, plus 1.1 liters of spirits and 200 cigarettes.

Returning to the United Kingdom: U.K. citizens are permitted to import goods worth up to £200, plus 200 cigarettes, 50 cigars, and two liters of spirits.

Returning to Australia and New Zealand: Australian citizens may import A$400 of goods, plus 250 cigarettes or 50 cigars, and 1.125 liters of spirits. New Zealand citizens can import NZ$700 worth of goods, 200 cigarettes or 50 cigars and 1.125 liters of spirits.

INTERNATIONAL AIRLINE OFFICES IN HAVANA

The following have offices in the Hotel Tryp Habana Libre, Calle L, e/ 23 y 25, Vedado:

Air Europa   tel. 07/204-6904, ofic.cuba@air-europa.com
Taca   tel. 07/833-3114, fax 07/833-3728

The following have offices at Calle 23 #64, e/ P y Infanta, Vedado:

Aerocaribbean   tel. 07/879-7525, fax 07/836-5016
Aeropostal   tel. 07/55-4000, fax 07/55-4128
Air France   tel. 07/833-2642, www.airfarnce.com/cu
Air Jamaica   tel. 07/833-8011, fax 07/66-2449, havanaventas@airjamaica.com
Cubana   tel. 07/834-4446, 07/834-4447, 07/834-4448, 07/834-4449
LanChile   tel. 07/831-6186, lanchile@enet.cu
Lloyd Aero Boliviano   tel. 07/833-1261
LTU   tel. 07/833-3525
Mexicana   tel. 07/833-3532
TAAG   tel. 07/833-3528

The following have offices at the Miramar Trade Center, 5ta Av. y 76, Miramar:

Aero Caribe   tel. 07/873-3621, fax 07/873-3871
Aeroflot   tel. 07/204-5593
COPA   tel. 07/204-1111
Iberia   tel. 07/204-3444
Virgin Atlantic   tel. 07/204-0747, fax 07/204-4094

The following also have offices in Havana:

Air Europe   La Lonja del Comercio, Plaza de San Francisco, Habana Vieja, tel. 07/866-9237
Martinair   Calle 23, esq. E, Vedado, tel. 07/833-3729, fax 07/833-3732, martinair@enet.cu

Immigration and Customs

DOCUMENTS AND REQUIREMENTS
Cuban Tourist Visas

A passport valid for six months from date of entry is required. Virtually every visitor needs a Cuban visa or tourist card valid for a single trip of 30 days; for most visitors, including U.S. citizens, a tourist card (*tarjeta de turista*) will suffice. No tourist visa is required for transit passengers continuing their journey to a third country within 72 hours. Tourist cards are issued outside Cuba by tour agencies or the airline or charter company providing travel to Cuba. In some cases, tourist cards are issued at an airport upon arrival within Cuba. They cost US$25 (CAN$36 in Canada, or £15 in the U.K.), but commercial agencies sometimes charge US$35 or more. If you're traveling with an organized group, the organization will obtain your visa.

Don't list your occupation as journalist, police, military personnel, or government employer, as the Cuban government is highly suspicious of anyone with these occupations.

Extensions: You can request a 30-day extension (*prórroga*) to your tourist visa. Multiple extensions are permitted up to six months; an exit permit is required of anyone staying 90 days or longer (CUC25). Extensions cost CUC25, payable in stamps purchased from branches of the Banco de Comercio y Crédito. To request a *prórroga,* you must visit the local immigration office in major cities, or in Havana at **Ministerio de Inmigración** (Calle Factor y Final, off Tulipán, Plaza de la Revolución).

If you're staying in a *casa particular,* you may need to provide a receipt for the house. Immigration officials don't look kindly on tourists staying in *casas particulares.* To ease your being issued a *prórroga,* consider telling the official that you'll be traveling around the island staying at state hotels; then you won't need to name a lodging in Havana.

Warning: There have been reports of visitors who overstay their visa being held in custody until reports are received on their activities in the country. In such an event, you are billed CUC20 daily for the privilege of being jailed! Plus, you miss your flight and will have to buy a new ticket. *Do not overextend your stay.* Foreign embassies also report that travelers have been jailed because their passports were torn or damaged.

Are U.S. Citizens Welcome? The Cubans have no restrictions on U.S. tourists. The Cubans are savvy—they stamp your tourist card, not your passport. The U.S. government recommends that its citizens arriving in Cuba register at the U.S. Interests Section (see the *Embassies and Consulates* section later in this chapter). *Warning:* All U.S. citizens traveling with a U.S. Treasury Dept. license are now suspect in the eyes of the Cuban government, and there are recent reports of innocent U.S. travelers being investigated and even jailed. Licensed U.S. travelers should assume that they may be under suspicion and surveillance and should avoid engaging in any activities that heighten such suspicion.

Cuban Émigrés: Cuban-born individuals who permanently left Cuba after December 31, 1970, must have a valid Cuban passport to enter and leave Cuba (you will also need your U.S. passport to depart and enter the United States). Cuban passports can be obtained from the **Cuban Interests Section** (2639 16th St. NW, Washington, DC 20009, 202/797-8518, fax 202/797-8521, www.eda.admin.ch/washington_emb/e/home/cuban.html), or any Cuban embassy or consulate in other countries (see *Cuban Embassies and Consulates*); as of 2005, the passport costs US$350. As of June 1, 2004, Cuban émigrés holding Cuban passports no longer need to apply for a visa or prior permission from the Cuban government to travel to Cuba.

However, Uncle Sam permits Cuban-Americans to visit Cuba only once every three years and only for reasons of extreme family hardship. And Cuba does not recognize dual citizenship for Cuban citizens who are also U.S. citizens; Cuban-born citizens are thereby denied representation through the U.S. Interests Section in the event of arrest.

Non-Tourist Visas

Journalists must enter on a journalists' D-6 visa (US$60). Ostensibly these should be obtained in advance from Cuban embassies, and in the United States from the **Cuban Interests Section** (2639 16th St. NW, Washington, DC 20009, 202/797-8518, fax 202/797-8521, www.eda.admin.ch/washington_emb/e/home/cuban.html). However, processing can take months while your credentials are vetted. If you enter on a tourist visa and intend to exercise your profession, you must register for a D-6 visa at the **Centro de Prensa Internacional** (International Press Center, Calle 23 #152, e/ N y O, Vedado, Havana, tel. 07/832-0526, cpi@cpi.minrex.gov.cu). Ask for an Acreditación de Prensa Extranjera (Foreign Journalist's Accreditation). You'll need to supply passport photos. Here, the process of getting a journalist's visa can be done in a day, although you might not get your passport back for a week!

A commercial visa is required for individuals traveling to Cuba for business. These must also be obtained in advance from Cuban embassies, or the Cuban Interests Section in Washington, D.C.

If you wish to enter using a tourist visa and

then, while within Cuba, change your visa status, contact the **Ministerio de Relaciones Exteriores** (Ministry of Foreign Affairs; MINREX, Calle Calzada #360, e/ G y H, Vedado, tel. 07/55-3537 or 07/55-3260, fax 07/33-3460, www.cubaminrex.cu), which handles immigration issues relating to foreigners.

Other Documentation Considerations

Visitors need a return ticket, adequate finances for their proposed stay, and proof that they have pre-booked accommodations for at least three nights.

The law requires that you carry your passport or tourist card with you at all times during your stay. Make photocopies of all your important documents, including your passport, and keep them separate from the originals, which you can keep in your hotel safe.

Cuban Embassies and Consulates

Cuba has representation in most major nations, including:

Australia: 128 Chalmers St., Surry Hills, NSW 2010, tel. 02/9698-9797, fax 02/8399-1106, consulcu@bigpond.com.

Canada: (Embassy) 388 Main St., Ottawa K1S 1E3, tel. 613/563-0141, fax 613/540-0068, embacuba@embacuba.ca; (Consulate) 5353 Dundas St. W., Suite 401, Etobicoke, Ontario M9B 6H8, 416/234-8181, fax 416/234-2754, cubaconl@on.aibn.com; (Consulate) 4542 Decarie Blvd., Montreal H4A 3P2, Quebec, tel. 514/843-8897, fax 514/845-1063, cnsulgralcuba@bellnet.ca.

France: 16 rue de Presles, Paris, tel. 1/45-67-55-35, fax 1/45-66-80-92, embacu@amba-cuba.fr.

Germany: (Embassy) Stavangertrasse 20, D-10439 Berlin, tel. 30/9161-1813, fax 30/916-4553, embacuba-berlin@t-online.de; (Consulate) Kennedyallee 22-24, Bad Godesberg 53175, Bonn, tel. 228/309225, fax 228/309244, ofidip-bonn@t-online.de.

Italy: (Consulate) Via Pirelli #30, 20121 Milano, tel. 02/6739-1344, fax 02/6671-2694, concubmi@tiscalinet.it; (Embassy) Via Licinia

7, 00153 Rome, tel. 06/571-7241, fax 06/574-5445, embajada@ecuitalia.it.

Spain: (Embassy) Paseo de La Habana #194, C.P. 28036, Madrid, tel. 34/359-2500, fax 91/359-6145, ecubamad@comunired.com; (Consulate) Calle Conde de Peñalver #38, 28006, Madrid, tel. 91/401-0579, fax 91/402-1948, camig@infonegocio.com.

United Kingdom: 167 High Holborn, London WC1V 6PA, tel. 020/7240-2488, fax 020/7836-2602, embacuba@cubaldn.com.

In the **United States,** the **Cuban Interests Section** (2639 16th St. NW, Washington, DC 20009, 202/797-8518, fax 202/797-8521, www.eda.admin.ch/washington_emb/e/home/cuban.html) is under the aegis of the Swiss embassy.

For a complete list of Cuban embassies and consulates, visit www.cubaminrex.cu/consulares/directorio_deCuba.htm.

CUSTOMS

Cuban airports have the international two-zone system: red (items to declare), and green (nothing to declare). Visitors to Cuba are permitted 20 kilos of personal effects plus "other articles and equipment depending on their profession," all of which must be re-exported. A "Welcome Tax" of CUC25 per kilo on excess baggage over 20 kilos applies for tourists arriving in Cuba; an additional two kilos of gifts are permitted, if packed separately.

In addition, visitors are allowed up to 10 kilos of medicines, 200 cigarettes, 50 cigars, 250 grams of pipe tobacco, and up to three liters of wine and alcohol, plus a reasonable quantity of items deemed for personal use. An additional US$200 of "objects and articles for non-commercial use" can be imported, subject to a tax equal to 100 percent of the declared value (you must fill out a customs form and use the red zone), but this applies mostly to Cubans and returning foreign residents. Most electrical goods are banned, including videocassette recorders. Laptops must be declared; you will need to fill out a customs declaration, and the laptop *must* depart Cuba with you. "Obscene and pornographic" literature is also banned—

the definition of "obscene" includes politically unacceptable tracts that are critical, explicitly or implicitly, of the Castro regime.

If for whatever reason you must leave some items with customs authorities, make sure that you obtain a signed receipt to enable you to reclaim the items upon departure.

Your carry-on baggage will be X-rayed upon arrival at the Havana airport.

For further information, contact the **Aduana** (Customs, Calle 6, esq. 39, Plaza de la Revolución, Havana, tel. 07/55-5466, fax 07/33-5222, adm@agr.aduana.cu, www.aduana.islagrande.com).

EMBASSIES AND CONSULATES

The **U.S. Interests Section** (USINT, Calzada, e/ L y M, Vedado, Havana, tel. 07/833-3551 to 07/833-3559, emergency/after hours tel. 07/833-3026, infousis@pd.state.gov, http://havana.usinterestsection.gov/; Mon.–Fri. 8:30 A.M.–5:00 P.M.) is the equivalent of an embassy but lacks an ambassador. The Interests Section represents U.S. citizens and the U.S. government in Cuba, and operates under the legal protection of the Swiss government. Readers report that it has been helpful to Americans in distress, and that its staff is not overly concerned about policing

> # EMBASSIES AND CONSULATES IN HAVANA
>
> The following nations have embassies/consulates in Havana. Additional countries can be found in the local telephone directory under Embajadas.
>
> **Australia:** c/o Canadian Embassy
> **Canada:** Calle 30 #518, esq. 7ma, Miramar, tel. 07/204-2516, fax 07/204-2044, emergency tel. 07/204-2516.
> **Germany:** Calle 13 #652, esq. B, Vedado, tel. 07/833-2569, fax 07/833-1586.
> **Italy:** Avenida 5ta #402, Miramar, tel.07/204-5615.
> **United Kingdom:** Calle 34 #702, e/ 7ma y 17-A, Miramar, tel. 07/204-1771, fax 204-8104.
> **United States:** Interests Section, Calzada, e/ L y M, Vedado, Havana, tel. 07/833-3551 to 07/833-3559, emergency/after hours tel. 07/833-3026, http://havana.usinterestsection.gov.

potential infractions of Treasury Department regulations.

See the sidebar *Embassies and Consulates in Havana* for more information.

Outdoor Recreation

Most outdoor recreational activities are under the bailiwick of two state entities: **Cubamar Viajes** (3ra Av., e/ 12 y Malecón, Havana, tel. 07/66-2523, fax 07/33-3111, www.cubamarviajes.cu) and **Rumbos** (Línea #60, esq. M, Vedado, Havana, tel. 07/66-2113 or 204-9626, fax 07/33-3110).

BICYCLING

Bicycle touring offers a chance to explore the island alongside the Cubans themselves. The roads are little trafficked, but potholes and stray animals are a consistent problem, as is

the horrendous pollution from cars and trucks. Wear a helmet!

Cubana treats bicycles as a piece of luggage, which counts towards your weight allowance (30 kg per person), and will accept bicycles unboxed.

Bring essential spares, as there are very few spare parts to be found. Bring some sturdy locks and a cover for the bike, as bicycle theft is a huge problem.

Bicycles Without Borders (685 Queen St. West, Toronto, Ontario M6J 1E6, tel. 416/364 5329, www.bikestocuba.org) trains

Cuban men and women to be mechanics and has a bike repair workshop and bike rental agency (the only one in Cuba) in Havana. You can reserve a bicycle in advance. (Also see *By Bicycle* in the *Getting Around* section of the *Havana* chapter.)

If planning an all-Cuba trip, touring is best done in a westerly direction to take advantage of prevailing east–west winds.

The **Club Nacional de Cicloturismo Gran Caribe** (Lonja del Comercio #6D, Calle Oficios, Habana Vieja, tel. 07/96-9193, fax 07/66-9908, trans@ip.etecsa.cu) offers cycle trips. Most foreign tour entities offering bicycle tours do so through the club.

A good resource is *Bicycling Cuba* by Barbara and Wally Smith (see *Suggested Reading* in the *Resources* section).

BIRD-WATCHING

Wherever you travel in Cuba, you're surrounded by the calls and whistles of exotic species. The swampy Zapata Peninsula is one of the best bird-watching arenas in the Caribbean—203 species are found here, including 18 of the nation's 21 endemics—as is Cayo Coco, with more than 200 species. With luck you might spot the smallest hummingbird in the world (the *pájaro mosca*), the *tocororo* or Cuban trogon, and flamingos, which can also be seen on the northern cays. The cays are also favored nesting sites for scores of migratory species. Isla de la Juventud has Cuba's largest population of parrots. The Sierra del Rosario and mountains of Oriente are also superb bird-watching sites, especially Reserva de la Biosfera Baconao and Reserva de la Biosfera Cuchillas de Toa.

The state agency **Cubatur** (Calle 23, esq. L, Vedado, Havana, tel. 07/833-3569, www.cubatur.cu) publishes a bird-watching brochure and offers bird-watching excursions.

ECOTOURISM

Cuba has very few naturalist guides, and so-called "eco-lodges" are mere lodges set in wilderness areas. But a beginning has been made, and eco-reserves, trails, and trained guides are being introduced.

Sportfishing in the Gulf Stream is world-class. Blue marlin is the species of choice.

Cubamar Viajes (3ra Av., e/ 12 y Malecón, Havana, tel. 07/66-2523, fax 07/33-3111, www.cubamarviajes.cu) and **EcoTur, S.A.** (Av. Independencia #116, esq. Santa Catalina, Cerro, Havana, tel. 07/41-0306, fax 07/53-9909, ecoturhabana@miramar.co.cu) offer eco-oriented tours.

FISHING
Freshwater and Inshore Fishing
Cuba's freshwater *lagos* (lakes) and *lagunas* (lagoons) almost boil with tarpon, bonefish, snook, and bass. The star of the show is largemouth bass, which is best at Lago Hanabanilla and neighboring Lago Granizo in the Sierra Escambray; Lago Cuyaguatoje in Pinar del Río; and Lago Zaza in Sancti Spíritus Province. Lago Redonda, near Morón in Ciego de Ávila Province, is another good site, as is Cayo Largo. The best months for bass fishing are the colder months.

Trout fishing is particularly good at Presa Alacranes, in Villa Clara. Lago Zaza and Lago La Redonda, which has the highest concentration of trout per square kilometer, are also good. As for bonefish, few (if any) destinations can compare. Angling maestro Joe Brooks wrote glowingly of fishing Cuba's Isle of Pines (today's Isla de la Juventud) in the 1950s, when he and his angling pals landed 31 bones on their best day.

Light-tackle enthusiasts will also find shallow-water bonefish and tarpon in abundance off Cayo Largo, and in the Jardines de la Reina archipelago south of Ciego de Ávila Province. Maspotón, a dedicated hunting and fishing resort on the south shore of Pinar del Río, is also a popular spot to catch tarpon, as are Laguna del Tesoro and the brackish coastal lagoons of Zapata Peninsula and Cayo Largo. These "silver rockets" can reach up to 75 kilograms. When you tire of wrestling these snappy fighters, you can take on snook—another worthy opponent. Tarpon and snook are caught year-round.

The only centers currently developed for inshore fishing are **Casa Batida Fishing Club** on Cayo Largo (see the *Isla de la Juventud Special Municipality* chapter), and live-aboard boats in the Jardines de la Reina (see the *Ciego de Ávila and Camagüey* chapter).

Cubatur publishes brochures on fishing in Cuba and can arrange licenses and compulsory fishing guides.

Deep-Sea Fishing

So many game fish run offshore, streaming through the Gulf Stream that Ernest Hemingway called his "great blue river," that hardly a season goes by without some IGFA record being broken. The big marlin run begins in May, when they swim against the Gulf Stream current close to the Cuban shore. No fishermen was ever so knowledgeable as Ernest Hemingway, who returned to Cuba year after year and reputedly became the first sportsman to fish marlin with rod and reel in Cuban waters. The Cubans aren't yet into tag-and-release, preferring to let you sautée the trophy (for a cut of the steak). The best months for spearfish are May–August.

Fishing expeditions are offered from Marina Hemingway, Playas del Este, Varadero, and other marinas along the north coast. Other good spots are the Archipiélago de los Canarreos (which includes Isla de la Juventud and Cayo Largo).

Fishing Tournaments

Cuba hosts several sportfishing tournaments. The big three competitions are based in Havana's Marina Hemingway. The Ernest Hemingway International Billfishing Tournament is held each June and may well be the world's most sought-after fishing trophy; the International Blue Marlin Fishing Tournament is held each September; and the International Wahoo Fishing Tournament is held each November.

GOLF

Before the Revolution, Cuba had several golf courses. After 1959, they were closed and/or fell into ruin. Cuba is investing in its future as a golfing destination, with courses planned for Jibacoa, Cayo Coco, Cayo Santa Lucía, and Guardalavaca. The Havana Golf Club is a nine-hole course, and Varadero has an 18-hole championship course.

HIKING, SPELUNKING, AND ROCK CLIMBING

Cuba has the potential to be a hiker's paradise, though organized hiking is virtually undeveloped. Notable exceptions are the trails in Parque Nacional Pico Turquino (Cuba's highest peak) in the Sierra Maestra. You can also head for the foothills of the Sierra del Rosario, and Sierra Maestra and Cuchillas de Toa in Oriente, where trails lace the mountains. Parque Nacional Península de Guanahacabibes also has marked trails. Pinares de Mayarí (in Holguín Province), El Saltón (in Santiago Province), and Moka Hotel (in Pinar del Río) are all eco-resorts with hiking trails. Guides are compulsory for many trails.

Cuba is riddled with caverns and caving (speleology) is growing in popularity, organized through the **Sociedad Espeleológica de Cuba** (tel. 07/209-2885), which also has a climbing division (c/o Anibal Fernández, Calle Águila #367, e/Neptuno y San Miguel,

Centro Habana, tel. 07/862-0401, anibalpiaz@yahoo.com). And many climbing routes have been established in Viñales. Climbing routes are open and no permission is necessary. Visit www.cubaclimbing.com. Cuban-American climber Armando Menocal (tel. 307/734-6034 in US, armandomenocal@wyoming.com) leads tours.

SAILING

For cruising, you'll need to register your boat upon arrival and receive a cruising permit called a *Permiso especial de navegación* (CUC50 or more, depending on the length of your boat). You'll need an official clearance—a *despacho*—to depart for your next, and each and every, stop. Authorities will usually ask for a planned itinerary, but hold to your guns and insist on flexibility to cruise at random toward your final destination. A *Permiso de Salida* will be issued listing your final destination and possible stops en route. Simon Charles, in his *Cruising Guide to Cuba*, recommends noting on the *permiso* any plans to scuba dive or anchor offshore at any of Cuba's zillion cays. Be patient! Official proceedings are always courteous but time consuming.

Cubanacán Náutica (Calle 184 #123, e/ 1ra y 5ta, Rpto. Flores, Havana, tel. 07/33-7969, www.cubanacan.cu) operates 18 marinas and dive centers. Only a few are up to international par, although most offer fresh water, 110-volt electrical hookups, plus diesel and gasoline. Yachts and catamarans can be rented at most.

An English company, **Sunsail** (tel. 0870/777-0313, www.sunsail.com), based at Playa Ancón, offers charter yachts for cruising the Jardines de la Reina.

SCUBA DIVING

Cuba is a diver's paradise. There are dozens of Spanish galleons and even U-boats sunk off the south coast, while the north coast also has some splendid sites. Visibility ranges from 15 to 35 meters. Water temperatures average 27–29°C.

Many large beachside hotels offer diving programs (typically CUC27 per dive; CUC37 for night dives) and certification courses (typically about CUC324), although this is usually an American & Canadian Underwater Certification (ACUC). Cuban dive masters are all trained by internationally recognized organizations and are highly skilled. However, the standard of equipment is not generally up to Western par, and it's a good idea to bring your own equipment, but leave tanks and weight belts at home. Dive shops are meagerly equipped. Tank fittings and equipment in Cuba are both European and North American.

Cuba has developed four principal dive areas: the Archipiélago de Las Colorados, off the north coast of Pinar del Río; the Jardines de la Rey archipelago, off the north coast of Ciego de Ávila and Camagüey Provinces; the Jardines de la Reina archipelago off the southern coast of Ciego de Ávila and Camagüey Provinces, where dedicated dive boats operate; and the Isla de la Juventud and Cayo Largo. The so-called "Blue Circuit" east of Havana also has prime sites, as do the waters off the tip of Cabo de Corrientes, at the westernmost point of Cuba. Isla de la Juventud, with many of the best wrecks and walls, is primarily for experienced divers. Varadero is of only modest interest for experienced divers, although it offers cave diving (nor is Varadero particularly good for snorkeling). Waters off the south and west coasts tend to be calmer than those of the north and east in winter (Nov.–Apr.), while those of the north coast are calmer in summer (May–Sept.).

The traditional critters of the Caribbean abound. Even whale sharks are commonly seen, notably from María la Gorda, in Pinar del Río Province.

Spearfishing is strictly controlled. Spearguns and gigs are *not* allowed through customs.

Divers should consult *Diving and Snorkeling Guide to Cuba* by Diana Williams.

SURFING AND SAILBOARDING

Surfing hasn't yet come to Cuba, and there are no boards to be rented. The north coast shores offer great possibilities, notably December–April, when the trade winds kick up good breaks. The south shore is generally placid except during summer, when frequent but unpredictable storms push the rollers ashore.

A good starting point is the website www .havanasurf-cuba.com.

Many resorts at Varadero, Cayo Largo del Sur, Guardalavaca, and in other resort areas rent sailboards.

Entertainment and Events

Cuba pulsates with the Afro-Latin spirit, be it energy-charged musical sessions or someone's home-based celebration (called *cumbanchas,* or rumbas), where drummers beat out thumping rhythms and partners dance overtly sexual *changüí* numbers.

Every city has at least one Casa de la Trova and a Casa de la Cultura, where movies, art exhibitions, and traditional music and other cultural events are hosted. The local UNEAC (National Union of Cuban Writers and Artists, www.uneac.com) will plug you into local life just as sweetly. Major cities also have ongoing music concerts, choral recitals, and art and sculpture exhibits. Virtually every town also has a theater, a movie house, and at least one disco or *centro nocturno.* Almost all boast live music, everything from salsa bands to folkloric trios. Romantic crooners are a staple, wooing local crowds with dead-on deliveries of Benny Moré classics. And *noches cubanas* take place in most towns on Saturday nights, when bars are set up, meals prepared alfresco, and the street is cleared for dancing and no small amount of drunkenness (a major problem in Cuba).

That said, Cuba's nocturnal entertainment scene is a far cry from days of yore and in many locales you are hard-pressed to find any signs of life.

Paradiso (Calle 19 #560, esq. C, Vedado, Havana, tel. 07/832-6928, fax 07/33-3921, paradis@paradiso.artex.com.cu) promotes artistic and cultural events, festivals, courses, seminars, and workshops.

FESTIVALS

The annual calendar is filled with cultural events held throughout the island and ranging from "high culture," such as the International Ballet Festival, to purely local, down-to-earth affairs, such as the year-end *parrandas* of Villa Clara Province, where the townsfolk indulge in massive fireworks battles. A highlight is Carnaval, held in Havana (February) and Santiago (July).

Cuba, though nominally atheist, hosts a number of religious parades, such as the Procession of the Miracles (December 17), when hundreds of pilgrims—many of them dragging stones or crawling on their knees—make their way to the Santuario de San Lázaro, at Rincón, on the outskirts of Santiago de las Vegas in suburban Havana. The old Spanish holiday El Día de los Reyes Magos (Three King's Day), on January 6, is the most important religious observance.

For a list of forthcoming conferences, symposiums, and events, contact the **Buró de Convenciones** (Hotel Neptuno, 3ra y 70, Miramar, Havana, tel. 07/204-8162, www .loseventos.cu).

THEATER

Theater is the least developed of Cuba's cultural media. Theaters are used mostly for operatic, symphonic, and other concerts. Theater was usurped by the Revolution as a medium for mass consciousness-raising. As such it became heavily politicized. In recent years, however, an avant-garde theater offering veiled political criticism has begun to evolve.

Comic theater is popular with Cubans. It is considered part of the national culture and was an important element in 19th-century life. However, you'll need to be fluent in Spanish to get many giggles out of the shows, which although heavy on easy-to-understand burlesque

MAJOR FESTIVALS

FESTIVAL/EVENT	MONTH	LOCATION
Havana Cigar Festival	February	Havana
Festival de Semana Santa (Easter)	April	Trinidad
International Percussion Festival	April	Havana
Carnaval de la Habana	July	Havana
Festival of Caribbean Culture (Carnaval)	July	Santiago de Cuba
Benny Moré International Festival	August	Cienfuegos
Festival of Contemporary Music	October	Havana
Festival of Latin American Culture	October	Holguín
International Ballet Festival	October	Havana
International Festival of New Latin American Cinema	November	Havana
International Steam Train Festival	November	Maltiempo (Cienfuegos)
International Jazz Festival	December	Havana

are also full of subtly hidden references to politically sensitive third-rail issues. Women, blacks, and homosexuals are the constant butt of crude jokes based on well-known stereotypes.

CINEMAS

Cubans are passionate moviegoers, and the entire island is blessed with cinemas, although most are extremely run-down. The old film-roll projectors still in use are no less in need of repair (remember the days when the celluloid would stick and burn?). Entrance usually costs a single peso—foreigners are rarely charged in dollars—and the menu is surprisingly varied and hip. Leading Hollywood productions (classic and contemporary) and cartoons are shown, as are westerns, kung-fu flicks, and other foreign productions, particularly those of socially redeeming quality. Movies are often subtitled in Spanish (others are dubbed; you'll need to be fluent in Spanish). Adult films are banned, as are certain politically "offensive" movies.

No children under 16 are admitted to cinemas. Most towns have special children's screenings.

Many cinemas and Casas de Cultura have *salas de videos*—tiny screening rooms. Often the movies have been pirated from satellite TV and are sometimes of dubious quality.

FOLKLORIC MUSIC VENUES

In Cuba, *música folklórica* (folkloric music) usually refers to Afro-Cuban music, the staple of the entertainment scene. Every town has a Casa de la Trova where you can hear traditional ballad-style *trova* (love songs rendered with the aid of guitar and drum), often blended with revolutionary themes; and a Casa de la Cultura, which hosts folkloric music and dance, plus movies, art exhibitions, and other cultural events for the locals.

Most major cities have a performance group supported by the national umbrella body. Look for performances by the Conjunto Folklórico Nacional (National Folklore Dance Group), which performs nationwide. The group was founded in 1962 to revive Cuban folk traditions because it was thought that the populace had lost touch with its folkloric past.

LOCO POR BÉISBOL

Béisbol (or *pelota*) is as much an obsession in Cuba as it is in the United States – more so, in fact. Baseball was introduced to Cuba in the 1860s, the island's first professional team – the Habana Baseball Club – was formed in 1872, and the first league was formed six years later. In 1909, Ralph Estep, a salesman for Packard, journeyed through Cuba and found the country to be "baseball crazy." Baseball terminology found its way into the Cuban lexicon, while many aspiring young Cubans fulfilled their dreams of making it to the big leagues; prior to the Revolution, many Cubans found positions in the U.S. leagues. The flow went both ways. Babe Ruth and Willie Mays played for Cuban clubs, for example, as did Tommy Lasorda, who played five seasons in Cuba.

Just watch Cuban kids – playing, writes author Randy Wayne White, "without spikes, hitting without helmets, sharing their cheap Batos gloves, but playing like I have never seen kids play before. It wasn't so much the skill – though they certainly had skill – as it was the passion with which they played, a kind of controlled frenzy." No wonder Cuba traditionally beats the pants off the U.S. team in the Olympic Games.

Players who make the Cuban national team and barnstorm the Olympics earn about 400 pesos a month – about the same as the average laborer – and it's not surprising that many are still tempted by the prospect of riches in the U.S. professional leagues. More than 40 Cuban baseball stars have fled Cuba since 1991, when Rene Arocha (who became a star pitcher for the St. Louis Cardinals) split from the Cuban national team during a stopover in Miami. In 1996, the defection of Livan Hernández (who was snatched up for US$4.5 million by the Florida Marlins) so rankled Castro that in a fit of spite, Livan's half-brother, Orlando "El Duque" Hernández, one of the world's greatest pitchers, was barred from playing and relegated to work in the Havana Psychiatric Hospital. Understandably, in January 1998 he fled Cuba on a homemade raft and was signed by the Yankees for US$6.6 million.

Still, not every player is eager to leave. In 1995, Omar Linares, slugging third baseman for the Pinar del Río team and considered to be one of the best amateur baseball players in the world, rejected a US$1.5 million offer to play for the New York Yankees. In 2002,

BARS

Take your pick between dollars-only haunts, where drinks will set you back at least CUC3 a pop, to earthy bars for locals, where *one peso* will buy a beer. However, Cuban cities are relatively devoid of the kind of lively sidewalk bars that make Rio de Janeiro buzz and South Beach hum. Tourist-only hotel bars are with few exceptions pretty dead, while most bars serving locals for pesos are run-down to the point of dilapidation and typically serve shots of *aguardiente* (cheap rum; your glass will likely be a sawn-off beer bottle) or beer served in 1.5-liter bottles.

Bars do not offer cigars for sale—bring your own.

DISCOS

Western-style discos are few and most are money-milking machines serving well-heeled foreigners and dollar-rich Cubans. Males can expect to be solicited outside the entrance to these dollars-only discos: Cuban women take a stranger's arm and beg to be escorted in because the cover charge is beyond their means and/or because the venue only permits couples to enter. Drink prices can give you sticker shock. The best bet is usually to buy a bottle of rum and a Coca-Cola. Earthy discos (called cabarets) and *centros nocturnos* (open-air discotheques) serve the locals and are cheap, usually run-down, unpretentious affairs, often with kitschy prerevolutionary decor. Be prepared for *merengue,* salsa, and

however, Linares and third baseman Omar Kindelan signed to play with Japanese teams for US$4,000 monthly, with the Cuban government taking a slice of the salary.

Cuba is led by a sports fanatic. In the early years of power, Castro would often drop in at Havana's Gran Stadium (in 1971 it was renamed Estadio Latinoamericano) in the evening to pitch a few balls at the Sugar Kings' batters. And everyone knows the story of how Castro once tried out as a pitcher for the old Washington Senators. Who knows? Had the story been true, Fidel might have become a Senator and not a dictator.

Cuba's stars play more than 100 games a season on regional teams under the supervision of the best coaches, sports doctors, and competition psychologists outside the U.S. big leagues. Each province has a team on the national league (Liga Nacional), and two provinces and the city of Havana have two teams each, making 16 teams in all. They're divided into two zones – Occidente and Oriente – with two groups of four teams each. The last game of every three-game series is played in a *pueblo* away from the provincial capital so that fans in the country can see the teams live. The season runs October–March. The teams play a 39-game season, with the top seven teams going on to compete in the 54-game National Series, culminating when the top Oriente team battles the top Occidental team in a seven-game battle.

Stadiums are oases of relaxation and amusement. There are no exploding scoreboards or dancing mascots, and beer and souvenir hawkers are replaced by old men wandering among the seats selling thimble-size cups of sweet Cuban espresso. Spam sandwiches replace hot dogs in the stands, where the spectators, being good socialists, also cheer for the opposition's base-stealers and home-run hitters. Balls (knocked out of the field by aluminum Batos bats made in Cuba) are even returned from the stands, because fans understand they're too valuable to keep as souvenirs.

Cubaball Tours (4772 Narvaez Dr., Vancouver, BC V6L 2J2, Canada, tel. 604/266-4664, www.cubaballtours.com) offers baseball trips to Cuba, as has **Baseball Adventures** (P.O. Box 707, Mendocino, CA 95460, 707/937-4478, www.cubabaseball.net) in past years.

even sexier *timba* dancing hot enough to fry the chicken! Few discos get their groove on before midnight. There's little point in arriving early.

Many clubs apply a *consumo mínimo* (minimum charge) policy that applies regardless of how many drinks you consume. The system is rife with *estafas* (swindles). For example, if a CUC5 *consumo mínimo* applies to your first purchase and you order several beverages during the evening, be sure that the first drink you order is a more expensive drink—you'll be charged CUC5 even for a mineral water—and that any inexpensive item you might order later in the evening doesn't appear as the first drink on your bill.

CABARETS

One of the first acts of the revolutionary government was to kick out the Mafia and close down the casinos and brothels. "It was as if the Amish had taken over Las Vegas," wrote Kenneth Tynan in a 1961 edition of *Holiday*. Not quite! Sure, the strip clubs and live sex shows are gone. But sexy cabarets (called *shows*) remain a staple of Cuban entertainment; every town has at least one. Although the term sometimes refers to a disco, more frequently, it refers to *cabarets espectáculos*, Las Vegas–style song-and-dance routines highlighted by long-legged dancers wearing high heels and g-strings, with lots of sequins, feathers, and frills, and who gyrate their glistening bodies into an erotic frenzy. Singers, magicians,

TURNING OUT CHAMPIONS

Tiny Cuba is one of the top five sports powers in the world, excelling in baseball, volleyball, boxing, and track and field. Cuba is by far the strongest Olympic power in Latin America, and took 11th place at the 2004 Olympic Games in Athens.

Cuba's international success is credited to its splendid sports training system. When the Revolution triumphed, sports became a priority alongside land reform, education, and health care. In 1964 the Castro government opened a network of sports schools – Escuelas de Iniciación Deportiva (EIDE) – as part of the primary and secondary education system, with the job of preparing young talent for sports achievement. There are 15 EIDE schools throughout Cuba. The island also has 76 sports academies and an athletic "finishing" school in Havana, the Escuela Superior de Perfeccionamiento Atlético.

Sports training is incorporated into every school curriculum. School Games are held is- landwide every year and help identify talent to be selected for specialized coaching. For example, María Colón Rueñes was identified as a potential javelin champion when she was only seven years old; she went on to win the gold medal at the Moscow Olympics. Many of Cuba's sports greats have passed through these schools – track-and-field stars such as world-record-holding high jumper Javier Sotomayor, world-record sprinters Leroy Burrel and Ana Fidelia Quirot, and volleyball legends such as Jel Despaigne and Mireya Luis.

Sports figures are considered workers and "part of the society's productive efforts." As such, sports stars are paid a pitiful salary on a par with other workers, although most national team members also receive special perks, such as access to new cars. Not surprisingly, scores of athletic stars have turned their backs on the island, and almost every international competition outside Cuba results in at least one defection.

---

acrobats, and comedians are often featured. Cuban couples delight in these razzmatazz spectacles and shake their heads at any puritan's concept that they are sexist.

Outshining all other venues is the Tropicana (see the sidebar *Paradise under the Stars* in the *Havana* chapter), with outlets in Havana, Matanzas, and Santiago de Cuba.

SPECTATOR SPORTS

Cuba is a world superstar in sports and athletics—out of all proportion to its diminutive size—as it was even before the Revolution, especially in baseball and boxing. Following the Revolution, the state took over all sports and professional sports were abolished. In 1971, the Cuban government formed the **Instituto**

Nacional del Deportivo y Recreo (National Institute for Sport, Physical Education, and Recreation, INDER, tel. 07/832-6082, www .inder.co.cu).

The Cuban calendar is replete with national and international sporting events, from fencing, tennis, and wrestling to badminton, sportfishing, and even motorcycle races and car rallies. The **Cubadeportes** (Calle 20 #710, e/ 7 y 9, Miramar, tel. 07/204-0904, www .cubadeportes.cu) specializes in sports tourism and arranges visits to international sporting events and training facilities.

See the *Sports and Recreation* section of the *Havana* chapter for information on venues in the capital and for contact information for individual sports federations.

Shopping

You don't come to Cuba for factory outlets or designer boutiques. But for high-quality arts and crafts, the island is unrivaled in the Caribbean. You're not going to find anything of interest in peso stores, which are meagerly stocked with shoddy Cuban-made plastic and tin wares.

Department stores and shopping malls are mostly restricted to Havana. These, and smaller outlets in every town, sell Western goods from toiletries, Levis, and Reeboks to Chinese toys and Japanese electronics sold for CUC or hard currency at vastly inflated prices. You must leave your handbags and backpacks at the *guardabolsas.*

Most stores selling dollar goods accept foreign credit cards except those issued by U.S. banks. However, processing can take forever, and frequently the credit card machines aren't working. Take sufficient cash. Prices for identical items are usually higher in tourist venues than they are in comparative outlets selling to Cubans.

A good rule for buying in Cuba... if you see something you want, *buy it!* If you dally, it most likely will disappear.

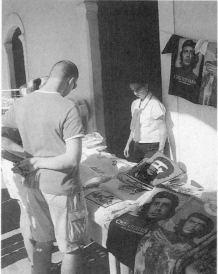

Che Guevara T-shirts are one of the most popular souvenirs of a visit to Cuba.

© CHRISTOPHER P. BAKER

ARTS AND CRAFTS

Cuba's strong suit is arts and crafts, sold by artisans at street stalls and also in stores by state agencies such as the Fondo Cubano de Bienes Culturales and ARTEX. In recent years, art has been patronized by the tourist dollar, so Cuban cities on the tourist map are overflowing with cheap canvas scenes, busty cigar-chomping ceramic mulattas, kitschy erotic carvings, and papier-mâché vintage Yankee cars. There is also plenty of true-quality art, ranging from paintings and tapestries to hand-worked leather goods and precious wood carvings representing a solid investment. You'll also see *muñequitas* (dolls) representing the goddesses of the *santería* religion. Cuban women are great doll collectors and often keep their childhood dolls into late adulthood. The best stuff is sold in the gift stores of the upscale hotels, which mark up accordingly.

Cuban jewelry can be quite stunning. Most open-air markets offer silver-plated jewelry at bargain prices (a favorite form is old cutlery shaped into bracelets), while most upscale hotels have *joyerías* (jewelry stores) selling international-quality silver jewelry, much of it in a distinctly contemporary style. Avoid buying black coral jewelry, as well as turtle shell jewelry. The Cuban government doesn't seem particularly conscientious in this regard, but European and North American customs officials may seize the offending items. The same goes for mounted butterflies and other animal "craft" items, including crocodile-skin products and appalling *ceniceros* (ashtrays) made of stuffed frogs performing acrobatic or obscene maneuvers.

A limited amount of bargaining is normal at street markets. However, most prices are very

CUBAN CIGARS

There is no substitute for our tobacco anywhere in the world. It's easier to make good cognac than to achieve the quality of Cuban tobacco.

— Fidel Castro

It seems ironic that Cuba – scourge of the capitalist world – should have been compelled by history and geography to produce one of the most blatant symbols of capitalist wealth and power. Yet it does so with pride. The unrivaled reputation of Cuban cigars as the best in the world transcends politics, transubstantiating a weed into an object capable of evoking rapture. Cubans guard the unique reputation scrupulously.

Cuban cigars – *habanos* or *puros* – are not only a source of hard currency; they're part and parcel of the national culture. Although Castro gave up smoking in 1985 (after what he called a "heroic struggle"), Cubans still smoke 250 million cigars domestically every year. Another 160 million or so are exported annually. Although some 20 percent of Cuban cigars are machine-made, the best are still hand-rolled.

HOW CIGARS GOT THEIR START

The cigar tradition was first documented among the indigenous tribes by Christopher Columbus. The Taíno made monster cigars – at the very least, they probably kept the mosquitoes away – called *cohibas*. The word "cigar" originated from *sikar*, the Mayan word for smoking, which in Spanish became *cigarro*.

The popular habit of smoking cigars – as opposed to tobacco in pipes, first introduced to Europe by Columbus – began in Spain, where cigars made from Cuban tobacco were first made in Seville in 1717. Demand for higher-quality cigars grew, and *Sevillas* (as Spanish cigars were called) were superseded by Cuban-made cigars. Soon, tobacco was Cuba's main export and received a boost after the Peninsula Campaign (1806-12) of the Napoleonic wars, when British and French veterans returned home with the cigar habit, creating a fashion in their home countries and launching Cubans cigars to international fame. "No lover of cigars can imagine the voluptuous pleasure of sitting in a café sipping slowly a strong magnificent coffee and smoking rhythmically those divine leaves of Cuba," wrote American pianist Arthur Rubinstein.

BUNDLED, BOXED, AND BOYCOTTED

The banking firm of H. Upmann initiated

---

low to begin with, and artisans are scratching to earn a few dollars. Don't bargain simply to win a battle. If the quoted price seems fair—and it usually is—then pay up and feel blessed that you already have a bargain.

Exporting Arts and Antiques

In 2003, the government stopped issuing permits for antiques, including antiquarian books, stamp collections, furniture, and porcelain. The security staff at Cuba's international airport checks all artwork and antiques (the Cuban government sure doesn't want you walking off with that rare Wilfredo Lam somebody sold you in desperation). An export permit is required for all quality artwork (you'll be required to show this to customs on leaving

Cuba); the regulation generally doesn't apply to kitschy tourist art bought at street markets.

State-run commercial galleries and *expo-ventas* (galleries representing freelance artists) will issue an export permit or arrange authorization for any items you buy. Export permits for items for which you have not received an official receipt must be obtained from the **Registro Nacional de Bienes Culturales** (National Registry of Cultural Goods, Calle 13 #810, e/ 6 y 8, Vedado, tel. 07/833-4193; Mon.–Fri. 8:30–11:30 A.M.), in the Centro de Patrimonio Cultural. The permit is good for up to five works of art and costs CUC10–30. You must bring the object for inspection, or a photo if the object is too large. Allow several hours for the visit and up to two days for processing.

export in cedar boxes in 1830, when it imported cigars for its directors in London. Later, the bank decided to enter the cigar business, and introduced the embossed cedar box complete with colorful lithographic label for each specific brand.

The Montecristo was the fashionable cigar of choice. In the 1930s, any tycoon or film director worth the name was seen with a whopping Montecristo A in his mouth. Half of all the Havanas sold in the world in the 1930s were Montecristos, by which time much of Cuba's tobacco industry had passed into U.S. ownership. Among the devotees of Cuban cigars was President Kennedy, who smoked Petit Upmanns. In 1962, at the height of the Cuban Missile Crisis, Kennedy asked his press secretary, Pierre Salinger, to obtain as many Upmanns as he could. Next day, reported Salinger, Kennedy asked him how many he had found. Twelve hundred, replied his aide. Kennedy then pulled out and signed the decree establishing a trade embargo with Cuba. Ex-British premier Winston Churchill also stopped smoking Havanas and started smoking Jamaican cigars, but after a time he forgot about politics and went back to Havanas. His brand was Romeo y Julieta.

The embargo dealt a crushing blow to Cuba's cigar industry. Castro nationalized the industry and founded a state monopoly, Cubatabaco. Many dispossessed cigar factory owners immigrated to the Dominican Republic, Mexico, Venezuela, and Honduras, where they started up again, often using the same brand names they had owned in Cuba. Today, the Dominican Republic produces 47 percent of the handmade cigars imported into the United States. Experts agree, however, that these foreign "Cuban" brands are inferior to their Havana counterparts.

CRACKING THE CODES
The code printed as a series of letters underneath each cigar box tells you a lot about the cigars inside. Even novices can determine the provenance and date of cigars, the quality of which varies markedly between factory and year, if they know the codes. However, the code system keeps changing (four times in the past eight years) to throw buyers off, so that cigars of different ages have different codes. The first three letters usually refer to the factory where the cigars were made, followed by four letters that give the date of manufacture.

CIGARS

Cuba's claim to shopping fame must be as the place to buy the best cigars in the world. Prices have jumped considerably in reason years, but you can still buy *habanos* or *puros* (the local terms for cigars) at prices anywhere from one-half to two-thirds the price of similar cigars in London.

There are about 40 brands and 500 cigar varieties—a single brand usually comes in various sizes and even shapes. Only eight factories make handmade export-quality cigars in Cuba today, compared to 120 at the beginning of the century. All cigar factories produce various brands. Some factories specialize in particular flavors, others in particular sizes—of which there are no fewer than 60 standard

variations, with minor variations from brand to brand; sizes are given specific names, such as Corona (142mm) and Julieta (178mm). Several of Cuba's 42 factories might be producing any one brand *simultaneously,* so quality can vary markedly even though the label is the same. Experts consider cigars produced in Havana's El Laguito and Romeo y Julieta factories to be the best. The source is marked in code on the underside of the box. The year of production is also indicated there. As with fine wines, the quality of cigars varies from year to year.

Since 1985, handmade Cuban cigars have carried the Cubatabaco stamp plus a factory mark and, since 1989, the legend *"Hecho en Cuba. Totalmente a Mano"* (Made in Cuba. Completely by Hand). If it reads *"Hecho a*

© CHRISTOPHER P. BAKER

Casas del Habano sell cigars to tourists. There's usually one in most major towns.

Mano," the cigars are most likely hand *finished* (i.e., the wrapper was put on by hand) rather than hand *made*. If it states only *"Hecho en Cuba,"* they are assuredly machine made. As of 2005, all boxes feature a holographic seal (any other boxes are subject to seizure by Cuban Customs).

Fatter cigars—the choice of connoisseurs—are more fully flavored and smoke more smoothly and slowly than those with smaller ring gauges. As a rule, darker cigars are also more full-bodied and sweeter. The expertise and care expressed in the cigar factory determine how well a cigar burns and tastes. Cigars, when properly stored, continue to ferment and mature in their boxes—an aging process similar to good wines. Rules on when to smoke a cigar don't exist, but many experts claim that the prime cigars are those aged for six to eight years. Everyone agrees that a cigar should be smoked either within three months of manufacture or not for at least a year; the interim is known as a "period of sickness."

Cigars should be slightly soft when gently squeezed, and should have a fresh, robust smell (a stale smell may indicate a fake, low-quality, or poorly stored cigar). Each cigar should be tightly-rolled, smooth and silky in texture, and free of any protuberances or air pockets, and the cigars should be of near identical color and shape.

The Cuban government permits you to leave Cuba with up to CUC2,000 worth of cigars with purchase receipts, which you also need for any more than 23 loose or unwrapped cigars. However, you can buy additional cigars in the airport duty-free lounge after passing through customs controls.

Cigars can be bought at virtually every hotel and store that welcomes tourists, or at dedicated Casas del Habano or Casas del Tabaco nationwide. Most shop clerks know little about *tabacos* (the Cuban term for Habanos). Your best bet is to buy at a serious outlet; those in the deluxe hotels are usually trustworthy. Prices can vary up to 20 percent from store to store, so shop around. If one store doesn't have what you desire, another surely will. You should inspect your cigars before committing to a purchase. Most shops don't allow this, but the best shops do.

Street Deals

In cities, *jiniteros* will offer you cigars at discount prices. You'll be tempted by what seems the deal of the century. Forget it! You might get lucky and get the real thing, but the vast majority are low-quality, machine-made cigars sold falsely as top-line cigars to unsuspecting travelers. Don't be taken in by the sealed counterfeit box, either. The hustlers use empty boxes and seals stolen by colleagues who work in the cigar factories, so the unknowing buyer is easily convinced that this is the real McCoy at a bargain. Not!

You can buy inferior domestic cigars—called *torpedoes*—for about one peso (less than CUC1) on the street.

LITERATURE

Books are severely restricted by the government, which controls access to all information and maintains an iron fist over what may be read. Alas, this is also true of periodicals. There are *no* newsstands or newsagents. Foreign periodicals are not for sale except in the lobbies of upscale tourist hotels, and even here the range is meager.

Most tourist outlets sell a limited range of English-language coffee-table books, travel-related books, and political treatises that have been approved by the censors. Otherwise the few bookstores that exist stock mostly Spanish-language texts. Most works are socialist texts glorifying the Revolution. Castro's own writings are the most ubiquitous works, alongside those of Che Guevara and José Martí.

THE *GUAYABERA*

The traditional *guayabera*, Cuba's all-purpose gift to menswear, was created in Central Cuba more than 200 years ago and is the quintessential symbol of Latin masculinity. Despite the infusion of New York fashion, this four-pocket, straight-bottom shirt remains the essence of sartorial style. The *guayabera*, thought Kimberley Cihlar, "is possessed of all the sex appeal any Latin peacock could want." Nonetheless, younger Cubans shun the shirt as a symbol of someone who works for the government.

The *guayabera*, which comes short sleeved or long, is made of light cotton perfect for weathering the tropical heat. In shape, it resembles a short-sleeved jacket or extended shirt and is worn draped outside the pants, usually as an outer garment with a T-shirt beneath. Thus it fulfills the needs of summertime dressing with the elegance of a jacket and the comfort of, well, a shirt. It is embellished with patterned embroidery running in parallel stripes down the front and is usually outfitted with pockets – with buttons – to stow enough *habanos* for a small shop.

Accommodations

RESERVATIONS

Officially, it's de rigueur to book at least three nights' accommodation prior to arrival. Cuban immigration officials are assiduous in ensuring that arriving visitors have pre-booked rooms. If you can't produce a voucher, you may be marched to the tour desk to make a booking and to pay for it. For this reason, do not leave the address line on your tourist visa blank.

Even if you don't have *any* reservation, it's best to fill in the name of a mid-price hotel. You can give a private address if you have reservations at a *casa particular*. Some immigration officials don't seem clear about this or, being loyal revolutionaries, attempt to force tourists to book a hotel room regardless. If this happens to you, point out that registered *casas particulares* pay taxes and are legal; stick to your guns!

FAWLTY TOWERS?

Cuba's hotel foibles conjure up déjà vu for viewers of *Fawlty Towers*, the BBC's hilarious sitcom. Most hotels have a few petty annoyances. For example, after a hot, sticky day, you return to your room to find no hot water – for which you're supposed to get 10 percent off your bill. No running water at all? Twenty percent off. In theory, you're entitled to a well-defined refund for each such contingency. A sorry mattress is worth a 10 percent discount, according to the State Prices Commission.

The number of faults in hotels is generally in inverse proportion to price. Away from Havana, things deteriorate quickly. At the cheapest places, you'll find gurgling pipes, no toilet seat (quite likely), no bathplugs (virtually guaranteed), and short – and sometimes sunken – mattresses (guaranteed). "Staying in less-than-two-star hotels... means passing below the rock bottom of comfort, to the point where involuntary abuse of guests begins," wrote Isadora Tattlin. In bare-bones hotels, shower units are often powered by electric heater elements, which you switch on for the duration of your shower. Beware! It's easy to give yourself a shock from any metal objects nearby.

Far too many hotels have abysmal service. Castro agreed: "Cubans are the most hospitable, friendly, and attentive people in the world. But as soon as you put a waiter's uniform on them, they become terrible."

To be fair, things are improving. Cuba has set up hotel-management training schools run by Austrians – world leaders in the hospitality industry. However, hotel management still leaves much to be desired. It's enough to make you wonder if Basil Fawlty is running the show.

make your reservation. Most of the tour agencies listed in the *By Organized Tour* section in this chapter can make bookings for you, often at a wholesalers' discount. Insist on receiving written confirmation, and be sure to take copies of such with you to Cuba, as Cuban hotels are notorious for not honoring reservations. And you should pay in advance for all nights you intend on staying; otherwise you might be asked to check out to make room for someone who just made a reservation.

You can keep costs down by buying a charter package tour with airfare and hotel included, although often the less notable hotels are used. If you book your hotels from abroad, you'll be issued hotel vouchers that you present upon arrival in Cuba.

PRICES

The Cuban government has a monopoly and charges outrageous prices, which usually vary for low and high season. Low season is May–June and September–November, high season is December–April and July–August. Some hotels have four rates, adding peak high season and low low season. Cuba imposes no room tax or service charge to guests' bills.

Often it's cheaper to pay as you go, rather than prepaying hotel rooms in advance. The same goes for meals. A "modified American plan" (MAP), meaning room rates that includes breakfast and dinner, might be a bargain at beach resorts, as ordering meals individually at hotel restaurants often costs considerably more. Alternately, if you're not intent on exploring much beyond the confines of your resort, consider an all-inclusive property, where the cost of all meals, drinks, and most activities is included in the room rate. In Havana, you're better off with a European plan (EP, room with breakfast only).

Budget hotels are the norm away from the tourist beat and exist to serve a Cuban clientele. They usually have two prices: a peso price for Cubans and a dollar price for foreigners.

The best way to keep costs down is to rent a *casa particular,* a private room in a family

The Christmas and New Year's season is particularly busy, as is July in Santiago de Cuba for Carnaval. Make reservations well ahead of time. Don't rely on mail. Call direct, send a fax or email, or have a Cuban state tour agency or a tour operator abroad

home. If you insist on a hotel, you can usually get considerably lower rates than the over-the-counter rack rates that we quote in this guidebook by booking online direct through the hotel company website, or with a package tour operator.

WHAT TYPE OF ACCOMMODATION?

Camping

Cuba is not geared for camping, and tent sites are virtually nonexistent. That said, Cuba is replete with *campismos,* basic holiday camps built for Cubans, but with cabins instead of tents. Many are in marginal locales. Facilities are often basic: Many have bunk beds only, sheets and towels are often worn, swimming pools often lack water, and restaurants are usually far below Western standards. Some sites have been upgraded for tourists. Foreigners are usually charged CUC5 per person, but if you're alone you may be charged for all the beds in a room. Often camps are closed Monday–Thursday and off-season; during summer they're often full.

The national system is operated by **Empresa Nacional de Campismo Popular** (Calle 13 #857, Vedado, Havana, tel. 07/831-3645), which has booking offices islandwide.

You will require permission to camp "wild." The government is paranoid about foreigners on the loose. Hence, you can expect that local police and MININT officials will inquire about you. While urbanites are savvy about the rules, rural folks may not be and you potentially expose farmers to the possibility of ruinous fines equivalent of several years' earnings merely for having you on their land—the system assumes guilt unless the farmer can prove that he has not or was not going to accept money.

Peso Hotels

Peso hotels cater to Cubans and are extremely cheap—usually the equivalent of less than US$1. You cannot book peso hotels through any state tourism organization; you will have to do this face-to-face in Cuba, but very few

---

HOTEL CHAINS

Cubanacán (Calle 23 #156, e/ O y P, Vedado, Havana, tel. 07/833-4090, www.cubanacan.cu) has more than 50 hotels ranging from two to five stars.

Gaviota (Calle 70, e/ 5ta y 7ma, Miramar, Havana, tel. 07/206-9595, fax 07/206-9912, www.gaviota-grupo.com), a branch of the Cuban military, owns special-interest properties, including eco-lodges, as well as deluxe city hotels and all-inclusive beach resorts.

Gran Caribe (7ma #4210, e/ 42 y 44, Miramar, Havana, tel. 07/204-0575, fax 07/204-0238, www.grancaribe.cu) has 29 hotels ranging from two to five stars.

Hoteles Habaguanex (Calle Oficios #110, e/ Lamparilla and Amargura, Habana Vieja, tel. 07/867-1039, fax 07/860-9761, www.habaguanex.com) operates historic hotels in Habana Vieja.

Islazul (Malecón and G, Vedado, tel. 07/857-1286, fax 07/833-3458, www.islazul.cu) operates relatively inexpensive hotels accepting both Cubans (who pay in pesos) and tourists. Several of its properties are splendid bargains.

---

accept foreigners. Those that still accept foreign travelers now charge in dollars (usually about CUC10–25), although most are overpriced at that standard. A few properties well off the tourist path may accept you for pesos at a pinch.

Most are dour by Western standards. Check the rooms, including for running water (cold water is normal; hot water is a luxury), functioning electricity, and flushing toilets, before agreeing to a reservation. Be especially wary for theft, and for scams by hotel staff.

An exception is the Islazul properties, which cater to both Cubans and foreigners and are more properly considered "tourist" hotels. Many are quite attractive and represent good bargains. Usually there's no problem finding a room, except in July–August, when Cubans take their vacations. Islazul properties can be noisy, however, and rooms often lack light bulbs and other essential accoutrements.

Tourist Hotels

All hotels in Cuba are owned by state enterprises. Five Cuban hotel entities compete for business (in 2004, the Horizontes company was eliminated), some in cooperative management agreements with foreign hotel groups; see the sidebar *Hotel Chains*. Throughout this guidebook, the relevant hotel chain is indicated in parentheses at the end of each hotel listing. Especially noteworthy are the splendidly restored colonial-era hotels of Habana Vieja.

Cuban hotels are graded by the conventional star system, but the ratings they give themselves are far too generous; most fall one or two categories below their international equivalents. Most towns have one or two older hotels around the central park, and a larger, concrete Bauhaus-era Soviet hotel on the outskirts. Hotels built in recent years reflect standards necessary to attract a foreign clientele, though few would be considered deluxe by international standards. Even the best suffer from poor design, shoddy construction, and sometimes apathetic and unethical staff. Most hotels supply towels and soap, but usually only top-line hotels provide shampoo and toiletries; also, bring your own sink plug and face cloth for budget hotels.

Hotels under foreign management are generally of a higher standard than their purely Cuban equivalents. That said, even the more upscale hotels are not entirely free of Cuban quirks, which makes the often unduly high prices doubly annoying. Even in top hotels, no one thinks to clean the fixtures, for example, so that hotels only one or two years old quickly become grimy.

Many hotels use both 220-volt and 110-volt outlets (usually marked), often in the same room. Check before plugging in any electrical appliances, or you could blow a fuse.

Upon registering, you'll be issued a *tarjeta de huésped* (guest card) at each hotel, identifying you as a hotel guest. Depending on your hotel, the card may have to be presented when ordering and signing for meals and drinks, when changing money, and often when entering the elevator to your room.

Though Cubans are barred from staying at most tourist hotels, many such hotels open their swimming pools to Cubans, who often turn the areas into raucous venues in summer and on weekends. Avoid rooms near hotel discos, which are also open to Cubans.

(At last visit, many tourist hotels were being used exclusively to house patients for Operación Milagro; see *Into the New Millennium* in the *History* section of the *Background* chapter.)

Aparthotels and *Protocolos*

Aparthotels offer rooms with kitchens or kitchenettes. Most are characterless. Many are linked to regular hotels, giving you access to broader facilities.

You can also stay in *protocolos*—special houses reserved for foreign dignitaries. Most of them are in splendid mansions in the Cubanacán region of Havana (they include Frank Sinatra's former home), but most other towns have at least one. *Protocolos* can be booked through **Cubanacán** (Calle 23 #156, e/ O y P, Vedado, Havana, tel. 07/833-4090, www.cubanacan.cu) and **Gran Caribe** (Av. 7ma #4210, e/ 42 y 44, Miramar, Havana, tel. 07/204-0575, fax 07/204-0565, www.grancaribe.cu).

All-Inclusive Resorts

Cuba has recently cottoned to the runaway success of the all-inclusive concept elsewhere in the Caribbean. Most beach resorts are now run as all-inclusives: cash-free, self-contained properties where your room rate theoretically includes all meals and beverages, entertainment, and water sports at no additional fee. Standards vary. Properties managed by international name-brand hotel chains are preferred to the purely Cuban-run affairs.

Nature Lodges

About half a dozen quasi-"ecotourism" properties can be found in mountain areas or close to nature reserves. However, Cuba has no eco-lodges to international standards. The most prominent is La Moka (Pinar del Río), though Cuba's promoting this as an "eco-lodge" is a stretch; others include Villa Soroa (Pinar del Río), Pinares del Mayarí and Cayo Saetía (Holguín Province), and Villa El Saltón (Santiago de Cuba); see the destination chapters for details on these lodgings.

Casas Particulares

My favorite way to go is to seek out a *casa particular* (literally, private house)—a room in a family home, granting you a chance to gain a perspective on the realities of Cuban living. This can be anything from a single room with a live-in family to a self-sufficient apartment. The going room rate in Havana is CUC20–300 (the latter price for entire houses in upscale neighborhoods, often with swimming pools and fabulously maintained 1950s modernist furnishings), and CUC10–35 outside Havana.

Many more *casas particulares* exist than it is possible to list in this book. The government has recently rescinded the licenses of many *casas* and the situation is fluid. As this book went to press a new, much more restrictive law was introduced and I anticipate that many *casas particulares* listed in this edition will be forced to close.

Legally licensed houses post a blue Arrendador Divisa sign, like an inverted anchor, on the front door (those with a red sign are licensed to rent only to Cubans, in pesos). There are also many illegal, unlicensed *casas particulares,* which should be avoided, not least because the legal houses have a tough time of things and get nothing back in return for the excessive taxation charged by the government. Many legal houses prefer not to post their Arrendador signs on the street, so ask around.

Compare several before making a decision, as conditions vary remarkably. Often you might arrive at a narrow doorway with a staircase of grime-stained, broken tiles and perhaps even a scent of urine. Don't let this put you off, as often the *casa particular* itself is clean and gracious. Check to see if hot water is available 24 hours, or only at specific times. Avoid rooms facing busy thoroughfares, although even rooms tucked discreetly away at the backs

Casa de Jorge Coalla Potts, a *casa particular* in Havana's Vedado district

© CHRISTOPHER P. BAKER

CASA PARTICULAR OWNERS' BURDENS

Since the triumph of the Revolution, the Urban Reform Law explicitly prohibited the rental of housing, despite which casas particulares (or hospedajes) began to blossom in the mid-1990s following the restrictions on having Cuban guests in hotel rooms – foreign guests turned to renting private rooms for their liaisons. With tourism booming, the government faced a room shortage. Hence, in 1996 the law was begrudgingly reformed: Cubans are now permitted to rent out up to two rooms, albeit under rigid and ever-tighter state regulations.

The government frowns upon the businesses and seemingly wants to squeeze casas particulares out of business. In 2004 it stopped granting licenses and began taking many away, while a stiff tax code is intended to sting casas particulares as much as possible. The tax varies according to district – in Havana, CUC150 monthly in a nontourist zone, and CUC325 in a tourist zone – and is payable whether the homeowner receives guests or not. An additional tax on income is paid at the end of the year and additional fees apply for signs outside the house, on-site parking, and a miscellany of attributes. Meal service is now obligatory.

The owner of a casa particular may not operate any other business, including car rental or guide services. And the owner must remain open 365 days a year; no vacation is permitted. Nor can they close in slow season, when they must continue to pay set taxes; if they close, they lose their license.

Inspectors visit regularly to check the books and property. The slightest infractions are dealt with harshly: a CUC1,500 fine is standard. And a three-strike rule applies: after three infractions, the house is seized by the government!

---

of buildings can hold an unpleasant surprise in the pre-dawn hours, when all manner of noises from hidden *solares* (communal slums) can intrude on your happy slumber.

Competition is fierce and sometimes aggressive touts do a brisk business trying to steer travelers to specific *casas*. If you're guided to a particular *casa particular* by someone, his or her commission will be added to your rent. Touts may try to guide you to specific houses, and are not above telling independent travelers lies, such as that a particular house you might be seeking has closed. Many such touts pose as hitchhikers on roads into major cities.

Reservations are recommended, especially in high season, when it can be difficult to find a room. If you arrive in a town without a reservation, owners of *casas particulares* are usually happy to call around on your behalf.

Meal service is obligatory: Breakfasts usually cost CUC3–5; expect to pay CUC5–10 for a belly-filling dinner. Don't agree to any services you don't need or want. Spell out all the prices involved before settling your initial discussion

with the owner of the home of your choice. Bargain if the price seems high, but remember that most home owners have cut their rates to the bare bones while facing punitive taxes. Honor regulations and avoid attracting undue attention to your host's home, as the legal repercussions of even the hint of an infraction can be serious. (See the sidebar *Casa Particular Owners' Burdens*.)

Many *casa particular* owners have grouped together in renters' cooperatives, referring clients to each other and cooperating in marketing on the Internet. Good websites include www.casaconfort.com, www.cubaparticular.com, www.havana-rentals.com, and www.cubaccommodation.com.

Your host must record your passport details, to be presented to the Ministry of the Interior within 24 hours (hence, MININT is always abreast of every foreigner's whereabouts).

Unauthorized Accommodation: Tourists must receive express permission from immigration authorities to stay anywhere other than a hotel or "authorized accommodation" (i.e., *casa particular*). If you're staying with friends, for example, you must present yourself to the nearest immigration office within 24 hours to convert from a tourist visa to an A2 visa (CUC25). You must be accompanied by the person you wish to stay with. Don't try to get around this, as you expose your Cuban host to a potentially ruinous risk. If an unregistered foreigner is found in a house (or camping), the Cuban host must prove that the foreigner is not a paying guest—an almost impossible situation. Thus, the Cuban is automatically found guilty of renting illegally. The regulations are strictly enforced, and fines are ruinous!

Posadas

The government is sensitive to the needs of every man and woman and has created state-run, 24-hour "love hotels," also known as *posadas* (or "motels"), which exist to provide relief for the large numbers of Cubans who live together with other family members, often in conditions in which rooms are subdivided by curtains. At these hotels, couples can enjoy an intimate moment together. In most, conditions are modest to say the least. More congenial facilities have gardens, air-conditioning, and music in the rooms, which are usually rented for three hours, typically for five pesos (US$0.25), for which the state thoughtfully provides a bottle of rum by the bed. Foreigners are usually turned away if accompanied by Cuban partners.

Budget travelers might find these handy places to bed down for the night, as will anyone forced to spend a night in remote communities that otherwise lack hotels.

SECURITY

Most tourist hotel lobbies have security staff. They were posted following the spate of bombs planted in Havana's hotels in 1997 and serve to prevent a repeat performance, but also do double duty to keep Cubans from slipping upstairs with foreign guests. Unfortunately, they don't seem entirely to trust foreigners and are not above bothering or even following hotel guests and their legitimate friends.

Theft is an issue in *every* tourist hotel. If your hotel has a safe deposit box, I recommend you use it. Before accepting a room, ensure that the door is secure and that your room can't be entered by someone climbing in through the window. *Always* lock your door. Keep your suitcase locked when you're not in your room, as maids (who are paid a pittance) have been known to make off with clothing and other items. One of their tricks is to spread your items around drawers so you don't know where anything is.

CUBAN GUESTS

There are strictures against Cubans entering many hotel lobbies alone and no Cubans are permitted in guest rooms in tourist hotels, without exception. Unless you can prove that a Cuban companion is your spouse, rest assured that hotel staff will turn your friend away, although in some hotels a significant tip to a doorman or elevator staff might get your friend in.

Cubans and foreigners *are* allowed to share hotels run by Islazul (where the clientele is primarily Cuban), while some rooms in a few other hotels are reserved for *la vanguardia* (i.e., workers receiving a reward, or *estímulo*, for productivity or revolutionary fervor). Here, foreigners and Cubans generally come and go and interact without restriction in public arenas. However, even these hotels go to sometimes absurd lengths to prevent Cuban guests entering the rooms of foreign hotel guests, and vice versa.

Nonetheless, for a CUC150 fee, a foreigner can get a permit called a *Poder Especial de Matrimonio@* permitting him or her to host a Cuban partner in a hotel. Ostensibly you need to prove that your partner is a long-term boyfriend or girlfriend. Any office of Bufete Internacional or Consultoría Jurídica Internacional can issue the same-day permit, good for the duration of said relationship.

Foreigners staying in *casas particulares* are permitted to share their bed with Cubans of either gender (at last visit, this included the provinces of Sancti Spíritus, Ciego de Ávila, Camagüey, and Isla de la Juventud, all of which had previously banned all such sexual relations). The sole exception is Varadero and environs. In all cases, your host must record your guest's name and *cédula* (ID) details for presentation to MININT within 24 hours. MININT runs the Cuban partners' names through a computer database; if the name of a woman appears three times with a different man, she is arrested as a "prostitute" and gets a mandatory jail term (four years, as of 2004), while in Varadero, a single "offense" is good for a jail term.

The rules keep changing. At last visit, a foreigner was permitted to host only one Cuban partner during his or her stay in any single *casa particular*. Multiple partners in the same *casa* were not permitted unless three months had elapsed since the last visit, in which case a new partner (but only one) was permitted.

Woe betide any *casa particular* owner whose guest is discovered with an unrecorded Cuban in his or her bed, let alone underage, or a series of different partners. In such cases, the owner of the *casa particular* can lose his or her home and license, and receive a hefty jail term to boot.

Food and Drink

A standing joke in Cuba is: What are the three biggest failures of the Revolution? Breakfast, lunch, and dinner. The paucity and poor quality of food is a constant source of exasperation. Before the Revolution, Cuba boasted many world-class restaurants. Alas, after 1959 many of the middle-and upper-class clientele fled Cuba along with the restaurateurs and chefs, taking their custom, knowledge, and entrepreneurship with them (Cuba's culinary landscape suffered for lack of international connections during four decades; let's face it: What could the Soviets offer?). In 1967 all remaining restaurants were taken over by the state, with bureaucrats calling the shots. It was downhill from there.

The blasé socialist attitude to dining, tough economic times, and general inefficiencies of the system are reflected in boring (usually identical) menus, abysmal standards (tablecloths rarely get washed), and lack of availability. Don't assume that you get what you pay for. Some of the lousiest service and dishes can be had for the most outrageous prices. And don't assume that a restaurant serving good dishes one day will do so the next. Restaurants rely upon the dysfunctional state distribution system to deliver daily supplies, which often don't arrive or are of vastly varying quality.

In the provinces eating can be a real challenge. Shortages are everywhere—a refrigerator in Cuba is called a *coco* because it has a hard shell on the outside and nothing but water inside—it can be a wearying experience trying to find somewhere with palatable food. Throughout the island you'll pass mile after mile of rich cultivated land growing produce, but when you arrive at your hotel you'll often find that the only vegetables on the menu are canned. After a while you'll be sick to death of fried chicken, *bocaditos,* and vegetables of dubious quality. As a foreign visitor, you're privileged to get the best that's available. Plan ahead. Stock up on sodas, biscuits, and other packaged snacks at dollars-only stores before setting out each day.

Now the good news: The country has begun to invest in culinary (and management) training in order to resolve the deplorable inadequacy of restaurant food. Today, Havana has some fine restaurants catering to foreign travelers, with more opening all the time. In general, the best meals are served in the upscale hotels. Most restaurants serve *criollo* (traditional Cuban) food, but only a few restaurants truly excel in native Cuban cuisine. The more expensive places tend toward "continental" cuisine, at which even fewer excel.

Take a sweater—many restaurants have the

RESTAURANT SCAMS

The creativity that Cubans apply to wheedle dollars from foreign travelers has been turned into an art form in restaurants. Here are a few tricks to beware:

Added Items: Bread and butter is often served without asking, but you are charged extra. Mineral water, coffee, and even beer often appear on your bill, even though you didn't ask for them... or they never arrived.

À la Carte Be Damned!: The restaurant has a fixed price for a set menu but your bill charges separately for itemized dishes, which add up to considerably more. When you challenge it, you're told that you were given the "lunch menu," say. Beware menus that don't list prices.

Bait and Switch: You ask for a cola and are brought an imported Coca-Cola (CUC2) instead of Tropicola (CUC0.50), a perfectly adequate Cuban equivalent.

Commissions: The *jinitero* who leads you to a recommended *paladar* gets his commission added to your bill... even if he's merely picked you up outside the *paladar* you've already chosen and "guided" you to the door.

Dollars or Pesos?: The "$" sign is used for both dollars and pesos. If you eat in a peso restaurant, you may be told that the "$" prices are in dollars. Sometimes this is legitimate. Even so, change may be given in pesos.

¡No Hay!: You're dying for a Hatüey beer but are told *ino hay!* (there is none). The waiter brings you a Heineken. Then you notice that the *habaneros* are drinking Hatuey. When you question this, you're told that the Hatueys aren't cold... or that Heineken (which is more expensive) is better.

Overpricing: Compare the prices on your bill against those on the menu. One or two items on your bill may be inflated.

Short Change: Count your change carefully. Cubans are normally pretty good mathematicians... except when it comes to giving change to foreign travelers.

Variable Pricing: Always ask for a printed menu with prices. Some places charge according to how much they think you are worth. If you're dressed in Gucci, expect to pay more than your neighbor who's wearing faded jeans.

air-conditioning cranked up to freezing. And be relaxed about dining. Sometimes the service is swift and friendly, sometimes protracted and surly. You can wait 20 minutes for a waiter, another half hour for the meal to arrive, 15 minutes for the bill, and another 10 for the change. You're likely to be serenaded by musicians, who usually hit up any available tourists for a tip (or to sell a CD or cassette recording).

Check your bill carefully, as several dastardly tricks are used to separate you from your dollars. (See the sidebar *Restaurant Scams*.)

Eating in Cuba doesn't present the health problems associated with many other destinations in Latin America. However, hygiene at streetside stalls is often questionable, as is shellfish. In February 1999, for example, at least 14 people died in Matanzas after eating from an unlicensed street stall.

Breakfasts

Few places serve breakfast other than hotel restaurants, most of which serve variations on the same dreary buffets: ham, cheese, boiled eggs, and an array of fruits and unappetizing cakes and biscuits. The variety is usually limited, and presentation often leaves much to be desired. Fruits—mangoes, papayas, pineapples—are often frozen overnight and thawed (barely) for breakfast, thereby destroying the pulp and flavor. Top-class hotels under foreign management usually do a bit better.

Peso Eateries

Pesos-only restaurants aim at Cubans. Food availability tends to be hit or miss and the cuisine undistinguished at best. Many restaurants offer an *oferta especial* (special offer), usually a set meal of the day.

State-run *merenderos* and private roadside snack stalls—the staple for local dining—display their meager offerings in glass cases. A signboard indicates what's available, with items noted on strips that can be removed as particular items sell out. These stalls accept pesos from foreigners and are an incredibly cheap way of appeasing your stomach with snacks, if you can stomach the not-always-hygienic conditions. You can eat for an entire day on US$3 or less—note that the "$" sign at peso eateries refers to Cuban pesos, not U.S. dollars.

The staple of the street stalls are basic *pizzetas* (pizza), usually costing five pesos per slice. Most Cuban pizzas are dismal by North American standards—usually a bland doughy base covered with a thin layer of tomato paste and a smattering of cheese and ham. Other staples are fatty pork *bocaditos, pan con queso* (basic but tasty cheese sandwich), *fritura de maíz* (corn fritters), *pay de coco* (coco flan), *refrescos,* and *batidos.*

Cajitas, sold at little restaurants, offer bargain-priced meals for a few pesos. You'll need your own utensils.

Paladares

The way to go is to eat at private restaurants—*paladares*—permitted since September 1994 to help resolve the food crisis. The word means "palate," and comes from the name of the restaurant of the character Raquel, a poor woman who makes her fortune cooking, in a popular Brazilian TV soap opera, *Vale Todo.* Here you can fill up for CUC5–15, usually with simple, albeit bloat-inducing, meals that usually include a salad and dessert as well as beer. The owners put great energy into their enterprises, often displaying an inventiveness in preparing good food and service that Castro himself has complained about with regard to state restaurants (Castro also says that the *paladares* are "enriching" their owners and has refused to dine at them). Some *paladares* offer bargain prices; many are open 24 hours. Others are rip-offs; if you think you're being hustled, feel free to up and away in search of somewhere

more amenable. Lack of a written menu listing prices can be a warning sign.

Paladares are fettered by onerous taxation and rigorous restrictions that are usually honored in the breach. For example, *paladares* are not allowed to sell shrimp or lobster (a state monopoly) or, since October 2004, potatoes! Nonetheless, most do, so ask: It's easy enough to find a huge lobster meal for CUC10, including beer or soft drink, although such meals are often served in a second dining room hidden away to the rear of the house. Beef is also illegal: The state maintains a monopoly and anyone found selling beef can face a lengthy spell in jail (only a few politically favored *paladares* sell beef). Though relatives can assist, the owners cannot hire salaried workers. And restaurant owners are also allowed to serve only up to 12 people at one seating (again, politically favored owners brazenly cram far more guests in than are legally allowed).

At press time, no new licenses for *paladares* were being issued, and the crippling monthly licensing fee and taxes had put many *paladares* out of business. You should not balk at tipping in private restaurants, as the little extra can make all the difference to the hard-pressed family. (Even here, however, scams are frequent. Don't ever order food without seeing the menu, or the price is likely to be jacked up.)

Taxi drivers may offer recommendations for *paladares,* as will touts on the street. Normally they're getting a commission, so their recommendations should be taken with a grain of salt. The commission will be added to your bill.

Food Chains

There are as yet no McDonald's or KFCs in Havana. However, the Cuban government has established a chain of tacky equivalents, including KFC-style fried-chicken joints called El Rápido. Food often runs out or is severely limited, and the quality is ho-hum at best. Cuba's answer to McDonald's is Burgui, open 24 hours. Are you sure that's *meat?*

The government has done a better job in recent years with seafoods. The Dimar chain has roadside restaurants (actually more like glorified glass booths) in major cities selling grilled shrimp, lobster, and other seafood at fair prices. And the Baturro chain of Spanish-style *bodegas* has outlets in major cities, with charming ambience and fare of acceptable standard.

Self-Catering

Shopping for food for the average Cuban is a dismal activity, especially outside Havana. There are scant groceries and no roadside 7-Elevens. The state-run groceries, called *puestos,* where fresh produce—often of questionable quality—is sold, can make Westerners cringe. Cuba's best fruits and vegetables are exported for hard currency or turned into juices. Cheese, which Cuba made in many varieties prior to the Revolution, is a precious scarcity. And count yourself lucky to find anywhere serving fresh milk. As a result, most Cubans are forced to rely on the black market.

Since 1994, when free trading was legalized for farmers, Cuba has sprouted farmers markets (*mercados agropecuarios,* or *agros* for short) where private farmers sell meats, fruits, and vegetables. Carrots, cucumbers, chard, and pole beans are about the only vegetables available year-round; tomatoes disappear about May and reappear around November, when beets, eggplants, cabbages, and onions are also in season. Every town has at least one *agro.* Don't expect to find potatoes, the sale of which is restricted to the *libreta* (ration book), nor many exotic fruits that may be familiar to you from other Caribbean islands. Chicken and pork are sold at *agros,* but not beef. Meat is very scarce, as is fish. The government-run *pescaderías especiales* sell fish and other seafood.

You can purchase imported packaged and canned goods (at vastly inflated prices) at dollars-only stores in every town.

Cafés and Bakeries

Havana has plenty of sidewalk cafés, although most of the prerevolutionary *cafeterías* (coffee stands) that used to make coffee on every corner have vanished, as have most of the former tea shops (*Casas de Té* or *Casas de Infusiones*).

Most cafés are really snack bars-cum-restaurants; there are few in the purist Parisian tradition, and as of yet, no Starbucks-style coffee shops. There are few cafés beyond Havana.

Most towns have bakeries serving sweet and tasty confections and Cuba's infamously horrible bread (most often served as buns or twisted rolls). Cuba's reputation for lousy bread predates the Revolution ("Why can't the Cubans make decent bread?" Che Guevara is reported to have asked). To be fair, some hotels and restaurants serve excellent bread, and the situation has improved following the arrival of French expertise to run the Pain de Paris bakery chain (Monday and Tuesday are usually best; after that the selection diminishes). The Doña Neli bakery chain competes.

Vegetarians

Few Cubans understand the concept of vegetarianism. Since colonial days meat has been at the very center of Cuban cooking. Cubans disdain greens, preferring an unhealthy sugar and starch-heavy diet (farmers markets have relatively few leafy greens). Only a few restaurants serve vegetarian dishes (the only true vegetarian restaurants are in Havana), and servers in restaurants may tell you that a particular dish is vegetarian, even though it may contain chunks of meat. Most beans are cooked in pork fat, and most *congrí* (rice with red beans) dishes contain meat.

"Protein vegetal" translates as "soy product."

WHAT TO EAT
Cuban Dishes

Cuban food is mostly peasant fare, usually lacking in sauces and spices. *Cerdo* (pork) and *pollo* (chicken) are the two main protein staples, usually served with *frijoles negros* (rice and black beans) and *plátanos* (fried banana or plantain). *Cerdo asado* (succulent roast pork), *moros y cristianos* (Moors and Christians—rice and black beans), and *arroz congrí* (rice with red beans) are the most popular dishes. *Congrí oriental* is rice and red beans cooked together. *Frijoles negros dormidos* are black beans cooked and allowed to stand till the next day. Another national dish is *ajiaco* (hotchpotch), a stew of meats and vegetables.

Cubans love *pollo frito* (fried chicken) and *pollo asado* (grilled chicken). Another favorite dish is *conejo*, rabbit. Grilled pork chops are also common. Beef is virtually unknown outside the tourist restaurants, where filet mignon and prime rib are often on the menu. Most steaks tend to be far below Western standards—often overcooked and fatty.

Meat finds its way into snacks such as *empanadas de carne*, pies or flat pancakes enclosing meat morsels; *ayacas*, a kind of corn tortilla filled with meat and spices; *picadillo*, a snack of spiced beef, onion, and tomato; and *bistec de palomilla*, fillet of steak, often cooked as an *empanada*. Crumbled pork rinds find their way into *fufu*, mixed with cooked plantain, a popular dish in Oriente. And ham and cheese find their way into fish and stuffed inside steaks as *bistec uruguayo*.

Fish had never been a major part of the Cuban diet and has made its way onto the national menu only in recent years. *Corvina* (sea bass), *filet de emperador* (swordfish), and *pargo* (red snapper) are the most commonly eaten species. Fish dishes are often zealously overcooked, with lots of bones for good measure. State restaurants charge CUC10–35 for lobster dishes, but you can enjoy a whole lobster meal with trimmings and beer for CUC10 at most *paladares*, although legally they're not supposed to serve shrimp or lobster. However, tales of stomach problems are legion, and I recommend staying clear of Cuban lobster.

Vegetables

Fresh vegetables rarely find their way onto menus, other than in salads. *Ensaladas mixtas* (mixed salads) usually consist of a plate of lettuce or *pepinos* (cucumbers) and tomatoes (often served green, yet sweet) with oil and vinaigrette dressing. *Palmito*, the succulent heart of palm, is also common. Often you'll receive canned vegetables. Sometimes you'll receive shredded *col* (cabbage), often alone.

Plátano (plantain), a relative of the banana, is the main staple and almost always served fried. Though technically a fruit, it's used as a vegetable in a variety of ways, including as *tostones*, fried green plantains eaten as a snack. Yucca is also popular: it resembles a stringy potato in look, taste, and texture and is prepared and served like a potato in any number of ways. A popular side dish is *boniato* (sweet potato), and other root vegetables such as *malanga*, a bland root crop rich in starch, are used in many dishes.

Vegetables are often used in soups and stews, such as *ajiaco*, a popular and tasty soup made with yucca, malanga, turnips, and herbs. Another common soup is made of garbanzos.

Fruits

Elsewhere in the Caribbean and Latin America, you can't drive around a bend without having someone selling a bunch of ripe bananas or handfuls of papayas, mangoes, or coconuts. Not so in Cuba. You'll pass fields of pineapples, melons, oranges, and grapefruits, but you won't have easy access to any outside of hotel restaurant buffets or farmers markets. Virtually the entire fruit harvest goes to produce fruit juice.

Local *mercado agropecuarios* sell well-known fruits such as papayas, plus such lesser-known types as the furry *mamey colorado*, an oval, chocolate-brown fruit with a custardy texture and taste; the cylindrical, orange-colored *marañon*, or cashew-apple; the oval, coarse-skinned *zapote*, a sweet granular fruit most commonly found in Oriente; and the large, irregular-shaped *guanábana*, whose pulp is sweet and "soupy," with a hint of vanilla. *Canitel* (familiar to travelers to Jamaica as ackee) is also grown, through rarely found.

You should refer to the papaya fruit as *fruta bomba* because in Cuba, "papaya" is a slang term for vagina.

Surprisingly, coconuts are rare, except in sweets. However, in eastern Cuba, around Baracoa, the juice and meat find their way into the cuisine peculiar to the region—eastern Cuba boasts the nation's only real regional cuisine.

Cubans love confections. Sponge cakes are the favorite, lavishly topped with cream.

Desserts

Cubans have a sweet tooth, as befits the land of sugar. They are especially fond of sickly sweet sponge cakes (*kek* or *ke*) covered in soft "shaving-foam" icing and sold for a few centavos at *panaderías* (bakeries) islandwide. Look for them being delivered by hand—often by bicycle with the huge flat cake perched precariously atop a board held waiter-like over the passenger's shoulder.

Flan, a caramel custard, is also popular (a variant is a delicious pudding called *natilla*), as is marmalade and cheese. Also try *tatianoff,* chocolate cake smothered with cream; *chu,* bite-size puff pastries stuffed with an almost-bitter cheesy meringue; and *churrizo,* deep-fried doughnut rings sold at every bakery and streetside stalls, where you can also buy *galletas,* ubiquitous sweet biscuits sold loose.

The many coconut-based desserts include *coco quemado* (coconut pudding), *coco rallado y queso* (grated coconut with cheese in syrup), and the *cucurucho,* a regional specialty of Baracoa made of pressed coconut and cocoa.

Cubans are renowned lovers of ice cream, sold for *pesos convertibles* in restaurants and *heladerías* (ice-cream stores), and for pesos at Coppelia and from street stalls. Cubans use specific terms for different kinds of scoops. *Helado,* which means "ice cream," also means a single large scoop; two large scoops are called *jimagua;* several small scoops is an *ensalada;* and *sundae* is ice cream served with fruit.

DRINKING
Nonalcoholic Drinks

Water is not always reliable, and many water pipes are contaminated through decay. Stick to bottled mineral water, readily available carbonated (*con gas*) or non-carbonated (*sin gas*). Coca-Cola and Pepsi (or their Cuban-made equivalent, Tropicola), Fanta (or Cuban-made Najita), and other soft drinks are also widely available. *Malta Caracas* is a popular nonalcoholic drink from Venezuela that resembles a dark English stout but tastes like root beer.

Far more thirst quenching and energy

CUBA'S COCKTAILS

Cuba's cocktails are legendary. Many were created in the Roaring Twenties, such as the Mary Pickford (white rum, pineapple juice, grenadine, maraschino cherry, and ice), the *ron collins* (white rum, lemon juice, club soda, sugar, and ice, garnished with a cherry and orange slice), the *presidente* (white rum, vermouth, grenadine, and ice), and *Havana especial* (white rum, pineapple juice, lemon juice, maraschino, and ice).

Dark rums are used in cocktails such as the *mulatta* (rum, cocoa liqueur, lemon juice, and crushed ice), the almost forgotten *sacao* (rum, coconut water, and ice), and the *Isla de Pinos* (rum, grapefruit juice, and ice).

Refreshing and simple to make, the "big three" below are the hit of any party.

CUBA LIBRE

Who can resist the killer kick of a rum and Coke? Supposedly, the simple concoction was named more than a century ago after the war cry of the independence army: "Free Cuba!"

The Perfect Cuba Libre: Place ice cubes in a tall glass, then pour in 2 ounces of seven-year-old Havana Club *añejo* rum. Fill with Coca-Cola, topped off with 1 ounce of lemon juice. Decorate the rim with a slice of lemon. Serve with a stirrer.

DAIQUIRI

The daiquiri is named for a Cuban hamlet 16 miles east of Santiago de Cuba, near a copper mine where the mining firm's chief engineer, Jennings S. Cox, first created the now world-famous cocktail that Hemingway immortalized in his novels. Cox had arrived in 1898, shortly after the Spanish-American War, to find workers at the mines anxious about putatively malarial drinking water. Cox added a heartening tot of local Bacardi rum to boiled water, then decided to give his mixture added snap and smoothness by introducing lime juice and sugar.

The concoction was soon duplicated, and within no time had moved on to conquer every high-life watering hole in Havana. It is still most notably associated with El Floridita, and

Hemingway's immortal words: *"Mi mojito en La Bodeguita, mi daiquirí en El Floridita."*

Shaved ice, which gave the drink its final touch of enchantment, was added by Constante Ribailagua, El Floridita's bartender, in the 1920s. The frozen daiquiris, "the great ones that Constante made," wrote Hemingway, "had no taste of alcohol and felt, as you drank them, the way downhill glacier skiing feels running through powder snow and, after the sixth and eighth, felt like downhill glacier skiing feels when you are running unroped."

A daiquiri should include all of Cox's original ingredients (minus the water, of course). It may be shaken and strained, or frappéed to a loose sherbet in a blender and served in a cocktail glass or poured over the rocks in an old-fashioned glass. The "Papa Special," which Constante made for Hemingway, contained a double dose of rum, no sugar, and a half ounce of grapefruit juice.

The Perfect Daiquiri: In an electric blender, pour half a tablespoon of sugar, the juice of half a lemon, and 1.5 ounces of white rum. Serve semi-frozen blended with ice (or on the rocks) in a tall martini glass with a maraschino cherry.

MOJITO

The *mojito* supposedly originated as a lowly drink favored by slaves. It is now considered the classic drink of Cuba, favored by tourists today as it has been since the 1940s, when Ángel Martínez, then owner of La Bodeguita del Medio, hit upon the idea of giving credit to writers, who popped in to sup, establishing a bohemian scene that promoted the bar and its drink.

The Perfect *Mojito*: With a stirrer, mix half a tablespoon of sugar and the juice of half a lime in an eight-inch highball glass. Add a sprig of yerba buena (mint), crushing the stalk to release the juice; two ice cubes; and 1.5 ounces of Havana Club Light Dry Cuban rum. Fill with soda water, add a small splash of angostura, then dress with a mint sprig. *¡Salud!*

giving, however, is *guarapo,* fresh-squeezed sugarcane juice sold at roadside *guaraperías.* And *prú,* a refreshing soft drink concocted from fruit, herbs, roots, and sugar, is common in Oriente. Occasionally you'll come across small bars selling fresh-squeezed orange juice (usually 20–50 centavos a glass). Another great way to beat the heat is by downing *batidos,* delicious and refreshing fruit drinks blended with milk and ice; and *refrescos naturales,* chilled fruit juices that you can buy at roadside stalls, usually for 50 centavos or one peso (but avoid the sickly sweet water-based *refrescos* and *limonadas*).

Cubans take frequent coffee breaks, and no home visit is complete without being offered a *cafecito.* Cubans love it thick and strong, like espresso, served black in tiny cups, and heavily sweetened. Unfortunately, much of Cuban domestic coffee has been adulterated—*café mezclado*—with other roasted products. Stick with Cubita, the export brand sold vacuum packed.

Café con leche (coffee with milk) is served in tourist restaurants, usually at a ratio of 50:50, with hot milk. Don't confuse this with *café americano,* which is usually diluted Cuban coffee.

Alcoholic Drinks

Cuba makes several excellent German-style beers, usually served just a little above freezing (CUC0.75–3, depending on where you drink). One of the best is Hatuey, Cuba's flagship beer. Bucanero is a heavy-bodied lager that comes light or dark. Cristal (the most commonly available), Manacas, and Lagarto are lighter. You'll also find regional beers as well as the duller Clara, the rough-brewed beer for domestic consumption (typically one peso). Harder-to-find brews include the new Caribbean Ice and Polar Bear, brewed in Camagüey since 1911. Heineken and Canadian and Mexican brands are sold in dollar stores and tourist hotel bars.

Most villages have *cervecerías,* beer dispensaries that are boisterous social centers. Local authorities distribute roadside dispensers on wheels where you can buy beer in paper cups or bottles sawed in half for a few centavos.

About one dozen rum distilleries operate in Cuba today, producing some 60 brands of rum. They vary widely—the worst can taste like paint thinner. Cuban rums resemble Bacardi rums, not surprisingly, as several factories were originally owned by the Bacardi family. Each brand generally has three types of rum: clear "white rum," labeled *Carta Blanca,* which is aged three years and costs less than CUC5 a bottle; the more asserting "golden rum," labeled *Dorado* or *Carta Oro,* aged five years, and costing about CUC6; and *"añejo,"* aged seven years and costing CUC10 or more.

The best in all three categories are Havana Club's rums, topped only by Matusalem Añejo Superior, described by a panel of tasting experts as showing "a distinctive Scotch whisky-like character, with peaty and smoky aromas and flavors accented by orange-peel notes dry on the palate and long in the finish." A few limited-production rums, such as Ron Santiago 45 Aniversario and the 15-year-old Havana Club Gran Reserva, approach the harmony and finesse of fine Cognacs.

In touristy nightclubs, a bottle of rum can set you back four or five times what it would cost in a store. In nontouristy clubs, a *trago* (shot) of rum will cost about CUC0.50, and in peso joints 50 centavos. Beware bottles of rum sold on the street—it may be bootleg rum. Impecunious Cubans drink *tragos* (shots) of *aguardiente*—cheap, overproof white rum.

Golden and aged rums are best enjoyed straight. White rum is ideal for cocktails such as a piña colada (rum, pineapple juice, coconut cream, and crushed ice) and, most notably, the daiquiri and the *mojito*—both favorites of Ernest Hemingway, who helped launch both drinks to world fame. And recalling the Andrews Sisters' song, "Drinking Rum and Coca-Cola," you'll want to try a Cuba libre on its home turf. (See the sidebar *Cuba's Cocktails.*)

The major rum manufacturers make liqueurs, including from coffee, crème de menthe, cocoa, guava, lemon, pineapple, and other fruits. Certain regions are known for unique liqueurs, such as *guayabita,* a drink made from rum and guava and exclusive to Pinar del Río.

Wine lists have improved in recent years, and imported South American, French, and even Californian wines are a relative bargain, though often "disturbed" by poor storage. You might even try the local *vino,* a sweet and unsophisticated Italian wine blended with local grapes from Soroa, Pinar del Río, and sold under the Soroa label.

Tourist Information

TOURIST INFORMATION OFFICES

Cuba's **Ministerio de Turismo** (Av. 3ra y F, Vedado, Havana, tel. 07/832-7535, www .cubatravel.cu) is in charge of tourism. It has representative offices in about a dozen countries, including Canada (1200 Bay St., Suite 305, Toronto, ON M5R 2A5, tel. 416/362-0700, fax 416/362-6799, www.gocuba.ca; and 2075 rue University, Bureau 460, Montreal, H3A 2L1, tel. 514/875-8004, fax 514/875-8006), Germany (Kaiserstrasse 8, Frankfurt D-60313, tel. 069/288322, www.cubainfo. de), Italy (Vía Fara #30, Milano 20124, tel. 02/6698-1463, www.cuba-si.it), and the United Kingdom (154 Shaftesbury Ave., London WC 2H8JT, tel. 020/7240-6655, tourism@cubasi.info). There is no such office in the United States; however, the Canadian offices will provide information and mail literature to U.S. citizens.

Publicitur (Calle 19 #60, e/ M y N, Vedado, tel. 07/55-2826, www.publicitur.cu) is responsible for publishing and disseminating tourism literature.

Cuba is a member of the **Caribbean Tourism Organization** (CTO, 80 Broad St., 32nd Floor, New York, NY 10004, 212/635-9530, www.doitcaribbean.com), which is a handy information source; and the **Caribbean Hotel Association** (CHA, 1000 Ponce de León Ave., San Juan, PR 00907, tel. 787/725-9139), both of which are barred under U.S. law from promoting tourism to Cuba in the United States. The CTO has offices in Canada (130 Bloor St. West, Suite 301, Toronto, Ontario M5S 1N5, tel. 416/935-0767) and the United Kingdom (22 The Quadrant, Richmond, Surrey TW9 1BP, tel. 0208/948-0057).

Infotur (Calle 28 #303, e/ 3ra y 5ta, Miramar, tel. 07/204-0624 or 204-6635, www.infotur.cu), the government tourist information bureau, operates Palacios de Turismo (tourist information booths) in key tourist areas in Cuba. It stocks only a limited range of tourist literature and maps.

Every tourist hotel has a *buró de turismo.*

Other Information Bureaus

Agencia de Información Nacional (Calle 23 #358, esq. J, Vedado, Havana, tel. 07/832-5541, www.ain.cubaweb.cu) dispenses information about virtually every aspect of Cuba, but serves primarily as a "news" bureau. The **Oficina Nacional de Estadísticas** (Paseo #60, e/ 3ra y 5ra, Vedado, Havana, tel. 07/866-2273 or 830-5021, www.cubagob.cu/ingles/otras_info/estadisticas.htm) provides all manner of statistics on Cuba, although foreigners are made to jump through hoops to gain access.

MAPS

Before You Go: A 1:250,000 topographical road map produced by Kartografiai Vallalat, of Hungary, and a similar map by Freytag & Berndt are recommended; both feature street maps of Havana. Likewise, Cuba's own Ediciones Geo produces a splendid 1:250,000 *La Habana Tourist Map,* plus a 1:20,000 *Ciudad de la Habana* map, sold in Cuba.

You can buy these and other Cuba maps in the United States from **Omni Resources** (P.O. Box 2096, Burlington, NC 72160, tel. 336/227-8300, www.omnimap.com); in

KEY ORGANIZATIONS TO KNOW

IN THE UNITED STATES

Alamar Associates: 2300 M St. NW, Suite 800, Washington, DC 20037, 202/530-5234, fax 202/530-5235, www.alamar-cuba.com. Arranges Cuba-related business summits and offers consultation regarding doing business with Cuba.

Association of Travel-Related Industry Professionals: 2300 M St. NW, Suite 800, Washington, DC 20037, 202/872-5071, www.atripusa.org. Works to promote freedom of travel to Cuba.

Caribbean American Children Foundation: P.O. Box 35393, Palm Coast, FL 32135, 386/446-2444, cacf2@aol.com. Provides humanitarian aid and sponsors cultural and medical assistance programs.

Center for a Free Cuba: 1320 19th St. NW, Suite 201, Washington, DC 20036, 202/463-8430, fax 202/463-8412, www.cubacenter.org. An anti-Castro organization that defines itself as "an independent, non-partisan institution dedicated to promoting human rights and a transition to democracy and the rule of law on the island."

Center for Cuban Studies: 124 W. 23rd St., New York, NY 10011, 212/242-0559, fax 212/242-1937, www.cubaupdate.org. Sponsors educational forums on Cuba, organizes study tours, and sells books and videos on Cuba. It has an art gallery and the largest research library on Cuba in North America.

Cuban American Alliance Education Fund: P.O. Box 5113, San Luis Obispo, CA 93403, tel./fax 805/627-1959, www.cubamer.org. A national network of Cuban-Americans sponsors an end to travel restrictions, specifically those that cause hardships for Cuban Americans and their families in Cuba; and for engagement with Cuba.

Cuban American National Foundation: CANF, 1312 SW 27th St., Miami, FL 33145, 305/592-7768, fax 305/592-7889, www.canfnet.org. A conservative and highly influential lobbying group dedicated to the overthrow of Fidel Castro.

Cuban Liberty Council: P.O. Box 352735, Miami, FL 33135, 305/642-0610, fax 305/642-0410, www.cubanlibertycouncil.org. An anti-Castro organization representing Cuban-Americans in exile dedicated to a democratic government through "free and fair elections."

Cuba Policy Foundation: 2300 M St. NW, Washington, DC 20037, 202/835-0200, fax 202/835-0291, www.cubapolicyfoundation.org. This nonpartisan organization works to end the U.S. ban on travel to Cuba, lift the U.S. embargo against Cuba, and foster democratic change in Cuba. It is led by former senior diplomats in Republican administrations.

Fund for Reconciliation and Development: 355 W. 39th St., New York, NY 10018, 212/760-9903, www.ffrd.org. Works to foster cooperation between the United States and Cambodia, Laos, Vietnam, and Cuba.

IFCO/Pastors for Peace: 620 West 28th St., Minneapolis, MN 55408, 612/670-7121 or 612/378-0062, fax 612/870-7109 or 612/378-0134, www.ifconews.org. Organizes the U.S. Friendshipment Caravans to Cuba, challenging the embargo by traveling with vehicles filled with donations of humanitarian aid. Also has study tours and organizes work brigades to assist in community projects in Cuba.

Latin America Working Group: 424 C St. NE, Washington, DC 20002, 202/546-7010, www.lawg.org. A coalition of nongovernmental religious, humanitarian, and grassroots organizations. It works to end the Cuba trade embargo and travel ban and to encourage U.S. policies that promote human rights, justice, and peace.

USA*Engage: 1625 K St. NW, Washington, DC 20006, 202/887-0278, ext. 115, www.usaengage.org. A broad-based coalition representing American business and agriculture interests that lobby for an end to the embargo and for open trade with Cuba.

(continued on next page)

KEY ORGANIZATIONS TO KNOW (continued)

U.S.-Cuba Sister City Association: 320 Lowenhill St., Pittsburgh, PA 15216, 412/563-1519, fax 412/563-1945, www.usc-sca.org. Exists to foster ties between U.S. and Cuban cities. Typically this involves regular exchanges of delegations, including scholars, artists, religious figures and musicians, and local politicians.

U.S.-Cuba Trade and Economic Council: 30 Rockefeller Plaza, New York, NY 10112, 212/246-1444, fax 212/246-2345, www.cubatrade.org. This nonpartisan business organization provides accurate, up-to-the-minute information on every aspect regarding U.S.-Cuban commercial relations.

U.S.-Cuba Trade Association: 2300 M St. NW, Suite 800, Washington, DC 20037, 202/530-5236, fax 202/530-5235, www.uscuba.org. Comprising more than 30 companies, state agencies, and organizations, this organization works to protect existing trade with Cuba and to promote full normalization of commercial relations with Cuba.

OUTSIDE THE UNITED STATES
The following "solidarity" organizations work to support Cuban socialism.

Association Cuba Sí: 20 Rue Denis-Papin, 94200 Ivry-sur-Seine, France, tel. 1/4515-1143, fax 1/4515-1144.

Associazione di Amicizia Italia-Cuba: Via Foscolo 3, 20121 Milano, Italy, tel. 02/8646-3493, http://web.tiscali.it/ItaliaCuba.

Australia-Cuba Friendship Society: P.O. Box 1051, Collingwood, Victoria 3066, Australia, tel. 3/9857-9249, fax 3/9857-6598.

Canadian-Cuba Friendship Association: P.O. Box 743, Station F, Toronto M4Y 2N6, Canada, tel. 416/742-6931, fax 416/744-6134, ccfatoronto@lefca.com.

Cuban Friendship Society: 3 Oakdale St., Christchurch, New Zealand tel./fax 3/365-6055, 100250.1511@compuserve.com.

Cuba Solidarity Campaign: c/o Red Rose Club, 129 Seven Sisters Rd., London N7 7QG, England, tel. 020/7263-6452, fax 020/7561-0191, www.cuba-solidarity.org.uk.

Canada from **ITMB Publishing** (530 W. Broadway, Vancouver BC V5Z 1E9, tel. 604/879-3621, www.itmb.com); in the United Kingdom at **Stanford's** (12-14 Long Acre, London WC2E 9LP, tel. 020/7836-1321, www.stanfords.co.uk), and in Australia at **The Map Shop** (6-10 Peel St., Adelaide, SA 5000, tel. 0618/8231-2033, www.mapshop.net.au).

In Cuba: The **Tienda de las Navegantes** (Calle Mercaderes #115, e/ Obispo y Obrapía, Habana Vieja, tel. 07/861-3625, fax 07/33-2869; Mon.–Fri. 8 A.M.–5 P.M., Sat. 8 A.M.–1 P.M.) has a wide range of tourist maps.

The *Guía de Carreteras* is a pocket-size road map atlas covering all Cuba. It can be purchased from tour desks and souvenir outlets.

Media Resources

NEWSPAPERS AND MAGAZINES
Before You Go

The Center for Cuban Studies (124 W. 23rd St., New York, NY 10011, 212/242-0559, fax 212/242-1937, www.cubaupdate.org) maintains the **Lourdes Casal Library,** with more than 5,000 books on Cuba, plus back issues of Cuban journals. The Center publishes the quarterly *Cuba Update.*

The **Casa Cuba Resource Center** (6501 Telegraph Ave., Oakland, CA 94609, 510/658-3984, www.cubaresource.org) also maintains a library.

Cuban Daily News Digest (P.O. Box 30003, North Vancouver, BC, Canada V7H 2Y8, tel. 604/929-9694, fax 604/929-3694, www.cubaninvestments.com) is a daily compilation of news articles about Cuba from various news sources, available free online. The same organization also publishes *Cuban Investment Letter* (US$125 subscription).

Serving investors are *CubaNews* (10454 Parthenon Ct., Bethesda, MD 20817, 301/365-1745, www.cubanews.org; annual subscription US$429) and *Cuba Trade & Investment News* (P.O. Box 13752, Tampa, FL 33681, 813/839-6988, www.cubatradenews.com; annual subscription US$300), and the website of the **U.S.-Cuba Trade and Economic Council** (www.cubatrade.org/eyeon.html) provides economic updates on Cuba.

Cuban Review (Global Reflexion, Sloterkade 20, 1058 HE Amsterdam, The Netherlands, tel. 020/615-1122, www.cubanreview.org) is a bimonthly journal that covers the spectrum, from politics and social issues to general interest. Although published in English, the editorial offices are in Havana (Calle 2 #209, e/ Línea y 11, Apto 41, Vedado, tel./fax 07/866-2258) and it presents too rosy a picture. Subscriptions cost €25 (€28 outside Europe).

La Alborada is a monthly newsletter published by the Cuban American Alliance Education Fund (1010 Vermont Ave. NW, Suite 620, Washington, DC 20005, 805/627-1959, www.cubamer.org) and representing the perspectives of moderate Cuban-Americans.

In Cuba

Foreign Newspapers and Magazines: Foreign magazines are sold only in some tourist hotel lobbies. Availability is limited to a small selection of leading international newspapers and carefully selected consumer magazines. There are no newsagents or newsstands on the streets. Foreign publications are distributed in Cuba through **World Services Publications** (5ta Av. #1808, Flores, Havana, tel. 07/33-3002, fax 07/33-3066, mayra.aguila@cimex.com.cu).

Cuban Publications: Pre-Castro Cuba had a vibrant media sector, with 58 daily newspapers of differing political hues. The Castro government closed them all down. Today domestic media is entirely state controlled—the Inter-American Press Association lists Cuba as the worst violator of press freedoms in the hemisphere—and subject to what Maurice Halperin refers to as "the self-righteous and congratulatory monotony of the Cuban propaganda machine." The Cuban populace has no access to foreign publications and is starved for unbiased news reporting. There is no independent press, and the few independent journalists that exist do so under constant surveillance and fear of touching a third rail.

The most important publication, and virtually the sole mouthpiece of international news, is *Granma* (www.granma.cu), the cheaply produced official outlet of the Communist Party. It focuses on profiling a daily succession of victories in the building of socialism (no negatives are reported about domestic affairs—a serial killer could be loose in Havana, but it would never be reported; instead, *habaneros* rely for news on *radio bemba,* the inordinately accurate and fast-moving street gossip or grapevine). Its other leitmotif is to denigrate the United States at every turn. You can buy *Granma* at streetside kiosks, but they rapidly run out, as many

INDEPENDENT LIBRARIES

President Fidel Castro's statement, at the International Book Fair in Havana City in February 1998, that "In Cuba no books are forbidden, there is just no money to buy them," sparked several Cubans with a passion for literature and learning to create an independent library system to offer publications that are not available in state-run bookstores or libraries. By 2003 the initiative had grown to more than 100 independent libraries nationwide, consisting of small collections of books housed in private homes. The libraries are entirely dependent on donations from abroad. The government considers them illegal and counterrevolutionary and has referred to the librarians as "mercenaries" since the U.S. Interests Section has provided assistance.

According to Amnesty International, independent librarians have been subject to intense persecution. The founders of the **Independent Libraries of Cuba** (tel. 305/441-0770, fax 305/441-1770, www.bibliocuba.org),

Berta Mexidor Vázquez and her husband, Dr. Ramón Humberto Colas Castillo, were fired from their jobs then evicted from their home (Amnesty International adopted Colas as a Prisoner of Conscience) and eventually forced to leave Cuba. Other librarians have been imprisoned (several have received prison terms of 25 years) and/or received beatings, and their books and magazines have been confiscated. Ironically, prohibited material includes copies of the United Nations Universal Declaration of Human Rights.

For further information, contact **Friends of Cuban Libraries** (474 48th Ave., #3-C, Long Island City, NY 11109, 718/340-8494, www.friends-ofcubanlibraries.org), which provides stockpiled books to people traveling to Cuba for delivery to the libraries. Note, however, that tourists who visit the libraries face potential consequences: One reader who visited five libraries wrote to report "a suspicious brush with the police wanting to question [him] on a 'drug' charge."

Cubans—seriously—stand in line to take *Granma* home to use as toilet paper (*leer el culo,* or "put the butt to read," is a favorite Cuban joke). A weekly edition published in Spanish, English, and French is sold at hotel gift stores.

Juventud Rebelde is the evening paper of the Communist Youth League published Wednesday–Sunday. It echoes *Granma,* although it does have a strong arts section and tends to probe more questioningly into international and social affairs. **Opciones** is a weekly serving the business, commercial, and tourist sectors, aimed at foreign businesspeople in Cuba. Similar mouthpieces include the less easily found *El Habanero* (Tues. and Fri.); *Tribuna de la Habana* (Sun.); *Trabajadores* (Mon.); and *Mujeres,* a monthly magazine for women. Magazines focusing on the arts and culture include *Habanera,* a monthly magazine about Havana; *Prisma,* an English-language bimonthly covering politics, economics, travel, and general subjects on Cuba and the Americas; the weekly *Bohemia;* and *Revolución y Cultura.*

BOOKS

For a list of recommended reading, see *Suggested Reading* in the *Resources* section.

Two publishers of leftist books on Cuba are **Ocean Press** (GPO Box 3279, Melbourne, Victoria 3001, Australia, tel. 03/9326-4280; or P.O. Box 1186, Old Chelsea Station, New York, NY 10113-1186, 212/260-3690, www .oceanbooks.com.au), which supplies most of the English-language books distributed in Cuba; and **Pathfinder Press** (P.O. Box 162767, Atlanta, GA 30321-2767, 404/669-0600, www.pathfinderpress.com).

Cuban Libraries

Cuba's *bibliotecas* have been neglected since the Revolution and are poorly stocked. Depending on the library, books—most of which are in tatterdemalion condition—may be stocked in closed areas, with library access limited to a few privileged Cubans who are granted special permits. The **International Federation of Library Associations &**

Institutions (P.O. Box 95312, 2509 CH The Hague, Netherlands, tel. 070/314-0884, www.ifla.org) reports monitoring of borrowers by the state. Many books by internationally respected authors are banned and are not represented. And access for foreigners can be difficult to obtain.

ONLINE RESOURCES

There are dozens of Internet sites on Cuba. All Cuban-hosted sites are state-owned.

See the *Internet Resources* section in the back of this book for a list of select websites and portals.

RADIO AND TELEVISION

All broadcast media in Cuba are state-controlled.

Television

Most tourist hotel rooms have satellite TVs showing international channels such as HBO, ESPN, CNN, VH1, TV España, and so on. (the Cuban government pirates foreign satellite signals using a dish mounted on the Hotel Tryp Habana Libre, then retransmits to other tourist hotels). Ordinary Cubans must make do with the four national TV networks: Canal 6: CubaVisión and Canal 2: Tele Rebelde, plus Canal Educativo and Canal Educativo-Dos, two educational channels. There is also one provincial station in Oriente. Tele Rebelde features selections from CNN España international news coverage. Otherwise, no foreign TV station is permitted to sully the airwaves. No Cuban (except the Communist elite) is permitted access to satellite TV—although illegal, a few jerrybuilt satellite dishes do festoon Cuban rooftops, risking the wrath of authorities.

Nonetheless, virtually every home has a TV, and Cubans are addicted to television, especially the immensely popular Latin American *telenovelas* (soap operas): You can walk through Havana when the *novela* is showing and follow the show as you walk.

Programming is largely an organ of political education, dominated by dreary reports on socialist progress; Fidel's lengthy speeches (which always take precedence over all other programming); and the daily *mesa redonda* (roundtable) political discussions—wicked Uncle Sam is the most common topic—in which no one in his right mind dares ask a probing question. However, Cuban television also has some very intelligent programming, emphasizing science and culture, sports, and foreign movies. Cartoons aim to teach Cuban youth sound morals, and educational shows have a broadly internationalist focus. There are no advertisements, but five-minute educative slots teach citizens about good behavior and might inveigh against abortions, exhort Cubans to work hard, or call for their participation in important festivals. Cubavisión shows movies every Saturday night.

Radio

Cuba ranked eighth in the world in number of radio stations in 1958. Today it has only five national radio stations, all government run: Radio Enciclopedia (94.1 FM) and Radio Musical Nacional (590 AM and 99.1 FM) offer classical music; Radio Rebelde (640 and 710 AM, and 96.7 FM) and Radio Reloj (950 AM and 101.5 FM) both report news; and Radio Progreso (640 AM and 90.3 FM) features traditional music. In addition, Havana is served by Radio Habana (106.9 FM), which specializes in cultural information; and Cadena Habana (1140 AM and 99.9 FM) and Radio Metropolitana (910 AM and 98.3 FM), both specializing in mostly traditional music and culture. Radio Ciudad de la Habana (820 AM and 94.9 FM) caters to a younger crowd. Radio Taíno (1290 AM and 93.3 FM) caters to tourists with programs in English, French, and Spanish.

There are also provincial and local stations. In Havana and along the northwest coast, you can tune in to radio stations from southern Florida; on the south coast, to stations from Jamaica; and in Oriente, to the American Forces Network (AM 1340 or FM 102.1), broadcast from Guantánamo naval base. However, in much of the countryside you can put your car radio onto "scan" and it will just go round and round without ever coming up with a station.

Health Issues

MEDICAL SERVICES

Sanitary standards in Cuba are generally good. As long as you take appropriate precautions and use common sense, you're not likely to incur a serious illness or disease. Cuba's much-vaunted public health system is geared to preventive medicine. The system faces severe shortages of medicines and equipment and with few exceptions, facilities and standards are not up to those of North America or northern Europe.

Facilities for Foreigners

Foreigners receive special treatment through **Cubanacán Turismo y Salud** (Av. 43 #1418, esq. 18, Miramar, Havana, tel. 07/204-4811, www.cubanacan.cu), which offers everything from "stress breaks" to advanced treatments such as eye, open-heart, and plastic surgery—even silicon breast implants are available. (However, respected Cuban doctor Hilda Molina is highly critical of the medical standards applied; see *Cuba Brief,* Summer 1998, www .cubacenter.org). Most major cities and resort destinations have 24-hour international clinics (*clínicas internacionales*) staffed by English-speaking doctors and nurses. (Don't expect privacy. Your *historial,* or descriptive interview of your problem, may happen in front of a curious crowd of nurses and patients.) The larger tourist hotels have nurses on duty. Other hotels can request a doctor for in-house diagnoses and treatment for minor ailments.

You pay in CUC or foreign currency—credit cards are acceptable unless they're issued on a U.S. bank. You'll get a receipt with which to make an insurance claim once you return home. U.S. citizens should note that even if visiting Cuba legally, payment for "nonemergency medical services" is prohibited. You can call your insurance company in advance, however, of receiving medical treatment. If approved, the company can pay direct to Asistur (see the *Travel Insurance* section), which then pays the Cuban clinic.

International pharmacies (*farmacias internacionales*) cater to foreigners only and are stocked with a full range of Western drugs and pharmaceuticals imported from Central America, Canada, and Europe. Local pharmacies are meagerly stocked and medicines are hard to find away from key tourist spots (*turnos regulares* pharmacies are open 8 A.M.– 5 P.M.; *turnos permanentes*—also known as *pilotos*—are open 24 hours).

Óptica Miramar (7ma Av., e/ 24 y 26, Miramar, tel. 07/204-2269, direccion@opticam .cha.cyt.cu) provides optician services and sells contact lenses and spectacles at prices comparable with the United States and United Kingdom. It has outlets nationwide.

Medical Evacuation

Uncle Sam has deemed that even U.S. emergency evacuation services cannot fly to Cuba to evacuate U.S. citizens without a license from the Treasury Department. Of course, the rules keep changing, so it may be worth checking the latest situation with such companies as **Traveler's Emergency Network** (P.O. Box 668, Millersville, MD 21108, 800/275-4836, www.tenweb.com) and **International SOS Assistance** (3600 Horizon Blvd., Suite 300, Philadelphia, PA 19053, 215/942-8000, www.internationalsos.com), which provide worldwide ground and air evacuation as well as medical assistance.

In Cuba, insurance packages sold by **Aseguradora del Turismo La Isla** (Calle 14 #301, esq. 3ra Av., Miramar, tel. 07/204-7490, fax 07/204-7494, www.cuba.cu/laisla/islaesp .html) include US$5,000 coverage for repatriation in the need of medical evacuation.

Swiss-based **Assist-Card** (in the U.S. 305/381-9959 or 800/874-2223, www.assist-card.com), with offices worldwide, provides emergency services in Cuba, even for U.S. citizens, including arranging doctor's visits to your hotel and even emergency evacuation. It works in conjunction with **Asistur** (Prado

#208, Havana, tel. 07/866-4499, www.asistur.cu). If you have difficulty in Cuba, you can call the Assist-Card regional office in Miami.

BEFORE YOU GO

Dental and medical checkups are advisable before departing home. Take along any medications; keep prescription drugs in their original bottles to avoid suspicion at customs. I had my spectacles stolen in Cuba—a reminder to take a spare pair (or at least a prescription for eyewear). If you suffer from a debilitating health problem, wear a medical alert bracelet.

A basic health kit is a good idea and should include alcohol swabs and medicinal alcohol, antiseptic cream, Band-Aids, aspirin or painkillers, diarrhea medication, sunburn remedy, antifungal foot powder, calamine and/or antihistamine, water-purification tablets, surgical tape, bandages and gauze, and scissors.

In the United States, information on health concerns can be answered in advance of travel by the **Department of State Citizens Emergency Center** (202/647-5226, http://travel.state.gov), the **Centers for Disease Control and Prevention** (1600 Clifton Rd., Atlanta, GA 30333, 404/639-3534 or 800/311-3435, www.cdc.gov), and the **International Association for Medical Assistance to Travellers** (IAMAT, 1623 Military Rd. #279, Niagara Falls, NY 14304, 716/754-4883, www.iamat.org), with offices worldwide. In the United Kingdom, you can get information, inoculations, and medical supplies from the **British Airways Travel Clinic** (213 Piccadilly, London W1J 9HQ, tel. 0845/600-2236).

Travel Insurance

Travel insurance is highly recommended. Travel agencies can sell you traveler's health and baggage insurance, as well as insurance against cancellation of a prepaid tour. Travelers should check to see if their health insurance or other policies cover for medical expenses while abroad—and specifically in Cuba.

Swiss-based **Assist-Card** (in the U.S. 305/381-9959 or 800/874-2223, www.assist-card.com) offers travel assistance with everything from tracking lost luggage and finding medical, legal, and technical services to emergency transfers and repatriation. You can obtain insurance in Cuba through its affiliate, **Asistur,** which represents about 160 insurance companies of 40 countries; **Aseguradora del Turismo La Isla, S.A.** (Calle 14 #301, esq. 3ra Av., Miramar, tel. 07/204-7490, fax 07/204-7494, www.cuba.cu/laisla/islaesp.html); and **ESEN** (5ta Calle #306, e/ C y D, Vedado, tel. 07/832-2508, www.esen.com.cu).

Vaccinations

No vaccinations are required to enter Cuba unless visitors are arriving from areas of cholera and yellow fever infection, in which case they must have valid vaccinations. Epidemic diseases have mostly been eradicated throughout the country. However, viral meningitis and dengue fever occasionally break out.

Consult your physician for recommended vaccinations. At the least, you should consider vaccinations against tetanus and infectious hepatitis (Hepatitis A), which is common, particularly in summer. The main symptoms are stomach pains, loss of appetite, yellowing skin and eyes, and extreme tiredness. Hepatitis A is contracted through unhygienic foods or contaminated water (salads and unpeeled fruits are major culprits). The much rarer Hepatitis B is usually contracted through unclean needles, blood transfusions, or unsafe sex.

HEALTH PROBLEMS

Cuba *is* a tropical country and the health hazards are many: filthy public fixtures, garbage rotting in the streets, vehicle fumes, stagnant water, polluted watercourses, broken sewer pipes, holes in sidewalks, dilapidated buildings, flies on food, and so on. In addition, molds, fungus, and bacteria thrive. The slightest scratch can fester quickly. Treat promptly with antiseptic and keep any wounds clean.

Intestinal Problems

Cuba's tap water is questionable, especially after heavy storms, which may render water supplies unsafe (hence, many tourist hotels receive fresh water daily, delivered by tanker truck). Play it safe and drink bottled mineral water (*agua mineral*), which is widely available. Remember that ice cubes are water, too, and don't brush your teeth using suspect water. Milk is pasteurized, so you're not likely to encounter any problems with dairy products. Most tourists who suffer intestinal bouts do so after eating at streetside stalls.

Diarrhea: The change in diet may briefly cause diarrhea or constipation (in case of the latter, eat lots of fruit). Most cases of diarrhea, however, are caused by microbial bowel infections resulting from contaminated food. Common-sense precautions include not eating uncooked fish or shellfish, uncooked vegetables, unwashed salads, or unpeeled fruit. Diarrhea is usually temporary, and many doctors recommend letting it run its course. If that's not preferable, medicate with Lomotil or another antidiarrheal product. Drink lots of liquid to replace the water and salts lost. Avoid alcohol and milk products. If conditions don't improve after three days, seek medical help.

Dysentery: Diarrhea accompanied by severe abdominal pain, blood in your stool, and fever is a sign of dysentery. Seek immediate medical diagnosis. Tetracycline or ampicillin is normally used to cure bacillary dysentery. More complex professional treatment is required for amoebic dysentery. The symptoms of both are similar.

Other Infections: Giardiasis, acquired from infected water, is another intestinal complaint. It causes diarrhea, bloating, persistent indigestion, and weight loss. Again, seek medical advice. Intestinal worms can be contracted by walking barefoot on infested beaches, grass, or earth.

Sunburn and Skin Problems

The tropical sun can fry you in minutes and even burn you through light clothing or while you're lying in the shade. Use a suncream or sunblock of at least SPF 15. Zinc oxide provides almost 100 percent protection. Bring sunscreens with you; they're not readily available in Cuba. If you're intent on a tan, have patience. Build up gradually, and use an aloe gel after sunbathing;

it helps repair any skin damage. The tops of feet and backs of knees are particularly susceptible. Wear a wide-brimmed hat. Calamine lotion and aloe gel will soothe light burns; for more serious burns, use steroid creams.

Sun glare can cause conjunctivitis. Use sunglasses. Prickly heat is an itchy rash, normally caused by clothing that is too tight or in need of washing. This, and athlete's foot (a fungal infection) are best treated by airing out the body and washing your clothes. Ringworm, another fungal infection, shows up as a ring of itchy spots, typically about one to two inches wide, most commonly on the scalp and groin; it's treated with over-the-counter ointments.

Dehydration and Heat Problems

The tropical humidity and heat can sap your body fluids like blotting paper, especially in summer. Leg cramps, exhaustion, dizziness, and headaches are signs of dehydration. Drink lots of water to avoid dehydration. Avoid alcohol, which processes water in the body.

Excessive exposure to too much heat can cause potentially fatal heat stroke. Excessive sweating, extreme headaches, and disorientation leading to possible convulsions and delirium are symptoms. Emergency medical care is essential. If hospitalization is not possible, place the victim in the shade, cover him with a wet cloth, and fan continually to cool him down.

Don't be alarmed if your ankles and legs get puffy. It's the heat. When you rest, keep your feet higher than your head.

Many tourists come down with colds (*gripe*—pronounced GREE-pay—or *catarro cubano*), often brought on by the debilitating effects of constantly shifting from icily air-conditioned restaurants and hotels to sultry outdoor heat. A more serious ailment is bronchitis, easily acquired in Cuba, and which can be left to run its course, though some strains may need to be treated with antibiotics.

Snakes, Scorpions, and Crocodiles

Snakes (*culebras*) are common in Cuba. Fortunately, they're not venomous. Scorpions (*alacranes*) also exist; their venom can cause nausea and fever but is not usually serious. Watch where you're treading or putting your hands in the wild.

Fortunately, most areas inhabited by crocodiles, such as the Zapata swamps, are off-limits to foreigners without guides. Don't go wading in swampland.

Insects and Arachnids

Bites can easily become infected in the tropics, so avoid scratching! Treat with antiseptics or antibiotics. Antihistamine, hydrocortisone, and calamine lotion can help relieve itching.

Coastal flatlands are noted for mosquitoes, as is the waterfront region of Miramar in Havana. Repellent sprays and lotions are a must for moist areas. A fan over your bed and mosquito coils (*espirales,* which are rarely sold in Cuba) also help keep mosquitoes at bay. Citronella candles may help, too.

Fortunately, malaria isn't present in Cuba. However, mosquitoes *do* transmit dengue fever, which *is* present on the island (a sudden explosion in the incidence of dengue hit Havana in 2000–2002; fumigation is ongoing, but occupants are rarely warned and go about their business amid the clouds of poison as if nothing was amiss). The illness can be fatal (death usually results from internal hemorrhaging). Its symptoms are similar to those for malaria, with severe headaches and high fever and, unlike malaria, additional severe pain in the joints and bones, for which it is sometimes called "breaking bones disease." Unlike malaria, it is not recurring. There is no cure. Dengue fever must run its course. In the unlikely event you contract it, have plenty of aspirin or other painkillers on hand. Drink lots of water.

Chiggers (*coloradillas*) inhabit grasslands, particularly in dry areas favored by cattle. Their bites itch like hell. Mosquito repellent won't deter them. Nail polish apparently works (over the bites, not on the nails) by suffocating the beasts. And ticks hang out near livestock and can burrow headfirst into your skin.

CUBA'S WAR ON AIDS

Cuba has one of the world's most aggressive and successful campaigns against AIDS. The World Health Organization (WHO) and the Pan-American Health Organization have praised as exemplary Cuba's AIDS surveillance system and prevention program. The program has stemmed an epidemic that rages only 50 miles away in Haiti and kept the spread of the disease to a level that no other country in the Americas can equal. As of January 2005, about 1,160 people had died of AIDS in Cuba, which has an adult prevalence rate of 0.05 percent, compared to four percent in the Bahamas, and nearly six percent in Haiti. Although in Cuba in the early years it was predominantly a heterosexual disease, today over 70 percent of AIDS sufferers are gay men (the number of HIV positive cases has tripled since 1998).

Cuba's unique response to the worldwide epidemic that began in the early 1980s was to initiate mass testing of the population and a "mandatory quarantine" of everyone testing positive. Twelve AIDS sanatoriums were developed throughout the island. By 1994, when the policy of mandatory testing and confinement were ended, about 98 percent of the adult population had been tested. Voluntary testing continues. An outpatient program was implemented so that sufferers could continue to lead a normal life; residents live in small houses or apartments, alone or as couples (straight or gay).

Cuba's biogenetic engineering industry has been at the forefront of research for an AIDS vaccine and cure (in 2001, for example, Cuba began manufacturing anti-retrovirals, which it supplies free of charge to all patients).

The **Cuba AIDS Project** (500 West Leota St., Suite 200, P.O. Box 1289, North Platte, NE 69103-1289, 308/532-4700, www.cubaaids-project.com) delivers medications to Cubans who suffer from HIV/AIDS.

Extract a tick by gripping it with tweezers as close to the head as you can get and pulling it gently out. Be careful not to pull the body—you'll snap their bodies off, leaving their heads in your flesh, where they'll fester.

Tiny, irritating *jejenes* (known worldwide as "no-see-ums"), sand flies about the size of a pinpoint, inhabit beaches and marshy coastal areas. This nuisance is active only around dawn and dusk, when you should avoid the beach. They're not fazed by bug repellent with DEET, but Avon's Skin-So-Soft works (Avon Skin-So-Soft oil is such an effective bug repellent—especially against "no-see-ums"—that U.S. Marines use it by the truckload).

Many Cubans live in poor hygienic conditions that are a perfect breeding ground for scabies (a microscopic mite) and lice. Fortunately, both are extremely rare in Cuba. Infestation is possible if you're sleeping in unhygienic conditions or engaging in sex with people already infested.

Sea Creatures

Portuguese man-o'-war jellyfish (*agua mala*), with their long trailing, are common along the Atlantic shoreline, especially in winter and spring. They can give a painful, even dangerous, welt that leaves a permanent scar. Dousing in vinegar can help neutralize the stingers, while calamine and antihistamines should be used to soothe the pain.

In Caribbean waters, a miscroscopic mollusk that locals call *caribe* can induce all manner of illnesses, from diarrhea and severe fever to itching. It, too, is more frequent in winter.

Sea urchins (*erizos*) are common beneath the inshore water line and around coral reefs.

These softball-size creatures are surrounded by long spines that will pierce your skin and break off if you touch or step on them. Excruciatingly painful! You'll have to extract the spines.

AIDS and Sexually Transmitted Diseases

Cubans are promiscuous, and sexually transmitted diseases are common, although the risk of contracting AIDS in Cuba is relatively minor (the rate of infection is among the world's lowest). If you succumb to the mating urge, use condoms (*preservativos*), which can be purchased at dollar stores, although the selection is limited.

Fungal infections of the skin, such as ringworm (see *Sunburn and Skin Problems* in this section), are also common and can be passed sexually, as well as from towels and shared clothing.

Gynecological Problems

Travel, hot climates, and a change of diet or health regimen can play havoc with your body, leading to yeast and other infections. A douche of diluted vinegar or lemon juice can help alleviate yeast infections. Loose, cotton underwear may help prevent infections such as candida, typified by itching and a white, cheesy discharge. A foul-smelling discharge accompanied by a burning sensation may indicate trichomoniasis, usually caught through intercourse but also by contact with unclean towels.

Other Problems

Rabies, though rare in Cuba, can be contracted through the bite of an infected dog or other animal. It's always fatal unless treated.

Safety

CRIME AND HUSTLING

All the negative media hype sponsored by Washington has left many people with a false impression that Cuba is unsafe. Far from it. In rural areas many residents still say they can hardly remember the last time a crime was committed. However, the material hardships of Cubans combined with the influx of wealthy tourists *has* fostered a resurgence of crime. Pickpockets (*carteristas*) and purse slashers work the streets. Chambermaids pilfer items from guests' luggage. Theft from luggage during baggage handling has been reported at the airport, where bogus tour agents and taxis operate (the British Embassy also report attempted robberies from vehicles on the Havana airport road). Muggings have escalated. Car-related crime is on the increase, notably by bogus hitchhikers and staged punctures (if you get a puncture, drive on several kilometers, preferably to a town, before stopping). Sexual assault appears to be rare. However, there have been several unreported murders of tourists in recent years. Most, but not all, have involved sexual relations between foreigners and Cubans, for which reason you should *never* go to a *casa clandestina* (an illegal room rental, usually rented by the hour); and *always* check a Cuban partner's *carnet* (ID) and leave a copy with someone you trust if possible.

Most crime is opportunistic snatch-and-grab. Caution is required when walking city streets, especially at night (few streets have lights). Crowded places are the happy hunting grounds of crafty crooks. If you sense yourself being squeezed or jostled, don't hold back—elbow your way out of there immediately. Better safe than sorry.

The **U.S. State Department** (888/407-4747, or 202/501-4444 from overseas, www.travel.state.gov) publishes travel advisories warning U.S. citizens of trouble spots; as does the **British Foreign & Commonwealth Office** (tel. 020/7008-1500, from overseas 020/7008-0210, www.fco.gov.uk).

DRUGS

Cuba's role in the international drug trade is controversial. In *Castro's Final Hour* Andres Oppenheimer documents Cuban complicity in the drug trade in the 1980s. However, during the past decade or so Cuba has been cooperative in the battle against international narcotics trading, even sharing information with the U.S. Coast Guard.

Few countries are so drug free. You may occasionally come across homegrown marijuana, but serious drug use is unknown. Nonetheless, drug use has increased in recent years with the blossoming of tourism and as Colombian and Jamaican drug lords take advantage of Cuba's remote, scattered cays to make transshipments en route to the United States.

In January 2003, the Cuban government initiated a nationwide campaign against possession and trafficking in drugs. Draconian laws are strictly enforced and foreigners receive no special favors. Cuban law allows for the death penalty, and sentences in excess of 20 years are the norm.

Hustling

Your biggest problem will probably be hustling by *jiniteros* (see the sidebar *Jiniterismo*), plus the persistent scams pulled by restaurants, hotels, and other tourist entities. And the *consumo mínimo* charge in many bars and nightclubs is an invitation to fleece you. Be prepared for charges for things you didn't consume or which didn't materialize, and for higher charges than you were quoted in the first place. Insist on an itemized bill at restaurants, add it up diligently, and count your change.

Car rental companies and their employees are particularly adept at scams. Cuban tour agencies aren't above the same. You pay for a deluxe hotel, say, on a package to Cayo Largo but are told when you arrive that the hotel in question

JINITERISMO

Jiniteros (male hustlers) and jiniteras (females who trade sex for money) are a persistent presence in tourist zones, where they pester foreigners like flies around fish. Many work in tandem, in syndicates.

Jineteros try to sell you cigars, tout places to stay or eat, or even a good time with their sisters for chump change. In provincial cities, touts on bicycles descend on tourists at traffic lights and will trail you through town, sometimes merely in the hope that you'll give them money to go away. If you're a female tourist, expect to be hustled by Cuban males touting themselves as potential boyfriends.

Jineteras work the streets and discos. Many an unsuspecting male has been robbed.

The best defense is to completely ignore them. Don't say a word. Don't look them in the eye. Don't even acknowledge their presence. Just keep walking.

surance policy, and driver's license. Carry the photocopies with you, and leave the originals along with your other valuables in the hotel safe whenever possible. If this isn't possible, carry the originals with you in a secure inside pocket. Don't put all your eggs in one basket. Prepare an "emergency kit" that includes photocopies of your documents and an adequate sum of money to tide you over if your wallet gets stolen.

Never carry more cash than you need for the day. The rest should be kept in the hotel safe. Never carry your wallet in your back pocket. Spread your money around your person. Most practical is to wear a secure money belt. The strap of fanny packs should be threaded through the belt loops of your pants. Wear an inexpensive watch. Don't flaunt jewelry or walk unescorted around urban slum districts with a purse or an expensive camera loosely slung over your shoulder. And be particularly wary after cashing money at a bank, or if doing a deal with a *jinitero* (several tourists have been murdered by *jiniteros* in *casas particulares* in recent years). Insist that credit card imprints are made in your presence. Make sure any imprints incorrectly completed are torn up, and destroy the carbons yourself.

Never leave items unattended. Always keep a wary eye on your luggage on public transportation. Don't carry more luggage than you can adequately manage; limit your baggage to *one* suitcase or duffel. And have a lock for each luggage item. Purses should have a short strap (ideally, one with metal woven in) that fits tightly against the body and snaps closed or has a zipper. *Always* keep purses fully zipped and luggage locked, even in your hotel room. Don't leave *anything* within reach of an open window nor in your car, which should always be parked in a secure area overnight.

doesn't honor such packages. You're then fobbed off to the cheapest hotel. When you return to Havana to request a refund, you're plain out of luck, as the documents relating to your trip can't be found. Rarely is there a manager available, and usually they also say there is nothing that can be done about it (even when a manager or employee acknowledges a mistake, you may be expected to pay anyway).

If the scam amounts to outright theft, as with rental car scams, take the staffer's name and threaten to report him or her to the head office and police. Don't pay cash in such conditions. Pay with a credit card and challenge the bill. Or simply refuse to pay. Good luck! The Cuban government treats individual travelers with almost as much disdain as it treats its own citizens and once it has your money it is not about to give refunds under virtually any condition.

Common-Sense Precautions

Make photocopies of all important documents: your passport, airline ticket, credit cards, in-

OTHER PROBLEMS
Traffic and Pedestrians

Traffic is perhaps the greatest danger. Be especially wary when crossing the streets in Havana. Stand well away from the curb—especially on corners, where buses often mount the sidewalk.

BITE YOUR TONGUE!

As Pico Iyer wrote in *Cuba and the Night:* "The whole city is a circle of informers." Cubans are a paranoid people, never sure who might be a *chivato,* a finger pointer for the CDR or MININT, the much-loathed Ministry of the Interior. In this regard, Cuba doesn't seem to have changed much since the 1930s, when Hemingway told Arnold Samuelson, "Don't trust anybody. That fellow might have been a government spy trying to get you in bad. You can never tell who they are."

Many visitors take the fact that you never hear a bad word about the system or the Bearded One expressed in public as a tacit expression that Cubans overwhelmingly support their government. In fact, no one in his or her right mind would dare to criticize the government or Fidel Castro in public. Irreverence (*desacato,* or criticism of the government) is defined as a crime against the Revolution and is punishable by law, as is *peligrosidad* (dangerousness), a general term that encompasses whatever the government wishes. Dissenting or being considered unsupportive risks being labeled a "counterrevolutionary," with loss of privileges such as employment, or even being jailed, however trivial the infraction. With so many people employed as informers, there is a culture of mistrust summed up in the Cuban saying: "You can swim safely if you keep your mouth closed." If you open your mouth, you might swallow water and drown.

Sometimes a diatribe against the government (usually offered in hushed tones) will end in mid-stream as the speaker taps his two forefingers on his opposite shoulder, signifying the presence of a member of State Security. Hence, Cubans have developed a cryptic, elliptical way of talking where nuance and meaning is hidden from casual tourists.

Even foreigners are not above surreptitious surveillance; those in sensitive occupations, such as embassy staff, are *muy bien acompañados* (well accompanied) by agents of State Security, sometimes identifiable by their imitation Lacoste shirts or *guayaberas,* pressed pants or stonewashed jeans, mirrored glasses, and well-groomed moustaches. Foreign journalists may even be assigned specific hotel rooms (which may be bugged) while journalists staying in *casas particulares* are sure to be kept an eye on. Be wary, too, of the beautiful *cubana* or *cubano* too eager to be your lover; and of what you say to drivers of licensed taxis available outside tourist hotels, as many are driven by security agents or by drivers who report to the General Directorate for State Security (DGSE).

Unfortunately, the situation worsened significantly in 2005 in response to the Bush administration's hardened posture intended to "transition" Cuba to a new government. The Cuban government now looks with suspicion on U.S. travelers entering on religious or humanitarian licenses. In some cases, individuals have been detained in Cuba, then deported, without any reason given.

Fortunately, you, the average tourist, are free to roam wherever you wish without hindrance or a need to look over your shoulder. That said, you can be sure that nay-saying the Revolution or you-know-who in public can swiftly land you in trouble. Cuban authorities have zero tolerance for foreigners who become involved in political activity, especially with known dissidents. Be circumspect about what you say, especially to anyone you do not implicitly trust. Avoid making inflammatory or derogatory comments; otherwise you could well find yourself on the next plane home.

Sidewalks are full of gaping potholes and tilted curbstones. Watch your step! And drive cautiously. Cuba presents unique dangers, from treacherous potholes and wayward bicyclists to cattle and ox-drawn carts wandering across four-lane freeways. Use extra caution when passing tractors and trucks, which without warning tend to make sweeping turns across the road.

Racial Discrimination

Despite all the hype about Cuba being a color-blind society, racial discrimination still exists.

EMERGENCY TELEPHONE NUMBERS

Cuba is slowly introducing a single number system for emergencies. At press time, most calls were still placed direct to regional service providers.

	AMBULANCE	FIRE	POLICE
HAVANA			
Ciudad de la Habana	07/55-1185	105	106
HAVANA PROVINCE			
Artemisa	063/36-2597	063/36-3300	116, 063/36-3153
Batabanó	062/85335	105	106
Mariel	–	063/92444	063/92321
Santa Cruz del Norte	0692/83158	0692/83310	0692/83306
San Antonio de los Baños	0650/38-2781	0650/38-2225	0650/38-2111
CAMAGÜEY			
Camagüey	032/29-2860	115	116
Nuevitas	032/42227	115	116
Playa Santa Lucía	032/33-6294	115, 032/33-6482	032/33-6225
Santa Cruz del Sur	032/32-2873	115, 032/32-2936	116, 032/32-2914
CIEGO DE ÁVILA			
Cayo Coco	–	033/30-9102	033/30-8107
Ciego de Ávila	185	115	116
Morón	0335/4469	115	116
CIENFUEGOS			
Cienfuegos	0432/51-5019	115	116
GRANMA			
Bartolomé Masó	023/56-5448	–	023/56-5441
Bayamo	023/42-6121	115	116
Manzanillo	118	115	116
Pilón	23/59-4261	23/59-4524	23/59-4493
GUANTÁNAMO			
Baracoa	021/42472	115	021/42472
Guantánamo	021/32-5720	115	116, 021/32-7162
HOLGUÍN			
Banes	024/82727	115	116
Gibara	–	024/34539	024/34248
Holguín	104	105	106
Moa	024/66432	105	106, 024/66243
ISLA DE LA JUVENTUD			
Cayo Largo	045/48238	045/48247	045/39-9406
Nueva Gerona	046/32-4170	115	116, 046/32-2462
LAS TUNAS			
Las Tunas	031/42073	115	116

	AMBULANCE	FIRE	POLICE
MATANZAS			
Cárdenas	196	105	106
Jagüey Grande	045/2414	105	106
Matanzas	045/24-2337	105	106
Playa Girón	045/94196	105	106
San Miguel de los Baños	045/89-6117	–	106
Varadero	045/61-2950	105	106
PINAR DEL RÍO			
Bahía Honda	086/66-8565	086/66-8241	086/66-8243
Consolación del Sur	08/82383	115	08/82121
Pinar del Río City	082/76-2317	115, 082/72-2291	116, 082/75-2525
Viñales	–	–	08/79-3124
SANCTI SPÍRITUS			
Sancti Spíritus	041/24462	115	116
Trinidad	0419/2362	115	116
SANTIAGO DE CUBA			
Santiago de Cuba	185, 022/62-2848	115	116
VILLA CLARA			
Caibarién	042/36-3888	115	116, 042/36-3635
Remedios	042/39-5149	115	116, 042/39-5218
Santa Clara	042/20-3965	115	116, 042/20-6976

Non-white tourists can expect to be mistaken for Cubans and hassled on the streets by police requesting ID. Likewise, tourists of non-European descent are more likely to be stopped at the entrances to hotel lobbies and other tourist venues where Cubans are barred. Mixed-race couples can expect to draw unwanted attention from the police.

Officialdom

Cuba has an insufferable bureaucracy, and working with government entities can be a perplexing and frustrating endeavor. Very few people have the power to say, "Yes," but everyone is allowed to say, "No!" Finding the person who can say "Yes" is the key. Ranting gets you nowhere. Logical arguments count for little; charm, romantic *piropos* (witty compliments), or a gift of chocolate work better.

The Policía Revolucionario Nacional (National Revolutionary Police, or PNR) are a branch of the Ministry of the Interior (MININT) and a major role is to enforce revolutionary purity. Uniformed Cuban policemen also perform the same functions as uniformed police officers in other countries, although they operate with far less professionalism than you may be used to in the United States or Europe. You may witness petty harassment of everyday Cubans on the streets, and you may even be subject to such petty police harassment. Cuban policemen tend to treat foreigners with disdain—they've been trained to be paranoid about Western imperialists. Hence, never attempt to photograph police officers or military figures without their permission.

If you are stopped by policemen wanting to search you, insist on it being done in front of a neutral witness—*"solamente con testigos."* If at all possible, do *not* allow an official to confiscate or walk away with your passport. You should always carry a copy of your passport and tourist card with you at all times to verify your identity. Tell as little as circumspection dictates—unlike priests, policemen rarely offer absolution for confessions.

Never pay a policeman money. If a policeman asks for money, get his name and badge number and file a complaint with the Ministry of Foreign Relations.

IF TROUBLE STRIKES

In emergencies, call 116 for the police, 114 for an ambulance, and 115 for fire.

If things turn dire, you should contact **Asistur** (tel. 07/866-4499 for emergencies, www.asistur.cu), which provides assistance to tourists in trouble. It has a 24-hour "alarm center" (Prado #212, e/ Trocadero y Colón, Habana Vieja, tel. 07/866-8527 or 866-8920, fax 07/866-8087, asisten@asisten.cu; Mon.–Fri. 9 A.M.–5 P.M.). It has outlets in Camagüey, Ciego de Ávila, Cienfuegos, Guardalavaca, Santiago de Cuba, and Varadero; see regional chapters.

You should also contact your embassy or consulate. Consulate officials can't get you out of jail, but they can help you locate a lawyer, alleviate unhealthy conditions, or arrange for funds to be wired if you run short of money. They may be able to authorize a reimbursable loan while you arrange for cash to be forwarded, or even lend you money to get home (the U.S. State Department hates to admit this, but even U.S. citizens in Cuba can request help in an emergency).

If you're robbed, immediately file a police report with the **Policía Revolucionaria Nacional** (PNR, in Havana, Calle Picota, e/ Leonor Pérez y San Isidro, tel. 07/867-0496 or 07/862-0116). You'll receive a statement (*denuncia*) for insurance purposes, which you should make sure is dated and stamped. There is no special unit responsible for pursuing thefts from tourists and proceedings can take hours (readers report Kafkaesque experiences). If you're involved in a car accident, call the **Tránsitos** (transit police, tel. 07/862-0116 in Havana, 116 outside Havana).

If you are charged with a crime, you should request that a representative of your embassy be present, and that any deposition be made in front of an independent witness (*testigo*).

Warning: There are reports of the Cuban police jailing victims of passport theft while the crime and the victim are investigated. Several foreign embassies recommend reporting to your embassy *before* reporting ID theft to the police.

Help for U.S. Citizens

Travelers report that the **U.S. Interests Section** (Calzada, e/ L y M, Vedado, tel. 07/833-3551 to 07/833-3559, emergency/after hours tel. 07/833-3026, http://usembassy .state.gov/havana) has a good record in helping U.S. citizens in need in Cuba. The U.S. Department of State has a **Hotline for American Travelers** (tel. 202/647-5225), and you can call the **Overseas Citizen Service** (OCS, Room 4811, Department of State, 2201 C St. NW, Washington, DC 20520, 888/407-4747, from overseas 317/472-2328 or 202/647-4000 for after-hours emergencies, http://travel.state .gov; Mon.–Fri. 8 A.M.–8 P.M.) if things go awry. However, the United States does not have full diplomatic representation in Cuba, and its tapestry of pullable strings is understandably threadbare. If arrested, U.S. citizens should ask Cuban authorities to notify the U.S. Interests Section. A U.S. consular officer will then try to arrange regular visits, at the discretion of the Cuban government. Cuba does not recognize dual citizenship for Cuban citizens who are also U.S. citizens; Cuban-born citizens are—according to the U.S. State Department—thereby denied representation through the U.S. Interests Section in the event of arrest.

Legal Assistance

The **Consultoría Jurídica Internacional** (International Judicial Consultative Bureau, Calle 16 #314, e/ 3ra y 5ta, Miramar, Havana, tel. 07/204-1318, fax 07/204-2303, www.cji.co.cu; Mon.–Fri. 8:30 A.M.–noon and 1:30–5:30 P.M.), with branches nationwide, provides legal services regarding all aspects of Cuban law, from marriages and notarization to advising on the constitutionality of business ventures. It can assist travelers, including those who lose their passports or have them stolen.

The **Bufete Internacional** (Av. 5ta #16202, esq. 162, Miramar, Havana, tel. 07/204-6749, fax 07/204-6750, bufete@bufete.cha.cyt.cu) offers similar services and also has branches in major cities.

Money

CURRENCY
Convertible Pesos
All prices in this book are quoted in Cuban Convertible Pesos (*pesos convertibles*), denominated by "CUC" (pronounced "say-ooh-say") and often, within Cuba, by "$." As of November 2004, transactions in U.S. dollars (the former currency for all tourist transactions) ceased. Also, in April 2005, Cuba revalued the CUC, which no longer operates at parity with the U.S. dollar: at press time one dollar was worth CUC0.89. Currently, U.S. dollars are no longer accepted in shops or elsewhere and foreigners must now exchange their foreign currency for CUC. Convertible peso bills are issued in the following denominations: 1, 2, 5, 10, 20, 50, and 100 pesos.

You should always carry a wad of small bills, as change for larger bills is often hard to come by. Counterfeit US$100 bills are in circulation (printed in Colombia, apparently), and Cubans are wary of these. Also, U.S. dollar notes with certain serial numbers are not accepted in Cuba.

Cuban Currency
The Cuban currency (*moneda nacional*), in which state salaries are paid, is the peso, which is worth about four U.S. cents (the exchange rate at press time was about 25 pesos to the dollar). It is designated "$" and should not be confused with the CUC or U.S. "$" (to make matters worse, the dollar is sometimes called the peso). The peso is divided into 100 *centavos* (also called pesetas).

There is very little that you will need pesos for. Exceptions are if you want to travel on local trains and buses, hang out at local bars

and restaurants not normally frequented by tourists, or buy snacks from street stalls.

Exchanging Currency
Foreign currency can be changed for CUC at tourist hotels, banks, and official *burós de cambios* (exchange bureaus) operated by **Cadeca, S.A.** (Av. 26, esq. 45, Nuevo Vedado, tel. 07/55-57010), which operates exchange booths throughout Cuba. Tourists and Cubans exchanging U.S. dollars are charged 11 percent commission; other foreign currencies are not charged a commission.

Jiniteros may offer to change foreign currency illegally on the streets. Many tourists are ripped off during the deal and muggings have been reported. *It ain't worth it!*

BANKS
All banks in Cuba are state entities. No foreign banks are present. The most important of the banks catering to foreigners is the **Banco Financiero Internacional,** which offers a full range of banking services, including currency exchange services at free-market rates. The branches, nationwide, are open Monday–Saturday 8 A.M.–3 P.M. (but 8 A.M.–noon only on the last working day of each month). The state-controlled **Banco de Crédito y Comercio** (Bandec) is the main commercial bank with outlets island-wide (most are open weekdays 8:30 A.M.–3 P.M.). The **Banco Popular** caters mainly to Cubans, but also provides foreign transaction services. The **Banco Internacional de Comercio** primarily caters to foreign businesses.

Warning: Cuban banks have been known to pass off counterfeit CUC50 and CUC100 bills to foreigners. When receiving such bills, always check for watermarks.

ATM Cards

Automated teller machines (ATMs) at major banks dispense CUC to Cubans with cash cards either issued in Cuba (see *Money Transfers* in this section) or sent from relatives abroad and used to cull money wired into accounts in Canada, Europe, or Latin America. Very few ATMs are linked to international systems such as Cirrus or Switch.

CREDIT CARDS

Most hotels, car rental companies, and travel suppliers, as well as larger restaurants, will accept credit card payments, as long as the cards are not issued or processed by U.S. banks—the U.S. Treasury Department forbids U.S. financial institutions to process transactions involving Cuba (British travelers should check that their cards can be used, as about 20 percent of British-issued cards are outsourced to U.S. companies that are barred from processing such transactions). Credit card transactions are subject to local commission charges of 11 percent.

You can use your non-U.S. credit card to obtain a cash advance up to CUC5,000 (CUC100 minimum) at branches of Banco Financiero Internacional (BFI).

Often, no vouchers are available to process transactions. And the centralized computer systems often fail for hours at a time, affecting every credit card machine in the country.

If you have a problem with your card while in Cuba, contact **Fincimex** (Calle L, e/ 23 y 25, Vedado, Havana, tel. 07/55-4466 or 07/55-4024; Mon.–Fri. 8:30 A.M.–noon and 1–4:30 P.M.).

U.S. citizens must travel on a cash-only basis. However, Rex Limousines accepts U.S. MasterCard payment for car rentals. Note that U.S. citizens are prohibited from using credit cards in Cuba, period, including those issued by foreign banks.

TRAVELERS CHECKS

Travelers checks (unless issued by U.S. banks) are accepted in some tourist restaurants, hotels, and foreign-goods stores. They can also be cashed at most hotel cashier desks, as well as at banks. Travelers checks issued by American Express *can* be used for payment in Cuban hotels and to get cash at branches of CADECA, plus major banks. You should *not* enter the date or the place when signing your checks—a quirky Cuban requirement.

MONEY TRANSFERS

Western Union (800/325-6000 in the U.S., www.westernunion.com) is licensed to handle wire transfers to Cuba, permitting Cuban-American residents only to send up to US$300 every three months, but only to immediate family members (and not to Cuban officials or government entities). Only designated Western Union offices are permitted to handle such transactions, which in Cuba are handled by Fincimex at locations throughout Cuba. Canadian money transfers are not accepted by Western Union in Cuba.

You can use an **Amigo Travel Card** (1600 Steeles Ave., Suite 400, Concord, Ontario L4K 4M2, Canada, tel. 905/660-5558 or 800/724-5685, www.amigotravelcard.com), which operates like a debit card using an account where you deposit funds to secure accounts in Canada, permitting you to withdraw cash in Cuba or to pay for goods and services at more than 6,000 locations. You can apply for a card online or in Cuba through **Fincimex** (Calle 2 #302, esq. 3ra, Miramar, Havana, tel. 07/204-4823; and 3ra Av., esq. 6, Miramar, tel. 07/204-2259; Mon.–Fri. 8:15 A.M.–4 P.M.). The same Canadian company also offers **Quickcash** (www.quickcash.com) money transfer service, permitting transfers via your Visa or MasterCard account online.

Non U.S.-citizens have several other options, including the Swiss company **AWS Technologies** (P.O. Box 47, 3960 Sierre, Switzerland, tel. 7/881-5599, www.aws-transaction.com).

COSTS

The Cuban government has overpriced almost everything in its greed to cull foreign currency. Without competition to regulate the market, the state has jacked up prices to levels that are often nothing less than extortion. Plus, you'll pay 11 percent commission on credit card purchases and to exchange U.S. dollars.

If you get around on public transport, rent rooms with Cuban families, dine on the street at *paladares* (private restaurants) and peso snack bars, and keep your entertainment to nontouristy venues, then you may be able to survive on as little as CUC40 a day in Havana (slightly less elsewhere), with your room taking the lion's share. If you want at least a modicum of comforts, then budget *at least* CUC100 a day.

Accommodations in Havana cost CUC25–300 per night. Meals average CUC5–15, but at the priciest (although not necessarily the best) restaurants meals may cost upward of CUC30 per person. Entrance to a cabaret or disco will cost CUC2 to CUC65, plus drinks, depending on venue. Day tours featuring sightseeing and meals average CU35–50. Taxis average about CUC1.50 per mile. Budget CUC55 upward per day for a rental car. And be prepared for extra expenses for minor services that you may be used to getting for free at home. The Cuban government gives nothing for free, not even the bread and butter that arrives with your meal without you asking.

Tipping

Regardless of occupation, Cubans receive slave-rate wages. Don't be stingy! Your waiter dressed in a tux probably lives in a slum and is being paid less than CUC1 day. In better restaurants, waiters expect to be tipped 10 percent, even where a service charge has been added to your bill (waiters and staff see only a small fraction of the service charge, if any, which the government pockets). However, many Cuban waiters haven't yet figured out that a tip is meant to reward good service; instead they perform poorly and rely on good will.

Museum guides and others in tourist venues often follow you around and offer unnecessary services in the hope of soliciting a tip. If you don't welcome the service, it's best to state so upfront, rather than refuse to tip after the fact. Similarly, musicians in bars and restaurants will usually hover by your table until you've tipped them; if you don't welcome the attention, tip after the first song and they'll usually move on to the next table.

Communications

POSTAL SERVICE

Correos de Cuba operates the Cuban postal service, which is terminally slow but relatively efficient, although delivery is never guaranteed. International mail is read by Cuba's censors; avoid any politically sensitive comments. *Never* send cash.

International airmail (*correo aereo*) averages about one month each way (to save time, savvy Cubans usually hand their letters to foreigners to mail outside Cuba). When mailing from Cuba, it helps to write the country destination in Spanish: England is *Inglaterra* (use this for Wales and Scotland also, on the line below either country); France is *Francia;* Italy is *Italia;* Germany is *Alemania;* Spain is *España;* Switzerland is *Suiza;* and the United States is *Estados Unidos* (often referred to in Cuba by "EE.UU.").

Major tourist hotels have small post offices and will accept your mail for delivery. Post offices (*correos*) are usually open weekdays 10 A.M.–5 P.M. and Saturday 8 A.M.–3 P.M.

Rates: International postcards cost CUC0.50 to all destinations; letters cost CUC0.80. Prepaid postcards (CUC0.50) are sold at tourist outlets and post offices. Within Cuba, letters cost from 15 centavos (20 grams or less) to 2.05 pesos (up to 500 grams); postcards cost 10 *centavos.* Stamps are called *sellos* (SAY-yos).

Parcels: All parcels to be mailed from Cuba must be delivered to the post office *unwrapped* for inspection. It is far better to send packages through an express courier service (see below), although the same regulation applies.

Receiving Mail: You can receive mail in Havana by having letters and parcels addressed to you using your name as it appears on your passport or other ID for general delivery to: "c/o *Espera* [your name], Ministerio de Comunicaciones, Avenida Independencia and 19 de Mayo, Habana 6, Cuba." To collect mail poste restante, go to the **Correos de Cuba,** (Av. Rancho Boyeros, Havana, tel. 07/879-6824 or 879-8654; Mon.–Sat. 8 A.M.–6 P.M.) for pickup. The names of people who have received mail are posted. Also consider having incoming mail addressed *"Espera"* [your name] c/o [your embassy].

Express Mail

DHL Worldwide Express (www.dhl.com) has offices in post offices in most major cities. The main offices are in Havana (1ra Av., esq. 26, Miramar, tel. 07/204-1578, fax 07/204-0999, comercial@dhl.cutisa.cu; weekdays 8 A.M.–8 P.M., Sat. 8 A.M.–4 P.M.). DHL offers daily door-to-door pickup and delivery service at no charge for both international and domestic delivery. DHL packages mailed to or from the United States typically take more than a week to arrive.

Cubapost (Calle 21 #10099, e/ 10 y 12, Vedado, Havana, tel. 07/831-3328; Mon.–Fri. 8 A.M.–5 P.M., Sat. 8 A.M.–noon) offers international express mail service.

Restrictions

Uncle Sam restricts what may be mailed to Cuba from the United States. Letters and literature can be mailed without restriction. Gift parcels can be "sent or carried by an authorized traveler" to an individual or religious or educational organization if the domestic retail value does not exceed US$200. Only one parcel per month is allowed, and contents are limited to food, vitamins, seeds, medicines, medical supplies, clothing, personal hygiene items, and a few other categories. All other parcels are subject to seizure. Don't think you can skirt around this by sending by DHL. Your pack-

---

SENDING FLOWERS TO CUBA

Want to surprise family or friends with a bouquet of roses? It's easily done through Swiss-based Interflora (www.fleurop.com), which handles requests online and can deliver to Cuba within 48 hours, worldwide. A bouquet of 12 red roses costs €67-73 and is delivered to the addressee's door.

---

age will either be returned or seized. If mailing to the United States, don't try mailing Uncle Fred a box of Cohibas for Christmas. They'll go up in smoke all right—on the U.S. Customs 24-hour pyre!

Online Mail

Want your mail to be delivered to Cuba within seconds? You can write online and send letters, postcards, telegrams, or phone messages using **E-scriba** (www.escriba.com). Content is printed and delivered by hand to recipients from an E-scriba distribution center. A package of 10 stamps costs CUC11. Letters cost one stamp for up to 500 words, and one stamp per 100 words extra. You can opt for express service (four stamps), Spanish translation (one stamp), and even perfume (one stamp). You can pay by money order, certified check, or wire transfer.

TELEPHONE SERVICE

Cuba's telephone system is the responsibility of the **Empresa de Telecomunicaciones de Cuba** (Etecsa, tel. 07/266-6666, www.etecsa.cu), headquartered in the Miramar Trade Center in Havana. It has a central office (*telepunto*) with international phone service (and often Internet) in all major towns.

Modern telephones linked to a modern digital system and fiber-optic network have almost entirely replaced the antediluvian relics that performed like something from a Hitchcock movie. Yet, there are still quirks, with some days better than others. And phones are scarce: Cuba has one of the lowest rates of telephones per capita in Latin America: only 5.4 per 100 people (placing it 14th out of 20 Latin American countries).

Cubans usually answer the phone by saying either *"¡Oigo!"* (I'm listening!) or *"¡Dígame!"* (Speak to me!). It sounds abrupt, but they're not being rude.

Call 113 for directory inquiries. The national telephone directory is available on CD-ROM and online at www.etecsa.cu. Etecsa also publishes a dandy little Yellow Page For Tourists (*Páginas Amarillas Para el Turista*). Telephone numbers change with exasperating regularity. Trying to determine a correct number can be problematic because many entities have several numbers and rarely publish the same number twice. If you get a wrong number, a recorded message will say: *"Este número no existe por ningún o nada."*

Most commercial entities have a switchboard (*pizarra*).

Online Calling: You can activate online calls from anywhere in the world either direct or via an operator at www.calls2cuba.com. Call packages start at US$34 for four 10-minute calls.

Public Phone Booths

Etecsa operates glass-enclosed telephone kiosks called *micropuntos* (*telecorreos* where they combine with postal services) throughout Cuba. They utilize phone cards and do not accept collect or incoming calls. Tourist hotels, *micropuntos,* certain restaurants, and miscellaneous other outlets sell phone cards in pesos (for calls within Cuba only) and in CUC (CUC10 and CUC25) for international calls. If it expires, you can replace it with a new one without interrupting your call by pushing button C and inserting a new card.

Stand-alone public phones tend to be on noisy street corners. Some are modern and take phone cards. Others are older and can only be used for local calls; they take five-centavo coins. When you hear the "time-up" signal (a short *blip*), you must *immediately* put in another coin to avoid being cut off. Newer public phones also take 20-centavo coins and can be used for long distance calls as well.

Etecsa telephone booths are in every town and village.

© CHRISTOPHER P. BAKER

International Calls

When calling Cuba from abroad, dial 011 (the international dialing code), then 53 (the Cuba country code) followed by the city code and the number. For direct international calls from Cuba, dial 119, then the country code (for example, 44 for the U.K.), followed by the area code and number. For the international operator, dial 0, wait 30 seconds for the tone; then dial 9. For operator-assisted calls to the United States, dial 07/66-1212. (Using a Cuban telephone operator can be a Kafkaesque experience, as many do not speak English. In the United States, AT&T has a "language line" that will connect you with an interpreter, 800/843-8420; US$3.50 per minute.)

Cost per minute varies depending on time of day and location from which you're calling. At last visit, typical per-minute rates were: CUC2.75 to the United States; CUC2.40 to Canada; CUC3.40 to Central America and Caribbean countries; CUC4.45 to South America; CUC4.80 to France, Germany, Italy, and Spain; and CUC5.30 to Europe and the rest of the world. You can use calling cards for international calls. Rates are about 40 percent higher for operator-assisted calls. (Most upscale tourist hotels have direct-dial telephones in guest rooms for international calls; others will connect you via the hotel operator. Expect to pay through the nose.)

Domestic Calls

For local calls in the same area code, simply dial the number you wish to reach. To dial a number outside your area code, dial 0, then wait for a tone before dialing the local city code and the number you wish to reach. For the local operator, dial 0. Local calls in Havana cost approximately five centavos (about a quarter of a cent). Rates for calls beyond Havana range from 30 centavos to three pesos and 15 centavos for the first three minutes, depending on zone—tourist hotels and Etecsa booths charge in U.S. dollar equivalent (CUCs).

Cellular Phones

Cubacel (Calle 28 #510, e/ 5 y 7, Miramar, tel. 05/264-2266 or 07/880-2222, www.cubacel .com; daily 8:30 A.M.–7:30 P.M., Sat. 8 A.M.– noon) provides cellular phone service. It also has offices elsewhere in Havana and in Varadero and most major cities.

You can bring your own cellular phone into the country; Cubacel will activate it and provide you with a local line for CUC120 (air time costs CUC0.30 to CUC0.50 per minute). It offers service for both TDMA and GSM standards.

FAX AND TELEGRAM

You can send faxes from most tourist hotels, usually for a fee slightly more than the comparable telephone charge.

Etecsa offers 24-hour "telegram by telephone" service (tel. 07/81-8844), including at its *telecorreo* offices.

ONLINE SERVICE IN CUBA

Computer communications are tightly controlled by the government, and access for the average citizen is severely restricted. Few individuals are permitted to own a computer or modem. Cubans are permitted to send and receive emails, but government authorization is needed to access the Internet; everyone else is limited to the Intranet of local, government-sanctioned websites (although many Cubans log onto the Internet illegally using borrowed or stolen log-on identities and passwords on the black market).

Etecsa offers Internet service at most *telepuntos* (typically a prepaid card costs CUC6 for one hour; some outlets charge CUC0.05 per minute additional).

Most tourist hotels have either cybercafés or business centers with online access. Some upscale hotels also have dataports in guest rooms. You can call your Internet provider, although there are no local access numbers for AOL, Yahoo, and other non-Cuban ISPs. Yahoo works much better in Cuba than, say, Hotmail (if you want to use Hotmail, sign on using www.msn.com).

Tourists are permitted to bring laptop computers, which must be declared and may not be left behind in Cuba. *Bring a surge protector!* Since Internet time in Cuba is expensive, you can save money by typing emails in advance on your laptop and saving them to a disk, which you can then use to paste messages into an email composition at a cybercafé.

Email may be read by security personnel reading directly off the server. Secret police have even been known to make house calls to check up on guests traveling with computers.

Miscellaneous Practicalities

WEATHER FORECASTS

The *Granma* newspaper prints a weather forecast, as does *Cartelera,* the weekly tourist newspaper. Cuban TV newscasts feature weather forecasts (in Spanish). The **Instituto de Meteorología** (Meterological Institute, www.met.inf.cu) provides weather information in Spanish online.

FILM AND PHOTOGRAPHY

You are rarely denied access to anything you wish to photograph (except military and industrial installations, airports, and officials in uniform, who are under strict instructions not to allow themselves to be photographed). However, you will normally be charged for photographing inside museums.

Official permission is needed to bring "professional" camera equipment. Otherwise, visitors to Cuba are allowed to bring two cameras (either digital or analog). Video cameras for tourist use are not restricted, although you may have to declare it upon arrival. Bring spare batteries and tapes.

If you're shooting with film, note that Cuban airport officials rarely permit hand inspection. Bring all the film you need with you, and keep it out of the sun. Film is sold at most tourist hotels and at Foto Video and Photo Service stores: Only print film is available. Often this is old, or has been exposed to heat for long periods of time.

Most Photo Service stores also sell instamatic and small digital cameras. However, there are *no* camera stores as we know them in North America or Europe, and 35mm SLRs, lenses, flash units, filters, and other types of equipment are unavailable.

Most Foto Video and Photo Service stores offer processing services and passport photos.

Never turn your back on your camera gear, and guard against snatch and grab of cameras from your shoulders.

Photo Etiquette

Cubans love to ham for your camera and will generally cooperate willingly. However, never assume an automatic right to take a personal photograph. If you come across individuals who don't want to be photographed, honor their wishes. It's a common courtesy, too, to ask permission to photograph what might be considered private situations.

Many children will request money for being photographed, as will the mulattas dressed in traditional costume in the plazas of Habana Vieja. Increasingly, many Cubans now expect to be paid for posing. Whether you pay is a matter of conscience. If they insist on being paid and you don't want to pay, don't take the shot. In markets, it is considered a courtesy to buy a small trinket from vendors you wish to photograph. And don't forget to send photographs to anyone you promise to send to, as few Cubans own cameras and they cherish being gifted highly treasured photos.

Several foreigners have been arrested and deported in recent years for filming "pornography." The Cuban government defines it fairly broadly (nude photography is forbidden) and keeps a strict watch for such illicit use of cameras.

BUSINESS HOURS

Banks are usually open Monday–Friday 8:30 A.M.–noon and 1:30–3 P.M., Saturday 8:30–10:30 A.M. Offices usually open Monday–Friday 8:30 A.M.–12:30 P.M. and 1:30–5:30 P.M. and every second Saturday 8:30 A.M.–noon. Pharmacies generally open daily 8 A.M.–8 P.M. (*turnos permanentes* stay open 24 hours). Post offices are usually open Monday–Saturday 8 A.M.–10 P.M., Sunday 8 A.M.–6 P.M. Shops are usually open Monday–Saturday 8:30 A.M.–5:30 P.M., although many remain open later, including all day Sunday. Museums vary widely (and change frequently), although most are closed on

NATIONAL HOLIDAYS

January 1	Liberation Day (Día de la Liberación)
January 2	Victory Day (Día de la Victoria)
January 28	José Martí's birthday
February 24	Anniversary of the Second War of Independence
March 8	International Women's Day (Día de la Mujer)
March 13	Anniversary of the students' attack on the presidential palace
April 19	Bay of Pigs Victory (Victoria del Playa Girón)
May 1	Labor Day (Día de los Trabajadores)
July 26	National Revolution Day (anniversary of the attack on the Moncada barracks)
July 30	Day of the Martyrs of the Revolution
October 8	Anniversary of Che Guevara's death
October 10	Anniversary of the First War of Independence
October 28	Memorial day to Camilo Cienfuegos
December 2	Anniversary of the landing of the *Granma*
December 7	Memorial day to Antonio Maceo

Monday; typically they open Tuesday–Saturday 9 A.M.–5 P.M., and Sunday 8 A.M.–noon.

Most banks, businesses, and government offices close during national holidays.

Cubans still honor the *merienda,* coffee breaks usually taken at about 10 A.M. and 3 P.M. They also like to dine late. Many restaurants are open until midnight, and some stay open 24 hours.

ELECTRICITY

Cuba operates on 110-volt AC (60-cycle) nationwide, although a few hotels operate on 220 volts (many have both). Most outlets use U.S. plugs: flat, parallel two-pins, and three rectangular pins. A two-prong adapter is a good idea (take one with you; they're impossible to come by in Cuba). Many electrical outlets are faulty and darn-right dangerous. Electricity blackouts (*apagones*) are common. Take a flashlight, spare batteries, and candles plus matches or lighter.

TIME

Cuban time is equivalent to U.S. Eastern Standard Time: five hours behind Greenwich Mean Time, the same as New York and Miami, and three hours ahead of the U.S. west coast. There is little seasonal variation in dawn. However, Cuba has daylight saving time May–October.

TOILETS

Public toilets are a rarity in Cuba. The few that exist are disgustingly foul. Most hotels and restaurants will let you use their facilities, though most lack toilet paper, which gets stolen. An attendant usually sits outside the door, dispensing pieces of toilet paper (usually for CUC0.50 or CUC1). *Always carry a small packet of toilet tissue with you!*

WEIGHTS AND MEASURES

Cuba operates on the metric system. Liquids are sold in liters, fruits and vegetables by the kilo. Distances are given in meters and kilometers. See the chart at the back of the book for metric conversions.

PERSONAL CONDUCT

Cubans are immensely respectful and courteous, with a deep sense of integrity and exemplary morals. Politeness is greatly appreciated, and you can ease your way considerably by being both courteous and patient. Always greet your host with *"¡Buenos días!"* (morning) or *"¡Buenas tardes!"* (afternoon). And never neglect to say, *"Gracias."* Honor local dress codes as appropriate. Topless and nude bathing are neither allowed nor accepted, except at key tourist resorts. For men, short shorts should be relegated to beachwear.

Cubans are extremely hygienic and have an understandable natural prejudice against anyone who ignores personal hygiene.

Respect the natural environment. Take only photographs, leave only footprints.

Since February 2005, smoking is prohibited in theaters, stores, buses, taxis, restaurants, and enclosed public areas, but the prohibition is rarely enforced.

Tips for Travelers

MALE TRAVELERS

It doesn't take the average male visitor long to discover that Cuban woman have an open attitude towards sexuality. True, they like being romanced, but they're also much more aggressive than foreign men may be used to, displaying little equivocation (especially toward foreign men).

Most Cuban women count themselves lucky to have found a foreigner's acceptance and are happy to accept whatever comes their way. However, Cuba is not free of the kind of scams pulled by good-time girls in other countries, and such liaisons require prudence. Petty robbery (your paramour steals your sunglasses or rifles your wallet while you take a shower) is common. Muggings by accomplices are a rare possibility, and even drugging and robbery occurs—in 2002, a ring of high-class prostitutes was robbing tourists by drugging their drinks, according to police. Several tourists have even been murdered during sexual encounters!

Men in "sensitive" occupations (journalists and government employees) should be aware that the femme fatale who sweeps you off your feet may be in the employ of Cuba's state security.

For more details see the sidebar *Prostitution, or Merely Permissive?* and the *Sexual Mores* section under *Cuban Society* in the *Background* chapter.

FEMALE TRAVELERS

With few exceptions, Cuban men treat women with great respect and, for the most part, as equals. True, Cuba remains a macho society,

GETTING MARRIED IN CUBA

It's fairly easy to get married in Cuba if you have the correct documents in place. Civil marriages are handled by the **Bufete Internacional** (5ta Av. #16202, esq. 162, Rpto. Flores, Havana, tel. 07/273-6824, fax 07/204-6750, www.bufeteinternacional.cu), the "International Lawyer's Office," which has an office in most major cities. The marriage certificate costs CUC525, plus there are other expenses. Foreigners need to produce their birth certificate, proof of marital status if single, and a divorce certificate (if relevant). These need to be translated into Spanish, and authenticated by the Cuban consulate in the country in which they were issued. Marriages in Cuba are recognized in the United States.

but postrevolutionary political correctness is everywhere. And sexual assault of women is unheard of. It is hard to imagine a safer place for women to travel. If you do welcome the amorous overtures of men, Havana is heaven. The art of gentle seduction is to Cuban men a kind of national pastime—a sport and a trial of manhood. They will hiss like serpents in appreciation from a distance, and call out *piropos*—affectionate and lyrical epithets that, in general, Cuban women encourage (see *Feminism and Machismo* in the *Cuban Society* section of the *Background* chapter). Take effusions of love with a grain of salt; while swearing eternal devotion, your Don Juan may conveniently forget to mention he's married. While the affection may be genuine, you are assuredly the moneybags in the relationship. Plenty of Cuban men earn their living giving pleasure to foreign women looking for love beneath the palms or, like their female counterparts, taking advantage of such an opportunity when it arises.

If you're not interested in love in the tropics, simply pretend not to notice advances and avoid eye contact; a longing stare is part of the game. You can help prevent these overtures by dressing modestly.

The **Federation of Women's Travel Organizations** (P.O. Box 466, Av. Palma de Mallorca 15, Spain, tel. 95/205-7060, fax 95/205-8418, www.ifwto.org) is a useful resource, as is Cuba's **Federación de Mujeres Cubanas** (Cuban Women's Federation, Paseo #260 e/ 11 y 13, Vedado, Havana, tel. 07/55-2771, fmc.cu@ceniai.inf.cu), which sponsors forums and acts to promote the interests of women; and *Mujeres* (Galiano #264, e/ Neptuno y Concordia, Havana, www.mujeres.cubaweb.cu), a women's magazine.

GAY AND LESBIAN TRAVELERS

Cuba is schizophrenic when it comes to homosexuality. The situation blows hot and cold and significant discrimination still exists at the official level. The gay community is fairly overt in Havana, but less so elsewhere; the lesbian scene is much less evolved and remains largely hidden. Gays—especially *jiniteros*—who befriend foreigners often fall afoul of the law of *peligrosidad,* which declares as "dangerous" anyone who acts against the norms of socialist morality.

At last visit the law had been revised to permit two people of the same gender to share the same bed in *casas particulares.*

See *Homosexuality* in the *Cuban Society* section of the *Background* chapter. Also see the sidebar *Havana's Gay Scene* in the *Havana* chapter.

Useful resources include the **International Gay & Lesbian Travel Association** (4431 N. Federal Hwy. #304, Fort Lauderdale, FL 33308, 954/776-2626 or 800/448-8550, www.iglta.org); and **Odysseus: The International Gay Travel Planner** (P.O. Box 1548, Port Washington, NY 11050, 516/944-5330 or 800/257-5344, www.odyusa.com).

Coda Tours (12794 Forest Hill Blvd., Suite 1A, W. Palm Beach, FL 33414, 561/791-9890 or 888/677-2632, www.coda-tours.com) has offered gay tours to Cuba in the past.

In Cuba, gay organizations are illegal. The **Centro Nacional de Educación Sexual** (Calle 10 #460, Vedado, Havana, tel. 07/55-5529, www.cenesex.sld.cu) may be of assistance. A website of interest is www.gay-cuba.com.

STUDENT AND YOUTH TRAVELERS

Cuban students receive discounts for entry to many museums and other sights, as do foreign students with the **International Student Identity Card** (ISIC) or similar student ID. Students can obtain an ISIC at any student union. Alternately, in the United States, contact the **Council on International Educational Exchange** (CIEE, 7 Custom House St., Portland, ME 04101, 207/553-7600 or 800/40-STUDY, www.ciee.org). In Canada, cards (C$13) can be obtained through **Travel Cuts** (tel. 866/246-9762, www.travelcuts.com). In the United Kingdom, students can obtain an ISIC from any student union.

The U.S. government permits academic exchanges with Cuba, and students can enroll at Cuban universities. (See the sidebar *Studying in Cuba* in this chapter.)

The **Federación Estudiantil Universitario** (Calle 23, esq. H, Vedado, Havana, tel. 07/832-4646) is Cuba's national student federation.

SENIOR TRAVELERS

Cuba treats its senior citizens with honor, and discounts are offered for entry to museums and other sights. Again, this may apply to foreign seniors in a few instances.

A useful resource is the **American**

Association of Retired Persons (AARP, 601 E. St. NW, Washington, DC 20049, 888/687-2277, www.aarp.org).

Canadian company **ElderTreks** (597 Markham St., Toronto, Ontario M6G 2L7, tel. 416/588-5000 or 800/741-7956, www.eldertreks.com) offers 14-day trips to Cuba.

TRAVELERS WITH DISABILITIES

Cubans go out of their way to assist travelers with disabilities, although few allowances have been made in infrastructure.

The **Asociación Cubana de Limitados Físicos y Motores** (Cuban Association for Physically-Motor Disabled People, ACLIFIM, Ermita #213, e/ San Pedro y Lombillo, Plaza de la Revolución, CP 10600, Havana, tel. 07/881-0911, fax 07/204-3787, aclifim@informed.sld.cu) can be of assistance.

In the United States, the **Society for Accessible Travel & Hospitality** (347 5th Ave. #610, New York, NY 10016, 212/447-7284, www.sath.org) and the **American Foundation for the Blind** (11 Penn Plaza #300, New York, NY 10001, 212/502-7600 or 800/232-5463, www.afb.org) are good resources.

TRAVELERS WITH CHILDREN

Cubans adore children and will dote on yours.

Children under the age of two travel free on airlines; children between 2 and 12 are offered special discounts (check with individual airlines). Children under 16 usually stay free with parents at hotels, although an extra-bed rate may be charged. And children under 12 are normally given free (or half-price) entry to museums.

Children's items such as diapers (nappies) and baby foods are very scarce in Cuba. Bring cotton swabs, diapers, Band-Aids, baby foods, and a small first-aid kit with any necessary medicines for your child. Children's car seats are not offered in rental cars.

The equivalent of the Boy and Girl Scouts and Girl Guides is the **Pioneros José Martí** (Calle F #352, Vedado, Havana, tel. 07/832-5292), which has chapters throughout the country. Its main focus is instilling youth with revolutionary correctness and civil responsibility. Having your children interact would be a fascinating education.

RESOURCES
Glossary

ache luck, positive vibe

aduana customs

agua mala jellyfish

alfarje Moorish-inspired ceiling layered with geometric and star patterns

aljibe well

altos upstairs unit (used in street addresses)

americano/a citizen of the Americas (from Alaska to Tierra del Fuego); see *gringo*

animación entertainment activity involving guests (at hotels)

apagón electricity blackout

Astro national bus company

autopista freeway

azotea rooftop terrace

babalawo *santería* priest

bajos downstairs unit (used in street addresses)

baño toilet, bathroom

bárbaro awesome, cool

batido milkshake

biblioteca library

bici-taxi bicycle taxi

bodega grocery store distributing rations; Spanish-style inn

bohío thatched rural homestead

bomba gasoline station (rarely used)

bombo lottery for U.S. visas

bosque woodland

botella hitchhike, graft

buceo scuba dive

caballería antiquated Spanish land measurement (about 13 hectares)

caballero sir, respectful address for a male

caballito motorcycle police

cabaret espectáculo Las Vegas-style cabaret

cabildo colonial-era town council

cacique Taíno chief

Cadeca foreign-exchange agency

cajita boxed meal

calle street

camarera maid or waitress

camello Metro bus in Havana and Santiago de Cuba

camión truck, often with bench seats welded onto the flatbed

campesino/a peasant, country person

campismo campsite (normally with cabins, not tents)

candela hot (as in a party scene, "promiscuous," or "deep trouble;" literally means "flame")

cañonazo cannon-firing (performed nightly at El Morro castles in Havana and Santiago de Cuba)

carne de res beef

carnet de identidad ID card that all Cubans must carry at all times

carpeta reception

carretera road

carro automobile

cartelera cultural calendar

casa de la cultura "culture house" hosting music and other cultural events

casa de la trova same as a *casa de la cultura*

casa particular literally "private house"; used to denote licensed room rental in a private home

casco histórico historic center of a city

cayo coral cay
CDR Comité Para la Defensa de la Revolución; neighborhood watch committees
cenote flooded cave
central sugar mill
ciego blind
cigarillo cigarette
cimarrón runaway slave
circunvalación ring road around a city
claves rhythm sticks
coche horse-drawn taxi
coco-taxi egg-shaped, three-wheeled open-air taxis
cola line, queue
colectivo collective taxi (usually an old Yankee car) that runs along a fixed route and operates like a bus
comemierda literally "shit-eater"; often used to refer to Communist or MININT officials (foreign travelers should avoid using this term, which can invite trouble)
compañero/a companion, used as a Revolutionary address for another person
congrí rice with red beans
correo post or post office
coño literally "cunt" (the most utilized cuss word in Cuba)
criollo Creole, used for Cuban food, or a person born in Cuba during the colonial era
cristianos y moros rice with black beans
Cuba libre "free cuba," or rum and Coke
cuenta propista self-employed person
custodio guard (as in parking lots)
daiquiri rum cocktail served with crushed ice
diente de perro jagged rock, as along unpaved coastal roads
divisa U.S. dollars
edificio building
efectivo cash
"el señor" colloquial term for Fidel Castro
el último last person in a queue
embajada embassy
embalse reservoir
embori snitch
encomienda colonial form of slavery giving landowners usufruct rights to Indian labor
entronque crossroads
escabeche ceviche, marinated raw fish

escuela school
esquina caliente literally "hot corner," used for a place where baseball fans heatedly debate the sport
estación station
fábrica factory
FAR Fuerza Revolucionaria Militar, or armed forces
farmacia pharmacy
faro lighthouse
ferrocarril railway
fiesta de quince girl's fifteenth birthday party, also *quinceañera*
filin "feeling" music, usually romantic ballads
finca farm
flota Spanish treasure fleet
FMC Federación de Mujeres Cubanas (Federation of Cuban Women)
fruta bomba papaya (see *papaya*, below)
fula U.S. dollars; also a messy situation
gasolinera gas station
gobernador colonial-era Spanish governor
golpe military coup
Granma yacht that carried Fidel Castro and his guerrilla army from Mexico to Cuba in 1956
gringo/a person from the United States, but can also apply to any Caucasian
guagua bus
guajiro/a peasant or country bumpkin; also used for a type of traditional country song
guanguancó traditional, sensual dance in which the male attempts to touch the female genitals
guaracha satirical song
guarapo fresh-squeezed sugarcane juice
guarapería place selling *guarapo*
guayabera pleated, buttoned men's shirt popular with Communist Party members
habanero/a person from Havana
habano export-quality cigar
heladería ice-cream store
iglesia church
ingenio colonial-era sugar mill
inmigración immigration
jaba plastic bag, as at a supermarket
jefe de sector Communist *vigilante* (see below) in charge of several street blocks
jefe de turno shift manager

jejénes minuscule sand fleas that pack a mean bite

jinitera female seeking a foreign male for pecuniary or other gain

jinitero male hustler who hassles tourists

joder to fuck, also to mess up

libreta ration book

luchar to fight; common term used to describe the difficulty of daily life

M-26-7 "26th of July Movement," Fidel Castro's underground revolutionary movement named for the date of the attack on the Moncada barracks

machetero sugarcane cutter/harvester

Mambí rebels fighting for independence from Spain; sometimes referred to as Mambises

mango slang term for a beautiful woman

maqueta scale model

máquina old Yankee automobile

mausoleo mausoleum

mediopunto half-moon stained-glass window

mercado market

mercado agropecuario produce market or farmers market

microbrigadista brigades of unskilled volunteer labor, usually utilized to built apartment blocks

MININT Ministry of the Interior

mirador lookout point or tower

mogote limestone monoliths, especially associated with Viñales

mojito rum cocktail served with mint and sugar

moneda coins

moneda nacional Cuban pesos

Mudejar Moorish (as in architecture)

muelle pier, wharf

mulatto/a mixed-blood person with both black and white heritage

negro/a black person

norteamericano/a U.S. or Canadian citizen

Oriente eastern provinces of Cuba

orisha *santería* deity

paladar private restaurant

palenque thatched structure

palestino derogatory term for a migrant to Havana from Oriente

papaya tropical fruit, but in Cuba also a slang term for vagina

parada bus stop

parque de diversiones amusement park

PCC Partido Comunista de Cuba

pedraplén causeway connecting offshore islands to the Cuban mainland

peninsular Spanish-born colonialist in Cuba in pre-independence days

peña social get-together for cultural enjoyment, such as a literary reading

piropo witty or flirtatious comment

pizarra switchboard

ponchero/a puncture repair person

presa dam

prórroga visa extension

puro export-quality cigar

quinceañera girl's fifteenth birthday celebration and rite of passage

quinta country house of nobility or wealthy person in colonial days

quintal Spanish colonial measure

rancheador a hunter of escaped slaves during colonial days

refresco "refreshment," usually freshsqueezed orange juice

resolver to resolve or fix a problem; daily grind of making ends meet

ropa vieja shredded beef dish

rumba a traditional Afro-Cuban dance; also a party involving such

sala room or gallery

salsa popular modern dance music derived from *son*

salsero/a performer of salsa

santería Afro-Cuban religion that is a syncretization of the African Yoruba and Catholic religions

santero/a adherent of *santería*

santiagüero/a person from Santiago de Cuba

sello postage or similar stamp

sendero walking trail

servicentro gasoline station

SIDA AIDS

son traditional music as popularized by Buena Vista Social Club

Taíno name of the predominant Indian inhabit-

ants of Cuba at the time of the Spanish conquest
taquilla ticket window
taller workshop
tarjeta card, such as a credit card
telenovela soap opera
telepunto main telephone exchange, sometimes with Internet service
temporada alta/baja high/low season
terminal de ómnibus bus station
tienda shop
tráfico traffic cop
trago a shot of rum
trova traditional poetry-based music
UJC Unión de Jóvenes Comunistas; politically oriented youth communist group

UNEAC Unión Nacional de Escritores y Artistas de Cuba; National Union of Cuban Writers and Artists
vaquero cowboy
vega patch of land where tobacco is grown
vigilante community-watch person, on behalf of the Revolution
verde slang for U.S. dollar
Víazul company offering daily bus service geared to tourists
vitral stained-glass window
Yoruba a group of peoples and a pantheistic religion from Nigeria
yuma slang for the United States
zafra sugarcane harvest

Cuban Spanish

Learning the basics of Spanish will aid your travels considerably. In key tourist destinations, however, you should be able to get along fine without it. English is now required of all university students and hotel staff, and is now compulsory in high schools. Most larger hotels have bilingual desk staff, and English is widely spoken by the staff of car rental agencies and tour companies. Cubans are exceedingly keen to practice their English and you will be approached often by such individuals. Away from the tourist path, far fewer people speak English.

Use that as an excuse to learn some Spanish. Cubans warm quickly to those who make an effort to speak their language. Don't be bashful. Use what Spanish you know and you'll be surprised how quickly you become familiar with the language.

See the sidebar *Spanish-Language Courses* in the *Essentials* chapter.

Pronunciation

In its literary form, Cuban Spanish is pure, classical Castilian (the Spanish of Spain). Alas, in its spoken form Cuban Spanish is the most difficult to understand in all of Latin America.

Cubans speak more briskly than other Latin Americans, blurring their rapid-fire words together. The diction of Cuba is lazy and unclear. Thought Richard Henry Dana Jr. in 1859: "it strikes me that the tendency here is to enfeeble the language, and take from it the openness of the vowels and the strength of the consonants." The letter "s," for example, is usually swallowed altogether, especially in plurals. Thus, the typical greeting *¿Como estás?* is usually pronounced como-TAH. (The swallowed "s"s are apparently accumulated for use in restaurants, where they are released to get the server's attention—*"S-s-s-s-s-st!"* Because of this, a restaurant with bad service can sound like a pit full of snakes.) The final consonants of words are also often deleted, as are diphthongs such as "d" and, often, the entire last syllable of words ("If they dropped any more syllables, they would be speechless," suggests author Tom Miller).

Cubanisms to Know

Cubans are long-winded and full of flowery, passionate, rhetorical flourishes. Fidel Castro didn't inherit his penchant for long speeches from dour, taciturn Galicia—it's a purely

Cuban characteristic. Cubans also spice up the language with little affectations and teasing endearments—*piropos*—given and taken among themselves without offense.

Many English (or "American") words have found their way into Cuban diction. Cubans go to *béisbol* (and use Cubanized American terms at the game) and today eat *hamburgesas*. Like the English, Cubans are clever in their use of words, imbuing their language with double entendres and their own lexicon of similes. Cubans are also great cussers. The two most common cuss words are *cojones* (balls) and *coño* (cunt), while one of the more common colloquialisms is *ojalá*, which loosely translated means "I wish" or "if only!" but which most commonly is used to mean "Some hope!"

Formal courtesies are rarely used when greeting someone. Since the Revolution, everyone is a *compañero* or *compañera* (*señor* and *señora* are considered too bourgeois), although the phrase is disdained by many Cubans as indicating approval of the Communist system. Confusingly, *¡ciao!* (used as a long-term good-bye, and spelled "chao" in Cuba) is also used as a greeting in casual passing—the equivalent of "Hi!" You will also be asked *¿Como anda?* ("How goes it?"), while younger Cubans prefer *¿Que bola?* (the Cuban equivalent of "Wassup?") rather than the traditional *¿Que pasa?* ("What's happening?").

Cubans speak to each other directly, no holds barred. Even conversations with strangers are laced with *"¡Ay, muchacha!"* ("Hey, girl!"), *"¡Mira, chica!"* ("Look, girl!"), and *"¡Hombre!"* ("Listen, man!") when one disagrees with the other. Cubans refer to one another in straightforward terms, often playing on their physical or racial characteristics: *El chino, la mulata, el nose hairs, la plucked eyebrows.* Thus, explains Isadora Tattlin, black people with kinky hair are called *negros de pasas* (raisin blacks); those with straight hair are *negros de pelo* (literally, blacks with hair). Cubans do not refer to themselves with a single definition of "white" or "black." There are a zillion gradations of skin color and features, from *negro azul y trompudo* (blue-black and thick-lipped) and *muy negro* (very black), for example, to *leche con una gota de café* (milk with a drop of coffee). Whites, too, come in shades. *Un blanco* is a blonde- or light-haired person with blue, green, or gray eyes. *Un blanquito* is a "white" with dark hair and dark eyes.

Bárbaro is often used to attribute a positive quality to someone, as in *él es un bárbaro* ("he's a great person"). It can also be used to express appreciation of something, as can *está en talla!* ("this is excellent"). The opposite would be *está en llamas* (literally "on fire"), figuratively used to express a negative opinion of something, as in "that's awful." *Está en candela* ("a flame") is it's equivalent, but more commonly used to describe an alarming or complicated situation, or excess, as in something that's "hot" (such as a promiscuous person); or to signify "I'm broke!" Young Cubans fortunate to have some money might slap the pocket of their jeans and say *tengo guano* ("I've got some palm leaf").

Marinovia defines a live-in girlfriend (from *marido*, for spouse, and *novia*, for girlfriend). An *asere* is one's close friend, though this street term is considered a low-class word, especially common with blacks. A *flojo* (literally, "loose guy") is a lounger who pretends to work. Cubans also have no shortage of terms referring to spies, informers, and untrustworthy souls. For example, *embori* refers to an informer in cahoots with the government. *Fronterizo* is a half-mad person. *Chispa* ("spark") is someone with vitality. To become "Cubanized" is to be *aplatanado*.

Spanish Phrasebook

PRONUNCIATION GUIDE

Spanish pronunciation is much more regular than that of English, but there are still occasional variations.

Consonants

c as 'c' in "cat," before 'a,' 'o,' or 'u'; like 's' before 'e' or 'i'

d as 'd' in "dog," except between vowels, then like 'th' in "that"

g before 'e' or 'i,' like the 'ch' in Scottish "loch"; elsewhere like 'g' in "get"

h always silent

j like the English 'h' in "hotel," but stronger

ll like the 'y' in "yellow"

ñ like the 'ni' in "onion"

r trilled 'r' at the beginning of words; in between vowels pronounced like the 'tt' in "butter"

rr trilled 'r'

v similar to the 'b' in "boy" (not as English 'v')

y similar to English, but with a slight 'j' sound. When standing, alone it's pronounced like the 'e' in "me."

z like 's' in "same"

b, f, k, l, m, n, p, q, s, t, w, x as in English

Vowels

a as in "father," but shorter

e as in "hen"

i as in "machine"

o as in "phone"

u usually as in "rule"; when it follows a 'q' the 'u' is silent; when it follows an 'h' or 'g,' it's pronounced like 'w,' except when it comes between 'g' and 'e' or 'i,' when it's also silent (unless it has an umlaut, when it again pronounced as English 'w'

Stress

Native English speakers frequently make errors of pronunciation by ignoring stress—all Spanish vowels—a, e, i, o, and u—may carry accents that determine which syllable of a word gets emphasis. Often, stress seems unnatural to nonnative speakers—the surname Chávez, for instance, is stressed on the first syllable—but failure to observe this rule may mean that native speakers may not understand you.

NUMBERS

0 *cero*
1 *uno (masculine)*
1 *una (feminine)*
2 *dos*
3 *tres*
4 *cuatro*
5 *cinco*
6 *seis*
7 *siete*
8 *ocho*
9 *nueve*
10 *diez*
11 *once*
12 *doce*
13 *trece*
14 *catorce*
15 *quince*
16 *dieciseis*
17 *diecisiete*
18 *dieciocho*
19 *diecinueve*
20 *veinte*
21 *veintiuno*
30 *treinta*
40 *cuarenta*
50 *cincuenta*
60 *sesenta*
70 *setenta*
80 *ochenta*
90 *noventa*
100 *cien*
101 *ciento y uno*
200 *doscientos*
1,000 *mil*
10,000 *diez mil*
1,000,000 *un millón*

DAYS OF THE WEEK

Sunday *domingo*
Monday *lunes*
Tuesday *martes*
Wednesday *miércoles*
Thursday *jueves*
Friday *viernes*
Saturday *sábado*

TIME

While Latin Americans mostly use the 12-hour clock, in some instances, usually associated with plane or bus schedules, they may use the 24-hour military clock. Under the 24-hour clock, for example, *las nueve de la noche* (9 P.M.) would be *las 21 horas* (2100 hours).

What time is it? *¿Qué hora es?*
It's one o'clock *Es la una.*
It's two o'clock *Son las dos.*
At two o'clock *Á las dos.*
It's ten to three *Son tres menos diez.*
It's ten past three *Son tres y diez.*
It's three fifteen *Son las tres y cuarto.*
It's two forty five *Son tres menos cuarto.*
It's two thirty *Son las dos y media.*
It's six A.M. *Son las seis de la mañana.*
It's six P.M. *Son las seis de la tarde.*
It's ten P.M. *Son las diez de la noche.*
today *hoy*
tomorrow *mañana*
morning *la mañana*
tomorrow morning *mañana por la mañana*
yesterday *ayer*
week *la semana*
month *mes*
year *año*
last night *anoche*
the next day *el día siguiente*

USEFUL WORDS AND PHRASES

Most Spanish-speaking people consider formalities important. Whenever approaching anyone for information or some other reason, do not forget the appropriate salutation—good

morning, good evening, etc. Standing alone, the greeting *hola* (hello) can sound brusque.

Hello. *Hola.*
Good morning. *Buenos días.*
Good afternoon. *Buenas tardes.*
Good evening. *Buenas noches.*
How are you? *¿Cómo está?*
Fine. *Muy bien.*
And you? *¿Y usted?*
So-so. *Más o menos.*
Thank you. *Gracias.*
Thank you very much. *Muchas gracias.*
You're very kind. *Muy amable.*
You're welcome. *De nada* (literally, "It's nothing").
yes *sí*
no *no*
I don't know. *No sé.*
It's fine; okay *Está bien.*
Good; okay. *Bueno.*
please *por favor*
Pleased to meet you. *Mucho gusto.*
Excuse me (physical) *Perdóneme.*
Excuse me (speech) *Discúlpeme.*
I'm sorry. *Lo siento.*
Goodbye. *Adios.*
See you later. *Hasta luego* (literally, "until later").
more *más*
less *menos*
better *mejor*
much, a lot *mucho*
a little *un poco*
large *grande*
small *pequeño, chico*
quick, fast *rápido*
slowly *despacio*
bad *malo*
difficult *difícil*
easy *fácil*
He/She/It is gone (as in "She left," "He's gone"). *Ya se fue.*
I don't speak Spanish well. *No hablo bien el español.*
I don't understand. *No entiendo.*

How do you say. . . in Spanish? *¿Cómo se dice. . . en español?*
Do you understand English? *¿Entiende el inglés?*
Is English spoken here? (Does anyone here speak English?) *¿Se habla inglés aquí?*

TERMS OF ADDRESS

When in doubt, use the formal *usted* (you) as a form of address. If you wish to dispense with formality and feel that the desire is mutual, you can say *Me puedes tutear* (you can call me "tú").

I *yo*
you (formal) *usted*
you (familiar) *tú*
he/him *él*
she/her *ella*
we/us *nosotros*
you (plural) *ustedes*
they/them (all males or mixed gender) *ellos*
they/them (all females) *ellas*
Mr., sir *señor*
Mrs., madam *señora*
Miss, young lady *señorita*
wife *esposa*
husband *marido or esposo*
friend *amigo* (male), *amiga* (female)
sweetheart *novio* (male), *novia* (female)
son, daughter *hijo, hija*
brother, sister *hermano, hermana*
father, mother *padre, madre*
grandfather, grandmother *abuelo, abuela*

GETTING AROUND

Where is. . . ? *¿Dónde está. . . ?*
How far is it to. . . ? *¿A cuánto está. . . ?*
from. . . to. . . *de. . . a. . .*
highway *la carretera*
road *el camino*
street *la calle*
block *la cuadra*
kilometer *kilómetro*
north *norte*
south *sur*

west *oeste; poniente*
east *este; oriente*
straight ahead *al derecho; adelante*
to the right *a la derecha*
to the left *a la izquierda*

ACCOMMODATIONS

Is there a room? *¿Hay cuarto?*
May I (we) see it? *¿Puedo (podemos) verlo?*
What is the rate? *¿Cuál es el precio?*
Is that your best rate? *¿Es su mejor precio?*
Is there something cheaper? *¿Hay algo más económico?*
single room *un sencillo*
double room *un doble*
room for a couple *matrimonial*
key *llave*
with private bath *con baño*
with shared bath *con baño general; con baño compartido*
hot water *agua caliente*
cold water *agua fría*
shower *ducha*
electric shower *ducha eléctrica*
towel *toalla*
soap *jabón*
toilet paper *papel higiénico*
air conditioning *aire acondicionado*
fan *abanico; ventilador*
blanket *frazada; manta*
sheets *sábanas*

PUBLIC TRANSPORT

bus stop *la parada*
bus terminal *terminal de buses*
airport *el aeropuerto*
launch *lancha; tiburonera*
dock *muelle*
I want a ticket to. . . *Quiero un pasaje a. . .*
I want to get off at. . . *Quiero bajar en. . .*
Here, please. *Aquí, por favor.*
Where is this bus going? *¿Adónde va este autobús?*
round-trip *ida y vuelta*
What do I owe? *¿Cuánto le debo?*

FOOD

menu *la carta, el menú*
glass *taza*
fork *tenedor*
knife *cuchillo*
spoon *cuchara*
napkin *servilleta*
soft drink *agua fresca*
coffee *café*
cream *crema*
tea *té*
sugar *azúcar*
drinking water *agua pura, agua potable*
bottled carbonated water *agua mineral con gas*
bottled uncarbonated water *agua sin gas*
beer *cerveza*
wine *vino*
milk *leche*
juice *jugo*
eggs *huevos*
bread *pan*
watermelon *sandía*
banana *banano, guineo*
plantain *plátano*
apple *manzana*
orange *naranja*
meat (without) *carne (sin)*
beef *carne de res*
chicken *pollo; gallina*
fish *pescado*
shellfish *mariscos*
shrimp *camarones*
fried *frito*
roasted *asado*

barbecued *a la parrilla*
breakfast *desayuno*
lunch *almuerzo*
dinner (often eaten in late afternoon) *comida*
dinner, or a late night snack *cena*
the check, or bill *la cuenta*

MAKING PURCHASES

I need. . . *Necesito. . .*
I want. . . *Deseo. . . or Quiero. . .*
I would like. . . (more polite) *Quisiera. . .*
How much does it cost? *¿Cuánto cuesta?*
What's the exchange rate? *¿Cuál es el tipo de cambio?*
May I see. . . ? *¿Puedo ver. . . ?*
this one *ésta/éste*
expensive *caro*
cheap *barato*
cheaper *más barato*
too much *demasiado*

HEALTH

Help me please. *Ayúdeme por favor.*
I am ill. *Estoy enfermo.*
pain *dolor*
fever *fiebre*
stomach ache *dolor de estómago*
vomiting *vomitar*
diarrhea *diarrea*
drugstore *farmacia*
medicine *medicina*
pill, tablet *pastilla*
birth control pills *pastillas anticonceptivas*
condom *condón, preservativo*

Suggested Reading

ART AND CULTURE

Pérez, Louis A. *On Becoming Cuban: Nationality, Identity and Culture.* New York: Harper Perennial, 2001. Seminal and highly readable account of the development of Cuban culture from colonialism through communism.

Robinson, Eugene. *Last Dance in Havana.* New York: Free Press, 2004. One man's insightful impressions of contemporary Cuba, and the importance of music and dance as an expression of Cuban culture and as a palliative to the harsh realities of life under a Communist dictator.

BIOGRAPHY

Anderson, Jon Lee. *Che Guevara: A Revolutionary Life.* New York: Grove Press, 1997. This definitive biography reveals heretofore unknown details of Che's life and presents an astounding profile that shows the dark side of this revolutionary icon.

Castro, Fidel. *My Early Years.* New York: Ocean Press, 1998. Fidel Castro reflects on his childhood, youth, and student activism, with an introduction by Gabriel García Márquez.

Geyer, Georgie Anne. *Guerrilla Prince: The Untold Story of Fidel Castro.* Boston: Little Brown, 1991. This sobering profile of the Cuban leader strips Castro bare, revealing his charisma and cunning, pride and paranoia, and megalomania and myth.

Gimbel, Wendy. *Havana Dreams: A Story of Cuba.* London: Virago, 1998. The moving story of Naty Revuelta's tormented love affair with Fidel Castro and the terrible consequences of a relationship as heady as the doomed romanticism of the Revolution.

Quirk, Robert E. *Fidel Castro.* New York: W. W. Norton, 1993. A detailed, none-too-complimentary profile of the Cuban leader.

Szulc, Tad. *Fidel: A Critical Portrait.* New York: Morrow, 1986. A riveting profile of the astounding life of this larger-than-life figure. This marvelous read is the most thorough of the Castro biographies.

CIGARS

Perelman, Richard B. *Perelman's Pocket Cyclopedia of Havana Cigars.* Perelman, Pioneer & Co, 1998. More than 160 pages with over 25 color photos providing a complete list of cigar brands and shapes. Handy 4- by 6-inch size makes it easy to carry in the coat pocket and invaluable as a reference source when shopping.

Stout, Nancy. *Habanos: The Story of the Havana Cigar.* New York: Rizzoli, 1997. Beautifully illustrated coffee table book that tells you all you want to know about the growing and processing of tobacco and its metamorphosis into fine Habanos cigars.

COFFEE-TABLE

Baker, Christopher P. *Cuba Classics: A Celebration of Vintage American Automobiles.* Northampton, MA: Interlink Books, 2004. This lavishly illustrated coffee table book pays homage to Cuba's astonishing wealth of antique cars, revealing the time-worn splendor of classic American automobiles spanning eight decades. The text traces the long love affair between Cubans and the U.S. automobile and offers a paean to the owners who keep their weary *cacharros* running with resourcefulness, ingenuity, and indefatigable good humor.

Barclay, Juliet (photographs by Martin Charles). *Havana: Portrait of a City.* London: Cassell, 1993. A well-researched and abundantly illustrated coffee table volume especially emphasizing the city's history.

Carley, Rachel. *Cuba: 400 Years of Architectural Legacy.* New York: Whitney Library of

Design, 1997. Beautifully illustrated coffee table book that spans the island in tracing the development of architectural styles, from early colonial days to the Communist aesthetic hiatus and post-Soviet renaissance.

Cushing, Lincoln. ¡*Revolución! Cuban Poster Art*. San Francisco: Chronicle Books, 2003. This splendid book assembles nearly 150 powerful examples of popular art from the 1950s through 1980s, providing a window into a truly revolutionary chapter in graphic design.

Evans, Walker. *Walker Evans: Cuba*. New York: Getty Publications, 2001. Recorded in 1933, these 60 beautiful black-and-white images capture the "eternal Cuba" in Evans's portraits, which portray in stark clarity the misery and hardships of life in the era. Andrei Codrescu wrote an accompanying essay.

Harvey, David Alan, and Elizabeth Newhouse. *Cuba*. Washington, D.C.: National Geographic, 2000. An acclaimed photographer and a *National Geographic* editor brilliantly display their passion for Cuba in this poignant and stunningly illustrated book that puts a human face on the rich culture.

Kenny, Jack. *Cuba*. Ann Arbor, MI: Corazon Press, 2005. Beautiful black-and-white images that capture the essence of Cuba and provide an intimate portrait into its soul.

Llanes, Lillian. *Havana Then and Now*. San Diego: Thunder Bay Press, 2004. A delightful collection of images wedding centenary black-and-whites to color photos showing the same locales as they are now.

GENERAL

Cabrera Infante, Guillermo. ¡*Mea Cuba!* New York: Farrar, Straus & Giroux, 1994. An acerbic, indignant, raw, wistful, and brilliant set of essays in which the author pours out his bile at the Castro regime.

Fuentes, Norberto. *Hemingway in Cuba*. Secaucus, NY: Lyle Stuart, 1984. The seminal,

lavishly illustrated study of the Nobel Prize–winner's years in Cuba.

Martínez-Fernández, Luis, et al. *Encyclopedia of Cuba: People, History, Culture*. Westport, CT: Greenwood Press, 2004. Comprehensive twin-volume set with chapters arranged by themes, such as History, Plastic Arts, and Sports. Indispensable for serious students of Cuba.

Shnookal, Deborah, and Mirta Muñiz, eds. *José Martí Reader*. New York: Ocean Press, 1999. An anthology of writings, poetry, and letters of one of the most brilliant and impassioned Latin American intellectuals of the 19th century.

HISTORY, ECONOMICS, AND POLITICS

Bardach, Ann Louise. *Cuba Confidential*. New York: Random House, 2002. A brilliant study of the failed politics of poisoned Cuban–U.S. relations that exposes the tragedy of families torn asunder by the Revolution, and the spiteful, self-seeking power plays and grand hypocrisies of the warring factions in Washington, Miami, and Havana.

Gott, Richard. *Cuba: A New History*. New Haven, CT: Yale University Press, 2005. Erudite, entertaining, and concise, yet with all the masterful detail that commends a tour de force.

Latell, Brian. *After Fidel: The Inside Story of Castro's Regime and Cuba's Next Leader*. New York: Palgrave Macmillan, 2005. A former senior CIA intelligence analyst brilliantly profiles the personalities of Fidel and Raúl Castro, providing fascinating insights into their quixotic, mutually dependent relationship and the motivations that have shaped their antagonistic relationship with the United States.

Oppenheimer, Andres. *Castro's Final Hour*. New York: Simon & Schuster, 1992. A sobering, in-depth exposé of the uglier side of both Fidel Castro and the state system, including controversial topics such as drug trading.

Smith, Wayne. *The Closest of Enemies.* New York: W. W. Norton, 1987. Essential reading, this personal account of the author's years serving as President Carter's man in Havana during the 1970s is a moving and entertaining account providing key insights into the complexities that haunt U.S. relations with Cuba.

Thomas, Hugh. *Cuba: The Pursuit of Freedom, 1726–1969.* New York: Harper & Row, 1971. A seminal work—called a "magisterial conspectus of Cuban history"—tracing the evolution of conditions that eventually engendered the Revolution.

Thomas, Hugh. *The Cuban Revolution.* London: Weidenfeld and Nicolson, 1986. The definitive work on the Revolution offering a brilliant analysis of all aspects of the country's diverse and tragic history.

Wyden, Peter. *Bay of Pigs: The Untold Story.* New York: Simon and Schuster, 1979. An in-depth and riveting exposé of the CIA's ill-conceived mission to topple Castro.

LITERATURE

Cabrera Infante, Guillermo. *Three Trapped Tigers.* New York: Avon, 1985. A poignant and comic novel that captures the essence of life in Havana before the ascendance of Castro.

García, Cristina. *Dreaming in Cuban.* New York: Ballantine Books, 1992. A brilliant, poignant, languid, and sensual tale of a family divided politically and geographically by the Cuban revolution and the generational fissures that open on each side.

Greene, Graham. *Our Man in Havana.* New York: Penguin, 1971. The story of Wormold, a conservative British vacuum-cleaner salesman in prerevolutionary Havana. Recruited by British intelligence, Wormold finds little information to pass on, and so invents it. Full of the sensuality of Havana and the tensions of Batista's last days.

Gutiérrez, Pedro Juan. *Dirty Havana Trilogy.*

New York: Farrar, Straus & Giroux, 2001. A bawdy, hilarious, and depressing semi-biographical take on the gritty life of Havana's underclass—begging, whoring, escaping hardship through sex and *santería*—during the harshest years of the Special Period.

Hemingway, Ernest. *Islands in the Stream.* New York: Harper Collins, 1970. An exciting triptych. The second and third parts are set in Cuba during the war and draw heavily on the author's own experience hunting Nazi U-boats at sea.

Hemingway, Ernest. *The Old Man and the Sea.* New York: Scribner's, 1952. The simple yet profound story of an unlucky Cuban fisherman, the slim novel won the author the Nobel Prize for Literature.

Smith, Martin Cruz. *Havana Bay.* New York: Random House, 1999. Smith engages us in a best-selling murder mystery as Russian Cold War spy Renko returns, this time to the "faded, lovely, dangerous" Cuban capital.

TRAVEL GUIDES

Calder, Nigel. *Cuba: A Cruising Guide.* St. Ives, England: Imray Laurie Norie & Wilson, 1999. A superb navigational guide for yachters.

Charles, Simon. *The Cruising Guide to Cuba.* St. Petersburg, FL: Cruising Guide Publications, 1997. Invaluable reference guide for every sailor wishing to charter sailing or motorized craft. Charles gives it to you straight. His goal is "to seek only to ensure the safe passage of all who would use the seas to travel where they will."

Lightfoot, Claudia. *Havana: A Cultural and Literary Companion.* Northampton, MA: Interlink Publishing, 2001. The author leads you through Havana past and present using literary quotations and allusions to add dimension to the sites and experiences.

Rodríguez, Eduardo Luis. *The Havana Guide: Modern Architecture 1925–65.* New York: Princeton Architectural Press, 2000. A marvelous guide to individual structures—

homes, churches, theaters, government buildings—representing the best of modern architecture (1925–65) throughout Havana.

Smith, Barbara and Walter. *Bicycling Cuba.* Woodstock, VT: Backcountry Guides, 2002. A detailed and practical guide to cycling in Cuba, with routes and maps spanning the entire country.

TRAVEL LITERATURE

Aschkenas, Lea. *Es Cuba: Life and Love on an Illegal Island.* Emeryville, CA: Seal Press, 2006. A beautiful story of true love straight from the heart. Told with gentle compassion for a culture and country, *Es Cuba* reveals with exquisite honesty how the possibilities and hopes of the heart can surmount even the most obdurate personal hardships and political barriers.

Baker, Christopher P. *Mi Moto Fidel: Motorcycling through Castro's Cuba.* Washington, D.C.: National Geographic's Adventure Press, 2001. Winner of both the Lowell Thomas Award Travel Book of the Year and the North American Travel Journalist Association's Grand Prize, this erotically charged tale of the author's 7,000-mile adventure by motorcycle through Cuba offers a bittersweet look at the last Marxist "utopia."

Codrescu, Andrei, and David Graham. *¡Ay, Cuba!* New York: St Martin's Press, 1999. A trenchant and witty social criticism that takes a scything view of Castroism while reflecting the author's affection and sensitivity for the Cuban culture and people.

Corbett, Ben. *This is Cuba: An Outlaw Culture Survives.* Cambridge, MA: Westview Press,

2002. A stinging indictment of the havoc, despair, and restraints wrought by four decades of *fidelismo,* this first-person account of life in Castro's Cuba beautifully but tragically exposes the harsh realities of a people struggling to survive.

Guillermoprieto, Alma. *Dancing With Cuba.* New York: Vintage, 2005. Poignant memoir of the author's life teaching dance in Havana during the Revolution.

Miller, Tom. *Trading with the Enemy: A Yankee Travels Through Castro's Cuba.* New York: Basic Books, 1996. Told by a famous author who lived in Cuba for almost a year, this travelogue is thoughtful, engaging, insightful, compassionate, and told in rich narrative.

Miller, Tom, ed. *Travelers' Tales: Cuba.* San Francisco: Travelers' Tales, 2001. Extracts from the contemporary works of 38 authors provide a lively and entertaining account of Cuba that is at times hilarious, cautionary, and inspiring.

Ryan, Alan, ed. *The Reader's Companion to Cuba.* New York: Harcourt Brace & Co., 1997. A gathering of some of the best travel writing about Cuba dating from the mid-1800s, spanning an eclectic menu of authors from John Muir and Graham Greene to mob lawyer Frank Ragano and baseball's Tommy Lasorda.

Tattlin, Isadora. *Cuba Diaries: An American Housewife in Havana.* Chapel Hill, NC: Algonquin Books, 2002. A fascinating and marvelous account of four years in Havana spent raising two children, entertaining her husband's clients (including Fidel), and contending with chronic shortages. A must-read.

Suggested Viewing

Before Night Falls. Fine Line Features, 2000. A potent and poignant adaptation of Reinaldo Arenas's autobiography, in which the persecuted Cuban novelist and poet recounts his life, first in Castro's Cuba and then in exile in the United States. Says film critic Lucas Hilderbrand, "It's an intoxicating, intensely erotic account of sexual discovery and liberation, and a devastating record of the artist's persecution under the Castro regime."

Buena Vista Social Club. Artisan Entertainment, 1999. A magnificent, adorable documentary look at the reemergence from obscurity of veteran performers Ruben González, Omara Portuondo, Ibrahim Ferrer, Eliades Ochoa, and Compay Segundo culminating in their sellout concert at Carnegie Hall. The performers tell their stories directly to the camera as they wander the decayed streets of Havana and gather to record and perform.

Death of a Bureaucrat. New Yorker Films, 1966. Tomás Gutiérrez Alea's questioning portrait of the absurdities of the Cuban bureaucratic system and people's propensity to conform to absurd Kremlin-style directives that cause misery to others.

Guantanamera. New Yorker Films, 1997. A road movie with a twist, this rueful romantic comedy by Tomás Gutiérrez Alea and Juan Carlos Tabio begins to unfold after an elderly dame dies from an excess of sexual stimulation. The farce of returning her body to Havana for proper burial provides the vehicle for a cutting yet comic parody of an overly-bureaucratic contemporary Cuba, and a lighthearted admonishment to live for the moment.

Memories of Underdevelopment. New Yorker Films, 1968. Director Tomás Gutiérrez Alea's intellectual and sensual, wide-ranging, stream-of-consciousness masterpiece revolves around an erotically charged, intellectual "playboy" existence in early 1960s Cuba, pinned by the tragedy of the central character's alienation from the "underdeveloped" people around him and his own inability to attain a more fulfilled state.

Miel para Ochún. ICAIC, 2003. Humberto Solas's "Honey for Oshún" tells the tale of a Cuban-American who, aided by a taxi driver, embarks on a wild road trip through Cuba to search for the mother he thought had abandoned him as a child.

Paradise Under the Stars. Vanguard Cinema, 1999. Set around a star-struck woman's dream of singing at the Tropicana nightclub, this buoyantly witty comedy combines exuberant musical numbers, bedroom farce, and some light-hearted satiric jabs at Cuban machismo.

¡Soy Cuba! Milestone Films, 1964. Filmed by great Russian director Mikhail Kalatozov, "I Am Cuba" is a brilliant, melodramatic, agit-prop black-and-white, anti-American epic to Communist kitsch that exposes the grinding poverty, oppression, and decadence of Batista's Havana, told in four didactic tales.

Strawberry and Chocolate. Miramax, 1995. Legendary Cuban director Tomás Gutiérrez Alea's famous skit about the evolving friendship between a gay man and an ardent revolutionary is a classic comedic drama and the first Cuban film to be nominated for an Oscar (Best Foreign Language Film). David, the young Communist, is selected by Diego, an artist, as a potential target for seduction. The tale that unfolds in derelict Havana is an indictment of the treatment of homosexuals in Cuba.

Suite Habana. ICAIC, 2003. The hit of the 25th Havana Film Festival and the official Cuban nomination to the Oscars, this silent documentary by Fernando Pérez records a simple day in the life of 10 ordinary Cubans in Havana.

Internet Resources

GENERAL INFORMATION

Cuban Government
www.cubagob.cu
Official website of the Cuban government.

Cubanos.org
www.cubanos.org
Excellent resource directory with links to Cuba-related websites on all themes.

Cubasí
www.cubasi.cu
Generic Cuban government site with sections on travel, culture, news, etc.

Cubaweb
www.cubaweb.cu
Similar to the Cubasí site, with sections on travel, culture, news, etc.

Latin American Network Information Center
http://lanic.utexas.edu/la/cb/cuba
Superb portal for dozens of links relating to Cuba.

TRAVEL INFORMATION

Caribbean Tourist Organization
www.doitcaribbean.com
Generic information on traveling in the Caribbean, including Cuba.

Cuba Central
www.cubacentral.com
Action center for efforts to end the travel ban for U.S. citizens and residents.

Cubalinda Interactive Travel
www.cubalinda.com
Online reservation agency for flights, hotels, etc.

Cuba Mapa
www.cubamapa.com
Maps, maps, and more maps about Cuba.

Directorio Turístico de Cuba (Tourism Directory of Cuba)
www.dtcuba.com
Cuban travel-related portal, with online reservation capability.

Ministerio de Turismo (Ministry of Tourism)
www.cubatravel.cu
Another lookalike tourism-related website from the Cuban government.

Rex
www.rexrentacar.com
Website of the only trustworthy Cuban car rental company (i.e., the best of a bad bunch).

U.S. Treasury Department (OFAC)
www.treas.gov/ofac
What you need to know about U.S. law and Cuba, direct from the horse's mouth.

Víazul
www.viazul.com
Website of Cuba's tourist bus company, with online reservation capability.

ART AND CULTURE
AfroCuba Web
www.afrocubaweb.com
Excellent source of information on Afro-Cuban culture and related themes.

Cuba Now
www.cubanow.net
Cuban government's website dedicated to arts and culture.

Cubarte, Portal of Cuban Culture
www.cubarte.cult.cu
Another Cuban government site dedicated to the arts.

BUSINESS-RELATED INFORMATION
U.S.-Cuba Trade & Economic Council
www.cubatrade.org
This site provides information on trade with Cuba and related business and political aspects.

HAVANA-SPECIFIC INFORMATION
Havana supersite
www.lahabana.com
Cuban government site dedicated to the capital city.

Hoteles Habaguanex
www.habaguanex.cu
Website of Cuba's Habaguanex corporation, with profiles on its more than a dozen boutique hotels.

Infotur
www.infotur.cu
Information on tourist information centers in Havana.

Oficina del Historiador de la Ciudad Habana (Office of the City Historian)
www.ohch.cu
Quality Spanish-only site relating to restoration projects, museums, hotels, and sites of interest in Habana Vieja.

TELEPHONE DIRECTORIES
Etecsa
www.etecsa.cu
Website of Cuba's telephone corporation, with a link to Cuba's online telephone directory.

Paginas Amarillas (Yellow Pages)
www.paginasamarillas.cu
Yes, Cuba has a Yellow Pages for commercial entities...this one online!

Index

BEACHES

CIGARS/TOBACCO

Acknowledgments

Researching a guidebook is fun, but it's no small task, and this fourth edition could not have been accomplished without the assistance of a coterie of selfless and supportive folk. Above all, I am indebted beyond words to my dearest friend Lynetta Cornelius for her selfless support and understanding.

Thanks go to all my friends, acquaintances, and others who kindly forwarded clips on Cuba, and especially to those readers who took the trouble to write with recommendations, warnings, and general comments. Alas, they are too numerous to be acknowledged individually, although I would be remiss if I failed to single out Ted Henken for his extensive and kind contributions. Rick Muñoz, of Chabot College, and Rick Schwag, of Caribbean Medical Transport, also deserve credit.

I am also extremely grateful for the support of everyone who contributed in ways large or small to the production of the prior editions, helping lay the foundation of this all-new edition. Not least, I wish to express appreciation to a number of area specialists from whose writings I have drawn heavily, notably Ann Louise Bardach (*Cuba Confidential*), Hugh Thomas (*Cuba: The Pursuit of Freedom*), Tom Miller (*Trading with the Enemy: A Yankee Travel's Through Castro's Cuba*), and Tad Szulc (*Fidel: A Critical Portrait*).

¡Gracias! too to the countless Cubans who shared insights and shone the light on obscure issues, displayed selfless hospitality, welcomed me into their hearts and homes, and with unequaled verve, virtue, charity, patience, and grace taught me that I, and the world, have much to learn. As always on my lengthy research trips, Cubans everywhere embraced and welcomed me, touching my heart. Among them, Jorge Mezerene and his wife, Liba, in Holguín, deserve special praise and now count among my true friends in Cuba. In Trinidad, Julio Muñoz Cocina and his wife, Rosa, continue to offer me the very best of friendship and support. In Havana, I wish to thank Hector Higueras, of *paladar* Le Chansonnier; Maurits Luytens, of NH Hotel Parque Central; and above all Jorge Coalla Potts and his wife, Marisel, and daughter, Jessica. No words can express the devotion I have for this wonderful family, nor the appreciation I feel for their genuine affection, generosity, and support.

Yet again, I came away feeling like my friend Stephanie Gervassi-Levin, who on her first visit to Cuba began dancing uncontrollably in a *casa de la trova*. The Cubans formed a line and, "like a diplomat," took her hand, kissed her cheek. As I set out to write the first edition, she implored, "Chris, bring your genuine feeling into your pages. Breathe the innocence and beauty of Cuba without castrating Castro and his revolution." She set me a difficult task.

Ernest Hemingway, who loved Cuba and lived there for the better part of 20 years, once warned novice writer Arnold Samuelson against "a tendency to condemn before you completely understand. You aren't God, and you never judge a man. You present him as he is and you let the reader judge."

This book is dedicated to my dear friend Ralph Martell, cubaphile, bon vivant, and victim of a most egregious injustice.

www.moon.com

For helpful advice on planning a trip, visit www.moon.com for the **TRAVEL PLANNER** and get access to useful travel strategies and valuable information about great places to visit. When you travel with Moon, expect an experience that is uncommon and truly unique.

 HANDBOOKS | METRO | OUTDOORS | LIVING ABROAD

MAP SYMBOLS

Expressway		**(**	Highlight	✗	Airfield	⚲	Golf Course
Primary Road		○	City/Town	✗	Airport	**P**	Parking Area
Secondary Road		⊙	State Capital	▲	Mountain	⛰	Archaeological Site
Unpaved Road		⊛	National Capital	✛	Unique Natural Feature	⌂	Church
Trail		★	Point of Interest				
Ferry		•	Accommodation	⚐	Waterfall	⛽	Gas Station
Railroad		▼	Restaurant/Bar	▲	Park		Glacier
Pedestrian Walkway		■	Other Location	▮	Trailhead		Mangrove
Stairs		Λ	Campground	⛷	Skiing Area		Reef
							Swamp

CONVERSION TABLES

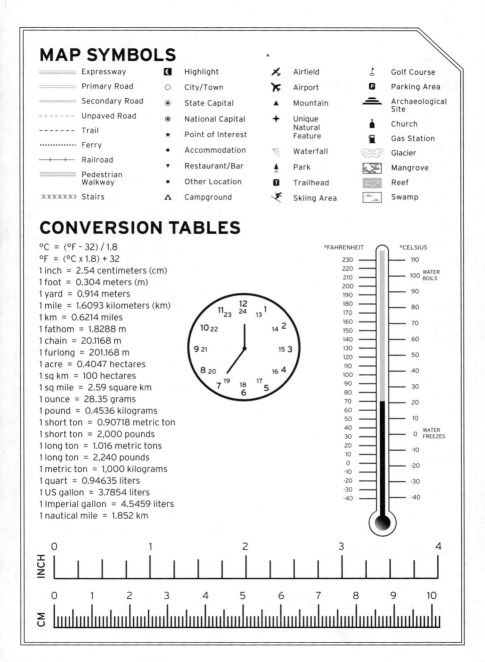

°C = (°F - 32) / 1.8
°F = (°C x 1.8) + 32
1 inch = 2.54 centimeters (cm)
1 foot = 0.304 meters (m)
1 yard = 0.914 meters
1 mile = 1.6093 kilometers (km)
1 km = 0.6214 miles
1 fathom = 1.8288 m
1 chain = 20.1168 m
1 furlong = 201.168 m
1 acre = 0.4047 hectares
1 sq km = 100 hectares
1 sq mile = 2.59 square km
1 ounce = 28.35 grams
1 pound = 0.4536 kilograms
1 short ton = 0.90718 metric ton
1 short ton = 2,000 pounds
1 long ton = 1.016 metric tons
1 long ton = 2,240 pounds
1 metric ton = 1,000 kilograms
1 quart = 0.94635 liters
1 US gallon = 3.7854 liters
1 Imperial gallon = 4.5459 liters
1 nautical mile = 1.852 km

MOON CUBA

Avalon Travel Publishing
An Imprint of
Avalon Publishing Group, Inc.

AVALON
publishing group incorporated

1400 65th Street, Suite 250
Emeryville, CA 94608, USA
www.moon.com

Editors: Kathryn Ettinger, Kay Elliott
Series Manager: Kathryn Ettinger
Acquisitions Manager: Rebecca K. Browning
Copy Editor: Amy Scott
Graphics Coordinator: Domini Dragoone
Production Coordinator: Domini Dragoone
Cover & Interior Designer: Gerilyn Attebery
Cartography Manager: Mike Morgenfeld
Map Editor: Kat Smith
Cartographers: Kat Bennett, Suzanne Service
Proofreader: Karen Gaynor Bleske
Indexer: Rachel Kuhn

ISBN-10: 1-56691-802-2
ISBN-13: 978-1-56691-802-2
ISSN: 1531-4170

Printing History
1st Edition – 1997
4th Edition – November 2006
5 4 3 2 1

KEEPING CURRENT

If you have a favorite gem you'd like to see included in the next edition, or see anything that needs updating, clarification, or correction, please drop us a line. Send your comments via email to feedback@moon.com, or use the address above.